W9-AAZ-392

THE GERMAN ORDER OF BATTLE

PANZERS

AND

ARTILLERY

IN WORLD WAR II

THE GERMAN ORDER OF BATTLE

PANZERS

AND

ARTILLERY

IN WORLD WAR II

George F. Nafziger

GREENHILL BOOKS, LONDON
STACKPOLE BOOKS, PENNSYLVANIA

This work is dedicated to
my dear friend Warren Worley,
whose pen may finally have run out of red ink.

Greenhill Books

The German Order of Battle: Panzers and Artillery in World War II
first published 1999 by Greenhill Books, Lionel Leventhal Limited,
Park House, 1 Russell Gardens, London NW11 9NN
and
Stackpole Books, 5067 Ritter Road, Mechanicsburg, PA 17055, USA

British Library Cataloguing in Publication Data
The German order of battle: panzers and artillery in World War II
1. Germany. Heer - Artillery - History - 20th century 2. Tank warfare -
Germany - History - 20th century 3. World War, 1939–1945 - Germany -
Tank warfare
I. Title
355.8'21'0943'09044

ISBN 1-85367-359-5

Library of Congress Cataloging-in-Publication Data
Nafziger, George F.
The German order of battle / by George F. Nafziger.
p. cm.
Contents: [1] panzers and artillery in World War II.
ISBN 1-85367-359-5
1. World War, 1939–1945 — Germany. 2. Tank warfare — History.
3. Germany. Heer — Armored troops. 4. Artillery — Germany — History
— 20th century. 5. World War, 1939–1945 — Artillery operations, German.
6. Germany — Armed Forces — Organization. 7. Germany — Armed
Forces — History World War, 1939–1945.
I. Title.
D757.54.N34 1999
940.54'1343 — dc21   98-47381 CIP

Publishing History
This book is based upon the author's privately published 'German Order
of Battle in World War II: An Organizational History of the Divisions and
Independent Brigades of the German Army. Volume I: Panzer, Motorized,
and Panzer Grenadier Divisions; and Volume V: Independent Artillery
Formations, Army and Luftwaffe Flak Artillery, and Nebelwerfer Formations.' This is the first trade publication of this revised material.

Printed and bound in Great Britain

Contents

CONTENTS

Introduction

World War II was marked by technical and tactical innovations. None was more of a shock to the world than the concept of armored warfare that the Germans developed, and there is little in the field of military history that has created more interest and excitement than the gray and sand colored panzers charging into battle.

The concept of armored warfare developed by the Germans was built from their experiences in World War I. Though the German army was not the creator of the armored land fighting vehicle, various individuals in its ranks saw its potential and combined it with a purely German innovation, the shock troops and their tactics. These tactics consisted of infiltration, bypassing strong points to be handled by the infantry, and the very Napoleonic concept of *manoeuvre sur les derrières*.

Napoleon's famous *manoeuvre sur les derrières* is a theory of the indirect approach to defeating your enemy. Camon provides the following list of advantages of the tactic:

1. It gives the attacking army a direction.
2. It provides the attacking army with reliable information on the enemy's army.
3. It places the enemy's parks and magazines in the control of the attacking army.
4. It permits large economies on the forces that are left behind to guard the attacker's territories.
5. If it succeeds, the results are decisive.
6. If it is only partially successful, it will cost the enemy large amounts of supplies and hurt his morale.

In the first instance, providing the attacking army with direction, at the beginning of each campaign the questions posed to the two opposing armies is which will have the initiative and where will the attacking forces be directed. The panzers were a weapon of the initiative as well as the defensive, but they were in their glory on the offense.

The second point, certain information on the enemy, comes as a result of the capture of their headquarters and other means of communication that are less secure from attack and interception in the rear of the army than they are from a position in front of the enemy's army. The German war records are filled with captured documents and discussions of those documents captured in these great armored thrusts.

The capture of the magazines and parks is obvious. These sit behind the enemy's defensive lines. The capture of magazines and parks denies the enemy both food and munitions. In addition, the capturing army is certainly capable of sustaining itself with the food captured, though it cannot always use the munitions. It is worth noting that the Soviet army made special efforts to be able to use captured ammunition, but to deny the use of their munitions by their enemies. Many of the standard German munitions could be used in Soviet equipment because, for example, the German 80mm mortar shells could be fired from the 82mm Soviet mortar, but not *vice versa*. The Soviets deliberately made their munitions slightly larger than their enemy's so that they could make use of captured munitions but their own munitions, if captured, could not be used in sinilar fashion. The Germans solved this problem by capturing so many Soviet guns and munitions that they were able to equip large portions of their infantry with captured Soviet artillery.

The minimization of the forces retained in the rear results from the enemy army being unable to pursue a successful frontal assault, because, by the time he has pushed particularly far forward, he will learn that his own lines of communication have been cut, his magazines have fallen, and he has been cut off from all resupply. His reaction will be an immediate withdrawal to reestablish his supply lines. This action was seen repeatedly on the Soviet front, and even the withdrawal of the Germans from France in 1944 can be seen in this light.

The decisive results, if they occur, do so because the enemy has lost his supply system and his ability to fight with 100 per cent of his capability, which will steadily erode as the encirclement continues. In addition, the cut-off army's morale will collapse as its troops discover their predicament. Should the enemy, however, be able maneuver and escape the decisive battle sought by the maneuvering army, at the very least he will have to abandon his existing lines of communication and attempt to establish others. This movement will strip him of his supply system. In addition, not only will it severely damage his army's morale and reduce its fighting ability in any future combats, but during its precipitous retreat his army will begin a process of disintegration as soldiers abandon the ranks. This type of disintegration, however, can quickly be recovered if the pursuit is not maintained as close and as hotly as possible. Should the withdrawing army be allowed to stop and reorganize, it will steadily recover what it has lost and soon be able to respond to attacks with vigor.

This process of disintegration can be found in many of the panzer battles of World War II. The French army collapsed because of this and the great battles in the early stages of the 1941 Russian campaign around Kiev and the other pockets clearly demonstrate the same process of collapse. Instead of the pursuit advocated by Napoleon, the process turned into one of encirclement of the slower moving infantry and other elements of the enemy's army. Napoleon had always advocated that the destruction of the enemy's army was the principal goal of war and this process of the panzers in forming great pockets of enemy troops led to the destruction of hundreds of Soviet divisions and the capture of millions of Soviet soldiers.

To do all this, however, in the day of the machine gun required armor, and that is where the armored vehicle came into the picture. The genius shown by such men as Heinz Guderian came by the blending of the British invention of the tank with the tactics of the storm trooper and Napoleon. This combination of man, machine and tactic has set the tone for warfare since 1 September 1939 when the word "*Blitzkrieg*" was born on the plains of Poland. The latest example was the stunning Coalition victory over the Iraqis in the 1990–91 Gulf War.

There are hundreds of books on the battles and campaigns of the German panzer divisions. There are numerous divisional histories. There many more filled with pictures of the tanks, armored cars and half-tracks that were used. There are, however, very few works that chronicle the organization of these forces and no single work that examines that organizational history from the beginning of the panzer division in the late 1930s to 1945. It is the goal of this book to provide as thorough a review of the organizational development of those divisions and brigades as possible. In addition, there are several formations that were armored, but were outside of the scope of the panzer division. Among these are the panzergrenadier divisions, which as the war was ending began to lose their distinctiveness from the panzer division as the two types of formation began to blend into one. There were also the various sturmgeschütz and other armored anti-tank units, some of which contained the most famous tanks of the war (the Tiger and King Tiger) and others some of the most obscure (for example, the Ferdinand).

Because the panzers worked in conjunction with the corps and army artillery and the famous nebelwerfers in order to achieve the Germans' goals, it had been felt necessary to explore the organizational history of the various artillery formations through the war. This study, however, forced an investigation into two extremes of organizational size. At the large end of the organizational spectrum there were a small number of artillery and nebelwerfer brigades, divisions, and even corps; at the other end there were literally hundreds of independent army artillery regiments and brigades. There are far too many of the latter to attempt any thorough documentation as was done with the larger formations, but, in the hope of providing some of the organizational history of these units, as many as could be identifed and have their structure determined have been included.

But why undertake such a compilation of data? How often has the reader read an account of some action, some skirmish or a major battle and seen a reference to a a brigade, a regiment, or a battalion and wondered how it fitted into its parent division? How often has one wondered what size of guns existed within a given battalion? And how often has a reader wished that the author provided just a little more detail? This work is intended to fill that niche. It is not intended to be read as one might a novel: instead, it is intended as a reference work that will be consulted by the historian and student of military history, to fill in those little details that are otherwise lost or for ever remain a mystery.

It is necessary to point out the contributions of two individuals who have made this work possible. Steve Sandman provided a tremendous amount of information from his collection of data, as well as reading and commenting on early versions of the manuscript. Bill Russ graciously loaned me numerous microfilms that he had bought from the US National Archives. My appreciation and thanks to both of them.

George F. Nafziger

Glossary of Terms

AC	Armored car
AOK	Armeeoberkommando (Command of an army in the field)
Arko	Artillerie Kommando (brigade level staff)
AT	anti-tank
btry	battery
btrys	batteries
co	company
col	column
cos	companies
Feldersatz	Replacement
fG	freie Gliederung (unit with a variable role, not strictly regulated)
FK	Feldkanone (field gun)
HMG	heavy machine gun
hvy	heavy
Inf Sup Plat	Infantry support platoon
KwK	Kampfwagenkanone (tank mounted gun; the main tank armament)
kz	kurz (short); short-barreled gun
leFH	105mm light field howitzer
leIG	75mm light infantry support gun
lFK	light field gun (generally 75mm lFK)
lg	lang (long); long-barreled gun
LMG	light machine gun
lt	light
maint	maintenance
Mk	Mark (equipment model designator)
mot	motorized
motZ	fully motorized
Mrs	Mörser or 210mm howitzer assigned at the army level
mtg	mounting (as in weapons mounted on a half-track)
Nebelwerfer	multiple-barreled rocket launcher
OKH	Oberkommando des Heeres (Supreme Army Command)
PAK	Panzerabwehrkanone (anti-tank gun)
plat	platoon
Pz I	Panzer Mk I, Sd Kfz 101
Pz II	Panzer Mk II, Sd Kfz 121
Pz III	Panzer Mk III, Sd Kfz 141 L/45
Pz III (50)	Panzer Mk III, Sd Kfz 141 L/42 with 50mm gun
Pz III (lg)	Panzer Mk III J, Sd Kfz 141/1 L/60 50mm gun
Pz IV	Panzer Mk IV, Sd Kfz 161 L/24 short 75mm gun
Pz IV (lg)	Panzer Mk IV, Sd Kfz 161 L/43 long 75mm gun
Pz VI	Panzer Mk VI, Sd Kfz 181 L/56 88mm gun
PzBu39	light anti-tank rifle Model 39
PzBu41	heavy anti-tank rifle Model 41 (28mm)
regt	regiment
sFH	heavy howitzer (generally the 150mm K18)
sfl	selbstfahrlafette (self propelled gun carriage)
sIG	150mm heavy infantry support gun
SP	self propelled
sPzB	schwere Panzerbüchse (heavy anti-tank rifle)
std	standard
StuG	Sturmgeschütz (assault gun)
StuK	Sturmkanone (assault gun mounted cannon)
sup	supply
tmot	teil motorisiert (partially motorized)
z.b.V.	zur besondere Verwendung (for special purposes)

1

Organizational History of the German Armored Formation 1939–1945

History of the German Panzer Forces

The genesis of the tank and of armored warfare was on the fields of Flanders. The first concentrated use of armor began with the Battle of Cambrai. As a result, the history of the German panzer forces began in the First World War. All of the men who were to form the German panzer arm were soldiers in this war and were greatly impressed by the possibilities of the tank. The first steps towards a modern German armored force began during the winter of 1923–24, when Oberstleutnant von Brauchitsch organized Germany's first maneuvers to explore the possibilities of employing motorized troops in a joint exercise with aircraft. This exercise attracted the attention of the German Army's Training Department and resulted in Heinz Guderian's appointment as an instructor in tactics and military history under the command of Oberst von Natzmer.

While Guderian was in this position a number of exercises, both on ground and on paper, were held to explore the potential of mobile and armored warfare. These experiments were successful enough that a modest amount of motorization began occurring in Weimar Germany's army.

In the autumn of 1928, Guderian was assigned to the command of the 3rd (Prussian) Motorized Battalion. While in this command, Guderian was forbidden to exercise with other units by a myopic Inspector of Transportation Troops, under whom he served.

As time passed, attitudes changed, and thus began the steady growth process that would lead to the formation of the panzer division. During the summer of 1932, General Lutz organized exercises involving cavalry, infantry, and simulated armored units. The first German armored reconnaissance cars appeared in these exercises—a bold experiment, as the Treaty of Versailles still forbade Germany from owning tanks. Though no accelerated decision process occurred in the upper echelons, many junior cavalry officers were greatly enamored of the new idea.

In 1933 Hitler rose to power and with his rise the tide of change quickened. Hitler tore up the Treaty of Versailles. On 16 March 1935 the Germans reintroduced universal military service. On 15 October 1935 the first three panzer divisions were formed.

As a result of the politics of the cavalry establishment for greater control over motorized troops, three "Light Divisions" were formed in place of a further expansion of the panzer divisions. They were to consist of two motorized cavalry rifle regiments, a reconnaissance regiment, an artillery regiment, a tank battalion, and supporting units. Internal German military politics was to have a considerable, and not necessarily positive, influence on the development of the panzer forces of the German army. Indeed, it would only be from the crucible of combat that, in 1945, the organization of the panzer division originally envisioned by Guderian would finally be accepted and ordered into existence. In 1937 the Germans began live fire field exercises to test in their concepts of armored warfare, courtesy of the Spanish Civil War. As part of the Condor Legion, Germany sent the Imker Armored Group to Spain. Initially two companies of Mk I tanks were sent to Spain. They were joined by a third company in October 1937. They took an active part in the campaign and operated with the air wing of the Condor Legion. Blitzkrieg was born as General Franco fought to take control of Spain.

When Germany invaded Poland in 1939 it did so with the 1st through 5th Panzer Divisions and the 1st through 4th Light Divisions. Between the Polish and French campaigns the 1st through 4th Light Divisions were reorganized and used to form the 6th through 9th Panzer Divisions. The 10th Panzer Division and the second infantry regiment of the 4th Panzer Division were formed using the 33rd, 69th and 86th Infantry Regiments. At the same time the Kavallerie-Schützen Regiments were redesignated as Schützen Regiments. In March 1940 the Panzerabwehr Battalions changed their names to Panzerjäger Battalions. On 15 April 1940 the Pioneer Battalions became Panzer Pioneer Battalions.

During the fall of 1940 the number of panzer divisions was doubled with the formation of the 11th through 20th Panzer Divisions. This did not mean that there were now twice as many tanks in the German army, only that the existing numbers of tanks were distributed among more divisions and the tank-to-infantry ratio in a panzer division was diluted. The 21st Panzer Division was organized in 1941 by the German Army in Africa. During the winter of 1941/42 the 22nd, 23rd, and 124th Panzer Divisions were formed from new drafts.

On 23 March 1942 the artillery regiments in the panzer divisions were renamed "Panzer Artillery Regiments". On 5 June 1942 the Schützen Regiments of the Panzer Divisions were renamed as Panzergrenadier Regiments. The panzergrenadier battalions were reorganized with four companies, rather than the former five companies. A 9th (Machine Gun) Company was formed, as were the 10th (Light Flak) and 11th (Light Infantry Gun) Companies. In June 1942 the army flak battalions assigned to the panzer divisions were officially redesignated as the division's 4th Artillery Battalion. This, however, was reversed on 1 May 1943 when the artillery battalions reverted to their former names.

In 1942 the 25th and 26th Panzer Divisions were formed in Germany. During the same year, the 27th Panzer Division was organized in southern Russia from part of the 22nd Panzer Division.

With the twin disasters of Stalingrad and North Africa, Germany found it had lost the 10th, 15th, 14th, 16th, 21st, 22nd, 24th, and 27th Panzer Divisions. All of these divisions were rebuilt, with the exception of the 10th Panzer Division. In addition, the 15th Panzer Division was re-formed as a panzergrenadier division, not as a panzer division. On 24 March 1943 the divisional *Kradschützen Bataillon* (Motorcycle Reconnaissance Battalion) was redesignated as *Panzer Aufklarung Bataillon* (Reconnaissance Battalion).

As the war progressed the following panzer divisions and brigades were formed:

1st through 27th Panzer Divisions
116th Panzer Division
178th (Reserve) Panzer Division
179th (Reserve) Panzer Division
223rd (Reserve) Panzer Division
233rd Panzer Division
273rd (Reserve) Panzer Division
Clausewitz Panzer Division
1st Feldherrnhalle Panzer Division
2nd Feldherrnhalle Panzer Division
Grossdeutschland Panzer Ersatz Brigade
Holstein Panzer Division
Jüterbog Panzer Division
Müncheberg Panzer Division
Norwegen (Norway) Panzer Division
Schlesien (Silesian) Panzer Division
Tatra Panzer Division
Panzer Lehr Panzer Division
Führer Begleit (Escort) Panzer Division
Hermann Göring Panzer Division
101–113th Panzer Brigades
Norwegen (Norway) Panzer Brigade

Oberschliesen Panzer Brigade
West Schnelle Panzer Brigade
West Panzerjägd Panzer Brigade
Hermann Göring Parachute Panzer Recruit and Training Brigade
2nd Hermann Göring Parachute Panzer Recruit and Training Brigade

In addition, there were a number of miscellaneous recruit and training "verbände" of various sizes, some quite large.

The panzer troops underwent a continual stream of reorganizations, with Type 43 and Type 44 Panzer Divisions being developed. The reorganization of the divisions, however, was not a smooth process and generally occurred when the divisions were withdrawn from combat as a bloody shambles desperately needing rebuilding.

The Type 43 Panzer Division organization was ordered for all divisions on 24 September 1943, with the exception of the 21st Panzer Division and the Norway Panzer Division. In this reorganization the panzergrenadier battalions were reorganized with three rifle companies each. Each rifle company had four heavy and 18 light machine guns. The fourth company in each battalion was now a heavy support company (*Schwere Panzer Grenadier Kompanie*), equipped with four 80mm mortars, three anti-tank guns, and three machine guns. The 9th Company remained the infantry support gun company and was equipped with six self-propelled guns. The 10th Company was a light flak company with 12 20mm self-propelled guns. In 1944 this company was replaced by a pioneer company with 12 machine guns and 18 flamethrowers.

Only one of the panzergrenadier battalions of each division was equipped with half-tracks. This battalion had three rifle companies with four heavy machine guns, 39 light machine guns, two 80mm mortars, two 75mm guns and three 37mm guns. It had a fourth heavy company with 21 light machine guns, three 75mm PAK, two 75mm leIG and six 75mm field guns. At one point this last company had an engineer platoon with 13 light machine guns, one 37mm PAK 36, and six flamethrowers, but this company was quickly deleted from the organization. The 1/1st, 1/2nd, 1/3rd, 1/4th, 1/5th, 1/6th, 1/8th, 1/9th, 1/10th, 1/12th, 1/13th, 1/21st, 1/40th, 1/59th, 1/64th, 1/66th, 1/73rd, 1/103rd, 1/110th, 1/126th, and 1/46th Panzergrenadier Regiments were equipped with half-tracks.

During 1943–44 the 25th Panzer Division was rebuilt and the 18th Panzer Division was disbanded after the battles around Orel and Kiev, in southern Russia. On 1 March 1944 the Panzer Lehr Division was formed. In addition, three reserve panzer divisions were organized in 1944—155th, 273rd and 179th Reserve Panzer Divisions.

In 1944 the 101st through 113th Panzer Brigades were formed. These units were of regimental strength and represented the final step in the integration of the panzergrenadiers and panzer troops. They consisted of a panzergrenadier battalion in half-tracks and a panzer battalion. The brigade staff also generally had some platoon-sized reconnaissance elements. This same formation was also to occur in the Type 45 Panzer Divisions. Records show it also in the Feldherrnhalle and 13th Panzer Divisions.

During the summer of 1944 the German panzer forces had suffered huge losses. The 13th Panzer Division, which was totally obliterated in Russia, was rebuilt from scratch. The other divisions were rebuilt and reorganized. In addition, three all-panzer corps were formed by merging pairs of divisions and adding a number of corps troops. The Grossdeutschland Panzer Corps was formed from the Grossdeutschland and Brandenburg Panzergrenadier Divisions. The Feldherrnhalle Panzer Corps was formed with the 1st and 2nd Feldherrnhalle Panzer Divisions. The XXIV Panzer Corps was formed with the 16th and 17th Panzer Divisions.

The Type 45 Panzer Division was developed at this time and the difference between a Panzergrenadier Division and a Panzer Division vanished. However, because of the lack of vehicles and fuel, the level of mechanization of the panzergrenadier battalions fell dramatically. They became little more than foot infantry. The German Panzer Division was coming full cycle due to the collapse of the German war industry and the mounting allied victories.

Another aspect of the German panzer forces that is always fascinating to the reader is the equipment. There were a number of unusual armored vehicles produced during the war. It is not my intention to provide technical details on those vehicles, but some of the more fascinating vehicles were not part of the panzer divisions' equipment. These vehicles were the Panther Mk V, the Tiger (Mk VI), the King Tiger (Tiger II), the Porsche Ferdinand, and the Goliath. All but the panthers were usually assigned only to independent battalions.

The Panther tank began its appearance in late 1943. Each panzer division would eventually be equipped with only one battalion of Panther tanks. The dates and the numbers of tanks assigned per company were as follows:

Battalions	Division	Date if Known	Number per Company
1/Grossdeutschland	Grossdeutschland	8 Feb. 1944	17 tanks
1/1st	1st Panzer Div	9 Nov. 1943*	19 tanks
1/3rd	2nd Panzer Div	4 Oct. 1943*	17 tanks
1/3rd	2nd Panzer Div	mid-April 1944	22 tanks
1/6th	3rd Panzer Div	13 Dec. 1943*	19 tanks
2/35th	4th Panzer Div	15 Jan. 1944	17 tanks
1/31st	5th Panzer Div	25 Sept. 1943*	17 tanks
		14 Nov. 1943*	14 tanks
1/11th	6th Panzer Div	15 Jan. 1944	22 tanks
1/25th	7th Panzer Div	30 Jan. 1944	17 tanks
2/33rd	9th Panzer Div		22 tanks
1/29th	12th Panzer Div	30 Dec. 1943	22 tanks
1/4th	13th Panzer Div	23 Dec. 1943	18 tanks
1/36th	14th Panzer Div	25 June 1944	unknown
1/2nd	16th Panzer Div	12 Sept. 1943*	17 tanks
		8 Dec. 1943*	18 tanks
1/27th	19th Panzer Div	30 Mar. 1944	17 tanks
2/23rd	23rd Panzer Div	28 Dec. 1943	17 tanks
1/24th	24th Panzer Div	30 May 1944	unknown
1/26th	26th Panzer Div	25 Nov. 1943	19 tanks
Lehr Regiment	Panzer Lehr Div	3 Jan. 1944	unknown
SS Wiking	Wiking SS Panzer Div	18 Dec. 1943*	19 tanks

* Date that production was dispatched from the factory to the division. Numbers of tanks per company were determined by dividing total number of tanks shipped by four companies.

The combat debut of the Porsche Ferdinands was at the battle of Kursk, where nearly all of them were destroyed. Of the ninety built, sixty-eight Ferdinands were assigned to the 656th Jagdpanzer Regiment, which was formed with the 653rd and 654th Panzer Jagdpanzer Battalions. Each battalion had three companies of 14 Ferdinands, a maintenance company, and a staff and staff battery that had

three more Ferdinands and three self-propelled quad 20mm flak guns. The 653rd Panzerjäger Battalion later served in Italy with the 1st Company being disbanded in September 1944 and the 2nd Company redesignated as the 614th Panzerjäger Company.

The Tiger tanks (Mk VI) were assigned to independent battalions and to some divisions. Their incorporation into the divisions is discussed in the following text, but the independent battalions, which were numbered 501st through 510th Panzer Battalions, are not. In addition, the 3/Grossdeutschland Panzer Regiment was equipped with Tigers and it is possible that the 104th Panzer Battalion was also equipped with Tigers.

The first King Tigers were assigned to the 503rd Panzer Battalion, which arrived on the battlefield in France on 17 June 1944. As a result of heavy fighting, by early August it had already lost all its tanks. The next instance of King Tigers in combat comes during the British assault on Arnhem, when the 506th Panzer Unit was encountered. The first King Tiger rolled off the production lines in March 1944 and by 1 March 1945 a total of 489 had apparently been built.

The Goliaths were unusual vehicles. They were basically tracked bombs that moved up to a fortified position and were detonated. They were assigned to the 301st, 302nd, and 303rd Panzer Battalions and 311th through 317th Panzer Companies.

Note: In the following text, the dates given for changes are generally the dates that the change was ordered and do not necessarily reflect the date that the change was implemented, if it was implemented at all.

Tactical Organization
of the Panzer Companies

The internal organization of the panzer regiment underwent almost constant change as the war progressed. The organization of a Panzer regiment on 1 October 1938 was theoretically:

Regimental Staff
    Panzer Command Troop (2 PzBefWg and 1 PzMk III tank)
    Panzer Signals Platoon (5 PzMk II tanks)
  2 Battalions, each with:
    Panzer Battalion Staff Company
    Panzer Signals Platoon (2 PzBefWg and 1 PzMk III tank)
    Panzer Signals Platoon (5 Mk II tanks)
    Command Squadron (1 PzMk IV, 3 PzMk III and 2 PzMk II tanks)
  3 Light Panzer Companies, each with:
    Command Troop (2 PzMk III tanks)
    Light Platoon (5 PzMk II tanks)

    1st–3rd Platoons (5 PzMk III tanks ea)

The medium panzer companies were to contain:
    Command Troop (2 PzMk III tanks)
    Light Platoon (5 PzMk II tanks)
    1st–3rd Platoons (5 PzMk IV tanks ea)

In addition an "ersatz" company was organized as follows:
    1st Platoon (1 PzMk I PzBefWg and 5 PzMk I tanks)
    2nd Platoon (3 PzMk II tanks)
    3rd Platoon (3 PzMk III tanks)
    4th Platoon (3 PzMk IV tanks)

However, despite this "theoretical" organization the practical world of inventories of vehicles prevented these structures from being organized. The numbers and types of tanks varied from division to division and are discussed on that basis. The actual inventories of tanks held by the Germans up to the date of the invasion of Poland were as follows:

Panzer Inventories 1935–39

	Tanks						Command	Command
	PzMk I	PzMk II	PzMk III	PzMk IV	35t	38t	Light	Heavy
1 Aug. 1935	318							
1 Jan. 1936	720							
1 June 1936	1065							
1 Oct. 1936	1212	5					40	
1 May 1937	1411	115					72	
1 Oct. 1937	1468	238	12				163	
1 Jan. 1938	1469	314	23	3			180	
1 Apr. 1938	1468	443	43	30			180	
1 July 1938	1468	626	56	46			180	
1 Oct. 1938	1468	823	59	76			180	2
1 Mar. 1939	1446	1094	60	137			180	30
1 Sept. 1939	1445	1223	98	211	202	78	180	35
1 September 1939								
with field army	1026	1151	87	197	164	57	177 total command tanks	
with reserves	260	67	11	11	34	5	20 total command tanks	

On 1 March 1939 the organization of a panzer regiment was once again reorganized, most likely reflecting the reality of equipment.

Regimental Staff
Panzer Command Troop (2 PzBefWg Command tanks and 1 PzMk III tank)
Panzer Signals Platoon (5 PzMk II tanks)
2 Battalions, each with
Panzer Battalion Staff Company
Panzer Signals Platoon (2 PzBefWg and 1 PzMk III tank)
Panzer Signals Platoon (5 PzMk II tanks)
Command Squadron (1 PzMk IV, 3 PzMk III and 2 PzMk II tanks)
3 Light Panzer Companies, each with
Command Troop (1 PzBefWg, 1 PzMk II and 2 PzMk I tanks)
1st–3rd Platoons (2 PzMk I and 3 PzMk II tanks ea)
4th Platoon (5 PzMk II tanks)

In addition, there was a "Light Panzer Company a" which contained:

Command Troop (1 PzBefWg, 7 PzMk I and 3 PzMk III tanks)
1st Platoon (3 PzMk III tanks)
2nd Platoon (3 PzMk IV tanks)
3rd Platoon (3 PzMk IV tanks)

A new "special" organization was issued on 1 September 1939, though it had been drafted in July, which authorized the 1st, 2nd, and 11th Panzer Regiments and the 65th Panzer Battalion to be equipped with Czech tanks.

On 1 September 1939 a new series of organizations was issued for the formations equipped with German tanks that were as follows:

Signals Platoon, for a Panzer Regimental Staff
3 PzMk III PzBefWg
Light Panzer Platoon, for a Panzer Regimental Staff
5 PzMk II tanks
Staff Company, for a Panzer Battalion
Signals Platoon (2 PzMk III PzBefWg and 1 PzMk III tank)
1st Platoon (5 PzMk II tanks)
Staff Squadron, of a Panzer Battalion
(1 PzMk IV, 3 PzMk III and 2 PzMk II tanks)
Light Panzer Company
Command Troop (2 PzMk III tanks)
Light Platoon (5 PzMk II tanks)
1st–3rd Platoons (5 PzMk III tanks ea)
Medium Panzer Company
Command Troop (2 PzMk IV tanks)
Light Platoon (5 PzMk II tanks)
1st–3rd Platoons (5 PzMk IV tanks ea)
Light Panzer Ersatz (replacement) Company
1st Platoon (1 PzBefWg and 5 PzMk I tanks)
2nd Platoon (3 PzMk II tanks)
3rd Platoon (3 PzMk III tanks)
4th Platoon (3 PzMk IV tanks)

The next organizational change occurred on 21 February 1940. At that time the theoretical organizations changed to:

Light Panzer Company
Command Troop (1 PzMk III, 2 PzMk II and 1 PzBefWg tank)
1st–2nd Platoons (3 PzMk II and 2 PzMk I tanks)
3rd–4th Platoons (3 PzMk III tanks ea)
Medium Panzer Company
Command Troop (1 PzMk IV, 1 PzMk I and 1 PzBefWg tank)
Light Platoon (5 PzMk II tanks)
1st Platoon (4 PzMk IV tanks)
2nd Platoon (3 PzMk IV tanks)

In 1939 the organization of a German Panzer Division was typically as follows:

1 Panzer Brigade
2 Panzer Regiments, each with:
2 Panzer Battalions, each with:
2 Light Panzer Companies
1 Mixed Panzer Company
Light Armored Column
1 Armored Repair Shop Company
Schützen Brigade, (4th and 5th Pz had no schützen brigade staff)
1 (mot) Schützen Regiment, with
2 Battalions, each with:
2 Schützen Companies (Infantry companies) (9 LMGs, 2 HMGs, 3 50mm Mortars ea)
1 Motorcycle Company, with (9 LMGs, 2 HMGs, 3 50mm Mortars)
1 Machine Gun Company (8 HMGs, 6 80mm Mortars)
1 (mot) Infantry Column
1 Motorcycle Battalion, with
3 Motorcycle Companies (9 LMGs, 2 HMGs, 3 50mm Mortars ea)
1 Motorcycle Machine Gun Company (8 HMGs and 6 80mm Mortars)
1 Heavy Company
1 (mot) Anti-Tank Platoon (3 37mm PAK 36)
1 (mot) Infantry Gun Platoon (2 75mm leIG)
1 (mot) Pioneer Platoon
1 (mot) Reconnaissance Battalion, with
2 Armored Car Squadrons

1 Motorcycle Squadron, with
(9 LMGs, 2 HMGs and 3 50mm Mortars)
1 Heavy Motorcycle Squadron (8 HMGs and 6 80mm
Mortars)
1 (mot) Supply Column

1 Anti-Tank Battalion (4th and 5th Pz Div had 2
Panzerjäger Bns)
3 (mot) Anti-Tank Companies (12 37mm PAK 36 ea)
1 (mot) Heavy Machine Gun Company (not in 2nd and
5th Pz Divs)
(12 20mm Flak guns)

1 (mot) Artillery Regiment
1 (mot) Heavy Artillery Battalion, with
2 (mot) Batteries (4 150mm sFH ea)
1 (mot) Battery (4 100mm guns)
1 (mot) Light Artillery Battalion, with
3 (mot) Batteries (4 105mm leFH 18 ea)
(In 2nd Pz Div 1 light and 1 heavy Artillery Bn, Heavy
having 150mm howitzers)

1 (mot) Pioneer Battalion, with
3 (mot) Light Pioneer Companies (9 LMGs ea)
1 (mot) Bridge Column K or B
1 (mot) Light Pioneer Column
(4th Pz had 1 Pioneer Co, 1 Bridge Column, 1 (mot)
Pioneer Column—5th Pz like 4th Pz, but with 2 Pioneer cos.)

1 (mot) Signals Battalion, with
1 (mot) Radio Company
1 (mot) Signals Company
1 Light Signals Column

Medical Service
2 (mot) Medical Companies
3 Ambulance Platoons

Supply Services
6 Light Small Motor Transport Columns
3 Large Motor Transport Columns for Fuel
2 (mot) Repair Shops
1 (mot) Supply Company

Administrative Services
1 (mot) Bakery Company
1 (mot) Butcher Platoon
1 (mot) Rations Office

Other
1 (mot) Military Police Detachment
1 (mot) Field Post Office

After the successful invasion of France the German army
went into a period of reorganization and even some de-
mobilization of units. The panzer units had shown their
value in an overwhelming manner. Now that the German
tank industry had a pause in the action it was able to begin
the serious replacement of the inferior and obsolete tanks
in the field units. A new series of organizations were, as a
result, issued. On 16 July 1940 the Light Panzer Companies were given a new organization:

Light Panzer Company
Command Troop (2 PzMk III and 4 PzMk II tanks)
1st–2nd Platoons (5 PzMk III tanks ea)
3rd Platoon (4 PzMk IV tanks)

On 1 February 1941 every armored element of the panzer regiments changed. They now consisted of:

Panzer Regimental Staff
Signals Platoon (2 PzMk III PzBefWg and 1 PzMk III
tank)
Light Panzer Platoon (5 PzMk II tanks)

Panzer Battalion Staff
Signals Platoon (2 PzMk III PzBefWg and 1 PzMk III
tank)
Light Panzer Platoon (5 PzMk II tanks)
Command Squadron (1 PzMk IV, 3 PzMk III and 2
PzMk II tanks)

Light Panzer Company
Command Troop (2 PzMk III tanks)
Light Platoon (5 PzMk II tanks)
1st–3rd Platoons (5 PzMk III tanks ea)

Medium Tank Company
Command Troop (2 PzMk IV tanks)
Light Platoon (5 PzMk II tanks)
1st–3rd Platoons (4 PzMk IV tanks ea)

The organization of the panzer divisions changed again
after France and from 10 February through 15 May 1941
they were generally organized as follows:

1st Panzer Division
1st Panzer Regiment
1 Armored Signals Platoon
1 Light Armored Platoon
1 Regimental Band
1 (mot) tank Maintenance Company
2 Armored Battalions, each with
1 Staff Company (2 PzBefWg III and 5 PzMk II)
1 Medium Armored Company (14 PzMk IV and 5
PzMk II)
2 Light Armored Companies (17 PzMk III and 5
PzMk II ea)
1 tank Maintenance Company
1 Light (mot) Armored Supply Column
1st Schützen Brigade
1st and 113th Schützen Regiments, each with:
1 (mot) Staff Company, with
1 (mot) Signals Platoon
1 (mot) Engineer Platoon (3 LMGs)
1 Motorcycle Platoon
1 Regimental Band
2 (mot) Battalions, each with
3 Infantry Companies (18 LMGs, 2 HMGs, 3
50mm mortars ea)

1 Machine Gun Company (6 80mm mortars and 8 HMGs)

1 Heavy Company, with:

    1 Infantry Gun Section (2 75mm leIG)

    1 Engineer Platoon (3 LMGs)

    1 Panzerjäger Platoon (3 37mm PAK 36 and 1 LMG)

1 (mot) Infantry Gun Company (2 150mm sIG and 4 75mm leIG)

702nd Heavy Self-Propelled Gun Battery

(6 150mm guns in Mk I tank Chassis)

1st Motorcycle Battalion, with

    3 Motorcycle Companies (3 50mm mortars, 2 HMGs and 18 LMGs ea)

    1 Motorcycle Machine Gun Company (12 HMGs and 6 80mm mortars)

    1 (mot) Support Company, with:

        1 Infantry Support Gun Section (2 75mm leIG)

        1 Engineer Platoon (3 LMGs)

        1 Panzerjäger Platoon (3 37mm PAK 36 and 1 LMG)

73rd Artillery Regiment

    1 (mot) Signals Platoon

    1 (mot) Weather Section

    1 Regimental Band

    2 (mot) Battalions, each with:

        1 (mot) Signals Platoon

        1 (mot) Artillery Survey Detachment

        3 (mot) Batteries (4 105mm leFH 18 howitzers and 2 LMGs ea)

    1 (mot) Battalion, with

        1 (mot) Signals Platoon

        1 (mot) Survey Detachment

        3 (mot) Batteries (4 150mm sFH 18 howitzers and 2 LMGs ea)

    330th (mot) Observation Battery

4th Reconnaissance Battalion

    1 (mot) Signals Platoon (2 LMGs)

    1 Light Armored Car Company (10 20mm KwK and 25 LMGs)

    1 (mot) Heavy Company, with:

        1 Infantry Gun Section (2 75mm leIG)

        1 Engineer Platoon (3 LMGs)

        1 Panzerjäger Platoon (3 37mm PAK 36 and 1 LMG)

    1 Small (mot) AA Supply Column (3 LMGs)

37th Panzerjäger Battalion

    1 (mot) Signals Platoon

    3 (mot) Panzerjäger Companies (9 37mm PAK 36, 2 50mm PAK 38 and 6 LMGs ea)

    2/59th (self-propelled) Flak Battalion (2 quad 20mm and 8 37mm AA guns)

37th Panzer Pioneer Battalion

    3 (mot) Pioneer Companies (9 LMGs ea)

    1 (mot) "B" Bridging Train

1 (mot) "K" Bridging Train (added later)

1 Small (mot) Engineering Supply Column

37th Signals Battalion

    1 (mot) Radio Company

    1 (mot) Telephone Company

    1 Small (mot) Signals Supply Column

81st Feldersatz Battalion

    3 Rifle Companies

81st Supply Train

    1–7th/81st Small (mot) Supply Columns

    11/, 12th/81st Small (mot) Supply Columns (added later)

    8/, 9/, 10th/81st Large (mot) POL Supply Columns

    13/, 14/81st Large (mot) Supply Columns (added later)

    1/, 2/, 3/81st (mot) Maintenance Companies

    81st (mot) Supply Company

81st Medical

    1/, 2/, 3/81st Ambulance Columns

    1/, 2/81st (mot) Field Hospitals

Other

    81st (mot) Military Police Detachment

    81st (mot) Field Post Office

Between 16 May 1941 and 15 October 1942 the typical panzer division was organized as follows:

Panzer Division

    Division Headquarters (2 LMGs)

    1 (mot) Mapping Section

1 Armored Regiment

    Regimental Headquarters

        Signals Section

        Armored Reconnaissance Section

        Regimental Band

    1 Armored Maintenance Company

1 to 3 Armored Battalions, each with

    1 Armored Staff Company

    1 Medium Armored Company

    2–3 Light Armored Companies

1 Panzergrenadier Brigade, with

    2 Panzergrenadier Regiments, each with

    HQ Company with

        1 Signals Platoon

        1 Panzerjäger Platoon (3 50mm PAK 38 and 3 LMGs)

        1 Motorcycle Section (6 LMGs)

        1 Regimental Band

    2 (mot) Infantry Battalions, each with

        3 (mot) Infantry Companies (18 LMGs, 4 HMGs, 2 80mm mortars and 3 PzBu39 ea)

        1 (mot) Heavy Infantry Company, with

        1 Engineer Platoon (4 LMGs)

        1 Panzerjäger Platoon (3 50mm PAK 38, 6 LMGs, 3 28mm sPzB 41)

        2 Infantry Gun Sections (2 75mm leIG ea)

2 (mot) Heavy Infantry Gun Sections (2 150mm sIG each)

Self-Propelled Heavy Infantry Gun Section
(6 SdKfz138/1 150mm sIG 33/1 and 3 LMGs)

Panzerjäger Battalion
HQ Section (2 LMGs)
1 SP Panzerjäger Company (Marder) (6 75mm and 6 LMGs)
1 (mot) Panzerjäger Company (6 50mm PAK 38, 4 37mm PAK 36 and 6 LMGs)
1 Self-Propelled Flak Battery (12 20mm AA and 4 LMGs)

Motorcycle Battalion
1 Heavy Armored Car Company (18 37mm and 24 LMGs)
3 Motorcycle Companies (2 80mm mortars, 4 HMGs, 18 LMGs and 3 PzBu39 ea)
1 (mot) Heavy Company, with:
1 Engineer Platoon (4 LMGs)
1 Panzerjäger Platoon (3 50mm PAK 38 and 3 LMGs)
1 Panzerjäger Platoon (3 28mm sPzB 41 and 3 LMGs)
1 Infantry Gun Section (2 75mm leIG)

Artillery Regiment
1 (mot) Regimental Staff (2 LMGs)
1 (mot) Observation Battery
2 (mot) Artillery Battalions, each with
1 (mot) Battalion Staffs (2 LMGs)
Light Munition Supply Column
3 Batteries, each with (3 105mm leFH 18 and 2 LMGs ea)
1 (mot) Artillery Battalion, with
1 (mot) Artillery Battalion HQ (2 LMGs)
2 Batteries, each with (3 150mm sFH 18 and 2 LMGs ea)
1 Battery, with (3 100mm K18 guns and 2 LMGs)

Armored Signals Battalion
1 Armored Radio Company (6 LMGs)
1 Armored Telephone Company (6 LMGs)
1 Light (mot) Signals Supply Column

Panzer Pioneer Battalion
1 Armored Pioneer Company (23 LMGs and 3 PzBu39)
2 (mot) Pioneer Companies (18 LMGs and 3 PzBu39 ea)
1 (mot) "K" Bridging Train (2 LMGs)
1 Light (mot) Engineering Supply Column (2 LMGs)

Administrative Service
1 (mot) Divisional Quartermaster Platoon
1 (mot) Butcher Company
1 (mot) Bakery Company

Supply Train
12 Light (mot) Supply Columns (2 LMGs ea)

3 Light POL Supply Columns (2 LMGs ea)
1 Light (mot) Supply Company (2 LMGs)
3 (mot) Maintenance Companies
Medical
3 (mot) Medical Companies (2 LMGs ea)
3 Ambulance Columns
Other
1 (mot) Military Police Platoon (2 LMGs)
1 (mot) Field Post Office

The quantities of equipment and the lessons learned during the beginning of the invasion of Russia brought about yet another reorganization of the regimental and battalion staffs and the companies on 1 November 1943.

Panzer Regimental Staff and Staff Company
Signals Platoon (2 Mk III PzBefWg and 1 Mk III tank)
Panzer Battalion Staff Company
Signals Platoon (2 Mk III PzBefWg and 1 Mk III tank)
1st Platoon (5 Mk II tanks)
Pioneer Platoon (3 Mk II tanks)
Panzer Battalion Staff
(1 Mk IV , 3 Mk III and 2 Mk II tanks)
Light Panzer Company
Command Troop (3 Mk III tanks)
Light Platoon (5 Mk II tanks)
1st–3rd Platoons (5 Mk III tanks ea)
Medium Panzer Company
Command Troop (2 Mk IV tanks)
Light Platoon (5 Mk II tanks)
1st–3rd Platoons (4 Mk IV tanks ea)

On 1/25/43 yet another change in the authorized organization of the panzer units was issued. The new organizations were:

Panzer Battalion Staff Company
Signals Platoon (2 Mk IV PzBefWg and 1 Mk III tank)
Reconnaissance Platoon (5 Mk IV tanks)
Flame Panzer Platoon (7 Mk III Flame Panzers)
Medium Panzer Company a
Troop Command (2 Mk IV tanks)
1st–4th Platoon (5 Mk IV tanks ea)

On 24 September 1943 an entirely new organization was issued for the panzer divisions. This new structure was known as the Panzer Division 43. This new organization applied to all the panzer divisions except the Grossdeutschland, Norwegen and 21st Panzer Divisions. When the panther battalions were formed and returned to their divisions they were to organize a regimental staff, if the regiment did not already have one. The tank companies were authorized 17 tanks. Only the 21st Panzer Division would remain with three panzer battalions. The Type 43 division had: *(see over)*

ORGANIZATION OF A TYPE 43 PANZER DIVISION, 24 SEPTEMBER 1943

Division Headquarters
1 Division Staff
1 (mot) Mapping Detachment

Panzer Battalion
1 Regimental Staff and Staff Company
3 Panzer Companies (14 tanks ea)
1 Panzer Maintenance Company

2 Panzergrenadier Divisions, each with
1 Regimental Staff
1 (mot) Regimental Staff Company
  1 Motorcycle Platoon (3 LMGs)
  1 Panzerjäger Platoon (3 75mm PAK 40)
  1 Signals Platoon
3 Panzergrenadier Battalions, each with:
  3 Rifle Companies (4 HMGs, 18 LMGs and 2 80mm mortars ea)
  1 Heavy Company
    1 Panzerjäger Platoon (3 75mm PAK 40, 3 LMGs)
    1 mortar Platoon (2 LMGs and 4 120mm mortars)
1 (mot) Infantry Gun Company (2 150mm sIG and 6 75mm leIG)
1 Self-Propelled Flak Company (12 20mm and 4 LMG)
1 (mot) Pioneer Company (12 LMGs and 18 flamethrowers)

1 Panzerjäger Company
1 Self-Propelled Staff Company (6 LMGs)
  1 Self-Propelled Panzerjäger Platoon (3 75mm PAK 40)
2 Self-Propelled Panzerjäger Companies (14 75mm PAK 40 and 14 LMGs ea)
1 Self-Propelled Flak Company (12 20mm and 12 LMGs)

1 Panzer Reconnaissance Company
3 Motorcycle Companies (2 80mm mortars, 18 LMGs ea)
1 Armored Car Company (24 LMGs and 18 20mm)
1 (mot) Heavy Company
  1 Pioneer Platoon (4 LMGs and 6 flamethrowers)
  1 Panzerjäger Platoon (3 LMGs and 3 75mm PAK 40)
  1 Infantry Gun Platoon (2 75mm leIG)
1 (mot) Light Supply Column

1 Flak Battalion
1 (mot) Light Flak Battery (12 20mm and 4 LMGs) plus a Searchlight Squadron
2 (mot) Heavy Flak Batteries (4 88mm, 3 20mm and 2 LMGs ea)
1 (mot) Light Flak Supply Column

1 Panzer Artillery Regiment
1 Regimental Staff and Staff Battery (2 LMGs)
2 (mot) Medium Artillery Battalions
  1 Battalion Staff and Staff Battery (2 LMGs)
  3 (mot) Batteries (4 105mm leFH and 2 LMGs ea)
1 (mot) Heavy Artillery Battalion
  1 Battalion Staff and Staff Battery (2 LMGs)
  3 (mot) Batteries (4 150mm sFH and 2 LMGs ea)

1 Ersatz Battalion
4 Companies

1 (mot) Pioneer Battalion
1 (mot) Battalion Staff
3 (mot) Pioneer Companies (2 HMGs, 18 LMGs, 2 80mm mortars and 6 flamethrowers ea)
1 (mot) Pioneer Supply Column

1 (mot) Signals Battalion
1 (mot) Telephone Company (6 LMGs)
1 (mot) Radio Company (4 LMGs)
1 (mot) Light Supply Column (2 LMGs)

Supply Troops
2 (mot) 120 ton Transportation Companies (6 LMGs ea)
3 (mot) 90 ton Transportation Companies (6 LMGs ea)
1 (mot) Supply Company (8 LMGs)
2 (mot) Maintenance Companies (4 LMGs ea)
1 (mot) Heavy Supply Column (4 LMGs)

Other
2 (mot) Medical Companies (4 LMGs ea)
3 Ambulance Companies (1 LMG)
1 (mot) Field Bakery (6 LMGs)
1 (mot) Butcher Company (4 LMGs)
1 (mot) Division Administration (2 LMGs)
1 (mot) Military Police Troop (2 LMGs)
1 (mot) Field Post Office (1 LMG)

With the introduction of Panther tanks into the field divisions, a new organization was issued. The formations equipped with MkV Panther tanks were issued on 10 January 1943.

Staff and Staff Company, Panzer Battalion "Panther"
Signals Platoon (3 Mk V PzBefWg)
Reconnaissance Platoon (5 Mk V tanks)

Medium Panzer Company "Panther"
Command Troop (2 Mk V tanks)
1st–4th Platoons (5 Mk V tanks ea)

The formations equipped with Mk IV tanks were issued on 1 November 1943.

Staff and Staff Company, Panzer Regiment
Signals Platoon
  3 Sd Kfz 171 Panther tanks 75mm L 70 PzBefWg
Reconnaissance Platoon
  4 Sd Kfz 171 Panther tanks 75mm 42 L70
Reconnaissance and Pioneer Platoon
Flak Platoon
  3 Sd Kfz 7/1 with quad 20mm Flak gun

Staff and Staff Company, Panzer Battalion
Signals Platoon

3 Mk III Panzer tanks (Sd Kfz 141 – 50mm L 42)
Reconnaissance Platoon
  5 Mk IV Panzer tanks (Sd Kfz 161/1 – 75mm 40 L 43)
Reconnaissance and Pioneer Platoon
  3 Sd Kfz 251/7 pioneer half-track
Flak Platoon
  1 Sd Kfz 7/1 with quad 20mm Flak gun
Medium Panzer Company
Command Troop (2 Mk IV tanks)
1st–4th Platoons (5 Mk IV tanks ea)

When the Panther tanks were incorporated into full armored regiments, new organizations were formulated and released on 1 November 1943.

Staff and Staff Company, Panzer Regiment "Panther"
Signals Platoon
  3 Sd Kfz 171 Panther tanks 75mm L 70 PzBefWg

Reconnaissance Platoon
  4 Sd Kfz 171 Panther tanks 75mm 42 L70
Reconnaissance and Pioneer Platoon
Flak Platoon
  3 Sd Kfz 7/1 with quad 20mm Flak gun
Staff and Staff Company, Panzer Battalion "Panther"
Signals Platoon (3 Mk V PzBefWg)
Reconnaissance Platoon (5 Mk V tanks)
Medium Panzer Company "Panther"
Command Troop (2 Mk V tanks)
1st–4th Platoons (5 Mk V tanks)

On 1 August 1944 the Panzer Divisions underwent a massive reorganization. Not only were new organizations issued for the armored regiments, battalions, and companies, but an entirely new divisional organization, known as the Type 44 Panzer Division, was issued. The Type 44 Panzer Division was organized as follows:

ORGANIZATION OF A TYPE 44 PANZER DIVISION, 1 AUGUST 1944

Division Headquarters (23/10/51/76)[1]
  1 Divisional Staff (2 LMGs)
  1 (mot) Panzer Division Escort Company (3/0/32/153)
    1 Heavy Platoon (4 HMGs and 6 LMGs)
    1 Self-Propelled Flak Platoon (4 SP 20mm guns)
    1 Motorcycle Platoon (6 LMGs)
  1 (mot) Mapping Detachment (0/0/1/7)
  1 (mot) Feldgendarme Troop (3/0/41/20)
1 Armored Regiment (59/7/750/1,190)
  1 Regimental Staff and Staff Company (8/0/63/105; 5 Pz Mk IV with 75mm KwK 40 and 3 PzBefWg V with 75mm KwK 42)
    1 Flak Platoon
      4 Groups (2 37mm Flak 43 on Mk IV Chassis ea)
1st Battalion
  1 Armored Battalion Staff (fG) (4/0/3/7)
  1 Armored Battalion Staff Company (fG) (3/0/38/104; 5 Pz Mk V and 3 PzBefWg V with 75mm KwK 40 or 42, 5 Sd Kfz 251 and 3 quad 20mm self-propelled guns)
  4 Armored Companies (fG) (3/0/57/43ea; 17 or 22 Panther MkV tanks with 75mm KwK 40 or 42 guns ea)
  1 Armored Maintenance Company (3/3/39/185; 4 LMGs)
  1 Armored Supply Company, Panzer Bn Panther (fG) (5/2/59/211)
2nd Battalion
  1 Armored Battalion Staff (fG)

  1 Armored Battalion Staff Company (fG) (5 Pz Mk IV and 3 PzBefWg IV with 75mm guns, 5 Sd Kfz 251 and 3 quad 20mm self-propelled guns)
  4 Armored Companies (fG) (17 or 22 Mk IV tanks ea)
  1 Armored Maintenance Company
  1 Armored Supply Company, Panzer Bn Pz IV (fG) (5/2/51/123)
  1 Armored Maintenance Company (Pz Mk IV)
1 (armored) Panzergrenadier Regiment (56/7/428/1,796)
  1 Panzergrenadier Regimental Staff and Staff Company (8/1/29/111; 9 Sd Kfz 251 and 6 LMGs)
    1 Signals Platoon
    1 Motorcycle Platoon (6 LMGs)
1st Panzergrenadier Battalion
  1 (half-track) Panzergrenadier Battalion Staff (5/0/11/27; 6 Sd Kfz 251 and 6 LMGs)
  3 (half-track) Panzergrenadier Companies (3/0/36/151ea; 23 Sd Kfz 251, 3 HMGs, 30 LMGs, 2 80mm mortars, 2 75mm KwK 37 and 7 20mm Flak guns ea)
  1 (half-track) Heavy Company (3/0/23/72; 17 Sd Kfz 251, 11 LMGs)
    1 Infantry Gun Platoon (6 75mm KwK 37 guns)
    1 Mortar Platoon (2 LMGs and 4 120mm mortars)
  1 (half-track) Panzergrenadier Supply Company (4/3/37/119; 5 LMGs)

---

[1] Numbers are officers, warrant officers, NCOs, and men.

2nd Panzergrenadier Battalion

1 (mot) Panzergrenadier Battalion Staff (3/0/29/165; 5 LMGs)

3 (mot) Panzergrenadier Companies (3/0/29/165 ea; 4 HMGs, 18 LMGs, 2 80mm mortars ea)

1 (mot) Heavy Company (3/0/22/79)
    1 Engineer Platoon (deleted) (13 LMGs, 1 37mm PAK 36 and 6 flamethrowers)
1 Heavy Panzerjäger Platoon (3 75mm PAK and 9 LMGs)
    1 Infantry Gun Platoon (2 75mm leIG and 4 LMGs)
    1 Gun Battery (6 75mm Stuk 37 in Sd Kfz 251/9 and 8 LMGs)

1 Self-Propelled Heavy Infantry Gun Company (3/0/31/108; 6 Sd Kfz138/1 150mm sIG 33/1 and 7 LMGs)

1 (mot) Pioneer Company (14 Sd Kfz 251; strength unknown)
    1 Pioneer Company Staff (1 LMG)
    1 (half-track) Platoon (6 flamethrowers and 6 LMGs)
    1 (mot) Mortar Platoon (2 HMGs and 2 80mm mortars)
    1 (mot) Engineer Platoon (8 LMGs and 12 flamethrowers)
    1 (half-track) Engineer Platoon (12 LMGs, 1 20mm gun and 6 flamethrowers)

1 (mot) Panzergrenadier Regiment (54/6/383/1,776)
    1 Panzergrenadier Regimental Staff and Staff Company
        1 Signals Platoon
        1 Motorcycle Platoon (6 LMGs)

2 (mot) Panzergrenadier Battalions, each with
    1 (mot) Panzergrenadier Battalion Staff
    3 (mot) Panzergrenadier Companies (4 HMGs, 18 LMGs, 2 80mm mortars ea)
    1 (mot) Heavy Company
        1 (mot) Heavy Company Staff
        1 Flak Platoon (6 20mm Flak guns motZ)
        1 Mortar Platoon (2 LMGs and 4 120mm mortars motZ)
    1 (mot) Panzergrenadier Supply Company (5 LMGs)

1 Self-Propelled Heavy Infantry Gun Company (6 Sd Kfz138/1 150mm sIG 33/1 and 7 LMGs)

1 (mot) Pioneer Company (3/0/34/180)
    1 Pioneer Company Staff (1 LMG)
    1 (half-track) Platoon (6 flamethrowers and 6 LMGs)
    1 (mot) Mortar Platoon (2 HMGs and 2 80mm mortars)
    1 (mot) Engineer Platoon (8 LMGs and 12 flamethrowers)
    1 (half-track) Engineer Platoon (12 LMGs, 1 20mm gun and 6 flamethrowers)

1 (self-propelled) Panzerjäger Battalion (17/3/145/310)
    1 (self-propelled) Battalion Staff and Staff Company (fG) (6 LMGs)

    1 Panzerjäger Platoon (3 PzJg IV with 75mm PAK 39)
    1 (motZ) Panzerjäger Company (fG) (12 75mm PAK 40 and 12 LMGs)
    2 Self-Propelled Anti-Tank Companies (fG) (14 PzJg IV – 75mm PAK 39 ea)
    1 (mot) Mixed Panzerjäger Supply Company (fG) (3 LMGs)

Armored Reconnaissance Battalion (Variant 1)

Staff and Staff Company (10 Sd Kfz 251, 16 Armored Cars, 26 LMG, 13 20mm KwK, 3 75mm KwK 37)

1st Armored (Luchs) Reconnaissance Company (16 Luchs light tanks and 25 LMGs)

2nd Armored (Half-Track) Reconnaissance Company (2 75mm, 2 80mm mortars and 44 LMGs)

3rd Armored (Half-Track) Reconnaissance Company (2 75mm, 7 20mm, 2 80mm mortars, 3 HMGs and 30 LMGs)

4th Armored (Half-Track) Reconnaissance Company
    1 Staff (1 LMG)
    1 Half-Track Infantry Gun Platoon (6 75mm, 2 LMGs)
    1 Mortar Platoon (6 80mm mortars and 2 LMGs)
    1 Engineer Platoon (13 LMGs)

1 (mot) Armored Reconnaissance Supply Company (4 LMGs)

Armored Reconnaissance Battalion (Variant 2) (24/3/222/696)

Staff and Staff Company (7/0/39/92; 10 Sd Kfz 251, 16 Armored Cars, 26 LMG, 13 20mm KwK, 3 75mm KwK 37)

1 Armored Car Company (3/0/29/53; 25 Sd Kfz 250 mounting 25 LMGs and 16 20mm KwK)

1 Light Armored Reconnaissance Company (3/0/39/125; 30 Sd Kfz 250 mounting 26 LMGs, and 2 75mm KwK 37; plus 2 HMGs)

1 Panzergrenadier Company (3/0/36/151; 23 Sd Kfz 251 mounting 12 HMGs, 7 20mm and 2 75mm KwK 37, plus 18 LMGs, 3 HMGs and 2 80mm mortars)

1 Armored Heavy Company
    Heavy Gun Platoon (6 Sd Kfz 251/9 with 6 75mm KwK 37)
    Mortar Platoon (6 Sd Kfz 251/2 with 6 80mm mortars)
    Pioneer Platoon (13 Sd Kfz 251 with 13 LMGs)

1 (mot) Supply Company (4 LMGs)

Panzer Artillery Regiment

1 Panzer Artillery Regimental Staff and Staff Battery (7/2/22/61; 2 LMGs)

1st (self-propelled) Armored Battalion (17/3/129/365)
    1 (self-propelled) Battalion Staff and Battery (8/3/39/131; 1 Sd Kfz 251, 3 artillery observation vehicles with 3 LMGs and 3 20mm mountain Flak guns)
    2 Light Self-Propelled 105mm Batteries (3/0/30/74 ea; 6 105mm leFH Sd Kfz 124 Wespe, 1 Sd Kfz 251, 1 artillery observation vehicle and 5 LMGs ea)

1 Heavy Self-Propelled 150mm Battery (3/0/30/86; 6 150mm sFH Sd Kfz 165 Hummel)

2nd (mot) Battalion (15/3/56/162)

1 (mot) Battalion Staff and Battery (1 Sd Kfz 251, 3 artillery observation vehicles with 3 LMGs and 3 20mm mountain Flak guns)

2 (motZ) Light 105mm leFH Batteries (3/0/26/81 ea; 6 105mm leFH 18 and 4 LMGs ea)

3rd (mot) Battalion (17/3/109/344)

1 (motZ) Battalion Staff and Battery (1 Sd Kfz 251, 3 artillery observation vehicles with 3 LMGs and 3 20mm mountain Flak guns)

2 (motZ) Heavy 150mm Batteries (3/0/25/81 ea; 4 150mm sFH 18 and 4 LMGs ea)

1 (motZ) 100mm Gun Battery (3/0/25/81; 4 100mm K 18 and 4 LMGs)

Army Flak Battalion (Variant 1 18/3/131/483, Variant 2 18/3/129/457)

1 (mot) Flak Battalion Staff and Staff Battery (9/3/27/83; 2 LMGs)

2 (motZ) Heavy Flak Batteries (3/0/33/126; 4 88mm, 3 20mm and 2 LMGs ea)

plus (Variant 1)

1 (mot or self-propelled) Light Flak Battery (3/0/38/144; 9 37mm Flak 43 and 3 quad 20mm Flak guns)

or (Variant 2)

1 (mot or self-propelled) Light Flak Battery (3/0/37/123; 11 20mm Flak guns)

(organization as of 1 January 1944)

Armored Pioneer Battalion (19/5/120/730)

1 Pioneer Battalion Staff and Staff Company (7/5/25/136; 6 Sd Kfz 251, 14 LMGs)

2 (mot) Pioneer Companies, each with: (3/0/26/166; 2 HMGs, 18 LMGs, 2 80mm mortars)

1 (armored) Pioneer Company (4/0/29/184; 25 Sd Kfz 251 mounting 25 LMGs and 3 20mm Flak; 2 HMGs, 18 LMGs, 6 flamethrowers and 2 80mm mortars)

1 (mot) Light Panzer Bridging Column (2/0/14/79; 3 LMGs)

Armored Signals Battalion (13/3/99/348)

1 Armored Signals Battalion Staff (4/2/6/8)

1 Armored Telephone Company (4/0/35/119; 5 LMGs, 6 Sd Kfz 251 mounting 6 LMGs)

1 Armored Radio Company (4/0/48/178; 5 LMGs, 2PzBefWg IV and 8 Sd Kfz 251 mounting 14 LMGs)

1 (mot) Signals Supply Column (1/1/10/43; 2 LMGs)

Feldersatz Battalion (17/1/91/64 + 800-man replacement squad)

4 companies (50 LMGs, 12 HMGs, 6 80mm mortars, 2 120mm mortars, 1 75mm PAK, 1 20mm Flak, 2 flamethrowers and 1 105mm leFH total)

Panzer Supply Troop (21/2/118/640)

1 Panzer Supply Troop Regimental Staff and Staff Company (2 LMGs) (new organization)

5 (mot) 120 ton Transportation Companies (8 LMGs ea)

1 (mot) Weapons Maintenance Company (new organization)

Vehicle Maintenance Troop (7/9/62/339)

3 (mot) Maintenance Companies (4 LMGs ea) (2 with organization as of 1 Nov. 1943) (1 with organization as of 1 July 1944)

1 (mot) 75 ton Maintenance Supply Column (4 LMGs)

Administrative Services (1/7/33/192)

1 (mot) Battalion Staff

1 (mot) Bakery Company (6 LMGs)

1 (mot) Butcher Company (4 LMGs)

1 (mot) Administration Company (2 LMGs)

Medical Troops (17/4/83/426)

2 (mot) Medical Companies (4 LMGs ea)

3 Ambulance Companies (new organization)

Other (0/3/7/8)

1 (mot) Field Post Office

1 (mot) Military Police Detachment

On 1 November 1944 yet another organizational change occurred and the "freie Gliederung" forms of the various armored units were altered once again. These changes reflected two things. The first was the limited numbers of tanks available and the second reflected operational changes. These new organizations were:

Regimental Staff and Staff Company

Staff

Staff Company

3 Panther Mk V tanks (Sd Kfz 171) with 75mm 42 L/70 guns

Reconnaissance Platoon

5 Panzer Mk IV, Sd Kfz 161/2, 75mm 40 (L/48) guns

Battalion Staff and Staff Company (Panzer IV Battalion)

Staff

Staff Company

3 Panzer IV (75mm cm 40 (L/48) (Sd Kfz 161/2)

2 Sd Kfz 251/8

Reconnaissance Platoon

5 Panzer IV (75mm cm 40 (L/48) (Sd Kfz 161/2)

Reconnaissance and Pioneer Platoon

3 Sd Kfz 3 or 3-ton truck

3 Sd Kfz 251/7 half-track

Anti-Aircraft Platoon

3 quad 20mm Flak guns

3 Sd Kfz 7/1 half-tracks

Battalion Staff and Staff Company (Panther Battalion)

Staff

Staff Company

3 Mk V Panther tank Sd Kfz 171 – 75mm KwK 41 (L/70)
2 Sd Kfz 251/8
Reconnaissance Platoon
  5 MkV Panther tank Sd Kfz 171 - 75mm KwK 41 (L/70)
Reconnaissance and Pioneer Platoon
  3 Sd Kfz 3 or 3-ton truck
  3 Sd Kfz 251/7 half-track
Anti-Aircraft Platoon
  3 quad 20mm Flak guns
  3 Sd Kfz 7/1 half-tracks
Medium Panzer Company (17 tanks)
Staff
  2 Panther tanks, Sd Kfz 171, 75mm 42 (L/70)
  or 2 Panzer Mk IV, Sd Kfz 161/2, 75mm 40 (L/48)
  or 2 Panzer 604/9 75mm 42 (L 70) (also known as Pz.IV/70(A))

1st–4th Platoons
  5 Panther tanks, Sd Kfz 171, 75mm 42 (L/70)
  or 5 Panzer Mk IV, Sd Kfz 161/2, 75mm 40 (L/48)
  or 5 Panzer 604/9 75mm 42 (L 70) (also known as Pz.IV/70(A))

In the 14-tank company the number of tanks per platoon was reduced to four. In a third form, the 10-tank company, the staff contained only one MkV tank and there were three platoons, each with three Mk V tanks.

The last reorganizational gasp was the issuance on 25 March 1945 of the organization for the Type 45 Panzer Division. It was to go into effect immediately for all panzer and panzergrenadier divisions. The distinction between the two divisions was, in fact, to disappear. The divisions that did not have sufficient forces were to assume the Type 45 Panzer Division Kampfgruppe organization.

ORGANIZATION OF A TYPE 45 PANZER DIVISION

Division Headquarters (420 men total)
  1 Division Staff (2 LMGs)
  1 (mot) Divisional Mapping Section
  1 (mot) Military Police Troop (5 LMGs)
  1 (mot) Division Escort Company
  1 Motorcycle Messenger Platoon (6 LMGs)
  1 (mot) Panzergrenadier Platoon (2 HMGs, 6 LMGs and 2 80mm mortars)
  1 Self-Propelled Flak Platoon (4 20mm Flak guns)
Mixed Panzer Regiment (1,361 men total)
  1 (Armored) Panzer Regiment Staff (126 men; 6 LMGs and 2 75mm KwK)
  1 (mot) Panzer Regiment Staff Company
  1 Staff Platoon
  1 Staff Signals Platoon
  1st (Panzer) Battalion (767 men total)
  Staff (1 LMG)
  Staff Company (12 LMGs)
    Staff Platoon
    Armored Pioneer Platoon
  2 Panzer Companies (10 Mk IV tanks ea)
  2 Panzer Companies (10 Mk V tanks ea)
  1 Armored Flak Company
    1 Panzer Flak Platoon (8 37mm Pz Flak 43 and 8 LMGs)
    1 Self-Propelled Flak Platoon (3 quad 20mm)
  1 Panzer Maintenance Company (1 LMG)
  1 (mot) Panzer Supply Company (3 LMGs)
  2nd (Panzergrenadier) Battalion (488 men total)
  1 Armored Staff (4 LMGs)
  1 Armored Staff Company (7 LMGS and 6 75mm PAK 40)

3 (armored) Panzergrenadier Companies (21 LMGs, 3 Sd Kfz 25/21 with triple 20mm guns and 1 sturm platoon with Sturmgewehr 44 ea)
  1 Armored Heavy Gun Platoon (6 75mm KwK and 1 LMG)
  1 (mot) Supply Company (1 LMG and 3 panzerschrecke)
2 (mot) Panzergrenadier Regiments, each with
  1 (mot) Staff (48 men total; 3 panzerschrecke)
  1 Staff Company (4 LMGs)
  1 Signals Platoon
  1 Motorcycle Messenger Platoon (4 LMGs)
  1 (mot) Battle Column
  2 (tmot) Panzergrenadier Battalions (724 men total)
  (mot) Staff (3 panzerschrecke)
  3 Panzergrenadier Companies (117 men per co,pany; 12 LMGs, 3 panzerschrecke and 1 sturm platoon with Sturmgewehr 44 ea)
  1 (mot) Machine Company (121 men; 8 HMGs, 6 20mm Flak and 1 LMG)
  1 (mot) Heavy Company (127 men)
  Medium Mortar Platoon (8 80mm mortars and 6 LMGs)
  Heavy Mortar Platoon (4 120mm and 2 LMGs)
  1 (mot) Supply Company (77 men; 2 LMGs and 3 panzerschrecke)
  1 (motZ) Heavy Infantry Gun Company (102 men; 4 150mm sIG)
  1 (mot) Pioneer Company (144 men; 9 LMGs and 9 panzerschrecke)
Panzer Reconnaissance Battalion (648 men)
  1 (mot) Staff (1 LMG and 1 20mm KwK)

1 (armored) Mixed Armored Car Company (10 75mm KwK, 2 Sd Kfz 251/21 with triple 20mm, 8 20mm KwK, 18 LMGs)

2 Light (mot) Reconnaissance Companies (Volkswagen) (4 HMGs, 9 LMGs and 2 80mm mortars ea)

1 (mot) Supply Company (1 LMG)

Mixed Panzerjäger Battalion (522 men)

Staff and Staff Company (2 Jagdpanzers and 1 LMG)

2 Jagdpanzer Companies, each with

1 Panzergrenadier Escort Platoon (10 Jagdpanzer and 10 LMGs)

1 Self-Propelled Panzerjäger Company (9 75mm PAK and 1 LMG)

1 (mot) Supply Company)

Panzer Artillery Regiment (1,367 men)

1 Panzer Artillery Regimental Staff and Staff Battery (2 LMGs)

1st (self-propelled) Armored Battalion

1 (self-propelled) Battalion Staff and Battery (2 LMGs and 3 20mm mountain Flak guns)

2 Light Self-Propelled 105mm Batteries (6 105mm leFH Sd Kfz 124 Wespe and 4 LMGs ea)

1 Heavy Self-Propelled 150mm Battery (6 150mm sFH Sd Kfz 165 Hummel and 4 LMGs)

2nd (mot) Battalion

1 (mot) Battalion Staff and Battery (2 LMGs and 3 (motZ) 20mm mountain Flak guns)

2 (motZ) Light 105mm leFH Batteries (6 105mm leFH 18 and 5 LMGs ea)

3rd (mot) Battalion (17/3/109/344)

1 (mot) Battalion Staff and Battery (1 Sd Kfz 251, 3 artillery observation vehicles with 3 LMGs and 3 20mm mountain Flak guns)

2 (motZ) Heavy 150mm Batteries (4 150mm sFH 18 and 4 LMGs ea)

1 (motZ) 100mm Gun Battery (4 100mm K 18 and 4 LMGs)

Army Flak Battalion (440 men)

1 (mot) Flak Battalion Staff and Staff Battery (2 LMGs)

2 (motZ) Heavy Flak Batteries (6 88mm, 3 20mm and 2 LMGs ea)

1 (motZ) Light Flak Battery (9 37mm Flak 43 and 3 self-propelled quad 20mm Flak guns)

Armored Pioneer Battalion (716 men)

1 Pioneer Battalion Staff (9 LMGs)

1 (mot) Staff and Supply Company (4 LMGs)

1 Bridging Column

2 (mot) Pioneer Companies (2 HMGs, 18 LMGs, 2 80mm mortars ea)

1 (armored) Pioneer Company (19 LMGs and 2 HMGs)

Armored Signals Battalion (378 men)

1 (mot) Armored Signals Battalion Staff

1 Armored Telephone Company (11 LMGs)

1 Armored Radio Company (19 LMGs)

1 (mot) Signals Supply Column (2 LMGs)

Feldersatz Battalion (173 men)

4 companies (50 LMGs, 12 HMGs, 6 80mm mortars, 2 120mm mortars, 1 20mm Flak, 2 flamethrowers and 1 105mm leFH total)

Panzer Supply Troop (702 men)

1 Panzer Supply Troop Regimental Staff and Staff Company (2 LMGs)

4 (mot) 120 ton Transportation Companies (4 LMGs ea)

3 (mot) 30 ton Transportation Squadrons (2 LMGs ea)

1 (mot) Weapons Maintenance Company (2 LMGs)

Vehicle Maintenance Troop (277 men)

2 (mot) Maintenance Companies (2 LMGs ea)

1 (mot) 75 ton Maintenance Supply Column

Administrative Services (206 men)

1 (mot) Administrative Service Company (3 LMGs)

1 (mot) Bakery Platoon

1 (mot) Butcher Platoon

1 (mot) Administration Platoon

Medical Troops (334 men)

1 (mot) Medical Company (2 LMGs)

1 Ambulance Company (1 LMG)

Other

1 (mot) Field Post Office (18 men)

ORGANIZATION OF A TYPE 45 PANZER DIVISION KAMPFGRUPPE

Division Headquarters

1 Division Staff (2 LMGs)

1 (mot) Divisional Mapping Section

1 (mot) Military Police Troop (5 LMGs)

1 (mot) Division Escort Company

1 Motorcycle Messenger Platoon (6 LMGs)

1 (mot) Panzergrenadier Platoon (2 HMGs, 6 LMGs and 2 80mm mortars)

1 Self-Propelled Flak Platoon (4 20mm Flak guns)

Mixed Panzer Regiment

1 (Armored) Panzer Regiment Staff (6 LMGs and 2 75mm KwK)

1 (mot) Panzer Regiment Staff Company

1 Staff Platoon

1 (mot) Staff Signals Platoon

1st (Panzer) Battalion

Staff (1 LMG)

Staff Company (12 LMGs)

Staff Platoon (4 LMGs)
Armored Pioneer Platoon (6 LMGs)
2 Panzer Companies (10 Mk IV tanks ea)
2 Panzer Companies (10 Mk V tanks ea)
1 Armored Flak Company
1 Panzer Flak Platoon (8 37mm Pz Flak 43 and 8 LMGs)
1 Self-Propelled Flak Platoon (3 quad 20mm)
1 Panzer Maintenance Company (1 LMG)
1 (mot) Panzer Supply Company (3 LMGs)

2nd (Panzergrenadier) Battalion

1 Armored Staff (4 LMGs)
1 Armored Staff Company (7 LMGS and 6 75mm PAK 40)
3 (armored) Panzergrenadier Companies (21 LMGs, 3 Sd Kfz 25/21 with triple 20mm guns and 1 sturm platoon armed with Sturmgewehr 44 ea)
1 Armored Heavy Gun Platoon (6 75mm KwK and 1 LMG)
1 (mot) Supply Company (1 LMG and 3 panzer-schrecke)

1 (mot) Panzergrenadier Regiment

1 (mot) Staff (48 men total; 3 panzerschrecke)
1 Staff Company (4 LMGs)
1 Signals Platoon
1 Motorcycle Messenger Platoon (4 LMGs)
1 (mot) Battle Column

2 (tmot) Panzergrenadier Battalions

(mot) Staff (3 panzerschrecke)
3 Panzergrenadier Companies (12 LMGs, 3 panzer-schrecke and 1 sturm platoon with Sturmgewehr 44 ea)
1 (mot) Machine Company (121 men; 8 HMGs, 6 20mm Flak and 1 LMG)
1 (mot) Heavy Company (127 men)
Medium Mortar Platoon (8 80mm mortars and 6 LMGs)
Heavy Mortar Platoon (4 120mm and 2 LMGs)
1 (mot) Supply Company (2 LMGs and 3 panzerschrecke)
1 (motZ) Heavy Infantry Gun Company (4 150mm sIG)
1 (mot) Pioneer Company (9 LMGs and 9 panzer-schrecke)

Panzer Reconnaissance Battalion (648 men)

1 (mot) Staff (1 LMG and 1 20mm KwK)
1 (armored) Mixed Armored Car Company (10 75mm KwK, 2 Sd Kfz 251/21 with triple 20mm, 8 20mm KwK, 18 LMGs)
2 Light (mot) Reconnaissance Companies (Volkswagen) (4 HMGs, 9 LMGs and 2 80mm mortars)
1 (mot) Supply Company (1 LMG)

Mixed Panzerjäger Battalion (522 men)

Staff and Staff Company (2 Jagdpanzers and 1 LMG)
2 Jagdpanzer Companies, each with
1 Panzergrenadier Escort Platoon (10 Jagdpanzer and 10 LMGs)
1 Self-Propelled Panzerjäger Company (9 75mm PAK and 1 LMG)

1 (mot) Supply Company)

Panzer Artillery Regiment (1,367 men)

1 Panzer Artillery Regimental Staff and Staff Battery (2 LMGs)

1st (self-propelled) Armored Battalion

1 (self-propelled) Battalion Staff and Battery (2 LMGs and 3 20mm mountain Flak guns)
2 Light Self-Propelled 105mm Batteries (6 105mm leFH Sd Kfz 124 Wespe and 4 LMGs ea)
1 Heavy Self-Propelled 150mm Battery (6 150mm sFH Sd Kfz 165 Hummel and 4 LMGs)

3rd (mot) Battalion

1 (mot) Battalion Staff and Battery (1 Sd Kfz 251, 3 Artillery observation Vehicle with 3 LMGs and 3 20mm mountain Flak guns)
2 (motZ) Heavy 150mm Batteries (4 150mm sFH 18 and 4 LMGs ea)
1 (motZ) 100mm Gun Battery (4 100mm K 18 and 4 LMGs)

Army Flak Battalion

1 (mot) Flak Battalion Staff and Staff Battery (2 LMGs)
2 (motZ) Heavy Flak Batteries (6 88mm, 3 20mm and 2 LMGs ea)
1 (motZ) Light Flak Battery (9 37mm Flak 43 and 3 self-propelled quad 20mm Flak guns)

Armored Pioneer Battalion (716 men)

1 Pioneer Battalion Staff (9 LMGs)
1 (mot) Staff and Supply Company (4 LMGs)
1 Bridging Column
2 (mot) Pioneer Companies (2 HMGs, 18 LMGs, 2 80mm mortars ea)
1 (armored) Pioneer Company (19 LMGs and 2 HMGs)

Armored Signals Battalion

1 Armored Signals Company (12 LMGs)

Feldersatz Battalion

4 companies

Panzer Supply Troop

1 Panzer Supply Troop Regimental Staff and Staff Company (2 LMGs)
1 (mot) 120 ton Transportation Companies (4 LMGs ea)
3 (mot) 30 ton Transportation Squadrons (2 LMGs ea)
1 (mot) Weapons Maintenance Company (2 LMGs)

Vehicle Maintenance Troop (277 men)

2 (mot) Maintenance Companies (2 LMGs)
1 (mot) 75 ton Maintenance Supply Column

Administrative Services (206 men)

1 (mot) Administrative Service Company (3 LMGs)
1 (mot) Bakery Platoon
1 (mot) Butcher Platoon
1 (mot) Administration Platoon

Medical Troops (334 men)

1 (mot) Medical Company (2 LMGs)
1 Ambulance Company (1 LMG)

Other

1 (mot) Field Post Office (18 men)

3

Divisional Histories

1st Panzer Division

Organized 15 October 1935, it had:

1st Schützen Brigade
  1/, 2/1st Schützen Regiment
  1st Motorcycle Battalion
1st Panzer Brigade
  1/, 2/1st Panzer Regiment
  1/, 2/2nd Panzer Regiment
4th Reconnaissance Battalion
1/, 2/73rd Artillery Regiment
37th Divisional Support Units
81st Supply Troops

On 6 October 1936, the armored portion of the division was organized as follows:

1/, 2/1st Panzer Regiment
  1 Regimental Staff Signals Platoon
  1 Regimental Staff Light Panzer Platoon
  Each Battalion had
    1 Panzer Signals Platoon
    1 Light Panzer Staff Platoon
    4 Light Panzer Companies
1/, 2/2nd Panzer Regiment
  1 Regimental Staff Signals Platoon
  1 Regimental Staff Light Panzer Platoon
  Each Battalion had
    1 Panzer Signals Platoon
    1 Light Panzer Staff Platoon
    4 Light Panzer Companies
1/, 2/7th Panzer Regiment
  1 Regimental Staff Signals Platoon
  1 Regimental Staff Light Panzer Platoon
  Each Battalion had
    1 Panzer Signals Platoon
    1 Light Panzer Staff Platoon
    4 Light Panzer Companies

On 12 October 1936 this was reorganized as follows:

1/, 2/1st Panzer Regiment
  1 Regimental Staff Signals Platoon
  1 Regimental Staff Light Panzer Platoon
  Each Battalion had

    1 Panzer Signals Platoon
    1 Light Panzer Staff Platoon
    4 Light Panzer Companies
1/, 2/2nd Panzer Regiment
  1 Regimental Staff Signals Platoon
  1 Regimental Staff Light Panzer Platoon
  Each Battalion had
    1 Panzer Signals Platoon
    1 Light Panzer Staff Platoon
    4 Light Panzer Companies

A third reorganization occurred on 10 November 1938 and the armored portion of the division contained:

1/, 2/1st Panzer Regiment
  1 Regimental Staff Signals Platoon
  1 Regimental Staff Light Panzer Platoon
  Each Battalion had
    1 Panzer Signals Platoon
    1 Light Panzer Staff Platoon
    4 Light Panzer Companies
1/, 2/2nd Panzer Regiment
  1 Regimental Staff Signals Platoon
  1 Regimental Staff Light Panzer Platoon
  Each Battalion had
    1 Panzer Signals Platoon
    1 Light Panzer Staff Platoon
    4 Light Panzer Companies

Just prior to the invasion of Poland and on the day of the invasion, the inventory of tanks assigned to the division was as follows:

	15 Aug. 1939	1 Sept. 1939
1st Regiment		
PzMk I	48	39
PzMk II	62	60
PzMk III	16	20
PzMk IV	28	28
PzBefWg 265	5	⎫
PzBefWg 267	1	⎬ 6
PzBefWg 268	0	⎭
2nd Regiment		
PzMk I	63	54

PzMk II	62	62
PzMk III	8	6
PzMk IV	28	28
PzBefWg 265	5	⎫
PzBefWg 267	1	⎬ 6
PzBefWg 268	0	⎭

OKH records show that when the Germans invaded Poland on 1 September 1939 the 1st Panzer Division was organized and equipped as follows:

1st Panzer Division Generalleutnant Schmidt
  81st (mot) Mapping Detachment
  81st Motorcycle Messenger Platoon
1st Schützen Brigade
1st Schützen Regiment
    1 (mot) Signals Platoon
  1st and 2nd (mot) Battalions, each with
    1 Motorcycle Company (9 LMGs, 2 HMGs and 3 50mm mortars)
    2 (mot) Rifle Companies (9 LMGs, 2 HMGs and 3 50mm mortars ea)
    1 (mot) Heavy Company
      1 Infantry Gun Section (2 75mm leIG)
      1 Pioneer Platoon (3 LMGs)
      1 Panzer Abwehr Platoon (3 37mm PAK 36 and 1 LMG)
    1 (mot) Light Infantry Column
2nd Motorcycle Battalion
    3 Motorcycle Companies (9 LMGs, 2 HMGs and 3 50mm mortars ea)
    1 Motorcycle Heavy Machine Gun Company (8 HMGs and 6 80mm mortars)
    1 (mot) Heavy Company
      1 Infantry Gun Section (2 75mm leIG)
      1 Panzer Abwehr Platoon (3 37mm PAK 36 and 1 LMG)
      1 Pioneer Platoon (3 LMGs)
1st Panzer Brigade
1st Panzer Regiment
    1 Armored Signals Platoon
    1 Staff Light Tank Platoon
  1st and 2nd Panzer Battalions, each with
    1 Armored Signals Platoon
    1 Staff Light Tank Platoon
    3 Light Panzer Companies
    1 (mot) Reserve Platoon
    1 (mot) Panzer Supply Column
    1 (mot) Maintenance Company
1/, 2/2nd Panzer Regiment
  same as 3rd Panzer Regiment
4th (mot) Reconnaissance Battalion
  1 (mot) Signals Platoon
  2 Armored Car Platoons (10 20mm and 25 LMGs)

    1 Motorcycle Company (9 LMGs, 2 HMGs and 3 50mm mortars)
    1 (mot) Heavy Company
      1 Infantry Gun Section (2 75mm leIG)
      1 Panzer Abwehr Platoon (3 37mm PAK 36 and 1 LMG)
      1 Pioneer Platoon (3 LMGs)
    1 (mot) Light Reconnaissance Supply Column
37th Panzerabwehr (Anti-Tank) Battalion
  1 (mot) Signals Platoon
  3 (mot) Batteries (12 37mm PAK 36 and 6 LMGs ea)
73rd Artillery Regiment
  1 (mot) Signals Platoon
  1 (mot) Weather Detachment
  1st and 2nd (mot) Battalion
  1 (mot) Signals Platoon
  1 (mot) Calibration Detachment
  3 (mot) Batteries (4 105mm leFH and 2 LMGs ea)
37th Panzer Signals Battalion
  1 (mot) Panzer Signals Company (2 LMGs)
  1 (mot) Panzer Radio Company (12 LMGs)
  1 (mot) Panzer Signals Supply Column
37th Pioneer Battalion
  3 (mot) Pioneer Companies (9 LMGs ea)
  1 (mot) Brüko K
  1 (mot) Light Pioneer Supply Column
81st Divisional Support Units
  1–6/81st (mot) Light Supply Columns
  7/, 8/, 9/81st (mot) Heavy Fuel Columns
  1/, 2/81st (mot) Maintenance Companies
  81st (mot) Supply Company
Support Units
  81st (mot) Field Bakery
  81st (mot) Butcher Detachment
  81st Division Administration
  1/, 2/81st (mot) Medical Companies
  1/, 2/, 3/81st Ambulance Companies
  81st (mot) Military Police Troop
  81st (mot) Field Post Office

In addition, the division had two Luftwaffe formations attached to it. They were:

83rd Luftwaffe Light Flak Battalion
  1 (mot) Signals Platoon
  1 (mot) Medium Flak Battery (9 37mm guns)
  2 (mot) Light Flak Batteries (12 20mm guns)
2.(H)/23 Reconnaissance Staffel

On 25 September 1939 the division contained 25 PzMk I tanks, 29 PzMk II tanks, 11 PzMk III tanks, six PzMk IV tanks and four PzBefWg command tanks.

On 30 October 1939 the 3/69th (mot) Infantry Regiment assigned and on 1 April 1940 it became the 3/1st Schützen Regiment. On 1 April 1940 the cavalry gun platoon and panzer abwehr platoons from the 1st Cavalry Division were assigned as the 15th Company/1st Schützen Regiment, the 1/27th Panzer Abwehr Battalion became the 3/37th Panzerjäger Battalion, the 10/81st Light Supply Column was renumbered the 7/81st and the 7/81st Heavy Fuel Column was renumbered the 10/81st.

On 10 May 1940, the day of the invasion of France, the organization of the armored portions of the division and the inventory of tanks were as follows:

1/, 2/1st Panzer Regiment
  1 Regimental Staff Signals Platoon
  1 Regimental Staff Light Panzer Platoon
  Each Battalion had
    1 Panzer Staff Company
    1 Medium Panzer Company
    2 Light Panzer Companies
  Total tanks available:
    PzMk I   26
    PzMk II   49
    PzMk III   28
    PzMk IV   20
    PzBefWg   4
1/, 2/2nd Panzer Regiment
  1 Regimental Staff Signals Platoon
  1 Regimental Staff Light Panzer Platoon
  Each Battalion had
    1 Panzer Staff Company
    1 Medium Panzer Company
    2 Light Panzer Companies
  Total tanks available:
    PzMk I   26
    PzMk II   49
    PzMk III   30
    PzMk IV   20
    PzBefWg   4

On 20 October 1940 the 2nd Panzer Regiment was reassigned to the newly forming 16th Panzer Division. On 6 November 1940 the 113th Schützen Regiment was formed from the 3/1st Schützen Regiment and assigned to the division. On 15 February 1941 the 2/69th Schützen Regiment was used to form the 2/113th Schützen Regiment. The 73rd Artillery Regiment formed a 3rd Battalion from the 2/56th Artillery Regiment. On 21 June 1941, the eve of the invasion of Russia, the division's panzer forces and inventories were as follows:

1/, 2/1st Panzer Regiment
  1 Regimental Staff Signals Platoon
  1 Regimental Staff Light Panzer Platoon
  Each Battalion had
    1 Panzer Staff Company
    1 Medium Panzer Company
    2 Light Panzer Companies

PzMk II   43
PzMk III (50) 71
PzMk IV   20
PzBefWg   11

On 10 September 1941, after three months of battle, the inventory of tanks had been reduced to:

PzMk I   9 operational
PzMk II   8
PzMk III   43
PzMk IV   10
PzBefWg   9

In November 1941 the 4th Panzer Reconnaissance Battalion was absorbed into the 1st Motorcycle Battalion, placing one armored car company at the immediate disposal of the division. In 1941 the staff of the 1st Panzer Brigade was reassigned to the 18th Panzer Division. From 1941 through mid-1942 the division had the 1st Company, 83rd Flak Battalion attached to it. The division had:

1/, 2/1st Schützen Regiment
1/, 2/113rd Schützen Regiment
1/, 2/1st Panzer Regiment
1st Kradschützen (motorcycle) Battalion
4th Reconnaissance Battalion
1/, 2/, 3/73rd Artillery Regiment
37th Panzer Divisional (Einheiten) Support Units
81st Supply Troops

On 7/15/42 the panzer forces assigned to the division and tank inventories stood at:

2/1st Panzer Regiment
  1 Regimental Staff Signals
  Platoon 1 Regimental Staff Light Panzer Platoon
  Each Battalion had
    1 Panzer Staff Company
    1 Medium Panzer Company
    2 Light Panzer Companies
    PzMk II   2
    38 (t)   10
    PzMk III (50kz)   26
    PzMk IV (kz)   7
    PzBefWg   4

Four days earlier, on 11 July 1942, the 1st and 113rd Schützen Regiments were redesignated as Panzergrenadier Regiments. The 1/1st Panzer Regiment was detached to the 16th Panzergrenadier Division as the 116th Panzer Battalion, leaving the 1st Panzer Division with only the 2nd Battalion until 15 January 1943, when it became the 1st Battalion and a new 2nd Battalion was formed from the 1/203rd Panzer Regiment. The Army 299th Flak Battalion was transferred to the division. The staff of the 1st Schützen Brigade was disbanded in the fall of 1942.

On 1 March 1943 the remains of the 1st Kradschützen (motorcycle) Battalion, which had been destroyed in Stalingrad, were built into the 91st Panzer Reconnaissance Battalion. In December 1942 the remains of the 1st Panzer Division were withdrawn to Germany for reorganization and refitting. On 15 January 1943 the 2/1st Panzer Regiment was redesignated the 1/1st Panzer Regiment. A new 2/1st Panzer Regiment was organized from the 1/203rd Panzer Regiment on 27 January 1943. The 1st Panzer Regiment was expanded to a total of eight panzer companies.

The (mot) divisional escort company was formed in March 1943 with detachments of the 1st and 113th Panzergrenadier Regiments. This eventually became the 1st Panzer Reconnaissance Battalion. In addition, a fourth artillery battalion was added. The division had:

1/, 2/1st Panzergrenadier Regiment
1/, 2/113rd Panzergrenadier Regiment
1/, 2/1st Panzer Regiment
1st Panzer Reconnaissance Battalion
1/, 2/, 3/, 4/73rd Panzer Artillery Regiment
299th Flak Battalion
37th Panzer Divisional (Einheiten) Support Units
81st Supply Troops

The division's organization underwent almost constant change during 1943. The 113th Panzergrenadier Regiment seems to have added a motorcycle platoon (six LMGs) to its staff company. Both panzergrenadier regiments had (mot) pioneer companies (two 80mm mortars, six flame-throwers and 18 LMGs) when 1943 arrived, but these were eliminated on 2/12/43.

The 905th Assault Gun Battalion was added and deleted during the summer. While assigned, it had three batteries, each with 10 StuG. The 37th Panzerjäger Battalion underwent an extensive series of modifications. One of the self-propelled batteries was replaced by a battery with six self-propelled (Hornisse) 88mm guns. This may have happened as early as March 1943, but by the summer it appears to have reverted to self-propelled 75mm guns. All three 75mm companies, however, rose from nine to 10, then to 14 guns each.

The reconnaissance force was upgraded to a full regiment. Its organization started early 1943 with the following:

Staff
1 Staff
1 Staff Company
  1 Signals Platoon
  1 Panzerjäger Platoon (3 LMGs and 3 75mm PAK 40)
  1 Self-Propelled Flak Platoon (4 20mm guns)
  1 Motorcycle Platoon (6 LMGs)

1 Armored Car Company (24 LMGs and 18 20mm guns)
1 Light Armored Car Supply Column (3 LMGs)
1st (motorcycle) Battalion
2 Motorcycle Companies (4 HMGs, 18 LMGs, 2 80mm mortars and 3 PzBu39 ea)
1 Half-Track Company
  1 Pioneer Platoon (4 LMGs)
  1 Panzerjäger Platoon (3 LMGs and 3 75mm PAK 40)
  1 Infantry Section (2 75mm leIG)
2nd (motorized) Battalion
2 (mot) Reconnaissance Companies (2 80mm mortars, 3 sPzBu 41, 4 HMGs and 18 LMGs ea)
1 (mot) Heavy Reconnaissance Company
  1 Pioneer Platoon (4 LMGs)
  1 Panzerjäger Platoon (3 LMGs and 3 75mm PAK 40)
  1 Infantry Gun Platoon (4 75mm leIG)

It was planned to upgrade the 91st Reconnaissance Regiment further as follows, but this organization underwent several changes and may not have been fully realized. This organization dates from sometime after 12 February 1943, when the motorcycle companies were replaced by half-track companies.

Staff
1 Staff
1 Staff Company
  1 Signals Platoon
  1 Panzerjäger Platoon (3 LMGs and 3 75mm PAK 40)
  1 Self-Propelled Flak Platoon (4 20mm guns)
  1 Motorcycle Platoon (6 LMGs)
1 Armored Car Company (24 LMGs and 18 20mm guns)
1 Light Armored Car Supply Column (3 LMGs)
1st (motorcycle) Battalion
1 Armored Car (half-track) Company (25 LMGs and 16 20mm guns)
1 Half-Track Company (4 HMGs, 56 LMGs, 3 37mm PAK 36 and 2 80mm mortars)
1 Half-Track Company
  1 Pioneer Platoon (13 LMGs)
  1 Panzerjäger Platoon (3 LMGs and 3 75mm PAK 40)
  1 Infantry Section (2 75mm leIG)
  1 Half-Track Gun Platoon (6 75mm guns on half-tracks)
2nd (motorized) Battalion
2 (mot) Reconnaissance Companies (2 80mm mortars, 3 sPzBu 41, 4 HMGs and 18 LMGs ea)
1 (mot) Heavy Reconnaissance Company
  1 Pioneer Platoon (4 LMGs)
  1 Panzerjäger Platoon (3 LMGs and 3 75mm PAK 40)
  1 Infantry Gun Platoon (4 75mm leIG)

Indications are that in May the 2nd Battalion organization was disbanded, the heavy and one light company eliminated, and the other light company incorporated into the 1st Battalion. The regimental staff company was also eliminated.

The artillery regiment was scheduled for reorganization. The regimental staff battery was initially to receive a self-propelled Flak battery with four quad 20mm guns, but this was downgraded to four self-propelled 20mm guns. The 1st and 2nd Artillery Battalion were to have one heavy and two light self-propelled batteries. This ambitious plan, labeled as an "experimental organization", was downgraded to only the 1st Battalion being self-propelled. The 2nd Battalion remained (motZ) for the time being.

According to OKH records, as the summer of 1943 arrived, the 1st Panzer Division was organized as follows:

Division Staff
1 Staff (2 LMGs)
81st (mot) Mapping Detachment
1 Divisional Escort Company
  1 Infantry Platoon (4 HMGs, 6 LMGs and 2 80mm mortars)
  1 Panzerjäger Platoon (3 LMGs and 3 75mm PAK 40)
  1 Flak Platoon (1 LMG and 4 self-propelled 20mm Flak guns)
  1 Infantry Gun Section (2 75mm leIG)
  1 Motorcycle Platoon (3 LMGs)

1st Panzer Regiment
1 Regimental Staff
1 Regimental Band
1 Regimental Signals Platoon
1st and 2nd Battalion, each with
  1 Battalion Staff and Staff Company (received 7 PzMk III flame panzers on 18 June 1943)
  4 Panzer Companies (22 PzMk IV ea)
  1 Panzer Maintenance Company

1st Panzergrenadier Regiment
1 (mot) Regimental Staff Company
  1 Signals Platoon
  1 Panzerjäger Platoon (3 LMGs and 3 75mm PAK 40)
  1 Motorcycle Platoon (6 LMGs)
  1 Regimental Band
1st and 2nd Battalions, each with
  3 (mot) Companies (4 HMGs, 18 LMGs and 2 80mm mortars ea)
  1 (mot) Heavy Company
    1 Pioneer Platoon (4 LMGs and 6 flamethrowers)
    1 Panzerjäger Platoon (3 75mm PAK 40)
    1 Infantry Gun Platoon (4 75mm leIG)
    1 Mortar Platoon (6 80mm mortars)
  9th Self-Propelled Flak Company (12 20mm and 4 LMGs)
  10th Self-Propelled Infantry Gun Company (6 150mm sIG and 3 LMGs)

113th Panzergrenadier Regiment
1 (mot) Regimental Staff Company
  1 Signals Platoon
  1 Panzerjäger Platoon (3 LMGs and 3 75mm PAK 40)
  1 Pioneer Platoon (6 LMGs and 6 flamethrowers)
  1 Motorcycle Platoon (6 LMGs)
1st Battalion
  3 (half-track) Companies (4 HMGs, 34 LMGs, 2 80mm mortars and 3 37mm PAK 36 on half-tracks ea)
  1 (half-track) Heavy Company
    1 Pioneer Platoon (13 LMGs, 1 37mm PAK 36 and 6 flamethrowers)
    1 Self-Propelled Panzerjäger Platoon (3 75mm PAK 40 and 3 LMGs)
    1 Infantry Gun Platoon (4 LMGs and 4 75mm leIG)
    1 Half-Track Gun Platoon (6 75mm guns on half-tracks and 8 LMGs)
2nd Battalion
  3 (mot) Companies (4 HMGs, 18 LMGs and 2 80mm mortars ea)
  1 (mot) Heavy Company
    1 Pioneer Platoon (4 LMGs and 6 flamethrowers)
    1 Panzerjäger Platoon (3 75mm PAK 40)
    1 Infantry Gun Platoon (4 75mm leIG)
    1 Mortar Platoon (6 80mm mortars)
  9th Self-Propelled Flak Company (12 20mm and 4 LMGs)
  10th Self-Propelled Infantry Gun Company (6 150mm sIG and 3 LMGs)

37th Panzerjäger Battalion
3 Self-Propelled Companies (14 75mm PAK 40 ea and 14 LMGs ea)
Note: On 30 Aug. 1943 these companies are shown as having 10 75mm PAK 40 ea and 5 LMGs

1st Reconnaissance Battalion
1 Armored Car Company (6 LMGs and 6 75mm guns)
1st Armored Car Company (24 LMGs and 18 20mm guns)
2nd Armored Car (half-track) Company (25 LMGs and 16 20mm)
3rd and 4th (half-track) Reconnaissance Companies (4 HMGs, 56 LMGs, 3 37mm PAK 36 and 2 120mm mortars ea)
5th (half-track) Heavy Reconnaissance Company
  1 Half-Track Gun Platoon (8 LMGs and 6 75mm guns on half-tracks)
  1 Infantry Gun Section (4 LMGs and 2 75mm leIG)
  1 Panzerjäger Platoon (3 LMGs and 3 75mm PAK 40)
  1 Pioneer Platoon (13 LMGs, 1 37mm PAK 36 and 6 flamethrowers)
1 (mot) Light Reconnaissance Supply Column (3 LMGs)

37th Panzer Artillery Regiment

1 Regimental Staff
  1 Staff Battery (6 LMGs)
  1 (motZ) Flak Platoon (4 20mm Flak guns and 2 LMGs)
1 Regimental Band

1st Battalion

1 Battalion Staff and Staff Battery (6 LMGs)
2 Self-Propelled Batteries (6 105mm leFH SdKfz 124 Wespe and 4 LMGs ea)
1 Self-Propelled Battery (6 150mm sFH SdKfz 165 Hummel and 4 LMGs)

2nd and 3rd (mot) Battalions, each with

1 Battalion Staff
1 Battalion Staff Battery (6 LMGs)
3 (mot) Batteries (4 105mm leFH and 4 LMGs ea)

4th (mot) Battalion (4/73rd Artillery Regiment)

1 Battalion Staff
1 Battalion Staff Battery (6 LMGs)
2 (mot) Batteries (4 150mm sFH and 4 LMGs ea)
1 (mot) Battery (4 100mm K 18 guns and 4 LMGs)

73rd (mot) Observation Battery (12 LMGs)

299th Army Flak Battalion

1 Staff and (mot) Staff Battery (1 LMG)
2 (motZ) Heavy Flak Batteries (4 88mm, 3 20mm and 2 LMGs ea)
1 (motZ) Medium Flak Battery (9 20mm, 2 quad 20mm self-propelled guns and 2 LMGs)
1 (mot) Light (20 ton) Flak Supply Column

37th Panzer Pioneer Battalion

1 Staff (2 LMGs)
1 (half-track) Pioneer Company (40 LMGs, 3 PzBu39, 2 80mm mortars and 6 flamethrowers)
2 (mot) Pioneer Companies (18 LMGs, 3 PzBu39, 2 80mm mortars and 6 flamethrowers ea)
30th Brüko B Bridging Column (4 LMGs)
1 Brüko K Bridging Column (4 LMGs)
1 (mot) Light Pioneer Supply Column (4 LMGs)

37th Panzer Signals Battalion

1 Panzer Telephone Company (21 LMGs)
1 Panzer Radio Company (35 LMGs)
1 (mot) Light Signals Supply Column (4 LMGs)

81st Feldersatz Battalion

4 Companies

81st Supply Troop

1–7/81st (mot) (120 ton) Transportation Companies (4 LMGs ea)
8/81st (mot) (90 ton) Transportation Company (3 LMGs)
81st (mot) Supply Company (6 LMGs)

Truck Park

1–3/81st (mot) Maintenance Companies (4 LMGs ea)
1 (mot) Heavy (75 ton) Replacement Supply Column (4 LMGs)

Other

81st (mot) Bakery Company
81st (mot) Butcher Company
81st (mot) Administration Platoon
1/, 2/81st (mot) Medical Companies (2 LMGs ea)
1/, 2/, 3/81st Ambulances
81st (mot) Military Police Troop (2 LMGs)
81st (mot) Field Post Office

During most of 1943 the two battalions of tanks were equipped with PzMk IVs. Sometime in late 1943 the 1/1st Panzer Regiment was equipped with Panther tanks. In November 1943 the organization of the panzer forces and tank inventories were as follows:

1/, 2/1st Panzer Regiment
  1 Regimental Staff Signals Platoon
  1 Regimental Staff Light Panzer Platoon
  Each Battalion had
    1 Panzer Staff Company
    4 Medium Panzer Companies

PzMk IV (lg)	96
PzMk V	76
PzBefWg	7
Flamm	7
VK6.01	2
VK18.01	8

The 2/1st Panzer Regiment continued to be equipped with Panzer Mk IV tanks. On 28 September 1944 the 1009th Grenadier Ausbildung (Training) Battalion of the Tatra Panzer Division was merged into the division. The division surrendered to the Allies on 9 May 1945 in Styria.

2nd Panzer Division

Formed on 15 October 1935 in Würzburg. On 6 October 1936 the panzer forces assigned to the division were organized as follows:

1/, 2/3rd Panzer Regiment
  1 Regimental Staff Signals Platoon
  1 Regimental Staff Light Panzer Platoon
  Each Battalion had
    1 Panzer Signals Platoon
    1 Light Panzer Staff Platoon
    4 Light Panzer Companies
1/, 2/4th Panzer Regiment

1 Regimental Staff Signals Platoon
1 Regimental Staff Light Panzer Platoon
Each Battalion had
  1 Panzer Signals Platoon
  1 Light Panzer Staff Platoon
  4 Light Panzer Companies

On 12 October 1937 the panzer forces were reorganized as follows:

1/, 2/3rd Panzer Regiment
  1 Regimental Staff Signals Platoon
  1 Regimental Staff Light Panzer Platoon
  Each Battalion had
    1 Panzer Signals Platoon
    1 Light Panzer Staff Platoon
    4 Light Panzer Companies
1/, 2/4th Panzer Regiment
  1 Regimental Staff Signals Platoon
  1 Regimental Staff Light Panzer Platoon
  Each Battalion had
    1 Panzer Signals Platoon
    1 Light Panzer Staff Platoon
    4 Light Panzer Companies

In the spring of 1938 it went to Vienna. It mobilized on 8/19/39 with:

2nd Schützen Brigade
  1/, 2/2nd Schützen Regiment
  2nd Motorcycle Battalion
2nd Panzer Brigade
  1/, 2/3rd Panzer Regiment
  1/, 2/4th Panzer Regiment
1/74th Artillery Regiment
1/110th Artillery Regiment
5th (mot) Reconnaissance Battalion
38th Panzerjäger Battalion
38th Signals Battalion
38th Pioneer Battalion
38th Divisional (Einheiten) Support Units
82nd Supply Troops

On 10 November 1938 a third organization of the panzer forces was implemented:

1/, 2/3rd Panzer Regiment
  1 Regimental Staff Signals Platoon
  1 Regimental Staff Light Panzer Platoon
  Each Battalion had
    1 Panzer Signals Platoon
    1 Light Panzer Staff Platoon
    4 Light Panzer Companies
1/, 2/4th Panzer Regiment
  1 Regimental Staff Signals Platoon

1 Regimental Staff Light Panzer Platoon
Each Battalion had
  1 Panzer Signals Platoon
  1 Light Panzer Staff Platoon
  4 Light Panzer Companies

Just prior to the invasion of Poland and on the day of the invasion, the inventory of tanks assigned to the division was as follows:

	15 Aug. 1939	1 Sept. 1939
3rd Regiment		
PzMk I	84	62
PzMk II	81	78
PzMk III	3	3
PzMk IV	9	8
PzBefWg 26	10	⎫
PzBefWg 267	1	⎬ 9
PzBefWg 268	0	⎭
4th Regiment		
PzMk I	84	62
PzMk II	81	77
PzMk III	3	3
PzMk IV	9	9
PzBefWg 265	10	⎫
PzBefWg 267	1	⎬ 11
PzBefWg 268	0	⎭

OKH records show that when the Germans invaded Poland on 1 September 1939 the 2nd Panzer Division was organized and equipped as follows:

2nd Panzer Division Generalleutnant Veiel
  82nd (mot) Mapping Detachment
  82nd Motorcycle Messenger Platoon
2nd Schützen Brigade
2nd Schützen Regiment
  1 (mot) Signals Platoon
  1st and 2nd (mot) Battalions, each with
    1 Motorcycle Company (18 LMGs, 4 HMGs and 4 50mm mortars)
    2 (mot) Rifle Companies (18 LMGs, 4 HMGs and 4 50mm mortars ea)
    1 (mot) Heavy Company
      1 Infantry Gun Section (2 75mm leIG)
      1 Pioneer Platoon (3 LMGs)
      1 Panzer Abwehr Platoon (3 37mm PAK 36 and 1 LMG)
    1 (mot) Light Infantry Column
2nd Motorcycle Battalion
  3 Motorcycle Companies (9 LMGs, 2 HMGs and 3 50mm mortars ea)
  1 Motorcycle Heavy Machine Gun Company (8 HMGs and 6 80mm mortars)

1 (mot) Heavy Company
   1 Infantry Gun Section (2 75mm leIG)
   1 Panzer Abwehr Platoon (3 37mm PAK 36 and
     1 LMG)
   1 Pioneer Platoon (3 LMGs)

2nd Panzer Brigade
  3rd Panzer Regiment
   1 Armored Signals Platoon
   1 Staff Light Tank Platoon
   1st and 2nd Panzer Battalions, each with
     1 Armored Signals Platoon
     1 Staff Light Tank Platoon
     3 Light Panzer Companies
     1 (mot) Reserve Platoon
     1 (mot) Panzer Supply Column
     1 (mot) Maintenance Company
  1/, 2/4th Panzer Regiment
   same as 3rd Panzer Regiment

5th (mot) Reconnaissance Battalion
  1 (mot) Signals Platoon
  2 Armored Car Platoons (10 20mm and 25 LMGs)
  1 Motorcycle Company (9 LMGs, 2 HMGs and 3
    50mm mortars)
  1 (mot) Heavy Company
   1 Infantry Gun Section (2 75mm leIG)
   1 Panzer Abwehr Platoon (3 37mm PAK 36 and 1
    LMG)
   1 Pioneer Platoon (3 LMGs)
  1 (mot) Light Reconnaissance Supply Column

38th Panzerabwehr Battalion
  1 (mot) Signals Platoon
  3 (mot) Batteries (12 37mm PAK 36 and 6 LMGs ea)

1/74th Artillery Regiment
  1 (mot) Signals Platoon
  1 (mot) Weather Detachment
  1st (mot) Battalion
   1 (mot) Signals Platoon
   1 (mot) Calibration Detachment
   3 (mot) Batteries (4 105mm leFH and 2 LMGs ea)

1/110th Artillery Regiment
  1st (mot) Battalion
   1 (mot) Signals Platoon
   1 (mot) Calibration Detachment
   1 (mot) Battery (4 100mm guns and 2 LMGs)
   2 (mot) Batteries (4 150mm sFH and 2 LMGs ea)

38th Panzer Signals Battalion
  1 (mot) Panzer Signals Company (2 LMGs)
  1 (mot) Panzer Radio Company (12 LMGs)
  1 (mot) Panzer Signals Supply Column

38th Pioneer Battalion
  3 (mot) Pioneer Companies (9 LMGs ea)
  1 (mot) Brüko K
  1 (mot) Light Pioneer Supply Column

82nd Divisional Support Units
  1–6/82nd (mot) Light Supply Columns

7/, 8/, 9/82nd (mot) Heavy Fuel Columns
1/, 2/82nd (mot) Maintenance Companies
82nd (mot) Supply Company
Support Units
  82nd (mot) Field Bakery
  82nd (mot) Butcher Detachment
  82nd Division Administration
  1/, 2/82nd (mot) Medical Companies
  1/, 2/, 3/82nd Ambulance Companies
  82nd (mot) Military Police Troop
  82nd (mot) Field Post Office

In addition, the division had two Luftwaffe formations attached to it. They were:

1.(H)/14 Reconnaissance Staffel
92nd (mot) Light Flak Battalion
  1 (mot) Medium Flak Battery (9 37mm guns)
  2 (mot) Light Flak Batteries (12 20mm guns)
  20th (mot) Flak Supply Column

On 1 November 1939 the 1/33rd (mot) Infantry Regiment of the 13th Infantry Division was transferred to the division and on 1 April 1940 it became the 3/2nd Schützen Regiment. On 1 April 1940 the 1/13th Artillery Regiment was assigned to the division as the 2/74th Artillery Regiment. A squadron of the 10th Heavy Divisional Reconnaissance Battalion became the 15th Company/2nd Schützen Regiment, the 1/52nd Panzer Abwehr Battalion became the 3/38th Panzerjäger Battalion, the 4/6th Light Supply Column became the 7/82nd and the 7/82nd Heavy Fuel Column was renumbered the 10/82nd Heavy Fuel Column.

On the eve of the invasion of France, 10 May 1940, the organization of the armored portion of the division and its panzer inventory were:

1/, 2/3rd Panzer Regiment
  1 Regimental Staff Signals Platoon
  1 Regimental Staff Light Panzer Platoon
  Each Battalion had
    1 Panzer Staff Company
    1 Medium Panzer Company
    2 Light Panzer Companies
  Total tanks available:

PzMk I	22
PzMk II	55
PzMk III	29
PzMk IV	16
PzBefWg	8

1/, 2/4th Panzer Regiment
  1 Regimental Staff Signals Platoon
  1 Regimental Staff Light Panzer Platoon
  Each Battalion had
    1 Panzer Signals Platoon
    1 Light Panzer Staff Platoon

1 Medium Panzer Company
2 Light Panzer Companies
Total tanks available:

PzMk I	23
PzMk II	60
PzMk III	29
PzMk IV	16
PzBefWg	8

On 28 September 1940 the 4th Panzer Regiment was transferred to the 13th Panzer Division and the 304th Schützen Regiment was raised. The 304th's staff came from the 304th Infantry Regiment (209th Infantry Division), the 1st Battalion was formed from the 1/2nd Schützen Regiment, the 2nd Battalion was formed from the 1/243rd Infantry Regiment (60th Infantry Division), and the 3/2nd Schützen Regiment became the 1/2nd. The 74th Artillery Regiment organized its 2nd Battalion from the 1/13th Artillery Regiment and its 3rd Battalion from the 1/110th Artillery Regiment, already assigned to the division. The division had:

1/, 2/2nd Schützen Regiment
1/, 2/304th Schützen Regiment
2nd Motorcycle Battalion
1/, 2/3rd Panzer Regiment
1/, 2/, 3/74th Artillery Regiment
5th (mot) Reconnaissance Battalion
38th Panzerjäger Battalion
38th Signals Battalion
38th Pioneer Battalion
38th Divisional (Einheiten) Support Units
82nd Supply Troops

On 5 April 1941, during the invasion of Greece, the 2nd Panzer Division had a total of three command tanks, 45 PzMk II, 51 PzMk III and 20 PzMk IV. The division was organized and equipped as follows:

2nd Panzer Division
Divisional Staff (2 LMGs)
82nd Motorcycle Platoon
82nd (mot) Mapping Detachment
3rd Panzer Regiment
1 Panzer Singals Platoon
1 Light Panzer Platoon
1st and 2nd Battalions, each with
  1 Staff and Staff Panzer Company
  2 Light Panzer Companies
  1 Medium Panzer Company
  1 (mot) Replacement Platoon
  1 (mot) Panzer Supply Column
1 (mot) Panzer Maintenance Company
2nd Schützen Brigade
2nd Schützen Regiment
1 (mot) Staff Company

1 Signals Platoon
1 Pioneer Platoon (3 LMGS)
1 Motorcycle Platoon
1st and 2nd (mot) Battalions, each with
  3 (mot) Companies (18 LMGs, 2 HMGs and 3 50mm mortars ea)
  1 (mot) Machine Gun Company (8 HMGs and 6 80mm mortars)
  1 (mot) Support Company
    1 (mot) Infantry Gun Platoon (2 75mm leIG)
    1 Panzerjäger Platoon (3 37mm PAK 36 and 1 LMG)
    1 Pioneer Platoon (3 LMGs)
1 (mot) Infantry Gun Company (2 150mm sIG and 4 75mm leIG)
1 (mot) Light Supply Column
304th Schützen Regiment
same as 2nd Schützen Regiment
16th Motorcycle Battalion
3 Motorcycle Companies (3 50mm mortars, 2 HMGs and 18 LMGs ea)
1 (mot) Heavy Machine Gun Company (8 HMGs and 6 80mm mortars)
1 (mot) Reconnaissance Company
  1 (mot) Infantry Gun Section (2 75mm leIG)
  1 (mot) Panzerjäger Platoon (3 37mm PAK 36 and 1 LMG)
  1 (mot) Pioneer Platoon (3 LMGs)
38th Panzerjäger Battalion
1 (mot) Signals Platoon
3 (mot) Panzerjäger Companies (12 37mm PAK 36 and 6 LMGs ea)
2nd Company/47th Self-Propelled Heavy Machine Gun Battalion (10 20mm guns)
5th Reconnaissance Battalion
1 (mot) Signals Platoon (2 LMGs)
1 Armored Car Company (10 20mm and 25 LMGs)
1 Motorcycle Company (3 50mm mortars, 2 HMGs and 18 LMGs)
1 (mot) Heavy Reconnaissance Company
  1 Panzerjäger Platoon (3 37mm PAK 36 and 1 LMG)
  1 Pioneer Platoon (3 LMGs)
  1 Infantry Gun Section (2 75mm leIG)
1 (mot) Reconnaissance Supply Column
74th Artillery Regiment
1 (mot) Support Detachment
  1 (mot) Signals Platoon
  1 (mot) Weather Detachment
1st and 2nd (mot) Battalions, each with
  1 (mot) Calibration Detachment
  1 (mot) Signals Platoon
  3 (mot) Batteries (4 105mm leFH and 2 LMGs ea)
3rd (mot) Battalions
1 Calibration Detachment

1 Signals Platoon
1 (mot) Battery (4 100mm K18 and 2 LMGs)
2 (mot) Batteries (4 150mm sFH and 2 LMGs ea)
320th (mot) Panzer Observation Company

38th Signals Battalion
1 (mot) Panzer Telephone Company (2 LMGs)
1 (mot) Panzer Radio Company (13 LMGS)
1 (mot) Light Signals Supply Column

38th (mot) Pioneer Battalion
1 Armored Pioneer Company (35 LMGs and 2 PzBu39)
2 (mot) Pioneer Companies (9 LMGs ea)
1 (mot) Brüko B
1 (mot) Brüko K
1 (mot) Light Pioneer Supply Column

38th Supply Troop
1/, 2/, 3/, 4/, 5/, 6/, 7/38th (mot) Light Supply Columns
8/, 9/, 10/38th (mot) Heavy Fuel Column
1/, 2/, 3/38th (mot) Maintenance Company
38th (mot) Supply Company

Administration
38th (mot) Field Bakery
38th (mot) Butcher Company
38th (mot) Divisional Administration

Other
1/, 2/38th (mot) Medical Company
1/, 2/, 3/38th (mot) Ambulance Companies
38th (mot) Military Police Troop
38th (mot) Field Post Office

Attached
76th Flak Battalion
1/(H) 14th Panzer Observation Squadron

By September 1941 the armored portion of the division had been reorganized as follows:

1/, 2/3rd Panzer Regiment
1 Regimental Staff Signals Platoon
1 Regimental Staff Light Panzer Platoon
Each Battalion had
1 Panzer Staff Company
1 Medium Panzer Company
3 Light Panzer Companies
Total tanks available:

PzMk II	63
PzMk III (50)	105
PzMk IV (kz)	20
PzBefWg	6

In 1942 the 1/3rd Panzer Regiment was detached to the 33rd Panzer Regiment. The regiment retained only the 2nd Battalion. The 5th Reconnaissance Battalion was reorganized as the 24th Motorcycle Battalion and assigned to the 24th Panzer Division. On 20 June 1942 the organi-

zation of the armored portion of the division and its panzer inventory were as follows:

2/3rd Panzer Regiment
1 Regimental Staff Signals Platoon
1 Regimental Staff Light Panzer Platoon
Each Battalion had
1 Panzer Staff Company
1 Medium Panzer Company
2 Light Panzer Companies
Total tanks available:

PzMk II	22
38 (t)	33
PzMk III (50 kz)	20
PzMk IV (kz)	5
PzBefWg	2

In 1942 the division absorbed the 273rd Army Flak Artillery Battalion. On 25 March 1943 the 1/3rd Panzer Regiment was rebuilt. On 7 May 1943 it became the 507th Panzer Battalion (Tiger tanks) and on 30 June 1943 it again became the 1/3rd Panzer Regiment (Panther tanks). The 2nd Motorcycle Battalion became the 2nd Armored Reconnaissance Battalion. The division had:

1/, 2/2nd Panzergrenadier Regiment
1/, 2/304th Panzergrenadier Regiment
2nd Armored Reconnaissance Battalion
1/, 2/3rd Panzer Regiment
1/, 2/, 3/74th Panzer Artillery Regiment
273rd Army Flak Artillery Battalion
38th Armored Panzerjäger Battalion
38th Panzer Signals Battalion
38th Panzer Pioneer Battalion
38th Divisional Support Units
82nd Supply Troops

Early in 1943 the two panzergrenadier regiments each had (motZ) infantry gun companies (four 150mm sIG) attached to them. In addition, they shared the services of the 703rd (self-propelled) Infantry Gun Company. In June the 703rd appears to have been removed and the two (motZ) companies were each re-equipped with six self-propelled 150mm sIG guns. The 273rd Army Flak Battalion added a second heavy Flak battery on 15 April 1943 and the 4th (light) Self-Propelled battery on 5 May 1943.

On 1 July 1943 the organization of the armored portion of the division and its panzer inventory were as follows:

2/3rd Panzer Regiment
1 Regimental Staff Signals Platoon
1 Regimental Staff Light Panzer Platoon
Each Battalion had
1 Panzer Staff Company
2 Medium Panzer Companies

2 Light Panzer Companies
Total tanks available:

PzMk II	12
PzMk III (kz)	8
PzMk III (lg)	12
PzMk III (75)	20
PzMk IV (kz)	1
PzMk IV (lg)	59
PzBefWg	6

The 82nd Supply Troop underwent some major reorganization on 16 April 1943. Initially it had seven (mot) light supply columns and five (mot) heavy fuel columns. They were replaced with the organization shown below. OKH Records indicate that the division was organized and equipped as follows during the "summer" of 1943:

Division Staff
1 Division Staff (2 LMGs)
82nd (mot) Mapping Detachment

2/3rd Panzer Regiment
1 Regimental Staff and Staff Company (received 7 PzMk III flame panzers on 18 June 1943)
4 Panzer Companies (22 PzMk IV ea)
1 Panzer Maintenance Company

2nd Panzergrenadier Regiment
1 Regimental Staff
1 (mot) Regimental Staff Company
  1 Signals Platoon
  1 Panzerjäger Platoon (3 75mm PAK 40 and 3 LMGs)
  1 Pioneer Platoon (6 flamethrowers and 6 LMGs)
  1 Motorcycle Platoon (6 LMGs)
  1 Regimental Band

1st (half-track) Battalion
3 (half-track) Companies (4 HMGs, 34 LMGs, 2 80mm mortars, 3 37mm PAK 36 on half-tracks and 3 sPzBu 41 ea)
1 (half-track) Heavy Company
  1 Staff (2 LMGs)
  1 Pioneer Platoon (4 LMGs)
  1 Panzerjäger Platoon (3 50mm PAK 38 and 3 LMGs)
  1 Infantry Gun Platoon (4 LMGs and 4 75mm leIG)
  1 Panzerjäger Platoon (3 LMGs and 3 PzBu39)

2nd (mot) Battalion
3 (mot) Companies (4 HMGs, 18 LMGs and 2 80mm mortars ea)
1 (mot) Heavy Company
  1 Pioneer Platoon (4 LMGs and 6 flamethrowers)
  1 Panzerjäger Platoon (3 50mm PAK 38)
  1 Infantry Gun Platoon (4 LMGs and 4 75mm leIG)
  1 Panzerjäger Platoon (3 LMGs and 3 sPzBu 41)
1 Self-Propelled Infantry Gun Company (6 150mm sIG and 7 LMGs)

304th Panzergrenadier Regiment
1 Regimental Staff
1 (mot) Regimental Staff Company
  1 Signals Platoon
  1 Panzerjäger Platoon (3 75mm PAK 40 and 3 LMGs)
  1 Pioneer Platoon (6 flamethrowers and 6 LMGs)
  1 Motorcycle Platoon (6 LMGs)
  1 Regimental Band

1st and 2nd (mot) Battalions, each with
3 (mot) Companies (4 HMGs, 18 LMGs and 2 80mm mortars ea)
1 (mot) Heavy Company
  1 Pioneer Platoon (4 LMGs and 6 flamethrowers)
  1 Panzerjäger Platoon (3 50mm PAK 38)
  1 Infantry Gun Platoon (4 LMGs and 4 75mm leIG)
  1 Panzerjäger Platoon (3 LMGs and 3 sPzBu 41)
1 Self-Propelled Infantry Gun Company (6 150mm sIG and 7 LMGs)

2nd Reconnaissance Battalion (7/10/43 organization)
1 Armored Car Company (6 LMGs and 6 75mm guns) (added later in year)
1 Armored Car Company (24 LMGs and 18 20mm guns)
1 Armored Car (half-track) Company (25 LMGs and 16 20mm)
1 Motorcycle Company (2 80mm mortars, 4 HMGs, 18 LMGs and 3 PzBu39) (replaced by formation of second half-track reconnaissance company; date of change is unclear)
1 (half-track) Reconnaissance Company (4 HMGs, 56 LMGs, 3 37mm PAK 36 and 2 120mm mortars; 2nd company raised to replace motorcycle company)
1 (half-track) Heavy Reconnaissance Company
  1 Staff Platoon (2 LMGs)
  1 Infantry Platoon (9 LMGs)
  1 Half-Track Gun Platoon (8 LMGs and 6 75mm guns on half-tracks)
  1 Infantry Gun Section (2 75mm leIG)
  1 Panzerjäger Platoon (4 LMGs and 3 75mm PAK 40)
  1 Pioneer Platoon (13 LMGs, 1 37mm PAK 36 and 6 flamethrowers)
1 (mot) Light Reconnaissance Supply Column (3 LMGs)

74th Panzer Artillery Regiment
1 Regimental Staff
  1 Staff Battery (2 LMGs)

1st and 2nd (mot) Battalions, each with
1 Battalion Staff
1 Battalion Staff Battery (6 LMGs)
3 (mot) Batteries (4 105mm leFH and 4 LMGs ea)

Revised 1st Battalion (as appeared in July 1943)
1 Battalion Staff and Staff Battery (6 LMGs)
2 Self-Propelled Batteries (6 105mm leFH SdKfz 124 Wespe and 4 LMGs ea)
1 Self-Propelled Battery (6 150mm sFH SdKfz 165 Hummel and 4 LMGs)

3rd (mot) Battalion
1 Battalion Staff
1 Battalion Staff Battery (6 LMGs)
2 (mot) Batteries (4 150mm sFH and 4 LMGs ea)
1 (mot) Battery (4 100mm K 18 guns and 4 LMGs)
74th (mot) Observation Battery (2 LMGs)
38th Panzerjäger Battalion
2 (motZ) Panzerjäger Companies (10 75mm PAK 40 ea) (later made self-propelled)
1 Self-Propelled Panzerjäger Company (14 75mm PAK 40 and 14 LMGs ea)
273rd Army Flak Battalion
1 Staff and (mot) Staff Battery (1 LMG)
1st–2nd (motZ) Heavy Flak Batteries (4 88mm, 3 20mm and 2 LMGs ea)
3rd (motZ) Light Flak Battery (12 20mm and 2 LMGs)
4th Self-Propelled Battery (8 20mm and 2 quad 20mm Flak guns and 4 LMGs)
1 (mot) Light (20 ton) Flak Supply Column
38th Panzer Pioneer Battalion
1 Staff (2 LMGs)
1 (half-track) Pioneer Company (25 LMGs, 3 PzBu39, 2 80mm mortars and 6 flamethrowers)
2 (mot) Pioneer Companies (18 LMGs, 3 PzBu39, 2 80mm mortars and 6 flamethrowers ea)
1 Brüko K Bridging Column (3 LMGs)
1 (mot) Light Pioneer Supply Column (2 LMGs)
38th Panzer Signals Battalion
1 Panzer Telephone Company (6 LMGs)
1 Panzer Radio Company (16 LMGs)
1 (mot) Light Signals Supply Column (1 LMG)
82nd Feldersatz Battalion
5 Companies
82nd Ost Battalion (disbanded in July 1943)
1 Staff Company (4 LMGs)
2 Companies (12 LMGs, 1 80mm mortar and 2 50mm mortars ea)
82nd Supply Troop
1–2/82nd (mot) (120 ton) Transportation Companies (4 LMGs ea)
3rd–5th/82nd (mot) (90 ton) Transportation Company (3 LMGs ea)
6/82nd (horse-drawn) Light Supply Column (4 LMGs)
82nd (mot) Supply Company (6 LMGs)
Truck Park
1–3/82nd (mot) Maintenance Companies (4 LMGs ea)
1 (mot) Heavy (75 ton) Replacement Supply Column (4 LMGs)
Other
82nd (mot) Bakery Company
82nd (mot) Butcher Company
82nd (mot) Administration Platoon
1/, 2/82nd (mot) Medical Companies (2 LMGs ea)
1/, 2/, 3/82nd Ambulances

82nd (mot) Military Police Troop (2 LMGs)
82nd (mot) Field Post Office

During 1943 2/3rd Panzer Regiment contained four companies of Panzer PzMk IV tanks. The panzergrenadier regiments had no Flak companies. The 304th Panzergrenadiers had no organic infantry gun company and those services were provided by the 703rd Self-Propelled Heavy Infantry Gun Company. The 1/304th Panzergrenadiers and the 3rd and 4th Companies of the reconnaissance battalion were equipped with half-tracks. The 38th Panzerjäger Battalion had three self-propelled companies. In addition, the 276th Army Sturmgeschütz Battalion was assigned to the division. The 74th Panzer (mot) Observation Battery was assigned to the division. The 273rd (mot) Army Flak Battalion had a staff, staff battery, one light and two heavy Flak batteries. In addition, the 4th Light Battery was a (motZ) 20mm Flak Battery. The feldersatz battalion had five companies.

On 15 January 1944 the 2nd Panzer Division was withdrawn from combat and began refitting and rebuilding. The 1/3rd Panzer Regiment was rebuilt and operational as a Panther battalion, on 25 February 1944. The 2/1st Panzer Regiment continued to be equipped with Panzer PzMk IV tanks. When complete, the regiment was to have 79 Panthers and 101 PzMk IV Tanks. It was rebuilt and equipped as follows:

Division Staff
1 Division Staff (2 LMGs)
82nd (mot) Mapping Detachment
82nd (mot) Divisional Escort Company
1 Motorcycle Messenger Platoon
1 (mot) Infantry Gun Section (2 75mm leIG)
1 Self-Propelled Flak Company (4 20mm guns)
1 (mot) Panzerjäger Platoon (3 75mm PAK 40 and 3 OMGs)
1 (mot) Infantry Section (4 HMGs, 6 LMGs and 2 80mm mortars)
1/3rd Panzer Regiment
1 Regimental Staff and Staff Company
4 Panzer Companies (22 PzMk V ea)
1 Panzer Maintenance Platoon
2/3rd Panzer Regiment
1 Regimental Staff and Staff Company
4 Panzer Companies (22 PzMk IV ea)
1 Panzer Maintenance Company (lacking 2nd Platoon)
2nd Panzergrenadier Regiment
1 Regimental Staff
1 (half-track) Regimental Staff Company
1 Signals Platoon (7 LMGs)
1 Motorcycle Platoon (6 LMGs)
1 Panzerjäger Platoon (6 75mm PAK 40 and 6 LMGs)

44

1 Pioneer Platoon (6 flamethrowers and 6 LMGs)
1 Light Gun Section (3 20mm guns)

1st (half-track) Battalion
3 (half-track) Companies (4 HMGs, 39 LMGs, 2 80mm mortars, 7 20mm guns and 2 75mm KwK)
1 (half-track) Heavy Company
1 Panzerjäger Platoon (4 20mm guns and 3 75mm PAK 40)
1 Infantry Gun Platoon (4 LMGs and 2 75mm leIG)
1 Support Platoon (8 LMGs and 6 75mm KwK guns)

2nd (mot) Battalion
3 (mot) Companies (4 HMGs, 18 LMGs and 2 80mm mortars ea)
1 (mot) Heavy Company
1 Panzerjäger Platoon (3 75mm PAK 40 and 3 LMGs)
1 Flak Platoon (6 20mm guns)
1 Heavy Mortar Platoon (6 120mm mortars)
1 (mot) Pioneer Company
1 (half-track) Pioneer Platoon (13 LMGs and 6 flamethrowers)
1 Pioneer Platoon (8 LMGs and 6 flamethrowers)
1 Self-Propelled Infantry Gun Company (6 150mm sIG and 7 LMGs)

304th Panzergrenadier Regiment
same as 2nd Panzergrenadier Regiment

2nd Reconnaissance Battalion
1 Armored Car Company (24 LMGs and 18 20mm guns)
1 (half-track) Armored Car Company (25 LMGs and 16 20mm guns)
2 (half-track) Reconnaissance Companies (4 HMGs, 56 LMGs, 3 37mm PAK 36 guns and 2 80mm mortars)
1 (half-track) Heavy Reconnaissance Company
1 Pioneer Platoon (13 LMGs, 1 37mm and 6 flamethrowers)
1 Half-Track Gun Platoon (8 LMGs and 6 75mm KwK on half-tracks)
1 Infantry Gun Section (2 75mm leFH and 4 LMGS)
1 Panzerjäger Platoon (4 LMGs and 3 75mm PAK 40)
1 (mot) Light Reconnaissance Supply Column (3 LMGs)

38th Panzerjäger Battalion
1 Self-Propelled Staff Battery
1 Self-Propelled Panzerjäger Platoon (3 75mm PAK 40)
3 Self-Propelled Panzerjäger Companies (14 75mm PAK 40 and 14 LMGs ea)

74th Panzer Artillery Regiment
1 Regimental Staff
1 Staff Battery (2 LMGs)

1st Battalion
1 Battalion Staff and Staff Battery (2 LMGs)
2 Self-Propelled Batteries (6 105mm leFH SdKfz 124 Wespe and 6 LMGs ea)
1 Self-Propelled Battery (6 150mm sFH SdKfz 165 Hummel and 5 LMGs)

2nd (mot) Battalion
1 Battalion Staff
1 Battalion Staff Battery (2 LMGs)
3 (mot) Batteries (4 105mm leFH and 5 LMGs ea)

3rd (mot) Battalion
1 Battalion Staff
1 Battalion Staff Battery (2 LMGs)
2 (mot) Batteries (4 150mm sFH and 5 LMGs ea)
1 (mot) Battery (4 100mm K 18 guns and 5 LMGs)

273rd Army Flak Battalion
1 Staff and (mot) Staff Battery (2 LMGs)
1st–2nd (motZ) Heavy Flak Batteries (4 88mm, 3 20mm and 2 LMGs ea)
3rd (motZ) Light Flak Battery (12 20mm and 2 LMGs)
4th Self-Propelled Battery (9 20mm and 2 quad 20mm Flak guns and 4 LMGs)
1 (mot) Light (20 ton) Flak Supply Column

38th Panzer Pioneer Battalion
1 Staff (2 LMGs)
1 (half-track) Pioneer Company (43 LMGs, 3 PzBu39, 2 80mm mortars and 6 flamethrowers)
2 (mot) Pioneer Companies (1
1 Brüko K Bridging Column (3 LMGs)
1 (mot) Light Pioneer Supply Column (2 LMGs)

38th Panzer Signals Battalion
1 (half-track) Panzer Telephone Company (21 LMGs)
1 (half-track) Panzer Radio Company (35 LMGs)
1 (mot) Light Signals Supply Column (4 LMGs)

82nd Feldersatz Battalion
4 Companies

82nd Supply Troop
1–7/82nd (mot) (120 ton) Transportation Companies (8 LMGs ea)
82nd (mot) Supply Company (6 LMGs)

Truck Park
1–3/82nd (mot) Maintenance Companies (4 LMGs ea)
1 (mot) Heavy (75 ton) Replacement Supply Column (4 LMGs)

Other
82nd (mot) Bakery Company
82nd (mot) Butcher Company
82nd (mot) Administration Platoon
1/, 2/82nd (mot) Medical Companies (2 LMGs ea)
1/, 2/, 3/82nd Ambulance Companies
82nd (mot) Military Police Troop (2 LMGs)
82nd (mot) Field Post Office

The division was ordered to convert its panzer regiment to the "freie Gliderung" on 20 May 1944. In June 1944 the organization of the armored portion of the division and its panzer inventory were as follows:

1/, 2/3rd Panzer Regiment
1 Panzer Staff Company
4/301st Panzer Battalion (FKL)

1 Battalion
  1 Panzer Staff Company
  4 Medium Panzer Companies (PzMk V)
1 Battalion
  1 Panzer Staff Company
  4 Medium Panzer Companies (PzMk IV)
Total tanks available:
  PzMk IV (lg) 99
  PzMk V   79
  Flakpz38   12
  StuG   10

The division was destroyed in Normandy in August 1944 and only a small cadre remained. The division was reorganized with a panther battalion organized with four companies, each with 14 PzMk V Panther tanks. The second battalion was a mixed battalion, having two companies with 14 PzMk IV tanks and two sturm-geschütz companies, each with 14 sturmgeschütze.

The division was rebuilt again in November 1944, in time to fight in the Ardennes Offensive. The 1st Battalion was to be equipped with 60 PzMkV Panthers and the 2nd Battalion was to have two companies each with 14 PzMk IV tanks and two companies each with 14 StuG IIIs. On 14 December 1944 the organization of the armored portion of the division and its panzer inventory were as follows:

1/, 2/3rd Panzer Regiment
  1 Panzer Staff Company
  1st Battalion
    1 Panzer Staff Company
    4 Medium Panzer Companies (PzMk V)
  2nd Battalion
    1 Panzer Staff Company
    2 Medium Panzer Companies (PzMk IV)
    2 Sturmgeschütz Companies (StuG)
Total tanks available:
  StuG   24
  PzMk IV (lg)   28
  PzMk V   64
  Flakpz38   4
  FlakpzIV (2V)   4
  FlakpzIV (37)   4

The 2nd Panzer Division surrendered to the Allies on 7 May 1945.

3rd Panzer Division

Formed on 15 October 1935 in Berlin. On 6 October 1936 the organization of the armored portion of the division and its panzer inventory were as follows:

1/, 2/5th Panzer Regiment
  1 Regimental Staff Signals Platoon
  1 Regimental Staff Light Panzer Platoon
  Each Battalion had
    1 Panzer Signals Platoon
    1 Light Panzer Staff Platoon
    4 Light Panzer Companies
1/, 2/6th Panzer Regiment
  1 Regimental Staff Signals Platoon
  1 Regimental Staff Light Panzer Platoon
  Each Battalion had
    1 Panzer Signals Platoon
    1 Light Panzer Staff Platoon
    4 Light Panzer Companies
1/, 2/8th Panzer Regiment
  1 Regimental Staff Signals Platoon
  1 Regimental Staff Light Panzer Platoon
  Each Battalion had
    1 Panzer Signals Platoon
    1 Light Panzer Staff Platoon
    4 Light Panzer Companies

On 12 October 1937 the armored portion of the division was reorganized and consisted of:

1/, 2/5th Panzer Regiment
  1 Regimental Staff Signals Platoon
  1 Regimental Staff Light Panzer Platoon
  Each Battalion had
    1 Panzer Signals Platoon
    1 Light Panzer Staff Platoon
    4 Light Panzer Companies
1/, 2/6th Panzer Regiment
  1 Regimental Staff Signals Platoon
  1 Regimental Staff Light Panzer Platoon
  Each Battalion had
    1 Panzer Signals Platoon
    1 Light Panzer Staff Platoon
    4 Light Panzer Companies

On 10 October 1938 the armored portion of the division was again reorganized and consisted of:

1/, 2/5th Panzer Regiment
  1 Regimental Staff Signals Platoon
  1 Regimental Staff Light Panzer Platoon

Each Battalion had
  1 Panzer Signals Platoon
  1 Light Panzer Staff Platoon
  4 Light Panzer Companies
1/, 2/6th Panzer Regiment
  1 Regimental Staff Signals Platoon
  1 Regimental Staff Light Panzer Platoon
Each Battalion had
  1 Panzer Signals Platoon
  1 Light Panzer Staff Platoon
  4 Light Panzer Companies

The division was mobilized for the invasion of Poland on 1 August 1939. At that time it was organized and equipped as follows:

3rd Panzer Division
3rd Schützen Brigade
  3rd Schützen Regiment
    1 (mot) Signals Platoon
    1 Motorcycle Company
    1st and 2nd (mot) Battalions, each with
      2 (mot) Rifle Companies (9 LMGS, 2 HMGS and 3 50mm mortars ea)
      1 (mot) Machine Gun Company (8 HMGs and 6 80mm mortars)
      1 (mot) Heavy Company
      1 Infantry Gun Section (2 75mm leIG)
      1 Panzer Abwehr Platoon (3 37mm PAK 36 and 1 LMG)
      1 Pioneer Platoon (3 LMGS)
  3rd Motorcycle Battalion
    3 Motorcycle Companies (9 LMGs, 2 HMGS and 3 50mm mortars ea)
    1 Motorcycle Heavy Machine Gun Company (8 HMGs and 6 80mm mortars)
    1 (mot) Heavy Company
    1 Infantry Gun Section (2 75mm leIG)
    1 Panzer Abwehr Platoon (3 37mm PAK 36 and 1 LMG)
    1 Pioneer Platoon (3 LMGs)
3rd Panzer Brigade
  5th Panzer Regiment
    1 Armored Signals Platoon
    1 Staff Light Tank Platoon
    1st and 2nd Panzer Battalions, each with
      1 Armored Signals Platoon
      1 Staff Light Tank Platoon
      3 Light Panzer Companies
      1 (mot) Reserve Platoon
      1 (mot) Panzer Supply Column
    1 (mot) Maintenance Company
  Reinforced Panzer Lehr Battalion
    1 Staff Light Panzer Platoon

    2 Light Panzer Companies
    1 Medium Panzer Company
    1 (mot) Maintenance Company
    2 (mot) Light Supply Columns
  6th Panzer Regiment
    1 Armored Signals Platoon
    1 Staff Light Tank Platoon
    1st and 2nd Battalions, each with
      1 Armored Signals Platoon
      1 Staff Light Tank Platoon
      3 Light Panzer Companies
      1 (mot) Reserve Platoon
      1 (mot) Panzer Supply Column
    1 (mot) Maintenance Company
  75th Artillery Regiment
    1 (mot) Signals Platoon
    1 (mot) Weather Detachment
    1st and 2nd (mot) Battalions, each with
      1 (mot) Signals Platoon
      1 (mot) Calibration Detachment
      3 (mot) Batteries (4 105mm leFH and 2 LMGs ea)
  3rd (mot) Reconnaissance Battalion
    1 (mot) Signals Platoon
    2 Armored Car Platoons (10 20mm and 25 LMGs)
    1 Motorcycle Company (9 LMGs, 2 HMGs and 3 50mm mortars)
    1 (mot) Heavy Company
    2 Infantry Gun Sections (2 75mm leIG ea)
    1 Pioneer Platoon (3 LMGs)
    1 (mot) Light Reconnaissance Supply Column
  39th Panzerabwehr (AT) Battalion
    1 (mot) Signals Platoon
    3 (mot) Batteries (12 37mm PAK 36 and 6 LMGs ea)
    1 (mot) Heavy Machine Gun Company (12 20mm guns) (attached later)
  39th Panzer Division Signals Battalion
    1 (mot) Panzer Signals Company (2 LMGs)
    1 (mot) Panzer Radio Company (12 LMGs)
    1 (mot) Panzer Signals Supply Column
  39th Pioneer Battalion
    3 (mot) Pioneer Companies (9 LMGs ea)
    1 (mot) Brüko K
    1 (mot) Light Pioneer Supply Column
  83rd Divisional Support Units
    1–6/83rd (mot) Light Supply Columns
    7–8/83rd (mot) Light Fuel Columns
    1/, 2/83rd (mot) Maintenance Companies
    83rd (mot) Supply Company
    83rd (mot) Field Bakery
    83rd (mot) Butcher Detachment
    83rd Division Administration
    1/, 2/83rd (mot) Medical Companies
    1/, 2/, 3/83rd Ambulance Companies
    83rd (mot) Military Police Troop
    83rd (mot) Field Post Office

Just prior to the invasion of Poland and on the day of the invasion, the inventory of tanks assigned to the division was as follows:

	15 Aug. 1939	1 Sept. 1939
5th Regiment		
PzMk I	84	63
PzMk II	81	77
PzMk III	3	3
PzMk IV	9	9
Cmd 265	10	
Cmd 267	1	8
Cmd 268	0	
6th Regiment		
PzMk I	84	59
PzMk II	81	66
PzMk III	3	0
PzMk IV	9	6
Cmd 265	10	
Cmd 267	1	8
Cmd 268	0	
Panzer Lehr Bn		
PzMk I		0
PzMk II		20
PzMk III		37
PzMk IV		14
PzBefWg		2

On the day of the invasion of Poland the armored portion of the division was organized as follows:

1/, 2/5th Panzer Regiment
  1 Regimental Staff Signals Platoon
  1 Regimental Staff Light Panzer Platoon
  Each Battalion had
    1 Panzer Signals Platoon
    1 Light Panzer Staff Platoon
    3 Light Panzer Companies
1/, 2/6th Panzer Regiment
  1 Regimental Staff Signals Platoon
  1 Regimental Staff Light Panzer Platoon
  Each Battalion had
    1 Panzer Signals Platoon
    1 Light Panzer Staff Platoon
    3 Light Panzer Companies
Panzer Lehr Battalion
  1 Panzer Staff Signals Platoon
  1 Light Panzer Staff Platoon
  1 Medium Panzer Company
  2 Light Panzer Companies

On 1 November 1939 the 1/69th (mot) Infantry Regiment of the 20th (mot) Infantry Division was incorporated into the division and on 1 April 1940 it became the 3/3rd Schützen Regiment. Later the 394th Schützen Regiment was formed with the staff of the 394th Infantry Regiment, the 3/3rd Schützen Regiment, and the 3/243rd Infantry Regiment (60th Infantry Division).

On 1 April 1940 a squadron of the 46th Divisoinal Reconaissance Battalion was assigned as the 15th Company/3rd Schützen Regiment, the 4/30th Light Supply Column became the 7/83rd, and the 7/83rd Heavy Fuel Column became the 10/83rd.

On 10 May 1940, the day of the invasion of France, the organization of the armored portion of the division and its panzer inventory were as follows:

1/, 2/5th Panzer Regiment
  1 Regimental Staff Signals Platoon
  1 Regimental Staff Light Panzer Platoon
  Each Battalion had
    1 Panzer Signals Platoon
    1 Light Panzer Staff Platoon
    1 Medium Tank Company
    2 Light Panzer Companies
1/, 2/6th Panzer Regiment
  1 Regimental Staff Signals Platoon
  1 Regimental Staff Light Panzer Platoon
  Each Battalion had
    1 Panzer Staff Company
    1 Medium Tank Company
    2 Light Panzer Companies
Total tanks available:

PzMk I	117
PzMk II	129
PzMk III	42
PzMk IV	26
PzBefWg	27

In January 1941, in order to support the newly forming Afrika Korps, the division detached the 5th Panzer Regiment, the 3rd (mot) Reconnaissance Battalion, the 39th Panzerjäger Battalion, and the 1/75th Artillery Regiment to the 5th Light Division. By March the 1/28th Panzer Regiment (18th Panzer Division) was redesignated as the 3/6th Panzer Division, and the 2/49th Artillery Regiment became the 3/75th Artillery Regiment. The 1st (mot) Reconnaissance Battalion and the 543rd Panzerjäger Battalion were formed from army troops. The staff of the 5th Panzer Brigade was also newly reorganized. The division then had:

3rd Schützen Brigade
  1/, 2/3rd Schützen Regiment
  1/, 2/394th Schützen Regiment
  3rd Motorcycle Battalion
5th Panzer Brigade
  1/, 2/, 3/6th Panzer Regiment
2/, 3/75th Artillery Regiment
543rd Panzerjäger Battalion

1st Reconnaissance Battalion
39th Signals Battalion
39th Pioneer Battalion
83rd Supply Troops
39th Divisional Support Units

On 22 June 1941, the day of the invasion of Russia, the organization of the armored portion of the division and its panzer inventory were as follows:

1/, 2/, 3/6th Panzer Regiment
  1 Regimental Staff Signals Platoon
  1 Regimental Staff Light Panzer Platoon
  Each Battalion had
    1 Panzer Staff Company
    1 Medium Panzer Company
    3 Light Panzer Companies
  Total tanks available:
    PzMk II   58
    PzMk III (37)   29
    PzMk III (50)   81
    PzMk IV (kz)   32
    PzBefWg   15

By 4 September 1941 its panzer inventory had been reduced to:

    PzMk I   5 operational
    PzMk II   30
    PzMk III   6
    PzMk IV   5
    PzBefWg   8

On 27 June 1942 the organization of the armored portion of the division and its panzer inventory were as follows:

1/, 2/, 3/6th Panzer Regiment
  1 Regimental Staff Signals Platoon
  1 Regimental Staff Light Panzer Platoon
  Each Battalion had
    1 Panzer Staff Company
    1 Medium Panzer Company
    2 Light Panzer Companies
  Total tanks available:
    PzMk II   25
    PzMk III (50 kz) 66
    PzMk III (50 lg) 40
    PzMk IV (kz)   21
    PzMk IV (lg)   12

In 1942 the 714th Heavy Artillery Battalion and 314th Army Flak Artillery Battalion became the 1/, 4/75th Artillery Regiment respectively. In 1943 the 4/75th Artillery Regiment became the 314th Army Flak Battalion. The 3rd

Motorcycle Battalion was redesignated as the 3rd Panzer Reconnaissance Battalion and the 3/6th Panzer Regiment was disbanded. The division then had:

1/, 2/3rd Panzergrenadier Regiment
1/, 2/394th Panzergrenadier Regiment
3rd Panzer Reconnaissance Battalion
1/, 2/6th Panzer Regiment
1/, 2/, 3/75th Panzer Artillery Regiment
314th Army Flak Artillery Battalion
543rd Panzerjäger Battalion
39th Signals Battalion
39th Pioneer Battalion
39th Divisional Support Units
83rd Supply Troops

In early 1943 the 1/3rd Panzergrenadier Regiment was equipped with half-tracks. The 714th Army (motZ) Artillery Battalion was assigned to the division to replace the 1/75th. The 75th Panzer (mot) Observation Battery was assigned to the division. Sometime during the early part of the summer the 1/6th Panzer Regiment was renumbered as the 2/6th and a new 1/6th Panzer Regiment was organized. On 1 July 1943 the organization of the armored portion of the division and its panzer inventory were as follows:

2/6th Panzer Regiment
  1 Regimental Staff Signals Platoon
  1 Regimental Staff Light Panzer Platoon
  Each Battalion had
    1 Panzer Staff Company
    1 Medium Panzer Company
    3 Light Panzer Companies
  Total tanks available:
    PzMk II   7
    PzMk III (kz)   8
    PzMk III (lg)   34
    PzMk III (75) 17
    PzMk IV (kz)   2
    PzMk IV (lg)   21
    PzBefWg   1

OKH records indicate that the division was organized and equipped as follows during the "summer" of 1943.

Division Staff
  1 Division Staff (2 LMGs)
  83rd (mot) Mapping Detachment
6th Panzer Regiment
1st Battalion
  1 Regimental Staff and Staff Company (received 7 PzMk III flame panzers on 18 June 1943)
  4 Panzer Companies (22 PzMk V ea)
  1 Panzer Maintenance Company

2nd Battalion

1 Regimental Staff and Staff Company (received 7 PzMk III flame panzers on 18 June 1943)

4 Panzer Companies (22 PzMk IV ea)

1 Panzer Maintenance Company

3rd Panzergrenadier Regiment

1 Regimental Staff

1 (mot) Regimental Staff Company

  1 Signals Platoon

  1 Panzerjäger Platoon (3 75mm PAK 40 and 3 LMGs)

  1 (half-track) Pioneer Platoon (6 flamethrowers and 6 LMGs)

  1 Motorcycle Platoon (6 LMGs)

1st (half-track) Battalion

3 (half-track) Companies (4 HMGs, 34 LMGs, 2 80mm mortars, 3 37mm PAK 36 on half-tracks and 3 sPzBu 41 ea)

1 (half-track) Heavy Company

  1 Staff (2 LMGs)

  1 Pioneer Platoon (4, later 9 LMGs)

  1 Panzerjäger Platoon (3 50mm PAK 38 and 3 LMGs)

  1 Infantry Gun Platoon (4 LMGs and 4 75mm leIG)

  1 Panzerjäger Platoon (3 LMGs and 3 sPzBu 41)

2nd (mot) Battalion

3 (mot) Companies (4 HMGs, 18 LMGs and 2 80mm mortars ea)

1 (mot) Heavy Company

  1 Pioneer Platoon (4 LMGs)

  1 Panzerjäger Platoon (3 50mm PAK 38)

  1 Infantry Gun Platoon (4 LMGs and 4 75mm leIG)

  1 Panzerjäger Platoon (3 LMGs and 3 sPzBu 41)

1 (motZ) Infantry Gun Company (4 150mm sIG)

1 Self-Propelled Flak Company (12 20mm and 4 LMGs)

394th Panzergrenadier Regiment

1 Regimental Staff

1 (mot) Regimental Staff Company

  1 Signals Platoon

  1 Panzerjäger Platoon (3 75mm PAK 40 and 3 LMGs)

  1 Pioneer Platoon (6 flamethrowers and 6 LMGs)

  1 Motorcycle Platoon (6 LMGs)

  1 Regimental Band

1st and 2nd (mot) Battalion

same as 2/3rd Panzergrenadier Regiment

1 (motZ) Infantry Gun Company (4 150mm sIG)

1 Self-Propelled Flak Company (12 20mm and 4 LMGs)

75th Panzer Artillery Regiment

1 Regimental Staff

  1 Staff Battery (2 LMGs)

714th and 2nd/75th (mot) Battalions, each with

1 Battalion Staff

1 Battalion Staff Battery (6 LMGs)

3 (mot) Batteries (4 105mm leFH and 4 LMGs ea)

3rd (mot) Battalion

1 Battalion Staff

1 Battalion Staff Battery (6 LMGs)

2 (mot) Batteries (4 150mm sFH and 4 LMGs ea)

1 (mot) Battery (4 100mm K 18 guns and 4 LMGs)

75th (mot) Observation Battery (2 LMGs)

543rd Panzerjäger Battalion

1 (motZ) Panzerjäger Company (12 75mm PAK 40 and 12 LMGs)

1 Self-Propelled Panzerjäger Company (75mm PAK 40)

2nd Reconnaissance Battalion (early 1943 organization)

1st Armored Car Company (24 LMGs and 18 20mm guns)

2nd and 3rd Motorcycle Companies (2 80mm mortars, 4 HMGs, 18 LMGs and 3 PzBu39 ea)

4th (half-track) Reconnaissance Company (4 HMGs, 56 LMGs, 3 37mm PAK 36 and 2 120mm mortars)

5th (half-track) Heavy Reconnaissance Company

  1 Pioneer Platoon (4 LMGs)

  1 Infantry Gun Section (2 75mm leIG)

  1 Panzerjäger Platoon (3 LMGs and 3 75mm PAK 40)

  1 Panzerjäger Platoon (3 LMGs and 2 sPzBu 41)

1 (mot) Light Reconnaissance Supply Column (3 LMGs)

2nd Reconnaissance Battalion (as of 7/10/43)

1 Armored Car Company (24 LMGs and 18 20mm guns)

1 Armored Car (half-track) Company (25 LMGs and 16 20mm guns)

1 Motorcycle Company (2 80mm mortars, 4 HMGs, 18 LMGs and 3 PzBu39)

1 (half-track) Heavy Reconnaissance Company

  1 Staff (2 LMGs)

  1 Infantry Platoon (9 LMGs)

  1 Pioneer Platoon (1 37mm PAK 36, 6 flamethrowers and 13 LMGs)

  1 Panzerjäger Platoon (3 75mm PAK 40 and 4 LMGs)

  1 Infantry Gun Section (2 75mm leIG)

  1 Half-Track Gun Section (8 LMGs and 6 75mm guns)

1 (mot) Light Reconnaissance Supply Column (3 LMGs)

314th Army Flak Battalion

1 Staff and (mot) Staff Battery (1 LMG)

1st–2nd (motZ) Heavy Flak Batteries (4 88mm, 3 20mm and 2 LMGs ea)

3rd (motZ) Light Flak Battery (12 20mm and 2 LMGs)

4th Self-Propelled Battery (8 20mm and 2 quad 20mm Flak guns and 4 LMGs)

1 (mot) Light (20 ton) Flak Supply Column

39th Panzer Pioneer Battalion

1 Staff (2 LMGs)

1 (half-track) Pioneer Company (25 LMGs, 3 PzBu39 and 2 80mm mortars)

2 (mot) Pioneer Companies (18 LMGs, 3 PzBu39 and 2 80mm mortars ea)

1 Brüko K Bridging Column (3 LMGs)
1 (mot) Light Pioneer Supply Column (2 LMGs)

33rd Panzer Signals Battalion
1 Panzer Telephone Company (6 LMGs)
1 Panzer Radio Company (16 LMGs)
1 (mot) Light Signals Supply Column (1 LMG)

83rd Feldersatz Battalion
4 Companies

83rd Supply Troop
1–3/83rd (mot) (90 ton) Transportation Company (3 LMGs ea)
4–5/83rd (mot) (120 ton) Transportation Company (4 LMGs ea)
7/83rd (mot) Heavy Fuel Column (2 LMGs)
83rd (mot) Supply Company (6 LMGs)

Truck Park
1–3/83rd (mot) Maintenance Companies (4 LMGs ea)

Other
83rd (mot) Bakery Company
83rd (mot) Butcher Company
83rd (mot) Administration Platoon
1/, 2/83rd (mot) Medical Companies (2 LMGs ea)
1/, 2/, 3/83rd Ambulances
83rd (mot) Military Police Troop (2 LMGs)
83rd (mot) Field Post Office

On 9 August 1943 the OKH ordered twelve Wespe self-propelled 105mm guns sent to the division. On 25 January 1944 the 1/6th Panzer Regiment was equipped with Panther tanks. The 2/6th Panzer Regiment continued to be equipped with Panzer PzMk IV tanks. In December 1944 the division was reorganized. It was captured in Steyr/Enns and passed into American captivity on 9 May 1945.

4th Panzer Division

Formed on 10 November 1938 in Würzburg. On that day the organization of the armored portion of the division and its panzer inventory were as follows:

1/, 2/35th Panzer Regiment
  1 Regimental Staff Signals Platoon
  1 Regimental Staff Light Panzer Platoon
  Each Battalion had
    1 Panzer Signals Platoon
    1 Light Panzer Staff Platoon
    4 Light Panzer Companies
1/, 2/36th Panzer Regiment
  1 Regimental Staff Signals Platoon
  1 Regimental Staff Light Panzer Platoon
  Each Battalion had
    1 Panzer Signals Platoon
    1 Light Panzer Staff Platoon
    4 Light Panzer Companies

Just prior to the invasion of Poland and on the day of the invasion, the inventory of tanks assigned to the division was as follows:

	15 Aug. 1939	1 Sept. 1939
35th Regiment		
PzMk I	102	99
PzMk II	66	64
PzMk III		0
PzMk IV	6	6
PzBefWg 265	10	
PzBefWg 267	1	8
PzBefWg 268		

2nd Regiment		
PzMk I	101	84
PzMk II	66	66
PzMk III		0
PzMk IV	6	6
PzBefWg 265	10	
PzBefWg 267	1	8
PzBefWg 268		

The division was mobilized on 22 August 1939 with:

4th Schützen Brigade
  1/, 2/12th Schützen Regiment
5th Panzer Brigade
  1/, 2/35th Panzer Regiment
  1/, 2/36th Panzer Regiment
  1/, 2/103rd Artillery Regiment
7th Reconnaissance Battalion
49th Panzerabwehr (Anti-Tank) Battalion
79th Pioneer Battalion
79th Signals Battalion
79th Divisional Support Units
84th Supply Troops

OKH records show that when the Germans invaded Poland on 1 September 1939 the 4th Panzer Division was organized and equipped as follows:

4th Panzer Division Generalleutnant Reinhardt
  84th (mot) Mapping Detachment
  84th Motorcycle Messenger Platoon
  12th Schützen Regiment
    1 (mot) Signals Platoon

1 Motorcycle Messenger Platoon

1st and 2nd (mot) Battalions, each with

   3 (mot) Rifle Companies (9 LMGs, 2 HMGs and 3 50mm mortars ea)

   1 (mot) Heavy Company

      1 Infantry Gun Section (2 75mm leIG)

      1 Mortar Platoon (6 80mm mortars)

      1 Panzer Abwehr Platoon (3 37mm PAK 36 and 1 LMG)

   1 (mot) Light Infantry Column

5th Panzer Brigade

35th Panzer Regiment

   1 Armored Signals Platoon

   1 Staff Light Tank Platoon

   1st and 2nd Panzer Battalions, each with

      1 Armored Signals Platoon

      1 Staff Light Tank Platoon

      3 Light Panzer Companies

      1 (mot) Reserve Platoon

      1 (mot) Panzer Supply Column

      1 (mot) Maintenance Company

1/, 2/36th Panzer Regiment

same as 3rd Panzer Regiment

7th (mot) Reconnaissance Battalion

1 (mot) Signals Platoon

2 Armored Car Platoons (10 20mm and 25 LMGs)

1 Motorcycle Company (9 LMGs, 2 HMGs and 3 50mm mortars)

1 (mot) Heavy Company

   1 Infantry Gun Section (2 75mm leIG)

   1 Panzer Abwehr Platoon (3 37mm PAK 36 and 1 LMG)

   1 Pioneer Platoon (3 LMGs)

1 (mot) Light Reconnaissance Supply Column

49th Panzerabwehr Battalion

1 (mot) Signals Platoon

3 (mot) Batteries (12 37mm PAK 36 and 6 LMGs ea)

103rd Artillery Regiment

1 (mot) Signals Platoon

1 (mot) Weather Detachment

1st and 2nd (mot) Battalions

   1 (mot) Signals Platoon

   1 (mot) Calibration Detachment

   3 (mot) Batteries (4 105mm leFH and 2 LMGs ea)

79th Panzer Signals Battalion

1 (mot) Panzer Signals Company (2 LMGs)

1 (mot) Panzer Radio Company

1 (mot) Panzer Signals Supply Column

Engineering Units

3/79th Pioneer Battalion (9 LMGs ea)

79th (mot) Brüko K

79th (mot) Light Pioneer Supply Column

84th Divisional Support Units

1–6/84th (mot) Light Supply Columns

7/, 8/, 9/84th (mot) Heavy Fuel Columns

1/, 2/84th (mot) Maintenance Companies

84th (mot) Supply Company

Support Units

84th (mot) Field Bakery

84th (mot) Butcher Detachment

84th Division Administration

1/, 2/84th (mot) Medical Companies

1/, 2/, 3/84th Ambulance Companies

84th (mot) Military Police Troop

84th (mot) Field Post Office

In addition, the division had two Luftwaffe formations attached to it. They were:

4.(H)/13 Reconnaissance Staffel

77th Luftwaffe Light Flak Battalion

   1 (mot) Signals Platoon

   3 (mot) Light Flak Batteries (12 20mm)

   1 (mot) Light Flak Supply Column

On 9/25/39 the division's panzer inventory was as follows:

PzMk I	46
PzMk II	33
PzMk III	0
PzMk IV	6
PzBefWg	9

On 18 October 1939 it received the 2/, 3/33rd (mot) Infantry Regiment from the 13th (mot) Infantry Division. On 1 April 1940 those two battalions became the 33rd Schützen Regiment. At the same time the 6/35th Light Supply Column became the 7/84th and the 7/84th Heavy Fuel Column was renumbered as the 10/84th. On 10 May 1940 the organization of the armored portion of the division and its panzer inventory were as follows:

1/, 2/35th Panzer Regiment

   1 Regimental Staff Signals Platoon

   1 Regimental Staff Light Panzer Platoon

   Each Battalion had

      1 Panzer Staff Company

      1 Medium Panzer Company

      2 Light Panzer Companies

   Total tanks available:

PzMk I	69
PzMk II	50
PzMk III	20
PzMk IV	12
PzBefWg	5

1/, 2/36th Panzer Regiment

   1 Regimental Staff Signals Platoon

   1 Regimental Staff Light Panzer Platoon

   Each Battalion had

      1 Panzer Staff Company

1 Medium Panzer Company
2 Light Panzer Companies
Total tanks available:

PzMk I	66
PzMk II	55
PzMk III	20
PzMk IV	12
PzBefWg	5

On 11 November 1940 the 36th Panzer Regiment was detached to the 14th Panzer Division. On 21 January 1941 the 2/93rd Artillery Regiment became the 3/103rd Artillery Regiment. The 34th Motorcycle Battalion was formed from the 3/5th (mot) Infantry Regiment (2nd (mot) Infantry Division). The 3/33rd Infantry Regiment was redesignated as the 1/33rd Schützen Regiment. The division had:

4th Schützen Brigade 7th (mot)
1/, 2/12th Schützen Regiment
1/, 2/33rd Schützen Regiment
34th Motorcycle Battalion
3rd Panzer Brigade (formerly 5th)
1/, 2/35th Panzer Regiment
1/, 2/, 3/103rd Artillery Regiment
Reconnaissance Battalion
49th Panzerjäger Battalion
79th Pioneer Battalion
79th Signals Battalion
79th Divisional Support Units
84th Supply Troops

On 22 June 1941 the organization of the armored portion of the division and its panzer inventory were as follows:

1/, 2/35th Panzer Regiment
1 Regimental Staff Signals Platoon
1 Regimental Staff Light Panzer Platoon
Each Battalion had
  1 Panzer Staff Company
  1 Medium Panzer Company
  3 Light Panzer Companies
Total tanks available:

PzMk II	44
PzMk III (37)	31
PzMk III (50)	74
PzMk IV (kz)	20
PzBefWg	8

By 9 September 1941 the tank inventory had been reduced to:

PzMk I	8 operational
PzMk II	21
PzMk III	24

PzMk IV	11
PzBefWg	19

In 1942 the 7th Reconnaissance and the 34th Motorcycle Battalion were merged and used to form the 4th Panzer Reconnaissance Battalion on 7 June 1943. The 2/35th Panzer Regiment became the 3/15th Panzer Regiment in 1942, leaving the division with only one armored battalion. The 290th Army Flak Battalion was assigned to the division in 1942. On 1 July 1942 the organization of the armored portion of the division and its panzer inventory were as follows:

1/35th Panzer Regiment
1 Regimental Staff Signals Platoon
1 Regimental Staff Light Panzer Platoon
Each Battalion had
  1 Panzer Staff Company
  1 Medium Panzer Company
  3 Light Panzer Companies
Total tanks available:

PzMk II	13
PzMk III (50 kz)	28
PzMk IV (kz)	5
PzBefWg	2

On 1 February 1943 the 700th Panzer Verband was disbanded and its remnants were absorbed into the 35th Panzer Regiment. On 1 July 1943 the organization of the armored portion of the division and its panzer inventory were as follows:

1/35th Panzer Regiment
1 Regimental Staff Signals Platoon
1 Regimental Staff Light Panzer Platoon
Each Battalion had
  1 Panzer Staff Company
  4 Medium Panzer Companies
Total tanks available:

PzMk III (75)	15
PzMk IV (kz)	1
PzMk IV (lg)	79
PzBefWg	6

OKH records show that during the "summer" of 1943 the division was organized and equipped as follows:

Division Staff
1 Division Staff (2 LMGs)
84th (mot) Mapping Detachment
35th Panzer Regiment
1st Battalion (as of 6/14/43)
  1 Regimental Staff and Staff Company (received 7 PzMk III flame panzers on 18 June 1943)
  4 Panzer Companies (22 PzMk IV ea)

5th Panzer Company (organization unknown)

1 Panzer Maintenance Company

12th Panzergrenadier Regiment

1 Regimental Staff

1 (mot) Regimental Staff Company

  1 Signals Platoon

  1 Panzerjäger Platoon (3 75mm PAK 40 and 3 LMGs)

  1 (half-track) Pioneer Platoon (6 flamethrowers and 6 LMGs)

  1 Motorcycle Platoon (6 LMGs)

1st (half-track) Battalion

3 (half-track) Companies (4 HMGs, 39 LMGs, 2 80mm mortars, 3 37mm PAK 36 and 2 75mm guns on half-tracks ea)

1 (half-track) Heavy Company

  1 Staff (5 LMGs)

  1 Pioneer Platoon (13 LMGs, 1 37mm PAK 36 and 6 flamethrowers)

  1 Panzerjäger Platoon (3 75mm PAK 40 and 9 LMGs)

  1 Infantry Gun Platoon (4 LMGs and 2 75mm leIG)

  1 Half-Track Gun Platoon (8 LMGs and 6 75mm guns on half-tracks)

2nd (mot) Battalion

3 (mot) Companies (4 HMGs, 18 LMGs, 2 80mm mortars and 3 PzBu39 ea)

1 (mot) Heavy Company

  1 Pioneer Platoon (4 LMGs)

  1 Panzerjäger Platoon (3 LMGs and 3 50mm PAK 38)

  1 Infantry Gun Platoon (2 75mm leIG)

  1 Panzerjäger Platoon (3 LMGs and 3 sPzBu 41)

1 Self-Propelled Infantry Gun Company (4 150mm sIG)

33rd Panzergrenadier Regiment

1 Regimental Staff

1 (mot) Regimental Staff Company

  1 Signals Platoon

  1 Panzerjäger Platoon (3 75mm PAK 40 and 3 LMGs)

  1 (half-track) Pioneer Platoon (6 flamethrowers and 6 LMGs)

  1 Motorcycle Platoon (6 LMGs)

1st and 2nd (mot) Battalions, each with

3 (mot) Companies (4 HMGs, 18 LMGs, 2 80mm mortars and 3 PzBu39 ea)

1 (mot) Heavy Company

  1 Pioneer Platoon (4 LMGs)

  1 Panzerjäger Platoon (3 LMGs and 3 50mm PAK 38)

  1 Infantry Gun Platoon (2 75mm leIG)

  1 Panzerjäger Platoon (3 LMGs and 3 sPzBu 41)

1 Self-Propelled Infantry Gun Company (4 150mm sIG)

4th Reconnaissance Battalion (early 1943 organization)

1st, 2nd and 3rd Motorcycle Companies (2 80mm mortars, 4 HMGs, 18 LMGs, and 3 PzBu39 ea)

4th Armored Car Company (24 LMGs and 18 20mm guns)

5th (half-track) Heavy Reconnaissance Company

  1 Pioneer Platoon (4 LMGs)

  1 Infantry Gun Section (2 75mm leIG)

  1 Panzerjäger Platoon (3 LMGs and 3 75mm PAK 40)

  1 Panzerjäger Platoon (3 LMGs and 3 sPzBu 41)

1 (mot) Light Reconnaissance Supply Column (3 LMGs)

4th Reconnaissance Battalion (Sept. organization)

4th Armored Car Company (24 LMGs and 18 20mm guns)

3rd Armored Car Company (6 LMGs and 6 75mm guns) (assigned on 17 Sept. 1943; replaced 3rd Motorcycle Company on 15 Sept. 19/43)

2nd Armored Car Company (29 LMGs and 29 20mm guns) (replaced 2nd Motorcycle Company on 15 Sept. 1943)

1st (half-track) Company (2 80mm mortars, 4 HMGs, 56 LMGs and 3 37mm PAK 36) (replaced 1st Motorcycle Company in Aug. 1943)

1 (half-track) Heavy Reconnaissance Company (as of Aug. 1943)

  1 Staff (2 LMGs)

  1 Infantry Platoon (9 LMGs)

  1 Pioneer Platoon (1 37mm PAK 36, 6 flamethrowers and 13 LMGs)

  1 Panzerjäger Platoon (3 75mm PAK 40 and 4 LMGs)

  1 Infantry Gun Section (2 75mm leIG)

  1 Half-Track Gun Section (8 LMGs and 6 75mm guns)

1 (mot) Light Reconnaissance Supply Column (3 LMGs)

49th Panzerjäger Battalion

1 (motZ) Panzerjäger Company (75mm PAK) (became self-propelled in Aug. 1943)

2 Self-Propelled Panzerjäger Companies (14 75mm PAK 40 and 14 LMGs ea)

103rd Panzer Artillery Regiment

1 Regimental Staff

  1 Staff Battery (2 LMGs)

1st and 3nd (mot) Battalions, each with

1 Battalion Staff

1 Battalion Staff Battery (6 LMGs)

3 (mot) Batteries (3 105mm leFH and 2 LMGs ea)

3rd (mot) Battalion

1 Battalion Staff

1 Battalion Staff Battery (6 LMGs)

2 (mot) Batteries (3 150mm sFH and 2 LMGs ea)

1 (mot) Battery (3 100mm K 18 guns and 2 LMGs)

103rd (mot) Observation Battery (2 LMGs)

290th Army Flak Battalion

1 Staff and (mot) Staff Battery

1st–2nd (motZ) Heavy Flak Batteries (4 88mm, 3 20mm and 2 LMGs ea)

3rd (motZ) Light Flak Battery (9 20mm, 2 quad 20mm and 2 LMGs) (upgraded to self-propelled in Aug. 1943)

4th Self-Propelled Battery (8 20mm and 2 quad 20mm Flak guns and 4 LMGs) (reorganized to 12 20mm guns in Aug. 1943)

1 (mot) Light (20 ton) Flak Supply Column

79th Panzer Pioneer Battalion

1 Staff (2 LMGs)

1 (half-track) Pioneer Company (25 LMGs, 3 PzBu39 and 2 80mm mortars)

2 (mot) Pioneer Companies (18 LMGs, 3 PzBu39 and 2 80mm mortars ea)

1 Brüko K Bridging Column (3 LMGs)

1 (mot) Light Pioneer Supply Column (2 LMGs)

79th Panzer Signals Battalion

1 Panzer Telephone Company (6 LMGs)

1 Panzer Radio Company (16 LMGs)

1 (mot) Light Signals Supply Column (1 LMG)

84th Feldersatz Battalion

2 Companies

84th Supply Troop

1–3/84th (mot) (120 ton) Transportation Companies (4 LMGs ea)

4/84th (mot) (90 ton) Transportation Company (3 LMGs)

5/84th (mot) (90 ton) Transportation Company (3 LMGs) (added Aug. 1943)

84th (mot) Supply Company (6 LMGs)

Truck Park

1–3/84th (mot) Maintenance Companies (4 LMGs ea)

84th (mot) Heavy Replacement Supply Column (added Aug. 1943)

Other

84th (mot) Bakery Company

84th (mot) Butcher Company

84th (mot) Administration Platoon

1/, 2/84th (mot) Medical Companies (2 LMGs ea)

1/, 2/, 3/84th Ambulances

84th (mot) Military Police Troop (2 LMGs)

84th (mot) Field Post Office

On 14 November 1943 the 2/35th Panzer Regiment was formed. The division had:

1/, 2/12th Panzergrenadier Regiment

1/, 2/33rd Panzergrenadier Regiment

4th Panzer Reconnaissance Battalion

1/, 2/35th Panzer Regiment

1/, 2/, 3/103rd Panzer Artillery Regiment

290th Army Flak Battalion

49th Panzerjäger Battalion

103rd Feldersatz Battalion

79th Panzer Pioneer Battalion

79th Panzer Signals Battalion

79th Divisional (Einheiten) Support Units

84th Supply Troops

In 1943 the 1/35th Panzer Regiment was equipped with three companies of Pz PzMk III and one company of Pz PzMk IV tanks, but was gradually totally equipped with PzMk IV tanks. The 2/103rd Panzer Artillery Regiment was initially equipped with three (motZ) 105mm batteries, but by August 1943 it had been upgraded to two self-propelled 105mm leFH batteries and one battery equipped with self-propelled 150mm sFH. In August the division added the 1st and 2nd Companies/84th Ost Battalion.

On 25 April 1944 the 2/35th Panzer Regiment was equipped with Panther tanks. The 1/35th Panzer Regiment continued to be equipped with Panzer PzMk IV tanks.

On 3 August 1944 the 1071st Grenadier Regiment was absorbed into the division. In January 1945 the division was again re-formed, and it was captured by the Russians on 8 May 1945.

5th Panzer Division

Officially established on 24 November 1938 in Oppeln. On 10 November 1938 the organization of the armored portion of the division and its panzer inventory were:

1/, 2/15th Panzer Regiment

1 Regimental Staff Signals Platoon

1 Regimental Staff Light Panzer Platoon

Each Battalion had

    1 Panzer Signals Platoon

    1 Light Panzer Staff Platoon

    4 Light Panzer Companies

1/, 2/31st Panzer Regiment

1 Regimental Staff Signals Platoon

1 Regimental Staff Light Panzer Platoon

Each Battalion had

    1 Panzer Signals Platoon

    1 Light Panzer Staff Platoon

    4 Light Panzer Companies

The division was mobilized on 18 August 1939 with:

5th Schützen Brigade

    1/, 2/13th Schützen Regiment

    1/, 2/14th Schützen Regiment

8th Panzer Brigade

    1/, 2/15th Panzer Regiment

1/, 2/31st Panzer Regiment
1/, 2/116th Artillery Regiment
8th (mot) Reconnaissance Battalion
53rd Panzerabwehr (AT) Battalion
77th Panzer Division Signals Battalion
89th Pioneer Battalion
85th Divisional Support Units

Just prior to the invasion of Poland and on the day of the invasion, the inventory of tanks assigned to the division was as follows:

	15 Aug. 1939	1 Sept. 1939
15th Regiment		
PzMk I	84	57
PzMk II	81	74
PzMk III	3	3
PzMk IV	6	7
PzBefWg 265	10	
PzBefWg 267	1	9
PzBefWg 268		
31st Regiment		
PzMk I	84	80
PzMk II	66	63
PzMk III	3	0
PzMk IV	6	6
PzBefWg 265	10	
PzBefWg 267	1	11
PzBefWg 268		

On 1 August 1939 the organization of the armored portion of the division was as follows:

1/, 2/15th Panzer Regiment
 1 Regimental Staff Signals Platoon
 1 Regimental Staff Light Panzer Platoon
 Each Battalion had
  1 Panzer Signals Platoon
  1 Light Panzer Staff Platoon
  3 Light Panzer Companies
1/, 2/31st Panzer Regiment
 1 Regimental Staff Signals Platoon
 1 Regimental Staff Light Panzer Platoon
 Each Battalion had
  1 Panzer Signals Platoon
  1 Light Panzer Staff Platoon
  3 Light Panzer Companies

OKH records show that when the Germans invaded Poland on 1 September 1939 the 5th Panzer Division was organized and equipped as follows:

5th Panzer Division Generalleutnant von Vietinghoff
 85th (mot) Mapping Detachment

85th Motorcycle Messenger Platoon
5th Schützen Brigade
13th Schützen Regiment
 1 (mot) Signals Platoon
 1 Motorcycle Company
 1st and 2nd (mot) Battalions, each with
  1 Motorcycle Company (18 LMGs, 4 HMGs and 4 50mm mortars)
  2 (mot) Rifle Companies (18 LMGs, 4 HMGs and 4 50mm mortars ea)
  1 (mot) Heavy Company
  2 Infantry Gun Sections (2 75mm leIG ea)
  1 Mortar Platoon (6 80mm mortars)
  1 Panzer Abwehr Platoon (3 37mm PAK 36 and 1 LMG)
1/, 2/14th Schützen Regiment
 same as 13th Schützen Regiment
 1 (mot) Light Infantry Column
8th Panzer Brigade
15th Panzer Regiment
 1 Armored Signals Platoon
 1 Staff Light Tank Platoon
 1st and 2nd Panzer Battalions, each with
  1 Armored Signals Platoon
  1 Staff Light Tank Platoon
  3 Light Panzer Companies
  1 (mot) Reserve Platoon
  1 (mot) Panzer Supply Column
  1 (mot) Maintenance Company
1/, 2/31st Panzer Regiment
 same as 15th Panzer Regiment
8th (mot) Reconnaissance Battalion
 1 (mot) Signals Platoon
 2 Armored Car Platoons (10 20mm and 25 LMGs)
 1 Motorcycle Company (9 LMGs, 2 HMGs and 3 50mm mortars)
 1 (mot) Heavy Company
  2 Infantry Gun Sections (2 75mm leIG ea)
  1 Pioneer Platoon (3 LMGs)
 1 (mot) Light Reconnaissance Supply Column
116th Artillery Regiment
 1 (mot) Signals Platoon
 1 (mot) Weather Detachment
 1st and 2nd (mot) Battalions, each with
  1 (mot) Signals Platoon
  1 (mot) Calibration Detachment
  3 (mot) Batteries (4 105mm leFH and 2 LMGs ea)
53rd Panzerabwehr Battalion
 1 (mot) Signals Platoon
 3 (mot) Batteries (12 37mm PAK 36 and 6 LMGs ea)
77th Panzer Signals Battalion
 1 (mot) Panzer Signals Company (2 LMGs)
 1 (mot) Panzer Radio Company (12 LMGs)
 1 (mot) Panzer Signals Supply Column

89th Pioneer Battalion
2 (mot) Pioneer Companies (9 LMGs ea)
1 (mot) Brüko H
1 (mot) Light Pioneer Supply Column

85th Divisional Support Units
1–6/85th (mot) Light Supply Columns
7/, 8/, 9/85th (mot) Heavy Fuel Columns
1/, 2/85th (mot) Maintenance Companies
85th (mot) Supply Company

Support Units
85th (mot) Field Bakery
85th (mot) Butcher Detachment
85th Division Administration
1/, 2/85th (mot) Medical Companies
1/, 2/, 3/85th Ambulance Companies
85th (mot) Military Police Troop
85th (mot) Field Post Office

In addition, the division had two Luftwaffe units attached to it. They were:

2.(H)/31 Luftwaffe Reconnaissance Staffel
1/38th Flak Regiment
1 (mot) Signals Platoon
3 (mot) Heavy Flak Batteries (4 88mm guns ea)
2 (mot) Light Flak Batteries (12 20mm guns ea)
42nd (mot) Flak Column

OKH documents dated 7 February 1940 indicate that the division had undergone very few changes. The significant changes were the assignment of a (mot) light infantry supply column to each schützen regiment, the elimination of a light panzer company in each panzer battalion, the assignment of a panzerabwehr platoon to the reconnaissance battalion's heavy company, and the equipping of a pioneer company with half-tracks. In addition, the division had the following units attached to it:

2.(H)/31st Panzer Reconnaissance Staffel
1/93rd Flak Battalion
1 (mot) Signals Platoon
2 (mot) Flak Batteries (12 20mm guns ea)
1 (mot) Flak Battery (9 37mm guns)
6th Btry/48th Flak Battalion (12 20mm guns)
2nd Btry/55th Flak Battalion (12 20mm guns)

On 1 April 1940 the 1/8th Light Supply Column became the 7/85th and the 7/85th Heavy Fuel Column became the 10/85th.

On 12 April 1940 the regiment had 38 PzMk I, 59 PzMk II, 18 PzMk III, 16 PzMk IV and 12 command tanks. On 5 April 1941, during the invasion of Greece, the 5th Panzer Division had a total of three heavy command tanks, two light command tanks, 20 PzMk I, 41 PzMk II, 51 PzMk III and 16 PzMk IV. The division was organized and equipped as follows:

5th Panzer Division
Divisional Staff (2 LMGs)
85th Motorcycle Platoon
85th (mot) Mapping Detachment

31st Panzer Regiment
1 Panzer Singals Platoon
1 Light Panzer Platoon
1st and 2nd Battalions, each with
  1 Staff and Staff Panzer Company
  2 Light Panzer Companies
  1 Medium Panzer Company
  1 (mot) Replacement Platoon
  1 (mot) Panzer Supply Column
1 (mot) Panzer Maintenance Company

5th Schützen Brigade
13th Schützen Regiment
1 (mot) Staff Company
  1 Signals Platoon
  1 Pioneer Platoon (3 LMGS)
  1 Motorcycle Platoon
1st and 2nd (mot) Battalions, each with
  3 (mot) Companies (18 LMGs, 2 HMGs and 3 50mm mortars ea)
  1 (mot) Machine Gun Company (8 HMGs and 6 80mm mortars)
  1 (mot) Support Company
    1 (mot) Infantry Gun Platoon (2 75mm leIG)
    1 Panzerjäger Platoon (3 37mm PAK 36 and 1 LMG)
    1 Pioneer Platoon (3 LMGs)
  1 (mot) Infantry Gun Company (2 150mm sIG and 4 75mm leIG)
  1 (mot) Light Supply Column
14th Schützen Regiment
same as 13th Schützen Regiment
55th Motorcycle Battalion
3 Motorcycle Companies (3 50mm mortars, 2 HMGs and 18 LMGs ea)
1 (mot) Heavy Machine Gun Company (8 HMGs and 6 80mm mortars)
1 (mot) Reconnaissance Company
  1 (mot) Infantry Gun Section (2 75mm leIG)
  1 (mot) Panzerjäger Platoon (3 37mm PAK 36 and 1 LMG)
  1 (mot) Pioneer Platoon (3 LMGs)
53rd Panzerjäger Battalion
1 (mot) Signals Platoon
1 (mot) Panzerjäger Company (3 50mm PAK 38, 9 37mm PAK 36 and 6 LMGs)
2 (mot) Panzerjäger Company (12 37mm PAK 36 and 6 LMGs ea)

2nd Btry/55th Self-Propelled Heavy Machine Gun Battalion (10 20mm guns; inc. 2 motZ quads)

8th Reconnaissance Battalion
1 (mot) Signals Platoon (2 LMGs)
1 Armored Car Company (10 20mm and 25 LMGs)
1 Motorcycle Company (3 50mm mortars, 2 HMGs and 18 LMGs)
1 (mot) Heavy Reconnaissance Company
  1 Panzerjäger Platoon (3 37mm PAK 36 and 1 LMG)
  1 Pioneer Platoon (3 LMGs)
  1 Infantry Gun Section (2 75mm leIG)
1 (mot) Reconnaissance Supply Column

116th Artillery Regiment
1 (mot) Support Detachment
1 (mot) Signals Platoon
1 (mot) Weather Detachment
1st and 2nd (mot) Battalions, each with
  1 (mot) Calibration Detachment
  1 (mot) Signals Platoon
  3 (mot) Batteries (4 105mm leFH and 2 LMGs ea)
3rd (mot) Battalion
  1 Calibration Detachment
  1 Signals Platoon
  3 (mot) Batteries (4 150mm sFH and 2 LMGs ea)

Feldersatz Battalion
3 Companies

77th Signals Battalion
1 (mot) Panzer Telephone Company (2 LMGs)
1 (mot) Panzer Radio Company (13 LMGS)
1 (mot) Light Signals Supply Column

89th (mot) Pioneer Battalion
1 Panzer Pioneer Comapny (15 LMGs)
2 (mot) Pioneer Companies (9 LMGs ea)
1 (mot) Brüko B
543rd (mot) Brüko K
1 (mot) Light Pioneer Supply Column

85th Supply Troop
1/, 2/, 3/, 4/, 5/, 6/, 7/85th (mot) Light Supply Columns
8/, 9/, 10/85th (mot) Heavy Fuel Column
1/, 2/, 3/85th (mot) Maintenance Company
85th (mot) Supply Company

Administration
85th (mot) Field Bakery
85th (mot) Butcher Company
85th Divisional Administration

Other
1/, 2/85th (mot) Medical Company
1/, 2/, 3/85th (mot) Ambulance Companies
85th (mot) Miltiary Police Troop
85th (mot) Field Post Office

Attached
84th Flak Battalion
2/(H)31st Pz. Luftwaffe Observation Staffel

On 10 May 1940, the day of the invasion of France, the organization of the armored portion of the division and its panzer inventory were as follows:

1/, 2/15th Panzer Regiment
  1 Regimental Staff Signals Platoon
  1 Regimental Staff Light Panzer Platoon
  Each Battalion had
    1 Panzer Staff Company
    1 Medium Panzer Company
    2 Light Panzer Companies
  Total tanks available:

PzMk I	51
PzMk II	61
PzMk III	24
PzMk IV	16
PzBefWg	15

1/, 2/31st Panzer Regiment
  1 Regimental Staff Signals Platoon
  1 Regimental Staff Light Panzer Platoon
  Each Battalion had
    1 Panzer Staff Company
    1 Medium Panzer Company
    2 Light Panzer Companies
  Total tanks available:

PzMk I	45
PzMk II	59
PzMk III	28
PzMk IV	16
PzBefWg	11

On 4 September 1940 the 15th Panzer Regiment was detached to the 11th Panzer Division. The 55th Motorcycle Battalion was formed on 10 August 1940 with the 2/14th Schützen Regiment, which was replaced by the 3/243rd Infantry Regiment (60th Infantry Division). The 2/48th Artillery Regiment then became the 3/116th Artillery Regiment. The division then had:

5th Schützen Brigade
  1/, 2/13th Schützen Regiment
  1/, 2/14th Schützen Regiment
  55th Motorcycle Battalion
1/, 2/31st Panzer Regiment
1/, 2/, 3/116th Artillery Regiment
8th (mot) Reconnaissance Battalion
53rd Panzerabwehr (AT) Battalion
77th Panzer Signals Battalion
89th Pioneer Battalion
85th Signals Battalion
85th Divisional Support Units

In September 1941 a single company and the 8th Reconnaissance Battalion was detached, as the 23rd Motorcycle Battalion, to the 23rd Panzer Division in France and replaced by the 56th Reconnaissance Battalion. In September 1941 the organization of the armored portion of the division and its panzer inventory were as follows:

1 Regimental Staff Signals Platoon
1 Regimental Staff Light Panzer Platoon
Each Battalion had
   1 Panzer Staff Company
   1 Medium Panzer Company
   3 Light Panzer Companies
Total tanks available:
   PzMk II   55
   PzMk III (50) 105
   PzMk IV (kz) 20
   PzBefWg   6

In 1942 the 228th (mot) Army Flak Artillery Battalion was assigned to the division. The division then had:

1/, 2/13th Panzergrenadier Regiment
1/, 2/14th Panzergrenadier Regiment
5th Panzer Reconnaissance Battalion
1/, 2/31st Panzer Regiment
1/, 2/, 3/116th Artillery Regiment
56th Reconnaissance Battalion
53rd Panzerjäger Battalion
77th Signals Battalion
89th Pioneer Battalion
85th Divisional Support Units

On 25 June 1941, three days after the invasion of Russia had begun, the organization of the armored portion of the division and its panzer inventory were as follows:

1/, 2/31st Panzer Regiment
1 Regimental Staff Signals Platoon
1 Regimental Staff Light Panzer Platoon
Each Battalion had
   1 Panzer Staff Company
   1 Medium Panzer Company 3 Light Panzer Companies
Total tanks available:
   PzMk II   26
   PzMk III (50 kz) 55
   PzMk IV (kz)   13
   PzBefWg   9

The 1/31st Panzer Regiment was sent to Germany and on 25 September 1943 it was equipped with Panther tanks. The 2/31st Panzer Regiment continued to be equipped with four companies of Panzer PzMk IV tanks. In June 1943 the 1/14th Panzergrenadier Regiment was reorganized and equipped with half-tracks.

Prior to that it was organized as the following chart shows for the other three panzergrenadier battalions. The regimental staff the 14th Panzergrenadiers was changed at the same time to what is shown below. Prior to that it was like that of the 13th. OKH records show that the division was organized and equipped as follows during 1943:

Division Staff
  1 Division Staff (2 LMGs)
  85th (mot) Mapping Detachment
31st Panzer Regiment
  2nd Battalion
    1 Regimental Staff and Staff Company (received 7 PzMk III flame panzers on 18 June 1943)
    3 Panzer Companies (22 PzMk III tanks ea; slowly equipped with PzMk IV tanks during the course of the year)
    1 Panzer Company (22 PzMk IV tanks)
    1 Panzer Maintenance Company
14th Panzergrenadier Regiment
  1 Regimental Staff
  1 (mot) Regimental Staff Company
    1 Signals Platoon
    1 Panzerjäger Platoon (3 75mm PAK 40 and 3 LMGs)
    1 (half-track) Pioneer Platoon (6 flamethrowers and 6 LMGs)
    1 Motorcycle Platoon (6 LMGs)
  1st (half-track) Battalion
    3 (half-track) Companies (4 HMGs, 34 LMGs, 2 75mm guns in half-tracks, 3 37mm PAK 36 on half-tracks and 3 sPzBu 41 ea)
    1 (half-track) Heavy Company
    1 Pioneer Platoon (13 LMGs, 1 37mm PAK 36 and 6 flamethrowers)
    1 Panzerjäger Platoon (3 75mm PAK 40 and 9 LMGs)
    1 Infantry Gun Platoon (4 LMGs and 2 75mm leIG)
    1 Half-Track Gun Platoon (8 LMGs and 6 75mm guns)
  2nd (mot) Battalion
    3 (mot) Companies (4 HMGs, 18 LMGs, 2 80mm mortars and 3 PzBu39 ea)
    1 (mot) Heavy Company
    1 Pioneer Platoon (4 LMGs)
    1 Panzerjäger Platoon (3 50mm PAK 38)
    1 Infantry Gun Platoon (4 75mm leIG)
    1 Panzerjäger Platoon (3 LMGs and 3 sPzBu 41)
  1 Self-Propelled Infantry Gun Company (4 150mm sIG)
13th Panzergrenadier Regiment
  1 Regimental Staff
  1 (mot) Regimental Staff Company
    1 Signals Platoon
    1 Panzerjäger Platoon (3 75mm PAK 40 and 3 LMGs)

1 Pioneer Platoon (6 flamethrowers and 6 LMGs)
1 Motorcycle Platoon (6 LMGs)
1 Regimental Band

1st and 2nd (mot) Battalion

3 (mot) Companies (4 HMGs, 18 LMGs, 2 80mm mortars and 3 PzBu39 ea)
1 (mot) Heavy Company
  1 Pioneer Platoon (4 LMGs)
  1 Panzerjäger Platoon (3 50mm PAK 38)
  1 Infantry Gun Platoon (4 75mm leIG)
  1 Panzerjäger Platoon (3 LMGs and 3 sPzBu 41)
1 Self-Propelled Infantry Gun Company (4 150mm sIG)

53rd Panzerjäger Battalion

1 (motZ) Panzerjäger Company (75mm PAK 40)
1 Self-Propelled Panzerjäger Company (14 75mm PAK 40 and 14 LMGs ea)

2nd Reconnaissance Battalion (early 1943 organization)

1st Armored Car Company (24 LMGs and 18 20mm guns)
2nd, 3rd and 4th Motorcycle Companies (2 80mm mortars, 4 HMGs, 18 LMGs and 3 PzBu39 ea)
5th (mot) Heavy Reconnaissance Company
  1 Pioneer Platoon (4 LMGs)
  1 Infantry Gun Section (2 75mm leIG)
  1 Panzerjäger Platoon (3 LMGs and 3 75mm PAK 40)
  1 Panzerjäger Platoon (3 LMGs and 3 sPzBu 41)
1 (mot) Light Reconnaissance Supply Column (3 LMGs)

2nd Reconnaissance Battalion (as of May–June 1943)

1 Armored Car Company (24 LMGs and 18 20mm guns)
1 (mot) Reconnaissance Company (2 80mm mortars, 4 HMGs, 18 LMGs and 3 PzBu39)
1 (half-track) Reconnaissance Company (2 80mm mortars, 4 HMGs, 56 LMGs and 3 PzBu39)
1 Motorcycle Company (2 80mm mortars, 4 HMGs, 18 LMGs and 3 PzBu39)
1 (half-track) Heavy Reconnaissance Company
  1 Staff (2 LMGs)
  1 Infantry Platoon (9 LMGs)
  1 Pioneer Platoon (1 37mm PAK 36, 6 flamethrowers and 13 LMGs)
  1 Panzerjäger Platoon (3 75mm PAK 40 and 4 LMGs)
  1 Infantry Gun Section (2 75mm leIG)
  1 Half-Track Gun Section (8 LMGs and 6 75mm guns)
1 (mot) Light Reconnaissance Supply Column (3 LMGs)

2nd Reconnaissance Battalion (as of 10 July 1943)

1 Armored Car Company (24 LMGs and 18 20mm guns)
1 (half-track) Armored Car Company (25 LMGs and 16 20mm guns)
1 (half-track) Reconnaissance Company (2 80mm mortars, 4 HMGs, 56 LMGs and 3 37mm PAK 36)

1 Motorcycle Company (2 80mm mortars, 4 HMGs, 18 LMGs and 3 sPzBu)
1 (half-track) Heavy Reconnaissance Company
  1 Staff (2 LMGs)
  1 Infantry Platoon (9 LMGs)
  1 Pioneer Platoon (1 37mm PAK 36, 6 flamethrowers and 13 LMGs)
  1 Panzerjäger Platoon (3 75mm PAK 40 and 4 LMGs)
  1 Infantry Gun Section (2 75mm leIG)
  1 Half-Track Gun Section (8 LMGs and 6 75mm guns)
1 (mot) Light Reconnaissance Supply Column (3 LMGs)

116th Panzer Artillery Regiment

1 Regimental Staff
1 Staff Battery (2 LMGs)

1st and 2nd Battalions, each with

1 Battalion Staff
1 Battalion Staff Battery (6 LMGs)
3 (mot) Batteries (3 105mm leFH and 2 LMGs ea)

1st (self-propelled) Battalion (as of Aug. 1943)

1 Battalion Staff
1 Self-Propelled Battalion Staff Battery (2 LMGs)
2 Self-Propelled Batteries (6 105mm leFH SdKfz 124 Wespe and 4 LMGs ea)
1 Self-Propelled Battery (6 150mm sFH SdKfz 165 Hummel and 4 LMGs)

3rd (mot) Battalion

1 Battalion Staff
1 Battalion Staff Battery (6 LMGs)
2 (mot) Batteries (3 150mm sFH and 2 LMGs ea)
1 (mot) Battery (3 100mm K 18 guns and 2 LMGs)

116th (mot) Observation Battery (2 LMGs)

288th Army Flak Battalion

1 Staff and (mot) Staff Battery (1 LMG)
1st–2nd (motZ) Heavy Flak Batteries (4 88mm, 3 20mm and 2 LMGs ea)
3rd (motZ) Light Flak Battery (12 20mm and 2 LMGs)
4th Self-Propelled Battery (8 20mm and 2 quad 20mm Flak guns and 4 LMGs)
1 (mot) Light (20 ton) Flak Supply Column

39th Panzer Pioneer Battalion

1 Staff (2 LMGs)
1 (half-track) Pioneer Company (25 LMGs, 3 PzBu39 and 2 80mm mortars)
2 (mot) Pioneer Companies (18 LMGs, 3 PzBu39 and 2 80mm mortars ea)
1 Brüko K Bridging Column (3 LMGs)
1 (mot) Light Pioneer Supply Column (2 LMGs)

77th Panzer Signals Battalion

1 Panzer Telephone Company (6 LMGs)
1 Panzer Radio Company (16 LMGs)
1 (mot) Light Signals Supply Column (1 LMG)

85th Feldersatz Battalion

4 Companies

85th Supply Troop
  1/, 2/, 4/, 5/85th (mot) (90 ton) Transportation Company (3 LMGs ea)
  3/, 6/85th (mot) (120 ton) Transportation Company (4 LMGs ea)
  85th (mot) Supply Company (6 LMGs)
Truck Park
  1–3/85th (mot) Maintenance Companies (4 LMGs ea)
Other
  85th (mot) Bakery Company
  85th (mot) Butcher Company
  85th (mot) Administration Platoon
  1/, 2/85th (mot) Medical Companies (2 LMGs ea)
  1/, 2/, 3/85th Ambulances
  85th (mot) Military Police Troop (2 LMGs)
  85th (mot) Field Post Office

On 1 July 1943 the organization of the armored portion of the division and its panzer inventory were as follows:

2/31st Panzer Regiment
  1 Regimental Staff Signals Platoon
  1 Regimental Staff Light Panzer Platoon
  Each Battalion had
    1 Panzer Staff Company
    1 Medium Panzer Company
    3 Light Panzer Companies
  Total tanks available:
    PzMk III (75)   17
    PzMk IV (lg)   76
    PzBefWg   9

From November 1943 to September 1944 the 31st Panzer Regiment had the Italian 3rd Armored Battalion attached to it. On 8 November 1944 the 103rd Panzer Brigade and the 2103rd Panzergrenadier Battalion were absorbed into the division. The division was taken prisoner by the Russians on 16 April 19/45.

6th Panzer Division

Formed from the 1st Light Division between 12 September and 18 October 1939 with:

  6th Schützen Brigade
    1/, 2/, 3/4th Schützen Regiment
    6th Motorcycle Battalion (former 4/4th Schützen Regiment)
  1/, 2/, 11th Panzer Regiment
  65th Panzer Battalion
  1/, 2/76th Artillery Regiment
  41st Panzerabwehr (AT) Battalion
  57th Pioneer Battalion
  82nd Signals Battalion
  57th Divisional Support Units

The division was the only German panzer unit equipped with the Pz.Kpfw 35(t) and they were in the 65th Panzer Battalion. On 10 May 1940 the organization of the armored portion of the division and its panzer inventory were as follows:

1/, 2/11th Panzer Regiment
  1 Regimental Staff Signals Platoon
  1 Regimental Staff Light Panzer Platoon
  Each Battalion had
    1 Panzer Staff Company
    1 Medium Panzer Company
    2 Light Panzer Companies
  65th Panzer Battalion
    1 Panzer Staff Company
    1 Medium Panzer Company
    2 Light Panzer Companies

Total tanks available:
  PzMk II   60
  35 (t)   118
  PzMk IV   31
  PzBefWg 35(t)   14

On 1 August 1940 it was used to help the 16th Infantry Division to form the 16th Panzer Division. The 3/4th Schützen Regiment was disbanded and the 1/76th Artillery Regiment was transferred out of the division. The 6th Schützen Brigade was expanded to include the 114th Schützen Regiment, the 1st Battalion newly formed from the 3/64th (16th Infantry Division). The 4th was newly formed from the Staff/243rd Infantry Regiment, with the 2/79th Infantry Regiment (16th Infantry Division), as the 2nd Battalion and the 1/4th Schützen Regiment became the 1st Battalion. The 1/76th Artillery Regiment was formed from the 3/16th Artillery Regiment and the 3/76th was formed from the 605th Artillery Battalion. The division then had:

  6th Schützen Brigade
    1/, 2/4th Schützen Regiment
    1/, 2/114th Schützen Regiment
  6th Motorcycle Battalion
  1/, 2/11th Panzer Regiment
  65th Panzer Battalion
  1/, 2/, 3/76th Artillery Regiment
  41st Panzerjäger Battalion
  57th Pioneer Battalion
  82nd Signals Battalion
  57th Divisional Support Units

On 1 April 1940 the 1/6th (mot) Reconnaissance Regiment became the 57th Reconnaissance Battalion, the 5/32nd Light Supply Column became the 7/57th and the 7/57th Heavy Fuel Column became the 10/57th.

On 22 June 1941 the organization of the armored portion of the division and its panzer inventory were as follows:

1/, 2/11th Panzer Regiment
  1 Regimental Staff Signals Platoon
  1 Regimental Staff Light Panzer Platoon
  Each Battalion had
    1 Panzer Staff Company
    1 Medium Panzer Company
    2 Light Panzer Companies
65th Panzer Battalion
  1 Panzer Staff Company
  1 Medium Panzer Company
  2 Light Panzer Companies
Total tanks available:

PzMk II	47
35 (t)	155
PzMk IV (kz)	30
PzBefWg 35 (t)	5
PzBefWg	8

By 10 September 1941 the armor inventory had been reduced to:

PzMk I	9 operational
PzMk II	38
PzMk III	102
PzMk IV	21
PzBefWg	11

On 3 June 1942 the 65th Panzer Battalion was disbanded and its forces were merged into the 11th Panzer Regiment, and the 6th Motorcycle Battalion was merged into the 57th Reconnaissance Battalion. The 298th (Army) Flak Battalion was assigned to the division. In February 1943 the remains of the 22nd Panzer Division were merged into the division. The division then had:

1/, 2/4th Panzergrenadier Regiment
1/, 2/114th Panzergrenadier Regiment
1/, 2/11th Panzer Regiment
6th Panzer Reconnaissance Battalion
1/, 2/, 3/76th Artillery Regiment
298th Flak Battalion
41st Panzerjäger Battalion
57th Panzer Pioneer Battalion
82nd Panzer Signals Battalion
57th Divisional Support Units

In November 1942 the organization of the armored portion of the division and its panzer inventory were as follows:

1/, 2/11th Panzer Regiment
  1 Regimental Staff Signals Platoon
  1 Regimental Staff Light Panzer Platoon
  Each Battalion had
    1 Panzer Staff Company
    1 Medium Panzer Company
    3 Light Panzer Companies
Total tanks available:

PzMk II	21
PzMk III (50 lg)	73
PzMk III (75)	32
PzMk IV (lg)	24
PzBefWg	9

When the 22nd Panzer Division was disbanded on 10 February 1943 the remains of its 204th Panzer Regiment were absorbed into the 11th Panzer Regiment. OKH records show that the division was organized and equipped as follows during 1943.

Division Staff
  1 Division Staff (2 LMGs)
  57th (mot) Mapping Detachment
11th Panzer Regiment
  Regimental Staff
  1 Signals Platoon
  1 Regimental Band
2nd Battalion
  1 Regimental Staff and Staff Company (received 7 PzMk III flame panzers on 18 June 1943)
  3 Panzer Companies (22 PzMk III ea; changed to PzMk IV by June)
  1 Panzer Company (22 PzMk IV ea)
  1 Panzer Maintenance Company
4th Panzergrenadier Regiment
  1 Regimental Staff
  1 Regimental Band
  1 (mot) Regimental Staff Company
    1 Signals Platoon
    1 Panzerjäger Platoon (3 50mm PAK 38 and 3 LMGs)
    1 Motorcycle Platoon (6 LMGs)
1st and 2nd (mot) Battalion, each with
  3 (mot) Companies (4 HMGs, 18 LMGs, 2 80mm mortars and 3 PzBu39 ea)
  1 (mot) Heavy Company
    1 Pioneer Platoon (4 LMGs)
    1 Panzerjäger Platoon (3 LMGs and 3 50mm PAK 38)
    1 Infantry Gun Platoon (4 75mm leIG)
    1 Panzerjäger Platoon (3 LMGs and 3 sPzBu 41 ea)
  1 Self-Propelled Infantry Gun Company (6 150mm sIG and 7 LMGs)
114th Panzergrenadier Regiment
  1 Regimental Staff

1 Regimental Band
1 (mot) Regimental Staff Company
  1 Signals Platoon
  1 Panzerjäger Platoon (3 50mm PAK 38 and 3 LMGs)
  1 Motorcycle Platoon (6 LMGs)

1st (mot) Battalion
  3 (mot) Companies (4 HMGs, 18 LMGs, 2 80mm mortars and 3 PzBu39 ea)
  1 (mot) Heavy Company
    1 Pioneer Platoon (4 LMGs)
    1 Panzerjäger Platoon (3 LMGs and 3 50mm PAK 38)
    1 Infantry Gun Platoon (4 75mm leIG)
    1 Panzerjäger Platoon (3 LMGs and 3 sPzBu 41 ea)

2nd (half-track) Battalion
  3 (half-track) Companies (4 HMGs, 34 LMGs, 2 80mm mortars and 3 75mm leIG ea)
  1 (half-track) Heavy Company
    1 Pioneer Platoon (4 LMGs)
    1 Panzerjäger Platoon (3 50mm PAK 38 and 3 LMGs)
    1 Infantry Gun Platoon (8 LMGs and 4 75mm leIG)
    1 Panzerjäger Platoon (3 LMGs and 3 sPzBu 41 ea)
  1 Self-Propelled Infantry Gun Company (6 150mm sIG and 7 LMGs)

6th Reconnaissance Battalion (early 1943 organization)
  1 Armored Car Company (24 LMGs and 18 20mm guns)
  1 Armored Car Platoon (6 LMGs and 6 75mm guns)
  2 Motorcycle Companies (2 80mm mortars, 4 HMGs, 18 LMGs and 3 PzBu39 ea)
  5th (mot) Heavy Reconnaissance Company
    1 Pioneer Platoon (4 LMGs)
    1 Infantry Gun Section (4 75mm leIG)
    1 Panzerjäger Platoon (3 LMGs and 3 75mm PAK 40)
    1 Panzerjäger Platoon (3 LMGs and 3 sPzBu 41)
  1 (mot) Light Reconnaissance Supply Column (3 LMGs)

6th Reconnaissance Battalion (as of 7/10/43)
  1 Armored Car Company (24 LMGs and 18 20mm guns)
  1 Armored Car (half-track) Company (25 LMGs and 16 20mm guns)
  1 Motorcycle Company (2 80mm mortars, 4 HMGs, 18 LMGs and 3 PzBu39)
  1 (half-track) Heavy Reconnaissance Company
    1 Staff (2 LMGs)
    1 Infantry Platoon (9 LMGs)
    1 Pioneer Platoon (1 37mm PAK 36, 6 flamethrowers and 13 LMGs)
    1 Panzerjäger Platoon (3 75mm PAK 40 and 4 LMGs)
    1 Infantry Gun Section (2 75mm leIG)
    1 Half-Track Gun Section (8 LMGs and 6 75mm guns)
  1 (mot) Light Reconnaissance Supply Column (3 LMGs)

76th Panzer Artillery Regiment
  1 Regimental Staff
    1 Staff Battery (2 LMGs)
  1st and 2nd Battalions, each with
    1 Battalion Staff
    1 Battalion Staff Battery (6 LMGs)
    3 (mot) Batteries (3 105mm leFH and 2 LMGs ea)
  3rd (mot) Battalion
    1 Battalion Staff
    1 Battalion Staff Battery (6 LMGs)
    2 (mot) Batteries (3 150mm sFH and 2 LMGs ea)
    1 (mot) Battery (3 100mm K 18 guns and 2 LMGs)
  76th (mot) Observation Battery (2 LMGs)

41st Panzerjäger Battalion
  1 (motZ) Panzerjäger Company (75mm PAK 40)
  1 Self-Propelled Panzerjäger Company (14 75mm PAK 40 and 14 LMGs ea)

298th Army Flak Battalion
  1 Staff and (mot) Staff Battery (1 LMG)
  1st–2nd (motZ) Heavy Flak Batteries (4 88mm, 3 20mm and 2 LMGs ea)
  3rd (motZ) Light Flak Battery (12 20mm and 2 LMGs)
  4th Self-Propelled Battery (8 20mm and 2 quad 20mm Flak guns and 4 LMGs)
  1 (mot) Light (20 ton) Flak Supply Column

57th Panzer Pioneer Battalion
  1 Staff (2 LMGs)
  2 (half-track) Pioneer Companies (25 LMGs, 3 PzBu39 and 2 80mm mortars ea)
  1 (mot) Pioneer Company (18 LMGs, 3 PzBu39 and 2 80mm mortars ea)
  1 Brüko K Bridging Column (3 LMGs)
  1 (mot) Light Pioneer Supply Column (2 LMGs)

82nd Panzer Signals Battalion
  1 Panzer Telephone Company (6 LMGs)
  1 Panzer Radio Company (16 LMGs)
  1 (mot) Light Signals Supply Column (1 LMG)

57th Feldersatz Battalion
  4 Companies

57th Supply Troop
  1/, 3/, 4/57th (mot) (90 ton) Transportation Company (3 LMGs ea)
  2/, 5/57th (mot) (120 ton) Transportation Company (4 LMGs ea)
  57th (mot) Heavy Fuel Column (2 LMGs)
  57th (mot) Supply Company (6 LMGs)

Truck Park
  1–3/57th (mot) Maintenance Companies (4 LMGs ea)

Other
  57th (mot) Bakery Company
  57th (mot) Butcher Company
  57th (mot) Administration Platoon
  1/, 2/57th (mot) Medical Companies (2 LMGs ea)
  1/, 2/, 3/57th Ambulances

57th (mot) Military Police Troop (2 LMGs)
57th (mot) Field Post Office

On 1 July 1943 the organization of the armored portion of the division and its panzer inventory were as follows:

2/11th Panzer Regiment
  1 Regimental Staff Signals Platoon
  1 Regimental Staff Light Panzer Platoon
  Each Battalion had
    1 Panzer Staff Company
    1 Medium Panzer Company
    3 Light Panzer Companies
  Total tanks available:

PzMk II	13	
PzMk III (lg)	34	
PzMk III (75)	18	
PzMk IV (lg)	32	
Flammpanzer	14	(in 8th Company)
PzBefWg	6	

During the course of late 1943 one of the light artillery battalions was scheduled to be reorganized as follows:

  1 Battalion Staff
  1 Self-Propelled Battalion Staff Battery (2 LMGs)
  2 Self-Propelled Batteries (6 105mm leFH SdKfz 124 Wespe and 4 LMGs ea)
  1 Self-Propelled Battery (6 150mm sFH SdKfz 165 Hummel and 4 LMGs)

On 15 January 1944 the 1/11th Panzer Regiment was equipped with Panther tanks. The 2/11th Panzer Regiment continued to be equipped with Panzer PzMk IV tanks. In March 1944 the organization of the armored portion of the division and its panzer inventory were as follows:

1/11th Panzer Regiment
  1 Panzer Staff Company
  4 Panzer Companies
  PzMk V   76 total

The division was decimated by the spring of 1944 and had been withdrawn to Germany to rest and refit by May 1944. The rebuilding was completed in June 1944. In July the organization of the armored portion of the division and its panzer inventory were as follows:

2/11th Panzer Regiment
  1 Panzer Staff Platoon
  1 Battalion
    1 Panzer Staff Company
    4 Medium Panzer Companies (PzMk IV)
  Total tanks available:
    PzMk IV (lg)   81
    FlakpzIV (37)   8

On 8 May 1945 the division was captured by the Russians.

7th Panzer Division

The division was formed on 10/18/39 using the 2nd Light Division and the assignment of the 66th Panzer Battalion and the 25th Panzer Regiment. Starting in February 1940, the 25th Panzer Regiment began equipping its light panzer companies with 17 PzKpfw 38 (t) each. This conversion was not, however, completed by the time of the invasion of France.

The 6th and 7th Kavallerieschützen (Cavalry Rifle) Regiments became Schützen Regiments on 20 March 1940. The 7th Reconnaissance Regiment was broken into the 7th Motorcycle Battalion and the 37th Reconnaissance Battalion on 1 November 1939. The 25th Panzer Regiment (only Staff and 1st Battalion) were joined by the 1/23rd Panzer Regiment which became the 2/25th Panzer Regiment on 1 April 1940. Oddly, OKH records from this period show the 66th Panzer Battalion as if it were the 3/25th Panzer Regiment. The division was organized and equipped as follows:

7th Panzer Division
  Divisional Staff (2 HMGs)
  58th Motorcycle Platoon
  58th (mot) Mapping Detachment
1/, 2/, 3/25th Panzer Regiment
  1 Panzer Signals Platoon
  1 Light Panzer Staff Platoon
  1 Regimental Band
3 Battalions, each with
  1 (mot) Staff Company
    1 Panzer Signals Platoon
    1 Light Tank Platoon
    1 Motorcycle Messenger Platoon
    1 Pioneer Platoon
    1 Machine Gun Platoon (8 HMGs)
  2 Light Panzer Companies
  1 Medium Panzer Company
  1 (mot) Panzer Maintenance Platoon
  1 (mot) Panzer Supply Column
Total tanks:
  17 PzBef, 44 PzMk, I, 96 PzMk II, 30 38(T) and 23 PzMk IV

7th Schützen Brigade
1/, 2/6th Schützen Regiment
1 (mot) Signals Platoon
2 Battalions, each with
  1 (mot) Pioneer Platoon (3 LMGs)
  3 (mot) Companies (3 50mm mortars, 4 HMGs and 18 LMGs ea)
  1 (mot) Heavy Company
    2 Infantry Gun Platoons (2 75mm leIG ea)
    1 Mortar Platoon (6 80mm mortars)
    1 Panzerabwehr Platoon (3 37mm PAK 36 and 1 LMG)
1 (mot) Light Infantry Supply Column
1/, 2/7th Schützen Regiment
same as 6th Schützen Regiment
7th Motorcycle Battalion
2 Motorcycle Companies (3 50mm mortars, 4 HMGs and 8 LMGs)
1 (mot) Heavy Company
  1 Mortar Platoon (6 80mm mortars)
  1 Panzerabwehr Platoon (3 37mm PAK 36 and 1 LMG)
  2 Infantry Gun Platoons (2 75mm leIG)
1 (mot) Light Infantry Supply Column
37th Panzer Reconnaissance Battalion
1 (mot) Signals Platoon (2 LMGs)
2 Armored Car Companies (10 20mm and 25 LMGs)
1 Motorcycle Company (3 50mm mortars, 4 HMGs and 8 LMGs)
1 (mot) Heavy Company
  1 Pioneer Platoon
  1 Infantry Gun Platoon (2 75mm leIG)
1 (mot) Light Reconnaissance Supply Column (3 LMGs)
1/, 2/78th (mot) Artillery Regiment
1 (mot) Signals Platoon
1 (mot) Weather Detachment
1st and 2nd (mot) Battalions, each with
  1 (mot) Signals Platoon
  1 (mot) Calibration Detachment
  3 (mot) Batteries (4 105mm leFH and 2 LMGs ea)
42nd Panzerabwehr Battalion
1 (mot) Signals Platoon
2 (mot) Panzerabwehr Companies (12 37mm PAK 36 and 6 LMGs ea)
3rd Btry/59th Flak Battalion (12 20mm guns)
83rd (mot) Signals Battalion
1 (mot) Panzer Telephone Company (2 LMGs)
1 (mot) Panzer Radio Company (6 LMGs)
1 (mot) Panzer Light Signals Supply Column
58th (mot) Pioneer Battalion
1 (half-track) Pioneer Company
2 (mot) Pioneer Companies (9 LMGs ea)
1 (mot) Brüko B
1 (mot) Light Pioneer Supply Column

85th Supply Troop
1/, 2/, 3/, 4/, 5/, 6/58th (mot) Light Supply Columns
7/, 8/, 9/, 10/58th (mot) Heavy Fuel Columns
1/, 2/, 3/58th Maintenance Companies
1/, 2/(mot) Supply Platoons
Administration
58th (mot) Bakery Company
58th (mot) Butcher Company
58th (mot) Administration
Other
1/, 2/58th (mot) Medical Companies
1/, 2/, 3/58th Ambulances
58th (mot) Field Post Office
58th (mot) Military Police Troop
Attached
86th Flak Battalion
  3 Batteries (12 20mm ea)
1.(H)/11th Reconnaissance Staffel

On 1 April 1940 the 3/28th and 4/12th Light Supply Columns became the 2/, 7/58th and the 7/58th Heavy Fuel Column was renumbered the 9/58th. In addition, the 2/405th and 2/12th Light Fuel Columns were merged to form the 10/58th Heavy Fuel Column.

On 12 April 1940 the 25th Panzer Regiment had 24 PzMk I, 51 PzMK II, no PzMk III, 15 PzMk 16, and 48 38(t) tanks. At the same time the 66th Panzer Battalion had 13 PzMk I, 21 PzMk II, no PzMk III, 7 PzMk IV, and 24 38(t) tanks. On 10 May 1940, the eve of the invasion of France, the organization of the armored portion of the division and its panzer inventory were as follows:

1/, 2/25th Panzer Regiment
  1 Regimental Staff Signals Platoon
  1 Regimental Staff Light Panzer Platoon
  Each Battalion had
    1 Panzer Staff Company
    1 Medium Panzer Company
    2 Light Panzer Companies
66th Panzer Battalion
  1 Panzer Staff Company
  1 Medium Panzer Company
  2 Light Panzer Companies
Total tanks available:

PzMk I	34
PzMk II	68
38 (t)	91
PzMk IV	24
PzBefWg 38(t)	8

In 1940 the division was assigned to be part of the invasion forces scheduled for Operation "Sealion". On 9 August 1940 the division was organized and equipped as follows: *(see over)*

7th Panzer Division

58th Motorcycle Platoon
58th (mot) Mapping Detachment
25th Panzer Regiment
  1/25th Panzer Regiment
    1 Medium Panzer Company
    2 Light Panzer Companies
    1 (mot) Munitions Column
  2/25th Panzer Regiment
    1 Medium Panzer Company
    2 Light Panzer Companies
    1 (mot) Munitions Column
  66th Panzer Battalion
    1 Medium Panzer Company
    2 Light Panzer Companies
    1 (mot) Munitions Column

7th Schützen Brigade

6th Schützen Regiment

1 (mot) Signals Battalion
1st and 2nd Battalions, each with
  1 (mot) Pioneer Platoon (3 LMGs)
  3 (mot) Schützen Companies (18 LMGs, 2 HMGs, 3 50mm mortars and 2 80mm mortars ea)
  1 (mot) Heavy Company
    1 Machine Gun Platoon (6 HMGs)
    1 Panzerjäger Platoon (3 37mm PAK 36 and 1 LMG)
    2 (mot) Infantry Gun Sections (2 75mm leIG ea)
  1 (mot) Light Supply Column

7th Schützen Regiment

1 (mot) Signals Staff
1st and 2nd Battalions, each with
  1 (mot) Pioneer Platoon (3 LMGs)
  3 (mot) Schützen Companies (18LMGs, 2 HMGs, 3 50mm mortars and 2 80mm mortars ea)
  1 (mot) Heavy Company
    1 Machine Gun Platoon (6 HMGs)
    1 Panzerjäger Platoon (3 37mm PAK 36 and 1 LMG)
    2 (mot) Infantry Gun Sections (2 75mm leIG ea)
  1 (mot) Light Supply Column
1 (mot) Infantry Gun Company (5 150mm sIG)

37th Panzer Reconnaissance Battalion

2 Armored Car Companies (10 HMGs and 25 LMGs ea)
1 Motorcycle Company (3 50mm mortars, 3 HMGs and 18 LMGs)
1 (mot) Heavy Company
  1 Pioneer Platoon (3 LMGs)
  1 Mortar Platoon (2 80mm mortars)
  1 Infantry Gun Section (2 75mm leIG)

78th (mot) Artillery Regiment

1 (mot) Signals Platoon
1 (mot) Weather Detachment
1 Regimental Band

1st and 2nd Battalions

1 (mot) Signals Platoon
1 (mot) Calibration Detachment
3 (mot) Batteries (4 105mm leFH and 2 LMGs ea)

3rd Battalion

1 (mot) Signals Platoon
1 (mot) Calibration Detachment
3 (mot) Batteries (4 150mm sFH and 2 LMGs ea)

42nd Panzerjäger Battalion

1 (mot) Signals Platoon
2 (mot) Companies (12 37mm PAK 36 and 6 LMGs ea)

58th (mot) Pioneer Battalion

2 (mot) Pioneer Companies (9 LMGs ea)
1 (mot) Bridging Company
  2 Pioneer Platoons
  3 Bridging Sections
1 Brüko B Bridging Train
1 Brüko K Bridging Train
1 (mot) Light Pioneer Supply Column

83rd (mot) Signals Battalion

1 (mot) Telephone Company (6 LMGs)
1 (mot) Radio Company (2 LMGs)
1 (mot) Light Supply Column

7th Motorcycle Battalion

2 Motorcycle Companies (2 80mm mortars, 3 50mm mortars, 2 HMGs and 18 LMGs ea)
1 (mot) Heavy Company
  1 Pioneer Platoon (3 LMGs)
  1 Machine Gun Platoon (4 HMGs)
  1 Panzerjäger Platoon (3 37mm PAK 36 and 1 LMG)
  2 Infantry Gun Sections (2 75mm leIG ea)

86th (mot) Flak Battalion

1 (mot) Signals Platoon
1 Battalion Band
3 (mot) Flak Companies (12 20mm ea)
1 (mot) Light Supply Column

58th Vehicle Battalion

8/, 9/, 10/58th (mot) Heavy Fuel Columns
1/, 2/, 3/58th Maintenance Companies
1/, 2/(mot) Supply Platoons

58th Munition Battalion

1/, 2/, 3/, 4/, 5/, 6/, 7/58th (mot) Light Supply Columns

Other

1/, 2/58th (mot) Medical Companies
1, 2/, 3/58th Ambulances
58th (mot) Field Post Office
58th (mot) Bakery Company
58th (mot) Butcher Company
1/, 2/58th (mot) Administration Platoons
58th (mot) Military Police Troop

The 3/78th Artillery Regiment was formed from the 2/45th Artillery Regiment on 2 January 1941. The 66th Panzer Battalion became the 3/25th Panzer Regiment on 19 February 1941. On 22 June 1941, the day of the invasion of Russia, the organization of the armored portion of the division and its panzer inventory were as follows:

1/, 2, /, 3/25th Panzer Regiment
  1 Regimental Staff Signals Platoon
  1 Regimental Staff Light Panzer Platoon
  Each Battalion had
    1 Panzer Staff Company
    1 Medium Panzer Company
    3 Light Panzer Companies
  Total tanks available:

PzMk II	53
38 (t)	167
PzMk IV (kz)	30
38 (t)	7
PzBefWg	8

By 6 September 1941 the tank inventory had been reduced to:

PzMk I	9 operational
PzMk II	37
PzMk III	62
PzMk IV	14
PzBefWg	8

On 15 March 1942 the 3/25th Panzer Regiment was disbanded, reducing the division to only 2 panzer battalions. The 37th Reconnaissance Battalion was merged with the 7th Motorcycle Battalion in 1943, to form the 7th Panzer Reconnaissance Battalion. In January 1943 the organization of the armored portion of the division and its panzer inventory were as follows:

1/, 2/25th Panzer Regiment
  1 Regimental Staff Signals Platoon
  1 Regimental Staff Light Panzer Platoon
  Each Battalion had
    1 Panzer Staff Company
    1 Medium Panzer Company
    3 Light Panzer Companies
  Total tanks available:

PzMk II	21
PzMk III (50 lg)	91
PzMk III (75)	14
PzMk IV (kz)	2
PzMk IV (lg)	18
PzBefWg	9

The 296th Army Flak Battalion was assigned to the division in February 1943, as were the remains of the now destroyed 27th Panzer Division. In 1943 the division had:

1/, 2/6th Panzergrenadier Regiment
1/, 2/7th Panzergrenadier Regiment
7th Panzer Reconnaissance Battalion
1/, 2/25th Panzer Regiment
1/, 2/, 3/78th Panzer Artillery Regiment
296th Army Flak Battalion
42nd Panzerjäger Battalion
83rd Panzer Signals Battalion
58th Panzer Pioneer Battalion
58th Divisional Support Units

On 15 February 1943 the 127th Panzer Battalion, of the 27th Panzer Division, was disbanded and its remains were incorporated into the 25th Panzer Regiment. This probably occurred when the 1/25th Panzer Division was sent to Germany to be re-equipped with Panther PzMk V tanks. This left the 2/25th Panzer Regiment, which began with three companies of Panzer PzMk III and one company of Panzer PzMk IV, but was slowly totally re-equipped with Panzer PzMk IV tanks. The 2/25th may have been renumbered as the 1/25th Panzer Regiment. OKH records show that the division was organized and equipped as follows during 1943:

Division Staff
  1 Division Staff (2 LMGs)
  58th (mot) Mapping Detachment
25th Panzer Regiment
  Regimental Staff
  1 Signals Platoon
  1 Regimental Band
1st Battalion
  1 Regimental Staff and Staff Company (received 7 PzMk III flame panzers on 18 June 1943)
  4 Panzer Companies (22 PzMk IV ea)
  1 Panzer Maintenance Company
6th Panzergrenadier Regiment
  1 Regimental Staff
  1 Regimental Band
  1 (mot) Regimental Staff Company
    1 Signals Platoon
    1 Panzerjäger Platoon (3 50mm PAK 38 and 3 LMGs)
    1 Motorcycle Platoon (6 LMGs)
1st (mot) Battalion
  3 (mot) Companies (4 HMGs, 18 LMGs, 2 80mm mortars and 3 PzBu39 ea)
  1 (mot) Heavy Company
    1 Pioneer Platoon (4 LMGs)
    1 Panzerjäger Platoon (3 LMGs and 3 50mm PAK 38)
    1 Infantry Gun Platoon (4 75mm leIG)
    1 Panzerjäger Platoon (3 LMGs and 3 sPzBu 41)
2nd (half-track) Battalion
  3 (half-track) Companies (4 HMGs, 34 LMGs, 2 80mm mortars and 3 75mm leIG ea)

1 (half-track) Heavy Company
  1 Pioneer Platoon (4 LMGs)
  1 Panzerjäger Platoon (3 50mm PAK 38 and 3 LMGs)
  1 Infantry Gun Platoon (8 LMGs and 4 75mm leIG)
  1 Panzerjäger Platoon (3 LMGs and 3 sPzBu 41)
1 Self-Propelled Infantry Gun Company (6 150mm sIG and 7 LMGs)

7th Panzergrenadier Regiment
1 Regimental Staff
1 Regimental Band
1 (mot) Regimental Staff Company
  1 Signals Platoon
  1 Panzerjäger Platoon (3 50mm PAK 38 and 3 LMGs)
  1 Motorcycle Platoon (6 LMGs)

1st and 2nd (mot) Battalions
same as 1/6th Panzergrenadier Regiment
1 Self-Propelled Infantry Gun Company (6 150mm sIG and 7 LMGs)

42nd Panzerjäger Battalion
1 (motZ) Panzerjäger Company (75mm PAK 40)
1 Self-Propelled Panzerjäger Company (14 75mm PAK 40 and 14 LMGs ea)

7th Reconnaissance Battalion (early 1943 organization)
1 Armored Car Platoon (6 LMGs and 6 75mm guns)
1 Armored Car Company (24 LMGs and 18 20mm guns)
2 Motorcycle Companies (2 80mm mortars, 4 HMGs, 18 LMGs and 3 PzBu39 ea)
1 (half-track) Reconnaissance Company (2 80mm mortars, 4 HMGs, 56 LMGs and 3 75mm leIG)
1 (mot) Heavy Reconnaissance Company
  1 Pioneer Platoon (4 LMGs)
  1 Infantry Gun Section (4 75mm leIG)
  1 Panzerjäger Platoon (3 LMGs and 3 75mm PAK 40)
  1 Panzerjäger Platoon (3 LMGs and 3 sPzBu 41)
1 (mot) Light Reconnaissance Supply Column (3 LMGs)

7th Reconnaissance Battalion (as of 10 July 1943)
1 Armored Car Company (24 LMGs and 18 20mm guns)
1 Armored Car (half-track) Company (25 LMGs and 16 20mm guns)
1 Motorcycle Company (2 80mm mortars, 4 HMGs, 18 LMGs and 3 PzBu39)
1 (half-track) Heavy Reconnaissance Company
  1 Staff (2 LMGs)
  1 Infantry Platoon (9 LMGs)
  1 Pioneer Platoon (1 37mm PAK 36, 6 flamethrowers and 13 LMGs)
  1 Panzerjäger Platoon (3 75mm PAK 40 and 4 LMGs)
  1 Infantry Gun Section (2 75mm leIG)
  1 Half-Track Gun Section (8 LMGs and 6 75mm guns)
1 (mot) Light Reconnaissance Supply Column (3 LMGs)

78th Panzer Artillery Regiment
1 Regimental Staff
  1 Staff Battery (2 LMGs)

1st and 2nd Battalions, each with
1 Battalion Staff
1 Battalion Staff Battery (6 LMGs)
3 (mot) Batteries (3 105mm leFH and 2 LMGs ea)

1st (self-propelled) Battalion (as of Aug. 1943)
1 Battalion Staff
1 Self-Propelled Battalion Staff Battery (2 LMGs)
2 Self-Propelled Batteries (6 105mm leFH SdKfz 124 Wespe and 4 LMGs ea)
1 Self-Propelled Battery (6 150mm sFH SdKfz 165 Hummel and 4 LMGs)

3rd (mot) Battalion
1 Battalion Staff
1 Battalion Staff Battery (6 LMGs)
2 (mot) Batteries (3 150mm sFH and 2 LMGs ea)
1 (mot) Battery (3 100mm K 18 guns and 2 LMGs)

78th (mot) Observation Battery (2 LMGs)

296th Army Flak Battalion
1 Staff and (mot) Staff Battery (1 LMG)
1st–2nd (motZ) Heavy Flak Batteries (4 88mm, 3 20mm and 2 LMGs ea)
3rd (motZ) Light Flak Battery (12 20mm and 2 LMGs)
4th Self-Propelled Battery (8 20mm and 2 quad 20mm Flak guns and 4 LMGs)
1 (mot) Light (20 ton) Flak Supply Column

58th Panzer Pioneer Battalion
1 Staff (2 LMGs)
2 (half-track) Pioneer Companies (25 LMGs, 2 80mm mortars and 3 PzBu39 ea)
1 (mot) Pioneer Company (18 LMGs, 3 PzBu39) and 2 80mm mortars ea
1 Brüko K Bridging Column (3 LMGs)
1 (mot) Light Pioneer Supply Column (2 LMGs)

83rd Panzer Signals Battalion
1 Panzer Telephone Company (6 LMGs)
1 Panzer Radio Company (16 LMGs)
1 (mot) Light Signals Supply Column (1 LMG)

58th Feldersatz Battalion
4 Companies

58th Supply Troop
1–6/58th (mot) (90 ton) Transportation Company (3 LMGs ea)
58th (mot) Heavy Fuel Column (2 LMGs)
58th (mot) Supply Company (6 LMGs)

Truck Park
1–3/58th (mot) Maintenance Companies (4 LMGs ea)

Other
58th (mot) Bakery Company
58th (mot) Butcher Company
58th (mot) Administration Platoon
1/, 2/58th (mot) Medical Companies (2 LMGs ea)
1/, 2/, 3/58th Ambulances

58th (mot) Military Police Troop (2 LMGs)
58th (mot) Field Post Office

In July 1943 the organization of the armored portion of the division and its panzer inventory were as follows:

1/, 2/25th Panzer Regiment
  1 Regimental Staff Signals Platoon
  1 Regimental Staff Light Panzer Platoon
  Each Battalion had
    1 Panzer Staff Company
    1 Medium Panzer Company
    2 Light Panzer Companies
  Total tanks available:

PzMk II	12
PzMk III (lg)	43
PzMk III (75)	12
PzMk IV (kz)	1
PzMk IV (lg)	37
PzBefWg	7

On 5 May 1944 the 1/25th Panzer Regiment was equipped with Panther tanks. The 2/25th Panzer Regiment continued to be equipped with Panzer PzMk IV tanks. In a major battle on 23 January 1945 near Deutsch-Eylau the 25th Panzer Regiment engaged the Russians with 20 combat veicles against 200. It was obliterated, only to be quickly rebuilt. On 1 April 1945 the 4th Company/11th Panzer Regiment was equipped with infra-red equipment and attached to the rebuilt 25th Panzer Regiment. The division refitted on 19 April 1945 and absorbed the Panzer Auffrischungs Verband Krampnitz. Reduced to a kampfgruppe, it contained a single panzer battalion from the 25th Panzer Regiment with 10 PzMk V Panther and 13 PzMk IV tanks. The division was taken into British captivity on 3 May 1945.

8th Panzer Division

Formed on 16 October 1939 from the 3rd Light Division. It retained the 67th Panzer Battalion and received the newly formed 1/10th Panzer Regiment. On 20 October 1939 the 2/10th Panzer Regiment and the necessary staff units were organized. The light companies of all three battalions began equipping with 17 Pz.Kpfw. 38(t) each and the conversion was substantially completed by the time of the invasion of France.

On 1 April 1940 the 2/8th (mot) Reconnaissance Regiment became the 59th Panzer Reconnaissance Battalion, the 2/9th Motorcycle Regiment became the 8th Motorcycle Battalion, the Staff/, 1/9th Cavalry Schützen Regiment became the Staff/, 3/8th Schützen Regiment, the 17th Company/9th Cavalry Schützen Regiment became the 13th Company/8th Schützen Regiment, the 6/156th Light Supply Column became the 7/59th, the 7/59th Heavy Fuel Column was renumbered as the 9/59th, and the 5/156th and 6/20th Light Supply Columns were reorganized into the 10/59th Heavy Fuel Column. The remainder of the 8th (mot) Reconnaissance Regiment became the 90th Reconnaissance Battalion and was sent to the 10th Panzer Division. The division consisted of:

8th Schützen Brigade
  1/, 2/, 3/8th Schützen Regiment
  8th Motorcycle Battalion
1/, 2/10th Panzer Regiment
67th Panzer Battalion
1/, 2/80th Artillery Regiment
59th Reconnaissance Battalion
43rd Panzerjäger Battalion
59th Pioneer Battalion
84th Signals Battalion
59th Divisional Support Units

On 10 May 1940 the organization of the armored portion of the division and its panzer inventory were as follows:

1/, 2/10th Panzer Regiment
  1 Regimental Staff Signals Platoon
  1 Regimental Staff Light Panzer Platoon
  Each Battalion had
    1 Panzer Staff Company
    1 Medium Panzer Company
    2 Light Panzer Companies
67th Panzer Battalion
  1 Panzer Staff Company
  1 Medium Panzer Company
  2 Light Panzer Companies
  Total tanks available:

PzMk II	58
38 (t)	116
PzMk IV	23
PzBefWg38(t)	15

On 1 January 1941 the 67th Panzer Battalion became the 3/10th Panzer Regiment and the 28th Schützen Regiment was formed. The 80th Artillery Regiment formed a third battalion from the 645th Heavy Artillery Battalion. The division now consisted of:

8th Schützen Brigade
  1/, 2/8th Schützen Regiment
  1/, 2/28th Schützen Regiment
  8th Motorcycle Battalion
  1/, 2/, 3/10th Panzer Regiment

1/, 2/, 3/80th Artillery Regiment
43rd Panzerjäger Battalion
59th Reconnaissance Battalion
84th Signals Battalion
59th Pioneer Battalion
59th Divisional Support Units

On 6 April 1941 the organization of the armored portion of the division and its panzer inventory were as follows:

1/, 2/, 3/10th Panzer Regiment
  1 Regimental Staff Signals Platoon
  1 Regimental Staff Light Panzer Platoon
  Each Battalion had
    1 Panzer Staff Company
    1 Medium Panzer Company
    2 Light Panzer Companies
  Total tanks available:
    PzMk II   49
    38 (t)   125
    PzMk IV   30

By 22 June 1941, the time of the invasion of Russia, the organization of the armored portion of the division and its panzer inventory were as follows:

1/, 2/, 3/10th Panzer Regiment
  1 Regimental Staff Signals Platoon
  1 Regimental Staff Light Panzer Platoon
  Each Battalion had
    1 Panzer Staff Company
    1 Medium Panzer Company
    2 Light Panzer Companies
  Total tanks available:
    PzMk II   49
    38 (t)   118
    PzMk IV (kz) 30
    38 (t) cmd   7
    PzBefWg   8

By 10 September 1941 the tank inventory had been reduced to:

    PzMk I   8 operational
    PzMk II   36
    PzMk III   78
    PzMk IV   17
    PzBefWg   15

On 22 June 1942 the organization of the armored portion of the division and its panzer inventory stood as follows:

1/, 2/10th Panzer Regiment
  1 Regimental Staff Signals Platoon

1 Regimental Staff Light Panzer Platoon
Each Battalion had
  1 Panzer Staff Company
  1 Medium Panzer Company
  2 Light Panzer Companies
Total tanks available:
  Mk II   1
  38 (t)   65
  Mk IV (kz)   2

The 2/10th Panzer Regiment was detached on 8 May 1942 and became the 3/2nd Panzer Regiment. The Staff/, 3/10th Panzer Regiment were transferred out of the division on 16 September 1942. They were to become the Staff/10th Panzer Brigade and 302nd Panzer Battalion. At the same time the 286th Army Flak Battalion was assigned to the division. The division then consisted of:

1/, 2/8th Panzergrenadier Regiment
1/, 2/28th Panzergrenadier Regiment
8th Panzer Reconnaissance Battalion
1/10th Panzer Regiment
1/, 2/, 3/80th Panzer Artillery Regiment
286th Army Flak Battalion
43rd Panzerjäger Battalion
84th Panzer Signals Battalion
59th Panzer Pioneer Battalion
59th Divisional Support Units

On 1 July 1943 the inventory of tanks with the division was as follows:

    PzMk II   14
    38 (t)   3
    PzMk III (kz) 25
    PzMk III (lg) 30
    PzMk III (75) 4
    PzMk IV (kz)   8
    PzMk IV (lg) 14
    PzBefWg   6

During 1943 the 1/10th Panzer Regiment was organized with three companies of PzMk III tanks and one company of Mk IV tanks. However, the Mk III tanks were gradually replaced with Mk IV tanks. OKH records show that the division was organized and equipped as follows during 1943:

Division Staff
  1 Division Staff (2 LMGs)
  59th (mot) Mapping Detachment
10th Panzer Regiment
  Regimental Staff
  1 Signals Platoon
  1 Regimental Band

1st Battalion

- 1 Regimental Staff and Staff Company (received 7 PzMk III flame panzers on 18 June 1943)
- 3 Panzer Companies (22 PzMk III ea; changed to PzMk IV by June)
- 1 Panzer Company (22 PzMk IV ea)
- 1 Panzer Maintenance Company

8th Panzergrenadier Regiment

- 1 Regimental Staff
- 1 Regimental Band
- 1 (mot) Regimental Staff Company
  - 1 Signals Platoon
  - 1 Panzerjäger Platoon (3 50mm PAK 38 and 3 LMGs)
  - 1 Motorcycle Platoon (6 LMGs)

1st and 2nd (mot) Battalions, each with

- 3 (mot) Companies (4 HMGs, 18 LMGs, 2 80mm mortars and 3 PzBu39 ea)
- 1 (mot) Heavy Company
  - 1 Pioneer Platoon (4 LMGs)
  - 1 Panzerjäger Platoon (3 LMGs and 3 50mm PAK 38)
  - 1 Panzerjäger Platoon (3 LMGs and 3 sPzBu 41)
  - 1 Infantry Gun Platoon (4 75mm leIG)
- 1 (motZ) Infantry Gun Company (4 150mm sIG)

28th Panzergrenadier Regiment

same as 8th Panzergrenadier Regiment

43rd Panzerjäger Battalion

- 2 Self-Propelled Panzerjäger Companies (14 75mm PAK 40 and 14 LMGs ea)

8th Reconnaissance Battalion (early 1943 organization)

- 1 Armored Car Company (24 LMGs and 18 20mm guns)
- 3 Motorcycle Companies (2 80mm mortars, 4 HMGs, 18 LMGs and 3 PzBu39 ea)
- 1 (mot) Heavy Reconnaissance Company
  - 1 Pioneer Platoon (4 LMGs)
  - 1 Infantry Gun Section (4 75mm leIG)
  - 1 Panzerjäger Platoon (3 LMGs and 3 75mm PAK 40)
  - 1 Panzerjäger Platoon (3 LMGs and 3 sPzBu 41)
- 1 (mot) Light Reconnaissance Supply Column (3 LMGs)

8th Reconnaissance Battalion (as of 10 July 1943)

- 1 Armored Car Company (24 LMGs and 18 20mm guns)
- 1 Armored Car (half-track) Company (25 LMGs and 16 20mm guns)
- 1 Motorcycle Company (2 80mm mortars, 4 HMGs, 18 LMGs and 3 PzBu39)
- 1 (half-track) Heavy Reconnaissance Company
  - 1 Staff (2 LMGs)
  - 1 Infantry Platoon (9 LMGs)
  - 1 Pioneer Platoon (1 37mm PAK 36, 6 flamethrowers and 13 LMGs)
  - 1 Panzerjäger Platoon (3 75mm PAK 40 and 4 LMGs)
  - 1 Infantry Gun Section (2 75mm leIG)
- 1 Half-Track Gun Section (8 LMGs and 6 75mm guns)
- 1 (mot) Light Reconnaissance Supply Column (3 LMGs)

80th Panzer Artillery Regiment

- 1 Regimental Staff
  - 1 Staff Battery (2 LMGs)

1st and 2nd Battalions, each with

- 1 Battalion Staff
- 1 Battalion Staff Battery (2 LMGs)
- 3 (mot) Batteries (3 105mm leFH and 2 LMGs ea)

3rd (mot) Battalion

- 1 Battalion Staff
- 1 Battalion Staff Battery (2 LMGs)
- 2 (mot) Batteries (3 150mm sFH and 2 LMGs ea)
- 1 (mot) Battery (3 100mm K 18 guns and 2 LMGs)

76th (mot) Observation Battery (2 LMGs)

286th Army Flak Battalion

- 1 Staff and (mot) Staff Battery (1 LMG)
- 1st–2nd (motZ) Heavy Flak Batteries (4 88mm, 3 20mm and 2 LMGs ea)
- 3rd (motZ) Light Flak Battery (12 20mm and 2 LMGs)
- 4th Self-Propelled Battery (8 20mm and 2 quad 20mm Flak guns and 4 LMGs)
- 1 (mot) Light (20 ton) Flak Supply Column

59th Panzer Pioneer Battalion

- 1 Staff (2 LMGs)
- 1 (half-track) Pioneer Company (25 LMGs, 3 PzBu39 and 2 80mm mortars)
- 1 (mot) Pioneer Companies (18 LMGs, 2 80mm mortars and 3 PzBu39 ea)
- 1 Brüko K Bridging Column (3 LMGs)
- 1 (mot) Light Pioneer Supply Column (2 LMGs)

84th Panzer Signals Battalion

- 1 Panzer Telephone Company (6 LMGs)
- 1 Panzer Radio Company (16 LMGs)
- 1 (mot) Light Signals Supply Column (1 LMG)

59th Ost Company

weapons unknown

59th Supply Troop

- 1/, 2/, 4/, 5/59th (mot) (90 ton) Transportation Company (3 LMGs ea) (4th and 5th Companies converted to 120 ton Companies in late 1943)
- 3/59th (mot) (120 ton) Transportation Company (4 LMGs ea) (converted to 90 ton Company in late 1943)
- 59th (mot) Supply Company (6 LMGs)

Truck Park

- 1–3/59th (mot) Maintenance Companies (4 LMGs ea)

Other

- 59th (mot) Bakery Company
- 59th (mot) Butcher Company
- 59th (mot) Administration Platoon
- 1/, 2/59th (mot) Medical Companies (2 LMGs ea)
- 1/, 2/, 3/59th Ambulances
- 59th (mot) Military Police Troop (2 LMGs)
- 59th (mot) Field Post Office

On 27 August 1944 it was ordered to reorganize into a Type 44 Panzer Division. After this reorganization the division was as follows:

Staff
1 Divisional Staff (2 LMGs)
1 Divisional Band
1 (mot) Mapping Detachment
1 (mot) Escort Company
  1 Infantry Platoon (4 HMGs and 6 LMGs)
  1 Motorcycle Platoon (6 LMGs)
  1 Flak Platoon (4 self-propelled 20mm Flak guns)
1 (mot) Military Police Troop (2 LMGs)

Panzer Battalion
1 Battalion Staff
1 Battalion Staff Company (12 LMGs)
1 Flak Platoon (3 self-propelled quad 20mm Flak guns)
2 Panzer Companies (22 PzMk IV tanks ea)
2 Panzer Companies (22 PzMk V Panther tanks ea)
1 Armored Maintenance Company
1 (mot) Armored Supply Company (5 LMGs)

Combined Panzergrenadier Regiment
1 (half-track) Regimental Staff
1 (half-track) Regimental Staff Company
  1 Signals Platoon (7 LMGs)
  1 Motorcycle Platoon (6 LMGs)

1st (half-track) Battalion
1 Battalion Staff (5 LMGs)
1 (mot) Panzergrenadier Supply Company (5 LMGs)
3 (half-track) Panzergrenadier Companies (4 HMGs, 29 LMGs, 2 80mm mortars, 2 75mm and 7 20mm Flak ea)
1 (half-track) Heavy Company
  1 Platoon (2 LMGs and 4 120mm mortars)
  1 Platoon (4 LMGs and 6 75mm guns)

2nd (mot) Battalion
1 Battalion Staff
1 Panzergrenadier Supply Company (4 LMGs)
3 (mot) Panzergrenadier Companies (4 HMGs, 18 LMGs and 2 80mm mortars ea)
1 (mot) Heavy Company (6 20mm, 2 LMGs and 4 120mm mortars)

3rd (Bicycle) Battalion
1 Battalion Staff
1 (mot) Panzergrenadier Supply Company (4 LMGs)
3 Panzergrenadier Companies (4 HMGs, 18 LMGs and 2 80mm mortars ea)
1 (mot) Heavy Company (6 20mm, 2 LMGs and 4 120mm mortars)

1 Self-Propelled Infantry Gun Company (6 150mm sIG and 7 LMGs)

1 (mot) Pioneer Company
1 Company Staff (1 LMG)
1 (half-track) Pioneer Platoon (6 flamethrowers, 1 20mm and 12 LMGs)
1 (mot) Pioneer Platoon (12 flamethrowers, 8 LMGs, 2 HMGs and 2 80mm mortars)
1 (half-track) Pioneer Platoon (6 flamethrowers and 6 LMGs)

43rd Panzerjäger Battalion
1 Panzerjäger Battalion Staff (3 StuG)
1 (mot) Panzerjäger Staff Battery (1 LMG)
2 Sturmgeschütz Batteries (14 StuG ea)
1 (motZ) Panzerjäger Battery (12 heavy PAK and 12 LMGs)
1 (mot) Panzerjäger Supply Company (3 LMGs)

Panzer Reconnaissance Battalion
1 Panzer Reconnaissance Battalion Staff (3 LMGs)
1 (mot) Staff Company
  1 (mot) Signals Platoon (7 LMGs)
  1 Armored Car Platoon (3 cars with 1 75mm and 1 LMG and 13 Cars with 1 20mm and 1 LMG)
1 (half-track) Reconnaissance Company (9 SdKfz 250/1 with 1 LMG and 16 SdKfz 250/9 with 1 LMGs and 1 20mm ea)
1 (half-track) Reconnaissance Company (40 SdKfz 250/1 with 1 LMG ea, 4 SdKfz 250/7 with 1 LMG and 1 80mm mortar, and 2 SdKfz 250/8 with 1 75mm KwK L24 and 1 LMG)
1 (half-track) Reconnaissance Company (4 HMGs, 20 SdKfz 250/1 with 1 LMG, 7 SdKfz 250/9 with 1 LMG and 1 20mm ea, and 2 SdKfz 250/8 with 1 75mm KwK L24 and 1 LMG)
1 (half-track) Reconnaissance Company
  1 Staff Section (1 LMG)
  1 Platoon (6 SdKfz 250/9 with 1 LMG and 1 20mm)
  1 Mortar Platoon (2 LMGs and 6 80mm mortars)
  1 Pioneer Platoon (13 LMGs)

80th Panzer Artillery Regiment
1 Regimental Staff
1 (mot) Regimental Staff Battery (2 LMGs)

1st (self-propelled) Battalion
1 Battalion Staff
1 Self-Propelled Battalion Staff Battery (2 LMGs and 3 20mm Flak)
2 Self-Propelled Batteries (6 105mm leFH SdKfz 124 Wespe and 4 LMGs ea)
1 Self-Propelled Battery (6 150mm sFH SdKfz 165 Hummel and 4 LMGs)

2nd (mot) Battalion
1 Battalion Staff
1 Battalion Staff Battery (2 LMGs and 3 20mm Flak)
2 (mot) Batteries (6 105mm leFH and 4 LMGs ea)

3rd (mot) Battalion
1 Battalion Staff
1 Battalion Staff Battery (2 LMGs and 3 20mm Flak)
2 (mot) Batteries (4 150mm sFH and 4 LMGs ea)
1 (mot) Battery (4 100mm K 18 guns and 4 LMGs)

286th Army Flak Battalion

1 Battalion Staff

1 (mot) Battalion Staff Battery (2 LMGs)

2 (mot) Flak Batteries (6 88mm, 3 20mm and 2 LMGs ea)

1 (mot) Flak Battery (9 37mm and 4 LMGs)

1 Self-Propelled Flak Platoon (3 quad 20mm guns)

1 (mot) Sound Ranging Platoon (4 sound ranging systems)

Feldersatz Battalion

(50 LMGs, 12 HMGs, 6 80mm mortars, 2 120mm mortars, 1 75mm PAK, 1 20mm Flak, 2 flamethrowers and 1 105mm leFH 18)

84th Panzer Signals Battalion

1 Armored Telephone Company (11 LMGs)

1 Armored Radio Company (19 LMGs)

1 (mot) Signals Supply Column (2 LMGs)

59th Panzer Pioneer Battalion

1 (half-track) Pioneer Battalion Staff Company (12 LMGs)

2 (mot) Pioneer Companies (2 HMGs, 18 LMGs and 2 80mm mortars ea)

1 (half-track) Pioneer Company (2 HMGs, 43 LMGs, 6 flamethrowers and 2 80mm mortars)

1 (mot) Bridging Section (3 LMGs)

59th Divisional Supply Units

1 (mot) Divisional Supply Staff

3 (mot) 120 ton Transportation Companies (8 LMGs ea)

1 (mot) Maintenance Company

Truck Park

3 (mot) Maintenance Companies (4 LMGs)

1 Heavy (mot) Truck Park Column (4 LMGs)

Administrative Troops

1 (mot) Bakery Company (6 LMGs)

1 (mot) Butcher Company (4 LMGs)

1 (mot) Administrative Company (2 LMGs)

Medical

2 (mot) Medical Companies (4 LMGs ea)

1 (mot) Medical Supply Company (4 LMGs)

Other

1 (mot) Field Post Office (1 LMG)

The OKH records show that the divisional units were renumbered on 17 November 1944. The 2/, 3/8th Panzergrenadier Regiment became the 1/, 2/28th. The 13th Heavy Infantry Gun Company, 8th Panzergrenadiers, became the 9th Heavy Infantry Gun Company of the 28th Panzergrenadiers, and the 14th Pioneer Company, 8th Panzergrenadiers, was assigned as the 10th Pioneer Company, 28th Panzergrenadiers. Though the OKH records do not show it, it appears as if the 8th Panzergrenadiers were being disbanded.

On 1 December 1944 the motorized grenadier regiments of the panzergrenadier divisions were redesignated as panzergrenadier regiments. This required a renumbering of the 8th Panzergrenadier Regiment assigned to this division, and it was redesignated as the 98th Panzergrenadier Regiment. In addition, the Staff/, 2/10th Panzer Regiment were rebuilt.

On 8 May 1945 the division passed into Russian captivity.

9th Panzer Division

Formed on 1 March 1940 from the 4th Light Division. The 33rd Panzer Regiment was formed on 2 February 1940 from the Staff/Conze Panzer Regiment (Panzer Lehr Regiment) and the 3/5th Panzer Regiment. The 33rd Panzer Battalion became the 2/33rd Panzer Regiment. On 1 April 1940 the 3/354th Light Supply Column became the 7/60th, the 7/60th Heavy Fuel Column was renumbered as the 60th, and the 10/60th Heavy Fuel Column was organized from the 7/13th and 7/29th Light Supply Columns.

The 10th and 11th Cavalry Schützen Regiments became Schützen Regiments. The 9th Reconnaissance Regiment was disbanded on 1 August 1940 and formed into the 59th Motorcycle Battalion and the 9th Reconnaissance Battalion. The division had:

9th Schützen Brigade
  1/, 2/10th Schützen Regiment
  1/, 2/11th Schützen Regiment
  59th Motorcycle Battalion

1/, 2/33rd Panzer Regiment
1/, 2/102nd Artillery Regiment
9th Reconnaissance Battalion
50th Panzerjäger Battalion
85th Signals Battalion
86th Pioneer Battalion
60th Divisional Support Units

On 10 May 1940 the organization of the armored portion of the division and its panzer inventory were as follows:

1/, 2/33rd Panzer Regiment
  1 Regimental Staff Signals Platoon
  1 Regimental Staff Light Panzer Platoon
  Each Battalion had
    1 Panzer Staff Company
    1 Medium Panzer Company
    2 Light Panzer Companies

Total tanks available:

PzMk I	30
PzMk II	54
PzMk III	41
PzMk IV	16
PzBefWg	12

During the fall of 1940, the 3/102nd Artillery Regiment was formed from the 2/50th Artillery Regiment. On 5 April 1941, during the invasion of Greece, the 9th Panzer Division had a total of three heavy command tanks, two light command tanks, nine PzMk 1a, 36 PzMk II, 51 PzMk III (28 with 50mm guns) and 20 PzMk IV. The division was organized and equipped as follows:

9th Panzer Division
Divisional Staff (2 LMGs)
60th Motorcycle Platoon
60th (mot) Mapping Detachment

33rd Panzer Regiment
1 Panzer Singals Platoon
1 Light Panzer Platoon

1st and 2nd Battalions, each with
1 Staff and Staff Panzer Company
2 Light Panzer Companies, (4 PzMk II, 7 PzMk III ea)
1 Medium Panzer Company (5 PzMk II, 5 PzMk IV)
1 (mot) Replacement Platoon
1 (mot) Panzer Supply Column
1 (mot) Panzer Maintenance Company

9th Schützen Brigade
10th Schützen Regiment
1 (mot) Staff Company
1 Signals Platoon
1 Pioneer Platoon (3 LMGS)
1 Motorcycle Platoon

1st and 2nd (mot) Battalions, each with
3 (mot) Companies (18 LMGs, 2 HMGs and 3 50mm mortars ea)
1 (mot) Machine Gun Company (8 HMGs and 6 80mm mortars)
1 (mot) Support Company
1 (mot) Infantry Gun Platoon (2 75mm leIG)
1 Panzerjäger Platoon (3 37mm PAK 36 and 1 LMG)
1 Pioneer Platoon (3 LMGs)
1 (mot) Infantry Gun Company (2 150mm sIG and 4 75mm leIG)
1 (mot) Light Supply Column

11th Schützen Regiment
same as 2nd Schützen Regiment

59th Motorcycle Battalion
3 Motorcycle Companies (3 50mm mortars, 2 HMGs and 18 LMGs ea)
1 (mot) Heavy Machine Gun Company (8 HMGs and 6 80mm mortars)

1 (mot) Reconnaissance Company
1 (mot) Infantry Gun Section (2 75mm leIG)
1 (mot) Panzerjäger Platoon (3 37mm PAK 36 and 1 LMG)
1 (mot) Pioneer Platoon (3 LMGs)

50th Panzerjäger Battalion
1 (mot) Signals Platoon
3 (mot) Panzerjäger Companies (12 37mm PAK 36 and 6 LMGs ea)
3rd Btry/47th Self-Propelled Heavy Machine Gun Battalion (10 20mm guns)

9th Reconnaissance Battalion
1 (mot) Signals Platoon (2 LMGs)
1 Armored Car Company (7 20mm and 25 LMGs)
1 Motorcycle Company (3 50mm mortars, 2 HMGs and 18 LMGs)
1 (mot) Heavy Reconnaissance Company
1 Panzerjäger Platoon (3 37mm PAK 36 and 1 LMG)
1 Pioneer Platoon (3 LMGs)
1 Infantry Gun Section (2 75mm leIG)
1 (mot) Reconnaissance Supply Column

102nd Artillery Regiment
1 (mot) Support Detachment
1 (mot) Signals Platoon
1 (mot) Weather Detachment

1st and 2nd (mot) Battalions, each with
1 (mot) Calibration Detachment
1 (mot) Signals Platoon
3 (mot) Batteries (4 105mm leFH and 2 LMGs ea)

3rd (mot) Battalion
1 Calibration Detachment
1 Signals Platoon
3 (mot) Batteries (4 150mm sFH and 2 LMGs ea)
321st (mot) Panzer Observation Company

85th Signals Battalion
1 (mot) Panzer Telephone Company (2 LMGs)
1 (mot) Panzer Radio Company (13 LMGS)
1 (mot) Light Signals Supply Column

86th (mot) Pioneer Battalion
1 Armored Pioneer Company (35 LMGs and 2 PzBu39)
2 (mot) Pioneer Companies (9 LMGs ea)
1 (mot) Brüko B
1 (mot) Brüko K (only part present)
1 (mot) Light Pioneer Supply Column

60th Supply Troop
1/, 2/, 3/, 4/, 5/, 6/, 7/60th (mot) Light Supply Columns
8/, 9/, 10/60th (mot) Heavy Fuel Column
1/, 2/, 3/60th (mot) Maintenance Company
60th (mot) Supply Company

Administration
60th (mot) Field Bakery

60th (mot) Butcher Company
60th (mot) Divisional Administration
Other
1/, 2/60th (mot) Medical Company
1/, 2/, 3/60th (mot) Ambulance Companies
60th (mot) Miltiary Police Troop
60th (mot) Field Post Office
Attached
Light Btry/86th Flak Battalion
1/(H) 23rd Panzer Observation Squadron

By 22 June 1941 the organization and tank inventory stood at:

1/, 2/33rd Panzer Regiment
1 Regimental Staff Signals Platoon
1 Regimental Staff Light Panzer Platoon
Each Battalion had
1 Panzer Staff Company
1 Medium Panzer Company
2 Light Panzer Companies
Total tanks available:

PzMk I	8
PzMk II	32
PzMk III (37)	11
PzMk III (50)	60
PzMk IV (kz)	20
PzBefWg	12

However, by 5 September 1941 the inventory of operational tanks had been reduced to:

PzMk I	4 operational
PzMk II	14
PzMk III	31
PzMk IV	6
PzBefWg	7

In 1942 the 3/33rd Panzer Regiment was formed from the 2/3rd Panzer Regiment. During 1942 the artillery regiment formed its 4th Battalion from the 287th Army Flak Battalion. On 22 June 1942 the organization of the armored portion of the division and its panzer inventory were as follows:

1/, 2/, 3/33rd Panzer Regiment
1 Regimental Staff Signals Platoon
1 Regimental Staff Light Panzer Platoon
Each Battalion had
1 Panzer Staff Company
1 Medium Panzer Company
2 Light Panzer Companies
Total tanks available:

PzMk II	22
PzMk III (50 kz)	38
PzMk III (50 lg)	61
PzMk IV (kz)	9
PzMk IV (lg)	12
PzBefWg	2

On 1 July 1942 the division contained:

Panzer Division
Division Headquarters (2 LMGs)
1 (mot) Mapping Section
33rd Armored Regiment
Regimental Headquarters
Signals Section
Armored Reconnaissance Section
Regimental Band
1 Armored Maintenance Company
3 Armored Battalions, each with
1 Armored Staff Company
1 Medium Armored Company
2 Light Armored Companies
9th Schützen Brigade, with
10th and 11th Schützen Regiments, each with
1 Staff Company with
1 Signals Platoon
1 Panzerjäger Platoon (3 50mm PAK 38 and 3 LMGs)
1 Motorcycle Section (6 LMGs)
1 Regimental Band
2 (mot) Infantry Battalions, each with
3 (mot) Infantry Companies (18 LMGs, 4 HMGs, 2 80mm mortars and 3 PzBu39 ea)
1 (mot) Infantry Support Company, with
1 Engineer Platoon (4 LMGs)
1 Panzerjäger Platoon (3 50mm PAK 38, 6 LMGs, 3 28mm sPzB 41)
2 Infantry Support Gun Sections (2 75mm ea)
2 (motZ) Infantry Support Sections (2 150mm sIG)
Self-Propelled Flak Battery (12 20mm AA guns and 2 LMGs)
50th Panzerjäger Battalion
Staff Section (2 LMGs)
2 (motZ) Panzerjäger Company (9 50mm PAK 38 and 6 LMGs)
1 Self-Propelled Flak Battery (12 20mm AA and 4 LMGs)
59th Motorcycle Battalion
1 Heavy Armored Car Company (18 37mm and 24 LMGs)
3 Motorcycle Companies (2 80mm mortars, 4 HMGs,
18 LMGs and 3 PzBu39 ea)
1 (mot) Support Company, with
1 Engineer Platoon (4 LMGs)
1 Panzerjäger Platoon (3 50mm PAK 38 and 3 LMGs)

1 Panzerjäger Platoon (3 28mm sPzB 41 and 3 LMGs)

1 Infantry Support Gun Section (2 75mm guns)

102nd Artillery Regiment

1 (mot) Regimental Staff (2 LMGs)

1 (mot) Observation Battery

2 (mot) Artillery Battalions, each with

  1 (mot) Battalion Staff (2 LMGs)

    1 Light Munition Supply Column

  3 Batteries (3 105mm leFH and 2 LMGs ea)

1 (mot) Artillery Battalion, with

  1 (mot) Battalion Staff (2 LMGs)

  2 (motZ) Batteries (3 150mm sFH and 2 LMGs ea)

  1 (motZ) Battery (3 100mm K18 guns and 2 LMGs)

85th Armored Signals Battalion

1 Armored Radio Company (16 LMGs)

1 Armored Telephone Company (6 LMGs)

1 Light (mot) Signals Supply Column

15th Feldersatz Battalion

4 Companies (no heavy weapons)

86th (mot) Pioneer Battalion

1 Armored Pioneer Company (18 LMGs)

2 (mot) Pioneer Companies (18 LMGs ea)

1 (mot) "K" Bridging Train

1 Light (mot) Engineering Supply Column

Food Service

60th (mot) Divisional Quartermaster Platoon

60th (mot) Butcher Company

60th (mot) Bakery Company

60th Supply Train

1st–9th Light (mot) Supply Columns (2 LMGs ea)

13th and 14th Heavy (mot) Supply Columns (2 LMGs ea)

10th–12th Light Fuel Supply Columns

60th Light (mot) Supply Company

1/, 2, /, 3/60th (mot) Maintenance Companies

Medical

1/, 2/60th (mot) Medical Companies (2 LMGs)

1/, 2/, 3/60th Ambulance Columns

Other

60th (mot) Military Police Platoon (2 LMGs)

60th (mot) Field Post Office

The reconnaissance and motorcycle battalions were merged and became the 9th Panzer Reconnaissance Battalion on 13 April 1943. The 2/33rd Panzer Regiment became the 51st Panzer Battalion (Army Troops) and later the 506th Panzer Battalion (equipped with PzMk VI Tiger tanks). The 1/33rd Panzer Regiment had a staff and battalion with three companies of PzMk III tanks and one of PzMk IV tanks. However, it was slowly totally re-equipped with PzMk IV tanks. On 1 July 1943 the organization of the armored portion of the division and its panzer inventory were as follows:

1/33rd Panzer Regiment

1 Regimental Staff Signals Platoon

1 Regimental Staff Light Panzer Platoon

Each Battalion had

  1 Panzer Staff Company

  1 Medium Panzer Company

  3 Light Panzer Companies

Total tanks available:

PzMk II	14
38 (t)	3
PzMk III (kz)	25
PzMk III (lg)	30
PzMk III (75)	4
PzMk IV (kz)	8
PzMk IV (lg)	14
PzBefWg	6

OKH records show that the division was organized and theoretically equipped as follows during 1943:

Division Staff

1 Division Staff (2 LMGs)

60th (mot) Mapping Detachment

33rd Panzer Regiment

Regimental Staff

1 Signals Platoon

1 Regimental Band

1st Battalion

1 Regimental Staff and Staff Company (received 7 PzMk III flame panzers on 18 June 1943)

4 Panzer Companies (22 PzMk IV ea)

1 Panzer Maintenance Company

10th Panzergrenadier Regiment

1 Regimental Staff

1 Regimental Band

1 (mot) Regimental Staff Company

  1 Signals Platoon

  1 Panzerjäger Platoon (3 50mm PAK 38 and 3 LMGs)

  1 Motorcycle Platoon (6 LMGs)

1st (half-track) Battalion

3 (half-track) Companies (4 HMGs, 34 LMGs, 2 80mm mortars and 3 75mm leIG ea)

1 (half-track) Heavy Company

  1 Pioneer Platoon (4 LMGs)

  1 Panzerjäger Platoon (3 50mm PAK 38 and 3 LMGs)

  1 Infantry Gun Platoon (8 LMGs and 4 75mm leIG)

  1 Panzerjäger Platoon (3 LMGs and 3 sPzBu 41)

2nd (mot) track) Battalion

3 (mot) Companies (4 HMGs, 18 LMGs, 2 80mm mortars and 3 PzBu39 ea)

1 (mot) Heavy Company

  1 Pioneer Platoon (4 LMGs)

  1 Panzerjäger Platoon (3 LMGs and 3 50mm PAK 38)

1 Infantry Gun Platoon (4 75mm leIG)

1 Panzerjäger Platoon (3 LMGs and 3 sPzBu 41)

1 (motZ) Infantry Gun Company (4 150mm sIG)

1 Self-Propelled Flak Company (12 20mm guns and 4 LMGs)

11th Panzergrenadier Regiment

1 Regimental Staff

1 Regimental Band

1 (mot) Regimental Staff Company

  1 Signals Platoon

  1 Panzerjäger Platoon (3 50mm PAK 38 and 3 LMGs)

  1 Motorcycle Platoon (6 LMGs)

1st and 2nd (mot) Battalion, each with

same as 2/10th Panzergrenadier Regiment

1 (motZ) Infantry Gun Company (4 150mm sIG)

1 Self-Propelled Flak Company (12 20mm guns and 4 LMGs)

701st Self-Propelled Infantry Gun Company (disbanded 13 June 1943) (6 150mm sIG and 3 LMGs)

50th Panzerjäger Battalion

1 (motZ) Panzerjäger Company (10 75mm PAK 40) (became self-propelled in August 1943)

1 Self-Propelled Panzerjäger Company (14 75mm PAK 40 and 14 LMGs ea)

1 Self-Propelled Flak Company (8 20mm, 2 quad 20mm and 4 LMGs)

59th Reconnaissance Battalion (early 1943 organization)

1 Armored Car Platoon (6 LMGs and 6 75mm guns)

2 (half-track) Reconnaissance Companies (2 80mm mortars, 4 HMGs, 56 LMGs and 3 75mm leIG ea)

1 (Luchs) Company (29 SdKfz 123)

1 (mot) Heavy Reconnaissance Company

  1 Pioneer Platoon (13 LMGs)

  1 Half-Track Gun Section (6 75mm guns)

  1 Infantry Gun Platoon (2 75mm leIG)

  1 Panzerjäger Platoon (3 LMGs and 3 75mm PAK 40)

1 (mot) Light Armored Supply Column (3 LMGs)

9th Reconnaissance Battalion (as of 29 Apr. 1943)

1 Armored Car Platoon (6 LMGs and 6 75mm guns)

2 (half-track) Reconnaissance Companies (2 80mm mortars, 4 HMGs, 56 LMGs and 3 75mm leIG ea)

5/59th (Luchs) Company (29 SdKfz 123) (became 2/9th in Aug. 1943)

1 Armored Car Company (24 LMGs and 18 20mm guns) (added 10 July 1943)

1 (mot) Heavy Reconnaissance Company

  1 Pioneer Platoon (13 LMGs)

  1 Half-Track Gun Section (6 75mm guns)

  1 Infantry Gun Platoon (2 75mm leIG)

  1 Panzerjäger Platoon (3 LMGs and 3 75mm PAK 40)

1 (mot) Light Reconnaissance Supply Column (3 LMGs)

76th Panzer Artillery Regiment

1 Regimental Staff

  1 Staff Battery (2 LMGs)

1st and 2nd Battalions, each with

1 Battalion Staff

1 Battalion Staff Battery (6 LMGs)

3 (mot) Batteries (4 105mm leFH and 2 LMGs ea)

2nd (self-propelled) Battalion (as of Aug. 1943)

1 Battalion Staff

1 Self-Propelled Battalion Staff Battery (2 LMGs and 3 20mm Flak)

2 Self-Propelled Batteries (6 105mm leFH SdKfz 124 Wespe and 4 LMGs ea)

1 Self-Propelled Battery (6 150mm sFH SdKfz 165 Hummel and 4 LMGs)

3rd (mot) Battalion

1 Battalion Staff

1 Battalion Staff Battery (6 LMGs)

2 (mot) Batteries (4 150mm sFH and 2 LMGs ea)

1 (mot) Battery (3 100mm K 18 guns and 2 LMGs)

102nd (mot) Observation Battery (2 LMGs)

287th Army Flak Battalion

1 Staff and (mot) Staff Battery (1 LMG)

1st–2nd (motZ) Heavy Flak Batteries (4 88mm, 3 20mm and 2 LMGs ea)

3rd (motZ) Light Flak Battery (12 20mm and 2 LMGs)

4th Self-Propelled Battery (8 20mm and 2 quad 20mm Flak guns and 4 LMGs) (added on 20 Apr. 1943)

1 (mot) Light (20 ton) Flak Supply Column

86th Panzer Pioneer Battalion

1 Staff (2 LMGs)

1 (half-track) Pioneer Company (25 LMGs, 2 80mm mortars and 3 PzBu39)

2 (mot) Pioneer Companies (18 LMGs, 2 80mm mortars and 3 PzBu39 ea)

1 Brüko K Bridging Column (3 LMGs)

1 (mot) Light Pioneer Supply Column (2 LMGs)

85th Panzer Signals Battalion

1 Panzer Telephone Company (6 LMGs)

1 Panzer Radio Company (16 LMGs)

1 (mot) Light Signals Supply Column (1 LMG)

60th Supply Troop

1–3/60th (mot) (120 ton) Transportation Company (4 LMGs ea)

4/, 5/60th (mot) (90 ton) Transportation Company (3 LMGs ea)

6/60th Transportation Company (6 LMGs) (added 1 Aug. 1943)

60th (mot) Supply Company (6 LMGs)

Truck Park

1–3/60th (mot) Maintenance Companies (4 LMGs ea)

60th (mot) Heavy (75 ton) Replacement Column (4 LMGs)

Other

60th (mot) Bakery Company

60th (mot) Butcher Company
60th (mot) Administration Platoon
1/, 2/60th (mot) Medical Companies (2 LMGs ea)
1/, 2/, 3/60th Ambulances
60th (mot) Military Police Troop (2 LMGs)
60th (mot) Field Post Office

On 16 June 1943 the (motZ) infantry gun companies in the panzergrenadier regiments were converted into self-propelled infantry gun companies, each equipped with with 6 150mm sIG and 7 LMGs

On 3 January 1944 the 51st Panzer (Panther) Battalion again became the 2/33rd Panzer Regiment. The 1/33rd Panzer Regiment continued to be equipped with Panzer PzMk IV tanks. The order of 18 March 1944 sent the division to Carcassone, in southern France, where it was rebuilt from the 155th Reserve Panzer Division. The panzergrenadier regiments were re-formed as follows:

10th Panzergrenadier from the 5th Reserve Panzergrenadier Regiment (86th and 35th Battalions)
11th Panzergrenadier from the 25th (mot) Reserve Panzergrenadier Regiment (119th and 215th Battalions)

The division was reorganized with a panther battalion now having four companies, each with 17 PzMk V Panther tanks. The second battalion was a mixed battalion, having two companies with 22 PzMk IV tanks and one sturmgeschütz company with 14 sturmgeschütze. The organization of the 2nd Battalion appears to have been temporary. In August 1944 the organization of the armored portion of the division and its panzer inventory were as follows:

1/, 2/33rd Panzer Regiment
1 Panzer Staff Company
2nd Battalion
1 Panzer Staff Company
4 Medium Panzer Companies (PzMk V)

1st Battalion
1 Panzer Staff Company
4 Medium Panzer Companies (PzMk IV)

PzMk IV (lg)	78
PzMk V	79
FlakpzIV (37)	8

On 27 September the 105th Panzer Brigade (2105th Panzergrenadier Battalion and 2105th Panzer Battalion) was absorbed into the division. On 14 December 1944 the organization of the armored portion of the division and its panzer inventory were as follows:

1/, 2/33rd Panzer Regiment
1 Panzer Staff Company
2nd Battalion
1 Panzer Staff Company
4 Medium Panzer Companies (PzMk V)
1st Battalion
1 Panzer Staff Company
3 Medium Panzer Companies (PzMk IV)
1 Sturmgeschütz Company (StuG)
Total tanks available:

StuG	14
PzMk IV (lg)	28
PzMk V	57
FlakpzIV (2V)	4
FlakpzIV (37)	4

On 7 April 1945 the division was ordered to form a kampfgruppe with a single panzer battalion. This battalion was to have two Panther Companies (10 tanks each) and a Panzer Company (10 PzMk IV tanks) by 11 April 1945. On 9 April 1945 orders were issued to form a new 2/33rd Panzer Regiment from the remains of the panzer and sturmgeschütz companies. It was formed with one panzer company from the 116th Kampfgruppe, one company with Jagdpanzer 38s, one company with StuG III, and one company with 10 Pz.IV/70 (V). The division was captured in the Ruhr pocket by the Americans on 17 April 1945.

10th Panzer Division

Formed on 1 April 1939 in Prague with a divisional staff and units exchanged from other panzer and motorized formations. At the beginning of the war it contained:

86th (mot) Infantry Regiment (from 29th Infantry Division)
8th Panzer Regiment (from Independent 4th Panzer Brigade)

1/8th Reconnaissance Regiment (from 3rd Light Division)
2/29th Artillery Regiment (from 29th Infantry Division)

The division was reinforced by parts of the Kempf Panzer Detachment, the Staff/4th Panzer Brigade, and the 7th Panzer Regiment on 11 October 1939. 1 April 1940 was a very big day in the formation of the division. On that date the following units were assigned and/or renamed:

Old Unit Designation	New Unit Designation
69th (mot) Infantry Regiment	69th Schützen Regiment
86th (mot) Infantry Regiment	86th Schützen Regiment
1/86th (mot) Infantry Regiment	1/69th Schützen Regiment
1/8th (mot) Reconnaissance Regt	90th Panzer Reconnaissance Battalion
1/20th Artillery Regiment	1/90th Artillery Regiment
2/29th Artillery Regiment	1/90th Artillery Regiment
2/24th Panzer Abwehr Bn	2/Lehr Panzerjäger Battalion
? Company, 9th Panzer Abwehr Bn	3/Lehr Panzerjäger Battalion
8/20th Light Supply Column	4/90th Light Supply Column
4/9th Light Supply Column	5/90th Light Supply Column
5/9th Light Supply Column	6/90th Light Supply Column
8/6th Light Supply Column	7/90th Light Supply Column
1/619th Hvy Fuel Column	8/90th Hvy Fuel Column
2/619th Hvy Fuel Column	9/90th Hvy Fuel Column
1/608th Hvy Fuel Column	10/90th Hvy Fuel Column
3/29th Maintenance Company	2/90th Maintenance Company
3/90th Maintenance Company	1/90th Maintenance Company
1/609th (mot) Supply Company	90th (mot) Supply Company
631st (mot) Field Bakery	90th (mot) Field Bakery
608th (mot) Butcher Platoon	90th (mot) Butcher Platoon
630th (mot) Medical Company	2/90th (mot) Medical Company
90th (mot) Medical Company	1/90th (mot) Medical Company
90th Maintenance Platoon	1/90th Maintenance Company
605th Maintenance Platoon	2/90th Maintenance Company
617th Maintenance Platoon	3/90th Maintenance Company
624th (mot) Field Post Office	90th (mot) Field Post Office
unnumbered (mot) Military Police Troop	90th Military Police Troop

After the incorporations of troops on 1 April 1940 the overall divisional organization was as follows:

10th Schützen Brigade (newly formed)
    1/, 2/69th Schützen Regiment
    1/, 2/86th Schützen Regiment
4th Panzer Brigade
    1/, 2/7th Panzer Regiment
    1/, 2/8th Panzer Regiment
1/, 2/90th Artillery Regiment
90th Panzerjäger Battalion
10th Reconnaissance Battalion
49th Panzer Pioneer Battalion
90th Signals Battalion
90th Divisional Support Units

On 10 May 1940, the eve of the invasion of France, the organization of the armored portion of the division and its panzer inventory were as follows:

1/, 2/7th Panzer Regiment
    1 Regimental Staff Signals Platoon
    1 Regimental Staff Light Panzer Platoon
    Each Battalion had
        1 Panzer Staff Company
        1 Medium Panzer Company
        2 Light Panzer Companies
    Total tanks available:

PzMk I	22
PzMk II	58
PzMk III	29
PzMk IV	16
PzBefWg	9

1/, 2/8th Panzer Regiment
    1 Regimental Staff Signals Platoon
    1 Regimental Staff Light Panzer Platoon
    Each Battalion had
        1 Panzer Staff Company
        1 Medium Panzer Company
        2 Light Panzer Companies
    Total tanks available:

PzMk I	22
PzMk II	55
PzMk III	29
PzMk IV	16
PzBefWg	9

On 18 January 1941 the 8th Panzer Regiment was detached and assigned to the 15th Panzer Division. The 10th Motorcycle Battalion was formed from drafts from within

the division and the 3/90th Artillery Regiment was formed from the 1/105th Artillery Regiment. On 22 June 1941 the organization of the armored portion of the division and its panzer inventory were as follows:

1/, 2/7th Panzer Regiment
  1 Regimental Staff Signals Platoon
  1 Regimental Staff Light Panzer Platoon
  Each Battalion had
    1 Panzer Staff Company
    1 Medium Panzer Company
    3 Light Panzer Companies
  Total tanks available:
    PzMk II   45
    PzMk III (50) 105
    PzMk IV (kz) 20
    PzBefWg   12

By 4 September 1941 the inventory of operational tanks was reduced to nine operational Pz I, 38 Pz II, 75 Pz III, eight Pz IV and 13 command tanks.

In 1942 the 7th Panzer Regiment raised a 3rd Battalion, but soon transferred it to the 36th Panzer Regiment. The 90th Reconnaissance Battalion (formerly the 1/8th Reconnaissance Regiment) was merged with the 10th Motorcycle Battalion and in 1943 became the 10th Panzer Reconnaissance Battalion. In 1942 the 302nd Army Flak Battalion became the 4/90th Artillery Regiment. On 1 January 1943, as the Allies closed in on the Germans around Tunis, the division was organized as follows:

Division Command
1/, 2/7th Panzer Regiment
501st Heavy Panzer Battalion
190th Panzer Battalion
1/, 2/69th Panzergrenadier Regiment
1/, 2/86th Panzergrenadier Regiment
10th Motorcycle Battalion
A24 Field Battalion
1/, 2/, 3/90th Panzer Artillery Regiment
4/(Flak) 90th Panzer Artillery Regiment
5/(StuG) 90th Panzer Artillery Regiment
2/190th Artillery Regiment
322nd Panzer Observation Battery
90th Panzerjäger Battalion
49th Panzer Pioneer Battalion
90th Panzer Signals Battalion
90th Division Supply Troop
Medical Company
Work Station Company
1/, 2/, 3/Koch Fallschirmjäger Battalion

On 4 March 1943 OKH records indicate that the division was organized and equipped as follows:

10th Panzer Division
  1 (mot) Mapping Detachment
69th Panzergrenadier Regiment
  1 (mot) Staff Battery
1st Battalion
  3 Companies (18 LMGs, 4 HMGs, 2 50mm mortars and 3 28mm PzBu 41)
  1 Company
    1 Pioneer Platoon (10 LMGs)
    1 Panzerjäger Platoon (3 50mm PAK 40)
    1 Panzerjäger Platoon (3 28mm PzBu41)
    1 Mortar Platoon (2 50mm mortars)
2nd Battalion
  1 Company (23 LMGs, 4 HMGs, 2 50mm mortars and 3 28mm PzBu 41)
  1 Company (23 LMGs, 4 HMGs, 2 50mm mortars, 3 28mm PzBu 41 and 1 75mm PAK 40)
  1 Company (18 LMGs, 4 HMGs, 2 50mm mortars and 3 28mm PzBu 41)
  1 Company
    1 Pioneer Platoon (10 LMGs)
    1 Panzerjäger Platoon (3 50mm PAK 40)
    1 Panzerjäger Platoon (5 28mm PzBu41)
    1 Mortar Platoon (4 50mm mortars)
  1 (mot) Infantry Gun Company (4 75mm leIG and 2 LMGs)
86th Panzergrenadier Regiment
  1 (mot) Staff Battery
1st Battalion
  1 Company (18 LMGs, 4 HMGs, 2 50mm mortars and 3 28mm PzBu 41)
  1 Company (17 LMGs, 3 HMGs, 2 50mm mortars and 3 28mm PzBu 41)
  1 Company (17 LMGs, 4 HMGs, 2 50mm mortars and 3 28mm PzBu 41)
  1 Company
    1 Pioneer Platoon (10 LMGs)
    1 Panzerjäger Platoon (3 50mm PAK 40)
    1 Panzerjäger Platoon (3 28mm PzBu41)
    1 Mortar Platoon (4 75mm leIG)
2nd Battalion
  3 Companies (18 LMGs, 4 HMGs, 2 50mm mortars and 3 28mm PzBu 41)
  1 Company
    1 Pioneer Platoon (10 LMGs)
    1 Panzerjäger Platoon (3 50mm PAK 40)
    1 Panzerjäger Platoon (3 28mm PzBu41)
    1 Mortar Platoon (4 50mm mortars)
  1 (mot) Infantry Gun Company (4 75mm leIG and 2 LMGs)
10th Motorcycle Battalion
  2 Motorcycle Companies (4 HMGs, 18 LMGs, 3 28mm PzBu41, and 2 80mm mortars ea)
  1 Half-Track Company (43 LMGs, 4 HMGs, 9 80mm mortars and 2 75mm leIG)

1 Armored Car Company (22 LMGs, 2 HMGS, 14 20mm and 6 self-propelled 20mm guns)
1 Heavy (mot) Company
Staff (4 LMGs)
Pioneer Platoon (3 LMGs)
Panzerjäger Platoon (3 75mm PAK 40)
Infantry Gun Platoon (3 75mm leIG and 3 LMGs)

90th (mot) Artillery Regiment
1 (mot) Staff Battery

1st Battalion
1 (mot) Staff Battery
1st, 2nd and 3rd Batteries (4 105mm leFH and 2 LMGs ea)

2nd Battalion
1 (mot) Staff Battery
4th, 5th and 6th Batteries (4 105mm leFH and 2 LMGs ea)

3rd Battalion
1 (mot) Staff Battery
7th Battery (4 105mm leFH and 2 LMGs)
8th and 9th Batteries (4 150mm sFH and 2 LMGs ea)

4th Battalion
1 (mot) Staff Battery
10th, 11th and 12th Batteries (3 20mm and 4 88mm guns ea)

13th Battery
(4 sturmgeschütze)

14th Battery
(4 British 25pdrs and 2 LMGs)
1 (mot) Observation Battery
1 (mot) Light Supply Column

7th Panzer Regiment
1 Panzer Staff Platoon
1 Panzer Signals Platoon

1st and 2nd Battalions, each with
1 Panzer Staff Company
4 Panzer Companies
1 Captured Tank Recovery Copmany

90th Panzerjäger Battalion
1 Self-Propelled Battery (9 Russian 76.2mm and 9 LMGs)
1 (motZ) Battery (7 75mm PAK 40 and 9 LMGs)
1 Self-Propelled Flak Battery (10 LMgs, 8 20mm and 2 quad 20mm)
Winkler (motZ) Battery (6 75mm PAK 40 and 6 LMGs)

49th Pioneer Battalion
1 (half-track) Pioneer Company (30 LMGs, 2 HMGs and 3 28mm PzBu41)
2 Pioneer Companies (16 LMGs, 2 HMGs and 3 28mm PzBu41 ea)
1 (mot) Bridging Column
1 (mot) Light Pioneer Supply Column

90th Signals Company
1 Panzer Radio Company (13 LMGs)
1 Panzer Telephone Company (6 LMGs)
1 (mot) Light Signals Supply Column

14th Company/104th Panzergrenadier Regiment
1 (mot) Reconnaissance Platoon
3 Panzerjäger Platoons (6 50mm PAK 38 ea)

Supply Troop
1/, 2/, 3/, 4/, 5/, 6/, 7/(mot) Light Supply Columns
8/, 9/(mot) Heavy Supply Columns
13/, 14/(mot) Light Supply Columns
10/, 11/, 12/(mot) Light Fuel Columns
1/, 2/, 3/(mot) Maintenance Companies
1 (mot) Supply Company
1 (mot) Maintenance Company
1 (mot) Butcher Company
1 (mot) Field Bakery
1 (mot) Divisional Administration
1 (mot) Miltary Police Troop
1 (mot) Field Post Office
2 (mot) Medical Companies
1 (mot) Ambulance

The 4/90th Artillery Regiment was redesignated as the 302nd Flak Battalion on 20 April 1943, though it was still referred to as the 4/90th. At that time the division had:

10th Panzergrenadier Brigade
  1/, 2/69th Panzergrenadier Regiment
  1/, 2/86th Panzergrenadier Regiment
10th Panzer Reconnaissance Battalion
1/, 2/7th Panzer Regiment
1/, 2/, 3/90th Artillery Regiment
302nd Army Flak Battalion
90th Panzerjäger Battalion
90th Reconnaissance Battalion
49th Panzer Pioneer Battalion
90th Signals Battalion
90th Divisional Support Units

The division was sent to North Africa and reorganized. Only part of reorganization was completed. The major change was the absorption of the 501st Tiger Tank Battalion as the 3/7th Panzer Regiment. It had a staff and three companies each with ten tanks. The 1/69th Panzergrenadier Regiment was to be equipped with halftracks, while the 2/69th and 1/, 2/86th Panzergrenadiers were still motorized. The 90th Reconnaissance Battalion was re-established, but as the 10th Reconnaissance Battalion. Otherwise the division's organization was unchanged. In November and December 1942 the organization of the armored portion of the division and its panzer inventory were as follows:

1/, 2/7th Panzer Regiment
  1 Regimental Staff Signals Platoon
  1 Regimental Staff Light Panzer Platoon

Each Battalion had
1 Panzer Staff Company
1 Medium Panzer Company
3 Light Panzer Companies

PzMk II	21
PzMk III (50 lg)	105
PzMk IV (kz)	4
PzMk IV (lg)	16
Cmd	9

On 26 February 1943 the panzer battalions were authorized to have four medium tank companies, each with 22 Pz IV tanks. The 1/, 2/501st Panzer Battalion was also directed to become the 3/7th Panzer Regiment. The division was destroyed in Tunis in May 1943. Its losses included:

Division Staff and Mapping Detachment
7th Panzer Regiment
  Staff, staff company, 2 battalions (each with staff, staff company, 4 panzer companies) and 1 armored repair company
501st (Tiger) Panzer Battalion
  Staff, 2 Tiger companies and 1 armored repair company
69th Panzergrenadier Regiment
  Staff, staff company, 2 battalions (each with staff, staff company, 4 panzergrenadier companies) and 9th Infantry Gun Company
86th Panzergrenadier Regiment
  Staff, staff company, 2 battalions, (each with staff, staff company, 4 panzergrenadier companies), and 9th Infantry Gun Company
10th Motorcycle Battalion
  Staff, 5 companies, 1 armored car platoon and 1 light supply column
90th Panzerjäger Battalion
  Staff and 3 companies
90th Panzer Artillery Regiment
  Staff, staff battery, observation company and 3 battalions, each with staff battery and 3 batteries
4/90th Afrika Artillery Regiment (302nd Army Flak Battalion)
  Staff, staff battery and 3 batteries
49th Panzer Pioneer Battalion
  Staff and 3 companies
90th Signals Battalion
  Staff and 2 companies

It was disbanded on 30 June 1943 and never re-formed.

11th Panzer Division

The division was formed on 1 August 1940 from the independent 11th Schützen Brigade and other units assigned from various active divisions. The 1/11th Schützen Regiment was transferred to the 14th Panzer Division. On 4 September 1940 the 15th Panzer Regiment was detached from the 5th Panzer Division to join the newly forming 11th Panzer Division. The 51st Motorcycle Battalion, 231st Reconnaissance Battalion, and 61st Panzerjäger Battalion were newly built, partially with drafts from the 231st Infantry Division. The 341st Signals Battalion came from the 311th Infantry Division. The 209th Pioneer Battalion came from the 209th Infantry Division. The 119th Artillery Regiment, initially known as the 231st Artillery Regiment, was formed from the Staff/746th, 1/4th, 3/677th, and 1/643rd Artillery Regiments. The 1/111th Schützen Regiment was organized from the 1/103rd Infantry Regiment of the 4th Infantry Division.

11th Schützen Brigade
  1/, 2/110th Schützen Regiment
  1/, 2/111th Schützen Regiment
61st Motorcycle Battalion
1/, 2/15th Panzer Regiment
1/, 2/, 3/119th Artillery Regiment
231st Reconnaissance Battalion
61st Panzerjäger Battalion
209th Panzer Pioneer Battalion
341st Signals Battalion
61st Divisional Support Units

On 5 April 1941, during the invasion of Greece, the 11th Panzer Division had a total of three heavy command tanks, 11 light command tanks, 45 PzMk II, 51 PzMk III and 16 PzMk IV. The division was organized and equipped as follows:

11th Panzer Division
  Divisional Staff (2 LMGs)
  61st Motorcycle Platoon
  61st (mot) Mapping Detachment
33rd Panzer Regiment
  1 Panzer Signals Platoon
  1 Light Panzer Platoon
  1st and 2nd Battalions, each with
    1 Staff and Staff Panzer Company
    2 Light Panzer Companies
    1 Medium Panzer Company
    1 (mot) Replacement Platoon
    1 (mot) Panzer Supply Column
    1 (mot) Panzer Maintenance Company
11th Schützen Brigade
  110th Schützen Regiment
    1 (mot) Staff Company

1 Signals Platoon
1 Pioneer Platoon (3 LMGS)
1 Motorcycle Platoon

1st and 2nd (mot) Battalions, each with

3 (mot) Companies (18 LMGs, 2 HMGs and 3 50mm mortars ea)

1 (mot) Machine Gun Company (8 HMGs and 6 80mm mortars)

1 (mot) Support Company

    1 (mot) Infantry Gun Platoon (2 75mm leIG)

    1 Panzerjäger Platoon (3 37mm PAK 36 and 1 LMG)

    1 Pioneer Platoon (3 LMGs)

1 (mot) Infantry Gun Company (2 150mm sIG and 4 75mm leIG)

1 (mot) Light Supply Column

111th Schützen Regiment

same as 2nd Schützen Regiment

61st Motorcycle Battalion

3 Motorcycle Companies (3 50mm mortars, 2 HMGs and 18 LMGs ea)

1 (mot) Heavy Machine Gun Company (8 HMGs and 6 80mm mortars)

1 (mot) Reconnaissance Company

    1 (mot) Infantry Gun Section (2 75mm leIG)

    1 (mot) Panzerjäger Platoon (3 37mm PAK 36 and 1 LMG)

    1 (mot) Pioneer Platoon (3 LMGs)

61st Panzerjäger Battalion

1 (mot) Signals Platoon

1 (mot) Panzerjäger Company (3 50mm PAK 38, 9 37mm PAK 36 and 6 LMGs)

2 (mot) Panzerjäger Company (12 37mm PAK 36 and 6 LMGs ea)

1st Btry/608th Self-Propelled Heavy Machine Gun Battalion (10 20mm guns; inc. 2 quads)

231st Reconnaissance Battalion

1 (mot) Signals Platoon (2 LMGs)

1 Armored Car Company (10 20mm and 25 LMGs)

1 Motorcycle Company (3 50mm mortars, 2 HMGs and 18 LMGs)

1 (mot) Heavy Reconnaissance Company

    1 Panzerjäger Platoon (3 37mm PAK 36 and 1 LMG)

    1 Pioneer Platoon (3 LMGs)

    1 Infantry Gun Section (2 75mm leIG)

1 (mot) Reconnaissance Supply Column

119th Artillery Regiment

1 (mot) Support Detachment

    1 (mot) Signals Platoon

    1 (mot) Weather Detachment

1st and 2nd (mot) Battalions, each with

1 (mot) Calibration Detachment

1 (mot) Signals Platoon

3 (mot) Batteries (4 105mm leFH and 2 LMGs ea)

3rd (mot) Battalion

1 Calibration Detachment

1 Signals Platoon

3 (mot) Batteries (4 150mm sFH and 2 LMGs ea)

85th Signals Battalion

1 (mot) Panzer Telephone Company (2 LMGs)

1 (mot) Panzer Radio Company (13 LMGS)

1 (mot) Light Signals Supply Column

86th (mot) Pioneer Battalion

3 (mot) Pioneer Companies (9 LMGs ea)

1 (mot) Brüko B

1 (mot) Brüko K

1 (mot) Light Pioneer Supply Column

61st Supply Troop

1/, 2/, 3/, 4/, 5/, 6/, 7/61st (mot) Light Supply Columns

8/, 9/, 10/61st (mot) Heavy Fuel Column

1/, 2/, 3/61st (mot) Maintenance Company

61st (mot) Supply Company

Administration

61st (mot) Field Bakery

61st (mot) Butcher Company

61st (mot) Divisional Administration

Other

1/, 2/61st (mot) Medical Company

1/, 2/, 3/61st (mot) Ambulance Companies

61st (mot) Miltiary Police Troop

61st (mot) Field Post Office

Attached

71st Flak Battalion

2/(H)21st Pz. Luftwaffe Observation Staffel

On 22 June 1941 that had changed to:

1/, 2/15th Panzer Regiment

1 Regimental Staff Signals Platoon

1 Regimental Staff Light Panzer Platoon

Each Battalion had

    1 Panzer Staff Company

    1 Medium Panzer Company

    2 Light Panzer Companies

Total tanks available:

PzMk II	44
PzMk III (37)	24
PzMk III (50)	47
PzMk IV (kz)	20
PzBefWg	9

By 5 September 1941 the operational inventory of tanks had been reduced to:

PzMk I	2 operational
PzMk II	18
PzMk III	21

PzMk IV 4
PzBefWg 15

On 25 June 1942 the organization of the armored portion of the division and its panzer inventory were as follows:

1/, 2/, 3/15th Panzer Regiment
  1 Regimental Staff Signals Platoon
  1 Regimental Staff Light Panzer Platoon
  Each Battalion had
    1 Panzer Staff Company
    1 Medium Panzer Company
    2 Light Panzer Companies
  Total tanks available:
    PzMk II   15
    PzMk III (50 kz) 14
    PzMk III (50 lg) 110
    PzMk IV (kz)   1
    PzMk IV (lg)   12
    PzBefWg   3

On 1 July 1942 the division had:

11th Panzer Division
  Division Headquarters (2 LMGs)
  61st (mot) Mapping Section
15th Armored Regiment
  Regimental Headquarters
    Signals Section
    Armored Reconnaissance Section
    Regimental Band
  1 Armored Maintenance Company
  1/, 2/, 3/15th Armored Battalions, each with
    1 Armored Staff Company
    1 Medium Armored Company
    2 Light Armored Companies
11th Schützen Brigade, with
  110th Schützen Regiment, with
    1 Staff Company with
      1 Signals Platoon
      1 Panzerjäger Platoon (3 50mm PAK 38 and 3 LMGs)
      1 Motorcycle Section (6 LMGs)
    2 Schützen Battalions, each with
      1 (half-track) Infantry Company (3 50mm PAK 38, 34 LMGs, 4 HMGs, 2 80mm mortars and 3 PzBu39)
      1 (mot) Infantry Company (18 LMGs, 4 HMGs, 2 80mm mortars and 3 PzBu39)
      1 (mot) Infantry Support Company, with
        1 (half-track) Engineer Platoon (5 LMGs)
        1 (half-track) Panzerjäger Platoon (3 50mm PAK 38, 8 LMGs and 3 28mm sPzB 41)
        2 Infantry Support Gun Sections (2 75mm leIG)

1 (mot) Infantry Support Section (4 150mm sIG)
3/31st Self-Propelled Flak Battalion (12 20mm guns and 4 LMGs)
111th Schützen Regiment, with
  1 Staff Company with
    1 Signals Platoon
    1 Panzerjäger Platoon (3 50mm PAK 38 and 3 LMGs)
    1 Motorcycle Section (6 LMGs)
  2 (mot) Infantry Battalions, each with
    3 (mot) Infantry Companies (18 LMGs, 4 HMGs, 2 80mm mortars and 3 PzBu39 ea)
    1 (mot) Infantry Support Company, with
      1 Engineer Platoon (4 LMGs)
      1 Panzerjäger Platoon (3 50mm PAK 38, 6 LMGs and 3 28mm sPzB 41)
      2 Infantry Support Gun Sections (2 75mm leIG)
  1 (mot) Infantry Support Section (4 150mm sIG)
  2/59th Self-Propelled Flak Battalion (12 20mm guns and 4 LMGs)
61st Panzerjäger Battalion
  1 Staff (2 LMGs)
  608th (self-propelled) Flak Company (12 20mm and 4 LMGs)
  2 (motZ) Panzerjäger Company (9 50mm PAK 38 6 LMGs)
61st Motorcycle Battalion
  1 Heavy Armored Car Company (18 37mm and 24 LMGs)
  2 Motorcycle Companies (2 80mm mortars, 4 HMGs, 18 LMGs and 3 PzBu39 ea)
  1 (mot) Support Company, with
    1 Engineer Platoon (4 LMGs)
    1 Panzerjäger Platoon (3 50mm PAK 38 and 3 LMGs)
    1 Panzerjäger Platoon (3 28mm sPzB 41 and 3 LMGs)
    1 Infantry Support Gun Section (2 75mm guns)
  1 Armored Car Supply Column (3 LMGs)
119th Artillery Regiment
  1 (mot) Regimental Staff (2 LMGs)
  1 (mot) Observation Battery
  2 (mot) Artillery Battalions, each with
    1 (mot) Artillery Battalion Staff (2 LMGs)
      1 Light Munition Supply Column
    3 Batteries (4 105mm leFH and 2 LMGs ea)
  1 (mot) Artillery Battalion, with
    1 (mot) Artillery Battalion Staff (2 LMGs)
    2 Batteries (4 150mm sFH and 2 LMGs ea)
    1 Battery (3 100mm K18 guns and 2 LMGs)
Motorcycle Lehr Battalion
  1 Armored Car Company
  1 Kettenkrad Company
  1 Schützen Company

1 Heavy Support Company	PzMk II 8
1 Volkswagen Company	PzMk III (kz) 11

341st Armored Signals Battalion

PzMk III (lg) 51

1 Armored Radio Company (16 LMGs)

PzMk IV (kz) 1

1 Armored Telephone Company (6 LMGs)

PzMk IV (lg) 25

1 Light (mot) Signals Supply Column

Flammpanzer 13

209th (mot) Pioneer Battalion

PzBefWg 4

1 (half-track) Pioneer Company (23 LMGs and 3 PzBu39)

OKH records show that the division was organized and equipped as follows during the "summer" of 1943:

2 (mot) Pioneer Companies (18 LMGs and 3 PzBu39)

1 (mot) "K" Bridging Train (3 LMGs)

Division Staff

1 Light (mot) Engineering Supply Column (2 LMGs)

1 Division Staff (2 LMGs)

61st (mot) Mapping Detachment

61st Food Service

15th Panzer Regiment

61st (mot) Divisional Quartermaster Platoon

Regimental Staff and Band

61st (mot) Butcher Company

1 Signals Platoon

61st (mot) Bakery Company

2nd and 3rd Battalions, each with

61st Supply Train

1 Battalion Staff and Staff Company (received 7 PzMk III flame panzers on 18 June 1943)

1st–9th Light (mot) Supply Columns (2 LMGs ea)

2 Panzer Companies (22 PzMk III ea)

13th and 14th Heavy (mot) Supply Columns (2 LMGs ea)

1 Panzer Company (22 PzMk IV ea)

10th–12th Heavy Fuel Supply Columns (2 LMGs ea)

1 Panzer Maintenance Company

61st Light (mot) Supply Company (2 LMGs)

110th Panzergrenadier Regiment

1/, 2/, 3/61st (mot) Maintenance Companies

1 Regimental Staff

Medical

1 Regimental Band

1/, 2/61st (mot) Medical Companies (2 LMGs)

1 (mot) Regimental Staff Company

1/, 2/, 3/61st Ambulance Columns

1 Signals Platoon

Other

1 Panzerjäger Platoon (3 50mm PAK 38 and 3 LMGs)

61st (mot) Military Police Platoon(2 LMGs)

1 Motorcycle Platoon (6 LMGs)

61st (mot) Field Post Office

1st (half-track) Battalion

3 (half-track) Companies (4 HMGs, 34 LMGs, 2 80mm mortars, 3 75mm leIG and 3 PzBu39 ea)

The division was destroyed in January 1943 at Stalingrad. Hitler quickly ordered the division rebuilt. In 1943 the 15th Panzer Regiment formed a 3rd Battalion from the 2/35th Panzer Regiment (4th Panzer Division). Very early in 1943 the 4/119th Artillery Regiment was organized from the 277th Army Flak Battalion. The 231st Reconnaissance Battalion was merged with the 61st Motorcycle Battalion and on 29 April 1943 this became the 11th Panzer Reconnaissance Battalion. At that time the 4/119th Artillery Regiment again became the 277th Army Flak Battalion (20 April 1943) and the 1/15th Panzer Regiment became the 52nd Panzer (Panther) Battalion. On 1 July 1943 the organization of the armored portion of the division and its panzer inventory were as follows:

1 (half-track) Heavy Company

1 Pioneer Platoon (4, later 9 LMGs)

1 Panzerjäger Platoon (3 50mm PAK 38 and 3 LMGs)

1 Infantry Gun Platoon (8 LMGs and 4 75mm leIG)

1 Panzerjäger Platoon (3 LMGs and 3 sPzBu 41)

2nd (mot) Battalion

3 (mot) Companies (4 HMGs, 18 LMGs, 2 80mm mortars and 3 PzBu39 ea)

1 (mot) Heavy Company

1 Pioneer Platoon (4 LMGs)

1 Panzerjäger Platoon (3 LMGs and 3 50mm PAK 38)

2/, 3/25th Panzer Regiment

1 Regimental Staff Signals Platoon

1 Regimental Staff Light Panzer Platoon

Each Battalion had

1 Infantry Gun Platoon (4 75mm leIG)

1 Panzerjäger Platoon (3 LMGs and 3 sPzBu 41)

1 (motZ) Infantry Gun Company (4 150mm sIG) (converted on 15 June 1943 to a self-propelled infantry gun company—6 150mm sIG and 7 LMGs)

1 Panzer Staff Company

1 Medium Panzer Company

1 Self-Propelled Flak Company (12 20mm and 4 LMGs)

2 Light Panzer Companies

4th Panzergrenadier Regiment

Total tanks available:

1 Regimental Staff

1 Regimental Band
1 (mot) Regimental Staff Company
  1 Signals Platoon
  1 Panzerjäger Platoon (3 50mm PAK 38 and 3 LMGs)
  1 Motorcycle Platoon (6 LMGs)
1st and 2nd (mot) Battalion, each with
  3 (mot) Companies (4 HMGs, 18 LMGs, 2 80mm mortars and 3 PzBu39 ea)
  1 (mot) Heavy Company
    1 Pioneer Platoon (4 LMGs)
    1 Panzerjäger Platoon (3 LMGs and 3 50mm PAK 38)
    1 Infantry Gun Platoon (4 75mm leIG)
    1 Panzerjäger Platoon (3 LMGs and 3 sPzBu 41)
  1 (motZ) Infantry Gun Company (4 150mm sIG) (converted on 16 June 1943 to a self-propelled infantry gun company—6 150mm sIG and 7 LMGs)
  1 Self-Propelled Flak Company (12 20mm and 4 LMGs)
61st Panzerjäger Battalion
  1 (motZ) Panzerjäger Company (9 75mm PAK 40 and 9 LMGs)
  1 Self-Propelled Panzerjäger Company (9 75mm PAK 40 and 9 LMGs)
11th Reconnaissance Battalion (early 1943 organization)
  1 Armored Car Company (24 LMGs and 18 20mm guns)
  1 (half-track) Company (2 80mm mortars, 4 HMGs, 56 LMGs and 3 75mm leIG)
  2 Motorcycle Companies (2 80mm mortars, 4 HMGs, 18 LMGs and 3 PzBu39 ea)
  1 (mot) Heavy Reconnaissance Company
    1 Pioneer Platoon (4 LMGs)
    1 Infantry Gun Section (4 75mm leIG)
    1 Panzerjäger Platoon (3 LMGs and 3 75mm PAK 40)
    1 Panzerjäger Platoon (3 LMGs and 3 sPzBu 41)
  1 (mot) Light Armored Car Supply Column (3 LMGs)
11th Reconnaissance Battalion (as of 10 July 1943)
  1 Armored Car Company (24 LMGs and 18 20mm guns)
  1 Armored Car (half-track) Company (25 LMGs and 16 20mm guns)
  1 Motorcycle Company (2 80mm mortars, 4 HMGs, 18 LMGs and 3 PzBu39)
  1 (half-track) Heavy Reconnaissance Company
    1 Staff (2 LMGs)
    1 Infantry Platoon (9 LMGs)
    1 Pioneer Platoon (1 37mm PAK 36, 6 flamethrowers and 13 LMGs)
    1 Panzerjäger Platoon (3 75mm PAK 40 and 4 LMGs)
    1 Infantry Gun Section (2 75mm leIG)
    1 Half-Track Gun Section (8 LMGs and 6 75mm guns)

1 (mot) Light Reconnaissance Supply Column (3 LMGs)
76th Panzer Artillery Regiment
  1 Regimental Staff
  1 Staff Battery (2 LMGs)
1st and 2nd Battalions, each with
  1 Battalion Staff
  1 Battalion Staff Battery (6 LMGs)
  3 (mot) Batteries (4 105mm leFH and 2 LMGs ea)
1st (self-propelled) Battalion (as of 1 Aug. 1943)
  1 Battalion Staff
  1 Self-Propelled Battalion Staff Battery (2 LMGs and 3 20mm Flak)
  2 Self-Propelled Batteries (6 105mm leFH SdKfz 124 Wespe and 4 LMGs ea)
  1 Self-Propelled Battery (6 150mm sFH SdKfz 165 Hummel and 4 LMGs)
3rd (mot) Battalion
  1 Battalion Staff
  1 Battalion Staff Battery (6 LMGs)
  2 (mot) Batteries (4 150mm sFH and 2 LMGs ea)
  1 (mot) Battery (4 100mm K 18 guns and 2 LMGs)
119th (mot) Observation Battery (2 LMGs)
277th Army Flak Battalion
  1 Staff and (mot) Staff Battery (1 LMG)
  1st–2nd (motZ) Heavy Flak Batteries (4 88mm, 3 20mm and 2 LMGs ea)
  3rd (motZ) Light Flak Battery (12 20mm and 2 LMGs)
  4th Self-Propelled Battery (8 20mm and 2 quad 20mm Flak guns and 4 LMGs)
  1 (mot) Light (20 ton) Flak Supply Column
209th Panzer Pioneer Battalion
  1 Staff (2 LMGs)
  1 (half-track) Pioneer Company (25 LMGs, 3 PzBu39 and 2 80mm mortars)
  2 (mot) Pioneer Companies (18 LMGs, 2 80mm mortars and 3 PzBu39 ea)
  1 Brüko K Bridging Column (3 LMGs)
  1 (mot) Light Pioneer Supply Column (2 LMGs)
89th Panzer Signals Battalion
  1 Panzer Telephone Company (6 LMGs)
  1 Panzer Radio Company (16 LMGs)
  1 (mot) Light Signals Supply Column (1 LMG)
61st Feldersatz Battalion
  6 Companies
61st Supply Troop
  1–6/61st (mot) (90 ton) Transportation Company (3 LMGs ea)
  61st (mot) Light Supply Column (2 LMGs)
  61st (mot) Supply Company (6 LMGs)
Other
  1–3/61st (mot) Maintenance Companies (4 LMGs ea)
  61st (mot) Bakery Company
  61st (mot) Butcher Company
  61st (mot) Administration Platoon

1/, 2/61st (mot) Medical Companies (2 LMGs ea)
1/, 2/, 3/61st Ambulances
61st (mot) Military Police Troop (2 LMGs)
61st (mot) Field Post Office

In the fall of 1943 the 3/15th was redesignated as the 1/15th Panzer Regiment. On 8 November 1943 the 356th Infantry Division detached the 3/869th to the 11th Panzer Division to rebuild its panzergrenadiers. Sometime in late 1943 the 1/15th Panzer Regiment was equipped with Panther tanks. The 2/15th Panzer Regiment continued to be equipped with Panzer PzMk IV tanks.

During 1943 the 1/110th Panzergrenadier Regiment was equipped with half-tracks. The reconnaissance battalion was restructured with a staff, a light armored car company, two motorcycle companies, a heavy reconnaissance company, and a supply column. The panzerjäger battalion was reorganized with a staff, a (motZ) company, and a self-propelled company.

In February 1944, while in France, the division was reorganized and rebuilt by troops from the 273rd Reserve Panzer Division. The Panther companies were equipped with 17 Panther tanks each and the companies equipped with PzMk IV tanks had 22 each. After the Normandy campaign the division's panzer regiment was reduced such that each company had only 14 tanks. On 23 September 1944 the division was rebuilt using the 113th Panzer Brigade (Panzergrenadier Regiment and 2113th Panzer Battalion). In August the organization of the armored portion of the division and its panzer inventory were as follows:

1/15th Panzer Regiment
  1 Panzer Signals Platoon
  1 Battalion
    1 Panzer Staff Company
    4 Medium Panzer Companies (PzMk V)
  Total tanks available:
  PzMk V   79
  FlakpzIV 37   8

In November 1944 the division was ordered refreshed. The 1/15th Panzer Battalion was to have four companies, each with 14 PzMk V Panther tanks, and the 2/15th was to have four companies, each with 14 PzMk IV Tanks. The division was taken into American captivity in the Bavarian forests on 4 May 1945.

12th Panzer Division

Formed on 5 October 1940 from the 2nd (mot) Infantry Division with:

12th Schützen Brigade (newly formed)
  1/, 2/5th Schützen Regiment (formed from the 5th Infantry Regiment)
  1/, 2/25th Schützen Regiment (formed from the 25th Infantry Regiment)
22nd Motorcycle Battalion
1/, 2/, 3/29th Panzer Regiment (newly formed)
1/, 2/, 3/2nd Artillery Regiment (1st and 2nd from 1/, 3/2nd and the 3/2nd Artillery Regiment from the 1/38th Artillery Regiment)
2nd Panzerjäger Battalion
32nd Pioneer Battalion
2nd Signals Battalion
2nd Divisional Support Units

On 22 June 1941, the eve of the invasion of Russia, the organization of the armored portion of the division and its panzer inventory were as follows:

1/, 2, /, 3/29th Panzer Regiment
  1 Regimental Staff Signals Platoon
  1 Regimental Staff Light Panzer Platoon
  Each Battalion had
    1 Panzer Staff Company

    1 Medium Panzer Company
    2 Light Panzer Companies
  Total tanks available:
  PzMk I   40
  PzMk II   33
  38 (t)   109
  PzMk IV (kz) 30
  38 (t) cmd   8

By 26 August 1941 the inventory of operational tanks stood at:

  PzMk I   7
  PzMk II   25
  PzMk III   42
  PzMk IV   14
  PzBefWg   8

On 1 July 1942 the organization of the armored portion of the division and its panzer inventory were as follows:

1/, 2/29th Panzer Regiment
  1 Regimental Staff Signals Platoon
  1 Regimental Staff Light Panzer Platoon
  Each Battalion had
    1 Panzer Staff Company
    1 Medium Panzer Company

2 Light Panzer Companies
Total tanks available:

PzMk III (50 kz)   48
PzMk IV (kz)   6
PzMk IV (lg)   4

In 1942 the 3/29th Panzer Regiment was transferred to the 13th Panzer Division and became the 3/4th Panzer Regiment. At that time the 303rd Army Flak Battalion was raised and assigned to the division. and the 2nd Reconnaissance Battalion was merged into the 22nd Motorcycle Battalion. The motorcycle battalion became the 12th Panzer Reconnaissance Battalion on 20 April 1943. The division then had:

1/, 2/5th Panzergrenadier Regiment
1/, 2/25th Panzergrenadier Regiment
12th Panzer Reconnaissance Battalion
1/, 2/29th Panzer Regiment
1/, 2/, 3/2nd Artillery Regiment
303rd Army Flak Battalion
2nd Panzerjäger Battalion
32nd Panzer Pioneer Battalion
2nd Signals Battalion
2nd Divisional Support Units

As a temporary measure, the 1/29th Panzer Regiment was redesignated as the 508th Panzer Battalion from 11 May to 8 July 1943. During 1943 the 2/29th Panzer Regiment was slowly equipped with PzMk IV tanks. Keilig indicates that both the 1/2nd and 3/2nd Panzer Artillery Regiment were eventually equipped with self-propelled guns. However, the OKH records through September do not show the 3/2nd so equipped, indicating that the change occurred later in the year. The 2nd Panzer (mot) Observation Battery was assigned to the division in 1943. On 1 July 1943 the organization of the armored portion of the division and its panzer inventory were as follows:

2/29th Panzer Regiment
1 Regimental Staff Signals Platoon
1 Regimental Staff Light Panzer Platoon
8th Medium Panzer Company
1 Panzer Battalion with
  1 Panzer Staff Company
  1 Medium Panzer Company
  2 Light Panzer Companies
Total tanks available:

PzMk II   6
PzMk III (kz)   15
PzMk III (lg)   15
PzMk III (75)   6
PzMk IV (kz)   1
PzMk IV (lg)   36
PzBefWg   4

OKH records show that the division was organized and equipped as follows during the spring and summer of 1943:

Division Staff
1 Division Staff (2 LMGs)
2nd (mot) Mapping Detachment
29th Panzer Regiment
Regimental Staff
1 Signals Platoon
1 Regimental Band
2nd Battalion
1 Battalion Staff and Staff Company (7 PzMk III flame panzers assigned by 18 June 1943)
2 Panzer Companies (22 PzMk III ea; changed to PzMk IV 15 June 1943)
2 Panzer Companies (22 PzMk IV ea)
1 Panzer Maintenance Company
5th Panzergrenadier Regiment
1 Regimental Staff
1 Regimental Band
1 (mot) Regimental Staff Company
1 Signals Platoon
1 Panzerjäger Platoon (3 50mm PAK 38 and 3 LMGs)
1 Motorcycle Platoon (6 LMGs)
1st and 2nd (mot) Battalions, each with
3 (mot) Companies (4 HMGs, 18 LMGs, 2 80mm mortars and 3 sPzBu 41 ea)
1 (mot) Heavy Company
  1 Pioneer Platoon (4 LMGs)
  1 Panzerjäger Platoon (3 LMGs and 3 50mm PAK 38)
  1 Infantry Gun Platoon (4 75mm leIG)
  1 Panzerjäger Platoon (3 LMGs and 3 sPzBu 41)
1 (motZ) Infantry Gun Company (4 150mm sIG)
25th Panzergrenadier Regiment
same as 5th Panzergrenadier Regiment
12th Reconnaissance Battalion (early 1943 organization)
1 Armored Car Company (24 LMGs and 18 20mm guns)
3 Motorcycle Companies (2 80mm mortars, 4 HMGs, 18 LMGs and 3 PzBu39 ea)
5th (mot) Heavy Reconnaissance Company
  1 Pioneer Platoon (4 LMGs)
  1 Infantry Gun Section (2 75mm leIG)
  1 Panzerjäger Platoon (3 LMGs and 3 75mm PAK 40)
  1 Panzerjäger Platoon (3 LMGs and 3 sPzBu 41)
1 (mot) Light Reconnaissance Supply Column (3 LMGs)
12th Reconnaissance Battalion (as of 10 July 1943)
1 Armored Car Company (24 LMGs and 18 20mm guns)
1 Armored Car (half-track) Company (25 LMGs and 16 20mm guns)

1 (half-track) Reconnaissance Company (2 80mm mortars, 3 37mm PAK 36, 4 HMGs and 56 LMGs)

1 Motorcycle Company (2 80mm mortars, 4 HMGs, 18 LMGs and 3 PzBu39)

1 (half-track) Heavy Reconnaissance Company
   1 Staff (2 LMGs)
   1 Infantry Platoon (9 LMGs)
   1 Pioneer Platoon (1 37mm PAK 36, 6 flamethrowers and 13 LMGs)
   1 Panzerjäger Platoon (3 75mm PAK 40 and 4 LMGs)
   1 Infantry Gun Section (2 75mm leIG)
   1 Half-Track Gun Section (8 LMGs and 6 75mm guns)
   1 (mot) Light Reconnaissance Supply Column (3 LMGs)

2nd Panzerjäger Battalion
   1 (motZ) Panzerjäger Company (75mm PAK 40)
   1 Self-Propelled Panzerjäger Company (14 75mm PAK 40 and 14 LMGs ea)

303rd Army Flak Battalion
   1 Staff and (mot) Staff Battery (1 LMG)
   1st–2nd (motZ) Heavy Flak Batteries (4 88mm, 3 20mm and 2 LMGs ea)
   3rd (motZ) Light Flak Battery (12 20mm and 2 LMGs)
   4th Self-Propelled Battery (8 20mm and 2 quad 20mm Flak guns and 4 LMGs)
   1 (mot) Light (20 ton) Flak Supply Column

2nd Panzer Artillery Regiment
   1 Regimental Staff
   1 Staff Battery (2 LMGs)
  1st and 2nd Battalions, each with
   1 Battalion Staff
   1 Battalion Staff Battery (6 LMGs)
   3 (mot) Batteries (3 105mm leFH and 2 LMGs ea)
  1st Battalion (self-propelled in mid-Aug. 1943)
   1 Battalion Staff and Staff Battery (6 LMGs)
   2 Self-Propelled Batteries (6 105mm leFH SdKfz 124 Wespe and 4 LMGs ea)
   1 Self-Propelled Battery (6 150mm sFH SdKfz 165 Hummel and 4 LMGs)
  3rd (mot) Battalion
   1 Battalion Staff

1 Battalion Staff Battery (6 LMGs)
2 (mot) Batteries (3 150mm sFH and 2 LMGs ea)
1 (mot) Battery (3 100mm K 18 guns and 2 LMGs)
  2nd (mot) Observation Battery (2 LMGs)

2nd Panzer Signals Battalion
   1 Panzer Telephone Company (6 LMGs)
   1 Panzer Radio Company (16 LMGs)
   1 (mot) Light Signals Supply Column (1 LMG)

32nd Panzer Pioneer Battalion
   1 Staff (2 LMGs)
   1 (half-track) Pioneer Company (25 LMGs, 2 80mm mortars and 3 PzBu39)
   2 (mot) Pioneer Companies (18 LMGs, 2 80mm mortars and 3 PzBu39 ea)
   1 Brüko K Bridging Column (3 LMGs)
   1 (mot) Light Pioneer Supply Column (2 LMGs)

2nd Supply Troop
   1–5/2nd (mot) (90 ton) Transportation Companies (3 LMGs ea)
   2nd (mot) Supply Company (6 LMGs)

Truck Park
   1–3/2nd (mot) Maintenance Companies (4 LMGs ea)
   32nd (mot) Heavy (75 ton)Replacement Supply Column (added 1 Aug. 1943)

Other
   2nd (mot) Bakery Company
   2nd (mot) Butcher Company
   2nd (mot) Administration Platoon
   1/, 2/2nd (mot) Medical Companies (2 LMGs ea)
   1/, 2/, 3/2nd Ambulances
   2nd (mot) Military Police Troop (2 LMGs)
   2nd (mot) Field Post Office

On 17 April 1944 the reconnaissance battalion was reorganized with the 1st Company as armored cars, the 2nd and 3rd Companies as armored reconnaissance companies, and the 4th as a motorcycle company. On 30 April 1944 the 1/29th Panzer Regiment was equipped with Panther tanks. The 2/29th Panzer Regiment continued to be equipped with Panzer PzMk IV tanks. The division was captured in Courland on 8 May 1945 by the Russians.

13th Panzer Division

Formed on 11 October 1940 from the 13th (mot) Infantry Division and the 4th Panzer Regiment, which was reassigned from the 2nd Panzer Division. The division had:

13th Schützen Brigade
   1/, 2/66th Schützen Regiment
   1/, 2/93rd Schützen Regiment

43rd Motorcycle Battalion
1/, 2/4th Panzer Regiment
1/, 2/, 3/13th Artillery Regiment
13th Panzerjäger Battalion
4th Pioneer Battalion
13th Signals Battalion
13th Divisional Support Units

Indications are that, initially, the 13th Panzer Division was a Lehr or school division used to train soldiers in Rumania. Every regiment, battalion and support unit's name was prefaced with the term "Lehr" or "instruction". On 22 June 1941 the organization of the armored portion of the division and its panzer inventory were as follows:

1/, 2/4th Panzer Regiment
  1 Regimental Staff Signals Platoon
  1 Regimental Staff Light Panzer Platoon
  Each Battalion had
    1 Panzer Staff Company
    1 Medium Panzer Company
    2 Light Panzer Companies
  Total tanks available:
    PzMk II   45
    PzMk III (37)   27
    PzMk III (50)   44
    PzMk IV (kz)   20
    PzBefWg   13

By 28 August 1941 the operational tank inventory was reduced to:

    PzMk I   3
    PzMk II   35
    PzMk III   37
    PzMk IV   9
    PzBefWg   9

In 1942 the 4th Panzer Regiment formed a 3rd Battalion from the 1/29th Panzer Regiment, the 13th Artillery Regiment formed a 4th Battalion from the 275th Army Flak Battalion, and the 13th Reconnaissance Battalion and the 43rd Motorcycle Battalion were merged. In 1943 the 43rd Motorcycle Battalion became the 13th Panzer Reconnaissance Battalion and the 274th Army Flak Battalion (the 4/13th Artillery Regiment) was replaced by the 271st Army Flak Battalion. The 3/4th Panzer Regiment was detached, reducing the regiment to two battalions. The division then had:

1/, 2/66th Panzergrenadier Regiment
1/, 2/93rd Panzergrenadier Regiment
13th Panzer Reconnaissance Battalion
1/, 2/4th Panzer Regiment
1/, 2/, 3/13th Panzer Artillery Regiment
271st Army Flak Battalion
13th Panzerjäger Battalion
4th Pioneer Battalion
13th Signals Battalion
13th Divisional Support Units

On 22 June 1942 the organization of the armored portion of the division and its panzer inventory were as follows:

1/, 2/, 3/4th Panzer Regiment
  1 Regimental Staff Signals Platoon
  1 Regimental Staff Light Panzer Platoon
  Each Battalion had
    1 Panzer Staff Company
    1 Medium Panzer Company
    2 Light Panzer Companies
  Total tanks available:
    PzMk II   15
    PzMk III (50 kz) 41
    PzMk III (50 lg) 30
    PzMk IV (kz)   12

During 1943 the 2/4th Panzer Regiment reequipped itself with Panzer PzMk IVs, discarding the remaining PzMk III tanks. The 1/4th Panzer Regiment was sent to Germany to re-equip with Tiger PzMk VI tanks and would be redesignated the 507th Panzer Battalion. OKH records show that the division was organized and equipped as follows during the spring and summer of 1943:

Division Staff
  1 Division Staff (2 LMGs)
  13th (mot) Mapping Detachment
4th Panzer Regiment
  Regimental Staff
  1 Signals Platoon
  1 Regimental Band
1st and 2nd Battalions, each with
  1 Battalion Staff and Staff Company
  2 Panzer Companies (PzMk III tanks)
  1 Panzer Company (PzMk IV tanks)
  1 Panzer Maintenance Company
66th Panzergrenadier Regiment
  1 Regimental Staff
  1 Regimental Band
  1 (mot) Regimental Staff Company
    1 Signals Platoon
    1 Panzerjäger Platoon (3 50mm PAK 38 and 3 LMGs)
    1 Motorcycle Platoon (6 LMGs)
    1 (half-track) Pioneer Platoon (LMGs and flamethrowers) (added 28 May 1943)
1st (half-track) Battalion
  3 (half-track) Companies (4 HMGs, 34 LMGs, 2 80mm mortars, 3 75mm leIG and 3 PzBu39 ea)
  1 (half-track) Heavy Company
    1 Pioneer Platoon (9 LMGs)
    1 Panzerjäger Platoon (3 50mm PAK 38 and 3 LMGs)
    1 Infantry Gun Platoon (8 LMGs and 4 75mm leIG)
    1 Panzerjäger Platoon (3 LMGs and 3 sPzBu 41)
2nd (mot) Battalion
  3 (mot) Companies (4 HMGs, 18 LMGs, 2 80mm mortars and 3 PzBu39 ea)

1 (mot) Heavy Company
  1 Pioneer Platoon (4 LMGs)
  1 Panzerjäger Platoon (3 LMGs and 3 50mm PAK 38)
  1 Infantry Gun Platoon (4 75mm leIG)
  1 Panzerjäger Platoon (3 LMGs and 3 sPzBu ea)
1 (motZ) Infantry Gun Company (4 150mm sIG)
1 Flak Company (8 self-propelled 20mm, 4 motZ 20mm guns and 4 LMGs)

93rd Panzergrenadier Regiment
1 Regimental Staff
1 Regimental Band
1 (mot) Regimental Staff Company
  1 Signals Platoon
  1 Panzerjäger Platoon (3 50mm PAK 38 and 3 LMGs)
  1 Motorcycle Platoon (6 LMGs)
1st and 2nd (mot) Battalions, each with
  3 (mot) Companies (4 HMGs, 18 LMGs, 2 80mm mortars and 3 PzBu39 ea)
  1 (mot) Heavy Company
    1 Pioneer Platoon (4 LMGs)
    1 Panzerjäger Platoon (3 LMGs and 3 50mm PAK 38)
    1 Infantry Gun Platoon (4 75mm leIG)
    1 Panzerjäger Platoon (3 LMGs and 3 sPzBu 41)
  1 (motZ) Infantry Gun Company (4 150mm sIG)
  1 Flak Company (8 self-propelled 20mm, 4 motZ 20mm guns and 4 LMGs)

13th Panzerjäger Battalion
1 (motZ) Panzerjäger Company (9 75mm PAK 40 and 9 LMGs)
1 Self-Propelled Panzerjäger Company (9 75mm PAK 40 and 9 LMGs)

13th Reconnaissance Battalion (early 1943 organization)
1 Armored Car Company (24 LMGs and 18 20mm guns)
2 Motorcycle Companies (2 80mm mortars, 4 HMGs, 18 LMGs and 3 PzBu39 ea)
1 (half-track) Reconnaissance Company (2 80mm mortars, 4 HMGs, 56 LMGs and 3 75mm leIG)
1 (mot) Heavy Reconnaissance Company
  1 Pioneer Platoon (4 LMGs)
  1 Infantry Gun Section (4 75mm leIG)
  1 Panzerjäger Platoon (3 LMGs and 3 75mm PAK 40)
  1 Panzerjäger Platoon (3 LMGs and 3 sPzBu 41)
1 (mot) Light Armored Car Supply Column (3 LMGs)

13th Panzer Artillery Regiment
1 Regimental Staff
1 Staff Battery (2 LMGs)
1st and 2nd Battalions, each with
1 Battalion Staff

1 Battalion Staff Battery (6 LMGs)
3 (mot) Batteries (3 105mm leFH and 2 LMGs ea)
3rd (mot) Battalion
1 Battalion Staff
1 Battalion Staff Battery (6 LMGs)
2 (mot) Batteries (3 150mm sFH and 2 LMGs ea)
1 (mot) Battery (3 100mm K 18 guns and 2 LMGs)
76th (mot) Observation Battery (2 LMGs)

271st Army Flak Battalion
1 Staff and (mot) Staff Battery (1 LMG)
1st–2nd (motZ) Heavy Flak Batteries (4 88mm, 3 20mm and 2 LMGs ea)
3rd (motZ) Light Flak Battery (12 20mm and 2 LMGs)
4th Self-Propelled Battery (8 20mm and 2 quad 20mm Flak guns and 4 LMGs)
1 (mot) Light (20 ton) Flak Supply Column

Montfort Panzergrenadier Battalion (forming in July 1943)
1 Staff
3 Companies (equipment unknown)

4th Panzer Pioneer Battalion
1 Staff (2 LMGs)
2 (half-track) Pioneer Companies (25 LMGs, 2 80mm mortars and 3 PzBu39 ea)
1 (mot) Pioneer Company (18 LMGs, 3 PzBu39 and 2 80mm mortars ea)
1 Brüko K Bridging Column (3 LMGs)
1 (mot) Light Pioneer Supply Column (2 LMGs)

13th Panzer Signals Battalion
1 Panzer Telephone Company (6 LMGs)
1 Panzer Radio Company (16 LMGs)
1 (mot) Light Signals Supply Column (1 LMG)

13th Feldersatz Battalion
4 Companies

13th Supply Troop
1–6/13th (mot) (90 ton) Transportation Company (3 LMGs ea)
13th (mot) Heavy Fuel Column (2 LMGs)
13th (mot) Supply Company (6 LMGs)

Truck Park
1–3/13th (mot) Maintenance Companies (4 LMGs ea)
Other
13th (mot) Bakery Company
13th (mot) Butcher Company
13th (mot) Administration Platoon
1/, 2/13th (mot) Medical Companies (2 LMGs ea)
1/, 2/, 3/13th Ambulances
13th (mot) Military Police Troop (2 LMGs)
13th (mot) Field Post Office

On 1 July 1943 the organization of the armored portion of the division and its panzer inventory were as follows:

1/, 2/4th Panzer Regiment
  1 Regimental Staff Signals Platoon

1 Regimental Staff Light Panzer Platoon
Each Battalion had
  1 Panzer Staff Company
  3 Medium Panzer Companies
Total tanks available:

PzMk II	5
PzMk III (kz)	4
PzMk III (lg)	10
PzMk III (75)	0
PzMk IV (kz)	0
PzMk IV (lg)	50
PzBefWg	2

On 25 January 1944 the 1/4th Panzer Regiment was equipped with Panther tanks. The 2/4th Panzer Regiment continued to be equipped with Panzer PzMk IV tanks. In May 1944 the 1030th (Feldherrnhalle) Panzergrenadier Regiment joined the division, but it was destroyed in the southern Ukraine in August. The division was re-formed in 1944 with the Ersatz Brigade Feldherrnhalle.

The 13th Panzer Division was reorganized using the 110th Panzer Brigade (2110th Panzer Battalion and 2110th Panzergrenadier Regiment). On 19 July 1944 the 13th Panzer Division was totally destroyed in Budapest.

In March 1945 the division re-formed and reorganized as the 2nd Feldherrnhalle Panzer Division. It surrendered to the Allies on 8 May 1945.

14th Panzer Division

Formed on 15 August 1940 from the 4th Infantry Division. It contained:

14th Schützen Brigade
  1/, 2/103rd Schützen Regiment
  1/, 2/108th Schützen Regiment
64th Motorcycle Battalion
1/, 2/36th Panzer Regiment
1/, 2/, 3/4th Artillery Regiment
4th Panzerjäger Battalion
40th Reconnaissance Battalion
13th Pioneer Battalion
4th Divisional Support units

On 6 April 1941 the organization of the armored portion of the division and its panzer inventory were as follows:

1/, 2/36th Panzer Division
  1 Regimental Staff Signals Platoon
  1 Regimental Staff Light Panzer Platoon
  Each Battalion had
    1 Panzer Staff Company
    1 Medium Panzer Company
    2 Light Panzer Companies
  Total tanks available:

PzMk II	45
PzMk III (37)	16
PzMk III (50)	35
PzMk IV	20
PzBefWg	8

By 22 June 1941 the organization and tank inventory stood at:

1/, 2/36th Panzer Regiment
  1 Regimental Staff Signals Platoon
  1 Regimental Staff Light Panzer Platoon
  Each Battalion had
    1 Panzer Staff Company
    1 Medium Panzer Company
    2 Light Panzer Companies
  Total tanks available:

PzMk II	45
PzMk III (37)	15
PzMk III (50)	56
PzMk IV (kz)	20
PzBefWg	11

By 6 September 1941 the operational tank inventory stood at:

PzMk I	5
PzMk II	35
PzMk III	49
PzMk IV	15
PzBefWg	8

In 1942 the 3/36th Panzer Regiment was formed using the 3/7th Panzer Regiment (10th Panzer Division). The 4/4th Artillery Regiment was formed from the 276th Army Flak Battalion and the 40th Reconnaissance Battalion was merged into the 64th Motorcycle Battalion. On 20 June 1942 the organization of the armored portion of the division and its panzer inventory were as follows:

1/, 2/, 3/36th Panzer Regiment
  1 Regimental Staff Signals Platoon
  1 Regimental Staff Light Panzer Platoon

Each Battalion had
  1 Panzer Staff Company
  1 Medium Panzer Company
  2 Light Panzer Companies
Total tanks available:
  PzMk II   14
  PzMk III (50 kz)   41
  PzMk III (50 lg)   19
  PzMk IV (kz)   20
  PzMk IV (lg)   4
  PzBefWg   4

In February 1943 the division was destroyed at Stalingrad. The division was re-formed in March 1943 and had:

1/, 2/103rd Panzergrenadier Regiment
1/, 2/108th Panzergrenadier Regiment
14th Panzer Reconnaissance Battalion
1/, 2/, 3/36th Panzer Regiment
1/, 2/, 3/4th Panzer Artillery Regiment
276th Army Flak Battalion
4th Panzerjäger Battalion
13th Panzer Pioneer Battalion
4th Panzer Signals Battalion
4th Divisional Support Units

The panzer regiment was re-formed on 17 February 1943 with two battalions, each with four companies. Orders were cut on 3 March 1943 directing the addition of a 3rd (Tiger) Battalion equipped with three heavy panzer companies and an independent sturmgeschütz Battalion with three batteries. However, on 20 March 1943 these plans were abandoned and the 3rd Battalion was ordered to be organized with sturmgeschütze. This battalion contained four companies and 22 sturmgeschütze.

The division was savaged during the Stalingrad battles and reduced to a kampfgruppe. On 7 February 1943 that kampfgruppe was organized and equipped as follows:

Divisional Staff
Panzer Battalion
  3 Panzer Companies (22 PzMk IV Tanks ea)
  1 Armored Maintenance Platoon
(mot) Panzergrenadier Battalion
  3 (mot) Panzergrenadier Companies (4 HMGs, 18 LMGs and 2 80mm mortars ea)
  1 (mot) Heavy Company
    1 Pioneer Platoon (4 LMGs)
    1 Infantry Gun Section (4 75mm leIG and 6 LMGs)
    1 Panzerjäger Platoon (3 75mm PAK 40)
Armored Battalion
  1 (motZ) Heavy Battery (4 150mm sFH and 2 LMGs)
  1 (motZ) Medium Battery (4 105mm leFH and 2 LMGs)
  1 Self-Propelled Battery (4, later 6 105mm leFH SdKfz 124 Wespe and 2 LMGs)

1 (mot) Observation Battery (2 LMGs) (added 2/11/43)
(mot) Pioneer Company (18 LMGs, 2 80mm mortars and 6 flamethrowers, plus 3 light anti-tank guns, added 20 Feb. 1943)
Self-Propelled Flak Company (12 20mm Flak guns and 4 LMGs)
Assault Gun Battery (10 StuG) (removed 2/23/43)
Panzer Mixed Signals Company (16 LMGs)

OKH records show that the division was organized and equipped as follows on 22 February 1943.

Division Staff
  1 Division Staff (2 LMGs)
  1 (mot) Mapping Detachment
  1 (mot) Escort Company
    1 Motorcycle Platoon (6 LMGs)
    1 Infantry Gun Section (2 75mm leIG)
    1 Self-Propelled Flak Platoon (4 20mm Flak guns)
    1 Panzerjäger Platoon (3 LMGs and 3 75mm PAK 40)
    1 Infantry Platoon (4 HMGs, 6 LMGs and 2 80mm mortars)
36th Panzer Regiment
  Regimental Staff
  1 Signals Platoon
  1 Regimental Band
1st Battalion
  1 Staff and Staff Company
    1 Pioneer Platoon
    1 Flak Platoon
  4 Panzer Companies (22 PzMk IV ea)
  1 Panzer Maintenance Company
2nd Battalion
  1 Staff and Staff Company
  4 Panzer Companies (22 PzMk IV ea)
  1 Panzer Maintenance Company
3rd Battalion (detached on 18 Mar. 1943)
  1 Staff and Staff Company
    1 Pioneer Platoon
    1 Flak Platoon
  3 Panzer Companies (10 PzMk VI Tiger Tanks ea)
  1 Panzer Maintenance Company
103rd Panzergrenadier Regiment
  1 Regimental Staff
  1 Regimental Band
  1 (mot) Regimental Staff Company
    1 Signals Platoon
    1 Pioneer Platoon (6 LMGs and 6 flamethrowers)
    1 Panzerjäger Platoon (3 75mm PAK 40 and 3 LMGs)
    1 Motorcycle Platoon (6 LMGs)
1st (half-track) Battalion
  3 (half-track) Companies (4 HMGs, 33 LMGs, 2 80mm mortars and 4 37mm PAK 36 ea) (upgraded

to 4 HMGs, 39 LMGs, 3 PzBu39, 3 75mm leIG, 2 80mm mortars and 2 75mm guns ea but date unknown)

1 (half-track) Heavy Company
    1 (half-track) Pioneer Platoon (9 LMGs, 1 37mm PAK and
    6 flamethrowers)
    1 Panzerjäger Platoon (3 75mm PAK 40 and 3 LMGs)
    1 Infantry Gun Platoon (8 LMGs and 4 75mm leIG)
    1 Half-Track Gun Platoon (6 75mm guns)

2nd (mot) Battalion
3 (mot) Companies (4 HMGs, 18 LMGs and 2 80mm mortars ea)
1 (mot) Heavy Company
    1 Pioneer Platoon (4 LMGs and 6 flamethrowers)
    1 Panzerjäger Platoon (3 LMGs and 3 75 PAK 40)
    1 Infantry Gun Platoon (4 75mm leIG)
    1 Panzerjäger Platoon (3 LMGs and 3 sPzBu 41)
1 Self-Propelled Flak Company (12 20mm and 4 LMGs)
1 Self-Propelled Infantry Gun Company (6 150mm sIG and 7 LMGs)

Assault Gun Battalion (detached Mar. 1943)
1 Battalion Staff and Staff Battery
3 Sturmgeschütz Batteries (10 StuG ea)

108th Panzergrenadier Regiment
1 Regimental Staff
1 Regimental Band
1 (mot) Regimental Staff Company
    1 Signals Platoon
    1 Panzerjäger Platoon (3 50mm PAK 38 and 3 LMGs)
    1 Motorcycle Platoon (6 LMGs)

1st and 2nd (mot) Battalions, each with
3 (mot) Companies (4 HMGs, 18 LMGs and 2 80mm mortars ea)
1 (mot) Heavy Company
    1 Pioneer Platoon (4 LMGs)
    1 Panzerjäger Platoon (3 LMGs and 3 50mm PAK 38)
    1 Infantry Gun Platoon (4 75mm leIG)
    1 Panzerjäger Platoon (3 LMGs and 3 sPzBu 41)
1 Self-Propelled Flak Company (12 20mm and 4 LMGs)
1 Self-Propelled Infantry Gun Company (6 150mm sIG and 7 LMGs)

64th (14th as of 29 Apr. 1943) Reconnaissance Battalion
1 Armored Car Company
    3 Armored Car Platoons (25 LMGs and 18 20mm guns)
    1 Armored Car Platoon (6 LMGs and 6 75mm guns)
1 (half-track) Armored Car Company (25 LMGs and 16 20mm guns)
2 (half-track) Reconnaissance Companies (2 120mm mortars, 3 37mm PAK 36, 4 HMGs and 56 LMGs ea)

1 (mot) Heavy Reconnaissance Company
    1 Pioneer Platoon (9, later 13 LMGs, 6 flamethrowers and 1 75mm gun)
    1 Infantry Gun Section (1 LMG and 2 75mm leIG)
    1 Panzerjäger Platoon (3 LMGs and 3 75mm PAK 40)
    1 Half-Track Gun Platoon (8 LMGs and 6 75mm guns)
1 (mot) Light Armored Car Supply Column (3 LMGs)

4th Panzer Artillery Regiment
1 Regimental Staff
1 Staff Battery (6 LMGs)
1 (mot) Observation Battery (12 LMGs)
1 Self-Propelled Flak Battery (4 quad 20mm) (this was reduced to 4 (motZ) 20mm guns on 3/9/43)

1st Battalion
1 Battalion Staff and Staff Battery (6 LMGs)
2 Self-Propelled Batteries (6 105mm leFH SdKfz 124 Wespe and 4 LMGs ea)
1 Self-Propelled Battery (6 150mm sFH SdKfz 165 Hummel and 4 LMGs)

2nd Battalion
1 Battalion Staff
1 Battalion Staff Battery (6 LMGs)
3 (mot) Batteries (3 105mm leFH and 2 LMGs ea)

3rd (mot) Battalion
1 Battalion Staff
1 Battalion Staff Battery (6 LMGs)
2 (mot) Batteries (3 150mm sFH and 2 LMGs ea)
1 (mot) Battery (3 100mm K 18 guns and 2 LMGs)

276th Army Flak Battalion (was 4/4th Panzer Artillery Regiment until 26 Apr. 1943)
1 Staff and (mot) Staff Battery (1 LMG)
1st–2nd (motZ) Heavy Flak Batteries (4 88mm, 3 20mm and 2 LMGs ea)
3rd (motZ) Light Flak Battery (9 20mm, 2 self-propelled quad 20mm guns and 2 LMGs)
1 (mot) Light (20 ton) Flak Supply Column

13th Panzer Pioneer Battalion
1 Staff (7 LMGs)
1 (half-track) Pioneer Company (2 HMGs, 43 LMGs, 3 PzBu39, 6 flamethrowers and 2 80mm mortars)
2 (mot) Pioneer Companies (2 HMGs, 18 LMGs, 3 PzBu39, 2 80mm mortars, and 6 flamethrowers ea)
1 Brüko K Bridging Column (3 LMGs)
1 (mot) Light Pioneer Supply Column (2 LMGs)

4th Panzer Signals Battalion
1 Panzer Telephone Company (21 LMGs)
1 Panzer Radio Company (35 LMGs)
1 (mot) Light Signals Supply Column (4 LMGs)

4th Supply Troop
1–8/4th (mot) (120 ton) Transportation Company (4 LMGs ea)
4th (mot) Supply Company (6 LMGs)

Truck Park
1–3/4th (mot) Maintenance Companies (4 LMGs ea)

1 (mot) Heavy (75 ton) Replacement Supply Column (4 LMGs)

Other

4th (mot) Bakery Company

4th (mot) Butcher Company

4th (mot) Administration Platoon

1/, 2/4th (mot) Medical Companies (2 LMGs ea)

1/, 2/, 3/4th Ambulances

4th (mot) Military Police Troop (2 LMGs)

4th (mot) Field Post Office

On 11 June 1943 the 1/108th Panzergrenadier Regiment was renamed the 1/108th (Jäger) Panzergrenadier Regiment. During 1943 the 1/36th Panzer Regiment contained four companies of PzMk IV tanks and the 2/36th contained two companies of PzMk IV tanks and two companies of sturmgeschütze. The 1/103rd Panzergrenadier Regiment and the 3rd and 4th Companies of the reconnaissance battalion were equipped with half-tracks. The division did not have a panzerjäger or feldersatz battalion at this time.

By August 1943 OKH records show that the division had not only been significantly rebuilt, but its structure had been modified. The division, now bearing the sobriquet "Stalingrad Division", was organized and equipped as follows:

Division Staff

1 Division Staff (2 LMGs)

1 (mot) Mapping Detachment

1 (mot) Escort Company

  1 Motorcycle Platoon (6 LMGs)

  1 Infantry Gun Section (2 75mm leIG)

  1 Self-Propelled Flak Platoon (4 20mm Flak guns)

  1 Panzerjäger Platoon (3 LMGs and 3 75mm PAK 40)

  1 Infantry Platoon (4 HMGs, 6 LMGs and 2 80mm mortars)

36th Panzer Regiment

Regimental Staff

1 Signals Platoon

1 Regimental Band

1st Battalion

1 Battalion Staff and Staff Company

4 Panzer Companies (22 PzMk IV ea) (apparently it was originally intended to equip these companies with PzMk V Panthers)

2nd Battalion (detached on 18 July 1943)

1 Battalion Staff and Staff Company

4 Panzer Companies (22 PzMk IV ea)

3rd (Assault Gun) Battalion (detached on 18 Mar. 1943)

1 Battalion Staff and Staff Company

2 Panzer Companies (22 PzMk IV tanks ea; originally intended to be equipped with StuG)

2 Sturmgeschütz Companies (22 StuG ea)

1 Panzer Maintenance Company

103rd Panzergrenadier Regiment

1 Regimental Staff

1 Regimental Band

1 (mot) Regimental Staff Company

  1 Signals Platoon

  1 Pioneer Platoon (6 LMGs and 6 flamethrowers)

  1 Panzerjäger Platoon (3 75mm PAK 40 and 3 LMGs)

  1 Motorcycle Platoon (6 LMGs)

1st (half-track) Battalion

3 (half-track) Companies (4 HMGs, 39 LMGs, 3 PzBu39 3 75mm leIG, 2 80mm mortars and 2 75mm guns ea)

1 (half-track) Heavy Company

  1 (half-track) Pioneer Platoon (9 LMGs, 1 37mm PAK and 6 flamethrowers)

  1 Panzerjäger Platoon (3 75mm PAK 40 and 9 LMGs)

  1 Infantry Gun Platoon (8 LMGs and 4 75mm leIG)

  1 Half-Track Gun Platoon (6 75mm guns)

  1 Staff Platoon (5 LMGs)

2nd (mot) Battalion

3 (mot) Companies (4 HMGs, 18 LMGs and 2 80mm mortars ea)

1 (mot) Heavy Company

  1 Pioneer Platoon (4 LMGs and 6 flamethrowers)

  1 Panzerjäger Platoon (3 LMGs and 3 75 PAK 40)

  1 Infantry Gun Platoon (4 75mm leIG)

  1 Mortar Platoon (6 80mm mortars, with talk of upgrading to 120mm mortars)

9th (Self-Propelled Flak) Company (12 20mm and 4 LMGs)

10th (Self-Propelled Infantry Gun) Company (6 150mm sIG and 7 LMGs)

108th Panzergrenadier Regiment

1 Regimental Staff

1 Regimental Band

1 (mot) Regimental Staff Company

  1 Signals Platoon

  1 Panzerjäger Platoon (3 50mm PAK 38 and 3 LMGs)

  1 Motorcycle Platoon (6 LMGs)

1st and 2nd (mot) Battalions, each with

3 (mot) Companies (4 HMGs, 18 LMGs and 2 80mm mortars ea)

1 (mot) Heavy Company

  1 Pioneer Platoon (4 LMGs and 6 flamethrowers)

  1 Panzerjäger Platoon (3 LMGs and 3 75 PAK 40)

  1 Infantry Gun Platoon (4 75mm leIG)

  1 Mortar Platoon (6 80mm mortars, with talk of upgrading to 120mm mortars)

9th (Self-Propelled Flak) Company (12 20mm and 4 LMGs)

10th (Self-Propelled Infantry Gun) Company (6 150mm sIG and 7 LMGs)

14th Reconnaissance Battalion

1 Armored Car Company (25 LMGs and 18 20mm guns)

1 Armored Car Platoon (6 LMGs and 6 75mm guns)

1 (half-track) Armored Car Company (25 LMGs and 16 20mm guns)

2 (half-track) Reconnaissance Companies (2 120mm mortars, 3 37mm PAK 36, 4 HMGs and 56 LMGs ea)

1 (mot) Heavy Reconnaissance Company

1 Pioneer Platoon (13 LMGs, 6 flamethrowers and 1 75mm gun)

1 Infantry Gun Section (1 LMG and 2 75mm leIG)

1 Panzerjäger Platoon (3 LMGs and 3 75mm PAK 40)

1 Half-Track Gun Platoon (8 LMGs and 6 75mm guns)

1 (mot) Light Armored Car Supply Column (3 LMGs)

4th Panzer Artillery Regiment

1 Regimental Staff

1 Staff Battery (6 LMGs)

1 (mot) Observation Battery (12 LMGs)

1 Self-Propelled Flak Battery (4 quad 20mm) (this was reduced to 4 (motZ) 20mm guns on 9 Mar. 1943)

1st Battalion

1 Battalion Staff and Staff Battery (6 LMGs)

2 Self-Propelled Batteries (6 105mm leFH SdKfz 124 Wespe and 4 LMGs ea)

1 Self-Propelled Battery (6 150mm sFH SdKfz 165 Hummel and 4 LMGs)

2nd Battalion

1 Battalion Staff

1 Battalion Staff Battery (6 LMGs)

3 (mot) Batteries (3 105mm leFH and 2 LMGs ea)

3rd (mot) Battalion

1 Battalion Staff

1 Battalion Staff Battery (6 LMGs)

2 (mot) Batteries (3 150mm sFH and 2 LMGs ea)

1 (mot) Battery (3 100mm K 18 guns and 2 LMGs)

276th Army Flak Battalion (was 4/4th Panzer Artillery Regiment until 26 Apr. 1943)

1 Staff and (mot) Staff Battery (1 LMG)

1st–2nd (motZ) Heavy Flak Batteries (4 88mm, 3 20mm and 2 LMGs ea)

3rd (motZ) Light Flak Battery (9 20mm, 2 self-propelled quad 20mm guns and 2 LMGs)

1 (mot) Light (20 ton) Flak Supply Column

13th Panzer Pioneer Battalion

1 Staff (2 LMGs)

1 (mot) Reconnaissance Platoon (6 50mm PAK 38 and 4 LMGs) (removed 7 Apr. 1943)

1 (half-track) Pioneer Company (40 LMGs, 3 PzBu39, 6 flamethrowers and 2 80mm mortars)

2 (mot) Pioneer Companies (18 LMGs, 3 PzBu39, 2 80mm mortars and 6 flamethrowers ea)

1 Brüko K Bridging Column (3 LMGs)

1 (mot) Light Pioneer Supply Column (2 LMGs)

4th Panzer Signals Battalion

1 (mot) Telephone Company (5 LMGs) (on 9 Mar. 1943 became a panzer telephone company with 21 LMGs)

1 Panzer Radio Company (35 LMGs)

1 (mot) Light Signals Supply Column (4 LMGs)

4th Supply Troop

1–8/4th (mot) (120 ton) Transportation Company (4 LMGs ea)

4th (mot) Supply Company (6 LMGs)

Truck Park

1–3/4th (mot) Maintenance Companies (4 LMGs ea)

1 (mot) Heavy (75 ton) Replacement Supply Column (4 LMGs)

Other

4th (mot) Bakery Company

4th (mot) Butcher Company

4th (mot) Administration Platoon

1/, 2/4th (mot) Medical Companies (2 LMGs ea)

1/, 2/, 3/4th Ambulances

4th (mot) Military Police Troop (2 LMGs)

4th (mot) Field Post Office

Though the 3/36th Panzer Regiment is shown in the preceding table, it may not have arrived until October, at which time it is shown as having the following organization and equipment:

3/36th Panzer Regiment

Regimental Staff Signals Platoon

Regimental Staff Panzer Platoon

1 Battalion with:

1 Battalion Staff Company

2 Medium Panzer Companies

2 Sturmgeschütz Companies

PzMk IV (lg)	49
StuG	44
Flammpanz	7
PzBefWg	9

The 2/36th Panzer Regiment was disbanded during the division's refitting and on 8 May 1945 the entire division was taken prisoner in Courland.

15th Panzer Division

Formed on 1 November 1940 from the 33rd Infantry Division. Organization was complete on 15 March 1941. It contained:

15th Schützen Brigade
  1/, 2/104th Schützen Regiment
  1/, 2/115th Schützen Regiment
15th Motorcycle Battalion
1/, 2/8th Panzer Regiment
1/, 2/, 3/33rd Artillery Regiment
33rd Panzerjäger Battalion
33rd Pioneer Battalion
33rd Signals Battalion
33rd Divisional Support units

The organization of the armored portion of the division and its panzer inventory were as follows:

1/, 2/8th Panzer Regiment
  1 Regimental Staff Signals Platoon
  1 Regimental Staff Light Panzer Platoon
  Each Battalion had
    1 Panzer Staff Company
    1 Medium Panzer Company
    2 Light Panzer Companies
  Total tanks available:
    PzMk II   45
    PzMk III (50)   71
    PzMk IV   20
    PzBefWg   10

The 33rd Signals Battalion was sunk en route to Africa and replaced by the 78th Signals Battalion. On 26 March 1941 the division contained:

Headquarters
  33rd (mot) Mapping Detachment
  1 Motorcycle Platoon
  2 LMGs
8th Panzer Regiment
  1st Panzer Battalion
    HQ Section
      HQ Armored Platoon (10 LMGs and 2 Pz II)
      Armored Signals Platoon (2 LMGs)
      1 Armored Pioneer Platoon (2 LMGs)
      1 Motorcycle Platoon (4 LMGs)
      1 Self-Propelled 20mm Battery (6 guns)
    1st Medium Company (31 LMGs, 6 Pz II and 8 Pz IV)
    1st Light Company (47 LMGs, 6 Pz II, 7 Pz III and 5 Pz IV)
    2nd Light Company (45 LMGs, 6 Pz II, 7 Pz III and 4 Pz IV)

1 (mot) Reserve Platoon
2nd Panzer Battalion
  HQ Section
    HQ Armored Platoon (10 LMGs and 2 Pz II)
    Armored Signals Platoon (2 LMGs)
    1 Armored Pioneer Platoon (2 LMGs)
    1 Motorcycle Platoon (4 LMGs)
    1 Self-Propelled 20mm Battery (6 guns)
  1st Medium Panzer Company (23 LMGs, 6 Pz II and 8 Pz IV)
  1st Light Panzer Company (45 LMGs, 6 Pz II, 7 Pz III and 8 Pz IV)
  2nd Light Company (46 LMGs, 6 Pz II, 8 Pz III and 4 Pz IV)
  1 (mot) Reserve Platoon
15th (mot) (Schützen) Brigade
104th Schützen Regiment
  1/104th (mot) Infantry Regiment
  (mot) HQ Company
    1 Signals Platoon
    1 Pioneer Platoon (3 LMGs)
    1 Motorcycle Platoon
    1 Panzerjäger Platoon (3 37mm PAK)
  3 Companies (18 LMGs, 2 HMGs and 3 50mm mortars ea)
  1 Machine Gun Company (8 HMGs and 6 80mm mortars)
  1 Heavy Company
    1 (mot) Infantry Gun Section (2 75mm leIG)
    (mot) Panzerjäger Platoon (3 37mm PAK and 1 LMG)
    Panzerjäger Section (1 28mm PzBu39 41)
    (mot) Pioneer Platoon (3 LMGs)
  2/104th (mot) Infantry Regiment
  (mot) HQ Company
    1 Signals Platoon
    1 Pioneer Platoon (3 LMGs)
    1 Motorcycle Platoon
    1 Panzerjäger Platoon (3 37mm PAK)
  3 Companies (18 LMGs, 2 HMGs and 3 50mm mortars ea)
  1 Machine Gun Company (8 HMGs and 6 80mm mortars)
  1 Heavy Company
    1 (mot) Infantry Gun Section (2 75mm leIG)
    (mot) Panzerjäger Platoon (3 37mm PAK and 1 LMG)
    Panzerjäger Section (1 28mm PzBu41)
    (mot) Pioneer Platoon (3 LMGs)
  11th Company, 104th Infantry Regiment (2 150mm sIG guns and 4 75mm leIG)
115th Schützen Regiment
  1/115th Schützen Regiment

(mot) HQ Company
1 Signals Platoon
1 Pioneer Platoon (3 LMGs)
1 Motorcycle Platoon
1 Panzerjäger Platoon (3 37mm PAK)
3 Companies (18 LMGs, 2 HMGs and 3 50mm mortars ea)
1 Machine Gun Company (8 HMGs and 6 80mm mortars)
1 Heavy Company
1 (mot) Infantry Gun Section (2 75mm leIG)
(mot) Panzerjäger Platoon (3 37mm PAK and 1 LMG)
Panzerjäger Section (1 28mm PzBu41)
(mot) Pioneer Platoon (3 LMGs)
2/115th Schützen Regiment
(mot) HQ Company
1 Signals Platoon
1 Pioneer Platoon (3 LMGs)
1 Motorcycle Platoon
1 Panzerjäger Platoon (3 37mm PAK)
3 Companies (18 LMGs, 2 HMGs and 3 50mm mortars ea)
1 Machine Gun Company (8 HMGs and 6 80mm mortars)
1 Heavy Company
1 (mot) Infantry Gun Section (2 75mm leIG)
(mot) Panzerjäger Platoon (3 37mm PAK and 1 LMG)
Panzerjäger Section (1 28mm PzBu41)
(mot) Pioneer Platoon (3 LMGs)
11th Company, 115th Infantry Regiment (2 150mm sIG and 4 75mm leIG)

15th Motorcycle Battalion
3 Motorcycle Companies (18 LMGs, 8 HMGs and 3 50mm mortars ea)
1 Motorcycle Machine Gun Company (8 HMGs and 6 80mm mortars)
1 Support Company
1 (mot) Infantry Gun Section (2 75mm leIG)
1 Panzerjäger Platoon (3 37mm PAK and 1 LMG)
1 Pioneer Platoon (3 LMGs)

33rd Reconnaissance Battalion
HQ Section
1 (mot) Signals Platoon (2 LMGs)
1 Armored Car Reconnaissance Company (26 LMGs and 10 75mm guns)
1 Motorcycle Company (18 LMGs, 2 HMGs and 3 50mm mortars)
1 Heavy Weapons Company
Infantry Gun Section (2 75mm leIG)
1 Panzerjäger Platoon (3 37mm PAK 36)
Panzerjäger Section (1 28mm PzBu41)
1 Pioneer Platoon (3 LMGs)
1 Light (mot) Supply Column

33rd Artillery Regiment, with
HQ Section
(mot) Signals Platoon
1st and 2nd Battalions, each with
HQ Section
(mot) Signals and Calibration Company
3 (mot) Batteries (4 105mm leFH 18 and 2 LMGs ea)
3rd Battalion, with
HQ Section
(mot) Signals and Calibration Company
3 Batteries (4 150mm sFH 18 and 2 LMGs ea)
326th (mot) Observation Company
33rd Panzerjäger Battalion
Panzerjäger Platoon (unknown number of 28mm PzBu41)
3 (mot) Panzerjäger Companies (3 50mm PAK 38, 8 37mm PAK 36 and 6 LMGs ea)
33rd Pioneer Battalion
1 (armored) Pioneer Company (in half-tracks)
1 (mot) Pioneer Company (9 LMGs)
1 Light (mot) Pioneer Supply Column
33rd Signals Battalion
1 (mot) Signals Company (2 LMGs)
1 (mot) Radio Company (13 LMGs)
1 Light (mot) Signals Supply Column
Support Units
33rd (mot) Field Post Office
33rd (mot) Military Police Platoon
1/, 2/, 3/33rd Ambulance Companies
1/, 2/33rd (mot) Medical Companies
33rd (mot) Division Quartermaster Company
33rd (mot) Bakery Company
33rd (mot) Butcher Platoon
33rd Supply Battalion
33rd (mot) Light Supply Company
1/, 2/, 3/33rd (mot) Maintenance Companies
1st–7th Light (mot) Supply Columns
8th–10th Heavy (mot) Fuel Supply Columns
11th–13th Light (mot) Supply Column
16th Heavy (mot) Fuel Supply Columns

On 1 September 1941 the 104th Schützen Regiment was transferred to the 21st Panzer Division In its place the 2nd Machine Gun Battalion was assigned to the division and on 1 April 1942 it became the 3/115th Panzergrenadier Regiment. The 15th Motorcycle Battalion was also transferred to the 21st Panzer Division, where it became the 3/104th Panzergrenadier Regiment. The 15th Panzer Division had:

1/, 2/, 3/115th Panzergrenadier Regiment
1/, 2/8th Panzer Regiment
1/, 2/, 3/33rd Panzer Artillery Regiment
33rd Reconnaissance Battalion

33rd Panzerjäger Battalion
33rd Panzer Pioneer Battalion
78th Signals Battalion
33rd Divisional Support Units

On 25 May 1942 the organization of the armored portion of the division and its panzer inventory were as follows:

1/, 2/8th Panzer Regiment
  1 Regimental Staff Signals Platoon
  1 Regimental Staff Light Panzer Platoon
  Each Battalion had
    1 Panzer Staff Company
    1 Medium Panzer Company
    3 Light Panzer Companies
  Total tanks available:
    PzMk II   29
    PzMk III (50) 131
    PzMk III (lg)   3
    PzMk IV (kz)   22
    PzBefWg   4

During the attack on Sidi Azeiz, 20 November 1941, the 15th Panzer Division was broken into kampfgruppen, as was the German standard practice. These kampfgruppe were organized to deal with the problems posed by their targets. In this instance the panzer division was broken into three kampfgruppen, with the 1st Kampfgruppe containing all of the armor. The other two kampfgruppen were infantry units and all three kampfgruppen were supported by a single artillery battalion.

1st Kampfgruppe
Commander, 8th Panzer Regiment: Oberstleutnant Cramer
8th Panzer Regiment, with
  38 Pz II
  76 Pz III
  21 Pz IV
  5 heavy command vehicles (Pz III Befl)
  4 light command vehicles (Pz I Befl)
1/33rd Artillery Regiment (reinforced)
3rd Company, 33rd Flak Battalion
1st Company, 33rd Panzerjäger Battalion
3rd Company, 33rd Panzer Pioneer Battalion

2nd Kampfgruppe
Commander, 15th Schützen Brigade: Oberst Menny
115th Schützen Regiment
33rd Panzerjäger Battalion (less two companies)
  3rd Company, 33rd Panzerjäger Battalion
2/33rd Artillery Regiment

3rd Kampfgruppe
Commander, 200th z.b.V. Regiment: Oberstleutnant Geissler
33rd Panzer Pioneer Battalion (3rd Company detached)

2nd Company, 33rd Panzerjäger Battalion
3/33rd Artillery Regiment (less 1 battery)

By 23 October 1942 the organization and panzer inventory stood as follows:

1/, 2/8th Panzer Regiment
  1 Regimental Staff Signals Platoon
  1 Regimental Staff Light Panzer Platoon
  Each Battalion had
    1 Panzer Staff Company
    1 Medium Panzer Company
    3 Light Panzer Companies
  Total tanks available:
    PzMk II   14
    PzMk III (50 kz) 43
    PzMk III (50 lg) 44
    PzMk IV (kz)   3
    PzMk IV (lg)   15
    PzBefWg   2

On 22 November 1941, during the drive on Tobruk, the 15th Panzer Division was again operating in Kampfgruppen. They were organized as follows:

Kampfgruppe A
Commander, 8th Panzer Regiment: Oberstleutnant Cramer
Staff/, 1/, 3/33rd Artillery Regiment (reinforced)
3rd Company, 33rd Flak Battalion
79th Panzer Signals Battalion
8th Panzer Regiment (38 Pz II, 76 Pz III 21 Pz IV, 5 heavy command vehicles and 4 light command vehicles)

Kampfgruppe B
Commander, 15th Schützen Brigade: Oberst Menny
115th Schützen Regiment
33rd Panzerjäger Battalion (on 8 Dec. 1941 the battalion had 11 50mm PAK 38, 5 37mm PAK 36 and 3 PzBu3941)
33rd Panzer Pioneer Battalion
2/33rd Artillery Regiment

Kampfgruppe C
Commander, 200th z.b.V. Regiment: Oberstleutnant Geissler
2nd Machine Gun Battalion
15th Motorcycle Battalion

As of 2 February 1942 its theoretical organization and allocated equipment was as follows (although casualties and equipment breakdowns and losses had severely reduced its strength):

Divisional Headquarters
1 Motorcycle Company

33rd (mot) Mapping Section

8th Panzer Regiment

1st Panzer Battalion

1 Battalion HQ

  1 Panzer Company (1 Pz III, 5 Pz II, 1 recovery tank)

  1 Panzer Maintenance Company

4th Medium Panzer Company (7 Pz IV, 5 Pz II)

3rd Light Panzer Company (16 Pz III)

2nd Light Panzer Company (15 Pz III)

1st Light Panzer Company (15 Pz III)

2nd Panzer Battalion

1 Battalion HQ

  1 Self-Propelled AA Section (20mm guns)

  1 Panzer Company (1 Pz III, 5 Pz II, 1 recovery tank)

  1 Panzer Maintenance Company

8th Medium Panzer Company (7 Pz IV, 5 Pz II)

7th Light Panzer Company (17 Pz III)

6th Light Panzer Company (15 Pz III)

5th Light Panzer Company (15 Pz III)

15th Schützen Brigade

115th Schützen Regiment

HQ Section

  1 Armored Company (5 half-tracks, 8 LMGs, 3 HMGs)

  1 (mot) Support Company, with

    1 (mot) Signals Platoon

    1 (mot) Pioneer Platoon (2 LMGs)

    1 (mot) Panzerjäger Platoon (1 50mm PAK 38 and 3 37mm PAK 36)

1st (mot) Battalion

  1st Company (8 LMGs)

  7th Company (4 LMGs, 1 PzBu39 and 1 50mm PAK 38)

  9th Company (6 LMGs, 2 HMGs, 2 PzBu39 and 2 50mm mortars)

  5th (mot) Support Company, with

    1 Mortar Section (3 80mm mortars)

    1 Panzerjäger Platoon (3 37mm and 2 LMGs)

    1 Infantry Support Platoon (2 75mm guns and 1 HMG)

2nd (mot) Battalion

  6th Company (8 LMGs, 2 PzBu39 and 1 50mm mortar)

  9th Company (2 LMGs, 2 HMGs, 2 PzBu39 and 1 50mm mortar)

  1 (mot) Support Company, with

    1 Pioneer Platoon (2 LMGs)

    1 Panzerjäger Platoon (2 50mm, 1 37mm, 1 PzBu39 and 2 LMGs)

2nd Machine Gun Battalion

  1 (mot) HQ Section

    2 Motorcycle Companies (1 37mm PAK 36 and 4 LMGs ea)

1 (mot) Signals Section

1 (mot) Company (2 LMGs, 7 HMGs, 1 50mm PAK 38 and 1 50mm mortar)

1 Company (4 LMGs and 4 HMGs)

1 Company (1 LMG and 6 HMGs)

1 (mot) Support Company

  1 Panzerjäger Company (4 50mm PAK 38 and 1 LMG)

  1 Mortar Platoon (3 80mm mortars)

33rd Reconnaissance Battalion

1 (mot) Signals Platoon

1 Armored Car Company (6 20mm guns)

1 (mot) Support Company

  1 (mot) Pioneer Platoon (1 LMG)

  1 (mot) Panzerjäger Gun (1 37mm gun)

  1 (mot) Support Gun Platoon (2 75mm guns)

  1 (mot) Infantry Platoon (4 LMGs)

1 Panzerjäger Section (2 AT guns)

1 Light (mot) Supply Columns (3 LMGs)

33rd Artillery Regiment

1 HQ section

1 (mot) Signals Platoon

1st (mot) Battalion

1 Battalion HQ

  1 (mot) Signals Platoon

  1 (mot) Calibration Platoon

2 Batteries, each with

  3 105mm leFH 18 and 2 LMGs

1 Battery, with

  4 105mm leFH 18 and 2 LMGs

2nd (mot) Battalion

1 Battalion HQ

  1 (mot) Signals Platoon

  1 (mot) Calibration Platoon

2 Batteries, each with

  3 105mm leFH 18 and 2 LMGs

3rd (mot) Battalion

1 Battalion HQ

  1 (mot) Signals Platoon

  1 (mot) Calibration Platoon

1 Battery (3 150mm sFH 18 and 4 LMGs)

33rd Panzerjäger Battalion

1 HQ Section

  1 (mot) Signals Platoon

  1 Panzerjäger section (PzBu41)

  1 LMG Section (2 LMGs)

2 (mot) Panzerjäger Companies, each with

  1 PzBu39, 4 LMGs, 3 37mm PAK 36 guns and 7 50mm PAK 38

1 (mot) Panzerjäger Company, with

  4 LMGs, 3 37mm PAK 36 and 7 50mm PAK 38

33rd (mot) Pioneer Battalion

1 Armored Pioneer Company (4 LMGs and 3 PzBu39)

1 Pioneer Company (4 LMGs and 2 PzBu39)

1 Pioneer Company (3 LMGs and 3 PzBu39)
1 Light (mot) Pioneer Supply Column

78th (mot) Signals Battalion

1 Radio Company (7 LMGs)
1 Telephone Company (1 LMG)
1 Light (mot) Signals Supply Column

Support Units

33rd (mot) Field Post Office
33rd (mot) Military Police Platoon
1/, 2/, 3/33rd Ambulance Companies
2/33rd (mot) Medical Companies
36th (mot) Field Hospital
33rd (mot) Division Quartermaster Company
33rd (mot) Bakery Company
33rd (mot) Butcher Platoon

33rd Supply Battalion

33rd (mot) Light Supply Company
1/, 2/, 3/33rd (mot) Maintenance Companies
1st–7th Light (mot) Supply Columns
8th–10th Heavy (mot) Fuel Supply Columns
12th Light (mot) Supply Column
2 (mot) Armored Replacement Platoons
1 Light (mot) Water Supply Column

Documents dated 6 February 1942 relating to a proposed organization of the 15th and 21st Panzer Divisions are labeled "Many Weapons, Few Men". Apparently the major problem being experienced by the Afrika Korps at that time was the loss of manpower, not the absence of weapons and ammunition. As a result the following proposed weapons allocations were provided for both the 15th and 21st Panzer Divisions. As can be seen, both divisions became an incredibly heavily armed force, with anti-tank weapons assigned to almost every formation that might see combat.

15th Panzer Division

Headquarters
33rd (mot) Mapping Detachment (2 LMGs)

8th Panzer Regiment

Armored Signals Platoon
1 Light Armored Platoon
1 Regimental Band
1 Armored Maintenance Company

1st and 2nd Battalions

1 Armored Staff Company
1 Medium Armored Company
3 Light Armored Companies
1 Armored Reserve Detachment (added during period)

15th Schützen Brigade

115th Schützen Regiment:

1 (mot) Headquarters Company
1 Signals Platoon
1 Pioneer Platoon (3 LMGs)

1 Motorcycle Platoon
1 Panzerjäger Platoon (3 50mm PAK 38)
1 Regimental Band

Attached

1 (mot) Infantry Support Gun Section (2 150mm sIG and 4 75mm leIG guns)

1st, 2nd and 3rd Battalions

3 (mot) Infantry Companies, each with
(13 MP, 18 LMGs, 2 HMGs, 3 80mm mortars, 3 28mm PzBu41 and 6 50mm PAK 38)
1 Pioneer Company
(13 MP, 18 LMGs, 2 HMGs, 3 80mm mortars, 3 28mm PzBu41 and 6 50mm PAK 38)
1 Heavy Infantry Gun Company, with
(3 150mm self-propelled guns)

33rd Artillery Regiment

HQ Company
1 (mot) Staff Battery
1st and 2nd Battalions, each with
1 (mot) Staff Battery
3 (mot) Batteries (4 105mm leFH 18 and 2 LMGs ea)
3rd Battalion, with
1 (mot) Staff Battery
3 (mot) Batteries (4 150mm leFH 18 and 2 LMGs ea)
1 (mot) Observation Company

33rd Reconnaissance Battalion

1 (mot) Signals Platoon (2 LMGs)
2 Armored Car Companies
1 Armored Car Company (25 half-tracks)
(13 MP, 18 LMGs, 2 HMGs, 3 80mm mortars, 3 28mm PzBu41 and 6 50mm PAK 38)
1 Light Battery
1 (mot) Support Company, with
1 Signals Platoon
1 Pioneer Platoon
1 Panzerjäger Platoon

33rd Panzerjäger Battalion

1 (mot) Signals Platoon
3 (mot) Companies (9 50mm self-propelled ea)

33rd (mot) Pioneer Battalion

3 (mot) Companies
(13 MP, 18 LMGs, 2 HMGs, 3 80mm mortars, 3 28mm PzBu41 and 6 50mm PAK 38 total)
1 Light (mot) Pioneer Supply Column

78th Signals Battalion

6 Signals Troops

Service Forces

33rd Supply Battalion

9 Light (mot) Supply Columns (one deleted later)
2 Heavy (mot) Supply Columns
1 (mot) Panzer Replacement Column
3 Heavy (mot) POL Supply Columns
3 (mot) Maintenance Companies

33rd (mot) Supply Company

Food Service

33rd (mot) Quartermaster Detachment

33rd (mot) Bakery Company

33rd (mot) Butcher Company

Medical

1/, 2/33rd (mot) Medical Companies

36th (mot) Field Hospital

1/, 2/, 3/Ambulance Companies

Other

33rd (mot) Military Police Detachment

33rd (mot) Field Post Office

The organizational debate continued, and on 1 March 1942 two new proposals for the revised organization of the 15th Panzer Division were developed. The two proposals were as follows:

1ST PROPOSAL

Divisional HQ

33rd (mot) Mapping Section

1 Motorcycle Platoon (1/2 Volkswagens and 1/2 motorcycles)

1 (mot) Reconnaissance Platoon

8th Panzer Regiment

Headquarters Section

1 Panzer Platoon

1 Armored Signals Section

1 (mot) Reconnaissance Platoon

1 Panzer Maintenance Company

3 Work Platoons

1 Recovery Platoon

3 Panzer Battalions, each with

1 Battalion HQ Section, with

1 Light Panzer Platoon

1 Panzer Signals Platoon

1 Panzer Pioneer Platoon

1 (mot) Reconnaissance Platoon

1 20mm Flak Section

3 Light Panzer Companies

1 Medium Panzer Company

1 Panzer Replacement Platoon

15th Schützen Brigade

Brigade HQ Section

1 (mot) Signals Section

1 Armored Car Platoon (2 troops)

1 (mot) Reconnaissance Platoon

115th Regiment

Regimental HQ Section

1 (mot) Pioneer Platoon (3 LMGs)

1 (mot) Panzerjäger Platoon(3 50mm, 1 37mm and 1 LMG)

1 Motorcycle Platoon

1 (mot) Signals Platoon

1st (mot) Battalion (in half-tracks)

3 (mot) Companies (18 LMGs, 2 HMGs, 2 50mm mortars ea)

1 (mot) Machine Gun Company (8 HMGs)

1 (mot) Support Company, with

1 Pioneer Platoon (3 LMGs)

1 (mot) Panzerjäger Platoon (3 50mm, 1 37mm and 1 LMG)

1 Infantry Support Section (2 75mm guns)

2nd (mot) Battalion (in trucks)

3 (mot) Companies (18 LMGs, 2 HMGs and 2 50mm mortars)

1 (mot) Machine Gun Company (8 HMGs)

1 (mot) Support Company, with

1 Pioneer Platoon (3 LMGs)

1 (mot) Panzerjäger Platoon (3 50mm, 1 37mm and 1 LMG)

1 Infantry Support Section (2 75mm guns)

1 (mot) Heavy Infantry Support Gun Company (6 150mm guns)

15th Machine Gun Battalion

3 Motorcycle Companies (18 LMGs, 2 HMGs and 2 80mm Mortars ea)

1 (mot) Heavy Machine Gun Company (8 HMGs)

1 (mot) Support Company, with

1 Pioneer Platoon (3 LMGs)

1 Panzerjäger Platoon (3 50mm, 1 37mm PAK and 1 LMG)

1 Infantry Support Section (2 75mm guns)

2nd Machine Gun Battalion

3 (mot) Machine Gun Companies (20 LMGs and 2 80mm mortars ea)

1 (mot) Support Company, with

1 Pioneer Platoon (3 LMGs)

1 Panzerjäger Platoon (6 50mm, 2 37mm PAK and 1 LMG)

1 Infantry Support Section (2 75mm guns)

33rd Artillery Regiment

Regimental HQ Section

1 (mot) Observation Company

1 (mot) Staff Company

1 Calibration Section

1st and 2nd (mot) Battalions

1 (mot) Staff Company

1 Calibration Section

3 (mot) Batteries (4 105mm leFH 18 and 2 LMGs)

3rd (mot) Battalion

1 (mot) Staff Company

1 Calibration Section

2 (mot) Batteries (4 150mm sFH 18 and 2 LMGs)

1 (mot) Battery (4 100mm K17 and 2 LMGs)

4th (mot) Battalion

1 (mot) Staff Company

1 Calibration Section

3 Batteries (4 105mm leFH 18s or British 25pdrs)

33rd Signals Battalion

1 (mot) Telephone Company

1 (mot) Radio Company

33rd Reconnaissance Battalion

1 Armored Car Company, with

  6 heavy ACs, 14 Light ACs, 4 Radio ACs and 1 Heavy Radio (8 wheel) AC

1 (mot) Infantry Platoon

1 Light Panzer Company (24 Pz II)

1 (mot) Support Company, with

  1 Infantry Support Section (2 75mm guns)

  1 Panzerjäger Platoon (1 LMG, 1 37mm and 3 50mm PAK)

  1 Heavy Weapons Platoon (6 LMGs and 2 80mm mortars)

  1 Pioneer Platoon (3 LMGs)

1 Light Armored Car Supply Column

33rd (mot) Pioneer Battalion

1 (mot) Panzerjäger Company (2 28mm PzBu41and 3 50mm PAK 38)

3 (mot) Pioneer Companies (9 LMGs ea) (1 in half-tracks)

1 Light (mot) Supply Column

33rd Panzerjäger Battalion

1 (mot) Signals Platoon

1 Panzerjäger Section (3 28mm PzBu41)

1 Panzerjäger (half-track) Company (9 50mm PAK and 6 LMGs)

2 (mot) Panzerjäger Companies (9 50mm PAK 38 and 3 37mm PAK 36, 3 28mm PzBu41 and 6 LMGs ea)

I/43rd Flak Regiment

3 (mot) Batteries (4 88mm guns each)

2 (mot) Batteries (12 20mm guns each)

Support Units

33rd (mot) Field Post Office

33rd (mot) Military Police Platoon

1/, 2/, 3/33rd Ambulance Companies

1/, 2/, 3/33rd (mot) Medical Companies

33rd (mot) Field Hospital

33rd (mot) Division Quartermaster Company

33rd (mot) Bakery Company

33rd (mot) Butcher Platoon

33rd Supply Battalion

33rd (mot) Light Supply Company

1/, 2/, 3/33rd (mot) Maintenance Companies

1st–7th Heavy (mot) Supply Columns (1 LMG ea)

8th Light (mot) Fuel Supply Columns (1 LMG)

9th–14th Light (mot) POL Supply Columns (1 LMG ea)

1 Light (mot) Water Supply Column

3 Heavy Panzer Supply Columns

2 Heavy Panzer Replacement Columns

2nd Proposal

Divisional HQ

33rd (mot) Mapping Section

1 Motorcycle Platoon (1/2 Volkswagens and 1/2 motorcycles)

1 Motorcycle Platoon

8th Panzer Regiment

Headquarters Section

  1 Panzer Platoon

  1 Armored Signals Section

  1 (mot) Reconnaissance Platoon

1 Panzer Maintenance Company

2 Work Platoons

2 Recovery Platoons

3 Panzer Battalions, each with

  1 Battalion HQ Section, with

    1 Light Panzer Platoon

    1 Panzer Signals Platoon

    1 Panzer Pioneer Platoon

    1 (mot) Reconnaissance Platoon

    1 20mm Flak Section

  3 Light Panzer Companies

  1 Medium Panzer Company

  1 Panzer Replacement Platoon

15th Schützen Brigade

Brigade HQ Section

  1 (mot) Signals Section

  1 Armored Car Platoon (2 troops)

  1 (mot) Reconnaissance Platoon

115th Regiment

Regimental HQ Section

1 (mot) Support Company

  1 (mot) Pioneer Platoon (3 LMGs)

  1 (mot) Panzerjäger Platoon (3 50mm, 1 37mm, 2 28mm PzBu41 and 1 LMG)

  1 Motorcycle Platoon

  1 (mot) Signals Platoon

1st (half-track) Battalion

  3 (mot) Companies (18 LMGs, 2 HMGs, 2 50mm mortars ea)

  1 (mot) Machine Gun Company (8 HMGs)

  1 (mot) Support Company, with

    1 Pioneer Platoon (3 LMGs)

    1 (mot) Panzerjäger Platoon (3 50mm, 1 37mm and 1 LMG)

    1 Infantry Support Section (2 75mm guns)

2nd (half-track) Battalion

  3 (mot) Companies (18 LMGs, 2 HMGs, 2 50mm mortars ea)

  1 (mot) Machine Gun Company (8 HMGs)

  1 (mot) Support Company, with

    1 Pioneer Platoon (3 LMGs)

    1 (mot) Panzerjäger Platoon (3 50mm, 1 37mm and 1 LMG)

1 Infantry Support Section (2 75mm guns)

1 (mot) Heavy Infantry Support Gun Company (6 150mm guns)

15th Machine Gun Battalion

3 Motorcycle Companies (18 LMGs, 2 HMGs and 2 80mm Mortars ea)

1 (mot) Heavy Machine Gun Company (8 HMGs)

1 (mot) Support Company, with
  1 Pioneer Platoon (3 LMGs)
  1 Panzerjäger Platoon (3 50mm, 1 37mm PAK and 1 LMG)
  1 Infantry Support Section (2 75mm guns)

2nd Machine Gun Battalion

3 (mot) Machine Gun Companies (20 LMGs and 2 80mm mortars ea)

1 (mot) Support Company, with
  1 Pioneer Platoon (3 LMGs)
  1 Panzerjäger Platoon (6 50mm, 2 37mm PAK and 1 LMG)
  1 Infantry Support Section (2 75mm guns)

33rd Artillery Regiment

Regimental HQ Section
  1 (mot) Observation Company
  1 (mot) Staff Company
  1 Calibration Section

1st and 2nd (mot) Battalions
  1 (mot) Staff Company
  1 Calibration Section
  3 (mot) Batteries (4 105mm leFH 18 and 2 LMGs)

3rd (mot) Battalion
  1 (mot) Staff Company
  1 Calibration Section
  3 (mot) Batteries (4 150mm sFH 18 and 2 LMGs)
  1 (mot) Battery (4 100mm K17 and 2 LMGs)

4th (mot) Battalion
  1 (mot) Staff Company
  1 Calibration Section
  3 Batteries (4 105mm leFH 18 or British 25pdrs)

33rd Signals Battalion

1 (mot) Telephone Company

1 (mot) Radio Company

33rd Reconnaissance Battalion

1 Armored Car Company, with
  (6 heavy ACs, 14 light ACs, 4 radio ACs, 1 heavy radio (8 wheel) AC)

1 (mot) Infantry Company

1 Light Panzer Company (24 Pz II) or

1 Armored Car Company (6 heavy, 14 light and 4 radio AC)

1 (mot) Support Company, with
  1 Infantry Support Section (2 75mm guns)
  1 Panzerjäger Platoon (1 LMG, 1 37mm and 3 50mm PAK)
  1 Heavy Weapons Platoon (6 LMGs and 2 80mm mortars)

1 Pioneer Platoon (3 LMGs)

1 Light Armored Car Supply Column

33rd (mot) Pioneer Battalion

1 (mot) Panzerjäger Company (2 28mm PzBu41 and 3 50mm PAK)

3 (half-track) Pioneer Companies (9 LMGs ea)

1 Light (mot) Supply Column

33rd Panzerjäger Battalion

1 (mot) Signals Platoon

1 Panzerjäger Section (3 28mm PzBu41)

1 Panzerjäger (half-track) Company (9 50mm PAK and 6 LMGs)

2 (mot) Panzerjäger Companies (9 50mm PAK 38 and 3 37mm PAK 36, 3 28mm PzBu41 and 6 LMGs ea)

I/43rd Flak Regiment

3 (mot) Batteries (4 88mm guns each)

2 (mot) Batteries (12 20mm guns each)

Support Units

33rd (mot) Field Post Office

33rd (mot) Military Police Platoon

1/, 2/, 3/33rd Ambulance Companies

1/, 2/, 3/33rd (mot) Medical Companies

33rd (mot) Field Hospital

33rd (mot) Division Quartermaster Company

33rd (mot) Bakery Company

33rd (mot) Butcher Platoon

33rd Supply Battalion

33rd (mot) Light Supply Company

1/, 2/, 3/33rd (mot) Maintenance Companies

1st–7th Heavy (mot) Supply Columns (1 LMG ea)

8th Light (mot) Fuel Supply Columns (1 LMG)

9th–14th Light (mot) POL Supply Columns (1 LMG ea)

1 Light (mot) Water Supply Column

3 Heavy Panzer Supply Columns

2 Heavy Panzer Replacement Columns

The actual reorganization resulting from this discussion took the following form and was ordered to be implemented on 10 March 1942. To effect it, the 2nd Machine Gun Battalion, then in the 21st Panzer Division, became the 3/115th Panzergrenadier Regiment.

Divisional Headquarters

1 Motorcycle Company

33rd (mot) Mapping Section

8th Panzer Regiment

1 Regimental HQ
  1 Panzer Company (5 20mm and 5 LMGs)
  1 Armored Signals Platoon (1 50mm PAK and 4 LMGs)
  1 Regimental Band
  1 Armored Maintenance Company

1st Panzer Battalion
1 Battalion HQ
  1 Panzer Staff Company
4th Medium Panzer Company (14 Pz IV and 5 Pz II)
3rd Light Panzer Company (17 Pz III J and 5 Pz II)
2nd Light Panzer Company (17 Pz III J and 5 Pz II)
1st Light Panzer Company (17 Pz III J and 5 Pz II)
1 (mot) Armored Replacement Company

2nd Panzer Battalion
1 Battalion HQ
  1 Panzer Staff Company (5 20mm and 5 LMGs)
8th Medium Panzer Company (14 Pz IV and 5 Pz II)
7th Light Panzer Company (17 Pz III J and 5 Pz II)
6th Light Panzer Company (17 Pz III J and 5 Pz II)
5th Light Panzer Company (17 Pz III J and 5 Pz II)
1 (mot) Armored Replacement Company

115th Panzergrenadier Regiment
HQ Section
  1 (mot) Support Company, with
    1 (mot) Signals Platoon
    1 (mot) Pioneer Platoon (3 LMGs)
    1 Motorcycle Platoon
    1 (mot) Panzerjäger Platoon (3 50mm and 3 LMGs)
1st (mot) Battalion
  4 Companies (18 LMGs, 2 HMGs, 3 28mm PzBu41, 3 80mm mortars and 3 50mm PAK 38 ea)
2nd (mot) Battalion
  4 Companies (18 LMGs, 2 HMGs, 3 28mm PzBu41, 3 80mm mortars and 3 50mm PAK 38 ea)
3rd (mot) Battalion
  4 Companies (18 LMGs, 2 HMGs, 3 28mm PzBu41, 3 80mm mortars and 3 50mm PAK 38 ea)
1 (mot) Infantry Support Gun Company (6 150mm)
1 (mot) Pioneer Company (10 LMGs, 3 28mm PzBu41, 3 80mm mortars, 3 50mm PAK 38)

33rd Reconnaissance Battalion
1 Armored Car Company (20 20mm and 40 LMGs)
1 (mot) Infantry Company (18 LMGs, 2 HMGs, 3 28mm PzBu41 and 4 50mm PAK 38)
1 (mot) Support Company
  1 (mot) Pioneer Platoon (3 LMGs)
  1 (mot) Panzerjäger Gun (3 50mm PAK 38 and 1 LMG)
  1 (mot) Signal Platoon
1 Light (mot) Supply Column (3 LMGs)

33rd Artillery Regiment
1 HQ section
1 (mot) Observation Company
1 Light (mot) Supply Column

1st and 2nd (mot) Battalions, each with
1 (mot) Staff Company
3 Batteries (4 105mm leFH K18 and 2 LMGs ea)

3rd (mot) Battalion
1 (mot) Staff Company

2 Batteries (4 150mm sFH K18 and 2 LMGs ea)
1 Battery (4 100 K17 guns and 2 LMGs)

33rd Feldersatz Battalion
4 Replacement Infantry Companies

78th (mot) Signals Battalion
1 Armored Radio Company
1 Armored Telephone Company
1 Light (mot) Signals Supply Column

33rd (mot) Pioneer Battalion
3 (mot) Pioneer Companies (9 LMGs, 3 28mm PzBu41 and 3 50mm PAK 38 ea)
1 Light (mot) Pioneer Supply Column

33rd Panzerjäger Battalion
1 HQ Section
  1 (mot) Signals Platoon
1 (mot) Panzerjäger Company (9 50mm PAK and 6 LMGs ea)
1 (mot) Panzerjäger Company (6 76.2mm PAK and 6 LMGs)

33rd Supply Battalion
33rd (mot) Light Supply Company
1/, 2/, 3/33rd (mot) Maintenance Companies
1st–9th Light (mot) Supply Columns
13th–14th Heavy (mot) Supply Columns
33rd (mot) Panzer Replacement Supply Column
10/, 11/, 12/33rd Heavy (mot) POL Supply Columns
33rd (mot) Supply Company
578th (mot) LW Company

Support Units
33rd (mot) Field Post Office
33rd (mot) Military Police Platoon
1/, 2/, 3/33rd Ambulance Companies
2/33rd (mot) Medical Companies
36th (mot) Field Hospital
33rd (mot) Division Quartermaster Company
33rd (mot) Bakery Company
33rd (mot) Butcher Platoon

A message from the AOK Ia dated 10 March 1942 directed equipping the mixed schützen companies with six 50mm PAK 38 guns. Pioneer companies for the schützen regiments were to be formed from the pioneer platoons of the schützen and machine gun companies.

On 1 April 1942 the 2nd Machine Gun Battalion became the 3/115th Panzergrenadier Regiment. The 15th Motorcycle Battalion was also transferred to the 21st Panzer Division where it became the 3/104th Panzergrenadier Regiment. The organization, however, remained fluid and on 16 April 1942 the division was organized as follows:

Divisional Headquarters
Panzer Command Staffel
33rd (mot) Mapping Section

8th Panzer Regiment
1 Regimental HQ

1 Panzer Platoon
1 Light Panzer Platoon
1 Regimental Band
1 Armored Maintenance Company

1st Panzer Battalion
1 Battalion HQ
1 Panzer Staff Company
4th Medium Panzer Company
3rd Light Panzer Company
2nd Light Panzer Company
1st Light Panzer Company
1 (mot) Armored Replacement Company

2nd Panzer Battalion
1 Battalion HQ
1 Panzer Staff Company
8th Medium Panzer Company
7th Light Panzer Company
6th Light Panzer Company
5th Light Panzer Company
1 (mot) Armored Replacement Company

115th Panzergrenadier Regiment
HQ Section
1 (mot) Support Company, with
1 (mot) Signals Platoon
1 (mot) Pioneer Platoon (3 LMGs)
1 Motorcycle Messenger Platoon
1 (mot) Panzerjäger Platoon (3 50mm and 3 LMGs)
1st (mot) Battalion
4 Companies (18 LMGs, 2 HMGs, 3 28mm PzBu41, 3 80mm mortars and 3 50mm PAK 38 ea)
2nd (mot) Battalion
4 Companies (18 LMGs, 2 HMGs, 3 28mm PzBu41, 3 80mm mortars and 3 50mm PAK 38 ea)
3rd (mot) Battalion
4 Companies (18 LMGs, 2 HMGs, 3 28mm PzBu41, 3 80mm mortars and 3 50mm PAK 38 ea)
1 (mot) Infantry Support Gun Company (2 150mm sIG and 4 75mm leIG)
1 (mot) Pioneer Company (10 LMGs, 2 HMGs, 3 28mm PzBu41, 3 80mm mortars and 3 50mm PAK 38)

33rd Reconnaissance Battalion
unchanged from March 1942

33rd Artillery Regiment
unchanged from March 1942, except for 326th (mot) Artillery Observation Company

33rd Feldersatz Battalion
4 Replacement Infantry Companies

78th (mot) Signals Battalion
1 Armored Radio Company
1 Armored Telephone Company

1 Light (mot) Signals Supply Column

33rd (mot) Pioneer Battalion
unchanged from March 1942

33rd Panzerjäger Battalion
1 HQ Section
1 (mot) Signals Platoon
1 (mot) Panzerjäger Company (6 50mm PAK and 6 LMGs)
1 Self-Propelled Panzerjäger Company (6 76.2mm (r) PAK and 6 LMGs)

33rd Supply Battalion
unchanged from March 1942

Support Units
unchanged from March 1942

On 1 May 1942 the 15th Panzer Division was theoretically organized as follows:

Divisional Headquarters
1 Motorcycle Company
33rd (mot) Mapping Section
1 Light Panzer Platoon (deleted in pencil in original manuscript)

8th Panzer Regiment
1 Regimental HQ
1 Panzer Company (5 Pz II, 1 Pz III and 2 heavy command vehicles)
1 Armored Maintenance Company

1st Panzer Battalion
1 Battalion HQ
1 Panzer Pioneer Platoon (2 Pz II)
1 Panzer Platoon (5 Pz II, 1 Pz III and 1 heavy command vehicle)
1 Panzer Replacement Platoon (5 Pz III)
4th Medium Panzer Company (11 Pz IV and 5 Pz II)
3rd Light Panzer Company (20 Pz III J)
2nd Light Panzer Company (20 Pz III J)
1st Light Panzer Company (20 Pz III J)

2nd Panzer Battalion
1 Battalion HQ
1 Self-Propelled Platoon (4 HMGs)
1 Panzer Pioneer Platoon (2 Pz II)
1 Panzer Platoon (5 Pz II, 1 Pz III and 1 heavy command vehicle)
1 Panzer Replacement Platoon (5 Pz III)
8th Medium Panzer Company (11 Pz IV and 5 Pz II)
7th Light Panzer Company (20 Pz III J)
6th Light Panzer Company (20 Pz III J)
5th Light Panzer Company (20 Pz III J)

115th Panzergrenadier Regiment
HQ Section
1 (mot) Support Company, with
1 (mot) Signals Platoon
1 (mot) Pioneer Platoon (3 LMGs)
1 Motorcycle Platoon

1 (mot) Panzerjäger Platoon (3 50mm PAK)

1st (mot) Battalion

  1st Company (6 LMGs, 2HMGs, 2 80mm mortars, 2 37mm and 1 50mm PAK)

  2nd Company (14 LMGs, 2 HMGs, 3 80mm mortars and 3 50mm PAK)

  3rd Company (8 LMGs, 2 HMGs, 1 28mm PzBu41, 3 80mm mortars and 2 50mm PAK 38)

  4th Company (5 LMGs, 2 HMGs, 1 28mm PzBu41, 3 80mm mortars and 2 37mm PAK)

2nd (mot) Battalion

  5th Company (6 LMGs, 2 HMGs, 3 80mm mortars and 3 50mm PAK)

  6th Company (18 LMGs, 4 HMGs, 2 80mm mortars, 1 37mm PAK and 3 50mm PAK)

  7th Company (16 LMGs, 2 HMGs, 2 80mm mortars and 2 50mm PAK)

  8th Company (8 LMGs, 2 HMGs, 2 80mm mortars and 2 50mm PAK)

3rd (mot) Battalion

  9th Company (12 LMGs, 2 HMGs, 2 80mm mortars, 1 37mm and 2 50mm PAK)

  10th Company (14 LMGs, 2 HMGs, 2 80mm mortars and 3 50mm PAK)

  11th Company (14 LMGs, 2 HMGs, 1 37mm PAK, 3 80mm mortars and 2 50mm PAK)

  12th Company (10 LMGs, 2 HMGs, 2 80mm mortars, 2 37mm PAK and 2 50mm PAK)

15th (mot) Heavy Infantry Support Gun Company (2 150mm Infantry Support Howitzers and 2 LMGs)

14th (mot) Pioneer company (3 37mm PAK and 4 LMGs)

1 (mot) Heavy Infantry Support Gun Company (5 150mm howitzers) (in Naples)

33rd Reconnaissance Battalion

1 Armored Car Company (15 20mm KwK and 17 LMGs) (only 2 armored cars with radios)

1 (mot) Infantry Company (6 LMGs, 2 self-propelled 37mm PAK)

1 (mot) Support Company

1 (mot) Pioneer Platoon (2 LMGs)

1 (mot) Panzerjäger Gun (3 50mm PAK)

1 (mot) Signal Platoon

1 (mot) Support Gun Section (1 75mm gun)

1 Light (mot) Supply Column (3 LMGs)

33rd Artillery Regiment

1 (mot) Staff Company

1 (mot) Observation Company

1 Light (mot) Supply Column

1st (mot) Battalion

1 (mot) Staff Company

3 (mot) Batteries (4 105mm leFH K18 and 2 LMGs ea)

2nd (mot) Battalion

1 (mot) Staff Company

3 (mot) Batteries (4 105mm leFH K18 and 2 LMGs ea)

3rd (mot) Battalion

1 (mot) Staff Company

2 (mot) Batteries (4 150mm sFH K18 and 2 LMGs ea)

1 (mot) Battery (4 100 K17 guns and 2 LMGs)

33rd Feldersatz Battalion

4 Replacement Infantry Companies

78th (mot) Signals Battalion

1 Armored Radio Company

1 Armored Telephone Company

1 Light (mot) Signals Supply Column

33rd (mot) Pioneer Battalion

2 (mot) Pioneer Companies (4 LMGs ea)

1 (mot) Pioneer Company (6 LMGs and 1 28mm PzBu41)

1 Light (mot) Pioneer Supply Column

33rd Panzerjäger Battalion

1 HQ Section

  1 (mot) Signals Platoon

2 (mot) Panzerjäger Companies (9 50mm PAK and 6 LMGs ea)

3/617th Flak Battalion

(12 Self-Propelled 20mm Flak 30 guns)

5/18th (mot) Flak Battalion

(12 20mm Flak 30 guns)

Support Units

33rd (mot) Field Post Office

33rd (mot) Military Police Platoon

1/, 2/, 3/33rd Ambulance Companies

2/33rd (mot) Medical Companies

36th (mot) Field Hospital

33rd (mot) Division Quartermaster Company

33rd (mot) Bakery Company

33rd (mot) Butcher Platoon

33rd Supply Battalion

33rd (mot) Light Supply Company

1/, 2/, 3/33rd (mot) Maintenance Companies

1st–9th Light (mot) Supply Columns (the 3rd and 4th Columns have been deleted in pencil and may not be present)

13th–14th Heavy (mot) Supply Columns (deleted in pencil from original document and may not be present)

641st Heavy Water column

10th, 11th, 12th Heavy (mot) POL Supply Column

1/, 2/, 3/33rd (mot) Maintenance Companies

33rd (mot) Supply Company

578th (mot) LW Company

On 25 May 1942 the organization of the armored portion of the division and its panzer inventory were as follows: *(see over)*

1/, 2/8th Panzer Regiment
  1 Regimental Staff Signals Platoon
  1 Regimental Staff Light Panzer Platoon
  Each Battalion had
    1 Panzer Staff Company
    1 Medium Panzer Company
    3 Light Panzer Companies

The regiment had a total of 29 Pz II, 131 Pz III (50), three Pz III (lg), 22 Pz IV (kz), and four command tanks. Afrika Korps records show another reorganization, and on 15 August 1942 the division was organized as follows:

Divisional Headquarters

  Panzer Command Staffel (4 20mm Flak guns, 3 20mm KwK and 3 50mm PAK 38)
  33rd (mot) Mapping Section

8th Panzer Regiment (60 officers/1, 942 men)

  1 Regimental HQ
    1 Panzer Platoon
    1 Light Panzer Platoon
    1 Regimental Band
  1 Armored Maintenance Company

1st Panzer Battalion

  1 Battalion HQ
    1 Panzer Staff Company
  3 Panzer Companies
  1 (mot) Armored Replacement Company

2nd Panzer Battalion

  1 Battalion HQ
    1 Panzer Staff Company
  3 Panzer Companies
  1 (mot) Armored Replacement Company

Total tanks: 15 Pz II, 51 Pz III, 29 Pz III (lg), 3 Pz IV, 8 Pz IV (lg) and 1 command tank

115th Panzergrenadier Regiment (75 officers/2, 400 men)

  HQ Section
    1 (mot) Support Company, with
      1 (mot) Signals Platoon
      1 (mot) Pioneer Platoon (3 LMGs)
      1 Motorcycle Messenger Platoon
      1 (mot) Panzerjäger Platoon (3 50mm and 3 LMGs)
    1st (mot) Battalion
      4 Companies (35 LMGs, 9 HMGs, 0 28mm PzBu41, 6 80mm mortars and 4 50mm PAK 38 total)
    2nd (mot) Battalion
      4 Companies (38 LMGs, 9 HMGs, 0 28mm PzBu41, 4 80mm mortars and 4 50mm PAK 38 total)
    3rd (mot) Battalion
      4 Companies (39 LMGs, 9 HMGs, 0 28mm PzBu41, 5 80mm mortars and 3 50mm PAK 38 total)
    1 (mot) Infantry Support Gun Company (8 British 25pdrs)

1 (mot) Pioneer Company (10 LMGs, 2HMGs, 3 28mm PzBu41, 3 80mm mortars and 3 50mm PAK 38)

33rd Reconnaissance Battalion (17 officers/492 men)

  1 (mot) Signals Platoon (taken from mot recon company)
  1 Armored Car Company
  1 (half-track) Reconnaissance Company (45 LMGs, 2 HMGs and 5 50mm PAK 38)
  1 (mot) Artillery Battery (6 British 25pdrs)
  1 (mot) Reconnaissance Column (3 LMGs)

33rd (mot) Artillery Regiment (71 officers/1, 563 men)

  1 (mot) Regimental Staff Battery

1st (mot) Battalion

  1 (mot) Staff Battery
  2 Batteries (4 105mm K18)
  1 Battery (3 105mm K18)

2nd (mot) Battalion

  1 (mot) Staff Battery
  3 Batteries (4 105mm K18)

3rd (mot) Battalion

  1 (mot) Staff Battery
  1 Battery (3 100mm K17 guns)
  1 Battery (5 150mm sFH K18)
  1 Battery (4 150mm sFH K18)
  33rd (mot) Artillery Observation Battery
  1 (mot) Heavy Artillery Supply Column

33rd Panzerjäger Battalion (4 officers/365 men)

  1 HQ Section
    1 (mot) Signals Platoon
  1 (mot) Panzerjäger Company (9 50mm PAK and 6 LMGs)
  1 Self-Propelled Panzerjäger Company (4 76.2mm (r) PAK and 6 LMGs)

33rd (mot) Pioneer Battalion (17 officers/382 men)

  3 (mot) Pioneer Companies (4 50mm PAK 38, 3 28mm PzBu41 and 39 LMGs total)
  1 (mot) Pioneer Supply Column

78th (mot) Signals Battalion

  1 Armored Radio Company
  1 Armored Telephone Company
  1 Light (mot) Signals Supply Column

33rd Feldersatz Battalion

  4 Companies (no heavy weapons)

Support Units

  33rd (mot) Field Post Office
  33rd (mot) Military Police Platoon
  1/, 2/, 3/33rd Ambulance Companies
  2/33rd (mot) Medical Companies
  36th (mot) Field Hospital
  33rd (mot) Division Administration
  33rd (mot) Bakery Company
  33rd (mot) Butcher Platoon

33rd Supply Battalion

  1/, 2/, 3/33rd (mot) Maintenance Companies

1st–8th Light (mot) Supply Columns
13th–14th Heavy (mot) Supply Columns
33rd (mot) Panzer Replacement Supply Column
10/, 11/, 12/33rd Heavy (mot) POL Supply Column
33rd (mot) Supply Company
33rd (mot) Panzer Replacement Company
641st (mot) Heavy Water Column

The process of reorganization continued, and on 1 September 1942 the 15th Panzer Division was organized as follows:

Divisional Headquarters
2 LMGs
1 Motorcycle Company
33rd (mot) Mapping Section
8th Panzer Regiment
Armored Signals Section (1 50mm PAK 38 and 7 LMGs)
1 Light Armored Section (5 20mm and 5 LMGs)
1 Regimental Band
1 (mot) Armored Repair Company (2 PzBu39)
1st and 2nd Panzer Battalions, each with
1 Battalion HQ
  1 Self-Propelled AA Gun Platoon (6 20mm guns)
  1 Motorcycle Company (4 LMGs)
  1 Panzer Pioneer Section
  1 Panzer Signals Section (1 50mm PAK 38 and 4 LMGs)
  1 Light Armored Section (5 37mm PAK 36 and 5 LMGs)
  1 Medium Panzer Company (10 Pz IV (75mm), 5 Pz II and 17 Pz III (37mm))
  1 Light Panzer Company (5 Pz II (20mm), 17 Pz III (37mm) and 19 Pz I)
  1 Light Panzer Company (5 Pz II (20mm) and 39 Pz III (37mm))
  1 Light (mot) Armored Replacement Platoon
15th Schützen Brigade
115th Schützen Regiment
HQ Section
  2 28mm anti-tank guns
  1 (mot) Support Company, with
    1 Signals Platoon
    1 Pioneer Platoon (3 LMGs)
    1 Motorcycle Platoon
    1 (mot) Panzerjäger Platoon (3 37mm PAK 36)
1st Battalion
  3 (mot) Infantry Companies (18 LMGs, 2 HMGs and 3 50mm mortars ea)
  1 Machine Gun Company (6 80mm mortars and 8 HMGs)
  1 (mot) Support Company, with
    1 Pioneer Platoon (3 LMGs)
    1 Panzerjäger Platoon (3 50mm and 1LMG)

    1 Infantry Support Platoon (2 75mm leIG)
2nd Battalion
  3 (mot) Infantry Companies (18 LMGs, 2 HMGs and 3 50mm mortars ea)
  1 Machine Gun Company (6 80mm mortars and 8 HMGs)
  1 (mot) Support Company, with
    1 Pioneer Platoon (3 LMGs)
    1 Panzerjäger Platoon (3 50mm and 1 LMG)
    1 Infantry Support Platoon (2 75mm guns)
33rd Reconnaissance Battalion
1 (mot) Signals Platoon
1 Motorcycle Company (3 50mm mortars, 2 HMGs and 18 LMGs)
1 Armored Car Company (25 LMGs and 10 20mm guns)
1 (mot) Support Company
  1 Pioneer Platoon (3 LMGs)
  1 Panzerjäger Platoon (3 37mm PAK 38 and 1 LMG)
  1 Support Gun Platoon (2 75mm leIG)
1 AT Rifle Section (2 PzBu39)
1 Light (mot) Supply Columns (3 LMGs)
33rd Artillery Regiment
1 HQ section
1 (mot) Signals Platoon
1st and 2nd (mot) Battalions
1 Battalion HQ
  1 (mot) Signals Platoon
  1 (mot) Calibration Platoon
3 Batteries (4 105mm leFH 18 and 2 LMGs ea)
3rd (mot) Battalion
1 Battalion HQ
  1 (mot) Signals Platoon
  1 (mot) Calibration Platoon
3 Batteries (4 150mm sFH 18 and 2 LMGs ea)
1 (mot) Observation Company
78th (mot) Signals Battalion
1 (mot) Radio Company (13 LMGs)
1 (mot) Telephone Company (2 LMGs)
1 Light (mot) Signals Supply Column
33rd (mot) Pioneer Battalion
1 Armored Pioneer Company
2 (mot) Pioneer Companies
1 Light (mot) Pioneer Supply Column
33rd Panzerjäger Battalion
1 HQ Section
  1 (mot) Signals Platoon
2 Self-Propelled Panzerjäger Companies (6 76.2mm (r) PAK and 6 LMGs ea)
Support Units
33rd (mot) Field Post Office
33rd (mot) Military Police Platoon
1/, 2/, 3/33rd Ambulance Companies
1/, 2/33rd (mot) Medical Companies

36th (mot) Field Hospital
33rd (mot) Division Quartermaster Company
33rd (mot) Bakery Company
33rd (mot) Butcher Platoon
33rd Supply Battalion
33rd (mot) Light Supply Company
1/, 2/, 3/33rd (mot) Maintenance Companies
1–7th Light (mot) Supply Columns
8–10th Heavy (mot) Supply Columns
11–12th Light (mot) Supply Columns

The anti-tank guns of the pioneer companies were raised from three to six 50mm PAK 38 by Pz.AOK Ia Nr 2092 issued on 20 September 1942 in the 15th and 21st Panzer Divisions. The same order directed that the Panzerjäger Battalions be equipped with Russian 76.2mm guns and that the 50mm PAK 38s removed be distributed to the schützen and pioneer companies. In late August or early September the reconnaissance battalions were stripped out of the two panzer divisions.

On 24 September 1942 the division was once again reorganized and its equipment allowances changed. It was now organized as follows:

Divisional Headquarters
Panzer Command Staffel
33rd (mot) Mapping Section
8th Panzer Regiment
1 Regimental HQ
1 Panzer Platoon
1 Light Panzer Platoon
1 Regimental Band
1 Armored Maintenance Company
1st and 2nd Panzer Battalions, each with
1 Battalion HQ
1 Panzer Staff Company
1 Medium Panzer Company
3 Light Panzer Companies
1 (mot) Armored Replacement Company
1 (mot) Armored Replacement Company
Theoretical total of tanks: 25 Pz II, 111 Pz III, 30 Pz IV and 6 command vehicles)
115th Panzergrenadier Regiment
HQ Section
1 (mot) Support Company, with
1 (mot) Signals Platoon
1 (mot) Pioneer Platoon (3 LMGs)
1 Motorcycle Messenger Platoon (6 LMGs)
1 (mot) Panzerjäger Platoon (3 50mm and 3 LMGs)
3 (mot) Battalions, each with
4 Companies (18 LMGs, 2 HMGs, 3 28mm PzBu41, 3 80mm mortars and 6 50mm PAK 38 ea)
707th Self-Propelled Infantry Support Gun Company (6 105mm sIG and 3 LMGs)

1 (mot) Pioneer Company (10 LMGs, 2HMGs, 3 28mm PzBu41, 3 80mm mortars and 3 50mm PAK 38)
33rd Reconnaissance Battalion
organization not indicated
33rd Artillery Regiment
1 (mot) Regimental Staff Battery
1st and 2nd Battalions
1 (mot) Staff Battery
3 (mot) Batteries (4 105mm leFH 18 and 2 LMGs ea)
3rd Battalion
1 (mot) HQ Company
2 (mot) Batteries (4 150mm sFH and 2 LMGs ea)
1 (mot) Battery (4 100 K18 guns and 2 LMGs)
1 (mot) Heavy Munitions Supply Column (60t)
1 (mot) Artillery Observation Battery
1 Self-Propelled Flak Battery (15 20mm guns)
33rd Feldersatz Battalion
4 Replacement Infantry Companies (6 LMGs and 1 50mm PAK 38 ea)
78th (mot) Signals Battalion
1 Armored Radio Company (28 LMGs)
1 Armored Telephone Company (6 LMGs)
1 Light (mot) Signals Supply Column (3 LMGs)
33rd (mot) Pioneer Battalion
3 (mot) Pioneer Companies (9 LMGS, 3 28mm PzBu41 and 6 50mm PAK 38 ea)
33rd Panzerjäger Battalion
1 HQ Section
1 (mot) Signals Platoon
2 Self-Propelled Panzerjäger Companies (6 76.2mm (r) PAK and 6 LMGs ea)
33rd Supply Battalion
unchanged from Mar. 1942
Support Units
unchanged from Mar. 1942

Before El Alamein, on 23 October 1942, the division was broken into Kampfgruppen as follows:

Kampfgruppe Nord Oberst Crasemann
Staff/33rd Panzer Artillery Regiment (with Staff Battery)
1/115th Panzergrenadier Regiment
2/33rd Panzer Artillery Regiment
3rd Company, 617th Flak Battalion
II/133rd Italian Panzer Battalion
Division Reserve Hauptman Hinrichs
33rd Panzer Pioneer Battalion
3rd Panzerjäger Battalion
10th Company, 33rd Panzer Artillery Regiment
Kampfgruppe Mitte Major Schemel
Staff/115th Panzergrenadier Regiment (with Staff Company)

2/8th Panzer Regiment

3/115th Panzergrenadier Regiment

13th (Inf Sup Guns) Company, 115th Panzergrenadier Regiment

15th Company, 115th Panzergrenadier Regiment (captured guns)

3/33rd Panzer Artillery Regiment

1/133rd Italian Panzer Regiment

23rd Company, 12th Italian Besaglieri Regiment

29th Company, 3rd Italian Artillery Regiment

556th Italian Sturmgeschütz Battalion

Kampfgruppe Süd Oberst Tegge

Staff/8th Panzer Regiment

1/8th Panzer Regiment

2/115th Panzergrenadier Regiment

1/33rd Panzer Artillery Regiment

Staff/13th Italian Besaglieri Regiment

3/133rd Italian Panzer Battalion

36th Company, 13th Italian Besaglieri Regiment

2/3rd Italian Artillery Regiment

554th Italian Assault Gun Battalion

70 50mm PAK

8 88mm Flak

4 100mm K17

24 100mm howitzers

8 150mm howitzers

4 150mm heavy infantry guns

5 87.6mm (captured British 25pdrs)

4 57mm (captured British 6pdrs)

16 76.2mm Sfl (Marder I)

8 150mm Howitzer Sfl (Self-Propelled)

41 Italian guns

At that time the organization of the overall division and its weapons inventory were as follows:

Divisional HQ

33rd (mot) Mapping Section

8th Panzer Regiment

Headquarters Section

  1 Light Panzer Platoon (4 20mm and 2 LMGs)

  1 Armored Signals Section (2 50mm PAK and 2 LMGs)

1 Panzer Maintenance Company

1 Panzer Battalion, with

  1 Battalion HQ Section, with

    1 Light Panzer Platoon

    1 Panzer Signals Platoon

    1 Panzer Pioneer Platoon

    1 Motorcycle Platoon

    1 20mm Flak Section

  3 Light Panzer Companies

  1 Medium Panzer Company

    Total 3 Pz II, 23 Pz III, 14 Pz III J and 8 Pz IV F2

1 Panzer Battalion, with

  1 Battalion HQ Section, with

    1 Light Panzer Platoon

    1 Panzer Signals Platoon

    1 Panzer Pioneer Platoon

    1 Motorcycle Platoon

    1 20mm Flak Section

  3 Light Panzer Companies

  1 Medium Panzer Company

    Total 5 Pz II, 14 Pz III, 18 Pz III J, 2 Pz IV and 7 Pz IV F2

115th Panzergrenadier Regiment

Regimental HQ Section

1 (mot) Support Company

  1 (mot) Pioneer Platoon (3 LMGs)

  1 (mot) Panzerjäger Platoon (3 50mm PAK 38 and 1 LMG)

  1 Motorcycle Platoon

  1 (mot) Signals Platoon

  1 Regimental Band

3 (mot) Battalions, each with

  4 (mot) Companies

  Total 178 MGs, 15 80mm mortars, 1 28mm PzBu41, 2 37mm PAK 36 and 4 50mm PAK 38)

13th Company (4 20mm SP Flak guns and 3 LMGs)

15th (mot) Heavy Infantry Support Gun Company (5 150mm guns)

33rd Artillery Regiment

Regimental HQ Section

  1 (mot) Staff Company

  1 Regimental Band

1st and 2nd (mot) Battalions

  1 (mot) Staff Company

  1 Calibration Section

  3 (mot) Batteries (4 105mm leFH 18 and 2 LMGs ea)

3rd (mot) Battalion

  1 (mot) Staff Company

  1 Calibration Section

  3 (mot) Batteries (4 150mm sFH 18 and 2 LMGs ea)

  1 (mot) Battery (4 100mm K17 and 2 LMGs)

4th Self-Propelled Battalion

  8 Self-Propelled 150mm sFH guns

I/33rd (mot) Flak Regiment

2 (mot) Batteries (4 88mm guns ea)

2 (mot) Batteries (12 20mm guns ea)

33rd (mot) Pioneer Battalion

1 (half-track) Pioneer Company (2 37mm PAK 36 and 9 LMGs)

1 (half-track) Pioneer Company (1 37mm PAK 36 and 9 LMGs)

1 (half-track) Pioneer Company (1 37mm PAK 36, 1 28mm PzBu41 and 9 LMGs)

1 Light (mot) Supply Column

33rd Panzerjäger Battalion
1 (mot) Signals Platoon (2 LMGs)
1 Panzerjäger (mot) Company (12 50mm PAK and 12 LMGs)
1 SP Panzerjäger Company (9 76.2mm and 34 LMGs) (9 Marder I on Czech 38t chassis)

33rd Reconnaissance Battalion
1 Armored Car Company (18 37mm and 24 LMGs)
1 (half-track) Infantry Company (5 SP 50mm PAK 38, 2 HMGs and 3 80mm mortars)
1 (mot) Support Company, with
1 Signals Section
1 Pioneer Platoon (2 LMGs)
1 Heavy Weapons Platoon 5 37mm and 3 50mm PAK)
1 Light Armored Car Supply Column
1 (mot) 105mm leFH Battery (4 guns and 2 LMGs)
1 Light Reconnaissance Supply Column

33rd Signals Battalion
1 (mot) Telephone Company
1 (mot) Radio Company
1 Light (mot) Signals Supply Column

33rd Feldersatz Battalion
4 Infantry Companies

Support Units
33rd (mot) Field Post Office
33rd (mot) Military Police Platoon
1/, 2/, 3/33rd Ambulance Companies
2/33rd (mot) Medical Companies
33rd (mot) Field Hospital
33rd (mot) Division Quartermaster Company
33rd (mot) Bakery Company
33rd (mot) Butcher Platoon

33rd Supply Battalion
33rd (mot) Light Supply Company
1st–8th Light (mot) Supply Columns (1 LMG ea)
9th–11th Light (mot) POL Supply Columns (1 LMG ea)
1 (mot) Maintenance Company
12th–13th Heavy (mot) Supply Columns (1 LMG ea)
2 (mot) Motor Vehicle Repair Companies

On 17 January 1943 the 2/5th Panzer Regiment, with all the tanks in the 5th Panzer Regiment, was transferred to the 8th Panzer Regiment and redesignated as the 2/8th Panzer Regiment, 15th Panzer Division. On 26 February the division was ordered re-formed. The 3/8th Panzer Regiment was organized at this time from the 504th (Tiger) Panzer Battalion and the 115th Schützen and 3/47th Infantry Regiments were to be reorganized into two Panzergrenadier Regiments, each with two battalions. On 29 April the 33rd Reconnaissance Battalion was ordered to become the 15th Panzer Reconnaissance Battalion, but this was apparently not done. The division was destroyed in Tunis in May 1943. Its losses were:

Division Staff
33rd Mapping Detachment
33rd Print Shop
8th Panzer Regiment
Staff, 2 battalions (each with staff, staff company and 4 companies) and armored maintenance company
504th (Tiger) Panzer Battalion
1 company (staff and 2 companies still in Italy)
115th Panzergrenadier Regiment
Staff, staff company, 3 battalions (each with staffs, staff company, 4 panzergrenadier companies) and 13th and 14th Companies
3/47th Panzergrenadier Regiment
Staff and 4 companies
15th Reconnaissance Battalion
Staff, 3 companies and 1 light column
33rd Panzerjäger Battalion
Staff, 3 companies, signals platoon
33rd Artillery Regiment
Staff, staff and observation battery and 3 battalions, each with staff, staff battery and 3 batteries
33rd Panzer Pioneer Battalion
Staff, 3 companies, 1 light supply column
78th Panzer Signals Battalion
2 companies and 1 light supply column
33rd Feldersatz Battalion
4 companies

On 1 July 1943 the Sizilien Division was reorganized into the 15th Panzer Division (the grenadier regiments becoming panzergrenadier regiments). On 15 July 1943 the name was changed to the 15th Panzergrenadier Division, but the regiments retained the title Panzergrenadier Regiments instead of (mot) Grenadier Regiments as with the other panzergrenadier divisions. The division had:

1/, 2/, 3/104th Panzergrenadier Regiment (from 1st Sizilien Grenadier Regiment)
1/, 2/, 3/115th Panzergrenadier Regiment (from 2nd Sizilien Grenadier Regiment)
1/, 2/, 3/129th Panzergrenadier Regiment (from 3rd Sizilien Grenadier Regiment)
Reggio Panzergrenadier Battalion
215th Panzer Battalion
1/, 2/, 3/, 4/33rd Panzer Artillery Regiment
315th Flak Battalion (formerly Sizilien Flak Battalion)
33rd Reconnaissance Battalion
33rd Panzerjäger Battalion
33rd Panzer Pioneer Battalion
999th Signals Battalion
33rd Divisional Support Troops

16th Panzer Division

Formed on 1 November 1940 from the 16th Infantry Division with:

1/, 2/64th Schützen Regiment (from 1/, 2/64th Infantry Regiment)

1/, 2/79th Schützen Regiment (from 1/, 2/79th Infantry Regiment)

16th Motorcycle Battalion (from 1st Machine Gun Battalion)

1/, 2/2nd Panzer Regiment (detached from 1st Panzer Division)

1/, 2/, 3/16th Artillery Regiment (from Staff/, 2/16th Artillery Regiment, 1/76th Artillery Regiment and 644th Heavy Artillery Battalion)

16th Panzerjäger Battalion

16th Pioneer Battalion

16th Signals Battalion

16th Divisional Support Troops

On 5 April 1941, during the invasion of Greece, the 16th Panzer Division was organized and equipped as follows:

16th Panzer Division
Divisional Staff (2 LMGs)
16th (mot) Mapping Detachment
2nd Panzer Regiment
1 Panzer Singals Platoon
1 Light Panzer Platoon
1 Regimental Band
1st and 2nd Battalions, each with
1 Staff and Staff Panzer Company
2 Light Panzer Companies
1 Medium Panzer Company
1 (mot) Replacement Platoon
1 (mot) Panzer Supply Column
16th Schützen Brigade
64th Schützen Regiment
1 (mot) Staff Company
1 Signals Platoon
1 Pioneer Platoon (3 LMGS)
1 Motorcycle Platoon
1 Regimental Band
1st and 2nd (mot) Battalions, each with
3 (mot) Companies (18 LMGs, 2 HMGs and 3 50mm mortars ea)
1 (mot) Machine Gun Company (8 HMGs and 6 80mm mortars)
1 (mot) Support Company
1 (mot) Infantry Gun Platoon (2 75mm leIG)
1 Panzerjäger Platoon (3 37mm PAK 36 and 1 LMG)
1 Pioneer Platoon (3 LMGs)

1 (mot) Infantry Gun Company (2 150mm sIG and 4 75mm leIG)
1 (mot) Light Supply Column
76th Schützen Regiment
same as 64th Schützen Regiment
16th Motorcycle Battalion
3 Motorcycle Companies (3 50mm mortars, 2 HMGs and 18 LMGs ea)
1 (mot) Heavy Machine Gun Company (8 HMGs and 6 80mm mortars)
1 (mot) Reconnaissance Company
1 (mot) Infantry Gun Section (2 75mm leIG)
1 (mot) Panzerjäger Platoon (3 37mm PAK 36 and 1 LMG)
1 (mot) Pioneer Platoon (3 LMGs)
16th Panzerjäger Battalion
1 (mot) Signals Platoon
3 (mot) Panzerjäger Companies (12 37mm PAK 36 and 6 LMGs ea)
6th Company/66th Self-Propelled Heavy Machine Gun Battalion (10 20mm guns)
16th Reconnaissance Battalion
1 (mot) Signals Platoon (2 LMGs)
1 Armored Car Company (10 HMGs and 25 LMGs)
1 Motorcycle Company (3 50mm mortars, 2 HMGs and 18 LMGs)
1 (mot) Heavy Reconnaissance Company
1 Panzerjäger Platoon (3 37mm PAK 36 and 1 LMG)
1 Pioneer Platoon (3 LMGs)
1 Infantry Gun Section (2 75mm leIG)
1 (mot) Reconnaissance Supply Column
16th Artillery Regiment
1 (mot) Support Detachment
1 (mot) Signals Platoon
1 (mot) Weather Detachment
1st and 2nd (mot) Battalions, each with
1 (mot) Calibration Detachment
1 (mot) Signals Platoon
3 (mot) Batteries (4 105mm leFH and 2 LMGs ea)
3rd (mot) Battalion
1 Calibration Detachment
1 Signals Platoon
1 (mot) Battery (4 100mm K18 and 2 LMGs)
2 (mot) Batteries (4 150mm sFH and 2 LMGs ea)
16th Signals Battalion
1 (mot) Panzer Telephone Company (2 LMGs)
1 (mot) Panzer Radio Company (16 LMGS)
1 (mot) Light Signals Supply Column
16th (mot) Pioneer Battalion
3 (mot) Pioneer Companies (9 LMGs ea)
1 (mot) Brüko T

1 (mot) Light Pioneer Supply Column
16th Supply Troop
  1/, 2/, 3/, 4/, 5/, 6/, 7/16th (mot) Light Supply Columns
  8/, 9/, 10/16th (mot) Heavy Fuel Column
  1/, 2/, 3/16th (mot) Maintenance Company
  16th (mot) Supply Company
Administration
  16th (mot) Field Bakery
  16th (mot) Butcher Company
  16th (mot) Divisional Administration
Other
  1/, 2/16th (mot) Medical Company
  1/, 2/, 3/16th (mot) Ambulance Companies
  16th (mot) Miltiary Police Troop
  16th (mot) Field Post Office

On 22 June 1941 the organization of the armored portion of the division and its panzer inventory were as follows:

1/, 2/2nd Panzer Regiment
  1 Regimental Staff Signals Platoon
  1 Regimental Staff Light Panzer Platoon
  Each Battalion had
    1 Panzer Staff Company
    1 Medium Panzer Company
    2 Light Panzer Companies
  Total tanks available:
    PzMk II   45
    PzMk III (37)   23
    PzMk III (50)   48
    PzMk IV (kz)   20
    PzBefWg   10

By 22 August 1941 the operational tank inventory had been reduced to:

    PzMk I   4
    PzMk II   18
    PzMk III   26
    PzMk IV   9
    PzBefWg   4

In 1942 the 3/2nd Panzer Regiment was formed from the 2/10th Panzer Regiment, while the 16th Motorcycle Battalion and the 16th Reconnaissance Battalion were merged. The 4/16th Artillery Regiment was formed from the 274th Army Flak Battalion. The division had:

1/, 2/64th Panzergrenadier Regiment
1/, 2/79th Panzergrenadier Regiment
16th Motorcycle Battalion
1/, 2/, 3/2nd Panzer Regiment
1/, 2/, 3/, 4/16th Panzer Artillery Regiment

16th Panzerjäger Battalion
16th Pioneer Battalion
16th Signals Battalion
16th Divisional Support Troops

On 1 July 1942 the organization of the armored portion of the division and its panzer inventory were as follows:

1/, 2/, 3/2nd Panzer Regiment
  1 Regimental Staff Signals Platoon
  1 Regimental Staff Light Panzer Platoon
  Each Battalion had
    1 Panzer Staff Company
    1 Medium Panzer Company
    2 Light Panzer Companies
  Total tanks available:
    PzMk II   13
    PzMk III (50 kz)   39
    PzMk III (50 lg)   18
    PzMk IV (kz)   15
    PzMk IV (lg)   12
    PzBefWg   3

The division was destroyed in January 1943 at Stalingrad. The 2nd Panzer Regiment was re-formed on 17 February 1943 with two battalions, each with four companies. Orders were cut on 3 March 1943 specifying the addition of a 3rd (Tiger) Battalion equipped with three heavy panzer companies and an independent sturmgeschütz Battalion with three batteries. However, plans for building the Tiger and sturmgeschütz battalions were abandoned in favor of organizing a 3rd Battalion with sturmgeschütze by the issuance of a new order dated 20 March 1943. This battalion contained four companies and 22 sturmgeschütze.

In March 1943 the 890th (mot) Grenadier Regiment Reinforced, less its staff and 2nd Battalion, was absorbed into the rebuilding division. The newly re-formed division contained:

1/, 2/64th Panzergrenadier Regiment
1/, 2/79th Panzergrenadier Regiment
16th Motorcycle Battalion (became 16th Panzer Reconnaissance Battalion on 1 Apr. 1943)
1/, 2/, 3/2nd Panzer Regiment
1/, 2/, 3/, 4/16th Panzer Artillery Regiment (4/16th Artillery Regiment reverted to the 274th Army Flak Battalion on 26 Apr. 1943)
16th Divisional Support Troops

During 1943 the 2nd Panzer Regiment was re-formed, with the 1st and 2nd Battalions having four companies of PzMk IV tanks and the 3rd Battalion having sturmgeschütze. The 2/64th Panzergrenadier Regiment and the 3rd and 4th Companies of the panzer reconnaissance battalion were equipped with half-tracks. The division was destroyed during the Stalingrad battles and reduced to a kampfgruppe. On 7 February 1943 that kampfgruppe was organized and equipped as follows:

Divisional Staff
Panzer Battalion:
   3 Panzer Companies (22 PzMk IV tanks ea)
   1 Armored Maintenance Platoon
(mot) Panzergrenadier Battalion
   3 (mot) Panzergrenadier Companies (4 HMGs, 18 LMG and 2 80mm mortars ea)
   1 (mot) Heavy Company
     1 Pioneer Platoon (4 LMGs)
     1 Infantry Gun Section (4 75mm leIG and 6 LMGs)
     1 Panzerjäger Platoon (3 75mm PAK 40)
Armored Battalion
   1 (motZ) Heavy Battery (4 150mm sFH and 2 LMGs)
   1 (motZ) Medium Battery (4 105mm leFH and 2 LMGs)
   1 Self-Propelled Battery (4, later 6 105mm leFH SdKfz 124 Wespe and 2 LMGs)
   1 (mot) Observation Battery (2 LMGs) (added 11 Feb. 1943)
(mot) Pioneer Company (18 LMGs, 2 80mm mortars and 6 flamethrowers, plus 3 light anti-tank guns, added 20 Feb. 1943)
Self-Propelled Flak Company (12 20mm Flak guns and 4 LMGs)
Assault Gun Battery (removed 23 Feb. 1943) (10 StuG)
Panzer Mixed Signals Company (16 LMGs)

OKH records show that by 22 February 1943 the division had not only been significantly rebuilt, but its structure had been modified. The division, now bearing the sobriquet "Stalingrad Division", was organized and equipped as follows (the division appears to have retained this organization until 1 October 1943):

Division Staff
   1 Division Staff (2 LMGs)
   1 (mot) Mapping Detachment (2 LMGs)
   1 (mot) Escort Company
     1 Motorcycle Platoon (6 LMGs)
     1 Infantry Gun Section (2 75mm leIG)
     1 Self-Propelled Flak Platoon (4 20mm Flak guns)
     1 Panzerjäger Platoon (3 LMGs and 3 75mm PAK 40)
     1 Infantry Platoon (4 HMGs, 6 LMGs and 2 80mm mortars)
2nd Panzer Regiment
   Regimental Staff
   1 Signals Platoon
   1 Regimental Band
  1st Battalion
     1 Staff and Staff Company

     1 Pioneer Platoon
     4 Panzer Companies (22 PzMk V Panther tanks ea)
     1 Panzer Maintenance Company
  2nd Battalion
     1 Staff and Staff Company
     4 Panzer Companies (22 PzMk IV ea)
     1 Panzer Maintenance Company
  3rd Battalion (detached on 18 Mar. 1943)
     1 Staff and Staff Company
     1 Pioneer Platoon
     3 Panzer Companies (10 PzMk VI Tiger tanks ea; replaced on 18 Feb. 1943 by 4 Sturmgeschütz Companies—22 StuG ea)
     1 Panzer Maintenance Company
64th Panzergrenadier Regiment
   1 Regimental Staff
   1 Regimental Band
   1 (mot) Regimental Staff Company
     1 Signals Platoon
     1 Pioneer Platoon (6 LMGs and 6 flamethrowers)
     1 Panzerjäger Platoon (3 75mm PAK 40 and 3 LMGs)
     1 Motorcycle Platoon (6 LMGs)
  1st (half-track) Battalion
     3 (half-track) Companies (4 HMGs, 33 LMGs, 2 80mm mortars and 4 37mm PAK 36 ea; upgraded to 4 HMGs, 39 LMGs, 3 PzBu39, 3 75mm leIG, 2 80mm mortars and 2 75mm guns ea—date unknown)
     1 (half-track) Heavy Company
       1 (half-track) Pioneer Platoon (13 LMGs, 1 37mm PAK and 6 flamethrowers)
       1 Panzerjäger Platoon (3 75mm PAK 40 and 3 LMGs)
       1 Infantry Gun Platoon (4 LMGs and 4 75mm leIG)
       1 Half-Track Gun Platoon (8 LMGs and 6 75mm guns) (this platoon was added on 28 Feb. 1943)
  2nd (mot) Battalion
     3 (mot) Companies (4 HMGs, 18 LMGs and 2 80mm mortars ea)
     1 (mot) Heavy Company
       1 Pioneer Platoon (4 LMGs and 6 flamethrowers)
       1 Panzerjäger Platoon (3 LMGs and 3 75 PAK 40)
       1 Infantry Gun Platoon (4 75mm leIG)
       1 Panzerjäger Platoon (3 LMGs and 3 sPzBu 41)
   1 Self-Propelled Flak Company (12 20mm and 4 LMGs)
   1 Self-Propelled Infantry Gun Company (6 150mm sIG and 7 LMGs)
79th Panzergrenadier Regiment
   1 Regimental Staff
   1 Regimental Band
   1 (mot) Regimental Staff Company
     1 Signals Platoon
     1 Panzerjäger Platoon (3 50mm PAK 38 and 3 LMGs)

1 Motorcycle Platoon (6 LMGs)

1st and 2nd (mot) Battalions, each with

3 (mot) Companies (4 HMGs, 18 LMGs and 2 80mm mortars ea)

1 (mot) Heavy Company

1 Pioneer Platoon (4 LMGs and 6 flamethrowers)

1 Panzerjäger Platoon (3 LMGs and 3 75 PAK 40)

1 Infantry Gun Platoon (4 75mm leIG)

1 Panzerjäger Platoon (3 LMGs and 3 sPzBu 41)

1 Self-Propelled Flak Company (12 20mm and 4 LMGs)

1 Self-Propelled Infantry Gun Company (6 150mm sIG and 7 LMGs)

Assault Gun Battalion (reassigned to the panzer regiment on 18 Feb. 1943)

1 Staff and Staff Company

4 Sturmgeschütz Companies (10 StuG ea)

1 Panzer Maintenance Company

16th Reconnaissance Battalion

1 Armored Car Company

3 Armored Car Platoons (25 LMGs and 18 20mm guns)

1 Armored Car Platoon (6 LMGs and 6 75mm guns)

1 (half-track) Armored Car Company (25 LMGs and 16 20mm guns)

2 (half-track) Reconnaissance Companies (2 120mm mortars, 3 37mm PAK 36, 4 HMGs and 56 LMGs ea)

1 (mot) Heavy Reconnaissance Company

1 Pioneer Platoon (9, later 13 LMGs, 6 flamethrowers and 1 75mm gun)

1 Infantry Gun Section (2 75mm leIG, adding later 4 LMGs)

1 Panzerjäger Platoon (3 LMGs and 3 75mm PAK 40)

1 Half-Track Gun Platoon (6 75mm guns, adding later 8 LMGs)

1 (mot) Light Armored Car Supply Column (3 LMGs)

16th Panzer Artillery Regiment

1 Regimental Staff

1 Staff Battery (6 LMGs)

1 (mot) Observation Battery (12 LMGs)

1 Self-Propelled Flak Battery (4 quad 20mm) (this was reduced to 4 (motZ) 20mm guns on 9 Mar. 1943)

1st Battalion

1 Battalion Staff and Staff Battery (6 LMGs)

2 Self-Propelled Batteries (6 105mm leFH SdKfz 124 Wespe and 4 LMGs ea)

1 Self-Propelled Battery (6 150mm sFH SdKfz 165 Hummel and 4 LMGs)

2nd Battalion

1 Battalion Staff

1 Battalion Staff Battery (6 LMGs)

3 (mot) Batteries (3 105mm leFH and 2 LMGs ea)

3rd (mot) Battalion

1 Battalion Staff

1 Battalion Staff Battery (6 LMGs)

2 (mot) Batteries (3 150mm sFH and 2 LMGs ea)

1 (mot) Battery (3 100mm K 18 guns and 2 LMGs)

274th Army Flak Battalion (was 4/4th Panzer Artillery Regiment until 26 Apr. 1943)

1 Staff and (mot) Staff Battery (1 LMG)

1st–2nd (motZ) Heavy Flak Batteries (4 88mm, 3 20mm and 2 LMGs ea)

3rd (motZ) Light Flak Battery (9 20mm, 2 self-propelled quad 20mm guns and 2 LMGs)

1 (mot) Light (20 ton) Flak Supply Column

16th Panzer Pioneer Battalion

1 Staff (7 LMGs)

1 (mot) Reconnaissance Platoon (6 50mm PAK 38 and 4 LMGs) (deleted on 20 Mar. 1943)

1 (half-track) Pioneer Company (2 HMGs, 43 LMGs, 3 PzBu39, 6 flamethrowers and 2 80mm mortars)

2 (mot) Pioneer Companies (2 HMGs, 18 LMGs, 3 PzBu39, 2 80mm mortars and 6 flamethrowers ea)

1 Brüko K Bridging Column (3 LMGs)

1 (mot) Light Pioneer Supply Column (2 LMGs)

16th Panzer Signals Battalion

1 (mot) Telephone Company (5 LMGs) (became Panzer Telephone Company with 21 LMGs on 9 Mar. 1943)

1 Panzer Radio Company (35 LMGs)

1 (mot) Light Signals Supply Column (4, later 1 LMG)

16th Supply Troop

1–8/16th (mot) (120 ton) Transportation Company (4 LMGs ea)

16th (mot) Supply Company (6 LMGs)

Truck Park

1–3/16th (mot) Maintenance Companies (4 LMGs ea)

1 (mot) Heavy (75 ton) Replacement Supply Column (4 LMGs)

Other

16th (mot) Bakery Company

16th (mot) Butcher Company

16th (mot) Administration Platoon

1/, 2/16th (mot) Medical Companies (2 LMGs ea)

1/, 2/, 3/16th Ambulances

16th (mot) Military Police Troop (2 LMGs)

16th (mot) Field Post Office

There were a few minor changes to the division's organization over the summer of 1943. On 8 September 1943 the panzer regimental staff company was equipped with PzMk IV tanks. The battalion staff companies were equipped with PzMk III flame panzers during July 1943. In June the artillery regiment downgraded the 1st Battalion to (motZ) status and upgraded the 2nd Battalion to self-propelled status. In October 1943 the division received the rebuilt 1/2nd Panzer Regiment, which was organized and equipped as follows:

1/2nd Panzer Regiment
1 Panzer Staff Company
4 Medium Panzer Companies (71 PzMk V tanks total)

An OKH order dated 16 November 1943 directed that the 3/2nd Panzer Regiment be stripped of its tanks and re-equipped with three companies of sturmgeschütze. Each company was to have 14 StuG, giving thebattalion a total of 45 StuG. In December 1943 the organization of the armored portion of the division and its panzer inventory were as follows:

2nd Panzer Regiment
1 Regimental Staff Signals Platoon
1 Regimental Staff Light Panzer Platoon
2nd Battalion, with
  1 Panzer Staff Company
  4 Medium Panzer Companies
3rd Battalion, with
  1 Panzer Staff Company
  3 Sturmgeschütz Companies
Total tanks available:
  StuG   42
  PzMk IV (lg) 98
  PzBefWg   12

On 20 August 1944 the organization of the armored portion of the division and its panzer inventory were as follows:

2/, 3/2nd Panzer Regiment
1 Panzer Signals Platoon
1 Battalion
  1 Panzer Staff Company
  4 Medium Panzer Companies
1 Battalion
  1 Panzer Staff Company
  4 Sturmgeschütz Companies
Total tanks available:
  PzMk IV (lg) 92
  StuG   40
  PzBefWg   12
  Flammpanz   7

In December 1944 the 79th Panzergrenadier Regiment was detached to become part of the 79th Corps Fusilier Regiment, XXIV Panzer Corps (the 1st Battalion from the 1/79th, the 2nd Battalion with the 2/63rd from the 17th Panzer Division). The 2/79th became the 3/64th Panzergrenadier Regiment. The division then had only the 1/, 2/, 3/64th Panzergrenadier Regiment.

Sometime in late 1943 the 1/2nd Panzer Regiment was equipped with Panther tanks. The 2/2nd Panzer Regiment continued to be equipped with Panzer PzMk IV tanks. On 22 April 1944 the division was organized and equipped as follows:

16th Panzer Division
1 Division Staff (2 LMGs)
16th (mot) Mapping Detachment
16th (mot) Military Police Detachment (5 LMGs)
16th Escort Company
  1 Machine Gun Platoon (4 HMGs and 6 LMGs)
  1 Motorcycle Platoon (5 LMGs)
  1 Flak Platoon (4 20mm self-propelled guns)
2nd Panzer Regiment
1 Panzer Regimental Staff
1 Panzer Regimental Staff Company
  1 Armored Signals Platoon
  1 Armored Platoon
  1 Armored Flak Platoon (8 self-propelled 20mm guns)
1st Battalion
1 Panzer Battalion Staff and Staff Company
4 Panzer Companies (17 Panther tanks ea)
1 (mot) Panzer Supply Company
2nd Battalion
1 Panzer Battalion Staff and Staff Company (12 LMGs and 3 self-propelled quad 20mm Flak guns)
4 Panzer Companies (17 PzMk IV Tanks ea)
1 (mot) Panzer Supply Company
1 Armored Maintenance Company
64th Panzergrenadier Regiment
1 Panzergrenadier Regimental Staff
1/, 3/64th Panzergrenadier Regiment
1 Panzergrenadier Battalion Staff
1 Panzergrenadier Battalion Supply Company (4 LMGs)
3 (mot) Panzergrenadier Companies (4 HMGs, 18 LMGs and 2 80mm mortars ea)
1 (mot) Heavy Panzergrenadier Company (6 20mm guns, 1 LMG and 4 120mm mortars)
2/64th Panzergrenadier Regiment
1 Panzergrenadier Battalion Staff (5 LMGs)
1 Panzergrenadier Battalion Supply Company (4 LMGs)
3 (half-track) Panzergrenadier Companies (4 HMGs, 29 LMGs, 7 20mm Flak and 2 75mm guns ea)
1 (half-track) Heavy Panzergrenadier Company
  1 Mortar Platoon (2 LMGs and 4 120mm mortars)
  1 Infantry Gun Platoon (4 LMGs and 6 75mm leIG)
(mot) Pioneer Company
1 Company Staff (1 LMG)
2 (mot) Pioneer Platoons (6 LMGs and 6 flame-throwers ea)
1 (half-track) Pioneer Platoon (6 LMGs and 6 flamethrowers)
1 (mot) Mortar Platoon (2 LMGs and 2 80mm mortars)
1 (half-track) Pioneer Platoon (12 LMGs, 1 20mm Flak and 6 flamethrowers)

Self-Propelled Infantry Support Gun Company
(6 SdKfz138/1 150mm sIG 33/1 and 8 LMGs)

16th Panzerjäger Battalion
1 Panzerjäger Battalion Staff
1 (mot) Panzerjäger Battalion Staff Company (1 LMG)
   1 Sturmgeschütz Platoon (3 StuG)
2 Sturmgeschütz Companies (14 StuG ea)
1 (motZ) Panzerjäger Company (12 75mm PAK and 12 LMGs)
1 (mot) Panzerjäger Supply Company (3 LMGs)

16th Panzer Reconnaissance Battalion
1 Panzer Reconnaissance Battalion Staff
1 Panzer Reconnaissance Battalion Staff Company
   1 (mot) Signals Platoon (7 LMGs)
   1 Armored Car Platoon (16 LMGs, 13 20mm and 3 75mm guns)
1st (Luchs) Reconnaissance Company (25 LMGs and 16 20mm guns)
2nd (half-track) Reconnaissance Company (44 LMGs, 2 80mm mortars and 2 75mm guns)
3rd (half-track) Reconnaissance Company (4 HMGs, 29 LMGs 2 80mm mortars, 7 20mm Flak and 2 75mm guns)
4th (half-track) Reconnaissance Company
   1 Company Staff (1 LMG)
   1 Engineer Platoon (13 LMGs)
   1 Mortar Platoon (2 LMGs and 6 80mm mortars)
   1 Support Gun Platoon (2 LMGs and 6 75mm guns)
1 (mot) Reconnaissance Supply Company

16th Panzer Artillery Regiment
1 Regimental Staff and Staff Battery (2 LMGs)

1st Battalion (motZ)
1 Battalion Staff and Staff Battery (2 LMGs and 3 20mm Flak guns)
2 (motZ) Light Howitzer Batteries (6 105mm leFH 18 and 4 LMGs ea)

2nd Battalion, Self-Propelled
1 Battalion Staff and Staff Battery (2 LMGs and 3 20mm Flak guns)
2 Self-Propelled Light Howitzer Batteries (6 105mm leFH SdKfz 124 Wespe and 4 LMGs ea)
2 Self-Propelled Heavy Howitzer Battery (6 150mm sFH SdKfz 165 Hummel and 4 LMGs ea)

3rd Battalion (motZ)
1 Battalion Staff and Staff Battery (2 LMGs and 3 20mm Flak guns)
3 (motZ) Heavy Howitzer Batteries (4 150mm sFH and 4 LMGs ea)

16th Panzer Signals Battalion
1 Signals Battalion Staff
1 Panzer Telephone Company (11 LMGs)
1 Panzer Radio Company (19 LMGs)
1 (mot) Signals Supply Company (2 LMGs)

16th Panzer Pioneer Battalion
1 (half-track) Pioneer Battalion Staff (12 LMGs)
2 (mot) Pioneer Companies (2 HMGs, 18 LMGs, 2 80mm mortars)
1 (half-track) Pioneer Company (2 HMGs, 43 LMGs, 6 flamethrowers and 2 80mm mortars)

Other
1/16th (mot) Medical Company (2 LMGs)
16th (mot) Medical Supply Company
16th (mot) Field Post Office

On 26 February 1945 the Jüterbog Panzer Division was disbanded and its troops were used to rebuild the 16th Panzer Division. In addition, the division was ordered to rebuild the 2nd Panzer Regiment with two battalions. On 5 March 1945 the organization of the armored portion of the division and its panzer inventory were as follows:

1/, 2/2nd Panzer Regiment
1 Panzer Staff Company
1 Battalion
   1 Panzer Staff Company
   3 Medium Panzer Companies (PzMk V)
   1 Medium Panzer Company (PzMk IV)
1 Battalion
   1 Panzer Staff Company
   1 Medium Panzer Company (PzMk IV)
   3 Sturmgeschütz Companies (StuG)
Total tanks available:

StuG	37
PzMk IV (lg)	7
PzMk V	15
PzMk IV/70 (V)	10

17th Panzer Division

Formed on 1 November 1940 from the 27th Infantry Division. On 15 March 1941 it had:

17th Schützen Brigade
   1/, 2/40th Schützen Regiment (from 1/, 2/40th Infantry Regiment)
   1/, 2/63rd Schützen Regiment (from 1/, 3/63rd Infantry Regiment)
17th Motorcycle Battalion (from 2/63rd Infantry Regiment)
1/, 2/39th Panzer Regiment (formed from 4th and 33rd Panzer Ersatz Battalions)

1/, 2/, 3/27th Artillery Regiment (from 27th and 1/63rd
  Artillery Regiment)
27th Panzerjäger Battalion
27th Pioneer Battalion
27th Signals Battalion
27th Divisional Support Units

Between 1 June 1941 and 16 August 1941 the 3/39th
Panzer Regiment was formed from the 1/Panzer Lehr Regiment. On 22 June 1941 the organization of the armored
portion of the division and its panzer inventory were as
follows:

1/, 2/, 3/39th Panzer Regiment
  1 Regimental Staff Signals Platoon
  1 Regimental Staff Light Panzer Platoon
  Each Battalion had
    1 Panzer Staff Company
    1 Medium Panzer Company
    2 Light Panzer Companies
  Total tanks available:
    PzMk I   12
    PzMk II   44
    PzMk III (50)   106
    PzMk IV (kz)   30
    PzBefWg   10

By 10 September 1941 the operational tank inventory
had been reduced to:

    PzMk I   4
    PzMk II   19
    PzMk III   20
    PzMk IV   4
    PzBefWg   5

In 1942 the 1/39th Panzer Regiment became the 129th
Panzer Battalion and was transferred to the 29th Panzergrenadier Division. The division had only one panzer battalion during 1942. On 29 June 1942 the organization of
the armored portion of the division and its panzer inventory were as follows:

2/39th Panzer Regiment
  1 Regimental Staff Signals Platoon
  1 Regimental Staff Light Panzer Platoon
  Each Battalion had
    1 Panzer Staff Company
    1 Medium Panzer Company
    2 Light Panzer Companies
  Total tanks available
    PzMk II   17
    PzMk III (50 kz) 38
    PzMk IV (kz)   16
    PzBefWg   2

The 27th Reconnaissance Battalion was merged with
the 17th Motorcycle Battalion. In 1943 the 17th Motorcycle Battalion became the 17th Panzer Reconnaissance
Battalion and the 297th Army Flak Battalion joined the
division. During 1943 the 2/39th Panzer Regiment had
three companies of Panzer PzMk III tanks and one company of PzMk IV tanks. The panzergrenadier regiments
had no Flak companies and neither had any half-tracks.
OKH records show that the division was organized and
equipped as follows in early 1943:

Division Staff
  1 Division Staff (2 LMGs)
  27th (mot) Mapping Detachment
39th Panzer Regiment
  Regimental Staff
  1 Signals Platoon
  1 Regimental Band
2nd Battalion
  1 Regimental Staff and Staff Company
  2 Panzer Companies (22 PzMk III ea; changed to
    PzMk IV by June)
  1 Panzer Company (22 PzMk IV ea) (a second PzMk
    IV company was added on 14 June 1943)
  1 Panzer Maintenance Company
40th Panzergrenadier Regiment
  1 Regimental Staff
  1 Regimental Band
  1 (mot) Regimental Staff Company
    1 Signals Platoon
    1 Panzerjäger Platoon (3 50mm PAK 38 and 3
      LMGs)
    1 Motorcycle Platoon (6 LMGs)
  1st and 2nd (mot) Battalions, each with
    3 (mot) Companies (4 HMGs, 18 LMGs, 2 80mm
      mortars and 3 PzBu39 ea)
    1 (mot) Heavy Company
      1 Pioneer Platoon (4 LMGs)
      1 Panzerjäger Platoon (3 LMGs and 3 50mm PAK
        38)
      1 Infantry Gun Platoon (4 75mm leIG)
      1 Panzerjäger Platoon (3 LMGs and 3 sPzBu 41)
    1 Self-Propelled Infantry Gun Company (6 150mm sIG
      and 7 LMGs)
63rd Panzergrenadier Regiment
  same as 40th Panzergrenadier Regiment
27th Panzerjäger Battalion
  3 Self-Propelled Panzerjäger Companies (14 75mm PAK
    40 and 14 LMGs ea)
6th Reconnaissance Battalion (early 1943 organization)
  1 Armored Car Company (24 LMGs and 18 20mm
    guns)
  3 Motorcycle Companies (2 80mm mortars, 4 HMGs,
    18 LMGs and 3 PzBu39 ea)
  1 (mot) Heavy Reconnaissance Company

1 Pioneer Platoon (4 LMGs)
1 Infantry Gun Section (4 75mm leIG)
1 Panzerjäger Platoon (3 LMGs and 3 75mm PAK 40)
1 Panzerjäger Platoon (3 LMGs and 3 sPzBu 41)
1 (mot) Light Reconnaissance Supply Column (3 LMGs)

27th Panzer Artillery Regiment
1 Regimental Staff
1 Staff Battery (2 LMGs)

1st Battalion
1 Battalion Staff and Staff Battery (6 LMGs)
2 Self-Propelled Batteries (6 105mm leFH SdKfz 124 Wespe and 4 LMGs ea)
1 Self-Propelled Battery (6 150mm sFH SdKfz 165 Hummel and 4 LMGs)

2nd Battalion
1 Battalion Staff
1 Battalion Staff Battery (6 LMGs)
3 (mot) Batteries (3 105mm leFH and 2 LMGs ea)

3rd (mot) Battalion
1 Battalion Staff
1 Battalion Staff Battery (6 LMGs)
3 (mot) Batteries (3 150mm sFH and 2 LMGs ea)

27th (mot) Observation Battery (2 LMGs)

297th Army Flak Battalion
1 Staff and (mot) Staff Battery (1 LMG)
1st–2nd (motZ) Heavy Flak Batteries (4 88mm, 3 20mm and 2 LMGs ea)
3rd (motZ) Light Flak Battery (12 20mm and 2 LMGs)
4th Self-Propelled Battery (8 20mm and 2 quad 20mm Flak guns and 4 LMGs)
1 (mot) Light (20 ton) Flak Supply Column

27th Panzer Pioneer Battalion
1 Staff (2 LMGs)
1 (half-track) Pioneer Company (25 LMGs, 2 80mm mortars and 3 PzBu39)
1 (mot) Pioneer Companies (18 LMGs, 2 80mm mortars and 3 PzBu39 ea)
1 Brüko K Bridging Column (3 LMGs)
1 (mot) Light Pioneer Supply Column (2 LMGs)

82nd Panzer Signals Battalion
1 Panzer Telephone Company (6 LMGs)
1 Panzer Radio Company (16 LMGs)
1 (mot) Light Signals Supply Column (1 LMG)

27th Feldersatz Battalion
4 Companies

27th Supply Troop
1/, 2/, 3/27th (mot) (90 ton) Transportation Company (3 LMGs ea)
10/, 11/, 12/27th (mot) Light Supply Columns (2 LMGs ea)
27th (mot) Supply Company (6 LMGs)

Truck Park
1–3/27th (mot) Maintenance Companies (4 LMGs ea)

Other
27th (mot) Bakery Company
27th (mot) Butcher Company
27th (mot) Administration Platoon
1/, 2/27th (mot) Medical Companies (2 LMGs ea)
1/, 2/, 3/27th Ambulances
27th (mot) Military Police Troop (2 LMGs)
27th (mot) Field Post Office

On 1 July 1943 the organization of the armored portion of the division and its panzer inventory were as follows:

2/39th Panzer Regiment
1 Regimental Staff Signals Platoon
1 Regimental Staff Light Panzer Platoon
1 Battalion with:
1 Panzer Staff Company
2 Medium Panzer Companies
2 Light Panzer Companies
Total tanks available:

PzMk II	4
PzMk III (kz)	1
PzMk III (lg)	19
PzMk III (75)	9
PzMk IV (kz)	1
PzMk IV (lg)	31
PzBefWg	2

During the summer and fall there were several changes made to the division. On 15 September 1943 two of the motorcycle companies in the reconnaissance regiment were replaced by half-track companies (two 80mm mortars, three 37mm PAK 36, four HMGs and 56 LMGs each). By 7 October 1943 it was reorganized into the standard formation for reconnaissance battalions and contained:

1 Armored Car Company (24 LMGs and 18 20mm guns)
1 Armored Car (half-track) Company (25 LMGs and 16 20mm guns)
1 Motorcycle Company (2 80mm mortars, 4 HMGs, 18 LMGs and 3 PzBu39)
1 (half-track) Heavy Reconnaissance Company
1 Staff (2 LMGs)
1 Infantry Platoon (9 LMGs)
1 Pioneer Platoon (1 37mm PAK 36, 6 flamethrowers and 13 LMGs)
1 Panzerjäger Platoon (3 75mm PAK 40 and 4 LMGs)
1 Infantry Gun Section (2 75mm leIG)
1 Half-Track Gun Section (8 LMGs and 6 75mm guns)
1 (mot) Light Reconnaissance Supply Column (3 LMGs)

During the summer, probably August, the (motZ) artillery batteries were brought back to four guns per battery, and one of the 150mm sFH batteries was equipped with four 100mm K18 guns. In August 1943 the 297th Army Flak Battalion reorganized its (motZ) Light Flak Battery with nine 20mm guns and two quad 20mm guns. In August the 27th Supply Troop replaced the three light (mot) supply columns with two (mot) (90 ton) transportation companies (three LMGs ea).

In 1944 the Staff/39th Panzer Regiment was detached to become the Staff/108th Panzer Brigade. In December 1944 the 63rd Panzergrenadier Regiment was disbanded. The staff was assigned to the 63rd Panzer Feldersatz Regiment, and the 2nd Battalion was detached to become the 2/79th Panzer Fusilier Regiment. The 1/63rd Panzergrenadier Regiment became the 3/40th. The division had, as a result, only a single panzergrenadier regiment with three battalions. The 39th Panzer Regiment was re-formed into a two-battalion regiment using the 108th Panzer Brigade's staff and the 2103rd Panzer Battalion (103rd Panzer Brigade). In 1944 the division was equipped as follows:

17th Panzer Division
- 1 Division Staff (2 LMGs)
- 27th (mot) Mapping Detachment
- 27th (mot) Military Police Detachment (5 LMGs)
- 27th Escort Company
  - 1 Machine Gun Platoon (4 HMGs and 6 LMGs)
  - 1 Motorcycle Platoon (5 LMGs)
  - 1 Flak Platoon (4 20mm self-propelled guns)

39th Panzer Regiment
- 1 Panzer Regimental Staff
  - 1 Armored Signals Platoon
  - 1 Armored Platoon
  - 1 Armored Flak Platoon (8 self-propelled 20mm guns)

1st Battalion
- 1 Panzer Battalion Staff and Staff Company (12 LMGs and 3 self-propelled quad 20mm Flak guns)
- 4 Panzer Companies (17 PzMk V Panther tanks ea)
- 1 (mot) Panzer Supply Company

2nd Battalion
- 1 Panzer Battalion Staff and Staff Company (12 LMGs and 3 self-propelled quad 20mm Flak guns)
- 4 Panzer Companies (17 PzMk IV tanks ea)
- 1 (mot) Panzer Supply Company

1 Armored Maintenance Company

40th Panzergrenadier Regiment
- 1 Panzergrenadier Regimental Staff

1/40th Panzergrenadier Regiment
- 1 Panzergrenadier Battalion Staff (5 LMGs)
- 1 Panzergrenadier Battalion Supply Company (4 LMGs)
- 3 (half-track) Panzergrenadier Companies (4 HMGs, 29 LMGs, 7 20mm Flak and 2 75mm guns ea)
- 1 (half-track) Heavy Panzergrenadier Company
  - 1 Mortar Platoon (2 LMGs and 4 120mm mortars)
  - 1 Anti-Tank Platoon (4 LMGs and 6 75mm PAK)

2/, 3/40th Panzergrenadier Regiment
- 1 Panzergrenadier Battalion Staff
- 1 Panzergrenadier Battalion Supply Company (4 LMGs)
- 3 (mot) Panzergrenadier Companies (4 HMGs, 18 LMGs and 2 80mm mortars ea)
- 1 (mot) Heavy Panzergrenadier Company (6 20mm guns, 1 LMG and 4 120mm mortars)

(mot) Pioneer Company
- 1 Company Staff (1 LMG)
- 2 (mot) Pioneer Platoons (6 LMGs and 6 flamethrowers ea)
- 1 (half-track) Pioneer Platoon (6 LMGs and 6 flamethrowers)
- 1 (mot) Mortar Platoon (2 LMGs and 2 80mm mortars)
- 1 (half-track) Pioneer Platoon (12 LMGs, 1 20mm Flak and 6 flamethrowers)

Self-Propelled Infantry Support Gun Company
(6 SdKfz 138/1 150mm sIG 33/1 and 8 LMGs)

27th Panzerjäger Battalion
- 1 Panzerjäger Battalion Staff
- 1 (mot) Panzerjäger Battalion Staff Company (1 LMG)
  - 1 Sturmgeschütz Platoon (3 StuG)
- 2 Sturmgeschütz Companies (14 StuG ea)
- 1 (motZ) Panzerjäger Company (12 75mm PAK and 12 LMGs)
- 1 (mot) Panzerjäger Supply Company (3 LMGs)

27th Panzer Reconnaissance Battalion
- 1 Panzer Reconnaissance Battalion Staff
- 1 Panzer Reconnaissance Battalion Staff Company
  - 1 (mot) Signals Platoon (7 LMGs)
  - 1 Armored Car Platoon (16 LMGs, 13 20mm and 3 75mm guns)
- 1st (Luchs) Reconnaissance Company (25 LMGs and 16 20mm guns)
- 2nd (half-track) Reconnaissance Company (44 LMGs, 2 80mm mortars and 2 75mm guns)
- 3rd (half-track) Reconnaissance Company (4 HMGs, 29 LMGs 2 80mm mortars, 7 20mm Flak and 2 75mm guns)
- 4th (half-track) Heavy Reconnaissance Company
  - 1 Company Staff (1 LMG)
  - 1 Engineer Platoon (13 LMGs)
  - 1 Mortar Platoon (2 LMGs and 6 80mm mortars)
  - 1 Support Gun Platoon (2 LMGs and 6 75mm guns)

1 (mot) Reconnaissance Supply Company

27th Panzer Artillery Regiment
 1 Regimental Staff and Staff Battery (2 LMGs)

1st (self-propelled) Battalion
 1 Battalion Staff and Staff Battery (2 LMGs and 3 20mm Flak guns)
 2 Self-Propelled Light Howitzer Batteries (6 105mm leFH SdKfz 124 Wespe and 4 LMGs ea)
 2 Self-Propelled Heavy Howitzer Batteries (6 150mm sFH SdKfz 165 Hummel and 4 LMGs ea)

2nd Battalion (motZ)
 1 Battalion Staff and Staff Battery (2 LMGs and 3 20mm Flak guns)
 2 (motZ) Light Howitzer Batteries (6 105mm leFH 18 and 4 LMGs ea)

3rd Battalion (motZ)
 1 Battalion Staff and Staff Battery (2 LMGs and 3 20mm Flak guns)
 3 (motZ) Heavy Howitzer Batteries (4 150mm sFH and 4 LMGs ea)

297th Army Flak Battalion
 1 (mot) Flak Battalion Staff and Staff Battery (2 LMGs)
 2 (motZ) Heavy Flak Batteries (6 88mm, 3 20mm and 2 LMGs ea)
 1 (motZ) Light Battery
  1 (motZ) Battery (9 37mm and 4 LMGs)
  1 Self-Propelled Battery (3 quad 20mm)
  1 Searchlight Section (4 searchlights)

27th Panzer Signals Battalion
 1 Signals Battalion Staff
 1 Panzer Telephone Company (11 LMGs)
 1 Panzer Radio Company (19 LMGs)
 1 (mot) Signals Supply Company (2 LMGs)

27th Panzer Pioneer Battalion
 1 (half-track) Pioneer Battalion Staff (12 LMGs)
 2 (mot) Pioneer Companies
 1 (half-track) Pioneer Company (2 HMGs, 43 LMGs, 6 flamethrowers and 2 80mm mortars)

Other
 1/27th (mot) Medical Company (2 LMGs)
 27th (mot) Medical Supply Company
 27th (mot) Field Post Office

After heavy losses on the Vistula in January 1945 the division stood as a Kampfgruppe with:

Division Staff
 1 Divisional Staff (2 LMGs)
 1 (mot) Mapping Detachment
 1 Armored Car Reconnaissance Platoon (3 SdKfz 234/3 with 75mm and 13 SdKfz 234/1 with 1 20mm and 1 LMG ea)

Panzer Battalion
 1 Panzer Battalion Staff (1 LMG) and Staff Company (8 LMGs and 3 self-propelled quad 20mm guns)
 3 Panzer Companies (14 PzMk IV tanks ea)
 1 Panzer Maintenance Company (4 LMGs)
 1 Panzer Supply Company (4 LMGs)

Panzergrenadier Regiment
 1 Regimental Staff (2 LMGs)
 1 (mot) Regimental Staff Company
  1 Signals Platoon
  1 Motorcycle Platoon (4 LMGs)

1st and 2nd (mot) Battalions, each with
 1 Battalion Staff (2 LMGs)
 1 (mot) Regimental Staff Company (3 panzerschrecke and 4 LMGs)
 3 (mot) Companies (12 LMGs, 3 panzerschrecke and 30 MP 44 ea)
 1 (mot) Heavy Company (12 HMGs, 1 LMG and 6 20mm Flak)
 1 (mot) Heavy Company (6 LMGs, 8 80mm mortars and 4 120mm mortars)

3rd (bicycle) Battalion
 1 Battalion Staff (2 LMGs)
 1 (mot) Regimental Staff Company (3 panzerschrecke and 4 LMGs)
 3 (bicycle) Companies (12 LMGs, 3 panzerschrecke and 30 MP 44 ea)
 1 (mot) Heavy Company (12 HMGs, 1 LMG and 6 20mm Flak)
 1 (mot) Heavy Company (6 LMGs, 8 80mm mortars and 4 120mm mortars)

Panzerjäger Battalion
 1 Battalion Staff
 1 Battalion Staff Company (1 LMG)
 1 Staff Sturmgeschütz Platoon (3 StuG)
 2 Jagdpanzer Batteries (14 Jagdpanzer ea)
 1 Half-Track Company (12 SdKfz 251/22 with 75mm PAK)
 1 (mot) Supply Company (3 LMGs)

1/39th Artillery Regiment
 1 Battalion Staff
 1 (mot) Battalion Staff Battery (2 LMGs and 3 20mm Flak)
 3 (motZ) Batteries (6 105mm leFH and 4 LMGs ea)

(mot) Pioneer Company (2 HMGs, 16 LMGs and 2 80mm mortars)

Other
 1 Panzer Signals Company
 1 (mot) Supply Troop Staff
 1 (mot) (120 ton) Transportation Company (8 LMGs)
 2 (mot) Maintenance Companies (4 LMGs ea)
 1 (mot) Mixed Supply Troop (3 LMGs)
 1 (mot) Medical Company (2 LMGs)
 1 (mot) Medical Supply Company (2 LMGs)
 1 (mot) Field Post Office (1 LMG)

On 6 February 1945 Army Group Center was ordered to rebuild the 17th Panzer Division (Kampfgruppe) with the 1/39th Panzer Regiment. One company was to have 17 PzMk IV, one company was to have 17 PzMk IV/70, and the staff was to consist of three command tanks. Twenty-eight PzMk IV/70(V) were shipped to the division on 7 February 1945, followed by 16 PzMk IV on 9 February 1945. On 9 February 1945 the organization of the armored portion of the division and its panzer inventory were as follows:

Kampfgruppe
  1/39th Panzer Regiment
    1 Battalion Staff Company
    1 Medium Panzer Company
    2 Jagdpanzer Companies
  Total tanks available:
    PzMk IV   16
    PzMk IV/70 (V)   28

On 8 May 1945 the division surrendered to the Allies.

18th Panzer Division

Formed on 26 October 1940 from parts of the 4th and 14th Infantry Division. On 1 May 1941 it had:

18th Schützen Brigade
  1/, 2/52nd Schützen Regiment (from 2/, 3/52nd Infantry Regiment)
  1/, 2/101st Schützen Regiment (from 2/, 3/101st Infantry Regiment)
  18th Motorcycle Battalion (from 1/52nd Infantry Regiment)
  1/, 2/18th Panzer Regiment (from "A" and "B" Panzer Battalions on 6 Dec. 1940) (diving and wading panzers)
  1/, 2/28th Panzer Regiment (from "C" and "D" Panzer Battalions on 6 Dec. 1940) (diving and wading panzers)
  1/, 2/, 3/88th Artillery Regiment (from Staff/209th Artillery Battalion,
  2/14th Artillery Regiment, 630th Heavy and 741st Light Artillery Battalions)
  88th Divisional Support Units, including
    98th Pioneer Battalion

On 1 March 1941 the staff of the 28th Panzer Regiment was disbanded, the 2/28th Panzer Regiment became the 3/18th, and the 1/28th became the 3/6th Panzer Regiment. On 22 June 1941 the organization of the armored portion of the division and its panzer inventory were as follows:

1/, 2/, 3/18th Panzer Regiment
  1 Regimental Staff Signals Platoon
  1 Regimental Staff Light Panzer Platoon
  Each Battalion had
    1 Panzer Staff Company
    1 Medium Panzer Company
    2 Light Panzer Companies
  Total tanks available:
    PzMk I   6
    PzMk II   50

PzMk III (37)	99
PzMk III (50)	15
PzMk IV (kz)	36
PzBefWg	12

By 9 September 1941 the division's inventory of operational tanks was:

PzMk I	12
PzMk II	27
PzMk III	30
PzMk IV	16
PzBefWg	2

On 15 May 1942 the 18th Panzer Regiment was disbanded. Its staff became the Staff/18th Panzer Brigade, the 1/18th became the 160th Panzer Battalion and the 2/18th became the 103rd Panzer Battalion. Only the 3/18th remained, and it was redesignated as the 18th Panzer Battalion. The division received the 292nd Army Flak Battalion. The 88th Reconnaissance Battalion was merged with the 18th Motorcycle Battalion and on 29 April 1942 became the 18th Panzer Reconnaissance Battalion. On 29 June 1942 the organization of the armored portion of the division and its panzer inventory were as follows:

18th Panzer Battalion
  1 Panzer Staff Company
  1 Medium Panzer Company
  2 Light Panzer Companies
  Total tanks available:
    PzMk II   11
    PzMk III (50 kz)   26
    PzMk IV (kz)   8
    PzBefWg   2

On 28 March 1943 the 292nd Army Flak Battalion was reduced by one battery and later in the year it was detached. OKH records show that the division was organized and equipped as follows in late 1943: (see over)

Division Staff
1 Division Staff (2 LMGs)
88th (mot) Mapping Detachment

18th Panzer Regiment
Regimental Staff
1 Signals Platoon
1 Regimental Band

1st Battalion
1 Regimental Staff and Staff Company
2 Panzer Companies (22 PzMk III ea; changed to PzMk IV on 18 June 1943)
1 Panzer Company (22 PzMk IV ea)
1 Panzer Company (22 PzMk IV ea; added 26 June 1943)
1 Panzer Maintenance Company

52nd Panzergrenadier Regiment
1 Regimental Staff
1 Regimental Band
1 (mot) Regimental Staff Company
  1 Signals Platoon
  1 Panzerjäger Platoon (3 50mm PAK 38 and 3 LMGs)
  1 Motorcycle Platoon (6 LMGs)

1st and 2nd (mot) Battalions, each with
2 (mot) Companies (4 HMGs, 18 LMGs, 2 80mm mortars and 3 PzBu39 ea)
1 (half-track) Company (4 HMGs, 18 LMGs, 2 80mm mortars and 3 PzBu39)
1 (mot) Heavy Company
  1 Pioneer Platoon (4 LMGs)
  1 Panzerjäger Platoon (3 LMGs and 3 50mm PAK 38)
  1 Infantry Gun Platoon (4 75mm leIG)
  1 Panzerjäger Platoon (3 LMGs and 3 sPzBu 41)
1 (motZ) Infantry Gun Company (4 150mm sIG)

101st Panzergrenadier Regiment
same as 52nd Panzergrenadier Regiment

88th Panzerjäger Battalion
2 (motZ) Panzerjäger Companies (12 75mm PAK 40 ea)
1 Self-Propelled Panzerjäger Company (14 75mm PAK 40 and 14 LMGs ea)
1 Self-Propelled Flak Company (8 self-propelled 20mm, 4 (motZ) 20mm and 4 LMGs)

6th Reconnaissance Battalion (early 1943 organization)
1 Armored Car Company (24 LMGs and 18 20mm guns)
3 Motorcycle Companies (2 80mm mortars, 4 HMGs, 18 LMGs and 3 PzBu39 ea)
1 (mot) Heavy Reconnaissance Company
  1 Pioneer Platoon (4 LMGs)
  1 Infantry Gun Section (4 75mm leIG)
  1 Panzerjäger Platoon (3 LMGs and 3 75mm PAK 40)
  1 Panzerjäger Platoon (3 LMGs and 3 sPzBu 41)

1 (mot) Light Reconnaissance Supply Column (3 LMGs)

88th Panzer Artillery Regiment
1 Regimental Staff
1 Staff Battery (2 LMGs)

1st and 2nd Battalions, each with
1 Battalion Staff
1 Battalion Staff Battery (6 LMGs)
3 (mot) Batteries (3 105mm leFH and 2 LMGs ea)

3rd (mot) Battalion
1 Battalion Staff
1 Battalion Staff Battery (6 LMGs)
2 (mot) Batteries (3 150mm sFH and 2 LMGs ea)
1 (mot) Battery (3 100mm K 18 guns and 2 LMGs)
10/88th Flak Regiment (12 20mm and 2 LMGs)

88th (mot) Observation Battery (2 LMGs)

98th Panzer Pioneer Battalion
1 Staff (2 LMGs)
1 (half-track) Pioneer Company (25 LMGs, 2 80mm mortars and PzBu39)
1 (mot) Pioneer Companies (18 LMGs, 2 80mm mortars and 3 PzBu39 ea)
1 Brüko K Bridging Column (3 LMGs)
1 (mot) Light Pioneer Supply Column (2 LMGs)

88th Panzer Signals Battalion
1 Panzer Telephone Company (6 LMGs)
1 Panzer Radio Company (16 LMGs)
1 (mot) Light Signals Supply Column (1 LMG)

88th Feldersatz Battalion
3 Companies

88th Supply Troop
1/, 2/, 5/, 6/88th (mot) (90 ton) Transportation Company (3 LMGs ea)
3/, 4/88th (mot) (120 ton) Transportation Company (4 LMGs ea)
88th (mot) Supply Company (6 LMGs)

Truck Park
1–3/88th (mot) Maintenance Companies (4 LMGs ea)

Other
534th (mot) Bakery Company
88th (mot) Butcher Company
88th (mot) Administration Platoon
1/, 2/88th (mot) Medical Companies (2 LMGs ea)
1/, 2/, 3/88th Ambulances
88th (mot) Military Police Troop (2 LMGs)
88th (mot) Field Post Office

As 1943 progressed the division began undergoing various changes. The artillery regiment was to have converted one of its light battalions to a self-propelled battalion with one heavy and two light batteries. This did not, apparently, happen. The reconnaissance battalion did, however, undergo a major reorganization and was, by 10 July 1943, reorganized with:

18th Reconnaissance Battalion

1 Armored Car Company (24 LMGs and 18 20mm guns)

1 Armored Car (half-track) Company (25 LMGs and 16 20mm guns)

1 (half-track) Reconnaissance Company (2 80mm mortars, 3 37mm PAK 36, 4 HMGs and 56 LMGs)

1 Motorcycle Company (2 80mm mortars, 4 HMGs, 18 LMGs and 3 PzBu39)

1 (half-track) Heavy Reconnaissance Company

1 Staff (2 LMGs)

1 Infantry Platoon (9 LMGs)

1 Pioneer Platoon (1 37mm PAK 36, 6 flamethrowers and 13 LMGs)

1 Panzerjäger Platoon (3 75mm PAK 40 and 4 LMGs)

1 Infantry Gun Section (2 75mm leIG)

1 Half-Track Gun Section (8 LMGs and 6 75mm guns)

1 (mot) Light Reconnaissance Supply Column (3 LMGs)

On 1 July 1943 the organization of the armored portion of the division and its panzer inventory were as follows:

18th Panzer Battalion

1 Panzer Staff Company

1 Medium Panzer Company

3 Light Panzer Companies

Total tanks available:

PzMk II	5
PzMk III (kz)	10
PzMk III (75)	20
PzMk IV (kz)	5
PzMk IV (lg)	29
PzBefWg	3

On 29 September 1943 it was disbanded. The division staff, artillery regiment, signals battalion, reconnaissance battalion and panzerjäger battalion were used to build the 18th Artillery Division. The 18th Panzer Battalion became the 504th Panzer Battalion.

19th Panzer Division

Formed on 1 November 1940 from the 19th Infantry Division. It had:

19th Schützen Brigade

1/, 2/73rd Schützen Regiment (from 2/, 3/73rd Infantry Regiment)

1/, 2/74th Schützen Regiment (from 2/, 3/74th Infantry Regiment)

19th Motorcycle Battalion (from 1/73rd Infantry Regiment)

1/, 2/, 3/27th Panzer Regiment (from 10th, 11th and 25th Ersatz Panzer Battalions)

1/, 2/, 3/19th Artillery Regiment (from 19th Artillery Regiment, 3/19th from 446th Artillery Battalion)

19th Panzerjäger Battalion

19th Pioneer Battalion

19th Signals Battalion

19th Divisional Support Units

On 22 June 1941 the organization of the armored portion of the division and its panzer inventory were as follows:

1/, 2/, 3/27th Panzer Regiment

1 Regimental Staff Signals Platoon

1 Regimental Staff Light Panzer Platoon

Each Battalion had

1 Panzer Staff Company

1 Medium Panzer Company

2 Light Panzer Companies

Total tanks available:

PzMk I	42
PzMk II	35
38 (t)	110
PzMk IV (kz)	30
38 (t) PzBefWg	11

By 25 August 1941 the division's tank inventory was reduced to:

PzMk I	6 operational
PzMk II	20
PzMk III	57
PzMk IV	9
PzBefWg	10

On 10 August 1941 the 3/27th Panzer Regiment was disbanded. On 31 March 1942 the 1/27th Panzer Regiment was disbanded, leaving only the 2/27th Panzer Regiment with the division, which was then renamed the 1/27th Panzer Regiment. On 27 March 1943 the 138th Panzer Battalion was assigned, and in October 1943 became the 2/27th Panzer Regiment.

On 156 July 1942 the organization of the armored portion of the division and its panzer inventory were as follows:

1/27th Panzer Regiment

1 Regimental Staff Signals Platoon

1 Regimental Staff Light Panzer Platoon

Each Battalion had
1 Panzer Staff Company
1 Medium Panzer Company
3 Light Panzer Companies
Total tanks available:
PzMk II   6
38 (t)   35
PzMk III (50 kz) 12
PzMk IV (kz)   4

By 1 July 1943 the organization and inventory had been revised to:

1/, 2/27th Panzer Regiment
1 Regimental Staff Signals Platoon
1 Regimental Staff Light Panzer Platoon
1st Battalion
1 Panzer Staff Company
2 Medium Panzer Companies
1 Light Panzer Company
2nd Battalion
1 Panzer Staff Company
2 Medium Panzer Companies
2 Light Panzer Companies
Total tanks available:
PzMk II   2
PzMk III (kz)   5
PzMk III (lg)   22
PzMk III (75)   11
PzMk IV (kz)   2
PzMk IV (lg)   36
PzBefWg   3

The 19th Reconnaissance and the 19th Motorcycle Battalions were formed on 1 November 1940. The 19th Motorcycle Battalion was disbanded on 14 August 1941, and absorbed by the 19th Panzer Reconnaissance Battalion. The 19th Panzer Reconnaissance Battalion was redesignated as the 19th Motorcycle Battalion on 1 May 1942 and on 24 March 1943 it again became the 19th Panzer Reconnaissance Battalion. In addition, the 272nd Army Flak Battalion was assigned to the division. The division then had:

1/, 2/27th Panzer Regiment
1/, 2/73rd Grenadier Regiment
1/, 2/74th Grenadier Regiment
1/, 2/27th Panzer Regiment
19th Panzer Reconnaissance Battalion
1/, 2/, 3/19th Panzer Artillery Regiment
272nd Army Flak Battalion
19th Panzerjäger Battalion
19th Pioneer Battalion
19th Signals Battalion
19th Divisional Support Units

During 1943 the 2/27th Panzer Regiment contained two companies of Panzer PzMk III and two of PzMk IV tanks. The PzMk III were steadily replaced by PzMk IV tanks during the year. The panzergrenadier regiments had no Flak companies and no half-tracks. The 19th Panzer Artillery Regiment contained two (motZ) 105mm leFH Battalions, with a total of five batteries, a mixed heavy battalion (150mm sFH and 100mm K18), and the 19th Panzer (mot) Observation Battalion. Later in 1943 OKH records show the division to be organized and equipped as follows:

Division Staff
1 Division Staff (2 LMGs)
19th (mot) Mapping Detachment
27th Panzer Regiment
Regimental Staff
1 Signals Platoon
1 Regimental Band
1st Battalion
1 Regimental Staff and Staff Company
3 Panzer Companies (22 PzMk III ea; changed to PzMk IV by June)
1 Panzer Company (22 PzMk IV ea)
1 Panzer Maintenance Company (added on 26 June 1943)
2nd Battalion (detached on 14 June 1943)
1 Regimental Staff and Staff Company
3 Panzer Companies (22 PzMk IV tanks)
1 Panzer Maintenance Company (disbanded on 26 June 1943)
73rd Panzergrenadier Regiment
1 Regimental Staff
1 Regimental Band
1 (mot) Regimental Staff Company
1 Signals Platoon
1 Panzerjäger Platoon (3 50mm PAK 38 and 3 LMGs)
1 Motorcycle Platoon (6 LMGs)
1st and 2nd (mot) Battalions, each with
3 (mot) Companies (4 HMGs, 18 LMGs, 2 80mm mortars and 3 PzBu39 ea)
1 (mot) Heavy Company
1 Pioneer Platoon (4 LMGs)
1 Panzerjäger Platoon (3 LMGs and 3 50mm PAK 38)
1 Infantry Gun Platoon (4 75mm leIG)
1 Panzerjäger Platoon (3 LMGs and 3 sPzBu 41)
1 (mot) Infantry Gun Company (4 150mm sIG)
74th Panzergrenadier Regiment
same as 73rd Panzergrenadier Regiment
19th Panzerjäger Battalion
1 (motZ) Panzerjäger Company (75mm PAK 40)
1 Self-Propelled Panzerjäger Company (14 75mm PAK 40 and 14 LMGs ea)

19th Reconnaissance Battalion (early 1943 organization)

1 Armored Car Company (24 LMGs and 18 20mm guns)
3 Motorcycle Companies (2 80mm mortars, 4 HMGs, 18 LMGs and 3 PzBu39 ea)
1 (mot) Heavy Reconnaissance Company
  1 Pioneer Platoon (4 LMGs)
  1 Infantry Gun Section (4 75mm leIG)
  1 Panzerjäger Platoon (3 LMGs and 3 75mm PAK 40)
  1 Panzerjäger Platoon (3 LMGs and 3 sPzBu 41)
1 (mot) Light Reconnaissance Supply Column (3 LMGs)

19th Panzer Artillery Regiment

1 Regimental Staff
1 Staff Battery (2 LMGs)

1st and 2nd Battalions, each with
1 Battalion Staff
1 Battalion Staff Battery (6 LMGs)
3 (mot) Batteries (3 105mm leFH and 2 LMGs ea)

3rd (mot) Battalion
1 Battalion Staff
1 Battalion Staff Battery (6 LMGs)
2 (mot) Batteries (3 150mm sFH and 2 LMGs ea)
1 (mot) Battery (3 100mm K 18 guns and 2 LMGs)

19th (mot) Observation Battery (2 LMGs)

272nd Army Flak Battalion

1 Staff and (mot) Staff Battery (1 LMG)
1st–2nd (motZ) Heavy Flak Batteries (4 88mm, 3 20mm and 2 LMGs ea)
3rd (motZ) Light Flak Battery (9 20mm, 2 quad 20mm and 2 LMGs)
1 (mot) Light (20 ton) Flak Supply Column

19th Panzer Pioneer Battalion

1 Staff (2 LMGs)
1 (half-track) Pioneer Company (25 LMGs, 2 80mm mortars and 3 PzBu39)
2 (mot) Pioneer Companies (18 LMGs, 2 80mm mortars and 3 PzBu39 ea)
1 Brüko K Bridging Column (3 LMGs)
1 (mot) Light Pioneer Supply Column (2 LMGs)

19th Panzer Signals Battalion

1 Panzer Telephone Company (6 LMGs)
1 Panzer Radio Company (16 LMGs)
1 (mot) Light Signals Supply Column (1 LMG)

19th Feldersatz Battalion

4 Companies

19th Supply Troop

1/, 2/, 3/19th (mot) (90 ton) Transportation Company (3 LMGs ea)
4/, 5/, 6/19th (mot) (120 ton) Transportation Company (4 LMGs ea)
19th (mot) Supply Company (6 LMGs)

Truck Park

1–3/19th (mot) Maintenance Companies (4 LMGs ea)

Other

19th (mot) Bakery Company
19th (mot) Butcher Company
19th (mot) Administration Platoon
1/, 2/19th (mot) Medical Companies (2 LMGs ea)
1/, 2/, 3/19th Ambulances
19th (mot) Military Police Troop (2 LMGs)
19th (mot) Field Post Office

On 14 June 1943 the 1/27th Panzer Regiment was renumbered as the 2/27th, and the original 1/27th was assigned as an Army Heavy Tank Troop. On 10 July 1943 the reconnaissance battalion was reorganized as follows:

19th Reconnaissance Battalion

1 Armored Car Company (24 LMGs and 18 20mm guns)
1 Armored Car (half-track) Company (25 LMGs and 16 20mm guns)
1 (half-track) Reconnaissance Company (2 80mm mortars, 3 37mm PAK 36, 4 HMGs and 56 LMGs)
1 Motorcycle Company (2 80mm mortars, 4 HMGs, 18 LMGs and 3 PzBu39)
1 (half-track) Heavy Reconnaissance Company
  1 Staff (2 LMGs)
  1 Infantry Platoon (9 LMGs)
  1 Pioneer Platoon (1 37mm PAK 36, 6 flamethrowers and 13 LMGs)
  1 Panzerjäger Platoon (3 75mm PAK 40 and 4 LMGs)
  1 Infantry Gun Section (2 75mm leIG)
  1 Half-Track Gun Section (8 LMGs and 6 75mm guns)
1 (mot) Light Reconnaissance Supply Column (3 LMGs)

On 9 August 1943 the OKH ordered twelve Wespe self-propelled 105mm guns sent to the division. On 14 August 1943 the artillery regiment reorganized itself with two standard 105mm leFH howitzer battalions and a self-propelled battalion that was as follows:

1 Battalion Staff and Staff Battery (6 LMGs)
2 Self-Propelled Batteries (6 105mm leFH SdKfz 124 Wespe and 4 LMGs ea)
1 Self-Propelled Battery (6 150mm sFH SdKfz 165 Hummel and 4 LMGs)

On 30 March 1944 the 1/27th Panzer Regiment was equipped with Panther tanks. The 2/1st Panzer Regiment continued to be equipped with Panzer PzMk IV tanks. In June 1944 the division was sent to the Netherlands where it re-formed as a Type 44 Panzer Division. In August the organization of the armored portion of the division and its panzer inventory were as follows: *(see over)*

1/, 2/27th Panzer Regiment
  1 Panzer Staff Company
  1st Battalion
    1 Panzer Staff Company
    4 Medium Panzer Companies (PzMk V)
  2nd Battalion
    1 Panzer Staff Company
    4 Medium Panzer Companies (PzMk IV)

Total tanks available:

PzMk IV (lg)	81
PzMk V	79
FlakpzIV (37)	8

20th Panzer Division

Formed on 15 October 1940 with forces drawn from the 19th Infantry Division when it was reorganized into the 19th Panzer Division. On 1 May 1941 the division had:

20th Schützen Brigade
  1/, 2/59th Schützen Regiment (from 1/, 3/59th Infantry Regiment)
  1/, 2/112th Schützen Regiment (from 3/74th and 2/59th Infantry Regiment)
  20th Motorcycle Battalion (from 3/115th Infantry Regiment)
  1/, 2/, 3/21st Panzer Regiment (from 7th and 35th Panzer Ersatz Battalions)
  1/, 2/, 3/92nd Artillery Regiment (from 3/19th, 3/697th and 648th Heavy Artillery Battalion)
  92nd Panzerjäger Battalion
  92nd Pioneer Battalion
  92nd Signals Battalion
  92nd Divisional Support Units

On 22 June 1941 the organization of the armored portion of the division and its panzer inventory were as follows:

1/, 2/, 3/21st Panzer Regiment
  1 Regimental Staff Signals Platoon
  1 Regimental Staff Light Panzer Platoon
  Each Battalion had
    1 Panzer Staff Company
    1 Medium Panzer Company
    2 Light Panzer Companies
  Total tanks available:

PzMk I	44
PzMk II	31
38 (t)	121
PzMk IV (kz)	31
38 (t) cmd	2

By 25 August 1941 the operational tank inventory had fallen to:

PzMk I	4
PzMk II	19
PzMk III	52
PzMk IV	11
PzBefWg	2

In early 1942 the 1/, 2/21st Panzer Regiment, the 2/112th Schützen Regiment, and the 92nd Reconnaissance Battalions were disbanded. The Staff/21st Panzer Regiment became the Staff/21st Panzer Brigade. The division then had only the 3/21st Panzer Regiment. On 20 April 1943 the Staff/, 2/112th Schützen Regiment were reformed with the 890th (mot) Grenadier Regiment. On 30 June 1942 the organization of the armored portion of the division and its panzer inventory were as follows:

3/21st Panzer Regiment
  1 Regimental Staff Signals Platoon
  1 Regimental Staff Light Panzer Platoon
  Each Battalion had
    1 Panzer Staff Company
    1 Medium Panzer Company
    2 Light Panzer Companies
  Total tanks available:

PzMk II	8
38 (t)	39
PzMk III (37)	20
PzMk IV (kz)	13
PzBefWg	7

In 1943 the 3/21st Panzer Regiment had three companies of PzMk III and one company of PzMk IV tanks. The panzergrenadier regiments had no Flak companies and no half-tracks. The 2/92nd Panzer Artillery Regiment was now (motZ) and equipped with three batteries, and it contained a 10th (motZ) Flak Battery and the 92nd Panzer (mot) Observation Battery. The division had no army Flak battery. OKH records show that the division was organized and equipped as follows during early 1943.

Division Staff
  1 Division Staff (2 LMGs)
  92nd(mot) Mapping Detachment

1/21st Panzer Regiment

Regimental Staff
1 Signals Platoon
1 Regimental Band

1st Battalion

1 Regimental Staff and Staff Company (flame panzer PzMk III tanks added on 14 June 1943)
3 Panzer Companies (22 PzMk III ea; changed to PzMk IV by June)
1 Panzer Company (22 PzMk IV ea)
1 Panzer Maintenance Company

59th Panzergrenadier Regiment

1 Regimental Staff
1 Regimental Band
1 (mot) Regimental Staff Company
 1 Signals Platoon
 1 Panzerjäger Platoon (3 50mm PAK 38 and 3 LMGs)
 1 Motorcycle Platoon (6 LMGs)

1st and 2nd (mot) Battalion, each with

3 (mot) Companies (4 HMGs, 18 LMGs, 2 80mm mortars and 3 PzBu39 ea)
1 (mot) Heavy Company
 1 Pioneer Platoon (4 LMGs)
 1 Panzerjäger Platoon (3 LMGs and 3 50mm PAK 38)
 1 Infantry Gun Platoon (4 75mm leIG)
 1 Panzerjäger Platoon (3 LMGs and 3 sPzBu 41)
1 (mot) Infantry Gun Company (4 150mm sIG)

112th Panzergrenadier Regiment

same as 59th Panzergrenadier Regiment

92nd Panzerjäger Battalion

1 (motZ) Panzerjäger Company (12 75mm PAK 40 and 12 LMGs)
2 Self-Propelled Panzerjäger Companies (14 75mm PAK 40 and 14 LMGs ea)
1 Self-Propelled Flak Company (8 20mm, 2 quad 20mm and 4 LMGs)

92nd Reconnaissance Battalion

1 Armored Car Company (24 LMGs and 18 20mm guns)
3 Motorcycle Companies (2 80mm mortars, 4 HMGs, 18 LMGs and PzBu39 ea)
1 (mot) Heavy Reconnaissance Company
 1 Pioneer Platoon (4 LMGs)
 1 Infantry Gun Section (4 75mm leIG)
 1 Panzerjäger Platoon (3 LMGs and 3 75mm PAK 40)
 1 Panzerjäger Platoon (3 LMGs and 3 sPzBu 41)
1 (mot) Light Reconnaissance Supply Column (3 LMGs)

92nd Panzer Artillery Regiment

1 Regimental Staff
1 Staff Battery (2 LMGs)

1st and 2nd Battalions, each with

1 Battalion Staff

1 Battalion Staff Battery (6 LMGs)
3 (mot) Batteries (3 105mm leFH and 2 LMGs ea)

3rd (mot) Battalion

1 Battalion Staff
1 Battalion Staff Battery (6 LMGs)
2 (mot) Batteries (3 150mm sFH and 2 LMGs ea)
1 (mot) Battery (3 100mm K 18 guns and 2 LMGs)
10/92nd (mot) Flak Battery (12 20mm and 2 LMGs)

92nd (mot) Observation Battery (2 LMGs)

92nd Panzer Pioneer Battalion

1 Staff (2 LMGs)
1 (half-track) Pioneer Company (25 LMGs, 2 80mm mortars and 3 PzBu39)
1 (mot) Pioneer Companies (18 LMGs, 2 80mm mortars and 3 PzBu39 ea)
1 Brüko K Bridging Column (3 LMGs)
1 (mot) Light Pioneer Supply Column (2 LMGs)

92nd Panzer Signals Battalion

1 Panzer Telephone Company (6 LMGs)
1 Panzer Radio Company (16 LMGs)
1 (mot) Light Signals Supply Column (1 LMG)

92nd Feldersatz Battalion

4 Companies

92nd Supply Troop

1/, 2/, 3/92nd (mot) (90 ton) Transportation Company (3 LMGs ea)
4/, 5/, 6/92nd (mot) (120 ton) Transportation Company (4 LMGs ea)
92nd (mot) Supply Company (6 LMGs)

Truck Park

1–3/92nd (mot) Maintenance Companies (4 LMGs ea)
92nd (mot) Heavy (75 ton) Replacement Column (4 LMGs) (added 22 Sept. 1943)

Other

92nd (mot) Bakery Company
92nd (mot) Butcher Company
92nd (mot) Administration Platoon
1/, 2/92nd (mot) Medical Companies (2 LMGs ea)
1/, 2/, 3/92nd Ambulances
92nd (mot) Military Police Troop (2 LMGs)
92nd (mot) Field Post Office

On 14 June 1943 the 3/21st Panzer Regiment was redesignated as the 21st Panzer Battalion. On 1 July 1943 the organization of the armored portion of the division and its panzer inventory were as follows:

21st Panzer Battalion
1 Panzer Staff Company
1 Medium Panzer Company
2 Light Panzer Companies
Total tanks available:

38 (t)	9
PzMk III (kz)	2
PzMk III (lg)	10

PzMk III (75)   5
PzMk IV (kz)   9
PzMk IV (lg)   40
PzBefWg   7

On 10 July 1943 the reconnaissance battalion was re-organized as follows:

20th Reconnaissance Battalion

1 Armored Car Company (24 LMGs and 18 20mm guns)
1 Armored Car (half-track) Company (25 LMGs and 16 20mm guns)
1 (half-track) Reconnaissance Company (2 80mm mortars, 3 37mm PAK 36, 4 HMGs and 56 LMGs)
1 Motorcycle Company (2 80mm mortars, 4 HMGs, 18 LMGs and 3 PzBu39)
1 (half-track) Heavy Reconnaissance Company
1 Staff (2 LMGs)
1 Infantry Platoon (9 LMGs)
1 Pioneer Platoon (1 37mm PAK 36, 6 flamethrowers and 13 LMGs)
1 Panzerjäger Platoon (3 75mm PAK 40 and 4 LMGs)
1 Infantry Gun Section (2 75mm leIG)
1 Half-Track Gun Section (8 LMGs and 6 75mm guns)

1 (mot) Light Reconnaissance Supply Column (3 LMGs)

On 9 August 1943 the OKH ordered twelve Wespe self-propelled 105mm guns sent to the division. On 14 August 1943 the artillery regiment organized a self-propelled battalion as follows:

1 Battalion Staff and Staff Battery (6 LMGs)
2 Self-Propelled Batteries (6 105mm leFH SdKfz 124 Wespe and 4 LMGs ea)
1 Self-Propelled Battery (6 150mm sFH SdKfz 165 Hummel and 4 LMGs

In 1944, during the battles around Kholm and Lublin, the division was badly mauled and reduced to the strength of a Kampfgruppe. Other portions were pulled out of the line and reorganized. The reorganized division fought on the Rumanian front. The 21st Panzer Regiment was re-formed when the 2101st Panzer Battalion became the 2/21st Panzer Regiment. The 21st Panzer Battalion became the 1/21st Panzer Regiment. The Staff/21st Panzer Regiment was formed from the Staff/101st Panzer Brigade. The division surrendered to the Allies on 5/8/45.

21st Panzer Division

Formed on 1 August 1941 in Africa from the 5th Light Division. The division had:

1/, 2/104th Schützen Regiment (from 15th Pz.Div)
15th Motorcycle Battalion (from 15th Pz.Div)
1/, 2/5th Panzer Regiment
1/, 2/, 3/155th Artillery Regiment (1st Bn from 864th Artillery Battalion, 2nd Bn from 1/75th Artillery Regiment and 3rd Battalion from 911th Heavy Artillery Battalion)
3rd Reconnaissance Battalion
39th Panzerjäger Battalion
200th Signals Battalion
200th Divisional Support Units

Both battalions of the 104th Regiment were transferred to the 5th Light Division when it was converted into the 21st Panzer Division. During June/July 1941 the division was organized and equipped as follows:

21st Panzer Division
Headquarters
  200 (mot) Mapping Detachment
  200th (mot) Communication Section
  200th Construction Section

5th Panzer Regiment
Headquarters
  1 Armored HQ Company
  1 Light Armored Platoon
  1 Regimental Band
Support Units
  1 Armored Maintenance Company
1st and 2nd Battalions, each with
  1 Armored HQ Company
  1 Light Armored Platoon
  1 Medium Armored Company
  2 Light Armored Companies
104th Schützen Regiment
  1 (mot) HQ Company
    1 (mot) Signals Platoon
    1 Motorcycle Platoon
    (2nd motorcycle platoon added later)
  1 Panzerjäger Platoon (3 50mm PAK 38)
  1 Regimental Band
2nd Machine Gun Battalion
  (mot) Battalion HQ Company with
    2 Motorcycle Platoons (4 LMGs ea)
    1 Signals Platoon
  3 (mot) Machine Gun Companies (12 HMGs, 3 50mm mortars and 3 PzBu39 ea)

1 (mot) Support Company, with
  1 Panzerjäger Platoon (3 37mm PAK 36, 3 50mm PAK 38)
  1 Mortar Platoon (6 80mm mortars)
Support Companies reorganized as follows on 27 Aug. 1941:
  1 (mot) Support Company, with
    1 Pioneer Platoon (3 LMGs)
    1 Panzerjäger Platoon (1 28mm PzBu41 and 2 50mm PAK 38)
    1 Panzerjäger Platoon (3 37mm PAK 36 and 1 LMG)
    1 Mortar Platoon (6 80mm mortars)

8th Machine Gun Battalion
1 (mot) HQ Company, with
  1 Signals Platoon
  2 Motorcycle Platoons (4 LMGs ea)
3 (mot) Machine Gun Companies (12 HMGs, 3 50mm mortars and 3 PzBu39 ea)
1 (mot) Support Company, with
  1 Panzerjäger Platoon (3 37mm PAK 36, 3 50mm PAK 38)
  1 Mortar Platoon (6 80mm mortars)
Support Companies reorganized as follows on 27 Aug. 1941:
  1 (mot) Support Company, with
    1 Pioneer Platoon (3 LMGs)
    1 Panzerjäger Platoon (1 28mm PzBu39 41 and 2 50mm PAK 38)
    1 Panzerjäger Platoon (3 37mm PAK 36 and 1 LMG)
    1 Mortar Platoon (6 80mm mortars)
1 (mot) Panzerjäger Company (9 50mm PAK 38 and 3 LMGs)

155th Artillery Regiment (formed in Aug.)
1/155th Artillery Regiment, with
  1 (mot) HQ Company
  3 (mot) Batteries (4 105mm leFH 18 and 2 LMGs ea)
2/155th Artillery Regiment
  1 (mot) Signals Platoon
  1 (mot) Calibration Detachment
  3 Batteries (4 105mm leFH 18 and 2 LMGs ea)
3/155th Artillery Regiment
  1 (mot) HQ Company
  2 (mot) Batteries (4 150mm sFH and 2 LMGs ea)
  1 (mot) Battery (4 100 K18 guns and 2 LMGs)

3rd Reconnaissance Battalion
1 (mot) Signals Platoon
1 Light (mot) Armored Supply Column
1 Armored Car Company (19 37mm guns and 41 LMGs
1 Motorcycle Company (3 50mm mortars, 2 HMGs and 18 LMGs)
1 (mot) Support Company, with
  1 Pioneer Platoon (3 LMGs)
  1 Panzerjäger Platoon (3 37mm PAK 36, 2 50mm PAK 38 and 1 LMG) (50mm PAK 38 later formed into separate platoon)

1 Infantry Support Platoon (2 75mm leIG)
200th Feldersatz Battalion
4 Companies (no heavy weapons)
200th Pioneer Battalion
3 (mot) Pioneer Companies (9 LMGs ea)
200th Signals Battalion
1 Armored Radio Company
1 Armored Signals Company
1 Light (mot) Signals Supply Column
39th Panzerjäger Battalion
1 (mot) Signals Platoon
3 (mot) Companies (9 37mm PAK 36 and 6 LMGs ea)
Service Forces
3/, 4/, 5/, 6/, 7/, 8/, 12/200th Light (mot) Supply Columns
1/, 2/, 10/, 11/Heavy (mot) Supply Columns
9/200th Heavy (mot) POL Supply Column
1/200th (mot) Maintenance Company
2/, 3/200th (mot) Motor Vehicle Repair Companies
200th (mot) Supply Company
200th (mot) Panzer Replacement Transport Column
200th (later 579th) (mot) "LW" Company
589th Light Filtration Column (may have been deleted)
Food Service
200th (mot) Bakery Company
200th (mot) Butcher Company
200th Divisional Quartermaster Detachment
Medical
1/82nd and 2/200th (mot) Medical Companies
200th (mot) Field Hospital
1/, 2/200th Ambulance Columns
Other
309th (mot) Military Police Detachment
735th (mot) Field Post Office

On 18 November 1941 the division was organized and equipped as follows:

21st Panzer Division
Headquarters
  200 (mot) Mapping Detachment
  200th (mot) Communication Section
  200th Construction Section
5th Panzer Regiment
Headquarters
  1 Armored HQ Company
  1 Light Armored Platoon
  1 Regimental Band
Support Units
  1 Armored Maintenance Company
1st and 2nd Battalions, each with
  1 Armored HQ Company
  1 Light Armored Platoon

1 Medium Armored Company

3 Light Armored Companies

Total (as of 18 Nov.): 35 Pz II, 58 Pz III and 17 Pz IV

104th Schützen Regiment

1 (mot) HQ Company

  1 (mot) Signals Platoon

  1 Motorcycle Platoon

  (2nd motorcycle platoon added later)

  1 Panzerjäger Platoon (3 50mm PAK 38)

  1 Regimental Band

2nd Machine Gun Battalion

(mot) Battalion HQ Company with

  2 Motorcycle Platoons

3 (mot) Machine Gun Companies

1 (mot) Support Company, with

  1 Panzerjäger Platoon (3 37mm PAK36 and 3 50mm PAK38)

  1 Mortar Platoon (6 80mm mortars)

1 (mot) Support Company, with

  1 Pioneer Platoon

  1 Panzerjäger Platoon (1 28mm PzBu41 and 2 50mm PAK 38)

  1 Panzerjäger Platoon (3 37mm PAK 36)

  1 Mortar Platoon

8th Machine Gun Battalion

1 (mot) HQ Company, with

  1 Signals Platoon

  2 Motorcycle Platoons

3 (mot) Machine Gun Companies

1 (mot) Support Company, with

  1 Panzerjäger Platoon (3 37mm PAK36 and 3 50mm PAK38)

  1 Mortar Platoon

1 (mot) Support Company

  1 Pioneer Platoon

  1 Panzerjäger Platoon (1 28mm PzBu41 and 2 50mm PAK38)

  1 Panzerjäger Platoon (3 37mm PAK36)

  1 Mortar Platoon

1 (mot) Panzerjäger Company (9 50mm PAK 38)

155th Artillery Regiment

1/155th Artillery Regiment, with

  1 (mot) HQ Company

  3 (mot) Batteries (4 105mm leFH 18 ea)

2/155th Artillery Regiment

  1 (mot) Signals Platoon

  1 (mot) Calibration Detachment

  3 Batteries (4 105mm leFH 18 ea)

3/155th Artillery Regiment

  1 (mot) HQ Company

  2 (mot) Batteries (4 150mm sFH ea)

  1 (mot) Battery (4 100 K18 guns)

3rd Reconnaissance Battalion

1 (mot) Signals Platoon

1 Light (mot) Armored Supply Column

1 Armored Car Company (19 armored cars)

1 Motorcycle Company

1 (mot) Support Company, with

  1 Pioneer Platoon

  1 Panzerjäger Platoon (3 37mm PAK36 and 2 50mm PAK38)

  1 Infantry Support Platoon (2 75mm leIG)

200th Feldersatz Battalion

4 Companies (no heavy weapons)

200th Pioneer Battalion

3 (mot) Pioneer Companies

200th Signals Battalion

1 Armored Radio Company

1 Armored Signals Company

1 Light (mot) Signals Supply Column

39th Panzerjäger Battalion

1 (mot) Signals Platoon

3 (mot) Companies (9 37mm PAK 36 ea)

Service Forces

3/, 4/, 5/, 6/, 7/, 8/, 12/200th Light (mot) Supply Columns

1/, 2/, 10/, 11/Heavy (mot) Supply Columns

9/200th Heavy (mot) POL Supply Column

1/200th (mot) Maintenance Company

2/, 3/200th (mot) Motor Vehicle Repair Companies

200th (mot) Supply Company

200th (mot) Panzer Replacement Column

200th (later 579th) (mot) "LW" Company

589th Light Filtration Column (may have been deleted)

Food Service

200th (mot) Bakery Company

200th (mot) Butcher Company

200th Divisional Quartermaster Detachment

Medical

1/82nd and 2/200th (mot) Medical Companies

200th (mot) Field Hospital

1/, 2/200th Ambulance Columns

Other

309th (mot) Military Police Detachment

735th (mot) Field Post Office

The "many weapons—few men" organization was also applied to the 21st Panzer Division in February 1942. The proposed organization for it was as follows:

21st Panzer Division

Headquarters

  200 (mot) Mapping Detachment

  200th (mot) Communication Section

5th Panzer Regiment

Headquarters

  1 Armored HQ Company

  2 Light Armored Platoons

1 Regimental Band

Support Units

1 Armored Maintenance Company

1st and 2nd Battalions, each with

1 Armored HQ Company

1 Light Armored Platoon

1 Medium Armored Company

3 Light Armored Companies

1 Armored Reserve Detachment

104th Schützen Regiment

1 (mot) HQ Company

1 (mot) Signals Platoon

1 Motorcycle Platoon

1 Panzerjäger Platoon (3 50mm PAK 38)

1 Regimental Band

1st, 2nd and 3rd Battalions

3 (mot) Infantry Companies (13 MP, 18 LMGs, 2 HMGs, 3 80mm mortars, 3 28mm PzBu41 and 6 50mm PAK 38 ea)

1 Pioneer Company (13 MP, 18 LMGs, 2 HMGs, 3 80mm mortars, 3 28mm PzBu41 and 6 50mm PAK 38)

1 (mot) Heavy Infantry Gun Company (3 150mm self-propelled guns)

155th Artillery Regiment

HQ Company

1 (mot) HQ Company

1st and 2nd Battalions, each with

1 (mot) HQ Company

3 (mot) Batteries (4 105mm leFH 18 and 2 LMGs ea)

3rd Battalion, with

1 (mot) HQ Company

3 (mot) Batteries (4 150mm leFH 18 and 2 LMGs ea)

1 (mot) Observation Company

3rd Reconnaissance Battalion

1 (mot) Signals Platoon (2 LMGs)

2 Armored Car Companies

1 Armored Car Company (25 half-tracks, 13 MP, 18 LMGs, 2 HMGs, 3 80mm mortars, 3 28mm PzBu41 and 6 50mm PAK 38)

1 Light Battery

1 (mot) Support Company, with

1 Signals Platoon

1 Pioneer Platoon

1 Panzerjäger Platoon

200th Feldersatz Battalion

4 Companies (no heavy weapons)

200th Panzerjäger Battalion

1 (mot) Signals Platoon

3 (mot) Companies (9 50mm self-propelled)

200th Pioneer Battalion

3 (mot) Companies (13 MP, 18 LMGs, 2 HMGs, 3 80mm mortars, 3 28mm PzBu41 and 6 50mm PAK 38)

1 Light (mot) Pioneer Supply Column

200th Signals Battalion

6 Signals Troops

Service Forces

3/, 4/, 5/, 6/, 7/, 8/, 12/200th Light (mot) Supply Columns

1/, 2/, 10/, 11/Heavy (mot) Supply Columns

9/200th Heavy (mot) POL Supply Column

1/200th (mot) Maintenance Company

2/, 3/200th (mot) Motor Vehicle Repair Companies

200th (mot) Supply Company

200th (mot) Panzer Replacement Column

579th (mot) "LW" Company

589th Light Filtration Column

Food Service

200th (mot) Bakery Company

200th (mot) Butcher Company

200th Divisional Quartermaster Detachment

Medical

1/, 2/200th (mot) Medical Companies

200th (mot) Field Hospital

1/, 2/200th Ambulance Columns

Other

309th (mot) Military Police Detachment

735th (mot) Field Post Office

The new organization for the 21st Panzer Division was ordered to be implemented on 10 March. The 2nd Machine Gun Battalion would become the 3/115th Panzergrenadier Regiment, and the 8th Machine Gun and the 15th Motorcycle Battalions became the 1/, 2/104th Panzergrenadier Regiment, respectively. The structure was as follows:

21st Panzer Division

Headquarters

Panzer Staff Staffel

200th (mot) Mapping Detachment

200th Motorcycle Messenger Platoon

5th Panzer Regiment

Headquarters

1 Armored HQ Company

2 Light Armored Platoons

1 Regimental Band

Support Units

1 Armored Maintenance Company

1st and 2nd Battalions, each with

1 Armored HQ Company

1 Light Armored Platoon

1 Medium Armored Company

3 Light Armored Companies

1 Panzer Replacement Platoon

104th Schützen Regiment

1 (mot) HQ Company

1 (mot) Signals Platoon

1 (mot) Pioneer Platoon (3 LMGs)
1 Motorcycle Messenger Platoon
1 Panzerjäger Platoon (3 50mm PAK 38 and 2 LMGS)

1st, 2nd and 3rd Battalions, each with
4 (mot) Infantry Companies (18 LMGs, 2 HMGs, 3 80mm mortars, 3 28mm PzBu41 and 3 50mm PAK 38 ea)

1 (mot) Infantry Gun Company
(2 150mm sIG and 4 75mm leIG)

1 (mot) Pioneer Company
(3 PzBu39, 3 50mm PAK 38, 19 LMGs and 3 80mm mortars)

155th Artillery Regiment
1 (mot) Regimental Staff Battery
1/155th Artillery Regiment, with
1 (mot) Staff Battery
3 (mot) Batteries (4 105mm leFH 18 and 2 LMGs ea)
2/155th Artillery Regiment
1 (mot) Signals Platoon
1 (mot) Calibration Detachment
3 Batteries (4 105mm leFH 18 and 2 LMGs ea)
3/155th Artillery Regiment
1 (mot) HQ Company
2 (mot) Batteries (4 150mm sFH and 2 LMGs ea)
1 (mot) Battery (4 100 K18 guns and 2 LMGs)
1 (mot) Heavy Munitions Supply Column (60t)
1 (mot) Artillery Observation Battery

3rd Reconnaissance Battalion
1 Armored Car Company (20 37mm guns and 40 LMGs)
1 (mot) Reconnaissance Company (18 LMGs, 2 HMGs, 3 28mm PzBu41 and 4 50mm PAK 38)
1 (mot) Support Company, with
1 Signals Platoon
1 Pioneer Platoon (3 LMGs)
1 Panzerjäger Platoon (3 50mm PAK 38 and 1 28mm PzBu41)
1 (mot) Battery (4 105mm leFH and 2 LMGs)
1 Reconnaissance Supply Column

200th Feldersatz Battalion
4 Companies (no heavy weapons)

200th Pioneer Battalion
3 (mot) Pioneer Companies (9 LMGs, 3 PzBu39 and 2 50mm PAK 38)
1 (mot) Light Supply Column

200th Signals Battalion
1 Armored Radio Company
1 Armored Signals Company
1 Light (mot) Signals Supply Column

39th Panzerjäger Battalion
1 (mot) Signals Platoon
2 (mot) Companies (9 50mm PAK 38 and 6 LMGs ea)
1 Self-Propelled (6 76.2mm (r) and 6 LMGs)

Service Forces
3/, 4/, 5/, 6/, 7/, 8/, 12/200th Light (mot) Supply Columns
1/, 2/, 10/, 11/Heavy (mot) Supply Columns
9/200th Heavy (mot) POL Supply Column
1/200th (mot) Maintenance Company
2/, 3/200th (mot) Motor Vehicle Repair Companies
200th (mot) Supply Company
200th (mot) Tank Replacement Transport Column
579th (mot) "LW" Company
589th (mot) Light Water Filtration Column

Food Service
200th (mot) Bakery Company
200th (mot) Butcher Company
200th Divisional Quartermaster Detachment

Medical
1/, 2/200th (mot) Medical Companies
200th (mot) Field Hospital
1/, 2/200th Ambulance Columns

Other
200th (mot) Military Police Detachment
200th (mot) Field Post Office z.b.V.

A message from the AOK Ia dated 10 March 1942 directed equipping the mixed schützen companies with six 50mm PAK 38 guns. Pioneer companies for the schützen regiments were to be formed from the pioneer platoons of the schützen and machine gun companies. The 1/104th Schützen Regiment was to be rebuilt in Germany.

The March organization did not last long, and on 16 April 1942 the division was reorganized as follows:

21st Panzer Division
Headquarters
Panzer Staff Staffel
200th (mot) Mapping Detachment
200th Motorcycle Messenger Platoon

5th Panzer Regiment
unchanged from March 1942

104th Schützen Regiment
unchanged from March 1942

155th Artillery Regiment
unchanged from March 1942

3rd Reconnaissance Battalion
unchanged from March 1942

39th Panzerjäger Battalion
1 (mot) Signals Platoon
1 (mot) Company (6 50mm PAK 38 and 6 LMGs)
1 Self-Propelled Company (6 76.2mm (r) PAK and 6 LMGs)

200th Feldersatz Battalion
4 Companies (no heavy weapons)

200th Pioneer Battalion (at about 50% strength)
3 (mot) Pioneer Companies (9 LMGs, 3 PzBu39 and 3 50mm PAK 38)

1 (mot) Light Supply Column

200th Signals Battalion

unchanged from March 1942

Service Forces

unchanged from March 1942

On 17 January 1942 the 1/104th Schützen Regiment was captured, and it was replaced on 1 April 1942 by the 8th Machine Gun Battalion. At the same time the 15th Motorcycle Battalion became the 3/104th Schützen Regiment. In 1943 the 305th Army Flak Battalion, formerly the 609th Flak Battalion, became the 4/155th Artillery Regiment. On 25 May 1942 the organization of the 5th Panzer Regiment was as follows:

1/, 2/5th Panzer Regiment

  1 Regimental Staff Signals Platoon

  1 Regimental Staff Light Panzer Platoon

  Each Battalion had

    1 Panzer Staff Company

    1 Medium Panzer Company

    3 Light Panzer Companies

  Total tanks available:

    PzMk II   29

    PzMk III (50 kz) 107

    PzMk III (50 lg) 15

    PzMk IV (kz)   19

    PzBefWg   4

On 15 August 1942 the division was once again reorganized and now it contained:

21st Panzer Division

  Headquarters

    Panzer Staff Staffel

    200th (mot) Mapping Detachment

    200th Motorcycle Messenger Platoon

  5th Panzer Regiment (42 officers/1, 274 men)

    Headquarters

      1 Armored HQ Company

      2 Light Armored Platoons

      1 Regimental Band

    Support Units

      1 Armored Maintenance Company

  1st and 2nd Battalions, each with

    1 Armored HQ Company

    1 Medium Armored Company

    3 Light Armored Companies

    1 Panzer Replacement Platoon

  Total tanks: 14 Pz II, 54 Pz III, 33 Pz III (lg), 8 Pz IV, 10 Pz IV (lg) and 2 command vehicles

  104th Schützen Regiment (69 officers/2, 715 men)

    1 (mot) HQ Company

      1 (mot) Signals Platoon

      1 (mot) Pioneer Platoon (3 LMGs)

      1 Motorcycle Messenger Platoon

      1 Panzerjäger Platoon (3 50mm PAK 38 and 2 LMGS)

  1st Battalion

    4 (mot) Infantry Companies (total equipment: 20 LMGs, 14 HMGs, 4 80mm mortars, 0 28mm PzBu41 and 9 50mm PAK 38)

  2nd Battalion

    4 (mot) Infantry Companies (total equipment: 36 LMGs, 6 HMGs, 3 80mm mortars, 0 28mm PzBu41 and 7 50mm PAK 38)

  3rd Battalion

    4 (mot) Infantry Companies (total equipment: 42 LMGs, 7 HMGs, 5 80mm mortars, 0 28mm PzBu41 and 5 50mm PAK 38)

  1 (mot) Infantry Gun Company

    (1 150mm sIG and 3 75mm leIG)

  1 (mot) Pioneer Company)

    (equipment unknown)

  155th Artillery Regiment (83 officers/1, 553 men)

    1 (mot) Regimental Staff Battery

    1/155th Artillery Regiment, with

      1 (mot) Staff Battery

      3 (mot) Batteries (4 105mm leFH 18 and 2 LMGs ea)

    2/155th Artillery Regiment

      1 (mot) Signals Platoon

      1 (mot) Calibration Detachment

      2 Batteries (4 105mm leFH 18 and 2 LMGs ea)

      1 Battery (4 British 25pdrs)

    3/155th Artillery Regiment

      1 (mot) HQ Company

      1 (mot) Battery (4 150mm sFH and 2 LMGs)

      1 (mot) Battery (3 150mm sFH and 2 LMGs)

      1 (mot) Battery (4 100 K18 guns and 2 LMGs)

    1 (mot) Heavy Munitions Supply Column (60t)

    155th (mot) Artillery Observation Battery

  3rd Reconnaissance Battalion (21 officers/724 men)

    1 Armored Car Company (10 armored cars)

    1 (half-track) Reconnaissance Company (13 LMGs, 2 HMGs, 2 28mm PzBu41 and 4 50mm PAK 38)

    1 (mot) Support Company, with

      1 Signals Platoon

      1 Pioneer Platoon (no heavy weapons)

      1 Panzerjäger Platoon (12 50mm PAK 38 and 9 LMGs)

    1 (mot) Battery (6 British 25pdrs)

    1 Reconnaissance Supply Column

  39th Panzerjäger Battalion (10 officers/326 men)

    1 (mot) Signals Platoon

    2 (mot) Companies (14 50mm PAK 38 total)

    1 Self-Propelled (4 76.2mm (r) PAK)

  200th Feldersatz Battalion

    4 Companies (no heavy weapons)

  200th Pioneer Battalion

    3 (mot) Pioneer Companies (15 LMGs, 3 PzBu39, 2 50mm PAK 38 total)

1 (mot) Light Supply Column

200th Signals Battalion
1 Armored Radio Company
1 Armored Signals Company
1 Light (mot) Signals Supply Column

Service Forces
1–8/, 12/200th Light (mot) Supply Columns
10/, 11/Heavy (mot) Supply Columns
200th Panzer Replacement Column
9/200th Heavy (mot) POL Supply Column
1/200th (mot) Maintenance Company
2/, 3/200th (mot) Motor Vehicle Repair Companies
200th (mot) Supply Company
579th (mot) Filtration Company
646th (mot) Water Column

Food Service
200th (mot) Bakery Company
200th (mot) Butcher Company
200th (mot) Divisional Quartermaster Detachment

Medical
1/, 2/200th (mot) Medical Companies
200th (mot) Field Hospital
1/, 2/200th Ambulance Columns

Other
200th (mot) Military Police Detachment
200th (mot) Field Post Office

The number of anti-tank guns of the pioneer companies was raised from three to six 50mm PAK 38 by Pz AOK Ia Nr 2092 issued on 20 September 1942 in the 15th and 21st Panzer Divisions. The same order directed that the panzerjäger battalions be equipped with Russian 76.2mm guns and that the 50mm PAK 38s removed be distributed to the schützen and pioneer companies. In late August or early September the reconnaissance battalions were stripped out of the two panzer divisions for a special assignment.

On 24 September 1942 the division underwent yet another reorganization and now consisted of:

Divisional Headquarters
Panzer Command Staffel
200th (mot) Mapping Section
Light Panzer Platoon

5th Panzer Regiment
1 Regimental HQ
1 Panzer Platoon
2 Light Panzer Platoons
1 Regimental Band
1 Armored Maintenance Company

1st and 2nd Panzer Battalions, each with
1 Battalion HQ
1 Panzer Staff Company
1 Light Panzer Platoon
1 Medium Panzer Company

3 Light Panzer Companies
1 (mot) Armored Replacement Company
1 (mot) Armored Replacement Company
Theoretical total of tanks: 46 Pz II, 111 Pz III, 30 Pz IV and 6 command vehicles)

104th Panzergrenadier Regiment
HQ Section
1 (mot) Support Company, with
1 (mot) Signals Platoon
1 (mot) Pioneer Platoon (3 LMGs)
1 Motorcycle Messenger Platoon (6 LMGs)
1 (mot) Panzerjäger Platoon (3 50mm and 3 LMGs)
3 (mot) Battalions, each with
4 Companies (18 LMGs, 2 HMGs, 3 28mm PzBu41, 3 80mm mortars and 6 50mm PAK 38 ea)
708th Self-Propelled Infantry Support Gun Company (6 105mm sIG and 3 LMGs)
1 (mot) Pioneer Company (10 LMGs, 2 HMGs, 3 28mm PzBu41, 3 80mm mortars, 3 50mm PAK 38)

155th Artillery Regiment
1 (mot) Regimental Staff Battery
1st and 2nd Battalions
1 (mot) Staff Battery
3 (mot) Batteries (4 105mm leFH 18 and 2 LMGs ea)
3rd Battalion
1 (mot) HQ Company
2 (mot) Batteries (4 150mm sFH and 2 LMGs ea)
1 (mot) Battery (4 100 K18 guns and 2 LMGs)
1 (mot) Heavy Munitions Supply Column (60t)
1 (mot) Artillery Observation Battery
1 Self-Propelled Flak Battery (15 20mm guns)

200th Feldersatz Battalion
4 Replacement Infantry Companies (6 LMGs and 1 50mm PAK 38 ea)

200th (mot) Signals Battalion
1 Armored Radio Company (28 LMGs)
1 Armored Telephone Company (6 LMGs)
1 Light (mot) Signals Supply Column (3 LMGs)

200th (mot) Pioneer Battalion
3 (mot) Pioneer Companies (9 LMGS, 3 28mm PzBu41 and 6 50mm PAK 38 ea)

200th Panzerjäger Battalion
1 HQ Section
1 (mot) Signals Platoon
2 Self-Propelled Panzerjäger Companies (6 76.2mm (r) PAK and 6 LMGs ea)

200th Supply Battalion
unchanged from March 1942

Support Units
unchanged from March 1942

On 23 October 1942 the organization stood at:

1/, 2/5th Panzer Regiment
  1 Regimental Staff Signals Platoon
  1 Regimental Staff Light Panzer Platoon
  Each Battalion had
    1 Panzer Staff Company
    1 Medium Panzer Company
    3 Light Panzer Companies
  Total tanks available:
    PzMk II   19
    PzMk III (50 kz)   53
    PzMk III (50 lg)   43
    PzMk IV (kz)   7
    PzMk IV (lg)   15
    PzBefWg   6

OKH records show that on 7 January 1943 the division containing the following units:

Division Command
200th Supply Command
200th Panzer Signals Battalion
200th Light Signals Column
Division Reconnaissance Platoon
1/5th Panzer Regiment
Panzer Maintenance Company
1/, 2/, 3/, 4/104th Panzergrenadier Regiment
1/, 2/, 3/155th Panzer Artillery Regiment
580th Reconnaissance Battalion
220th Panzer Pioneer Battalion
2/15th Flak Regiment
609th Flak Battalion
200th Feldersatz Battalion
Kuhn Kampfgruppe
1/, 2/200th Transportation Platoons
1/200th Heavy Transportation Platoon
1/200th Maintenance Company
2/, 3/200th Vehicle Recovery Companies
200th Division Administration
200th Field Bakery
200th Butcher Company
200th Field Post Office

On 17 January 1943 the 2/5th Panzer Regiment, with all the tanks in the 5th Panzer Regiment, was transferred to the 8th Panzer Regiment and redesignated as the 2/8th Panzer Regiment, 15th Panzer Division. A new 1/5th Panzer Regiment, initially known as the Grün Panzer Battalion, was organized in Tunis by 15 January 1943. It was equipped with 13 Pz III (lg), eight Pz III (75), and 17 Pz IV (lg) tanks. The 190th Panzer Battalion, with all its tanks except for two command tanks, became the new 2/5th Panzer Regiment on 6 February.

On 26 February 1943 the division was reorganized. The division detached the 3rd Reconnaissance Battalion to the 90th Light Division in return for the 580th Reconnais-

sance Battalion, and the 200th Panzer Pioneer Battalion to the 164th Light Afrika Division for the 220th Panzer Pioneer Battalion. At the same time the panzer battalions were authorized to have four medium companies, each with 22 Pz IV tanks. On 4 March 1943 the division was organized and equipped as follows:

21st Panzer Division
  1 (mot) Panzer Pioneer Platoon
  1 Armored Car Platoon (4 armored cars)
104th Panzergrenadier Regiment
  1st and 2nd (mot) Battalions, each with 4 companies (the weapon make-up was undetermined, as the battalions had just been rebuilt from March battalions)
  3rd and 4th Battalions, each with 4 companies (the weapon make-up was undetermined, as the battalions had just been rebuilt from March battalions)
155th Artillery Regiment
  1st (mot) Battalion
    1st (mot) Battery (4 105mm leFH)
    2nd (mot) Battery (4 105mm leFH)
  2nd (mot) Battalion
    4th (mot) Battery (4 105mm leFH)
    5th (mot) Battery (4 105mm leFH)
    6th (mot) Battery (3 British 25pdrs)
  3rd (mot) Battalion
    7th (mot) Battery (4 105mm leFH)
    8th (mot) Battery (4 150mm sFH)
    9th (mot) Battery (3 150mm sFH)
  609th Flak Battalion
    1 Self-Propelled Company (10 20mm guns)
    1 Self-Propelled Company (10 20mm guns)
5th Panzer Regiment
  1st "Grün" Battalion
    4 Companies (2 missing)
  2nd (190th) Battalion
    4 Companies
200th (mot) Signals Battalion
  1 (mot) Panzer Telephone Company
  1 (mot) Panzer Radio Company
  1 (mot) Light Signals Supply Column
220th (mot) Panzer Pioneer Battalion
  2 (mot) Panzer Pioneer Companies
590th Reconnaissance Battalion
  Staff Company
    1 Panzer Signals Platoon
    1 Infantry Gun Platoon
    1 Panzerjäger Platoon (2 AT guns)
  1 Armored Car Company (3 armored cars)
  1 (mot) Reconnaissance Company (3 AT guns and 3 LMGs)
  1 (mot) Battery (4 British 25pdr guns)
  1 Self-Propelled Flak Company (8 20mm guns)
2/25th (mot) Flak Battalion
  1 (mot) Battery (2 88mm and 2 20mm guns)

1 (mot) Battery (3 88mm and 2 20mm guns)
1 (mot) Battery (4 88mm and 2 20mm guns)
1 (mot) Battery (4 88mm and 2 20mm guns)
1 (mot) Battery (10 20mm guns)

200th Supply Troop
1/, 2/, 3/, 4/, 5/, 6/, 7/200th (mot) Light Supply Columns
1//200th (mot) Supply Company
1/, 2/, 3/200th (mot) Companies
1 (mot) Water Column
1 (mot) Field Bakery
1 (mot) Butcher Company
1 (mot) Divisional Administration
1/200th Medical Company
1/200th Ambulance
1 Field Post Office

It is worth noting that the two panzergrenadier regiments were being completely rebuilt, as a result of casualties, using a number of March battalions. The equipment was, as a result, totally unknown to OKH. It is also interesting to note that a battery of captured British 25pdr guns was formally incorporated into the division.

On 29 April 1943 the 580th Panzer Reconnaissance Battalion became the 21st Panzer Reconnaissance Battalion. In addition, the division's panzergrenadier element was dramatically changed. The 47th and 104th Panzergrenadier Regiments were replaced by the 192nd Panzergrenadier Regiment, which was expanded to four battalions. The panzerjäger battalion became the 39th and the 305th Flak Battalion was added. The division was destroyed when the Allies recaptured North Africa. Its losses were:

Division Staff
200th Mapping Detachment
200th Print Shop
5th Panzer Regiment
Staff, staff company, 2 battalions each with staff, staff company and 4 companies and 1 armored repair company
192nd (104th) Panzergrenadier Regiment
Staff, staff company, 4 battalions and 13th Company
21st (580th) Panzer Reconnaissance Battalion
Staff and 3 companies
39th Panzerjäger Battalion
Staff and 3 companies
305th Army Flak Battalion (609th Flak Battalion)
Staff, staff battery, 3 batteries and 1 light supply column

155th Panzer Artillery Regiment
Staff, staff battery, 3 Battalions (each with staff, staff battery and total of 5 (9) batteries)
200th Panzer Signals Battalion
2 companies and 1 light supply column

220th Panzer Pioneer Battalion
3 companies and 1 light supply column
200th Feldersatz Battalion
4 companies

The 21st Panzer Division was re-formed on 15 July 1943 in France, near Rennes, by the reorganization of the 931st Fast Brigade and other forces. The 100th Panzer Regiment was assigned to the division and expanded to eight companies. The division was drawn together as follows:

1/, 2/125th Panzergrenadier Regiment (from West Fast Brigade)
1/, 2/192nd Panzergrenadier Regiment (newly formed)
21st Panzer Reconnaissance Battalion (from 1st and 2nd Companies, 931st Motorcycle Battalion and built up from Panzer Reconnaissance Lehr Battalion)
1/, 2/100th Panzer Regiment (from 223rd Panzer Battalion, Paris Panzer Company and Panzer Company of the LXXXI Army Corps—captured French tanks)
1/, 2/, 3/155th Panzer Artillery Regiment (from the 931st Panzer Artillery Regiment)
305th Army Flak Battalion (newly formed)
200th Divisional Support Troops, including
220th Pioneer Battalion

OKH records show that the newly formed division was to be organized and equipped as follows:

Division Staff
1 Division Staff (2 LMGs)
200th (mot) Mapping Detachment
100th Panzer Regiment
Regimental Staff
1 Signals Platoon
1 Regimental Band
1st and 2nd Battalions, each with
1 Regimental Staff and Staff Company
3 Panzer Companies (22 PzMk III ea)
1 Panzer Company (22 PzMk IV)
1 Panzer Maintenance Company
125th and 192nd Panzergrenadier Regiments, each with
1 Regimental Staff
1 Regimental Band
1 (mot) Regimental Staff Company
1 Signals Platoon
1 Panzerjäger Platoon (3 50mm PAK 38 and 3 LMGs)
1 Motorcycle Platoon (6 LMGs)
1st (half-track) Battalion
3 (half-track) Companies (4 HMGs, 15 LMGs and 4 80mm mortars ea)
1 (half-track) Heavy Company

1 Panzerjäger Platoon (4 75mm on half-tracks and 4 LMGs)

1 Nebelwerfer Platoon (1 half-track launcher)

1 Flak Platoon (4 20mm on half-tracks and 3 LMGs)

2nd (mot) Battalion

3 (mot) Companies (4 HMGs, 15 LMGs and 4 80mm mortars ea)

1 (half-track) Heavy Company

1 Panzerjäger Platoon (4 75mm on half-tracks and 4 LMGs)

1 Nebelwerfer Platoon (1 half-track launcher)

1 Flak Platoon (4 20mm on half-tracks and 3 LMGs)

1 Self-Propelled Infantry Gun Company (6 150mm sIG and 6 LMGs)

200th Panzerjäger Battalion

2 (motZ) Panzerjäger Companies (12 75mm PAK 40 and 12 LMGs ea)

200th Sturmgeschütz Battalion

1 Staff and Staff Battery (4 half-track mounted nebelwerfers)

4 Companies (4 leFH 16 and 6 75mm PAK 40 ea)

155th Panzer Artillery Regiment

1 Regimental Staff

1 Staff Battery (2 LMGs)

1st Battalion

1 Battalion Staff and Staff Battery (6 LMGs)

2 Self-Propelled Batteries (6 105mm leFH SdKfz 124 Wespe and 4 LMGs ea)

1 Self-Propelled Battery (6 150mm sFH SdKfz 165 Hummel and 4 LMGs)

2nd Battalion

1 Battalion Staff and Staff Battery (6 LMGs)

3 Self-Propelled Batteries (6 105mm leFH SdKfz 124 Wespe and 4 LMGs ea)

3rd Battalion

1 Battalion Staff and Staff Battery (6 LMGs)

3 Self-Propelled Batteries (6 150mm sFH SdKfz 165 Hummel and 4 LMGs ea)

21st Reconnaissance Battalion (early 1943 organization)

2 Motorcycle Companies (2 120mm mortars, 4 HMGs and 18 LMGs ea)

305th Army Flak Battalion

1 Staff and (mot) Staff Battery (1 LMG)

1st–3rd (half-track) Flak Batteries (4 88mm and 2 20mm on half-tracks ea)

200th Feldersatz Company

220th Panzer Pioneer Battalion

1 Staff (2 LMGs)

2 (half-track) Pioneer Companies (43 LMGs and 3 PzBu39 ea)

1 Brüko K Bridging Column (3 LMGs) (added 6 Aug. 1943)

1 (mot) Light Pioneer Supply Column (2 LMGs)

200th Panzer Signals Battalion

1 Panzer Telephone Company (6 LMGs)

1 Panzer Radio Company (35 LMGs)

1 (mot) Light Signals Supply Column (1 LMG)

200th Supply Troop

1/, 2/, 3/, 4/200th (mot) (120 ton) Transportation Company (4 LMGs ea)

200th (mot) Supply Company (6 LMGs)

Truck Park

200th (mot) Maintenance Company (4 LMGs ea)

Other

200th (mot) Bakery Company

200th (mot) Butcher Company

200th (mot) Administration Platoon

200th (mot) Medical Company (2 LMGs)

1/, 2/200th Ambulances

200th (mot) Military Police Troop (2 LMGs)

200th (mot) Field Post Office

Keilig indicates that the 1/, 2/100th Panzer Regiment both contained three companies of captured French light tanks and one of captured French medium tanks. The tanks, however, were quickly replaced with PzMk IV tanks. The panzergrenadier regiment's Flak companies or infantry gun companies were replaced with Flak and infantry gun platoons in the regiment's heavy company. The 1/125th and 1/192nd Panzergrenadier Regiments and the 3rd and 4th Companies of the 200th Panzer Reconnaissance Battalion were equipped with half-tracks. The 200th Sturmgeschütz Battalion contained a staff, a staff company and four sturmgeschütz companies. Keilig indicates that the artillery regiment was organized as shown above; however, in a letter from Oberkommando Herresgruppe B, found in T-311, Roll 44, the 21st Panzer Division is shown as having 24 105mm leFH, eight 122mm Russian guns, 12 150mm sFH, and four 100mm K18 guns. This is the traditional, non-self-propelled organization of a panzer division's artillery, but it has the two additional batteries of Russian 122mm guns. At best, it indicates that the 1/, 2/155th were equipped totally with 105mm guns, possibly Wespes. It suggests that the 3/155th was a normal (motZ) heavy battalion with four 100mm K18 guns and eight 150mm howitzers. The two batteries of Russian 122mm guns were probably assigned as independent batteries. On 1 March 1944 the division was organized and equipped as follows:

Division Staff

1 Division Staff (2 LMGs)

200th (mot) Mapping Detachment

1 Divisional Band

100th Panzer Regiment

Regimental Staff

1 Signals Platoon (2 LMGs

1 Regimental Staff Panzer Platoon (2 Pz III and 1 Pz III Command)

1st Battalion
1 Regimental Staff
1 Staff
1 Staff Company (2 Pz II, 5 Pz lg, 19 LMGs, 2 50mm KwK and 5 75mm KWK)
1 Self-Propelled Flak Company (12 20mm and 3 LMGs)
4 Panzer Companies (17 Pz IV lg ea)

2nd Battalion
1 Regimental Staff
1 Staff
1 Staff Company (2 Pz II, 5 Pz lg)
1 Panzer Company (18 Somua tanks)
1 Panzer Company (10 Hotchkiss and 6 Somua tanks)
1 Panzer Company (18 Somua tanks)
1 Panzer Company (17 Pz V lg)
1 Panzer Maintenance Company (2 LMGs)

125th Panzergrenadier Regiment
1 Regimental Staff
1 (mot) Regimental Staff Company
1 Signals Platoon
1 Panzerjäger Platoon (3 50mm PAK 38 and 3 LMGs)
1 Pioneer Platoon
1 Motorcycle Platoon (6 LMGs)
9th Self-Propelled Infantry Gun Company (6 150mm sIG and 2 LMGs)
10th Half-Track Nebelwerfer Company (4 half-tracks with launchers and 4 LMGs)

1st (half-track) Battalion
3 (half-track) Companies (4 HMGs, 39 LMGs and 1 88mm panzerschreck ea)
1 (half-track) Heavy Company
1 Panzerjäger Platoon (4 75mm KwK on half-tracks)
1 Flak Platoon (3 20mm on half-tracks)
1 Panzerzerstörer Section (1 88mm panzerschreck)

2nd (mot) Battalion
3 (mot) Companies (4 HMGs, 18 LMGs and 1 88mm panzerschreck ea)
1 (half-track) Heavy Company
1 Panzerjäger Platoon (4 75mm KwK on half-tracks)
1 Flak Platoon (3 20mm on half-tracks)
1 Panzerzerstörer Section (1 88mm panzerschreck)

200th Panzer Reconnaissance Battalion
1st (half-track) Company (16 SdKfz 250s, 25 LMGs and 2 75mm KwK)
2nd Armored Car Company
Armored Car Platoon (6 SdKfz 234/2—75mm gun)
Armored Car Detachment (8 SdKfz 234/1 and 16 SdKfz 222)
3rd (half-track) Company (2 SdKfz 250/3, 28 SdKfz 250/1, 2 SdKfz 251/2 (80mm mortar) and 5 SdKfz 251/10 (37mm gun))

4th (half-track) Company (2 SdKfz 250/3, 28 SdKfz 250/1, 2 SdKfz 251/2 (80mm mortar) and 5 SdKfz 251/10 (37mm gun))
5th (half-track) Company (27 SdKfz 251-2 flame-throwers, 2 75mm KwK, 3 75mm PAK 40, 1 37mm PAK 36 and 36 LMGs)

200th Sturmgeschütz Battalion
1 Staff and Staff Battery (1 Stug and 15 LMGs)
4 Companies (8 StuG III Ausf 6 with 105mm gun and 4 StuG with 75mm PAK 40)

200th Panzerjäger Battalion
2 (motZ) Panzerjäger Companies (12 88mm PAK 43 and 12 LMGs ea)

155th Panzer Artillery Regiment
1 Regimental Staff
1 Staff Battery (2 LMGs)

1st (motZ) Battalion
1 Battalion Staff and Staff Battery (6 LMGs)
2 (motZ) Batteries (4 122mm (r) howitzers and 5 LMGs ea)
1 (motZ) Battery (4 100mm K18 guns and 5 LMGs)

2nd and 3rd Battalions, each with
1 Battalion Staff and Staff Battery (6 LMGs)
2 Self-Propelled Batteries (6 105mm leFH SdKfz 124 Wespe and 4 LMGs ea)
1 Self-Propelled Battery (6 150mm sFH SdKfz 165 Hummel and 4 LMGs)

305th Army Flak Battalion
1 Staff and (mot) Staff Battery (2 LMGs)
1st–2nd (half-track) Flak Batteries (4 88mm and 3 20mm on half-tracks ea)
3rd (half-track) Flak Battery (9 37mm and 2 quad 20mm)
1 Searchlight Battery (4 searchlights and 1 LMG)

200th Feldersatz Company
4 Companies (2 LMGs ea)

220th Panzer Pioneer Battalion
1 Staff (2 LMGs)
2 (half-track) Pioneer Companies (43 LMGs, 2 HMGs and 1 88mm panzerschreck)
1 (mot) Panzerzerstörer Company (1 88mm panzerschreck)
1 Brüko K Bridging Column (3 LMGs)

200th Panzer Signals Battalion
1 Panzer Telephone Company (14 LMGs)
1 Panzer Radio Company (1 47mm French gun and 20 LMGs)
1 (mot) Light Signals Supply Column (1 LMG)

200th Supply Troop
1/, 2/, 3/, 4/, 5/, 6/, 7/200th (mot) (120 ton) Transportation Company (8 LMGs ea)
200th (mot) Supply Company (6 LMGs)

Truck Park
1/, 2/200th (mot) Maintenance Company (4 LMGs ea)
200th (mot) Heavy Maintenance Supply Column

Other

200th (mot) Bakery Company (6 LMGs)
200th (mot) Butcher Company (4 LMGs)
200th (mot) Administration Platoon (2 LMGs)
1/, 2/200th (mot) Medical Company (4 LMGs ea)
1/, 2/200th Ambulances (1 LMG ea)
200th (mot) Military Police Troop (2 LMGs)
200th (mot) Field Post Office

On 20 May 1944 the 100th Panzer Regiment was ordered to reorganize into the "freie Gliderung" and was immediately renamed the 22nd Panzer Division. The 1/22nd was outfitted with four companies of 17 PzMk IV tanks and the 2/22nd was directed to discard its captured tanks and outfit each of its four companies with 14 PzMk IV tanks.

In June the organization of the armored portion of the division and its panzer inventory were as follows:

1/, 2/22nd Panzer Regiment
  1 Panzer Signals Platoon
  1 Panzer Staff Platoon
  315th (FKL) Panzer Company (10 sturmgeschütze)
  1 Battalion
    1 Panzer Staff Company
    1 Self-Propelled Flak Platoon
    4 Medium Panzer Companies
  1 Battalion
    1 Panzer Staff Company
    4 Panzer Companies
  Total tanks available:

PzMk III (75)	4
PzMk IV (kz)	21
PzMk IV (lg)	96
Flakpz38	12
PzBefWg	2

In August 1944 the infantry of the 16th Luftwaffe Field Division was absorbed into the division. The 21st Division was later destroyed in the Falaise Pocket. The division was re-formed in September 1944 in Lorraine from the 112th Panzer Brigade (2112th Panzer Battalion and 2112th Panzergrenadier Regiment). In November 1944 the division's panzer regiment was once again ordered reformed. The 1/100th Panzer Regiment was to have two companies each with 17 PzMk V Panthers, and two companies each with PzMk IV tanks. In addition, the second battalion was ordered replaced by the 655th Army Panzerjäger Battalion, which had three companies, each equipped with 14 SdKfz 164 Hornisse. This may or may not have happened as Jentz indicates that on 29 December 1944 the organization of the armored portion of the division and its panzer inventory were as follows:

1/22nd Panzer Regiment
  1 Panzer Staff Company
  1st Battalion
    1 Panzer Staff Company
    2 Medium Panzer Companies (PzMk V)
    2 Medium Panzer Companies (PzMk IV)
  Total tanks available:

PzMk IV (lg)	34
PzMk V	38
FlakpzIV (2V)	5
FlakpzIV (37)	3

In early 1945 the 22nd Panzer Regiment was re-formed using the 22nd Panzer Battalion (former 2112th Panzer Battalion) as the 1st Battalion and a newly formed 2nd Battalion. On 2 February 1945 the 21st Panzer Division was ordered reorganized as a Type 44 Panzer Division. The 22nd Panzer Regiment was organized with a staff and staff company, supported by a Flak platoon. It consisted of a single mixed battalion, formed with a staff company, two companies equipped with PzMk IV tanks, and two companies equipped with PzMk V Panther tanks. On 7 February 16 PzMk IV tanks were shipped to the division and seven Panthers followed on 9 February. The division surrendered to the Allies on 29 April 1945.

22nd Panzer Division

Formed on 25 September 1941 in France from the 204th Panzer Regiment and two newly formed schützen regiments. It had:

22nd Schützen Brigade
  1/, 2/129th Schützen Regiment
  1/, 2/140th Schützen Regiment
24th Motorcycle Battalion
1/, 2/204th Panzer Regiment
1/, 2/, 3/140th Artillery Regiment (from 3/337th, 2/44th and 4/227th Artillery Regiments)
50th Panzer Pioneer Battalion
140th Reconnaissance Battalion
140th Panzerjäger Battalion
140th Signals Battalion
140th Supply Troop

In February the organization of the armored portion of the division and its panzer inventory were as follows: *(see over)*

1/, 2/204th Panzer Regiment
  1 Regimental Staff Signals Platoon
  1 Regimental Staff Light Panzer Platoon
  Each Battalion had
    1 Panzer Staff Company
    1 Medium Panzer Company
  Total tanks available:
  2 Light Panzer Companies
    PzMk II   45
    38 (t)   77
    PzMk IV (kz)   20
  3/204th Panzer Regiment (formed later)
    1 Panzer Staff Company
    1 Medium Panzer Company
    2 Light Panzer Companies
  Total tanks available:
    PzMk II   15
    38 (t)   37

In 1942 the 3/204th Panzer Regiment was formed. At the same time the 289th Army Flak Battalion became the 4/140th Artillery Regiment. During the summer of 1942 the 140th Panzergrenadier Regiment, 3/204th Panzer Regiment, and 1/140th Artillery Regiment were detached to the Michalik Group, 2nd Army. On 1 July 1942 the organization of the armored portion of the division and its panzer inventory were as follows:

1/, 2/204th Panzer Regiment
  1 Regimental Staff Signals Platoon
  1 Regimental Staff Light Panzer Platoon

Each Battalion had
  1 Panzer Staff Company
  1 Medium Panzer Company
  2 Light Panzer Companies
Total tanks available:
  PzMk II   28
  38 (t)   114
  PzMk III (50 lg)   12
  PzMk IV (kz)   11
  PzMk IV (lg)   11

On 5 September 1942 the 27th Panzer Division was organized from the Michalik Group. The order of 9 February 1943 disbanded the division. It was initially to be absorbed into the 6th Panzer Division, but ended up going into the 23rd Panzer Division. The rest of the division was used to form Kampfgruppe Burgsthaler. Kampfgruppe Burgsthaler consisted of the 1/129th Panzergrenadier Regiment (5 companies), 204th Armored Group (one panzer and one half-track company), 24th Motorcycle Company, 140th Panzerjäger Company, 140th Signals Company, and 140th Flak Battery. On 7 April 1943 it was absorbed into the 23rd Panzer Division. The staff 1/129th Panzergrenadiers became the Staff/Field Lehr Battalion of the 23rd Panzer Division.

What was not absorbed by the 23rd Panzer Division was distributed as followed: Staff/204th Panzer Regiment became the 509th Panzer Battalion, Staff/140th Artillery Regiment became the Staff/732nd Army Artillery Brigade, and the 3/140th Artillery Regiment became the 1/959th Army Artillery Brigade.

23rd Panzer Division

Formed on 21 September 1941 in France by the 1st Army from the 101st Panzer Brigade, which consisted of the 203rd and 204th Captured Panzer Regiments, two newly formed schützen regiments, and the Staff/23rd Panzer Division. The division had:

23rd Schützen Brigade
  1/, 2/126th Schützen Regiment
  1/, 2/128th Schützen Regiment
1/, 2/, 3/201st Panzer Regiment
23rd Motorcycle Battalion
1/, 2/, 3/128th Artillery Regiment (from 3/335th, 847th
  and 863rd Artillery Battalions)
128th Panzerjäger Battalion
128th Signals Battalion
51st Pioneer Battalion
128th Divisional Support Troops

In March 1942 the organization of the armored portion of the division and its panzer inventory were as follows:

1/, 2/, 3/201st Panzer Regiment
  1 Regimental Staff Signals Platoon
  1 Regimental Staff Light Panzer Platoon
  Each Battalion had
    1 Panzer Staff Company
    1 Medium Panzer Company
    2 Light Panzer Companies
  Total tanks available:
    PzMk II   34
    PzMk III   112
    PzMk IV (kz)   32
    PzBefWg   3

In 1942 the 4/128th Artillery Regiment was formed from the 278th Army Flak Battalion and the schützen regiments were designated as panzergrenadier regiments. On 28 June 1942 the organization of the armored portion of the division and its panzer inventory were as follows:

1/, 2/, 3/201st
   1 Regimental Staff Signals Platoon
   1 Regimental Staff Light Panzer Platoon
   Each Battalion had
      1 Panzer Staff Company
      1 Medium Panzer Company
      2 Light Panzer Companies
   Total tanks available:
      PzMk II   32
      PzMk III (50 kz)   54
      PzMk III (50 lg)   56
      PzMk IV (kz)   20
      PzMk IV (lg)   12
      PzBefWg   7

In 1943 the 4/128th Artillery once again became the 278th Army Flak Battalion, the 3/201st Panzer Regiment was disbanded, and the motorcycle battalion was converted into the 23rd Panzer Reconnaissance Battalion. The 201st Panzer Regiment was renamed the 23rd Panzer Regiment on 16 August 1943. On 1 July 1942 the organization of the armored portion of the division and its panzer inventory were as follows:

1/201st Panzer Regiment
   1 Regimental Staff Signals Platoon
   1 Regimental Staff Light Panzer Platoon
   1 Sturmgeschütz Battery
   1 Battalion with:
      1 Panzer Staff Company
      2 Medium Panzer Companies
      2 Light Panzer Companies
   Total tanks available:
      PzMk II   1
      PzMk III (kz)   7
      PzMk III (lg)   17
      PzMk III (75)   3
      PzMk IV (lg)   50
      PzBefWg   1
      StuG   7

OKH records show that the division was organized and equipped as follows during early 1943:

Division Staff
   1 Division Staff (2 LMGs)
   128th (mot) Mapping Detachment
201st Panzer Regiment
   Regimental Staff

   1 Signals Platoon
   1 Regimental Band
1st Battalion
   1 Regimental Staff and Staff Company (7 PzMk III flame panzers)
   4 Panzer Companies (22 PzMk IV tanks ea)
   1 Panzer Maintenance Company
2nd Battalion
   1 Regimental Staff and Staff Company (7 PzMk III flame panzers)
   4 Panzer Companies (22 PzMk V Panther tanks ea)
   1 Panzer Maintenance Company
126th Panzergrenadier Regiment
   1 Regimental Staff
   1 Regimental Band
   1 (mot) Regimental Staff Company
      1 Signals Platoon
      1 Panzerjäger Platoon (3 50mm PAK 38 and 3 LMGs)
      1 Motorcycle Platoon (6 LMGs)
1st (half-track) Battalion
   3 (half-track) Companies (4 HMGs, 34 LMGs, 2 80mm mortars and 3 75mm leIG ea)
   1 (half-track) Heavy Company
      1 Pioneer Platoon (4 LMGs)
      1 Panzerjäger Platoon (3 50mm PAK 38 and 3 LMGs)
      1 Infantry Gun Platoon (8 LMGs and 4 75mm leIG)
      1 Panzerjäger Platoon (3 LMGs and 3 sPzBu 41)
2nd (mot) Battalion
   3 (mot) Companies (4 HMGs, 18 LMGs, 2 80mm mortars and 3 PzBu39 ea)
   1 (mot) Heavy Company
      1 Pioneer Platoon (4 LMGs)
      1 Panzerjäger Platoon (3 LMGs and 3 50mm PAK 38)
      1 Infantry Gun Platoon (4 75mm leIG)
      1 Panzerjäger Platoon (3 LMGs and 3 sPzBu 41)
   1 Self-Propelled Infantry Gun Company (6 150mm sIG and 7 LMGs)
   1 Self-Propelled Flak Company (12 20mm and 4 LMGs)
128th Panzergrenadier Regiment
   1 Regimental Staff
   1 Regimental Band
   1 (mot) Regimental Staff Company
      1 Signals Platoon
      1 Panzerjäger Platoon (3 50mm PAK 38 and 3 LMGs)
      1 Motorcycle Platoon (6 LMGs)
1st and 2nd (mot) Battalion, each with
   same as 2/126th Panzergrenadier Regiment
   1 Self-Propelled Flak Company (12 20mm and 4 LMGs)
   1 Self-Propelled Infantry Gun Company (6 150mm sIG and 7 LMGs)
128th Panzerjäger Battalion
   1 (motZ) Panzerjäger Company (12 75mm PAK 40 and 12 LMGs ea)

1 Self-Propelled Panzerjäger Company (14 75mm PAK 40 and 14 LMGs ea)

23rd Reconnaissance Battalion (early 1943 organization)

1 Armored Car Company (24 LMGs and 18 20mm guns)

1 (half-track) Reconnaissance Company (2 80mm mortars, 4 HMGs, 56 LMGs and 3 75mm leIG)

2 Motorcycle Companies (2 80mm mortars, 4 HMGs, 18 LMGs and 3 PzBu39 ea)

1 (mot) Heavy Reconnaissance Company
  1 Pioneer Platoon (4 LMGs)
  1 Infantry Gun Section (2 75mm leIG)
  1 Panzerjäger Platoon (3 LMGs and 3 75mm PAK 40)
  1 Panzerjäger Platoon (3 LMGs and 3 sPzBu 41)

1 (mot) Light Reconnaissance Supply Column (3 LMGs)

128th Panzer Artillery Regiment

1 Regimental Staff

1 Staff Battery (2 LMGs)

1st and 2nd Battalions, each with
  1 Battalion Staff
  1 Battalion Staff Battery (6 LMGs)
  3 (mot) Batteries (3 105mm leFH and 2 LMGs ea)

3rd (mot) Battalion
  1 Battalion Staff
  1 Battalion Staff Battery (6 LMGs)
  2 (mot) Batteries (3 150mm sFH and 2 LMGs ea)
  1 (mot) Battery (3 100mm K 18 guns and 2 LMGs)

128th (mot) Observation Battery (2 LMGs)

278th Army Flak Battalion

1 Staff and (mot) Staff Battery (1 LMG)

1st–2nd (motZ) Heavy Flak Batteries (4 88mm, 3 20mm and 2 LMGs ea)

3rd (motZ) Light Flak Battery (9 20mm, 2 quad 20mm and 2 LMGs)

4th Self-Propelled Battery (8 20mm and 2 quad 20mm Flak guns and 4 LMGs)

1 (mot) Light (20 ton) Flak Supply Column

51st Panzer Pioneer Battalion

1 Staff (2 LMGs)

1 (half-track) Pioneer Company (25 LMGs, 2 80mm mortars and 3 PzBu39)

2 (mot) Pioneer Companies (18 LMGs, 2 80mm mortars and 3 PzBu39 ea)

151st Brüko K Bridging Column (3 LMGs)

1 (mot) Light Pioneer Supply Column (2 LMGs)

128th Panzer Signals Battalion

1 Panzer Telephone Company (6 LMGs)

1 Panzer Radio Company (16 LMGs)

1 (mot) Light Signals Supply Column (1 LMG)

128th Supply Troop

1/, 2/, 3/128th (mot) (120 ton) Transportation Company (4 LMGs ea)

4/, 5//128th (mot) (90 ton) Transportation Company (3 LMGs ea)

128th Heavy (mot) Supply Column (2 LMGs)

128th (mot) Supply Company (6 LMGs)

Truck Park

1–3/128th (mot) Maintenance Companies (4 LMGs ea)

Other

128th (mot) Bakery Company

128th (mot) Butcher Company

128th (mot) Administration Platoon

1/, 2/128th (mot) Medical Companies (2 LMGs ea)

1/, 2/, 3/128th Ambulances

128th (mot) Military Police Troop (2 LMGs)

128th (mot) Field Post Office

On 31 July 1943 the 201st Panzer Regiment was replaced by the 23rd Panzer Regiment. A note in OKH records indicates that in August a self-propelled infantry gun battery was added to the panzer regiment. It also indicates that the battalion staff companies had added Flak platoons. The panzer reconnaissance battalion was reorganized and on 10 July 1943 it was as follows:

23rd Reconnaissance Battalion

1 Armored Car Company (24 LMGs and 18 20mm guns)

1 Armored Car (half-track) Company (25 LMGs and 16 20mm guns)

1 (half-track) Reconnaissance Company (2 80mm mortars, 3 37mm PAK 36, 4 HMGs and 56 LMGs)

1 Motorcycle Company (2 80mm mortars, 4 HMGs, 18 LMGs and 3 PzBu39)

1 (half-track) Heavy Reconnaissance Company
  1 Staff (2 LMGs)
  1 Infantry Platoon (9 LMGs)
  1 Pioneer Platoon (1 37mm PAK 36, 6 flamethrowers and 13 LMGs)
  1 Panzerjäger Platoon (3 75mm PAK 40 and 4 LMGs)
  1 Infantry Gun Section (2 75mm leIG)
  1 Half-Track Gun Section (8 LMGs and 6 75mm guns)

1 (mot) Light Reconnaissance Supply Column (3 LMGs)

In August 1943 the 128th Panzerjäger Battalion replaced its (motZ) company with a self-propelled company. The artillery regiment was to equip one of its battalions as a self-propelled battalion. Notes indicate that it was to happen on 14 August 1943. It was to be organized as follows:

1 Battalion Staff and Staff Battery (6 LMGs)

2 Self-Propelled Batteries (6 105mm leFH SdKfz 124 Wespe and 4 LMGs ea)

1 Self-Propelled Battery (6 150mm sFH SdKfz 165 Hummel and 4 LMGs)

The division formed a feldersatz battalion, which on 1 May 1943 had five companies and a Hiwi company (Russian volunteers in the German army). In 1944 the 128th Panzergrenadier Regiment was disbanded, merged with the 126th Panzergrenadier Regiment and then re-formed from the 1031st (mot) Grenadier Regiment. The division then had:

1/, 2/126th Panzergrenadier Regiment
1/, 2/128th Panzergrenadier Regiment
1/, 2/23rd Panzer Regiment
23rd Panzer Reconnaissance Battalion

278th Army Flak Battalion
1/, 2/, 3/128th Panzer Artillery Regiment
128th Panzerjäger Battalion
128th Signals Battalion
51st Pioneer Battalion
128th Divisional Support Troops

Sometime in September 1943 the 2/201st Panzer Regiment was equipped with 86 Panther tanks. The 1/201st Panzer Regiment continued to be equipped with Panzer PzMk IV tanks. It surrendered to the Allies on 8/9 May 1945.

24th Panzer Division

Formed on 28 November 1941 by the conversion of the 1st Cavalry Division into a panzer division. In February 1942 the division had:

24th Schützen Brigade
  1/, 2/21st Schützen Regiment (formerly 1st Reiter Regiment)
  1/, 2/26th Schützen Regiment (formerly 22nd Reiter Regiment)
1/, 2/24th Panzer Regiment (formerly 2nd and 21st Reiter Regiment)
4th Motorcycle Battalion (formerly 1st Bicycle Battalion)
1/, 2/, 3/89th Artillery Regiment (from 1st Cavalry Artillery Regiment)
40th Reconnaissance Battalion
40th Panzerjäger Battalion
40th Pioneer Battalion
86th Signals Battalion
40th Divisional Support Troops

In May 1942 the organization of the armored portion of the division and its panzer inventory were as follows:

1/, 2, /, 3/24th Panzer Regiment
  1 Regimental Staff Signals Platoon
  1 Regimental Staff Light Panzer Platoon
Each Battalion had
  1 Panzer Staff Company
  1 Medium Panzer Company
  2 Light Panzer Companies
Total tanks available:

PzMk II	32
PzMk III (50kz)	55
PzMk III (50lg)	56
PzMk IV (kz)	20
PzMk IV (lg)	12
PzBefWg	7

On 28 June 1942 the organization and inventory were:

1/, 2/, 3/24th Panzer Regiment
  1 Regimental Staff Signals Platoon
  1 Regimental Staff Light Panzer Platoon
Each Battalion had
  1 Panzer Staff Company
  1 Medium Panzer Company
  2 Light Panzer Companies
Total tanks available:

PzMk II	32
PzMk III (50 kz)	54
PzMk III (50 lg)	56
PzMk IV (kz)	20
PzMk IV (lg)	12
PzBefWg	7

In 1942 the artillery regiment formed a 4th Battalion from the 283rd Army Flak Battalion and the schützen were renamed panzergrenadiers. The division was destroyed in January 1943 at Stalingrad.

The process of rebuilding the division began almost immediately. The 24th Panzer Regiment was re-formed on 17 February 1943 with two battalions, each with four companies. Orders were cut on 3 March 1943 ordering the addition of a 3rd (Tiger) Battalion equipped with three heavy panzer companies and an independent sturmgeschütz Battalion with three batteries. However, plans for building the Tiger and sturmgeschütz battalions were abandoned in favor of organizing a 3rd Battalion equipped only with sturmgeschütze with the issuance of a new order dated 20 March 1943. This battalion contained four companies and 22 sturmgeschütze. The division was re-formed in France and had:

1/, 2/21st Panzergrenadier Regiment (from 891st Panzergrenadier Regiment)
1/, 2/26th Panzergrenadier Regiment (from 891st Panzergrenadier Regiment)

1/, 2/, 3/24th Panzer Regiment
24th Panzer Reconnaissance Battalion
1/, 2/, 3/89th Panzer Artillery Regiment
283rd Flak Battalion
86th Panzer Signals Battalion
40th Panzerjäger Battalion
40th Panzer Pioneer Battalion
89th Feldersatz Battalion
40th Divisional Support Troops

The 24th Panzer Regiment had a staff and a staff company, its 1st Battalion had four companies of Panzer PzMk IV tanks, and its 2nd Battalion had two companies of Panzer PzMk IV tanks and two companies of sturmgeschütze. The 1/26th Panzergrenadier Regiment and 3rd and 4th Companies of the 24th Panzer Reconnaissance Battalion were equipped with half-tracks. OKH records show that the division was organized and equipped as follows on 22 February 1943.

Division Staff
1 Division Staff (2 LMGs)
40th (mot) Mapping Detachment
24th Panzer Regiment
Regimental Staff
1 Signals Platoon
1 Regimental Band
1st Battalion
1 Regimental Staff and Staff Company
4 Panzer Companies (22 PzMk V Panthers ea)
2nd Battalion
1 Regimental Staff and Staff Company
4 Panzer Companies (22 PzMk IV ea)
1 Panzer Maintenance Company (shared by 1st and 2nd Bns)
3rd Battalion (apparently detached on 18 Mar. 1943)
1 Regimental Staff and Staff Company
3 Panzer Companies (10 PzMk VI Tiger tanks ea)
1 Panzer Maintenance Company
21st Panzergrenadier Regiment
1 Regimental Staff
1 Regimental Band
1 (mot) Regimental Staff Company
1 Signals Platoon
1 Panzerjäger Platoon (3 50mm PAK 38 and 3 LMGs)
1 Motorcycle Platoon (6 LMGs)
1st (half-track) Battalion
3 (half-track) Companies (4 HMGs, 33 LMGs, 2 80mm mortars and 3 37mm PAK 36; up-gunned to 4 HMGs, 39 LMGs, 3 PzBu39, 3 37mm PAK 36, 2 80mm mortars and 2 75mm guns on 23 May 1943)
1 (half-track) Heavy Company
1 Pioneer Platoon (6, later 13 LMGs, 1 75mm gun, and 6 flamethrowers)

1 Panzerjäger Platoon (3 75mm PAK 40 and 3 LMGs)
1 Infantry Gun Platoon (2 75mm leIG and 4 LMGs)
1 Gun Platoon (6 75mm guns and 8 LMGs)
2nd (mot) Battalion
3 (mot) Companies (4 HMGs, 18 LMGs and 2 80mm mortars ea)
1 (mot) Heavy Company
1 Pioneer Platoon (4 LMGs and 6 LMGs)
1 Panzerjäger Platoon (3 LMGs and 3 50mm PAK 38)
1 Infantry Gun Platoon (4 75mm leIG)
1 Mortar Platoon (6 80mm mortars)
1 Self-Propelled Flak Company (12 20mm and 4 LMGs)
1 Self-Propelled Infantry Gun Company (6 150mm sIG and 5, later 7 LMGs)
26th Panzergrenadier Regiment
1 Regimental Staff
1 Regimental Band
1 (mot) Regimental Staff Company
1 Signals Platoon
1 Panzerjäger Platoon (3 50mm PAK 38 and 3 LMGs)
1 Motorcycle Platoon (6 LMGs)
1st and 2nd (mot) Battalion, each with
3 (mot) Companies (4 HMGs, 18 LMGs and 2 80mm mortars ea)
1 (mot) Heavy Company
1 Pioneer Platoon (4 LMGs and 6 LMGs)
1 Panzerjäger Platoon (3 LMGs and 3 50mm PAK 38)
1 Infantry Gun Platoon (4 75mm leIG)
1 Mortar Platoon (6 80mm mortars)
1 Self-Propelled Flak Company (12 20mm and 4 LMGs)
1 Self-Propelled Infantry Gun Company (6 150mm sIG and 5, later 7 LMGs)
89th Panzer Artillery Regiment
1 Regimental Staff
1 Staff Battery (2 LMGs)
1 Staff Self-Propelled Flak Battery (4 20mm and 2 LMGs)
1 (mot) Observation Battery (12 LMGs)
1st Battalion
1 Battalion Staff and Staff Battery (6 LMGs)
2 Self-Propelled Batteries (6 105mm leFH SdKfz 124 Wespe and 4 LMGs ea)
1 Self-Propelled Battery (6 150mm sFH SdKfz 165 Hummel and 4 LMGs
2nd (mot) Battalion
1 Battalion Staff
1 Battalion Staff Battery (6 LMGs)
3 (mot) Batteries (3 105mm leFH and 2 LMGs ea)
3rd (mot) Battalion
1 Battalion Staff
1 Battalion Staff Battery (6 LMGs)

2 (mot) Batteries (3 150mm sFH and 2 LMGs)
1 (mot) Battery (3 100mm K 18 guns and 2 LMGs)

24th Reconnaissance Battalion
1 Armored Car Company
   3 Platoons (24 LMGs and 18 20mm guns)
   1 Platoon (6 75mm guns and 6 LMGs)
1 (half-track) Armored Car Platoon (16 20mm and 25 LMGs)
2 (half-track) Reconnaissance Companies (2 120mm mortars, 3 37mm PAK 36, 4 HMGs and 56 LMGs ea)
1 (mot) Heavy Reconnaissance Company
   1 Pioneer Platoon (9, later 13 LMGs, 1 75mm gun and 6 flamethrowers)
   1 Infantry Gun Section (2 75mm leIG)
   1 Panzerjäger Platoon (3 LMGs and 3 75mm PAK 40)
   1 Gun Platoon (6 75mm guns and 8 LMGs)
1 (mot) Light Reconnaissance Supply Column (3 LMGs)

283rd Army Flak Battalion
1 Staff and (mot) Staff Battery (1 LMG)
1st–2nd (motZ) Heavy Flak Batteries (4 88mm, 3 20mm and 2 LMGs ea)
3rd (motZ) Medium Flak Battery (9 37mm, 2 quad 20mm and 2 LMGs; the 20mm were made self-propelled on 7 Mar. 1943)
1 (mot) Light (20 ton) Flak Supply Column

Sturmgeschütz Battalion (detached on 20 Mar. 1943)
1 Battalion Staff and Staff Battery (2 LMGs)
3 Sturmgeschütz Batteries (10 StuG ea)

40th Panzer Pioneer Battalion
1 Staff (2 LMGs)
1 (mot) Reconnaissance Platoon (6 50mm PAK 38, 4 LMGs) (deleted on 20 Mar. 1943)
1 (half-track) Pioneer Company (43 LMGs, 3 PzBu39, 2 80mm mortars and 6 flamethrowers)
2 (mot) Pioneer Companies (18 LMGs, 3 PzBu39, 2 80mm mortars and 6 flamethrowers ea)
1 Brüko K Bridging Column (3 LMGs)
1 (mot) Light Pioneer Supply Column (2 LMGs)

86th Panzer Signals Battalion
1 (mot) Telephone Company (5 LMGs) (replaced on 14 Mar. 1943 by a panzer signals company with 21 LMGs)
1 Panzer Radio Company (16 LMGs)
1 (mot) Light Signals Supply Column (1 LMG)

40th Supply Troop
1–8/40th (mot) (120 ton) Transportation Company (4 LMGs ea)
40th (mot) Supply Company (6 LMGs)

Truck Park
1–3/40th (mot) Maintenance Companies (4 LMGs ea)
40th (mot) Heavy (75 ton) Replacement Column (4 LMGs)

Other
40th (mot) Bakery Company
40th (mot) Butcher Company
40th (mot) Administration Platoon
1/, 2/40th (mot) Medical Companies (2 LMGs ea)
1/, 2/, 3/40th Ambulances
40th (mot) Military Police Troop (2 LMGs)
40th (mot) Field Post Office

Indications are that on 18 March 1943 the Tiger tank battalion was detached from the panzer regiment and each battalion was then equipped with a panzer maintenance company. The staff companies were apparently without either the pioneer or Flak platoons, but on 19 May 1943 they were equipped with PzMk III flame panzers. The sturmgeschütz battalion or 3rd Battalion of the panzer regiment apparently was operational on 2 April 1943. Indications are that at least two of the companies may have had Mk IV tanks. The changes to the panzer continued and the 2/24th Panzer Regiment was detached, possibly in August or September. The 3/24th Panzer Regiment, still a combination of two companies of StuG and two companies of PzMk IV tanks, then became the 2nd Battalion. At that point the battalion staff companies acquired both pioneer and Flak platoons.

On 7 April 1943 the reconnaissance battalion's armored car company broke out the six SdKfz 233 armored cars (75mm guns) and formed them as a separate platoon. At the same time all of the four-wheeled armored cars were replaced by eight-wheeled cars. The Flak battalion changed the quad 20mm guns of the 3rd Company for self-propelled models on 7 March 1943.

In October 1943 the division received the rebuilt 3/24th Panzer Regiment, equipped and organized with:

3/24th Panzer Regiment
Regimental Staff Signals Platoon
Regimental Staff Panzer Platoon
1 Flame Panzer Company
   Flammpanz   14
1 Battalion with:
   1 Battalion Staff Company
   2 Medium Panzer Companies
   2 Sturmgeschütz Companies
   PzMk IV (lg)   49
   StuG   44
   PzBefWg   9

In December 1943 the 2/24th Panzer Regiment was disbanded and the 3/24th was renumbered 2/24th. In September 1944 the 40th Panzerjäger Battalion was rebuilt from the 471st Panzer Destroyer Battalion.

On 30 May 1944 the 1/24th Panzer Regiment was equipped with Panther tanks. The 2/24th Panzer Regiment continued to be equipped with Panzer PzMk IV tanks. In the middle of

1944 the 1/24th Panzer Regiment was detached to the 1st Panzer Division. On 19 July 1944 the 15th (L) Panzerjäger Battalion of the disbanded 15th Luftwaffe Feld Division was redesignated as the 40th Panzerjäger Battalion and assigned to the 24th Panzer Division. On 20 August 1944 the organization of the armored portion of the division and its panzer inventory were as follows:

3/24th Panzer Regiment
  1 Panzer Staff Company
  1 Flame Panzer Company
  1 Battalion
    1 Panzer Staff Company
    2 Medium Panzer Companies

2 Sturmgeschütz Companies
Total tanks available:
  PzMk IV (lg)   49
  StuG   42
  PzBefWg   9
  Flammpanz   14

In January 1945 the 24th Panzer Division consisted of a kampfgruppe with only the 21st Panzergrenadier Regiment, two Panzer Companies (V), and the 40th Panzerjäger Battalion. In March 1945 the division was supported by the 9th Grenadier Regiment (1/, 2/9th and 1/68th) from the 23rd Infantry Division. It surrendered to the Allies on 4 May 1945.

25th Panzer Division

Formed on 25 February 1942 in Norway from the Schützen Verband Oslo, the division had:

1/, 2/, 3/146th Schützen Regiment
214th Panzer Battalion
514th Panzerjäger Company
91st 100mm Cannon Battery
91st Self-Propelled (88mm) Battery

The Staff/9th Panzer Regiment was assigned on 25 November 1942 and was redesignated as the Staff/9th Panzer Division. The 40th Panzer Battalion z.b.V. became the 2/9th Panzer Regiment on 5 December 1942 and the 214th Panzer Battalion became the 1/9th Panzer Regiment on 16 December 1942. OKH records show that the division was organized and equipped as follows on 5 April 1943:

Division Staff
  1 Division Staff (2 LMGs)
  1 (mot) Mapping Detachment
9th Panzer Regiment
  Regimental Staff
  1 Panzer Signals Platoon
1st Battalion
  1 Regimental Staff and Staff Company
  3 Panzer Companies (22 PzMk IV ea)
2nd Battalion
  1 Regimental Staff and Staff Company
  3 Panzer Companies (14 PzMk IV ea)
  1 Panzer Maintenance Company (2 platoons)
146th Panzergrenadier Regiment
  1 Regimental Staff
  1 Regimental Band
  1 (mot) Regimental Staff Company
    1 Signals Platoon

  1 Panzerjäger Platoon (3 50mm PAK 38 and 3 LMGs)
  1 Motorcycle Platoon (6 LMGs)
1st and 2nd (mot) Battalions, each with
  3 (mot) Companies (4 HMGs, 18 LMGs, 2 80mm mortars and 3 PzBu39 ea)
  1 (mot) Heavy Company
    1 Pioneer Platoon (4 LMGs)
    1 Panzerjäger Platoon (3 LMGs and 3 50mm PAK 38)
    1 Infantry Gun Platoon (4 75mm leIG)
    1 Panzerjäger Platoon (3 LMGs and 3 sPzBu 41)
  1 (motZ) Infantry Gun Company (4 150mm sIG)
147th Panzergrenadier Regiment
  same as 146th Panzergrenadier Regiment
87th Panzerjäger Battalion
  2 (motZ) Panzerjäger Companies (9, later 10 75mm PAK 40 and 6 LMGs ea)
  1 Sturmgeschütz Battery (10 StuG)
87th (later 25th) Reconnaissance Battalion
  1 Armored Car Company (24 LMGs and 18 20mm guns)
  2 Motorcycle Companies (2 80mm mortars, 4 HMGs, 18 LMGs and 3 PzBu39)
  1 (mot) Heavy Reconnaissance Company
    1 Pioneer Platoon (4 LMGs)
    1 Infantry Gun Section (2 75mm leIG)
    1 Panzerjäger Platoon (3 LMGs and 3 50 PAK 38)
    1 Panzerjäger Platoon (3 LMGs and 3 sPzBu 41)
91st Panzer Artillery Regiment
  1 Regimental Staff
  1 Staff Battery (2 LMGs)
1st and 2nd Battalions, each with
  1 Battalion Staff
  1 Battalion Staff Battery (6 LMGs)
  3 (mot) Batteries (3 105mm leFH and 2 LMGs ea)

3rd (mot) Battalion
1 Battalion Staff
1 Battalion Staff Battery (6 LMGs)
2 (mot) Batteries (3 150mm sFH and 2 LMGs ea)
1 (mot) Battery (3 100mm K 18 guns and 2 LMGs)

87th Panzer Pioneer Battalion
1 Staff (2 LMGs)
3 (mot) Pioneer Companies (18 LMGs, 2 80mm mortars and 3 PzBu39 ea)
1 Brüko K Bridging Column (3 LMGs)
1 (mot) Light Pioneer Supply Column (2 LMGs)

87th Panzer Signals Battalion
1 Panzer Telephone Company (6 LMGs)
1 Panzer Radio Company (16 LMGs)
1 (mot) Light Signals Supply Column (1 LMG)

87th Feldersatz Battalion
4 Companies

87th Supply Troop
3/, 4/, 5/87th (mot) (90 ton) Transportation Company (3 LMGs ea)
1/, 2/87th (mot) (120 ton) Transportation Company (4 LMGs ea)
87th (mot) Supply Company (6 LMGs)

Truck Park
1–2/87th (mot) Maintenance Companies (4 LMGs ea)

Other
87th (mot) Bakery Company
87th (mot) Butcher Company
87th (mot) Administration Platoon
1/, 2/87th (mot) Medical Companies (2 LMGs ea)
1/, 2/, 3/87th Ambulances
87th (mot) Military Police Troop (2 LMGs)
87th (mot) Field Post Office

On 15 June 1943 the division was brought to full strength with:

1/, 2/146th Schützen Regiment
1/, 2/147th Schützen Regiment
87th Motorcycle Battalion
1/, 2/9th Panzer Regiment
1/, 2/, 3/91st Panzer Artillery Regiment
279th Army Flak Battalion
87th Pioneer Battalion
87th Panzerjäger Battalion
87th Panzer Signals Battalion
87th Divisional Support Troops

Indications are that on or by 8 September 1943 the 1/9th Panzer Regiment was detached and the 2/9th expanded to four full companies, each with 22 PzMk IV tanks. The regimental staff companies of the panzergrenadier regiments added a pioneer platoon with 6 LMGs and 6 flamethrowers in mid-September 1943. At some point during the summer the sturmgeschütz company was detached from the panzerjäger battalion; it was gone by 25 August 1943. By that date the reconnaissance battalion had re-equipped one of its motorcycle companies with half-tracks, forming it as a half-track reconnaissance company (25 LMGs and 16 20mm guns). In addition, an independent heavy armored car platoon (six 75mm and six LMGs) was added on 19 September 1943. The 3/91st Artillery Regiment (heavy battalion) was either lost or detached during the summer.

The 284th Army Flak Battalion was added on 4 August 1943. It consisted of a staff, staff battery, two heavy (motZ) batteries (four 88mm, three 20mm and two LMGs), a (motZ) light battery (12 20mm and two LMGs) and a light (mot) Flak supply column.

In August 1943 the division was sent to France to prepare for battle in Russia. What remained in Norway was reorganized into a brigade-sized formation that was designated as the Panzer Division Norwegen. The 1/, 2/91st Artillery Regiment both had three (motZ) batteries of 105mm leFH. The 3/93rd contained three (motZ) batteries of captured Russian 122mm howitzers. The division had no feldersatz battalion.

On 6 September 1943 the 1/9th Panzer Regiment was detached and designated as the Panzer Battalion Norwegen. In November 1943 the organization of the armored portion of the division and its panzer inventory were as follows:

2/9th Panzer Regiment
1 Regimental Staff Signals Platoon
1 Regimental Staff Light Panzer Platoon
1 Battalion with
1 Panzer Staff Company
4 Medium Panzer Companies
Total tanks available:
PzMk IV (lg)   93
PzBefWg   8

In February 1944 the division was destroyed in the northern Ukraine. On 10 May 1944 it was re-formed in Denmark with the Norwegian Panzer Division, and the 104th Panzer Brigade was merged on 14 June 1944. The division had:

1/, 2/146th Schützen Regiment (from 2/146th and 3/ Norwegian Panzergrenadier Regiment)
1/, 2/147th Schützen Regiment (from Krampnitz Panzer Troop School, later replaced by 2104th Panzergrenadier Battalion, and new drafts)
25th Panzer Reconnaissance Battalion
1/, 2/9th Panzer Regiment (from 2104th and 2111th Panzer Battalions)
1/, 2/, 3/91st Panzer Artillery Regiment (from 3/2nd Artillery Lehr Regiment, 1/91st, Norwegian Panzer Artillery Battalion)

279th Army Flak Battalion
81st Pioneer Battalion
87th Panzerjäger Battalion
87th Panzer Signals Battalion
91st Feldersatz Battalion
87th Divisional Support Troops

On 5 August 1944 the 25th Panzer Division was organized as follows:

Staff
Divisional Staff
505th (mot) Mapping Detachment
Divisional Escort Company
  Flak Platoon (4 self-propelled 20mm Flak guns)
  Motorcycle Platoon (6 LMGs)
  Infantry Platoon (4 HMGs and 6 LMGs)
87th (mot) Feldgendarmerie Troop
146th Panzergrenadier Regiment
Regimental Staff
(mot) Regimental Staff Company
  Signals Platoon
  Motorcycle Platoon
2 Battalions, each with
  1 Battalion Staff
  1 (mot) Supply Company (4 LMGs)
  3 (mot) Panzergrenadier Companies (4 HMGs, 18 LMGs and 2 80mm mortars ea)
  1 (mot) Heavy Company (6 20mm Flak, 2 LMGs and 4 120mm mortars)
  1 (mot) Panzerjäger Company (4 heavy PAK and 7 LMGs)
  1 (mot) Pioneer Company (18 flamethrowers, 2 80mm mortars, 2 HMGs and 12 LMGs)
87th Panzerjäger Battalion
1 (mot) Staff
1 (mot) Staff Battery (4 LMGs)
1 (mot) Supply Company (3 LMGs)
2 Sturmgeschütz Companies (14 StuG and 14 LMGs ea)
1 Jagdpanzer Company (14 Jagdpanzer IV)
1 (motZ) Panzerjäger Company (12 75mm PAK 40 and 12 LMGs)
25th Panzer Reconnaissance Battalion
1 (Armored) Reconnaissance Staff
1 (mot) Staff Company
  1 (mot) Signals Platoon (7 LMGs)
  1 Armored Car Platoon (13 armored cars with 20mm and 3 armored cars with 75mm guns)
1st (half-track) Reconnaissance Company (2 75mm, 2 80mm mortars and 44 LMGs)
2nd (half-track) Reconnaissance Company (2 75mm, 2 80mm mortars and 44 LMGs)
3rd (half-track) Reconnaissance Company
  Staff (1 LMG)
  1 Platoon (6 75mm and 2 LMGs)

1 Platoon (6 80mm mortars and 2 LMGs)
1 Pioneer Platoon (13 LMGs)
1 (mot) Supply Company (4 LMGs)
91st Panzer Artillery Detachment
1 (mot) Regimental Staff Battery (2 LMGs)
1st Battalion
1 (mot) Staff Battery
3 Batteries (4 105mm leFH and 4 LMGs ea)
2nd Battalion
1 (mot) Staff Battery
2 Batteries (4 150mm sFH and 4 LMGs ea)
1 Battery (4 100mm K 18 and 4 LMGs)
1/279th (motZ) Army Flak Battalion (6 88mm and 6 20mm Flak guns)
87th Panzer Pioneer Battalion
1 (mot) Pioneer Staff (10 LMGs)
1 (mot) Pioneer Supply Company (4 LMGs)
3 (mot) Pioneer Companies (2 HMGs, 18 LMGs and 2 80mm mortars ea)
1 (mot) Panzer Bridging Section
87th Panzer Signals Battalion
1 Armored Radio Company (19 LMGs)
1 Armored Telephone Company (11 LMGs)
1 (mot) Signals Supply Platoon (2 LMGs)
87th Supply Detachment
1 (mot) Supply Staff Company
2 (120 ton) (mot) Transportation Companies
1/87th (mot) Maintenance Company
87th Maintenance Platoon
87th Maintenance Column
87th Administration Troops
87th (mot) Bakery Company
87th (mot) Butcher Company
87th (mot) Administration Company
Medical
1/87th (mot) Medical Company
2/87th (mot) Medical Company
87th Ambulance
Other
87th (mot) Field Post Office

The battles of late 1943 and early 1944 had dramatically reduced the division's strength. Elements of the division were used to create the independent army panzer brigades, and on 5 August 1944 the rest were organized into a kampfgruppe. Initially, this kampfgruppe had only a single panzer company, equipped with 14 PzMk IV tanks, and was assigned to the panzerjäger battalion. In October the organization of the armored portion of the division and its panzer inventory were as follows:

Kampfgruppe
1 Medium Panzer Company
1 Jagdpanzer Company
Total tanks available:

PzMk IV   15
JagdpzIV (V)   17

On 5 November 1944 the division absorbed the 104th Panzer Brigade. In early 1945 the 25th Panzer Division was greatly reduced by combat and was reorganized into a kampfgruppe. This kampfgruppe was organized as follows:

Division Staff
1 Divisional Staff (2 LMGs)
1 (mot) Mapping Detachment
1 Armored Car Reconnaissance Platoon (3 SdKfz 234/3 with 75mm and 13 SdKfz234/1 with 1 20mm and 1 LMG ea)

Panzer Battalion
1 Panzer Battalion Staff (1 LMG)
1 Panzer Battalion Staff Company (8 LMGs and 3 self-propelled quad 20mm guns)
3 Panzer Companies (14 PzMk IV tanks ea)
1 Panzer Maintenance Company (4 LMGs)
1 Panzer Supply Company (4 LMGs)

Panzergrenadier Regiment
1 Regimental Staff (2 LMGs)
1 (mot) Regimental Staff Company
   1 Signals Platoon
   1 Motorcycle Platoon (4 LMGs)

1st and 2nd (mot) Battalions, each with
1 Battalion Staff (2 LMGs)
1 (mot) Regimental Staff Company (3 panzerschrecke and 4 LMGs)
3 (mot) Companies (12 LMGs, 3 panzerschrecke and 30 MP 44 ea)
1 (mot) Heavy Company (12 HMGs, 1 LMG and 6 20mm Flak)
1 (mot) Heavy Company (6 LMGs, 8 80mm mortars and 4 120mm mortars)

3rd (bicycle) Battalion
1 Battalion Staff (2 LMGs)
1 (mot) Regimental Staff Company (3 panzerschrecke 4 LMGs)
3 (bicycle) Companies (12 LMGs, 3 panzerschrecke and 30 MP 44 ea)
1 (mot) Heavy Company (12 HMGs, 1 LMG and 6 20mm Flak)

1 (mot) Heavy Company (6 LMGs, 8 80mm mortars and 4 120mm mortars)

Panzerjäger Battalion
1 Battalion Staff
1 Battalion Staff Company (1 LMG)
1 Staff Sturmgeschütz Platoon (3 StuG)
2 Jagdpanzer Batteries (14 Jagdpanzer ea)
1 Half-Track Company (12 SdKfz 251/22 with 75mm PAK)
1 (mot) Supply Company (3 LMGs)

Artillery Battalion
1 Battalion Staff
1 (mot) Battalion Staff Battery (2 LMGs and 3 20mm Flak)
3 (motZ) Batteries (6 105mm leFH and 4 LMGs ea)

(mot) Pioneer Company
(2 HMGs, 16 LMGs and 2 80mm mortars)

Panzer Signals Company
Other
1 (mot) Supply Troop Staff
1 (mot) (120 ton) Transportation Company (8 LMGs)
2 (mot) Maintenance Companies (4 LMGs ea)
1 (mot) Mixed Supply Troop (3 LMGs)
1 (mot) Medical Company (2 LMGs)
1 (mot) Medical Supply Company (2 LMGs)
1 (mot) Field Post Office (1 LMG)

On 11 February 1945 Army Group Center was ordered to refurbish the 25th Panzer Division as a kampfgruppe. The 1/9th Panzer Regiment was to contain two PzMk IV Companies (14 tanks each), one Jagdpanzer Company (14 Pz IV/70), and two command tanks for the command staff. On 19 February 1945 the organization of the armored portion of the division and its panzer inventory were as follows:

Kampfgruppe
   2 Medium Panzer Company
   1 Jagdpanzer Company
Total tanks available:
   PzMk IV   21
   JagdpzIV (V)   10

It surrendered to the Allies on 9 May 1945.

26th Panzer Division

Formed on 14 September 1942 in France from the 23rd Infantry Division. It had:

26th Panzergrenadier Brigade
   1/, 2/9th Panzergrenadier Regiment (from 9th Infantry Regiment)

1/, 2/67th Panzergrenadier Regiment (from 67th Infantry Regiment)
26th Motorcycle Battalion (from 23rd Bicycle Battalion)
1/, 2/26th Panzer Regiment (from 2/, 3/202nd Panzer Regiment)

1/, 2/, 3/93rd Panzer Artillery Regiment (from 23rd Panzer Artillery Regiment)
304th Army Flak Battalion
93rd Panzerjäger Battalion
93rd Panzer Pioneer Battalion
93rd Panzer Signals Battalion
93rd Divisional Support Troops

The 202nd Panzer Regiment was redesignated as the 26th Panzer Regiment on 5 January 1943. The 2/202nd Panzer Regiment became the 2/26th Panzer Regiment and the 3/202nd Panzer Regiment became the 1/26th Panzer Regiment. The 1/202nd Panzer Regiment became the 202nd Panzer Battalion and was retained in the Balkans to fight partisans. In January 1943 the 1/26th Panzer Regiment was organized and equipped with one panzer staff company, four panzer companies, and a total of 76 PzMk V tanks.

Later in 1943 the 26th Panzer Regiment was rebuilt and contained a staff, a staff company, a 1st Battalion with four companies of Panther PzMk V tanks, and a 2nd Battalion with four companies of Panzer PzMk IV tanks. OKH records show that the division was organized and equipped as follows in early 1943:

Division Staff
1 Division Staff (2 LMGs)
93rd (mot) Mapping Detachment
26th Panzer Regiment
Regimental Staff
1 Signals Platoon
1 Regimental Band
1st Battalion
1 Regimental Staff and Staff Company (1 PzMk III flame panzer platoon)
2 Light Panzer Companies (14 PzMk III ea)
1 Panzer Company (14 PzMk IV)
2nd Battalion
1 Regimental Staff and Staff Company
2 Light Panzer Companies (14 PzMk III ea)
1 Panzer Company (14 PzMk IV)
1 Panzer Maintenance Company
9th Panzergrenadier Regiment
1 Regimental Staff
1 Regimental Band
1 (mot) Regimental Staff Company
1 Signals Platoon
1 Panzerjäger Platoon (3 50mm PAK 38 and 3 LMGs)
1 Motorcycle Platoon (6 LMGs)
1 Panzer Pioneer Platoon (6 flamethrowers)
1st (half-track) Battalion
3 (half-track) Companies (4 HMGs, 34 LMGs, 2 80mm mortars and 3 75mm leIG ea)
1 (half-track) Heavy Company

1 Pioneer Platoon (4 LMGs; upgraded to 9 LMGs and 6 flamethrowers, replacing the self-propelled flamethrower platoon)
1 Self-Propelled Flamethrower Platoon (deleted)
1 Gun Platoon (8 LMGs and 6 75mm guns)
1 Panzerjäger Platoon (3 50mm PAK 38 and 3 LMGs)
1 Infantry Gun Platoon (8 LMGs and 4 75mm leIG)
1 Panzerjäger Platoon (3 LMGs and 3 sPzBu 41)
2nd (mot) Battalion
3 (mot) Companies (4 HMGs, 18 LMGs, 2 80mm mortars and 3 PzBu39 ea)
1 (mot) Heavy Company
1 Pioneer Platoon (4 LMGs)
1 Panzerjäger Platoon (3 LMGs and 3 50mm PAK 38)
1 Infantry Gun Platoon (4 75mm leIG)
1 Panzerjäger Platoon (3 LMGs and 3 sPzBu 41)
1 Self-Propelled Infantry Gun Company (6 150mm sIG and 3 LMGs)
67th Panzergrenadier Regiment
1 Regimental Staff
1 Regimental Band
1 (mot) Regimental Staff Company
1 Signals Platoon
1 Panzerjäger Platoon (3 50mm PAK 38 and 3 LMGs)
1 Motorcycle Platoon (6 LMGs)
1st and 2nd (mot) Battalions, each with same as 2/9th Panzergrenadiers
1 Self-Propelled Infantry Gun Company (6 150mm sIG and 3 LMGs)
93rd Panzerjäger Battalion
2 (motZ) Panzerjäger Company (12 75mm PAK 40 and 12 LMGs ea)
1 Self-Propelled Panzerjäger Company (14 75mm PAK 40 and 14 LMGs ea)
26th Reconnaissance Battalion (early 1943 organization)
1 Armored Car Company (24 LMGs and 18 20mm guns)
3 (half-track) Reconnaissance Companies (2 80mm mortars, 4 HMGs, 56 LMGs and 3 37mm PAK 36 ea)
1 (half-track) Heavy Reconnaissance Company
1 Pioneer Platoon (4, later 13 LMGs)
1 (half-track) Gun Section (6 75mm and 8 LMGs)
1 Infantry Gun Section (4 75mm leIG, later adding 4 LMGs)
1 Panzerjäger Platoon (3, later 9 LMGs and 3 75mm PAK 40)
1 Panzerjäger Platoon (3 LMGs and 3 sPzBu 41)
1 (mot) Light Reconnaissance Supply Column (3 LMGs)
93rd Panzer Artillery Regiment
1 Regimental Staff

1 Staff Battery (2 LMGs)

1st Battalion

1 Battalion Staff and Staff Battery (6 LMGs)

2 Self-Propelled Batteries (6 105mm leFH SdKfz 124 Wespe and 4 LMGs ea)

1 Self-Propelled Battery (6 150mm sFH SdKfz 165 Hummel and 4 LMGs)

2nd Battalion

1 Battalion Staff

1 Battalion Staff Battery (6 LMGs)

3 (mot) Batteries (3 105mm leFH and 2 LMGs ea)

3rd (mot) Battalion

1 Battalion Staff

1 Battalion Staff Battery (6 LMGs)

2 (mot) Batteries (3 150mm sFH and 2 LMGs ea)

1 (mot) Battery (3 100mm K 18 guns and 2 LMGs)

93rd (mot) Observation Battery (2 LMGs)

93rd Panzer Pioneer Battalion

1 Staff (2 LMGs)

1 (half-track) Pioneer Company (25 LMGs, 2 80mm mortars and 3 panzerschrecke ea)

1 (mot) Pioneer Companies (18 LMGs, 2 80mm mortars and 3 panzerschrecke)

1 Brüko K Bridging Column (3 LMGs)

1 (mot) Light Pioneer Supply Column (2 LMGs)

82nd Panzer Signals Battalion

1 Panzer Telephone Company (6 LMGs)

1 Panzer Radio Company (16 LMGs)

1 (mot) Light Signals Supply Column (1 LMG)

93rd Feldersatz Company

93rd Supply Troop

5/93rd (mot) (90 ton) Transportation Company (3 LMGs ea)

1/, 2/, 3/, 4/93rd (mot) (120 ton) Transportation Company (4 LMGs ea)

93rd (mot) Supply Company (6 LMGs)

Truck Park

1–3/93rd (mot) Maintenance Companies (4 LMGs ea)

Other

93rd (mot) Bakery Company

93rd (mot) Butcher Company

93rd (mot) Administration Platoon

1/, 2/93rd (mot) Medical Companies (2 LMGs ea)

1/, 2/, 3/93rd Ambulances

93rd (mot) Military Police Troop (2 LMGs)

93rd (mot) Field Post Office

Prior to July 1943 the 26th Panzer Regiment underwent significant changes, though unfortunately the dates of those changes are not known. The battalion staffs added pioneer platoons, but not Flak platoons. The light panzer companies were initially upgraded to medium companies with PzMk IV tanks. From there the two battalions added a fourth company, and all companies were upgraded to 22 tanks each. Then the 1/26th was re-equipped with PzMk

V Panther tanks. When the battalions equipped with PzMk IV tanks it appears that a second maintenance company was added and each battalion had an assigned maintenance company.

On 16 June 1943 the panzerjäger battalion was to have undergone a major reorganization and re-equipment. All three companies were to be equipped with 14 Hornisse SdKfz 14 88mm PAK 43/1 L/71 and 16 LMGs. In addition, the staff added three self-propelled quad 20mm guns. The new staff battery had three Hornissen and 10 LMGs. However, notes dating from 31 August 1943 indicate that this organization was scrapped, and there is no indication of what replaced it.

On 23 July 1943 the 93rd Panzerjäger Battalion was detached and became an independent army unit. On 25 November 1943 the 1/26th Panzer Regiment was equipped with Panther tanks. Shortly afterwards it seems to have been assigned to the Grossdeutschland Division and was replaced by the 1/4th Panzer Regiment (13th Panzer Division) until early 1945.

On 20 August 1943 the organization of the armored portion of the division and its panzer inventory were as follows:

2/26th Panzer Regiment

1 Panzer Staff Platoon

1 Panzer Signals Platoon

1 Battalion

  1 Panzer Staff Company

  4 Medium Panzer Companies

Total tanks available:

PzMk III (75)	16
PzMk IV (kz)	17
PzMk IV (lg)	36
Flammpanzer	14
PzBefWg	9

On 17 October 1944 the 51st Panzerjäger Battalion was assigned to the division. In 1944 the 6th Panzer Division received the 1/26th Panzer Regiment. This battalion would become the 1/Brandenburg Panzer Regiment in 1945, and the 1(Panther)/4th Panzer Regiment replaced the 1/26th in April. On 11 June 1944 the division was reinforced by the absorption of the 1027th (mot) Grenadier Brigade, and in November 1944 the 20th Field Division (L) was absorbed into the division. It surrendered to the Allies on 9 May 1945.

27th Panzer Division

Formed on 1 October 1942 in southern Russia by the renaming of the Michalek Panzer Group (detached from the 22nd Panzer Division). The division had:

1/, 2/140th Panzergrenadier Regiment (from 22nd Panzer Division)
127th Panzer Battalion (from 3/204th Panzer Regiment)
1/, 2/127th Panzer Artillery Regiment (from staff/677th Artillery Regiment, 1/140th Panzer Artillery Regiment and 2/51st Artillery Regiment)
127th Schnelle Battalion
127th Panzer Reconnaissance Battalion

127th Panzer Pioneer Battalion
127th Panzer Signals Battalion
127th Divisional Support Troops

The 127th Schnelle Battalion was formed from the 560th Panzerjäger Battalion and the 127th Pioneer Battalion was formed from the 260th Pioneer Battalion. On 15 February 1943 the division was disbanded and absorbed into the 7th Panzer Division. The 1/140th Panzergrenadier Regiment became the 2/7th Panzergrenadier Regiment, and the 127th Panzer Battalion was absorbed into the 24th Panzer Division as the 3/24th Panzer Regiment.

116th Panzer Division

Formed on 28 March 1944 in France from the remains of the 16th Panzergrenadier Division and the 179th Reserve Panzer Division. The division had:

1/, 2/16th Panzer Regiment (from Staff/69th Panzer Regiment, 116th Panzer
Battalion and 1st Reserve Panzer Battalion (179th Reserve Panzer Division)
1/, 2/60th Panzergrenadier Regiment (from 60th (mot) Grenadier Regiment)
1/, 2/156th Panzergrenadier Regiment (from 156th (mot) Grenadier Regiment)
116th Panzer Reconnaissance Battalion (from 1st Reserve Panzer Reconnaissance Battalion)
1/, 2/, 3/146th Panzer Artillery Regiment
281st Army Flak Battalion
228th Panzerjäger Battalion
675th Pioneer Battalion
228th Signals Battalion
66th Supply Units

The Panther companies were equipped with 17 Panther tanks and the companies equipped with PzMk IV tanks had 22 each. In July 1944 the organization of the armored portion of the division and its panzer inventory were as follows:

1/24th Panzer Regiment
  1 Panzer Staff Company
  1 Battalion
    1 Panzer Staff Company
    4 Medium Panzer Companies (PzMk V)
2/16th Panzer Regiment
  1 Battalion
    1 Panzer Staff Company
    4 Medium Panzer Companies (PzMk IV)

Total tanks available:

PzMk III (lg)	6
PzMk IV (lg)	73
PzMk V	79
Flakpz IV (37)	8

After heavy losses in Normandy, the division was rebuilt in the Eifel by incorporating the XII, XIII, and XIX Luftwaffe Fortress Battalions. On 13 October 1944 it absorbed the 108th Panzer Brigade. The division was reorganized with a panther battalion organized with four companies, each with 14 PzMk V Panther tanks. The second battalion was a mixed battalion, having two companies with 14 PzMk IV tanks and one sturmgeschütz company with 14 sturmgeschütze. On 16 December 1944 the organization of the armored portion of the division and its panzer inventory were as follows:

1/, 2/16th Panzer Regiment
  1 Panzer Staff Company
  1st Battalion
    1 Panzer Staff Company
    4 Medium Panzer Companies (PzMk V)
  2nd Battalion
    1 Panzer Staff Company
    2 Medium Panzer Companies (PzMk IV)
    1 Sturmgeschütz Company (StuG)

Total tanks available:

StuG	14 (en route)
PzMk IV (lg)	21 (+5 en route)
PzMk V	41 (+23 en route)
FlakpzIV (2V)	3

On 14 April 1945 the division formed a kampfgruppe. This kampfgruppe had a single panzer company with 14 Panther MI V tanks and a platoon with 4 Sturmtigers. The division was taken prisoner in the Ruhr pocket on 17 April 1945.

Panzer Division Nr 155

The Division (mot) Nr 155 was reorganized into the Panzer Division Nr 155 on 5 April 1943, and on 1 August 1943 it was again reorganized into the 155th Reserve Panzer Division. In December 1943 it had:

7th Reserve Panzer Battalion
5th Reserve Panzergrenadier Regiment (86th and 215th Battalions)
25th Reserve (mot) Grenadier Regiment (35th and 119th Battalions)
260th Reserve (mot) Artillery Battalion
5th Reserve Panzerjäger Battalion
1055th Reserve Panzer Signals Company
9th (mot) Reserve Reconnaissance Battalion

In January 1944 the division was assigned to the 7th AOK and is shown to have contained:

7th Reserve Panzer Battalion
   1st Battalion: 6 medium companies
   2nd Battalion: 4 medium companies
   1 Maintenance Company
9th Reserve Panzer Reconnaissance Battalion
   1 Armored Car Platoon (11 armored cars)
   2 Half-Track Reconnaissance Companies
   1 Motorcycle Company
   1 Infantry Company
5th Reserve Panzergrenadier Regiment
   86th (half-track) Reserve Panzergrenadier Battalion (4 companies)
   215th (half-track) Reserve Panzergrenadier Battalion (4 companies)
   1 Heavy Company (no vehicles)
   1 (mot) Infantry Gun Company (4 150mm sIG)
   1 (mot) Panzerjäger Company (7 37mm, 1 47mm, 1 50mm and 1 75mm guns)
25th Reserve (mot) Grenadier Regiment
   36th (mot) Panzergrenadier Battalion (4 companies)
   1 Heavy Company (no vehicles)
   119th (mot) Panzergrenadier Battalion (4 companies)
   1 Heavy Company (no vehicles)
260th Reserve (mot) Artillery Battalion
   1 (mot) Panzergrenadier Company
   1 (motZ) Artillery Battery (3 150mm sFH and 2 LMGs)
   1 (motZ) Artillery Battery (4 105mm leFH and 2 LMGs)
5th Reserve Panzerjäger Battalion
   1 (motZ) Company (4 LMGs, 2 HMGs, 1 75mm PAK 40, 2 75mm PAK 97/38, 1 50mm PAK 38 and 7 37mm PAK 36)
   1 Self-Propelled Company (4 LMGs, 4 HMGs, 1 50mm PAK 38, 4 75mm PAK 40, 2 47mm and 1 self-propelled gun)
   1 Self-Propelled Company (8 LMGs, 1 HMG, 1 20mm KWK, 3 37mm PAK 36, 1 47mm self-propelled, 3 75mm PAK 40 self-propelled and 1 StuG)
   1 Self-Propelled Company (1 20mm KWK, 3 HMGs, 6 LMGs, 1 50mm PAK 38, 1 75mm PAK 40, 1 75mm PAK 97/38, 3 75mm PAK 40 self-propelled and 1 StuG)
   3 Training Companies

The order of 19 March 1944 directed it be used to reform the 9th Panzer Division. It was disbanded on 30 April 1944. The 7th Reserve Panzer battalion was used to form the Norwegian Panzer brigade.

Panzer Division Nr 178

Formed on 5 April 1943 from the 178th (mot) Division. It contained:

15th Panzer Ersatz and Ausbildungs Battalion
85th Panzergrenadier Ausbildungs Regiment (13th, 110th Battalions)
128th (mot) Grenadier Ausbildungs Regiment (30th and 51st Battalions)
55th Panzer Reconnaissance Ersatz and Ausbildungs Battalion
8th Panzerjäger Ersatz and Ausbildungs Battalion

In December 1944 the division was disbanded. The 85th Panzergrenadier. Ersatz und Ausbildungs Regiment, the 13th Panzergrenadier Ersatz und Ausbildungs Battalions, and the 30/51st Combined Battalion were sent to the Tatra Panzer (Feldausbildungs) Division. The 128th Panzergrenadier Ersatz and Ausbildungs Regiment remained in Silesia.

Panzer Division Nr 179

Formed in Weimar on 5 April 1943 from the 179th (mot) Division. On 30 July 1943 it became the 179th Reserve Panzer Division.

179th Reserve Panzer Division

Formed in France on 30 July 1943 with:

1st Reserve Panzer Battalion
81st Reserve Panzergrenadier Regiment (1st, 6th and 59th Battalions)
29th Reserve Grenadier Regiment (mot) (15th and 71st Battalions)
29th Reserve Artillery Battalion
1st Reserve Armored Reconnaissance Battalion
9th Reserve Panzerjäger Battalion

In January 1944 the 179th Reserve Panzer Division was assigned to the 7th AOK, whose records show that the division was organized and equipped as follows:

1st Reserve Panzer Battalion (9 companies)
1st Reserve Armored Reconnaissance Battalion
  1 Armored Car Company (15 LMGs, 12 20mm KWK and 1 75mm KWK)
  1 (half-track) Reconnaissance Company (1 37mm and 9 LMGs)
  1 (half-track) Reconnaissance Company (8 LMGs)
  1 Motorcycle Company (10 LMGs and 2 HMGs)
  1 Training Company (3 LMGs)
81st (half-track) Reserve Panzergrenadier Regiment
  1 (motZ) Panzerjäger Company (5 75mm PAK 40 and 4 LMGs)
  1 (mot) Signals Platoon
  1 (mot) Pioneer Platoon (9 LMGs)
  1 (mot) Escort Company (2 HMGs and 11 LMGs)
1st (half-track) Reserve Panzergrenadier Battalion
  4 Companies (4 LMGs and 3 HMGs ea on average)
  1 Training Company (4 LMGs and 5 HMGs)
6th (half-track) Reserve Panzergrenadier Battalion
  4 Companies (6 LMGs and 4 HMGs ea on average)
  1 Training Company (4 LMG and 5 HMGs)
59th (half-track) Reserve Panzergrenadier Battalion
  4 Companies (6 LMGs and 4 HMGs ea on average)
  1 Training Company (1 LMG and 5 HMGs)

29th (mot) Reserve Grenadier Regiment
  1 (mot) Escort Company (3 LMGs)
  1 (mot) Signals Company (1 LMG)
  1 (motZ) Infantry Gun Company (2 150mm sIG and 4 75mm leIG)
  1 (motZ) Panzerjäger Company (8 37mm PAK 36, 4 LMGs, 1 50mm PAK 36 and 2 75mm PAK 40)
15th Reserve Grenadier Battalion
  4 (mot) Companies
  2 (mot) Training Companies
71st Reserve Grenadier Battalion
  4 (mot) Companies
  2 (mot) Training Companies
29th Reserve Artillery Battalion
  1 (mot) Signals Platoon
  1 (mot) Battery (4 105mm leFH, 3 LMGs and 3 HMGs)
  1 (mot) Battery (4 150mm sFH, 3 LMGs and 3 HMGs)
  1 (mot) Training Company
  2 Training Companies
9th Reserve Panzerjäger Battalion
  1 (motZ) Company (2 37mm PAK 36, 2 50mm PAK 38 and 6 LMGs)
  1 Self-Propelled Company (1 37mm PAK 36 and 2 LMGs)
  1 Self-Propelled Company (1 37mm PAK 36 and 2 LMGs)
  1 Self-Propelled Company (1 37mm PAK 36, 2 47mm, 5 LMGs, ? 75mm PAK 40 and 4 76.2mm)
  1 Self-Propelled Company (2 37mm PAK 36, 4 50mm PAK 38, 9 75mm PAK 40 and 8 LMGs)
  1 Training Company (2 37mm PAK 36 and 2 LMGs)
  1 Sturmgeschütz Company (2 37mm PAK 36 and 2 LMGs)

The 179th Reserve Panzer Division and the 16th Panzergrenadier Division were used to form the 116th Panzer Division. The 179th was disbanded on 1 May 1944. The remainder of the division was sent back to Germany and reabsorbed into the system.

232nd Reserve Panzer Division

Formed in February 1945 in Slovakia, from the Tatra Panzer Feldausbildungs Division. It contained:

101st Panzergrenadier Regiment (from 82nd Panzergrenadier Replacement and Training Regiment)
102nd Panzergrenadier Regiment (from 85th Panzergrenadier Replacement and Training Regiment)

The division was destroyed in the Raab bridgehad in late March 1945.

233rd Reserve Panzer Division

Formed on 5 April 1943 from the 233rd Reserve Panzergrenadier Division. When organized, the 9th Bicycle Ersatz Battalion was redesignated the 9th Ersatz Reconnaissance Battalion. The division was organized as follows:

233rd Reserve Panzer Division
1 Divisional Staff

5th Reserve Panzer Regiment
1 Regimental Staff
1 Panzer Signals Platoon
1 Panzer Battalion
  6 Panzer Companies
1 Panzer Battalion
  3 Panzer Medium Companies

83rd Reserve Panzergrenadier Regiment
  1 Regimental Headquarters
  3rd Reserve (half-track) Panzergrenadier Battalion
    1 (half-track) Battalion Headquarters
    4 (half-track) Companies
    1 (mot) Company
  8th Reserve (half-track) Panzergrenadier Battalion
  same as 3rd Reserve Panzergrenadier Regiment
  9th Reserve (half-track) Panzergrenadier Battalion
  same as 3rd Reserve Panzergrenadier Regiment
  83rd Reserve (mot) Panzerjäger Company
  83rd Reserve (mot) Signals Company
  83rd Reserve (mot) Pioneer Company

3rd Reserve Panzergrenadier Regiment
  1 Regimental Headquarters
  8th Reserve Panzergrenadier Battalion
    1 (mot) Battalion Headquarters
    3 (mot) Companies
    1 (mot) Machine Gun Company
    1 (mot) Company
  8th Reserve (mot) Panzergrenadier Battalion
  same as 8th Reserve Panzergrenadier Regiment
  50th Reserve (half-track) Panzergrenadier Battalion
  same as 3rd Reserve Panzergrenadier Regiment
  3rd Reserve (motZ) Panzerjäger Company
  3rd Reserve (mot) Signals Company
  3rd Reserve (mot) Machine Gun Company
  3rd Reserve (mot) Pioneer Company

59th Reserve (motZ) Artillery Battalion
1 (mot) Signals Platoon
1 (motZ) Battery (105mm leFH)
1 (motZ) Battery (150mm sFH)
1 (mot) Training Battery
1 Training Company

3rd Reserve Panzer Reconnaissance Battalion
1 Panzer Reconnaissance Battalion Headquarters
1 (mot) Signals Platoon
1 Armored Car Company

2 (half-track) Reconnaissance Companies
1 Motorcycle Reconnaissance Company
1 Training Company

5th Reserve (mot) Panzerjäger Battalion
3 Self-Propelled Panzerjäger Batteries
1 (motZ) Panzerjäger Battery
1 Training Company

208th Reserve Panzer Pioneer Battalion
1 Panzer Pioneer Headquarters
1 Panzer Signals Platoon
3 Panzer Pioneer Companies
1/2 (mot) Bridging Column

Medical
1233rd (mot) Medical Company
1233rd Ambulance

OKH records show that on 1 December 1944 the division was organized and equipped as follows:

233rd Reserve Panzer Division
1 Divisional Staff (3 LMGs and 3 37mm PAK 36)
1233rd (mot) Military Police Detachment

5th Reserve Panzer Regiment
1 Regimental Staff (8 LMGs)
1 Regimental Staff Company (16 LMGs, 1 command PzMk IV and 8 PzMk I flame)
1 Panzer Battalion
  Panzer Company (2 PzMk III 50mm, 8 Mk III short 75mm and 11 Mk IV L/43)
  Panzer Company (1 PzMk III 50mm, 10 PzMk III short 75mm, 1 PzMk IV L/24 and 11 Mk IV L/43)
  Panzer Company (1 PzMk III 50mm, 4 PzMk III short 75mm, 2 PzMk IV L/24 and 6 PzMk IV L/43)
  Panzer Company (PzMk I PzBefWg)
1 Panzergrenadier Battalion
  83rd (half-track) Company (2 50mm guns, 2 80mm mortars, 4 HMGs and 44 LMGs)
  208th (half-track) Company (5 LMGs, 3 37mm PAK 36 and 2 20mm)
  1st Btry/59th Self-Propelled Artillery Battalion (2 105mm leFH 189 and 2 150mm sFH 18)
  3rd Btry/3rd Panzerjäger Company (13 75mm PAK 40, 10 LMGs and 1 panzerschreck)

3rd Panzer Reconnaissance Battalion
1 Staff (1 LMG)
1 (mot) Signals Platoon (2 LMGs)
1 Armored Car Company (19 LMGs, 1 75mm gun, 2 20mm guns and 1 panzerschreck)
1 (mot) Company
  1 Half-Track Platoon (4 HMGs, 27 LMGs and 3 panzerschrecke)
  1 Gun Platoon (2 73mm PAK 36 and 2 20mm guns)
1 Motorcycle Company (4 HMGs and 12 LMGs)

1 (mot) Infantry Company (4 80mm mortars, 2 LMGs and 2 37mm PAK 36)

83rd Reserve Panzergrenadier Regiment

1 Regimental Staff (2 LMGs and 1 20mm gun)

1 Regimental Staff Company

  1 Gun Platoon (2 panzerschrecke and 3 20mm guns)

  1 Signals Platoon

  1 Motorcycle Platoon

  1 Mortar Platoon (3 120mm mortars)

  1 (half-track) Platoon (10 LMGs and 2 75mm guns)

8th Reserve (half-track) Panzergrenadier Battalion

1 (mot) Battalion Staff and Staff Company (3 motZ 50mm PAK 38 and 2 motZ 75mm leIG)

1 (mot) Signals Platoon

3 (mot) Companies (9 HMGs, 18 LMGs, 2 80mm mortars and 2 panzerschrecke ea)

1 (mot) Reserve Company

1 (mot) Company

9th Reserve (half-track) Panzergrenadier Battalion

same as 3rd Reserve Panzergrenadier Regiment

83rd Reserve (motZ) Panzerjäger Company (11 75mm PAK 40, 3 75mm PAK 97/38 (French), 1 panzerschreck and 4 LMGs)

83rd (mot) Reserve Company (3 LMGs)

83rd (mot) Reserve Pioneer Company (12 LMGs, 2 panzerschrecke and 12 flamethrowers)

3rd Reserve Panzergrenadier Regiment

1 Regimental Staff

1 Regimental Staff Company

  1 Signals Platoon

  1 Panzerjäger Platoon (3 LMGs and 2 panzerschrecke)

1 Motorcycle Platoon

1 (mot) Reserve Platoon

3rd Reserve (half-track) Panzergrenadier Battalion

1 (mot) Battalion Staff and Staff Company (3 motZ 75mm leIG and 2 motZ 50mm PAK 38)

1 (mot) Panzerjäger Platoon (2 panerschreck)

1 (mot) Signals Platoon

3 (mot) Companies (9 HMGs, 18 LMGs, 2 80mm mortars and 3 panzerschrecke ea) (one company on bicycles)

1 (mot) Reserve Company

1 (mot) Company

50th Reserve (half-track) Panzergrenadier Battalion

1 (mot) Battalion Staff and Staff Company (4 motZ 50mm PAK 38, 2 75mm leIG and 1 panzerschreck)

1 (mot) Signals Platoon

1 (mot) Panzerjäger Platoon (2 panerschreck)

3 (mot) Companies (9 HMGs, 18 LMGs, 2 80mm mortars and 3 panzerschrecke ea) (one company on bicycles)

1 (mot) Reserve Company

1 (mot) Company

3rd Reserve (motZ) Panzerjäger Company (6 75mm PAK 40, 7 50mm PAK 38, 13 LMGs and 2 20mm guns)

3rd (motZ) Infantry Gun Company (4 120mm sIG, 2 75mm leIG, 4 120mm mortars and 2 LMGs)

3rd (mot) Reserve Pioneer Company (12 LMGs and 16 flamethrowers)

59th Reserve (motZ) Artillery Battalion

1 (mot) Staff (8 LMGs and 1 panzerschreck)

1 (mot) Staff Battery

  1 Signals Platoon

  1 Calibration Platoon

  1 Reserve Platoon

1 (motZ) Battery (4 105mm leFH 18, 4 LMGs and 2 panzerschrecke)

1 (motZ) Battery (4 150mm sFH 18, 4 LMGs and 2 panzerschrecke)

3rd Reserve Panzerjäger Battalion

1 Panzerjäger Battalion Staff (2 LMGs)

1 (mot) Signals Platoon

1 (motZ) Panzerjäger Company (11 75mm PAK 40, 1 panzerschreck and 3 LMGs)

1 Self-Propelled Panzerjäger Company (3 75mm PAK 40, 3 76.2mm Russian guns, 1 panzerschreck and 4 LMGs)

1 (mot) Sturmgeschütz Escort Company (5 StuG and 9 LMGs)

1 Reserve Company (1 panzerschreck and 3 LMGs)

208th Reserve Panzer Pioneer Battalion

1 Panzer Pioneer Headquarters

1 (mot) Signals Platoon

2 (mot) Pioneer Companies (1 HMG, 9 LMGs, 2 80mm mortars and 3 panzerschrecke ea)

1 (mot) Pioneer Company (1 HMG and 9 LMGs)

1 (mot) "K" Bridging Column (1 LMG)

1 (mot) "B" Bridging Column (1 LMG)

1 (mot) Reserve Company

1233rd Panzer Signals Troop

(5 LMGs)

1233rd Panzer Supply Troop

1 Staff (1 37mm PAK 36 and 1 LMG)

1 (mot) Transportation Company (1 37mm PAK 36 and 6 LMGs)

1 (mot) Light Fuel Column (1 LMG)

1 (mot) Supply Platoon (1 LMG)

Medical

1233rd (mot) Medical Company

1233rd Ambulance

Other

1233rd Ordnance Platoon

1233rd Panzer Maintenance Company (2 LMGs)

1233rd (tmot) Maintenance Company

1233rd (tmot) Administration Platoon (1 LMG)

233rd Panzer Division

On 21 February 1944 the 233rd Reserve Panzer Division was redesignated as the 233rd Panzer Division. With this change, the 5th Reserve Panzer Battalion became the 55th Panzer Battalion. On 20 April 1945 the division contained two PzMk III (kz), 18 PzMk III (75), three PzMk IV (kz), two PzMk IV (L/43), and four 37mm Flak panzers. The division remained in Denmark, and on 7 May 1945 it contained:

42nd Panzergrenadier Regiment (3 battalions)
50th Panzergrenadier Regiment (2 battalions) (former 3rd Reserve Panzer Ersatz Regiment)

83rd Panzergrenadier Regiment (2 battalions)
55th Panzer Battalion
233rd Panzer Reconnaissance Battalion
1033rd Panzerjäger Battalion
1233rd Artillery Regiment (only 1233rd Artillery Battalion)
1233rd Panzer Pioneer Battalion
1233rd Panzer Signals Company
1233rd Support Battalion

273rd Reserve Panzer Division

The division was formed on 1 November 1943 with:

25/35th Panzer Regiment (25th and 35th Reserve Panzer Battalions)
92nd Reserve Panzergrenadier Regiment (12th and 40th Battalions)
73rd (mot) Reserve Grenadier Regiment (20th and 41st Battalions)
42nd Panzergrenadier Ersatz und Ausbildungs Regiment
167th Reserve Artillery Battalion
7th Reserve Panzer Reconnaissance Battalion
7th Reserve Panzerjäger Battalion

10th Reserve Panzerjäger Battalion
19th Reserve Panzer Pioneer Battalion

The staff of the combined 25/35th Panzer Regiment and the 92nd Reserve Panzergrenadier Regiments was formed in France in 1944. The two reserve panzer battalions were then assigned to it.

The order of 15 March 1944 directed that the division be used to re-form the 10th Panzergrenadier Regiment, and on 5 May 1944 it was ordered to rebuild the 11th Panzer Division. As a result, the division was completely dismembered.

Feldherrnhalle Panzer Division

The division was formed in October 1944 using the 109th Panzer Brigade. On 27 November 1944 the division contained:

Feldherrnhalle Panzer Division
Feldherrnhalle Panzer Division Staff (2 LMGs)
Feldherrnhalle Panzer Division Staff Escort Company
  1 Machine Gun Platoon (4 HMGs, 6 LMGs)
  1 Motorcycle Platoon (6 LMGs)
  1 Self-Propelled Flak Platoon (4 20mm guns)
  1 Mortar Platoon (2 80mm mortars)
Feldherrnhalle (mot) Mapping Detachment
Feldherrnhalle (mot) Military Police Detachment (5 LMGs)
Feldherrnhalle Panzer Regiment
Feldherrnhalle Panzer Regimental Staff
Feldherrnhalle Panzer Regimental Staff Company
  1 Signals Platoon
  1 Pioneer Platoon
  1 Self-Propelled Flak Platoon (3 37mm Flak guns)

1 Armored Maintenance Company
1st Battalion
  1 Panzer Battalion Staff (1 LMG)
  1 Panzer Battalion Staff Company (12 LMGs)
  4 Panzer Companies (17 PzMk V Panther tanks ea)
  1 (self-propelled) Armored Flak Company (3 quad 20mm Flak guns)
  1 (mot) Supply Company (5 LMGs)
2nd Battalion
  1 Panzer Battalion Staff (1 LMG)
  1 Panzer Battalion Staff Company (8 LMGs)
  4 Panzer Companies (17 PzMk IV tanks ea)
  1 (self-propelled) Armored Flak Company (3 quad 20mm Flak guns)
  1 (mot) Supply Company (5 LMGs)
Feldherrnhalle Panzergrenadier Regiment
Feldherrnhalle Panzergrenadier Regimental Staff
Feldherrnhalle Panzergrenadier Regimental Staff Company

1 Staff Platoon (1 LMG)

1 Signals Platoon (7 LMGs)

1 Motorcycle Platoon (6 LMGs)

1st (half-track) Panzergrenadier Battalion

1 Panzergrenadier Battalion Staff (6 LMGs)

1 (mot) Panzergrenadier Battalion Supply Company (5 LMGs)

3 (half-track) Panzergrenadier Companies (4 HMGs, 29 LMGs, 20mm and 2 75mm guns ea)

1 (half-track) Heavy Panzergrenadier Company

  1 Mortar Platoon (2 LMGs and 4 120mm mortars)

  1 leIG Platoon (4 LMGs and 6 75mm leIG)

2nd and 3rd Panzergrenadier Battalions, each with

1 Battalion Staff

1 Battalion Supply Company (4 LMGs)

3 (mot) Panzergrenadier Companies (4 HMGs and 18 LMGs ea)

1 (mot) Heavy Panzergrenadier Company

  1 Mortar Platoon (2 LMGs and 4 120mm mortars)

  1 Flak Platoon (6 20mm Flak guns)

16th (Infantry Support) Company (motZ)

(4 150mm sIG guns and 2 LMGs)

17th (Pioneer) Company (motZ)

1 Half-Track Staff (1 LMG)

1 Half-Track Platoon (6 flamethrowers, 1 20mm and 12 LMGs)

1 Half-Track Platoon (12 flamethrowers and 6 LMGs)

1 Half-Track Platoon (2 80mm mortars and 2 HMGs)

1 Half-Track Platoon (6 flamethrowers and 6 LMGs)

Feldherrnhalle Panzerjäger Battalion

1 Panzerjäger Battalion Staff

1 Panzerjäger Battalion Staff Battery (1 LMG)

1 Sturmgeschütz Staff Platoon (3 StuG)

2 Sturmgeschütz Companies (14 StuG ea)

1 (motZ) Panzerjäger Company (12 75mm PAK and 12 LMGs)

1 (mot) Panzerjäger Supply Company (3 LMGs)

Feldherrnhalle Reconnaissance Battalion

1 Reconnaissance Battalion Staff (3 75mm, 13 20mm and 16 LMG)

  1 (mot) Signals Platoon

1st Armored Car (half-track) Company (16 20mm and 25 LMGs)

2nd Half-Track Reconnaissance Company (2 75mm, 2 80mm mortars and 44 LMGs)

3rd Half-Track Reconnaissance Company (2 75mm and 7 20mm, 2 80mm mortars, 4 HMGs and 29 LMGs)

4th Half-Track Reconnaissance Company

  1 Staff Platoon (1 LMG)

  1 Platoon (6 75mm and 2 LMGs)

1 Mortar Platoon (6 80mm and 2 LMGs)

1 Pioneer Platoon (13 LMGs)

1 (mot) Reconnaissance Supply Company (3 LMGs)

Feldherrnhalle Artillery Regiment

1 Artillery Regimental Staff

1 (mot) Artillery Regimental Staff Company (2 LMGs)

1st Battalion

1 (Self-Propelled) Artillery Battalion Staff

1 (Self-Propelled) Artillery Battalion Staff Battery (2 LMGs)

1 (Self-Propelled) Flak Platoon (3 20mm)

2 (Self-Propelled) Light Howitzer Batteries (6 105mm leFH SdKfz 124 Wespe and 4 LMGs ea)

1 (Self-Propelled) Heavy Howitzer Battery (6 150mm sFH SdKfz 165 Hummel and 4 LMGs)

2nd Battalion

1 (mot) Artillery Battalion Staff

1 (mot) Artillery Battalion Staff Company (2 LMGs)

1 (motZ) Flak Platoon (3 20mm)

2 (motZ) Light Howitzer Batteries (6 105mm leFH and 4 LMGs ea)

3rd Battalion

1 (mot) Artillery Battalion Staff

1 (mot) Artillery Battalion Staff Company (2 LMGs)

1 (motZ) Flak Platoon (3 20mm)

3 (motZ) Heavy Howitzer Batteries (6 150mm sFH and 4 LMGs ea)

Feldherrnhalle Flak Battalion

1 (mot) Flak Battalion Staff

1 (mot) Flak Battalion Staff Battery (2 LMGs)

2 (motZ) Flak Batteries (6 88mm, 3 20mm and 2 LMGs ea)

1 (motZ) Light Flak Battery

  1 (motZ) Flak Section (9 37mm Flak guns and 4 LMGs)

  1 Self-Propelled Section (3 quad 20mm Flak guns)

  1 (mot) Searchlight Section (4 searchlights)

Feldherrnhalle Pioneer Battalion

1 (motZ) Pioneer Battalion Staff

1 (half-track) Pioneer Battalion Staff Company (12 LMGs)

2 (mot) Pioneer Companies (2 HMGs, 18 LMGs and 2 80mm mortars ea)

1 (half-track) Pioneer Company (2 HMGs, 43 LMGs, 6 flamethrowers and 2 80mm mortars)

Feldherrnhalle Signals Battalion

1 Armored Signals Battalion Staff

1 Armored Telephone Company (11 LMGs)

1 Armored Radio Company (19 LMGs)

1 (mot) Signals Supply Column (2 LMGs)

Feldherrnhalle Supply Troop

1 (mot) Medical Company (2 LMGs)

1 (mot) Medical Supply Company (2 LMGs)

1 (mot) Field Post Office

On 25 February 1945 the division was ordered to undergo some major reorganizations. The panzer regiment became a hermaphroditic formation containing a panzer battalion and a panzergrenadier battalion mounted in half-tracks. The rest of the panzergrenadier regiment was truck-borne. There were also other minor changes, including the assignment of panzerschrecke anti-tank weapons to the organization:

Feldherrnhalle Panzer Division

Feldherrnhalle Panzer Division Staff (2 LMGs)
Feldherrnhalle Panzer Division Staff Escort Company
  1 Machine Gun Platoon (2 HMGs, 6 LMGs)
  1 Motorcycle Platoon (6 LMGs)
  1 Self-Propelled Flak Platoon (4 20mm guns)
  1 Mortar Platoon (2 80mm mortars)
Feldherrnhalle (mot) Mapping Detachment
Feldherrnhalle (mot) Military Police Detachment (5 LMGs)

Feldherrnhalle Panzer Regiment (formed from "Panzer Brigade 100 F")

Feldherrnhalle Panzer Regimental Staff and Staff Company

1st (Panzer) Battalion

1 Panzer Battalion Staff (1 LMG)
1 Panzer Battalion Staff Company (8 LMGs)
2 Panzer Companies (10 PzMk IV tanks ea)
2 Panzer Companies (10 Panther tanks ea)
1 (self-propelled) Armored Flak Company (3 37mm Flak and 6 20mm Flak guns)
1 Armored Maintenance Company (2nd Platoon detached)
1 (mot) Supply Company (3 LMGs)

2nd (half-track) Panzergrenadier Battalion

1 Panzergrenadier Battalion Staff (6 LMGs)
1 (mot) Panzergrenadier Battalion Supply Company (5 LMGs)
2 (half-track) Panzergrenadier Companies (3 triple 20mm gun mounts and 21 LMGs ea)
1 (half-track) Panzergrenadier Company (13 LMGs and 6 flamethrowers)
1 (half-track) Heavy Panzergrenadier Company (6 triple 20mm gun mounts, 6 75mm PAK and a pioneer platoon)

Feldherrnhalle Panzergrenadier Regiment

Feldherrnhalle Panzergrenadier Regimental Staff
Feldherrnhalle Panzergrenadier Regimental Staff Company
  1 Signals Platoon
  1 Panzerjäger (destroyer) Platoon (3 panzerschrecke)
  1 Motorcycle Platoon (4 LMGs)

2 Panzergrenadier Battalions, each with

1 Battalion Staff
1 Panzerjäger (destroyer) Platoon (3 panzerschrecke)
1 Battalion Supply Company (4 LMGs)
1 Panzerjäger (destroyer) Platoon (3 panzerschrecke)
3 (mot) Panzergrenadier Companies (12 LMGs and 3 panzerschrecke ea)
1 (mot) Panzergrenadier Flak Company (12 HMGs, 1 LMG, 8 20mm guns)
1 (mot) Heavy Panzergrenadier Company (6 LMGs 8 80mm mortars and 4 120mm mortars)

16th (motZ) Heavy Infantry Gun Company
(4 150mm sIG guns and 2 LMGs)

17th (Pioneer) Company (motZ)
(18 LMGs, 18 flamethrowers and 3 panzerschrecke)

Feldherrnhalle Panzerjäger Battalion

1 Panzerjäger Battalion Staff
1 Panzerjäger Battalion Staff Battery (1 LMG)
1 Sturmgeschütz Platoon (3 StuG)
2 Sturmgeschütz Companies (10 StuG ea)
2 Sturmgeschütz Supply Platoons
1 (motZ) Panzerjäger Company (9 75mm PAK 40)
1 (mot) Panzerjäger Supply Company

Feldherrnhalle Reconnaissance Battalion

1 Reconnaissance Battalion Staff (? 20mm and 1 LMG)
1 (mot) Signals Platoon
1 Armored Car Platoon (18 LMGs, 11 20mm and 2 75mm)
1 (mot) Reconnaissance Company (2 80mm mortars, 2 HMGs and 9 LMGs)
1 (mot) Reconnaissance Supply Company (3 LMGs)

Feldherrnhalle Pioneer Battalion

1 Pioneer Battalion Staff
1 (mot) Pioneer Battalion Staff Company
2 (mot) Pioneer Companies (2 HMGs, 18 LMGs and 2 80mm mortars ea)

Feldherrnhalle Artillery Regiment

1 Artillery Regimental Staff
  1 (mot) Artillery Regimental Staff Company (2 LMGs)

1st Battalion (formerly 3/818th Army Artillery Regiment)

1 (Self-Propelled) Artillery Battalion Staff
1 (Self-Propelled) Artillery Battalion Staff Company (2 LMGs)
1 (Self-Propelled) Flak Platoon (3 20mm)
2 (Self-Propelled) Light Howitzer Batteries (6 105mm leFH SdKfz 124 Wespe and 4 LMGs ea)
1 (Self-Propelled) Heavy Howitzer Battery (6 150mm sFH SdKfz 165 Hummel and 4 LMGs)

2nd Battalion (newly formed)

1 (mot) Artillery Battalion Staff
1 (mot) Artillery Battalion Staff Company (2 LMGs)
1 (motZ) Flak Platoon (3 20mm)
2 (motZ) Batteries (6 105mm leFH 18 and 4 LMGs ea)
1 (motZ) Battery (6 150mm sFH 18 and 4 LMGs)

Feldherrnhalle Signals Company
1 Armored Signals Company (12 LMGs)

Feldherrnhalle Supply Troop
1 (mot) Supply Staff
1 (mot) Supply Staff Company
1 (mot) Veterinary Detachment
2 (mot) (120 ton) Transportation Companies (4 LMGs ea)
1 (mot) (60ton)Transportation Companies (2 LMGs)
2 (horse-drawn) (60ton) Transportation Companies (4 LMGs ea)
1 (mot) Maintenance Company (3 LMGs)
1 (mot) (75 ton) Maintenance Supply Column
1 (mot) Administrative Service Company (bakery, butcher and administration) (3 LMGs)
1 (mot) Medical Company (2 LMGs)
1 (mot) Medical Supply Company (2 LMGs)
1 (mot) Field Post Office

When the division was ordered rebuilt in March 1945, the 208th Panzer Battalion was used to rebuild the division's panzer force. On 15 March 1945 the organization of the armored portion of the division and its panzer inventory were as follows:

1/FH Panzer Regiment
1 Battalion Staff Company
2 Medium Panzer Companies (PzMk V)
2 Medium Panzer Companies (PzMk IV)
Total tanks available:
PzMk IV/70(V)   3
PzMk IV (lg)   18
PzMk IV   19

On 25 March 1945 the division was ordered reorganized as a Type 45 Panzer Division. However, the war ended before this reorganization could take place.

Panzerkorps Feldherrnhalle

Formed on 27 November 1944 from the IV Panzer Corps in Army Group Center with the remains of the Feldherrnhalle Panzergrenadier Division and the 13th Panzer Division. On that date the corps had:

Artillery Commander FH
Staff/Pioneer Regiment FH
Heavy Panzer Battalion FH (from 503rd (Tiger) Panzer Battalion)
1/, 2/Corps Fusilier Regiment FH (not formed)
Panzer Corps Artillery Battalion (1/104th and 2/404th Artillery Regiment)
404th Panzer Pioneer Battalion
44th Panzer Signals Battalion
1/, 2/Panzer Feldersatz Regiment FH (not formed)
Panzer Corps Support Troops FH
Supply Battalion FH
Ordnance Battalion FH
Motor Vehicle Maintenance Battalion FH
Administrative Troops Battalion FH
404th Medical Battalion

On 27 November 1944 the corps contained:

Feldherrnhalle Corps
Feldherrnhalle Pioneer Regimental Staff
1 (half-track) Pioneer Company (2 75mm, 2 80mm mortars and 44 LMGs)
Feldherrnhalle Artillery Commander
Feldherrnhalle (mot) Observation Battery
Feldherrnhalle (mot) Mapping Detachment
Feldherrnhalle (mot) Escort Company

1 Motorcycle Platoon (6 LMGs)
1 Self-Propelled Flak Platoon (3 20mm quad guns)
404th (mot) Military Police Troop

Corps Fusilier Regiment FH
1 (mot) Regimental Staff
1 (mot) Regimental Staff Company
1 Signals Platoon
1 Motorcycle Platoon (4 LMGs)

1st and 2nd Battalions, each with
1 (mot) Battalion Staff
1 (mot) Supply Company (4 LMGs)
3 (bicycle) Fusilier Companies (4 HMGs, 18 LMGs and 2 80mm mortars ea)
1 (mot) Heavy Company
1 Flak Platoon (6 20mm)
1 Heavy Mortar Platoon (2 LMGs and 4 120mm mortars)

1 (motZ) Infantry Gun Company (4 150mm sIG and 2 LMGs)

Heavy Panzer Battalion FH
1 Panzer Battalion Staff (1 LMG)
1 Panzer Battalion Staff Company (31 LMGs)
1 Self-Propelled Flak Platoon (3 quad 20mm guns)
3 Tiger Tank Companies (14 PzMk VI Tiger tanks ea)
1 Panzer Maintenance Company
1 (mot) Supply Company (4 LMGs)

404th Artillery Regiment
1/404th Artillery Regiment
1 (mot) Battalion Staff
1 (mot) Battalion Staff Battery (2 LMGs)
3 (motZ) Heavy Batteries (4 150mm sFH and 4 LMGs ea)

2/404th Artillery Regiment
same as 1/404th

404th Panzer Pioneer Battalion
1 (mot) Pioneer Battalion Staff (2 LMGs)
1 (mot) Pioneer Battalion Staff Company (4 LMGs)
3 (mot) Pioneer Companies (2 HMGs, 18 LMGs and 2 80mm mortars ea)
1 (mot) Panzer Bridging Column (5 LMGs)
1 (mot) Panzer Bridging Column (3 LMGs)

44th Panzer Signals Battalion
1 Panzer Radio Company (7 LMGs)
1 (mot) Signals Company (6 LMGs)
2 (mot) Telephone Companies (5 LMGs ea)
1 (mot) Signals Supply Company (2 LMGs)

Panzer Feldersatz Regiment FH
2 Battalions, each with 4 companies

Panzer Corps Support Troops FH
Supply Battalion FH
1st–7th (120 ton) (mot) Transportation Columns (4 LMGs ea)
1st and 2nd (horse-drawn) (60 ton) Transportation Columns (6 LMGs ea)

Ordnance Battalion FH
2 (mot) Ordnance Companies
1 (mot) Maintenance Company
Motor Vehicle Maintenance Battalion FH
5 (mot) Maintenance Companies (3 LMGs ea)
2 Heavy (mot) Maintenance Supply Columns
Administrative Troops Battalion FH
1 (mot) Medical Company
1 (mot) Medical Supply Company
1 (mot) Field Hospital
404th Medical Battalion
1 (mot) Mixed Administration, Bakery, Butcher Company (3 LMGs)
1 (mot) Mixed Administration, Bakery, Butcher Company (3 LMGs)
404th (mot) Field Post Office

The corps later added the 429th Machine Gun Battalion as the Machine Gun Battalion Feldherrnhalle. The corps was first used in Hungary in February 1945. On 10 March 1945 Army Group South was ordered to rebuild the corps with the Feldherrnhalle and 13th Panzer Divisions.

2nd Feldherrnhalle Panzer Division

Formed in March 1945 by the renaming of the 13th Panzer Division. The renaming of the units were as follows:

Original Name	Became
1/, 2/, 3/66th Panzergrenadier Regiment	3rd FH Panzergrenadier Regiment
1/, 2/4th Panzer Regiment	2nd FH Panzer Regiment
13th Panzer Reconnaissance Bn (4 sqns)	not renamed
13th Panzerjäger Battalion (3 cos)	2nd FH Panzerjäger Battalion
1/, 2/, 3/13th Panzer Artillery Regiment	2nd FH Panzer Artillery Regiment
271st Army Flak Battalion (5 btrys)	2nd FH Army Flak Artillery Battalion
4th Panzer Pioneer Battalion (3 cos)	2nd FH Panzer Pioneer Battalion
13th Panzer Signals Battalion (2 cos)	not renamed

Initially the 93rd Panzergrenadier Regiment was to be absorbed into the 66th Panzergrenadier Regiment, but instead it was used to form the FH Corps Fusilier Regiment. On 25 March 1945 the division was ordered reorganized as a Type 45 Panzer Division. The 2nd Feldherrnhalle Division was taken into captivity by the Russians on 8 May 1945.

Generalkommando Grossdeutschland Panzer Corps

This corps was formed on 28 September 1944 from the 18th Artillery Division, the remains of the XXIII Army Corps, the Grossdeutschland Panzergrenadier Division and the Brandenburg Panzergrenadier Division. The 1/Grossdeutschland Panzer Regiment was reorganized with three companies of 17 PzMk V Panther tanks, the 2/Grossdeutschland Panzer Regiment had four companies of 17 PzMk IV tanks, and the 3/Grossdeutschland Panzer Regiment, which was equipped with PzMk VI Tiger tanks, became the Grossdeutschland Heavy Panzer Battalion. On 13 December 1944, it contained the following support units: *(see over)*

Grossdeutschland Corps Staff

Corps Staff
500th (mot) Mapping Detachment
500th Military Police Detachment (5 LMGs)
500th (half-track) Reconnaissance Company (2 75mm, 2 80mm mortars and 44 LMGs)
500th (mot) Sound Ranging Platoon
500th Escort Company
  1 Motorcycle Platoon (6 LMGs)
  1 Self-Propelled Flak Platoon (3 20mm Flak guns)
500th Artillery Brigade Staff
  500th (mot) Artillery (mot) Observation Battery
500th (mot) Pioneer Regimental Staff

Grossdeutschland Corps Troops

Corps Fusilier Regiment GD

1 (mot) Staff Company
1 Signals Platoon
1 Motorcycle Platoon (4 LMGs)

1st Battalion

1 (mot) Supply Company (4 LMGs)
3 (bicycle) Companies (12 LMGs ea)
1 (mot) Heavy Company (12 HMGs and 6 20mm Flak)
1 (mot) Heavy Company (4 120mm and 8 80mm mortars and 6 HMGs)

2nd Battalion

same as 1st Fusilier Battalion

1 (motZ) Infantry Gun Company (4 150mm sIG and 2 LMGs)

Heavy Panzer Battalion GD

1 Panzer Battalion Staff (1 LMG)
1 Panzer Battalion Staff Company (31 LMGs)
1 Self-Propelled Flak Platoon (3 quad 20mm guns)
3 Tiger Tank Companies (14 PzMk VI tanks ea)
1 Panzer Maintenance Company
1 (mot) Supply Company (4 LMGs)

500th Artillery Regiment

1/500th Artillery Regiment

1 (mot) Battalion Staff
1 (mot) Battalion Staff Battery (2 LMGs)
3 (motZ) Heavy Batteries (4 150mm sFH and 4 LMGs ea)

2/500th Artillery Regiment

same as 1/500th

500th Panzer Pioneer Battalion

1 (mot) Pioneer Battalion Staff (2 LMGs)
1 (mot) Pioneer Battalion Staff Company (4 LMGs)
3 (mot) Pioneer Companies (2 HMGs, 18 LMGs and 2 80mm mortars ea)
1 (mot) Panzer Bridging Column (5 LMGs)
1 (mot) Panzer Bridging Column (3 LMGs)

44th Panzer Signals Battalion

1 Panzer Radio Company (7 LMGs)
1 (mot) Signals Company (6 LMGs)
2 (mot) Telephone Companies (5 LMGs ea)
1 (mot) Signals Supply Company (2 LMGs)

Panzer Feldersatz Regiment GD

2 Battalions, each with 4 companies each

Panzer Corps Support Troops GD

Supply Battalion FH
  1st–8th (120 ton) (mot) Transportation Columns (4 LMGs ea)
  1st–2nd (horse-drawn) (60 ton) Transportation Columns (6 LMGs ea)
Ordnance Battalion GD
  2 (mot) Ordnance Companies
  1 (mot) Maintenance Company
Motor Vehicle Maintenance Battalion GD
  5 (mot) Maintenance Companies (3 LMGs ea)
  2 Heavy (mot) Maintenance Supply Columns
Administrative Troops Battalion GD
  1 (mot) Medical Company
  1 (mot) Medical Supply Company
  1 (mot) Field Hospital
500th Medical Battalion
  1 (mot) Mixed Administration, Bakery, Butcher Company (3 LMGs)
  1 (mot) Mixed Administration, Bakery, Butcher Company (3 LMGs)
500th (mot) Field Post Office

On 8 January 1945 the Grossdeutschland Panzergrenadier Division was ordered reorganized as a Type 44 Panzer Division, but without the PzMk IV Panzer Battalion. The 2/Grossdeutschland Panzer Regiment had already been transferred to the Führer Begleit Brigade.

On 14 December 1944 the Brandenburg Panzer Regiment was ordered raised. Its 1st Battalion was to have three Panther companies, each with 17 tanks. The 2nd Battalion was to have four companies, each with 17 PzMk IV tanks. On 13 December 1944 it had been ordered that the Grossdeutschland Sturmgeschütz Battalion be redesignated as the 2/Brandenburg Panzer Regiment. However, this had not proven successful, so the sturmgeschütz battalion remained with the division until the Brandenburg Panzer Regiment had been completed.

On 18 January 1945 the 1/26th Panzer Regiment had been ordered reorganized with three companies, 14 Panthers each, and a staff of three command Panthers. This reorganization was completed on 27 January 1945 and the battalion was renamed the 1/Brandenburg Panzer Regiment. The 45 Panther tanks for its organization were received between 27 January and 2 February 1945.

On 1 February 1945 the formation of the 2/Brandenburg Panzer Regiment was ordered. It was to have four companies, each with 14 PzMk IV tanks, and a staff of four PzMk IV tanks in its staff. It was organized by utilizing the 12th Panzer Battalion z.b.V., and the Gutschmidt Panzer Company.

On 2 February 1945 the 1/Brandenburg Panzer Regiment was ordered detached and reassigned to the Kurmark Panzergrenadier Division.

Grossdeutschland Ersatz Brigade

Formed on 1 June 1942 as a replacement training formation for the Grossdeutschland Division. It contained the Grossdeutschland (mot) Infantry Ersatz Regiment and the Grossdeutschland Artillery Ersatz Battalion.

Between 10 February 1943 and 1 January 1944 it also contained a Fast Troop Training Battalion, which, after 13 August 1943, was known as the Panzer Truppen Ersatz und Ausbildungs Abteilung. In early February 1945 the brigade was used as an Alarm Unit near Forst/Lausitz and on 10 March 1945 it was used to rebuild the Brandenburg Panzergrenadier Division. It was re-formed in Schleswig-Holstein as the Panzergrenadier Ersatz und Ausbildungs Brigade Grossdeutschland. On 4 April 1945 it was re-organized as the Panzer-Ausbildungs Verband Grossdeutschland. It had:

Grossdeutschland Panzer Ausbildungs Battalion (not formed)

1/, 2/, 3/Grossdeutschland Panzergrenadier Ausbildungs Regiment
Grossdeutschland Officer Candidate School
Grossdeutschland Panzer Artillery Ausbildungs Battalion
Grossdeutschland Panzer Pioneer Ausbildungs Battalion (2 companies)
Grossdeutschland Panzer Signals Ausbildungs Battalion (1 company)
20th Panzer Ausbildungs Battalion

The Panzer Ausbildungs Verband "GD" was supposed to be absorbed by the Clausewitz Panzer Division, but this was never carried out. Instead, it was absorbed by the 15th Panzergrenadier Division. It was captured by the British.

Panzer Lehr Division

The division was ordered formed on 30 December 1943, and it was assembled on 10 January 1944 in France near Nancy and Verdun, using troops drawn from various instructional schools. The division had:

1/6th Panzer Regiment (3 companies, each with 22 Panther PzMk V tanks and 1 company with 22 Jagdpanthers)
2/Panzer Lehr Regiment (4 companies, each with 22 PzMk IV tanks)
316th (FKL) Panzer Company
1/, 2/901st Panzergrenadier Lehr Regiment
1/, 2/902nd Panzergrenadier Lehr Regiment
130th Panzer Lehr Reconnaissance Battalion (5 companies)
130th Panzer Lehr Panzerjäger Battalion
1/, 2/, 3/130th Panzer Artillery Regiment
311th Army Flak Battalion
130th Panzer Pioneer Battalion
130th Panzer Signals Battalion
130th Feldersatz Battalion
130th Divisional Support Units

The Panzer Lehr Battalion became the 2/Panzer Lehr Regiment. On 3 February 1944 orders were issued to convert the 316th (FKL) Panzer Company into a Tiger II Panzer Company, equipping it with 14 Tiger II tanks. On 8 November 1944 the 1/6th Panzer Regiment was officially redesignated the 1/130th Panzer Regiment. OKH records show the division organized and equipped as follows on 22 March 1944:

Division Staff
Divisional Staff (2 LMGs)
130th (mot) Division Mapping Detachment
Divisional Escort Company
   Motorcycle Platoon (6 LMGs)
   Infantry Gun Platoon (2 75mm leIG)
   Self-Propelled Flak Platoon (4 20mm guns)
   Heavy Anti-Tank Platoon (3 LMGs and 3 75mm PAK 40)
   Mixed Panzergrenadier Platoon (4 HMGs, 6 LMGs and 2 80mm mortars)
130th Panzer Regiment
   1 Regimental Staff
   1 Regimental Staff Company
      1 Panzer Signals Platoon
      1 Panzer Flak Platoon (12 37mm Flak guns)
      1 Panzer Platoon
   1 Panzer Maintenance Company
   1st Panzer Battalion
   Staff
   Staff Signals Platoon
   Panzer Flak Platoon (7 37mm Flak 43)
   4 Panzer Companies (22 Panther PzMk V tanks ea)
   1 (mot) Panzer Supply Company (5 LMGs)
   2nd Panzer Battalion
   Staff
   Staff Signals Platoon
   Panzer Flak Platoon (7 37mm Flak 43)
   4 Panzer Companies (22 PzMk IV tanks ea)
   1 (mot) Panzer Supply Company (5 LMGs)

901st Panzergrenadier Lehr Regiment

1 Panzergrenadier Regimental Staff (2 LMGs)
1 (half-track) Staff Company
  1 (half-track) Signals Platoon (7 LMGs)
  1 Motorcycle Platoon (6 LMGs)

1st Battalion

1 (half-track) Battalion Staff (5 LMGs)
1 (mot) Supply Company (5 LMGs)
3 (half-track) Panzergrenadier Companies (4 HMGs, 29 LMGs, 2 80mm mortars, 6 20mm guns and 2 75mm guns ea)
1 (half-track) Heavy Company
  1 Mortar Platoon (2 LMGs and 4 120mm mortars)
  1 Gun Platoon (4 LMGs and 6 75mm guns)

2nd Battalion

same as 1st Battalion

Self-Propelled Infantry Gun Company

(6 150mm sIG and 7 LMGs)

(half-track) Pioneer Company

1 Staff Platoon (1 LMG)
1 Pioneer Platoon (6 LMGs and 6 flamethrowers)
1 Mortar Platoon (2 HMGs, 2 80mm mortars)
1 Pioneer Platoon (6 LMGs and 12 flamethrowers)
1 Pioneer Platoon (12 LMGs, 1 20mm gun and 6 flamethrowers)

130th Panzer Lehr Reconnaissance Battalion

Staff (12 LMGs)
1 (mot) Supply Company (4 LMGs)
1 (half-track) Armored Car Company (18 20mm and 24 LMGs)
1 Armored Car Company (25 SdKfz 234/2 with 50mm gun and 1 LMG ea)
2 (half-track) Heavy Reconnaissance Companies (49 LMGs, 2 80mm mortars and 3 75mm guns ea)
1 (half-track) Heavy Company
  1 Staff Platoon (1 LMG)
  1 Pioneer Platoon (13 LMGs and 6 flamethrowers)
  1 Panzerjäger Platoon (8 LMGs and 3 75mm PAK 40)
  1 Light Infantry Gun Section (4 LMGs and 2 75mm leIG)
  1 Gun Platoon (8 LMGs and 6 75mm guns)

130th Panzer Artillery Regiment

Staff and (mot) Staff Battery (2 LMGs)

1st Battalion

Staff and (self-propelled) Staff Battery (6 LMGs)
2 Self-Propelled leFH Batteries (6 105mm leFH SdKfz 124 Wespe ea)
1 Self-Propelled Battery (6 150mm sFH SdKfz 165 Hummel)

2nd Battalion

Staff and Staff Battery (2 LMGs)
3 (motZ) Batteries (4 105mm leFH and 2 LMGs ea)

3rd Battalion

Staff and (mot) Staff Battery (6 LMGs)

3 (motZ) Batteries (4 152mm Russian howitzers and 2 LMGs ea)

Panzerjäger Lehr Battalion

1 Staff and Staff Battery (3 StuG and 1 LMG)
2 Sturmgeschütz Companies (10 StuG ea)
1 (motZ) Panzerjäger Company (12 75mm PAK 40 and 12 LMGs)
1 (mot) Supply Company

331st Army Flak Battalions

Staff and Staff Battery
1/, 2/, 3/331st (motZ) Heavy Flak Batteries (4 88mm, 3 20mm Flak guns and 2 LMGs ea)

130th Panzer Pioneer Battalion

1 Battalion Staff (7 LMGs)
1 (mot) Staff Company
2 (half-track) Pioneer Companies (2 HMGs, 46 LMGs, 6 flamethrowers, 3 sPzBu 41, 2 80mm mortars and 3 75mm guns ea)
1 (mot) Pioneer Company (2 HMGs, 18 LMGs, 6 flamethrowers and 2 80mm mortars)
1 (mot) Heavy Panzer Bridging Train (4 LMGs)

130th Panzer Signals Battalion

1 Panzer Telephone Company (11 LMGs)
1 Panzer Radio Company (19 LMGs)
1 (mot) Supply Company

130th Supply Troop

1 Supply Troop Staff (2 LMGs)
1st–6th/130th (mot) 90 ton Transportation Column (6 LMGs ea)
130th Supply Company (8 LMGs)

130th Truck Park

1/, 2/, 3/130th (mot) Maintenance Companies (4 LMGs ea)
130th (mot) Heavy Maintenance Supply Column

Administration

130th (mot) Bakery Company (6 LMGs)
130th (mot) Butcher Company (4 LMGs)
130th (mot) Divisional Administration Company (2 LMGs)

Medical Battalion

1/, 2/130th (mot) Medical Companies (4 LMGs ea)
1/, 2/, 3/130th Ambulance Platoons

Other

130th (mot) Military Police Troop (2 LMGs)
130th (mot) Field Post Office (1 LMG)

On 4 April 1944 the Panzer Lehr Regiment, the Panzer Lehr Reconnaissance Battalion and the Panzerjäger Battalion were given the number 130th. On 5 June 1944 elements of the division, including the Panzer Lehr Regiment, were ordered to reorganize to the "freie gliederung" formation, as part of the reorganization into a Type 44 Panzer Division.

A letter from the Oberkommando Herresgruppe B indicates that on 21 June 1944 the division had 24 105mm howitzers, six 150mm howitzers, and 12 Russian 152mm guns. In June 1944 the organization of the armored portion of the division and its panzer inventory were as follows:

1/, 2/130th Panzer Regiment
  1 Panzer Staff Company
  1 Panzer FKL Company
  1 Battalion
    1 Panzer Staff Company
    4 Medium Panzer Companies (PzMk V)
  1 Battalion
    1 Panzer Staff Company
    4 Medium Panzer Companies (PzMk IV)
  Total tanks available:

StuG	9
PzMk IV (lg)	101
PzMk V	89
PzMk VI	3
Flakpz38	12

After heavy losses in Normandy, the division was refreshed on 15 October 1944. The division was reorganized with a single panzer battalion, with two companies each with 14 PzMk V Panther tanks and two companies each equipped with 14 PzMk IV tanks. Later, in 1945, when the division was again rebuilt, the 509th Fast Battalion was used to rebuild the 2/901st Panzergrenadier Regiment. In November 1944 the organization of the armored portion of the division and its panzer inventory were as follows:

2/130th Panzer Lehr Regiment
1 Panzer Staff Company
  1 Battalion
    1 Panzer Staff Company
    3 Medium Panzer Companies (PzMk V)
    1 Medium Panzer Company (PzMk IV)

Total tanks available:

PzMk IV (lg)	34
PzMk V	38
FlakpzIV 37	4
FlakpzIV (2V)	4

On 8 December 1944 the organization and equipment were as follows:

2/130th Panzer Lehr Regiment
  1 Panzer Staff Company
  1 Battalion
    1 Panzer Staff Company
    2 Medium Panzer Companies (PzMk V)
    2 Medium Panzer Companies (PzMk IV)
  Total tanks available:

PzMk IV (lg)	27 (+10 en route)
PzMk V	30 (+10 en route)
FlakpzIV 37	3
FlakpzIV (2V)	4

In February 1945 the division's armored units and tank inventory were as follows:

1/22nd Panzer Regiment
  1 Panzer Staff Company
  1 Battalion
    1 Panzer Staff Company
    2 Medium Panzer Companies (PzMk V)
    2 Medium Panzer Companies (PzMk IV)
Total tanks available:

PzMk IV (lg)	26 (plus 16 on 9 Feb.)
PzMk V	32 (plus 7 on 9 Feb.)
FlakpzIV	10

The division was taken prisoner in the Ruhr Pocket by the Americans on 16 April 1945.

General Göring Brigade

The history of the Hermann Göring Brigade begins with the formation of a special police unit, "an instrument, which in complete devotion to the "Führer", was "capable and ready to stamp out any spark of resistance before it could become dangerous to the young National Socialist revolution". On 23 February 1933 Major Wecke, of the Prussian Police force, was given the job of establishing this brigade, and two days later it was in place. It consisted of three police squads, a police motorcycle platoon, a police signals platoon, and two special vehicles. Each police squad had four officers and 106 sergeants. The motorcycle platoon had one officer

and 38 sergeants, and the signals platoon had one officer and 25 sergeants.

Nine months after its formation, the unit was authorized to wear the name "General Göring", and on 16 March 1935, upon the institution of general conscription, it became the "State Police Detachment General Göring" (Landespolizeigruppe General Göring). This regiment was incorporated into the Luftwaffe and, in addition to other duties, it became the nucleus for the Fallschirmjägers (paratroopers). The transition from the General Göring State Police Regiment to the General Göring Regiment occurred on 1 November 1935 and was effected as follows:

General Göring State Police Regiment		General Göring Regiment
Regimental Headquarters	became	Regimental Headquarters
Music Corps	became	Music Corps
Signals Platoon	became	Signals Platoon
1st Battalion	became	1st Light Infantry Battalion
Signals Platoon	became	Signals Platoon
	formed 1 Oct. 1936	Pioneer Platoon
1st–3rd Rifle Companies	became	1st–3rd Light Infantry Companies
4th Machine Gun Company	became	4th Machine Gun Company
2nd Battalion	became	2nd Light Infantry Battalion
Signals Platoon	became	Signals Platoon
	formed 1 Oct. 1936	Pioneer Platoon
5th–7th Rifle Companies	became	5th–7th Light Infantry Companies
8th Machine Gun Company	became	8th Machine Gun Company
3rd Battalion	became	3rd Light Flak Battalion
	newly formed	HQ Battery
	formed 1 Oct. 1936	10th Battery (12 20mm Flak guns)
13th MW Battery	became	11th Battery (9 37mm Flak guns)
14th Anti-Tank Company[1]	became	9th Battery (12 20mm Flak guns)
15th Special Purpose (3 armored cars)	became	13th Motorcycle Infantry Company with 3 armored cars
Pioneer Platoon	became	Pioneer Platoon
Cavalry Platoon	became	Cavalry Platoon
	formed 11 July 1936	15th Guard Company
	formed 1 Apr. 1936	16th Guard Company

[1] The anti-tank company was equipped with 9 37mm PAK 36 anti-tank guns.

The units of the 1st Battalion were designated "Parachute Rifle". A 12th Searchlight Battery (12 600mm searchlights) was formed sometime shortly afterwards. On 1 December 1935 the regiment was apparently re-formed and then contained:

Regimental Staff
  Regimental Signals Platoon
  1 Motorcycle Rifle Company
  1 Pioneer Company
  1 Cavalry Platoon
1 Jäger Battalion (Parachute)
  1 Headquarters Platoon
  1 Signals Platoon
  3 (parachute) Rifle Companies
  1 (parachute) Machine Gun
1 Jäger Battalion
  1 Headquarters Platoon
  1 Signals Platoon
  3 Rifle Companies
  1 Machine Gun
1 Flak Battalion
  1 Headquarters Platoon
  1 Signals Platoon
  2 Light Flak Batteries (12 20mm guns ea)
  1 Medium Flak Battery (9 37mm guns)

On 1 October 1937 the regiment was once again re-organized and had added several Flak formations. It was organized with:

Staff
HQ Battery
1st Heavy Flak Battalion
  Staff Battery
  1st–4th (mot) Batteries (4 88mm guns ea)
2nd Light Flak Battalion
  Staff Battery
  5th–7th (mot) Batteries (12 20mm guns ea)
3rd (Guard) Battalion
  8th (motorcycle) Company
  9th Guard Company
  10th Guard Company
4th (parachute) Light Battalion
  11th–15th Companies

In 1938 the fallschirmjägers were separated from the unit. The regiment participated in the occupation of Austria and Czechoslovakia. In August 1939 the regiment added:

14th (heavy) Flak Battery (105mm guns)
Reserve Searchlight Battalion
Replacement Battalion

Between 15 August 1939 and 1 March 1940 the regiment was organized as follows:

1st Battalion
  1 (mot) Staff Battery
  1 (mot) Light Flak Supply Column
  1st–3rd (motZ) Heavy Flak Batteries (4 88mm guns ea)
  4th–5th (motZ) Light Flak Batteries (12 20mm guns ea)

2nd Battalion
  1 (mot) Staff Battery
  1 (mot) Light Flak Supply Column
  6th (motZ) Medium Flak Battery (9 37mm guns)
  7th–8th Self-Propelled Light Flak Batteries (12 20mm guns ea)
  9th (motZ) Light Flak Battery (quad 20mm guns)

3rd Battalion
  1 (mot) Staff Battery
  11th–13th Searchlight Flak Batteries

4th Battalion
  1 (mot) Staff Battery
  1 (mot) Light Flak Supply Column
  15th (motZ) Medium Flak Battery (9 37mm guns)
  16th–17th (motZ) Light Flak Batteries (12 20mm guns ea)

Wach (Guard) Battalion
  1 (mot) Signals Platoon
  3 (mot) Guard Rifle Companies
  1 Cavalry Squadron
  1 Cavalry Squadron (added Mar. 1940)
  1 Motorcycle Company (added Mar. 1940)

Reserve Battalion
  1 Signals Platoon
  1st Reserve Searchlight Battery
  2nd Reserve Searchlight Battery
  3rd Reserve Searchlight Battery
14th (Railroad) Heavy Flak Battery (105mm guns)
Replacement Battalion
  1st Replacement (motZ) Heavy Flak Battery (4 88mm guns)
  2nd Replacement (motZ) Heavy Flak Battery (4 88mm guns)
  3rd Replacement (motZ) Medium Flak Battery (9 37mm guns)
  4th Replacement (motZ) Light Flak Battery (12 20mm guns)
  5th "Genes" Company
  6th (f) Heavy Flak Company
  7th (f) Heavy Flak Company
  8th (f) Heavy Flak Company

In the Polish campaign it remained at Göring's headquarters. In the spring of 1940 a special rifle battalion was formed from components of the Guard Battalion and the Motorcycle Company. This battalion took part in the invasion of Denmark and Norway. The remainder of the regiment remained on the Rhine facing Holland. On 10 May it invaded Belgium and its Flak units appear to have distinguished themselves in an engagement with French armor.

After the fall of France and a short spell providing Flak defenses for Paris, the regiment was withdrawn to Berlin to provide Flak defenses for that city. On 15 June 1941 the regiment was again significantly reorganized and now contained:

Regimental Units
  Headquarters (8/28/74)[1]
  Transport Group (1/5/26)
  Signals Platoon (1/12/64)
  Workshop Platoon (1/6/47)
1st Battalion
  Staff (7/28/129)
  1st–3rd Heavy Flak Batteries (4 88mm guns ea)
  4th Light Battery (12 20mm guns)
4th Battalion
  6th Battery (9 37mm guns)
  15th Battery (6 20mm and 6 37mm guns)
  16th Battery (12 20mm guns)
Rifle Battalion
  8th Battery (12 20mm guns)
  1st Rifle Company (4/32/160)
  3rd Rifle Company (4/31/155)
  Motorcycle Company (6/59/180)
2/43rd Luftwaffe Flak Regiment
  6th–8th Batteries (4 88mm guns ea)
  9th–10th Batteries (12 20mm guns ea)

During the Russian campaign the Flak units once again provided significant support in the tank battle of Dubno on 27 June 1941. Some parts of the regiment remained in Russia until April 1942. Of what returned from Russia, the Flak regiment's battalions became mixed battalions with three batteries of 88mm guns and two of 20mm guns. The former 2nd Battalion RGG was disbanded and the battalion headquarters became "Flak Sub-group Center", part of the Berlin Flak defenses. In March 1942 the regiment contained:

1st Battalion
  1st–3rd Batteries (4 88mm guns ea)
  4th (formerly 8th) Battery (12 20mm guns)
  5th Battery (12 20mm guns)
2nd Battalion (former 4th Battalion)
  6th Battery (4 88mm guns)
  7th and 8th Batteries (newly formed) (4 88mm guns ea)

---

[1] Numbers are officers, NCOs, and men.

9th Battery (former 15th Battery) (12 20mm guns)
10th Battery (12 20mm guns)
3rd Battalion
11th–13th Searchlight Batteries
Flak Replacement Battalion
  unchanged
Guard Battalion
  1st–3rd Guard Companies
  Cavalry Platoon

In the summer of 1942 the 3rd Battalion was re-designated the 528th Searchlight Battalion. The Flak Replacement Battalion was transferred to Utrecht, Holland, in May 1940. Its organization remained unchanged.

It appears that in March 1942 the Göring Brigade was formed in France. By October 1942 the brigade's organization was complete. The brigade was broken into three parts: the headquarters and main body of the troops were in France, the replacement training battalion was in Utrecht, Holland, and the Special Administrative Staff was in Berlin. The Hermann Göring Rifle Regiment was formed on 15 July 1942. In mid-1942 it was absorbed into the brigade, which was organized as follows:

In France:
Brigade Headquarters
  Headquarters Company
Rifle Regiment Hermann Göring (HG)
  1st Battalion
    1st–3rd Rifle Companies
    4th Machine Gun Company
    Trains
  2nd Battalion
    5th–7th Rifle Companies
    8th Machine Gun Company
    9th Infantry Gun Company (75mm leIG)
  3rd Battalion
    10th Motorcycle Company
    11th Pioneer Company
    12th Panzerjäger Company
    13th Panzer Company
    Tank Repair Shop Platoon
    Motor Transport Column
Flak Regiment HG
  1st Flak Battalion
    1st–3rd Batteries (37mm)
    4th–5th and 14th Batteries (20mm)
    Trains
  2nd Flak Battalion
    7th–8th Batteries (37mm)
    9th–10th Batteries (20mm)
    11th Battery (howitzer)
    Trains
  3rd Battalion
    (forming)

In Berlin:
Special Staff
Guard Battalion
  1st–3rd Guard Companies
4th Flak Battalion
  15th–16th Batteries

In Utrecht:
Replacement Battalion
  1st (Staff) Company
  2nd–3rd Companies (rifle)
  4th Company (75mm leIG)
  5th Company (motor transport)
  6th Company (motorcycle)
  7th Battery (37mm)
  8th Battery (20mm)
  9th Battery (howitzers)
  10th Battery (collective)

On 15 October 1942 the brigade was used to organize the General Göring Division. Five thousand volunteers were drawn from the Luftwaffe and trained for ground combat. In addition, the 5th Fallschirmjäger Regiment was assigned to the division. The 3rd Flak Battalion was re-equipped as a light field howitzer battalion, retaining the 11th, 12th and 13th Heavy Batteries. It would shortly become the 1st Battalion, 1st Armored Artillery Regiment HG. The 4/Hermann Göring Flak Regiment was newly formed and contained:

14th Battery (37mm guns) (formerly 4th Battery HG)
15th (Railway) Escort Battery (20mm guns) (formerly
  9th Battery RGG)
16th Battery (20mm guns) (formerly 17th Battery RGG)
17th Battery (20mm guns) (newly formed)

On 15 October the 1/, 2/Rifle Regiment HG were re-designated the 3/, 2/Grenadier Regiment HG respectively and the remaining elements of the 3rd (Heavy) Battalion were used to form the 13th (Infantry Gun) and 14th (Panzerjäger) Companies. The remaining elements of this battalion formed the 1/Panzer Regiment HG. The 10th (Motorcycle) Company was used to form the core of the Armored Reconnaissance Battalion HG.

In late 1942 elements of the 211th Flak Battery (11th–13th 88mm Batteries and 14th–15th 20mm Batteries) joined the Flak regiment of the Hermann Göring Brigade as its new 3rd Battalion. The 4th Flak Battalion, newly raised, contained the 14th Battery (37mm guns; formerly 4th Battery RGG), 15th (Railway) Escort Battery (20mm guns; formerly 9th Battery RGG), and the 16th Battery (20mm guns; formerly 17th Battery RGG), and 17th Battery (20mm guns).

Those elements of the Rifle Regiment that did not go to North Africa were reorganized as follows prior to the organization of the division:

1st Battalion
  1st–3rd Rifle Companies
  4th Heavy Company
  Trains
2nd Battalion
  5th–7th Rifle Companies
  8th Heavy Company
3rd Battalion
  9th Infantry Gun Company (75mm leIG)
  10th Motorcycle Company
  11th Pioneer Company

12th Panzerjäger Company
13th Panzer Company
Tank Repair Shop Platoon
Motor Transport Column

The 1/604th Flak Battalion had been assigned to defend Hitler's headquarters, the Wolfschanze. In 1942 it was renamed the Führer Flak Battalion and shortly afterwards it was redesignated the 4th Flak Battalion/Flak Regiment HG.

General Göring Division

Formed from the General Göring Brigade in November 1942. The 1st Hermann Göring Grenadier Regiment was formed from the 1/, 2/Hermann Göring Rifle Regiment. The 3/1st Hermann Göring Regiment was newly formed. The name was bestowed on the regiment on 14 November 1942. The division was formed as follows, with the sources of cadres noted:

1st Hermann Göring Grenadier Regiment (from Schützen Regiment HG)
2nd Hermann Göring Grenadier Regiment (new)
Hermann Göring Jäger Regiment (formed in Feb 1943 by renaming 5th Fallschirmjäger Regiment)
1/Artillery Regiment HG (former 11th–13th Batteries Flak Regiment HG)
1/Panzer Regiment HG (former 13th (Panzer) Company of Rifle Regiment HG plus new drafts)
Armored Reconnaissance Battalion HG (from 10th (motorcycle) Company of Rifle Regiment HG)
Pioneer Battalion HG (from 11th (Pioneer) Company, Rifle Regiment HG)

In the process of organizing the 1st Hermann Göring Grenadier Regiment the elements of the older Hermann Göring Rifle Regiment were as follows:

Units of Rifle Regiment	Units of Grenadier Regiment
1st Battalion	1st Battalion
1st Battalion	2nd Battalion
Armored Recon Plat/ 13th Company	3rd Co/Armored Recon Bn HG
10th Motorcycle Co	1st (Motorcycle) Co, Armored Recon Bn
2nd VW Company	2nd VW Co, Armored Recon Bn
11th Armored Pioneer Co	1st Co, Armored Pioneer Bn

The "Fallschirmjäger-Regiment 5 (Sturm-Regiment)", which became the "Jäger Regiment HG", appears formerly to have consisted of two separate parachute units, the "Fallschirmjäger Regiment 5" (1st Battalion) and the "Sturm-Regiment" (2nd Battalion). These two regiments had been engaged, at least in part, in the occupation of Crete and had fought in Russia, where they had suffered heavy losses. Between 11 January 1942 and 31 March 1942 the Kampfgruppe Koch (1st Battalion, "Sturm-Regiment") apparently lost 714 officers and men out of an original 880 men. It seems probable, therefore, that these two units were merged to form one unit, the combined "Fallschirmjäger Regiment 5 (Sturm-Regiment)". This unit was assigned to the division as the Hermann Göring Jäger Regiment on 19 February 1943.

A panzer regiment and divisional support troops were added to bring the division up to the strength of a panzer division while it was in southern France. By March 1943 the following units were ready for combat:

1 (half-track)/1st Grenadier Regiment HG
1 (mot)/1st Grenadier Regiment HG
13th (Infantry Gun) Company/2nd Grenadier Regiment HG
14th (Panzerjäger) Company/2nd Grenadier Regiment HG

In late 1942 the division contained:

Divisional Staff
  Staff
  Staff Company (organization as of Nov. 1942)
    Panzer Platoon
    Pioneer Platoon
    Reconnaissance Platoon
    Flak Platoon
1st Grenadier Regiment HG
  1st Battalion (half-track) (not ready until 1 Apr. 1943)

2nd and 3rd Battalions (mot)
13th Heavy Infantry Gun Company
14th Panzerjäger Company

2nd Grenadier Regiment HG (forming)
1st Battalion (half-track)
2nd and 3rd Battalions (mot)
13th Heavy Infantry Gun Company
14th Panzerjäger Company

1/, 3/Jäger Regiment HG (formerly 5th Fallschirmjäger Regiment)
1st Battalion
2nd Battalion
3rd Battalion (not ready until 1 April 1943)

Panzer Regiment HG
1st Battalion (1st–3rd Companies to be ready 1 Apr. 1943, 4th Company forming)
2nd Battalion (5th–7th Companies to be ready 1 Apr. 1943, 8th Company forming)

Flak Regiment
1st Flak Battalion (Staff, Staff Battery and 1st–5th Btrys)
2nd Flak Battalion (Staff, Staff Battery and 6th–9th Btrys)
10th Battery (forming)
3rd Flak Battalion (formerly 221st Flak Regiment) (Staff, Staff Battery and 11th–15th Btrys)
4th Flak Battalion (Staff, Staff Battery and 16th–18th Btrys)

Artillery Regiment HG
1st Battalion
  Staff, Staff Battery and 1st Battery
  2nd and 3rd Battery (not ready until 1 Apr. 1943)
2nd Battalion
  Staff, Staff Battery and 6th Battery
  7th and 8th Battery (not ready until 1 Apr. 1943)
3rd Battalion (forming)
4th Battalion (forming)
5th Assault Gun Battalion (later III Sturmgeschütz Abteilung/Panzer Regiment HG)
  Staff, Staff Btry, 16th, 17th and 19th Btrys (forming)
  18th Btry (ready)

Reconnaissance Battalion HG
Staff Company with armored car platoon
1st (Motorcycle) Company
2nd (Volkswagen) Company
3rd (Armored Car) Company (to be ready 1 Apr. 1943)
4th (Panzerjäger) Company
5th (Heavy Weapons) Company
6th (Flak) Company (20mm guns)

Panzer Pioneer Battalion HG
Staff Company
1st Panzer Pioneer Company
2nd–4th Panzer Pioneer Companies (forming)
Bridging Train

Panzer Signals Battalion HG
Staff Company
1st Panzer Radio Company
2nd Panzer Telephone Company

Medical Battalion HG
1st Medical Company
2nd and 3rd Medical Companies (2 forming)

Supply Regiment
2 Battalions
1 Battalion in planning stage
1 Vehicle Maintenance Battalion (forming)

Other
Ersatz und Ausbildungs Regiment HG
Wach Regiment (later Führer-Begleit-Regiment)
Military Police detachment
Field Post Office

In December 1942 the Flak Regiment was assigned to the air defense units in the Naples area. The Grenadier Regiment HG arrived in Italy in December 1942. By February 1943 much of the division was in the vicinity of S. Maria. The sturmgeschütz battalion had originally been designated as the 3rd Battalion, Artillery Regiment HG. However, around 7 December 1942 it was redesignated as the 5th Battalion.

The first portion of the division to go to Tunisia was the Jäger Regiment HG, which arrived there in early November 1942 in response to the Allied landings in North Africa. It had, attached to it, the 24th African Battalion, the 5th Tunisian Battalion, the 14th (Panzerjäger) Company, the 104th Panzergrenadier Regiment, and the 9th Company/69th Panzergrenadier Regiment.

In early 1943 those elements of the division and the attached support units that were serving in Africa were:

Divisional Units
1/, 3/Light Infantry Regiment, Hermann Göring
1/, 2/, 3/1st Panzergrenadier Regiment, Hermann Göring
1/, 2/Flak Regiment, Hermann Göring
1/, 2/Panzer Regiment, Hermann Göring
1/, 2/, 3/Panzer Artillery Regiment, Hermann Göring
Panzer Reconnaissance Battalion, Hermann Göring
Panzer Pioneer Battalion, Hermann Göring
Panzer Signals Battalion, Hermann Göring
Medical Battalion, Hermann Göring
Administration Unit

Attached
9th Company/69th Panzergrenadier Regiment
14th Company/104th Panzergrenadier Regiment
2nd and 4th Companies/90th Panzerjäger Battalion
Afrika Battalion T-4
Tunisia Battalion 5
1/, 2/90th Artillery Regiment
2nd Battery, 190th Artillery Regiment
von Bülow Nebelwerfer Battery
2nd Battery, 1st Nebelwerfer Battalion

Eventually the Kampfgruppe Schmidt was formed with units of the Hermann Göring Division. Two forms of this kampfgruppe are shown on the facing page:

13 March 1943
Staff/Kampfgruppe Schmidt
Grenadier Regiment HG
Jäger Regiment HG
1st Parachute Medical Company
Flak Regiment HG
Armored Signals Battalion
Trains

Attached
14th Company, 104th Panzergrenadier Regt
2nd Company/90th Panzerjäger Battalion
Det. 4th Company/90th Panzerjäger Battalion
9th Company/69th Panzergrenadier Regiment
2/190th Artillery Regiment
24th Africa Battalion

4 April 1943
Staff/Kampfgruppe Schmidt
2/, 3/Grenadier Regiment HG
1/, 2/Jäger Regiment HG
1/, 2/Flak Regiment HG
Armored Signals Battalion
Medical Battalion HG
1/Panzer Regiment HG
Trains

Attached
14th Company, 104th Panzergrenadier Regt
1/90th Artillery Battalion
2nd Company/1st Mortar Battalion
2/190th Artillery Regiment
24th Africa Battalion
5th Tunisian Battalion

Parts of the 1/Flak Regiment HG arrived in Tunisia in mid-February. The 2/, 3/1st Grenadier Regiment HG arrived there in early March, and the 1st, 5th, and 6th Companies and the armored scout car platoon of the Reconnaissance Battalion HG arrived in late March. The 1/Panzer Regiment arrived in April. In early April the Ewert Regiment was organized and consisted of those non-divisional units that were attached to the organic divisional elements in Tunisia. Between 22 and 27 April, the 5th, 6th and 6th Companies/2nd Grenadier Regiment HG and the 1st, 2nd and 3rd Companies/1st Grenadier Regiment HG arrived in Tunisia.

The Armored Reconnaissance Battalion HG arrived in North Africa in a complete state. It was organized as follows:

1st (Motorcycle) Company
2nd (VW) Company
3rd (Half-Track) Company
4th (Armored Scout Car) Company
5th (Pioneer) Company
6th (Flak) Company

In typical German fashion, the organization of Kampfgruppe Schmidt was quite flexible. The Armored Reconnaissance Battalion HG, the 3/1st Grenadier Regiment HG, and the 2/Flak Regiment HG were assigned to the Afrika Korps on 24 April 1943. The 5th Tunisia Battalion, 2/190th Artillery Regiment, and 1/199th Artillery Regiment were apparently detached from the kampfgruppe. The kampfgruppe appears, at this time, to have consisted of the following core units:

Organic Units
Jäger Regiment HG
2/Grenadier Regiment HG (reduced to two companies because of casualties)

13th Company/1st Grenadier Regiment HG
14th Company/1st Grenadier Regiment HG (two-thirds of company present)
5th, 6th and 7th Companies/2nd Grenadier Regiment HG
1st, 2nd and 3rd Companies/1st Grenadier Regiment HG
1/Flak Regiment HG
1st Company/Panzer Pioneers (reduced to one-third authorized strength by casualties)
18th Company/Flak Regiment HG
Attached Units
1/90th Panzer Artillery Regiment
Nebelwerfer Battery von Bülow

The records of the 5th Panzer Army show that Kampfgruppe Schmid had the following organization and equipment:

Kampfgruppe Schmid
  Divisional Staff Hermann Göring
Jäger Regiment Hermann Göring
  1 Signals Platoon
1st Battalion
  1 Company (12 LMGs, 2 HMGs, 2 50mm and 1 80mm mortar and 3 PzBu39)
  1 Company (12 LMGs, 2 HMGs, 1 50mm and 2 80mm mortars and 3 PzBu39)
  1 Company (8 LMGs, 4 HMGs, 8 120mm mortars, 3 75mm PAK 40 and 2 75mm leIG)
2nd Battalion
  2 Companies (20 LMGs, 2 HMGs, 3 50mm mortars and 2 PzBu39)
  1 Company (12 LMGs, 4 HMGs, 8 120mm mortars, 3 75mm PAK 40 and 2 75mm leIG)
3rd Battalion
  1 Company (12 LMGs, 2 HMGs, 3 50mm mortars and 2 PzBu39)

1 Company (12 LMGs, 2 HMGs, 1 50mm and 2 80mm mortars and 1 PzBu39)

1 Company (6 LMGs, 5 HMGs, 5 120mm mortars, 2 75mm PAK 40 and 1 75mm leIG)

Grenadier Regiment Hermann Göring
1st and 2nd Battalions, each with

4 Companies (8 LMGs, 6 HMGs, 2 50mm and 3 80mm mortars)

M(A)33 Battalion
4 Companies (8 LMGs, 6 HMGs, 2 50mm and 3 80mm mortars)

M(A)24 Battalion
4 Companies (8 LMGs, 6 HMGs, 2 50mm and 3 80mm mortars)

2/190th Artillery Regiment
1 (mot) Battalion Staff Battery

5th (mot) Battery (4 105mm leFH and 2 LMGs)

6th (mot) Battery (4 105mm leFH and 2 LMGs)

7th (mot) Battery (4 105mm leFH and 2 LMGs)

8th (mot) Battery (1 British 25pdr and 2 LMGs)

Flak Regiment Hermann Göring
1 (mot) Staff Battery

1st Battalion

1 (mot) Signals Platoon

1st Battery (4 88mm and 3 20mm guns)

2nd Battery (4 88mm and 3 20mm guns)

3rd Battery (4 88mm and 3 20mm guns)

4th Self-Propelled Battery (3 single and 3 quad 20mm guns)

5th Self-Propelled Battery (6 single and 3 quad 20mm guns)

2nd Battalion

1 (mot) Signals Platoon

6th Battery (4 88mm and 3 20mm guns)

7th Battery (3 88mm and 1 20mm guns)

8th Battery (3 88mm and 1 20mm guns)

9th Self-Propelled Battery (9 single guns)

In March the Kampfgruppe Schmidt had a combined strength of 6,954 officers and men. A report from the medical battalion estimates that on 1 May the division had an estimated strength of 11, 000 officers and men. There was, obviously, a continuous stream of new drafts into the division, as the Allies estimated that the division lost 13,000 casualties in North Africa. An undated organizational diagram from or after April 1943 provides the following picture of the division's actual organization and equipment:

Divisional Staff
Divisional Staff

1 (mot) Mapping Detachment

Jäger Regiment Hermann Göring
1st Battalion

1 Staff

1 Signals Platoon

1 Pioneer Platoon

1st–4th Companies (99 LMGs, 14 HMGs, 5 80mm mortars, 10 120mm mortars, 2 sPzBu 41, 1 37mm PAK 36, 7 50mm PAK 38, 6 75mm PAK 40 and 2 panzerfausts total; 12 officers, 160 NCOs and 654 men total)

2nd Battalion

1 Staff

1 Signals Platoon

1 Pioneer Platoon

5th–8th Companies (85 LMGs, 10 HMGs, 6 80mm mortars, 11 120mm mortars, 3 sPzBu 41, 10 50mm PAK 38 and 2 panzerfausts total; 12 officers, 160 NCOs and 661 men total)

Grenadier Regiment HG
1st Battalion

1 Staff

1 Signals Platoon

1 Pioneer Platoon

1st–4th Companies (94 LMGs, 11 HMGs, 3 80mm mortars, 6 120mm mortars, 3 sPzBu 41, 3 75mm PAK 40 and 2 75mm leIG; 12 officers, 163 NCOs and 634 men total)

2nd Battalion

1 Staff

1 Signals Platoon

1 Pioneer Platoon

5th–8th Companies (96 LMGs, 12 HMGs, 6 120mm mortars, 3 sPzBu41, 3 75mm PAK 40, and 2 panzerfausts total; 18 officers, 160 NCOs and 625 men total)

Ewert Regiment
5th Tunisia Battalion

1 Staff (1 captured British armored car and 1 infantry tank)

1st–5th Companies (60 LMGs, 54 HMGs, 16 120mm mortars, 2 panzerschrecke, 3 50mm PAK 38 and 3 75mm field guns ea; 13 officers, 123 NCOs and 878 men)

Reconnaissance Battalion HG
1st Motorcycle Company

2nd (mot) Reconnaissance Company

4th (motZ) Panzerjäger Company

5th Heavy Support Company

1 Pioneer Platoon

1 Panzerjäger Platoon (3 50mm PAK 38)

2 Infantry Sections (4 75mm leIG)

6th Flak Company (3 20mm guns, 67 LMGs, 8 HMGs, 2 panzerschrecke and 2 120mm mortars; 25 officers, 150 NCOs and 696 men)

1/Panzer Regiment HG
14th Self-Propelled Panzerjäger Company (9 SdKfz 131 Marder with 75mm PAK 40)

18th (half-track) Company (9 20mm and 19 LMGs)

Panzer Company (2 Pz PzMk III and 5 Pz PzMk IV tanks)

2/190th Artillery Regiment

1/999th Artillery Regiment

Unger Battery (4 87mm (British 24pdr) howitzers)

2 Batteries (4 105mm leFH 18 ea)

1/3rd Italian Artillery Regiment

1st, 2nd and 3rd Batteries (3 100mm Italian howitzers ea)

2/21st Italian Artillery Regiment

5th, 6th and 7th Batteries (4 105mm howitzers ea)

8th Battery (4 87mm captured British howitzers)

2 Batteries (3 100mm howitzers ea)

1/90th Artillery Regiment

2 Batteries (4 105mm leFH 18 ea)

Flak Regiment HG

Staff and Staff Battery (4 LMGs)

1st Battalion

1st–5th Flak Batteries (11 88mm, 28 20mm, 6 quad 20mm and 29 LMGs ea; 26 officers, 142 NCOs and 604 men)

2nd Battalion

6th–9th Flak Batteries (10 88mm, 18 20mm, 16 quad 20mm and 21 LMGs ea; 23 officers, 95 NCOs and 571 men)

Panzer Pioneer Company HG

Indicated as being in a tracked armored vehicle, not half-tracks

All formed units of the division sent to Africa were destroyed in the collapse of the German army in North Africa. Only scattered and broken survivors succeeded in escaping the disaster. What remained in continental Europe would be engaged in Sicily and later used to form the Hermann Göring Panzer Division.

Hermann Göring Panzer Division

Formed in June 1943 in Sicily from the survivors of the General Göring Division that had been destroyed in Tunisia or had not yet been shipped to Tunisia. Officially, on 10 July 1943 the division was organized with:

1/1st Hermann Göring Panzergrenadier Regiment

1st–3rd (armored) Panzergrenadier Companies

4th (armored) Heavy Company

2/1st Hermann Göring Panzergrenadier Regiment

5th–7th (motorized) Panzergrenadier Companies

8th (motorized) Heavy Company

1/Hermann Göring Panzer Regiment

1st–4th Panzer Companies

2/Hermann Göring Panzer Regiment

5th–8th Panzer Companies

Sturmgeschütz Battery HG

Hermann Göring Panzer Reconnaissance Battalion

1st Panzer Reconnaissance Company

2nd Motorcycle Company

3rd (armored) Grenadier Company

1/Hermann Göring Panzer Artillery Regiment

1st–2nd Batteries (4 105mm leFH ea)

2/Hermann Göring Panzer Artillery Regiment

3rd–5th Batteries (4 150mm sFH ea)

6th Battery (4 100mm K18 guns)

3/Hermann Göring Panzer Artillery Regiment

7th–8th Batteries (4 150mm sFH ea)

9th Battery (4 100mm K18 guns)

1/Hermann Göring Flak Regiment

1st–3rd Heavy Batteries (4 88mm guns ea)

4th–5th Light Batteries (12 20mm guns ea)

Hermann Göring Panzer Pioneer Battalion

1st–3rd Pioneer Companies

Hermann Göring Panzer Signals Battalion

1st (field telephone) Company

2nd (radio) Company

Hermann Göring Supply Battalion

1st–3rd Motor Transport Companies

Supply Company

Hermann Göring Maintenance Battalion

1st–2nd Repair Shop Companies

Equipment Distribution Center

Replacement Part Echelon

Hermann Göring Medical Battalion

1st–2nd Medical Squads

1st–3rd Ambulance Platoons

Administrative Units

Administration Company

Field Bakery Company

Butcher Company

Military Police Troop

Field Post Office

The part of the panzer battalion that had been sent to North Africa went without its equipment and was used as infantry. On 12 May, that portion of the battalion that remained in Sicily was merged with the 215th Panzer Battalion. A battalion of four companies was organized in Sicily. Further companies were organized in the Münsingen Troop Training Grounds and in southern France. As each of these additional companies was completed, it was forwarded to the newly organizing regiment. During the fighting in Italy, the personnel of the 2nd Company/504th Tiger Battalion were absorbed into the newly forming Hermann Göring Panzer Regiment after their last Tiger tanks had been lost in combat.

On 10 July 1943 the organization of the division and its panzer inventory were as follows:

Headquarters
HG Divisional Mapping Detachment
HG Military Band
HG Special Purpose Panzergrenadier Brigade
  1st Panzergrenadier Regiment HG
    1st (half-track) Battalion
      1st–3rd (half-track) Panzergrenadier Companies
      4th (heavy) Panzergrenadier Company
    2nd (mot) Battalion
      5th–7th (mot) Panzergrenadier Companies
      8th (heavy) (mot) Panzergrenadier Company
    3rd (Sturmgeschütz) Battalion
      9th–11th (Sturmgeschütz) Panzergrenadier Companies
      12th (heavy) (mot) Company
      1 Panzer Staff Company
      3 Sturmgeschütz Companies
      StuG (75mm)   20
      StuG (H) (105mm)   9
  1/, 2/, 3/HG Panzer Regiment
    1 Regimental Staff Signals Platoon
    1 Regimental Staff Light Panzer Platoon
    2 Battalions with:
      1 Panzer Staff Company
      1 Medium Panzer Company
      2 Light Panzer Companies
    Total tanks available:
      PzMk III (lg)   43
      PzMk III (75)   3
      PzMk IV (lg)   32
      PzBefWg   7
  Armored Reconnaissance Battalion HG
    Battalion Headquarters
    1st (armored) Reconnaissance Company
    2nd (motorcycle) Company
    3rd (half-track) Grenadier Company
  Hermann Göring Panzer Artillery Regiment
    1st (mot) Battalion
      1 Battalion Staff Battery
      1st–2nd Batteries (4 105mm leFH ea)
    2nd (mot) Battalion
      1 Battalion Staff Battery
      4th–5th Batteries (4 150mm sFH ea)
      6th Battery (4 100mm K18 guns)
    3rd (mot) Battalion
      1 Battalion Staff Battery
      7th–8th Batteries (4 150mm sFH ea)
      9th Battery (4 100mm K18 guns)

Hermann Göring Flak Regiment
  Regimental Headquarters
  1st Battalion
    Staff Battery
    1st–3rd Batteries (4 88mm Flak guns ea)
    4th–5th Batteries (12 20mm Flak guns ea)
Hermann Göring Panzer Pioneer Battalion
  Battalion Headquarters
  1st–3rd Panzer Pioneer Companies
Hermann Göring (mot) Signals Battalion
  1st (mot) Telephone Company
  2nd (mot) Radio Company
  Light (mot) Supply Column
Hermann Göring Divisional Supply Troop
  Battalion Headquarters
  1st–3rd Hermann Göring Transport Companies
  Hermann Göring Supply Company
Hermann Göring Maintenance Battalion
  Battalion Headquarters
  1st–2nd (mot) Maintenance Companies
  Equipment Distribution Point
  (mot) Replacement Part Supply Column
Medical Battalion
  1st–2nd Medical Companies
  1st–3rd Ambulances
Other
  Hermann Göring Divisional Administration Detachment
  Hermann Göring (mot) Field Bakery
  Hermann Göring (mot) Butcher Company
  Hermann Göring (mot) Military Police Troop
  Hermann Göring (mot) Field Post Office

On 21 July 1943 the division was in active combat in Sicily and was combined with a number of other formations and organized into a series of kampfgruppen. Those kampfgruppen were:

Kampfgruppe von Carnap
  1/3rd Fallschirmjäger Regiment
  4/Panzer Artillery Regiment HG
  923rd Fortress Battery
  5 Reconnaissance Squadrons
Kampfgruppe Schmalz
  115th Panzergrenadier Regiment
  3/Panzer Artillery Regiment HG
  3/Panzer Regiment HG
  Sachachtleben Battalion
  4th Fallschirmjäger Regiment
  Catania Flak Group (2 batteries)
  382nd Infantry Regiment (2 bns)
  804th Fortress Battalion
  1/Flak Regiment HG
Kampfgruppe Preuss
  2/Panzer Regiment HG

1 unknown Flak unit
Kampfgruppe Kluge
1/Panzergrenadier Regiment HG
1/Panzer Artillery Regiment HG
1/Panzer Regiment HG (from divisional reserve)
Oria Tank Battalion
10 Reconnaissance Squads
Kampfgruppe Rebholz
Panzer Reconnaissance Battalion HG
2/Panzer Artillery Regiment HG
2/Panzergrenadier Regiment HG
Reggio Fortress Battalion
9 Reconnaissance Squads
Divisional Reserve
1/Panzer Regiment HG (from divisional reserve)
2/, 3/3rd Fallschirmjäger Regiment

On 9 August 1943 the OKH ordered twelve Wespe self-propelled 105mm guns sent to the division. On 20 August 1943 the organization of the armored portion of the division and its panzer inventory were as follows:

1/, 2/, 3/HG Panzer Regiment
1 Panzer Staff Company
2 Battalion, each with
1 Panzer Staff Company
4 Medium Panzer Companies
1 Battalion
1 Panzer Staff Company
3 Sturmgeschütz Companies

Total tanks available:

PzMk III (lg)	25
PzMk III (75)	3
PzMk IV (lg)	31
StuG	16
PzBefWg	3
StuG H	6

In November 1943 the Hermann Göring Panzer Reconnaissance Battalion was reorganized as follows:

Headquarters and Signals Platoon
1st (half-track) Panzer Reconnaissance Company
2nd Motorcycle Reconnaissance Company
3rd (half-track) Panzergrenadier Company
4th (mot) Panzergrenadier Company (VW Schwimmwagen)
5th (half-track) Panzer Pioneer Company
Reconnaissance Supply Column

On 4 May 1944 the Hermann Göring Panzer Regiment was reorganized. The 2nd Battalion was to have four companies, each with 17 PzMk IV tanks. The 3rd Battalion was converted to a Panzerjäger Battalion with two companies equipped with 21 Jagdpanzer IV 75mm Pak 39 (L/48)—SdKfz 162—and a third, towed panzerjäger company. The re-equipping of the 1st Battalion with Panther tanks seems to have occurred in the fall of 1943. The division was reorganized in August 1944 as the Hermann Göring Parachute (Fallschirmjäger) Panzer Division.

Hermann Göring Parachute (Fallschirm) Panzer Division

Formed by renaming the Hermann Göring Panzer Division. On 4 June 1944 the division OKH records show the division to have been organized as follows:

Fallschirm Panzer Division Hermann Göring
1 Panzer Division Staff (2 LMGs)
1 (mot) Mapping Detachment
1 (mot) Divisional Band
1 (mot) Escort Company
1 Motorcycle Platoon (6 LMGs)
1 Infantry Gun Section (2 75mm leIG)
1 Light Self-Propelled Flak Platoon (4 20mm Flak guns)
1 Panzerjäger Platoon (3 LMGs and 3 75mm PAK 40)
1 Infantry Company (4 HMGs, 6 LMGs, 2 80mm mortars)
Fallschirm Panzer Regiment HG
1 Panzer Regiment Staff
1 Panzer Signals Platoon (4 LMGs)
1 Panzer Regiment Staff Company

1 Panzer Platoon
1 Self-Propelled Flak Platoon (12 20mm Flak guns)
1st Panzer Battalion
1 Panzer Battalion Staff
1 Panzer Battalion Staff Company
1 Panzer Flak Platoon (37mm Flak 43)
4 Panzer Companies (22 PzMk V tanks ea)
1 Panzer Maintenance Platoon
2nd Panzer Battalion
1 Panzer Battalion Staff
1 Panzer Battalion Staff Company
1 Panzer Flak Platoon (37mm Flak 43)
4 Panzer Companies (22 PzMk IV tanks ea)
1 Panzer Maintenance Company
3rd Sturmgeschütz Battalion
1 Sturmgeschütz Battalion Staff (1 LMG)
1 Sturmgeschütz Battalion Staff Company (2 LMGs)
2 Sturmgeschütz Batteries (10 StuG ea)
1 (motZ) Panzerjäger Company (12 75mm PAK 40 and 12 LMGs)

1 (mot) Supply Company (3 LMGs)

1st Fallschirm Panzergrenadier Regiment HG

1 (half-track) Regimental Staff

1 (half-track) Regimental Staff Company

  1 Staff Platoon (1 LMG)

  1 Motorcycle Platoon (8 LMGs)

  1 Pioneer Platoon (6 LMGs and 6 flamethrowers)

  1 Panzerjäger Platoon (9 LMGs and 3 50mm PAK 38)

  1 Signals Platoon (7 LMGs)

1st Battalion

1st–3rd (half-track) Companies (4 HMGs, 39 LMGs, 2 75mm guns, 2 80mm mortars and 3 37mm guns ea)

4th (half-track) Heavy Company

1 Staff Platoon (2 LMGs)

1 Pioneer Platoon (13 LMGs and 1 37mm PAK 36)

2 Infantry Gun Sections (4 LMGs and 2 75mm leIG ea)

1 Panzerjäger Platoon (8 LMGs and 3 75mm PAK 40)

1 Gun Platoon (8 LMGs and 6 75mm guns)

2nd Battalion

5th–7th (mot) Companies (4 HMGs, 18 LMGs, 2 80mm mortars and 13 panzerschrecke ea)

8th (mot) Heavy Company

  1 Pioneer Platoon (4 LMGs)

  1 Panzerjäger Platoon (3 LMGs and 3 75mm PAK 40)

  2 Infantry Gun Sections (4 LMGs and 2 75mm leIG ea)

  1 Mortar Platoon (2 LMGs and 6 120mm mortars)

3rd Battalion

same as 2nd Battalion

Self-Propelled Support Gun Battery (6 150mm sIG)

(motZ) Panzerjäger Company

(13 75mm PAK 40 and 13 LMGs)

2nd Fallschirm Panzergrenadier Regiment HG

1 (mot) Regimental Staff (2 LMGs)

1 (mot) Regimental Staff Company

  1 Signals Platoon

  1 Motorcycle Platoon (6 LMGs)

  1 Panzerjäger Platoon (3 LMGs and 3 75mm PAK 40)

1st Battalion

same as 2/2nd Fallschirm Panzergrenadier Regiment

2nd Battalion

same as 2/2nd Fallschirm Panzergrenadier Regiment

HG Fallschirm Panzer Reconnaissance Battalion

1 Panzer Reconnaissance Battalion Staff

1 Panzer Reconnaissance Battalion Staff Company

  1 Signals Platoon (7 LMGs)

  1 Armored Car Platoon (6 SdKfz 234/3 with 75mm StuK L/24 and 1 LMG)

1st (Armored Car) Company (6 LMGs and 18 SdKfz 234/1 with 20mm and 1 LMG)

2nd (Armored Car) Company (7 LMGs and 18 SdKfz 250/9 with 20mm and 1 LMG)

3rd Light (half-track) Reconnaissance Company (4 HMGs, 56 LMGs, 2 80mm mortars and 3 37mm PAK 36)

4th (mot) Reconnaissance Company (4 HMGs, 18 LMGs, 3 PzBu39 and 2 80mm mortars)

5th (half-track) Reconnaissance Company

  1 Staff (2 LMGs)

  1 Pioneer Platoon (13 LMGs and 1 37mm PAK 36)

  2 Infantry Gun Sections (4 LMGs and 2 75mm leIG ea)

  1 Panzerjäger Platoon (8 LMGs and 3 75mm PAK 40)

  1 Gun Platoon (8 LMGs and 6 75mm guns)

1 (mot) Reconnaissance Supply Column (2 LMGs)

HG Fallschirm Panzer Artillery Regiment

1 (mot) Regimental Staff

1 (mot) Regimental Staff Battery (2 LMGs)

1 (mot) Observation Battery (12 LMGs)

13th Nebelwerfer Battery (9 280/320mm launchers and 2 LMGs)

1st Battalion

1 (mot) Staff

1 (mot) Staff Battery (2 LMGs and 3 20mm mountain Flak guns)

3 (motZ) Batteries (4 105mm leFH and 5 LMGs ea)

2nd Battalion

1 (mot) Staff

1 (mot) Staff Battery (2 LMGs and 3 20mm mountain Flak guns)

3 (motZ) Batteries (4 150mm sFH and 5 LMGs ea)

3rd Battalion

same as 2nd Battalion

4th Battalion

Staff and (self-propelled) Staff Battery (2 LMGs)

2 Self-Propelled leFH Batteries (6 105mm leFH SdKfz 124 Wespe ea)

1 Self-Propelled sFH Battery (6 150mm sFH SdKfz 165 Hummel)

HG Panzer Flak Regiment

1 Battalion Staff (6 LMGs)

1 (mot) Signals Platoon

1 (mot) Weather Section

1 (mot) Range Correction Section

1st Battalion

1 Battalion Staff (1 LMG)

1 (mot) Signals Platoon

1 (mot) Heavy (60 ton) Flak Supply Column (2 LMGs)

3 (motZ) Heavy Flak Batteries (4 88mm, 3 20mm and 2 LMGs ea)

2 Self-Propelled Flak Batteries (9 20mm, 3 quad 20mm and 2 LMGs ea)

2nd Battalion

1 Battalion Staff (1 LMG)

1 (mot) Signals Platoon

1 (mot) Heavy (60 ton) Flak Supply Column (2 LMGs)

3 (motZ) Heavy Flak Batteries (4 88mm, 3 20mm and 2 LMGs ea)

2 Self-Propelled Flak Batteries (9 20mm, 3 quad 20mm and 2 LMGs ea)

2 Self-Propelled Flak Batteries (12 20mm and 2 LMGs ea)

3rd Battalion

1 Battalion Staff (1 LMG)

1 (mot) Signals Platoon

1 (mot) Heavy (60 ton) Flak Supply Column (2 LMGs)

3 (motZ) Heavy Flak Batteries (4 88mm, 3 20mm and 2 LMGs ea)

1 Self-Propelled Flak Battery (8 37mm and 2 LMGs)

1 Self-Propelled Flak Battery (9 20mm, 3 quad 20mm and 5 LMGs)

HG Fallschirm Panzer Pioneer Battalion

1 Panzer Pioneer Battalion Staff (7 LMGs)

1 (mot) Pioneer Battalion Staff Company (14 LMGs)

1 Panzer (half-track) Pioneer Company (43 LMGs, 2 80mm mortars, 3 panzerschrecke and 6 flame-throwers)

2 Panzer (mot) Pioneer Companies (18 LMGs, 2 80mm mortars and 6 flamethrowers ea)

1 (mot) Heavy Panzer Bridging Train

1 (mot) Light Panzer Bridging Train (3 LMGs)

HG Aircraft Liaison Detachment

no weapons

HG Panzer Signals Battalion

1 Panzer Battalion Staff

1 (mot) Supply Company (1 LMG)

1 Panzer Radio Company (20 LMGs)

1 Panzer Signals Company (21 LMGs)

HG Feldersatz Battalion

3 Companies (4 HMGs, 18 LMGs and 2 80mm mortars ea)

1 Company

2 Pioneer Platoons (4 LMGs)

1 Mortar Platoon (6 120mm mortars)

1 Panzerjäger Platoon (3 LMGs and 3 75mm guns)

HG Ersatz und Ausbildungs Battalion

HG Liaison Staff

HG Escort Regiment

HG Supply Troops

1st–8th/HG (mot) 120 ton Transportation Companies (8 LMGs ea)

HG (mot) Supply Company

HG Truck Park

1/, 2/, 3/HG (mot) Maintenance Companies (4 LMGs ea)

HG (mot) Ordnance Company (4 LMGs)

HG (mot) Heavy Maintenance Supply Train

HG (mot) Flak Instruction Platoon (2 LMGs)

HG (mot) Flak Ordnance Platoon

HG Administration Troops

HG (mot) Bakery Company (6 LMGs)

HG (mot) Butcher Company (4 LMGs)

HG (mot) Administration Company (2 LMGs)

HG Fallschirm Medical Battalion

1/, 2/, 3/HG (mot) Medical Companies (2 LMGs ea)

1/, 2/, 3/HG Ambulance Platoons

Other

HG Military Police Troop (2 LMGs)

HG Field Post Office

When the organization of the Hermann Göring Fallschirm Panzer Corps was well under way, the Führer Flak Battalion was detached from the Hermann Göring Fallschirm Panzer Division and became the Führer Flak Regiment in the newly forming Führer Escort Division. A new 4th Battalion was formed and the Hermann Göring Fallschirm Flak Regiment became a corps unit organized as follows:

1st Battalion

1st–3rd Batteries (88mm)

4th–5th Batteries (20mm and quad 20mm)

6th Battery (quad 20mm)

2nd Battalion

7th–9th Batteries (88mm)

10th Battery (37mm)

11th Battery (20mm and quad 20mm)

12th Battery (quad 20mm)

3rd Battalion

13th–15th Batteries (88mm)

16th Battery (37mm and 20mm)

17th Battery (20mm)

18th Battery (quad 20mm)

4th Battalion

19th–21st Batteries (88mm)

22nd Battery (37mm)

23rd and 24th Batteries (20mm)

On 12 July 1944 the division was ordered to pull out of Italy and move to the Russian front. It was to leave all its tanks behind in Italy and was to be refitted with 64 PzMk IV tanks in the 2nd Battalion (14 per company) and 31 Jagdpanzer IV in the 3/Hermann Göring Panzer Regiment. In August 1944 the organization of the armored portion of the division and its panzer inventory were as follows:

2/, 3/Hermann Göring Panzer Regiment

1 Panzer Flak Platoon

3rd Battalion

1 Panzer Staff Company

3 Panzerjäger Companies (Jagdpz IV)

2nd Battalion

1 Panzer Staff Company

4 Medium Panzer Companies (PzMk IV)
Total tanks available:

PzMk IV (lg)	64
Jagdpz IV	31
Flakpz38	8

On 24 September 1944 the division and the newly form-ing 2nd Hermann Göring Parachute Panzergrenadier Di-vision were organized into the Hermann Göring Fall-schirmjäger Panzer Corps. At that point the original divi-sion was renamed the Fallschirm Panzer Division Her-mann Göring. The following OKH organizational chart, dating from 24 September 1944, is significantly different from that of 4 June 1944. This strongly suggests that the original division was stripped for cadres and units to be used to organize the 2nd Hermann Göring Parachute Panzergrenadier Division.

Fallschirm Panzer Division Hermann Göring

1 Panzer Division Staff
1 (mot) Field Post Office
1 (mot) Military Police Detachment
1 (mot) Mapping Detachment
1 (mot) Escort Company
  1 Light Self-Propelled Flak Platoon (4 20mm Flak guns)
  1 Motorcycle Platoon (6 LMGs)
  1 Infantry Company (4 HMGs and 6 LMGs)

Fallschirm Panzer Regiment HG

1 Panzer Regiment Staff
1 Panzer Regiment Staff Company
  1 Signals Platoon
  1 Panzer Platoon
  1 Self-Propelled Flak Platoon (37mm Flak guns)
1 Panzer Maintenance Company

1st Panzer Battalion

1 Panzer Battalion Staff
1 Panzer Battalion Staff Company (12 LMGs and 3 self-propelled quad 20mm guns)
4 Panzer Companies (22 PzMk V tanks ea)
1 (mot) Panzer Supply Company (5 LMGs)

2nd Panzer Battalion

1 Panzer Battalion Staff
1 Panzer Battalion Staff Company (12 LMGs and 3 self-propelled quad 20mm guns)
4 Panzer Companies (22 PzMk IV tanks ea)
1 (mot) Panzer Supply Company (5 LMGs)

1st Fallschirm Panzergrenadier Regiment HG

1 (half-track) Regimental Staff (2 LMGs)
1 (half-track) Regimental Staff Company
  1 Signals Platoon (7 LMGs)
  1 Motorcycle Platoon (6 LMGs)
  1 Self-Propelled Flak Platoon (3 quad 20mm guns)

1st Battalion

1st–3rd (half-track) Companies (4 HMGs, 20 LMGs, 2 75mm guns, 2 80mm mortars and 2 20mm guns ea)

4th (half-track) Heavy Company
  1 Mortar Platoon (2 LMGs and 4 120mm mortars)
  1 leIG Platoon (2 LMGs and 6 75mm guns)

2nd Battalion

5th–7th (mot) Companies (4 HMGs, 18 LMGs and 2 80mm mortars ea)
8th (mot) Heavy Company
  1 Flak Platoon (6 20mm Flak guns)
  1 Mortar Platoon (2 LMGs and 4 120mm mortars)

(mot) Pioneer Company

2 (half-track) Platoons (LMGs and flamethrowers)
1 (mot) Pioneer Platoon (5 LMGs and ? 80mm mor-tars)

Self-Propelled Support Gun Battery (150mm sIG)
(motZ) Panzerjäger Company (12 75mm PAK)
2nd Fallschirm Panzergrenadier Regiment HG

1 (mot) Regimental Staff (2 LMGs)
1 (mot) Regimental Staff Company
  1 Signals Platoon (7 LMGs)
  1 Motorcycle Platoon (6 LMGs)
  1 Self-Propelled Flak Platoon (3 quad 20mm guns)

1st Battalion

same as 2/2nd Fallschirm Panzergrenadier Regiment
1st–3rd (mot) Companies
4th (mot) Heavy Company

2nd Battalion

same as 2/2nd Fallschirm Panzergrenadier Regiment
5th–7th (mot) Companies
8th (mot) Heavy Company

1st Fallschirm Panzer Pioneer Battalion HG

1 Panzer Pioneer Battalion Staff
1 Panzer (half-track) Pioneer Battalion Supply Com-pany
1 Panzer (half-track) Pioneer Company (2 HMGs, 45 LMGs, 2 80mm mortars and 6 flamethrowers)
2 Panzer (mot) Pioneer Companies (2 HMGs, 18 LMGs, 2 80mm mortars and 3 panzerschrecke)

1st Fallschirm Panzer Reconnaissance Battalion HG

1 Panzer Reconnaissance Battalion Staff
1 Panzer Reconnaissance Battalion Staff Company
  1 Signals Platoon (7 LMGs)
  1 Armored Car Platoon (3 75mm guns, 15 20mm guns and 16 LMGs)
1st (Armored Car) Company (16 Luchs tanks with 20mm guns and 25 LMGs)
2nd Light (half-track) Reconnaissance Company (2 75mm, 2 80mm mortars and 44 LMGs)
3rd (half-track) Reconnaissance Company (2 75mm, 7 20mm guns, 2 80mm mortars, 4 HMGs and 29 LMGs)
4th (half-track) Reconnaissance Company
  1 Staff (1 LMG)
  1 leIG Platoon (6 75mm and 2 LMGs)
  1 Mortar Platoon (6 80mm mortars and 2 LMGs)
  1 Pioneer Platoon (13 LMGs)

1 (mot) Reconnaissance Supply Column (4 LMGs)

1st Fallschirm Panzer Artillery Regiment HG
1 (mot) Regimental Staff
1 (mot) Regimental Staff Battery
1 (mot) Observation Battery

1st Battalion
1 Self-Propelled Staff
1 Self-Propelled Staff Battery (2 LMGs and 3 20mm mountain Flak guns)
3 Self-Propelled Batteries (6 105mm leFH Wespe and 6 LMGs ea)

2nd Battalion
1 (mot) Staff
1 (mot) Staff Battery (2 LMGs and 3 20mm mountain Flak guns)
2 (motZ) Batteries (6 105mm leFH and 5 LMGs)
1 (motZ) Battery (6 150mm sFH and 5 LMGs)

3rd Battalion
1 (mot) Staff
1 (mot) Staff Battery (2 LMGs and 3 20mm mountain Flak guns)

3 (motZ) Batteries (6 105mm leFH and 5 LMGs)

1st Panzer Signals Battalion HG
1 Panzer Battalion Staff
1 Panzer Battalion Staff Supply Company (2 LMGs)
1 Panzer Radio Company
1 Panzer Signals Company

1st Feldersatz Battalion HG
4 Companies

1st Fallschirm Medical Battalion HG
2 (mot) Medical Companies (4 LMGs ea)
2 (mot) Medical Supply Companies (4 LMGs ea)
1 (mot) Medical "Eg" Company

In November 1944 the division received a reinforcement in the form of:

1/Hermann Göring Panzer Regiment
1 Battalion
1 Panzer Staff Company
4 Medium Panzer Companies (PzMk V)
PzMk V   60

1st Hermann Göring Parachute (Fallschirm) Panzer Division

Formed by renaming the Hermann Göring Parachute (Fallschirm-jäger) Division after the 2nd Division was formed. By the end of the war it stood as a Kampfgruppe in the 4th Panzer Army.

General Command Fallschirm-Panzer Corps Hermann Göring

Formed in October 1944 by the merging of the Fallschirm-Panzer Division Hermann Göring and the 2nd Fallschirm-Panzergrenadier Division Hermann Göring. The corps was formed by pulling together fragments of existing units rather than by assigning complete units. It became operational on 1 October 1944 and was organized as follows:

Corps Headquarters
Commanding Officer: Generalmajor Schmalz
Corps Troops
Hermann Göring Corps Assault Battalion
Hermann Göring Panzerjäger Battalion
Hermann Göring Corps Signals Battalion
Hermann Göring Pioneer Battalion
Hermann Göring Parachute-Flak Regiment (4 bns)
I Hermann Göring Supply Battalion
II Hermann Göring Maintenance Battalion
Hermann Administration Göring Battalion
Hermann Göring Medical Battalion
Hermann Göring Field Post Office

1st Hermann Göring Fallschirm-Panzer Division
Commanding Officer: Oberst von Necker (until Feb. 1945)
1/, 2/Hermann Göring Panzer Regiment
1/, 2/1st Hermann Göring Fallschirm-Panzergrenadier Regiment
1/, 2/2nd Hermann Göring Fallschirmjäger-Panzergrenadier Regiment
1st Hermann Göring Fallschirm-Panzer Fusilier Battalion
1st Hermann Göring Panzer Reconnaissance Battalion
1st Hermann Göring Fallschirm-Pioneer Battalion
1/, 2/, 3/1st Hermann Göring Fallschirm-Panzer Artillery Regiment
1st Hermann Göring Fallschirm-Panzer Signals Battalion
1st Hermann Göring Feldersatz Battalion
1st Hermann Göring Medical Battalion
1st Hermann Göring Field Post Office
2nd Hermann Göring Fallschirm-Panzergrenadier Division
Commanding Officer: Oberst Walther

Hermann Göring Sturmgeschütz Battalion

1/, 2/, 3/3rd Hermann Göring Fallschirm-Panzer-grenadier Regiment

1/, 2/, 3/4th Hermann Göring Fallschirm-Panzer-grenadier Regiment

2nd Hermann Göring Fallschirm-Panzer Fusilier Battalion

2nd Hermann Göring Panzer Reconnaissance Battalion

1/, 2/, 3/2nd Hermann Göring Fallschirm-Panzer Artillery Regiment

2nd Hermann Göring Fallschirm-Panzer Signals Battalion

2nd Hermann Göring Feldersatz Battalion

2nd Hermann Göring Medical Battalion

2nd Hermann Göring Field Post Office

Other Units Assigned

Führer Flak Battalion (only initial period)

"Reichsmarschall" Begleit (Escort) Battalion

1st Hermann Göring Fallschirm-Panzer Replacement and Training Brigade

    1st HG Fallschirm-Panzer Replacement and Training Regiment

    2nd HG Fallschirm-Panzer Replacement and Training Regiment

The 1st Hermann Göring Fallschirm-Panzer Replacement and Training Brigade was assigned until March 1945, when it was replaced by the 2nd Hermann Göring Fallschirm-Panzer Replacement and Training Brigade, which had the 3rd and 4th Hermann Göring Fallschirm-Panzer Replacement and Training Regiments.

In January 1945 the Grossdeutschland Panzergrenadier Division and the 2nd Fallschirmjäger Panzergrenadier Division were assigned to the Corps. The Luftwaffe portions of the Corps were:

Fallschirm-Panzer Korps Hermann Göring

Corps Staff

1 (mot) Mapping Detachment

1 (mot) Field Post Office

1 (mot) Military Police Detachment

Corps Panzer Signals Battalion HG

1 Panzer Radio Company

2 (mot) Telephone Companies

1 (mot) Light Signals Supply Column

Corps Panzer Pioneer Battalion HG

1 (mot) Pioneer Company

2 (mot) Light Panzer Bridging Columns

Sturm Battalion HG

1 (mot) Battalion Staff

1 (mot) Battalion Supply Company

3 (mot) Companies (4 HMGs, 18 LMGs and 2 80mm mortars ea)

1 Heavy Company (6 20mm Flak 4 120mm mortars and 2 LMGs)

1 Pioneer Platoon

1 Panzerjäger Section

Fallschirm Flak Regiment HG

1 (mot) Regimental Staff

1 (mot) Signals Platoon

1 (mot) Calibration Detachment

1st Battalion

3 (motZ) Flak Batteries (6 88mm and 3 20mm guns ea)

1 Self-Propelled Company (12 37mm guns)

1 Self-Propelled Company (9 20mm and 3 quad 20mm guns)

1 Self-Propelled Company (12 quad 20mm guns)

1 (mot) 60 ton Supply Column

2nd and 3rd Battalions

same as 1st Battalion

4th Battalion

4 (motZ) Flak Batteries (6 88mm and 3 20mm guns ea)

1 (motZ) Flak Battery (12 37mm guns)

1 (motZ) Flak Battery (12 quad 20mm guns)

1 (mot) Signals Platoon

1 (mot) 60 ton Supply Column

Fallschirm Truck Park Troop, HG

3 (mot) Maintenance Companies

2 (mot) Ordnance Companies

1 75 ton (mot) Supply Column

1 (mot) Park Company

1 (mot) Flak Ordnance Platoon

1 (mot) Flak Instruction Platoon

1 (mot) Butcher Company

1 (mot) Baker Company

1 (mot) Supply Company

Corps Supply Troop

9 (120 ton) (mot) Transportation Columns

1 (mot) Fuel Column

Fallschirm-Panzer Division 1 HG

see Hermann Göring Fallschirmjäger Panzer Division

Fallschirm-Panzergrenadier Division 2 HG

see Fallschirm-Panzergrenadier Division 2 Hermann Göring

Hermann Göring Fallschirm-Panzer Replacement and Training Brigade

When the Hermann Göring Fallschirm-Panzer Division was expanded into a full corps on 24 September 1944 orders were issued for the formation of the Hermann Göring Fallschirm-Panzer Replacement and Training Brigade. Its organization appears to have begun in Holland, but shortly afterwards, in late September, Rippin, in West Prussia, was selected for its principal organizational location. The brigade was entirely formed from volunteers and contained both 16-year-olds and veterans of World War I. Units known to have been assigned were:

1/HG Fallschirm-Panzer Replacement and Training Regiment
Det/HG Fallschirm-Flak Replacement and Training Battalion
Det/HG Fallschirm-Artillery Replacement and Training Battalion
Det/21st Luftwaffe Feld Division
Det/25th Airbase Garrison Headquarters/VIII(Silesia)
10622nd Special Purpose Heavy Flak Battery
Det/5th Luftwaffe Special Purpose Light Infantry Battalion
Det/608th Grenadier Security Regiment
Det/HG Special Purpose Grenadier Battalion
Det/16th Heavy Machine Gun Company
Paratrooper Platoon (forced to cease training as Ramm on 16 December 1944)

The brigade soon grew to 2, 000–3, 000 men and was organized as follows:

Brigade Headquarters
Headquarters Company
Headquarters Signals Company
Headquarters Medical Company
Headquarters Infantry Gun Company
Training and Conversion Battalion
1st HG Fallschirm-Panzer Replacement and Training Regiment
Headquarters
1st Supply Company
3 Battalions, each with
    4 Companies (5 platoons ea)
HG Fallschirm-Panzer Pioneer Replacement and Training Unit
2nd HG Fallschirm-Panzer Replacement and Training Regiment
Headquarters
1st Supply Company
1 (mixed) Flak Battalion
    1st 88mm Flak Battery (4 88mm guns)
    2nd 88mm Flak Battery (2 88mm guns)
    4th 20mm Flak Battery (6 20mm guns)
    5th 20mm Flak Battery (6 20mm guns)
1 Artillery Battalion
    1 Light Battery (105mm leFH 18 howitzers)
    1 Heavy Battery (150mm sFH 18 howitzers)
HG Fallschirm-Panzer Pioneer Replacement and Training Unit

The brigade was committed to battle in Graudenz in February 1945 and it surrendered to the Russians on 6 March 1945.

2nd Göring Parachute Panzer Replacement and Training Brigade

Formed on 14 March 1945 in Velten and Joachimsthal with the 3rd and 4th Hermann Göring Parachute Panzer Replacement and Training Regiments and the remains of the destroyed Fallschirmjäger Panzer Replacement and Training Support Units, from Graudenz.

Nord Armored Brigade

Indications are that the Nord Armored Brigade was organized on 5 January 1944. It consisted of two medium panzer companies (30 Panthers each) and one armored maintenance platoon. Its fate is not known.

On 5 March 1945 a Panzerkampfgruppe Nord was formed with a four-company battalion. Its staff company had a Flak platoon with three quad 20mm guns and four 37mm Flak guns, all mounted on PzMk III chassis. A mixed company from Bergen consisted of 10 PzMk V Panther tanks and six PzMkVI Tiger I tanks. The light panzer company from Bergen contained 22 PzMk IV tanks, while the Putlos Gunnery School mixed panzer company had 12 Panther PzMk V and two PzMk VI Tiger I tanks. Putlos Gunnery School light company contained 7 PzMk IV tanks. The two companies from the Putlos Gunnery School were later designated the Putlos Panzer Battalion and assigned to the Clausewitz Panzer Division.

Norway Panzer Brigade

Formed on 13 July 1944 from drafts and various existing units, it replaced the Panzer Division Norway. It contained the Norway Panzer Battalion (four companies) and the Norway Panzergrenadier Battalion (from Norway Sturm Battalion). The brigade was apparently also known as the Sturmbrigade Norwegen. A structural diagram dated 28 June 1944 indicates that it was organized as follows:

Sturmbataillon Norwegen
2 (mot) Heavy Company
1 Pioneer Platoon (3 HMGs, 4 20mm Flak guns, 3 75mm PAK, 8 LMGs and 2 flamethrowers)
4 (bicycle) Companies (14 LMGs, 2 80mm mortars and 1 50mm mortar)

1 (mot) Supply Company
1 Panzer Platoon (3 French light tanks with 37mm guns)
Panzer Abteilung Norwegen
1 Staff Company
4 Panzer Companies
1 (mot) Supply Company
1 Armored Maintenance Platoon
Sturmbrigade Norwegen
1 Sturmgeschütz Battery (10 sturmgeschütze with 75mm guns)
Norwegen Lehr Battery
(4 105mm leFH 16 with 3 LMGs)

Norwegen (Norway) Panzer Division

Formed on 1 October 1943 using the staff of the 21st Panzer Brigade. The division had:

Norway Panzer Battalion
Staff Company
3 Panzer Companies
1/, 2/, 3/Norway Panzergrenadier Regiment
3 Panzer Companies
Norway Panzerjäger Battalion
2 (motZ) Panzerjäger Companies
1 Sturmgeschütz Company
Norway Panzer Artillery Battalion
1 Light Howitzer Battery (French guns)
2 Heavy Howitzer Batteries (French guns)
Norway Panzer Pioneer Company
Norway Panzer Signals Company

The division was formed from units left in Norway when the 25th Panzer Division departed. The division staff was formed from the former Staff/21st Panzer Brigade. The Norwegen Panzergrenadier Regiment contained a staff, staff company, and three (tmot) panzergrenadier battalions. What was not motorized was on bicycles. The Norwegen Panzer Battalion contained a staff, staff company, and three panzer companies, each apparently with 12 tanks. The Norwegen Panzerjäger Battalion contained a staff, staff company, two (motZ) panzerjäger companies, and a sturmgeschütz company. The Norwegen (mot) Panzer Artillery Regiment contained a staff, staff battery, a light howitzer battery equipped with French guns, a heavy howitzer battery equipped with French guns, and a battery equipped with heavy French guns. The pioneer company and panzer signals company were motorized.

An OKH order dated 17 November 1943 ordered the formation of a 13th (motorcycle) Company for the panzergrenadier regiment and set the supply and administrative troops at one heavy truck column, a motorized supply platoon, a divisional administrative detachment, a bakery platoon, and a butcher company. The panzer battalion added a panzer work shop platoon and a truck work shop platoon. On 1 July 1944 the division was disbanded and re-established as the 25th Panzer Division Kampfgruppe. At that time it had:

Panzer Battalion became 2103rd Panzer Battalion (103rd Panzer Brigade)
3/Panzergrenadier Regiment became 2/146th Panzergrenadier Regiment
Panzerjäger Battalion became 87th Panzerjäger Battalion
Panzer Artillery Battalion became 3/91st Panzer Artillery Battalion

OKH records show that in January 1945 the division was organized and equipped as follows:

Division Staff
1 (mot) Staff Company
Norwegen Panzer Battalion
1 Staff Company (5 PzMk III SdKfz 141/1 with 50mm KwK 39L/60 and 4 PzMk III SdKfz 141/2 with 75mm KwK L/24)
4 Panzer Companies (5 PzMk III SdKfz 141/1 with 50mm KwK 39L/60 and 8 PzMk III SdKfz 141/2 with 75mm KwK L/24 ea)
Norwegen Sturmgeschütz Battery (10 SdKfz 142 with 75m gun)

1 (mot) Panzer Maintenance Platoon
1 (mot) Panzer Supply Company
1 Grenadier Escort Platoon
Lehr (motZ) Battery (4 105mm leFH and 3 LMGs)
Panzergrenadier Battalion
1 Staff (2 HMGs and 3 LMGs)
1 Supply Company (2 LMGs)
3 Companies (2 HMGs and 15 LMGs)
1 Machine Gun Company
1 Mortar Platoon (6 LMGs and 4 120mm mortars)
1 Mortar Platoon (6 80mm mortars)
1 (motZ) Panzerjäger Platoon (3 75mm PAK 40)
1 (motZ) Flak Platoon (4 20mm Flak guns)
1 Infantry Gun Section (2 75mm leIG)
2/517th Infantry Regiment
1 Pioneer Platoon (3 LMGs)
3 Companies (2 HMGs, 9 LMGs and 2 (motZ) Russian 45mm guns ea)
1 Bicycle Company (9 LMGs)
Armored Troops
1 Panzer Platoon (1 French tank, 1 37mm French gun and 1 French LMG)
1 Armored Train (1 quad 20mm, 1 88mm gun, 1 20mm gun, 1 37mm PAK 36, 2 50mm British mortars, 2 80mm mortars, 2 HMGs and 12 LMGs)
Sturm Pioneer Company Norwegen (2 HMGs and 18 LMGs)
4th Company/762nd Pioneer Battalion (no heavy weapons)
710th (mot) Field Hospital

Its organization appears to have been rather fluid, because in January 1945 the division was organized and equipped as follows:

Norwegian Panzer Division
Norwegian Panzer Battalion
Staff Company (5 PzMk III 50mm L and 4 PzMk III 75mm K)

1st Company (5 PzMk III 50mm L and 3 PzMk III 75mm K)
2nd Company (5 PzMk III 50mm L and 3 PzMk III 75mm K)
3rd Company (5 PzMk III 50mm L and 3 PzMk III 75mm K)
4th Company (5 PzMk III 50mm L and 3 PzMk III 75mm K)
Norwegian Sturmgeschütz Battery (10 75mm StuG and 8 PzMk III 75mm Kz)
1 (mot) Maintenance Platoon
1 (mot) Supply Company
1 Escort Grenadier Platoon
Norwegian Panzergrenadier Battalion
Staff Company (2 HMGs and 3 LMGs)
Supply Company (2 LMGs)
3 Companies (2 HMGs and 16 LMGs ea)
1 Heavy Company
1 Mortar Platoon (4 120mm mortars and 6 LMGs)
1 Mortar Platoon (6 80mm mortars)
1 (motZ) Panzerjäger Platoon (3 75mm PAK 40)
1 (motZ) Flak Platoon (4 20mm Flak guns)
1 Infantry Gun Platoon (2 75mm leIG)
Training Battery (4 105mm leFH 16 and 3 LMGs)
2/517th Infantry Regiment
1 Pioneer Platoon (3 LMGs)
1 Company (2 HMGs, 10 LMGs and 2 45mm (motZ) Russian PAK)
2 Companies (2 HMGs, 9 LMGs and 2 45mm (motZ) Russian PAK ea)
Norwegian Armored Train (1 quad 20mm Flak gun, 1 88mm Flak gun, 1 37mm PAK, 2 British 50mm mortars, 2 80mm mortars, 2 HMGs, 12 LMGs and 1 French tank with 37mm gun and 1 LMG)
Norwegian Sturm Pioneer Company (2 HMGs and 18 LMGs)
4th Company/762nd Pioneer Battalion
710th (mot) Medical Company
Independent Battery (4 75mm PAK 40)

Oberschleisen Panzerjäger Brigade

Formed with three battalions in April 1945. Nothing is known of its organization or fate.

Panzer Ausbildungs Verband Böhmen

Formed on 28 March 1945 near Bautzen. It contained:

Staff (from Silesian Panzer Division)
Panzer Ausbildungs Regiment (from Milowitz Panzer Training Detachment)

7th Panzer Ausbildungs Battalion
18th Panzer Ausbildungs Battalion
1st and 2nd Panzergrenadier Ausbildungs Regiment, with
13th Panzergrenadier Ausbildungs Battalion

40th Panzergrenadier Ausbildungs Battalion
108th Panzergrenadier Ausbildungs Battalion
413th Panzergrenadier Ausbildungs Battalion
55th Panzer Reconnaissance Ausbildungs Battalion
124th Panzer Pioneer Ausbildungs Battalion

124th Panzer Signals Ausbildungs Battalion

It later absorbed a number of training formations. In April 1945 it was serving with the Grossdeutschland Panzer Corps.

Clausewitz Panzer Division

Formed on 6 April 1945 from the Panzer Ausbildungs Verband Grossdeutschland, the division had:

Staff (from Panzer Division Holstein), with
  "Holstein" Begleit (Escort) Company
106th Panzer Brigade
2/Feldherrnhalle Panzer Regiment (equipped with half-tracks)
Feldherrnhalle Panzergrenadier Replacement and Training Regiment
42nd Panzergrenadier Regiment Grossdeutschland
  Panzerjäger Battalion

On 4/7/45 the Grossdeutschland Panzerjäger Battalion, with two companies plus one from the Potsdam Panzer Battalion and a total of 31 sturmgeschütze, was ordered to join the division. Tanks were shipped to the division as follows: 31 StuG III on 13 April, 10 PzMk V Panthers on 14 April, five Jagdpanthers on 14 April, and 10 Pz IV/70(V) on 15 April 1945.

On 13 April 1945 the Putlos Kampfgruppe was ordered to the division, and it was renamed the Putlos Panzer Battalion on 17 April. It had a staff with two PzMk V, the 1st Company had two PzMk VI Tiger I and 10 Panther PzMk V, and the 2nd Company had seven PzMk IV, 1 Jagdpz VI, one StuG, and four Pz IV/70.

On 4/15/45 10 Panthers and five Jagdpanthers arrived and were given to the Panther Company/2106th Panzer Battalion.

Later the various detachments had their names changed, i.e. from "Feldherrnhalle" to "Clausewitz". The division was destroyed on 21 April 1945 by Fallersleben and the remnants moved to the Elbe. On 17 April 1945 the organization of the armored portion of the division and its panzer inventory were as follows:

2106th Panzer Battalion
  1 Jagdpanther Company
  1 Medium Panzer Company (PzMk V)
  Total tanks available:
  PzMk IV/70 (V)   10
  PzMk V   10
  Jagdpanther   5
Putlos Panzer Battalion
  1 Jagdpanther Company
  1 Medium Panzer Company (PzMk V)
  Total tanks available:
  PzMk IV (lg)   7
  PzMk IV/70 (V)   4
  PzMk V   12
  Jagdpz IV   1
  StuG   1

Donau Panzer Ausbildungs Verband

Formed on 30 March 1945, it contained:

Staff (perhaps from Staff/Holstein Panzer Division)
Panzer Regiment
  4th Panzer Ausbildungs Battalion
  17th Panzer Ausbildungs Battalion
  Panzergrenadier Ausbildungs Regiment
  12th Panzergrenadier Ausbildungs Battalion
  20th Panzergrenadier Ausbildungs Battalion
  2nd Panzergrenadier Ausbildungs Battalion
  10th Panzergrenadier Ausbildungs Battalion
81st (half) Panzer Signals Battalion

While forming it absorbed a number of training formations. The 12th and 20th Panzergrenadier Ausbildungs Battalions were assigned initially, but were later replaced by the 119th and 215th Panzergrenadier Ausbildungs Battalions. The 17th Panzer Ausbildungs Battalion appears to have merged with the Böhmen Panzer Ausbildungs Verband. Towards the end of the war the Donau Panzer Ausbildungs Verband was disbanded and used to rebuild the 1st, 6th and 13th Panzer Divisions.

Holstein Panzer Division

Formed on 10 February 1945 in Denmark by the mobilization of the 233rd Reserve Panzer Division. It consisted of:

44th Panzer Battalion (from 5th Reserve Panzer Battalion)

1/, 2/139th Panzergrenadier Regiment (from 8th and 9th Panzergrenadier Battalion)

1/, 2/142nd Panzergrenadier Regiment (from 50th and 93rd Reserve Panzergrenadier Battalions)

44th Panzer Reconnaissance Battalion (from 5th Reserve Panzer Reconnaissance Battalion)

144th Panzerjäger Battalion (from 3rd Reserve Panzerjäger Battalion)

144th Panzer Artillery Battalion (from 59th Reserve Panzer Artillery Battalion)

144th Panzer Pioneer Battalion (from 208th Reserve Panzer Pioneer Battalion)

144th Panzer Signals Company (from 1233rd Reserve Panzer Signals Battalion)

144th Panzer Supply Command Troops (from 1233rd Supply Troops)

The 44th Panzer Battalion was formed on 2 February 1945 with three companies of PzMk IV tanks and one company of self-propelled anti-tank guns. Shortly afterwards it received 29 PzMk IV from the 233rd Reserve Panzer Division. A further 29 were received from Denmark and 14 more from Stettin. Three command tanks were received on 11 February 1945. As of 10 February 1945 the division had a total authorized strength of 7,028 men, including 198 hiwi. It was organized as follows:

Holstein Panzer Division Staff
1 Divisional Staff (3 LMGs)
1 (mot) Mapping Detachment
44th Panzer Battalion
1 Panzer Battalion Staff (3 LMGs)
1 Panzer Battalion Staff Company (3 PzMk IV tanks and 3 LMGs)
2 Panzer Companies (9 PzMk IV tanks ea)
1 Panzer Company (7 PzMk IV tanks)
1 Panzer Maintenance Platoon
1 (mot) Panzer Supply Company
144th Panzerjäger Battalion
1 (motZ) Panzerjäger Battery (12 75mm PAK)
1 (motZ) Flak Battery (mixed 20mm and 37mm Flak guns)
1 Self-Propelled sIG Company
  1 Self-Propelled sIG Platoon (9 150mm sIG)
  1 Sturmgeschütz Battery (5 StuG)
139th Panzergrenadier Regiment
1 Panzergrenadier Regimental Staff

1 (mot) Panzergrenadier Regimental Staff Company
1 Signals Platoon
1 Motorcycle Platoon (3 LMGs)
1st (bicycle) Battalion
1 Battalion Staff
1 Battalion Staff Company
  1 (mot) Signals Platoon
  1 (mot) Infantry Gun Platoon (2 75mm leIG)
3 (bicycle) Companies (4 HMGs, 18 LMGs and 2 80mm mortars ea)
2nd (mot) Battalion
1 Battalion Staff
1 Battalion Staff Company
  1 (mot) Signals Platoon
  1 (mot) Infantry Gun Platoon (2 75mm leIG)
3 (mot) Companies (4 HMGs, 18 LMGs and 2 80mm mortars ea)
(motZ) Heavy Platoon
1 (motZ) Panzerjäger Section (2 PAK)
1 (motZ) Mortar Section (4 120mm mortars and 3 LMGs)
(motZ) Infantry Gun Company (6 150mm sIG, 2 20mm Flak and 4 LMGs)
Bicycle Pioneer Company (12 flamethrowers and 12 LMGs)
142nd Panzergrenadier Regiment
1 Panzergrenadier Regimental Staff
1 (mot) Panzergrenadier Regimental Staff Company
1 Signals Platoon
1 Motorcycle Platoon
2 (mot) Platoons (3 20mm Flak, 11 LMGs and 3 120mm mortars)
1st (bicycle) Battalion
same as 1/139th Panzergrenadier Regiment
2nd (mot) Battalion
same as 2/139th Panzergrenadier Regiment
(motZ) Heavy Platoon
1 (motZ) Panzerjäger Section (2 PAK)
1 (motZ) Mortar Section (4 120mm mortars and 3 LMGs)
(motZ) Infantry Gun Company (11 150mm sIG, 2 20mm Flak and 4 LMGs)
(mot) Pioneer Company (12 flamethrowers and 12 LMGs)
144th Panzer Artillery
144th Panzer Artillery Battalion
1 Panzer Artillery Battalion Staff
1 (mot) Panzer Artillery Battalion Staff Battery (4 LMGs)
1 Self-Propelled Battery (2 150mm sFH SdKfz 165 Hummels and 2 105mm leFH SdKfz 124 Wespe)
1 (motZ) Battery (4 105mm leFH and 4 LMGs)
1 (motZ) Battery (4 150mm sFH and 4 LMGs)

Luftwaffe Flak Battalion
1 Flak Battalion Staff
1 (mot) Flak Battalion Staff Battery (4 LMGs)
3 (motZ) Flak Batteries (4 88mm, 2 20mm and 2 LMGs ea)

44th Reconnaissance Battalion
1 Motorcycle Company
1 Armored Car Company (1 SdKfz 234/3 with 75mm, 5 SdKfz 234/1 with 1 20mm and 1 LMG ea, 2 80mm mortars and 33 LMGs)

144th Panzer Pioneer Battalion
1 Pioneer Battalion Staff (2 LMGs)
1 (mot) Pioneer Battalion Staff Company
1 Signals Platoon
1 (half-track) Pioneer Platoon
1 Supply Platoon
2 (mot) Pioneer Companies (2 HMGs, 9 LMGs and 2 80mm mortars ea)

144th Panzer Signals Company (no heavy weapons)
Administrative Units
144th (mot) (120 ton) Transportation Company

144th (mot) Supply Company
144th (mot) Maintenance Company
144th (mot) Medical Supply Company
144th (mot) Medical Company

On 8 February 1945 the organization of the armored portion of the division and its panzer inventory were as follows:

44th Panzer Battalion
1 Panzer Staff Company
3 Medium Panzer Companies (PzMk IV)
Total tanks available:
PzMk IV (lg)   29 (+17 arriving 11 Feb. 1945)

The division and the Schlesien Panzer Division were merged on 26 March 1945 to re-form the 18th Panzergrenadier Division. On 6 April 1945 the division's staff was used to rebuild the Clausewitz Panzer Division.

Jüterbog Panzer Division

Formed on 25 February 1945 from the remains of Army Group units from Army Group Center. It contained:

Staff
1 Panzer Divisional Staff (2 LMGs)
1 (mot) Mapping Detachment
1 (mot) Escort Company
1 Infantry Platoon (4 HMGs and 6 LMGs)
1 Motorcycle Platoon (6 LMGs)
1 Self-Propelled Flak Platoon (4 20mm Flak guns)
1 (mot) Military Police Detachment (5 LMGs)

Jüterbog Panzer Battalion
1 Panzer Battalion Staff (1 LMG and 2 command tanks)
1 Panzer Battalion Staff Company (8 LMGs and 3 quad 20mm Flak guns)
2 Panzer Companies (10 PzMk IV tanks ea)
1 Panzer Company (10 PzMk IV L tanks)
1 Panzer Maintenance Platoon (4 LMGs)
1 Panzer Supply Company (4 LMGs)

Jüterbog Panzer (tmot) Grenadier Regiment
1 Regimental Staff
1 (tmot) Regimental Staff Company
1 Signals Platoon
1 Motorcycle Platoon (4 LMGs)

1st (tmot) Battalion
1 Battalion Staff
1 (tmot) Battalion Supply Company (4 LMGs)
2 (half-track) Companies (3 HMGs, 30 LMGs, 2 80mm mortars, 7 20mm and 2 75mm guns ea)

1 (tmot) Company (4 HMGs, 18 LMGs and 2 80mm mortars)
1 (tmot) Heavy Company (6 20mm Flak, 2 LMGs and 4 120mm mortars)

2nd (tmot) Battalion
1 Battalion Staff
1 (tmot) Battalion Supply Company (4 LMGs)
3 (tmot) Companies (3 HMGs, 18 LMGs and 2 80mm mortars ea)
1 (tmot) Heavy Company (6 20mm Flak, 2 LMGs and 4 120mm mortars)
1 (tmot) Heavy Infantry Gun Company (4 150mm sIG and 2 LMGs)
1 (tmot) Pioneer Company (18 flamethrowers, 2 HMGs, 12 LMGs, and 2 80mm mortars)

Jüterbog Mixed Panzer Company
1 Jagdpanzer Battery (10 Jagdpanzer)
1 (half-track) Panzerjäger Company (6 SdKfz 251/22 with 75mm PAK)

Jüterbog Reconnaissance Company (3 SdKfz 250/8 with 75mm gun and 12 SdKfz 234/1 with 20mm guns)

Jüterbog Artillery Regiment
1 Regimental Staff
1 Regimental Staff Battery (2 LMGs)

1/Jüterbog Artillery Regiment (formerly 510th Artillery Battalion)
1 Battalion Staff
1 (mot) Battalion Staff Battery (2 LMGs and 3 20mm Flak guns)

3 (motZ) Batteries (4 105mm leFH and 4 LMGs ea)

Luftwaffe Flak Battalion
1 Flak Battalion Staff
1 (mot) Flak Battalion Staff Battery (4 LMGs)
3 (motZ) Flak Batteries (4 88mm, 2 20mm and 2 LMGs ea)

Jüterbog Pioneer Company (2 HMGs, 18 LMGs and 2 80mm mortars)
Jüterbog Panzer Signals Company (12 LMGs)
Jüterbog (mot) (120 ton) Transportation Company

Jüterbog (mot) Maintenance Company (3 LMGs)
Jüterbog (mot) Mixed Administration Company (3 LMGs)
Jüterbog (mot) Medical Company
Jüterbog (mot) Medical Supply Company
Jüterbog (mot) Field Post Office

On 26 February 1945 the division was merged into the 16th Panzer Division's Kampfgruppe and was brought to full strength as a division. It was disbanded in March.

Müncheberg Panzer Division

Formed on 8 March 1945. Its staff was formed from the Staff/103rd Panzer Brigade. The division had:

1/, 2/1st Müncheberg Panzergrenadier Regiment
1/, 2/2nd Müncheberg Panzergrenadier Regiment
Kummersdorf Panzer Battalion (later renamed Münchenburg Panzer Bn)
  1 Medium Panzer Company (PzMk IV)
  2 Medium Panzer Companies (PzMk V)
1 Independent Heavy Panzer Company (PzMk VI)
  PzMk IV (lg)   4
  PzMk V   11 (+10 on 25 March and +10 on 10 April)
  PzMk VI   11
Staff/, 1/Müncheberg Panzer Artillery Regiment
Müncheberg Reconnaissance Company
Müncheberg Panzerjäger Company
Müncheberg Pioneer Company
Müncheberg Signals Company
Müncheberg Feldersatz Battalion
Müncheberg Supply Troops

An OKH order dated 18 April 1945 shows that the Kummersdorf Battalion and the 1/29th Panzer Regiment were organized into an *ad hoc* regiment. The Kummersdorf, or 1st, Battalion had a staff, a staff company, a Tiger company (formerly 3/Kummersdorf Panzer Battalion), a Panther company, a mixed panzer company, and a supply company. The 1/29th or 2nd Battalion had a staff, a staff company, a Panther company, a "special equipment" panzer company, a panzergrenadier company in half-tracks, a "special equipment" panzergrenadier company, a supply company, and a maintenance company.

On 20 March 1945 the 1/29th Panzer Regiment was ordered reorganized with four companies. The 1st, 2nd and 4th Companies were to be organized with ten tanks, and the 3rd Company was organized with 14 PzMk VI Tigers. However, indications are that only Panther MI V tanks were shipped to the division. Orders were issued on 7 April 1945 for a Panther Company of the 1/29th Panzer Regiment and a company of the 25th Panzergrenadier Regiment, then in Wunsdorf, to join the division. Both companies were equipped with infra-red equipment.

The division was destroyed in Berlin and its survivors passed into Russian captivity on 3 May 1945.

Schlesien (Silesian) Panzer Division

Formed on 20 February 1945, initially as the Döberitz Panzer Division, it was renamed on 22 February and contained:

Staff
1 Panzer Divisional Staff (2 LMGs)
1 (mot) Mapping Detachment
1 (mot) Escort Company
  1 Infantry Platoon (4 HMGs and 6 LMGs)
  1 Motorcycle Platoon (6 LMGs)
  1 Self-Propelled Flak Platoon (4 20mm Flak guns)
1 (mot) Military Police Detachment (5 LMGs)

Schleisen Panzer Battalion (formerly 303rd Panzer Battalion)
  1 Panzer Battalion Staff (1 LMG and 2 command tanks)
  1 Panzer Battalion Staff Company (8 LMGs and 3 quad 20mm Flak guns)
  2 Panzer Companies (10 PzMk IV tanks ea)
  1 Panzer Company (10 PzMk IV L tanks)
  1 Panzer Maintenance Platoon (4 LMGs)
  1 Panzer Supply Company (4 LMGs)
Schleisen Panzer (tmot) Grenadier Regiment
  1 Regimental Staff

1 (tmot) Regimental Staff Company
1 Signals Platoon
1 Motorcycle Platoon (4 LMGs)

1st (tmot) Battalion
1 Battalion Staff
1 (tmot) Battalion Supply Company (4 LMGs)
2 (half-track) Companies (3 HMGs, 30 LMGs, 2 80mm mortars, 7 20mm and 2 75mm guns ea)
1 (tmot) Company (4 HMGs, 18 LMGs and 2 80mm mortars)
1 (tmot) Heavy Company (6 20mm Flak, 2 LMGs and 4 120mm mortars)

2nd (tmot) Battalion
1 Battalion Staff
1 (tmot) Battalion Supply Company (4 LMGs)
3 (tmot) Companies (3 HMGs, 18 LMGs and 2 80mm mortars ea)
1 (tmot) Heavy Company (6 20mm Flak, 2 LMGs and 4 120mm mortars)
1 (tmot) Heavy Infantry Gun Company (4 150mm sIG and 2 LMGs)
1 (tmot) Pioneer Company (18 flamethrowers, 2 HMGs, 12 LMGs and 2 80mm mortars)

Schleisen Mixed Panzer Company
1 Jagdpanzer Battery (10 Jagdpanzer)
1 (half-track) Panzerjäger Company (6 SdKfz 251/22 with 75mm PAK)

Schleisen Reconnaissance Company (3 SdKfz 250/8 with 75mm gun and 12 SdKfz 234/1 with 20mm guns)

Schleisen Artillery Regiment
1 Regimental Staff
1 Regimental Staff Battery (2 LMGs)

1/Schleisen Artillery Regiment (formerly 510th Artillery Battalion)
1 Battalion Staff

1 (mot) Battalion Staff Battery (2 LMGs and 3 20mm Flak guns)
3 (motZ) Batteries (4 105mm leFH and 4 LMGs ea)

Luftwaffe Flak Battalion
1 Flak Battalion Staff
1 (mot) Flak Battalion Staff Battery (4 LMGs)
3 (motZ) Flak Batteries (4 88mm, 2 20mm and 2 LMGs ea)

Schleisen Pioneer Company (2 HMGs, 18 LMGs and 2 80mm mortars)
Schleisen Panzer Signals Company (12 LMGs)
Schleisen (mot) (120 ton) Transportation Company
Schleisen (mot) Maintenance Company (3 LMGs)
Schleisen (mot) Mixed Administration Company (3 LMGs)
Schleisen (mot) Medical Company
Schleisen (mot) Medical Supply Company
Schleisen (mot) Field Post Office

It would appear that a Flak battalion and a full panzer pioneer battalion were formed, each with three companies. Later the 2nd Silesian Panzergrenadier Regiment was formed. However, it had only 1 battalion with four companies.

The Döbritz, later Schlesien, Panzer Battalion, was ordered formed with three companies, each with 10 PzMk IV tanks. A total of 21 were shipped to the division on 21 February 1945, followed by 10 PzMk IV/70(V) on 21 February and a further 10 PzMk IV on 2 March. On 26 February 1945 the division was ordered transferred to Army Group Vistula. A 4/Schlesien Panzer Battalion was assigned to the division on 9 March 1945, but its equipment is unknown.

On 30 March 1945 the division was disbanded and absorbed into the Holstein Panzer Division, which was itself later used to rebuild the 18th Panzergrenadier Division.

Tatra Panzer Division

Formed in August 1944 in Czechoslovakia from troops in the recruit forces. The division had:

1/, 2/82nd Panzergrenadier Replacement and Training Regiment
1/, 2/85th Panzergrenadier Replacement and Training Regiment
Panzer Company (from 4th Panzer Replacement and Training Battalion)
Panzerjäger Company (from 8th Panzerjäger Replacement and Training Battalion)
Tatra Artillery Battalion (3 self-propelled batteries)
2 Pioneer Companies
1st and 2nd Companies/1st Battalion, 482nd Grenadier Training Battalion

Field Replacement Battalion (after December 1944)

In December the division became the Tatra Panzer Field Training Division and was assigned to the field army. In March 1945 it became the 232nd Panzer Division.

Führer Begleit (Escort) Brigade

Formed originally as a battalion, in 1939 it actually performed escort duties for Adolf Hitler. It contained:

Headquarters
Führer Operations Company
  Guard Platoon
1st Rifle Company
2nd Fast Company
  3 Motorcycle Platoons
3rd Heavy Company (20mm Flak and 37mm PAK 36 guns)
Führer Escort Battery (7th Btry/Regiment General Göring)
1st Railway Flak Platoon Battery (9th Btry/Regiment General Göring) (2 quad 20mm railroad guns)
2nd Railway Flak Platoon Battery (9th Btry/Regiment General Göring) (2 quad 20mm railroad guns)

In 1941, when Hitler and the Führer Escort Battalion moved to the Wolfsschanze headquarters, an additional force of Flak, the 604th Flak Regiment, was assigned to protect Hitler against air attack. At the end of 1942 this battalion was redesignated the Führer Flak Battalion. The Führer Escort Battery (7/RGG) was assigned to this battalion and the 2nd Company, Guard Battalion HG, joined it as the 8th (Guard) Company.

The two railway platoons were not incorporated as they had, since 1942, been redesignated the 15th (Railway) Battery Flak Regiment HG. Despite this, they remained under the operational control of the Führer Headquarters. In the fall of 1944 the Führer Flak Battalion was expanded into the Führer Flak Regiment. The Führer Flak Regiment contained:

1st Battalion
  1st Battery (88mm guns)
  2nd Battery (88mm guns)
  3rd Battery (88mm guns)
  4th Battery (88mm guns)
2nd Battalion
  5th Battery (Self-Propelled 20mm guns)
  6th Battery (Self-Propelled 20mm guns)
  7th Battery (Self-Propelled 37mm guns)

At the end of 1944 the regiment expanded into 14 companies. The evolution and lineage of the Flak elements through 1943 was as follows:

Incorporated at end of 1942	In Führer Battalion as	To 4/Flak Regiment HG	Weapons
1st Co/604th	1st Company	1st Co/4th Bn	88mm
2nd Co/604th	2nd Company	2nd Co/4th Bn	88mm
3rd Co/604th	3rd Company	3rd Co/4th Bn	88mm
6th Co/604th	4th Company	4th Co/4th Bn	88mm
4th Co/604th	5th Company	5th Co/4th Bn	88mm
7th Co/RGG	6th Company	6th Co/4th Bn	20mm
5th Co/604th	7th Company	7th Co/4th Bn	88mm
2nd Co/Guard Bn HGG	8th Company	8th Co/4th Bn	Guard Co
7th Co/604th (formerly 4/321st)	9th Company	9th Co/4th Bn	20mm
8th Co/604th (formerly 5/321st)	10th Company	10th Co/4th Bn	20mm
New Formation	11th Company	11th Co/4th Bn	Fire fighting
New Formation	12th Company	12th Co/4th Bn	Fire fighting
New Formation	13th Company	13th Co/4th Bn	Fire fighting
New Formation	14th Company	14th Co/4th Bn	Fire fighting

On 1 June 1944, the Führer Escort Battalion was expanded into a regiment. Immediately prior to becoming a regiment it contained:

1 Staff Company
  1 (mot) Signals Platoon
  1 (mot) Maintenance Platoon
1 Mixed Light/Medium Armored Company

1 (mot) Infantry Support Company
  1 Panzerjäger Platoon (2 LMGs and 4 50mm PAK 38)
  1 Flak Platoon (8 20mm AA guns and 6 LMGs)
2 (mot) Infantry Companies (12 LMGs, 2 HMGs and 4 88mm panzerschrecke)
1 (mot) Infantry Company (9 armored cars with 9 20mm and 9 LMGs and 3 cars with 3 LMGs and 3 88mm panzerschrecke)

This was expanded into a regiment, and on 28 November 1944 the regiment was formed into a brigade. The brigade contained:

Brigade Staff
Staff (half-track) (10/10/22)[1]
Panzer (half-track) Escort Company (3/41/162; 2 panzerschrecke and 18 LMGs)
  1 (mot) Supply Column
  1 Maintenance Platoon
  1 Signals Platoon

1st Panzergrenadier Battalion Führer Begleit Brigade
1st, 2nd and 3rd SS (half-track) Companies[2] (5/43/208; 2 HMGs, 39 LMGs, 2 80mm mortars, 6 20mm and 2 75mm leIG ea)
4th (half-track) Heavy Company (3/27/119; 6 HMGs, 16 LMGs, 6 120mm mortars and 6 75mm guns)
5th Panzer Company (6/96/157; 46 LMGs, 17 PzMk IV tanks and 10 sturmgeschütze)
6th Self-Propelled Flak Company (5/36/184; 1 20mm gun, 4 37mm, 4 quad 20mm, 8 20mm Flak and 13 LMGs)

2nd (mot) Panzergrenadier Battalion Führer Begleit Brigade
7th (mot) Infantry Company (5/41/219; 2 HMGs, 18 LMGs and 2 80mm mortars)
8th (mot) Reconnaissance Company (5/40/215; 2 HMGs, 18 LMGs and 2 80mm mortars)
9th (mot) Sturm Pioneer Company (5/53/208; 12 flamethrowers)
10th (mot) Heavy Company (8 LMGs, 4 150mm sIG, 4 75mm PAK)

928th Bicycle Battalion
Staff (4 flamethrowers and 1 LMG; 5/17/56)
1 Bicycle Company (2/25/139; 6 HMGs, 12 LMGs, 2 80mm and 3 50mm mortars)
2 Bicycle Companies (2/25/136; 5 HMGs, 12 LMGs, 2 80mm and 3 50mm mortars ea)
1 Heavy Company (2/30/122; 8 HMGs, 2 LMGs, 2 75mm PAK, 2 75mm leIG, 3 80mm mortars)

Führer Begleit Brigade Artillery Battalion
(mot) Staff (2 LMGs)
(mot) Staff Company
  87 ton Supply Column
  Medical Group
  Signals Platoon
1st (mot) Battery (2/21/120)
  3 Gun Sections (6 88mm guns)
  Flak Platoon (3 self-propelled 20mm quad guns)
  Sound Ranging Platoon (4 self-propelled sound ranging vehicles)

2nd, 3rd and 4th (mot) Batteries (2/29/148 ea)
  3 Gun Sections (6 88mm guns total)
  Flak Platoon (3 self-propelled 20mm quad guns)
  Sound Ranging Platoon (1 self-propelled sound ranging vehicle)
5th (mot) Battery (2/24/135)
  12 Self-Propelled 37mm Flak guns
  5 (mot) 600mm searchlights
6th and 7th Batteries
  12 Self-Propelled 20mm Flak guns each
  5 (mot) 600mm searchlights

200th Sturmgeschütz Brigade (army troops)
organization unknown

Reconnaissance Company (1/32/80)
2 Armored Car Platoons (13 20mm guns and 13 LMGs)
1 Motorcycle Platoon (5 LMGs)

Feldersatz Battalion
organization unknown

(mot) Field Hospital (9/21/146)

In December, for the Battle of the Bulge, the brigade contained:

Brigade Staff
1 Brigade Staff Company
  1 Half-Track Mounted Infantry Platoon
  1 Half-Track 20mm Flak Platoon
1 Armored Car Reconnaissance Company
1 Signals Company
1 20mm Flak Company
  FlakpzIV (2V)   4
  FlakpzIV (37)   4
1 (Half-Track) Pioneer Company
1 Self-Propelled Infantry Gun Company (150mm sIG)
1 Self-Propelled Panzerjäger Company

Führer Begleit Panzergrenadier Regiment
1 (Half-Track) Staff Company

Panzer Fusilier Battalion
1 (Half-Track) Battalion Staff
3 (Half-Track) Rifle Companies
1 (Half-Track) Heavy Company
1 (mot) Supply Company

(mot) Panzergrenadier Battalion
1 Battalion Staff
3 (mot) Rifle Companies
1 (mot) Machine Gun Company
1 (mot) Support Company (75mm leIG)
1 (mot) Supply Company

829th Infantry Battalion z.b.V.
1 (mot) Battalion Staff
3 (bicycle) Rifle Companies
1 (mot) Heavy Company
1 (mot) Supply Company

Führer Begleit Panzer Battalion
1 (mot) Battalion Staff

---

[1] Strength figures are officers, NCOs, and men.
[2] The 3rd SS Company was assigned on 1 December 1944.

1st Panzer Company (Panther tanks)
2nd Panzer Company (Panther tanks)
3rd Panzer Company (Jagdpanther tanks)
4th Panzerjäger Company (self-propelled PAK)
5th Sturmgeschütz Company (10 StuG)
1 (mot) Supply Company
1 (mot) Maintenance Company

Führer Begleit Sturmgeschütz Brigade
1 Staff and Staff Battery
3 Sturmgeschütz Batteries (10 StuG ea)

Führer Begleit Artillery Regiment
1 Regiment Staff
1st and 2nd Battalions, each with
1 Battalion Staff and Staff Battery
1st and 2nd (half-track) Batteries (105mm leFH)
3rd (half-track) Battery (150mm sFH)
1 (mot) Supply Battery

Führer Begleit Flak Battalion
1st Flak Battery (20mm guns)
2nd Flak Battery (37mm guns)
3rd Flak Battery (88mm guns)

Führer Begleit Battle School
1 (mot) Staff
3 (mot) Companies

Other
2 Ambulance Platoons
1 (mot) Medical Company
1 (mot) Maintenance Company
1 Army Transportation Column
1 "OT" Transportation Column

On 18 January 1945 it was ordered expanded to form the Führer Begleit (Escort) Division. On 1/25/45 the Staff/102nd Panzer Regiment was raised and the 2/Grossdeutschland Panzer Regiment was assigned as the 2/102nd Panzer Regiment.

Division Staff
1 Division Staff (2 LMGs)
120th (mot) Mapping Detachment
120th (mot) Military Police Detachment (5 LMGs)

102nd Panzer Regiment
1 Panzer Regimental Staff
1 Panzer Regimental Staff Company
1 Panzer Signals Platoon (6 LMGs)
1 Panzer Platoon (10 LMGs)
1 Self-Propelled Flak Platoon (8 37mm Flak guns)
2/102nd Panzer Regiment (formerly 2/Grossdeutschland Panzer Regiment)
1 Panzer Battalion Staff
1 Self-Propelled Flak Platoon (3 quad 20mm Flak guns and 12 LMGs)
2 Panzer Companies (14 PzMk V Panther tanks ea)
2 Panzer Companies (14 PzMk IV tanks ea)
1 Panzer Maintenance Platoon

1 (mot) Panzer Supply Company (5 LMGs)

99th Panzergrenadier Regiment
1 (half-track) Regimental Staff
1 (half-track) Regimental Staff Company
1 Signals Platoon (7 LMGs)
1 Motorcycle Platoon (4 LMGs)
1 Staff Platoon (1 LMG)
1st Battalion
1 (half-track) Battalion Staff (6 LMGs)
1 (mot) Supply Company (5 LMGs)
3 (half-track) Companies (3 HMGs, 30 LMGs, 2 80mm mortars, 2 SdKfz 251/9 with 75mm gun and 7 20mm guns ea)
1 (half-track) Heavy Company
1 Staff Platoon (2 LMGs)
1 Infantry Gun Platoon (6 SdKfz 251/9 with 75mm guns)
1 Mortar Platoon (7 LMGs and 4 120mm mortars)
2nd Battalion
1 Battalion Staff
1 (mot) Supply Company (4 LMGs)
3 (mot) Companies (4 HMGs, 18 LMGs and 2 80mm mortars ea)
1 (mot) Heavy Company
1 Platoon (6 20mm)
1 Mortar Platoon (2 LMGs and 4 120mm mortars)
3rd Battalion
1 Battalion Staff
1 (mot) Supply Company (4 LMGs)
3 (bicycle) Companies (4 HMGs, 18 LMGs and 2 80mm mortars ea)
1 (mot) Heavy Company
1 Platoon (6 20mm)
1 Mortar Platoon (2 LMGs and 4 120mm mortars)

120th Panzer Artillery Regiment (formed from 1036th Regimental Artillery Staff z.b.V., FGB Artillery Battalion, 423rd Army Artillery Battalion and 2/500th Panzer Artillery Regiment)
1 Regimental Staff
1 (mot) Regimental Staff Battery (2 LMGs)
1st Battalion (formerly 1/234th Artillery Regiment)
1 Battalion Staff
1 (mot) Battalion Staff Battery (2 LMGs and 3 20mm mountain Flak guns)
3 (motZ) Batteries (4 105mm leFH and 4 LMGs ea)
2nd Battalion (formerly 2/5th Artillery Regiment) same as 1st Battalion
3rd Battalion (formerly 3/184th Artillery Regiment)
1 Battalion Staff
1 (mot) Battalion Staff Battery (2 LMGs and 3 20mm mountain Flak guns)
3 (motZ) Batteries (4 150mm sFH and 4 LMGs ea)

673rd Panzerjäger Battalion
1 Battalion Staff 1 Battalion Staff Company (12 LMGs and 3 quad 20mm)

3 Jagdpanzer Companies (10 jagdpanzers ea)
1 (mot) Supply Company (5 LMGs)

Mixed Luftwaffe Flak Battalion
1 Battalion Staff
1 (mot) Battalion Staff (2 LMGs)
2 (motZ) Heavy Flak Batteries (4 88mm, 3 self-propelled 20mm, 4 LMGs and 1 self-propelled searchlight ea)
2 (motZ) Heavy Flak Batteries (4 88mm, 3 20mm, 4 LMGs and 1 self-propelled searchlight ea)
1 Self-Propelled Medium Flak Battery (9 37mm and 5 self-propelled searchlights)
1 (motZ) Light Flak Battery (12 20mm and 5 self-propelled searchlights)

102nd (mixed) Panzer Reconnaissance Company (18 LMGs and 13 20mm guns)

124th Panzer Pioneer Battalion
1 Pioneer Battalion Staff (10 LMGs)
1 (half-track) Pioneer Battalion Staff Company (4 LMGs)
1 (half-track) Pioneer Company (2 HMGs, 43 LMGs, 6 flamethrowers and 2 80mm mortars)
2 (mot) Pioneer Companies (2 HMGs, 18 LMGs, 6 flamethrowers and 2 80mm mortars ea)

120th Panzer Signals Battalion
1 Panzer Radio Company (19 LMGs)
1 Panzer Telephone Company (11 LMGs)
1 (mot) Supply Company (2 LMGs)

120th Panzer Feldersatz Battalion
1 Supply Company
4 Feldersatz Companies (50 LMGs, 12 HMGs, 6 80mm mortars, 2 120mm mortars, 1 75mm PAK, 1 20mm Flak, 2 flamethrowers and 1 105mm leFH 18 total)

124th Panzer Supply Troop
1 Panzer Supply Troop Staff (2 LMGs)
1 (mot) Staff Company
1/, 2/, 3/124th (mot) (120 ton) Transportation Companies (4 LMGs ea)
124th (mot) Supply Platoon

Other
1/, 2/124th Maintenance Company (2 LMGs ea)
120th (mot) (50 ton) Maintenance Supply Column
120th Mixed Administration Company (Bakery, Butcher and Divisional Administration)
1/120th (mot) Medical Company (2 LMGs)
1/120th (mot) Medical supply Company (1 LMG)
120th (mot) Field Post Office

Thirty Panther tanks were delivered between 8 and 10 February. The 1/102nd Panzer Regiment was ordered formed on 16 February 1945. It was to have two Panther Companies, with 14 tanks each, and two PzMk IV Companies, also with 14 tanks each. The 2/Grossdeutschland Panzer Regiment was then formally renamed the 2/1st Führer Panzer Regiment, and a 673rd Panzerjäger Battalion was assigned to serve as the regiment's 2nd Battalion.

Führer Grenadier Brigade

Formed in July 1944 in East Prussia from the reinforced Führer Grenadier Battalion. Correspondence dated 28 June 1944 ordered it to have, on 1 September 1944, the following organization:

Brigade Staff
1 (half-track) Staff (2 LMGs)
1 (half-track) Staff Company
1 Signals Platoon (7 LMGs)
1 Motorcycle Messenger Platoon (6 LMGs)

1st Battalion (former Führer Grenadier Battalion) (1st–4th Companies)
1 (half-track) Staff Platoon (5 LMGs)
1 (mot) Supply Company (5 LMGs)
1 (mot) Escort Company
1 (half-track) Pioneer Platoon
1 (half-track) Signals Platoon (2 heavy rocket launchers, 4 light flamethrowers, 1 37mm leIG and 16 LMGs)
2 (half-track) Companies (21 LMGs, 2 HMGs, 5 37mm guns and 2 80mm mortars ea)

1 (mot) Company (2 50mm mortars, 21 LMGs and 2 HMGs)
1 (half-track) Company (4 leIG, 4 sIG, 4 80mm mortars and 4 75mm PAK, 4 HMGs and 7 LMGs)

3rd Battalion (armored) (9th–12th Companies)
1 (mot) Staff (5 LMGs)
1 (mot) Supply Company (5 LMGs)
3 (half-track) Companies (2 75mm PAK, 6 20mm Flak, 2 50mm mortars, 29 LMGs and 4 HMGs ea)
1 (half-track) Company (6 75mm PAK, 6 LMGs and 4 120mm mortars)

4th Battalion (newly formed) (Grenadier Battalion) (13th–16th Companies)
1 (mot) Supply Company (4 LMGs)
3 (mot) Companies (2 50mm mortars, 18 LMGs and 4 HMGs ea)
1 (mot) Company (6 20mm Flak, 4 120mm mortars and 2 LMGs)

5th Company
1 Armored Car Platoon (12 armored cars with 20mm guns)

1 Panzer Company (17 PzMk IV tanks and 5 sturm-geschütze)

6th (mot) Company
1 Self-Propelled Flak Company (4 37mm and 8 20mm Flak guns)
1 leIG Company (7 37mm guns and 8 LMGs)

7th (mot) Heavy Infantry Company (19 LMGs, 2 HMGs, 2 80mm mortars)

17th sIG Company (6 Self-Propelled 150mm sIG)

18th Flak Company (12 self-propelled 20mm Flak guns and 4 LMGs)

1st Führer Grenadier Sturmgeschütz Brigade
1 Sturmgeschütz Battery (14 sturmgeschütze and 12 LMGs)

2nd Führer Grenadier Sturmgeschütz Brigade
1 Sturmgeschütz Battery (14 sturmgeschütze and 12 LMGs)

(mot) Maintenance Platoon (no heavy weapons assigned)

On 2 August 1944 the brigade was to be reorganized, by 1 October 1944, as follows:

Brigade Staff
1 (half-track) Staff (2 LMGs)
1 (half-track) Staff Company
  1 Signals Platoon (7 LMGs)
  1 Motorcycle Messenger Platoon (1 HMG and 4 LMGs)

1st Battalion (1st–4th Companies)
1 (half-track) Staff Platoon (6 LMGs)
1 (mot) Supply Company (4 LMGs)
1 (mot) Escort Company
  1 (half-track) Pioneer Platoon
  1 (half-track) Signals Platoon (16 LMGs, 1 37mm leIG, 4 LMGs and 2 heavy flamethrowers)
2 (half-track) Companies (21 LMGs, 2 HMGs, 5 37mm guns and 2 80mm mortars ea)
1 (mot) Company (2 50mm mortars, 21 LMGs and 2 HMGs)
1 (half-track) Company (4 leIG, 4 sIG, 4 80mm mortars and 4 75mm PAK, 4 HMGs and 7 LMGs)

5th Company (53 LMGs)
1 Armored Car Platoon (12 armored cars with 20mm guns)
1 Panzer Company (17 PzMk IV tanks and 5 sturm-geschütze)

6th (mot) Company
1 Self-Propelled Flak Company (4 37mm and 8 20mm Flak guns)
1 leIG Company (7 37mm guns and 8 LMGs)

7th (mot) Heavy Infantry Company
(19 LMGs, 2 HMGs and 2 80mm mortars)

3rd Battalion (armored) (9th–12th Companies)
1 (mot) Staff (6 LMGs)

1 (mot) Supply Company (4 LMGs)
3 (half-track) Companies (2 75mm PAK, 6 20mm Flak, 2 50mm mortars, 29 LMGs and 4 HMGs ea)
1 (half-track) Company (6 75mm PAK, 6 LMGs and 4 120mm mortars)

4th Battalion (13th–16th Companies)
3 (mot) Companies (2 50mm mortars, 18 LMGs and 4 HMGs ea)
1 (mot) Company (6 20mm Flak, 4 120mm mortars and 2 LMGs)
1 (mot) Supply Company (4 LMGs)

5th Battalion
17th–19th Panzer Companies (11 Panther PzMkV tanks ea)
20th Panzer Company (11 Jagdpanzer IV L70)
21st (mot) Supply Company (4 LMGs)
Self-Propelled Flak Platoon (3 quad 20mm Flak guns)

23rd sIG Company
(6 Self-Propelled 150mm sIG and 8 LMGs)

24th Flak Company
(12 self-propelled 20mm Flak guns and 2 LMGs)

25th Panzer Pioneer Company
(6 flamethrowers, 2 HMGs, 6 LMGs and 2 80mm mortars)

26th (mot) Reconnaissance Company
2 Reconnaissance Platoons (6 LMGs ea)
1 Armored Car Platoon (6 armored cars)

27th Panzer Signals Company
(12 LMGs)

28th Panzer Maintenance Platoon
(no heavy weapons assigned)

29th (mot) Transportation Company
(8 LMGs)

However, on 8 August 1944 the organization was revised such that the 5th, 6th, and 7th Companies were incorporated into the 1st Battalion, the 3rd Battalion was redesignated as the 2nd Battalion, and the 5th (panzer) Battalion was redesignated as the 3rd (panzer) Battalion. The support units were redesignated with the 14th sIG Company, 15th Flak Company, 16th Panzer Pioneer Company, 17th Reconnaissance Company, 18th Signals Company, 19th Panzer Maintenance Company, and 20th (mot) Transportation Company. On 14 September 1944 the organization was directed to be reorganized yet again. This new organization was as follows:

Brigade Staff
Staff (2 LMGs)
(mot) Escort Company
  Staff (4 HMGs, 2 LMGs)
  Motorcycle Messenger Platoon (6 LMGs)
  Panzerjäger Platoon (3 75mm PAK and 3 LMGs)
  Flak Platoon (4 20mm Flak guns)

1st (half-track) Battalion (1st–4th Companies)
1 (half-track) Staff Platoon (6 LMGs)

1 (half-track) Supply Company (4 LMGs)

3 (half-track) Companies (30 LMGs, 3 HMGs, 2 80mm mortars, 7 20mm Flak and 2 75mm leIG ea)

1 (half-track) Company

Company Staff (2 LMGs)

Panzerjäger Platoon (6 75mm PAK and 2 LMGs)

Mortar Platoon (4 120mm mortars and 7 LMGs)

2nd (mot) Battalion (5th–8th Companies)

1 (mot) Staff Platoon

1 (mot) Supply Company (4 LMGs)

3 (mot) Companies (18 LMGs, 4 HMGs and 2 80mm mortars ea)

1 (mot) Company (6 20mm Flak, 4 120mm mortars and 2 LMGs)

3rd Panzer Battalion

9th–11th Panzer Companies (11 Panther PzMk V tanks ea)

12th Panzer Company (11 Jagdpanzer IV L70)

13th (mot) Supply Company (4 LMGs)

Self-Propelled Flak Platoon (3 quad 20mm Flak guns)

14th sIG Company

(6 Self-Propelled 150mm sIG and 8 LMGs)

15th Flak Company

(12 self-propelled 20mm Flak guns and 2 LMGs)

16th Panzer Pioneer Company

Platoon (6 flamethrowers and 12 LMGs)

Platoon (43 LMGs, 6 flamethrowers and 2 80mm mortars)

19th Panzer Maintenance Platoon

(4 LMGs)

20th (mot) Transportation Company

(8 LMGs)

21st (mot) Medical Company

(4 LMGs)

In December 1944, prior to the Ardennes offensive, the staffs of the grenadier and panzer regiments were organized and the 929th z.b.v. Grenadier (Bicycle) Battalion was assigned to the brigade.

Führer Grenadier Division

Formed on 26 January 1945 from the Führer Grenadier Brigade. On 25 January 1945 the 101st Panzer Regiment was ordered formed with a single battalion. It was organized and equipped as follows:

Division Staff

1 Division Staff

1 Divisional Escort Company

1 Infantry Platoon (4 HMGs and 6 LMGs)

1 Motorcycle Platoon (6 LMGs)

1 Self-Propelled Flak Platoon (4 20mm Flak)

124th (mot) Military Police Detachment (5 LMGs)

101st Panzer Regiment (from 3rd FGB)

1 Panzer Regimental Staff

1 Panzer Regimental Staff Company

1 Panzer Signals Platoon (6 LMGs)

1 Panzer Platoon (10 LMGs)

1 Self-Propelled Flak Platoon (8 37mm Flak guns)

1/101st Panzer Regiment

1 Panzer Battalion Staff

1 Self-Propelled Flak Platoon (3 quad 20mm Flak guns and 12 LMGs)

2 Panzer Companies (14 PzMk V Panther tanks ea)

2 Panzer Companies (14 PzMk IV tanks ea)

1 Panzer Maintenance Platoon

1 (mot) Panzer Supply Company (3 LMGs)

99th Panzergrenadier Regiment (formed from 1/, 2/ FGB and 929th Grenadier Battalion)

1 (half-track) Regimental Staff

1 (half-track) Regimental Staff Company

1 Signals Platoon (7 LMGs)

1 Motorcycle Platoon (4 LMGs)

1 Staff Platoon (1 LMG)

1st Battalion

1 (half-track) Battalion Staff (6 LMGs)

1 (mot) Supply Company (5 LMGs)

3 (half-track) Companies (3 HMGs, 30 LMGs, 2 80mm mortars, 2 SdKfz 251/9 with 75mm gun and 7 20mm guns ea)

1 (half-track) Heavy Company

1 Staff Platoon (2 LMGs)

1 Infantry Gun Platoon (6 SdKfz 251/9 with 75mm guns)

1 Mortar Platoon (7 LMGs and 4 120mm mortars)

2nd Battalion

1 Battalion Staff

1 (mot) Supply Company (4 LMGs)

3 (mot) Companies (4 HMGs, 18 LMGs and 2 80mm mortars ea)

1 (mot) Heavy Company

1 Platoon (6 20mm)

1 Mortar Platoon (2 LMGs and 4 120mm mortars)

3rd Battalion

1 Battalion Staff

1 (mot) Supply Company (4 LMGs)

3 (bicycle) Companies (4 HMGs, 18 LMGs and 2 80mm mortars ea)

1 (mot) Heavy Company

1 Platoon (6 20mm)

1 Mortar Platoon (2 LMGs and 4 120mm mortars)

911th Army Assault Artillery Brigade
1 Sturm Artillery Brigade Staff (1 LMG)
1 Sturm Artillery Brigade Staff Company (2 LMGs)
3 Sturmgeschütz Companies (10 StuG and 12 LMGs ea)
1 (mot) Sturm Artillery Escort Company (1 LMG)

101st (mixed) Panzer Reconnaissance Company
(16 LMGs and 16 20mm guns)

124th Panzer Artillery Regiment
1 Regimental Staff
1 (mot) Regimental Staff Battery (2 LMGs)

1st Battalion
1 Battalion Staff
1 Self-Propelled Battalion Staff Battery (2 LMGs and 3 20mm mountain Flak guns)
1 Self-Propelled Battery (6 105mm SdKfz 124 Wespe and 4 LMGs)
2 Self-Propelled Batteries (6 150mm SdKfz 165 Hummel and 4 LMGs ea)

2nd Battalion
1 Battalion Staff
1 (mot) Battalion Staff Battery (2 LMGs and 3 20mm mountain Flak guns)
3 (motZ) Batteries (4 105mm leFH and 4 LMGs ea)

3rd Battalion
1 Battalion Staff
1 (mot) Battalion Staff Battery (2 LMGs and 3 20mm mountain Flak guns)
3 (motZ) Batteries (4 150mm sFH and 4 LMGs ea)

Mixed Luftwaffe Flak Battalion
1 Battalion Staff
1 (mot) Battalion Staff (2 LMGs)
3 (motZ) Heavy Flak Batteries (4 88mm, 3 20mm and 4 LMGs ea)
1 (motZ) Medium Flak Battery (9 37mm and 5 LMGs)
1 (motZ) Light Flak Battery (12 20mm and 2 LMGs)

124th Panzer Pioneer Battalion:
1 Pioneer Battalion Staff (10 LMGs)
1 (half-track) Pioneer Battalion Staff Company (4 LMGs)
1 (half-track) Pioneer Company (2 HMGs, 43 LMGs, 6 flamethrowers and 2 80mm mortars)
2 (mot) Pioneer Companies (2 HMGs, 18 LMGs, 6 flamethrowers and 2 80mm mortars ea)

124th Panzer Signals Battalion
1 Panzer Radio Company (19 LMGs)
1 Panzer Telephone Company (11 LMGs)
1 (mot) Supply Company (2 LMGs)

124th Panzer Feldersatz Battalion
1 Supply Company
4 Feldersatz Companies (50 LMGs, 12 HMGs, 6 80mm mortars, 2 120mm mortars, 1 75mm PAK, 1 20mm Flak, 2 flamethrowers and 1 105mm leFH 18 total)

124th Panzer Supply Troop
1/, 2/, 3/124th (mot) (120 ton) Transportation Companies (4 LMGs ea)
124th (mot) Supply Platoon

Other
1/124th Maintenance Platoon (1 LMG)
2/124th Maintenance Company (2 LMGs)
124th Mixed Administration Company (Bakery, Butcher and Divisional Administration)
1/124th (mot) Medical Company (2 LMGs)
1/124th (mot) Medical supply Company (1 LMG)
124th (mot) Field Post Office

On 15 February 1945 ten jagdpanthers were shipped to the division and on 17 February 16 PzMkV Panther tanks were delivered. In April it was renamed and the units were as follows:

1/, 2/, 3/3rd Führer-Panzergrenadier Regiment (from 2, 3/99th)
1/, 2/, 3/4th Führer-Panzergrenadier Regiment (from Staff/Sommer Bicycle Regiment, 124th Feldersatz Battalion and 3/Ersatz und Ausbildungs Regiment Grossdeutschland)
1/, 2/Führer-Panzer Regiment (from 1/101st and 1/99th)
1/, 2/, 3/, 2nd Führer-Panzer Artillery Regiment (from 124th)
Führer-Panzer Division (mixed) Flak Battalion (from the Luftwaffe)
124th Divisional Support Unit

The division was taken into American captivity in Zwettl, on the Lower Donau, then handed over to the Russians.

West Schnelle Brigade

Formed in France during the summer of 1943 as a reinforced brigade, it had:

1/, 2/West Brigade Panzergrenadier Regiment
West Brigade Sturmgeschütz Battalion (3 batteries)

1st and 2nd West Brigade Motorcycle Companies
West Brigade Pioneer Company
West Brigade Signals Company
West Brigade Division Support Units
West Brigade Feldersatz Company

OKH records show that the brigade was ordered to assume the following organization on 16 February 1943:

931st Brigade Staff
1 Brigade Staff
1 (mot) Mapping Detachment (2 LMGs)
435th Panzergrenadier Regiment
1 Regimental Staff
1 (half-track) Pioneer Company (4 HMGs, 3 LMGs and 3 panzerschrecke)
1 Motorcycle Company (18 LMGs, 4 HMGs and 2 120mm mortars)
1 Signals Platoon
1 (half-track) Panzergrenadier Battalion
4 (half-track) Panzergrenadier Companies (3 HMGs, 11 LMGs and 3 80mm mortars ea)
1 (mot) Panzergrenadier Battalion
4 (mot) Panzergrenadier Companies (3 HMGs, 11 LMGs and 3 80mm mortars ea)
931st (mot) Feldersatz Company
(no heavy weapons)
931st Self-Propelled Panzerjäger Battalion
1st and 2nd Companies, each with
1 (self-propelled) Heavy Platoon (3 88mm guns)
1 (self-propelled) Platoon (4 105mm leFH)
1 (half-track) Flak Platoon (4 20mm and 10 LMGs)
3rd Company
1 (self-propelled) Heavy Platoon (7 88mm guns)
1 (half-track) Flak Platoon (4 20mm and 10 LMGs)
4th and 5th (half-track) Companies (7 76.2mm guns and 7 LMGs ea)
1 (mot) Maintenance Platoon
931st Panzer Artillery Regiment
1 (mot) Signals Platoon
1 (mot) Calibration Detachment
1st Battalion
1 Battalion Staff and Staff Battery (6 LMGs)
2 Self-Propelled Batteries (6 105mm leFH SdKfz 124 Wespe and 4 LMGs ea)
1 Self-Propelled Battery (6 150mm sFH SdKfz 165 Hummel and 4 LMGs)
2nd Battalion
1 Battalion Staff and Staff Battery (6 LMGs)
3 Self-Propelled Batteries (6 150mm sFH SdKfz 165 Hummel and 4 LMGs ea)

Supply Troop
1/, 2/931st (mot) (120 ton) Transportation Companies
Other
931st (mot) Mixed Signals Company (2 LMGs)
931st (mot) Administration Platoon
931st (mot) Medical Company
931st (mot) Ambulance

This organization did not last long and was quickly changed. By March 1943 the panzergrenadier regiment gave up its half-track pioneer and motorcycle companies as independent companies (numbered 931st). For a short time the brigade was numbered the 931st Schnelle Brigade, the Panzergrenadiers were numbered 433rd, and the brigade support units were numbered the 931st. On 12 March 1943 the sturmgeschütz battalion was renumbered the 931st. The two panzergrenadier battalions took one of their companies and rebuilt it as follows:

Heavy (half-track) Company
1 Platoon (4 half-track mounted heavy anti-tank guns and 4 LMGs)
1 Platoon (3 half-track mounted 20mm Flak guns and 3 LMGs)

The artillery regiment underwent significant reorganization. The 4th Battalion was detached as an independent battalion. The 5th Battalion was disbanded. The 1st, 2nd, and 3rd Batteries had the four self-propelled 105mm howitzers replaced by four StuG. Their Flak detachments were reduced to four 20mm guns on half-tracks and eight LMGs.

The organization continued to change and by 14 March 1943 it had added a brigade band. The 435th Panzergrenadier Regiment added a (motZ) Infantry Gun Company (4 150mm sIG).

On 15 July 1943 the brigade was sent to Rennes, France, to re-form the 21st Panzer Division. The 433rd Panzergrenadier Regiment became the 125th Panzergrenadier Regiment, the two motorcycle companies became the 21st Reconnaissance Battalion, and the 931st Panzer Artillery Regiment became the 155th Panzer Artillery Regiment.

West Schnelle Division

The West Schnelle Brigade was originally to be expanded into a division on 6 May 1943. This did not happen: the unit was disbanded, and its elements were used to rebuild the 21st Panzer Division. However, the plans for its reorganization show that it was to be organized and equipped as follows:

Division Staff
1 Division Staff
1 (mot) Mapping Detachment
931st Motorcycle Company (2 120mm mortars, 4 HMGs and 18 LMGs)

436th and 1 other Panzergrenadier Regiment, each with
- 1 Regimental Staff
- 1 (half-track) Pioneer Company (4 HMGs, 3 LMGs and 3 panzerschrecke)
- 1 Motorcycle Company (18 LMGs, 4 HMGs and 2 120mm mortars)
- 1 Signals Platoon

1 (half-track) Panzergrenadier Battalion
- 3 (half-track) Panzergrenadier Companies (3 HMGs, 11 LMGs and 3 80mm mortars ea)
- 1 Heavy (half-track) Company
  - 1 Platoon (4 half-track mounted heavy anti-tank guns and 4 LMGs)
  - 1 Platoon (3 half-track mounted 20mm Flak guns and 3 LMGs)

1 (mot) Panzergrenadier Battalion
- 3 (mot) Panzergrenadier Companies (3 HMGs 11 LMGs and 3 80mm mortars ea)
- 1 Heavy (half-track) Company
  - 1 Platoon (4 half-track mounted heavy anti-tank guns and 4 LMGs)
  - 1 Platoon (3 half-track mounted 20mm Flak guns and 3 LMGs)

931st (mot) Feldersatz Company

Reinforced Panzerjäger Battalion
- 1st Self-Propelled Panzerjäger Company (10 75mm PAK 40 and 8 LMGs)
- 2nd Self-Propelled Panzerjäger Company (10 75mm PAK 40 and 8 LMGs)
- 3rd Sturmgeschütz Company (10 StuG)
- 4th (half-track) Flak Company (6 20mm mounted on half-tracks and 8 LMGs)

Pioneer Battalion
- 931st (half-track) Pioneer Company (40 LMGs, 2 80mm mortars and 6 flamethrowers)
- 1 (mot) Pioneer Company (18 LMGs, 2 80mm mortars and 6 flamethrowers)
- 1 (mot) Light Pioneer Supply Column (2 LMGs)

Signals Battalion
- 931st (mot) Mixed Signals Company (2 LMGs)
- 1 (mot) Radio Company
- 1 (mot) Signals Supply Column

931st Panzer Artillery Regiment
- 1 (mot) Signals Platoon
- 1 (mot) Calibration Detachment

1st Battalion
- 1 Battalion Staff and Staff Battery (6 LMGs)
- 2 Self-Propelled Batteries (6 105mm leFH SdKfz 124 Wespe and 4 LMGs ea)
- 1 Self-Propelled Battery (6 150mm sFH SdKfz 165 Hummel and 4 LMGs)

2nd Battalion
- 1 Battalion Staff and Staff Battery
- 3 (motZ) Batteries (4 105mm leFH and 2 LMGs ea)

3rd Battalion
- 1 Battalion Staff and Staff Battery (6 LMGs)
- 3 Self-Propelled Batteries (6 150mm sFH SdKfz 165 Hummel and 4 LMGs ea)

Supply Troop
- 1–4/931st (mot) (120 ton) Transportation Companies
- 931st (mot) Supply Company
- 931st (mot) Maintenance Company

Other
- 931st (mot) Bakery Company
- 931st (mot) Butcher Company
- 931st (mot) Administration Platoon
- 931st (mot) Medical Company
- 1/, 2/931st (mot) Ambulances
- 931st (mot) Field Post Office

Grossdeutschland Panzer Training Verband

The division was formed on 4 April 1945 and had:

Grossdeutschland Panzer Training Battalion (not formed)
1/, 2/, 3/Grossdeutschland Panzergrenadier Training Regiment
Grossdeutschland OB School
Grossdeutschland Panzer Artillery Training Battalion
Grossdeutschland Pioneer Training Battalion (2 companies)
Grossdeutschland Signals Training Battalion (1 company)
20th Panzer Training Battalion

With the incorporation of the formation into the Clausewitz Panzer Division, the Wackernagel (Panzergrenadier Regiment) and the Poerschmann (OB School) Regiments were sent to the Ems and Weser. The latter was incorporated into the 15th Panzer Division and passed into British captivity.

Krampnitz Panzer Refitting Verband (Detachment)

Formed on 28 March 1945 in Krampnitz with personnel from a variety of sites. The detachment had:

Krampnitz Mixed Panzer Battalion (from 2108th Panzer Battalion, 218th Sturmpanzer Battalion and Potsdam Panzer Battalion)
1/, 2/1st Krampnitz Panzergrenadier Regiment
1/, 2/2nd Krampnitz Panzergrenadier Regiment

Krampnitz Panzerjäger Battalion (from Deiss Panzerjäger Battalion)
Krampnitz Armored Car Company
Krampnitz Pioneer Company
Krampnitz Signals Company Krampnitz Supply Troops

On 19 April 1945 the detachment was sent to rebuild the 7th Panzer Division near Hela.

Ostsee Panzer Ausbildungs Verband

Formed on 28 March 1945 with:

Staff/227th Infantry Division
Staff/Coburg Regiment
5th Panzer Ausbildungs Battalion
13th Panzer Ausbildungs Battalion
Staff/1st Panzergrenadier Ausbildungs Regiment
Staff/2nd Panzergrenadier Ausbildungs Regiment
5th Panzergrenadier Ausbildungs Battalion
73rd Panzergrenadier Ausbildungs Battalion
76th Panzergrenadier Ausbildungs Battalion

90th Panzergrenadier Ausbildungs Battalion
3rd Panzer Reconnaissance Ausbildungs Battalion
6th Panzer Reconnaissance Ausbildungs Half Battalion
208th Panzer Pioneer Ausbildungs Battalion
82nd (half) Panzer Signals Ausbildungs Battalion

The division was intended to absorb the Sharpshooter Instruction Course, Wehrkreis X, the Army Panzergrenadier NCO School from Putlos, and the 2nd Fahnenjunker School for armored troops in Munsterlager.

Panzer Verband Stegemann

Formed in February 1945 in Wehrkreise VIII. It contained:

30th Grenadier Ersatz und Ausbildungs (mot) Battalion
55th Panzer Reconnaissance Ausbildungs Battalion
15th Panzer Ersatz und Ausbildungs Battalion
48th Army Flak Ersatz und Ausbildungs Battalion

116/54th Light Field Howitzer Battery
8th Panzerjäger Ersatz und Ausbildungs Battalion

This formation was responsible for the training of troops in the VIII Wehrkreise. In February 1945 it was serving near Görlitz and Ohlau, at which time it vanishes from German records.

Thüringian Panzer Ausbildungs Verband

Formed on 28 March 1945, the division had:

Staff/Panzer Troop School Bergen
Panzer Ausbildungs Regiment
  Bergen Panzer Lehr Battalion
  1st Panzer Ausbildungs Battalion
  300th Panzer Ausbildungs Battalion
1st and 2nd Panzergrenadier Ausbildungs Regiments
  1st Panzergrenadier Ausbildungs Battalion
  15th Panzergrenadier Ausbildungs Battalion
  59th Panzergrenadier Ausbildungs Battalion
  71st Panzergrenadier Ausbildungs Battalion

Bergen Panzer Reconnaissance Lehr Company
Putlos Panzer Reconnaissance Schiess-Lehr Company
29th Panzer Pioneer Ausbildungs Battalion
81st Panzer Signals Ausbildungs Half Battalion

The division also absorbed the Sharpshooter Lehrgang IX Wildflecken, the Panzergrenadier Field NCO School, Wildflecken, the Ravensberg Army NCO school, and the 3rd Landshut Panzer Troop Fahnenjunker School. The 508th Army Flak Brigade was attached to the division.
OKH records for 3 March 1945 show it as having the following units:

Staff/2nd Panzergrenadier Ausbildungs Battalion
Putlos Panzer Reconnaissance FiringTraining Company
Panzergrenadier Flak Company, Lehrgängen Panzer-
grenadiers
Panzergrenadier Flak Company, 204th Panzer Flak Bat-
talion
Wildflecken Sharpshooter School
HUS Ravenensburg
3rd Fhj. School, Landshut Panzer Troop

Bergen Panzergrenadier Training Battalion
9th Panzerjäger Ausbildungs Battalion
39th Infantry Signals Ausbildungs Battalion
81st Panzergrenadier Ausbildungs Battalion
29th and 81st Gun Ausbildungs Company
9th Construction Pioneer Battalion
69th Heavy Artillery Ausbildungs Battalion
29th Light Artillery Ausbildungs Battalion
18th Officer Artillery Ausbildungs Battalion

Westfalen Panzer Ausbildungs Verband

Formed on 28 March 1945 with Ausbildungs (training)
units, it had:

Panzer Ausbildungs Regiment
11th Panzer Ausbildungs Battalion
500th Panzer Ausbildungs Battalion
1st and 2nd Panzergrenadier Ausbildungs Regiments
4th Panzergrenadier Ausbildungs Battalion
60th Panzergrenadier Ausbildungs Battalion
64th Panzergrenadier Ausbildungs Battalion

361st Panzergrenadier Ausbildungs Battalion
6th Panzer Reconnaissance Ausbildungs Half Battalion
16th Panzer Pioneer Ausbildungs Battalion
26th Panzer Signals Ausbildungs Battalion

The division incorporated the Officer Candidate School
for Panzer Reconnaissance in Mainz, the Eisenach Panzer
Schützen Army NCO School, and the Sharpshooter
Instruction Course from Wehrkries VI. Part of this formation joined the 11th Panzer Division.

Franken Panzer Training Formation

Formed on 28 March 1945, the detachment had:

Staff
Staff/Panzer Training (Ausbildungs) Regiment (from
Grafwöhr Pz School)
35th Panzer Training Battalion
1st and 2nd Panzergrenadier Training Regiments
104th Panzergrenadier Training Battalion
115th Panzergrenadier Training Battalion
119th Panzergrenadier Training Battalion
215th Panzergrenadier Training Battalion
9th Panzer ReconnaissanceTraining Battalion (only half-
battalion)

19th Panzer Pioneer Training Battalion
26th Panzer Signals Training Battalion (only 1/2 battalion)

The division later absorbed the following units:

Scharfschützen (Sharpshooter) Instruction Course
Army NCO School for Panzergrenadiers at Eisenach
Erlangen OB School for Panzer Schützen
Weimar OB School for Panzergrenadiers

The formation was sent the the front, where it was absorbed by other units.

4

The Independent Army Panzer Brigades

On 2 July 1944 Adolf Hitler was in a meeting with the Chef des Herresstabes beim Chef OKW. While considering the fate of Army Group Center, Hitler suggested that it would be useful to have small, mobile, fast, armored kampfgruppe available that could move into action quickly, and surround and destroy the Russian armored spearheads. Hitler proposed that they contain an armored half-track battalion, a panzer group of 30–40 tanks, an anti-tank company or Pak 37 towed by half-tracks, and a number of 20mm and 37mm Flak guns. Hitler went on to request that a dozen of these "brigades", as he called them, be raised.

On 3 July the OKH staff proposed that these twelve formations be organized by converting elements from the 6th, 9th, 11th, 19th, 25th, and 116th Panzer Divisions, which were then in Germany refitting. However, this proposal was not accepted. Instead, a new order was issued on 11 July 1944 that directed the formation of ten panzer brigades, numbered 101st through 110th. Each of these brigades was to have a panzer battalion, organized with three panzer companies, each company having 11 Panthers, and a panzerjäger Company, equipped with 11 Panzer IV/70(V). The battalion staff contained three PzMk V Panthers and four Flak panzers.

On 24 July 1944 the order was modified. It now directed that the 101st–104th Panzer Brigades be ready for action by 15 August, the 105th and 106th by 31 August, the 107th and 108th by 15 September and the 108th and 110th by 25 September.

The 106th and 110th were to be named the 106th (Feldherrnhalle) Panzer Brigade and the 110th (Feldherrnhalle) Panzer Brigade respectively. Personnel for the 101st–104th, 108th, and 109th Panzer Brigades were drawn from the Replacement Army (Ersatz Heeres) and the 25th Panzer Division. Those for the 110th Panzer Brigade came from the Feldherrnhalle Ersatz Brigade, and the 107th was formed using drafts from the Feldherrnhalle Division. The 105th and 107th were created from the useful remaining elements of the 18th and 25th Panzergrenadier Divisions.

Three additional panzer brigades, the 111th–113th, were raised in early September from the "Walkuere" draft. Their armored battalions were equipped with 45 PzMk IV tanks: three PzMk IV in the staff and 14 in each of the three companies.

100th Panzer Brigade

Formed on 1 March 1941 with the staff/8th Panzer Brigade in France. It contained:

201st Panzer (Captured Tank) Regiment
202nd Panzer (Captured Tank) Regiment
301st Panzer Battalion

It absorbed a number of other small armored formations, including the Versailles Company Leader School of Panzer Troops.

101st Panzer Brigade

Formed on 5 July 1941 in France with captured tanks. The brigade had:

203rd Panzer (Captured Tank) Regiment
204th Panzer (Captured Tank)Regiment

On 21 September 1941 it was used to form the staff of the 23rd Panzer Division.

It was again ordered formed on 11 July 1944, but was not in fact formed until 15 August 1944. It contained:

2101st Panzer Battalion (4 companies)
  1 Panzer Flak Platoon
  3 Medium Panzer Companies
  PzMk IV (lg)   36
  FlakpzIV (37)   4

2101st Panzergrenadier Battalion (3 companies)
2101st Brigade Support Units

The standard organization of the ten panzer brigades (numbered 101st–110th) ordered raised on 11 July 1944 was as follows:

Brigade Staff

1 (armored) Brigade Staff (2 LMGs)
1 (mot) Escort Company
  1 Company Staff (1 LMG)
  1 Signals Platoon (7 LMGs)
  1 Reconnaissance Platoon (14 LMGs)
  1 Motorcycle Messenger Platoon (6 LMGs)

Armored Battalion

1 (armored) Battalion Staff (6 LMGs)
1 Self-Propelled Flak Platoon (4 37mm and 4 LMGs)
3 Panzer Companies (11 Panther PzMk V tanks ea)
1 Jagdpanzer Company (11 Jagdpanzer PzMk IV/L70 ea)
1 (armored) Maintenance Platoon
1 (mot) Supply Company (5 LMGs)
  2 Self-Propelled Quad 20mm Flak guns

Panzergrenadier Battalion

1 (armored) Battalion Staff (6 LMGs)
1 (mot) Supply Company (4 LMGs)
3 (armored) Panzergrenadier Companies (7 20mm, 2 75mm guns, 2 80mm mortars, 3 HMGs and 30 LMGs)
1 (armored) Pioneer Company
  1 Pioneer Platoon (6 flamethrowers, 6 LMGs)
  1 Pioneer Platoon (6 flamethrowers, 1 20mm and 12 LMGs)
  1 Pioneer Platoon (6 flamethrowers, 1 20mm and 12 LMGs)

Other

1 (mot) 60 ton Transportation Company

On 6 August 1944 the organization of the brigades was ordered to be changed again. Now it was to contain:

Brigade Staff

1 (half-track) Brigade Staff (2 LMGs)
1 (mot) Escort Company

  1 Company Staff (1 LMG)
  1 Signals Platoon (7 LMGs)
  1 Reconnaissance Platoon (14 LMGs)
  1 Motorcycle Messenger Platoon (6 LMGs)

Armored Battalion

1 (armored) Battalion Staff (6 LMGs)
1 (armored) Flak Platoon (4 37mm and 4 LMGs)
1 Flak Platoon (one triple 20mm gun on truck)
3 Panzer Companies (11 Panther PzMk V tanks ea)
1 Jagdpanzer Company (11 Jagdpanzer PzMk V/L70 ea)
1 (armored) Maintenance Platoon
1 (mot) Supply Company (5 LMGs)
  2 Self-Propelled Quad 20mm Flak guns

Panzergrenadier Battalion

1 (half-track) Battalion Staff (8 LMGs)
1 (mot) Supply Company (4 LMGs)
2 (half-track) Panzergrenadier Companies (2 75mm, 6 triple 20mm on SdKfz 251/21, 2 80mm mortars and 11 LMGs)
1 (half-track) Pioneer Company
2 Platoons (11 LMGs and 6 triple 20mm SdKfz 251/21 ea)
1 (half-track) Pioneer Company (3 LMGs)
3 Platoons (6 triple 20mm SdKfz 251/21 ea)
1 (half-track) Heavy Company
  1 Platoon (2 HMGs, 7 LMGs and 4 120mm mortars)
  1 Platoon (7 LMGs and 4 120mm mortars)
  1 Platoon (6 75mm and 2 LMGs)

Panzer (half-track) Pioneer Company (6 flamethrowers and 37 LMGs)

Panzer (armored) Maintenance Platoon (2 LMGs)

1 (mot) 60 ton Transportation Company (2 LMGs)

In October 1944 the 101st Brigade was re-formed near Bobruisk, then it was merged with the remains of the destroyed 20th Panzer Division. The brigade staff formed the Staff/21st Panzer Regiment, the armored battalion became the 2/21st Panzer Regiment, while the Panzergrenadier Battalion became a Jagd-Kommando in the 20th Panzer Division.

102nd Panzer Brigade

Ordered formed on 11 July 1944, but not in fact formed until 15 August 1944. It contained:

2102nd Panzer Battalion (4 Panther tank companies)
  1 Panzer Flak Platoon
  3 Medium Panzer Companies
  PzMk V   36
  FlakpzIV (37)   4

2102nd Panzergrenadier Battalion (3 half-track companies)
2102nd Brigade Support Units
2102nd Pioneer Company

The brigade was disbanded on 27 November 1944 and absorbed into the 7th Panzer Division.

103rd Panzer Brigade

Ordered formed on 11 July 1944, it was not in fact formed until 15 August 1944. It contained:

2103rd Panzer Battalion (from Panzer Battalion Norway)
  1 Panzer Flak Platoon
  3 Medium Panzer Companies
  PzMk V   36
  FlakpzIV (37)   4
2103rd Panzergrenadier Battalion (3 half-track companies)
2103rd Brigade Support Units

The brigade was disbanded in November 1944. The Panzergrenadier Battalion was disbanded and the armored battalion became the 1/39th Panzer Regiment in the 17th Panzer Division.

Despite the "official" disbanding, another 103rd Panzer Brigade appears in OKH records in late 1944 and it appears to have existed until January 1945, and perhaps longer. It was apparently pieced together from several divisions and formations. The following organizational and equipment listing comes from OKH records and the sources of the various units are indicated:

103rd Panzer Brigade Staff
1 Brigade Staff
1 Signals Platoon (9 LMGs)

Panzer Regiment
  1 Regimental Staff
  1 Regimental Staff Company
    1 Signals Platoon
    1 Pioneer Platoon (12 LMGs)

1/29th Panzer Regiment
1 Battalion Staff
1 Battalion Staff Company
  1 Infantry Platoon (12 LMGs)
  1 Self-Propelled Flak Platoon (3 quad 20mm guns)
1 Jagdpanther Company (14 Jagdpanthers)
1 Panzer Company (14 PzMk IV Long)
1 (mot) Supply Company (3 LMGs)
1 Panzer Maintenance Company

2/9th Panzer Regiment
1 Battalion Staff
1 Battalion Staff Company
  1 Infantry Platoon (12 LMGs)
1 Panzer Company (14 PzMk IV)
2 Panzer Companies (14 PzMk IV Long ea)
1 (mot) Supply Company (3 LMGs)
1 Panzer Maintenance Company

1/39th Panzer Regiment
1 Battalion Staff
1 Battalion Staff Company

  1 Infantry Platoon (12 LMGs)
  1 Self-Propelled Flak Platoon (3 quad 20mm guns)
3 Panzer Companies (14 PzMk V Panthers each)
1 (mot) Supply Company (3 LMGs)
1 Panzer Maintenance Company

Panzergrenadier Regiment
1 Regimental Staff and Staff Company
  1 (mot) Signals Platoon
  1 Motorcycle Platoon

1st (Neuhammer) Battalion
1 (mot) Supply Company
3 (half-track) Panzergrenadier Companies (12 20mm guns, 4 flamethrowers and 12 LMGs on 12 SdKfz 251/21, 4 SdKfz 251/16, 5 SdKfz 251/1 and 2 SdKfz 251/3 ea)

2nd (Kamenz) Battalion
1 (mot) Supply Company
1 (mot) Pioneer Company
2 (half-track) Panzergrenadier Companies (3 HMGs, 30 LMGs, 2 80mm mortars, 7 20mm guns and 2 75mm guns ea)
1 (mot) Panzergrenadier Company (4 HMGs, 18 LMGs and 2 80mm mortars)

Hirschberg Panzer Reconnaissance Battalion
1st Armored Car Company (15 LMGs, 13 20mm and 3 75mm guns)
2nd and 3rd (half-track) Reconnaissance Companies (44 LMGs, 2 80mm mortars and 2 75mm guns ea)
4th (mot) Reconnaissance Company (2 80mm mortars, 4 HMGs and 9 LMGs)
1 (mot) Supply Company (4 LMGs)

Sternberg Panzer Reconnaissance Battalion
1st Armored Car Company (6 8-wheeled and 9 4-wheeled armored cars)
2nd and 3rd (half-track) Reconnaissance Companies (8 medium and 14 light half-tracks ea)
4th (mot) Reconnaissance Company
1 (mot) Supply Company

Notes indicate that the weapons of the Sternberg Panzer Reconnaissance Battalion were not fixed.

On 24 January 1945 the Staff/103rd Panzer Brigade was assigned to command a Panzer Kampfgruppe consisting of panzer regimental staff with the 2/9th Panzer Regiment, 1(Panther)/29th Panzer Regiment, and 1(Panther)/39th Panzer Regiment. The 2/9th was ordered organized with two companies, each with 13 PzIV/70 and three PzMk IV command tanks. On 19 January 1945 14 PzMk IV tanks were shipped to the battalion and on 22 February a further 26 Pz.IV/70(V) were shipped. On 21 January 1945 the 1/29th Panzer Regiment consisted of a company of 14 Jagdpanthers and a company of 14 Pz.IV/70(A). The 1/39th Panzer Regiment was ordered completed on 22 January 1945 with a battalion staff and three Panther companies, each with 14 PzMkV Panther tanks. The 45 Panthers necessary for this were shipped between 16 and 22 January. After heavy losses in battle against the Russians, the brigade was ordered disbanded on 5 March 1945. The staff was used to form the division staff of the Munchenberg Panzer Division. The 1/29th was stripped of its tanks and sent to the Munchenberg Division. Four of its PzMk IV tanks were given to the 17th Panzer Division, 12 Pz.IV/70 went to the 20th Panzer Division, and six Jagdpanthers went to the 8th Panzer Division.

104th Panzer Brigade

Ordered formed on 11 July 1944, but not in fact formed until 15 August 1944. In September 1944 it contained:

2104th Panzer Battalion
  1 Panzer Flak Platoon
  3 Medium Panzer Companies
  PzMkV   36
  FlakpzIV (37)   4

2104th Panzergrenadier Battalion (3 half-track companies)
2104th Brigade Support Units (inc. a pioneer company)

It was disbanded on 5 November 1944 and incorporated into the 25th Panzer Division. The 2104th Panzer Battalion became the 1/9th Panzer Regiment and the grenadiers became the 1/147th Panzergrenadier Regiment.

105th Panzer Brigade

Ordered formed on 11 July 1944, but not formed until 31 August 1944. It absorbed the remnants of the 18th Panzergrenadier Division and in September it contained:

2105th Panzer Battalion
  1 Staff Platoon
  1 Panzer Flak Platoon
  3 Medium Panzer Companies (PzMk V)
  1 Panzerjäger Company (PzMk IV/L70)
  PzMkV   36
  PzMk IV/L40   11
  FlakpzIV 37   4

2105th Panzergrenadier Battalion (5 half-track companies)
2105th Brigade Support Units

On 31 August 1944 the brigade was sent to Belgium. On 12 September 1944 it was equipped with 11 PzMk IV long, 36 Panther PzMk V, and 157 SdKfz 251 half-tracks. On 23 September 1944 it was disbanded on the lower Rhine and used to re-form the 9th Panzer Division that was decimated in Normandy. The panzergrenadiers became the 2/11th Panzergrenadier Regiment and the panzer battalion became the 2/10th Panzer Regiment of the 9th Panzer Division.

106th Panzer Brigade

Ordered formed on 11 July 1944, but not actually formed until 31 August 1944. It contained the remnants of the Feldherrnhalle Panzergrenadier Division In September 1944 it contained:

2106th Panzer Battalion (4 Panther tank companies)
  1 Staff Platoon
  1 Panzer Flak Platoon
  3 Medium Panzer Companies (PzMk V)
  1 Panzerjäger Company (PzMk IV/L70)
  PzMkV   36
  PzMk IV/L40   11
  FlakpzIV 37   4
2106th Panzergrenadier Battalion (5 half-track companies)

2106th Brigade Support Units
2106th Pioneer Battalion

On 11 July 1944 the brigade was redesignated the 106th Panzer Brigade (Feldherrnhalle). On 12 September 1944 it was equipped with 11 PzMk IV (lg), 36 Panther Mk V, and 157 SdKfz 251 half-tracks. It was captured in the Ruhr Pocket in 1945. On 8 December 1944 it contained:

2106th Panzer Battalion
  1 Staff Platoon
  1 Panzer Flak Platoon
  3 Medium Panzer Companies (PzMk V)

1 Panzerjäger Company (PzMk IV/L70)

PzMk IV (lg)	2
PzMk V	10
PzMk IV/L40	4
FlakpzIV 37	4

107th Panzer Brigade

Ordered formed on 11 July 1944, but not in fact formed until 15 September 1944. It contained the remnants of the 25th Panzergrenadier Division:

2107th Panzer Battalion
  1 Staff Platoon
  1 Panzer Flak Platoon
  3 Medium Panzer Companies (PzMk V)
  1 Panzerjäger Company (PzMk IV/L70)

PzMk V	36
PzMk IV/70(V)	11
Flakpz IV37	4

2107th Panzergrenadier Battalion (5 half-track companies)
2107th Brigade Support Units
2107th Pioneer Battalion

On 5 November 1944 the brigade was disbanded and used to rebuild the 25th Panzergrenadier Kampfgruppe back up to the strength of a full division. The staff and panzergrenadier battalion became the Staff/, 1/119th Panzergrenadier Regiment and the armored battalion became the 5th Panzer Battalion, assigned to the division.

108th Panzer Brigade

Ordered formed on 11 July 1944, it was not in fact formed until 15 September 1944. It contained:

2108th Panzer Battalion
  1 Staff Platoon
  1 Panzer Flak Platoon
  3 Medium Panzer Companies (PzMk V)
  1 Panzerjäger Company (PzMk IV/L70)

PzMk V	36
PzMk IV/70(V)	11 (arrived on 19 Sept. 1944)
Flakpz IV37	4

2108th Panzergrenadier Battalion (5 half-track companies)
2108th Brigade Support Units

In November the brigade was disbanded. The brigade staff became the Staff/39th Panzer Regiment, the panzer battalion became part of the Coburg Panzer Regiment, and the panzergrenadier battalion was incorporated into the 116th Panzergrenadier Division.

109th Panzer Brigade

Ordered formed on 19 July 1944, it was, however, not formed until 25 September 1944. It was organized with the remains of the 25th Panzer Division and part of the 233rd Reserve Panzer Division. The brigade had:

2109th Panzer Battalion (4 Panther tank companies)
2109th Panzergrenadier Battalion (5 half-track companies)
2109th Brigade Support Units

In October 1944 it was used to rebuild the Feldherrnhalle Panzer Division.

110th Panzer Brigade

Ordered formed on 19 July 1944, but not formed until 25 September 1944, with the troops from the Feldherrnhalle Ersatz Battalion.

2110th Panzer Battalion (4 Panther tank companies)
2110th Panzergrenadier Battalion (5 half-track companies)

2110th Brigade Support Units
2110th Pioneer Company

On 11 July 1944 the brigade was redesignated the 110th Panzer Brigade (Feldherrnhalle). In September 1944 it was used to rebuild the destroyed 13th Panzer Division, later renamed the 2nd Feldherrnhalle Panzer Division.

111th Panzer Brigade

OKH documents indicate that it was formed on 4 September 1944. The brigade had:

2111th Panzer Battalion
  1 Staff Platoon
  1 Panzer Flak Platoon
  3 Medium Panzer Companies (PzMk V)
  2111th Sturmgeschütz Company
    StuG   10
    PzMk IV (lg)   45
    FlakpzIV 37   4
    FlakpzIV (2V)   4
1/16th Panzer Regiment
  1 Panzer Staff Company (3 PzMk V tanks and 4 FlakpzIV (2V))
  3 Medium Panzer Companies (14 PzMk V each)
1/, 2/2111th Panzergrenadier Regiment
2111th Brigade Support Units
2111th Armored Reconnaissance Company
2111th Flak Company

2111th Sturmgeschütz Battalion

The brigade was sent to Lorraine on 6 September 1944. On 12 September 1944 it was equipped with 45 PzMk IV, 45 Panther PzMk V, 10 StuG III, and eight SdKfz 251 half-tracks. OKH records indicate that a third battalion was initially envisaged for the 2111th Panzergrenadier Regiment. The Panzergrenadiers were supported by a self-propelled heavy infantry gun company (possibly not raised), the 2111th (mot) Pioneer Company, and the 2111th Reconnaissance Company with an armored car platoon (4 HMGs, 14 LMGs and 3 20mm guns) and half-track company.

On 25 September 1944 it was disbanded and incorporated into the 15th Panzergrenadier Division. There is also some indication that on 1 October 1944 it was incorporated into the 11th Panzer Division. The two armored battalions were re-formed, and in December 1944 the 2111th Panzer Battalion was used to rebuild the 2/9th Panzer Regiment (25th Panzer Division).

112th Panzer Brigade

Formed on 4 September 1944, the brigade had:

2112th Panzer Battalion
  1 Staff Platoon
  1 Panzer Flak Platoon
  3 Medium Panzer Companies (PzMk V)
  1 Sturmgeschütz Company
    StuG   10
    PzMk IV (lg)   46
    FlakpzIV 37   4
1/29th Panzer Regiment
  1 Panzer Staff Company (3 PzMk V tanks and 4 FlakpzIV (2V))
  3 Medium Panzer Companies (14 PzMk V each)
1/, 2/2112th Panzergrenadier Regiment
3 (mot) Panzergrenadier Companies per Battalion

1 (mot) Pioneer Company (2 HMGs, 12 LMGs, 2 80mm mortars and 18 flamethrowers)
1 (mot) Mortar Company (8 120mm mortars)
1 (motZ) Flak Company (2 platoons 20mm guns)
1 Panzerjäger Company
  1 (motZ) Platoon
  1 Self-Propelled Platoon
2112th Brigade Support Units
2112th Panzer Reconnaissance Battalion
2112th Sturmgeschütz Battalion (10 StuG and 12 LMGs)

On 6 September 1944 the brigade was sent to Epinal. On 12 September it was equipped with 45 PzMk IV, 45 Panther PzMk V, 10 StuG III, and eight SdKfz 251 half-tracks. On 23 September 1944 it was disbanded and incorporated into the 21st Panzer Division.

113th Panzer Brigade

Formed on 4 September 1944, the brigade had:

2113th Panzer Battalion
  1 Staff Platoon
  1 Panzer Flak Platoon
  3 Medium Panzer Companies (PzMk V)
  1 Sturmgeschütz Company

StuG	10
PzMk IV (lg)	45
FlakpzIV 37	4
FlakpzIV (2V)	4

1/130th Panzer Regiment
  1 Panzer Staff Company (3 PzMk V tanks and 4 FlakpzIV (2V))
  3 Medium Panzer Companies (14 PzMk V each)
1/, 2/2113th Panzergrenadier Regiment

2113th Brigade Support Units
2113th Panzer Reconnaissance Battalion
2113th Flak Company
2113th Sturmgeschütz Battalion (10 StuG and 12 LMGs)

The brigade also contained the 1/130th (Panther) Panzer Regiment from the Panzer Lehr Division. On 6 September 1944 the brigade was sent to Kolmar and on 16 September to Saarburg. On 12 September 1944 the brigade was equipped with 45 PzMk IV, 45 Panther PzMk V, 10 StuG III, and eight SdKfz 251 half-tracks. On 1 October 1944 it was used to reinforce the 15th Panzergrenadier Division. The two panzer battalions were detached, the 2113rd Panzer Battalion becoming the 2/10th Panzer Regiment, 11th Panzer Division.

150th Panzer Brigade

Orders for the formation of this brigade were issued on 4 November 1944. It was equipped with captured American equipment and intended for deceptive operations against the Americans. It contained only a single armored company, manned by men of the 1/11th Panzer Regiment, and was equipped with five PzMk V Panther tanks disguised to look like American M-10 tank destroyers.

5

Reserve and Replacement Panzer Formations

Panzer Division Nr 155

The Division (mot) Nr 155 was reorganized into the Panzer Division Nr 155 on 5 April 1943, and on 1 August 1943 it was reorganized into the 155th Reserve Panzer Division. In the summer of 1943 the division was activated from the Ersatzheer and transferred to OB West as a Reserve Panzer Division. In December 1943 it had:

Reserve Panzer Division Nr 155
1 Divisional Staff
7th Reserve Panzer Regiment:
1 Regimental Staff
1 Panzer Signals Platoon
1 Panzer Battalion
6 Panzer Companies (32 LMGs ea)
1 Panzer Battalion
6 Panzer Medium Companies
1 Panzer Maintenance Company
5th Reserve Panzergrenadier Regiment
1 Regimental Headquarters
88th Reserve Panzergrenadier Battalion
1 (half-track) Battalion Headquarters (2 80mm mortars)
2 (half-track) Companies (5 LMGs and 4 HMGs ea)
1 (half-track) Company (6 LMGs and 5 HMGs)
1 (half-track) Company (6 LMGs and 4 HMGs)
2 Training Companies
215th Reserve Panzergrenadier Battalion
1 (half-track) Battalion Headquarters (2 80mm mortars)
2 (half-track) Companies (6 LMGs and 4 HMGs ea)
1 (half-track) Company (5 LMGs and 9 HMGs)
1 (half-track) Company (5 LMGs and 3 HMGs)
1 Training Company
25th Reserve (mot) Panzergrenadier Regiment
35th (mot) Panzergrenadier Battalion
1 Battalion Headquarters (2 80mm mortars)
3 (mot) Companies (5 LMGs and 1 80mm mortar ea)

1 (mot) Heavy Company (10 HMGs and 3 80mm mortars)
1 Training Company
119th Reserve Panzergrenadier Battalion
same as 35th (mot) Panzergrenadier Battalion
25th Reserve (motZ) Infantry Support Gun Company
25th Reserve (motZ) Panzerjäger Company
260th Reserve (motZ) Artillery Battalion
1 (mot) Signals Platoon
1 (motZ) Battery (4 105mm leFH and 2 LMGs)
1 (motZ) Battery (4 150mm sFH and 2 LMGs)
1 (motZ) Battery (1 LMG and ? guns)
2 Artillery Training Companies
9th Reserve Panzer Reconnaissance Battalion
1 Panzer Reconnaissance Battalion Headquarters
1 (mot) Signals Platoon
1 Armored Car Company (6 LMGs)
2 (half-track) Reconnaissance Companies (9 LMGs, 2 HMGs and 1 80mm mortar ea)
1 Motorcycle Reconnaissance Company (3 HMGs and 6 LMGs)
1 Training Company
5th Reserve (mot) Panzerjäger Battalion
2 Self-Propelled Panzerjäger Companies (probably 14 75mm PAK 40
and 14 LMGs ea)
2 (motZ) Panzerjäger Companies (probably 12 75mm PAK 40 and 12 LMGs ea)
1 Heavy Company (2 37mm PAK, 1 50mm PAK, 2 45mm Russian PAK and 3 LMGs)

The order of 19 March 1944 directed it be used to reform the 9th Panzer Division. It was disbanded on 30 April 1944. The 7th Reserve Panzer battalion was used to form the Norwegian Panzer brigade.

Panzer Division Nr 178

Formed on 5 April 1943 from the 178th (mot) Division. It contained:

15th Panzer Ersatz and Ausbildungs Battalion

85th Panzergrenadier Ausbildungs Regiment (13th, 110th Battalions)
128th (mot) Grenadier Ausbildungs Regiment (30th and 51st Battalions)

55th Panzer Reconnaissance Ersatz and Ausbildungs Battalion

8th Panzerjäger Ersatz and Ausbildungs Battalion

In December 1944 the division was disbanded. The 85th Panzergrenadier Ersatz und Ausbildungs Regiment, the 13th Panzergrenadier Ersatz und Ausbildungs Battalions, and the 30/51st Combined Battalion were sent to the Tatra Panzer (Feldausbildungs) Division. The 128th Panzergrenadier Ersatz and Ausbildungs Regiment remained in Silesia.

Panzer Division Nr 179

Formed in Weimar on 5 April 1943 from the 179th (mot) Division. On 30 July 1943 it became the 179th Reserve Panzer Division. In the summer of 1943 the division was activated from the Ersatzheer and transferred to OB West as a Reserve Panzer Division.

179th Reserve Panzer Division

Formed in France on 30 July 1943 with:

179th Reserve Panzer Division
1 Divisional Staff
1st Reserve Panzer Regiment:
1 Regimental Staff
1 Panzer Signals Platoon (4 LMGs)
1 Panzer Battalion
  1 Panzer Company (4 LMGs)
  1 Panzer Company (6 LMGs)
  1 Panzer Company (10 LMGs)
  1 Panzer Company (12 LMGs)
  1 Panzer Company (15 LMGs)
  1 Panzer Company (18 LMGs)
1 Medium Panzer Battalion
  1 Panzer Company (22 LMGs)
  1 Panzer Company (7 LMGs)
  1 Panzer Company (4 LMGs)
81st Reserve Panzergrenadier Regiment
  1 (half-track) Panzergrenadier Regimental Staff
1st Reserve Panzergrenadier Battalion
  1 (half-track) Panzergrenadier Battalion Staff 4 (half-track)
  4 (half-track) Panzergrenadier Companies (4 LMGs and 4 HMGs ea)
  2 Training Companies
6th Reserve Panzergrenadier Battalion
  1 (half-track) Panzergrenadier Battalion Staff
  4 (half-track) Panzergrenadier Companies (4 LMGs and 4 HMGs ea)
  1 Training Company
59th Reserve Panzergrenadier Battalion
  1 (half-track) Panzergrenadier Battalion Staff
  4 (half-track) Panzergrenadier Companies (4 LMGs and 4 HMGs ea)
  2 Training Companies

81st Reserve Battalion
  1 (motZ) Panzerjäger Company (4 LMGs and ? PAK)
  1 (mot) Pioneer Company (13 LMGs, 2 HMGs and 1 80mm mortar)
  1 (mot) Signals Company (3 LMGs)
  1 (mot) Pioneer Company (1 80mm mortar and 4 LMGs)
29th Reserve Infantry Regiment
  1 Infantry Regimental Staff
15th (mot) Reserve Infantry Regiment
  3 (mot) Panzergrenadier Companies (6 LMGs and 1 80mm mortar ea)
  1 (mot) Machine Gun Company
  2 (non-mot) Training Companies
71st (mot) Reserve Infantry Regiment
  same as 15th (mot) Reserve Infantry Regiment
  71st Reserve (motZ) Panzerjäger Company
  71st Reserve (motZ) Infantry Gun Company
  29th Reserve (mot) Signals Company
29th Reserve (motZ) Artillery Battalion
  2 (mot) Artillery Batteries
  1 (motZ) Infantry Gun Battery
  2 Artillery Training Companies
1st Reserve Panzer Reconnaissance Battalion
  1 Panzer Reconnaissance Battalion Headquarters
  1 (mot) Signals Platoon
  1 Mortar Platoon
  1 Armored Car Company (10 LMGs)
  2 (half-track) Reconnaissance Companies (10 LMGs and 1 80mm mortar ea)
  2 Motorcycle Reconnaissance Companies (11 LMGs and 6 80mm mortars total)
9th Reserve (mot) Panzerjäger Battalion
  2 Self-Propelled Panzerjäger Companies (10 75mm PAK 40 and 4 LMGs ea)
  2 (motZ) Panzerjäger Companies (6 LMGs and ? 75mm PAK 40 ea)

1 Training Company (2 LMGs)

On 15 March 1944 the 179th Reserve Panzer Division was ordered to be used to rebuild the 16th Panzergrenadier Division. On 2 May 1944 the orders were changed and it was to be used to build the 116th Panzer Division. The 179th was disbanded on 1 May 1944. The remainder of the division was sent back to Germany and reabsorbed into the system.

232nd Reserve Panzer Division

Formed in February 1945 in Slovakia from the Tatra Panzer Feldausbildungs Division. It contained:

101st Panzergrenadier Regiment (from 82nd Panzergrenadier Replacement and Training Regiment)
102nd Panzergrenadier Regiment (from 85th Panzergrenadier Replacement and Training Regiment)

It did not have a panzer battalion and was only to receive a Panzerjäger Ausbildungs Battalion with two self-propelled anti-tank companies. On 21 February 1945 the division was renamed the 232rd Panzer Division. It was destroyed in the Raab bridgehead in late March 1945.

233rd Reserve Panzer Division

In the summer of 1943 Panzer Division 233 was activated from the Ersatzheer (Replacement Army) and transferred to OB West as the 233rd Reserve Panzer Division. The redesignation occurred on 10 August 1943. In December 1943 the division was organized as follows:

5th Reserve Panzer Battalion
83rd Reserve Panzergrenadier Regiment (3rd, 8th and 9th Battalions)
3rd (mot) Reserve Grenadier Regiment (8th, 39th Grenadiers and 50th Panzergrenadier Battalion)
59th Reserve Artillery Battalion
3rd Reserve Panzer Reconnaissance Battalion
3rd Reserve Panzerjäger Battalion
208th Reserve Panzer Pioneer Battalion

In May 1944 the division detached units to the re-forming of the 6th, 19th and 25th Panzer Divisions. It was then re-formed from the 155th, 179th and 255th Reserve Panzer Divisions. On 12 May 1944 the 1233rd Panzer Signals Company was formed. In December the division had:

Staff
5th Reserve Panzer Battalion (as an armored Kampfgruppe with 3rd Company, 3rd Panzerjäger, 1/59th Artillery Regiment, 1 pioneer and 1 heavy company)
83rd Reserve Panzergrenadier Regiment (8th, 9th, and 3rd Battalions)
3rd Reserve Grenadier (mot) Regt (8th, 50th and 29th Battalions)
3rd Reserve Panzerjäger Battalion
3rd Reserve Panzer Reconnaissance Battalion
59th Reserve Artillery Battalion

208th Reserve Panzer Pioneer Battalion
1233rd Reserve Panzer Signals Company
1233rd Supply Troops
2033rd (later 1233rd) Medical Troops

On 1 May 1944 the division contained:

Division
1 Divisional Staff
5th Reserve Panzer Regiment
1 Regimental Staff
1 Panzer Signals Platoon
1 Panzer Battalion
6 Panzer Companies
1 Panzer Battalion
3 Panzer Medium Companies
83rd Reserve Panzergrenadier Regiment
1 Regimental Headquarters
3rd Reserve (halftrack) Panzergrenadier Battalion
1 (half-track) Battalion Headquarters
4 (half-track) Companies
1 (mot) Company
8th and 9th Reserve (half-track) Panzergrenadier Battalion
both same as 3rd Reserve Panzergrenadier Regiment
83rd Reserve (motZ) Panzerjäger Company
83rd Reserve (mot) Signals Company
83rd Reserve (mot) Pioneer Company
3rd Reserve Panzergrenadier Regiment
1 Regimental Headquarters
8th Reserve Panzergrenadier Battalion
1 (mot) Battalion Headquarters
3 (mot) Companies

1 (mot) Machine Gun Company

1 (mot) Company

8th Reserve (mot) Panzergrenadier Battalion

same as 8th Reserve Panzergrenadier Regiment

50th Reserve (half-track) Panzergrenadier Battalion

same as 3rd Reserve Panzergrenadier Regiment

3rd Reserve (motZ) Panzerjäger Company

3rd Reserve (mot) Signals Company

3rd Reserve (mot) Machine Gun Company

3rd Reserve (mot) Pioneer Company

59th Reserve (motZ) Artillery Battalion

1 (mot) Signals Platoon

1 (motZ) Battery (105mm leFH)

1 (motZ) Battery (150mm sFH)

1 (mot) Training Battery

1 Training Company

3rd Reserve Panzer Reconnaissance Battalion

1 Panzer Reconnaissance Battalion Headquarters

1 (mot) Signals Platoon

1 Armored Car Company

2 (half-track) Reconnaissance Companies

1 Motorcycle Reconnaissance Company

1 Training Company

5th Reserve (mot) Panzerjäger Battalion

3 Self-Propelled Panzerjäger Batteries

1 (motZ) Panzerjäger Battery

1 Training Company

208th Reserve Panzer Pioneer Battalion

1 Panzer Pioneer Headquarters

1 Panzer Signals Platoon

3 Panzer Pioneer Companies

1/2 (mot) Bridging Column

Medical

1233rd (mot) Medical Company

1233rd Ambulance

The order of 5 February 1945 reorganized the 233rd Reserve Panzer Division as the Holstein Panzer Division. Its units were redesignated as follows:

5th Panzer Reserve Battalion became 44th Panzer Battalion

83rd Res Pzgren Regiment became 139th Panzergrenadier Regiment

3rd Res Gren Regiment became 142nd Panzergrenadier Regiment

Reconnaissance Battalion became 44th Panzer Reconnaissance Battalion

Support Units were numbered 144th

On 15 February 1945 the division was reorganized in Denmark and again as the 233rd Reserve Panzer Division. Its units were as follows:

3rd Reserve Panzergrenadier Regiment

83rd Reserve Panzergrenadier Regiment

8th Reserve Panzergrenadier Battalion

9th Reserve Panzergrenadier Battalion

50th Reserve Panzergrenadier Battalion

93rd Reserve Panzergrenadier Battalion

273rd Reserve Panzer Division

The division was formed on 25 October 1943 using the 25th and 35th Reserve Panzer Battalions. When it was activated it was transferred to OB West as a Reserve Panzer Division. It contained:

273rd Reserve Panzer Division

1 Divisional Staff

25th Reserve Panzer Battalion

1 Battalion Staff

1 Panzer Signals Platoon

1 Panzer Maintenance Platoon

6 Panzer Companies (total 5 PzMk IV, 12 PzMk III, 6 PzMk II and 19 PzMk I)

2 Training Companies

35th Reserve Panzer Battalion

1 Battalion Staff

1 Panzer Signals Platoon

6 Panzer Companies (total 4 PzMk IV, 14 PzMk III, 5 PzMk II, 25 PzMk I)

2 Training Companies

12th Reserve Panzergrenadier Battalion

1 (half-track) Battalion Headquarters (2 80mm mortars)

2 (half-track) Companies (2 LMGs and 3 HMGs ea)

1 (half-track) Heavy Company (4 HMGs, 2 LMGs and 1 80mm mortar)

1 (mot) Training Company

40th Reserve Panzergrenadier Battalion

1 (half-track) Battalion Headquarters (2 80mm mortars)

4 (half-track) Companies (4 HMGs, 9 LMGs and 2 80mm mortars ea)

2 (mot) Companies (2 LMGs ea)

167th Reserve (motZ) Artillery Battalion

1 (mot) Signals Platoon

1 (motZ) Battery (4 105mm leFH and 2 LMGs)

1 (motZ) Battery (4 150mm sFH and 2 LMGs)

1 (motZ) Battery (1 LMG and ? guns)

1 Artillery Training Company (2 100mm guns)

7th Reserve Panzer Reconnaissance Battalion

1 Panzer Reconnaissance Battalion Headquarters

1 (mot) Signals Platoon (2 LMGs)

1 Armored Car Company (? 75mm guns, 2 20mm guns and 7 HMGs)

2 (half-track) Reconnaissance Companies (7 LMGs and 1 80mm mortar ea)

1 Motorcycle Reconnaissance Company (3 HMGs, 8 LMGs and 3 80mm mortars)

1 (mot) Companies (4 HMGs total)

7th Reserve (mot) Panzerjäger Battalion

1 Panzerjäger Battalion Staff

1 (mot) Signals Platoon

2 Self-Propelled Panzerjäger Companies

1 (motZ) Panzerjäger Company

1 Sturmgeschütz Battery

2 Training Companies

10th Reserve (mot) Panzerjäger Battalion

3 Self-Propelled Panzerjäger Companies

1 (motZ) Panzerjäger Company

1 Training Company

9th Reserve Panzer Pioneer Battalion

1 Panzer Pioneer Battalion Staff

1 (mot) Signals Platoon

1 Panzer Pioneer Company (5 LMGs and 2 80mm mortars)

1 Panzer Pioneer Company (1 HMG and 4 LMGs)

1 Panzer Pioneer Company (1 HMG and 5 LMGs)

1 Panzer Pioneer Company (5 LMGs)

1/2 K Bridging Column

1/2 B Bridging Column

The staff of the combined 25th/35th Panzer Regiment and the 92nd Reserve Panzergrenadier Regiments were formed in France in 1944. The two reserve panzer battalions were assigned to it at that time.

The order of 15 March 1944 directed that the division be used to re-form the 10th Panzergrenadier Regiment, but on 5 May 1944 that formation was converted into the 11th Panzer Division.

6

Field Organization of Panzer Divisions

What follows is the detailed internal organization of panzer divisions through the course of the war. There were, in fact, three organizations for every formation in the German army. The first organization was the standardized theoretical organization. This was a theoretical description of how the division should be organized. This formation almost never occurred nor lasted very long. The second organization was the "authorized" variation from the theoretical organization, which might occur as a result of shortages of equipment or other problems. The third organization was what actually existed in the field on any given day. This latter organization also included such captured equipment that may have been pressed into service and casualties resulting from combat.

It should also be recognized that, though orders might be issued reorganizing a division, they were never executed immediately: several months might elapse between a division being ordered to assume a new formation and its actually reorganizing into that formation. This being the case, the decreed organization should not be assumed to have been implemented unless the division in question had been pulled back from the front and was being "refreshed".

Divisional Variations, 10 February–15 May 1941

2nd Panzer Division

Panzer Regiment	3rd
Schützen Brigade	2nd
Schützen Regiments	2nd and 304th
SP Infantry Gun Battery	703rd
Motorcycle Battalion	2nd
Artillery Regiment	74th
Reconnaissance Battalion	5th
Panzerjäger Battalion	38th
Flak Battery	2/47th Flak Battalion
Pioneer Battalion	38th
Signals Battalion	38th
Feldersatz Battalion	82nd
Supply Train	82nd
Medical	82nd
Other	82nd

3rd Panzer Division

Panzer Regiment	5th Brigade, 6th Regiment (had three battalions, vice the normal two)
Schützen Brigade	3rd
Schützen Regiments	3rd and 394th
SP Infantry Gun Battery	none
Motorcycle Battalion	3rd
Artillery Regiment	75th (3rd Bn had 1 100mm K 18 (mot) gun btry and 2 150mm sFH 18 (mot) btrys; 1st Bn was equipped with 3 100mm K 18 (mot) gun btrys, but later changed to 3 105mm leFH 18 btrys)
Reconnaissance Battalion	1st (Engineers were mounted, not motorized)
Panzerjäger Battalion	543rd
Flak Battery	6/59th Flak Battalion
Pioneer Battalion	39th
Signals Battalion	39th

Feldersatz Battalion	83rd
Supply Train	83rd
Medical	83rd
Other	83rd

4th Panzer Division

Panzer Regiment	35th
Schützen Brigade	4th
Schützen Regiments	12th and 33rd
SP Infantry Gun Battery	none
Motorcycle Battalion	34th
Artillery Regiment	103rd
Reconnaissance Battalion	7th
Panzerjäger Battalion	49th
Flak Battery	5/66th Flak Battalion
Pioneer Battalion	79th
Signals Battalion	79th
Feldersatz Battalion	84th
Supply Train	84th
Medical	84th
Other	84th

5th Panzer Division:

Panzer Regiment	31st
Schützen Brigade	5th
Schützen Regiments	13th and 14th
SP Infantry Gun Battery	704th
Motorcycle Battalion	55th
Artillery Regiment	116th
Reconnaissance Battalion	8th
Panzerjäger Battalion	53rd
Flak Battery	2/53rd Flak Battalion
Pioneer Battalion	89th
Signals Battalion	77th
Feldersatz Battalion	85th
Supply Train	85th
Medical	85th
Other	85th

6th Panzer Division

Panzer Regiment	11th
Panzer Battalion	65th (same organization as bns in panzer regiment)
Schützen Brigade	6th
Schützen Regiments	4th and 114th
SP Infantry Gun Battery	none
Motorcycle Battalion	6th
Artillery Regiment	76th
Reconnaissance Battalion	57th
Panzerjäger Battalion	41st
Flak Battery	3/46th Flak Battalion
Pioneer Battalion	57th
Signals Battalion	82nd
Feldersatz Battalion	57th
Supply Train	57th

Medical	57th
Other	57th

7th Panzer Division

Panzer Regiment	25th (3 battalions, vice only 2)
Schützen Brigade	7th
Schützen Regiments	6th and 7th
SP Infantry Gun Battery	705th
Motorcycle Battalion	7th
Artillery Regiment	78th (3rd Bn had 1 100mm K 18 (mot) gun btry and 2 150mm sFH 18 (mot) btrys; observation company added later)
Reconnaissance Battalion	37th
Panzerjäger Battalion	42nd
Flak Battery	3/59th Flak Battalion
Pioneer Battalion	58th
Signals Battalion	83rd
Feldersatz Battalion	58th
Supply Train	58th
Medical	58th
Other	58th

8th Panzer Division:

Panzer Regiment	10th (same as 7th Pz Division)
Schützen Brigade	8th
Schützen Regiments	8th and 28th
SP Infantry Gun Battery	none
Motorcycle Battalion	8th
Artillery Regiment	80th
Reconnaissance Battalion	59th (like 3rd Pz Div)
Panzerjäger Battalion	43rd
Flak Battery	4/48th Flak Battalion
Pioneer Battalion	59th
Signals Battalion	84th
Feldersatz Battalion	59th
Supply Train	59th
Medical	59th
Other	59th

9th Panzer Division:

Panzer Regiment	33rd
Schützen Brigade	9th
Schützen Regiments	10th and 11th
SP Infantry Gun Battery	701st
Motorcycle Battalion	59th
Artillery Regiment	102nd
Reconnaissance Battalion	9th
Panzerjäger Battalion	50th
Flak Battery	3/47th Flak Battalion
Pioneer Battalion	86th
Signals Battalion	85th
Feldersatz Battalion	60th
Supply Train	60th
Medical	60th
Other	60th

10th Panzer Division

Panzer Regiment	4th Brigade, 7th Regiment
Schützen Brigade	10th
Schützen Regiments	86th and 69th
SP Infantry Gun Battery	706th
Motorcycle Battalion	10th
Artillery Regiment	90th (3rd Bn had 1 100mm K 18 (mot) gun btry and 2 150mm sFH 18 (mot) btrys)
Reconnaissance Battalion	90th (like 3rd Pz Div)
Panzerjäger Battalion	90th
Flak Battery	3/55th Flak Battalion
Pioneer Battalion	49th
Signals Battalion	90th
Feldersatz Battalion	90th
Supply Train	90th
Medical	90th
Other	90th

11th Panzer Division

Panzer Regiment	15th
Schützen Brigade	11th
Schützen Regiments	110th and 111th
SP Infantry Gun Battery	none
Motorcycle Battalion	61st
Artillery Regiment	119th (like 10th Pz Div)
Reconnaissance Battalion	231st
Panzerjäger Battalion	61st
Flak Battery	1/608th Flak Battalion
Pioneer Battalion	209th
Signals Battalion	341st
Feldersatz Battalion	61st
Supply Train	61st
Medical	61st
Other	61st

12th Panzer Division

Panzer Regiment	29th (3 armored battalions, each with a mot maintenance company)
Schützen Brigade	12th
Schützen Regiments	5th and 25th
SP Infantry Gun Battery	none
Motorcycle Battalion	22nd
Artillery Regiment	2nd
Reconnaissance Battalion	2nd (had a second armored car company that was later deleted)
Panzerjäger Battalion	2nd (the 3 AT companies had 6 37mm PAK 36, 4 50mm PAK 38 and 6 LMGs each)
Flak Battalion	4/52nd Flak Battalion
Pioneer Battalion	32nd (1 of 3 pioneer companies had no LMGs)
Signals Battalion	2nd
Feldersatz Battalion	2nd
Supply Train	2nd
Medical	2nd
Other	2nd

13th Panzer Division

Panzer Regiment	4th

Schützen Brigade	13th
Schützen Regiments	66th and 93rd (battalions had no motorized support company; however, each regiment had a motorcycle platoon with 3 LMGs; regts each had a mot AT company with 12 50mm PAK 38 and 4 LMGs)
SP Infantry Gun Battery	none
Motorcycle Battalion	13th
Artillery Regiment	13th
Reconnaissance Battalion	13th
Panzerjäger Battalion	13th
Flak Battery	4/66th Flak Battalion
Pioneer Battalion	13th (the "K" bridging train appears to have been added later)
Signals Battalion	13th
Feldersatz Battalion	13th
Supply Train	13th
Medical	13th
Other	13th

14th Panzer Division

Panzer Regiment	36th
Schützen Brigade	14th
Schützen Regiments	103rd and 108th
SP Infantry Gun Battery	none
Motorcycle Battalion	64th
Artillery Regiment	4th (like 10th Pz Div)
Reconnaissance Battalion	40th
Panzerjäger Battalion	4th
Flak Battery	2/608th Flak Battalion
Pioneer Battalion	13th
Signals Battalion	4th
Feldersatz Battalion	4th
Supply Train	4th
Medical	4th
Other	4th

15th Panzer Division

Panzer Regiment	8th
Schützen Brigade	15th
Schützen Regiments	104th and 115th (each regiment appears to have had a motorized AT platoon added with 3 50mm PAK 38; this was later assigned to the regimental HQ company)
SP Infantry Gun Battery	none
Motorcycle Battalion	15th
Artillery Regiment	33rd (observation company added later)
Reconnaissance Battalion	33rd (light supply column later deleted)
Panzerjäger Battalion	33rd (50mm PAK 38 replaced by 28mm sPzB 41 AT guns)
Pioneer Battalion	33rd ("B" bridging train deleted; no "K" train ever assigned)
Signals Battalion	33rd
Feldersatz Battalion	33rd
Supply Train	33rd
Medical	33rd
Other	33rd

16th Panzer Division

Panzer Regiment	2nd
Schützen Brigade	16th

Schützen Regiments	64th and 79th
SP Infantry Gun Battery	none
Motorcycle Battalion	16th
Artillery Regiment	16th
Reconnaissance Battalion	16th (had a 2nd light (mot) supply column that was later deleted)
Panzerjäger Battalion	16th
Flak Battery	6/66th Flak Battalion
Pioneer Battalion	16th
Signals Battalion	16th
Feldersatz Battalion	16th
Supply Train	16th
Medical	16th
Other	16th

17th Panzer Division

Panzer Regiment	39th
Schützen Brigade	17th
Schützen Regiments	40th and 63rd
SP Infantry Gun Battery	none
Motorcycle Battalion	77th
Artillery Regiment	27th
Reconnaissance Battalion	27th
Panzerjäger Battalion	27th
Flak Battery	1/66th Flak Battalion (added later)
Pioneer Battalion	27th
Signals Battalion	27th
Feldersatz Battalion	27th
Supply Train	27th
Medical	27th
Other	27th

18th Panzer Division

Panzer Regiment	18th Brigade, 18th Regiment (3 battalions, each with maintenance company; no reserve tank detachments)
Schützen Brigade	18th
Schützen Regiments	52nd and 101st
SP Infantry Gun Battery	none
Motorcycle Battalion	18th
Artillery Regiment	88th
Reconnaissance Battalion	88th
Panzerjäger Battalion	88th
Flak Battery	631st Flak Battalion (added later)
Pioneer Battalion	88th
Signals Battalion	88th
Feldersatz Battalion	88th
Supply Train	88th
Medical	88th
Other	88th

19th Panzer Division

Panzer Regiment	27th (3 battalions, each with maintenance company and reserve tank detachment)
Schützen Brigade	19th
Schützen Regiments	73rd and 74th
SP Infantry Gun Battery	none

Motorcycle Battalion	19th
Artillery Regiment	19th
Reconnaissance Battalion	19th
Panzerjäger Battalion	19th (no Flak battery added)
Pioneer Battalion	19th (no "K" bridging train)
Signals Battalion	19th
Feldersatz Battalion	19th
Supply Train	19th
Medical	19th
Other	19th

20th Panzer Division

Panzer Regiment	21st
Schützen Brigade	20th
Schützen Regiments	59th and 112th
SP Infantry Gun Battery	none
Motorcycle Battalion	20th
Artillery Regiment	92nd
Reconnaissance Battalion	92nd (German armored cars replaced with French armored cars)
Panzerjäger Battalion	92nd (no independent Flak battery)
Pioneer Battalion	92nd (no "K" bridging train)
Signals Battalion	92nd
Feldersatz Battalion	92nd
Supply Train	92nd
Medical	92nd
Other	92nd

Divisional Variations, 16 May 1941–15 October 1942

1st Panzer Division

Armored Regiment	2/1st (1942 1 battalion only)
Panzergrenadier Brigade	1st
Panzergrenadier Regiments	1st and 113th (1st Regiment did not have (mot) Infantry Heavy Company)
SP Infantry Gun Section	702nd
Panzerjäger Battalion	37th
Motorcycle Battalion	1st
Artillery Regiment	73rd
Signals Battalion	37th
Pioneer Battalion	37th
Supply Train, etc	37th

2nd Panzer Division

Armored Regiment	2/3rd (1942 1 battalion only)
Panzergrenadier Brigade	2nd
Panzergrenadier Regiments	2nd and 304th
SP Infantry Gun Section	703rd
Panzerjäger Battalion	38th (2 mot AT, 2 SP AT and 1 SP 20mm AA Companies; AA Company had 8 20mm and 2 quad 20mm AA)
Motorcycle Battalion	2nd
Artillery Regiment	74th
Signals Battalion	38th
Pioneer Battalion	38th
Supply Train, etc	38th

3rd Panzer Division

Armored Regiment	1/, 2/, 3/6th (3 battalions)
Panzergrenadier Brigade	3rd
Panzergrenadier Regiments	3rd and 394th (1/3rd in half-tracks; 3 companies with34 LMGs, 4 HMGs, 2 80mm mortars, 3 37mm PAK 36 and 3 AT Rifles; 1 Heavy Company with 1 Engineer Platoon (9 LMGs), 1 AT Section (3 50mm PAK 38 and 3 LMGs), 1 AT Section (3 28mm sPzB 41 and 3 LMGs), 1 Inf Sup Platoon (4 75mm leIG and 8 LMGs); both Regiments had 1 SP AA Battery with 12 20mm AA, and 2 (mot) Hvy Inf Gun Co with 4 150mm sIG)
Panzerjäger Battalion	543rd (2 mot AT Companies with 9 50mm PAK 38 and 6 LMGs; 1 SP Flak Company with 8 20mm and 2 quad 20mm AA guns)
Motorcycle Battalion	3rd (2 standard Motorcycle Companies, 1 standard Heavy Armored Car Company, 1 standard Heavy Company, 1 Half-Track Company with 4 HMGs, 56 LMGs, 2 80mm mortars and 3 37mm PAK 36)
Artillery Regiment	75th (3 standard battalions, plus 4th (Flak) Bn with 1 (mot) AA Btry with 12 20mm and 4 LMGs; 2 (mot) Btrys with 4 88mm, 3 20mm and 4 LMGs; and Mot Bn HQ Company (1 LMG))
Signals Battalion	39th
Pioneer Battalion	39th
Supply Train, etc	39th (9 light columns and 2 heavy supply columns; rest same)

4th Panzer Division

Armored Regiment	1/35th (1942 1 battalion only)
Panzergrenadier Brigade	4th
Panzergrenadier Regiments	12th and 33rd
SP Infantry Heavy Section	none
Panzerjäger Battalion	49th (1 standard SP AT Company and 2 standard mot AT Companies; Flak Company had 8 SP 20mm, 2 quad SP 20mm and 2 LMGs)
Motorcycle Battalion	34th (standard, plus 1 light armored car platoon with 3 LMGs)
Artillery Regiment	103rd (1st and 2nd Bns standard organ.; 3rd Bn had 3 btrys with 3 150mm sFH 18 and 2 LMGs ea)
Signals Battalion	79th
Pioneer Battalion	79th
Supply Train, etc	79th

5th Panzer Division

Armored Regiment	1/, 2/31st (2 battalions)
Panzergrenadier Brigade	5th
Panzergrenadier Regiments	13th and 14th
SP Infantry Gun Section	704th
Panzerjäger Battalion	53rd (1 SP AT Co (Marder) with 6 75mm and 6 LMGs; 1 (mot) AT Co with 3 50mm PAK 38, 8 37mm PAK 36 and 9 LMGs; 1 SP Flak Co with 8 20mm and 2 quad 20mm)
Motorcycle Battalion	56th (standard bn, plus 1 lt Armored Car Co with 3 LMGs)
Artillery Regiment	116th
Signals Battalion	77th
Pioneer Battalion	89th (same as standard, but 2 (mot) companies had only 9 LMGs ea)
Supply Train, etc	85th (9 lt and 2 hvy (mot) sup columns, rest at standard organization)

6th Panzer Division

Armored Regiment	1/, 2/11th (2 bns)
Panzergrenadier Brigade	6th
Panzergrenadier Regiments	4th and 114th
SP Infantry Gun Section	none

Panzerjäger Battalion	41st (1 SP AT Co (Marder) with 6 75mm and 6 LMGs; 1 (mot) AT Company with 9 75mm PAK 40 and 6 LMGs; 1 SP Flak Company with 8 20mm, 2 quad 20mm and 4 LMGs)
Motorcycle Battalion	6th (2 standard Motorcycle Companies, 1 standard Heavy Armored Car Company, 1 Light Armored Car Company with 3 LMGs; 1 (mot) Sup Company with 1 Eng Platoon (4 LMGs), 1 AT Platoon (3 50mm PAK 38 and 3 LMGs), 1 AT Plat (3 28mm sPzB 41 AT and 3 LMGs), 2 Inf Sup Gun Sects (2 75mm leIG guns ea), 1 Half-Track Company with 4 HMGs, 56 LMGs, 2 80mm mortars and 3 37mm PAK 36)
Artillery Regiment	76th (standard organization, but each bn had a munition column integral to Bn HQ)
Signals Battalion	82nd
Pioneer Battalion	57th
Supply Train, etc	57th (like 5th Pz Div)

7th Panzer Division

Armored Regiment	1/, 2/25th (2 bns)
Panzergrenadier Brigade	7th
Panzergrenadier Regiments	6th and 7th (1/, 2/7th and 2/6th had the normal organization; the 1/6th was all half-track mounted and organized with 3 (mot) Infantry Companies (34 LMGs, 4 HMGs, 2 80mm mortars and 3 AT rifles each; and 1 (mot) Infantry Heavy Company, with 1 Engineer Platoon (9 LMGs), 1 AT Platoon (3 50mm PAK 38, 6 LMGs and 3 28mm sPzB 41 AT) and 2 Infantry Gun Sections (2 75mm leIG and 4 LMGs each))
SP Infantry Gun Section	none
Panzerjäger Battalion	42nd (same as 6th Pz Div)
Motorcycle Battalion	7th (2 standard Motorcycle Companies, 1 standard Heavy Armored Car Company, 1 Light Armored Car Company with 3 LMGs; 1 (mot) Sup Company, with 1 Eng Platoon (4 LMGs), 1 AT Platoon (3 50mm PAK 38 and 3 LMGs), 1 AT Sect (3 28mm sPzB 41 AT and 3 LMGs), 2 Inf Sup Gun Sects (2 75mm leIG ea), 1 Half-Track Company with 4 HMGs, 56 LMGs, 2 80mm mortars and 3 37mm PAK 36)
Artillery Regiment	7th (same as 6th Pz Div)
Signals Battalion	83rd
Pioneer Battalion	58th
Supply Train, etc	58th (same as 6th Pz. Div.)

8th Panzer Division

Armored Regiment	1/10th (1942 only 1 Bn)
Panzergrenadier Brigade	8th
Panzergrenadier Regiments	8th and 28th
SP Infantry Gun Section	none
Panzerjäger Battalion	43rd (1 SP AT Co (Marder) with 6 75mm and 6 LMGs; 1 (mot) AT Company with 9 50mm PAK 40 and 6 LMGs, 1 SP Flak Co with 8 20mm, 2 quad 20mm and 4 LMGs)
Motorcycle Battalion	8th (standard organization, plus 1 Light Armored Car Platoon with 3 LMGs)
Artillery Regiment	80th
Signals Battalion	84th
Pioneer Battalion	59th
Supply Train, etc	59th (same as 6th Pz Div)

9th Panzer Division

Armored Regiment	1/, 2/, 3/33rd (3 bns)
Panzergrenadier Brigade	9th
Panzergrenadier Regiments	10th and 11th (1/10th like 1/6th of 7th Panzer Division; both Pz Gren Rgts had an SP Flak Company with 12 20mm guns and 4 LMGs)

SP Infantry Gun Section	701st (6 150mm sIG)
Panzerjäger Battalion	50th (1 SP AT Company (Marder) with 9 75mm and 6 LMGs; 1 (mot) AT Company with 9 50mm PAK 38 and 6 LMGs; 1 SP Flak Company with 8 20mm, 2 quad 20mm and 4 LMGs)
Motorcycle Battalion	59th (2 standard Motorcycle Companies, 1 standard Heavy Armored Car Company, 1 Light Armored Car Company with 3 LMGs; 1 (mot) Sup Company, with 1 Eng Platoon (4 LMGs), 1 AT Platoon (3 50mm PAK 38 and 3 LMGs), 1 AT Sect (3 28mm sPzB 41 AT and 3 LMGs) and 2 Inf Sup Gun Sects (2 75mm leIG and 8 LMGs ea); and 1 Half-Track Company with 4 HMGs, 56 LMGs, 2 80mm mortars and 3 37mm PAK 36)
Artillery Regiment	102nd (3 standard bns , plus 4th (Flak) Bn with 1 (mot) AA Btry with 12 20mm and 4 LMGs; 2 (mot) Btrys with 4 88mm, 3 20mm and 4 LMGs; and Mot Bn HQ Co (1 LMG)
Signals Battalion	85th
Pioneer Battalion	86th
Supply Train, etc	60th (4 Heavy and 7 Light Mot Sup Columns; rest standard)

10th Panzer Division

Armored Regiment	1/, 2/7th (2 bns, each with 3 light and 1 medium company)
Panzergrenadier Brigade	10th
Panzergrenadier Regiments	69th and 86th (1/69th like 1/6th of 7th Panzer Division).
SP Infantry Gun Section	none
Panzerjäger Battalion	90th (like 9th Panzer Div)
Motorcycle Battalion	90th (like 9th Panzer Div)
Artillery Regiment	90th (like 9th Panzer Div)
Signals Battalion	90th
Pioneer Battalion	46th
Supply Train, etc	90th (2 Heavy and 9 Light Mot Sup Columns; rest standard)

11th Panzer Division

Armored Regiment	1/, 2/, 3/15th (3 bns)
Panzergrenadier Brigade	11th
Panzergrenadier Regiments	110th and 111th (1/110th like 1/6th of 7th Pz Div; each Pz Gren Regt had 1 SP Flak Company with 12 20mm AA and 4 LMGs)
SP Infantry Gun Section	none
Panzerjäger Battalion	61st (like 9th Panzer Div)
Motorcycle Battalion	61st (like 9th Panzer Div)
Artillery Regiment	119th (like 9th Panzer Div)
Signals Battalion	341st
Pioneer Battalion	209th
Supply Train, etc	61st (2 heavy and 9 light Mot Sup Columns; rest standard)

12th Panzer Division

Armored Regiment	12th (1 bn, plus 8th (medical) Company/29th Panzer Regiment)
Panzergrenadier Brigade	12th
Panzergrenadier Regiments	5th and 25th (normal organization)
SP Infantry Gun Section	none
Panzerjäger Battalion	2nd (1 SP AT Co (Marder) with 6 75mm and 6 LMGs; 1 (mot) AT Company with 9 50mm PAK 38 and 6 LMGs; 1 SP Flak Company with 8 20mm, 2 quad 20mm and 4 LMGs)
Motorcycle Battalion	22nd (like 9th Panzer Div)
Artillery Regiment	2nd (normal organization, but Bn HQs had integral light munition supply column)
Signals Battalion	2nd
Pioneer Battalion	32nd
Supply Train, etc	2nd (2 heavy and 7 light Mot Sup Columns; rest standard)

13th Panzer Division

Armored Regiment	1/, 2/, 3/4th (3 bns)
Panzergrenadier Brigade	13th
Panzergrenadier Regiments	66th and 93rd (like 9th Pz Div; 66th had 1 Flak Company with 8 SP 20mm, 4 (mot) 20mm and 4 LMGs; 93rd had 1 Flak with 12 SP 20mm AA and 4 LMGs)
SP Infantry Gun Section	none
Panzerjäger Battalion	13th (like 9th Pz Div)
Motorcycle Battalion	43rd (like 9th Pz Div)
Artillery Regiment	13th (like 9th Pz Div)
Signals Battalion	13th
Pioneer Battalion	4th
Supply Train, etc	13th (4 heavy and 7 light Mot Sup Columns; rest standard)

14th Panzer Division

Armored Regiment	1/, 2/, 3/36th (3 bns)
Panzergrenadier Brigade	14th
Panzergrenadier Regiments	103rd and 108th (1/103rd like 1/6th of 7th Pz Div; each Pz Gren Regt also had 1 SP Flak company with 12 20mm and 4 LMGs)
SP Infantry Gun Section	none
Panzerjäger Battalion	4th (1 SP AT Co (Marder) with 6 75mm and 6 LMGs; 1 (mot) AT Company with 9 50mm PAK 38 and 6 LMGs; and 1 SP Flak Company with 8 20mm, 2 quad 20mm and 4 LMGs)
Motorcycle Battalion	64th (like 9th Pz Div)
Artillery Regiment	4th (like 9th Pz Div; plus 1 mot Observer Company with 2 LMGs; 1 Light mot Munition Sup Column (20t) and 1st, 2nd and 3rd Bn HQ Companies had integral munition columns)
Signals Battalion	4th
Pioneer Battalion	13th
Supply Train, etc	4th (2 heavy and 9 light Mot Sup Columns; rest standard)

16th Panzer Division

Armored Regiment	1/, 2/, 3/2nd (3 bns)
Panzergrenadier Brigade	16th
Panzergrenadier Regiments	64th and 79th (1/64th like 1/6th of 7th Pz Div; 64th had 1 Flak Company with 8 SP 20mm, 4 (mot) 20mm and 4 LMGs; 79th had 1 Flak with 12 SP 20mm AA and 4 LMGs)
SP Infantry Gun Section	none
Panzerjäger Battalion	16th (like 14th Pz Div)
Motorcycle Battalion	16th (like 9th Pz Div)
Artillery Regiment	16th (like 9th Pz Div; plus 1 SP Artillery Btry with 6 105mm Wespe)
Signals Battalion	16th
Pioneer Battalion	16th
Supply Train, etc	16th (2 heavy and 9 light Mot Sup Columns; rest standard)

17th Panzer Division

Armored Regiment	1/39th (only 1 bn)
Panzergrenadier Brigade	17th
Panzergrenadier Regiments	40th and 63rd
SP Infantry Gun Section	none
Panzerjäger Battalion	27th (1 SP AT Company with 6 75mm and 6 LMGs; 2 AT Companies with 3 50mm PAK 38, 8 37mm PAK 36 and 6 LMGs; and 1 SP Flak Company with 8 20mm, 2 quad 20mm and 4 LMGs)
Motorcycle Battalion	17th (basic organization)
Artillery Regiment	27th (1st and 2nd Bns, 3 btrys ea, each btry 3 105mm lFH 18 and 2 LMGs; 3rd Bn 3 btrys, each with 3 150mm sFH 18 and 2 LMGs; Bn HQs had integral light munition columns; 1 (mot) Observation Cmpany with 2 LMGs)

Signals Battalion	27th
Pioneer Battalion	27th
Supply Train, etc	27th (2 heavy and 9 light Mot Sup Columns; rest standard)

18th Panzer Division

Armored Regiment	1/18th (only 1 bn)
Panzergrenadier Brigade	18th
Panzergrenadier Regiments	52nd and 101st
SP Infantry Gun Section	none
Panzerjäger Battalion	88th (like 17th Pz Div)
Motorcycle Battalion	18th (standard organization plus 1 Light Armored Car Platoon with 3 LMGs)
Artillery Regiment	88th (like 17th Pz Div)
Signals Battalion	88th
Pioneer Battalion	98th (no "K" Bridging Column)
Supply Train, etc	88th (1 heavy and 11 lt mot sup columns; rest standard organization)

19th Panzer Division

Armored Regiment	1/27th (1 bn with 3 light and 2 medium armored companies, plus 1 addtional light company)
Panzergrenadier Brigade	19th
Panzergrenadier Regiments	73rd and 74th
SP Infantry Gun Section	none
Panzerjäger Battalion	19th (2 SP AT Companies with 6 75mm and 6 LMGs, and 1 (mot) AT Company with 9 50mm PAK 38 and 6 LMGs)
Motorcycle Battalion	19th (like 18th Pz Div)
Artillery Regiment	19th (standard organization, plus 1 (mot) Observation Company)
Signals Battalion	19th
Pioneer Battalion	19th
Supply Train, etc	19th (1 heavy and 9 light mot sup columns, 5 light fuel columns, 3 mot maintenance companies and 1 light mot supply company)

20th Panzer Division

Armored Regiment	3/21st (1942 only 1 bn)
Panzergrenadier Brigade	20th
Panzergrenadier Regiments	59th and 1/112th (2/112th not present, nor was the mot inf sup company for the 112th Pz Gren Rgt)
SP Infantry Gun Section	none
Panzerjäger Battalion	92nd (1 mot AT Company with 6 50mm PAK 38, 4 37mm PAK 36 and 6 LMGs; 1 SP Flak Company with 12 20mm AA and 4 LMGs; and 2 SP AT Companies with 6 75mm (Marders) and 6 LMGs)
Motorcycle Battalion	20th (standard organization, plus 1 Light Armored Car Section with 3 LMGs.)
Artillery Regiment	92nd (standard organization)
Signals Battalion	92nd (standard organization)
Pioneer Battalion	92nd (standard organization)
Supply Train, etc	92nd (2 heavy and 7 light mot sup columns, only 1 fuel sup column, rest standard)

22nd Panzer Division

Armored Regiment	1/, 2/204th (2 bns)
Panzergrenadier Brigade	22nd
Panzergrenadier Regiments	1/, 2/129th (only 1 regt, organized like the 6th Pz Gren Regt, 7th Pz Division, including SP Flak Company.)
SP Infantry Gun Section	none
Panzerjäger Battalion	140th (2 mot AT Companies with 6 50mm PAK 38, 4 37mm PAK 36 and 6 LMGs; and 1 SP Flak Company with 12 20mm AA and 4 LMGs)

Motorcycle Battalion	24th (like 9th Pz Div)
Artillery Regiment	2/, 3/, 4/140th (2nd Bn with 3 btrys, each with 4 105mm lFH 18 and 2 LMGs; 3rd Bn with 2 btrys, each with 4 150mm sFH 18 and 2 LMGs and 1 btry with 4 100mm K18 guns and 2 LMGs; and 4th (Flak) Bn with 2 btrys, each with 4 88mm, 3 20mm and 4 LMGs, and 1 btry with 12 20mm and 2 LMGs; all bns motorized; HQ companies had integral light munitions supply column)
Signals Battalion	140th
Pioneer Battalion	50th
Supply Train, etc	140th (2 heavy and 6 light sup columns, only 2 fuel columns, rest standard; 1 ambulance column detached)

23rd Panzer Division

Armored Regiment	1/, 2/, 3/201st (3 bns)
Panzergrenadier Brigade	23rd
Panzergrenadier Regiments	126th and 128th (1/126th like 1/6th Pz GR; Each Pz GR had 1 SP Flak Company with 12 20mm and 4 LMGs)
SP Infantry Gun Section	none
Panzerjäger Battalion	128th (2 mot AT companies with 9 50mm PAK 38 and 6 LMGs, and 1 SP Flak Company with 8 20mm, 2 quad 20mm and 4 LMGs)
Motorcycle Battalion	23rd (2 motorcycle companies, 1 heavy armored car company, and 1 light armored car company with 3 LMGs; 1 (mot) Sup Company, with 1 Eng Platoon (4 LMGs), 1 AT Plat (3 50mm PAK 38 and 3 LMGs), 1 AT Sect (3 28mm sPzB 41 AT and 3 LMGs), 1 Inf Sup Gun Sect (2 75mm leIG and 8 LMGs); and 1 Half-Track Company with 4 HMGs, 56 LMGs, 2 80mm mortars and 3 37mm PAK 36)
Artillery Regiment	128th (3 bns, plus 4th (Flak) Bn with 1 (mot) AA Btry with 12 20mm and 4 LMGs; 2 (mot) Btrys with 4 88mm, 3 20mm and 4 LMGs; Mot. Bn HQ Company (1 LMG); and 1 light munitions sup column; 1st–3rd Bn HQs had munition supply column)
Signals Battalion	128th
Pioneer Battalion	51st
Supply Train, etc	128th (2 heavy and 9 light mot sup columns; rest standard organization)

24th Panzer Division

Armored Regiment	1/, 2/, 3/24th (3 bns)
Panzergrenadier Brigade	24th
Panzergrenadier Regiments	21st and 26th (1/26th like 1/6th of 7th Pz Div; each Pz Gren Regt had 1 SP Flak Company with 12 20mm and 4 LMGs)
SP Infantry Gun Section	none
Panzerjäger Battalion	40th (like 23rd Pz Div)
Motorcycle Battalion	4th (like 23rd Pz Div)
Artillery Regiment	89th (like 23rd Pz Div)
Signals Battalion	86th
Pioneer Battalion	40th
Supply Train, etc	40th

25th Panzer Division

Armored Regiment	1/214th (1 bn with 2 light and 2 medium armored companies)
Panzergrenadier Brigade	none
Panzergrenadier Regiments	1/, 2/, 3/, 146th (3 bns vice 2, normal organization; only 1 mot inf sup gun section (2 75mm leIG); also had 1 (mot) AT Company with 9 75mm PAK 40 and 6 LMGs)
SP Infantry Gun Section	none
Panzerjäger Battalion	514th Panzerjäger Company: 1 (mot) AT Co with 9 75mm PAK 40 and 6 LMGs
Motorcycle Battalion	87th (3 motorcycle companies, 1 motorized support company)

Artillery Regiment	1/91st (only 1 bn, with 4 btrys, 2 with 4 105mm lFH 18 and 2LMGs, 1 with 4 150mm French howitzers and 2 LMGs, and 1 with 4 100mm French field guns and 2 LMGs)
Signals Battalion	87th (standard organization)
Pioneer Battalion	87th (2 mot standard pioneer companies and 1 light mot engineer sup column)
Supply Train, etc	none

26th Panzer Division

Armored Regiment	2/, 3/202nd (2 bns)
Panzergrenadier Brigade	26th
Panzergrenadier Regiments	9th and 67th
SP Infantry Gun Section	none
Panzerjäger Battalion	23rd (1 mot AT Company with 9 50mm PAK 38 and 6 LMGs, 1 mot AT Company with 9 75mm 40 and 6 LMGs, and 1 SP AT company with 9 75mm and 6 LMGs)
Motorcycle Battalion	26th (like 23rd Pz Div)
Artillery Regiment	23rd
Signals Battalion	23rd
Pioneer Battalion	23rd (all pioneer companies mot)
Supply Train, etc	23rd (2 heavy and 9 light mot sup columns; rest standard organization)

27th Panzer Division

Armored Battalion	127th Panzer Battalion
Panzergrenadier Brigade	none
Panzergrenadier Regiments	1/, 2/140th Pz Gren Regt (standard organization, plus 1 SP Flak Company with 12 20mm and 4 LMGs)
SP Infantry Gun Section	none
Panzerjäger Battalion	127th (2 mot AT Companies with 9 75mm PAK 40 and 6 LMGs; and 1 SP AT Company with (Marder) 9 75mm and 6 LMGs)
Motorcycle Battalion	none
Artillery Regiment	127th (1st Bn with mot HQ platoon and 3 btrys each with 4 105mm lFH 18 and 2 LMGs; 2nd Bn mot HQ Company and 2 btrys each with 4 150mm sFH 18 and 2 LMGs; and 1 btry 4 100 K18 guns and 2 LMGs)
Signals Battalion	127th
Pioneer Battalion (mot)	127th (2 mot pioneer companies, each with 9 LMGs and 3 AT rifles; and 1 Lt Engineer Sup Column)
Supply Train, etc	1 Ambulance Column, 3 light mot sup columns, 1 lt fuel sup column, 1 mot maintenance company and 1 lt mot supply company)

Authorized Organization, 10th Panzer Division in Tunisia, 17 May 1943

7th Panzer Regiment
  1 Panzer Regimental Staff
  1 Panzer Regimental Staff Company
  1 Panzer Signals Company
  1/7th Panzer Regiment
    1 Battalion Staff and Staff Company
    4 Panzer Companies (22 PzMk IV ea)
  2/7th Panzer Regiment
    1 Battalion Staff and Staff Company
    4 Panzer Companies (22 PzMk IV ea)
    1 Armored Maintenance Company

3/7th Panzer Regiment (former 501st Panzer Battalion)
    1 Battalion Staff and Staff Company
    3 Panzer Companies (10 PzMk VI Tiger tanks ea)
    1 Armored Maintenance Company
10th Panzergrenadier Brigade
  1 Regimental Staff
  1 (mot) Regimental Staff Company
    1 Signals Platoon
    1 Infantry Gun Platoon (3 LMGs and 3 75mm leIG)
    1 Motorcycle Platoon (6 LMGs)

1/69th Panzergrenadier Regiment
1 Battalion Staff
3 (Half-Track) Companies (4 HMGs, 34 LMGs, 2 80 mortars, 3 75mm leIG and 3 PzBu ea)
1 (Half-Track) Company (3 75mm leIG, 3 28mm sPzB 41, 4 37mm PAK 36 and 14 LMGs)
1 Pioneer Platoon (9 LMGs)
2/69th Panzergrenadier Regiment
1 Battalion Staff
3 (mot) Companies (4 HMGs, 18 LMGs, 2 80 mortars and 3 PzBu ea)
1 (Half-Track) Company (3 75mm leIG, 3 28mm sPzB 41, 4 37mm PAK 36 and 6 LMGs)
1 Pioneer Platoon (4 LMGs)
1 (mot) Heavy Infantry Gun Company (4 150mm sIG)
1/, 2/86th Panzergrenadier Regiment
both organized like 2/69th

10th Panzer Reconnaissance Battalion
1 Light Armored Car Company (6 LMGs and 6 20mm)
1 Light Armored Car Company (24 LMGs and 18 20mm)
1 Half-Track Reconnaissance Company (3 75mm leIG, 2 80mm mortars, 4 HMGs and 56 LMGs)
2 Motorcycle Companies (2 80mm mortars, 4 HMGs, 18 LMGs and 3 PzBu ea)
1 (mot) Heavy Reconnaissance Company
1 Pioneer Platoon (4 LMGs)
1 Infantry Gun Platoon (3 75mm leIG and 3 LMGs)
1 Panzerjäger Platoon (3 28mm sPzB 41 and 3 LMGs)
2 Panzerjäger Platoons (3 37mm PAK 36 3 LMGs)

90th Panzerjäger Battalion
1 (mot) Panzerjäger Company (9 75mm PAK 40 and 6 LMGs)
1 Self-Propelled Panzerjäger Company (9 Marder II with 76.2mm guns and 6 LMGs)
3/90th Flak Battalion (8 20mm, 2 quad 20mm and 4 LMGs)
90th Sturmgeschütz Battery (formerly 1/242nd Bn) (10 Sturmgeschütz)
1/, 2/, 3/90th Artillery Regiment
1 Regimental Staff and Staff Battery (2 LMGs)
1 (mot) Observation Battery (2 LMGs)

1/90th Artillery Regiment
1 Battalion Staff and Staff Battery (2 LMGs)
3 Batteries (6 105mm SdKfz 124 Wespe and 2 LMGs ea)
2/90th Artillery Regiment
1 Battalion Staff and Staff Battery (2 LMGs)
3 (motZ) Batteries (4 105mm leFH 18 and 2 LMGs ea)
3/90th Artillery Regiment
1 Battalion Staff and Staff Battery (2 LMGs)
2 (motZ) Batteries (4 150mm sFH 18 and 2 LMGs ea)
1 (motZ) Battery (4 100mm K18 guns and 2 LMGs)
302nd Army Flak Battalion
1 Battalion Staff and Staff Battery (1 LMG)
2 (motZ) Flak Batteries (4 88mm, 3 20mm and 2 LMGs ea)
1 (motZ) Flak Battery (12 20mm and 4 LMGs)
1 Searchlight Squad
1 Light (mot) Flak Supply Column
49th Panzer Pioneer Battalion
1 Pioneer Battalion Staff (2 LMGs)
2 (mot) Pioneer Companies (18 LMGs and 3 PzBu ea)
1 Panzer Pioneer Company (25 LMGs and 3 PzBu ea)
1 (mot) Pioneer Supply Column
90th Signals Battalion
1 Signals Battalion Staff
1 Armored Radio Company (16 LMGs)
1 Armored Telephone Company (6 LMGs)
1 Light (mot) Signals Supply Column (1 LMG)
90th Divisional Support Units
1 Supply Battalion Staff (2 LMGs)
1st–9th/Light (mot) Supply Columns (2 LMGs ea)
13/, 14/Heavy (mot) Supply Columns (2 LMGs ea)
10/, 11/, 12/Heavy (mot) Fuel Columns (2 LMGs ea)
90th (mot) Supply Company (6 LMGs)
1/, 2/, 3/90th (mot) Maintenance Companies
Administrative Services
90th (mot) Bakery Company
90th (mot) Butcher Company
90th (mot) Administration Company
Other
1/, 2/90th (mot) Medical Companies
1/, 2/, 3/90th (mot) Ambulance Companies
90th (mot) Military Police Company
90th (mot) Field Post Office

ORGANIZATION OF PANZER DIVISIONS, SEPTEMBER–OCTOBER 1943

1st Panzer Division

Division Staff
Divisional Staff (2 LMGs)
81st (mot) Division Mapping Detachment
Divisional Escort Company

Motorcycle Platoon (3 LMGs)
Infantry Gun Platoon (2 75mm leIG)
Heavy Anti-Tank Platoon (3 LMGs and 3 75mm PAK 40)

Self-Propelled Flak Platoon (4 20mm guns)
Mixed Panzergrenadier Platoon (4 HMGs, 6 LMGs, and 2 80mm mortars)

1st Panzer Regiment

1st Panzer Battalion
Staff
Staff Signals Platoon
Panzer Flak Platoon (7 37mm Flak 43)
4 Panzer Companies (22 Panther PzMk V tanks ea)
1 Panzer Maintenance Company

2nd Panzer Battalion
Staff
Staff Signals Platoon
Panzer Flak Platoon (7 37mm Flak 43)
4 Panzer Companies (22 PzMk IV tanks ea)
1 Panzer Maintenance Company

1st Panzergrenadier Regiment
Regimental Staff
Regimental Band
Regimental Staff Company
Signals Platoon
Panzerjäger Platoon (3 LMGs and 3 75mm PAK 40)
Motorcycle Platoon (6 LMGs)

1st (mot) Battalion
3 Panzergrenadier Companies (4 HMGs, 18 LMGs and 2 80mm mortars ea)
1 Heavy Panzergrenadier Company
1 Pioneer Platoon (4 LMGs and 6 flamethrowers)
1 Panzerjäger Platoon (3 75mm PAK 40)
2 Infantry Gun Sections (2 75mm leIG ea)
1 Mortar Platoon (6 80mm mortars)

2nd (mot) Battalion
same as 1st Battalion

1 Self-Propelled Light Flak Company (12 20mm Flak and 4 LMGs)
1 Self-Propelled Infantry Gun Company (6 150mm sIG and 3 LMGs)

113th Panzergrenadier Regiment
same as 1st Panzergrenadier Regiment

37th Panzerjäger Battalion
Staff
3 Self-Propelled Heavy Panzerjäger Companies (14 75mm PAK 40 and 14 LMGs ea)

1st Panzer Reconnaissance Battalion
Staff (15 LMGs)
Heavy Platoon (6 SdKfz 234/3 with 75mm KwK and 6 LMGs)
1 Light Armored Car Company (18 20mm and 24 LMGs)
1 (half-track) Reconnaissance Company (16 20mm and 25 LMGs)
2 (half-track) Heavy Reconnaissance Companies (2 80mm mortars, 4 HMGs, 56 LMGs and 3 37mm PAK 36 ea)
1 (half-track) Heavy Company

1 Pioneer Platoon (13 LMGs, 1 20mm and 6 flame-throwers)
1 Panzerjäger Platoon (3 LMGs and 3 75mm PAK 40)
1 Light Infantry Gun Section (4 LMGs and 2 75mm leIG)
2 Platoons (4 LMGs and 3 SdKfz 251/9 with 75mm KwK ea)
1 Light Panzer Reconnaissance Battalion Column

73rd Panzer Artillery Regiment
Staff and (mot) Staff Battery (6 LMGs)
1 (motZ) Flak Platoon (4 20mm and 2 LMGs)

1st Battalion
Staff and (self-propelled) Staff Battery (6 LMGs)
2 Self-Propelled leFH Batteries (6 105mm leFH SdKfz 124 Wespe ea)
1 Self-Propelled sFH Battery (6 150mm sFH SdKfz 165 Hummel)

2nd Battalion
Staff and Staff Battery (2 LMGs)
3 (motZ) Batteries (4 105mm leFH and 2 LMGs ea)

3rd Battalion
same as 2nd Battalion

4th Battalion
Staff and (mot) Staff Battery (6 LMGs)
2 (motZ) Batteries (4 105mm leFH and 2 LMGs ea)
1 (motZ) Battery (4 100mm K18 and 2 LMGs)

299th Army Flak Battalion
Staff and Staff Battery
1/, 2/299th (motZ) Heavy Flak Batteries (4 88mm, 3 20mm Flak guns and 2 LMGs ea)
3/299th (motZ) Light Flak Battery (9 20mm guns, 2 self-propelled quad 20mm Flak guns and 2 LMGs)
1 (mot) Light (48 ton) Flak Column

1st Feldersatz Battalion
Staff
4 Companies

37th (mot) Pioneer Battalion
Staff (2 LMGs)
2 (mot) Pioneer Companies (18 LMGs, 2 80mm mortars, 6 flamethrowers and 3 PzBu ea)
1 (armored) Pioneer Company (40 LMGs, 2 80mm mortars, 6 flamethrowers and 3 PzBu)
1 Brüko K Bridging Column (4 LMGs)
1 Brüko B Bridging Column (4 LMGs)
1 (mot) Light Pioneer Column (4 LMGs)

37th Panzer Signals Battalion
Staff
1 Panzer Telephone Company (21 LMGs)
1 Panzer Radio Company (35 LMGs)
1 (mot) Light Signals Column (4 LMGs)

81st Supply Troops
Staff
1–7/81st (mot) (120 ton) Transportation Companies (4 LMGs ea)

8/81st (mot) (90 ton) Transportation Companies (3 LMGs ea)

81st (mot) Supply Company (6 LMGs)

81st Truck Maintenance Park

1/, 2/, 3/81st (mot) Maintenance Companies

1 (mot) (75 ton) Maintenance Supply Column

Administration

81st Divisional Administration Office

81st (mot) Bakery Company

81st (mot) Butcher Company

Medical Troops

1/, 2/81st (mot) Medical Companies

1/, 2/, 3/81st Ambulance Platoons

Other

81st (mot) Military Police Troop (2 LMGs)

81st (mot) Field Post Office

2nd Panzer Division

Division Staff

Divisional Staff (2 LMGs)

82nd (mot) Division Mapping Detachment

Divisional Escort Company

Motorcycle Platoon (3 LMGs)

Infantry Gun Platoon (2 75mm leIG)

Heavy Anti-Tank Platoon (3 LMGs and 3 75mm PAK 40)

Self-Propelled Flak Platoon (4 20mm guns)

Mixed Panzergrenadier Platoon (4 HMGs, 6 LMGs, and 2 80mm mortars)

3rd Panzer Regiment

1st Panzer Battalion

Detached to army, equipped with Panther PzMkV tanks

2nd Panzer Battalion

Staff

Staff Signals Platoon

Panzer Flak Platoon (7 37mm Flak 43)

4 Panzer Companies (22 PzMk IV tanks ea)

1 Panzer Maintenance Company

2nd Panzergrenadier Regiment

Regimental Staff

Regimental Band

Regimental Staff Company

Signals Platoon

Panzerjäger Platoon (3 LMGs and 3 75mm PAK 40)

Motorcycle Platoon (6 LMGs)

1st (mot) Battalion

3 Panzergrenadier Companies (4 HMGs, 18 LMGs, 3 PzBu and 2 80mm mortars ea)

1 Heavy Panzergrenadier Company

1 Pioneer Platoon (4 LMGs)

1 Panzerjäger Platoon (3 50mm PAK 38)

2 Infantry Gun Sections (2 75mm leIG ea)

1 Panzerjäger Platoon (3 LMGs and 3 sPzBu 41)

2nd (mot) Battalion

same as 1st Battalion

1 Self-Propelled Infantry Gun Company (6 150mm sIG and 7 LMGs)

304th Panzergrenadier Regiment

Regimental Staff

Regimental Band

Regimental Staff Company

Signals Platoon

Panzerjäger Platoon (3 LMGs and 3 75mm PAK 40)

Motorcycle Platoon (6 LMGs)

1st (half-track) Battalion

3 (half-track) Panzergrenadier Companies (4 HMGs, 34 LMGs, 3 PzBu, 3 37mm PAK 36 and 2 80mm mortars ea)

1 (half-track) Heavy Panzergrenadier Company

1 Staff Platoon (2 LMGs)

1 Pioneer Platoon (9 LMGs)

1 Panzerjäger Platoon (3 50mm PAK 38)

2 Infantry Gun Sections (4 LMGs 2 75mm leIG ea)

1 Panzerjäger Platoon (3 LMGs and 3 sPzBu 41)

2nd (mot) Battalion

3 Panzergrenadier Companies (4 HMGs, 18 LMGs, 3 PzBu and 2 80mm mortars ea)

1 Heavy Panzergrenadier Company

1 Pioneer Platoon (4 LMGs)

1 Panzerjäger Platoon (3 50mm PAK 38)

2 Infantry Gun Sections (2 75mm leIG ea)

1 Panzerjäger Platoon (3 LMGs and 3 sPzBu 41)

1 Self-Propelled Infantry Gun Company (6 150mm sIG and 7 LMGs)

38th Panzerjäger Battalion

Staff

3 Self-Propelled Heavy Panzerjäger Companies (equipment unknown)

2nd Panzer Reconnaissance Battalion

Staff (15 LMGs)

Heavy Platoon (6 SdKfz 234/3 with 75mm KwK and 6 LMGs)

1 Light Armored Car Company (18 20mm and 24 LMGs)

1 (half-track) Reconnaissance Company (16 20mm and 25 LMGs)

2 (half-track) Heavy Reconnaissance Companies (2 80mm mortars, 4 HMGs, 56 LMGs and 3 37mm PAK 36)

1 (half-track) Heavy Company
  1 Pioneer Platoon (13 LMGs, 1 20mm and 6 flame-throwers)
  1 Panzerjäger Platoon (3 LMGs and 3 75mm PAK 40)
  1 Light Infantry Gun Section (4 LMGs and 2 75mm leIG)
  2 Platoons (4 LMGs and 3 SdKfz 251/9 with 75mm KwK ea)
1 Light Panzer Reconnaissance Battalion Column

276th Sturmgeschütz Battalion
1 Staff and Staff Platoon
3 Sturmgeschütz Companies (14 StuG ea)

74th Panzer Artillery Regiment
Staff and (mot) Staff Battery (6 LMGs)
74th (motZ) (mot) Observation Battery (2 LMGs)

1st Battalion
Staff and (self-propelled) Staff Battery (6 LMGs)
2 Self-Propelled leFH Batteries (6 105mm leFH SdKfz 124 Wespe ea)
1 Self-Propelled sFH Battery (6 SdKfz 165 150mm sFH Hummel)

2nd Battalion
Staff and Staff Battery (2 LMGs)
3 (motZ) Batteries (4 105mm leFH and 2 LMGs ea)

3rd Battalion
Staff and (mot) Staff Battery (6 LMGs)
2 (motZ) Batteries (4 150mm sFH and 2 LMGs ea)
1 (motZ) Battery (4 100mm K18 and 2 LMGs)

273rd Army Flak Battalions
Staff and Staff Battery
1/, 2/273rd (motZ) Heavy Flak Batteries (4 88mm, 3 20mm Flak guns and 2 LMGs ea)
3/273rd (motZ) Light Flak Battery (12 20mm guns and 2 LMGs)
4/273rd Self-Propelled Light Battery (2 quad 20mm Flak guns, 8 20mm guns and 2 LMGs)
1 (mot) Light (48 ton) Flak Column

38th Feldersatz Battalion
Staff
5 Companies

38th Panzer Pioneer Battalion
Staff (2 LMGs)
2 (mot) Pioneer Companies (18 LMGs, 3 PzBu and 2 80mm mortars ea)
1 Panzer Pioneer Company (25 LMGs, 3 PzBu and 2 80mm mortars)
1 Brüko K Bridging Column (4 LMGs)
1 (mot) Light Pioneer Column (4 LMGs)

38th Panzer Signals Battalion
Staff
1 Panzer Telephone Company (6 LMGs)
1 Panzer Radio Company (16 LMGs)
1 (mot) Light Signals Column (4 LMGs)

82nd Supply Troops
Staff
1–2/82nd (mot) (120 ton) Transportation Companies (4 LMGs ea)
3–5/82nd (mot) (90 ton) Transportation Companies (3 LMGs ea)
6/82nd Light Supply Column (4 LMGs)
82nd (mot) Supply Company (6 LMGs)

82nd Truck Maintenance Park
1/, 2/, 3/81st (mot) Maintenance Companies
1 (mot) (75 ton) Maintenance Supply Column

Administration
82nd Divisional Administration Office
82nd (mot) Bakery Company
82nd (mot) Butcher Company

Medical Troops
1/, 2/82nd (mot) Medical Companies
1/, 2/, 3/82nd Ambulance Platoons

Other
82nd (mot) Military Police Troop (2 LMGs)
82nd (mot) Field Post Office

3rd Panzer Division

Division Staff
Divisional Staff (2 LMGs)
83rd (mot) Division Mapping Detachment

6th Panzer Regiment
1st Panzer Battalion
Staff
Staff Signals Platoon
Staff Panzer Platoon
4 Panzer Companies (22 Panther PzMk V tanks ea)
1 Panzer Maintenance Company

2nd Panzer Battalion
Staff
Staff Panzer Platoon
Panzer Flak Platoon (7 37mm Flak 43)
4 Panzer Companies (22 PzMk IV tanks ea)
1 Panzer Maintenance Company

3rd Panzergrenadier Regiment
Regimental Staff
Regimental Band
Regimental Staff Company
  Signals Platoon
  Panzerjäger Platoon (3 LMGs and 3 75mm PAK 40)
  Motorcycle Platoon (6 LMGs)

1st (half-track) Battalion

3 (half-track) Panzergrenadier Companies (4 HMGs, 34 LMGs, 3 PzBu, 3 37mm PAK 36 and 2 80mm mortars ea)

1 (half-track) Heavy Panzergrenadier Company
1 Staff Platoon (2 LMGs)
1 Pioneer Platoon (9 LMGs)
1 Panzerjäger Platoon (3 LMGs and 3 50mm PAK 38)
2 Infantry Gun Sections (4 LMGs and 2 75mm leIG ea)
1 Panzerjäger Platoon (3 LMGs and 3 sPzBu 41)

2nd (mot) Battalion

3 Panzergrenadier Companies (4 HMGs, 18 LMGs, 3 PzBu and 2 80mm mortars ea)

1 Heavy Panzergrenadier Company
1 Pioneer Platoon (4 LMGs)
1 Panzerjäger Platoon (3 50mm PAK 38)
2 Infantry Gun Sections (2 75mm leIG ea)
1 Panzerjäger Platoon (3 LMGs and 3 sPzBu 41)

1 Self-Propelled Light Flak Company (12 20mm Flak and 4 LMGs)

1 Self-Propelled Infantry Gun Company (6 150mm sIG and 3 LMGs)

394th Panzergrenadier Regiment

Regimental Staff
Regimental Band
Regimental Staff Company
Signals Platoon
Panzerjäger Platoon (3 LMGs and 3 75mm PAK 40)
Motorcycle Platoon (6 LMGs)

1st (mot) Battalion

3 Panzergrenadier Companies (4 HMGs, 18 LMGs and 2 80mm mortars ea)

1 Heavy Panzergrenadier Company
1 Pioneer Platoon (4 LMGs and 6 flamethrowers)
1 Panzerjäger Platoon (3 75mm PAK 40)
2 Infantry Gun Sections (2 75mm leIG ea)
1 Mortar Platoon (6 80mm mortars)

2nd (mot) Battalion

same as 1st Battalion

1 Self-Propelled Light Flak Company (12 20mm Flak and 4 LMGs)

1 Self-Propelled Infantry Gun Company (6 150mm sIG and 3 LMGs)

543rd Panzerjäger Battalion

Staff
1 (motZ) Panzerjäger Company (12 75mm PAK 40 and 12 LMGs)
1 Self-Propelled Panzerjäger Company (14 75mm PAK 40 and 14 LMGs)

3rd Panzer Reconnaissance Battalion

Staff (15 LMGs)
1 Light Armored Car Company (16 20mm and 24 LMGs)

1 (half-track) Heavy Reconnaissance Company (2 80mm mortars, 4 HMGs, 56 LMGs and 3 37mm PAK 36)

2 Motorcycle Companies (2 80mm mortars, 3 PzBu, 4 HMGs and 18 LMGs)

1 (half-track) Heavy Company
1 Pioneer Platoon (4 LMGs)
1 Panzerjäger Platoon (3 LMGs and 3 75mm PAK 40)
1 Panzerjäger Platoon (3 LMGs and 3 sPzBu 41)
1 Light Infantry Gun Section (2 75mm leIG)
1 Light Panzer Reconnaissance Battalion Column

75th Panzer Artillery Regiment

Staff and (mot) Staff Battery (6 LMGs)
75th (mot) Observation Battery

1st Battalion

Staff and Staff Battery (2 LMGs)
3 (motZ) Batteries (4 105mm leFH and 2 LMGs ea)

2nd Battalion

same as 1st Battalion

3rd Battalion

Staff and (mot) Staff Battery (6 LMGs)
2 (motZ) Batteries (4 150mm sFH and 2 LMGs ea)
1 (motZ) Battery (4 100mm K18 and 2 LMGs)

314th Army Flak Battalion

Staff and Staff Battery
1/, 2/314th (motZ) Heavy Flak Batteries (4 88mm, 3 20mm Flak guns and 2 LMGs ea)
3/314th (motZ) Light Flak Battery (12 20mm guns and 2 LMGs)
1 Self-Propelled Battery (2 quad 20mm, 8 20mm and 2 LMGs)
1 (mot) Light (20 ton) Flak Column

83rd Feldersatz Battalion

Staff
4 Companies

39th (mot) Pioneer Battalion

Staff (2 LMGs)
2 (mot) Pioneer Companies (18 LMGs, 3 PzBu and 2 80mm mortars ea)
1 (armored) Pioneer Company (40 LMGs, 3 PzBu and 2 80mm mortars)
1 Brüko K Bridging Column (4 LMGs)
1 (mot) Light Pioneer Column (4 LMGs)

39th Panzer Signals Battalion

Staff
1 Panzer Telephone Company (6 LMGs)
1 Panzer Radio Company (16 LMGs)
1 (mot) Light Signals Column (4 LMGs)

83rd Supply Troops

Staff
4/, 5/83rd (mot) (120 ton) Transportation Companies (4 LMGs ea)
1/, 2/, 3/83rd (mot) (90 ton) Transportation Companies (3 LMGs ea)
83rd (mot) Fuel Column (2 LMGs)

83rd (mot) Supply Company (6 LMGs)

83rd Truck Maintenance Park

1/, 2/, 3/81st (mot) Maintenance Companies

1 (mot) (75 ton) Maintenance Supply Column

Administration

83rd Divisional Administration Office

83rd (mot) Bakery Company

83rd (mot) Butcher Company

Medical Troops

1/, 2/522nd (mot) Medical Companies

1/, 2/, 3/522nd Ambulance Platoons

Other

83rd (mot) Military Police Troop (2 LMGs)

83rd (mot) Field Post Office

4th Panzer Division

Division Staff

Divisional Staff (2 LMGs)

84th (mot) Division Mapping Detachment

35th Panzer Regiment

1st Panzer Battalion

Staff

Staff Signals Platoon

Panzer Flak Platoon (7 37mm Flak 43)

4 Panzer Companies (22 Panther PzMk V tanks ea)

1 Panzer Maintenance Company

3rd Panzergrenadier Regiment

Regimental Staff

Regimental Band

Regimental Staff Company

Signals Platoon

Pioneer Platoon (6 LMGs and 6 flamethrowers)

Panzerjäger Platoon (3 LMGs and 3 75mm PAK 40)

Motorcycle Platoon (6 LMGs)

1st (half-track) Battalion

3 (half-track) Panzergrenadier Companies (4 HMGs, 39 LMGs, 3 PzBu, 3 37mm PAK 36, 2 75mm guns and 2 80mm mortars ea)

1 (half-track) Heavy Panzergrenadier Company

1 Staff Platoon (2 LMGs)

1 Pioneer Platoon (13 LMGs, 1 37mm PAK 36 and 3 flamethrowers)

1 Panzerjäger Platoon (9 LMGs and 3 75mm PAK 40)

1 Infantry Gun Section (4 LMGs and 2 75mm leIG)

1 Panzerjäger Platoon (5 HMGs, 8 LMGs, and 6 75mm guns)

2nd (mot) Battalion

3 Panzergrenadier Companies (4 HMGs, 18 LMGs, 3 PzBu and 2 80mm mortars)

1 Heavy Panzergrenadier Company

1 Pioneer Platoon (4 LMGs)

1 Panzerjäger Platoon (3 LMGs and 3 50mm PAK 38)

1 Infantry Gun Section (2 LMGs and 2 75mm leIG)

1 Panzerjäger Platoon (3 LMGs and 3 sPzBu 41)

1 Self-Propelled Infantry Gun Company (6 150mm sIG and 7 LMGs)

394th Panzergrenadier Regiment

Regimental Staff

Regimental Band

Regimental Staff Company

Signals Platoon

Panzerjäger Platoon (3 LMGs and 3 75mm PAK 40)

Motorcycle Platoon (6 LMGs)

1st (mot) Battalion

3 Panzergrenadier Companies (4 HMGs, 18 LMGs, 3 PzBu and 2 80mm mortars)

1 Heavy Panzergrenadier Company

1 Pioneer Platoon (4 LMGs)

1 Panzerjäger Platoon (3 LMGs and 3 50mm PAK 38)

1 Infantry Gun Section (2 LMGs and 2 75mm leIG)

1 Panzerjäger Platoon (3 LMGs and 3 sPzBu 41)

2nd (mot) Battalion

same as 1st Battalion

1 Self-Propelled Infantry Gun Company (6 150mm sIG and 7 LMGs)

49th Panzerjäger Battalion

Staff

3 Self-Propelled Heavy Panzerjäger Companies (75mm PAK 40)

1 (motZ) Panzerjäger Company (ordered formed, not formed yet)

4th Panzer Reconnaissance Battalion

Staff (3 LMGs)

1st (half-track) Heavy Reconnaissance Company (2 80mm mortars, 4 HMGs, 56 LMGs and 3 37mm PAK 36)

2nd Light Armored Car Company (29 20mm and 29 LMGs)

1 Armored Car Platoon (6 SdKfz 234/3 with 75mm KwK and 6 LMGs)

3rd (half-track) Heavy Company

1 Pioneer Platoon (4 LMGs)

1 Panzerjäger Platoon (3 LMGs and 3 75mm PAK 40)

1 Panzerjäger Platoon (3 LMGs and 3 sPzBu 41)

1 Light Infantry Gun Section (2 75mm leIG)

4th Light Armored Car Company (18 20mm and 24 LMGs)

5th Motorcycle Company (2 80mm mortars, 3 PzBu, 4 HMGs, and 18 LMGs)
1 Light Panzer Reconnaissance Battalion Column

103rd Panzer Artillery Regiment
Staff and (mot) Staff Battery (6 LMGs)
103rd (mot) Observation Battery
1st Battalion
Staff and Staff Battery (2 LMGs)
3 (motZ) Batteries (3 105mm leFH and 2 LMGs ea)
2nd Battalion
Staff and (self-propelled) Staff Battery (6 LMGs)
2 Self-Propelled leFH Batteries (6 105mm leFH SdKfz 124 Wespe ea)
1 Self-Propelled sFH Battery (6 SdKfz 165 150mm sFH Hummel)
3rd Battalion
Staff and (mot) Staff Battery (6 LMGs)
2 (motZ) Batteries (4 150mm sFH and 2 LMGs ea)
1 (motZ) Battery (4 100mm K18 and 2 LMGs)
290th Army Flak Battalion
Staff and Staff Battery
1/, 2/290th (motZ) Heavy Flak Batteries (4 88mm, 3 20mm Flak guns and 2 LMGs ea)
3/290th Self-Propelled Flak Battery (12 20mm guns and 2 LMGs)
4/290th Self-Propelled Battery (12 20mm and 2 LMGs)
1 (mot) Light (20 ton) Flak Column
84th Feldersatz Battalion
Staff
2 Companies
79th (mot) Pioneer Battalion
Staff (2 LMGs)

2 (mot) Pioneer Companies (18 LMGs, 3 PzBu and 2 80mm mortars ea)
1 (armored) Pioneer Company (25 LMGs, 3 PzBu and 2 80mm mortars)
1 Brüko K Bridging Column (4 LMGs)
1 (mot) Light Pioneer Column (4 LMGs)
79th Panzer Signals Battalion
Staff
1 Panzer Telephone Company (6 LMGs)
1 Panzer Radio Company (16 LMGs)
1 (mot) Light Signals Column (4 LMGs)
84th Supply Troops
Staff
1/, 2/, 3/84th (mot) (120 ton) Transportation Companies (3 LMGs ea)
4/, 5/84th (mot) (90 ton) Transportation Companies (4 LMGs ea)
84th (mot) Supply Company (6 LMGs)
84th Truck Maintenance Park
1/, 2/, 3/81st (mot) Maintenance Companies
1 (mot) (75 ton) Maintenance Supply Column
Administration
84th Divisional Administration Office
84th (mot) Bakery Company
84th (mot) Butcher Company
Medical Troops
1/, 2/522nd (mot) Medical Companies
1/, 2/, 3/522nd Ambulance Platoons
Other
84th (mot) Military Police Troop (2 LMGs)
84th (mot) Field Post Office

5th Panzer Division

Division Staff
Divisional Staff (2 LMGs)
85th (mot) Division Mapping Detachment
31st Panzer Regiment
1st Panzer Battalion
detached to army, equipped with Panther PzMkV tanks
2nd Panzer Battalion
Staff
Staff Signals Platoon
Panzer Flak Platoon (7 37mm Flak 43)
4 Panzer Companies (22 PzMk IV tanks ea)
1 Panzer Maintenance Company
13th Panzergrenadier Regiment
Regimental Staff
Regimental Band
Regimental Staff Company
Signals Platoon

Panzerjäger Platoon (3 LMGs and 3 75mm PAK 40)
Motorcycle Platoon (6 LMGs)
1st (mot) Battalion
3 Panzergrenadier Companies (4 HMGs, 18 LMGs, 3 PzBu and 2 80mm mortars ea)
1 Heavy Panzergrenadier Company
1 Pioneer Platoon (4 LMGs)
1 Panzerjäger Platoon (3 LMGs and 3 50mm PAK 38)
2 Infantry Gun Sections (2 75mm leIG ea)
1 Panzerjäger Platoon (3 LMGs and 3 sPzBu 41)
2nd (mot) Battalion
same as 1st Battalion
1 Self-Propelled Infantry Gun Company (6 150mm sIG and 7 LMGs)
14th Panzergrenadier Regiment
Regimental Staff
Regimental Band

Regimental Staff Company

Signals Platoon

Pioneer Platoon (6 LMGs and 6 flamethrowers)

Panzerjäger Platoon (3 LMGs and 3 75mm PAK 40)

Motorcycle Platoon (6 LMGs)

1st (half-track) Battalion

3 (half-track) Panzergrenadier Companies (4 HMGs, 39 LMGs, 3 PzBu, 3 37mm PAK 36, 2 80mm mortars and 2 75mm guns ea)

1 (half-track) Heavy Panzergrenadier Company

1 Staff Platoon

1 Pioneer Platoon (13 LMGs, 1 37mm PAK 36 and 6 flamethrowers)

1 Panzerjäger Platoon (9 LMGs and 3 75mm PAK 40)

1 Infantry Gun Section (4 LMGs and 2 75mm leIG)

1 Panzergrenadier Platoon (5 HMGs, 8 LMGs, and 6 75mm guns)

2nd (mot) Battalion

3 Panzergrenadier Companies (4 HMGs, 18 LMGs, 3 PzBu and 2 80mm mortars ea)

1 Heavy Panzergrenadier Company

1 Pioneer Platoon (4 LMGs)

1 Panzerjäger Platoon (3 LMGs and 3 50mm PAK 38)

2 Infantry Gun Sections (2 75mm leIG ea)

1 Panzerjäger Platoon (3 LMGs and 3 sPzBu 41)

1 Self-Propelled Infantry Gun Company (6 150mm sIG and 7 LMGs)

53rd Panzerjäger Battalion

Staff

1 Self-Propelled Heavy Panzerjäger Company (equipment unknown)

1 (motZ) Heavy Panzerjäger Company (equipment unknown)

5th Panzer Reconnaissance Battalion

Staff (3 LMGs)

1 Light Armored Car Company (24 20mm and 18 LMGs)

1 (half-track) Reconnaissance Company (2 80mm mortars, 3 PzBu, 4 HMGs and 56 LMGs)

1 (mot) Heavy Reconnaissance Company (2 80mm mortars, 3 PzBu, 4 HMGs and 18 LMGs)

1 Motorcycle Company (2 80mm mortars, 3 PzBu, 4 HMGs and 18 LMGs)

1 (mot) Heavy Company

1 Pioneer Platoon (13 LMGs, 1 20mm and 6 flamethrowers)

1 Panzerjäger Platoon (3 LMGs and 3 75mm PAK 40)

1 Panzerjäger Platoon (3 LMGs and 3 sPzBu 41)

1 Light Infantry Gun Section (4 LMGs and 2 75mm leIG)

1 Light Panzer Reconnaissance Battalion Column

116th Panzer Artillery Regiment

Staff and (mot) Staff Battery (6 LMGs)

116th (motZ) (mot) Observation Battery (2 LMGs)

1st Battalion

Staff and (self-propelled) Staff Battery (6 LMGs)

2 Self-Propelled leFH Batteries (6 105mm leFH SdKfz 124 Wespe ea)

1 Self-Propelled sFH Battery (6 150mm sFH SdKfz 165 Hummel)

2nd Battalion

Staff and Staff Battery (2 LMGs)

3 (motZ) Batteries (4 105mm leFH and 2 LMGs ea)

3rd Battalion

Staff and (mot) Staff Battery (6 LMGs)

2 (motZ) Batteries (4 150mm sFH and 2 LMGs ea)

1 (motZ) Battery (4 100mm K18 and 2 LMGs)

288th Army Flak Battalion

Staff and Staff Battery

1/, 2/288th (motZ) Heavy Flak Batteries (4 88mm, 3 20mm Flak guns and 2 LMGs ea)

4/288th Self-Propelled Light Battery (2 quad 20mm Flak guns, 8 20mm guns and 2 LMGs)

1 (mot) Light (20 ton) Flak Column

85th Feldersatz Battalion

Staff

4 Companies

89th Panzer Pioneer Battalion

Staff (2 LMGs)

2 (mot) Pioneer Companies (18 LMGs, 3 PzBu and 2 80mm mortars)

1 Panzer Pioneer Company (25 LMGs, 3 PzBu and 2 80mm mortars)

89th Brüko K Bridging Column (4 LMGs)

1 (mot) Light Pioneer Column (4 LMGs)

77th Panzer Signals Battalion

Staff

1 Panzer Telephone Company (6 LMGs)

1 Panzer Radio Company (16 LMGs)

1 (mot) Light Signals Column (4 LMGs)

85th Supply Troops

Staff

3/, 6/85th (mot) (120 ton) Transportation Companies (4 LMGs ea)

1/, 2/, 4/, 5//85th (mot) (90 ton) Transportation Companies (3 LMGs ea)

85th (mot) Supply Company (6 LMGs)

85th Truck Maintenance Park

1/, 2/, 3/85th (mot) Maintenance Companies

1 (mot) (75 ton) Maintenance Supply Column

Administration

85th Divisional Administration Office

85th (mot) Bakery Company

85th (mot) Butcher Company

Medical Troops

1/, 2/85th (mot) Medical Companies

1/, 2/, 3/85th Ambulance Platoons

Other

85th (mot) Military Police Troop (2 LMGs)

85th (mot) Field Post Office

6th Panzer Division

Division Staff
Divisional Staff (2 LMGs)
57th (mot) Division Mapping Detachment
11th Panzer Regiment
1st Panzer Battalion
detached to army, equipped with Panther PzMkV tanks
2nd Panzer Battalion
Staff
Staff Signals Platoon
Panzer Flak Platoon (7 37mm Flak 43)
4 Panzer Companies (22 PzMk IV tanks ea)
1 Panzer Maintenance Company
2nd Panzergrenadier Regiment
Regimental Staff
Regimental Band
Regimental Staff Company
Signals Platoon
Panzerjäger Platoon (3 LMGs and 3 75mm PAK 40)
Motorcycle Platoon (6 LMGs)
1st (mot) Battalion
3 Panzergrenadier Companies (4 HMGs, 18 LMGs, 3 PzBu and 2 80mm mortars ea)
1 Heavy Panzergrenadier Company
1 Pioneer Platoon (4 LMGs)
1 Panzerjäger Platoon (3 LMGs and 3 50mm PAK 38)
2 Infantry Gun Sections (2 75mm leIG ea)
1 Panzerjäger Platoon (3 LMGs and 3 sPzBu 41)
2nd (mot) Battalion
same as 1st Battalion
1 Self-Propelled Infantry Gun Company (6 150mm sIG and 7 LMGs)
114th Panzergrenadier Regiment
Regimental Staff
Regimental Band
Regimental Staff Company
Signals Platoon
Panzerjäger Platoon (3 LMGs and 3 50mm PAK 38)
Motorcycle Platoon (6 LMGs)
1st (half-track) Battalion
3 Panzergrenadier Companies (4 HMGs, 18 LMGs, 3 PzBu and 2 80mm mortars ea)
1 Heavy Panzergrenadier Company
1 Pioneer Platoon (4 LMGs)
1 Panzerjäger Platoon (3 50mm PAK 38)
2 Infantry Gun Sections (2 75mm leIG ea)
1 Panzerjäger Platoon (3 LMGs and 3 sPzBu 41)
2nd (mot) Battalion
3 (half-track) Panzergrenadier Companies (4 HMGs, 34 LMGs, 3 PzBu, 3 37mm PAK 36 and 2 80mm mortars ea)
1 (half-track) Heavy Panzergrenadier Company

1 Pioneer Platoon (9 LMGs)
1 Panzerjäger Platoon (3 LMGs and 3 50mm PAK 38)
2 Infantry Gun Sections (4 LMGs and 2 75mm leIG ea)
1 Panzerjäger Platoon (3 LMGs and 3 sPzBu 41)
1 Self-Propelled Infantry Gun Company (6 150mm sIG and 7 LMGs)
41st Panzerjäger Battalion
Staff
1 (motZ) Heavy Panzerjäger Company (75mm PAK 40)
1 Self-Propelled Heavy Panzerjäger Company (75mm PAK 40)
6th Panzer Reconnaissance Battalion
Staff (15 LMGs)
Heavy Platoon (6 SdKfz 234/3 with 75mm KwK and 6 LMGs)
1 Light Armored Car Company (18 20mm and 24 LMGs)
1 (half-track) Heavy Reconnaissance Company (2 80mm mortars, 4 HMGs, 56 LMGs and 3 37mm PAK 36)
2 Motorcycle Companies (2 80mm mortars, 3 PzBu, 4 HMGs, and 18 LMGs ea)
1 (mot) Heavy Company
1 Pioneer Platoon (4 LMGs)
1 Panzerjäger Platoon (3 LMGs and 3 75mm PAK 40)
1 Panzerjäger Platoon (3 LMGs and 3 sPzBu 41)
2 Light Infantry Gun Sections (2 75mm leIG ea)
1 Light Panzer Reconnaissance Battalion Column
76th Panzer Artillery Regiment
Staff and (mot) Staff Battery (6 LMGs)
76th (motZ) (mot) Observation Battery (2 LMGs)
1st Battalion
Staff and Staff Battery (2 LMGs)
3 (motZ) Batteries (3 105mm leFH and 2 LMGs ea)
2nd Battalion
same as 1st Battalion
3rd Battalion
Staff and (mot) Staff Battery (6 LMGs)
2 (motZ) Batteries (3 150mm sFH and 2 LMGs ea)
1 (motZ) Battery (3 100mm K18 and 2 LMGs)
298th Army Flak Battalion
Staff and Staff Battery
1/, 2/298th (motZ) Heavy Flak Batteries (4 88mm, 3 20mm Flak guns and 2 LMGs ea)
3/298th (motZ) Light Flak Battery (12 20mm guns and 2 LMGs)
4/298th Self-Propelled Light Battery (2 quad 20mm Flak guns, 8 20mm guns and 2 LMGs)
1 (mot) Light (48 ton) Flak Column
57th Feldersatz Battalion
organization unknown
57th Panzer Pioneer Battalion
Staff (2 LMGs)

2 (mot) Pioneer Companies (18 LMGs, 3 PzBu and 2 80mm mortars)

1 Panzer Pioneer Company (25 LMGs, 3 PzBu and 2 80mm mortars)

1 Brüko K Bridging Column (4 LMGs)

1 (mot) Light Pioneer Column (4 LMGs)

82nd Panzer Signals Battalion
Staff

1 Panzer Telephone Company (6 LMGs)

1 Panzer Radio Company (16 LMGs)

1 (mot) Light Signals Column (4 LMGs)

57th Supply Troops
Staff

2/, 5/57th (mot) (90 ton) Transportation Companies (4 LMGs ea)

1/, 3/, 4/57th (mot) (120 ton) Transportation Companies (3 LMGs ea)

57th Heavy Fuel Column (2 LMGs)

81st (mot) Supply Company (6 LMGs)

57th Truck Maintenance Park
1/, 2/, 3/57th (mot) Maintenance Companies

1 (mot) (75 ton) Maintenance Supply Column

Administration
57th Divisional Administration Office

57th (mot) Bakery Company

57th (mot) Butcher Company

Medical Troops
1/, 2/57th (mot) Medical Companies

1/, 2/, 3/57th Ambulance Platoons

Other
57th (mot) Military Police Troop (2 LMGs)

57th (mot) Field Post Office

7th Panzer Division

Division Staff
Divisional Staff (2 LMGs)

58th (mot) Division Mapping Detachment

25th Panzer Regiment
Regimental Staff

Regimental Staff Panzer Platoon

Panzer Signals Platoon

Regimental Band

1st Panzer Battalion
detached to army, equipped with Panther PzMkV tanks

2nd Panzer Battalion
Staff

Staff Signals Platoon

Panzer Flak Platoon (7 37mm Flak 43)

4 Panzer Companies (22 PzMk IV tanks ea)

1 Panzer Maintenance Company

6th Panzergrenadier Regiment
Regimental Staff

Regimental Band

Regimental Staff Company

Signals Platoon

Panzerjäger Platoon (3 LMGs and 3 75mm PAK 40)

Motorcycle Platoon (6 LMGs)

1st (mot) Battalion
3 Panzergrenadier Companies (4 HMGs, 18 LMGs, 3 PzBu and 2 80mm mortars ea)

1 Heavy Panzergrenadier Company

1 Pioneer Platoon (4 LMGs)

1 Panzerjäger Platoon (3 LMGs and 3 50mm PAK 38)

1 Panzerjäger Platoon (3 LMGs and 3 sPzBu 41)

2 Infantry Gun Sections (2 75mm leIG ea)

2nd (half-track) Battalion
3 (half-track) Panzergrenadier Companies (4 HMGs, 34 LMGs, 3 PzBu, 3 37mm PAK 36 and 2 80mm mortars ea)

1 (half-track) Heavy Panzergrenadier Company

1 Pioneer Platoon (9 LMGs and 6 flamethrowers)

1 Panzerjäger Platoon (3 LMGs, 3 50mm PAK 38 and 6 75mm guns)

2 Infantry Gun Sections (4 LMGs 2 75mm leIG ea)

1 Panzerjäger Platoon (3 LMGs and 3 sPzBu 41)

1 Self-Propelled Infantry Gun Company (6 150mm sIG and 7 LMGs)

7th Panzergrenadier Regiment
Regimental Staff

Regimental Band

Regimental Staff Company

Signals Platoon

Panzerjäger Platoon (3 LMGs and 3 75mm PAK 40)

Motorcycle Platoon (6 LMGs)

1st (mot) Battalion
same as 1/6th Panzergrenadier Regiment

2nd (mot) Battalion
same as 1/6th Panzergrenadier Regiment

1 Self-Propelled Infantry Gun Company (6 150mm sIG and 7 LMGs)

42nd Panzerjäger Battalion
Staff

1 Self-Propelled Heavy Panzerjäger Company (14 75mm PAK 40 and 14 LMGs)

1 (motZ) Heavy Panzerjäger Company (equipment unknown)

7th Panzer Reconnaissance Battalion
Staff (3 LMGs)

Heavy Platoon (6 SdKfz 234/3 with 75mm KwK and 6 LMGs)

1 Light Armored Car Company (18 20mm and 24 LMGs)

2 (half-track) Heavy Reconnaissance Company (2 80mm mortars, 4 HMGs, 56 LMGs and 3 37mm PAK 36)

2 Motorcycle Companies (2 80mm mortars, 3 PzBu, 4 HMGs and 18 LMGs)

1 (half-track) Heavy Company

1 Pioneer Platoon (4 LMGs)

1 Panzerjäger Platoon (3 LMGs and 3 75mm PAK 40)

1 Panzerjäger Platoon (3 LMGs and 3 sPzBu 41)

2 Light Infantry Gun Sections (2 75mm leIG ea)

1 Light Panzer Reconnaissance Battalion Column

78th Panzer Artillery Regiment

Staff and (mot) Staff Battery (6 LMGs)

78th (mot) Observation Battery (2 LMGs)

1st Battalion

Staff and (self-propelled) Staff Battery (6 LMGs)

2 Self-Propelled leFH Batteries (6 105mm leFH SdKfz 124 Wespe ea)

1 Self-Propelled sFH Battery (6 150mm sFH SdKfz 165 Hummel)

2nd Battalion

Staff and Staff Battery (2 LMGs)

3 (motZ) Batteries (4 105mm leFH and 2 LMGs ea)

3rd Battalion

Staff and (mot) Staff Battery (6 LMGs)

2 (motZ) Batteries (4 150mm sFH and 2 LMGs ea)

1 (motZ) Battery (4 100mm K18 and 2 LMGs)

296th Army Flak Battalion

Staff and Staff Battery

1/, 2/296th (motZ) Heavy Flak Batteries (4 88mm, 3 20mm Flak guns and 2 LMGs ea)

3/296th (motZ) Light Flak Battery (12 20mm guns and 2 LMGs)

4/296th Self-Propelled Light Battery (2 quad 20mm Flak guns, 8 20mm guns and 2 LMGs)

1 (mot) Light (20 ton) Flak Column

58th Feldersatz Battalion

Staff

5 Companies

58th Panzer Pioneer Battalion

Staff (2 LMGs)

2 Panzer Pioneer Companies (25 LMGs, 3 PzBu and 2 80mm mortars)

1 (mot) Pioneer Company (18 LMGs, 3 PzBu and 2 80mm mortars)

1 Brüko K Bridging Column (3 LMGs)

1 (mot) Light Pioneer Column (2 LMGs)

83rd Panzer Signals Battalion

Staff

1 Panzer Telephone Company (6 LMGs)

1 Panzer Radio Company (16 LMGs)

1 (mot) Light Signals Column (4 LMGs)

58th Supply Troops

Staff

1st–6th/58th (mot) (90 ton) Transportation Companies (3 LMGs ea)

58th (mot) Supply Company (6 LMGs)

58th Truck Maintenance Park

1/, 2/, 3/58th (mot) Maintenance Companies

1 (mot) (75 ton) Maintenance Supply Column

Administration

58th Divisional Administration Office

58th (mot) Bakery Company

58th (mot) Butcher Company

Medical Troops

1/, 2/58th (mot) Medical Companies

1/, 2/, 3/58th Ambulance Platoons

Other

58th (mot) Military Police Troop (2 LMGs)

58th (mot) Field Post Office

8th Panzer Division

Division Staff

Divisional Staff (2 LMGs)

59th (mot) Division Mapping Detachment

1/10th Panzer Regiment

1st Panzer Battalion

Staff

Staff Signals Platoon

Panzer Flak Platoon (7 37mm Flak 43)

4 Panzer Companies (22 PzMk IV tanks ea)

1 Panzer Maintenance Company

8th Panzergrenadier Regiment

Regimental Staff

Regimental Band

Regimental Staff Company

Signals Platoon

Panzerjäger Platoon (3 LMGs and 3 75mm PAK 40)

Motorcycle Platoon (6 LMGs)

1st (mot) Battalion

3 Panzergrenadier Companies (4 HMGs, 18 LMGs, 3 PzBu and 2 80mm mortars ea)

1 Heavy Panzergrenadier Company

1 Pioneer Platoon (4 LMGs)

1 Panzerjäger Platoon (3 LMGs and 3 50mm PAK 38)

2 Infantry Gun Sections (2 75mm leIG ea)
1 Panzerjäger Platoon (3 LMGs and 3 sPzBu 41)

2nd (mot) Battalion

same as 1st Battalion

1 (motZ) Infantry Gun Company (4 150mm sIG and 7 LMGs)

28th Panzergrenadier Regiment

same as 8th Panzergrenadier Regiment

43rd Panzerjäger Battalion

Staff

2 Self-Propelled Heavy Panzerjäger Company (75mm PAK 40)

8th Panzer Reconnaissance Battalion

Staff (15 LMGs)

1 Light Armored Car Company (18 20mm and 24 LMGs)

2 Motorcycle Companies (2 80mm mortars, 3 PzBu, 4 HMGs and 18 LMGs ea)

1 (half-track) Heavy Reconnaissance Company (2 80mm mortars, 4 HMGs, 56 LMGs and 3 37mm PAK 36)

1 (mot) Heavy Company

  1 Pioneer Platoon (4 LMGs)

  1 Panzerjäger Platoon (3 LMGs and 3 75mm PAK 40)

  1 Panzerjäger Platoon (3 LMGs and 3 sPzBu 41)

  1 Light Infantry Gun Section (2 75mm leIG)

1 Light Panzer Reconnaissance Battalion Column

80th Panzer Artillery Regiment

Staff and (mot) Staff Battery (6 LMGs)

80th (mot) Observation Battery (2 LMGs)

1st Battalion

Staff and Staff Battery (2 LMGs)

3 (motZ) Batteries (3 105mm leFH and 2 LMGs ea)

2nd Battalion

same as 1st Battalion

3rd Battalion

Staff and (mot) Staff Battery (6 LMGs)

2 (motZ) Batteries (3 150mm sFH and 2 LMGs ea)

1 (motZ) Battery (3 100mm K18 and 2 LMGs)

286th Army Flak Battalion

Staff and Staff Battery

1/, 2/286th (motZ) Heavy Flak Batteries (4 88mm, 3 20mm Flak guns and 2 LMGs ea)

3/286th (motZ) Light Flak Battery (12 20mm guns and 2 LMGs)

4/286th Self-Propelled Light Battery (2 quad 20mm Flak guns, 8 20mm guns and 2 LMGs)

1 (mot) Light (48 ton) Flak Column

59th Ost Company

(organization unknown)

59th Panzer Pioneer Battalion

Staff (2 LMGs)

2 (mot) Pioneer Companies (18 LMGs, 3 PzBu and 2 80mm mortars)

1 Panzer Pioneer Company (25 LMGs, 3 PzBu and 2 80mm mortars)

1 Brüko K Bridging Column (3 LMGs)

1 (mot) Light Pioneer Column (3 LMGs)

84th Panzer Signals Battalion

Staff

1 Panzer Telephone Company (6 LMGs)

1 Panzer Radio Company (16 LMGs)

1 (mot) Light Signals Column (4 LMGs)

59th Supply Troops

Staff

1/, 2/, 3/59th (mot) (90 ton) Transportation Companies (3 LMGs ea)

4/, 5//59th (mot) (120 ton) Transportation Companies (4 LMGs ea)

59th (mot) Supply Company (6 LMGs)

59th Truck Maintenance Park

1/, 2/, 3/59th (mot) Maintenance Companies

1 (mot) (75 ton) Maintenance Supply Column

Administration

59th Divisional Administration Office

59th (mot) Bakery Company

59th (mot) Butcher Company

Medical Troops

1/, 2/59th (mot) Medical Companies

1/, 2/, 3/59th Ambulance Platoons

Other

59th (mot) Military Police Troop (2 LMGs)

59th (mot) Field Post Office

9th Panzer Division

Division Staff

Divisional Staff (2 LMGs)

60th (mot) Division Mapping Detachment

33rd Panzer Regiment

Regimental Staff

Regimental Staff Panzer Platoon

Panzer Signals Platoon

Regimental Band

1st Panzer Battalion

Staff

Staff Signals Platoon

Panzer Flak Platoon (7 37mm Flak 43)

4 Panzer Companies (22 PzMk IV tanks ea)

1 Panzer Maintenance Company

2/33rd Panzer Regiment

detached to army as 51st Panzer Battalion (Panther PzMk V tanks)

3/33rd Panzer Regiment

detached to army as 506th Panzer Battalion (Tiger PzMk VI tanks)

10th Panzergrenadier Regiment

Regimental Staff

Regimental Band

Regimental Staff Company

Signals Platoon

Panzerjäger Platoon (3 LMGs and 3 75mm PAK 40)

Motorcycle Platoon (6 LMGs)

1st (half-track) Battalion

3 (half-track) Panzergrenadier Companies (4 HMGs, 34 LMGs, 3 PzBu, 3 37mm PAK 36 and 2 80mm mortars ea)

1 (half-track) Heavy Panzergrenadier Company

1 Pioneer Platoon (9 LMGs and 6 flamethrowers)

1 Panzerjäger Platoon (3 LMGs, 3 50mm PAK 38, and 6 75mm guns)

2 Infantry Gun Sections (4 LMGs 2 75mm leIG ea)

1 Panzerjäger Platoon (3 LMGs and 3 sPzBu 41)

2nd (mot) Battalion

3 Panzergrenadier Companies (4 HMGs, 18 LMGs, 3 PzBu and 2 80mm mortars ea)

1 Heavy Panzergrenadier Company

1 Pioneer Platoon (4 LMGs)

1 Panzerjäger Platoon (3 LMGs and 3 50mm PAK 38)

1 Panzerjäger Platoon (3 LMGs and 3 sPzBu 41)

2 Infantry Gun Sections (2 75mm leIG ea)

1 Self-Propelled Infantry Gun Company (6 150mm sIG and 7 LMGs)

1 Self-Propelled Flak Company (12 20mm and 4 LMGs)

7th Panzergrenadier Regiment

Regimental Staff

Regimental Band

Regimental Staff Company

Signals Platoon

Panzerjäger Platoon (3 LMGs and 3 75mm PAK 40)

Motorcycle Platoon (6 LMGs)

1st (mot) Battalion

same as 2/10th Panzergrenadier Regiment

2nd (mot) Battalion

same as 2/10th Panzergrenadier Regiment

1 Self-Propelled Infantry Gun Company (6 150mm sIG and 7 LMGs)

1 Self-Propelled Flak Company (12 20mm and 4 LMGs)

50th Panzerjäger Battalion

Staff

2 Self-Propelled Heavy Panzerjäger Company (75mm PAK 40)

9th Panzer Reconnaissance Battalion

Staff (3 LMGs)

1st Heavy Armored Car Platoon (6 SdKfz 234/3 with 75mm KwK and 6 LMGs)

2nd Light Armored Car Company (29 Luchs SdKfz 123 tanks)

3rd (half-track) Heavy Reconnaissance Company (2 80mm mortars, 4 HMGs, 56 LMGs and 3 37mm PAK 36)

4th (half-track) Heavy Reconnaissance Company (2 80mm mortars, 4 HMGs, 56 LMGs and 3 37mm PAK 36)

5th (half-track) Heavy Reconnaissance Company

1 Pioneer Platoon (4 LMGs)

1 Panzerjäger Platoon (3 LMGs and 3 75mm PAK 40)

1 Gun Platoon (8 LMGs and 6 75mm guns)

1 Light Infantry Gun Section (2 75mm leIG)

1 Light Panzer Reconnaissance Battalion Column

102nd Panzer Artillery Regiment

Staff and (mot) Staff Battery (6 LMGs)

102nd (mot) Observation Battery (2 LMGs)

1st Battalion

Staff and Staff Battery (2 LMGs)

3 (motZ) Batteries (4 105mm leFH and 2 LMGs ea)

2nd Battalion

Staff and (self-propelled) Staff Battery (2 LMGs)

2 Self-Propelled leFH Batteries (6 105mm leFH SdKfz 124 Wespe ea)

1 Self-Propelled sFH Battery (6 150mm sFH SdKfz 165 Hummel)

3rd Battalion

Staff and (mot) Staff Battery (2 LMGs)

2 (motZ) Batteries (4 150mm sFH and 2 LMGs ea)

1 (motZ) Battery (4 100mm K18 and 2 LMGs)

287th Army Flak Battalion

Staff and Staff Battery

1/, 2/287th (motZ) Heavy Flak Batteries (4 88mm, 3 20mm Flak guns and 2 LMGs ea)

3/287th (motZ) Light Flak Battery (12 20mm guns and 2 LMGs)

4/287th Self-Propelled Light Battery (2 quad 20mm Flak guns, 8 20mm guns and 2 LMGs)

1 (mot) Light (20 ton) Flak Column

60th Feldersatz Battalion

organization unknown

86th Panzer Pioneer Battalion

Staff (2 LMGs)

1 Panzer Pioneer Company (25 LMGs, 3 PzBu and 2 80mm mortars)

2 (mot) Pioneer Companies (18 LMGs, 3 PzBu and 2 80mm mortars)

1 Brüko K Bridging Column (3 LMGs)

1 (mot) Light Pioneer Column (2 LMGs)

85th Panzer Signals Battalion
Staff
1 Panzer Telephone Company (6 LMGs)
1 Panzer Radio Company (16 LMGs)
1 (mot) Light Signals Column (4 LMGs)

60th Supply Troops
Staff
1st–3rd/60th (mot) (120 ton) Transportation Companies (4 LMGs ea)
4/, 5/60th (mot) (90 ton) Transportation Companies (3 LMGs ea)
6/60th (60 ton) Transportation Company (6 LMGs)
60th (mot) Supply Company (6 LMGs)

60th Truck Maintenance Park
1/, 2/, 3/60th (mot) Maintenance Companies
1 (mot) (75 ton) Maintenance Supply Column

Administration
60th Divisional Administration Office
60th (mot) Bakery Company
60th (mot) Butcher Company

Medical Troops
1/, 2/60th (mot) Medical Companies
1/, 2/, 3/60th Ambulance Platoons

Other
60th (mot) Military Police Troop (2 LMGs)
60th (mot) Field Post Office

11th Panzer Division

Division Staff
Divisional Staff (2 LMGs)
61st (mot) Division Mapping Detachment

15th Panzer Regiment
Regimental Staff
Regimental Staff Panzer Platoon
Panzer Signals Platoon
Regimental Band

1st Panzer Battalion
Staff
Staff Signals Platoon
Staff Panzer Platoon
4 Panzer Companies (22 PzMk V Panther Tanks ea)
1 Panzer Maintenance Company

2nd Panzer Battalion
Staff
Staff Signals Platoon
Panzer Flak Platoon (7 37mm Flak 43)
4 Panzer Companies (22 PzMk IV Tanks ea)
1 Panzer Maintenance Company

110th Panzergrenadier Regiment
Regimental Staff
Regimental Band
Regimental Staff Company
Signals Platoon
Panzer Pioneer Platoon (6 LMGs and 6 flame-throwers)
Panzerjäger Platoon (3 LMGs and 3 75mm PAK 40)
Motorcycle Platoon (6 LMGs)

1st (half-track) Battalion
3 (half-track) Panzergrenadier Companies (4 HMGs, 34 LMGs, 3 PzBu, 3 37mm PAK 36 and 2 80mm mortars ea)
1 (half-track) Heavy Panzergrenadier Company
1 Pioneer Platoon (9 LMGs)

1 Panzerjäger Platoon (3 LMGs, 3 50mm PAK 38 and 6 75mm guns)
2 Infantry Gun Sections (4 LMGs and 2 75mm leIG ea)
1 Panzerjäger Platoon (3 LMGs and 3 sPzBu 41)

2nd (mot) Battalion
3 Panzergrenadier Companies (4 HMGs, 18 LMGs, 3 Pzbu and 2 80mm mortars ea)
1 Heavy Panzergrenadier Company
1 Pioneer Platoon (4 LMGs)
1 Panzerjäger Platoon (3 LMGs and 3 50mm PAK 38)
1 Panzerjäger Platoon (3 LMGs and 3 sPzBu 41)
2 Infantry Gun Sections (2 75mm leIG ea)

1 Self-Propelled Infantry Gun Company (6 150mm sIG and 7 LMGs)

1 Self-Propelled Flak Company (12 20mm and 4 LMGs)

111th Panzergrenadier Regiment
Regimental Staff
Regimental Band
Regimental Staff Company
Signals Platoon
Panzerjäger Platoon (3 LMGs and 3 75mm PAK 40)
Motorcycle Platoon (6 LMGs)

1st (mot) Battalion
same as 1/110th Panzergrenadier Regiment

2nd (mot) Battalion
same as 1/110th Panzergrenadier Regiment

1 Self-Propelled Infantry Gun Company (6 150mm sIG and 7 LMGs)

1 Self-Propelled Flak Company (12 20mm and 4 LMGs)

61st Panzerjäger Battalion
Staff

1 Self-Propelled Heavy Panzerjäger Company (75mm PAK 40)
1 (motZ) Heavy Panzerjäger Company (75mm PAK 40)

11th Panzer Reconnaissance Battalion
Staff (3 LMGs)
1 Light Armored Car Company (24 LMGs and 18 20mm guns)
1 (half-track) Heavy Reconnaissance Company (2 80mm mortars, 4 HMGs, 56 LMGs and 3 37mm PAK 36)
1 (half-track) Heavy Reconnaissance Company (2 80mm mortars, 4 HMGs, 56 LMGs and 3 37mm PAK 36)
2 Motorcycle Companies (2 80mm mortars, 3 PzBu, 4 HMGs and 18 LMGs ea)
1 (mot) Heavy Reconnaissance Company
1 Pioneer Platoon (4 LMGs)
1 Panzerjäger Platoon (3 LMGs and 3 75mm PAK 40)
1 Panzerjäger Platoon (3 LMGs and 3 sPzBu 41)
1 Light Infantry Gun Section (2 75mm leIG)
1 Light Panzer Reconnaissance Battalion Column

119th Panzer Artillery Regiment
Staff and (mot) Staff Battery (2 LMGs)
119th (mot) Observation Battery (2 LMGs)
1st Battalion
Staff and (self-propelled) Staff Battery (6 LMGs)
2 Self-Propelled leFH Batteries (6 105mm leFH SdKfz 124 Wespe ea)
1 Self-Propelled sFH Battery (6 150mm sFH SdKfz 165 Hummel)
2nd Battalion
Staff and Staff Battery (2 LMGs)
3 (motZ) Batteries (4 105mm leFH and 2 LMGs ea)
3rd Battalion
Staff and (mot) Staff Battery (2 LMGs)
2 (motZ) Batteries (4 150mm sFH and 2 LMGs ea)
1 (motZ) Battery (4 100mm K18 and 2 LMGs)
277th Army Flak Battalion
Staff and Staff Battery
1/, 2/277th (motZ) Heavy Flak Batteries (4 88mm, 3 20mm Flak guns and 2 LMGs ea)

3/277th (motZ) Light Flak Battery (12 20mm guns and 2 LMGs)
4/277th Self-Propelled Light Battery (2 quad 20mm Flak guns, 8 20mm guns and 2 LMGs)
1 (mot) Light (20 ton) Flak Column

61st Feldersatz Battalion
5 companies
209th Panzer Pioneer Battalion
Staff (2 LMGs)
1 Panzer Pioneer Company (25 LMGs, 3 PzBu and 2 80mm mortars)
2 (mot) Pioneer Companies (18 LMGs, 3 PzBu and 2 80mm mortars)
1 Brüko K Bridging Column (3 LMGs)
1 (mot) Light Pioneer Column (2 LMGs)
89th Panzer Signals Battalion
Staff
1 Panzer Telephone Company (6 LMGs)
1 Panzer Radio Company (16 LMGs)
1 (mot) Light Signals Column (4 LMGs)
61st Supply Troops
Staff
1–6/61st (mot) (90 ton) Transportation Companies (3 LMGs ea)
61st (mot) Light Supply Column (2 LMGs)
61st (mot) Supply Company (6 LMGs)
61st Truck Maintenance Park
1/, 2/, 3/61st (mot) Maintenance Companies
1 (mot) (75 ton) Maintenance Supply Column
Administration
61st Divisional Administration Office
61st (mot) Bakery Company
61st (mot) Butcher Company
Medical Troops
1/, 2/61st (mot) Medical Companies
1/, 2/, 3/61st Ambulance Platoons
Other
61st (mot) Military Police Troop (2 LMGs)
61st (mot) Field Post Office

12th Panzer Division

Division Staff
Divisional Staff (2 LMGs)
2nd (mot) Division Mapping Detachment
29th Panzer Regiment
Regimental Staff
Regimental Staff Panzer Platoon
Panzer Signals Platoon
Regimental Band
1st Panzer Battalion
detached to army as independent panther battalion

2nd Panzer Battalion
Staff
Staff Signals Platoon
Panzer Flak Platoon (7 37mm Flak 43)
4 Panzer Companies (22 PzMk IV tanks ea)
1 Panzer Maintenance Company
5th Panzergrenadier Regiment
Regimental Staff
Regimental Band
Regimental Staff Company

Signals Platoon
Panzerjäger Platoon (3 LMGs and 3 75mm PAK 40)
Motorcycle Platoon (6 LMGs)

1st (mot) Battalion
3 Panzergrenadier Companies (4 HMGs, 18 LMGs, 3 PzBu and 2 80mm mortars ea)
1 Heavy Panzergrenadier Company
1 Pioneer Platoon (4 LMGs)
1 Panzerjäger Platoon (3 LMGs and 3 50mm PAK 38)
1 Panzerjäger Platoon (3 LMGs and 3 sPzBu 41)
2 Infantry Gun Sections (2 75mm leIG ea)

2nd (mot) Battalion
same as 1/5th Panzergrenadier Regiment

1 (motZ) Infantry Gun Company (4 150mm sIG and 7 LMGs)

25th Panzergrenadier Regiment
same as 5th Panzergrenadier Regiment

2nd Panzerjäger Battalion
Staff
1 Self-Propelled Heavy Panzerjäger Company (14 75mm PAK 40 and 14 LMGs)
1 (motZ) Heavy Panzerjäger Company (75mm PAK 40)

12th Panzer Reconnaissance Battalion
Staff (3 LMGs)
Light Armored Car Company (24 LMGs and 18 20mm)
3 Motorcycle Companies (2 80mm mortars, 3 PzBu, 4 HMGs and 18 LMGs ea)
5th (half-track) Heavy Reconnaissance Company
1 Pioneer Platoon (4 LMGs)
1 Panzerjäger Platoon (3 LMGs and 3 75mm PAK 40)
1 Panzerjäger Platoon (3 LMGs and 3 sPzBu 41)
1 Gun Platoon (8 LMGs and 6 75mm guns)
1 Light Infantry Gun Section (2 75mm leIG)
1 Light Panzer Reconnaissance Battalion Column

2nd Panzer Artillery Regiment
Staff and (mot) Staff Battery (6 LMGs)
2nd (mot) Observation Battery (2 LMGs)

1st Battalion
Staff and Staff Battery (2 LMGs)
3 (motZ) Batteries (4 105mm leFH and 2 LMGs ea)

2nd Battalion
same as 1st Battalion

3rd Battalion
Staff and (mot) Staff Battery (2 LMGs)

2 (motZ) Batteries (4 150mm sFH and 2 LMGs ea)
1 (motZ) Battery (4 100mm K18 and 2 LMGs)

303rd Army Flak Battalion
Staff and Staff Battery
1/, 2/303rd (motZ) Heavy Flak Batteries (4 88mm, 3 20mm Flak guns and 2 LMGs ea)
3/303rd (motZ) Light Flak Battery (12 20mm guns and 2 LMGs)
4/303rd Self-Propelled Light Battery (2 quad 20mm Flak guns, 8 20mm guns and 2 LMGs)
1 (mot) Light (20 ton) Flak Column

2nd Feldersatz Battalion
organization unknown

32nd Panzer Pioneer Battalion
Staff (2 LMGs)
1 Panzer Pioneer Company (25 LMGs, 3 PzBu and 2 80mm mortars)
2 (mot) Pioneer Companies (18 LMGs, 3 PzBu and 2 80mm mortars)
1 Brüko K Bridging Column (3 LMGs)
1 (mot) Light Pioneer Column (2 LMGs)

2nd Panzer Signals Battalion
Staff
1 Panzer Telephone Company (6 LMGs)
1 Panzer Radio Company (16 LMGs)
1 (mot) Light Signals Column (4 LMGs)

2nd Supply Troops
Staff
1/, 2/2nd (mot) (120 ton) Transportation Companies (4 LMGs ea)
1/, 2/, 3//2nd (mot) (90 ton) Transportation Companies (3 LMGs ea)
2nd (mot) Supply Company (6 LMGs)

2nd Truck Maintenance Park
1/, 2/, 3/2nd (mot) Maintenance Companies
1 (mot) (75 ton) Maintenance Supply Column

Administration
2nd Divisional Administration Office
2nd (mot) Bakery Company
2nd (mot) Butcher Company

Medical Troops
1/, 2/2nd (mot) Medical Companies
1/, 2/, 3/2nd Ambulance Platoons

Other
2nd (mot) Military Police Troop (2 LMGs)
2nd (mot) Field Post Office

13th Panzer Division

Division Staff
Divisional Staff (2 LMGs)
13th (mot) Division Mapping Detachment

33rd Panzer Regiment
Regimental Staff
Regimental Staff Panzer Platoon

Panzer Signals Platoon
Regimental Band

1st Panzer Battalion

detached to Germany to become 507th Tiger Tank
Battalion

2nd Panzer Battalion

Staff

Staff Signals Platoon

Panzer Flak Platoon (7 37mm Flak 43)

4 Panzer Companies (22 PzMk IV tanks ea)

1 Panzer Maintenance Company

66th Panzergrenadier Regiment

Regimental Staff

Regimental Band

Regimental Staff Company

Signals Platoon

Panzerjäger Platoon (3 LMGs and 3 75mm PAK
40)

Motorcycle Platoon (6 LMGs)

1st (half-track) Battalion

3 (half-track) Panzergrenadier Companies (4 HMGs,
34 LMGs, 3 PzBu, 3 37mm PAK 36 and 2 80mm
mortars ea)

1 (half-track) Heavy Panzergrenadier Company

1 Pioneer Platoon (9 LMGs)

1 Panzerjäger Platoon (3 LMGs and 3 50mm PAK
38)

2 Infantry Gun Sections (4 LMGs and 2 75mm leIG
ea)

1 Panzerjäger Platoon (3 LMGs and 3 sPzBu 41)

2nd (mot) Battalion

3 Panzergrenadier Companies (4 HMGs, 18 LMGs,
3 PzBu and 2 80mm mortars ea)

1 Heavy Panzergrenadier Company

1 Pioneer Platoon (4 LMGs)

1 Panzerjäger Platoon (3 LMGs and 3 50mm PAK
38)

1 Panzerjäger Platoon (3 LMGs and 3 sPzBu 41)

2 Infantry Gun Sections (2 75mm leIG ea)

1 Self-Propelled Infantry Gun Company (6 150mm
sIG and 7 LMGs)

1 Self-Propelled Flak Company (12 20mm and 4
LMGs)

93rd Panzergrenadier Regiment

Regimental Staff

Regimental Band

Regimental Staff Company

Signals Platoon

Panzerjäger Platoon (3 LMGs and 3 75mm PAK
40)

Motorcycle Platoon (6 LMGs)

1st (mot) Battalion

same as 2/66th Panzergrenadier Regiment

2nd (mot) Battalion

same as 2/66th Panzergrenadier Regiment

1 Self-Propelled Infantry Gun Company (6 150mm
sIG and 7 LMGs)

1 Self-Propelled Flak Company (12 20mm and 4
LMGs)

13th Panzerjäger Battalion

Staff

2 Self-Propelled Heavy Panzerjäger Company (75mm
PAK 40)

1 (motZ) Heavy Panzerjäger Company (75mm PAK 40)

13th Panzer Reconnaissance Battalion

Staff (3 LMGs)

1 Light Armored Car Company (24 LMGs 18 and 18
20mm guns)

1 Light Armored Car (half-track) Company (25 LMGs
and 16 20mm)

2 Motorcycle Companies (2 80mm mortars, 3 PzBu, 4
HMGs and 18 LMGs)

1 (half-track) Heavy Reconnaissance Company

1 Staff Platoon (2 LMGs)

1 Pioneer Platoon (1 37mm PAK 36, 13 LMGs and 6
flamethrowers)

1 Panzergrenadier Platoon (9 LMGs)

1 Panzerjäger Platoon (4 LMGs and 3 75mm PAK 40)

1 Gun Platoon (8 LMGs and 6 75mm guns)

1 Light Infantry Gun Section (2 75mm leIG)

1 Light Panzer Reconnaissance Battalion Column

13th Panzer Artillery Regiment

Staff and (mot) Staff Battery (6 LMGs)

102nd (mot) Observation Battery (2 LMGs)

1st Battalion

Staff and (self-propelled) Staff Battery (2 LMGs)

2 Self-Propelled leFH Batteries (6 105mm leFH
SdKfz 124 Wespe ea)

1 Self-Propelled sFH Battery (6 150mm sFH SdKfz
165 Hummel)

2nd Battalion

Staff and Staff Battery (2 LMGs)

3 (motZ) Batteries (4 105mm leFH and 2 LMGs ea)

3rd Battalion

Staff and (mot) Staff Battery (2 LMGs)

2 (motZ) Batteries (4 150mm sFH and 2 LMGs ea)

1 (motZ) Battery (4 100mm K18 and 2 LMGs)

271st Army Flak Battalions

Staff and Staff Battery

1/, 2/271st (motZ) Heavy Flak Batteries (4 88mm, 3
20mm Flak guns and 2 LMGs ea)

3/271st (motZ) Light Flak Battery (12 20mm guns
and 2 LMGs)

4/271st Self-Propelled Light Battery (2 quad 20mm
Flak guns, 8 20mm guns and 2 LMGs)

1 (mot) Light (20 ton) Flak Column

13th Feldersatz Battalion

organization unknown

4th Panzer Pioneer Battalion

Staff (2 LMGs)

1 Panzer Pioneer Company (25 LMGs, 3 PzBu and 2 80mm mortars)

2 (mot) Pioneer Companies (18 LMGs, 3 PzBu and 2 80mm mortars ea)

1 Brüko K Bridging Column (3 LMGs)

1 (mot) Light Pioneer Column (2 LMGs)

13th Panzer Signals Battalion
Staff

1 Panzer Telephone Company (6 LMGs)

1 Panzer Radio Company (16 LMGs)

1 (mot) Light Signals Column (4 LMGs)

13th Supply Troops
Staff

1/, 2/, 3/13th (mot) (90 ton) Transportation Companies (3 LMGs ea)

4–6/13th (mot) (90 ton) Transportation Companies (3 LMGs ea) (authorized, not yet formed)

13th (mot) Supply Company (6 LMGs)

13th Truck Maintenance Park
1/, 2/, 3/13th (mot) Maintenance Companies

1 (mot) (75 ton) Maintenance Supply Column

Administration
13th Divisional Administration Office

13th (mot) Bakery Company

13th (mot) Butcher Company

Medical Troops
1/, 2/13th (mot) Medical Companies

1/, 2/, 3/13th Ambulance Platoons

Other
13th (mot) Military Police Troop (2 LMGs)

13th (mot) Field Post Office

14th Panzer Division

Division Staff
Divisional Staff (2 LMGs)

4th (mot) Division Mapping Detachment

Divisional Escort Company

Motorcycle Platoon (3 LMGs)

Infantry Gun Platoon (2 75mm leIG)

Self-Propelled Flak Platoon (1 LMG and 4 20mm guns)

Heavy Anti-Tank Platoon (3 LMGs and 3 75mm PAK 40)

Mixed Panzergrenadier Platoon (4 HMGs, 6 LMGs and 2 80mm mortars)

36th Panzer Regiment
Regimental Staff

Regimental Staff Panzer Platoon

Panzer Signals Platoon

Regimental Band

1st Panzer Battalion
Staff

Staff Signals Platoon

Staff Pioneer Platoon

Panzer Flak Platoon (7 37mm Flak 43)

4 Panzer Companies (22 PzMk IV tanks ea)

1 Panzer Maintenance Company

2nd Panzer Battalion
Staff

Staff Signals Platoon

Staff Pioneer Platoon

Panzer Flak Platoon (7 37mm Flak 43)

4 Panzer Companies (22 PzMk IV tanks ea)

1 Panzer Maintenance Company

103rd Panzergrenadier Regiment
Regimental Staff

Regimental Band

Regimental Staff Company

Signals Platoon

Pioneer Platoon (6 LMGs and 6 flamethrowers)

Panzerjäger Platoon (3 LMGs and 3 75mm PAK 40)

Motorcycle Platoon (6 LMGs)

1st (half-track) Battalion
3 (half-track) Panzergrenadier Companies (4 HMGs, 39 LMGs, 3 PzBu, 3 37mm PAK 36, 2 75mm guns and 2 80mm mortars ea)

1 (half-track) Heavy Panzergrenadier Company

1 Pioneer Platoon (13 LMGs, 1 37mm PAK 36 and 6 flamethrowers)

1 Panzerjäger Platoon (3 LMGs and 3 75mm PAK 40)

1 Infantry Gun Section (4 LMGs and 2 75mm leIG)

1 Panzerjäger Platoon (13 LMGs and 6 75mm guns)

2nd (mot) Battalion
3 Panzergrenadier Companies (4 HMGs, 18 LMGs and 2 80mm mortars ea)

1 Heavy Panzergrenadier Company

1 Pioneer Platoon (4 LMGs and 6 flamethrowers)

1 Panzerjäger Platoon (3 LMGs and 3 50mm PAK 38)

2 Infantry Gun Sections (2 75mm leIG ea)

1 Mortar Platoon (6 80mm mortars)

9th (Self-Propelled Infantry Gun) Company (6 150mm sIG and 7 LMGs)

10th (Self-Propelled Flak) Company (12 20mm and 4 LMGs)

108th Panzergrenadier Regiment
Regimental Staff

Regimental Band
Regimental Staff Company
  Signals Platoon
  Panzerjäger Platoon (3 LMGs and 3 75mm PAK 40)
  Motorcycle Platoon (6 LMGs)
1st (mot) Battalion
  same as 2/108th Panzergrenadier Regiment
2nd (mot) Battalion
  same as 2/208th Panzergrenadier Regiment
1 Self-Propelled Infantry Gun Company (6 150mm
  sIG and 7 LMGs)
1 Self-Propelled Flak Company (12 20mm and 4
  LMGs)
Panzerjäger Battalion
  none
14th Panzer Reconnaissance Battalion
  Staff (3 LMGs)
  1 Heavy Armored Car Platoon (6 SdKfz 234/3 with
    75mm KwK and 6 LMGs)
  1 Light Armored Car Company (25 LMGs and 18
    20mm)
  1 Light Armored Car (half-track) Company (25 LMGs
    and 16 20mm)
  2 (half-track) Heavy Reconnaissance Company (2
    120mm mortars, 4 HMGs, 56 LMGs and 3 37mm
    PAK 36)
  1 (half-track) Heavy Reconnaissance Company
    1 Pioneer Platoon (13 LMGs, 12 37mm PAK 36 and
      6 flamethrowers)
    1 Panzerjäger Platoon (9 LMGs and 3 75mm PAK
      40)
    1 Light Infantry Gun Section (4 LMGs and 2 75mm
      leIG)
    1 Gun Platoon (8 LMGs and 6 75mm guns)
  1 Light Panzer Reconnaissance Battalion Column
4th Panzer Artillery Regiment
  Staff and (mot) Staff Battery (6 LMGs)
  4th (mot) Observation Battery (2 LMGs)
  1st Battalion
    Staff and (self-propelled) Staff Battery (2 LMGs)
    2 Self-Propelled leFH Batteries (6 105mm leFH
      SdKfz 124 Wespe ea)
    1 Self-Propelled sFH Battery (6 150mm sFH SdKfz
      165 Hummel)
  2nd Battalion
    Staff and Staff Battery (2 LMGs)

3 (motZ) Batteries (4 105mm leFH and 2 LMGs ea)
  3rd Battalion
    Staff and (mot) Staff Battery (2 LMGs)
    2 (motZ) Batteries (4 150mm sFH and 2 LMGs ea)
    1 (motZ) Battery (4 100mm K18 and 2 LMGs)
276th Army Flak Battalion
  Staff and Staff Battery
  1/, 2/276th (motZ) Heavy Flak Batteries (4 88mm, 3
    20mm Flak guns and 2 LMGs ea)
  3/276th (motZ) Light Flak Battery (9 20mm guns, 2
    quad 20mm Flak guns and 2 LMGs)
  1 (mot) Light (20 ton) Flak Column
4th Feldersatz Battalion
  organization unknown
13th Panzer Pioneer Battalion
  Staff (2 LMGs)
  1 (half-track) Pioneer Company (4 HMGs, 43 LMGs,
    3 PzBu, 6 flamethrowers and 2 80mm mortars)
  2 (mot) Pioneer Companies (2 HMGs, 18 LMGs, 3
    PzBu, 6 flamethrowers and 2 80mm mortars)
  1 Brüko K Bridging Column (3 LMGs)
  1 (mot) Light Pioneer Column (2 LMGs)
4th Panzer Signals Battalion
  Staff
  1 Panzer Telephone Company (6 LMGs)
  1 Panzer Radio Company (16 LMGs)
  1 (mot) Light Signals Column (4 LMGs)
4th Supply Troops
  Staff
  1–8/4th (mot) (120 ton) Transportation Companies
    (4 LMGs ea)
  4th (mot) Supply Company (6 LMGs)
4th Truck Maintenance Park
  1/, 2/, 3/4th (mot) Maintenance Companies
  1 (mot) (75 ton) Maintenance Supply Column
Administration
  4th Divisional Administration Office
  4th (mot) Bakery Company
  4th (mot) Butcher Company
Medical Troops
  1/, 2/4th (mot) Medical Companies
  1/, 2/, 3/4th Ambulance Platoons
Other
  4th (mot) Military Police Troop (2 LMGs)
  4th (mot) Field Post Office

16th Panzer Division

Division Staff
  Divisional Staff (2 LMGs)
  16th (mot) Division Mapping Detachment
  Divisional Escort Company

  Motorcycle Platoon (3 LMGs)
  Infantry Gun Platoon (2 75mm leIG)
  Heavy Anti-Tank Platoon (3 LMGs and 3 75mm PAK
    40)

Self-Propelled Flak Platoon (4 20mm guns)
Mixed Panzergrenadier Platoon (4 HMGs, 6 LMGs and 2 80mm mortars)

2nd Panzer Regiment
Regimental Staff
Regimental Staff Panzer Platoon
Panzer Signals Platoon
Regimental Band

1st Panzer Battalion
Staff
Staff Signals Platoon
Staff Pioneer Platoon
Panzer Flak Platoon (7 37mm Flak 43)
4 Panzer Companies (22 PzMk V Panther tanks ea)
1 Panzer Maintenance Company

2nd Panzer Battalion
Staff
Staff Signals Platoon
Panzer Flak Platoon (7 37mm Flak 43)
4 Panzer Companies (22 PzMk IV tanks ea)
1 Panzer Maintenance Company

3rd Panzer Battalion
same as 2/2nd Panzer Regiment

64th Panzergrenadier Regiment
Regimental Staff
Regimental Band
Regimental Staff Company
Signals Platoon
Pioneer Platoon (6 LMGs and 6 flamethrowers)
Panzerjäger Platoon (3 LMGs and 3 75mm PAK 40)
Motorcycle Platoon (6 LMGs)

1st (mot) Battalion
3 (mot)Panzergrenadier Companies (4 HMGs, 18 LMGs and 2 80mm mortars ea)
1 (mot) Heavy Panzergrenadier Company
1 Pioneer Platoon (4 LMGs and 6 flamethrowers)
1 Panzerjäger Platoon (3 LMGs and 3 50mm PAK 38)
2 Infantry Gun Sections (2 75mm leIG ea)
1 Mortar Platoon (6 80mm mortars)

2nd (half-track) Battalion
3 (half-track) Grenadier Companies (4 HMGs, 39 LMGs, 3 PzBu, 3 37mm PAK 36, 2 75mm guns and 2 80mm mortars ea)
1 (half-track) Heavy Panzergrenadier Company
1 Pioneer Platoon (13 LMGs, 1 37mm PAK 36 and 6 flamethrowers)
1 Panzerjäger Platoon (9 LMGs and 3 75mm PAK 40)
1 Infantry Gun Section (4 LMGs and 2 75mm leIG)
1 Gun Platoon (13 LMGs and 6 75mm guns)

1 Self-Propelled Infantry Gun Company (6 150mm sIG and 7 LMGs)

1 Self-Propelled Flak Company (12 20mm and 4 LMGs)

79th Panzergrenadier Regiment
Regimental Staff

Regimental Band
Regimental Staff Company
Signals Platoon
Pioneer Platoon (6 LMGs and 6 flamethrowers)
Panzerjäger Platoon (3 LMGs and 3 75mm PAK 40)
Motorcycle Platoon (6 LMGs)

1st (mot) Battalion
same as 1/64th Panzergrenadier Regiment

2nd (mot) Battalion
same as 1/64th Panzergrenadier Regiment

1 Self-Propelled Infantry Gun Company (6 150mm sIG and 7 LMGs)

1 Self-Propelled Flak Company (12 20mm and 4 LMGs)

Panzerjäger Battalion
none

16th Panzer Reconnaissance Battalion
Staff (3 LMGs)
1 Heavy Armored Car Platoon (6 SdKfz 234/3 with 75mm KwK and 6 LMGs)
1 Light Armored Car Company (25 LMGs and 18 20mm)
1 Light Armored Car Company (25 LMGs and 16 20mm)
2 (half-track) Heavy Reconnaissance Companies (2 80mm mortars, 4 HMGs, 56 LMGs and 3 37mm PAK 36 ea)
1 (half-track) Heavy Reconnaissance Company
1 Pioneer Platoon (4 LMGs, 1 37mm PAK 36 and 6 flamethrowers)
1 Panzerjäger Platoon (3 LMGs and 3 75mm PAK 40)
1 Gun Platoon (8 LMGs and 6 75mm guns)
1 Light Infantry Gun Section (2 75mm leIG)
1 Light Panzer Reconnaissance Battalion Column

16th Panzer Artillery Regiment
Staff and (mot) Staff Battery (6 LMGs)
16th (mot) Observation Battery (2 LMGs)
1 (motZ) Flak Platoon (4 20mm and 2 LMGs)

1st Battalion
Staff and Staff Battery (2 LMGs)
3 (motZ) Batteries (4 105mm leFH and 2 LMGs ea)

2nd Battalion
Staff and (self-propelled) Staff Battery (2 LMGs)
2 Self-Propelled leFH Batteries (6 105mm leFH SdKfz 124 Wespe ea)
1 Self-Propelled sFH Battery (6 150mm sFH SdKfz 165 Hummel)

3rd Battalion
Staff and (mot) Staff Battery (2 LMGs)
2 (motZ) Batteries (4 150mm sFH and 2 LMGs ea)
1 (motZ) Battery (4 100mm K18 and 2 LMGs)

274th Army Flak Battalion
Staff and Staff Battery

1/, 2/274th (motZ) Heavy Flak Batteries (4 88mm, 3 20mm Flak guns and 2 LMGs ea)

3/274th (motZ) Light Flak Battery (9 20mm guns, 2 quad 20mm and 2 LMGs)

1 (mot) Light (20 ton) Flak Column

16th Feldersatz Battalion

5 companies

16th Panzer Pioneer Battalion

Staff (2 LMGs)

1 (half-track) Pioneer Company (2 HMGs, 43 LMGs, 3 PzBu, 6 flamethrowers and 2 80mm mortars)

2 (mot) Pioneer Companies (2 HMGs, 18 LMGs, 3 PzBu, 6 flamethrowers and 2 80mm mortars ea)

1 Brüko K Bridging Column (3 LMGs)

1 (mot) Light Pioneer Column (2 LMGs)

16th Panzer Signals Battalion

Staff

1 Panzer Telephone Company (21 LMGs)

1 Panzer Radio Company (35 LMGs)

1 (mot) Light Signals Column (1 LMG)

16th Supply Troops

Staff

1–8th/16th (mot) (120 ton) Transportation Companies (4 LMGs)

16th (mot) Supply Company (6 LMGs)

16th Truck Maintenance Park

1/, 2/, 3/16th (mot) Maintenance Companies

1 (mot) (75 ton) Maintenance Supply Column

Administration

16th Divisional Administration Office

16th (mot) Bakery Company

16th (mot) Butcher Company

Medical Troops

1/, 2/16th (mot) Medical Companies

1/, 2/, 3/16th Ambulance Platoons

Other

16th (mot) Military Police Troop (2 LMGs)

16th (mot) Field Post Office

17th Panzer Division

Division Staff

Divisional Staff (2 LMGs)

27th (mot) Division Mapping Detachment

39th Panzer Regiment

Regimental Staff

Regimental Staff Panzer Platoon

Panzer Signals Platoon

Regimental Band

1st Panzer Battalion

detached

2nd Panzer Battalion

Staff

Staff Signals Platoon

Panzer Flak Platoon (7 37mm Flak 43)

4 Panzer Companies (22 PzMk IV tanks ea)

1 Panzer Maintenance Company

40th Panzergrenadier Regiment

Regimental Staff

Regimental Band

Regimental Staff Company

Signals Platoon

Panzerjäger Platoon (3 LMGs and 3 75mm PAK 40)

Motorcycle Platoon (6 LMGs)

1st (mot) Battalion

3 (mot) Panzergrenadier Companies (4 HMGs, 18 LMGs, 3 PzBu and 2 80mm mortars ea)

1 (mot) Heavy Panzergrenadier Company

1 Pioneer Platoon (4 LMGs)

1 Panzerjäger Platoon (3 LMGs and 3 50mm PAK 38)

1 Panzerjäger Platoon (3 LMGs and 3 sPzBu 41)

1 Infantry Gun Section (2 75mm leIG)

2nd (mot) Battalion

same as 1/40th Panzergrenadier Regiment

1 Self-Propelled Infantry Gun Company (6 150mm sIG and 7 LMGs)

79th Panzergrenadier Regiment

same as 40th Panzergrenadier Regiment

27th Panzerjäger Battalion

1 Staff

3 Self-Propelled Panzerjäger Companies (14 75mm PAK 40 and 14 LMGs)

17th Panzer Reconnaissance Battalion

Staff (3 LMGs)

1 Light Armored Car Company (24 LMGs and 18 20mm)

1 Motorcycle Company (2 80mm mortars, 3 PzBu, 4 HMGs and 18 LMGs)

2 (half-track) Heavy Reconnaissance Companies (2 80mm mortars, 4 HMGs, 56 LMGs and 3 37mm PAK 36 ea)

1 (half-track) Heavy Reconnaissance Company

1 Pioneer Platoon (4 LMGs)

1 Panzerjäger Platoon (3 LMGs and 3 75mm PAK 40)

1 Panzerjäger Platoon (3 LMGs and 3 sPzBu 41)

1 Light Infantry Gun Section (2 75mm leIG)

1 Light Panzer Reconnaissance Battalion Column

27th Panzer Artillery Regiment

Staff and (mot) Staff Battery (6 LMGs)

27th (mot) Observation Battery (2 LMGs)

1st Battalion

Staff and (self-propelled) Staff Battery (2 LMGs)

2 Self-Propelled leFH Batteries (6 105mm leFH SdKfz 124 Wespe ea)

1 Self-Propelled sFH Battery (6 150mm sFH SdKfz 165 Hummel)

2nd Battalion

Staff and Staff Battery (2 LMGs)

3 (motZ) Batteries (4 105mm leFH and 2 LMGs ea)

3rd Battalion

Staff and (mot) Staff Battery (2 LMGs)

2 (motZ) Batteries (4 150mm sFH and 2 LMGs ea)

1 (motZ) Battery (4 100mm K18 and 2 LMGs)

297th Army Flak Battalion

Staff and Staff Battery

1/, 2/297th (motZ) Heavy Flak Batteries (4 88mm, 3 20mm Flak guns and 2 LMGs ea)

3/297th (motZ) Light Flak Battery (9 20mm guns, 2 quad 20mm and 2 LMGs)

4/297th Self-Propelled Light Flak Battery (8 20mm guns, 2 quad 20mm and 4 LMGs)

1 (mot) Light (20 ton) Flak Column

27th Feldersatz Battalion

5 companies

27th Panzer Pioneer Battalion

Staff (2 LMGs)

1 Panzer Pioneer Company (25 LMGs, 3 PzBu and 2 80mm mortars)

2 (mot) Pioneer Companies (18 LMGs, 3 PzBu and 2 80mm mortars ea)

1 (mot) Light Pioneer Column (2 LMGs)

27th Panzer Signals Battalion

Staff

1 Panzer Telephone Company (6 LMGs)

1 Panzer Radio Company (16 LMGs)

1 (mot) Light Signals Column (1 LMG)

27th Supply Troops

1–5/27th (mot) (90 ton) Transportation Companies (3 LMGs ea)

27th (mot) Supply Company (6 LMGs)

27th Truck Maintenance Park

1/, 2/, 3/27th (mot) Maintenance Companies

1 (mot) (75 ton) Maintenance Supply Column

Administration

27th Divisional Administration Office

27th (mot) Bakery Company

27th (mot) Butcher Company

Medical Troops

1/, 2/27th (mot) Medical Companies

1/, 2/, 3/27th Ambulance Platoons

Other

27th (mot) Military Police Troop (2 LMGs)

27th (mot) Field Post Office

19th Panzer Division

Division Staff

Divisional Staff (2 LMGs)

19th (mot) Division Mapping Detachment

27th Panzer Regiment

Regimental Staff

Regimental Staff Panzer Platoon

Panzer Signals Platoon

Regimental Band

1st Panzer Battalion

detached as an army troop

2nd Panzer Battalion

Staff

Staff Signals Platoon

Panzer Flak Platoon (7 37mm Flak 43)

4 Panzer Companies (22 PzMk IV tanks ea)

1 Panzer Maintenance Company

73rd Panzergrenadier Regiment

Regimental Staff

Regimental Band

Regimental Staff Company

Signals Platoon

Panzerjäger Platoon (3 LMGs and 3 75mm PAK 40)

Motorcycle Platoon (6 LMGs)

1st (mot) Battalion

3 (mot) Panzergrenadier Companies (4 HMGs, 18 LMGs, 3 PzBu and 2 80mm mortars ea)

1 (mot) Heavy Panzergrenadier Company

1 Pioneer Platoon (4 LMGs)

1 Panzerjäger Platoon (3 LMGs and 3 50mm PAK 38)

1 Panzerjäger Platoon (3 LMGs and 3 sPzBu 41)

1 Infantry Gun Section (2 75mm leIG)

2nd (mot) Battalion

same as 1/73rd Panzergrenadier Regiment

1 (motZ) Infantry Gun Company (4 150mm sIG)

79th Panzergrenadier Regiment

same as 73rd Panzergrenadier Regiment

19th Panzerjäger Battalion

1 Battalion Staff

2 Self-Propelled Panzerjäger Companies (14 75mm PAK 40 and 14 LMGs)

1 (motZ) Panzerjäger Company (12 75mm PAK 40 and 12 LMGs)

19th Panzer Reconnaissance Battalion

Staff (3 LMGs)

1 Light Armored Car Company (24 LMGs and 18 20mm)

3 Motorcycle Companies (2 80mm mortars, 3 PzBu, 4 HMGs and 18 LMGs ea)

1 (mot) Heavy Reconnaissance Company
  1 Pioneer Platoon (4 LMGs)
  1 Panzerjäger Platoon (3 LMGs and 3 75mm PAK 40)
  1 Panzerjäger Platoon (3 LMGs and 3 sPzBu 41)
  1 Light Infantry Gun Section (2 75mm leIG)

1 Light Panzer Reconnaissance Battalion Column

19th Panzer Artillery Regiment
Staff and (mot) Staff Battery (6 LMGs)
19th (mot) Observation Battery (2 LMGs)

1st Battalion
Staff and Staff Battery (2 LMGs)
3 (motZ) Batteries (4 105mm leFH and 2 LMGs ea)

2nd Battalion
Staff and Staff Battery (2 LMGs)
2 (motZ) Batteries (4 105mm leFH and 2 LMGs ea)

3rd Battalion
Staff and (mot) Staff Battery (2 LMGs)
2 (motZ) Batteries (4 150mm sFH and 2 LMGs ea)
1 (motZ) Battery (4 100mm K18 and 2 LMGs)

272nd Army Flak Battalion
Staff and Staff Battery
1/, 2/272nd (motZ) Heavy Flak Batteries (4 88mm, 3 20mm Flak guns and 2 LMGs ea)
3/272nd (motZ) Light Flak Battery (9 20mm guns, 2 quad 20mm and 2 LMGs)
1 (mot) Light (20 ton) Flak Column

19th Feldersatz Battalion
4 companies

19th Panzer Pioneer Battalion
Staff (2 LMGs)
1 Panzer Pioneer Company (25 LMGs, 3 PzBu and 2 80mm mortars)
2 (mot) Pioneer Companies (18 LMGs, 3 PzBu and 2 80mm mortars ea)
1 Brüko K Bridging Column (3 LMGs)
1 (mot) Light Pioneer Column (2 LMGs)

19th Panzer Signals Battalion
Staff
1 Panzer Telephone Company (6 LMGs)
1 Panzer Radio Company (16 LMGs)
1 (mot) Light Signals Column (1 LMG)

19th Supply Troops
Staff
1/, 2/, 3/19th (mot) (90 ton) Transportation Companies (3 LMGs ea)
4/, 5/, 6/19th (mot) (120 ton) Transportation Companies (4 LMGs ea)
19th (mot) Supply Company (6 LMGs)

19th Truck Maintenance Park
1/, 2/, 3/19th (mot) Maintenance Companies

Administration
19th Divisional Administration Office
19th (mot) Bakery Company
19th (mot) Butcher Company

Medical Troops
1/, 2/19th (mot) Medical Companies
1/, 2/, 3/19th Ambulance Platoons

Other
19th (mot) Military Police Troop (2 LMGs)
19th (mot) Field Post Office

20th Panzer Division

Division Staff
Divisional Staff (2 LMGs)
20th (mot) Division Mapping Detachment

21st Panzer Regiment

3rd Panzer Battalion
Staff
Staff Signals Platoon
Panzer Flak Platoon (7 37mm Flak 43)
4 Panzer Companies (22 PzMk IV tanks ea)
1 Panzer Maintenance Company

59th Panzergrenadier Regiment
Regimental Staff
Regimental Band
Regimental Staff Company
  Signals Platoon
  Panzerjäger Platoon (3 LMGs and 3 75mm PAK 40)
  Motorcycle Platoon (6 LMGs)

1st (mot) Battalion
3 (mot) Panzergrenadier Companies (4 HMGs, 18 LMGs, 3 PzBu and 2 80mm mortars ea)
1 (mot) Heavy Panzergrenadier Company
  1 Pioneer Platoon (4 LMGs)
  1 Panzerjäger Platoon (3 LMGs and 3 50mm PAK 38)
  1 Panzerjäger Platoon (3 LMGs and 3 sPzBu 41)
  1 Infantry Gun Section (2 75mm leIG)

2nd (mot) Battalion
same as 1/73rd Panzergrenadier Regiment

11th (motZ) Infantry Gun Company (4 150mm sIG)

112th Panzergrenadier Regiment
same as 73rd Panzergrenadier Regiment

92nd Panzerjäger Battalion
1 Battalion Staff
2 Self-Propelled Panzerjäger Companies (14 75mm PAK 40 and 14 LMGs ea)

1 (motZ) Panzerjäger Company (12 75mm PAK 40 and 12 LMGs)

1 Self-Propelled Flak Company (8 20mm, 2 quad 20mm and 4 LMGs)

20th Panzer Reconnaissance Battalion

Staff (3 LMGs)

1 Light Armored Car Company (24 LMGs and 18 20mm)

3 Motorcycle Companies (2 80mm mortars, 3 PzBu, 4 HMGs and 18 LMGs ea)

1 (mot) Heavy Reconnaissance Company

    1 Pioneer Platoon (4 LMGs)

    1 Panzerjäger Platoon (3 LMGs and 3 75mm PAK 40)

    1 Panzerjäger Platoon (3 LMGs and 3 sPzBu 41)

    1 Light Infantry Gun Section (2 75mm leIG)

1 Light Panzer Reconnaissance Battalion Column

92nd Panzer Artillery Regiment

Staff and (mot) Staff Battery (6 LMGs)

92nd (mot) Observation Battery (2 LMGs)

1st Battalion

Staff and Staff Battery (2 LMGs)

3 (motZ) Batteries (3 105mm leFH and 2 LMGs ea)

2nd Battalion

Staff and Staff Battery (2 LMGs)

3 (motZ) Batteries (3 105mm leFH and 2 LMGs ea)

3rd Battalion

Staff and (mot) Staff Battery (2 LMGs)

2 (motZ) Batteries (3 150mm sFH and 2 LMGs ea)

1 (motZ) Battery (3 100mm K18 and 2 LMGs)

Other

10th (motZ) Flak Battery (12 20mm and 2 LMGs)

Army Flak Battalions

92nd Feldersatz Battalion

4 companies

92nd Panzer Pioneer Battalion

Staff (2 LMGs)

1 Panzer Pioneer Company (25 LMGs, 3 PzBu and 2 80mm mortars)

2 (mot) Pioneer Companies (18 LMGs, 3 PzBu and 2 80mm mortars ea)

1 Brüko K Bridging Column (3 LMGs)

1 (mot) Light Pioneer Column (2 LMGs)

92nd Panzer Signals Battalion

Staff

1 Panzer Telephone Company (6 LMGs)

1 Panzer Radio Company (16 LMGs)

1 (mot) Light Signals Column (1 LMG)

92nd Supply Troops

Staff

1/, 2/, 3/92nd (mot) (90 ton) Transportation Companies (3 LMGs ea)

4/92nd (mot) (120 ton) Transportation Companies (4 LMGs)

92nd (mot) Supply Company (6 LMGs)

92nd Truck Maintenance Park

1/, 2/, 3/92nd (mot) Maintenance Companies

75 ton Heavy Maintenance Supply Column

Administration

92nd Divisional Administration Office

92nd (mot) Bakery Company

92nd (mot) Butcher Company

Medical Troops

1/, 2/92nd (mot) Medical Companies

1/, 2/92nd Ambulance Platoons

Other

92nd (mot) Military Police Troop (2 LMGs)

92nd (mot) Field Post Office

21st Panzer Division (Afrika Division)

Division Staff

Divisional Staff (2 LMGs)

200th (mot) Division Mapping Detachment (2 LMGs)

100th Panzer Regiment

Regimental Staff

Regimental Staff Panzer Platoon

Panzer Signals Platoon

1st Panzer Battalion

Staff

Staff Company

1 Panzer Company (medium French tanks)

3 Panzer Companies (light French tanks)

1 Panzer Maintenance Company

2nd Panzer Battalion

same as 1/100th Panzer Regiment

125th Panzergrenadier Regiment

Regimental Staff

Regimental Band

Regimental Staff Company

    Signals Platoon

    Panzerjäger Platoon (3 LMGs and 3 75mm PAK 40)

    Motorcycle Platoon (6 LMGs)

1st (half-track) Battalion

3 (half-track) Panzergrenadier Companies (4 HMGs, 15 LMGs and 4 80mm mortars ea)

1 (half-track) Heavy Panzergrenadier Company
  1 (half-track) Panzerjäger Platoon (4 75mm PAK 40 and 4 LMGs)
  1 (half-track) Nebelwerfer Platoon (1 half-track with 16 nebelwerfer tubes, probably on captured French Somua half-track chassis)
  1 (half-track) Flak Platoon (3 20mm and 3 LMGs)
  1 Mortar Platoon (3 120mm mortars)

2nd (mot) Battalion

3 (mot) Panzergrenadier Companies (4 HMGs, 15 LMGs and 4 80mm mortars ea)
1 (half-track) Heavy Panzergrenadier Company
  1 (half-track) Panzerjäger Platoon (4 75mm PAK 40 and 4 LMGs)
  1 (half-track) Nebelwerfer Platoon (1 half-track with 16 nebelwerfer tubes, probably on captured French Somua half-track chassis)
  1 (half-track) Flak Platoon (3 20mm and 3 LMGs)
1 Self-Propelled Artillery Battery (4 150mm sFH and 6 LMGs)

192nd Panzergrenadier Regiment

same as 125th Panzergrenadier Regiment

200th Panzerjäger Battalion

1 Battalion Staff
2 (motZ) Panzerjäger Companies (12 75mm PAK 40 and 12 LMGs)

200th Sturmgeschütz Battalion

Battalion Staff
Battalion Staff Company (StuG and 4 half-tracks with 16 nebelwerfer tubes, probably on captured French Somua half-track chassis)
4 Sturmgeschütz Companies (6 75mm SdKfz 142/1 and 4 105mm SdKfz 142/2)

21st Panzer Reconnaissance Battalion

Staff (3 LMGs)
1 Heavy Armored Car Platoon (6 SdKfz 234/3 with 75mm KwK and 6 LMGs)
1 Light Armored Car Company (24 LMGs and 18 20mm)
2 (half-track) Heavy Reconnaissance Companies (2 80mm mortars, 4 HMGs, 56 LMGs and 3 37mm PAK 36 ea)
1 (half-track) Heavy Reconnaissance Company
  1 Staff Platoon (2 LMGs)
  1 Pioneer Platoon (4 LMGs, 1 37mm PAK 36 and 6 flamethrowers)
  1 Panzerjäger Platoon (3 LMGs and 3 75mm PAK 40)
  1 Gun Platoon (8 LMGs and 6 75mm guns)
  1 Light Infantry Gun Section (4 LMGs and 2 75mm leIG)
1 Light Panzer Reconnaissance Battalion Column

155th Panzer Artillery Regiment

Staff and (mot) Staff Battery (6 LMGs)

1st Battalion

Staff and Staff Battery (2 LMGs)

2 Self-Propelled Batteries (6 105mm leFH SdKfz 124 Wespe ea)
1 Self-Propelled Battery (6 150mm sFH SdKfz 165 Hummel)

2nd Battalion

Staff and Staff Battery (2 LMGs)
3 Self-Propelled Batteries (6 105mm leFH SdKfz 124 Wespe ea)

3rd Battalion

Staff and (mot) Staff Battery (2 LMGs)
3 Self-Propelled Batteries (6 150mm sFH SdKfz 165 Hummel ea)

305th Army Flak Battalion

Staff and Staff Battery
1/, 2/305th (motZ) Heavy Flak Batteries (4 88mm, 3 20mm Flak guns and 2 LMGs ea)
3/305th (motZ) Light Flak Battery (9 20mm guns, 2 quad 20mm and 2 LMGs)
1 (mot) Light (20 ton) Flak Column

200th Feldersatz Company

organization unknown

220th Panzer Pioneer Battalion

Staff (2 LMGs)
2 (half-track) Pioneer Companies (43 LMGs, 3 PzBu and 2 80mm mortars ea)
220th Brüko K Bridging Column (3 LMGs)
1 (mot) Light Pioneer Column (2 LMGs)

200th Panzer Signals Battalion

Staff
1 Panzer Telephone Company (6 LMGs)
1 Panzer Radio Company (35 LMGs)
1 (mot) Light Signals Column (1 LMG)

200th Supply Troops

Staff
1–4/200th (mot) (120 ton) Transportation Companies (4 LMGs ea)
200th (mot) Supply Company (6 LMGs)

200th Truck Maintenance Park

200th (mot) Maintenance Company

Administration

200th Divisional Administration Office
200th (mot) Bakery Company
200th (mot) Butcher Company

Medical Troops

1/200th (mot) Medical Companies
1/, 2/200th Ambulance Platoons

Other

200th (mot) Military Police Troop (2 LMGs)
200th (mot) Field Post Office

23rd Panzer Division

Division Staff
Divisional Staff (2 LMGs)
128th (mot) Division Mapping Detachment

23rd Panzer Regiment
Regimental Staff
Regimental Staff Panzer Platoon
Panzer Signals Platoon
Regimental Band

1st Panzer Battalion
Staff
Staff Signals Platoon
Panzer Flak Platoon (7 37mm Flak 43)
4 Panzer Companies (22 PzMk IV tanks ea)
1 Panzer Maintenance Company

2nd Panzer Battalion
Staff
Staff Signals Platoon
Panzer Flak Platoon (7 37mm Flak 43)
4 Panzer Companies (22 PzMk V Panther tanks ea)
1 Panzer Maintenance Company

Attached
1 Self-Propelled Sturm Infantry Gun Battery

1236th Panzergrenadier Regiment
Regimental Staff
Regimental Band
Regimental Staff Company
Signals Platoon
Pioneer Platoon (6LMGs and 6 flamethrowers)
Panzerjäger Platoon (3 LMGs and 3 75mm PAK 40)
Motorcycle Platoon (6 LMGs)

1st (half-track) Battalion
3 (half-track) Panzergrenadier Companies (4 HMGs, 34 LMGs, 3 PzBu, 3 37mm PAK 36 and 2 80mm mortars ea)
1 (half-track) Heavy Panzergrenadier Company
1 Pioneer Platoon (9 LMGs)
1 Panzerjäger Platoon (3 LMGs and 3 50mm PAK 38)
1 Panzerjäger Platoon (3 LMGs and 3 sPzBu 41)
2 Infantry Gun Sections (4 LMGs and 2 75mm leIG ea)

2nd (mot) Battalion
3 (mot)Panzergrenadier Companies (4 HMGs, 18 LMGs, 3 PzBu and 2 80mm mortars ea)
1 (mot) Heavy Panzergrenadier Company
1 Pioneer Platoon (4 LMGs)
1 Panzerjäger Platoon (3 LMGs and 3 50mm PAK 38)
1 Panzerjäger Platoon (3 LMGs and 3 sPzBu 41)
2 Infantry Gun Sections (2 75mm leIG ea)

1 (motZ) Infantry Gun Company (4 150mm sIG)
1 Self-Propelled Flak Company (12 20mm and 4 LMGs)

79th Panzergrenadier Regiment
Regimental Staff
Regimental Band
Regimental Staff Company
Signals Platoon
Pioneer Platoon (6LMGs and 6 flamethrowers)
Panzerjäger Platoon (3 LMGs and 3 75mm PAK 40)
Motorcycle Platoon (6 LMGs)

1st (mot) Battalion
3 (mot)Panzergrenadier Companies (4 HMGs, 18 LMGs, 3 PzBu and 2 80mm mortars ea)
1 (mot) Heavy Panzergrenadier Company
1 Pioneer Platoon (4 LMGs)
1 Panzerjäger Platoon (3 LMGs and 3 50mm PAK 38)
1 Panzerjäger Platoon (3 LMGs and 3 sPzBu 41)
2 Infantry Gun Sections (2 75mm leIG ea)

2nd (mot) Battalion
same as 1st Battalion

128th Panzerjäger Battalion
1 Battalion Staff
2 Self-Propelled Panzerjäger Companies (14 75mm PAK 40 and 14 LMGs ea)

23rd Panzer Reconnaissance Battalion
Staff (3 LMGs)
1 Light Armored Car Company (24 LMGs and 18 20mm)
2 Motorcycle Companies (2 80mm mortars, 3 PzBu, 4 HMGs and 18 LMGs ea)
1 (half-track) Reconnaissance Company (2 80mm mortars, 3 37mm PAK 36, 4 HMGs, and 56 LMGs)
1 (mot) Heavy Reconnaissance Company
1 Pioneer Platoon (4 LMGs)
1 Panzerjäger Platoon (3 LMGs and 3 75mm PAK 40)
1 Panzerjäger Platoon (3 LMGs and 3 sPzBu 41)
1 Light Infantry Gun Section (2 75mm leIG)
1 Light Panzer Reconnaissance Battalion Column

128th Panzer Artillery Regiment
Staff and (mot) Staff Battery (6 LMGs)
128th (mot) Observation Battery (2 LMGs)

1st Battalion
Staff and Staff Battery (2 LMGs)
3 (motZ) Batteries (4 105mm leFH and 2 LMGs ea)

2nd Battalion
same as 1st Battalion

3rd Battalion
Staff and (mot) Staff Battery (2 LMGs)
2 (motZ) Batteries (4 150mm sFH and 2 LMGs ea)
1 (motZ) Battery (4 100mm K18 and 2 LMGs)

278th Army Flak Battalion
Staff and Staff Battery
1/, 2/278th (motZ) Heavy Flak Batteries (4 88mm, 3 20mm Flak guns and 2 LMGs ea)

3/278th (motZ) Light Flak Battery (9 20mm guns, 2 quad 20mm and 2 LMGs)

4/278th Self-Propelled Light Flak Battery (8 20mm guns, 2 quad 20mm and 4 LMGs)

1 (mot) Light (20 ton) Flak Column

128th Feldersatz Battalion
5 companies

1 Hiwi company

128th Panzer Pioneer Battalion
Staff (2 LMGs)

1 Panzer Pioneer Company (25 LMGs, 3 PzBu and 2 80mm mortars)

2 (mot) Pioneer Companies (18 LMGs, 3 PzBu and 2 80mm mortars ea)

1 Brüko K Bridging Column (3 LMGs)

1 (mot) Light Pioneer Column (2 LMGs)

128th Panzer Signals Battalion
Staff

1 Panzer Telephone Company (6 LMGs)

1 Panzer Radio Company (16 LMGs)

1 (mot) Light Signals Column (1 LMG)

128th Supply Troops
Staff

1/, 2/, 3/128th (mot) (120 ton) Transportation Companies (4 LMGs ea)

4/, 5/128th (mot) (90 ton) Transportation Companies (3 LMGs ea)

1 (mot) Heavy Supply Column (6 LMGs)

128th (mot) Supply Company (6 LMGs)

128th Truck Maintenance Park
1/, 2/, 3/128th (mot) Maintenance Companies

Administration
128th Divisional Administration Office

128th (mot) Bakery Company

128th (mot) Butcher Company

Medical Troops
1/, 2/128th (mot) Medical Companies

1/, 2/, 3/128th Ambulance Platoons

Other
128th (mot) Military Police Troop (2 LMGs)

128th (mot) Field Post Office

24th Panzer Division

Division Staff
Divisional Staff (2 LMGs)

40th (mot) Division Mapping Detachment

Motorcycle Platoon (3 LMGs)

Infantry Gun Platoon (2 75mm leIG)

Self-Propelled Flak Platoon (4 20mm guns)

Heavy Anti-Tank Platoon (3 LMGs and 3 75mm PAK 40)

Mixed Panzergrenadier Platoon (4 HMGs, 6 LMGs and 2 80mm mortars)

24th Panzer Regiment
Regimental Staff

Regimental Staff Panzer Platoon

Panzer Signals Platoon

Regimental Band

1 Panzer Maintenance Company

1st Panzer Battalion
Staff

Staff Signals Platoon

Staff Pioneer Platoon

Panzer Flak Platoon (7 37mm Flak 43)

4 Panzer Companies (22 PzMk IV tanks ea)

2nd Panzer Battalion
same as 1st Battalion

21st Panzergrenadier Regiment
Regimental Staff

Regimental Band

Regimental Staff Company

Signals Platoon

Panzerjäger Platoon (3 LMGs and 3 75mm PAK 40)

Motorcycle Platoon (6 LMGs)

1st (mot) Battalion
3 (mot) Panzergrenadier Companies (4 HMGs, 18 LMGs and 2 80mm mortars ea)

1 (mot) Heavy Panzergrenadier Company

1 Pioneer Platoon (4 LMGs and 6 flamethrowers)

1 Panzerjäger Platoon (3 LMGs and 3 50mm PAK 38)

1 Mortar Platoon (6 80mm mortars)

2 Infantry Gun Sections (2 75mm leIG ea)

2nd (mot) Battalion
same as 1/21st Panzergrenadier Regiment

1 Self-Propelled Infantry Gun Company (6 150mm sIG)

1 Self-Propelled Flak Company (12 20mm and 4 LMGs)

26th Panzergrenadier Regiment
Regimental Staff

Regimental Band

Regimental Staff Company

Signals Platoon

Panzerjäger Platoon (3 LMGs and 3 75mm PAK 40)

Motorcycle Platoon (6 LMGs)

1st (half-track) Battalion
3 (half-track) Panzergrenadier Companies (4 HMGs, 39 LMGs, 3 PzBu, 3 37mm PAK 36, 2 80mm mortars and 2 75mm guns ea)

1 (half-track) Heavy Panzergrenadier Company
   1 Pioneer Platoon (12 LMGs, 1 37mm PAK 36 and
     6 flamethrowers)
   1 Panzerjäger Platoon (9 LMGs and 3 75mm PAK 40)
   1 Gun Platoon (8 LMGs and 6 75mm guns)
   1 Infantry Gun Section (2 75mm leIG)

2nd (mot) Battalion
   same as 1/21st Panzergrenadier Regiment

1 Self-Propelled Infantry Gun Company (6 150mm
sIG)

1 Self-Propelled Flak Company (12 20mm and 4
LMGs)

24th Panzer Reconnaissance Battalion
   Staff (3 LMGs)
   1 Heavy Armored Car Platoon (6 SdKfz 234/3 with
     75mm KwK and 6 LMGs)
   1 Light Armored Car Company (7 LMGs and 18 SdKfz
     234/1 with 20mm and 1 LMG)
   1 (half-track) Heavy Reconnaissance Company (26
     LMGs and 16 20mm guns)
   2 (half-track) Heavy Reconnaissance Company (2 120mm
     mortars, 4 HMGs, 56 LMGs and 3 37mm PAK 36)
   1 (half-track) Heavy Reconnaissance Company
     1 Pioneer Platoon (13 LMGs, 1 37mm PAK 36 and 6
      flamethrowers)
     1 Panzerjäger Platoon (9 LMGs and 3 75mm PAK 40)
     1 Gun Platoon (8 LMGs and 6 75mm guns)
     2 Light Infantry Gun Sections (4 LMGs and 2 75mm
      leIG)
   1 Light Panzer Reconnaissance Battalion Column

89th Panzer Artillery Regiment
   Staff and (mot) Staff Battery (6 LMGs)
   89th (mot) Observation Battery (2 LMGs)

1st Battalion
   Staff and Staff Battery (2 LMGs)
   2 Self-Propelled Batteries (6 105mm leFH SdKfz 124
     Wespe ea)
   1 Self-Propelled sFH Battery (6 150mm sFH SdKfz
     165 Hummel)

2nd Battalion
   Staff and Staff Battery (2 LMGs)
   3 (motZ) Batteries (4 105mm leFH and 2 LMGs ea)

3rd Battalion
   Staff and (mot) Staff Battery (2 LMGs)
   2 (motZ) Batteries (4 150mm sFH and 2 LMGs ea)
   1 (motZ) Battery (4 100mm K18 and 2 LMGs)

283rd Army Flak Battalion
   Staff and Staff Battery
   1/, 2/283rd (motZ) Heavy Flak Batteries (4 88mm, 3
     20mm Flak guns and 2 LMGs ea)
   3/283rd (motZ) Light Flak Battery (9 20mm guns, 2
     quad 20mm and 2 LMGs)
   1 (mot) Light (20 ton) Flak Column

40th Panzer Pioneer Battalion
   Staff (2 LMGs)
   1 (half-track) Pioneer Company (2 HMGs, 43 LMGs,
     3 PzBu, 6 flamethrowers and 2 80mm mortars)
   2 (mot) Pioneer Companies (2 HMGs, 18 LMGs, 3
     PzBu, 6 flamethrowers and 2 80mm mortars ea)
   1 Brüko K Bridging Column (3 LMGs)
   1 (mot) Light Pioneer Column (2 LMGs)

86th Panzer Signals Battalion
   Staff
   1 Panzer Telephone Company (21 LMGs)
   1 Panzer Radio Company (35 LMGs)
   1 (mot) Light Signals Column (1 LMG)

40th Supply Troops
   Staff
   1–8/40th (mot) (120 ton) Transportation Companies
     (4 LMGs ea)
   40th (mot) Supply Company (6 LMGs)

40th Truck Maintenance Park
   1/, 2/, 3/40th (mot) Maintenance Companies
   1 (mot) (75 ton Heavy Maintenance Column

Administration
   40th Divisional Administration Office
   40th (mot) Bakery Company
   40th (mot) Butcher Company

Medical Troops
   1/, 2/40th (mot) Medical Companies
   1/, 2/, 3/40th Ambulance Platoons

Other
   40th (mot) Military Police Troop (2 LMGs)
   40th (mot) Field Post Office

25th Panzer Division

Division Staff
   Divisional Staff (2 LMGs)
   505th (mot) Division Mapping Detachment

9th Panzer Regiment
   Regimental Staff
   Panzer Signals Platoon

2nd Panzer Battalion
   Staff

   Staff Signals Platoon
   Panzer Flak Platoon (7 37mm Flak 43)
   4 Panzer Companies (22 PzMk IV tanks ea)
   1 Panzer Maintenance Company

146th Panzergrenadier Regiment
   Regimental Staff
   Regimental Staff Company
     Signals Platoon

Panzerjäger Platoon (3 LMGs and 3 75mm PAK 40)
Motorcycle Platoon (6 LMGs)

1st (mot) Battalion

3 (mot)Panzergrenadier Companies (4 HMGs, 18 LMGs, 3 PzBu and 2 80mm mortars ea)

1 (mot) Heavy Panzergrenadier Company

1 Pioneer Platoon (4 LMGs)

1 Panzerjäger Platoon (3 LMGs and 3 50mm PAK 38)

1 Panzerjäger Platoon (3 LMGs and 3 sPzBu 41)

2 Infantry Gun Sections (2 75mm leIG ea)

2nd (mot) Battalion

same as 1/146th Panzergrenadier Regiment

1 (motZ) Infantry Gun Company (4 150mm sIG)

147th Panzergrenadier Regiment

same as 146th Panzergrenadier Regiment

87th Panzerjäger Battalion

1 Battalion Staff

2 (motZ) Panzerjäger Companies (12 75mm PAK 40 and 12 LMGs ea)

25th Panzer Reconnaissance Battalion

Staff (3 LMGs)

1 Heavy Armored Car Platoon (6 SdKfz 234/3 with 75mm KwK and 6 LMGs)

1 Light Armored Car Company (6 LMGs and 18 SdKfz 234/1 with 20mm and 1 LMG)

1 (half-track) Heavy Reconnaissance Company (25 LMGs and 16 20mm guns)

2 Motorcycle Company (2 80mm mortars, 3 PzBu, 4 HMGs and 18 LMGs)

1 (half-track) Heavy Reconnaissance Company

1 Pioneer Platoon (4 LMGs)

1 Panzerjäger Platoon (3 LMGs and 3 50mm PAK 38)

1 Panzerjäger Platoon (3 LMGs and 3 sPzBu 41)

2 Light Infantry Gun Sections (4 LMGs and 2 75mm leIG)

1 Light Panzer Reconnaissance Battalion Column

91st Panzer Artillery Regiment

Staff and (mot) Staff Battery (6 LMGs)

1st Battalion

Staff and Staff Battery (2 LMGs)

3 (motZ) Batteries (4 105mm leFH and 2 LMGs ea)

2nd Battalion

same as 1st Battalion

3rd Battalion

Staff and (mot) Staff Battery (2 LMGs)

2 (motZ) Batteries (4 150mm sFH and 2 LMGs ea)

1 (motZ) Battery (4 100mm K18 and 2 LMGs)

284th Army Flak Battalion

Staff and Staff Battery

1/, 2/284th (motZ) Heavy Flak Batteries (4 88mm, 3 20mm Flak guns and 2 LMGs ea)

3/284th (motZ) Light Flak Battery (9 20mm guns, 2 quad 20mm and 2 LMGs)

1 (mot) Light (20 ton) Flak Column

19th Feldersatz Battalion

4 companies

87th Panzer Pioneer Battalion

Staff (2 LMGs)

3 (mot) Pioneer Companies (18 LMGs, 3 PzBu and 2 80mm mortars ea)

1 Brüko K Bridging Column (3 LMGs)

1 (mot) Light Pioneer Column (2 LMGs)

87th Panzer Signals Battalion

Staff

1 Panzer Telephone Company (6 LMGs)

1 Panzer Radio Company (16 LMGs)

1 (mot) Light Signals Column (1 LMG)

87th Supply Troops

Staff

1/, 2/, 3/87th (mot) (120 ton) Transportation Companies (4 LMGs ea)

4/, 5/87th (mot) (90 ton) Transportation Companies (3 LMGs ea)

87th (mot) Supply Company (6 LMGs)

87th Truck Maintenance Park

1/, 2/, 3/87th (mot) Maintenance Companies

Administration

87th Divisional Administration Office

87th (mot) Bakery Company

87th (mot) Butcher Company

Medical Troops

1/, 2/87th (mot) Medical Companies

1/, 2/, 3/87th Ambulance Platoons

Other

87th (mot) Military Police Troop (2 LMGs)

87th (mot) Field Post Office

26th Panzer Division

Division Staff

Divisional Staff (2 LMGs)

93rd (mot) Division Mapping Detachment

26th Panzer Regiment

Regimental Staff

Panzer Signals Platoon

Staff Panzer Platoon

Regimental Band

1st Panzer Battalion

Staff

Staff Signals Platoon
Staff Pioneer Platoon
Panzer Flak Platoon (7 37mm Flak 43)
4 Panzer Companies (22 PzMk V Panther tanks ea)
1 Panzer Maintenance Company

2nd Panzer Battalion
Staff
Staff Signals Platoon
Staff Pioneer Platoon
Panzer Flak Platoon (7 37mm Flak 43)
4 Panzer Companies (22 PzMk IV tanks ea)
1 Panzer Maintenance Company

9th Panzergrenadier Regiment
Regimental Staff
Regimental Staff Company
  Signals Platoon
  Half-track Pioneer Platoon (6 LMGs and 6 flame-throwers)
  Panzerjäger Platoon (3 LMGs and 3 75mm PAK 40)
  Motorcycle Platoon (6 LMGs)

1st (half-track) Battalion
3 (half-track) Panzergrenadier Companies (4 HMGs, 34 LMGs, 3 PzBu, 3 37mm PAK 36 and 2 80mm mortars ea)
1 (half-track) Heavy Panzergrenadier Company
  1 Pioneer Platoon (9 LMGs and 6 flamethrowers)
  1 Gun Platoon (8 LMGs and 6 75mm guns)
  1 Panzerjäger Platoon (3 LMGs and 3 50mm PAK 38)
  1 Panzerjäger Platoon (3 LMGs and 3 sPzBu 41)
  1 Infantry Gun Section (4 LMGs 2 75mm leIG)

2nd (mot) Battalion
3 (mot) Panzergrenadier Companies (4 HMGs, 18 LMGs, 3 PzBu and 2 80mm mortars ea)
1 (mot) Heavy Panzergrenadier Company
  1 Pioneer Platoon (4 LMGs)
  1 Panzerjäger Platoon (3 LMGs and 3 50mm PAK 38)
  1 Panzerjäger Platoon (3 LMGs and 3 sPzBu 41)
  1 Infantry Gun Section (2 75mm leIG)

1 Self-Propelled Infantry Gun Company (6 150mm sIG and 7 LMGs)

67th Panzergrenadier Regiment
Regimental Staff
Regimental Staff Company
  Signals Platoon
  Half-track Pioneer Platoon (6 LMGs and 6 flame-throwers)
  Panzerjäger Platoon (3 LMGs and 3 75mm PAK 40)
  Motorcycle Platoon (6 LMGs)

1st Battalion
1 (half-track) Panzergrenadier Companies (4 HMGs, 34 LMGs, 3 PzBu, 3 37mm PAK 36 and 2 80mm mortars)
2 (mot) Panzergrenadier Companies (4 HMGs, 18 LMGs, 3 PzBu and 2 80mm mortars ea)

1 (half-track) Heavy Panzergrenadier Company
  1 Pioneer Platoon (9 LMGs and 6 flamethrowers)
  1 Gun Platoon (8 LMGs and 6 75mm guns)
  1 Panzerjäger Platoon (3 LMGs and 3 50mm PAK 38)
  1 Panzerjäger Platoon (3 LMGs and 3 sPzBu 41)
  1 Infantry Gun Section (4 LMGs 2 75mm leIG)

2nd (mot) Battalion
same as 2/9th Panzergrenadier Regiment

1 Self-Propelled Infantry Gun Company (6 150mm sIG and 7 LMGs)

Panzerjäger Battalion
525th Panzerjäger Company (tactically assigned)

26th Panzer Reconnaissance Battalion
Staff (3 LMGs)
1 Light Armored Car Company (6 LMGs and 18 SdKfz 234/1 with 20mm and 1 LMG)
3 (half-track) Heavy Reconnaissance Companies (2 80mm mortars, 3 37mm PAK 36, 4 HMGs, and 56 LMGs ea)
1 (half-track) Heavy Reconnaissance Company
  1 Pioneer Platoon (13 LMGs)
  1 Panzerjäger Platoon (9 LMGs and 3 75mm PAK 40)
  1 Panzerjäger Platoon (3 LMGs and 3 sPzBu 41)
  1 Light Infantry Gun Section (4 LMGs and 2 75mm leIG)
  1 Gun Platoon (8 LMGs and 6 75mm guns)
1 Light Panzer Reconnaissance Battalion Column

93rd Panzer Artillery Regiment
Staff and (mot) Staff Battery (6 LMGs)
93rd (mot) Observation Battery (2 LMGs)

1st Battalion
Staff and Staff Battery (2 LMGs)
2 Self-Propelled Batteries (6 105mm leFH SdKfz 124 Wespe ea)
1 Self-Propelled sFH Battery (6 150mm sFH SdKfz 165 Hummel)

2nd Battalion
Staff and Staff Battery (2 LMGs)
3 (motZ) Batteries (4 105mm leFH and 2 LMGs ea)

3rd Battalion
Staff and (mot) Staff Battery (2 LMGs)
2 (motZ) Batteries (4 150mm sFH and 2 LMGs ea)
1 (motZ) Battery (4 100mm K18 and 2 LMGs)

Army Flak Battalions
none

26th Feldersatz Battalion
3 companies

93rd Panzer Pioneer Battalion
Staff (2 LMGs)
1 Panzer Pioneer Company (25 LMGs, 3 PzBu and 2 80mm mortars)
2 (mot) Pioneer Companies (18 LMGs, 3 PzBu and 2 80mm mortars ea)

1 Brüko K Bridging Column (3 LMGs)
1 (mot) Light Pioneer Column (2 LMGs)

93rd Panzer Signals Battalion

Staff
1 Panzer Telephone Company (6 LMGs)
1 Panzer Radio Company (16 LMGs)
1 (mot) Light Signals Column (1 LMG)

93rd Supply Troops

Staff
1/, 2/, 3/, 4/93rd (mot) (120 ton) Transportation Companies (4 LMGs ea)
5/93rd (mot) (90 ton) Transportation Companies (3 LMGs)
93rd (mot) Supply Company (6 LMGs)

93rd Truck Maintenance Park

1/, 2/, 3/93rd (mot) Maintenance Companies

Administration

93rd Divisional Administration Office
93rd (mot) Bakery Company
93rd (mot) Butcher Company

Medical Troops

1/, 2/93rd (mot) Medical Companies
1/, 2/, 3/93rd Ambulance Platoons

Other

93rd (mot) Military Police Troop (2 LMGs)
93rd (mot) Field Post Office

7

Organizational History of German Motorized and Panzergrenadier Divisions, 1939–1945

The motorized infantry arm of the German army began its life as part of the *Schnelle Truppen*, or "Fast Troops" of the German army. The *Schnelle Truppen* were officially established in 1938 and included the panzer, anti-tank, and cavalry troops. The motorized infantry began life as *Schützen* (riflemen), *Kavallerieschützen* (cavalry riflemen), and *Motorisierte Infantrie* (motorized infantry). On 5 July 1942 they were redesignated as *Panzertruppen* (armored troops), by which time the cavalry had long been deleted from this organization.

The term *Panzergrenadier* was adopted in 1943. However, despite the use of that name, there were invariably insufficient half-tracks to support their needs and they generally went into battle in trucks.

The Panzergrenadiers were the direct result of Heinz Guderian's concept of armored mobile warfare. They were an integral part of armored warfare and absolutely necessary if any tank formation was to survive long on the battlefield.

When first formed, not only was extensive use made of trucks, but entire battalions of motorcycles were organized. Though the numbers of motorcycles diminished as the war progressed, there were still formations that were designated as motorcycle battalions, even if they were heavily equipped with Volkswagen Kübelwagen scout cars or the SdKfz 2 Halbkettenkraftkrad and very few motorcycles. The riflemen who rode these motorcycles into battle were known as *Kradschützen* (motorcycle riflemen). These motorcycle formations continued in the German army until 1943, when the last ones were transferred to the panzer reconnaissance arm.

The organization of the panzergrenadier divisions varied considerably, as will be shown later. When the Polish campaign began Germany's motorized infantry consisted of the 2nd, 13th, 20th, and 29th (mot) Infantry Divisions. During the winter of 1939/1940 the Grossdeutschland (mot) Infantry Regiment was formed. However, it was in the fall of 1940 that the real increase in motorized infantry occurred. At this time the 3rd, 10th, 14th, 18th, 25th, 36th, and 60th Infantry Divisions were motorized. In addition, the 16th (mot) Infantry Division was formed from those portions of the 16th Infantry Division not used to form the 16th Panzer Division. On 1 April 1942 the Grossdeutschland Regiment was expanded into two regiments and began its growth into a full division.

The disaster at Stalingrad resulted in the destruction of the 3rd, 29th, and 60th (mot) Infantry Divisions. The 3rd and 29th were rebuilt in France using two Kriemhilde Divisions. The re-formation of the 60th (mot) Infantry Division was begun, but in July 1943 it became the Feldherrnhalle Panzergrenadier Division.

On 15 October 1942 the infantry regiments in the motorized infantry divisions were renamed "grenadier regiments". On 23 June 1943 the all of the (mot) infantry divisions, except the 14th and 36th, were renamed Panzergrenadier Divisions. These two exceptions were later demotorized and reverted to being simple infantry divisions. A total of 15 "panzer infantry" divisions were eventually formed. They were:

3rd Panzergrenadier Division
10th Panzergrenadier Division
15th Panzergrenadier Division
16th Panzergrenadier Division
18th Panzergrenadier Division
20th Panzergrenadier Division
25th Panzergrenadier Division
29th Panzergrenadier Division
90th Panzergrenadier Division
Brandenburg Panzergrenadier Division
Feldherrnhalle Panzergrenadier Division
Grossdeutschland Panzergrenadier Division
Kurmark Panzergrenadier Division
Führer Grenadier Division
Führer Escort Division

On 24 September 1943 the "Type 43" Panzergrenadier Division was developed. Each of the grenadier regiments in the divisions was raised to three full battalions. The 13th Companies were uniformly organized with two 150mm sIG and six 75mm leIG guns. In addition, if material was available, a light Flak company with 12 20mm guns on self-propelled carriages and a pioneer company with 16 flamethrowers was organized.

In May 1944 the 16th Panzergrenadier Division was used to form the 116th Panzer Division. The Feldherrnhalle Panzergrenadier Division was destroyed in January 1945 and rebuilt, as were the 10th, 18th and 25th Panzergrenadier Divisions.

In 1944 independent panzer brigades appeared. They were also occasionally known as panzergrenadier brigades. In fact, they were of regimental strength and consisted of a panzergrenadier battalion in half-tracks and a panzer battalion. The brigade staff also generally had some platoon sized reconnaissance elements. This same formation was also to occur in the Type 45 panzer divisions. Records show it in the Feldherrnhalle and 13th Panzer Divisions.

On 1 December 1944 the remaining (mot) Grenadier Regiments were renamed Panzergrenadier Regiments. However, despite the name change only one battalion in each division was actually equipped with half-tracks. In 1945 the Führer Escort Battalion was expanded into two brigades, the Führer Escort Brigade and the Führer Grenadier Brigade.

2nd (mot) Infantry Division

Mobilized in August 1939 and organized and equipped as follows:

2nd (mot) Infantry Division
1/, 2/, 3/5th (mot) Infantry Regiment
  1 (mot) Signals Platoon
  3 Battalions, each with
    3 (mot) Battalions, each with
      3 Rifle Companies (9 LMGs, 2 HMGs and 3 50mm mortars)
      1 Heavy Company (8 HMGs and 6 80mm mortars)
      1 (mot) Panzerabwehr Company (12 37mm PAK 36 and 4 LMGs)
      1 (mot) Infantry Support Gun Company (8 75mm leIG)
      1 Motorcycle Platoon (3 LMGs)
      1 Light Infantry Supply Column
1/, 2/, 3/25th (mot) Infantry Regiment
  same as 5th (mot) Infantry Regiment
1/, 2/, 3/92nd (mot) Infantry Regiment
  same as 5th (mot) Infantry Regiment
2nd (mot) Artillery Regiment
  1st, 2nd and 3rd (mot) Battalions, each with
    3 Batteries (4 105mm leFH and 2 LMGs ea)
  4th (mot) Artillery Battalion
    3 Batteries (4 150mm sFH and 2 LMGs ea)
    2nd Artillery Observation Battalion
2nd Panzer Abwehr Battalion
  1 (mot) Signals Platoon
  2 (mot) Panzer Abwehr Companies (12 37mm PAK 36 and 4 LMGs ea)
  5/32nd Heavy Machine Gun Battalion (12 20mm)
2nd Reconnaissance Battalion
  1 Motorcycle Company (9 LMGs, 2 HMGs and 3 50mm mortars)
  1 Armored Car Company (10 20mm and 25 LMGs)
2nd (mot) Pioneer Battalion
  3 (mot) Pioneer Companies (9 LMGs ea)
  1 (mot) Brüko B
  1 (mot) Pioneer Supply Column
2nd Signals Battalion
  1 (mot) Telephone Company

  1 (mot) Radio Company
  1 (mot) Signals Supply Column
2nd Supply Troop
  1–8/2nd (mot) Light Supply Columns
  9–10/2nd (mot) Light Fuel Columns
  1/, 2/, 3/2nd (mot) Maintenance Companies
  2nd (mot) Supply Company
Other
  2nd (mot) Field Bakery
  2nd (mot) Butcher Unit
  2nd Division Administration
  1/, 2/2nd (mot) Medical Companies
  2nd (mot) Field Hospital
  1/, 2/, 3/2nd Ambulance Companies
  2nd (mot) Military Police Troop
  2nd (mot) Field Post Office

On 15 October 1939 the 2/92nd became the 2/Grossdeutschland Infantry Regiment and the remainder of the 92nd Infantry Regiment was demotorized and sent to the 60th Infantry Division. In 1940 a motorcycle battalion was formed in the division:

  1/, 2/, 3/5th (mot) Infantry Regiment
  1/, 2/, 3/25th (mot) Infantry Regiment
  22nd Motorcycle Battalion
  1/, 2/, 3/2nd (mot) Artillery Regiment
  1/38th Artillery Regiment
  32nd Pioneer Battalion
  2nd Division Support Units

On 1 April 1940 the 7/, 8/2nd Light Supply Column were renumbered the 4/, 6/2nd and the 9/, 10/2 Heavy Fuel Columns were renumbered the 7/, 8/2nd.

On 5 October 19/40 the division was attached to the 12th Panzer Division. The 3/5th (mot) Infantry Regiment was sent to the 4th Panzer Division as the 34th Motorcycle Battalion and the 3/25th Infantry Regiment became the 30th Motorcycle Battalion in the 20th (mot) Infantry Division. The 2/2nd Artillery Regiment became the independent 154th Heavy Artillery Battalion. On 10 January 1941 the division was absorbed into the 12th Panzer Division.

3rd (mot) Infantry Division

Formed on 27 October 1940 from the 3rd Infantry Division by detaching the 50th Infantry Regiment, 3/3rd Artillery Regiment, and 1/39th Artillery Regiment to the 123rd Infantry Division. To the remainder was added a new heavy artillery battalion (3/3rd), which was formed on 12/15/40 from the 628th Heavy Artillery Battalion. The division was organized as follows:

1/, 2/, 3/8th (mot) Infantry Regiment
1/, 2/, 3/29th (mot) Infantry Regiment
53rd Motorcycle Battalion (from 2/50th Infantry Regiment)
1/, 2/, 3/3rd (mot) Artillery Regiment
53rd Motorcycle Battalion
3rd Divisional Service Units

On 15 March 1942 the 53rd Motorcycle Battalion was redesignated as the 386th Motorcycle Battalion. This battalion was later to become the 53rd Panzer Reconnaissance Battalion. The 4/3rd Artillery Regiment was formed in 1942 using the 312th Army Flak Artillery Battalion. In May 1942 the 14th Companies of the two (mot) Infantry Regiments were organized from the 6/47th Flak Machine Gun Battalion and 5/48th Flak Machine Gun Battalion. On 1 June 1942 the division contained:

Division Headquarters
1 (mot) Mapping Detachment
1 Escort Detachment (2 LMGs)
8th (mot) Infantry Regiment
1 (mot) Staff Company
1 Signals Detachment
1 Anti-Tank Platoon (3 50mm PAK 38 guns and 3 LMGs)
1 Engineer Platoon (3 LMGs)
1 Motorcycle Platoon (3 LMGs)
3 (mot) Infantry Battalions, each with
3 Infantry Companies (12 LMGs, 6 HMGs, 3 50mm mortars, 1 28mm sPzB 41 and 3 PzBu39 ea)
1 Heavy Company (12 HMGs, 6 80mm mortars, 3 37mm PAK 36 guns and 1 LMG)
1 (mot) Infantry Support Gun Company (2 150mm and 6 75mm leIG)
1 Self-Propelled Flak Company (12 20mm Flak guns)
29th (mot) Infantry Regiment
1 (mot) Staff Company
1 Signals Detachment
1 Anti-Tank Platoon (3 50mm PAK 38 guns and 3 LMGs)
1 Engineer Platoon (3 LMGs)
1 Motorcycle Platoon (3 LMGs)
3 (mot) Infantry Battalions, each with
3 Infantry Companies (12 LMGs, 6 HMGs, 3 50mm mortars, 1 28mm sPzBu41 and 3 PzBu39 ea)

1 Heavy Company (12 HMGs, 6 80mm mortars, 3 37mm PAK 36 guns and 1 LMG)
1 (mot) Infantry Support Gun Company (2 150mm and 6 75mm leIG)
1 Self-Propelled Flak Company (12 20mm Flak guns)
53rd Motorcycle Battalion
1 Armored Car Company (18 20mm and 24 LMGs)
3 Motorcycle Companies (2 80mm mortars, 4 HMGs, 18 LMGs and 3 PzBu39 ea)
1 (mot) Heavy Company
1 (mot) Engineer Platoon (4 LMGs)
1 (mot) Panzerjäger Platoon (3 50mm PAK 38 and 3 LMGs)
1 Panzerjäger Platoon (3 28mm sPzBu 41)
1 Infantry Support Platoon (2 75mm leIG)
1 Light Armored Car Supply Column (3 LMGs)
103rd Panzer Battalion
1 Armored Staff Company
1 Medium Armored Company
2 Light Armored Companies
1 Armored Maintenance Company
3rd Panzerjäger Battalion
2 Self-Propelled Anti-Tank Companies (6 75mm PAK 40 and 6 LMGs, probably Marder III Ausf M ea)
1 (mot) Anti-Tank Company (9 50mm PAK 38 and 9 LMGs)
3rd (mot) Artillery Regiment
1st Battalion
1 (mot) Staff Battery (2 150mm Infantry Support Guns and 2 LMGs)
3 Batteries (4 105mm leFH howitzers and 2 LMGs ea)
2nd Battalion
1 (mot) Staff Battery (2 150mm sFH 18 and 2 LMGs)
3 Batteries (4 105mm leFH howitzers and 2 LMGs ea)
3rd Battalion
1 (mot) Staff Battery (2 150mm Infantry Support Guns and 2 LMGs)
1 (mot) Heavy Battery (4 100mm guns and 2 LMGs)
1 (mot) Heavy Batteries (4 150mm howitzers and 2 LMGs)
1 (mot) Observation Company
4th Battalion
2 (mot) Heavy Flak Batteries (4 88mm guns, 2 self-propelled 20mm Flak guns and 2 LMGs)
1 (mot) Self-Propelled Flak Battery (12 37mm Flak guns)
1 (mot) Munitions Column
3rd (mot) Pioneer Battalion
3 (mot) Pioneer Companies (9 HMGs, 9 LMGs, 3 PzBu39 ea)
1 (mot) Pioneer Supply Column (2 LMGs)

3rd Signals Battalion
- 1 (mot) Radio Company
- 1 (mot) Telephone Company
- 1 (mot) Supply Column

3rd Supply Battalion
- 1–8/3rd Light (mot) Supply Columns (2 LMGs ea)
- 9/3rd Heavy (mot) Supply Column (2 LMGs)
- 10/, 11/3rd Heavy (mot) Fuel Column (2 LMGs ea)
- 1/, 2/3rd (mot) Maintenance Companies
- 1 (mot) Supply Company (2 LMGs)

Medical
- 1st and 2nd Medical Companies (2 LMGs ea)
- 1st, 2nd and 3rd Ambulance Columns (1 LMG ea)

Other
- 1 (mot) Field Bakery Company
- 1 (mot) Field Butcher Company
- 1 (mot) Divisional Administration Unit
- 1 (mot) Field Post Office
- 1 (mot) Military Police Detachment

On 28 June 1942 the organization of the armored portion of the division and its panzer inventory were as follows:

103rd Panzer Battalion
- 1 Panzer Staff Company
- 1 Medium Panzer Company
- 2 Light Panzer Companies

PzMk II	10
PzMk III (50 lg)	35
PzMk IV (lg)	8
Cmd	1

The division was destroyed at Stalingrad in January 1943. On 1 March 1943 the division was re-formed in France by redesignating the 386th (mot) Infantry Division and joining to it the few surviving fragments of the old division. It had:

- 1/, 2/, 3/8th (mot) Infantry Regiment (from 149th (mot) Grenadier Regiment)
- 1/, 2/, 3/29th (mot) Infantry Regiment (from 153rd Panzergrenadier Regiment)
- 103rd Panzer Battalion (from 386th Pz Battalion)
- 103rd Armored Reconnaissance Battalion (from 386th Motorcycle Battalion)
- 1/, 2/, 3/3rd (mot) Artillery Regiment (from staff and 1/ 386th Artillery Regiment)
- 312th Army Flak Artillery Battalion (from 2/386th Artillery Regiment; later became 4/3rd (mot) Artillery Regiment)
- 3rd Divisional Service Units

The division was renamed the 3rd Panzergrenadier Division on 23 June 1943.

3rd Panzergrenadier Division

Formed on 23 June 1943 from the 3rd (mot) Infantry Division. The infantry regiments were converted to motorized grenadier regiments on 15 October 1942. On 20 April 1943 the 53rd Panzer Reconnaissance Battalion became the 103rd Panzer Reconnaissance Battalion.

Keilig states that, after being rebuilt, the division had the 22nd Sound Ranging Troop attached to it. The 103rd Panzer Reconnaissance Battalion had staff, a heavy platoon with six SdKfz 251/9 with 75mm KwK, a light armored car company, a (half-track) reconnaissance company, a (half-track) heavy reconnaissance company, a (half-track) heavy company—containing a pioneer platoon, a panzerjäger platoon, a light infantry gun platoon (75mm leIG), and two platoons (SdKfz 251/9 with 75mm KwK)—and a light panzer reconnaissance battalion column. The 103rd Panzer Battalion was equipped with sturmgeschütze. The division had no panzerjäger battalion. The 1/3rd Artillery Regiment had staff, staff battery, two self-propelled leFH batteries (six SdKfz 124 Wespe with 105mm leFH ea), and one self-propelled sFH battery (six SdKfz 165 Hummel with 150mm sFH). The feldersatz battalion had two companies.

The division was destroyed in the battles around Stalingrad. The 103rd Panzer Battalion was rebuilt with four companies on 11 February 1943. OKH records indicate that sometime in July 1943 the 103rd Panzer Battalion was reorganized from four medium tank companies (22 tanks per company) to three assault gun batteries (14 StuG per battery). On 20 August 1943 the organization of the armored portion of the division and its panzer inventory were as follows:

103rd Panzer Battalion
1 Battalion
- 1 Panzer Staff Company
- 3 Sturmgeschütz Companies

StuG	42
Cmd	6

OKH records show that in September 1943 the division was organized and equipped as follows:

3rd Panzergrenadier Division
Divisional Staff
Staff

3rd (mot) Mapping Detachment
22nd Sound Ranging Troop (temporarily attached)

8th Panzergrenadier Regiment
Staff
Regimental Band
Staff Company
Signals Platoon
Pioneer Platoon (6 flamethrowers and 3 LMGs)
3 Battalions, each with
Staff
4 (mot) Grenadier Companies (4 HMGs, 18 LMGs, 3 PzBu39 and 2 80mm mortars ea)
1 Self-Propelled Heavy Infantry Gun Company (6 150mm sIG)
1 (motZ) Panzerjäger Company (3 75mm PAK 40, 6 50mm PAK 38 and 9 LMGs)

29th Panzergrenadier Regiment
same as 8th Panzergrenadier Regiment

103rd Panzer Reconnaissance Battalion
Staff (15 LMGs)
Heavy Platoon (6 SdKfz 234/3 with 75mm KwK and 6 LMGs)
1 Light Armored Car Company (18 20mm and 24 LMGs)
1 (half-track) Reconnaissance Company (16 20mm and 25 LMGs)
2 (half-track) Heavy Reconnaissance Companies (2 80mm mortars, 4 LMGs, 56 LMGs and 3 75mm leIG ea)
1 (half-track) Heavy Company
1 Pioneer Platoon (3 LMGs, 1 20mm and 6 flamethrowers)
1 Panzerjäger Platoon (3 LMGs and 3 75mm PAK 40)
1 Light Infantry Gun Section (4 LMGs and 2 75mm leIG)
2 Platoons (4 LMGs and 3 SdKfz 251/9 with 75mm KwK ea)
1 Light Panzer Reconnaissance Battalion Column

103rd Panzer Battalion
Staff and Staff Battery (3 StuG)
3 Sturmgeschütz Batteries (14 StuG ea)
1 Panzer Maintenance Platoon

3rd Flak Battalion
Staff and (mot) Staff Battery (1 LMG)
2 (motZ) Heavy Flak Batteries (4 88mm, 3 20mm and 2 LMGs ea)
1 (motZ) Light Flak Battery (9 20mm, 2 quad 20mm and 2 LMGs)
1 (mot) (20 ton) Supply Column

3rd Artillery Regiment
1 Regimental Staff and (mot) Staff Battery (2 LMGs)
1st Battalion
1 Battalion Staff and (self-propelled) Staff Battery (2 LMGs)
3 Self-Propelled Batteries (4 105mm leFH in Wespe and 2 LMGs ea)

2nd Battalion
1 Battalion Staff and (mot) Staff Battery (2 LMGs)
3 (motZ) Batteries (4 105mm leFh and 2 LMGs ea)
3rd Battalion
1 Battalion Staff and (mot) Staff Battery (2 LMGs)
2 (motZ) Batteries (4 150mm sFH and 2 LMGs ea)
1 (motZ) Battery (4 100mm K18 and 2 LMGs)

3rd Pioneer Battalion
Staff
3 (mot) Pioneer Companies (2 HMGs, 18 LMGs, 3 PzBu39, 2 80mm mortars and 6 flamethrowers ea)
1 (mot) Brüko K Bridging Column (3 LMGs)
1 (mot) Light Pioneer Column (2 LMGs)

3rd Signals Battalion
Staff
1 (mot) Telephone Company (5 LMGs)
1 (mot) Radio Company (4 LMGs)
1 (mot) Signals Column (1 LMG)

3rd Supply Troops
1/, 2/3rd (120 ton) Transportation Companies (4 LMGs ea)
3/, 4/, 5/3rd (90 ton) Transportation Companies (3 LMGs ea)
3rd (mot) Supply Company (6 LMGs)

Maintenance
1/, 2/3rd (mot) Maintenance Companies
3rd (75 ton) Maintenance Supply Column

Administration
3rd (mot) Administration Bureau
3rd (mot) Bakery Company
3rd (mot) Butcher Company

Medical Units
1/, 2/3rd (mot) Medical Companies
1/, 2/, 3/3rd Ambulance Platoons

Other
3rd (mot) Military Police Troop
3rd (mot) Field Post Office

On 28 April 1944 the division was reorganized. In June 1944 the panzerjäger battalion was equipped with two companies of Panzerjäger IV/38 and the 3rd Company with (motZ) 75mm PAK 40. A 4th Company was later organized with "Ofenrohren" tank destroyers. This battalion bore no relationship to the old 3rd Panzerjäger Battalion of the 3rd (mot) Infantry Division. The sturmgeschütz assigned to the division had the long 75mm gun. On 1 December 1944 the two motorized grenadier regiments were renamed panzergrenadier regiments. In August 1944 the organization of the armored portion of the division and its panzer inventory were as follows:

103rd Panzer Battalion
1 Sturmgeschütz Staff Company
3 Sturmgeschütz Companies

StuG   37
PzBefWgIII   2

In September 1944 the 1/3rd (mot) Artillery Regiment was equipped with the self-propelled 105mm Wespe gun carriages. On 10 December 1944 the organization of the armored portion of the division and its panzer inventory were as follows:

103rd Panzer Battalion
  1 Sturmgeschütz Staff Company
  3 Sturmgeschütz Companies
  StuG   41
  PzBefWg III   1
  PzBefWg IV   2

The division was destroyed in the 1945 battles for the Ruhr.

10th (mot) Infantry Division

Formed on 15 November 1940 from the 10th Infantry Division. The 85th Infantry Regiment was transformed into the 85th Mountain Regiment and transferred to the 5th Mountain Division along with the 3/10th Artillery Regiment. The division then had:

1/, 2/, 3/20th (mot) Infantry Regiment
1/, 2/, 3/41st (mot) Infantry Regiment
40th Motorcycle Battalion (formed from 6th Machine Gun Battalion)

1/, 2/, 3/10th Artillery Regiment (the 3rd Battalion was formed from the 649th Army Heavy Artillery Battalion.)
10th Divisional Service Units

The conversion was complete on 1 May 1941, and on 15 October 1942 the motorized infantry regiments were redesignated as motorized grenadier regiments.

10th Panzergrenadier Division

Formed on 13 June 1943 from the 10th (mot) Infantry Division. With this transformation, it consisted of:

1/, 2/, 3/20th Grenadier Regiment (motorized)
1/, 2/, 3/41st Grenadier Regiment (motorized)
7th Panzer Battalion
110th Panzer Reconnaissance Battalion (formed from the 40th Motorcycle Battalion)
1/, 2/, 3/10th Artillery Regiment
275th Army Flak Battalion
10th Divisional Service Units

Keilig states that in 1943 the 110th Panzer Reconnaissance Battalion contained a staff, one light armored car company, three motorcycle companies, a heavy company, and a reconnaissance supply column. The 7th Panzer Battalion was equipped with sturmgeschütze. The 10th Panzerjäger Battalion had a staff and three self-propelled panzerjäger companies. The 10th Pioneer Battalion had no bridging column. The feldersatz battalion had four companies. The 10th Ost Company was assigned to the division. This company was formed with Russian nationals who volunteered to serve in the German army.

In July 1943, as the division prepared for the Battle of Kursk, it is known to have had seven artillery battalions, a nebelwerfer regiment, a mortar battalion, and an assault gun battalion attached to it. However, if they were assigned

as organic units or merely assigned temporarily for the battle is not known. In September 1943 OKH records show that the division was organized and equipped as follows:

10th Panzergrenadier Division
Divisional Staff
  Staff
  10th (mot) Mapping Detachment
10th Panzer Battalion
  Staff
  Staff Battery (3 StuG)
  Flak Platoon (3 self-propelled quad 20mm guns)
  3 Sturmgeschütz Batteries (14 StuG ea)
  1 Panzer Maintenance Platoon
20th Panzergrenadier Regiment
  Staff
  Regimental Band
  Staff Company
    Panzerjäger Platoon (3 LMGs and 3 50mm PAK 38)
    Motorcycle Platoon (3 LMGs)
    Signals Platoon
    Pioneer Platoon (6 flamethrowers and 3 LMGs)
  3 Battalions, each with
    Staff
    3 (mot) Grenadier Companies (12 HMGs, 6 LMGs, 1 28mm sPzBu, 3 PzBu39 and 3 50mm mortars ea)

1 (mot) Machine Gun Company
  2 Machine Gun Platoons (6 HMGs ea)
  1 Panzerjäger Platoon (1 LMG and 3 37mm PAK 36)
  1 Mortar Platoon (6 80mm mortars)
1 (motZ) Infantry Gun Company (2 150mm sIG and 6 75mm leIG)

41st Panzergrenadier Regiment
same as 20th Panzergrenadier Regiment

10th Panzer Reconnaissance Battalion
Staff (3 LMGs)
1 Light Armored Car Company (18 20mm and 24 LMGs)
3 Motorcycle Companies (2 80mm mortars, 3 PzBu39, 4 HMGs, and 18 LMGs ea)
1 (mot) Heavy Company
  1 Pioneer Platoon (3 LMGs)
  1 Panzerjäger Platoon (3 LMGs and 3 PAK)
  1 Panzerjäger Platoon (3 LMGs and 3 sPzBu 41)
  1 Light Infantry Gun Section (2 75mm leIG)
1 Light Panzer Reconnaissance Battalion Column

10th Artillery Regiment
1 Regimental Staff and (mot) Staff Battery (2 LMGs)

1st Battalion
1 Battalion Staff and (mot) Staff Battery (2 LMGs)
3 (motZ) Batteries (3 105mm leFH and 2 LMGs ea)

2nd Battalion
same as 1st Battalion

3rd Battalion
1 Battalion Staff and (mot) Staff Battery (2 LMGs)
2 (motZ) Batteries (3 150mm sFH and 2 LMGs ea)
1 (motZ) Battery (3 100mm K18 and 2 LMGs)

10th Panzerjäger Battalion
3 Self-Propelled Panzerjäger Companies (14 75mm PAK 40 and 14 LMGs ea)
1 Self-Propelled Flak Company (12 20mm and 4 LMGs)

10th Pioneer Battalion
Staff
3 (mot) Pioneer Companies (2 HMGs, 9 LMGs, 3 PzBu39 and 2 80mm mortars ea)
1 (mot) Light Pioneer Column (2 LMGs)

10th Signals Battalion
Staff
1 (mot) Telephone Company (5 LMGs)
1 (mot) Radio Company (4 LMGs)
1 (mot) Signals Column (1 LMG)

10th Supply Troops
1/, 2/10th (90 ton) Transportation Companies (3 LMGs ea)
3/10th (100 ton) Transportation Company (4 LMGs)
4/10th Heavy Supply Column (2 LMGs)
10th (mot) Supply Company (6 LMGs)

Maintenance
1/, 2/10th (mot) Maintenance Companies

Administration
10th (mot) Administration Bureau

10th (mot) Bakery
10th (mot) Butcher

Medical Units
1/, 2/10th (mot) Medi
1/, 2/, 3/10th Ambuland

Other
10th (mot) Military Police
10th (mot) Field Post Offi

The division was destroyed i
formed by Army Group A on 15
built it contained:

1/, 2/, 3/20th Panzergrenadier R
1/, 2/, 3/41st Panzergrenadier Re
7th Panzer Battalion
110th Panzer Reconnaissance Batt
1/, 2/, 3/10th Artillery Regiment
10th Divisional Service Units

The newly reorganized division was sent into batt.
ary 1945 on the Vistula. By 6 February 1945 it was redu
the force of a Kampfgruppe and was organized as follows:

Divisional Staff
1 Panzergrenadier Division Staff (2 LMGs)
1 (mot) Mapping Detachment
1 (mot) Military Police Detachment (5 LMGs)
1 Armored Car Platoon (3 SdKfz 234/3 with 75mm and 1 LMG and 13 SdKfz 234/1 with 1 LMG and 1 20mm gun)

Panzer Battalion
1 Panzer Battalion Staff
1 Panzer Battalion Staff Company (1 StuG, 8 LMGs and 3 self-propelled 20mm Flak guns)
3 Sturmgeschütz Companies (10 StuG ea)
1 (mot) Supply Company
1 (mot) Maintenance Platoon

Panzergrenadier Regiment
1 Panzergrenadier Regimental Staff
1 (mot) Panzergrenadier Regimental Staff Company
  1 Signals Platoon
  1 Motorcycle Platoon (6 LMGs)
  1 Panzerjäger Platoon (3 75mm PAK 40 and 3 LMGs)

1st and 2nd Battalions, each with
1 Battalion Staff
1 (mot) Supply Company (4 LMGs)
3 (mot) Panzergrenadier Companies (12 LMGs, 30 MP 44 and 3 panzerschrecke ea)
1 (mot) Heavy Company (12 HMGs, 1 LMG, 6 20mm Flak)
1 (mot) Heavy Company (6 LMGs, 8 80mm mortars and 4 120mm mortars)

3rd Battalion
1 Battalion Staff

mpany (4 LMGs)

rgrenadier Companies (12 LMGs, 3 panzerschrecke ea)

Company (12 HMGs, 1 LMG and 6

y Company (6 LMGs, 8 80mm mortars 0mm mortars)

G Company (4 150mm sIG and 2 LMGs)

ioneer Company (16 flamethrowers, 2 12 LMGs and 2 80mm mortars)

er Battalion

erjäger Battalion Staff

t) Panzerjäger Battalion Staff Company

urmgeschütz Platoon

turmgeschütz Companies (10 StuG ea)

(motZ) Panzerjäger Battery (12 75mm PAK 40 and 12 LMGs)

1 (mot) Panzerjäger Supply Company (3 LMGs)

Panzer (mot) Reconnaissance Company
(4 HMGs, 9 LMGs and 2 80mm mortars)

Panzer Artillery Battalion
1 Panzer Artillery Battalion Staff
1 Panzer Artillery Battalion Staff Battery (2 LMGs and 3 20mm Flak)
2 (motZ) Batteries (6 105mm leFH and 4 LMGs ea)
1 (motZ) Battery (6 150mm sFH and 4 LMGs)

(mot) Pioneer Company
(2 HMGs, 18 LMGs and 2 80mm mortars)

(mot) Signals Company (5 LMGs)

Other
1 (mot) Supply Troop Staff (2 LMGs)
1 (mot) Supply Troop Staff Company (8 LMGs)
1 (mot) (120 ton) Transportation Company (8 LMGs)
1 (mot) Maintenance Company (4 LMGs)
1 (mot) Mixed Administration Company (2 LMGs)
1 (mot) Medical Company
1 (mot) Medical Supply Company
1 (mot) Field Post Office (1 LMG)

On 6 February 1945 the division was ordered rebuilt as a kampfgruppe. The 7th Panzer Battalion was equipped with 21 Sturmgeschütz III and 10 Jagdpanzer IV/70 (V). A 4th Company was formed in the 7th Panzer Battalion using personnel from the 2110th Panzerjäger Battalion. The division had only the panzer battalion, three panzergrenadier battalions, a panzerjäger battalion and a motorized artillery battalion. On 9 February 1945 the organization of the armored portion of the division and its panzer inventory were as follows

7th Panzer Battalion
1 Sturmgeschütz Staff Company
2 Sturmgeschütz Companies
2 Jagdpanzer Companies (PzMk IVL)
StuG 31 (arrived 9 February)
PzMk IV/70 (V) 10 (arrived in February)

The division was captured by the Russians around Olmütz and Deutsch Brod.

13th (mot) Infantry Division

Mobilized on 18 August 1939 with:

1/, 2/, 3/33rd (mot) Infantry Regiment
1/, 2/, 3/66th (mot) Infantry Regiment
1/, 2/, 3/93rd (mot) Infantry Regiment
1/, 2/, 3/13th Artillery Regiment
1/49th Artillery Regiment
13th Divisional Service Units
13th Feldersatz Battalion
13th Signals Battalion
4th Pioneer Battalion
13th Supply Troop

OKH records show that when the Germans invaded Poland on 1 September 1939 the 13th (mot) Infantry Division was organized and equipped as follows:

13th (mot) Infantry Division Generalleutnant Otto
13th (mot) (mot) Mapping Detachment
13th (mot) Motorcycle Messenger Platoon

33rd (mot) Infantry Regiment
1 Signals Platoon
3 (mot) Battalions, each with
3 Rifle Companies (9 LMGs, 2 HMGs and 3 50mm mortars ea)
1 Heavy Company (8 HMGs and 6 80mm mortars)
1 (mot) Panzerabwehr Company (12 37mm PAK 36 and 4 LMGs)
1 (mot) Infantry Support Gun Company (8 75mm leIG)
1 Motorcycle Platoon (3 LMGs)
1 Light Infantry Supply Column
66th (mot) Infantry Regiment
same as before
93rd (mot) Infantry Regiment
same as before
13th (mot) Panzerabwehr Battalion
1 (mot) Signals Platoon
3 (mot) Panzerabwehr Companies (12 37mm PAK 36 and 6 LMGs ea)

6/46th (mot) Heavy Machine Gun Battalion (12 20mm guns)

13th Reconnaissance Battalion
1 (mot) Signals Platoon (1 LMG)
1 Motorcycle Company (9 LMGs, 2 HMGs and 9 LMGs)
1 Armored Car Company (10 20mm and 25 LMGs)

13th Artillery Regiment
1st and 3rd (mot) Battalions, each with
   3 Batteries (4 105mm leFH and 2 LMGs ea)
1/49th (mot) Artillery Regiment, with
   3 Batteries (4 150mm sFH and 2 LMGs ea)
13th Artillery Observation Battalion

13th Feldersatz Battalion
3 Companies (9 LMGs, 2 HMGs and 3 50mm mortars ea)

13th Signals Battalion
1 (mot) Radio Company
1 (tmot) Telephone Company
1 (mot) Signals Supply Column

4th Pioneer Battalion
3 (mot) Pioneer Companies (9 LMGs ea)
1 (mot) Brüko B
1 (mot) Engineer Supply Column

13th Supply Troop
1st–8th (mot) Light Supply Columns
9/, 10/13th (mot) Heavy Fuel Column
13th (mot) Maintenance Platoon
13th (mot) Supply Company

Administration
13th Divisional Administration
13th (mot) Field Bakery

13th (mot) Butcher Detachment

Other
1/, 2/13th Medical Company
13th (mot) Field Hospital
1/, 2/13th Ambulance Companies
13th Veterinarian Company
13th (mot) Military Police Troop
13th (mot) Field Post Office

On 18 October 1939 the 33rd (mot) Infantry Regiment was transferred to the 4th Panzer Division, becoming the 33rd Schützen Regiment on 1 April 1940. The 1/33rd became the 3/2nd Schützen Regiment (2nd Panzer Division). The 1/13th Artillery Regiment became the 2/74th Artillery Regiment, the 3/13th Artillery Regiment became the 1/13th Artillery Regiment, and the 1/49th became the 3/13th Artillery Regiment. The 43rd Motorcycle Battalion was newly formed. The division had:

1/, 2/, 3/66th (mot) Infantry Regiment
1/, 2/, 3/93rd (mot) Infantry Regiment
43rd Motorcycle Battalion
1/, 2/, 3/13th Artillery Regiment
4th Pioneer Battalion
13th Divisional Service Units

On 1 April 1940 the 8/13th Light Supply Column was renumbered the 3/13th and the 9/, 10/13th Heavy Fuel Column were renumbered the 7/, 8/13th.

On 11 October 1940 the division became the 13th Panzer Division.

14th (mot) Infantry Division

Formed on 15 October 1940 when the 14th Infantry Division became motorized.

On 15 March 1941 the 101st Infantry Regiment became the 101st Schützen Regiment and was assigned to the 18th Panzer Division. The 1/101st Infantry Regiment remained with the 14th Infantry Division and became the 54th Motorcycle Battalion. The 2/14th Artillery Regiment became the 1/88th Artillery Regiment. The 3/14th Artillery Regiment was renumbered as the 2/14th and the 1/50th Artillery Regiment became the 3/14th. The division then had:

1/, 2/, 3/11th (mot) Infantry Regiment
1/, 2/, 3/53rd (mot) Infantry Regiment
54th Motorcycle Battalion
1/, 2/, 3/14th (mot) Artillery Regiment
14th Division Support Units

In 1943 the division was ordered to covert into the 14th Panzergrenadier Division. During that conversion the 54th Motorcycle Battalion was to become the 114th Panzer Reconnaissance Battalion. The conversion did not occur and the division was demotorized, reverting to the 14th Infantry Division.

Sizilien Panzergrenadier Division

Formed on 14 May 1943 as the Sizilien (Sicilian) Division from various "march" battalions destined for Tunis. On 1 May 1943 the Palermo Panzergrenadier Regiment (four battalions) was formed from the 46th, 47th, 48th, 50th, and 56th March Battalions. These units were organized into the Ens and Körner Regiments. The division had:

1/, 2/, 3/1st Sizilien Grenadier Regiment (formed from Ens Regiment; 2 battalions)

1/, 2/, 3/2nd Sizilien Grenadier Regiment (Körner Regiment; 2 battalions)

1/, 2/, 3/3rd Sizilien Grenadier Regiment (Fullriede Regiment; 2 battalions)

Reggio Panzergrenadier Battalion (69th March Battalion)

1/, 2/, 3/, 4/Sizilien Artillery Regiment (Staff/190th Artillery Regiment, 1/Hermann Göring Artillery Regiment, 557th Heavy Artillery Battalion and other troops)

Sizilien Flak Battalion (Naples Flak Battalion)

215th Panzer Battalion (from army troops)

Became the 15th Panzergrenadier Division on 7/1/43.

15th Panzergrenadier Division

On 1 July 1943 the Sizilien Panzergrenadier Division was reorganized into the 15th Panzer Division (the motorized grenadier regiments becoming panzergrenadier regiments). On 15 July 1943 the name was changed again to the 15th Panzergrenadier Division, but the regiments retained the title "Panzergrenadier Regiments" instead of "(mot) Grenadier Regiments", like the other panzergrenadier divisions. The division had:

Division Staff
999th (mot) Mapping Detachment
15th Armored Car Platoon

104th Panzergrenadier Regiment (1st Sizilien Grenadier Regiment)
1 (mot) Staff Company
1 Signals Platoon
1 Pioneer Platoon
1 Motorcycle Platoon
3 Battalions, each with
3 (mot) Rifle Companies (2 HMGS, 18 LMGs, 3 sPzBu41, 2 75mm PAK 40 and 2 80mm mortars ea)
1 (mot) Machine Gun Company (12 HMGs and 6 80mm mortars)
1 (motZ) Infantry Gun Company (2 150mm sIG and 4 75mm leIG)
1 (motZ) Panzerjäger Company (6 75mm PAK 40, 6 50mm PAK 38 and 12 LMGs)

1/, 2/, 3/115th Panzergrenadier Regiment (2nd Sizilien Grenadier Regiment)
same as 104th Panzergrenadier Regiment

1/, 2/, 3/129th Panzergrenadier Regiment (3rd Sizilien Grenadier Regiment)
same as 104th Panzergrenadier Regiment

Reggio Panzergrenadier Battalion
3 (mot) Rifle Companies (2 HMGs, 18 LMGs, 3 sPzBu41 and 2 80mm mortars ea)
1 (mot) Heavy Support Company
1 Pioneer Platoon
1 Panzerjäger Platoon (3 50mm PAK 38)
1 Mortar Platoon (6 80mm mortars)

215th Panzer Battalion
Staff
Staff Company
2/504th Heavy Panzer Battalion
3 Panzer Companies (PzMk IV tanks)
1 Sturmgeschütz Company
1 Maintenance Platoon

33rd Panzer Artillery Regiment
Staff and Staff Battery
1st Battalion
Staff and Staff Battery
3 (motZ) Batteries (4 150mm sFH guns ea)
2nd Battalion
Staff and Staff Battery
3 (motZ) Batteries (initially 4 170mm guns and 2 LMGs each, later changed to 4 100mm K17 guns ea)
3rd Battalion
Staff and Staff Battery
1 (motZ) Battery (initially 4 100mm K18, later 4 150mm sFH)
1 (motZ) Battery (210mm mörser)
1 (motZ) Battery (captured French 150mm guns)
2/53rd Artillery Regiment
Staff
3 (motZ) Batteries (4 105mm leFH and 2 LMGs ea—RSO)

Panzerjäger Battalion
1/33rd (motZ) Panzerjäger Battalion (12 75mm PAK 40)

1 (motZ) Flak Battery (added later)
  1 Flak Section (4 20mm guns)
  1 Flak Section (3 quad 20mm guns)

315th Flak Battalion (formerly Sizilien Flak Battalion)
  Staff
  1 Self-Propelled 37mm Flak Battery
  2 (motZ) 20mm Flak Companies
  2 (motZ) 20mm Quad Flak Platoons

999th Schnelle Battalion (added later)
  Staff
  Schützen Company
  1 Half-Track Platoon
  1 105mm leFH Battery
  1 Heavy Company/33rd Panzerjäger Battalion

33rd (mot) Pioneer Battalion
  Staff
  3 (mot) Pioneer Companies (18 LMGs, 3 sPzBu41 and
    6 flamethrowers ea)
  1 (mot) Pioneer Column (2 LMGs)

999th Signals Battalion
  1 (mot) Telephone Company (6 LMGs)
  1 (mot) Radio Company (4 LMGs)
  1 (mot) Signals Supply Column (1 LMG)

Divisional Support Troops
  1–3/33rd (120 ton) Transportation Companies (4 LMGs
    ea)
  4/33rd (90 ton) Transportation Company (3 LMGs)
  1 Vehicle Truck Park
  33rd (mot) Supply Company (6 LMGs)

Other
  1/, 2/33rd (mot) Medical Companies (2 LMGs ea)
  1/, 2/, 3/33rd Ambulances
  1 (mot) Maintenance Company
  1 (75 ton) Replacement Squadron
  33rd (mot) Bakery Company
  33rd (mot) Butcher Company
  33rd (mot) Administration Detachment
  33rd Military Police Troop (2 LMGs)
  999th Field Post Office

On 10 July 1943 the organization of the armored portion of the division and its panzer inventory were as follows:

215th Panzer Battalion
  1 Panzer Staff Company
  3 Medium Companies

PzMk III (lg)	6
PzMk IV (lg)	46
Cmd	1

On 20 August 1943 the organization of the armored portion of the division and its panzer inventory were revised as follows:

215th Panzer Battalion
  1 Panzer Staff Company
  3 Medium Panzer Companies

PzMk III (75)	1
PzMk IV (lg)	15

The 2/504th Heavy Panzer Battalion was apparently detached shortly after the division was formed. In September 1943 OKH records show that the division was organized and equipped as follows:

15th Panzergrenadier Division
Divisional Staff
  Staff
  999th (mot) Mapping Detachment
  15th Armored Car Platoon (5 LMGs)

Reggio Panzergrenadier Battalion
  Staff
  3 (mot) Grenadier Companies (2 HMGs, 18 LMGs,
    3 sPzBu41 and 2 80mm mortars ea)
  1 (mot) Machine Gun Company
  1 Pioneer Platoon
  1 Panzerjäger Platoon (3 50 PAK 38)
  1 Mortar Platoon (6 80mm mortars)

104th Panzergrenadier Regiment (1st Sizilien)
  Staff
  Regimental Band
  Staff Company
    Panzerjäger Platoon (3 LMGs and 3 50mm PAK
    38)
    Motorcycle Platoon (3 LMGs)
    Signals Platoon
    Pioneer Platoon (6 flamethrowers and 3 LMGs)
  3 Battalions, each with
    Staff
    3 (mot) Grenadier Companies (2 HMGs, 18 LMGs,
      3 sPzBu41, 2 150mm sIG and 2 80mm mortars ea)
    1 (mot) Machine Gun Company (12 HMGs and 6
      80mm mortars)
    1 (motZ) Infantry Gun Company (2 150mm sIG and 6
      75mm leIG)
    1 (motZ) Panzerjäger Company (6 75mm PAK 40, 6
      50mm PAK 38 and 12 LMGs)

115th and 129th Panzergrenadier Regiments (1st and
2nd Sizilien)
same as 104th Panzergrenadier Regiment

215th Panzer Battalion (detached to the army)
  1 Battalion Staff and Staff Company
  3 Panzer Companies (PzMk IV tanks)
  1 Sturmgeschütz Company
  1 Panzer Maintenance Company
1/33rd (motZ) Panzerjäger Company
(12 75mm PAK 40)

33rd Artillery Regiment
  1 Regimental Staff and (mot) Staff Battery

1st Battalion
1 Battalion Staff and (mot) Staff Battery
1 (motZ) Battery (4 150mm sFH and 2 LMGs)
2nd Battalion
1 Battalion Staff and (mot) Staff Battery
3 (motZ) Batteries (3 170mm guns and 2 LMGs ea)
3rd Battalion
1 Battalion Staff and (mot) Staff Battery
1 (motZ) Battery (4 150mm guns and 2 LMGs)
1 (motZ) Battery (4 150mm sFH and 2 LMGs)
1 (motZ) Battery (4 210mm mörsers and 2 LMGs)
2/53rd Artillery Regiment
1 Battalion Staff and (mot) Staff Battery
3 (motZ) Batteries (4 105mm leFH and 2 LMGs ea)
315th Flak Battalion
1 Self-Propelled Medium Flak Battery (12 37mm Flak guns)
2 (motZ) Light Flak Batteries (12 20mm Flak guns ea)
1 (motZ) Light Flak Battery (4 20mm and 3 quad 20mm Flak guns)
33rd Pioneer Battalion
Staff
3 (mot) Pioneer Companies (18 LMGs, 3 sPzBu41 and 6 flamethrowers ea)
1 (mot) Light Pioneer Column (2 LMGs)
999th Signals Battalion
Staff
1 (mot) Telephone Company (6 LMGs)
1 (mot) Radio Company (5 LMGs)
1 (mot) Signals Column (1 LMG)
33rd Supply Troops
1/, 2/, 3/33rd (120 ton) Transportation Companies (4 LMGs ea)
4/33rd (90 ton) Transportation Company (3 LMGs)
33rd (mot) Supply Company (6 LMGs)
Maintenance
33rd Maintenance Company
Administration
33rd (mot) Administration Bureau
33rd (mot) Bakery Company
33rd (mot) Butcher Company
Medical Units
1/, 2/33rd (mot) Medical Companies
1/, 2/, 3/33rd Ambulance Platoons
Other
33rd (mot) Military Police Troop
33rd (mot) Field Post Office

During the winter of 1943 the 33rd Panzer Reconnaissance Battalion was formed, the 2/33rd Artillery Regiment reverted to the 557th Heavy Artillery Battalion, and the 4/33rd Artillery Regiment became the 2/33rd Artillery Regiment. Sometime in late 1943 the 115th Panzergrenadier Regiment was disbanded, and on 14 April 1944

the 129th was renamed the 115th. The 215th Panzer Battalion became the 115th Panzer Battalion. On 12 January 1944 actual field returns of the division show that it contained:

15th Panzergrenadier Division
Divisional Staff
Staff (4 LMGs)
999th (mot) Mapping Detachment
33rd (mot) Military Police Troop
115th Panzergrenadier Regiment
Staff
Staff Company
Panzerjäger Platoon (2 75mm PAK 40)
Motorcycle Platoon (3 LMGs)
Signals Platoon
1st Battalion
Staff
1 (mot) Grenadier Company (3 HMGs, 8 LMGs and 2 80mm mortars)
1 (mot) Grenadier Company (2 HMGs, 4 LMGs and 2 80mm mortars)
1 (mot) Grenadier Company (3 HMGs, 8 LMGs and 2 80mm mortars)
1 (mot) Heavy Company (no HMGs, 3 120mm and 2 80mm mortars and 2 20mm guns)
2nd Battalion
Staff
1 (mot) Grenadier Company (1 HMG, 8 LMGs and 2 80mm mortars)
1 (mot) Grenadier Company (1 HMG, 5 LMGs and 2 80mm mortars)
1 (mot) Grenadier Company (1 HMG, 7 LMGs and 2 80mm mortars)
1 (mot) Heavy Company (1 HMG, 3 120mm and 2 80mm mortars and 2 20mm guns)
3rd Battalion
Staff
1 (mot) Grenadier Company (9 LMGs and 1 80mm mortar)
1 (mot) Grenadier Company (2 HMGs, 8 LMGs and 1 80mm mortar)
1 (mot) Grenadier Company (2 HMGs, 8 LMGs and 2 80mm mortars)
1 (mot) Heavy Company (no HMGs, 2 120mm and 2 80mm mortars and 2 20mm guns)
1 (motZ) Infantry Gun Company (4 150mm sIG and 8 75mm leIG)
1 (mot) Pioneer Company (2 80mm mortars, 2HMGs and 6 LMGs)
104th Panzergrenadier Regiment
Staff
Staff Company
Panzerjäger Platoon (2 75mm PAK 40 and 3 50mm PAK 38)

Mortar Platoon (2 120mm mortars)
Motorcycle Platoon
Signals Platoon (3 LMGs)

1st Battalion
Staff
1 (mot) Grenadier Company (2 HMGs and 7 LMGs)
1 (mot) Grenadier Company (2 HMGs and 4 LMGs)
1 (mot) Grenadier Company (1 HMG and 4 LMGs)
1 (mot) Heavy Company (1 HMG, 4 120mm and 4 80mm mortars and 4 20mm guns)

2nd Battalion
Staff
1 (mot) Grenadier Company (2 HMGs, 4 LMGs and 1 80mm mortar)
1 (mot) Grenadier Company (2 HMGs, 7 LMGs and 2 80mm mortars)
1 (mot) Grenadier Company (2 HMGs, 5 LMGs and 2 80mm mortars)
1 (mot) Heavy Company (2 HMGs, 2 120mm and 2 20mm guns)

3rd Battalion
Staff
1 (mot) Grenadier Company (2 HMGs and 3 LMGs)
1 (mot) Grenadier Company (1 LMG)
1 (mot) Grenadier Company (1 HMG and 1 LMG)
1 (mot) Heavy Company (no HMGs, 4 120mm and 6 80mm mortars and 2 20mm guns)
1 (motZ) Infantry Gun Company (4 150mm sIG and 2 75mm leIG)
1 (mot) Pioneer Company (10 LMGs)

115th Panzer Battalion
1 Battalion Staff
1 Staff Company (1 PzMk III, 1 PzMk IV and 2 self-propelled 20mm guns)
3 Panzer Companies (13 PzMk IV tanks ea)
1 (mot) Panzer Supply Company
1 Panzer Maintenance Company

(mot) Anti-Tank Battle Troop
1 Armored Panzerjäger Staff
1 (mot) Panzerjäger Staff Company (4 LMGs)
1 (mot) Signals Platoon
1 Armored Panzerjäger Platoon (3 Jagdpanzers)
1st Jagdpanther Company (10 Jagdpanzers)
2nd Jagdpanther Company (8 Jagdpanzers)
1 Sturmgeschütz Platoon (5 StuG)
3rd (motZ) Panzerjäger Company (8 75mm PAK 40 and 6 LMGs)
1 (motZ) Heavy Flak Battery (8 88mm guns)
1 (mot) Panzerjäger Supply Company (2 LMGs)

31st (mot) Heavy Flak Battalion
1 Flak Staff
1 (mot) Flak Staff Battery (2 LMGs)
1st and 2nd (motZ) Flak Batteries (8 88mm, 3 20mm and 2 LMGs ea)

3rd (motZ) Flak Batteries (7 88mm, 3 20mm, 2 self-propelled 20mm Flak guns and 3 LMGs ea)

33rd Panzergrenadier Feldersatz Battalion
1st–4th Panzergrenadier Companies
5th Panzer Replacement Company

33rd Reconnaissance Battalion
1 Staff
1 (mot) Staff Company
1 Armored Car Platoon (8 Sd Kfz 234, 3 Sd Kfz 221, 1 Sd Kfz 250/1, 1 unknown armored car and 1 signals armored car)
1st (mot) Reconnaissance Company
2nd (mot) Reconnaissance Company (2 HMGs, 4 LMGs and 2 80mm mortars)
3rd (mot) Reconnaissance Company (2 HMGs, 4 LMGs and 2 80mm mortars)
4th (mot) Heavy Reconnaissance Company
1 Pioneer Platoon (1 LMG)
1 Infantry Gun Platoon (2 75mm le IG)
1 Mortar Platoon (8 80mm mortars)
1 (mot) Reconnaissance Supply Company

33rd Artillery Regiment
1 Regimental Staff and (mot) Staff Battery

1st Battalion
1 Battalion Staff and (mot) Staff Battery
3 (motZ) Batteries (6 105mm leFH and 1 LMG ea)

2nd Battalion
1 Battalion Staff
1 (mot) Staff Battery (3 20mm Flak guns and 1 LMG)
3 (motZ) Batteries (6 105mm leFH and 1 LMG ea)

3rd Battalion
1 Battalion Staff
1 (mot) Staff Battery (2 20mm Flak guns and 1 LMG)
3 (motZ) Batteries (4 150mm sFH and 1 LMG ea)

33rd Pioneer Battalion
Staff
1 (mot) Pioneer Company (2 LMGs and 4 flamethrowers)
1 (mot) Pioneer Company (4 flamethrowers)
1 (mot) Pioneer Company (4 flamethrowers)
1 (mot) Light Pioneer Column (2 LMGs)

999th Signals Battalion
Staff
1st (mot) Telephone Company (2 LMGs)
2nd (mot) Radio Company (2 LMGs)
1 (mot) Signals Column
Battalion had 1 Sd Kfz 251/3 and 1 Sd Kfz 251/6

33rd Supply Troops
1/, 2/, 3/, 4/33rd (120 ton) Transportation Companies (5, 3, 4, and 2 LMGs respectively)
1 (mot) Maintenance Company)

Maintenance
1/, 2/33rd Maintenance Companies (2 LMGs ea)
33rd (mot) Maintenance Supply Company

Administration
33rd (mot) Administration Bureau

33rd (mot) Bakery Company (2 LMGs)

33rd (mot) Butcher Company (1 LMG)

Medical Units

1/33rd (mot) Medical Company (3 LMGs)

2/33rd (mot) Medical Company (4 LMGs)

33rd (mot) Medical Supply Company (1 LMG)

Other

33rd (mot) Field Post Office

The division had a mixture of German and captured weapons. The German weapons consisted of 8,081 rifles, 290 rifle grenade launchers, 6,998 sub-machine guns, 1,970 pistols, 14 MP43s, 12 Zf. Gew., 25 Italian pistols, 38 Italian sub-machine guns, and 40 British Sten guns. In April 1944 the division had:

1/, 2/, 3/104th Panzergrenadier Regiment

1/, 2/, 3/115th Panzergrenadier Regiment

115th Panzer Reconnaissance Battalion

115th Panzer Battalion

1/, 2/, 3/33rd Panzer Artillery Regiment

315th Flak Battalion

33rd Divisional Support Troops

In August 1944 the organization of the armored portion of the division and its panzer inventory were as follows:

115th Panzer Battalion

1 Sturmgeschütz Staff Company

3 Sturmgeschütz Companies

StuG	36
PzBefWgIII	1

The order of 23 September 1944 directed the 113th Panzer Brigade be incorporated into the division. On 9 December 1944 the organization of the armored portion of the division and its panzer inventory were as follows:

115th Panzer Battalion

1 Sturmgeschütz Staff Company

1 Medium Panzer Company

2 Sturmgeschütz Companies

StuG	30
PzMk IV (lg)	14
PzBefWg III	1
FlakpzIV (37)	2

With the German capitulation, the division passed into British captivity.

16th (mot) Infantry Division

Formed on 6 August 1940, the division had:

Staff (from Staff/228th Infantry Division)

1/, 2/, 3/60th (mot) Infantry Regiment (formed from 60th Infantry Regiment, 16th Infantry Division)

1/, 2/, 3/156th (mot) Infantry Regiment (formed from 1st Security Regiment and 3/10th Infantry Regiment from 4th Infantry Division)

165th Motorcycle Battalion (formed from 3rd Machine Gun Battalion)

1/, 2/, 3/146th Artillery Regiment (formed from Staff/ 331th Artillery Regiment, 1/16th Artillery Regiment, 1/697th Artillery Regiment and 621st Heavy Artillery Battalion)

341st Reconnaissance Battalion

228th Panzerjäger Battalion

675th Pioneer Battalion

228th Signals Battalion

66th Supply Support Troop

In 1942 the division added:

116th Panzer Battalion (formed from 1/1st Panzer Regiment)

4/146th Panzer Artillery Regiment (281st Army Flak Battalion)

On 28 June 1942 the organization of the armored portion of the division and its panzer inventory were as follows:

116th Panzer Battalion

1 Panzer Staff Company

1 Medium Panzer Company

2 Light Panzer Companies

PzMk II	10
PzMk III (50 lg)	35
PzMk IV (lg)	8
PzBefWg	1

On 23 June 1943 the 16th (mot) Infantry Division became the 16th Panzergrenadier Division.

16th Panzergrenadier Division

On 23 June 1943 the 16th (mot) Infantry Division was renamed as the 16th Panzergrenadier Division. The 165th Motorcycle Battalion became the 116th Panzer Reconnaissance Battalion and the 4/146th Panzer Artillery Regiment reverted to the 281st Army Flak Battalion.

1/, 2/, 3/60th Panzergrenadier Regiment
1/, 2/, 3/156th Panzergrenadier Regiment
116th Panzer Battalion
116th Panzer Reconnaissance Battalion
1/, 2/, 3/146th Artillery Regiment
281st Army Flak Battalion
228th Panzerjäger Battalion
675th Pioneer Battalion
228th Signals Battalion
66th Supply Support Troop

Keilig states that in 1943 the panzergrenadier regiments had only a medium anti-tank platoon. The 116th Panzer Reconnaissance Battalion contained a staff, one light armored car company, three motorcycle companies, a heavy company, and a reconnaissance column. The 228th Panzerjäger Battalion had a staff, a self-propelled company, and two (motZ) panzerjäger companies. The 236th Sturmgeschütz Battalion was also assigned to the division. The 675th (mot) Pioneer Battalion had no bridging column and the division had no feldersatz battalion. The division was used in March 1944 to form the 116th Panzer Division. On 1 July 1943 the organization of the armored portion of the division and its panzer inventory were as follows:

116th Panzer Battalion
  1 Panzer Staff Company
  1 Medium Panzer Company
  2 Light Panzer Companies

PzMk II	4
PzMk III (kz)	32
PzMk III (75)	5
PzMk IV (lg)	11
PzBefWg	1

In September 1943 OKH records show that the division was organized and equipped as follows:

16th Panzergrenadier Division
Divisional Staff
  Staff
  16th (mot) Mapping Detachment
60th Panzergrenadier Regiment
  Staff
  Regimental Band
  Staff Company

  Panzerjäger Platoon (3 LMGs and 3 50mm PAK 38)
  Motorcycle Platoon (3 LMGs)
  Signals Platoon
  Pioneer Platoon (3 LMGs)
3 Battalions, each with
  Staff
  3 (mot) Grenadier Companies (12 HMGs, 6 LMGs, 1 sPzBu 41, 3 PzBu39 and 3 50mm mortars ea)
  1 (mot) Machine Gun Company (12 HMGs, 1 LMG, 3 37mm PAK 36 and 6 80mm mortars)
  1 (motZ) Infantry Gun Company (2 150mm sIG and 6 75mm leIG)
  1 Self-Propelled Flak Company (12 20mm and 4 LMGs)
156th Panzergrenadier Regiment
  same as 60th Panzergrenadier Regiment
116th Panzer Reconnaissance Battalion
  Staff (3 LMGs)
  1 Light Armored Car Company (18 20mm and 24 LMGs)
  3 Motorcycle Companies (2 80mm mortars, 3 PzBu39, 4 HMGs and 18 LMGs ea)
  1 (mot) Heavy Company
    1 Pioneer Platoon (4 LMGs)
    1 Panzerjäger Platoon (3 LMGs and 3 75mm PAK 40)
    1 Panzerjäger Platoon (3 LMGs and 3 sPzBu41)
    1 Light Infantry Gun Section (2 75mm leIG)
  1 Light Panzer Reconnaissance Battalion Column
228th Panzerjäger Battalion
  2 Self-Propelled Panzerjäger Companies (equipment unknown)
  1 Self-Propelled Panzerjäger Company
116th Panzer Battalion
  Staff
  Staff Battery (3 StuG)
  1 Medium Panzer Company
  2 Light Panzer Companies
  1 Panzer Maintenance Platoon
146th Artillery Regiment
  1 Regimental Staff and (mot) Staff Battery (2 LMGs)
1st Battalion
  1 Battalion Staff and (mot) Staff Battery (2 LMGs)
  3 (motZ) Batteries (3 105mm leFh and 2 LMGs ea)
2nd Battalion
  same as 1st Battalion
3rd Battalion
  1 Battalion Staff and (mot) Staff Battery (2 LMGs)
  2 (motZ) Batteries (3 150mm sFH and 2 LMGs ea)
  1 (motZ) Battery (3 100mm K18 and 2 LMGs)
281st Army Flak Battalion
  1 Staff and Staff Battery (1 LMG)
  2 (motZ) Heavy Flak Batteries (4 88mm, 3 20mm and 2 LMGs ea)

1 (motZ) Light Flak Battery (12 20mm and 2 LMGs)
1 (Mot) Light (20 ton) Flak Supply Column
675th Pioneer Battalion
  Staff
  3 (mot) Pioneer Companies (2 HMGs, 9 LMGs, 3
  sPzBu41 and 2 80mm mortars ea)
  1 (mot) Light Pioneer Column (2 LMGs)
16th Signals Battalion
  Staff
  1 (mot) Telephone Company (5 LMGs)
  1 (mot) Radio Company (4 LMGs)
  1 (mot) Signals Column (1 LMG)
66th Supply Troops
  1/, 2/66th (90 ton) Transportation Companies (3 LMGs
  ea)

3/, 4/66th (120 ton) Transportation Companies (4
  LMGs ea)
16th (mot) Supply Company (6 LMGs)
Maintenance
  1/, 2/66th (mot) Maintenance Companies
Administration
  66th (mot) Administration Bureau
  66th (mot) Bakery Company
  66th (mot) Butcher Company
Medical Units
  1/, 2/66th (mot) Medical Companies
  1/, 2/, 3/66th Ambulance Platoons
Other
  66th (mot) Military Police Troop
  66th (mot) Field Post Office

18th (mot) Infantry Division

Formed on 1 November 1940 from the 18th Infantry Division. The 54th Infantry Regiment was transferred to the 100th Light Infantry Division, except for the 1/54th Infantry Regiment, which became the new 3/51st when the old 3/51st became the 38th Motorcycle Battalion. The 1/54th Artillery Regiment became the 3/18th Artillery Regiment. The division had:

1/, 2/, 3/30th (mot) Infantry Regiment
1/, 2/, 3/51st (mot) Infantry Regiment

1/, 2/, 3/18th (mot) Artillery Regiment
38th Motorcycle Battalion
18th Divisional Service Units

On 23 June 1943 the division was renamed the 18th Panzergrenadier Division.

18th Panzergrenadier Division

Formed on 23 June 1943 by renaming the 18th (mot) Infantry Division.

1/, 2/, 3/30th (mot) Grenadier Regiment
1/, 2/, 3/51st (mot) Grenadier Regiment
1/, 2/, 3/18th (mot) Artillery Regiment
118th Panzer Reconnaissance Battalion (from 38th
  Motorcycle Battalion)
118th Panzer Battalion (new)
1/, 2/, 3/18th Artillery Regiment
18th Divisional Service Units

Keilig states that in 1943 the panzergrenadier regiments had only a medium anti-tank platoon. The 118th Panzer Reconnaissance Battalion contained a staff, one light armored car company, three motorcycle companies, a heavy company, and a reconnaissance supply column. The 18th Panzer Battalion was equipped with sturmgeschütze. The 18th Panzerjäger Battalion had a staff, a self-propelled company, and two (motZ) panzerjäger companies. The 18th Artillery Regiment had an

additional battery formed with Polish 155mm howitzers and a second battery formed with French 155mm howitzers. The 18th Pioneer Battalion had no bridging column. In September 1943 OKH records show the division to be organized and equipped as follows:

18th Panzergrenadier Division
Divisional Staff
  Staff
  18th (mot) Mapping Detachment
30th and 51st Panzergrenadier Regiments, each with
  Staff and Staff Company
    Panzerjäger Platoon (3 LMGs and 3 50mm PAK
    38)
    Motorcycle Platoon (3 LMGs)
    Signals Platoon
    Pioneer Platoon (6 flamethrowers and 3 LMGs)
  Regimental Band
  3 Battalions, each with
    Staff

3 (mot) Grenadier Companies (12 HMGs, 6 LMGs, 1 sPzbu 41, 3 PzBu39 and 2 80mm mortars ea)

1 (mot) Machine Gun Company (12 HMGs, 1 LMG, 3 37mm PAK 36 and 4 120mm mortars)

1 (motZ) Infantry Gun Company (2 150mm sIG and 6 75mm leIG)

118th Panzer Reconnaissance Battalion

Staff (3 LMGs)

1 Light Armored Car Company (18 20mm and 24 LMGs)

3 Motorcycle Companies (2 80mm mortars, 3 PzBu39, 4 HMGs and 18 LMGs ea)

1 (mot) Heavy Company
1 Pioneer Platoon (4 LMGs)
1 Panzerjäger Platoon (3 LMGs and 3 75mm PAK 40)
1 Panzerjäger Platoon (3 LMGs and 3 sPzBu41)
1 Light Infantry Gun Section (2 75mm leIG)

1 Light Panzer Reconnaissance Battalion Column

118th Panzerjäger Battalion

2 Self-Propelled Panzerjäger Companies (14 75mm PAK 40 and 14 LMGs ea)

1 Self-Propelled Panzerjäger Company (75mm PAK 40)

118th Panzer Battalion

Staff and Staff Battery (3 StuG)

Flak Platoon (3 self-propelled quad 20mm guns)

3 Sturmgeschütz Batteries (14 StuG ea)

1 Panzer Maintenance Platoon

18th Artillery Regiment

1 Regimental Staff
1 (mot) Regimental Staff Battery (2 LMGs)
1 Regimental Band

1st Battalion

1 Battalion Staff and (mot) Staff Battery (2 LMGs)
3 (motZ) Batteries (3 105mm leFh and 2 LMGs ea)
1 (motZ) Battery (5 152mm Russian howitzers)

2nd Battalion

1 Battalion Staff and (mot) Staff Battery (2 LMGs)
3 (motZ) Batteries (3 105mm leFH and 2 LMGs ea)

3rd Battalion

1 Battalion Staff and (mot) Staff Battery (2 LMGs)
2 (motZ) Batteries (3 150mm sFH and 2 LMGs ea)
1 (motZ) Battery (3 100mm K18 and 2 LMGs)
1 (motZ) Battery (1 155mm French howitzer)

18th Pioneer Battalion

3 (mot) Pioneer Companies (2 HMGs, 9 LMGs, 3 PzBu39, 2 flamethrowers and 2 80mm mortars ea)

1 (mot) Light Pioneer Column (2 LMGs)

18th Signals Battalion

1 (mot) Telephone Company (5 LMGs)
1 (mot) Radio Company (4 LMGs)
1 (mot) Signals Column (1 LMG)

18th Supply Troops

1/, 2/18th (90 ton) Transportation Companies (3 LMGs ea)

3/18th (120 ton) Transportation Companies (4 LMGs)

18th (mot) Supply Company (6 LMGs)

Maintenance

1/, 2/18th (mot) Maintenance Companies

Administration

18th (mot) Administration Bureau
18th (mot) Bakery Company
18th (mot) Butcher Company

Medical Units

1/, 2/18th (mot) Medical Companies
1/, 2/, 3/18th Ambulance Platoons

Other

18th (mot) Military Police Troop
18th (mot) Field Post Office

The division was destroyed in June 1944 and the debris was incorporated into the 105th Panzer Brigade. The division was reconstituted on 7 September 1944 as Kampfgruppe 18th Panzergrenadier from the 105th Panzer Brigade. The reorganization was to have been completed by 1 November 1944. The division was to have:

Divisional Staff

Staff (2 LMGs)
1 Armored Car Platoon (4 20mm and 6 LMGs)

Panzergrenadier Division Regiment

1 Regimental Staff
1 (mot) Regimental Staff Company
1 Signals Platoon
1 Motorcycle Messenger Platoon (4 LMGs)

1 (mot) Battalion

1 Battalion Staff
1 Battalion Supply Company (4 LMGs)
3 (mot) Grenadier Companies (4 HMGs, 18 LMGs and 2 80mm mortars ea)
1 (motZ) Heavy Company
(motZ) Flak Platoon (6 20mm Flak)
(motZ) Mortar Platoon (4 120mm mortars and 2 LMGs)

1 Battalion

1 Battalion Staff
1 Battalion Supply Company (4 LMGs)
3 (bicycle) Grenadier Companies (4 HMGs, 18 LMGs and 2 80mm mortars ea)
1 (mot) Heavy Company (6 20mm Flak, 4 120mm mortars and 2 LMGs)

13th (motZ) (sIG) Company (4 150mm sIG 7 LMGs)

14th (motZ) (pioneer) Company (18 flame throwers, 2 80mm mortars, 2 HMGs and 12 LMGs)

15th (motZ) (Flak) Company (12 20mm mountain Flak guns)

1/118th Panzer Regiment

Staff and Staff Battery (3 MK IV
Flak Platoon (3 self-propelled quad 20mm guns)
3 Panzer Medium Companies (14 PzMk IV ea)
1 Panzer Maintenance Platoon

Panzerjäger Battalion
1 Battalion Staff
1 Battalion Staff Battery (1 LMG and 3 StuG)
2 Sturmgeschütz Batteries (14 LMGs and 14 StuG ea)
1 (motZ) Panzerjäger Battery (12 75mm PAK 40 and 12 LMGs)
1 (mot) Supply Company (3 LMGs)

Artillery Battalion
1 Battalion Staff
1 Battalion Staff Battery (2 LMGs and 3 20mm Flak)
3 (motZ) 105mm Batteries (4 105mm leFH 18 and 4 LMGs ea)

Other
1 Panzer Radio Company (12 LMGs)
1 (mot) Pioneer Company (2 HMGs, 18 LMGs and 2 80mm mortars)
1 (mot) Vehicle Maintenance Company (4 LMGs)
1 (mot) (120 ton) Supply Column (8 LMGs)
1 (mot) Medical Company (4 LMGs)
1 (mot) Medical Supply Company

A reorganization was to be carried out in September, but it was canceled, then reordered on 12 December 1944. The 105th Panzer Brigade was organized from elements of the 18th Panzergrenadier Division and the 18th Panzergrenadier Division was rebuilt using elements of the 103rd Panzer Brigade. The division then had:

1/, 2/30th Panzergrenadier Regiment
1/, 2/51st Panzergrenadier Regiment
118th Panzer Reconnaissance Battalion
118th Panzer Battalion
300th Army Artillery Battalion
1/, 2/18th Artillery Regiment
18th Divisional Support Troops

In January 1945 the 30th and 51st Panzergrenadier Regiments formed a 3rd Battalion, and the 3/18th Artillery Regiment was formed. In March 1945 the division was disbanded in East Prussia. On 21 March 1945 it was ordered re-formed

on the Vistula from the Schlesien and Holstein Panzer Divisions. The Holstein Panzer Division had been formed on 2 February 1945 from the 233rd Reserve Panzer Division and the Schlesien Panzer Division on 20 February 1945 in Döbritz. In February/March 1945 the organization of the armored portion of the division and its panzer inventory were as follows:

1/118th Panzer Regiment
1 Battalion Staff Company
3 Medium Panzer Companies (PzMk IV)
1 Jagdpanzer Company (PzMk IV/70 (V)
PzMk IV   9 (+26 on 27 Mar.)
PzMk IV/70 (V)   10 (+8 on 27 Mar.)

When re-formed, the division had:

Divisional Staff (former Staff/Schlesien Panzer Division)
1/, 2/30th Panzergrenadier Division (Staff Schlesien 2, 2/Schlesien 1 and 1/, 2/Schlesien 2)
1/, 2/51st Panzergrenadier Division (Staff 139th Panzergrenadier Regiment, 1/, 2/142nd and 1/, 2/139th of the Holstein Panzer Division)
118th Panzer Regiment (Panzer Gren Rgt Schlesien, 1st Panzer Battalion from Schlesien Panzer Battalion, 2nd Battalion from 1/Schlesien)
1/, 2/, 3/18th Artillery Regiment (Schlesien Artillery Battalion, Holstein Artillery Battalion and Schlesien Flak Battalion)
18th Panzerjäger Battalion
18th Panzer Reconnaissance Battalion
18th Pioneer Battalion
Feldersatz Battalion (from staff of 2/142nd Panzergrenadier Regiment)

On 30 March 1945 the division was ordered to form a mixed panzer regiment consisting of a panzer battalion and a panzergrenadier battalion. This was to be accomplished by consolidating the Holstein and Schlesien Panzer Divisions. The 1/18th was to have three companies of PzMk IV tanks and one company of PzMk IV/70.

20th (mot) Infantry Division

Mobilized on 20 August 1939, the division was organized and equipped with

20th (mot) Infantry Division
69th (mot) Infantry Regiment
1st, 2nd and 3rd Battalions, each with
3 (mot) Rifle Companies (9 LMGs, 2 HMGs and 3 50mm mortars ea)
1 (mot) Machine Gun Company (8 HMGs and 6 80mm mortars)

76th (mot) Infantry Regiment
same as 69th (mot) Infantry Regiment
1/, 2/20th (mot) Artillery Regiment, each with
1 (mot) Signals Platoon
1 (mot) Calibration Detachment
3 (mot) Batteries (4 105mm leFH and 2 LMGs ea)
Det/20th Reconnaissance Battalion
1 (mot) Signals Platoon
1 Motorcycle Company (9 LMGs, 2 HMGS and 3 50mm mortars)

1 Armored Car Company (10 20mm and 25 LMGs)
2/20th (mot) Panzerjäger Battalion
  1 Panzerjäger Company (12 37mm PAK 36 and 6
  LMGs)
  1 Company/Heavy Machine Gun Battalion (12 20mm)
20th Pioneer Battalion
  2 Pioneer Companies (9 LMGs ea)
20th Signals Battalion
  1 (mot) Radio Company
  1 (mot) Signals Light Supply Column
20th Supply Troop
  1–4/, 7/, 8/20th (mot) Light Supply Columns
  9/20th (mot) Light Fuel Column
  1/2nd (mot) Maintenance Company
Other
  20th Divisional Administration
  20th (mot) Field Bakery
  20th (mot) Butcher Company
  1/, 2/20th Medical Companies
  20th Field Hospital
  2/20th Ambulance Company
  20th (mot) Field Post Office

In early 1940 the division was organized and equipped
as follows:

Staff
  20th Motorcycle Messenger Platoon
  20th (mot) Mapping Detachment
76th (mot) Infantry Regiment
  1 (mot) Signals Platoon
  1 (mot) Regimental Band
  3 (mot) Battalions, each with
    3 (mot) Infantry Companies (9 LMGs, 2 HMGs and
    3 50mm mortars ea)
    1 (mot) Machine Gun Company (6 HMGs and 6
    80mm mortars)
  1 (mot) Infantry Gun Company (8 75mm leIG)
  1 Motorcycle Platoon (3 LMGs)
  1 Panzer Abwehr Company (12 37mm PAK 36 and 4
  LMGs)
  1 (mot) Light Infantry Column
80th (mot) Infantry Regiment
  same as 76th
20th Reconnaissance Battalion
  1 (mot) Signals Platoon
  1 Motorcycle Company (2 HMGs and 9 LMGs)
  1 Mortar Section (3 50mm mortars)
  1 Armored Car Company (10 20mm and 25 LMGs)
20th Panzer Abwehr Battalion
  1 (mot) Signals Platoon
  1st and 3rd (mot) Panzer Abwehr Companies (12 37mm
  PAK 36 and 6 LMGs ea)
  1/52nd (mot) Heavy Machine Gun Battalion (12 20mm
  guns)

20th (mot) Artillery Regiment
2/, 3/20th Artillery Regiment, each with
  1 (mot) Signals Platoon
  1 (mot) Calibration Detachment
  3 (mot) Batteries (4 105mm leFH and 2 LMGs ea)
1/58th (mot) Artillery Regiment
  1 (mot) Signals Platoon
  1 (mot) Calibration Detachment
  3 (mot) Batteries (4 150mm sFH and 2 LMGs ea)
20th (mot) Observation Battalion
  1 (mot) Signals Platoon
  1 (mot) Weather Platoon
  1 (mot) Flash Ranging Battery (2 LMGs)
  1 (mot) Sound Ranging Battery (2 LMGs)
  1 (mot) Survey Battery (2 LMGs)
20th Signals Battalion
  1 (mot) Telephone Company
  1 (mot) Radio Company
  1 (mot) Light Signals Column
20th (mot) Pioneer Battalion
  3 (mot) Pioneer Companies (9 LMGs ea)
  1 (mot) Brüko B Bridging Train
  1 Light Pioneer Column
20th Supply Troops
  1/, 2/, 3/, 4/, 5/, 6/, 7/20th (mot) Light Transportation
  Columns
  9/, 10/20th (mot) Light Fuel Columns
  1/, 2/20th (mot) Maintenance Companies
  20th (mot) Supply Company
Administration
  20th (mot) Field Bakery
  20th (mot) Field Butcher Company
  20th (mot) Administration Detachment
Medical
  20th (mot) Field Hospital
  1/, 2/20th (mot) Medical Companies
  1/, 2/, 3/20th Ambulance Companies
Other
  20th (mot) Military Police Detachment
  20th (mot) Field Post Office

Early in 1940 the 69th (mot) Infantry Regiment became
the 69th Schützen Regiment of the 10th Panzer Division
and the 1/56th Artillery Regiment was renumbered as the
4/20th Artillery Regiment.

On 1 April 1940 the Staff/56th Artillery Regiment be-
came the Staff/20th Artillery Regiment, the 7/20th Light
Supply Column became the 6/20th and the 9/, 10/20th
Heavy Fuel Columns became the 7/, 8/20th.

In the fall of 1940 the 1/20th Artillery Regiment was
transferred to the 10th Panzer Division as well, but it
was re-formed from the 3/20th Artillery Regiment. At
the same time the 1/56th Artillery Regiment became
the 3/20th Artillery Regiment. The 30th Motorcycle
Battalion was formed from the 3/25th (mot) Infantry

Regiment from the 2nd (mot) Infantry Division. The division now had:

1/, 2/, 3/76th (mot) Infantry Regiment
1/, 2/, 3/90th (mot) Infantry Regiment

1/, 2/, 3/20th (mot) Artillery Regiment
30th Motorcycle Battalion
20th Divisional Support Units

20th Panzergrenadier Division

Formed on 23 July 1943 by renaming the 20th (mot) Infantry Division. The newly formed 8th Panzer Battalion and the 284th Army Flak Battalion were assigned to the division.

Keilig states that in 1943 the division's two panzergrenadier regiments each had only a medium anti-tank platoon. The 5th Panzer Battalion was equipped with sturmgeschütze. The 20th Panzerjäger Battalion had a staff, a self-propelled panzerjäger company, two heavy (motZ) panzerjäger companies, and a self-propelled 20mm Flak company. The artillery regiment had an additional (motZ) battery of captured Russian 152mm howitzers. The 20th Pioneer Battalion had no bridging column. The division had no feldersatz battalion. In September 1943 OKH records show that the division was organized and equipped as follows:

20th Panzergrenadier Division
Divisional Staff
Staff
20th (mot) Mapping Detachment
76th Panzergrenadier Regiment
Staff
Regimental Band
Staff Company
Panzerjäger Platoon (3 LMGs and 3 50mm PAK 38)
Motorcycle Platoon (3 LMGs)
Signals Platoon
Pioneer Platoon (6 flamethrowers and 3 LMGs)
3 Battalions, each with
Staff
3 (mot) Grenadier Companies (12 HMGs, 6 LMGs, 1 sPzBu 41, 3 PzBu39 and 2 80mm mortars ea)
1 (mot) Machine Gun Company (12 HMGs, 1 LMG, 3 37mm PAK 36 and 6 80mm mortars)
1 (motZ) Infantry Gun Company (2 150mm sIG and 6 75mm leIG)
90th Panzergrenadier Regiment
same as 76th Panzergrenadier Regiment
120th Panzer Reconnaissance Battalion
Staff (3 LMGs)
1 Light Armored Car Company (120 20mm and 24 LMGs)
3 Motorcycle Companies (2 80mm mortars, 3 sPzBu41, 4 HMGs and 120 LMGs ea)

1 (mot) Heavy Company
1 Pioneer Platoon (4 LMGs)
1 Panzerjäger Platoon (3 LMGs and 3 75mm PAK 40)
1 Panzerjäger Platoon (3 LMGs and 3 sPzBu41)
1 Light Infantry Gun Section (2 75mm leIG)
1 Light Panzer Reconnaissance Battalion Column
20th Panzerjäger Battalion
2 Self-Propelled Panzerjäger Companies (12 75mm PAK 40 and 12 LMGs ea)
1 Self-Propelled Panzerjäger Company (14 75mm PAK 40 and 14 LMGs)
1 Self-Propelled Flak Company (12 20mm and 4 LMGs)
5th Panzer Battalion
Staff
Staff Battery (3 StuG)
Flak Platoon (3 self-propelled quad 20mm guns)
3 Sturmgeschütz Batteries (14 StuG ea)
1 Panzer Maintenance Platoon
20th Artillery Regiment
1 Regimental Staff
1 (mot) Regimental Staff Battery (2 LMGs)
1 Regimental Band
1st Battalion
1 Battalion Staff and (mot) Staff Battery (2 LMGs)
3 (motZ) Batteries (3 105mm leFH and 2 LMGs ea)
2nd Battalion
same as 1st Battalion
3rd Battalion
1 Battalion Staff and (mot) Staff Battery (2 LMGs)
2 (motZ) Batteries (3 150mm sFH and 2 LMGs ea)
1 (motZ) Battery (3 100mm K18 and 2 LMGs)
From Army
1 (motZ) Battery (4 152mm Russian howitzers and 2 LMGs ea)
20th Pioneer Battalion
Staff
3 (mot) Pioneer Companies (2 HMGs, 9 LMGs, 3 PzBu39, 2 flamethrowers and 2 80mm mortars ea)
1 (mot) Light Pioneer Column (2 LMGs)
20th Signals Battalion
Staff
1 (mot) Telephone Company (5 LMGs)
1 (mot) Radio Company (4 LMGs)
1 (mot) Signals Column (1 LMG)

20th Supply Troops
  1/, 2/, 3/20th (120 ton) Transportation Companies (4 LMGs ea)
  20th (mot) Supply Company (6 LMGs)
Maintenance
  1/, 2/20th (mot) Maintenance Companies
Administration
  20th (mot) Administration Bureau
  20th (mot) Bakery Company
  20th (mot) Butcher Company
Medical Units
  1/, 2/20th (mot) Medical Companies
  1/, 2/, 3/20th Ambulance Platoons
Other
  20th (mot) Military Police Troop
  20th (mot) Field Post Office

On 29 April 1944 the 20th (mot) Reconnaissance Battalion and the 30th Motorcycle Battalion were merged and became the 120th Panzer Reconnaissance Battalion. The 120th Panzer Reconnaissance Battalion contained a staff, one light armored car company, three motorcycle companies, a heavy company, and a reconnaissance column. On 1 December 1944 the motorized infantry became panzergrenadiers. The division had:

  1/, 2/, 3/76th Panzergrenadier Regiment
  1/, 2/, 3/90th Panzergrenadier Regiment
  1/, 2/, 3/20th Artillery Regiment
  120th Panzer Reconnaissance Battalion
  8th Panzer Battalion
  284th Army Flak Battalion
  20th Divisional Support Units

25th (mot) Infantry Division

Formed on 15 November 1940 by the renaming of the 25th Infantry Division. The 13th Infantry Regiment was detached to the 4th Mountain Division, along with the 1/25th Artillery Regiment, which became the 1/94th Mountain Artillery Regiment, and the 1/61st Artillery Regiment was disbanded. On 15 March 1941 the 3/40th Infantry Regiment (27th Infantry Division) became the 25th Motorcycle Battalion and the 626th Heavy Artillery Regiment became the 3/25th Artillery Regiment (the former 3/25th became the 1/25th Artillery Regiment). The division had:

  1/, 2/, 3/35th (mot) Infantry Regiment
  1/, 2/, 3/119th (mot) Infantry Regiment
  25th Motorcycle Battalion (from 3/40th Infantry Regiment)
  1/, 2/, 3/25th (mot) Artillery Regiment
  25th Divisional Service Units

The 292nd Army Flak Battalion was assigned to the division during the winter of 1942/1943. On 23 June 1943 it became the 25th Panzergrenadier Division.

25th Panzergrenadier Division

Formed on 23 June 1943 by redesignating the 25th (mot) Infantry Division. It added the 5th Panzer Battalion and the 125th Panzer Reconnaissance Battalion. The division had:

  1/, 2/, 3/35th (mot) Grenadier Regiment
  1/, 2/, 3/119th (mot) Grenadier Regiment
  5th Panzer Battalion
  125th Panzer Reconnaissance Battalion (from 25th Motorcycle Battalion)
  1/, 2/, 3/25th (mot) Artillery Regiment
  292nd Army Flak Battalion
  25th Divisional Service Units

Keilig states that in 1943 the 125th Panzer Reconnaissance Battalion had a staff, a motorcycle company, a heavy company, and a light reconnaissance column. The 28th Panzer Battalion was equipped with sturmgeschütze. The

25th Artillery Regiment had two (motZ) battalions, each with two batteries of 105mm leFH, and a heavy (motZ) battalion with three batteries of 150mm sFH. In addition, the 1st and 2nd Battalions had a (motZ) battery of 88mm PAK. The regiment also had two 220mm French howitzers and one French 105mm gun. The 25th Pioneer Battalion had no bridging column and the division had no feldersatz battalion. In September 1943 OKH records show the division to be organized and equipped as follows:

25th Panzergrenadier Division
Divisional Staff
  Staff
  25th (mot) Mapping Detachment
35th Panzergrenadier Regiment
  Staff
  Regimental Band

Staff Company
  Panzerjäger Platoon (3 LMGs and 3 50mm PAK 38)
  Motorcycle Platoon (3 LMGs)
  Signals Platoon
  Pioneer Platoon (6 flamethrowers and 3 LMGs)
3 Battalions, each with
Staff
  3 (mot) Grenadier Companies (12 HMGs, 6 LMGs, 1 sPzBu41, 3 PzBu39 and 2 80mm mortars ea)
  1 (mot) Machine Gun Company (12 HMGs, 1 LMG, 3 37mm PAK 36 and 6 80mm mortars)
  1 (motZ) Infantry Gun Company (2 150mm sIG and 6 75mm leIG)

119th Panzergrenadier Regiment
same as 35th Panzergrenadier Regiment

125th Panzer Reconnaissance Battalion
Staff (3 LMGs)
  1 Light Armored Car Company (18 20mm and 24 LMGs)
  3 Motorcycle Companies (2 80mm mortars, 3 PzBu39, 4 HMGs and 18 LMGs ea)
  1 (mot) Heavy Company
    1 Pioneer Platoon (4 LMGs)
    1 Panzerjäger Platoon (3 LMGs and 3 75mm PAK 40)
    1 Panzerjäger Platoon (3 LMGs and 3 sPzBu41)
    1 Light Infantry Gun Section (2 75mm leIG)
  1 Light Panzer Reconnaissance Battalion Column

125th Panzerjäger Battalion
  2 Self-Propelled Panzerjäger Companies (12 75mm PAK 40 and 12 LMGs ea)
  1 Self-Propelled Panzerjäger Company (12 75mm PAK 40 and 12 LMGs)
  1 Self-Propelled Flak Company (12 20mm Flak guns and 4 LMGs)

8th Panzer Battalion
  Staff and Staff Battery (3 StuG)
  Flak Platoon (3 self-propelled quad 20mm guns)
  3 Sturmgeschütz Batteries (14 StuG ea)
  1 Panzer Maintenance Platoon

25th Artillery Regiment
  1 Regimental Staff
  1 (mot) Regimental Staff Battery (2 LMGs)
  1 Regimental Band
1st Battalion
  1 Battalion Staff and (mot) Staff Battery (2 LMGs)
  2 (motZ) Batteries (3 105mm Czech howitzers and 2 LMGs ea)
  1 (motZ) Battery (3 88mm PAK 43/41)
2nd Battalion
  same as 1st Battalion
3rd Battalion
  1 Battalion Staff and (mot) Staff Battery (2 LMGs)
  2 (motZ) Batteries (3 150mm sFH and 2 LMGs ea)

  1 (motZ) Battery (3 100mm K18 and 2 LMGs)
  1 (motZ) Battery (2 220mm French mörsers and 1 105mm French gun)
25th Pioneer Battalion
Staff
  3 (mot) Pioneer Companies (2 HMGs, 9 LMGs, 3 PzBu39, 2 flamethrowers and 2 80mm mortars ea)
  1 (mot) Light Pioneer Column (2 LMGs)
25th Signals Battalion
Staff
  1 (mot) Telephone Company (5 LMGs)
  1 (mot) Radio Company (4 LMGs)
  1 (mot) Signals Column (1 LMG)
25th Supply Troops
  1/25th (120 ton) Transportation Company (4 LMGs)
  2/, 3/25th (90 ton) Transportation Companies (3 LMGs ea)
  25th (mot) Supply Company (6 LMGs)
Maintenance
  1/, 2/25th (mot) Maintenance Companies
Administration
  25th (mot) Administration Bureau
  25th (mot) Bakery Company
  25th (mot) Butcher Company
Medical Units
  1/, 2/25th (mot) Medical Companies
  1/, 2/, 3/25th Ambulance Platoons
Other
  25th (mot) Military Police Troop
  25th (mot) Field Post Office

The division was destroyed with Army Group Center in July 1944. Initially, its debris was incorporated into the 107th Panzer Brigade. It was ordered reconstituted as a kampfgruppe on 31 August 1944. When division was re-formed on 1 October 1944 as a kampfgruppe it contained:

Divisional Staff
  125th Armored Car Platoon (6 LMGs and 4 20mm guns)
  25th (mot) Military Police Detachment (5 LMGs)
35th Panzergrenadier Regiment
  1 Regimental Staff
  1 (mot) Staff Company
    1 Signals Platoon
    1 Motorcycle Platoon (4 LMGs)
1/35th Panzergrenadier Regiment
  1 Battalion Staff
  1 (mot) Supply Company (4 LMGs)
  3 (mot) Panzergrenadier Companies (4 HMGs, 18 LMGs and 2 80mm mortars ea)
  1 (mot) Heavy Company (6 20mm Flak guns, 2 LMGs and 4 120mm mortars)
2/35th Panzergrenadier Regiment
  1 Battalion Staff

1 (mot) Supply Company (4 LMGs)

3 (bicycle) Panzergrenadier Companies (4 HMGs, 18 LMGs and 2 80mm mortars ea)

1 (mot) Heavy Company (6 20mm Flak guns, 2 LMGs and 4 120mm mortars)

13th (mot) Infantry Gun Company (4 150mm sIG and 7 LMGs)

14th (mot) Pioneer Company (2 HMGS, 12 LMGs, 2 80mm mortars and 18 flamethrowers)

15th (mot) Flak Company (12 20mm Flak guns and 2 LMGs)

25th Panzerjäger Battalion

1 Staff and Staff Battery (1 LMG and 3 StuG)

2 Sturmgeschütz Batteries (14 StuG and 14 LMGs ea)

1 (motZ) Panzerjäger Battery (12 75mm PAK 40 and 12 LMGs)

1 (mot) Supply Company (3 LMGs)

25th Artillery Battalion

1 Staff and Staff Battery (2 LMGs and 3 20mm guns)

3 (motZ) Light Howitzer Batteries (4 105mm leFH and 4 LMGs ea)

25th (mot) Pioneer Company (2 HMGs, 18 LMGs and 2 80mm mortars)

25th Panzer Signals Company (12 LMGs)

25th (mot) Maintenance Company

25th (mot) Butcher Company

25th (120 ton) Transportation Company (8 LMGs)

1/, 2/25th (mot) Medical Companies (4 LMGs ea)

1/, 2/25th (mot) Medical Supply Companies

25th (mot) Field Post Office

On 7 November 1944 it was reorganized into a full division by the addition of the 107th Panzer Brigade. It was organized and equipped as follows:

Division

Divisional Staff (2 LMGs)

25th (mot) Mapping Detachment

25th (mot) Military Police Troop (5 LMGs)

5th Panzer Battalion

1 Panzer Battalion Staff

1 Panzer Flak Platoon (4 self-propelled 37mm Flak)

3 Panzer Companies (11 PzMk V Panthers ea)

1 Panzer Company (11 PzMk IV/L70 tanks)

1 Panzer Maintenance Platoon (2 LMGs)

1 (mot) Panzer Supply Company

35th Panzergrenadier Regiment

1 Panzergrenadier Regimental Staff

1 Panzergrenadier Regimental Staff Company

1 Signals Platoon

1 Motorcycle Platoon (4 LMGs)

1 Panzerjäger Platoon (3 75mm PAK 40)

1st (mot) Battalion

1 Battalion Staff

1 (mot) Panzergrenadier Supply Company (4 LMGs)

3 (mot) Panzergrenadier Companies (12 LMGs ea)

1 (mot) Heavy Company (12 HMGs, 1 LMG and 6 20mm Flak guns)

1 (mot) Heavy Company (6 LMGs, 8 80mm mortars, 4 120mm mortars)

2nd Battalion

1 Battalion Staff

1 (mot) Panzergrenadier Supply Company (4 LMGs)

3 (bicycle) Panzergrenadier Companies (12 LMGs ea)

1 (mot) Heavy Company (12 HMGs, 1 LMG and 6 20mm Flak guns)

1 (mot) Heavy Company (6 LMGs, 8 80mm mortars and 4 120mm mortars)

3rd Battalion

same as 2nd Battalion

1 (mot) Infantry Gun Company (4 150mm sIG and 2 LMGs)

1 (mot) Pioneer Company (2 HMGs, 12 LMGs, 2 80mm mortars and 18 flamethrowers)

119th Panzergrenadier Regiment

1 Panzergrenadier Regimental Staff

1 Panzergrenadier Regimental Staff Company

1 Signals Platoon (7 LMGs)

1 Motorcycle Platoon (4 LMGs)

1 Panzerjäger Platoon (1 LMG and 3 heavy PAK guns)

1st (mot) Battalion

1 Battalion Staff (5 LMGs)

1 (mot) Panzergrenadier Supply Company (5 LMGs)

3 (half-track) Panzergrenadier Companies (3 HMGs, 30 LMGs, 7 triple 20mm SdKfz 251/21 and 2 75mm SdKfz 251/9 ea)

1 (half-track) Heavy Company

1 Company Staff (2 LMGs)

1 Platoon (7 LMGs and 4 120mm mortars)

1 Platoon (2 LMGs and 2 75mm SdKfz 251/9)

2nd Battalion

same as 1/35th Panzergrenadier Regiment

3rd Battalion

same as 2/35th Panzergrenadier Regiment

1 (mot) Infantry Gun Company (4 150mm sIG and 2 LMGs)

1 (mot) Pioneer Company (2 HMGs, 12 LMGs, 2 80mm mortars and 18 flamethrowers)

125th Panzer Reconnaissance Battalion

1 Battalion Staff

1 (mot) Battalion Staff Company

1 Signals Platoon (7 LMGs)

1 Armored Car Platoon (13 SdKfz 231/1 and 3 SdKfz 231/3)

1st, 2nd and 3rd (mot) Reconnaissance Companies (4 HMGS, 9 LMGs and 2 80mm mortars ea)

4th (mot) Heavy Reconnaissance Company

1 Pioneer Platoon (4 LMGs)

1 Mortar Platoon (6 80mm mortars)

1 (mot) Reconnaissance Supply Company

25th Panzer Artillery Regiment

1 Regimental Staff

1 (mot) Regimental Staff Battery (2 LMGs)

1st (motZ) Battalion

1 Battalion Staff

1 (mot) Battalion Staff Battery (2 LMGs and 3 20mm Flak)

3 (motZ) Batteries (6 105mm leFH and 4 LMGs ea)

2nd (motZ) Battalion

same as 1st Battalion

3rd (motZ) Battalion

1 Battalion Staff

1 (mot) Battalion Staff Battery (2 LMGs and 3 20mm Flak)

2 (motZ) Batteries (6 150mm sFH and 4 LMGs ea)

1 (motZ) Battery (4 100mm K18 and 4 LMGs ea)

25th Panzerjäger Battalion

1 Battalion Staff

1 (mot) Battalion Staff Company

1 Sturmgeschütz Platoon (3 StuG)

2 Sturmgeschütz Batteries (10 StuG ea)

1 (motZ) Panzerjäger Battery (12 LMGs and 12 75mm PAK 40)

1 (mot) Sturmgeschütz Supply Company

292nd Army Flak Battalion

1 Flak Battalion Staff

1 Flak Battalion Staff Battery (2 LMGs)

2 (motZ) Heavy Flak Batteries (6 88mm, 3 20mm and 2 LMGs ea)

1 (motZ) Medium Flak Battery (9 37mm and 4 LMGs)

1 Self-Propelled (3 quad 20mm Flak guns)

25th Pioneer Battalion

1 (half-track) Pioneer Battalion Staff (3 LMGs)

1 (half-track) Pioneer Battalion Staff Company (4 LMGs)

1 (half-track) Pioneer Company (2 HMGs, 18 LMGs and 2 80mm mortars)

2 (mot) Pioneer Companies (2 HMGs, 18 LMGs and 2 80mm mortars ea)

25th Signals Battalion

1 (mot) Radio Company (6 LMGs)

1 (mot) Telephone Company (5 LMGs)

1 (mot) Signals Supply Company (2 LMGs)

25th Panzergrenadier Feldersatz Battalion

1 Supply Company

4 Ersatz Companies (50 LMGs, 12 HMGs, 6 80mm mortars, 2 120mm mortars, 1 75mm PAK 40, 1 20mm Flak, 2 flamethrowers and 1 105mm leFH total)

Supply Troops

1 (mot) Supply Battalion Staff (2 LMGs)

1 (mot) Supply Battalion Staff Company

1/, 2/, 3/25th (mot) (120 ton) Transportation Companies (4 LMGs ea)

4/, 5/25th (horse-drawn) (60 ton) Transportation Companies (4 LMGs ea)

25th (mot) Maintenance Platoon

Vehicle Park Troops

1/, 2/25th (mot) Maintenance Companies

1 (mot) Maintenance Supply Column

Medical

1 (mot) Medical Company (reinforced) (2 LMGs)

1 (mot) Medical Supply Company (1 LMG)

Other

25th (mot) Mixed Administration Company

25th (mot) Field Post Office

On 14 December 1944 the organization of the armored portion of the division and its panzer inventory were as follows:

5th Panzer Battalion

1 Panzer Staff Platoon

1 Panzer Flak Platoon

3 Medium Panzer Companies (PzMk V)

1 Panzerjäger Company (PzMk IV/L70)

PzMk IV/L70	6
PzMk V	11 (+30 en route)
FlakpzIV (37)	4

On 2/1/45 the division was ordered rebuilt as a Type 44 Panzergrenadier Division near Küstrin. By 1 February 1945 it contained:

5th Panzer Battalion

1 Panzer Staff Platoon

1 Panzer Flak Platoon

3 Medium Panzer Companies (PzMk V)

1 Panzerjäger Company (PzMk IV/L70)

PzMk IV/L70	10 (+10 on 17 Feb.)
PzMk V	26 (+10 on 17 Feb.)
FlakpzIV (37)	4

29th (mot) Infantry Division

On 24 August 1939 the division contained:

1/, 2/, 3/15th (mot) Infantry Regiment
1/, 2/, 3/71st (mot) Infantry Regiment
1/, 2/, 3/86th (mot) Infantry Regiment
1/, 2/, 3/29th (mot) Artillery Regiment
1/65th Artillery Regiment
29th Divisional Service Units

OKH records show that when the Germans invaded Poland on 1 September 1939 the 29th (mot) Infantry Division was organized and equipped as follows:

29th (mot) Infantry Division Generalleutnant Lemelsen
  29th (mot) (mot) Mapping Detachment
  29th (mot) Motorcycle Messenger Platoon
  15th (mot) Infantry Regiment
    1 Signals Platoon
    3 (mot) Battalions, each with
      3 Rifle Companies (9 LMGs, 2 HMGs and 3 50mm mortars ea)
      1 Heavy Company (8 HMGs and 6 80mm mortars)
    1 (mot) Panzerabwehr Company (12 37mm PAK 36 and 4 LMGs)
    1 (mot) Infantry Support Gun Company (8 75mm leIG)
    1 Motorcycle Platoon (3 LMGs)
    1 Light Infantry Supply Column
  71st (mot) Infantry Regiment
  same as before
  29th (mot) Panzerabwehr Battalion
    1 (mot) Signals Platoon
    3 (mot) Panzerabwehr Companies (12 37mm PAK 36 and 6 LMGs ea)
    6/46th (mot) Heavy Machine Gun Battalion (12 20mm guns)
  29th Reconnaissance Battalion
    1 (mot) Signals Platoon (1 LMG)
    1 Motorcycle Company (9 LMGs, 2 HMGs and 9 LMGs)
    1 Armored Car Company (10 20mm and 25 LMGs)
  29th Artillery Regiment
    1st and 3rd (mot) Battalions, each with
      3 Batteries (4 105mm leFH and 2 LMGs ea)
    1/65th (mot) Artillery Regiment
      3 Batteries (4 150mm sFH and 2 LMGs ea)
    29th Artillery Observation Battalion
  29th Feldersatz Battalion
    3 Companies (9 LMGs, 2 HMGs and 3 50mm mortars ea)
  29th Signals Battalion
    1 (mot) Radio Company

    1 (tmot) Telephone Company
    1 (mot) Signals Supply Column
  29th Pioneer Battalion
    3 (mot) Pioneer Companies (9 LMGs ea)
    1 (mot) Brüko B
    1 (mot) Engineer Supply Column
  29th Supply Troop
    1st–8th (mot) Light Supply Columns
    9/, 10/29th (mot) Heavy Fuel Column
    29th (mot) Maintenance Platoon
    29th (mot) Supply Company
  Administration
    29th Divisional Administration
    29th (mot) Field Bakery
    29th (mot) Butcher Detachment
  Other
    1/, 2/29th Medical Company
    29th (mot) Field Hospital
    1/, 2/29th Ambulance Companies
    29th Veterinarian Company
    29th (mot) Military Police Troop
    29th (mot) Field Post Office

After Poland the 86th (mot) Infantry Regiment and the 2/29th Artillery Regiment were transferred to the 10th Panzer Division. The 1/65th Artillery Regiment was attached to the 29th Artillery Regiment as, on 1 April 1940, the 3/29th and the old 3/29th became the 2/29th Artillery Regiment. In addition, again on 1 April 1940, the 9/, 10/29th Heavy Fuel Columns were renumbered the 7/, 8/29th Heavy Fuel Columns. In the fall of 1940 the 29th Division had:

1/, 2/, 3/15th (mot) Infantry Regiment
1/, 2/, 3/71st (mot) Infantry Regiment
29th Motorcycle Battalion
1/, 2/, 3/29th (mot) Artillery Regiment
29th Divisional Service Units

In 1942 the division had the 129th Panzer Battalion (from the 1/39th Panzer Regiment) and the 4/29th (mot) Artillery Regiment (from the 313th Army Flak Battalion) attached to it. On 28 June 1942 the organization of the armored portion of the division and its panzer inventory were as follows:

129th Panzer Battalion
  1 Panzer Staff Company
  1 Medium Panzer Company
  2 Light Panzer Companies
    PzMk II   12
    PzMk III (50 lg   36
    PzMk IV (lg)   8
    PzBefWg   2

The division was destroyed in the battles around Stalingrad. The 129th Panzer Battalion was rebuilt with four companies on 11 February 1943. The division was re-formed by the order of 11 February 1943 in France from the 345th (mot) Division and on 1 March 1943 the division had:

1/, 2/, 3/15th Grenadier Regiment (from 148th (mot) Grenadier Regiment)

1/, 2/, 3/71st Grenadier Regiment (from 152nd Panzer-grenadier Regiment)

129th Panzer Battalion (from 345th Panzer Battalion)

1/, 2/, 3/29th (mot) Artillery Regiment (from 345th Artillery Regiment and new drafts)

313th Army Flak Battalion (from 4/345th Artillery Regiment)

29th Divisional Service Units (from 345th Division Service Units)

On 23 June 1943 the division became the 29th Panzer-grenadier Division.

29th Panzergrenadier Division

Formed on 23 June 1943 by renaming the 29th (mot) Infantry Division. Keilig states that in 1943 the division had the 23rd Sound Ranging Troop attached to it. The 129th Panzer Reconnaissance Battalion had a staff, a heavy platoon with six SdKfz 251/9 with 75mm KwK, a light armored car company, a (half-track) reconnaissance company, a (half-track) heavy reconnaissance company, a (half-track) heavy company (containing a pioneer platoon, a panzerjäger platoon, a light infantry gun platoon with 75mm leIG, and two platoons with SdKfz 251/9 with 75mm KwK), and a light panzer reconnaissance battalion column. The 129th Panzer Battalion was equipped with sturmgeschütze. The 1/29th Artillery Regiment had a staff, staff battery, and two self-propelled leFH batteries (six SdKfz 124 Wespe with 105mm leFH ea), and one self-propelled sFH battery (six SdKfz 165 Hummel with 150mm sFH). The division had no feldersatz battalion.

On 10 July 1943 the organization of the armored portion of the division and its panzer inventory were as follows:

129th Panzer Battalion
  1 Panzer Staff Company
  4 Sturmgeschütz Companies
    StuG   43
    PzBefWg   3

On 20 August 1943 it was organized and equipped with:

129th Panzer Battalion
  1 Panzer Staff Company
  3 Sturmgeschütz Companies
    StuG   38
    PzBefWg   3

In September 1943 OKH records show that the division was organized and equipped as follows:

29th Panzergrenadier Division
Divisional Staff
Staff
29th (mot) Mapping Detachment
23rd Sound Ranging Troop (temporarily attached)
15th Panzergrenadier Regiment
  Staff
  Regimental Band
  Staff Company
    Signals Platoon
    Pioneer Platoon (6 flamethrowers and 3 LMGs)
3 Battalions, each with
  Staff
  4 (mot) Grenadier Companies (4 HMGs, 18 LMGs, 3 PzBu39 and 2 80mm mortars ea)
  1 Self-Propelled Heavy Infantry Gun Company (6 150mm sIG)
  1 (motZ) Panzerjäger Company (3 75mm PAK 40, 6 50mm PAK 38 and 9 LMGs)
71st Panzergrenadier Regiment
same as 15th Panzergrenadier Regiment
129th Panzer Reconnaissance Battalion
Staff (15 LMGs)
1 Heavy Platoon (6 SdKfz 234/3 with 75mm KwK and 6 LMGs)
1 Light Armored Car Company (18 20mm and 24 LMGs)
1 (half-track) Reconnaissance Company (16 20mm and 25 LMGs)
2 (half-track) Heavy Reconnaissance Companies (2 80mm mortars, 4 HMGs, 56 LMGs and 3 75mm leIG ea)
1 (half-track) Heavy Company
  1 Pioneer Platoon (3 LMGs, 1 20mm and 6 flamethrowers)
  1 Panzerjäger Platoon (3 LMGs and 3 75mm PAK 40)
  1 Light Infantry Gun Section (4 LMGs and 2 75mm leIG)

2 Platoons (4 LMGs and 3 SdKfz 251/9 with 75mm KwK ea)

1 Light Panzer Reconnaissance Battalion Column

129th Panzer Battalion

Staff and Staff Battery (3 StuG)

3 Sturmgeschütz Batteries (14 StuG ea)

1 Panzer Maintenance Platoon

29th Artillery Regiment

1 Regimental Staff and (mot) Staff Battery (2 LMGs)

1st Battalion

1 Battalion Staff and (self-propelled) Staff Battery (2 LMGs)

3 Self-Propelled Batteries (4 105mm leFH in Wespe and 2 LMGs ea)

2nd Battalion

1 Battalion Staff and (mot) Staff Battery (2 LMGs)

3 (motZ) Batteries (4 105mm leFh and 2 LMGs ea)

3rd Battalion

1 Battalion Staff and (mot) Staff Battery (2 LMGs)

2 (motZ) Batteries (4 150mm sFH and 2 LMGs ea)

1 (motZ) Battery (4 100mm K18 and 2 LMGs)

313th Army Flak Battalion

Staff and (mot) Staff Battery (1 LMG)

2 (motZ) Heavy Flak Batteries (4 88mm, 3 20mm and 2 LMGs ea)

1 (motZ) Light Flak Battery (9 20mm, 2 quad 20mm and 2 LMGs)

1 (mot) (20 ton) Supply Column

29th Pioneer Battalion

Staff

3 (mot) Pioneer Companies (2 HMGs, 18 LMGs, 3 PzBu39, 2 80mm mortars and 6 flamethrowers ea)

1 (mot) Brüko K Bridging Column (3 LMGs)

1 (mot) Light Pioneer Column (2 LMGs)

29th Signals Battalion

Staff

1 (mot) Telephone Company (5 LMGs)

1 (mot) Radio Company (4 LMGs)

1 (mot) Signals Column (1 LMG)

29th Supply Troops

1/, 2/29th (120 ton) Transportation Companies (4 LMGs ea)

3/, 4/, 5/29th (90 ton) Transportation Companies (3 LMGs ea)

29th (mot) Supply Company (6 LMGs)

Maintenance

1/, 2/29th (mot) Maintenance Companies

29th (75 ton) Maintenance Supply Column

Administration

29th (mot) Administration Bureau

29th (mot) Bakery Company

29th (mot) Butcher Company

Medical Units

1/, 2/29th (mot) Medical Companies

1/, 2/, 3/29th Ambulance Platoons

Other

29th (mot) Military Police Troop

29th (mot) Field Post Office

In April/May 1944 the division was at Anzio. The motorized grenadier regiments were redesignated as panzergrenadier regiments on 1 December 1944. By February 1945 the panzerjäger battalion had been finally rebuilt.

36th (mot) Infantry Division

Began forming on 1 November 1940 and finished forming on 1 May 1941 using the 36th Infantry Division as a cadre. The 70th Infantry Regiment was transferred to the 111th Infantry Division, along with the 2/36th Artillery Regiment (as the 2/117th Artillery Regiment). The 3/36th Artillery Regiment became the 2/36th and the 3/36th was formed from the 1/72nd Artillery Regiment. The 36th Motorcycle Battalion was formed from the 11th Machine Gun Battalion. The horse-drawn units of the division were transferred to the 126th Infantry Division. The division had:

1/, 2/, 3/87th (mot) Infantry Regiment

1/, 2/, 3/118th (mot) Infantry Regiment

36th Motorcycle Battalion (from 11th Machine Gun Battalion)

1/, 2/, 3/36th (mot) Artillery Regiment

36th Divisional Service Units

During the summer of 1943 the division became the 36th Panzergrenadier Division and the reconnaissance battalion became the 136th Armored Reconnaissance Battalion. The division was demotorized in June 1943 and reverted to the 36th Infantry Division. The division was apparently ordered redesignated as the 36th Panzergrenadier Division and the 36th Reconnaissance Battalion became the 136th Panzer Reconnaissance Battalion in the summer of 1943, but these changes apparently did not occur. On 27 March 1943 the division was ordered demotorized and the order was executed on 1 May 1943. After July 1943 the division operated as a normal infantry division.

60th (mot) Infantry Division

Established on 17 July 1940 from the 60th Infantry Division, the new motorized division had:

1/, 2/, 3/92nd (mot) Infantry Regiment (formerly 92nd Infantry Regiment)

1/, 2/, 3/120th (mot) Infantry Regiment (formerly 244th Infantry Regiment)

160th Motorcycle Battalion (formed from 15th Machine Gun Battalion)

1/, 2/, 3/160th Artillery Regiment

160th Divisional Service Units

On 5 April 1941, during the invasion of Greece, the 60th (mot) Infantry Division was organized and equipped as follows:

60th (mot) Infantry Division
Divisional Staff (2 LMGs)
160th (mot) Mapping Detachment
Motorcycle Messenger Platoon

92nd Infantry Regiment
1 (mot) Signals Platoon
1 (mot) Reconnaissance Company
  1 Motorcycle Platoon
  1 Pioneer Platoon (3 LMGs)
3 (mot) Infantry Battalions, each with
  3 (mot) Companies (12 LMGs and 3 50mm mortars ea)
  1 (mot) Machine Gun Company (12 HMGs and 6 80mm mortars)
1 Motorcycle Platoon
1 (mot) Infantry Gun Company (2 150mm sIG and 6 75mm leIG)
1 (mot) Panzerjäger Platoon (12 37mm PAK 36 and 4 LMGs)
1 (mot) Light Supply Column

120th Infantry Regiment
same as 92nd Infantry Regiment

160th Motorcycle Battalion
3 Motorcycle Companies (3 50mm mortars, 2 HMGs and 18 LMGs ea)
1 (mot) Heavy Machine Gun Company (8 HMGs and 6 80mm mortars)
1 (mot) Reconnaissance Company
  1 (mot) Infantry Gun Section (2 75mm leIG)
  1 (mot) Panzerjäger Platoon (3 37mm PAK 36 and 1 LMG)
  1 (mot) Pioneer Platoon (3 LMGs)

160th Panzerjäger Battalion
1 (mot) Signals Platoon
3 (mot) Panzerjäger Companies (12 37mm PAK 36 and 6 LMGs ea)

3rd Company/608th Self-Propelled Heavy Machine Gun Battalion (10 20mm guns)

160th Reconnaissance Battalion
1 (mot) Signals Platoon (2 LMGs)
1 Armored Car Company (10 HMGs and 25 LMGs)
1 Motorcycle Company (3 50mm mortars, 4 HMGs and 18 LMGs)
1 (mot) Heavy Reconnaissance Company
  1 Panzerjäger Platoon (3 37mm PAK 36 and 1 LMG)
  1 Pioneer Platoon (3 LMGs)
  1 Infantry Gun Section (2 75mm leIG)
1 (mot) Reconnaissance Supply Column

160th Artillery Regiment
1 (mot) Support Detachment
1 (mot) Signals Platoon
1 (mot) Weather Detachment

1st and 2nd (mot) Battalions, each with
1 (mot) Calibration Detachment
1 (mot) Signals Platoon
3 (mot) Batteries (4 105mm leFH and 2 LMGs ea)

3rd (mot) Battalion
1 Calibration Detachment
1 Signals Platoon
1 (mot) Battery (4 100mm K18 and 2 LMGs)
2 (mot) Batteries (4 150mm sFH and 2 LMGs ea)

160th Signals Battalion
1 (mot) Telephone Company (2 LMGs)
1 (mot) Radio Company (2 LMGs)
1 (mot) Light Signals Supply Column

160th (mot) Pioneer Battalion
3 (mot) Pioneer Companies (9 LMGs ea)
1 (mot) Brüko T
1 (mot) Light Pioneer Supply Column

160th Supply Troop
1–6/160th (mot) Light Supply Columns
7/, 8/160th (mot) Heavy Fuel Column
1/, 2/160th (mot) Maintenance Company
160th (mot) Supply Company

Administration
160th (mot) Field Bakery
160th (mot) Butcher Company
160th Divisional Administration

Other
1/, 2/160th (mot) Medical Company
160th (mot) Field Hospital
1/, 2/160th (mot) Ambulance Companies
160th (mot) Miltiary Police Troop
160th (mot) Field Post Office

Attached
74th Luftwaffe Flak Battalion

Later in 1941, most likely prior to the invasion of Russia in June, the 160th Motorcycle and 160th Reconnaissance

Battalions were merged and the 282nd Army Flak Battalion joined the division as the 4/160th Artillery Regiment. The 2/, 3/160th Artillery Regiment were formed from the 2/77th (mot) Army Artillery Battalion and the 601st (mot) Heavy Army Artillery Battalion. The 3/608th Flak Machine Gun Battalion became the 4/160th Panzerjäger Battalion. On 15 June 1942 the 1/18th Panzer Regiment (18th Panzer Division) became the 160th Panzer Battalion. The division was destroyed at Stalingrad. On 28 June 1942 the organization of the armored portion of the division and its panzer inventory were as follows:

160th Panzer Battalion
  1 Panzer Staff Company
  1 Medium Panzer Company
  2 Light Panzer Companies

PzMk II	17
PzMk III (50 lg)	35
PzMk IV (lg)	4
PzBefWg	1

After Stalingrad the division was rebuilt by the order of 17 February 1943 in southern France using the 271st Grenadier Regiment (93rd Infantry Division). The 160th Panzer Battalion was rebuilt with drafts and was brought to a strength of four panzer companies.

The rest of the division was organized on 15 March 1944. It was retitled the 60th Panzergrenadier Division, but the order of 14 June 1944 changed its name to the Feldherrnhalle Panzergrenadier Division. The 160th Panzer Battalion was redesignated the Feldherrnhalle Panzer Battalion on 20 June 1943.

90th Light Afrika Division

Formed on 26 November 1941 from the Division z.b.V. Afrika, the division had:

1/, 2/, 3/155th Schützen Regiment
1/, 2/361st (Afrika Regiment) Infantry Regiment
580th (mixed) Reconnaissance Company
361st Artillery Battalion
900th Pioneer Battalion
190th Signals Company

The "many weapons—few men" organization was also applied to the 90th Light Division in February 1942. The proposed organization for it was as follows:

90th Light Afrika Division
155th Infantry Regiment (8 companies)
  2 Battalions, each with 4 companies, each company to have 13 MP, 18 LMGs, 2 HMGs, 3 80mm mortars, 3 28mm PzBu41 and 6 76.2mm (r) or 75mm (f) anti-tank guns
  1 Self-Propelled Infantry Gun Company (3 platoons)
  1 Pioneer Company, with 13 MP, 18 LMGs, 2 HMGs, 3 80mm mortars, 3 28mm PzBu41 and 6 76.2mm (r) or 75mm (f) anti-tank guns
361st Afrika Regiment (5 companies)
  same as 155th proposed organization
288th Sonderverband (Special Unit) (8 companies, no vehicles)
361st Afrika Artillery Battalion (guns still in Italy; to be expanded to a full regiment, with two battalions, each battalion to have 2 105mm leFH batteries and 1 100mm K 17 gun battery)
3/255th Infantry Regiment (nearly totally destroyed)
3/347th Infantry Regiment (2½ companies)

1/3rd Mixed Signals Company z.b.V. Afrika

When the 3/255th Infantry Regiment was destroyed, its remnants were sent to the 288th Infantry Regiment, later becoming the 1/200th Infantry Regiment. Apparently the division was also to have also have the following units attached, but they were never organized:

1 Reconnaissance Battalion (with two mixed reconnaissance companies organized like the 580th)
1 Pioneer Battalion (2 companies, each with 13 MP, 18 LMGs, 2 HMGs, 3 80mm mortars, 3 28mm PzBu41 and 6 50mm PAK 38)
1 Mixed Signals Company (6 medium platoons)

On 10 March 1942, when the reorganization was completed, the new structure of the division was as follows:

90th Light Afrika Division
  259th (mot) Mapping Detachment
155th Schützen Regiment
  1 (mot) Staff Company
  1st and 2nd Battalions, each with
    4 (mot) Companies, each with 18 LMGs, 2 HMGs, 2 80mm mortars, 1 28mm PzBu41 and 2 50mm PAK 38)
200th Schützen Regiment
  1 (mot) Staff Company
  1st and 2nd Battalions, each with
    4 (mot) Companies, each with 18 LMGs, 2 HMGs, 2 80mm mortars, 1 28mm PzBu41 and 3 50mm PAK 38)
361st (mot) Infantry Regiment
  1 (mot) Staff Company

1st and 2nd Battalions, each with

4 (mot) Companies, each with 18 LMGs, 2 HMGs, 2 80mm mortars, 1 28mm PzBu41 and 2 75mm PAK 40)

707th Heavy Self-Propelled Infantry Gun Company (6 150mm sfl sIG guns)

708th Heavy Self-Propelled Infantry Gun Company (6 150mm sfl sIG guns)

190th Panzer Battalion

1 Panzer Staff Platoon

1 Panzer Platoon

1 Medium Panzer Company

3 Light Panzer Companies

1 Panzer Replacement Platoon

190th (mot) Artillery Regiment

1 (mot) Regimental Staff Battery

1st and 2nd (mot) Battalions, each with

1 Staff Battery

2 (mot) Batteries (4 105mm leFH 18 and 2 LMGs)

1 (mot) Battery (4 100mm K17 guns and 2 LMGs)

580th (mot) Reconnaissance Company

1 Pioneer Platoon (3 HMGs, 9 LMGs and 3 28mm PzBu41)

1 Armored Car Platoon (6 37mm and 6 LMGs)

1 Panzerjäger Platoon (3 50mm PAK 38)

1 Flak Battery (4 20mm and 2 LMGs)

190th Panzerjäger Battalion

2 (mot) Panzerjäger Companies (9 50mm PAK 38 and 6 LMGs ea)

190th (mot) Signals Company

Administrative Units

535th (mot) Bakery Company

517th (mot) Butcher company

(mot) Ambulance Company

(mot) Military Police Detachment

190th (mot) Field Post Office

On 1 April 1942 the division was renamed the 90th Light Infantry Division. The 200th Schützen Regiment, shown above, was actually not formed until 1 April 1942. The 190th Panzer Battalion, though assigned, was not in Africa. On 1 April 1942 the division was renamed the 90th Light Infantry Division and the 155th Schützen Regiment became the 155th Light Infantry Regiment. The 3/155th Schützen Regiment was reorganized as the 2/200th Panzergrenadiers and the 3/200th was organized from the 3/347th Infantry Regiment. Then the 361th, 155th, and 200th Infantry Regiments, became Schützen Regiments. On 16 April 1942 the division was reorganized and contained:

90th Light Afrika Division

259th (mot) Mapping Detachment

155th Schützen Regiment

1 (mot) Staff Company

1st and 2nd Battalions, each with

4 (mot) Companies (18 LMGs, 2 HMGs, 2 80mm mortars, 1 28mm PzBu41 and 2 75mm PAK 40 ea)

200th Schützen Regiment

1 (mot) Staff Company

1st and 2nd Battalions, each with

4 (mot) Companies (18 LMGs, 2 HMGs, 2 80mm mortars, 1 28mm PzBu41 and 2 75mm PAK 40 ea)

361st (mot) Schützen Regiment

1 (mot) Staff Company

1st and 2nd (mot) Battalions, each with

4 (mot) Companies (18 LMGs, 2 HMGs, 2 80mm mortars, 1 28mm PzBu41 and 2 75mm PAK 40 ea)

707th Heavy Self-Propelled Infantry Gun Company (6 150mm sIG sfl guns)

708th Heavy Self-Propelled Infantry Gun Company (6 150mm sIG sfl guns)

1 (mot) Infantry Gun Company (6 150mm sIG guns)

190th Panzer Battalion (not in Africa)

190th (mot) Artillery Regiment

1 (mot) Regimental Staff Battery

1st and 2nd (mot) Battalions, each with

1 Staff Battery

2 (mot) Batteries (4 105mm leFH 18 and 2 LMGs)

1 (mot) Battery (4 100mm K17 guns and 2 LMGs)

1/613th (mot) Light Flak Battalion (12 20mm Flak guns)

580th (mot) Reconnaissance Battalion

1 Pioneer Platoon (3 HMGs, 9 LMGs and 3 28mm PzBu41)

1 Armored Car Platoon (6 37mm, 6 LMGs)

1 Panzerjäger Platoon (3 50mm PAK 38)

1 Flak Battery (4 20mm)

190th Panzerjäger Battalion

2 (mot) Panzerjäger Companies (9 50mm PAK 38 and 6 LMGs ea)

190th Pioneer Battalion

2 (mot) Pioneer Companies (9 LMGs, 3 28mm PzBu41 and 3 50mm PAK 38 ea)

190th Panzer Signals Battalion

1 (mot) Telephone Company

1 (mot) Radio Company

1 (mot) Light Signals Supply Column

Administrative Units

566th (mot) Maintenance Company

535th (mot) Bakery Company

517th (mot) Butcher company

546th (mot) Munitions Company

Divisional Administration

638th (mot) Ambulance Company

(mot) Military Police Detachment

190th (mot) Field Post Office

On 26 July 1942 the 90th Light Afrika Division was a full division. The three regiments, however, became

ORGANIZATIONAL HISTORY OF GERMAN MOTORIZED AND PANZERGRENADIER DIVISIONS

Panzergrenadier Regiments. The division now consisted of:

1/, 2/155th Panzergrenadier Regiment
1/, 2/200th Panzergrenadier Regiment
1/, 2/361st Panzergrenadier Regiment
190th Panzer Battalion (not in Africa)
190th Panzerjäger Battalion
580th Reconnaissance Battalion
1/, 2/190th Artillery Regiment
900th Pioneer Battalion
190th Divisional Service Units

During 1942 the following units were assigned to the 90th Light Afrika Division and operational in Africa:

Divisional Staff
259th (mot) Divisional Mapping Detachment
155th (mot) Infantry Regiment
200th (mot) Infantry Regiment
361st (mot) Afrika Infantry Regiment
Afrika (mot) Panzergrenadier Regiment
Kolbeck Battalion
707th Heavy Infantry Gun Company (150mm sfl sIG guns)
708th Heavy Infantry Gun Company (150mm sfl sIG guns)
190th (mot) Panzerjäger Battalion
190th (mot) Artillery Regiment
580th (mot) Reconnaissance Company
(mot) Signals Battalion
900th (mot) Pioneer Battalion
Feldersatz Battalion
638th (mot) Ambulance Platoon
566th Maintenance Platoon
540th (mot) Munitions Administration Company
535th (mot) Bakery Company
517th (mot) Butcher company
(mot) Divisional Administration Bureau
(mot) Military Police Detachment
190th (mot) Field Post Office

The 259th (mot) Divisional Mapping Detachment was detached to the Staff of Panzer Army Afrika on 26 January 1942. The 200th (mot) Infantry Regiment was formed with one battalion of the 155th Infantry Regiment and the 3/347th Infantry Regiment on 24 March 1942. The 361st (mot) Afrika Infantry Regiment was formed with veterans of the French Foreign Legion. The Afrika (mot) Panzergrenadier Regiment, formerly the Sonderverband 288, was reorganized and renamed on 6 August 1942, though the formal redesignation occurred on 31 October 1942. The Kolbeck Battalion was formed on 25 November 1942 from the 90th Light Division transport and Flak transport personnel. It was reinforced by 500 men from the 361st Afrika Infantry Regiment who were rescued from a New Zealand POW camp. It was put under the com-

mand of Major Kolbeck on 28 November. The 707th and 708th Self-Propelled Infantry Gun Companies were detached to the division on 14 August 1942. The 190th (mot) Panzerjäger Battalion was formed by combining the 3/33rd Panzerjäger Battalion, 3/39th Panzerjäger Battalion, and 1/613th Flak Battalion on 24 March 1942. The 190th (mot) Artillery Regiment was formed from the 361st Artillery Regiment on 27 May 1942. The 580th (mot) Reconnaissance Company was reorganized as the 580th Reconnaissance Battalion on 23 May 1942.

When the rest of the Afrika Korps was reorganized on 15 August 1942 the 90th Light Afrika Division was also reorganized. Its new organization, actual head count and actual weapons present were as follows:

90th Light Afrika Division
  259th (mot) Mapping Detachment
155th Schützen Regiment (51 officers/1,145 men)
  1 (mot) Staff Company
1st Battalion
  4 (mot) Companies (total equipment 34 LMGs, 3 HMGs, 4 80mm mortars and 3 75mm PAK 40)
2nd Battalion
  4 (mot) Companies (total equipment 30 LMGs, 8 HMGs, 4 80mm mortars and 4 75mm PAK 40)
200th Schützen Regiment (30 officers/898 men)
  1 (mot) Staff Company
1st Battalion
  4 (mot) Companies (total equipment 44 LMGs, 7 HMGs, 5 80mm mortars, 3 28mm PzBu41 and 7 75mm PAK 40)
2nd Battalion
  4 (mot) Companies (total equipment 29 LMGs, 9 HMGs, 4 80mm mortars, 2 28mm PzBu41 and 9 75mm PAK 40)
361st (mot) Infantry Regiment (35 officers/919 men)
  1 (mot) Staff Company
1st Battalion
  4 (mot) Companies (total equipment 21 LMGs, 8 HMGs, 5 80mm mortars, 0 28mm PzBu41 and 5 75mm PAK 40)
2nd Battalion
  4 (mot) Companies (total equipment 30 LMGs, 8 HMGs, 7 80mm mortars, 0 28mm PzBu41 and 3 75mm PAK 40)
707th Heavy Self-Propelled Infantry Gun Company (5 150mm sIG sfl guns)
708th Heavy Self-Propelled Infantry Gun Company (4 150mm sIG sfl guns)
1 (mot) Infantry Gun Company (6 150mm sIG) (newly raised as of 1 Aug. 1942)
190th Panzer Battalion (newly raised as of 1 Aug. 1942; not in Africa)
  2 Light Panzer Platoons

3 Light Panzer Companies
1 Medium Panzer Company
1 Panzer Maintenance Platoon
1 Panzer Replacement Platoon
190th (mot) Artillery Regiment
1 (mot) Regimental Staff Battery
1st (mot) Battalion
1 Staff Battery
1 (mot) Battery (4 British 25pdrs)
1 (mot) Battery (3 British 25pdrs)
1 (mot) Battery (4 76.2mm (r) guns)
2nd (mot) Battalion (newly raised as of 1 Aug. 1942)
1 Staff Battery
2 (mot) Batteries (4 105mm leFH 18 and 2 LMGs ea)
1 (mot) Battery (4 100mm K17 and 2 LMGs ea)
190th (mot) Light Flak Battalion (7 20mm Flak guns)
580th (mot) Reconnaissance Battalion
1 Armored Car Platoon (2 armored cars, 4 MTW and 2 self-propelled gun carriages)
1 (mot) Reconnaissance Company (18 LMGs, 2 HMGs, 3 PzBu3939 and 4 50mm PAK 38)
1 (mot) Heavy Reconnaissance Company
1 Pioneer Platoon
1 Panzerjäger Platoon
1 Signals Platoon
(total 21 LMGs, 2 HMGs, 1 80mm mortar and 8 50mm PAK 38)
1 (mot) Battery (7 British 25pdrs)
1 (mot) Light Reconnaissance Supply Column
190th Panzerjäger Battalion (6 officers/219 men)
2 (mot) Panzerjäger Companies (7 50mm PAK 38)
190th Panzer Signals Battalion
1 Panzer Telephone Company (newly raised as of 1 Aug. 1942)
1 Panzer Radio Company
1 (mot) Light Signals Supply Column (newly raised as of 1 Aug. 1942)
90th Feldersatz Battalion
6 Companies (no heavy weapons)
190th Supply Battalion (appears to be organizing)
1–4/190th (mot) Light Supply Columns
566th (mot) Maintenance Company
190th (tmot) Supply Company
Administrative Units
190th (mot) Bakery Company
190th (mot) Butcher Company
190th Divisional Administration
546th (mot) Munitions Company
1/, 2/190th (mot) Ambulance Companies
2/92nd Medical Company
(mot) Military Police Detachment
190th (mot) Field Post Office

On 24 September 1942 the division was once again reorganized and now consisted of:

90th Light Afrika Division
259th (mot) Mapping Detachment
155th Schützen Regiment
1 (mot) Staff Company
1st and 2nd Battalions, each with
4 (mot) Companies (18 LMGs, 2 HMGs, 2 80mm mortars, 1 28mm PzBu41 and 6 50mm PAK 38 ea)
200th Schützen Regiment
1 (mot) Staff Company
1st and 2nd Battalions, each with
4 (mot) Companies (18 LMGs, 2 HMGs, 2 80mm mortars, 1 28mm PzBu41 and 6 50mm PAK 38 ea)
361st (mot) Infantry Regiment
1 (mot) Staff Company
1st and 2nd Battalions, each with
4 (mot) Companies (18 LMGs, 2 HMGs, 2 80mm mortars, 1 28mm PzBu41 and 6 75mm PAK 40 ea)
(mot) Infantry Gun Company (2 150mm sIG and 4 75mm leIG guns)
(mot) Heavy Infantry Gun Company (6 150mm sIG guns)
190th Panzer Battalion (not in Africa)
1 Panzer Staff Platoon
1 Panzer Platoon
1 Medium Panzer Company
3 Light Panzer Companies
1 Panzer Replacement Platoon
(theoretical totals 7 PzMk II, 55 PzMk III, 14 PzMk IV and 2 command tanks)
190th (mot) Artillery Regiment
1 (mot) Regimental Staff Battery
1st and 2nd (mot) Battalions, each with
1 Staff Battery
2 (mot) Batteries (4 105mm leFH 18 and 2 LMGs)
1 (mot) Battery (4 100mm K17 guns and 2 LMGs)
190th (mot) Flak Company (12 20mm Flak guns)
190th (self-propelled) Panzerjäger Battalion
2 Panzerjäger Companies (6 76.2mm (r) PAK and 6 LMGs ea)
190th (mot) Pioneer Battalion
2 (mot) Companies (9 LMGs, 3 28mm PzBu41 and 6 50mm PAK 38 ea)
190th (mot) Panzer Battalion
1 Panzer Telephone Company (6 LMGs)
1 Panzer Radio Company (28 LMGs)
1 (mot) Light Signals Supply Column (3 LMGs)
190th Feldersatz Battalion
6 Companies (6 LMGs and 1 50mm PAK 38 ea)
Administrative Units
535th (mot) Bakery Company
517th (mot) Butcher company
(mot) Ambulance Company
(mot) Military Police Detachment
190th (mot) Field Post Office

ORGANIZATIONAL HISTORY OF GERMAN MOTORIZED AND PANZERGRENADIER DIVISIONS

The 190th Panzer Battalion arrived in Africa between 8 and 22 November 1942. On 26 February 1943 the 580th Reconnaissance Battalion was assigned to the 21st Panzer Division as the 21st Panzer Reconnaissance Battalion and the 3rd Panzer Reconnaissance Battalion was assigned to the 90th Light Afrika Division as the 90th Panzer Reconnaissance Battalion. In May 1943 the division was captured in Tunisia, and it was formally disbanded on 30 June 1943. Its losses in Tunisia were:

Division Staff
190th Mapping Detachment
155th Panzergrenadier Regiment
    Staff, staff company, 2 battalions and 9th Infantry Gun Company
200th Panzergrenadier Regiment
    Staff, staff company, 2 battalions and 9th Infantry Gun Company

361st Panzergrenadier Regiment
    Staff, staff company, and 2 battalions
90th Panzer Reconnaissance Battalion
    3 companies and 1 battery
90th Panzerjäger Battalion
    3 companies (staff still in Italy)
190th Artillery Regiment
    Staff, 2 battalions (each with staff and 6 batteries; appears 2nd Battalion and staff company still in Italy)
2/22nd Artillery Regiment (3/190th)
    Staff and 3 batteries
190th Light Flak Battalion
190th Signals Battalion
    2 companies and light supply column
190th Pioneer Battalion
    Staff, 3 companies and light supply column
190th Feldersatz Battalion
    Staff and 3 (6) companies

Sardinien Division

Formed on 12 May 1943 in Sardinia from the Sturmbrigade XI, which had been formed in the XI Wehrkreise on 2 March 1943. It formed the 90th Panzergrenadier Division in the place of the 90th Light Afrika Division when that formation was destroyed in Tunis. It contained:

1st Sardinien Panzergrenadier Regiment
2nd Sardinien Panzergrenadier Regiment
Sardinien Panzer Battalion
1st–3rd Sardinien Panzerjäger Companies
Sardinien Artillery Regiment
Sardinien Signals Company

90th Panzergrenadier Division

The 90th Panzergrenadier Division was the re-formed 90th Light Afrika Division. It was formed on 6 July 1943 from units drawn from Sardinia, and had:

Divisional Headquarters
190th (mot) Mapping Detachment
Staff/90th (mot) Schützen Brigade
Divisional Escort Company
    1 Motorcycle Platoon
    1 Panzerjäger Platoon
    1 Pioneer Platoon
155th Panzergrenadier Regiment (from 1st Sardinian Grenadier Regiment)
Staff and Staff Company
1st (mot) Battalion
2nd (tmot) Battalion
1 (motZ) Infantry Gun Company
200th Panzergrenadier Regiment (from 2nd Sardinian Grenadier Regiment)
same as 155th Panzergrenadier Regiment

361st Panzergrenadier Regiment (from 853rd Sturm Regiment)
same as 155th Panzergrenadier Regiment
1 Mixed Gebirg (Mountain) Jäger Company
190th Panzer Battalion (from Sardinien Panzer Battalion)
Staff and Staff Company
2 Panzer Companies (PzMk IV Tanks)
1 Maintenance Platoon
3 Companies from Wege Command
242nd Army Sturmgeschütz Battalion
Staff and Staff Battery
3 Sturmgeschütz Batteries
1st Company, 190th Panzerjäger Battalion
190th Artillery Regiment (from Sardinian Artillery Regiment)
Staff and Staff Battery
1st (motZ) leFH Battalion
    Staff and Staff Battery
    3 (motZ) 105mm leFH Batteries

2nd (motZ) Mixed Heavy Battalion
  Staff and Staff Battery
  1 100mm K18 Battery
  2 150mm sFH Batteries
3rd Battalion
  Staff and Staff Battery
  2 Self-Propelled leFH Batteries (6 SdKfz 124 Wespe ea)
  1 Self-Propelled sFH Battery (6 SdKfz 165 6 Hummel)

2/5th Luftwaffe Flak Regiment
Staff
3 Heavy Flak Batteries (88mm guns)
2 Light Flak Batteries (20mm and 20mm quad guns)
1 (20 ton) Light Flak Column
190th Pioneer Battalion
Staff
3 (tmot) Pioneer Companies
190th Divisional Service Units

The panzergrenadier regiments were only partially motorized and the 3rd battalion was never formed. In place of the 3rd Battalion the artillery regiment formed the 247th Sturmgeschütz Battalion. The division formed the 190th Mountain Jäger Company, and the 2/361st Panzergrenadier Regiment became the 61st Panzergrenadier Battalion. The 2/5th Luftwaffe Flak Battalion was also attached.

On 20 August 1943 the organization of the armored portion of the division and its panzer inventory were as follows:

190th Panzer Battalion
  1 Panzer Staff Company
  1 Light Panzer Company
  2 Medium Panzer Companies
  PzMk III(50kz)   1
  PzMk III (75)   20
  PzMk IV (lg)   37

OKH records indicate that the division was envisioned by OKH as follows, for 21 December 1943. The 242nd Sturmgeschütz Battalion was not yet present, and the third battalions of the panzergrenadier regiments were envisioned as being raised:

90th Panzergrenadier Division
Divisional Staff
Staff
190th (mot) Mapping Detachment
Escort Company
  1 Pioneer Platoon
  1 Panzerjäger Platoon
  1 Motorcycle Platoon
361st Panzergrenadier Regiment (formerly 853rd Panzergrenadier Regiment)
1 Staff and Staff Company

1 Signals Platoon
1 Pioneer Platoon
1 Motorcycle Platoon
3 Battalions, each with
Staff
3 (mot) Grenadier Companies (2 HMGs, 18 LMGs, 3 sPzBu41, 2 150mm sIG, and 2 80mm mortars ea)
1 (mot) Machine Gun Company (12 HMGs and 6 80mm mortars)
1 (motZ) Infantry Gun Company (2 150mm sIG and 4 75mm leIG)
1 (motZ) Panzerjäger Company (6 75mm PAK 40, 6 50mm PAK 38 and 12 LMGs)
155th and 200th Panzergrenadier Regiments (formerly 1st and 2nd Sardinian)
both same as 361st Panzergrenadier Regiment
190th Panzer Battalion (formerly Sardinian Panzer Battalion)
1 Battalion Staff
2 Medium Panzer Companies (PzMk IV tanks)
1 Medium Panzer Company (PzMk IV tanks; not yet organized)
242nd Sturmgeschütz Battalion (assigned but not present)
Staff
Staff Battery (3 StuG)
3 Sturmgeschütz Batteries (10 StuG ea)
1 Panzer Maintenance Platoon
247th Sturmgeschütz Company (7 StuG)
190th Feldersatz Battalion
1 Gebirgsjäger Company with two rifle and 1 heavy platoon
190th Artillery Regiment
1 Regimental Staff and (mot) Staff Battery
1st Battalion
1 Battalion Staff and (self-propelled) Staff Battery (2 LMGs)
3 Self-Propelled Batteries (4 105mm leFH in Wespe and 2 LMGs ea)
2nd Battalion
1 Battalion Staff and (mot) Staff Battery (2 LMGs)
2 (motZ) Batteries (4 150mm sFH and 2 LMGs ea)
1 (motZ) Battery (4 100mm K18 and 2 LMGs)
3rd Battalion
1 Battalion Staff and Self-Propelled Staff Battery
2 Self-Propelled Batteries (6 105mm leFH Wespe and 2 LMGs ea)
1 Self-Propelled Battery (6 150mm sFH Hummel and 2 LMGs ea; this battery was not yet raised, but was envisioned)
2/5th Luftwaffe Flak Regiment
Staff and (mot) Staff Battery
3 (motZ) Heavy Flak Batteries (4 88mm, 3 20mm and 2 LMGs ea)

2 (motZ) Light Flak Battery (3 quad 20mm Flak guns)

1 (mot) (20 ton) Supply Column

190th Pioneer Battalion

Staff

3 (mot) Pioneer Companies (18 LMGs, 3 sPzBu41 and 6 flamethrowers ea)

1 (mot) Light Pioneer Column (2 LMGs)

190th Signals Battalion

Staff

1 (mot) Telephone Company (5 LMGs)

1 (mot) Radio Company (4 LMGs)

190th Supply Troops

1/, 2/, 3/190th (90 ton) Transportation Companies (3 LMGs ea)

190th (90 ton) Transportation Companies (4 LMGs)

190th (mot) Supply Company (6 LMGs)

Maintenance

1/, 2/190th (mot) Maintenance Companies

190th (75 ton) Maintenance Supply Column

Administration

190th (mot) Administration Bureau

190th (mot) Bakery Company

190th (mot) Butcher Company

Medical Units

1/, 2/190th (mot) Medical Companies

1/, 2/, 3/190th Ambulance Platoons

Other

190th (mot) Military Police Troop

190th (mot) Field Post Office

On 23 October the division was in Tuscany and was reorganized as a Type 43 Panzergrenadier Division. The 155th Panzergrenadier Regiment was disbanded and used to form the 3/200th and 3/361st Panzergrenadier Regiments. The 61st Panzergrenadier Battalion became the 2/361st. The 1/190th Panzerjäger Company became the 590th Panzejäger Battalion, an army troop. The 190th Panzer Reconnaissance Battalion was formed from the 190th Mountain Jäger Company, and the 190th Feldersatz Battalion was formed. The Panzergrenadier Regiments were now known as (mot) Grenadier Regiments. The division had:

1/, 2/, 3/200th (mot) Grenadier Regiment (Panzergrenadiers in 1945)

1/, 2/, 3/361st (mot) Grenadier Regiment (Panzergrenadiers in 1945)

190th Panzer Battalion

190th Panzer Reconnaissance Battalion

190th Panzerjäger Battalion (in Apr. 1945 became 90th Panzerjäger Battalion)

1/, 2/, 3/, 190th Artillery Regiment

190th Divisional Service Units

The division was taken prisoner by the Americans near Lake Garda in northern Italy.

Division (mot) Nr 155

Formed on 10 May 1942 from the Division Nr 155, it contained:

7th Panzer Ersatz Battalion

18th Panzer Ersatz Battalion

5th Schützen Ersatz Regiment (86th and 215th Battalions)

25th (mot) Infantry Ersatz Regiment (35th and 119th Battalions)

18th Cavalry Ersatz Battalion

5th Panzer Jäger Ersatz Battalion

260th (mot) Artillery Ersatz Battalion

5th Observation Ersatz Battalion

5th Panzer Pioneer Ersatz Battalion

5th Kraftfahr-Ersatz Battalion

25th Kraftfahr-Ersatz Battalion

Division (mot) Nr 155 was reorganized into the Panzer Division Nr 155 on 5 April 1943.

164th Light Afrika Division

Formed on 15 August 1942 in Africa for service with the Panzer Armee Afrika. The division was re-formed from the 164th Infantry Division.

After 22 September 1942 the division had three regiments, each with two battalions. Upon forming the division had:

1/, 2/, 3/125th Panzergrenadier Regiment

1/, 2/, 3/382nd Panzergrenadier Regiment

1/, 2/, 3/433rd Panzergrenadier Regiment

220th Artillery Regiment

220th Panzer Reconnaissance Battalion

220th Divisional Service Units

The 125th Panzergrenadier Regiment was organized using army troops, while the 382nd and 433rd Panzergrenadier Regiments were organized using forces from the Krete Fortress Division. On 26 February 1943 the division was rebuilt after heavy losses and the 125th Panzergrenadier Regiment was disbanded. The division had:

1/, 2/Afrika Panzergrenadier Regiment
1/, 2/382nd Panzergrenadier Regiment
1/, 2/433rd Panzergrenadier Regiment
1/, 2/220th (mot) Artillery Regiment
  (1st Battalion—3 btrys of 105mm leFH)
  (2nd Battalion—3 btrys of 150mm sFH)
220th (mot) Reconnaissance Battalion
220th Divisional Service Units
200th Pioneer Battalion (from 21st Panzer Division)

The 2/382nd Panzergrenadier Regiment was organized from the 1/125th Panzergrenadier Regiment. On 29 April 1943 the 220th (mot) Reconnaissance Battalion was redesignated as the 164th Panzer Reconnaissance Battalion. The division was destroyed in Tunis in May 1943 and on 30 June 1943 it was disbanded. Its losses in Tunisia were:

Division Staff
220th Mapping Detachment
125th ("Afrika") Panzergrenadier Regiment
  Staff, staff company and 2 battalions (each with 4 companies)
  13th and 14th Companies, 15th (Pioneer) Company, 16th (Signals) Company and light Flak battery
382nd Panzergrenadier Regiment
  Staff, staff company and 2 battalions (each with 4 companies), infantry gun, pioneer and PAK companies
433rd Panzergrenadier Regiment
  Staff, staff company and 2 battalions (each with 4 companies)
  13th, 14th and 15th (Pioneer) Companies
164th (220th) Reconnaissance Battalion
  Staff and 3 companies
220th Panzerjäger Battalion
220th Artillery Regiment
  2 battalions and staff batteries and total of 6 batteries
200th Panzer Pioneer Battalion
  Staff, 3 companies and light supply column
220th Panzer Signals Battalion
  Staff, 2 companies and light supply column
220th Feldersatz Battalion

179th (mot) Division

Formed on 27 April 1942 from the 179th Division. On 5 April 1943 it was reorganized into the 179th Panzer Division.

233rd (mot) Division

Formed in Frankfurt on 15 May 1942 for the training of motorized troops.

233rd Panzergrenadier Division

The 233rd (mot) Division was redesignated on 7 July 1942 and had:

5th Panzer Ersatz Battalion
83rd Panzergrenadier Ersatz Regiment (3rd, 8th, 9th and 50th Battalions)
3rd Infantry (mot) Ersatz Regiment (8th and 29th Battalions)
3rd Panzerjäger Ersatz Battalion
43rd Panzerjäger Ersatz Battalion
3rd Motorcycle Ersatz Battalion
4th Motorcycle Ersatz Battalion
9th Cavalry (later Bicycle) Ersatz Battalion
1/, 2/59th (mot) Artillery Ersatz Battalion

208th Panzer Pioneer Ersatz Battalion

On 5 April 1943 it was redesignated as the 233rd Panzer Division.

345th Infantry Division (mot)

Formed on 24 November 1942 during the call-up of the "Kriemhilde" Divisions. It contained:

1/, 2/, 3/148th (mot) Grenadier Regiment
1/, 2/, 3/152nd (mot) Grenadier Regiment
345th Panzer Battalion
345th Motorcycle Battalion
1/, 2/345th Artillery Regiment
345th Divisional Support Units

The division was to be sent to the Russian front, but ended up going to France in January 1943. On 1 March 1944 it was used to rebuild the 29th (mot) Infantry Division, which had been destroyed at Stalingrad. Its units were redesignated as follows:

Former Designation	New Designation
148th (mot) Grenadier Regiment	15th (mot) Grenadier Regiment
152nd (mot) Grenadier Regiment	71st (mot) Grenadier Regiment
345th Panzer Battalion	129th Panzer Battalion
345th Motorcycle Battalion	129th Panzer Reconnaissance Battalion
345th Artillery Regiment	1/29th Artillery Regiment
	313th Army Flak Battalion (new)
345th Divisional Support Units	29th Divisional Support Units

386th Infantry Division (mot)

Formed on 25 November 1942 during the call-up of the "Kriemhilde" Divisions. It contained:

1/, 2/, 3/149th (mot) Grenadier Regiment
1/, 2/, 3/153rd Panzergrenadier Regiment
386th Panzer Battalion
386th Motorcycle Battalion

1/, 2/386th Artillery Regiment
386th Divisional Support Units

In January 1943 the division was stationed in the West and on 1 March 1943 it was used to re-form the 3rd (mot) Infantry Division, which had been destroyed at Stalingrad. Its units were redesignated as follows:

Former Designation	New Designation
149th (mot) Grenadier Regiment	8th (mot) Grenadier Regiment
153rd Panzergrenadier Regiment	29th (mot) Grenadier Regiment
386th Panzer Battalion	103rd Panzer Battalion
386th Motorcycle Battalion	53rd Panzer Reconnaissance Battalion
386th Artillery Regiment	2/3rd Artillery Regiment
	312th Army Flak Battalion (new)
386th Divisional Support Units	3rd Divisional Support Units

900th (mot) Lehr Brigade

Formed on 17 June 1941, it contained:

1/, 2/900th (mot) Infantry Regiment
900th Panzerjäger Battalion (3 companies)
900th Artillery Battalion (4 batteries)
900th Pioneer Battalion (3 companies)
900th Signals Battalion
900th Administrative Services

On 7 April 1942 the brigade was ordered disbanded. The staff went to the Döberitz Infantry School and the remaining troops were sent on 28 May 1942 to various schools.

Brandenburg Panzergrenadier Division

Formed on 15 September 1944 from the Brandenburg Division, it had:

1/, 2/, 3/1st Brandenburg (mot) Jäger Regiment
1/, 2/, 3/2nd Brandenburg (mot) Jäger Regiment
1/, 2/, 3/, 4/Brandenburg Artillery Regiment
Brandenburg Divisional Support Units

A panzer battalion and a reconnaissance battalion were formed later. On 13 December 1944 the division contained:

Brandenburg Panzergrenadier Division

Brandenburg Panzergrenadier Division Staff (2 LMGs)
Brandenburg Panzergrenadier Division Staff Escort Company
  1 Machine Gun Platoon (4 HMGs, 6 LMGs)
  1 Motorcycle Platoon (6 LMGs)
  1 Self-Propelled Flak Platoon (4 20mm guns)
  1 Mortar Platoon (2 80mm mortars)
Brandenburg (mot) Mapping Detachment
Brandenburg (mot) Military Police Detachment (5 LMGs)

Brandenburg Panzer Regiment

Brandenburg Panzer Regimental Staff
Brandenburg Panzer Regimental Staff Company
  1 Signals Platoon
  1 Pioneer Platoon
  1 Self-Propelled Flak Platoon (3 37mm Flak guns)
1 Armored Maintenance Company

1st Battalion

1 Panzer Battalion Staff (1 LMG)
1 Panzer Battalion Staff Company (12 LMGs)
4 Panzer Companies (17 PzMk V Panther tanks ea)
1 (self-propelled) Armored Flak Company (3 quad 20mm Flak guns)
1 (mot) Supply Company (5 LMGs)

2nd Battalion

1 Panzer Battalion Staff (1 LMG)
1 Panzer Battalion Staff Company (8 LMGs)
4 Panzer Companies (17 PzMk IV tanks ea)
1 (self-propelled) Armored Flak Company (3 quad 20mm Flak guns)
1 (mot) Supply Company (5 LMGs)

1st Jäger Regiment Brandenburg

Regimental Staff
Regimental Staff Company
  1 Staff Platoon (2 LMGs)
  1 Signals Platoon (7 LMGs)
  1 Motorcycle Platoon (6 LMGs)

1st (half-track) Panzergrenadier Battalion

1 Panzergrenadier Battalion Staff (6 LMGs)

1 (mot) Panzergrenadier Battalion Supply Company (5 LMGs)
3 (half-track) Panzergrenadier Companies (4 HMGs, 30 LMGs, 20mm and 2 75mm guns ea)
1 (half-track) Heavy Panzergrenadier Company
  1 Staff Platoon (2 LMGs)
  1 Mortar Platoon (2 LMGs and 4 120mm mortars)
  1 leIG Platoon (4 LMGs and 6 75mm leIG)

2nd (mot) Jäger Battalion

1 Battalion Staff
1 Battalion Supply Company (4 LMGs)
3 (mot) Companies (12 LMGs ea)
1 (mot) Heavy Company (12 HMGs and 6 20mm Flak)
1 (mot) Heavy Company (4 120mm and 8 80mm mortars)

9th Self-Propelled sIG Company (8 150mm sIG guns and 6 LMGs)

10th (Pioneer) Company (motZ)

1 Half-Track Staff (1 LMG)
1 Half-Track Platoon (6 flamethrowers and 6 LMGs)
1 Half-Track Platoon (6 flamethrowers, 1 20mm and 12 LMGs)
1 Half-Track Platoon (12 flamethrowers and 8 LMGs)
1 Half-Track Platoon (2 80mm mortars and 2 HMGs)

2nd Jäger Regiment Brandenburg

Regimental Staff
Regimental Staff Company (4 LMGs)
  1 Staff Platoon
  1 Signals Platoon
  1 Motorcycle Platoon

1st and 2nd (mot) Jäger Battalions, each with

1 Battalion Staff
1 Battalion Supply Company (4 LMGs)
3 (mot) Companies (12 LMGs ea)
1 (mot) Heavy Company (12 HMGs and 6 20mm Flak)
1 (mot) Heavy Company (4 120mm and 8 80mm mortars)

9th Self-Propelled sIG Company (8 150mm sIG guns and 6 LMGs)

10th (Pioneer) Company (motZ) (18 flamethrowers, 2 HMGs, 12 LMGs, and 2 80mm mortars)

Brandenburg Panzerjäger Battalion

1 Panzerjäger Battalion Staff
1 Panzerjäger Battalion Staff Battery (1 LMG)
1 Sturmgeschütz Staff Platoon (3 StuG)
2 Sturmgeschütz Companies (14 StuG ea)

1 (motZ) Panzerjäger Company (12 88mm PAK and 12 LMGs)

1 (mot) Panzerjäger Supply Company (3 LMGs)

Brandenburg Reconnaissance Battalion

1 Reconnaissance Battalion Staff

   1 Armored Car Platoon (3 75mm, 13 20mm, 16 LMG)

   1 (mot) Signals Platoon (7 LMGs)

1st Armored Car (half-track) Company (16 20mm and 25 LMGs)

2nd Half-Track Reconnaissance Company (2 75mm, 2 80mm mortars and 44 LMGs)

3rd Half-Track Reconnaissance Company (2 75mm and 7 20mm, 2 80mm mortars, 4 HMGs and 29 LMGs)

4th Half-Track Reconnaissance Company

   1 Staff Platoon (1 LMG)

   1 Platoon (6 75mm and 2 LMGs)

   1 Mortar Platoon (6 80mm and 2 LMGs)

   1 Pioneer Platoon (13 LMGs)

1 (mot) Reconnaissance Supply Company (3 LMGs)

Brandenburg Artillery Regiment

1 Artillery Regimental Staff

1 (mot) Artillery Regimental Staff Company (2 LMGs)

1st Battalion

   1 (Self-Propelled) Artillery Battalion Staff

   1 (Self-Propelled) Artillery Battalion Staff Battery (2 LMGs)

   1 (Self-Propelled) Flak Platoon (3 20mm)

   2 (Self-Propelled) Light Howitzer Batteries (6 105mm howitzers in Wespe and 4 LMGs ea)

   1 (Self-Propelled) Heavy Howitzer Battery (6 150mm howitzers in Hummel and 4 LMGs)

2nd Battalion

   1 (motZ) Artillery Battalion Staff

   1 (motZ) Artillery Battalion Staff Company (2 LMGs)

   1 Flak Platoon (motZ) (3 20mm)

   2 Light Howitzer Batteries (motZ) (6 105mm leFH and 4 LMGs ea)

3rd Battalion

   1 (motZ) Artillery Battalion Staff

   1 (motZ) Artillery Battalion Staff Company (2 LMGs)

   1 Flak Platoon (motZ) (3 20mm)

   3 Heavy Howitzer Batteries (6 150mm sFH and 4 LMGs ea)

Brandenburg Army Flak Battalion

1 (motZ) Flak Battalion Staff

1 (mot) Flak Battalion Staff Battery (2 LMGs)

2 (motZ) Flak Batteries (6 88mm, 3 20mm and 2 LMGs ea)

1 (motZ) Light Flak Battery

   1 (motZ) Section (9 37mm Flak guns and 4 LMGs)

1 Self-Propelled Section (3 quad 20mm Flak guns)

1 (motZ) Searchlight Section (4 searchlights)

Brandenburg Pioneer Battalion

1 (motZ) Pioneer Battalion Staff

1 (half-track) Pioneer Battalion Staff Company (12 LMGs)

2 Pioneer Companies (motZ) (2 HMGs, 18 LMGs, 2 80mm mortars)

1 (half-track) Pioneer Company (2 HMGs, 43 LMGs, 6 flamethrowers and 2 80mm mortars)

Brandenburg Signals Battalion

1 Armored Signals Battalion Staff

1 Armored Telephone Company (11 LMGs)

1 Armored Radio Company (19 LMGs)

1 (mot) Signals Supply Column (2 LMGs)

Brandenburg Supply Troop

1 (mot) Medical Company (2 LMGs)

1 (mot) Medical Supply Company (2 LMGs)

1 (mot) Field Post Office

During their formation, on 20 December 1944, the Grossdeutschland Division and the Brandenburg Division were merged to form the Grossdeutschland Panzer Corps. The 3/1st Brandenburg Infantry Regiment became the 3/Corps Fusilier Regiment Grossdeutschland. The 3/2nd Brandenburg Infantry Regiment was disbanded. The 3/Brandenburg Panzer Artillery Regiment became the 2/Corps 500th Panzer Artillery Regiment, the 4th Battalion became the 3rd Battalion and the Brandenburg Panzer Regiment formed a second battalion using the Grossdeutschland Sturmgeschütz Battalion. The two Jäger Regiments were redesignated Panzer Jäger Regiments. The division had:

2/Brandenburg Panzer Regiment
1/, 2/1st Brandenburg Panzer Jäger Regiment
1/, 2/2nd Brandenburg Panzer Jäger Regiment
Brandenburg Panzer Reconnaissance Battalion (forming)
1/, 2/, 3/Brandenburg Panzer Artillery Regiment
Brandenburg Divisional Support Units

The division was heavily engaged and suffered heavy casualties after the Russians broke through the Vistula line. It was rebuilt on 10 March 1945 from the Grossdeutschland Ersatz Brigade and was taken prisoner by the Russians near Deutsch-Brod.

1030th (Feldherrnhalle) Panzergrenadier Brigade, Reinforced

It is not known when this brigade was organized or disbanded. It appears in OKH records on 3 December 1943 as having the following organization and equipment:

1030th (Feldherrnhalle) Panzergrenadier Regiment
1 Brigade Staff
1 Staff Company
  1 Signals Platoon
  1 Infantry Gun Platoon
  1 Motorcycle Platoon
2 (mot) Panzergrenadier Battalions, each with
  3 Panzergrenadier Companies (4 HMGs, 18 LMGs and 2 80mm mortars ea)
  1 Heavy Panzergrenadier Company (3 LMGs, 3 75mm PAK 40 and 6 80mm mortars)
  1 (motZ) Infantry Gun Company (2 150mm sIG, 6 75mm leIG and 3 LMGs)

1030th (Feldherrnhalle) Panzerjäger Battalion
1030th (Feldherrnhalle) Flak Company (mixed 20mm and 88mm guns and 4 LMG)
1030th (Feldherrnhalle) Panzerjäger Company (12 75mm PAK 40 and 12 LMGs)
1030th (Feldherrnhalle) Artillery Battalion
1 (mot) Staff Battery
1 (motZ) Light Battery (4 105mm leFH)
1 (motZ) Heavy Battery (4 150mm sFH)
1030th (Feldherrnhalle) (mot) Pioneer Company (18 LMGs, 2 80mm mortars and 6 flamethrowers)
1030th (Feldherrnhalle) (mot) Signals Company (1 LMG)
1030th (Feldherrnhalle) (mot) (90 ton) Transportation Company (6 LMGs)

Feldherrnhalle Panzergrenadier Division

Formed on 20 June 1943 from the 60th Panzergrenadier Division. It contained:

1/, 2/, 3/Feldherrnhalle Panzergrenadier Regiment (from 271st Grenadier Regiment)
1/, 2/, 3/Feldherrnhalle Fusilier Regiment (from 120th (mot) Grenadier Regiment)
Feldherrnhalle Panzer Battalion (from 160th Panzer Battalion)
Feldherrnhalle Panzer Reconnaissance Battalion (from 160th Panzer Reconnaissance Battalion)
1/, 2/, 3/Feldherrnhalle (mot) Artillery Regiment (from 160th Artillery Regiment)
Feldherrnhalle Divisional Support Units (from 160th Divisional Support Units)

Originally the armored battalion was to be equipped with four companies of medium tanks, 22 tanks per company. However, OKH records show it being reorganized into a three-battery assault gun battalion (14 StuG per battery) sometime in July.

On 17 July 1943 the 282nd Army Flak Battalion became the Feldherrnhalle Flak Battalion. In December the panzer battalion was expanded into a full regiment, with the existing battalion becoming the second battalion. In February 1944 the Staff/, 2/Feldherrnhalle Panzer Regiment became the Staff/, 2/69th Panzer Regiment. In June the staff formed the 16th Panzer Regiment of the 116th Panzer Division, while the 2nd Battalion joined later and became the 2/Feldherrnhalle Panzer Regiment. On 1 October 1943 OKH records show that the division was organized and equipped as follows:

Divisional Staff
Staff
FHH (mot) Mapping Detachment
FHH Fusilier Regiment
Staff
Regimental Band
Staff Company
  Signals Platoon
  Pioneer Platoon (6 flamethrowers and 3 LMGs)
3 Battalions, each with
Staff
4 (mot) Fusilier Companies (4 HMGs, 18 LMGs, 3 PzBu39 and 2 80mm mortars ea)
1 Self-Propelled Heavy Infantry Gun Company (6 150mm sIG)
1 (motZ) Panzerjäger Company (3 75mm PAK 40, 6 50mm PAK 38 and 9 LMGs)
FHH Grenadier Regiment
same as fusilier regiment
FHH Panzer Reconnaissance Battalion
Staff (15 LMGs)
Heavy Platoon (6 SdKfz 234/3 with 75mm KwK and 6 LMGs)
1 Light Armored Car Company (18 20mm and 24 LMGs)
1 (half-track) Reconnaissance Company (16 20mm and 25 LMGs)
2 (half-track) Heavy Reconnaissance Companies (2 80mm mortars, 4 HMGs, 56 LMGs and 3 75mm leIG ea)
1 (half-track) Heavy Company
  1 Pioneer Platoon (3 LMGs, 1 20mm and 6 flamethrowers)

1 Panzerjäger Platoon (3 LMGs and 3 75mm PAK 40)

1 Light Infantry Gun Section (4 LMGsand 2 75mm leIG)

2 Platoons (4 LMGs and 3 SdKfz 251/9 with 75mm KwK ea)

1 Light Panzer Reconnaissance Battalion Column

FHH Panzer Battalion

Staff

Staff Battery (3 StuG)

3 Sturmgeschütz Batteries (14 StuG ea)

1 Panzer Maintenance Platoon

FHH Artillery Regiment

1 Regimental Staff and (mot) Staff Battery (2 LMGs)

1st Battalion

1 Battalion Staff and (self-propelled) Staff Battery (2 LMGs)

3 Self-Propelled Batteries (4 105mm leFH in Wespe and 2 LMGs ea)

2nd Battalion

1 Battalion Staff and (mot) Staff Battery (2 LMGs)

3 (motZ) Batteries (4 105mm leFh and 2 LMGs ea)

3rd Battalion

1 Battalion Staff and (mot) Staff Battery (2 LMGs)

2 (motZ) Batteries (4 150mm sFH and 2 LMGs ea)

1 (motZ) Battery (4 100mm K18 and 2 LMGs)

FHH Flak Battalion

Staff and (mot) Staff Battery (1 LMG)

2 (motZ) Heavy Flak Batteries (4 80mm, 3 20mm and 2 LMGs ea)

1 (motZ) Light Flak Battery (12 20mm and 2 LMGs)

1 (mot) (20 ton) Supply Column

FHH Pioneer Battalion

Staff

3 (mot) Pioneer Companies (2 HMGs, 18 LMGs, 3 PzBu39, 2 80mm mortars and 6 flamethrowers ea)

1 (mot) Brüko K Bridging Column (3 LMGs)

1 (mot) Light Pioneer Column (2 LMGs)

FHH Signals Battalion

Staff

1 (mot) Telephone Company (6 LMGs)

1 (mot) Radio Company (4 LMGs)

1 (mot) Signals Column (1 LMG)

FHH Supply Troops

1/, 2/FHH (120 ton) Transportation Companies (4 LMGs ea)

3/, 4/, 5/FHH (90 ton) Transportation Companies (3 LMGs ea)

FHH (mot) Supply Company (6 LMGs)

Maintenance

1/, 2/FHH (mot) Maintenance Companies

FHH (75 ton) Maintenance Supply Column

Administration

FHH (mot) Administration Bureau

FHH (mot) Bakery Company

FHH (mot) Butcher Company

Medical Units

1/, 2/FHH (mot) Medical Companies

1/, 2/, 3/FHH Ambulance Platoons

Other

FHH (mot) Military Police Troop

FHH (mot) Field Post Office

An OKH order dated 6 November 1943 directed the reorganization of the division's panzer battalion. It was to have a staff, a staff company, two panzer companies equipped with PzMk IV tanks, two sturmgeschütz companies, and a workshop company, which lacked the 2nd Platoon. In December 1943 the organization of the armored portion of the division and its panzer inventory were as follows:

FHH Panzer Regiment

1 Regimental Staff Company

2 Medium Panzer Companies

2 Sturmgeschütz Companies

PzMk IV (lg)	17
StuG	42
PzBefWg	3

In June 1944 the Panzerjäger company was expanded into a full battalion. In July 1944 the division was destroyed near Minsk. On 20 August 1944 Hitler ordered the division rebuilt. It was reorganized as follows:

Divisional Staff

Staff (2 LMGs)

(mot) Mapping Detachment

(mot) Feld Gendarmerie Troop (2 LMGs)

1 (mot) Grenadier Regiment

1 (mot) Regimental Staff

1 (mot) Regimental Staff Company

1 (mot) Signals Platoon

1 Motorcycle Messenger Platoon (4 LMGs)

1st Battalion (former Kampfgruppe FH Fusilier Regiment)

1 (mot) Battalion Staff

1 (mot) Supply Company (4 LMGs)

3 (mot) Panzergrenadier Companies (4 HMGs, 18 LMGs and 2 80mm mortars ea)

1 (mot) Heavy Company (6 20mm, 2 LMGs, 4 120mm mortars)

2nd Battalion

same as 1st Battalion

1 (motZ) Panzerjäger Company (4 heavy PAK)

1 (mot) Pioneer Company (18 flamethrowers, 2 80mm mortars, 2 HMGS, and 12 LMGs)

Panzerjäger Battalion

Armored Staff

1 Sturmgeschütz Platoon

1 (mot) Staff Battery (1 LMG)

2 Sturmgeschütz Batteries (14 StuG ea)

1 (motZ) Panzerjäger Company (12 heavy PAK and 12 LMGs)

1 (mot) Panzerjäger Supply Company (3 LMGs)

Panzer Reconnaissance Battalion

1 (half-track) Reconnaissance Company (3 75mm, 2 80mm mortars and 49 LMGs)

1 Armored Car Platoon (6 armored cars with 1 20mm and 1 LMG ea)

Panzer Artillery Regiment

1 (mot) Staff

1 (mot) Staff Battery (2 LMGs)

1st Battalion

1 Self-Propelled Staff Battery (2 LMGs)

2 Self-Propelled Batteries (6 105mm leFH Wespe and 4 LMGs)

1 Self-Propelled Battery (6 150mm sFH Hummel and 4 LMGs)

2nd Battalion

1 Self-Propelled Staff Battery (2 LMGs)

2 Self-Propelled Batteries (6 150mm sFH Hummel and 4 LMGs ea)

1 Self-Propelled Battery (4 150mm sFH Hummel and 4 LMGs)

Army Flak Battalion

1 (mot) Staff Battery (2 LMGs)

2 (motZ) Flak Batteries (6 88mm, 3 20mm and 2 LMGs ea)

1 (motZ) Flak Battery (9 37mm and 4 LMGs, plus 3 quad 20mm self-propelled guns)

1 Sound Ranging Flak Battery (4 sound ranging sets)

Pioneer Battalion

1 Staff (3 LMGs)

1 Staff Company (1 LMG)

3 (mot) Pioneer Companies (18 LMGs, 6 flamethrowers and 2 80mm mortars ea)

1 (mot) Bridging Train (3 LMGs)

Signals Battalion

1 (mot) Telephone Company (5 LMGs)

1 (mot) Radio Company (6 LMGs)

1 (mot) Supply Platoon (2 LMGs)

Supply Troops

3 (mot) (120 ton) Transportation Companies (8 LMGs ea)

1st and 2nd (mot) Maintenance Companies (4 LMGs ea)

Administrative Troops

1 (mot) Bakery Company (4 LMGs)

1 (mot) Butcher Company (2 LMGs)

1 (mot) Administrative Company (2 LMGs)

Medical

1st and 2nd (mot) Medical Companies (4 LMGs ea)

1 (mot) Medical Supply Company (4 LMGs)

Other

1 (mot) Field Post Office (1 LMG)

It was re-formed on 1 September 1944. On 27 November 1944 the division was joined with the 13th Panzer Division to become the Panzerkorps Feldherrnhalle. The division itself became the Feldherrnhalle Panzer Division and had:

1/, 2/Feldherrnhalle Panzer Regiment

1/, 2/, 3/Feldherrnhalle Panzergrenadier Regiment

Feldherrnhalle Panzer Reconnaissance Battalion

Feldherrnhalle Panzerjäger Battalion

1/, 2, 3/Feldherrnhalle Panzer Artillery Regiment

Feldherrnhalle Divisional Support Units

On 27 November 1944 the division contained:

Feldherrnhalle Panzer Division

Feldherrnhalle Panzer Division Staff (2 LMGs)

Feldherrnhalle Panzer Division Staff Escort Company

1 Machine Gun Platoon (4 HMGs and 6 LMGs)

1 Motorcycle Platoon (6 LMGs)

1 Self-Propelled Flak Platoon (4 20mm guns)

1 Mortar Platoon (2 80mm mortars)

Feldherrnhalle (mot) Mapping Detachment

Feldherrnhalle (mot) Military Police Detachment (5 LMGs)

Feldherrnhalle Panzer Regiment

Feldherrnhalle Panzer Regimental Staff

Feldherrnhalle Panzer Regimental Staff Company

1 Signals Platoon

1 Pioneer Platoon

1 Self-Propelled Flak Platoon (3 37mm Flak guns)

1 Armored Maintenance Company

1st Battalion

1 Panzer Battalion Staff (1 LMG)

1 Panzer Battalion Staff Company (12 LMGs)

4 Panzer Companies (17 PzMk V Panther tanks ea)

1 (self-propelled) Armored Flak Company (3 quad 20mm Flak guns)

1 (mot) Supply Company (5 LMGs)

2nd Battalion

1 Panzer Battalion Staff (1 LMG)

1 Panzer Battalion Staff Company (8 LMGs)

4 Panzer Companies (17 PzMk IV tanks ea)

1 (self-propelled) Armored Flak Company (3 quad 20mm Flak guns)

1 (mot) Supply Company (5 LMGs)

Feldherrnhalle Panzergrenadier Regiment

Feldherrnhalle Panzergrenadier Regimental Staff

Feldherrnhalle Panzergrenadier Regimental Staff Company

1 Staff Platoon (1 LMG)

1 Signals Platoon (7 LMGs)

1 Motorcycle Platoon (6 LMGs)

1st (half-track) Panzergrenadier Battalion

1 Panzergrenadier Battalion Staff (6 LMGs)

1 (mot) Panzergrenadier Battalion Supply Company (5 LMGs)

3 (half-track) Panzergrenadier Companies (4 HMGs, 29 LMGs, 5 20mm and 2 75mm guns ea)

1 (half-track) Heavy Panzergrenadier Company
   1 Mortar Platoon (2 LMGs and 4 120mm mortars)
   1 leIG Platoon (4 LMGs and 6 75mm leIG)

2nd and 3rd Panzergrenadier Battalions, each with

1 Battalion Staff

1 Battalion Supply Company (4 LMGs)

3 (mot) Panzergrenadier Companies (4 HMGs and 18 LMGs ea)

1 (mot) Heavy Panzergrenadier Company
   1 Mortar Platoon (2 LMGs and 4 120mm mortars)
   1 Flak Platoon (6 20mm Flak guns)

16th (motZ) Infantry Gun Company (150mm sIG guns and 2 LMGs)

17th (Pioneer) Company (motZ)

1 Half-Track Staff (1 LMG)

1 Half-Track Platoon (6 flamethrowers, 1 20mm and 12 LMGs)

1 Half-Track Platoon (12 flamethrowers and 6 LMGs)

1 Half-Track Platoon (2 80mm mortars and 2 HMGs)

1 Half-Track Platoon (6 flamethrowers and 6 LMGs)

Feldherrnhalle Panzerjäger Battalion

1 Panzerjäger Battalion Staff

1 Panzerjäger Battalion Staff Battery (1 LMG)

1 Sturmgeschütz Staff Platoon (3 StuG)

2 Sturmgeschütz Companies (14 StuG ea)

1 Panzerjäger Company (motZ) (12 75mm PAK 40 and 12 LMGs)

1 (mot) Panzerjäger Supply Company (3 LMGs)

Feldherrnhalle Reconnaissance Battalion

1 Reconnaissance Battalion Staff (3 75mm, 13 20mm and 16 LMG)

1 (mot) Signals Platoon

1st Armored Car (half-track) Company (16 20mm and 25 LMGs)

2nd Half-Track Reconnaissance Company (2 75mm, 2 80mm mortars and 44 LMGs)

3rd Half-Track Reconnaissance Company (2 75mm and 7 20mm, 2 80mm mortars, 4 HMGs and 29 LMGs)

4th Half-Track Reconnaissance Company
   1 Staff Platoon (1 LMG)
   1 Platoon (6 75mm and 2 LMGs)
   1 Mortar Platoon (6 80mm and 2 LMGs)
   1 Pioneer Platoon (13 LMGs)

1 (mot) Reconnaissance Supply Company (3 LMGs)

Feldherrnhalle Artillery Regiment

1 Artillery Regimental Staff

1 (mot) Artillery Regimental Staff Company (2 LMGs)

1st Battalion

1 (self-propelled) Artillery Battalion Staff

1 (self-propelled) Staff Battery (2 LMGs)

1 (self-propelled) Flak Platoon (3 20mm)

2 (self-propelled) Light Howitzer Batteries (6 105mm howitzers in Wespe and 4 LMGs ea)

1 (Self-Propelled) Heavy Howitzer Battery (6 150mm howitzers in Hummel and 4 LMGs)

2nd Battalion

1 (motZ) Artillery Battalion Staff

1 (motZ) Artillery Battalion Staff Company (2 LMGs)

1 Flak Platoon (motZ) (3 20mm)

2 (motZ) Light Howitzer Batteries (6 105mm leFH and 4 LMGs ea)

3rd Battalion

1 (motZ) Artillery Battalion Staff

1 (motZ) Artillery Battalion Staff Company (2 LMGs)

1 Flak Platoon (motZ) (3 20mm)

3 Heavy Howitzer Batteries (6 150mm sFH and 4 LMGs ea)

Feldherrnhalle Flak Battalion

1 (motZ) Flak Battalion Staff

1 (mot) Flak Battalion Staff Battery (2 LMGs)

2 (motZ) Flak Batteries (6 88mm, 3 20mm and 2 LMGs ea)

1 (motZ) Light Flak Battery
   1 (motZ) Section (9 37mm Flak guns and 4 LMGs)
   1 Self-Propelled Section (3 quad 20mm Flak guns)
   1 (motZ) Searchlight Section (4 searchlights)

Feldherrnhalle Pioneer Battalion

1 (motZ) Pioneer Battalion Staff

1 (half-track) Pioneer Battalion Staff Company (12 LMGs)

2 (mot) Pioneer Companies (2 HMGs, 18 LMGs and 2 80mm mortars ea)

1 (half-track) Pioneer Company (2 HMGs, 43 LMGs, 6 flamethrowers and 2 80mm mortars)

Feldherrnhalle Signals Battalion

1 Armored Signals Battalion Staff

1 Armored Telephone Company (11 LMGs)

1 Armored Radio Company (19 LMGs)

1 (mot) Signals Supply Column (2 LMGs)

Feldherrnhalle Supply Troop

1 (mot) Medical Company (2 LMGs)

1 (mot) Medical Supply Company (2 LMGs)

1 (mot) Field Post Office

The 13th Panzer Division was later redesignated the 2nd Feldherrnhalle Panzer Division, so this division was renamed the 1st Feldherrnhalle Panzer Division. The division was again destroyed and in February 1945 it was reformed. It passed into Russian captivity.

Ersatz Brigade Feldherrnhalle

Formed on 1 September 1944, it contained:

PanzerTruppen Ersatz und Ausbildungs Battalion Feldherrnhalle Elbing

1/, 3/Ersatz und Ausbildungs Regiment (mot) Feldherrnhalle Danzig

Artillery Ersatz und Ausbildungs Battalion (mot) Feldherrnhalle Elbing

The brigade fought and was destroyed in West Prussia. It was re-formed in Parchim, and re-formed again in Magdeburg. On 6 April 1945 the Panzergrenadier Ersatz und Ausbildungs Regiment Feldherrnhalle was absorbed into the Clausewitz Division.

Grossdeutschland (mot) Infantry Division

The division started as a motorized infantry regiment and fought as such through the French campaign.

On 10 May 1940 the Grossdeutschland Regiment contained:

Regimental Headquarters
(mot) Signal Platoon
  Platoon Headquarters
  4 Light Telephone Sections
  4 Light Radio Sections
  6 Pack Radio Sections
  1 Motorcycle Messenger Platoon
  Platoon Headquarters
  5 Sections
1st, 2nd, and 3rd (mot) Infantry Battalions, each with
  Battalion Headquarters
    2 Light Telephone Sections
    4 Pack Radio Sections
    2 Pack Radio Sections
  3 (mot) Infantry Companies
    Company Headquarters
      Headquarters Section
    3 Infantry Platoons
      Headquarters Section
      4 Infantry Squads
      1 Mortar Section (1 50mm mortar)
  1 (mot) Machine Gun Company
    Company Headquarters
    3 Machine Gun Platoons
      Headquarters Sections
      2 Machine Gun Sections (2 HMGs ea)
    1 Mortar Platoon
      Headquarters Sections
      3 Mortar Sections (2 80mm mortars ea)
4th (mot) Battalion
  Battalion Headquarters
    2 Light Telephone Sections
    4 Pack Radio Sections
    2 Pack Radio Sections

(mot) Light Infantry Gun Company
  Company Headquarters
    Headquarters Section
    Light Telephone Section
  3 Light Infantry Gun Platoons
    Headquarters Section
    Light Telephone Section
    Ammunition Section
    Gun Section (2 75mm leIG)
(mot) Panzerjäger Company
  Company Headquarters
  4 Panzerjäger Platoons
    Headquarters Section
    Machine Gun Section (1 LMG)
    Ammunition Section
    Gun Section (3 37mm PAK 36)
(mot) Heavy Infantry Gun Company
  Company Headquarters
    Headquarters Section
    2 Light Telephone Sections
    2 Pack Radio Sections
  2 Heavy Infantry Gun Platoons, each with
    Headquarters Section
    Light Telephone Section
    Ammunition Section
    Gun Section (2 150mm sIG)
Assault Gun Battery
  Battery Headquarters
  3 Assault Gun Platoons
    Headquarters Section
    Ammunition Section
    Gun Section (2 Sturmgeschütz SdKfz 142)

On 5 April 1941, during the invasion of Greece, the regiment was organized and equipped as follows:

Grossdetuschland (mot) Infantry Regiment
  Regimental Staff Company
    1 Motorcycle Platoon
    1 Regimental Band

1st–3rd (mot) Infantry Battalions, each with
- 3 (mot) Infantry Companies (12 LMGs, 2 HMGs, and 3 50mm mortars ea)
- **1 (mot) Machine Gun Company** (12 HMGs and 6 80mm mortars)
- **1 (mot) Support Company,** with
  - 1 Pioneer Platoon (3 LMGs)
  - 1 Panzerjäger Platoon (3 37mm PAK 36 and 2 LMGs)
  - 1 Panzerjäger Platoon (3 50mm PAK 38 and 2 LMGs)
  - 1 Flak Platoon (4 20mm guns)

4th Battalion
- 13th (mot) Infantry Support Company (4 75mm leIG)
- 14th (mot) Panzerjäger Company (9 50mm PAK 38 and 4 LMGs)
- 15th (mot) Heavy Infantry Gun Company (4 150mm sIG)
- 16th Assault Gun Battery (6 75mm StuG)

5th Battalion
- 1 (mot) Signals Platoon
- 1 Self-Propelled Flak Battery (9 37mm guns)
- 1 Light Armored Car Company (4 37mm and 7 LMGs)
- 1 Motorcycle Company (3 50mm mortars, 2 HMGs and 9 LMGs)
- 1 (mot) Engineer Company (9 LMGs)

400th Artillery Battalion
- 1 (mot) Signals Platoon
- 1 (mot) Calibration Detachment
- 1 (mot) Weather Detachment
- 1 (mot) Battery (4 150mm sFH 18 and 2 LMGs)
- 2 (mot) Batteries (4 105mm leFH 18 and 2 LMGs ea)

40th Supply Train
- 1, /2/, 3/400th Light (mot) Supply Columns (30 ton)
- 4/400th Heavy (mot) Fuel Supply Column
- 400th (mot) Maintenance Company
- 400th (mot) Supply Platoon

It was planned to expand Grossdeutschland into a division on 14 December 1941. These plans would have organized the division as follows (it is not clear, however, whether the brigade was ever formed):

Brigade Staff
- 1 Brigade Staff
- 1 Mapping Detachment

1st–4th Battalions, each with
- 3 Companies (18 LMGs, 2 HMGs and 3 50mm mortars ea)
- 1 Machine Gun Company (12 HMGs and 6 80mm mortars)
- 1 (mot) Support Company
  - 1 Pioneer Platoon (3 LMGs)

- 1 Panzerjäger Platoon (4 50mm PAK 38 and 1 LMG)
- 1 Infantry Gun Section (2 75mm leIG)

5th Battalion
- 1 Self-Propelled Flak Company (8 20mm and 2 quad 20mm guns)
- 1 (mot) Infantry Gun Section (2 150mm sIG)
- 1 (mot) Infantry Gun Section (6 75mm leIG)
- 1 Self-Propelled Panzerjäger Company (9 75mm PAK 40 and 4 LMGs)

6th Battalion
- 1 (mot) Signals Platoon
- 3 Sturmgeschütz Batteries (7 StuG ea)

Grossdeutschland Panzer Battalion
- 1 Panzer Battalion Staff
- 3 Medium Panzer Companies
- 1 Panzer Maintenance Company

Grossdeutschland Reconnaissance Battalion
- 1 Armored Car Company
- 3 Motorcycle Companies (3 PzBu39, 18 LMGs, 2 HMGs and 2 80mm mortars ea)
- 1 (mot) Reconnaissance Support Company
  - 1 Pioneer Platoon (3 LMGs)
  - 1 Panzerjäger Platoon (3 75mm PAK 40 and 4 LMGs)
  - 1 Panzerjäger Platoon (3 sPzBu41)
  - 1 Infantry Gun Platoon (2 75mm leIG)

Grossdeutschland Artillery Regiment
- 1 (mot) Regimental Staff Battery
- 1 Regimental Band
- 1 (mot) Nebelwerfer Battery (6 launchers)
- 1st and 2nd Batteries, each with
  - 1 Battalion Staff Battery
  - 3 (motZ) Batteries (4 105mm leFH and 2 LMGs ea)
- 3rd Battery
  - 1 Battalion Staff Battery
  - 2 (motZ) Batteries (4 150mm sFH and 2 LMGs ea)
  - 1 (motZ) Battery (4 100mm K 18 guns and 2 LMGs)
- 4th Battery
  - 1 Signals Platoon
  - 3 (motZ) Heavy Flak Batteries (4 88mm and 3 20mm guns ea)
  - 1 Self-Propelled Light Flak Battery (12 20mm guns)
  - 1 Self-Propelled Medium Flak Battery (9 37mm guns)

Grossdeutschland (mot) Panzerjäger Battalion
- 1 (mot) Signals Platoon
- 3 (motZ) Panzerjäger Batteries (9 75mm Pak 40 and 6 LMGs ea)

Grossdeutschland (mot) Pioneer Battalion
- 1 Battalion Band
- 3 (mot) Pioneer Companies (9 LMGs ea)
- 1 (mot) Brüko B
- 1 (mot) Light Pioneer Supply Column

Grossdeutschland (mot) Signals Battalion
- 1 (mot) Telephone Company (6 LMGs)
- 1 (mot) Radio Company (4 LMGs)
- 1 (mot) Signals Supply Column

Grossdeutschland Brigade Supply Troop
1–7/GD (mot) Light Supply Columns
8–10/GD (mot) Heavy Fuel Columns
1/, 2/GD (mot) Maintenance Companies
GD (mot) Supply Company
Other
GD (mot) Medical Company
1/, 2/GD (mot) Ambulance Companies
GD (mot) Field Post Office

Grossdeutschland was expanded into a division in May 1942. Between 16 May and 15 October 1942 it was organized as follows:

Grossdeutschland (mot) Infantry Division
Divisional Staff (2 LMGs)
   Grossdeutschland (GD) (mot) Mapping Platoon
Grenadier Regiment GD and Fusilier Regiment GD (two regiments)
1 Regimental Staff, with
   1 Signals Platoon
   1 Engineer Platoon
   1 Motorcycle Platoon
3 Battalions each, with
   3 Infantry Companies (18 LMGs, 4 HMGs, 2 80mm mortars and 2 flamethrowers ea)
   1 Machine Gun Company (12 HMGs and 6 80mm mortars)
   1 Heavy Company with
      1 Engineer Platoon (3 LMGs)
      1 Infantry Gun Section (2 75mm leIG and 1 LMG)
      1 Panzerjäger Section (2 50mm PAK 38 and 3 28mm sPzBu 41)
1 Self-Propelled AA Company (8 20mm and 2 quad 20mm)
1 (mot) Heavy Infantry Gun Company (2 150mm sIG and 6 75mm leIG)
1 Self-Propelled Panzerjäger Company (9 75mm PAK 40 and 6 LMGs)
GD Sturmgeschütz Battalion
3 Batteries (7 Sturmgeschütz ea)
GD Panzer Troop
1 Armored Staff Company
3 Medium Armored Companies
1 Armored Maintenance Platoon
GD Motorcycle Battalion
1 Armored Car Platoon (3 LMGs)
1 Armored Car Company (18 20mm and 25 LMGs)
1 Half-Track Company (2 80mm mortars, 3 37mm PAK 36, 4 HMGs and 56 LMGs)
2 Motorcycle Companies (2 80mm mortars, 4 HMGs, 18 LMGs and 3 PzBu39 ea)
1 (mot) Heavy Company
   1 Engineer Platoon (1 flamethrower and 2 LMGs)

1 Panzerjäger Platoon (3 50mm PAK 38 and 3 LMGs)
1 Panzerjäger Section (3 PzBu39 and 3 LMGs)
1 Infantry Gun Section (2 75mm leIG and 1 LMG)
GD (mot) Artillery Regiment
1 Regimental Staff
   1 (mot) Staff Company
   1 (mot) Observation Company
      10th (mot) Nebelwerfer Battery (6 nebelwerfers, 1 50mm PAK 38 and 2 LMGs)
2 Battalions, with
   (Mot) Battalion Staff Companies
   2 Batteries (4 105mm leFH and 2 LMGs ea)
   1 Battery (4 150mm sFH and 2 LMGs)
1 Battalion, with
   2 Batteries (4 150mm sFH and 2 LMGs ea)
   1 Battery (4 100mm K18 guns and 2 LMGs)
1 Flak Battalion, with
   3 (mot) Batteries (4 88mm AA guns and 3 20mm AA guns ea)
   2 Self-Propelled Batteries (9 Self-Propelled 37mm AA guns ea)
GD Signals Battalion
1 Armored Radio Company
1 Armored Telephone Company
1 Light (mot) Signals Supply Column
GD Pioneer Battalion
3 (mot) Pioneer Companies (9 LMGs and 6 flamethrowers ea)
1 Light (mot) Bridging Column "K"
1 Light (mot) Engineer Supply Column
GD Panzerjäger Battalion
2 (mot) Companies (9 50mm PAK 38 and 6 LMGs ea)
1 Self-Propelled Company (6 75mm PAK 40 and 6 LMGs)
Supply Train
10 Light (mot) Supply Columns
4 Heavy (mot) Supply Columns
4 Light Fuel Supply Columns
3 (mot) Maintenance Companies
1 Light (mot) Supply Company
Administrative Services
1 (mot) Divisional Quartermaster Platoon
1 (mot) Butcher Company
1 (mot) Bakery Company
Medical
3 Ambulance Columns
2 (mot) Medical Companies
Other
GD (mot) Field Post Office
GD (mot) Military Police Company

The exact equipment of the Grossdeutschland Panzer Battalion is difficult to ascertain as sources vary. The OKH document indicate what is above, yet Jentz gives the following for May and July 1942:

May 1942
Grossdeutschland Panzer Battalion
  1 Panzer Staff Company
  1 Medium Panzer Company
  2 Light Panzer Companies
    PzMk II   12
    PzMk III (50kz)   2
    PzMk IV (kz)   18
    PzMk IV (lg)   12
    PzBefWg   1

July 1942
Grossdeutschland Panzer Battalion
  1 Panzer Staff Company
  3 Medium Panzer Companies
    PzMk II   12
    PzMk III (50kz)   2
    PzMk IV (kz)   18
    PzMk IV (lg)   12
    PzBefWg   1

The 203rd Panzer Regiment was pulled back to Germany in December 1942. The 2/203rd Panzer Regiment was redesignated the 2/Grossdeutschland Panzer Regiment on 13 January 1943 and organized with three medium panzer companies. On the same day the 13th Heavy Panzer Company/Grossdeutschland Panzer Regiment was created by renaming the 3rd Company/203rd Panzer Regiment. The Grossdeutschland Panzer Battalion was redesignated the 1/Grossdeutschland Panzer Regiment. The Grossdeutschland Panzer Regiment re-joined the division on the front on 1 March 1943. In February 1943 reinforcements were received that consisted of:

Grossdeutschland Panzer Regiment
  2nd Battalion
    1 Panzer Staff Company
    3 Medium Panzer Companies
    13th Heavy Panzer Company
  Total tank inventory:
    PzMk III (lg)   10
    PzMk IV (lg)   42
    PzMk VI   9
    Flammpanzer 28
    PzBefWg   6

Grossdeutschland Panzergrenadier Division

Formed on 19 May 1943 by the redesignation of the Grossdeutschland (mot) Infantry Division. During the early summer of 1943 1/Grossdeutschland Panzer Regiment was equipped with PzMk V (Panther) tanks. The 2/Grossdeutschland Panzer Regiment continued to be equipped with PzMk IV tanks. On 1 July 1943 the organization of the armored portion of the division and its panzer inventory were as follows:

Grossdeutschland Panzer Regiment
  1 Regimental Staff Signals Platoon
  1 Regimental Staff Light Panzer Platoon
  Each Battalion had:
    1 Panzer Staff Company
    3 Medium Panzer Companies
    13th Heavy Panzer Company
Total tank inventory:
  PzMk II   4
  PzMk III (kz)   1
  PzMk III (lg)   20
  PzMk III (75)   2
  PzMk IV (kz)   5
  PzMk IV (lg)   63
  PzMk VI   15
  PzBefWg   8
  Flammpanzer 14

At the Battle of Kursk the division had 45 PzMk IVs, 46 Panthers, 13 Tigers, and 35 assault guns. On 10 July 1943 the reconnaissance battalion was apparently reorganized. OKH records indicate that it was restructured as follows:

Original "summer" 1943 organization
  1 Armored Car Company (24 LMGs and 18 20mm)
  1 Half-Track Company (3 75mm leIG, 2 80mm mortars, 4 HMG and 56 LMGs)
  2 (mot) Companies (3 PzBu39, 2 80mm mortars, 4 HMGS and 18 LMGs ea)
  1 (mot) Company
    1 Infantry Gun Section (2 75mm leIG)
    1 Half-Track Gun Section (75mm guns on half-tracks)
    1 Panzerjäger Section (3 50mm PAK 38 and 3 LMGs)
    1 Pioneer Section (4 LMGs)
  1 (mot) Light Reconnaissance Supply Column (3 LMGs)

July 1943 organization
  1 Armored Car Company (24 LMGs and 18 20mm)
  1 Half-Track Reconnaissance Company (25 LMGs and 16 20mm guns)
  1 Half-Track Company (2 80mm mortars, 3 37mm PAK, 4 HMGs and 56 LMGs)
  1 Motorcycle Company (2 80mm mortars, 4 HMGs 18 LMGs and 3 PzBu39)

1 Half-Track Company
  1 Staff (2 LMGs)
  1 Pioneer Platoon (1 37mm PAK, 13 LMGs and 6 flamethrowers)
  1 Infantry Section (?) (9 LMGs)
  1 Panzerjäger Section (4 LMGs and 3 75mm PAK 40)
  1 Infantry Gun Section (2 75mm leIG)
  1 Half-Track Section (6 75mm guns and 8 LMGs)
1 (mot) Light Reconnaissance Supply Column (3 LMGs)

OKH records show that in September 1943 the division was organized and equipped as follows:

Division Staff
  (mot) Division Mapping Detachment
  Divisional Truck Column
  Divisional Escort Company
    Motorcycle Platoon (6 LMGs)
    Infantry Gun Platoon (2 75mm leIG)
    Heavy Anti-Tank Platoon (3 LMGs and 3 75mm PAK 40)
    Self-Propelled Flak Platoon (4 20mm guns)
    Mixed Panzergrenadier Platoon (4 HMGs, 6 LMGs and 2 80mm mortars)
GD Panzer Regiment
  1st Panzer Battalion
    Staff and Staff Company
    Staff Flak Tank Platoon (7 37mm Flak guns)
    4 Panzer Platoons (Panther PzMk V Tanks)
  2nd Panzer Battalion
    Staff and Staff Company
    Staff Flak Tank Platoon (7 37mm Flak guns)
    4 Panzer Platoons (Panzer PzMk IV tanks)
  3rd Panzer Battalion
    Staff and Staff Company
    3 Panzer Platoons (Tiger PzMk VI tanks)
  311th (FKL) Panzer Company
    assigned to 3/Grossdeutschland Panzer Regiment
GD Panzergrenadier and GD Fusilier Regiments, each with
    Regimental Staff and Staff Company
      Signals Platoon
      Pioneer Platoon (3 LMGs)
      Motorcycle Platoon (6 LMGs)
  1st (armored) Battalion
    Staff (6 LMGs)
    3 Panzergrenadier Companies (4 HMGs, 34 LMGs, 2 80mm mortars ea)
    1 Heavy Panzergrenadier Company
      1 Staff Platoon (2 LMGs)
      1 Mortar Platoon (2 LMGs and 4 120mm mortars)
      1 leIG Platoon (4 LMGs and 6 75mm leIG)
  2nd and 3rd (mot) Battalions, each with
    3 Panzergrenadier Companies (4 HMGs, 34 LMGs and 2 80mm mortars ea)

1 Machine Gun Company (12 HMGs and 6 80mm mortars)
1 Heavy Company
  1 Pioneer Platoon (3 LMGs)
  1 Panzerjäger Platoon (3 50mm PAK 38)
  1 Infantry Gun Section (2 75mm leIG)
4th Self-Propelled Heavy Battalion
  1 Self-Propelled Light Flak Company (12 20mm Flak and 4 LMGs)
  1 Self-Propelled Infantry Gun Company (8 150mm sIG and 3 LMGs)
  1 Self-Propelled Heavy Panzerjäger Company (9 75mm PAK 40 and 9 LMGs)
GD Panzer Reconnaissance Battalion
  Staff (3 LMGs)
  1 Self-Propelled Flak Platoon (4 20mm and 2 LMGs)
  1 Armored Car Company (18 20mm and 25 LMGs)
  1 (half-track) Reconnaissance Company (2 80mm mortars, 4 HMGs, 56 LMGs, and 3 75mm leIG)
  2 (Volkswagen) Reconnaissance Companies (2 80mm mortars, 4 HMGs, 18 LMGs and 3 PzBu39 ea)
  1 Heavy Panzer Reconnaissance Company
    1 Pioneer Platoon (3 LMGs)
    1 Medium Panzerjäger Platoon (3 LMGs and 3 50mm PAK 38)
    1 Panzerjäger Platoon (6 SdKfz 251/22 with 75mm PAK 40)
    1 Infantry Support Gun Section (2 75mm leIG)
  1 Light Panzer Reconnaissance Column
GD Panzerjäger Battalion
  1 Self-Propelled Heavy Panzerjäger Company (9 75mm PAK 40 and 9 LMGs)
  2 (motZ) Heavy Panzerjäger Companies (9 75mm PAK 40 and 9 LMGs ea)
GD Sturmgeschütz Battalion
  Staff and Staff Battery (2 LMGs)
  Staff Company (2 StuG)
  3 Sturmgeschütz Batteries (11 StuG ea)
GD Artillery Regiment
  Staff and (mot) Staff Battery (2 LMGs)
  Observation Battery
  Self-Propelled Light Flak Platoon
  1st Battalion
  Staff and Staff Battery (2 LMGs)
  2 (motZ) Batteries (4 105mm leFH and 2 LMGs ea)
  1 (motZ) Battery (4 150mm sFH and 2 LMGs)
  2nd Battalion
  Staff and (self-propelled) Staff Battery
  2 Self-Propelled leFH Batteries (6 105mm leFH SdKfz 124 Wespe ea)
  1 Self-Propelled sFH Battery (6 150mm sFH SdKfz 165 Hummel)
  3rd Battalion
  Staff and (mot) Staff Battery (2 LMGs)

1 (motZ) Battery (4 105mm leFH and 2 LMGs)

1 (motZ) Battery (4 150mm sFH and 2 LMGs)

1 (motZ) Battery (4 100mm K18 and 2 LMGs)

4th Battalion

Staff and (mot) Staff Battery (2 LMGs)

2 (motZ) Batteries (4 105mm leFH and 2 LMGs ea)

1 (motZ) Battery (6 150mm nebelwerfer, 1 50mm PAK 38 and 2 LMGs)

GD Army Flak Battalions

Staff and Staff Battery

1/, 2/, 3/GD Heavy Flak Batteries (4 88mm and 3 self-propelled 20mm Flak guns ea)

4/, 5/GD Self-Propelled Medium Flak Batteries (9 37mm guns and 4 LMGs ea)

6/GD Light Flak Battery (3 quad 20mm Flak guns)

1 (mot) Light (48 ton) Flak Column

GD Feldersatz Battalion

5 (tmot) Companies

GD (mot) Pioneer Battalion

Staff (2 LMGs)

1 (mot) Pioneer Reconnaissance Platoon (8 LMGs and 6 20mm Flak guns)

3 (mot) Pioneer Companies (25 LMGs and 6 flame-throwers ea)

1 (armored) Pioneer Company (40 LMGs and 6 flamethrowers)

1 Brüko K Bridging Column (4 LMGs)

1 (mot) Light Pioneer Column (4 LMGs)

GD Panzer Signals Battalion

Staff

1 (mot) Telephone Company (6 LMGs)

1 Panzer Radio Company (35 LMGs)

1 (mot) Light Signals Column (4 LMGs)

Supply Troops

Staff

1st–5th GD (mot) (120 ton) Transportation Companies (4 LMGs ea)

6th–8th GD (mot) (90 ton) Transportation Companies (3 LMGs ea)

GD (mot) Supply Company (6 LMGs)

3 (mot) Maintenance Companies

1–4/GD (mot) Maintenance Companies (4 LMGs ea)

1 (60 ton) Maintenance Supply Squadron

Administration

1 Divisional Administration Office (4 LMGs)

1 (mot) Bakery Company (4 LMGs)

1 (mot) Butcher Company (4 LMGs)

Medical Troops

1/, 2/GD (mot) Medical Companies

GD (mot) Field Hospital

1–3/GD Ambulance Platoons

Other

GD (mot) Military Police Troop

GD (mot) Field Post Office

In July 1944 the Grossdeutschland division was organized as follows:

Division Headquarters

Divisional Staff

Grossdeutschland (GD) (mot) Mapping Platoon

GD (mot) Military Police Company

Division Escort Company

2 Half-Track Mounted Panzergrenadier Platoons

20mm Self-Propelled Flak Platoon

GD Panzer Regiment

Staff and Staff Company

1st Battalion

Staff and Staff Company

4 Panther Tank Companies

1 (mot) Supply Company

1 (mot) Maintenance Company

2nd Battalion

Staff and Staff Company

4 Tank Companies (PzMk IV tanks)

1 (mot) Supply Company

1 (mot) Maintenance Company

3rd Battalion

Staff and Staff Company

3 Tiger Tank Companies

1 (mot) Supply Company

1 (mot) Maintenance Company

Grenadier Regiment GD

Regimental Staff and Staff Company

1st (Half-Track) Battalion

4 Infantry Companies

1 Supply Company

2nd (mot) Battalion

3 Infantry Companies

1 Heavy Company

1 Supply Company

3rd (mot) Battalion

4 Infantry Companies

1 Self-Propelled Flak Company

1 Supply Company

13th (self-propelled) Heavy Infantry Gun Company

(6 SdKfz138/1 150mm sIG 33/1)

14th (mot) Pioneer Company

15th (mot) Panzerjäger Company

16th Self-Propelled AA Company

Fusilier Regiment GD

same as Grenadier Regiment GD

GD Reconnaissance Battalion

Staff and Staff Squadron

1st (Hetzer) Squadron

2nd Half-Track Reconnaissance Squadron

3rd Half-Track Reconnaissance Squadron

4th Heavy Squadron

Army Flak Battalion

Staff and Staff Battery

1st–3rd (mot) Heavy Flak Batteries (88mm guns)
4th–5th (self-propelled) Medium Flak Battery
6th (self-propelled) Light Flak Battery (quad 20mm guns)

GD Panzer Artillery Regiment

Regimental Staff and Staff Battery
Observation Battery

1st Battalion

Staff and Staff Battery
2 (self-propelled) Batteries (105mm Wespe)
1 (self-propelled) Battery (150mm Hummel)

2nd Battalion

Staff and Staff Battery
2 Batteries (105mm lFH)
1 Battery (150mm sFH)

3rd Battalion

Staff and Staff Battery
2 Batteries (105mm lFH)
1 Battery (100mm K18 guns)

4th Battalion

Staff and Staff Battery
2 Batteries (105mm lFH)
1 Battery (150mm sFH)

GD Sturmgeschütz Brigade

Staff and Staff Battery
1 (mot) Supply Company
1st–3rd StuG Batteries

GD Pioneer Battalion

Staff and Staff Company
1 (Half-Track) Pioneer Company
3 (mot) Pioneer Companies
1 Light (mot) Bridging Column "K"
1 Light (mot) Engineer Supply Column

GD Signals Battalion

1 (mot) Radio Company
1 (mot) Telephone Company
1 Light (mot) Signals Supply Column

Supply Train

1st–6th (mot) (120 ton) Supply Columns
Light (mot) (60 ton) Supply Columns
1 (mot) Equipment Column
3 (mot) Maintenance Companies
1 (mot) Recovery Company
1 (mot) Weapons Repair Group

Administrative Services

1 (mot) Divisional Quartermaster Platoon
1 (mot) Butcher Company
1 (mot) Bakery Company

Feldersatz Battalion

1st–6th Companies

Other

2 (mot) Medical Companies
3 Ambulance Columns
GD Field Hospital
GD (mot) Field Post Office

On 13 December 1944 the division was organized and equipped as follows:

Grossdeutschland Panzergrenadier Division

Grossdeutschland Panzergrenadier Division Staff (2 LMGs)
Grossdeutschland Panzergrenadier Division Staff Escort Company
1 Machine Gun Platoon (4 HMGs and 6 LMGs)
1 Motorcycle Platoon (6 LMGs)
1 Self-Propelled Flak Platoon (4 20mm guns)
1 Mortar Platoon (2 80mm mortars)
Grossdeutschland (mot) Mapping Detachment
Grossdeutschland (mot) Military Police Detachment (5 LMGs)

Grossdeutschland Panzer Regiment

Grossdeutschland Panzer Regimental Staff
Grossdeutschland Panzer Regimental Staff Company
1 Pioneer Platoon
1 Panzer Signals Platoon
1 Self-Propelled Flak Platoon (3 20mm Flak guns)
1 Armored Maintenance Company

1st Battalion

1 Panzer Battalion Staff (1 LMG)
1 Panzer Battalion Staff Company (12 LMGs)
4 Panzer Companies (17 PzMk V Panther tanks ea)
1 (self-propelled) Armored Flak Company (3 quad 20mm Flak guns)
1 (mot) Supply Company (5 LMGs)

2nd Battalion

1 Panzer Battalion Staff (1 LMG)
1 Panzer Battalion Staff Company (8 LMGs)
4 Panzer Companies (17 PzMk IV tanks ea)
1 (self-propelled) Armored Flak Company (3 quad 20mm Flak guns)
1 (mot) Supply Company (5 LMGs)

Grossdeutschland Grenadier Regiment

Regimental Staff
Regimental Staff Company
1 Staff Platoon (2 LMGs)
1 Signals Platoon (7 LMGs)
1 Motorcycle Platoon (6 LMGs)

1st (half-track) Panzergrenadier Battalion

1 Panzergrenadier Battalion Staff (6 LMGs)
1 (mot) Panzergrenadier Battalion Supply Company (5 LMGs)
3 (half-track) Panzergrenadier Companies (4 HMGs, 30 LMGs, 5 20mm and 2 75mm guns ea)
1 (half-track) Heavy Panzergrenadier Company
1 Staff Platoon (2 LMGs)
1 Mortar Platoon (2 LMGs and 4 120mm mortars)
1 leIG Platoon (4 LMGs and 6 75mm leIG)

2nd (mot) Jäger Battalions

1 Battalion Staff

1 Battalion Supply Company (4 LMGs)

3 (mot) Companies (12 LMGs ea)

1 (mot) Heavy Company (12 HMGs and 6 20mm Flak guns)

1 (mot) Heavy Company (4 120mm and 8 80mm mortars)

9th Self-Propelled sIG Company (8 150mm sIG guns and 6 LMGs)

10th (Pioneer) Company (motZ)

1 Half-Track Staff (1 LMG)

1 Half-Track Platoon (6 flamethrowers and 6 LMGs)

1 Half-Track Platoon (6 flamethrowers, 1 20mm and 12 LMGs)

1 Half-Track Platoon (12 flamethrowers and 8 LMGs)

1 Half-Track Platoon (2 80mm mortars and 2 HMGs)

Grossdeutschland Fusilier Regiment

Regimental Staff

Regimental Staff Company (4 LMGs)

1 Staff Platoon

1 Motorcycle Platoon

1st and 2nd (mot) Battalions, each with

1 Battalion Staff

1 Battalion Supply Company (4 LMGs)

3 (mot) Companies (12 LMGs ea)

1 (mot) Heavy Company (12 HMGs and 6 20mm Flak guns)

1 (mot) Heavy Company (4 120mm and 8 80mm mortars)

9th Self-Propelled sIG Company (8 150mm sIG guns and 6 LMGs)

10th (Pioneer) Company (motZ) (18 flamethrowers, 2 HMGs, 12 LMGs, and 2 80mm mortars)

Grossdeutschland Panzerjäger Battalion

1 Panzerjäger Battalion Staff

1 Panzerjäger Battalion Staff Battery (1 LMG)

1 Sturmgeschütz Staff Platoon (3 StuG)

2 Sturmgeschütz Companies (14 StuG ea)

1 (motZ) Panzerjäger Company (12 88mm PAK and 12 LMGs)

1 (mot) Panzerjäger Supply Company (3 LMGs)

Grossdeutschland Reconnaissance Battalion

1 Reconnaissance Battalion Staff

1 Armored Car Platoon (3 75mm, 13 20mm and 16 LMGs)

1 (mot) Signals Platoon (7 LMGs)

1st Armored Car (half-track) Company (16 20mm and 25 LMGs)

2nd Half-Track Reconnaissance Company (2 75mm, 2 80mm mortars and 44 LMGs)

3rd Half-Track Reconnaissance Company (2 75mm and 7 20mm, 2 80mm mortars, 4 HMGs and 29 LMGs)

4th Half-Track Reconnaissance Company

1 Staff Platoon (1 LMG)

1 Platoon (6 75mm and 2 LMGs)

1 Mortar Platoon (6 80mm and 2 LMGs)

1 Pioneer Platoon (13 LMGs)

1 (mot) Reconnaissance Supply Company (3 LMGs)

Grossdeutschland Artillery Regiment

1 Artillery Regimental Staff

1 (mot) Artillery Regimental Staff Company (2 LMGs)

1st Battalion

1 (Self-Propelled) Artillery Battalion Staff

1 (Self-Propelled) Artillery Battalion Staff Battery (2 LMGs)

1 (Self-Propelled) Flak Platoon (3 20mm)

2 (Self-Propelled) Light Howitzer Batteries (6 105mm howitzers in Wespe and 4 LMGs ea)

1 (Self-Propelled) Heavy Howitzer Battery (6 150mm howitzers in Hummel and 4 LMGs)

2nd Battalion

1 (motZ) Artillery Battalion Staff

1 (motZ) Artillery Battalion Staff Company (2 LMGs)

1 Flak Platoon (motZ) (3 20mm)

2 Light Howitzer Batteries (motZ) (6 105mm leFH and 4 LMGs ea)

3rd Battalion

1 (motZ) Artillery Battalion Staff

1 (motZ) Artillery Battalion Staff Company (2 LMGs)

1 Flak Platoon (motZ) (3 20mm)

3 Heavy Howitzer Batteries (6 150mm sFH and 4 LMGs ea)

Grossdeutschland Army Flak Battalion

1 (motZ) Flak Battalion Staff

1 (mot) Flak Battalion Staff Battery (2 LMGs)

2 (motZ) Flak Batteries (6 88mm, 3 20mm and 2 LMGs ea)

1 (motZ) Light Flak Battery

1 (motZ) Section (9 37mm Flak guns and 4 LMGs)

1 Self-Propelled Section (3 quad 20mm Flak guns)

1 (motZ) Searchlight Section (4 searchlights)

Grossdeutschland Pioneer Battalion

1 (motZ) Pioneer Battalion Staff

1 (half-track) Pioneer Battalion Staff Company (12 LMGs)

2 Pioneer Companies (motZ) (2 HMGs, 18 LMGs and 2 80mm mortars ea)

1 (half-track) Pioneer Company (2 HMGs, 43 LMGs, 6 flamethrowers and 2 80mm mortars)

Grossdeutschland Signals Battalion

1 Armored Signals Battalion Staff

1 Armored Telephone Company (11 LMGs)

1 Armored Radio Company (19 LMGs)
1 (mot) Signals Supply Column (2 LMGs)

Grossdeutschland Supply Troop
1 (mot) Medical Company (2 LMGs)
1 (mot) Medical Supply Company (2 LMGs)
1 (mot) Field Post Office

The order of 20 december 1944 directed the formation of the Grossdeutschland Panzer Corps with the Grossdeutschland and Brandenburg Panzergrenadier Divisions. At that time the 3/Grossdeutschland Grenadier Regiment was detached to become the 1/Grossdeutschland Corps Fusilier Regiment and the 1/Grossdeutschland Fusilier Regiment became the Corps Escort Company and the 500th Corps Reconnaissance Company. The 3rd Fusilier Battalion was then redesignated as the 1st Battalion. The 3/Grossdeutschland Panzer Regiment was redesignated as the Grossdeutschland Heavy Panzer Battalion (corps troops). The 4/Grossdeutschland Artillery Regiment was redesignated as the 1/500th Corps Panzer Artillery Regi-

ment, as were the administrative troops and the feldersatz battalion. The Grossdeutschland Sturmgeschütz Battalion was to form the 2/Brandenburg Panzer Regiment, in the Brandenburg Division. The Grossdeutschland Division now had:

1/, 2/Grossdeutschland Panzer Regiment
1st (armored) and 2nd Battalions, Grossdeutschland Grenadier Regiment
1/, 2/Grossdeutschland Fusilier Regiment
Grossdeutschland Panzer Reconnaissance Battalion
Grossdeutschland Panzerjäger Battalion
1/, 2/, 3/Grossdeutschland Artillery Regiment
Grossdeutschland Army Flak Battalion
Grossdeutschland Pioneer Battalion
Grossdeutschland Signals Battalion
Grossdeutschland Administrative Troops

The division was captured by the British.

Fallschirmjäger Panzergrenadier Division Hermann Göring

Formed during the summer of 1944, the division contained:

Fallschirmjäger Panzergrenadier Division Hermann Göring
1 Panzergrenadier Division Staff (2 LMGs)
1 (mot) Field Post Office (1 LMG)
1 (mot) Military Police Detachment
1 (mot) Mapping Detachment (2 LMGs)

Fallschirmjäger Panzerjäger Battalion HG
1 Panzerjäger Battalion Staff
1 Panzerjäger Battalion Staff Company (1 LMG)
1 Sturmgeschütz Platoon (3 StuG)
2 Sturmgeschütz Batteries (14 StuG ea)
1 (motZ) Panzerjäger Battery (12 heavy PAK guns)
1 (mot) Supply Column

3rd Fallschirmjäger Grenadier Regiment HG
1 Regimental Staff
1 Regimental Staff Company
1 (mot) Regimental Staff Company
1 Signals Platoon (7 LMGs)
1 Motorcycle Platoon (6 LMGs)
1 Self-Propelled Flak Platoon (3 quad 20mm guns)

1st Battalion
1st–3rd (mot) Companies (4 HMGs, 18 LMGs and 2 80mm mortars ea)
4th (mot) Heavy Company
1 Flak Platoon (6 20mm Flak guns)
1 Mortar Platoon (2 LMGs and 4 120mm mortars)

2nd Battalion
same as 1/3rd Fallschirmjäger Panzergrenadier Regiment
5th–7th (mot) Companies
8th (mot) Heavy Company

(mot) Pioneer Company
2 (half-track) Platoons (? LMGs and ? flamethrowers)
1 (mot) Pioneer Platoon (5 LMGs and ? 80mm mortars)

Self-Propelled Support Gun Battery (150mm sIG)

4th Fallschirmjäger Grenadier Regiment HG
same as 3rd Fallschirmjäger Grenadier Regiment HG

2nd Fallschirmjäger Flak Battalion HG
same as 1 Fallschirmjäger Flak Battalion HG

2nd Fallschirmjäger Pioneer Battalion HG
1 (mot) Pioneer Battalion Staff
3 (mot) Pioneer Companies (18 LMGs, 6 flamethrowers and 2 80mm mortars ea)

2nd Fallschirmjäger Panzer Artillery Regiment HG
1 (mot) Regimental Staff
1 (mot) Regimental Staff Battery
1 (mot) Observation Battery

1st Battalion
1 Self-Propelled Staff
1 Self-Propelled Staff Battery (2 LMGs and 3 20mm mountain Flak guns)
2 (motZ) Batteries (6 105mm leFH and 5 LMGs ea)

1 (motZ) Battery (4 150mm sFH and 5 LMGs)
2nd Battalion
  1 (mot) Staff
  1 (mot) Staff Battery (2 LMGs and 3 20mm mountain Flak guns)
  2 (motZ) Batteries (6 105mm leFH and 5 LMGs ea)
  1 (motZ) Nebelwerfer Battery (6 launchers and 5 LMGs)
3rd Battalion
  same as 1st Battalion
1st Signals Battalion HG
  1 (mot) Battalion Staff
  1 (mot) Battalion Staff Supply Company (2 LMGs)

1 (mot) Radio Company
1 (mot) Signals Company
1st Feldersatz Battalion HG
  4 Companies
1st Fallschirmjäger Medical Battalion HG
  2 (mot) Medical Companies (4 LMGs ea)
  3 (mot) Medical Supply Companies (4 LMGs ea)
  1 (mot) Medical Decontamination Company

It was then combined with the Fallschirmjäger Panzer Division Hermann Göring to form the General Command Parachute-Panzer Corps Hermann Göring in October 1944.

Kurmark Panzergrenadier Division

Formed on 3 February 1945 from the Grossdeutschland Panzergrenadier Replacement Brigade. It was organized as a Type 44 Panzergrenadier Division, with its panzergrenadier battalions organized on the 1945 model, with three self-propelled gun companies equipped with Jagdpanzer 38 and one company with PzMk IV/70. The artillery battalion was organized from the 3/184th (mot) Artillery Regiment. The panzergrenadier regiment apparently had only a staff, a staff company, and two panzergrenadier battalions. The division was sometimes known as the Kurmark Panzer Division.

The order of 4 February 1945 gave the division an authorized strength of 4,559 men, including 128 Hiwis. It was organized and equipped as follows:

Division
  1 Brigade Staff (2 LMGs)
Kurmark Panzer Battalion
  1 Panzer Battalion Staff
  1 Panzer Battalion Staff Company
    1 Panzer Flak Platoon (3 self-propelled 37mm Flak guns)
    1 Panzer Platoon (3 StuG)
    1 Staff Platoon (4 LMGs)
  3 Panzer Companies (14 StuG ea)
  1 Panzer Company (10 PzMk IV tanks)
  1 Panzer Maintenance Platoon (2 LMGs)
  1 (mot) Panzer Supply Company (3 LMGs)
Kurmark Panzergrenadier Regiment
  1 Panzergrenadier Regimental Staff
  1 Panzergrenadier Regimental Staff Company
    1 Signals Platoon
    1 Motorcycle Platoon (6 LMGs)
    1 Panzerjäger Platoon (3 heavy PAK guns)
  1st (mot) Battalion
  1 Battalion Staff

1 (mot) Panzergrenadier Supply Company
3 (mot) Panzergrenadier Companies (11 LMGs ea)
1 (mot) Heavy Company (12 HMGs)
1 (mot) Heavy Company (? 120mm mortars and ? 150mm sIG)
2nd (mot) Battalion
  same as 1st Battalion
Kurmark Reconnaissance Battalion
  1 Reconnaissance Company (4 HMGs, 9 LMGs and 2 80mm mortars)
Kurmark Panzerjäger Battalion
  1 Panzerjäger Company (12 75mm PAK and 12 LMGs)
Kurmark Artillery Regiment
  1st Battalion
  1 Battalion Staff
  1 (mot) Battalion Staff Battery (2 LMGs and 3 20mm Flak guns)
  3 (motZ) Batteries (4 105mm leFH and 4 LMGs ea)
  2nd Battalion
  assigned, not present
Luftwaffe Flak Battalion
  1 Flak Battalion Staff
  1 (mot) Flak Battalion Staff Battery (2 LMGs)
  3 (motZ) Heavy Flak Companies (4 88mm, 2 20mm and ? LMGs ea)
  1 (motZ) Mixed Flak Battery (equipment unknown)
Kurmark Pioneer Battalion
  1 Pioneer Battalion Staff (3 LMGs)
  1 (mot) Pioneer Supply Company (4 LMGs)
  2 (mot) Pioneer Companies (2 HMGs, 18 LMGs and 2 80mm mortars ea)
Other
  1 Maintenance Platoon (3 LMGs)
  1 (mot) Mixed Signals Company

On 2 February 1945 the organization of the armored portion of the division and its panzer inventory were as follows:

1/Brandenburg Panzer Regiment
  1st Battalion
    1 Panzer Staff Company
    3 Medium Panzer Companies (PzMk V)
  1 Battalion
    1 Panzer Staff Company
    1 Medium Panzer Company (PzMk IV)
    3 Jagdpanzer Companies (Jagdpz IV)

Total tank inventory:
  MkV   45
  Jagdpz IV 28

On 5 February 1945 the panzer battalion was designated as the 51st Panzer Battalion and between 23 and 25 February 28 Jagdpanzer 38 were shipped to it. In addition, on 5 February 1945 the 1/Brandenburg Panzer Regiment was ordered to join the division. It received 45 Panther tanks that were shipped to the regiment between 27 January and 2 February. The division broke out of the Halbe pocket and was taken prisoner by the Americans near Jerichow.

150th or "Rabenhügel" Panzergrenadier Brigade

This brigade was formed in late 1944, but the precise date is uncertain. Its fate is equally unknown. However, on 20 November 1944 it was organized and equipped as follows:

Brigade Staff
  1 (half-track) Brigade Staff
  1 (half-track) Staff Company
    1 Signals Platoon (12 LMGs)
    1 Motorcycle Platoon (6 LMGs)
    1 Reconnaissance Platoon (6 LMGs)
  2150th (mot) Pioneer Company (2 HMGS, 18 LMGs, 2 80mm mortars)
  2150th Self-Propelled Light Howitzer Battery (6 105mm howitzers in Wespe and 4 LMGs ea)
  2150th (mot) Heavy (60 ton) Supply Column (1 LMG)
1/2150th Kampfabteilung
  1 (half-track) Battalion Staff
  1 (half-track) Signals Platoon (9 LMGs)
  1st Panzer Company (22 PzMk V Panther tanks)
  2nd (half-track) Panzergrenadier Company (4 HMGs, 40 LMGs, 2 80mm mortars, 7 20mm guns and 2 75mm guns)

3rd Armored Car Company (24 LMGs and 18 20mm guns)
4th–7th (mot) Panzergrenadier Companies (4 HMGs, 18 LMGs and 2 80mm mortars ea)
8th (motZ) Flak Company (6 88mm, 3 20mm and 4 LMGs)
2/2150th Kampfabteilung
  1 (half-track) Battalion Staff
  1 (half-track) Signals Platoon (9 LMGs)
  9th Sturmgeschütz Company (14 StuG and 16 LMGs)
  10th Armored Car Company (25 LMGs and 16 20mm guns)
  11th–14th (mot) Panzergrenadier Companies (4 HMGs, 18 LMGs and 2 80mm mortars ea)
  15th (motZ) Flak Company (6 88mm, 3 20mm and 4 LMGs)

In December 1944 the organization of the armored portion of the division and its panzer inventory were as follows:

9th Company/2150th Kampfabteilung (5 StuG)
1/2150th Kampfabteilung (5 Mk V tanks)

Von Werthen Panzergrenadier Brigade

Formed by order of Adolf Hitler on 4 July 1944, the brigade was organized from units drawn from the Führer Grenadier Battalion and the Führer Flak Battalion. It was to have:

Staff with signals detachment
2 Panzergrenadier Companies
1 Heavy Company
1 Panzer Company (12 PzMk IV and 5 StuG)
1 Mixed Flak Battery

In order to form this unit, the Führer Grenadier Battalion detached:

1 Panzergrenadier Company, with 3 schützen platoons
2 Heavy Platoons in half-tracks
1 Sturmgeschütz Platoon (5 StuG)
1 Panzer Platoon without Personnel (5 PzMk IV tanks)

The Führer Flak Battalion detached:

1 Flak Battery with 4 88mm guns
1 Self-Propelled 37mm Flak gun
2 Self-Propelled 20mm Flak guns

Kampfgruppe B provided:

Staff and Signals Detachment
1 Panzergrenadier Company (with 3 schützen platoons in half-tracks)
1 Heavy Company (with 1 sIG platoon, 1 37mm self-propelled Flak platoon and one self-propelled 75mm PAK 40 platoon)
1 Panzer Company (2 platoons, 1 without tanks and 1 StuG platoon)

OKH records show it having the following equipment:

1st (mot) Company (4 HMGs, 18 LMGs and 2 80mm mortars)

2nd (mot) Company (4 HMGs, 18 LMGs and 2 80mm mortars)
3rd (mot) Company
　1 (motZ) Heavy Panzerjäger Company (2 75mm PAK 40)
　1 Self-Propelled Heavy Panzerjäger Company (3 75mm PAK 40)
　1 Self-Propelled Flak Company (3 37mm Flak guns)
4th (Flak) Company
　1 (motZ) Flak Battery (4 88mm guns)
　1 Self-Propelled (3 37mm Flak guns)
　2 Self-Propelled (8 20mm Flak guns)
5th Company (12 PzMk IV tanks and 5 StuG)

The brigade was to be operational on 6 July 1944. Notes indicate that the 5th Company was detached on 7 October 1944. As mentioned earlier, its fate is unknown.

ORGANIZATION OF A (MOT) DIVISION, 1939

3 (mot) Infantry Regiments
　3 (mot) Infantry Battalions (21/3/136/704 each[1])
　　3 Schützen Companies (9 LMGs, 3HMGs and 3 50mm mortars ea)
　　1 Machine Gun Company (8 HMGs and 6 80mm Mortars)
　　Infantry Support Gun Company (8 75mm leIG guns)
Reconnaissance Battalion (15/3/58/310)
　Motorcycle Squadron (9 LMGs, 2 HMGs and 2 50mm mortars)
　1 Armored Car Squadron (10 armored cars)
　1 Heavy Squadron
　(mot) Anti-Tank Platoon (3 37mm PAK 36)
　Infantry Gun Platoon (2 75mm leIG)
Artillery Regiment
　1 (mot) Observation Battery (25/2/82/464)
　3 Light Artillery Battalions (18/3/69/450 ea), each with
　　3 Batteries (4 105mm leFH 18 ea)
　1 Heavy Artillery Battalion (19/3/69/463)
　　3 Batteries (4 150mm sFH 18 ea)
　(mot) Observation Battalion
Panzer Abwehr Battalion (18/3/103/395)
　3 (mot) Anti-Tank Companies (12 37mm PAK 36 ea)
　1 (mot) Heavy Machine Gun Company (12 20mm Flak guns)
Pioneer Battalion (22/2/91/716)
　2 Pioneer Companies (9 LMGs ea)
　1 (mot) Pioneer Company (9 LMGs ea)
　1 (mot) Bridge Column C or B
　1 (mot) Light Pioneer Column

Signals Battalion (14/3/74/333)
　1 (mot) Field Telephone Company
　1 (mot) Radio Company
　1 (mot) Light Signal Company
Quartermaster Service (25/23/102/834)
　Staff Divisional Quartermaster, with
　　8 Small Columns
　　2 Light Column for Operations Material
　　3 (mot) Repair Shop Company
　　1 (mot) Quartermaster Company
Administrative Service (3/10/328/167)
　1 (mot) Bakery Company
　1 (mot) Butcher Company
　1 (mot) Administrative Company
Medical Service (21/10/71/429)
　2 (mot) Medical Companies
　1 (mot) Field Hospital
　3 Ambulance Companies
Other
　1 (mot) Military Police Troop (1/0/35/1)
　1 (mot) Field Post Office (0/18/0/0)

---

[1] Numbers are officers, warrant officers, NCOs, and men.

ORGANIZATION OF A (MOT) INFANTRY DIVISION, 10 FEBRUARY–15 MAY 1941

(mot) Division
1 Division Staff (2 HMGs)
  1 (mot) Divisional Mapping Detachment
2 (mot) Regiments, each with
  1 Regimental Staff Company with
    1 Motorcycle Platoon
    1 Engineer Platoon (3 LMGs)
    1 Signals Platoon
    1 Regimental Band
  3 (mot) Battalions, each with
    3 Infantry Companies, (12 LMGs and 3 50mm mortars ea)
    1 Heavy Company (12 HMGs and 6 80mm mortars)
    1 (mot) Panzerjäger Company (12 37mm PAK 36 and 4 LMGs)
    1 (mot) Heavy Infantry Gun Company (2 150mm sIG and 6 75mm leIG)
    1 Motorcycle Platoon (3 LMGs)
    1 Light (mot) Supply Column (deleted later)
1 Motorcycle Battalion, with
  3 Motorcycle Companies (18 LMGs, 2 HMGs and 3 50mm mortars ea)
  1 (mot) Heavy Machine Gun Company (8 HMGs and 6 80mm mortars)
  1 (mot) Support Company, with
    1 Engineer Platoon (3 LMGs)
    1 Panzerjäger Platoon (3 37mm PAK 36 and 1 LMG)
    1 Infantry Support Gun Section (2 75mm leIG)
Artillery Regiment
  1 (mot) Staff Company
  1 Weather Detachment
  1 Signals Platoon
  1 Regimental Band
  2 (mot) Battalions, each with
    1 (mot) Signals Platoon
    1 (mot) Calibration Detachment
    3 (mot) Batteries (4 105mm leFH 18 howitzers and 2 LMGs ea)
  1 (mot) Battalion, with
    1 (mot) Signals Platoon
    1 (mot) Calibration Detachment
    3 (mot) Batteries (4 150mm sFH 18 and 2 LMGs ea)
Reconnaissance Battalion
  1 (mot) Staff Signals Platoon (2 LMGs)
  1 Armored Car Company (10 HMGs and 25 LMGs)
  1 Motorcycle Company (18 LMGs, 2 HMGs and 3 50mm mortars)
  1 (mot) Support Company, with
    1 Engineer Platoon (3 LMGs)

    1 Panzerjäger Platoon (3 37mm PAK 36 and 1 LMG)
    1 Infantry Support Gun Section (2 75mm leIG)
Feldersatz Battalion
  3 Companies (not motorized)
Panzerjäger Battalion
  1 (mot) Staff Signals Platoon
  3 (mot) Panzerjäger Companies (9 37mm PAK 36, 2 50mm PAK 38 and 6 LMGs ea)
Pioneer Battalion
  3 (mot) Pioneer Companies (9 LMGs ea)
  1 (mot) "B" Bridging Train
  1 Light (mot) Engineering Supply Column
Signals Battalion
  1 (mot) Telephone Company
  1 (mot) Radio Company
  1 Light (mot) Signals Supply Column
Supply Train
  6 Light (mot) Supply Columns
  2 Light (mot) Supply Columns (added later)
  2 Heavy (mot) Fuel Supply Columns
  2 (mot) Maintenance Companies
  1 (mot) Supply Company
Administrative Services
  1 (mot) Bakery Company
  1 (mot) Butcher Company
  1 Quartermaster Detachment
Medical
  3 Ambulance Columns
  1 (mot) Field Hospital
  2 (mot) Medical Companies
Other
  1 (mot) Military Police Platoon
  1 (mot) Field Post Office

Divisional Variations, 10 February–15 May 1941

3rd (mot) Infantry Division

Infantry Regiments	8th and 29th
Motorcycle Battalion	53rd
Artillery Regiment	3rd
Reconnaissance Battalion	53rd
Panzerjäger Battalion	3rd
Pioneer Battalion	3rd
Signals Battalion	3rd
Feldersatz Battalion	3rd
Other	3rd

10th (mot) Infantry Division

Infantry Regiments	20th and 41st
Motorcycle Battalion	40th
Artillery Regiment	10th
Reconnaissance Battalion	10th
Panzerjäger Battalion	10th
Pioneer Battalion	10th
Signals Battalion	10th
Feldersatz Battalion	10th
Other	10th

14th (mot) Infantry Division

Infantry Regiments	11th and 53rd
Motorcycle Battalion	54th
Artillery Regiment	14th
Reconnaissance Battalion	14th
Panzerjäger Battalion	14th
Pioneer Battalion	14th
Signals Battalion	14th
Feldersatz Battalion	14th
Other	14th

16th (mot) Infantry Division

Infantry Regiments	60th and 156th
Motorcycle Battalion	165th
Artillery Regiment	146th
Reconnaissance Battalion	341st
Panzerjäger Battalion	228th (6/31st Flak Regiment assigned, with self-propelled 8 37mm and 2 quad 20mm)
Pioneer Battalion	675th
Signals Battalion	228th
Feldersatz Battalion	16th
Other	66th

18th (mot) Infantry Division

Infantry Regiments	30th and 51st
Motorcycle Battalion	38th
Artillery Regiment	18th
Reconnaissance Battalion	18th
Panzerjäger Battalion	18th
Pioneer Battalion	18th
Signals Battalion	18th
Feldersatz Battalion	18th
Other	18th

20th (mot) Infantry Division

Infantry Regiments	76th and 90th
Motorcycle Battalion	30th
Artillery Regiment	20th
Reconnaissance Battalion	20th
Panzerjäger Battalion	20th (1/52nd Flak Regiment assigned, with self-propelled 8 37mm and 2 quad 20mm)
Pioneer Battalion	20th
Signals Battalion	20th
Feldersatz Battalion	20th
Other	20th

25th (mot) Infantry Division

Infantry Regiments	35th and 119th
Motorcycle Battalion	25th
Artillery Regiment	25th
Reconnaissance Battalion	25th
Panzerjäger Battalion	25th
Pioneer Battalion	25th
Signals Battalion	25th
Feldersatz Battalion	25th
Other	25th

29th (mot) Infantry Division

Infantry Regiments	15th and 71st
Motorcycle Battalion	29th
Artillery Regiment	29th
Reconnaissance Battalion	29th
Panzerjäger Battalion	29th (1/59th Flak Regiment assigned, with self-propelled 8 37mm and 2 quad 20mm)
Pioneer Battalion	29th
Signals Battalion	29th
Feldersatz Battalion	29th
Other	29th

36th (mot) Infantry Division

Infantry Regiments	87th and 118th
Motorcycle Battalion	36th
Artillery Regiment	36th
Reconnaissance Battalion	36th
Panzerjäger Battalion	36th
Pioneer Battalion	36th
Signals Battalion	36th
Feldersatz Battalion	36th
Other	36th

60th (mot) Infantry Division

Infantry Regiments	92nd and 120th
Motorcycle Battalion	160th
Artillery Regiment	160th
Reconnaissance Battalion	160th
Panzerjäger Battalion	160th (3/608th Flak Regiment assigned, with self-propelled 8 37mm and 2 quad 20mm)

Pioneer Battalion	160th
Signals Battalion	160th
Feldersatz Battalion	160th
Other	160th

ORGANIZATION OF A (MOT) INFANTRY DIVISION, 16 MAY 1941–15 OCTOBER 1942

(mot) Division
- 1 Divisional Staff
- 1 (mot) Mapping Section (2 LMGs)

2 (mot) Regiments, each with
- Regimental Staff
- 1 (mot) Staff Company, with
  - Signals Platoon
  - Panzerjäger Platoon (3 50mm PAK 38 and 3 LMGs)
  - Engineer Platoon (3 LMGs)
  - Motorcycle Platoon (6 LMGs)
  - Regimental Band
- **3 (mot) Infantry Battalions**
  - 3 (mot) Infantry Companies (18 LMGs, 3 PzBu39, 1 28mm sPzBu 41 and 3 50mm mortars ea)
  - 1 Heavy (mot) Infantry Company (12 HMGs, 3 37mm PAK 36 and 6 80mm mortars)
- **(mot) Heavy Infantry Gun Company** (2 150mm sIG and 6 75mm leIG)

Panzerjäger Battalion
- Battalion Staff (2 LMGs)
- 2 Self-Propelled Companies (9 50mm PAK 38 and 6 LMGs ea)
- 1 (mot) Company (9 50mm PAK 38 and 6 LMGs)

Panzer Battalion
- Armored Battalion Staff Company
- 1 Medium Armored Company
- 2 Light Armored Companies

Motorcycle Battalion
- 1 Light Armored Car Company (3 LMGs)
- 1 Heavy Armored Car Company (18 37mm PAK 36 and 24 LMGs)
- 3 Motorcycle Companies (2 50mm mortars, 4 HMGs, 18 LMGs and 3 PzBu39 ea)
- 1 (mot) Support Company, with
  - Engineering Platoon (4 LMGs)
  - Panzerjäger Platoon (3 50mm PAK 38 and 3 LMGs)
  - Support Platoon (2 75mm leIG)
  - Anti-Tank Rifle Section (3 PzBu39 and 3 LMGs)

Artillery Regiment
- **2 Light Battalions**
  - 1 (mot) Staff Company

- 1 Light Munitions Supply Column (2 LMGs)
- 3 (motZ) Batteries (4 105mm leFH 18 and 2 LMGs ea)

1 Heavy Battalion
- 1 (mot) Staff Company
- 1 Light Munitions Supply Column (2 LMGs)
- 2 (motZ) Batteries (4 150m sFH 18 and 2 LMGs ea)
- 1 (motZ) Battery (4 100mm K 18 guns and 2 LMGs)

1 Flak Battalion
- 1 (mot) Staff Company (1 LMG)
- 1 Battery (12 20mm and 2 LMGs)
- 2 Batteries (4 88mm, 3 20mm and 2 LMGs ea)
- 1 Light (mot) Munitions Supply Column

Signals Battalion
- 1 (mot) Radio Company (2 LMGs)
- 1 (mot) Telephone Company (5 LMGs)
- 1 Light (mot) Signals Supply Column (1 LMG)

Pioneer Battalion
- 3 (mot) Pioneer Companies (3 PzBu39 and 9 LMGs ea)
- 1 Light (mot) Engineer Supply Column (1 LMG)

Supply Train
- 8 Light (mot) Supply Columns (2 LMGs ea)
- 1 Heavy (mot) Supply Column (2 LMGs ea)
- 2 (mot) POL Supply Columns (2 LMGs ea)
- 2 (mot) Maintenance Companies
- 1 (mot) Light Supply Company (6 LMGs)

Medical
- 2 (mot) Medical Companies (2 LMGs ea)
- 3 Ambulance Columns

Other
- 1 (mot) Field Post Office
- 1 (mot) Military Police Platoon (2 LMGs)

Divisional Variations, 16 May 1941–15 October 1942

3rd (mot) Infantry Division

Infantry Regiments	8th and 29th (3 bns per regt; each regt also had 1 SP AA Company with 12 20mm and 4 LMGs)
Panzerjäger Battalion	3rd
Panzer Battalion	103rd
Motorcycle Battalion	53rd
Artillery Regiment	3rd
Signals Battalion	3rd
Pioneer Battalion	3rd
Supply Train	3rd
Administrative	3rd
Medical Service	3rd
Other	3rd

10th (mot) Infantry Division

Infantry Regiments	20th and 41st (3 bns per regt)
Panzerjäger Battalion	10th (3 mot AT companies, 8 50mm PAK 38 and 6 LMGs ea)
Panzer Battalion	none
Motorcycle Battalion	10th (no heavy armored car company)
Artillery Regiment	10th (no 4th; Flak Battalion)
Signals Battalion	10th
Pioneer Battalion	10th
Supply Train	10th (7 light and 2 heavy supply columns, rest the same)
Administrative	10th
Medical Service	10th
Other	10th

14th (mot) Infantry Division

Infantry Regiments	11th and 53rd
Panzerjäger Battalion	14th (same as 10th (Mot) Division)
Panzer Battalion	none
Motorcycle Battalion	54th (mot company had 3 additional LMGs)
Artillery Regiment	14th (same as 10th (mot) Division)
Signals Battalion	14th
Pioneer Battalion	14th
Supply Train	14th
Administrative	14th
Medical Service	14th
Other	14th

16th (mot) Infantry Division

Infantry Regiments	60th and 156th (3 bns per regt; each regt had 1 SP AA company with 12 20mm AA and 4 LMGs)
Panzerjäger Battalion	228th
Panzer Battalion	116th
Panzer Verband	700th (2 Staff Armored Companies; 3 Light Armored Companies, 1 Armored Maintenance Company; 1 heavy Armored Car Platoon with 75mm guns; 1 Light Armored Car Company with 18 HMGs and 24 LMGs)
Motorcycle Battalion	165th
Artillery Regiment	146th
Signals Battalion	288th
Pioneer Battalion	675th
Supply Train	66th
Administrative	66th
Medical Service	66th
Other	66th

18th (mot) Infantry Division

Infantry Regiments	30th and 51st (3 bns per regt)
Panzerjäger Battalion	18th (1 SP AT company with 6 75mm PAK 40 and 6 LMGs; 1 mot AT company with 9 50mm PAK 38 and 6 LMGs; 1 mot AT company with 3 50mm PAK 38, 8 37mm PAK 36 and 6 LMGs)
Panzer Battalion	none
Motorcycle Battalion	38th
Artillery Regiment	18th (2 bns with 3 btrys with 3 105mm leFH and 2 LMGs; 1 mot bn with 2 btrys with 3 150mm sFH and 2 LMGs and 1 btry with 3 100mm 18 guns and 2 LMGs)
Signals Battalion	18th
Pioneer Battalion	18th
Supply Train	18th
Administrative	18th
Medical Service	18th
Other	18th

20th (mot) Infantry Division

Infantry Regiments	76th and 90th (3 bns per regt)
Panzerjäger Battalion	20th (3 mot companies with 3 50mm PAK 38, 8 37mm PAK 36 and 6 LMGs; 1 AA company with 12 20mm SP Flak and 4 LMGs)
Panzer Battalion	30th

Motorcycle Battalion	20th
Artillery Regiment	20th (same as 18th (Mot) Infantry Division)
Signals Battalion	20th
Pioneer Battalion	20th
Supply Train	20th
Administrative	20th
Medical Service	20th
Other	20th

25th (mot) Infantry Division

Infantry Regiments	35th and 119th (3 bns per regt)
Panzerjäger Battalion	25th (2 SP Companies with 9 50mm PAK 38 and 6 LMGs)
Panzer Battalion	none
Motorcycle Battalion	25th
Artillery Regiment	25th (same as 18th (mot) Infantry Division)
Signals Battalion	25th
Pioneer Battalion	25th
Supply Train	25th
Administrative	25th
Medical Service	25th
Other	25th

29th (mot) Infantry Division

Infantry Regiments	15th and 71st (3 bns per regt; in addition, had 1 SP AA Company with 12 20mm with 71st; 15th had 8 single AA SP mounts and 2 quad SP mounts)
Panzerjäger Battalion	29th (1 mot AT company with 9 50mm PAK 38 and 6 LMGs; 2 SP AT companies with 6 75mm PAK 40 and 6 LMGs)
Panzer Battalion	129th
Motorcycle Battalion	29th
Artillery Regiment	29th (2 bns with 3 btrys with 3 105mm leFH and 2 LMGs; 1 bn with 2 btrys with 3 150mm sFH and 2 LMGs and 1 btry with 3 100mm 18 guns and 2 LMGs; 1 Flak bn with 2 btrys with 4 88mm AA, 3 20mm and 2 LMGs and 2 btrys with 12 88mm AA and 2 LMGs; 1 Light (mot) Munitions Column)
Signals Battalion	29th
Pioneer Battalion	29th
Supply Train	29th
Administrative	29th

Medical Service	29th
Other	29th

36th (mot) Infantry Division

Infantry Regiments	87th and 118th (3 bns per regt)
Panzerjäger Battalion	36th (3 mot AT companies with 9 50mm PAK 38 and 6 LMGs)
Panzer Battalion	none
Motorcycle Battalion	36th
Artillery Regiment	36th (same as 18th (Mot) Infantry Division)
Signals Battalion	36th
Pioneer Battalion	36th
Supply Train	36th
Administrative	36th
Medical Service	36th
Other	36th

60th (mot) Infantry Division

Infantry Regiments	92nd and 120th (3 bns per regt; additional 8 single AA SP mounts and 2 quad SP mounts)
Panzerjäger Battalion	160th (2 SP Companies with 6 75mm PAK 40 and 6 LMGs; 1 mot company with 9 50mm PAK 38 and 6 LMGs)
Panzer Battalion	160th
Motorcycle Battalion	160th
Artillery Regiment	160th (same as 29th (Mot) Infantry Division)
Signals Battalion	160th
Pioneer Battalion	160th
Supply Train	160th
Administrative	160th
Medical Service	160th
Other	160th

ORGANIZATION OF A TYPE 1943 PANZERGRENADIER DIVISION, 24 SEPTEMBER 1943

Division Headquarters
- 1 Divisional Staff (2 LMGs)
- 1 (mot) Mapping Detachment

2 Panzergrenadier Regiments, each with
- 1 Panzergrenadier Regimental Staff
- 1 Panzergrenadier Regimental Staff Company
  - 1 Signals Platoon
  - 1 Heavy Panzerjäger Platoon (3 75mm PAK 40 and 3 LMGs)
  - 1 Motorcycle Platoon (6 LMGs)
- **3 Panzergrenadier Battalions**, each with
  - 3 (mot) Panzergrenadier Companies (4 HMGs, 18 LMGs and 2 80mm mortars ea)
  - 1 (mot) Heavy Company
    - 1 Heavy Panzerjäger Platoon (3 75mm PAK 40 and 3 LMGs)
    - 1 Heavy Mortar Platoon (4 120mm mortars)
- **1 Self-Propelled Flak Company** (12 Self-Propelled 20mm Flak guns)
- **1 (mot) Heavy Infantry Gun Company** (2 150mm sIG, 4 75mm leIG and 4 LMGs)
- **(mot) Engineer Company**
  - 3 Platoons (4 LMGs and 6 flamethrowers ea)

1 Armored Battalion
- 1 Battalion Staff
- **1st Battalion**
  - 1 Armored Battalion Staff
  - 1 Armored Battalion Staff Company
  - **3 Sturmgeschütz Companies** (14 StuG ea)
  - **1 Armored Maintenance Company**

(Self-propelled) Panzerjäger Battalion
- 1 (self-propelled) Battalion Headquarters
- 1 (self-propelled) Battalion Headquarters Company (6 LMGs)
- 1 (self-propelled) Platoon (3 self-propelled 75mm PAK 40)
- 1 (mot) Panzerjäger Company (motZ) (12 75mm PAK 40)
- 2 (self-propelled) Panzerjäger Companies (14 Marder I or Marder II 75mm gun carriages and 14 LMGs ea)
- 1 (mot) Flak Company (motZ) (12 20mm Flak guns and 4 LMGs)

Armored Reconnaissance Battalion
- 1 Armored Reconnaissance Battalion Staff (3 LMGs)
- 1st Armored Reconnaissance Company (normal organization; 24 LMGs and 18 20mm guns in 18 armored cars)
- 2nd–4th Motorcycle Companies (4 HMGs, 18 LMGs and 2 80mm mortars ea)
- 5th (mot) Armored Reconnaissance Company
  - 1 (mot) Pioneer Platoon (4 LMGs and 6 flamethrowers)

- 1 (mot) Heavy Panzerjäger Platoon (3 75mm PAK 40)
- 1 (mot) Infantry Gun Platoon (3 75mm leIG)
- 1 (mot) Supply Column (3 LMGs)

1 (mot) Artillery Regiment
- 1 (mot) Artillery Regimental Staff
- 1 (mot) Artillery Regimental Staff Company (2 LMGs)
- **1st (motZ) Battalion**
  - 1 (mot) Battalion Staff
  - 1 (mot) Battalion Staff Company (2 LMGs)
  - 3 (motZ) Batteries (4 105mm leFH and 5 LMGs ea)
- **2nd (motZ) Battalion**
  - 1 (mot) Battalion Staff
  - 1 (mot) Battalion Staff Company (2 LMGs)
  - 3 (motZ) Batteries (4 105mm leFH and 5 LMGs ea)
- **3rd (mot) Battalion**
  - 1 (mot) Battalion Staff
  - 1 (mot) Battalion Staff Company (2 LMGs)
  - 3 (motZ) Batteries (4 150mm sFH and 5 LMGs ea)

Army Flak Battalion
- 1 (mot) Flak Battalion Staff
- 1 (mot) Flak Battalion Staff Company (2 LMGs)
- 2 (mot) Heavy Flak Batteries (4 88mm, 3 20mm and 2 LMGs ea)
- 1 (mot or self-propelled) Light Flak Battery (12 20mm Flak guns and 2 LMGs)
- 1 (mot) Light Flak Supply Column

Armored Pioneer Battalion
- 1 Pioneer Battalion Staff
- 1 Pioneer Battalion Staff Company
- 3 (mot) Pioneer Companies (18 LMGs, 6 flamethrowers and 2 80mm mortars ea)
- 1 (mot) Brüko K Bridging Train

Armored Signals Battalion
- 1 (mot) Signals Battalion Staff
- 1 (mot) Telephone Company (6 LMGs)
- 1 (mot) Radio Company (4 LMGs)
- 1 (mot) Signals Supply Column (1 LMG)

Feldersatz Battalion
- 4 companies

Panzer Supply Troop
- 1 (mot) Supply Troop Regimental Headquarters (2 LMGs)
- 2 (mot) 120 ton Transportation Companies (8 LMGs ea)
- 3 (mot) 90ton Transportation Companies (6 LMGs ea)
- 1 (mot) Supply Company (8 LMGs)

Vehicle Maintenance Troop
- 2 (mot) Maintenance Companies (4 LMGs ea)
- 1 (mot) 75 ton Maintenance Supply Column

Administrative Services
1 (mot) Bakery Company (6 LMGs)
1 (mot) Butcher Company (4 LMGs)
1 (mot) Administration Platoon (2 LMGs)
Medical
2 (mot) Medical Companies (4 LMGs ea)

3 (mot) Ambulance Platoons (1 LMG ea)
Other
1 (mot) Military Police Detachment (2 LMGs)
1 (mot) Field Post Office

ORGANIZATION OF A TYPE 1944 PANZERGRENADIER DIVISION, 1 AUGUST 1944

Division Headquarters (23/10/57/101)[1]
1 Divisional Staff (2 LMGs)
1 Divisional Band
1 (mot) Mapping Detachment (0/0/1/7)
1 (mot) Military Police Detachment (3/0/41/20; 2 LMGs)
2 Panzergrenadier Regiments (75/9/528/2,495 ea)
1 Panzergrenadier Regimental Staff and Staff Company (8/26/118/152)
  1 Signals Platoon
  1 Heavy Panzerjäger Platoon (motZ) (1/0/4/27; 3 75mm PAK 40 and 3 LMGs)
  1 Motorcycle Platoon (6 LMGs)
  3 Panzergrenadier Battalions (20/3/148/697 ea)
1 (mot) Panzergrenadier Staff (4/0/9/29)
1 (mot) Panzergrenadier Supply Company (4 LMGs)
3 (mot) Panzergrenadier Companies (3/0/29/165; 4 HMGs, 18 LMGs, 2 80mm mortars ea)
1 (mot) Heavy Company (3/0/22/79)
  1 Heavy Company Staff
  1 Flak Platoon (motZ) (6 20mm Flak guns)
  1 (motZ) Heavy Mortar Platoon (4 120mm mortars)
  1 (mot) Heavy Infantry Gun Company (3/0/20/79; 4 150mm sIG and 4 LMGs)
  1 (mot) Pioneer Company (3/0/34/180)
  3 Platoons (2 HMGs, 12 LMGs, 2 80mm mortars and 18 flamethrowers)
1 Armored Battalion (21/4/224/353)
  1 Battalion Staff and Staff Company (fG) (7/0/28/93; 3 self-propelled quad 20mm, 3 PzBefWg IV with 50mm KwK 39 (L/60) and 4 armored cars)
  3 Sturmgeschütz Companies (fG) (3/0/42/19 ea; 14 StuG with 75mm StuK 40 L/48 ea)
  1 Armored Maintenance Company (1/3/22/86)
  1 (mot) Assault Gun Supply Company (fG) (4/1/48/117)
1 (self-propelled) Panzerjäger Battalion (17/3/145/310)
  1 (self-propelled) Battalion Staff and Staff Company (fG) (5/0/16/32; 6 LMGs)

1 Panzerjäger Platoon (3 PzJg IV with 75mm PAK 40)
1 Panzerjäger Company (motZ) (fG) (3/0/20/94; 12 75mm PAK 40 and 12 LMGs)
2 SP Anti-Tank Companies (fG) (3/0/32/22; 14 PzJg IV 75mm PAK 40 ea)
1 (mot) Mixed Panzerjäger Supply Company (fG) (3/3/45/140; 3 LMGs)
1 Armored Reconnaissance Battalion (23/3/185/794)
1 Reconnaissance Battalion Staff and Staff Company (fG) (7/0/34/82; 3 LMGs)
  1 Signals Platoon (7 LMGs)
  1 Armored Car Platoon (17 heavy or 20 light armored cars with 16 LMGs, 13 20mm KwK and 3 75mm K37)
3 (mot) (Volkswagen) Reconnaissance Companies (fG) (3/0/31/164 ea; 2 80mm mortars, 4 HMGs and 9 LMGs ea)
1 (mot) Reconnaissance Company (3/0/24/97)
  1 Pioneer Staff (fG) (4 LMGs)
  1 Pioneer Platoon (fG) (4 LMGs)
  1 Mortar Platoon (fG) (6 80mm mortars)
1 (mot) Supply Column (fG) (4/3/34/123; 3 LMGs)

Note: The administrative service group was reorganized from a (mot) Supply, Bakery, and Butcher Companies and Supply Staff with a 1 April 1944 organization date to the indicated organization.

1 (mot) Artillery Regiment (48/11/370/1,141)
  1 (mot) Artillery Regimental Staff and Company (7/2/22/61; 2 LMGs))
1st (motZ) Battalion (17/3/118/348)
  1 (mot) Battalion Staff and Staff Company (fG) (8/3/34/105; 2 LMGs and 3 20mm guns)
  3 (motZ) Batteries (fG) (3/0/28/81ea; 6 105mm leFH and 4 LMGs ea)
2nd (motZ) Battalion
  1 (mot) Battalion Staff and Staff Company (fG) (2 LMGs and 3 20mm guns)
  3 (motZ) Batteries (fG) (6 105mm leFH and 4 LMGs ea)
3rd (mot) Battalion (17/3/112/384)
  1 (mot) Battalion Staff and Staff Company (fG) (2 LMGs and 3 20mm guns)

---

[1] Numbers are officers, warrant officers, NCOs, and soldiers.

2 Heavy (mot) 150mm Batteries (3/0/27/100 ea; 6 150mm sFH and 4 LMGs ea)

1 Heavy (mot) 100mm Batteries (3/0/24/79; 6 100mm gun and 4 LMGs)

1 Army Flak Battalion (*either* 18/3/131/483 *or* 18/3/129/457)

    1 (mot) Flak Battalion Staff and Staff Company (fG) (2 LMGs)

    2 (motZ) Heavy Flak Batteries (fG) (4 88mm, 3 20mm and 2 LMGs ea)

    either 1 (motZ) Light Flak Battery (fG) (9 37mm Flak guns, 4 LMGs and 3 SP 20mm guns)

    or 1 Self-Propelled Light Flak Battery (motZ) (fG) (11 self-propelled 20mm guns)

    1 (mot) Light Flak Supply Column

1 (mot) Pioneer Battalion (17/3/114/699)

    1 (mot) Pioneer Battalion Staff (fG)

    3 (mot) Pioneer Companies (fG) (18 LMGs and 2 80mm mortars ea)

    1 (mot) Light Panzer Bridging Train (3 LMGs)

1 (mot) Signals Battalion (13/3/87/324)

    1 (mot) Signals Battalion Staff

    1 (mot) Telephone Company (5 LMGs)

    1 (mot) Radio Company (6 LMGs)

1 (mot) Signals Supply Column (2 LMGs)

1 Feldersatz Battalion (17/1/91/864)

    4 Companies (50 LMGs, 12 HMGs, 6 80mm mortars, 2 120mm mortars, 1 75mm PAK 40, 1 20mm Flak, 2 flamethrowers and 1 105mm leFH total)

    1 (mot) Supply Troop Regimental Staff (2 LMGs)

    3 (mot) 120 ton Transportation Companies (4 LMGs ea)

    1 (horse-drawn) 60 ton Transportation Companies (4 LMGs ea)

    1 (mot) Maintenance Company

Vehicle Maintenance Troop (5/6/40/230)

    2 (mot) Maintenance Companies (3 LMGs ea)

    1 (mot) 75 ton Maintenance Supply Column

Administrative Services (1/7/33/192)

    1 (mot) Supply Troop (3 LMGs)

    1 Bakery Platoon

    1 Butcher Platoon

    1 Administration Platoon

Medical (17/4/83/426)

    2 (mot) Medical Company (2 LMGs)

    1 (mot) Medical Supply Company (1 LMG)

Other (0/3/7/8)

    1 (mot) Field Post Office

8

German Light Divisions, 1939–1940

The six Light Divisions were formed as a politically acceptable interim formation as the cavalry evolved completely into armored formations. It must be understood that the cavalry had been the senior arm of the German army since time immemorial. Theey had been the sole reserve of the nobility and were descended from the armored knights of the middle and dark ages. They were a symbol and an institution.

Despite the diminutive size of the cavalry arm, it contained all the aristocrats who were anyone of note. It was the senior arm of the Wehrmacht and fought tenaciously for its place. It would not be put aside by these upstarts in rolling steel boxes, no matter how good they thought they were. As a result of this intransigence, the Wehrmacht high command developed a compromise formation, the Light Division.

The Light Divisions fit nicely into the model of the dragoon. This was a cavalry man who rode into battle, but then dismounted and fought on foot. The cavalry regiments were converted into *"Kavallerie Schützen"* Regiments, simply replacing the dragoon's horse with a truck.

The Light Division satisfied the cavalry, but it was not permitted to last very long once the Polish campaign had been completed. The panzer division had proved its worth, and in October 1939 the Light Divisions were all quickly re-equipped as Panzer Divisions, ending the political experiment.

1st Light Division

In October 1937 the 1st Light Brigade was formed. On 1 April 1938 it became the 1st Light Division, but it was not formed until 10 November 1938 in Wuppertal. On that date the organization of the armored portion of the division was as follows:

65th Panzer Battalion
  1 (mot) Panzer Signals Platoon
  1 Light Panzer Staff Platoon
  4 Light Panzer Companies

On 1 August 1939 it mobilized and contained:

1/, 2/, 3/4th Kavallerie Schützen Regiment
6th Kradschützen (Motorcycle) Battalion
65th Panzer Battalion
1/, 2/76th Artillery Regiment
6th Reconnaissance Battalion
41st Panzerabwehr (AT) Battalion
82nd Signals Battalion
57th Pioneer Battalion
57th Divisional Service Units

OKH records show that when the Germans invaded Poland on 1 September 1939 the 1st Light Division was organized and equipped as follows:

1st Light Division Generalmajor von Loeper
  57th (mot) Mapping Detachment
  57th Motorcycle Platoon
4th Kavallerie Schützen Regiment
  1 (mot) Supply Column
  1 Motorcycle Platoon
  1st, 2nd and 3rd (mot) Battalions, each with
    1 (mot) Pioneer Platoon (3 LMGs)
    3 (mot) Rifle Companies (18 LMGs, 2 HMGs and
      3 50mm mortars ea)
    1 (mot) Heavy Company
      1 Machine Gun Platoon (8 HMGs)
      1 Mortar Platoon (6 80mm mortars)
      1 Panzerabwehr Platoon (3 37mm PAK 36 and 1
        LMG)
    1 (mot) Light Supply Column
6th Motorcycle Battalion
  3 Motorcycle Companies (18 LMGs, 2 HMGs and 3
    50mm mortars ea)
  1 (mot) Heavy Company
    1 Machine Gun Platoon (8 HMGs)
    1 Mortar Platoon (6 80mm mortars)
    1 Panzerabwehr Platoon (3 37mm PAK 36 and 1
      LMG)
  1 (mot) Light Supply Column
1/6th Reconnaissance Regiment
  1 (mot) Battalion Signals Platoon (2 LMGs)

1 Motorcycle Company (9 LMGs, 4 HMGs and 3 50mm mortars)

2 Armored Car Companies (10 20mm and 25 LMGs ea)

1 (mot) Heavy Company
  1 Infantry Gun Section (2 75mm leIG ea)
  1 Pioneer Platoon (3 LMGs)
  1 Panzerabwehr Platoon (3 37mm PAK 36 and 1 LMG)

1 (mot) Supply Column (3 LMGs)

65th Panzer Battalion

1 (mot) Signals Platoon
1 Staff Tank Platoon
3 Light Panzer Companies
1 (mot) Reserve Platoon
1 (mot) Maintenance Platoon
1 (mot) Light Panzer Supply Column

11th Panzer Regiment

1 Panzer Signals Platoon
1 Staff Tank Platoon
1st and 2nd Panzer Battalions, each with
  1 Panzer Signals Platoon
  1 Staff Tank Platoon
  3 Light Panzer Companies
  1 (mot) Reserve Platoon
  1 (mot) Maintenance Platoon
  1 (mot) Light Panzer Supply Column

76th Artillery Regiment

1 (mot) Signals Platoon
1 (mot) Weather Detachment
1st and 2nd (mot) Battalions, each with
  1 (mot) Signals Platoon
  1 (mot) Calibration Detachment
  3 (mot) Batteries (4 105mm leFH and 2 LMGs ea)

41st Panzerabwehr Battalion

1 (mot) Signals Platoon
3 (mot) Panzerabwehr Companies (12 37mm PAK 36 and 6 LMGs ea)
3/46th Heavy Machine Gun Battalion (12 20mm)

57th Pioneer Battalion

2 Pioneer Companies (9 LMGs ea)
1 (mot) Pioneer Company (9 LMGs)
1 (mot) Brüko B
1 (mot) Engineer Supply Column

82nd Signals Battalion

1 (mot) Panzer Radio Company (13 LMGs)
1 (mot) Panzer Signals Company (2 LMGs)
1 (mot) Light Signals Column

57th Divisional Service Units

1–6/57th (mot) Light Supply Columns
7–9/57th (mot) Heavy Fuel Columns
1–3/57th (mot) Maintenance Companies
57th (mot) Supply Column

Administration

57th Divisional Administration
57th (mot) Field Bakery
57th (mot) Butcher Detachment

Other

1/, 2/57th (mot) Medical Companies
57th (mot) Field Hospital
1/, 2/57th Ambulance Companies
57th Veterinarian Company
57th (mot) Military Police Troop
57th (mot) Field Post Office

The actual tank returns were as follows:

1/, 2/11th Panzer Regiment
PzMk II	45
38 (t)	74
PzMk IV	27
PzBefWg 35(t)	6

65th Panzer Battalion
PzMk II	20
35 (t)	37
PzMk IV	14
PzBefWg 35(t)	2

The tank inventory on 25 September 1939 was:

PzMk I	0
PzMk II	8
35 (t)	77
PzMk IV	9
PzBefWg	0

The division also had the 76th Luftwaffe Light Flak Battalion attached to it. The battalion contained:

76th Luftwaffe Light Flak Battalion
  1 (mot) Signals Platoon
  2 (mot) Light Flak Batteries (12 20mm ea)
  1 (mot) Medium Flak Batteries (9 37mm)
  1 (mot) Light Flak Supply Column

At full strength the division had 302 officers, 101 warrant officers, 1,485 NCOs, and 8,047 soldiers. On 18 October 1939 the division was reorganized into the 6th Panzer Division.

2nd Light Division

Formed 10 November 1938 in Gera. On 19 August 1939 it was mobilized with:

1/, 2/6th Kavallerie Schützen Regiment
1/, 2/7th Kavallerie Schützen Regiment
1/, 2/7th Reconnaissance Regiment
66th Panzer Battalion
  1 (mot) Panzer Signals Platoon
  1 Light Panzer Staff Platoon
  4 Light Panzer Companies
1/, 2/78th Artillery Regiment
58th Reconnaissance Battalion
42nd Panzerabwehr (AT) Battalion
83rd Signals Battalion
58th Pioneer Battalion
58th Divisional Service Units

At full strength the division had 353 officers, 106 warrant officers, 1,717 NCOs, and 9,336 men. OKH records show that when the Germans invaded Poland on 1 September 1939 the 2nd Light Division was organized and equipped as follows:

2nd Light Division Generalleutnant Stumme
  58th (mot) Mapping Detachment
  58th Motorcycle Platoon
6th Kavallerie Schützen Regiment
  1 (mot) Supply Column
  1 Motorcycle Platoon
  1st and 2nd (mot) Battalions, each with
    1 (mot) Pioneer Platoon (3 LMGs)
    3 (mot) Rifle Companies (12 LMGs, 4 HMGs and 3 50mm mortars ea)
    1 (mot) Heavy Company
    2 Infantry Gun Sections (2 75mm leIG ea)
    1 Mortar Platoon (6 80mm mortars)
    1 Panzerabwehr Platoon (3 37mm PAK 36 and 1 LMG)
    1 (mot) Light Supply Column
1/, 2/7th Kavallerie Schützen Regiment
same as 6th Kavallerie Schützen Regiment
1/7th (motorcycle) Reconnaissance Regiment
  1 (mot) Pioneer Platoon (3 LMGs)
  3 Motorcycle Companies (18 LMGs, 4 HMGs and 3 50mm mortars ea)
  1 (mot) Heavy Company
    2 Infantry Gun Sections (2 75mm leIG ea)
    1 Mortar Platoon (6 80mm mortars)
    1 Panzerabwehr Platoon (3 37mm PAK 36 and 1 LMG)
  1 (mot) Supply Column (3 LMGs)
2/7th (armored car) Reconnaissance Regiment
  1 (mot) Signals Platoon (2 LMGs)

3 Armored Car Companies (10 20mm and 25 LMGs ea)
33rd Panzer Battalion
  1 (mot) Signals Platoon
  1 Staff Tank Platoon
  3 Light Panzer Companies
  1 (mot) Reserve Platoon
  1 (mot) Maintenance Platoon
  1 (mot) Light Panzer Supply Column
102nd Artillery Regiment
  1 (mot) Signals Platoon
  1 (mot) Weather Detachment
  1st and 2nd (mot) Battalions, each with
    1 (mot) Signals Platoon
    1 (mot) Calibration Detachment
    3 (mot) Batteries (4 105mm leFH and 2 LMGs ea)
42nd Panzerabwehr Battalion
  1 (mot) Signals Platoon
  3 (mot) Panzerabwehr Companies (12 37mm PAK 36 and 6 LMGs ea)
  3/59th Heavy Machine Gun Battalion (12 20mm)
58th Pioneer Battalion
  2 Pioneer Companies (9 LMGs ea)
  1 (mot) Pioneer Company (9 LMGs)
  1 (mot) Brüko B
  1 (mot) Engineer Supply Column
Signals
  3/29th Signals Battalion
58th Divisional Service Units
  1–6/60th (mot) Light Supply Columns
  7/, 8/60th (mot) Heavy Fuel Columns
  1–3/60th (mot) Maintenance Companies
  60th (mot) Supply Column
Administration
  58th Divisional Administration
  58th (mot) Field Bakery
  58th (mot) Butcher Detachment
Other
  1/, 2/58th Medical Companies
  58th (mot) Field Hospital
  1/, 2/58th Ambulance Companies
  58th Veterinarian Company
  58th (mot) Military Police Troop
  58th (mot) Field Post Office

After Poland was crushed, on 18 October 1939, the division was reorganized into the 7th Panzer Division.

3rd Light Division

Formed on 10 November 1938 in Cottbus. On 28 August 1939 it mobilized with:

1/, 2/8th Kavallerie Schützen Regiment (less staff)
1/9th Kavallerie Schützen Regiment
2/9th (motorcycle) Kavallerie Schützen Regiment
1/, 2/8th Reconnaissance Regiment (1/8th detached to 10th Panzer Division)
67th Panzer Battalion
1/, 2/80th Artillery Regiment
43rd Panzerabwehr (AT) Battalion
84th Divisional Signals Battalion
59th Pioneer Battalion
59th Divisional Service Units

At full strength the division had 332 officers, 105 warrant officers, 1,616 NCOs, and 8,719 men. OKH records show that when the Germans invaded Poland, on 1 September 1939, the 3rd Light Division was organized and equipped as follows:

3rd Light Division Generalmajor Kuntzen
    59th (mot) Mapping Detachment
    59th Motorcycle Platoon
8th Kavallerie Schützen Regiment
    1 (mot) Supply Column
    1 Motorcycle Platoon
    1st and 2nd (mot) Battalions, each with
        1 (mot) Pioneer Platoon (3 LMGs)
        3 (mot) Rifle Companies (18 LMGs, 2 HMGs and 3 50mm mortars ea)
        1 (mot) Heavy Company
            1 Machine Gun Platoon (8 HMGs)
            1 Mortar Platoon (6 80mm mortars)
            1 Panzerabwehr Platoon (3 37mm PAK 36 and 1 LMG)
        1 (mot) Light Supply Column
9th Kavallerie Schützen Regiment
    1 (mot) Supply Column
    1 Motorcycle Platoon
    1st (mot) Battalion
        1 (mot) Pioneer Platoon (3 LMGs)
        3 (mot) Rifle Companies (18 LMGs, 2 HMGs and 3 50mm mortars ea)
        1 (mot) Heavy Company
            1 Machine Gun Platoon (8 HMGs)
            1 Mortar Platoon (6 80mm mortars)
            1 Panzerabwehr Platoon (3 37mm PAK 36 and 1 LMG)
        1 (mot) Light Supply Column
    2nd (Motorcycle) Battalion
        3 Motorcycle Companies (18 LMGs, 2 HMGs and 3 50mm mortars ea)

    1 (mot) Heavy Company
        1 Machine Gun Platoon (8 HMGs)
        1 Mortar Platoon (6 80mm mortars)
        1 Panzerabwehr Platoon (3 37mm PAK 36 and 1 LMG)
    1 (mot) Light Supply Column
1/8th (motorcycle) Reconnaissance Regiment
    1 (mot) Regimental Signals Platoon
    1 (mot) Battalion Signals Platoon
    1 Motorcycle Company (18 LMGs, 4 HMGs and 3 50mm mortars)
    2 Armored Car Companies (10 20mm and 25 LMGs ea)
    1 (mot) Heavy Company
        1 Infantry Gun Section (2 75mm leIG ea)
        1 Pioneer Platoon (3 LMGs)
        1 Panzerabwehr Platoon (3 37mm PAK 36 and 1 LMG)
    1 (mot) Supply Column (3 LMGs)
67th Panzer Battalion
    1 (mot) Signals Platoon
    1 Staff Tank Platoon
    3 Light Panzer Companies
    1 (mot) Reserve Platoon
    1 (mot) Maintenance Platoon
    1 (mot) Light Panzer Supply Column
80th Artillery Regiment
    1 (mot) Signals Platoon
    1 (mot) Weather Detachment
    1st and 2nd (mot) Battalions, each with
        1 (mot) Signals Platoon
        1 (mot) Calibration Detachment
        3 (mot) Batteries (4 105mm leFH and 2 LMGs ea)
43rd Panzerabwehr Battalion
    1 (mot) Signals Platoon
    3 (mot) Panzerabwehr Companies (12 37mm PAK 36 and 6 LMGs ea)
    4/48th Heavy Machine Gun Battalion (12 20mm)
59th Pioneer Battalion
    2 Pioneer Companies (9 LMGs ea)
    1 (mot) Pioneer Company (9 LMGs)
    1 (mot) Brüko B
    1 (mot) Engineer Supply Column
Signals
    4/3rd Signals Battalion
58th Divisional Service Units
    1–6/59th (mot) Light Supply Columns
    7/, 8/59th (mot) Heavy Fuel Columns
    1–3/59th (mot) Maintenance Companies
    59th (mot) Supply Column
Administration
    59th Divisional Administration
    59th (mot) Field Bakery

59th (mot) Butcher Detachment
Other
1/, 2/59th (mot) Medical Companies
59th (mot) Field Hospital
1/, 2/59th Ambulance Companies
59th Veterinarian Company
59th (mot) Military Police Troop
59th (mot) Field Post Office

In addition, the Luftwaffe had the 3.(H)/41 Reconnaissance Staffel assigned to the division to provide it with artillery observation and other reconnaissance support. The actual tank inventory on 1 September 1939 was:

67th Panzer Battalion
PzMk II   45
38 (t)   55
PzBefWg 35(t)   2

On 16 October 1939, after Poland had been crushed, the division was reorganized as the 8th Panzer Division.

4th Light Division

Formed in Vienna on 1 April 1938. On 19 August 1939 it mobilized with:

1/, 2/10th Kavallerie Schützen Regiment
1/, 2/11th Kavallerie Schützen Regiment
1/9th Reconnaissance Regiment
2/9th (motorcycle) Reconnaissance Regiment
33rd Panzer Battalion
  1 (mot) Panzer Signals Platoon
  1 Light Panzer Staff Platoon
  4 Light Panzer Companies
1/, 2/102nd Artillery Regiment
50th Panzerabwehr (AT) Battalion
86th Pioneer Battalion
85th Signals Battalion
60th Divisional Service Units

At full strength the division had 346 officers, 106 warrant officers, 1,685 NCOs, and 9,170 soldiers. OKH records show that when the Germans invaded Poland on 1 September 1939 the 4th Light Division was organized and equipped as follows:

4th Light Division Generalmajor Hubicki
  60th (mot) Mapping Detachment
  60th Motorcycle Platoon
10th Kavallerie Schützen Regiment
  1 (mot) Supply Column
  1 Motorcycle Platoon
  1st and 2nd (mot) Battalions, each with
    1 (mot) Pioneer Platoon (3 LMGs)
    3 (mot) Rifle Companies (12 LMGs, 4 HMGs and 3 50mm mortars ea)
    1 (mot) Heavy Company
    2 Infantry Gun Sections (2 75mm leIG ea)
    1 Mortar Platoon (6 80mm mortars)
    1 Panzerabwehr Platoon (3 37mm PAK 36 and 1 LMG)
    1 (mot) Light Supply Column

1/, 2/11th Kavallerie Schützen Regiment
  same as 10th Kavallerie Schützen Regiment
1/9th (motorcycle) Reconnaissance Regiment
  1 (mot) Pioneer Platoon (3 LMGs)
  3 Motorcycle Companies(18 LMGs, 4 HMGs and 3 50mm mortars)
  1 (mot) Heavy Company
    2 Infantry Gun Sections (2 75mm leIG ea)
    1 Mortar Platoon (6 80mm mortars)
    1 Panzerabwehr Platoon (3 37mm PAK 36 and 1 LMG)
  1 (mot) Supply Column (3 LMGs)
2/9th (armored car) Reconnaissance Regiment
  1 (mot) Signals Platoon (2 LMGs)
  3 Armored Car Companies (10 20mm and 25 LMGs ea)
33rd Panzer Battalion
  1 (mot) Signals Platoon
  1 Staff Tank Platoon
  3 Light Panzer Companies
  1 (mot) Reserve Platoon
  1 (mot) Maintenance Platoon
  1 (mot) Light Panzer Supply Column
102nd Artillery Regiment
  1 (mot) Signals Platoon
  1 (mot) Weather Detachment
  1st and 2nd (mot) Battalions, each with
    1 (mot) Signals Platoon
    1 (mot) Calibration Detachment
    3 (mot) Batteries (4 105mm leFH and 2 LMGs ea)
50th Panzerabwehr Battalion
  1 (mot) Signals Platoon
  3 (mot) Panzerabwehr Companies (12 37mm PAK 36 and 6 LMGs ea)
86th Pioneer Battalion
  2 Pioneer Companies (9 LMGs ea)
  1 (mot) Pioneer Company (9 LMGs)
  1 (mot) Brüko B
  1 (mot) Engineer Supply Column

Signals

3/38th Signals Battalion

60th Divisional Service Units

1–6/60th (mot) Light Supply Columns

7/, 8/60th (mot) Heavy Fuel Columns

1–3/60th (mot) Maintenance Companies

60th (mot) Supply Column

Administration

60th Divisional Administration

60th (mot) Field Bakery

60th (mot) Butcher Detachment

Other

1/, 2/60th Medical Companies

60th (mot) Field Hospital

1/, 2/60th Ambulance Companies

60th Veterinarian Company

60th (mot) Military Police Troop

60th (mot) Field Post Office

In addition, the 94th Luftwaffe Light Flak Battalion was attached to the division. It contained:

94th Luftwaffe Light Flak Battalion

1 (mot) Medium Flak Battery (9 37mm guns)

2 (mot) Light Flak Batteries (12 20mm guns ea)

20th (mot) Flak Supply Column

The actual tank inventory on 1 September 1939 was:

33rd Panzer Battalion

PzMk I   34

PzMk II   23

PzBefWg   5

On 3 January 1940 the division was reorganized as the 9th Panzer Division.

5th Light Division

The division was formed on 18 February 1941 from troops sent to Africa, part of the 3rd Panzer Division and the two army machine gun battalions. The division had:

Division Staff (from Staff 3rd Panzer brigade)

Infantry Regiment z.b.V. 200

2nd Army Machine Gun Battalion (army troops)

8th Army Machine Gun Battalion (army troops)

3rd Reconnaissance Battalion (from 3rd Panzer Division)

1/, 2/5th Panzer Regiment (from 3rd Panzer Division)

39th Panzerjäger Battalion (from 3rd Panzer Division)

1/75th Artillery Regiment (from 3rd Panzer Division)

605th Panzerjäger Battalion (from 3rd Army Troops)

606th Flak Battalion (from 3rd Army Troops)

The Infantry Regiment z.b.V. 200 was redesignated as the 200th Schützen (Rifle) Regiment shortly after the division was organized. When the division arrived in Africa it contained 25 Pz Ib, 45 Pz II, 75 Pz III, and 20 Pz IV tanks. In early February 1941 the 5th Light (mot) Division was organized as follows:

Divisional Staff

3/39th (Mot) Signals Battalion

1 (mot) Radio Company

200th (mot) Mapping Platoon

200th Printing Detachment

5th Panzer Regiment

2 Light Panzer Platoons (5 Pz I and 5 Pz II total)

1 Armored Signal Platoon (1 Pz III and 3 command tanks)

1 Regimental Band

1st Battalion

1 Staff Panzer Company (1 Pz III and 2 command tanks)

1 Light Panzer Platoon (5 Pz II)

1 Medium Panzer Company (5 Pz I, 5 Pz II and 10 Pz IV)

2 Light Panzer Companies (5 Pz II and 17 Pz III ea)

1 Light Panzer Supply Column

2nd Battalion

1 Staff Panzer Company (1 Pz III and 2 command tanks)

1 Light Panzer Platoon (5 Pz II)

1 Medium Panzer Company (5 Pz I, 5 Pz II and 10 Pz IV)

2 Light Panzer Companies (5 Pz II and 17 Pz III ea)

1 Light Panzer Supply Column

Attached

1 (mot) Reserve Detachment

1 (mot) Armored Maintenance Company

200th Schützen Regiment

1 (mot) Signals Platoon

2nd (mot) Machine Gun Battalion

1 (mot) Signals Platoon

1 Motorcycle Company (8 LMGs)

3 (mot) Machine Gun Companies (12 HMGs, 3 50mm mortars and 3 PzBu39 ea)

1 (mot) Heavy Company, with

1 Anti-Tank Platoon (6 37mm PAK 36 and 2 LMGs)

1 Mortar Section (6 80mm mortars)

2 (mot) Pioneer Companies (9 LMGs ea)

8th (mot) Machine Gun Battalion

1 (mot) Signals Platoon

1 Motorcycle Company (8 LMGs)

3 (mot) Machine Gun Companies (12 LMGs, 3 50mm Mortars and 3 PzBu39 ea)

1 (mot) Support Company (no heavy weapons)

1 Anti-Tank Company (6 37mm PAK 36 and 2 LMGs)

1 Mortar Section (6 80mm mortars)

1 (mot) Support Company (9 37mm PAK 36 and 3 LMGs)

1 (mot) Pioneer Company (9 LMGs)

3rd Reconnaissance Battalion

1 Light Armored Car Company (1 zug had Volkswagen kubelwagens) (10 37mm tank guns and 25 LMGs)

1 Motorcycle Company (3 50mm mortars, 2 PzBu39 and 18 LMGs)

1 (mot) Heavy Company, with
1 Pioneer Platoon (3 LMGs)
1 Panzerjäger Platoon (3 37mm PAK 36 and 1 LMG)

1 Infantry Support Gun Section (2 75mm guns)

1 (mot) Light Supply Column (3 LMGs)

1/75th Artillery Regiment

Battalion Headquarters
1 (mot) Signal Detachment
1 (mot) Calibration Detachment
3 (motZ) Batteries (4 105mm leFH18 guns)

1/33rd Flak Regiment

1 Battalion Staff Section
Signals Section
2 (mot) Light Batteries (4 20mm guns ea)
3 (mot) Heavy Batteries (4 88mm guns ea)
1 Light (horse-drawn) Supply Column

606th Self-Propelled Flak Battalion

1 Self-Propelled Staff Section
3 Self-Propelled Flak Companies (12 20mm ea)

Luftwaffe

2.(H)/14 Panzer Reconnaissance Staffel

605th Panzerjäger Battalion

1 Armored Staff Section
1 (mot) Signals Detachment
3 Self-Propelled Panzerjäger Companies (9 47mm Czech PAK guns on PzMk I chassis ea)

39th (Mot) Panzerjäger Battalion

1 (mot) Staff Section
3 (mot) Panzerjäger Companies (9 37mm, 2 50mm PAK 38 and 6 LMGs ea)

Support Troops

Staff/683rd (mot) Loading Special Employment Battalion

Staff/681st (mot) Unloading Special Employment Battalion

688th (mot) Supply Commander z.b.V.
1 (mot) Light Supply Column
641st (mot) Heavy Water Column
1 (mot) Panzer Replacement Column
588th (mot) Munition Column

129th (mot) Motor Vehicle Repair Company
122nd (mot) Motor Vehicle Repair Company
1 (mot) Supply Battalion (3 companies)
619th (mot) Supply Battalion
797th (mot) Light Supply Column
800th (mot) Light Supply Column
801st (mot) Light Supply Column
803rd (mot) Light Supply Column
804th (mot) Light Supply Column
822nd (mot) Light Supply Column
5/619th (mot) Heavy Supply Column
6/619th (mot) Heavy Supply Column
622nd (mot) Heavy Supply Column
533rd (mot) Supply Battalion
6 (mot) Heavy Supply Columns
1 (mot) Heavy Fuel Column
1 (mot) Maintenance Platoon
735th (mot) Field Post Office
309th (mot) Military Police Platoon
631st (mot) Ambulance Company
633rd (mot) Ambulance Company
4/572nd (mot) Field Hospital
1/83rd (mot) Medical Company
877th (mot) Medical Supply Column
645th (mot) Water Column
503rd (mot) Butcher Section
531st (mot) Bakery Section
341st (mot) Administration Section

On 31 March the division was organized as follows:

Division Staff

1 Intelligence Company
3/39th Reconnaissance Battalion (1 company)

5th Panzer Regiment

1st Panzer Abteilung
1 Medium Armored Company
2 Light Armored Companies
2nd Panzer Abteilung
1 Medium Armored Company
2 Light Armored Companies

Total tanks: 25 Pz Ib, 45 Pz II, 71 Pz III and 20 Pz IV

(mot) Infantry

200th Schützen Regimental Staff
2nd Machine Gun Battalion
3 Companies (12 HMGs, 3 50mm mortars and 3 PzBu39 ea)
Motorcycle Company (8 LMGs)
Intelligence Platoon
Heavy Weapons Company (6 37mm PAK 36, 6 80mm mortars and 2 LMGs)
Intelligence Platoon
8th Machine Gun Battalion
3 Companies (12 HMG, 3 50mm mortars and 3 PzBu39 ea)

Motorcycle Company (8 LMGs)

Intelligence Platoon

HeavyWeapons Company (6 37mm PAK 36, 6 80mm mortars and 2 LMGs)

Panzerjäger Company (9 37mm PAK 36 and 3 LMGs)

1/75th Artillery Regiment

3 Batteries (4 105mm guns ea)

39th Panzerjäger Battalion

3 Companies (3 50mm PAK 38, 8 37mm PAK 36 and 6 LMGs ea)

605th Self-Propelled Heavy Panzerjäger Battalion

3 Companies (9 47mm Czech AT guns mounted on Panzer Ib ea)

3rd Reconnaissance Battalion

1 Pioneer Platoon

Armored Car Company (10 heavy and 15 light armored cars ea)

1 VW platoon

1 Motorcycle Company (18 LMGs, 2 HMGs and 3 50mm mortars)

1 Heavy Support Company (2 75mm leIG and 3 37mm PAK 36 guns)

606th Flak Battalion

3 Companies (12 20mm AA guns ea)

Pioneer Battalion z.b.V. 200

5th Pioneer Company/2nd Machine Gun Battalion (on 12 Feb. 1942 became 2/39th Panzer Pioneer Battalion)

6th Pioneer Company/2nd Machine Gun Battalion (on 25 Feb. 1942 became 2/33rd Panzer Pioneer Battalion)

6th Pioneer Company/8th Machine Gun Battalion

Attached

1/33rd Luftwaffe AA Regiment, with

3 88mm AA Batteries (4 88mm guns ea)

2 20mm AA Batteries (12 20mm guns ea)

Support Troops

619th Supply Troop

3 large truck columns

6 small truck columns

2 water columns

1 filter column

532nd Supply Troop

3 Companies

Medical Service

2 Medical Companies

1 Field Hospital

2 Ambulance Sections

Ordinance Service Section

Field Post Office

The three (mot) pioneer companies were later organized into the 200th z.b.V. Pioneer Battalion. In May 1940 the organization of the 5th Panzer Regiment was as follows:

1/, 2/5th Panzer Regiment

1 Regimental Staff Signals Platoon

1 Regimental Staff Light Panzer Platoon

each Battalion had

1 Panzer Staff Company

1 Medium Panzer Company

2 Light Panzer Companies

Total tank inventory:

PzMk I	25
PzMk II	45
PzMk III (50)	71
PzMk IV	20
PzBefWg	7

On 1 August 1941 this force was formed into the 21st Panzer Division and the Staff 200th Infantry Regiment and the 2nd Machine Gun Battalion were sent to the 15th Panzer Division.

9

Organizational History of German Cavalry and Bicycle Formations, 1939–1945

Though technological innovation had made the cavalry charge obsolete by the time of the American Civil War, cavalry continued to exist and to operate as though time had not changed until the early days of World War I. True, on the eastern front cavalry could still operate much as it had in the previous century, but its day was clearly past. Germany entered the war with a Guard and nine sequentially numbered cavalry divisions. In 1914 a typical cavalry division was organized as follows:

5th Cavalry Division
  9th Cavalry Brigade
    1/, 2/, 3/, 4/4th Dragoon Regiment
    1/, 2/, 3/, 4/10th Uhlan Regiment
  10th Cavalry Brigade
    1/, 2/, 3/, 4/1st (Leib) Cuirassier Regiment
    1/, 2/, 3/, 4/8th Dragoon Regiment
  12th Cavalry Brigade
    1/, 2/, 3/, 4/4th Hussar Regiment
    1/, 2/, 3/, 4/6th Hussar Regiment
  Attached
    1st Machine Gun Battalion
    Guard Schützen Battalion
      Infantry Company
      Bicycle Company
      Machine Gun Section
  Artillery
    Horse Battalion, 5th Field Artillery Regiment (3 batteries; 4 77mm guns ea)
  Divisional Troops
    Signals Battalion
    Pioneer Battalion
    Vehicle Column

The Treaty of Versailles reduced the German cavalry to a single brigade. When Germany entered World War II it still had a single brigade of cavalry, but it was not mobilized until after the Polish campaign had been completed. When it was mobilized, on 14 February 1940, it was expanded into a full division. Its performance in the French campaign was modest, and, with the demand for the optimal utilization of manpower, it was converted into a Panzer Division in November 1941.

However, the cavalry was not to disappear from the German army. With the invasion of Russia cavalry once again had room to maneuver and could assume the role of dragoons. In fact, the shortage of motor vehicles and the large numbers of horses made mounting some units a reasonable proposition once again.

Germany responded by forming the 8th SS Cavalry Division "Florian Geyer" in September 1942. The SS would form the 22nd SS Freiwilligen Cavalry Division in April 1944 and the 27th SS Cavalry Division in February 1945. The next cavalry division formed in the Wehrmacht was, in fact, formed with Russians, or, to be more precise, Cossacks. The SS and Cossack divisions, however, will be covered in future volumes.

The Russian front continued to be a source for forming cavalry units. In 1942 the Cavalry Regiment Mitte was formed. It eventually expanded into a brigade and then the 3rd Cavalry Division, though the division was very short-lived and probably never fully formed. The same process produced a 4th Cavalry Division and the Nord Cavalry Division, though these were equally short-lived.

The search for mobility outside the confines of the gasoline-powered vehicle continued and even led to an extensive use of bicycles late in the war. Though most of the bicycles were assigned to the fusilier battalions of the infantry divisions, one larger formation, the Norwegian Bicycle Reconnaissance Brigade, was formed in April 1944.

1st Cavalry Brigade

Formed on 1 October 1934 as the 5th Reiter Brigade. On 1 April 1936, as it was the only cavalry brigade, it was renumbered as the 1st Cavalry Brigade. On 1 August 1939 it was mobilized with the 1st Reiter Regiment, 2nd Reiter

Regiment, 1st Bicycle Battalion, 1st Horse Artillery Battalion, and 40th Brigade Support Units. The brigade weapon allocations were as follows:

2 Reiter Regiments, each with
1 Staff and (tmot) Signals Platoon
1 (mot) Staff Squadron
  1 Cavalry Armored Car Platoon (3 armored cars)
  1 (mot) Pioneer Platoon (3 LMGs)
  1 (motZ) Panzer Abwehr Platoon (3 37mm PAK 36 and 1 LMG)
1–4th Reiter Squadrons (9 LMGs and 4 HMGs ea)
5th (heavy) Squadron
  2 Cavalry Gun Platoons (2 75mm leIG each)
  1 Cavalry Mortar Platoon (6 80mm mortars)
1 Light Cavalry Column

(tmot) Bicycle Battalion
1 (tmot) Staff and (mot) Signals Platoon
3 Bicycle Squadrons (9 LMGs, 4 HMGs and 3 50mm mortars ea)
1 (mot) Heavy Squadron
  2 (motZ) Cavalry Platoons (2 75mm leIG ea)
  1 (mot) Cavalry Mortar Platoon (6 80mm mortars)
  1 (mot) Cavalry Panzer Abwehr Platoon (3 37mm PAK 36 and 1 LMG)

(motZ) Panzer Abwehr Company (12 37mm PAK 36 and 6 LMGs)
(motZ) Machine Gun Company (12 20mm Flak guns)
Horse Artillery Battalion
1 Staff, Signals Platoon, Artillery Direction Troop and Weather Troop
3 Horse Batteries (4 75mm FK and 2 LMGs ea)
1 15 ton Light Artillery Column
(mot) Pioneer Company (9 LMGs), plus:
1 (mot) C Bridging Column
(tmot) Signals Company:
Supply Service:
1 Cavalry Brigade Supply Staff
2 Light (30 ton) Transportation Companies
2 Transportation Columns
1 Light Fuel Column
1 Vehicle Maintenance Platoon
1 Supply Platoon
Administrative Bureau
Medical Service
1 (mot) Medical Company
1 Ambulance
Other
1 Veterinary Company
1 (mot) Field Post Office

On 25 October 1939 the 1st Cavalry Brigade was expanded into a division-sized organization, though it was not formally called a division. It contained:

Division Command:
40th Motorcycle Messenger Platoon
40th (mot) Divisional Mapping Detachment
Brigade Command
Motorcycle Messenger Platoon
21st and 22nd Reiter (Cavalry) Regiments, each with
1 (semi-mot) Regimental Staff and Signals Platoon
1 (mot) Regimental Staff Squadron, with
  Cavalry Armored Car Detachment (3 armored cars)
  1 (mot) Cavalry Engineer Platoon (3 LMGs)
  1 (motZ) Cavalry Panzerjäger Platoon (3 37mm PAK 36 and 1 LMG)
4 Cavalry Squadrons (9 LMGs and 4 HMGs ea)
5th Heavy Cavalry Squadron
  2 Cavalry Gun Platoons (2 75mm leIG guns)
  1 Cavalry Mortar Platoon (6 80mm Mortars)
1 Light Cavalry Column

1 (tmot) Bicycle Battalion, with
1 (semi-mot) Staff and Signals Platoon
3 Bicycle Squadrons (9 LMGs, 4 HMGs, 3 50mm Mortars)
1 (mot) Heavy Squadron
  2 (mot) Infantry Gun Platoons (2 75mm leIG guns ea)
  1 Cavalry Mortar Platoon (6 80mm mortars)
  1 (mot) Cavalry Anti-Tank Platoon (3 37mm PAK 36)

2nd Reiter (Mounted) Artillery Battalion, with
1 Staff
1 Signals Platoon
1 Artillery Survey Detachment
1 (mot) Weather Detachment
3 Horse Batteries (4 75mm FK guns ea)
1 (mot) Anti-Tank Company (12 37mm PAK 36)
1 Heavy Machine Gun Company (12 20mm Flak guns)
1 (mot) Pioneer Company (9 LMGs)
1 Bridge Column C
1 (semi-mot) Signals Company
Quartermaster Service, with
  Staff Brigade Quartermaster, with
    2 Light Motor Transport Columns
    2 Supply Trains
    1 Small Column for Fuel
    1 Repair Shop Platoon
    1 Quartermaster Platoon
Administrative Service, with
Ratios Office
Medical Service, with
1 (mot) Medical Company
1 Ambulance Platoon
Other
Veterinary Company

1st Cavalry Division

On 14 February 1940 the 1st Cavalry Brigade was expanded into a full division, the 2/21st was disbanded and the three remaining regiments were brought to the same strength—two battalions, each of four squadrons. The 9th Squadron was the sIG (schwere Infanterie Geschütz, or 150mm heavy infantry gun) and the 10th Squadron was the headquarters. The division had:

Division Command
40th Motorcycle Messenger Platoon
40th (mot) Divisional Mapping Detachment
Reiter (Cavalry) Brigade (as of 2 Apr. 1941, 1st Reiter Brigade)
1 Motorcycle Messenger Platoon
1 Armored Car Section (2 armored cars)
1 (mot) Panzerabwehr Section (3 37mm PAK 36 and 1 LMG)
1st Reiter (Cavalry) Regiment
1 (mot) Signals Platoon
2 Cavalry Battalions, each with
  3 Squadrons (9 LMGs ea)
  1 Heavy Squadron (8 HMGs and 4 80mm mortars)
1 (mot) Heavy Company
  1 Armored Car Section (3 armored cars)
  1 Engineer Platoon (3 LMGs)
  1 Panzerabwehr Group (4 37mm PAK 36 and 1 LMG)
1 (mot) Infantry Gun Company (6 75mm leIG)
1 (tmot) Light Supply Column
1/, 2/2nd Reiter Regiment
same as 1st Reiter Regiment
1/, 2/22nd Reiter Regiment
same as 1st Reiter Regiment
1st Bicycle Battalion (added 5th Escort Battery in 1941)
1 (mot) Signals Platoon
3 Bicycle Squadrons (9 LMGs, 4 HMGs and 3 50mm mortars ea)
1 (mot) Heavy Company
1 Panzerabwehr Squad (3 37mm PAK 36 and 1 LMG)
2 Infantry Gun Sections (2 75mm leIG ea)
1 Mortar Detachment (6 80mm mortars)
1st Reiter (Horse) Artillery Regiment
1 (mot) Signals Platoon
1 (mot) Weather Detachment
1st and 2nd Battalions, each with
1 Signals Platoon
1 Calibration Detachment
3 Batteries (4 75mm guns and 2 LMGs ea)
1 (15 ton) Light Supply Column
40th (mot) Panzerabwehr Company (12 37mm PAK 36 and 6 LMGs)
40th (mot) PIoneer Battalion
1 Bicycle Pioneer Company (9 LMGs)

1 (mot) Pioneer Company (9 LMGs)
1 (mot) Bridging Company
86th (tmot) Signals Battalion
1 (tmot) Telephone Company
1 (tmot) Radio Company
1 (mot) Light Signals Supply Column
40th Supply Troops
1/, 2/, 5/40th Light (mot) Supply Columns
3/, 4/40th Light Supply Columns
6/40th Light (mot) Fuel Column
40th (mot) Supply Company
40th (mot) Maintenance Company
Other
40th (mot) Field Bakery
40th (mot) Butcher Company
40th (mot) Divisional Adminsitration
40th (mot) Medical Company
1/, 2/40th (mot) Ambulances
40th Veterinary Company
40th (mot) Veterinary Ambulance
509th (mot) Field Post Office

The 3/1st Reiter (Horse) Artillery Regiment was the heavy battalion and was organized in the fall of 1940. On 28 November 1941 the 1st Cavalry Division converted into the 24th Panzer Division. Prior to that, between 10 February 1941 and May 1941, the division had:

Division
Divisional Staff Company
  40th (mot) Mapping Detachment
1st Reiter (Cavalry) Brigade
Brigade Staff
  1 Light Armored Car Platoon (2 LMGs)
  1 (mot) Panzerjäger Platoon (3 37mm PAK 36and 1 LMG)
1st Reiter Regiment
Regimental Staff
  1 Mixed Mobility Signals Platoon (later fully motorized)
2 Battalions, each with
  3 Cavalry Squadrons (12 LMGs ea)
  1 Cavalry Squadron (4 80mm mortars and 8 HMGs)
  1 (horse-drawn) Panzerjäger Platoon (2 37mm PAK 36; 1 LMG added later)
  1 Close Support Horse Gun Company (6 75mm guns leIG)
1 (mot) Support Company, with
  1 Armored Car Platoon (3 LMGs)
  1 Engineer Platoon (3 LMGs)
  1 Panzerjäger Platoon (4 37mm PAK 36 and 1 LMG; later re-equipped with 3 37mm PAK 36 and 2 LMGs)

1 Light (horse-drawn) Supply Column

2nd Reiter Regiment

same as 1st Reiter Regiment

22nd Reiter Regiment:

same as 1st Reiter Regiment, except armored car platoon in motorized support company had only 2 LMGs)

21st Cavalry Regiment

Regimental Staff

1 Mixed Mobility Signals Platoon

1 (mot) Engineer Platoon (2 LMGs)

1 Battalion, with

3 Cavalry Squadrons (12 LMGs ea)

1 Cavalry Squadron (4 80mm mortars and 8 HMGs)

1 (horse-drawn) Panzerjäger Platoon (2 37mm PAK 36; 1 LMG added later)

1 Close Support Horse Gun Company (6 75mm leIG)

1 (mot) Support Company, with

1 Armored Car Platoon (2 LMGs)

2 Close Support Horse Gun Sections (2 75mm leIG ea)

1 Panzerjäger Platoon (3 37mm PAK 36 and 1 LMG; later re-equipped with 3 37mm PAK 36 and 2 LMGs)

1 Light (horse-drawn) Supply Column

1st Reiter (Horse) Artillery Regiment

1 (mot) Staff Company

3 Artillery Battalions, each with

1 (non-mot) Signals Platoon

1 (non-mot) Calibration Section

3 Horse Batteries (4 75mm FK 18 field guns and 2 LMGs ea)

1 Light (horse-drawn) Supply Column (15t)

1 (mot) Battery (4 105mm leFH 18 and 2 LMGs)

1st Bicycle Battalion

1 (mot) Signals Platoon

1 Light Armored Car Platoon (2 LMGs)

1 (mot) Engineer Platoon (3 LMGs)

3 Bicycle Companies (3 50mm mortars, 4 HMGs and 9 LMGs ea)

1 (mot) Support Company, with

1 Mortar Platoon (6 80mm mortars)

2 Support Gun Sections (2 75mm leIG guns ea)

1 Panzerjäger Platoon (3 37mm PAK 36 and 1 LMG)

86th Signals Battalion

1 (mixed mobility) Radio Company

1 (mixed mobility) Telephone Company

1 Light (mot) Supply Column

40th Pioneer Battalion

3 (mot) Pioneer Companies (9 LMGs ea)

1 (mot) "T" Bridging Train

1 Light (mot) Engineering Supply Column

40th Panzerjäger Battalion

1 (mot) Signals Platoon

3 (mot) Panzerjäger Companies (12 37mm PAK 36 and 6 LMGs ea)

40th Supply Train

1/, 2/, 3/, 6/40th Light (mot) Supply Columns

4/40th Light (horse-drawn) Supply Column

2/, 4/605th Light (horse-drawn) Supply Column

7/, 8/40th Light (mot) Fuel Supply Columns

5/40th Light (horse-drawn) Supply Column (added later)

40th (mot) Maintenance Company

40th (mot) Supply Company

Administrative Services

40th (mot) Bakery Platoon (later Company)

40th (mot) Butcher Platoon (later Company)

40th Quartermaster Section

Medical

1/, 2/, 3/40th Ambulance Columns

1/, 2/ (mot) Medical Companies

Other

40th Veterinary Company

1/, 2/40th (mot) Horse Transportation Columns

40th Military Police Platoon

509th (mot) Field Post Office

3rd Cavalry Brigade

Formed in March 1944 from the Cavalry Regiment Mitte and other existing units. The brigade contained:

1–3/31st Cavalry Regiment

1–3/32nd Cavalry Regiment

105th Light Artillery Battalion (formerly Horse Artillery Battalion Mitte)

177th Sturmgeschütz Battalion (later 5th StuG Brigade)

3rd Heavy Cavalry Battalion (later 3/870th Artillery Regiment)

1st Pioneer Company

2nd Pioneer Company

3rd Flugabwehr (Flak) Squadron

Panzer Squadron

Panzer Spähwagen (Armored Car) Squadron

3rd Cossack Battalion, 3rd Cavalry Brigade (3 squadrons)

3rd Cavalry Brigade (cossack battalion; later disbanded)

69th Feldersatz Battalion

238th (mot) Signals Brigade

69th Supply troops
69th (mot) Field Gendarme Troop

In July 1944 the brigade was reorganized and equipped as follows:

Divisional Staff
1 Divisional Staff
1 (mot) Military Police Detachment (1 LMG)
31st Reiter Regiment (formerly Mitte Cavalry Regiment)
1 Staff
1 (tmot) Staff Company
  1 Signals Platoon (3 LMGs)
  1 (mot) Reconnaissance Platoon (8 LMGs)
  1 Pioneer Platoon (4 LMGs)
  1 Panzerjäger Platoon (3 75mm PAK 40 and 3 LMGs)
1st Battalion
1 Battalion Staff
1 Signals Platoon (1 LMG)
3 Cavalry Squadrons (1 LMG ea)
1 Machine Gun Squadron (12 HMGs and 1 LMG)
1 Mortar Squadron (4 LMGs and 12 80mm mortars)
2nd Battalion
same as 1st Battalion
32nd Reiter Regiment (from Mitte Cavalry Regiment)
same as 31st Reiter Regiment
Artillery Battalion
1 Staff and Staff Battery
3 Horse Batteries (4 75mm guns and 2 LMGs ea)
1 (tmot) Mortar Battery (8 120mm mortars and 2 LMGs)
177th Sturmgeschütz Brigade
1 Staff (1 LMG)
1 Staff Battery (2 LMGs and 1 StuG)
3 Sturmgeschütz Batteries (12 LMGs and 10 StuGs ea)
3rd Heavy Battalion
1 Battalion Staff
1 (half-track) Squadron (49 LMGs)
1 (motZ) Cavalry Flak Company (12 20mm Flak and 2 LMGs)
1 (mot) Pioneer Company (2 80mm mortars, 3 PzBu, 2 HMGs, and 18 LMGs)
238th Signals Battalion
1 (tmot) Telephone Company (6 LMGs)
1 (mot) Radio Company (5 LMGs)
1 (mot) Light Supply Column (1 LMG)
69th Cossack Battalion (formerly Kossack Battalion, 3rd Cavalry Brigade)
5 Squadrons (no heavy weapons)
69th Feldersatz Battalion
5 Squadrons (no heavy weapons)
69th Supply Troop
1 Brigade Staff

1 Supply Detachment (60 men)
1 Administration Detachment (60 men)
1 (mot) 60 ton Transportation Company (4 LMGs)
2 60 ton Transportation Companies (8 LMGs ea)
69th (mot) Maintenance Company (3 LMGs)
Other
69th (mot) Medical Company (4 LMGs)
69th Ambulance (2 LMGs)
69th Veterinary Company (6 LMGs)
69th (mot) Field Post Office

On 4 November 1944 the brigade was significantly modified. The two cavalry regiments added a (tmot) regimental staff company that contained a signals platoon (three LMGs), a (mot) reconnaissance platoon (eight LMGs), a pioneer platoon (four LMGs), a panzerjäger platoon (three 75mm PAK 40 and three LMGs), and a staff platoon (one LMG). Each of the battalion staffs of the cavalry regiments added a panzerzerstörer platoon (one LMG and 18 panzerschreck). The cavalry squadrons raised the number of LMGs to six.

The artillery battalion was organized into the 869th Artillery Regiment. The 425th Army Artillery Battalion, with three RSO batteries (four 105mm leFH and two LMGs each) was assigned and reorganized into two batteries (six 105mm leFH and four LMGs each). It was apparently stripped of its RSOs. A second artillery battalion was organized with two batteries (six 105mm leFH and four LMGs each).

The 177th Sturmgeschütz Brigade was replaced by the 69th Panzerjäger Battalion. Initially this had a staff and (mot) staff company (one LMG and one StuG), two Sturmgeschütz Companies (later three), each with 10 StuGs and 12 LMGs, and a (mot) Supply Company (three LMGs).

The 3rd Heavy Cavalry Battalion lost its anti-tank rifles, and the half-track company was reduced from 49 to 43 LMGs. The 69th Cossack Battalion was detached. The (tmot) telephone company had its armament reduced to four LMGs and the (mot) radio company was reduced to three LMGs. The remainder of the units had their number of LMGs halved.

The 177th Sturmgeschütz Battalion became a brigade on 10 June 1944, and on 9 August 1944 it became the 69th Panzerjäger Battalion. On 6 January 1945 the 3rd Cavalry Brigade had a theoretical strength of 11,333 men, including 953 Hiwis (*Hilfsfreiwilliger*, or Russian volunteers). The strength figures for staff include strength of staff companies if no separate figure is given for staff company. The brigade was organized and equipped as follows:

Brigade Staff
Brigade Staff (20/0/24/51/95/0/95;[1] 2 LMGs)
1 (mot) Mapping Detachment (0/0/1/7/8/0/8)

---

[1] Numbers are theoretical numbers of officers, warrant officers, NCOs, soldiers, total strength, number of Hiwis and number of German personnel.

1 (mot) Military Police Troop (2/0/21/10/33/0/33; 3 LMGs)

31st Reiter Regiment

1 Regimental Staff (16/1/52/262/331/36/295)

1 (tmot) Regimental Staff Company

  1 Staff Platoon (1 LMG)

  1 Signals Platoon (1 LMG)

  1 (mot) Platoon (3 LMGs)

  1 Pioneer Platoon (4 LMGs)

  1 Infantry Gun Platoon (4 LMGs and 4 150mm sIG)

1st Battalion

1 Battalion Staff (10/1/20/81/112/18/94)

1 Signals Platoon (1 LMG)

1 Tank Destroyer Platoon (1/0/4/60/65/0/65; 1 LMG and 18 panzerschreck)

3 Reiter Squadrons (3/0/33/186/222/12/210; 6 LMGs)

1 Machine Gun Squadron (3/0/32/152/187/23/164; 12 HMGs and 1 LMG)

1 Mortar Squadron (3/0/39/192/234/29/205; 4 LMGs and 12 80mm mortars)

2nd Battalion

same as 1st Battalion

32nd Reiter Regiment

same as 31st Reiter Regiment

69th Panzer Reconnaissance Battalion

1 Panzer Reconnaissance Staff (7/0/37/82/126/0/126; 3 LMGs)

1 (mot) Reconnaissance Staff Company

1 (mot) Signals Platoon (3 LMGs)

1 Armored Car Platoon (16 LMGs, 12 20mm and 3 75mm guns)

1 Light Panzer Reconnaissance Company (Half-Track) (Freie Gliederung) (3/0/38/125/166/0/166; 2 75mm, 2 80mm mortars and 44 LMGs)

1 Panzer Reconnaissance Company (Half-Track) (Freie Gliederung) (3/0/36/151/190/0/190; 2 75mm, 7 20mm, 2 80mm mortars 3 HMGs and 30 LMGs)

1 (mot) Supply Company (2/3/59/94/158/28/130; 1 LMG)

69th Panzerjäger Battalion

1 Staff and Staff Company, Panzerjäger Battalion (5/0/16/32/53/0/53; 3 LMGs)

3 (motZ) Panzerjäger Companies (Freie Gliederung) (3/0/32/25/60/0/60 ea; 12 LMGs and 10 guns ea)

1 (motZ) Mountain Flak Company (2/0/34/112/148/9/139; 12 20mm and 2 LMGs)

1 (mot) Supply Company (3/2/46/140/191/21/170; 3 LMGs)

869th Artillery Regiment

1 Regimental Staff (6/0/19/59/84/5/79)

1 (mot) Regimental Staff Battery (2 LMGs)

1st (mot) Battalion (formerly 425th (RSO) Army Artillery Battalion)

  1 Battalion Staff (7/0/4/9/20/0/20)

  1 (mot) Battalion Staff Battery (3/2/26/87/118/7/111; 2 LMGs)

  2 (RSO) Batteries (3/0/28/86/117/7/110 ea; 6 105mm leFH and 4 LMGs ea)

2nd (mot) Battalion

  1 Battalion Staff

  1 (mot) Battalion Staff Battery (2 LMGs)

  2 (motZ) Batteries (6 105mm leFH and 4 LMGs ea)

3rd (mot) Battalion (formerly Artillery Battalion/Cavalry Regiment Mitte)

  1 Battalion Staff

  1 (mot) Battalion Staff Battery (2/1/17/71/91/9/82; 2 LMGs)

  3 Horse Batteries (3/0/25/113/141/35/106 ea; 4 75mm guns and 4 LMGs ea)

Attached

  1 (tmot) Heavy Mortar Company (8 120mm mortars)

69th (mot) Pioneer Squadron (3/0/27/172/202/4/198; 2 HMGs, 18 LMGs and 2 80mm mortars)

238th Signals Battalion

1 (tmot) Telephone Company (4 LMGs)

1 (mot) Radio Company (2 LMGs)

1 (mot) Supply Company (2 LMGs)

69th Feldersatz Battalion

4 Companies

69th Supply Troop

1 Brigade Staff

69th (mot) (60 ton) Transportation Company (2 LMGs)

1/, 2/69th (horse-drawn) (60 ton) Transportation Companies (4 LMGs ea)

Other

69th (mot) Maintenance Company (2 LMGs)

69th Mixed Administration Company (3 LMGs)

69th (mot) Medical Company (2 LMGs)

69th (mot) Medical Supply Company

69th Veterinary Troop (2 LMGs)

69th (mot) Field Post Office

3rd Cavalry Division

Formed in February 1945 from the 3rd Cavalry Brigade. It was captured near Graz in May 1945 by the Americans. Its organization is unknown.

4th Cavalry Brigade

Formed on 29 May 1944 by Army Group Middle as the Süd und Nord Cavalry Regiment. It had:

1/, 2/5th Reiter (Cavalry) Regiment (from Nord Cavalry Regiment)

1/, 2/41st Reiter (Cavalry) Regiment (from Sud Cavalry Regiment)

1/, 2/, 3/870th Artillery Regiment (staff and 1st Battalion in 1944)

70th Panzer Reconnaissance Battalion

189th Sturmgeschütz Battalion

387th Signals Battalion

70th Feldersatz Battalion

70th Supply Troops

70th (mot) Field Gendarme Troop

On 12 August 1944 the brigade was organized and equipped as follows:

Headquarters
1 Brigade Staff (1 LMG)

5th Cavalry Regiment
1 Regimental Staff
1 Regimental Staff Company
  1 Signals Platoon (2 LMGs)
  1 Engineer Platoon (6 LMGs)
  1 Heavy Panzerjäger Platoon (3 LMGsand 3 PAK)
  1 Reconnaissance Platoon (6 LMGs)

1st Battalion
1 Battalion Staff
1 Signals Platoon
2 Cavalry Squadrons (6 LMGs and 3 HMGs ea)
1 Heavy Squadron (4 HMGs and 4 80mm mortars)

2nd Battalion
1 Battalion Staff
1 Signals Platoon
1 Cavalry Squadron (6 LMGs and 3 HMGs)
1 Heavy Squadron (4 HMGs and 4 80mm mortars)

41st Reiter Regiment
1 Regimental Staff
1 Regimental Staff Company
  1 Signals Platoon (2 LMGs)
  1 Engineer Platoon (6 LMGs)
  1 Heavy Panzerjäger Platoon (3 LMGs and 3 PAK)

1st Battalion
1 Battalion Staff
1 Signals Platoon
3 Cavalry Squadrons (4 LMGs ea)
1 Machine Gun Squadron (9 HMGs)
1 Mortar Squadron (8 80mm mortars)

2nd Battalion
1 Battalion Staff
1 Signals Platoon

2 Cavalry Squadrons (4 LMGs ea)
1 Machine Gun Squadron (10 HMGs and 1 LMG)
1 Mortar Squadron (1 LMG and 8 80mm mortars)

4th Heavy Cavalry Battalion
1 Battalion Staff (3 LMGs)
1 Panzer Company
1st (Half-Track) Squadron (3 80mm mortars, 3 HMGs and 16 LMGs)
3rd (mot) Squadron (3 80mm mortars, 3 HMGs and 3 LMGs)

70th Heavy Mortar Battalion
1 Battalion Staff
1 Signals Platoon
3 Heavy Mortar Companies (8 120mm mortars and 2 LMGs ea)

Artillery Battalion Süd
1 Battalion Staff
1 Signals Platoon
3 Batteries (3 75mm FK 16 and 3 LMGs ea)

387th Signals Battalion
1 (mixed mobility) Telephone Company
1 (mot) Radio Company
1 (mixed mobility) Signals Supply Column

Other
70th (mot) 90 ton Supply Company
1 (horse-drawn) 30 ton Supply Column
70th Administration Platoon
70th (mot) Maintenance Company
70th (mot) Supply Company
70th (mot) Medical Company
70th (mot) Veterinary Company
70th (mot) Field Post Office
1 (mot) Military Police Detachment

A second artillery battalion was formed in 1945. The 3/870th Artillery Regiment was formed from the 70th Cavalry Granatwerfer (Mortar) Regiment. A third battalion was formed later. The 189th Sturmgeschütz Battalion was assigned to the brigade as the 70th Panzerjäger Battalion. On 6 January 1945 the brigade had a theoretical strength of 11,333 men, including 953 Hiwis. In the following list the strength figures for staff include strength of staff companies if no separate figure is given for staff company. The brigade was organized and equipped as follows:

Brigade Staff
Brigade Staff (20/0/24/51/95/0/95;[1] 2 LMGs)
  70th (mot) Mapping Detachment (0/0/1/7/8/0/8)
  70th (mot) Military Police Troop (2/0/21/10/33/0/33; 3 LMGs)

---

[1] Numbers are the theoretical numbers of officers, warrant officers, NCOs, soldiers, total strength, number of Hiwis and number of German personnel.

41st Reiter Regiment (formerly Süd Cavalry Regiment)
  1 Regimental Staff (16/1/52/262/331/36/295)
  1 (tmot) Regimental Staff Company
    1 Staff Platoon (1 LMG)
    1 Signals Platoon (1 LMG)
    1 (mot) Platoon (3 LMGs)
    1 Pioneer Platoon (4 LMGs)
    1 sIG Platoon (4 LMGs and 4 150mm sIG)
  1st and 2nd Battalions, each with
    1 Battalion Staff (10/1/20/81/112/18/94)
    1 Signals Platoon (1 LMG)
    1 Tank Destroyer Platoon (1/0/4/60/65/0/65; 1 LMG and 18 panzerschrecke)
    3 Reiter Squadrons (3/0/33/186/222/12/210 ea; 6 LMGs)
    1 Machine Gun Squadron (3/0/32/152/187/23/164; 12 HMGs and 1 LMG)
    1 Mortar Squadron (3/0/39/192/234/29/205; 4 LMGs and 12 80mm mortars)
5th Reiter Regiment "Feldmarschall von Mackenstein" (formerly Nord Cavalry Regiment)
    same as 41st Reiter Regiment
70th Panzer Reconnaissance Battalion
  1 Panzer Reconnaissance Staff (7/0/37/82/126/0/126; 3 LMGs)
  1 (mot) Reconnaissance Staff Company
  1 (mot) Signals Platoon (3 LMGs)
  1 Armored Car Platoon (16 LMGs, 12 20mm and 3 75mm guns)
  1 Light Panzer Reconnaissance Company (Half-Track) (Freie Gliederung) (3/0/38/125/166/0/166; 2 75mm, 2 80mm mortars and 44 LMGs)
  1 Panzer Reconnaissance Company (Half-Track) (Freie Gliederung) (3/0/36/151/190/0/190; 2 75mm, 7 20mm, 2 80mm mortars 3 HMGs and 30 LMGs)
  1 (mot) Supply Company (2/3/59/94/158/28/130; 1 LMG)
70th Panzerjäger Battalion
  1 (mot) Staff Battery (5/0/16/32/53/0/53; 3 LMGs)
  3 (motZ) Panzerjäger Companies (Freie Gliederung) (3/0/32/25/60/0/60 ea; 12 LMGs and 10 guns ea)
  1 (motZ) Mountain Flak Company (2/0/34/112/148/9/139; 12 20mm and 2 LMGs)
  1 (mot) Supply Company (3/2/46/140/191/21/170; 3 LMGs)
870th Artillery Regiment
  1 Regimental Staff (6/0/19/59/84/5/79)

  1 (mot) Regimental Staff Battery (2 LMGs)
1st (mot) Battalion
  1 Battalion Staff (7/0/4/9/20/0/20)
  1 (mot) Battalion Staff Battery (3/2/26/87/118/7/111; 2 LMGs)
  2 (RSO) Batteries (3/0/28/86/117/7/110; 6 105mm leFH and 4 LMGs ea)
2nd (mot) Battalion
  same as 1st Battalion
3rd (tmot) Battalion (formerly Artillery Battalion/Cavalry Regiment Nord)
  1 Battalion Staff (6/0/4/9/19/0/19)
  1 Battalion Staff Battery (8/2/25/103/138/14/124)
  3 (tmot) Heavy Mortar Companies (3/0/38/149/190/0/190 ea; 8 120mm mortars ea)
70th (mot) Pioneer Squadron (formerly 3rd Pioneer Company, 4th Heavy Cavalry Battalion, 4th Cavalry Brigade) (3/0/27/172/202/4/198; 2 HMGs, 18 LMGs, and 2 80mm mortars)
238th Signals Battalion
  1 (tmot) Telephone Company (4 LMGs)
  1 (mot) Radio Company (2 LMGs)
  1 (mot) Supply Company (2 LMGs)
70th Feldersatz Battalion
  4 Companies
70th Supply Troop
  1 Brigade Staff
  70th (mot) (60 ton) Transportation Company (2 LMGs)
  1/, 2/70th (horse-drawn) (60 ton) Transportation Companies (4 LMGs ea)
Other
  70th (mot) Maintenance Company (2 LMGs)
  70th Mixed Administration Company (3 LMGs)
  70th (mot) Medical Company (2 LMGs)
  70th (mot) Medical Supply Company
  70th Veterinary Troop (2 LMGs)
  70th (mot) Field Post Office

4th Cavalry Division

Formed in February 1945 from the 4th Cavalry Brigade. In May 1945 it went into British captivity. Its organization is unknown.

Nord Cavalry Division

Formed on 1 June 1943 by Army Group North from the cavalry squadrons of the 32nd and 132nd Infantry Divisions and the cavalry of the other reconnaissance and bicycle units assigned as army troops. On 23 November 1943 it formed a 9th Company from the 1st Company, 112nd Infantry Regiment. It was restructured on 23 April 1944, and an artillery battalion (2 battteries), two trench mortar squadrons, and a Flak squadron were formed. In the summer of 1944 it became the 5th Reiter Regiment.

Kavallerie Brigade z.b.V. beim Armeeoberkommando 9

Formed in April or May 1942 specifically to participate in Operation Seydlitz, the brigade was an *ad hoc* formation that did not outlast the operation, which ended on 12 July 1942. The brigade was from the mounted reconnaissance units of the infantry divisions, as much as possible, and entirely of veteran troops. It was organized and equipped as follows:

1st Cavalry Regiment (8/88/450)[1] Oberst Holste
  1st (Cavalry) Squadron (8 LMGs and 3 HMGs)
  2nd (Bicycle) Squadron (8 LMGs and 3 HMGs)
  3rd (Bicycle) Squadron (8 LMGs and 3 HMGs)
  4th (Heavy) Squadron
    Infantry Gun Platoon (6 75mm leIG)
    Pioneer Platoon
    Anti-Tank Platoon (equipment unknown)
    Mortar Platoon (equipment unknown)
2nd Cavalry Regiment (11/125/709) Oberstleutnant von Baath
  1st (Cavalry) Squadron (8 LMGs and 3 HMGs)
  2nd (Bicycle) Squadron (8 LMGs and 3 HMGs)
  3rd (Bicycle) Squadron (8 LMGs and 3 HMGs)
  4th (Heavy) Squadron
    Infantry Gun Platoon (6 75mm leIG)

    Pioneer Platoon
    Anti-Tank Platoon (equipment unknown)
    Mortar Platoon (equipment unknown)
  5th (Cavalry) Squadron (8 LMGs and 3 HMGs)
3rd Cavalry Regiment (8/95/581) Major Briegleb
  1st (Cavalry) Squadron (8 LMGs and 3 HMGs)
  2nd (Bicycle) Squadron (8 LMGs and 3 HMGs)
  3rd (Bicycle) Squadron (8 LMGs and 3 HMGs)
  4th (Heavy) Squadron
    Infantry Gun Platoon (6 75mm leIG)
    Pioneer Platoon
    Anti-Tank Platoon (equipment unknown)
    Mortar Platoon (equipment unknown)
1 Pioneer Company
1 Medical Company
1 (Horse-drawn) Supply Column
1 (mot) Supply Column (equipped with panje wagons)

The men and officers, as much as possible, were all equipped with sub-machine guns. The brigade had no integral field artillery. When the operation began a panzer company (with fourteen tanks) of the 5th Panzer Division and six batteries of artillery were attached to the brigade.

Mitte Cavalry Regiment

On 24 April 1942 Army Group Center issued orders directing the formation of a Army Cavalry Commando with the strength of a brigade. Its role was that of a security formation. It was to be organized as follows:

Kommando (Brigade)
  1 Kommando Staff
  1 (tmot) Staff Cavalry Squadron
    1 (tmot) Signals Platoon
    1 (tmot) Anti-Tank Rifle Platoon
3 Cavalry Regiments, each with
  1 Regimental Staff
  1 (tmot) Staff Cavalry Squadron
    1 (tmot) Signals Platoon

    1 (tmot) Anti-Tank Rifle Platoon
  1st Cavalry Squadron (2 HMGs and 9 LMGs)
  2nd and 3rd Bicycle Squadrons (2 HMGs, 12 LMGs and 2 50mm mortars)
  4th (tmot) Heavy Squadron
    1 Mortar Section (2 80mm mortars)
    1 Panzerjäger Section (3 37mm PAK 36 and 3 LMGs)
    1 Infantry Gun Section (2 75mm leIG)
    1 Pioneer Platoon (3 LMGs)
Independent Cavalry Squadron, z.b.V. (2 HMGs and 9 LMGs) (assigned to the 2nd Regiment)

---

[1] Strength figures are officers, NCOs, and men.

Supply and Support Troops

1 (horse-drawn) Light Supply Column
2 (mot) Light Supply Columns
1 (mot) Light Fuel Column
2 (mot) Maintenance Platoons
1 (mot) Administration Platoon
1 Medical Company

1 (mot) Ambulance
1 Veterinary Platoon
1 (mot) Veterinary Ambulance

Within the regiments, the strengths of the squadron, when raised, were as follows:

	Officers	NCOs	Men	Actual Equipment
1st Regiment				
1st Squadron	2	24	110	8 LMGs and 2 HMGs
2nd Squadron	2	25	130	9 LMGs, 2 HMGs and 2 50mm mortars
3rd Squadron	1	23	137	9 LMGs, 2 HMGs and 2 50mm mortars
4th Squadron	3	16	73	3 LMGs, 2 75mm cavalry guns
				3 37mm PAK 36 and 2 80mm mortars
2nd Regiment				
1st Squadron	3	32	166	9 LMGs, 2 HMGs and 2 50mm mortars
2nd Squadron	2	21	152	12 LMGs, 2 HMGs and 2 50mm mortars
3rd Squadron	2	22	100	8 LMGs, 2 HMGs and 2 50mm mortars
4th Squadron	1	23	101	2 LMGs, 2 HMGs, 2 75mm cavalry guns
				3 37mm PAK 36 and 2 80mm mortars
5th Squadron	3	27	190	8 LMGs and 2 HMGs
3rd Regiment				
1st Squadron	2	24	186	9 LMGs and 2 HMGs
2nd Squadron	2	29	174	9 LMGs, 2 HMGs and 2 50mm mortars
3rd Squadron	1	22	119	9 LMGs and 2 HMGs
4th Squadron	3	20	102	3 LMGs, 2 75mm cavalry guns
				3 37mm PAK 36 and 2 80mm mortars

In order to form this unit, the 6th, 26th, 102nd, 129th, and 251st Reconnaissance Battalions detached a staff, signals platoon, 1 cavalry squadron, 1 bicycle squadron and 1 heavy squadron. The 161st and 206th Reconnaissance Battalions each detached a bicycle squadron.

On 22 March 1943 Cavalry Regiment Mitte was organized and equipped as follows:

Cavalry Regiment "Mitte"[1]

1 (mot) Staff Squadron, with
  1 Motorcycle Platoon (3 LMGs)
  1 Engineering Platoon (3 LMGs)
  1 Panzerjäger Section (3 75mm PAK 40 and 3 LMGs)
  1 Armored Car Section (4 50mm and 6 LMGs)
1 Mixed Mobility Signals Company (3 LMGs)
3 Cavalry Battalions, each with
  3 Squadrons (2 HMGs, 18 LMGs and 2 80mm mortars ea)
  1 Squadron (6 HMGs, 4 LMGs and 6 80mm mortars)
1 Artillery Battalion, with
  3 Recoilless Rifle Batteries (4 Light Recoilless Rifles and 2 LMGs ea)

1 Nebelwerfer Battery (6 150mm nebelwerfer launchers and 2 LMGs)
1 Ambulance Company
1 (mot) Maintenance Platoon
1 (mixed mobility) Supply Column
1 Veterinary Company

It appears to have remained in this configuration until 7 April 1943, when it was reduced to:

Cavalry Regiment "Mitte"

1 Mixed Mobility Signals Company (3 LMGs)
2 Cavalry Battalions, each with
  3 Squadrons (2 HMGs, 18 LMGs and 2 80mm mortars ea)
  1 Squadron (6 HMGs, 4 LMGs and 6 80mm mortars)
9th Squadron (6 HMGs, 4 LMGs, and 6 80mm mortars)
13th (mot) Squadron
  1 Motorcycle Platoon (3 LMGs)

---

[1] This may also have been known as the 105th Cavalry Regiment.

THE GERMAN ORDER OF BATTLE

1 Engineering Platoon (3 LMGs)
1 Panzerjäger Section (3 75mm PAK 40 and 3 LMGs)
1 Armored Car Section (4 50mm and 6 LMGs)
14th Signals Squadron
1 Artillery Squadron (4 75mm field guns)

The organization was changed again, and on 16 July 1943 the Cavalry Regiment "Mitte" was restructured as follows:

Cavalry Regiment "Mitte"
1 (mixed mobility) Staff Company
  1 (mot) Reconnaissance Platoon (6 LMGs)
  1 Engineer Platoon (4 LMGs)
  1 Machine Gun Section (3 HMGs)
  1 Panzerjäger Section (3 PAK)
  1 Signals Platoon
3 Cavalry Battalions, each with
  3 Squadrons (2 HMGs, 18 LMGs and 2 80mm mortars ea)
  1 Squadron (8 HMGs and 6 80mm mortars)
1 Artillery Battalion
  1 Staff Battery
  3 Horse Batteries (4 75mm guns and 2 LMGs ea)
  1 Half-Track Light Artillery Supply Column
From OKH
1 Flak Platoon
1 Armored Car Platoon
1 Half-Track Platoon
1 Panzer Company
1 Signals Squadron
1 Light Cavalry Column

In January 1944 the Cavalry Regiment "Mitte" was organized and equipped as follows:

Cavalry Regiment "Mitte"
1 Staff (mixed mobility) Company
  1 (mot) Infantry Platoon (6 LMGs)
  1 Engineer Platoon (4 LMGs)
  1 Panzerjäger Platoon (3 LMGs and 3 75mm PAK 40)
  1 Signals Platoon
3 Cavalry Battalions, each with

1 Signals Platoon
3 Mounted Companies (2 HMGs, 18 LMGs and 2 80mm mortars ea)
1 Mounted Company (8 HMGs and 6 80mm mortars)
1 Artillery Battalion, with
  3 Horse Batteries (4 75mm guns and 2 LMGs ea)
  1 (mot) Light Artillery Train
1 Self-Propelled Flak Squadron (12 20mm AA guns and 2 LMGs)
Süd Cavalry Regiment
1 Staff (tmot) Company
  1 (mot) Infantry Platoon (6 LMGs)
  1 Engineer Platoon (4 LMGs)
  1 Panzerjäger Platoon (3 LMGs and 3 75mm PAK 40)
  1 Signals Platoon
2 Cavalry Battalions, each with
  1 Signals Platoon
  3 Mounted Companies (2 HMGs, 18 LMGs, 2 80mm mortars ea)
  1 Mounted Company (8 HMGs and 6 80mm mortars)
1 Artillery Battalion, with
  3 Batteries (4 75mm guns and 5 LMGs ea)
  1 (mot) Light Artillery Train
Nord Cavalry Regiment
1 Staff (mixed mobility) Company
  1 (mot) Infantry Platoon (6 LMGs)
  1 Engineer Platoon (4 LMGs)
  1 Panzerjäger Platoon (3 LMGs and 3 75mm PAK 40)
  1 Signals Platoon
2 Cavalry Battalions, each with
  1 Signals Platoon
  3 Mounted Companies (2 HMGs, 18 LMGs and 2 80mm mortars ea)
  1 Mounted Company (8 HMGs and 6 80mm mortars)
1 Artillery Battery (4 75mm guns and 2 LMGs)

In March 1944 it was used to organize the 3rd Cavalry Brigade.

Norwegian Bicycle Reconnaissance Brigade

Formed in April 1944 as a the Norwegian Bicycle Reconnaissance Regiment. It had two battalions, each with four companies. The 1st Battalion was formed from the 95th Reconnaissance Battalion, 3rd Mountain Division, and the 2nd Battalion from the 233rd Reconnaissance Battalion, 196th Division. In July 1944 it was renamed the Norwegian Bicycle Reconnaissance Brigade. In November 1944

it was assigned to the 20th Mountain Corps. It was ordered reorganized on 18 February 1945 to brigade strength and had:

Brigade Staff
1 Brigade Staff
1 Motorcycle Platoon

1/10th Bicycle Regiment (tactically attached, not assigned)

- 1 Battalion Staff
- 1 Battalion Staff Company
  - 1 Signals Platoon
  - 1 Armored Car Platoon (4 20mm and 4 LMGs)
  - 1 Self-Propelled Flak Platoon (4 20mm)
- 3 (bicycle) Companies (4 HMGs and 9 LMGs ea)
- 1 (bicycle) Machine Gun Company (12 HMGs, 1 LMG and 18 panzerschrecke)
- 1 (mot) Heavy Company
  - 1 Pioneer Platoon (4 LMGs)
  - 1 Panzerjäger Platoon (4 75mm PAK 40)
  - 1 leIG Platoon (2 75mm leIG)

2/10th Bicycle Regiment

- 1 Battalion Staff (1 LMG)
- 1 (mot) Battalion Staff Company (1 LMG)
- 3 (bicycle) Companies (9 LMGs ea)
  - 2 Sturm Platoons
  - 1 Panzer Zerstörer Platoon (1 LMG and 18 panzerschrecke)
- 1 (bicycle) Machine Gun Company (12 HMGs, 1 LMG and 18 panzerschrecke)
- 1 (bicycle) Heavy Company
  - 1 Mortar Platoon (1 LMG and 12 80mm mortars)
  - 1 Pioneer Platoon (3 LMGs)

510th Panzerjäger Battalion

- 1 Battalion Staff
- 1 (mot) Battalion Staff Company
  - 1 Staff Platoon (7 LMGs)
  - 1 Sturmgeschütz Platoon (3 jagdpanzers)
  - 1 Self-Propelled Flak Platoon (3 quad 20mm guns)
- 1/510th Battalion (formerly 1106th Company, 106th Infantry Division) (14 jagdpanzers and 16 LMGs)
- 2nd Company (tactically assigned from 73rd Infantry Division) (14 jagdpanzers and 16 LMGs)

510th (motZ) Artillery Battalion

- 1 Battalion Staff
- 1 (mot) Battalion Staff Company (2 LMGs)
- 3 (motZ) Batteries (4 105mm leFH 18 and 4 LMGs ea)

1510th (bicycle) Pioneer Company

(2 HMGs, 9 LMGs, 2 80mm mortars and 6 flamethrowers)

Other

- 1510th (mot) Signal Company (no weapons assigned)
- 510th Feldausbildungs Company (2 HMGs and 9 LMGs)
- 1510th (mot) (60 ton) Transportation Company
- 1510th (mot) (30 ton) Light Supply Column
- 1510th (mot) Medical Supply Company
- 1510th (mot) Field Post Office

10

The Sturmgeschütze

The Sturmgeschütze, or assault guns, were the one instance where the artillery branch seemingly stole a weapons system from another branch of the German armed forces. Indeed, the assignment of the assault guns to the artillery was the result of the political fight between the artillery and the armored factions of the Wehrmacht.

The first order for these weapons occurred on 15 June 1936 when the Artillery Weapons Department was asked to produce an armored artillery close support weapon for infantry and anti-tank purposes.

The first weapons were produced in 1940, with production rising to 50 per month in 1940. The first units were assigned to general headquarters units and distributed in time for a few to participate in the invasion of France in May 1940. As the war progressed the demand for armored vehicles rose, and, with the comparative ease of manufacture of assault guns—which lacked a turret when compared to tanks—heavy emphasis was placed on the production of these weapons.

On 10 February 1941 there were eleven independent sturmgeschütz battalions and six independent batteries. The 184th through 226th Battalions were organized with a staff battery and three sturmgeschütz batteries. Each battery had six sturmgeschütze. The following battalions and batteries were available to the German army on 10 February.

184th Sturmgeschütz Battalion
185th Sturmgeschütz Battalion
190th Sturmgeschütz Battalion
191st Sturmgeschütz Battalion
192nd Sturmgeschütz Battalion
197th Sturmgeschütz Battalion
201st Sturmgeschütz Battalion
203rd Sturmgeschütz Battalion
204th Sturmgeschütz Battalion[1]
210th Sturmgeschütz Battalion
226th Sturmgeschütz Battalion
600th Sturmgeschütz Battery (6 75mm StuG)
659th Sturmgeschütz Battery (6 75mm StuG)
660th Sturmgeschütz Battery (6 75mm StuG)
665th Sturmgeschütz Battery (6 75mm StuG)
666th Sturmgeschütz Battery (6 75mm StuG)
667th Sturmgeschütz Battery (6 75mm StuG)

By 16 May 1941 the number of battalions had been increased to nineteen and now comprised the 177th, 184th, 185th, 189th, 190th, 191st, 197th, 201st 202nd, 203rd, 209th, 210th, 226th, 243rd, 244th, 245th, 249th, 600th, and 667th Sturmgeschütz Battalions. Each battalion contained a staff battery and three sturmgeschütz batteries. The batteries now had seven sturmgeschütze.

The Sturmgeschütz Battalions appear to have been renumbered in 1943. All battalions appear to have been increased from seven to ten sturmgeschütze in February and March 1943.

Old Bn No	New Bn No	Date renumbered
177th	236th	1 June 1943
184th	237th	1 July 1943
185th	239th	1 July 1943
190th	259th	1 July 1943
191st	261st	1 Aug. 1943
201st	276th	1 Aug. 1943
202nd	277th	1 Aug. 1943
203rd	278th	1 Sept. 1943
203rd	278th	1 Sept. 1943
210th	280th	1 Sept. 1943
226th	281st	1 Oct. 1943
228th	286th	1 Oct. 1943
232nd	300th	1 Oct. 1943
243rd	301st	1 Oct. 1943
244th	303rd	1 Nov. 1943
245th	311th	1 Nov. 1943
249th	322nd	1 Nov. 1943
270th	325th	1 Dec. 1943
912th	341st	1 Dec. 1943

These battalions all consisted of a staff battery and three sturmgeschütz companies with 10 sturmgeschützen each. In addition there were a number of other sturmgeschütz formations organizations. They were:

242nd, 600th and 912th Sturmgeschütz Battalion[2]
  1 Sturmgeschütz (Armored) HQ Company
  3 Sturmgeschütz Companies (7 75mm and 3 105mm StuG ea)
393rd Sturmgeschütz Battery (10 StuG)

---

[1] Appears to have been renumbered the 200th Battalion

[2] The 600th, as shown below, was re-equipped to this in April 1943.

741st and 742nd Sturmgeschütz Companies (7 75mm and 3 105mm StuG ea)

393rd, 581st, 582nd, 583rd, and 584th Sturmgeschütz Companies (10 StuG ea)

393rd Sturmgeschütz Battalion

1 Sturmgeschütz (Armored) HQ Company

3 Sturmgeschütz Companies (7 75mm and 3 105mm StuG ea)

667th, 904th, 905th, 909th, and 911th Sturmgeschütz Battalions and 912th (redesignated as 341st on 1 Dec. 1943) StuG Battalion

1 Sturmgeschütz (Armored) HQ Company

3 Sturmgeschütz Companies (7 75mm and 3 105mm StuG ea)

197th, 600th and 190th Sturmgeschütz Battalions[1]

1 Sturmgeschütz (Armored) HQ Company

3 Sturmgeschütz Companies (10 88mm StuG ea)

1 (mot) Maintenance Company

On 1 November 1943 the organization of the Sturmgeschütz Battalions underwent a major change. The battalion staff battery had a three-man command staff, a signals platoon with 21 men and three Panzer PzMk III command vehicles (Sd Kfz 141), a reconnaissance and pioneer platoon with 48 men, a flak platoon with three Sd Kfz 7/1 with quad 20mm guns and 41 men, a maintenance troop with 44 men, a field train with 29 men, a supply troop with 27 men, a six-man administrative unit and a four-man baggage train. The staff battery had a total of four officers, one civil service employee, 43 NCOs, and 164 soldiers.

Each of the three sturmgeschütz companies was organized with a command staff of 12 men and two Sd Kfz 142 (75mm) Sturmgeschütze. The three platoons were organized with 16 men and four Sd Kfz 142 each. There was a small vehicle detachment with 26 men, a field train with 23 men, and a baggage train of four men. The company had three officers, 51 NCOs, and 59 soldiers. This gave the battalion a total of 36 sturmgeschütze, three Sd Kfz 141 command vehicles, 13 officers, one civil servant, 196 NCOs, and 341 soldiers.

On the same day an alternative company organization was established. This was probably for independent companies, but the source documentation does not indicate this and conflicts with other official documentation. These companies had a staff with two Sd Kfz 142 sturmgeschütz and 12 men. Each had four platoons, each with five Sd Kfz 142 sturmgeschütze and 20 men. The vehicle maintenance detachment had 26 men, the field train had 23 men, and the baggage train had four men. The company had three officers, 75 NCOs, and 67 soldiers.

By January 1944 there were 46 Sturmgeschütz Battalions. They were numbered as follows:

177th, 184th, 195th, 190th, 191st, 201st, 202nd, 203rd, 209th, 210th, 226th, 228th, 232nd, 236th, 237th, 239th, 242nd, 243rd, 244th, 245th, 249th, 259th, 261st, 276th, 277th, 278th, 279th, 280th, 281st, 286th, 300th, 301st, 303rd, 311th, 322nd, 325th, 341st, 600th, 667th, 902nd, 904th, 905th, 907th, 909th, 911th, 912th

On 1 February 1944 there was a minor reorganization of the companies. On 1 September 1944 the 150mm sturmgeschütz company formation was established. The staff had 16 men and two sturmgeschütze (Sd Kfz 166; 150mm Stu Haub. 43). The companies were organized with three platoons, each of which had four sturmgeschütze (Sd Kfz 166; 150mm Stu Haub. 43), one officer, 11 NCOs, and eight soldiers. There were no maintenance or other support staffs. The company had a total of three officers, 42 NCOs, and 32 men.

On 25 February 1944 the Sturmgeschütz (Abteilung)[2] Battalions were redesignated Sturmgeschütz Brigades. Each brigade had three batteries. At the same time the 2nd (StuG) Companies of the panzerjäger battalions were given numbers in the 1000 series. For example, in the 85th Panzerjäger Battalion, the 2nd Company was now designated as the 1085th Sturmgeschütz Abteilung.

On 10 June 1944 these new brigades were reorganized with an escort company equipped with half-tracks and containing a pioneer platoon. Their name was then changed to *Heeres-Sturmartillerie-Brigaden*. The escort company contained a signals platoon with two half-tracks, one officer, five NCOs and nine soldiers. The two flak platoons contained eight half-track mounted 20mm flak guns, one officer, 17 NCOs, and 62 soldiers. The pioneer platoon contained seven half-tracks, six NCOs and 45 soldiers. The complete brigades contained a foot escort company, one or two flak escort companies, and three sturmgeschütz batteries.

On 1 November 1944 the battalion staff for all the German armored formations was standardized. This included standardization not only of the tank-equipped battalions, but also of the sturmgeschütz and sturmpanzer battalions. The staff now had 15 men. The staff company had 26 men, Sturmgeschütz III 75mm StuK 40(L/48) Sd Kfz 142/1 command vehicles and one Sd Kfz 251/8 half-track. There was a combined reconnaissance and pioneer platoon that had a command of seven men, and four reconnaissance troops, each of five men. It also had three pioneer troops, each with 12 men, an Sd Kfz 251/7 half-track and either an Sd Kfz 3 or a 3 ton truck. The last part of the battalion staff was the anti-aircraft platoon, which had 35 men, three quad 20mm flak guns, and three Sd Kfz 7/1 half-tracks.

---

[1] Re-equipped on 3 April 1943

[2] The term "Abteilung" generally means battalion and was applied to any formation with two or more companies. It can, however, simply mean "detachment", and there were some exceptions where these "abteilungen" had a single company.

The company formation was also altered. The staff contained 15 men and two Sturmgeschütz III (75mm Stu. Kan 40 L 48; Sd Kfz 142/1). The 1st and 2nd Platoons each had 16 men and four Sturmgeschütz III (75mm Stu. Kan 40 L 48; Sd Kfz 142/1). The 3rd Platoon had one additional soldier. This gave the company a total of three officers, 42 NCOs, and 18 men.

There was an alternative formation in which the Sd Kfz 142/1 (75mm) were replaced by the Sd Kfz 166 Sturmgeschütz IV with the 150mm Stu. Haub 42 (L/12). The troop command had 17 men, the 1st and 2nd Platoons each had 19 men, the 3rd Platoon had 20 men, and the company had a total of one officer, 42 NCOs, and 32 men.

The assignment of Sturmgeschütz Battalions to infantry divisions on 25 May 1944 was as follows:

Division	StuG Battalion
1st Infantry	1001st
1st Mountain	none
2nd Mountain	none
3rd Mountain	1095th
4th Mountain	1094th
5th Jäger	1005th
6th Infantry	1085th
6th Mountain	1006th
7th Infantry	none
7th Mountain	1007th
8th Jäger	none
9th Infantry	1008th
11th Infantry	1011th
12th Infantry	1012th
14th Infantry	1014th
15th Infantry	1015th
17th Infantry	1017th
19th Luftwaffe Feld	1019th
21st Infantry	1021st
22nd Infantry	none
23rd Infantry	1023rd
24th Infantry	none
26th Infantry	1026th
28th Jäger	1028th
30th Infantry	1030th
31st Infantry	1031st
32nd Infantry	1032nd
34th Infantry	1034th
35th Infantry	1035th
36th Infantry	1036th
42nd Jäger	none
44th Grenadier	1040th
45th Infantry	1045th
47th Infantry	1052nd
48th Infantry	none
49th Infantry	none
50th Infantry	none
57th Infantry	1157th
58th Infantry	1158th
61st Infantry	1161st
65th Infantry	1165th
68th Infantry	none
69th Infantry	1169th
71st Infantry	1172nd
72nd Infantry	1172nd
73rd Infantry	none
75th Infantry	1175th
76th Infantry	1176th
77th Infantry	none
78th Infantry	none
79th Infantry	1179th
81st Infantry	1181st
83rd Infantry	none
84th Infantry	none
85th Infantry	none
87th Infantry	1187th
88th Infantry	1188th
89th Infantry	none
91st Infantry	none
92nd Infantry	1192nd
93rd Infantry	1193rd
94th Infantry	1194th
95th Infantry	1195th
96th Infantry	1196th
97th Infantry	1197th
98th Infantry	1198th
100th Jäger	1100th
101st Jäger	1101st
102nd Jäger	none
104th Jäger	none
105th Jäger	none
110th Infantry	1110th
111th Infantry	none
114th Jäger	1114th
117th Jäger	none
118th Jäger	none
121st Infantry	1121st
122nd Infantry	none
126th Infantry	1126th
129th Infantry	1129th
131st Infantry	1131st
132nd Infantry	none
134th Infantry	1134th
162nd Infantry	1236th
163rd Infantry	none
168th Infantry	1248th
169th Infantry	none
170th Infantry	1240th
181st Infantry	none
196th Infantry	none
197th Infantry	1197th
198th Infantry	none
199th Infantry	none

205th Infantry	none	337th Infantry	1337th
206th Infantry	1206th	338th Infantry	none
208th Infantry	1208th	340th Infantry	none
210th Infantry	none	342nd Infantry	1342nd
211th Infantry	none	343rd Infantry	none
212th Infantry	1212th	344th Infantry	1344th
214th Infantry	1214th	346th Infantry	1346th
215th Infantry	none	347th Infantry	none
218th Infantry	none	348th Infantry	1348th
225th Infantry	1225th	349th Infantry	1349th
227th Infantry	none	352nd Infantry	1352nd
230th Infantry	none	353rd Infantry	1353rd
252nd Infantry	none	356th Infantry	1356th
253rd Infantry	1253rd	357th Infantry	1357th
254th Infantry	none	359th Infantry	1359th
256th Infantry	none	361st Infantry	none
257th Infantry	1257th	362nd Infantry	1362nd
258th Infantry	none	363rd Infantry	none
260th Infantry	none	367th Infantry	1367th
263rd Infantry	none	370th Infantry	1370th
264th Infantry	none	371st Infantry	none
265th Infantry	none	376th Infantry	none
266th Infantry	none	383rd Infantry	none
267th Infantry	1267th	384th Infantry	none
269th Infantry	none	389th Infantry	1389th
270th Infantry	none	416th Infantry	none
271st Infantry	none	702nd Infantry	none
272nd Infantry	none	707th Infantry	none
274th Infantry	none	708th Infantry	none
275th Infantry	none	709th Infantry	none
276th Infantry	none	710th Infantry	none
277th Infantry	none	711th Infantry	none
278th Infantry	1278th	712th Infantry	none
280th Infantry	none	715th Infantry	none
282nd Infantry	none	716th Infantry	none
290th Infantry	1290th	719th Infantry	none
291st Infantry	none	Corps Detachment A	none
292nd Infantry	none	Corps Detachment C	1219th
294th Infantry	none	Corps Detachment D	1156th
295th Infantry	none	Corps Detachment E	1186th
296th Infantry	none	Corps Detachment F	none
297th Infantry	none		
299th Infantry	1299th		
302nd Infantry	none		
304th Infantry	none		
305th Infantry	1305th		
306th Infantry	none		
319th Infantry	none		
320th Infantry	1320th		
326th Infantry	1326th		
329th Infantry	1329th		
331st Infantry	1331st		
334th Infantry	1334th		
335th Infantry	1335th		
336th Infantry	none		

On 1 August 1944 the 177th Sturmgeschütz Brigade was absorbed into the 3rd Cavalry Brigade and the 270th Sturmgeschütz Brigade was absorbed into the organization of the 1st Skijäger Division. Both units were redesignated as Panzerjäger Battalions when they were absorbed into these two divisions.

An interesting document came to light in reviewing the plans for the 1944–1945 production requirements and levels of the *sturmartillerie*. What follows is a list of the numbers of sturmgeschütze produced from June to November 1944: *(see over)*

	June	July	Aug.	Sept.	Oct.	Nov.
Sturmgeschütz III	385	395	405	420	425	420
Sturmgeschütz IV	95	90	90	90	90	90
Sturmhowitzer	75	75	75	75	75	75
Sturmgeschütz 38t	100	175	250	330	400	450
Sturmgeschütz (new type)	120	130	140	150	160	170
Total	775	865	960	1,065	1,150	1,205
Needed for Artillery units	375	375	375	375	375	375
Available for Panzerjäger units	400	490	585	690	775	830

Sturmgeschütz Battalions in Panzer and Panzergrenadier Divisions

In order to increase the strength of the panzer divisions, Heinz Guderian requested that Sturmgeschütz Battalions be organized and assigned as the third battalion of the panzer regiments. These battalions were established in the newly reorganized 14th, 16th, and 24th Panzer Divisions as they were rebuilt after being destroyed at Stalingrad. They were raised as follows:

Battalion	Companies	Raised on	Raised from
3/2nd Panzer Regiment	4	5 April 1943	
3/24th Panzer Regiment	4	5 April 1943	127th Panzer Battalion
3/36th Panzer Regiment	4	25 April 1943	

On 20 June 1943 a new sturmgeschütz battalion organization was issued that contained three companies and a total of 45 StuG. This new organization did not apply to all existing sturmgeschütz battalions; initially, only eight battalions were affected:

StuG Bn	Converted on	Created From
103rd	21 July 1943	
129th	21 July 1943	
5th	25 August 1943	Remains 5th Panzer Regiment
7th	25 August 1943	Remains 7th Panzer Regiment
8th	25 August 1943	Remains 8th Panzer Regiment
118th	23 September 1943	
190th	9 October 1943	
3/2nd Panzer Regiment	12 November 1943	

The 5th, 7th, and 8th Sturmgeschütz Battalions were assigned to the 25th, 10th, and 20th Panzergrenadier Divisions. The 118th Sturmgeschütz Battalion was assigned to the 18th Panzergrenadier Division. The 190th Sturmgeschütz Battalion retained its PzMk IV tanks until it received its allocation of 42 StuG in February 1944. On 3 May 1944 the sturmgeschütz battalion of the Feldherrnhalle Panzergrenadier Division was ordered into a Panzer Battalion with three companies, each with 14 PzMk IV tanks. On 1 May 1944 a KstN was issued that converted the panzer grenadier divisions to "freie Gliederungen". Their sturmgeschütz battalions were organized with:

Staff and Staff Company
Command Group
   3 PzMk III (50mm L/42)(SdKfz 141)
3 Sturmgeschütz Companies, each with
Command Group
   3 Sturmgeschütz III (75mm Stu.Kan. 40 (L/48) Sd Kfz 142/1)
   3 Platoons, each with
      4 Sturmgeschütz III (75mm Stu.Kan. 40 (L/48) Sd Kfz 142/1)
Supply Company

On 20 August 1944 all the panzergrenadier divisions were to form Sturmgeschütz battalions with the preceding organization, plus a maintenance platoon added. The battalion had an authorized strength of 45 sturmgeschütze.

On 1 June 1944 the 4th, 16th, 17th, and 18th SS Panzergrenadier Divisions were refitted with three Sturmgeschütz companies, each with 14 StuG. During July 1944 the 18th, 25th and Feldherrnhalle Panzergrenadier Divisions were wiped out. The surviving portions of these divisions were used to establish the newly forming Army panzer brigades. The Feldherrnhalle Panzergrenadier Division was subsequently re-formed by absorbing the 107th Panzer Brigade in October 1944. The 25th Panzergrenadier Division was re-formed in November and its panzer battalions retained the panzer battalion organization that had existed in the now disbanded and absorbed panzer brigades—three panther companies. The 118th Panzer Battalion of the 18th Panzergrenadier Division was rebuilt, in late November, to the 45 StuG organization.

On 1 November 1944 a new KstN was issued for the Sturmgeschütz Battalions. These new battalions had:

Staff and Staff Company
  Staff Company
    3 Sturmgeschütz III 75mm StuK 40(L/48) Sd Kfz 142/1

1 Sd Kfz 251/8 half-track
Reconnaissance and Pioneer Platoon
  4 Reconnaissance Troops
  3 Pioneer Troop
    1 Sd Kfz 3 or 3-ton truck
    1 Sd Kfz 251/7 half-track
Anti-Aircraft Platoon
    3 Sd Kfz 7/1 half-tracks
3 Companies, each with:
Staff
    2 Assault Guns III (75mm Stu. Kan. 40 (L/48) Sd Kfz 142/1)
  3 Platoons, each with
    4 Assault Guns III (75mm Stu. Kan. 40 (L/48) Sd Kfz 142/1)

In an alternative organization, the Sd Kfz 142/1 (75mm) were replaced by the Sturmgeschütz IV (Sd Kfz 166) equipped with the 150mm Stu. Haub. 42 ((L/12). The details of these units are contained within the various histories of the divisions to which they were assigned.

11

Jagdpanzer and Panzerjäger Formations, 1944–1945

The discussion of the sturmgeschütz units logically leads to the discussion of the various German anti-tank formations. The topic of anti-tank formations in the German army is a very lengthy and complex topic. It also crosses normal boundaries between the artillery, infantry, and armored units, as was noted in the discussion of the sturmgeschütz formations. There were very few large formations, the anti-tank formations generally being seldom larger than battalions, but in 1944 this size barrier was finally broken. In addition, in 1943 a few very unusual formations were raised that deserve some comment and review. What follows is not intended as a complete review of anti-tank formations, but more a sampling of unusual formations or tidbits of information encountered in a review of OKH records.

An interesting note on the organization of new formations scheduled for 1944 indicates that the German army intended to raise 20 Panzerjäger Battalions (equipped with Mk V Panthers and Mk VI Tigers).

104th Panzerjagd Brigade

The existence of this formation was established by OKH records, and it appears to have been organized on 26 January 1945. On 2 February 1945 it was organized as follows:

1st Battalion ("Weichsel")
1 (mot) Staff Company (1 LMG)
1st Jagdpanzer Company (10 PzMk IV Jagdpanzers and 12 LMGs)
1 Escort Detachment
2nd Jagdpanzer Company (10 PzMk IV Jagdpanzers and 12 LMGs)
1 Escort Detachment
3rd (half-track) Panzergrenadier Company (3 Sd Kfz 251/1 (1 LMG), 2 Sd Kfz 251/2 half-tracks (1 LMG ea), 3 Sd Kfz 251/3 (radio), 1 Sd Kfz 251/7, 6 Sd Kfz 251/17 (20mm gun), 2 Sd Kfz 251/9 (1 75mm gun and 1 LMG ea), 13 88mm R Panzerbüsche 54, 8 LMGs, 4 HMGs and 2 80mm mortars Mk34)
4th Jagdpanzer Company (14 Marder III and 16 LMGs)
1 Escort Detachment (originally intended to be assigned, but may not have been)
5th (motZ) Panzerjäger Company (12 75mm PAK 40 and 12 LMGs; originally intended to be assigned, but may not have been)

2nd Battalion ("Herford")
1 (mot) Staff Company (1 LMG)
1st Jagdpanzer Company (10 PzMk IV Jagdpanzers and 12 LMGs)
1 Escort Detachment
2nd Jagdpanzer Company (14 Marder III and 16 LMGs)

1 Escort Detachment
3rd (half-track) Panzergrenadier Company
same as in 1st Battalion

3rd Battalion ("Landau")
1 (mot) Staff Company (1 LMG)
1st Jagdpanzer Company (equipment unknown)
1 Escort Detachment
2nd Jagdpanzer Company (equipment unknown)
1 Escort Detachment
3rd (half-track) Panzergrenadier Company
same as in 1st Battalion

4th Battalion ("Böblingen")
1 (mot) Staff Company (1 LMG)
1st Jagdpanzer Company (14 Marder III and 16 LMGs)
1 Escort Detachment
2nd Jagdpanzer Company (14 Marder III and 16 LMGs)
1 Escort Detachment
3rd (half-track) Panzergrenadier Company
same as in 1st Battalion

5th Battalion ("Freystadt")
1 (mot) Staff Company (1 LMG)
1st Jagdpanzer Company (14 Marder III and 16 LMGs)
1 Escort Detachment
2nd Jagdpanzer Company (14 Marder III and 16 LMGs)
1 Escort Detachment
3rd (half-track) Panzergrenadier Company
same as in 1st Battalion

6th Battalion ("Regensburg")
1 (mot) Staff Company (1 LMG)
1st Jagdpanzer Company (14 Marder III and 16 LMGs)
1 Escort Detachment

2nd Jagdpanzer Company (14 Marder III and 16 LMGs)
 1 Escort Detachment
3rd (half-track) Panzergrenadier Company
 same as in 1st Battalion

Tessin states that it was a brigade staff for the 6th Panzer Jagd Battalion and 1st Panzer Reconnaissance Battalion, employing the Staff/2102nd Panzer Battalion (1st–6th Panzer Jagd Battalions). It became the staff/General Münzel Kampfgruppe.

West Panzerjagd Brigade

This was planned for formation in April 1945 with:

1/, 2/Blücher Panzerjagd Regiment
1/, 2/Nürnberg Panzerjagd Regiment
1/, 2/Stuttgart Panzerjagd Regiment

Each battalion was to have three companies. It is questionable if the unit was actually formed.

Independent Jagdpanzer Battalions

Though nominally below the level of review in this series, these are exceptional and interesting formations that merit some review, especially since they contained some of the most exotic equipment of the German army. The following formations are known to have existed in late 1944 and early 1945. Little is otherwise known about their formation:

88th Heavy Army Panzerjäger Battalion (formed 1 Apr. 1943)
1 Staff and Staff Battery (3 Nashorn and 3 self-propelled quad 20mm guns)
3 Companies (14 SdKfz 164 Nashorn with 88mm PAK 43/1 L/71 and 16 LMGs ea)

93rd Heavy Army Panzerjäger Battalion (formed 23 July 1943)
1 Staff and Staff Company (3 Nashorn and 3 self-propelled quad 20mm guns)
3 Company (14 SdKfz 164 Nashorn with 88mm PAK 43/1 L/71 and 16 LMGs ea)

463rd Panzerjäger Battalion
1 (mot) Staff and Staff Company
3 (motZ) Panzerjäger Companies (12 75m PAK 40 and 12 LMGs ea)

The 463rd Panzerjäger Battalion was formed as part of the 199th Infantry Division and was later detached to become army troops. The 519th, 559th, 560th and 561st Battalions originally were to be equipped as the 88th Panzerjäger Battalion, shown above. This organization, however, was transitory and they were reorganized as follows:

519th Jagdpanther Battalion (formed 15 Sept. 1944)
1 Self-Propelled Staff and Staff Company (3 SdKfz 173)
1 Panzer Flak Platoon (4 37mm Flak guns and 4 LMGs; added 25 Nov. 1944)
1 Panzer Flak Platoon (4 20mm Flak guns and 4 LMGs; added 25 Nov. 1944)
3 Jagdpanther Companies (14 SdKfz 173 with 88mm PAK 41/1 L/71 and 14 LMGs ea)

525th Jagdpanther Battalion
1 Self-Propelled Staff and Staff Company (3 SdKfz 173)
1 Panzer Flak Platoon (4 37mm Flak guns and 4 LMGs; added 25 Nov. 1944)
1 Panzer Flak Platoon (4 20mm Flak guns and 4 LMGs; added 25 Nov. 1944)
3 Jagdpanther Companies (14 SdKfz 173 with 88mm PAK 41/1 L/71 and 14 LMGs ea)

560th Jagdpanther Battalion (formed 26 May 1944)
1 Self-Propelled Staff and Staff Company (3 SdKfz 173; included a pioneer platoon)
1 Panzer Flak Platoon (4 37mm Flak guns and 4 LMGs; added 25 Nov. 1944)
1 Panzer Flak Platoon (4 20mm Flak guns and 4 LMGs; added 25 Nov. 1944)
3 Jagdpanther Companies (14 SdKfz 173 with 88mm PAK 41/1 L/71 and 14 LMGs ea)

559th Jagdpanther Battalion
1 Self-Propelled Staff and Staff Company (3 SdKfz 173; included a pioneer platoon)
1 Panzer Flak Platoon (4 37mm Flak guns and 4 LMGs; added 25 Nov. 1944)

1 Panzer Flak Platoon (4 20mm Flak guns and 4 LMGs; added 25 Nov. 1944)

3 Jagdpanther Companies (14 SdKfz 173 with 88mm PAK 41/1 L/71 and 14 LMGs ea)

The 559th Jagdpanther Battalion was formed on 10 April 1944, but was reorganized with its 2nd and 3rd Companies being equipped with StuG on 20 August 1944.

561st Panzerjäger Battalion (became self-propelled on 13 Dec. 1942)

1 Staff and Staff Company

3 Panzerjäger Companies (14 self-propelled 75mm PAK 40 gun carriages ea)

563rd Jagdpanther Battalion

1 Self-Propelled Staff and Staff Company

1 Staff Escort Platoon (3 PzMk IV Jagdpanzers)

4 Panzerjäger Companies (14 self-propelled 75mm PAK 40 gun carriages ea)

The four panzerjäger companies were replaced by three jagdpanther companies (14 SdKfz 173 with 88mm PAK 41/1 L/71 and 14 LMGs each) on 25 November 1944.

590th Panzerjäger Battalion (formed 2 Oct. 1943)

1 (mot) Staff and Staff Company

3 (motZ) Panzerjäger Companies (6 75m PAK 40, 6 50mm PAK 38 and 12 LMGs ea)

616th Panzerjäger Battalion (formed 1 Apr. 1940)

1 Staff and Staff Company

3 Panzerjäger Companies (14 75mm PAK 40 on self-propelled carriages and 14 LMGs ea)

The 616th underwent major reorganization on 25 January 1945. It had three companies of Hetzers (10 Hetzers each), a company of Jagdpanthers (14 Jagdpanthers and 14 LMGs) and a (mot) maintenance company.

The 653rd and 654th Panzerjäger Battalions are among the most famous of these battalions. Originally they were equipped with the Ferdinand SdKfz 184 Elephant. When raised they were equipped as follows:

1 Staff

1 Staff Company

  1 Elephant Platoon (3 SdKfz 184)

  1 Self-Propelled Flak Platoon (3 quad 20mm guns)

3 Elephant Companies (14 SdKfz 184 and 14 LMGs ea)

1 Self-Propelled Maintenance Company

These two battalions were badly mauled during the Battle of Kursk in July 1943, but they remained active and were re-equipped. The 653rd was re-equipped with the 128mm Jagdtiger tank destroyers (SdKfz 186) on 13 De-

cember 1944 and the 654th was re-equipped with Jagdpanthers (SdKfz 173) on 15 March 1944 by OB West. They were organized as follows:

653rd Jagdtiger Battalion

1 Staff and Staff Company

3 Jagdtiger Companies (14 SdKfz 186 and 31 LMGs ea)

1 (mot) Maintenance Company

1 (mot) Supply Company

654th Jagdpanther Battalion

1 Self-Propelled Staff and Staff Company (3 SdKfz 173; included a pioneer platoon)

1 Panzer Flak Platoon (4 37mm Flak guns and 4 LMGs)

1 Panzer Flak Platoon (4 20mm Flak guns and 4 LMGs)

3 Jagdpanther Companies (14 SdKfz 173 with 88mm PAK 41/1 L/71 and 14 LMGs ea)

1 (mot) Maintenance Company

1 (mot) Supply Company

The 655th Panzerjäger Battalion, which began life operating with the Nashorn SdKfz 164, was organized and equipped as follows:

1 Staff and Staff Battery (3 Nashorn and 3 self-propelled quad 20mm guns)

521st, 611th and 670th Panzerjäger Companies (14 SdKfz 164 Nashorn with 88mm PAK 43/1 L/71 and 16 LMGs ea)

However, it was re-equipped as a Jagdpanther battalion sometime in late 1944 and then had:

1 Self-Propelled Staff and Staff Company (3 SdKfz 173; included a pioneer platoon)

1 Panzer Flak Platoon (4 37mm Flak guns and 4 LMGs)

1 Panzer Flak Platoon (4 20mm Flak guns and 4 LMGs)

3 Jagdpanther Companies (14 SdKfz 173 with 88mm PAK 41/1 L/71 and 14 LMGs ea)

1 (mot) Maintenance Company

1 (mot) Supply Company

The **673rd Panzerjäger Battalion** was ordered raised by Hitler on 25 January 1945. It was organized as follows:

1 Staff (1 LMG) and Staff Company (2 LMGs)

3 Panzerjäger Companies (10 PzMk IV Jagdpanzers (?) and 12 LMGs ea)

The **512th Jagdtiger Battalion** was raised on 15 February 1945 and organized and equipped as follows:

1 Staff and Staff Company

3 Jagdtiger Companies (10 SdKfz 186 and 31 LMGs ea)

1 (mot) Maintenance Company

1 (mot) Supply Company

The **614th Jagdtiger Compa**... ...d on 20 February 1945 and contained 10... ...**4th and 669th Panzerjäger Comp**... ...February 1945 and each had 1... ...he

1012nd, 1212th, 1258th, 1276th, 1352nd, 1363rd, and 1384th Panzerjäger Companies were each equipped with Hetzers and were assigned, respectively, to the 12th, 212th, unknown, 276th, 352nd, 363rd, and unknown Volks Grenadier Divisions.

...ttalions

In late 1944,
Germans c...
anti-tank...
bers of P...
estir...
of Panzers...

...5th, and 686th (motZ) Panzerjäger Battalions ...ed on 28 October 1944, 18 October 1944, ...n 1945 respectively. The first two appear to ...edesignated the 657th and 668th. All three had ...signals platoon and three (motZ) companies ...ed with nine 88mm PAK 43 guns and nine LMGs.

...e Germans also raised a large number of independ-...t companies. They were the 671st, Hadsten, Prag, Wien, Dresden, Cilli, Braunschweig, Brona, Straubing, Oppeln, Herning, Bergen, Hohensalza, Hamburg, and Eisenach (motZ) Companies. They all appear to have been organized between 10 November 1944 and 31 January 1945.

PAK Sperrverband

A most interesting o... ...exists in the OKH records that merits relatio... ...on 1 August 1944 the formation of the following un... ...sted their equipment:

1st Barrier Group
3rd Panzer AOK
664th Heavy Army Panzerjäger Battalion (2 companies, 8 88mm PAK 43 ea)
665th Heavy Army Panzerjäger Battalion (2 companies, 8 88mm PAK 43 ea)
3rd Medium PAK Sperr Company (12 76.2mm IKH 290 (r) guns)
4th Medium PAK Sperr Company (12 76.2mm IKH 290 (r) guns)
5th Medium PAK Sperr Company (12 76.2mm IKH 290 (r) guns)
6th Medium PAK Sperr Company (12 76.2mm IKH 290 (r) guns)
9th Medium PAK Sperr Company (12 76.2mm IKH 290 (r) guns)
11th Medium PAK Sperr Company (12 76.2mm IKH 290 (r) guns)

4th AOK
1st Medium PAK Sperr Company (12 76.2mm IKH 290 (r) guns)

2nd Medium PAK Sperr Company (12 76.2mm IKH 290 (r) guns)
10th Medium PAK Sperr Company (12 76.2mm IKH 290 (r) guns; ready to ship out on 4 Aug. 1944)

2nd AOK
13th Medium PAK Sperr Company (12 76.2mm IKH 290 (r) guns)
14th Medium PAK Sperr Company (12 76.2mm IKH 290 (r) guns; ready to ship out on 4 Aug. 1944)
15th Medium PAK Sperr Company (12 76.2mm IKH 290 (r) guns)
16th Medium PAK Sperr Company (12 76.2mm IKH 290 (r) guns)
17th Medium PAK Sperr Company (12 76.2mm IKH 290 (r) guns)

2nd Barrier Group
9th AOK
7th Medium PAK Sperr Company (12 76.2mm IKH 290 (r) guns)
8th Medium PAK Sperr Company (12 76.2mm IKH 290 (r) guns)
12th Medium PAK Sperr Company (12 76.2mm IKH 290 (r) guns; moving to Warka on 8 Feb. 91944)

Forming in Germany as of 27 July 1944

20th Medium PAK Sperr Company (12 76.2mm IKH 290 (r) guns)

21st Medium PAK Sperr Company (12 76.2mm IKH 290 (r) guns)

22nd Medium PAK Sperr Company (12 76.2mm IKH 290 (r) guns)

23rd Medium PAK Sperr Company (12 76.2mm IKH 290 (r) guns)

24th Medium PAK Sperr Company (12 76.2mm IKH 290 (r) guns)

25th Medium PAK Sperr Company (12 76.2mm IKH 290 (r) guns)

26th Medium PAK Sperr Company (12 76.2mm IKH 290 (r) guns)

Forming in Lamsdorf on 27 July 1944

28th Medium PAK Sperr Company (12 76.2mm IKH 290 (r) guns)

29th Medium PAK Sperr Company (12 76.2mm IKH 290 (r) guns)

30th Medium PAK Sperr Company (12 76.2mm IKH 290 (r) guns)

31st Medium PAK Sperr Company (12 76.2mm IKH 290 (r) guns)

32nd Medium PAK Sperr Company (12 76.2mm IKH 290 (r) guns)

33rd Medium PAK Sperr Company (12 76.2mm IKH 290 (r) guns)

34th Medium PAK Sperr Company (12 76.2mm IKH 290 (r) guns)

35th Medium PAK Sperr Company (12 76.2mm IKH 290 (r) guns)

18th Fortress PAK Company (12 76.2mm IKH 290 (r) guns)

19th Fortress PAK Company (12 88mm PAK 43)

Fortress PAK Units

The **I Fortress PAK Verband** was formed in August 1944 from the 762nd Fortress PAK Battalion. It was organized and equipped as follows:

I Fortress PAK Verband
1/I Company (12 76.2mm and 12 LMGs)
2/I Company (12 75mm PAK 40 and 12 LMGs)
3/I Company (12 FK 39 and 12 LMGs)
4/I Company (6 76.2mm, 6 88mm and 12 LMGs)
4/I Company (12 75mm PAK 40 and 12 LMGs)
6/I Company (12 76.2mm and 12 LMGs)
9/I Company (6 76.2mm, 6 88mm and 12 LMGs)
10/I Company (12 75mm PAK 40 and 12 LMGs)
11/I Company (6 76.2mm, 6 88mm and 12 LMGs)
13/I Company (12 75mm PAK 40 and 12 LMGs)
14/I Company (12 76.2mm and 12 LMGs)
15/I Company (12 75mm PAK 40 and 12 LMGs)
16/I Company (12 75mm PAK 40 and 12 LMGs)
17/I Company (12 75mm PAK 40 and 12 LMGs)

The **II Fortress PAK Verband** was formed in August 1944 based on OKH orders dated 27 August 1944 using the Special Oehmichen Staff with the 1–10/II and 12/II Fortress PAK Companies. In January 1945 the 11/II and 13–19/II Companies were formed. The staff became the XXI PAK Staff and was rebuilt from scratch. Its companies were all equipped with 12 75mm PAK 40 and 12 LMGs.

The **III Fortress PAK Verband** was formed in August using the 1–10/III Fortress PAK Companies formed from

the 28th–37th PAK Sperr Companies. Each company contained 12 75mm PAK 40 and 12 LMGs.

The **IV Fortress PAK Verband** was formed in August 1944 by orders from OKH issued on 16 August 1944. Initially it formed the 11–17/IV Companies (12 75mm PAK 40, 12 panzerschrecke and 12 LMGs each) and in December 1944 it formed the 38–47/IV Companies (12 76.2mm, 3 88mm and 15 LMGs each).

The **V Fortress PAK Verband** was formed in August through the Lippold Staff Organization in Wehrkreis XXI with the 1–15/V Companies (12 76.2mm, 3 88mm and 15 LMGs each). The 1st and 2nd Companies helped to form the 17th Company of the 8th and 88th Infantry Regiments of the Warschau Fortress Division.

The **VI Fortress PAK Verband** was formed in September 1944 in Wehrkreis XX and contained:

1–3/VI Companies (12 75mm PAK 40 and 12 LMGs ea)
4/VI Company (12 75mm FK 39 and 12 LMGs)
5–9/VI Companies (12 76.2mm, 3 88mm and 15 LMGs ea)

In January 1944 the 2/VI was used to form the 183rd Fortress Infantry Regiment of the **Warschau Fortress Division**.

The **VII Fortress PAK Verband** was formed in September 1944 in Wehrkreis I through the Gness Staff Formation and initially contained the 3/VII, 4/VII, 5/VII, and 6/VII Companies (12 75mm PAK 40 and 12 LMGs each) and the 7–21/VII Companies (8 76.2mm, 4 88mm and 12 LMGs each). In October 1944 it formed the 22–27/VII Companies (12 75mm PAK 40 (?) and 12 LMGs).

The **VIII Fortress PAK Verband** was formed in November and December 1944 in Wehrkreis XXI with:

1st–7th Companies (12 75mm PAK 40 and 12 LMGs ea)

8th–14th Companies (12 75mm PAK 40, 12 panzerschrecke and 12 LMGs ea)

The **IX Fortress PAK Verband** was formed in January 194 in Wehrkreis XX and contained the 1/IX–12/IX Companies (equipment unknown)

The **X Fortress PAK Verband** was formed in January 1945 in Wehrkreis X. The 1–97/X Companies were entirely deployed in the west, but were assigned to various other formations. When formed, the companies were equipped as follows:

1st–2nd Companies (unknown)
5th–6th Companies (12 88mm PAK 43 and 12 LMGs ea)
12th–21st Companies (12 75mm or 76.2mm PAK, 4 88mm PAK 43 and 16 LMGs ea)
22nd Company (30 75mm PAK 40)
23rd Company (9 76.2mm IKH 290 (r))
28th–62nd, 65th, 66th and 72nd Companies (equipment unknown)
53rd and 64th Companies (25 88mm PAK 43 ea)
57th Company (19 88mm PAK 43)
68th Company (19 75mm PAK 40)
69th Company (26 75mm PAK 40)
70th, 71st and 73rd Companies (27 75mm PAK 40)
74th–92nd Companies (equipment unknown)
93rd–97th Companies (75mm PAK 40)

The 1/X and 2/X Companies became the 8/X and 9/X; the 6/X and 7/X became the 20/X and 21/X; the 24/, 39/, 42/, 46/, 57/, 58/, 60, 66/ and 68/X later built the 1–3 and 5–10/XVIII, 25/, 31/, 41/, 43/ and 48/XVIII; the 36/, 37/, 55/ and 73/X joined the XXXX; and the 29/, 38/, 40/, 56/ and 67/X joined the XXXXII.

The **XI Fortress PAK Verband** was formed in December 1944 in Wehrkreis XI and deployed to the west on the lower Rhine. It consisted of only a staff.

The **XII Fortress PAK Verband** was formed in December 1944 in Wehrkreis V. Initially it consisted solely of a staff, but it later added the 1–8/XII Companies. Their organization is not known.

The **XIII Fortress PAK Verband** was formed in Wehrkreis XIII as a staff. It was apparently very short-lived, as in March 1945 it was created anew by redesignating the XXII Fortress PAK Verband.

The **XIV Fortress PAK Verband** consisted solely of a staff and was formed on 25 December 1944 in Wehrkreis VI.

The **XV Fortress PAK Verband** consisted solely of a staff and was formed in December 1944 in Wehrkreis VII.

The **XVI Fortress PAK Verband** consisted solely of a staff and was formed in December 1944 in Wehrkreis VIII.

The **XVII Fortress PAK Verband** was formed between 23 December 1944 and 5 January 1945 in Wehrkreis XVII using the 17th Panzer Jäger Ersatz Battalion. It was assigned, in April, the 1–10/XVIII Companies, formerly the 24/, 39/, 42/, 46/, 57/, 60/, 66/ and 68/X and the 1204th Fortress Panther Turm (Turret) Company.

The **XVIII Fortress PAK Verband** was formed as a staff in December 1944 in Wehrkreis XVIII. It was later assigned the 1–7/XVIII Companies formed from the former 31/, 38/, 41/, 43/ and 48/X and 1205th and 1206th Panther Fortress Turm Companies.

The **XIX Fortress PAK Verband** was formed solely as a staff in December 1944 in Wehrkreis IX.

The **XX Fortress PAK Verband** was formed in December 1944 in Wehrkreis XX. Tessin indicates that only ten companies were formed, but OKH records show that the 1–12/XX Companies (equipment unknown) were ordered formed.

The **XXI Fortress PAK Verband** was formed in January 1945 by renaming the II Fortress PAK Verband and was then assigned the 1–2/XX Companies (25 88mm PAK 43 each).

The **XXII Fortress PAK Verband** was formed in January 1945 in Wehrkreis XII and renamed the XIII. It was then recreated in March 1945 using the XXX Fortress PAK Verband and then contained the ten companies (1–10/XXII Companies; 12 88mm and 12 LMGs each) from Wehrkreis III.

The **XXIII Fortress PAK Verband** was formed on 10 January 1945 in Wehrkreis XVII and its formation was completed on 15 February 1945. In February 1945 it was assigned the 1–18/XXIII Companies from Wehrkreis XI.

The **XXIV Fortress PAK Verband** was formed in January 1945 in Wehrkreis XVIII. In February it was assigned the 1–15/XXIV Fortress PAK Companies.

The **XXV Fortress PAK Verband** was formed in Denmark in January 1945. Tessin indicates that in March it was assigned the 1–18/XXV Fortress PAK Companies from Wehrkreis XI. OKH records show the following as having been ordered:

1–15/XXV Companies (4 88mm and 8 75mm PAK 40)
16–19/XXV Companies (equipment unknown)

The **XXVI Fortress PAK Verband** was formed in January 1945 in Wehrkreis V. It was assigned the 1–10/XXVI Companies from Wehrkreis XXX. OKH records show the following as having been ordered.

1–10/XXVI Companies (10 88mm PAK 43, 7 panzerschrecke and ? LMGs ea)
11–12/XXVI Companies (equipment unknown)
13–14/XXVI Companies (12 75mm PAK 40 and 12 LMGs ea)

The **XXVII Fortress PAK Verband** was formed in January 1945 in Wehrkreis VII. In March 1945 it received the 1–10/XXVII Companies (4 88mm PAK, 8 75mm PAK 40, 6 panzerschrecke and ? LMGs each) from Wehrkreis III.

The dates of the formation of the **XXVIII Fortress PAK Verband** are not known, but it contained the 1–15/XXVIII Companies (12 75mm PAK 40 each).

The dates of the formation of the **XXIX Fortress PAK Verband** are not known, but it contained the 1–15/XXIX Companies (12 75mm PAK 40 each).

The **XXX Fortress PAK Verband** was formed in the winter of 1944/1945. It became the XXII Fortress PAK Verband and was re-formed sometime in early 1945. It was assigned the 1–3/XXX Companies (total 70 75mm PAK 40), drawn from Wehrkreis XI.

The dates of the formation of the **XXXI Fortress PAK Verband** are not known, but it contained the 1/XXXI Company (8 88mm PAK 40 and 4 88mm PAK 43).

OKH records also show three numbered fortress anti-tank battalions that were apparently formed in late 1944 or early 1945. They were:

501st Fortress PAK Battalion
3 Companies (12 75mm PAK 40 and 12 LMGs ea)
502nd Fortress PAK Battalion
3 Companies (12 75mm PAK 40 and 12 LMGs ea)
503rd Fortress PAK Battalion
3 Companies (12 75mm PAK 40 and 12 LMGs), changed to 3 Flak Companies (12 88mm Russian Flak guns and 12 LMGs ea)

Tank Destroyer Infantry Units

The 1st Feldherrnhalle Panzerjäger Brigade is listed in the OKH records as existing in early 1945. It consisted of five battalions, each with five companies. The companies were organized with six commandos each and apparently armed with the 88mm R Panzerbüchse 54.

The 470th, 471st, 472nd, 473rd, 474th, 475th, 476th, 477th, 478th, and 479th Panzerzerstörer Battalions were formed from late 1943 into early 1945. Very little is known about the 468th. The 470th appears to have been formed under Army Group A, but there is no confirmatory documentation. The 471st was formed in December 1943 by the 1st Panzer Army from Panzerjäger units from disbanded divisions. The staff and 1st Company came from the 333rd Infantry Division and the 2nd and 3rd Companies from the 1/, 2/138th Panzerjäger Battalion of the 38th Infantry Division. In September 1944 it became the 40th Panzerjäger Battalion of the 24th Panzer Division. However, by late 1944 it had been re-formed again.

The 472nd was formed in December with three companies drawn from disbanded divisions. Its staff was from the Staff/139th Panzerjäger Battalion and its 1st and 2nd Companies came from the 1/, 2/223rd Schnelle Battalion. It was destroyed in Bessarabia in August 1944 and disbanded on 6 October 1944.

The 473rd was formed in December 1943 in southern Russia from the remains of disbanded divisions. The staff came from the Staff/322nd Panzerjäger Battalion and its companies were formed from the 2/332nd, 2/219th, and 2/217th Panzerjäger Battalions. It was disbanded on 9 May 1944, but it still remained on OKH records in early 1945, indicating that the number was probably reissued to a new unit.

The 474th was formed in December 1943 by Army Group Center from the remains of disbanded divisions. The staff was formed from the Staff/216th Schnelle Battalion, and the 1st and 3rd Companies were formed from the 1/216th and 2/86th Panzerjäger Battalions. The 2nd Company was never formed.

The 475th was formed in December 1943 with three companies by Army Group Center using the staff and one company of the disbanded 268th Panzerjäger Battalion. The 476th was formed by Army Group Center at the same time, but nothing is known of its constituent units.

The 477th was formed on 29 September 1943 with four companies by Army Group North. It used the Staff/161st Schnelle Battalion, and the 2/11th, 2/23rd, 3/158th, and 2/161st Panzerjäger Battalions. It was disbanded in May 1944 and its elements returned to their newly reconstituted parent formations.

The 479th was formed on 29 September 1943 with four companies by Army Group North using the Staff/181st Schnelle Battalion and the 1/181st, 2/254th, 3/290th, and 4/126th Panzerjäger Battalions. It was disbanded in May 1944. It staff became the Staff/183rd Panzer Jäger Battalion; two companies went to the 753rd Panzerjäger Battalion and one became the 1290th Sturmgeschütz Battalion. However, the number was probably reissued, as it appears in OKH records for late 1944 and early 1945.

The 479th is thought to have been raised in late 1944 or early 1945, but there is not sufficient documentary evidence to do more than state that it was ordered formed.

Each of these battalions had four companies. These companies were each equipped with 54 88mm R Panzerbüchse 54 anti-tank rockets and three LMGs. There were also the 480th, 481st, 482nd 483rd, and 484th Independent Panzerzerstörer Companies, which also had 54 launchers and three LMGs each.

12

Independent Armored Battalions

Tiger Tanks

The first two Tiger units were the 501st and 502nd Heavy Panzer Companies. They were organized on 16 February 1942. On 10 May 1942 these two companies were reassigned to form the cadre of the 501st Heavy Panzer Battalion. The 502nd Heavy Panzer Battalion was organized on 25 May 1942 and the 503rd was organized on 5 May 1942. Each of these battalions was organized with a staff company and two heavy panzer companies. The 501st and 503rd were outfitted with the PzMk VI(P) (P = Porsche) and sent to North Africa. The 502nd was equipped with PzMk VI(H) (H = Henschel) and sent to Russia. The staff companies had two PzMk VI and one PzMk III (50mm) tank in their signals platoons and five PzMk III tanks in the light tank platoons. Each of the heavy tank companies were organized with a company troop (one PzMk VI and two PzMk III tanks) and four platoons (two PzMk VI and two PzMk III tanks each).

On 13 November 1942 orders were issued to raise three heavy panzer companies on 15 November. A company was to be assigned to the 1st, 2nd, and 3rd SS Panzer Regiments. These companies were organized with nine PzMk VIH (Sd Kfz 182) and ten PzMk III (50mm; Sd Kfz 141) tanks.

In December 1942 the 504th Heavy Panzer Battalion was ordered raised. It contained a staff, a staff company, three companies (eight PzMk VI and eight PzMk III tanks each) and a panzer maintenance company. On 17 January 1943 the existing heavy companies were changed to contain only PzMk VI tanks.

The 505th Heavy Panzer Battalion was ordered formed on 24 January 1943 and it was to be operational on 18 February. It was organized with the mixture of PzMk VI and PzMk III tanks, like the 504th Heavy Panzer Battalion. It had 20 PzMk VI (88mm L/56; SdKfz 181) and 25 PzMk III (50mm; Sd Kfz 141). It arrived in Russia in April 1943.

On 5 March 1943 the organization of the battalion staff company and the Tiger companies was altered. Each battalion was then organized with purely Tiger tanks and had three companies. Each company contained a signals platoon with two signals PzMk VI tanks and one conventional PzMk VI. The Company Command Troop contained two PzMk VI tanks and each of the three platoons contained four PzMk VI tanks.

A third heavy tank company was formed for the various heavy tank battalions in 1943:

Heavy Panzer Bn	Date formed
501st	6 Mar. 1943
504th	20 Mar. 1943
505th	3 Apr. 1943

The 2nd Company, 502nd Heavy Panzer Battalion became the 3rd Company in the 503rd. The 502nd then raised new 2nd and 3rd Companies on 1 April 1943.

Somewhat later, the elements of the 502nd, 503rd, and 504th Heavy Panzer Battalions serving in Russia were authorized to assume the pure Tiger structure and the PzMk III tanks were removed, bring each heavy company to 14 PzMk VI tanks.

The formation of Tiger battalions continued in 1943, with the following new battalions being formed and old ones rebuilt:

Heavy Panzer Bn	Date formed	Formed from
506th	8 May 1943	3/33rd Panzer Regt
509th	9 Sept. 1943	
501st	9 Sept. 1943	Remains of original bn
507th	23 Sept. 1943	1/4th Panzer Regt
508th	25 Sept. 1943	Remains of 8th Panzer Regt
504th	18 Nov. 1943	18th Panzer Bn

The 506th Heavy Panzer Battalion was built with 45 Tiger tanks and sent to Russia in the summer of 1943. The 508th also had 45 tanks and was sent to Russia in November 1943.

On 22 April 1943 orders were issued for the formation of a Tiger Battalion for the I SS Panzer Corps. A new staff was organized, but its three companies, previously raised on 15 November 1942 and distributed to the SS divisions, were to remain with those divisions. However, their internal organization was altered and the PzMk III tanks were withdrawn and replaced by PzMk VI tanks.

The I SS Panzer Corps became the II SS Panzer Corps on 1 June 1943. On 27 July 1943 the new I SS Panzer Corps Leibstandarte Adolf Hitler was ordered raised. Its new Tiger Battalion had been ordered raised earlier, on 19 July 1943. This battalion had the pure Tiger organization.

The Tiger Company serving with the 1st SS Panzergrenadier Division LSSAH, originally part of the II SS Panzer Corps Heavy Panzer Battalion, was reassigned to the I SS Panzer Corps Heavy Panzer Battalion as its 3rd Company. A new company was raised in the II SS Panzer Corps Heavy Panzer Battalion to replace this company.

On 22 October 1943 the SS Tiger Battalions were renamed by adding 100 to their numbers. The two SS Tiger Battalions became the 101st and 102nd Heavy SS Panzer Battalions. On 28 October 1943 the operational 1st and 2nd Companies, 101st Heavy SS Panzer Battalion, were assigned to the SS Panzer Division LSSAH and shipped to Russia with 27 PzMkVI tanks. The Staff and 3rd Company remained in the west.

The 3rd Heavy SS Panzer Battalion was ordered raised on 1 July 1943 as the II/11th SS Panzer Regiment. It served in Yugoslavia from August 1943 until January 1944, when it was reassigned to Holland. On 1 November 1943 it was renamed the 3rd Heavy SS Panzer Battalion. The accompanying reorganization was not completed until the end of November.

In 1943 the five heavy panzer battalions were brought to their full strength of 45 Tiger I tanks and deployed the as follows:

Battalion	Deployed to	Month
508th	Italy	February
507th E	ast	March
504th	Italy	June
101st SS	West	June
102nd SS	West	June

In July 1943 the 2/504th Heavy Panzer Battalion was assigned to the Herman Göring Panzer Division.

The 503rd Battalion was returned to Germany to refit on 25 May 1944. It received 12 Tiger II and 33 Tiger I tanks to bring it to the authorized strength of 45 tanks in June 1944. it was then sent to the West and entered action in July 1944. On 27 November 1944 it became the Heavy Panzer Battalion Feldherrnhalle.

The 510th Heavy Panzer Battalion was raised on 6 June 1944. It received 45 Tiger I tanks and was sent to Army Group Center in Russia on 19 July 1944. On 1 June 1944 a new organization of the Tiger Battalions was issued. It established the battalions with:

Staff
3 Tiger tanks Sd Kfz 181 (88mm 36 L/56) or Sd Kfz 182 (88mm 43 L/71) as command vehicles
4 Sd Kfz 251/5 reconnaissance half-tracks
6 Sd Kfz 251/1 half-tracks
3 Sd Kfz 251/7 pioneer half-tracks

3 Companies, each with
either 2 Tiger tanks Sd Kfz 181 (88mm 36 L/56)
or 2 Tiger tanks Sd Kfz 182 (88mm 43 L/71)
3 Platoons, each with
4 Tiger tanks Sd Kfz 181 (88mm 36 L/56)
or 4 Tiger tanks Sd Kfz 182 (88mm 43 L/71)

When the 501st Heavy Panzer Battalion was returned to Germany for refitting in 1944 it was re-established under this new organization. The 3rd Company/503rd and 1st Company/101st SS Heavy Panzer Battalions were withdrawn to Germany for refitting in July 1944 and re-equipped with Tiger II (King Tigers). The 505th was withdrawn from combat on 7 July 1944 and re-equipped with 45 Tiger II tanks. It returned to the Eastern Front, arriving in Nasielsk on 11 September 1944.

On 15 August 1944 the 506th Heavy Panzer Battalion was withdrawn from combat and equipped with 45 Tiger II tanks. On 22 September it was sent to Holland to fight the British thrust on Arnhem. On 8 December 1944 it absorbed the Hummel Heavy Panzer Company as a 4th Company.

On 9 September 1944 the 503rd Heavy Panzer Battalion was withdrawn from combat and re-equipped with Tiger II tanks. On 14 October 1944 it was unloaded in Budapest, Hungary.

The 101st Heavy SS Panzer Battalion, later redesignated as the 501st Heavy Panzer Battalion, was withdrawn and refitted with 45 Tiger II tanks. It returned to the Western Front on 5 December 1944.

On 1 November 1944 a new organizational KstN was issued and the structure of the battalions was changed to:

Battalion Staff Company
Tiger I Sd Kfz 181 88mm KwK 36 (L/56) or Sd Kfz 182 88mm KwK 43 (L/71)
1 Sd Kfz 251/8 half-track
Reconnaissance Platoon
1 Sd Kfz 251/5 reconnaissance vehicle
3 Groups, each with
3 Sd Kfz 251/1
3 Sd Kfz 251/3
Reconnaissance and Pioneer Platoon
3 Reconnaissance Troops
3 Pioneer Troops:
3 Sd Kfz 251/7 half-track
Anti-Aircraft Platoon
3 quad 20mm Flak guns
3 Sd Kfz 7/1 half-tracks
3–4 Companies, each with
Staff
2 Tiger tanks Sd Kfz 181 (88mm 36 L/56)
or 2 Tiger tanks Sd Kfz 182 (88mm 43 L/71)

3 Platoons, each with
4 Tiger tanks Sd Kfz 181 (88mm 36 L/56)
or 4 Tiger tanks Sd Kfz 182 (88mm 43 L/71)

Because of a level of confusion, the three SS Panzer Battalions were renamed from the 101st, 102nd, and 103rd to the 501st, 502nd, and 503rd Heavy Army Panzer Battalions. The existing 501st, 502nd and 503rd Battalions were renamed as follows:

Old name	New name	Date of change
501st	424th	27 Nov. 1944
502nd	511th	5 Jan. 1945
503rd	Feldherrnhalle	21 Dec. 1944

The 102nd SS Heavy Panzer Battalion, renamed the 502nd Heavy Panzer Battalion, was ordered to Sennelager on 9 September 1944 to refit. Six Tiger IIs were assigned, but reassigned on 27 December to the 503rd SS Heavy Panzer Battalion. Between 14 February and 6 March 1945 it received 31 Tiger II tanks. It was sent to Army Group Center in mid-March and committed to battle on 22 March.

In October 1944 the 503rd Heavy Panzer Battalion was used as a receiving units for Tiger I tanks removed from those units that were re-equipping with Tiger IIs. It received its first Tiger II tanks, four of them, on 29 October 1944. Six further were then received from the 502nd Heavy Panzer Battalion. Between 11 and 25 January 1945 a further 29 Tiger II were received. On 27 January 1945 it was sent to the Vistula Army Group on the Eastern Front.

The 507th Heavy Panzer Battalion, except for the 1st Company, was sent to Germany on 30 January 1945 to re-equip with Tiger II tanks. The 1st Company was ordered back on 20 February 1945. On 25 February orders were issued for the battalion to be re-equipped with 31 Tiger II tanks by 31 March. The last Tigers were received on 31 March 1945, with six coming from the 510th and 511th Heavy Panzer Battalions. It had a total strength of 27 Tiger II tanks at that time. When the battalion was ready for operations the war had arrived at its depot, where it was committed to the final defense of Germany.

As of the Battle of the Bulge in December 1944 the Tiger tanks units engaged in the German offensive were:

501st SS Heavy Panzer Battalion (30 PzMk VI King Tigers)
Mk VI Tiger: 45/15/15/30[1]
506th Heavy Panzer Battalion (8 PzMk VI King Tigers)
301th FKL Heavy Panzer Battalion (PzMk VI Tiger I)

Apparently 45 tanks were assigned to the 501st SS Heavy Panzer Battalion, but only 30 were operational on 17 December. A total of 30 King Tigers were assigned to the 506th Heavy Panzer Battalion, but only eight were present on 17 December. The rest were down for repair. The unit slowly gained strength and by 1 January it had 13 operational PzMk VI King Tigers.

In addition to the straight Tiger battalions, special battalions equipped with some Tiger tanks and known as Funklenk-Panzer Battalions were organized. When formed on 25 January 1943 they were equipped with PzMk III tanks and special explosive vehicles known as Sprengstoffträger (Sd Kfz 301). In late 1943 or early 1944 a few of these units were re-equipped with Tiger tanks to serve as the radio control vehicles for the Sprengstoffträger. On 1 February 1944 the Heavy Panzer Companies "Tiger" (FKL) were organized with a group command with two 88mm 36 L/56 Tigers (Sd Kfz 181) or two 88mm/43 L/71 Tigers (Sd Kfz 182) and three platoons, each with four Sd Kfz 181 or four Sd Kfz 182 and a special reserve with 12 Sprengstoffträger.

The 312th Panzer Company (FKL) became the 1/301st Panzer Battalion (FKL) on 7 April 1944. The 301st Panzer Battalion (FKL), equipped with Tigers, was dispatched to Russia on 5 June 1944, but the 4/301st Panzer Battalion remained in the West, attached to the 2nd Panzer Division. The 301st FKL Heavy Panzer Battalion had 27 Tiger I tanks, of which 14 were combat-ready during the Battle of the Bulge. In addition, it had 36 B-IV radio controlled tank bombs and five sturmgeschütze in "long-term repair". The B-IV tanks were loaded with explosives and designed to be driven, by radio, into a target and detonated. This radio-controlled program was a failure. At the end of the year, when the battalion was withdrawn, it had 20 operational Tiger I tanks.

On 16 April 1945 the 507th Heavy Panzer Battalion absorbed the remains of the 508th Heavy Panzer Battalion. On 17 April 1945 it was ordered converted into a panzerjäger battalion and was renamed the 507th Panzer Battalion. It was equipped with Jagdpanzer 38s on 25 April 1945.

The 508th Heavy Panzer Battalion turned in its 15 Tigers on 4 February 1945 and was sent back to Germany to receive Tiger II tanks.

In September 1944 the 509th Heavy Panzer Battalion was issued with 11 Tiger IIs, but turned them over to the 501st Heavy Panzer Battalion at a later date. Between 5 December 1944 and 1 January 1945 it was equipped with 45 Tiger II tanks.

The 3rd Companies of the 510th and 511th Heavy Panzer Battalions were assigned 13 Tiger II tanks on 31 March 1945, which brought each company to a strength of eight Tiger II tanks.

Tiger tanks were also assigned to units other than the independent heavy panzer battalions. On 12 January 1943

---

1 Numbers authorized, present, operational, and en route. These come from Jung, and are confirmed in T-311, Roll 18. They are indicated as "for the 10 December".

the 13th Heavy Panzer Company was organized for the Grossdeutschland Panzer Regiment. It was organized with nine PzMk VIH (Sd Kfz 182) and ten PzMk III (50mm; Sd Kfz 141) tanks. The 3rd Heavy Battalion/Grossdeutschland Panzer Regiment was raised on 1 July 1943 by absorbing the 13th Heavy Company/Grossdeutschland Panzer Regiment as the new 9th Company; the 3rd Company, 501st Heavy Panzer became the 10th Company/GD; and the 3rd Company/504th Heavy Panzer Regiment became the 11th Company/GD.

When the Generalkommando Grossdeutschland Panzer Corps was organized on 28 September 1944 the 3/Grossdeutschland Panzer Regiment, which was equipped with PzMk VI tanks, was redesignated the Grossdeutschland Heavy Panzer Battalion.

By 22 February 1943 the 3/36th Panzer Regiment (14th Panzer Division) was ordered equipped with three companies of Tiger tanks. Each company was to have had ten PzMk VI tanks. When the 16th Panzer Division was or-

dered rebuilt it was to have had the 3/2nd Panzer Regiment equipped with three companies of Tiger tanks, but this seems to have been changed and the battalion was equipped with four companies of sturmgeschütze on 18 February 1943. OKH records dated 22 February 1943 indicate that the 3/24th Panzer Regiment (24th Panzer Division) was equipped with three companies of PzMk VI tanks. Before it was destroyed in North Africa in May 1943 the 3/7th Panzer Regiment (10th Panzer Division) had three companies, each with 10 Tiger tanks.

There were a number of other small detachments of Tiger tanks. In June 1944 Panzer Lehr's 130th Panzer Regiment had three PzMk VI tanks. Late in the war Tigers were put in a number of units including the 3rd Company, 1/29th Panzer Regiment (Müncheberg Panzer Division), the 1st Company/Putlos Panzer Battalion (17 April 1945; Clausewitz Panzer Division), and the Nord Armored Brigade.

Panther Battalions

The first unit equipped with the PzMkV Panther tank was the 51st Panzer Battalion, which was formed from the 2/33rd Panzer Regiment. It was organized with:

Staff
  Signals Squad
    3 Sd Kfz 171 Panther 75mm L 70 command tanks
  Reconnaissance Platoon
    5 Panther tanks Sd Kfz 173
  Flak Platoon
    3 Sd Kfz 7/1 half-tracks with quad 20mm Flak gun
Staff Company
  Signals Squad
    3 Sd Kfz 171 Panther 75mm L 70 command tanks
  Reconnaissance Platoon
    5 Panther tanks Sd Kfz 173
4 Panzer Companies
  Company Troop
    2 Panther tanks Sd Kfz 173
  4 Platoons, each with
    5 Panther tanks Sd Kfz 173

This establishment gave a Panther-equipped regiment 96 Panther tanks. However, a second organization was authorized with 17 Panthers per company and a total strength of 76 Panthers.

The 1/15th Panzer Regiment was redesignated the 52nd Panzer Battalion on 6 February 1943 and equipped with Panther tanks. Two companies were drawn from the 1/1st Panzer Regiment when they were sent to Grafenwöhr to begin training in Panthers on 5 March 1943. The 2/201st

Panzer Regiment was equipped with Panthers on 5 May 1943 and was renamed the 2/23rd Panzer Regiment. The 1/31st Panzer Regiment, 1/11th Panzer Regiment and 3/4th Panzer Regiment (later renamed 1/4th) were the next equipped with Panthers. The 1/1st and 1/2nd SS Panzer Regiments detached personnel on 1 May 1943 and sent them to Germany to form two Panther-equipped battalions. On 25 August 1943 the 1/2nd Panzer Regiment converted to Panthers.

After the Battle of Kursk the surviving Panthers were incorporated into the 52nd Panzer Battalion. The 52nd Panzer Battalion was redesignated the 1/15th Panzer Regiment on 24 August 1943. The 51st Panzer Battalion was re-equipped with a full new allotment of 96 Panthers in August 1943 and assigned to the Grossdeutschland Panzergrenadier Battalion.

On 1 November 1943 a Panther Regiment structure was issued. The battalions had the same organization as before, but the regimental staff now had eight Panther tanks.

Determining when the various units were equipped with Panthers is difficult. The following table summarizes the dates that PzMkV were known to have been shipped from the factory (indicated thus *) to the various divisions or when they were ordered re-equipped with Panther tanks.

Panther Tank Battalions	Division	Date if known	No of tanks per Company
51st Panzer Bn	Independent bn	Jan./Feb. 1943	19[1]
52nd Panzer Bn	Independent bn	6 Feb. 1943	19
1/1st SS	Leibstandarte SS	Nov. 1943	19
1/2nd SS	Das Reich	Aug. 1943	unknown
SS Wiking	Wiking SS	18 Dec. 1943★	19
1/Grossdeutschland	Grossdeutschland	8 Feb. 1944	17
Lehr Regiment	Panzer Lehr Div	3 Jan. 1944	unknown
1/1st	1st Panzer Div	9 Nov. 1943★	19
1/2nd	16th Panzer Div	25 Aug. 1943	ordered
1/3rd	2nd Panzer Div	4 Oct. 1943★	17
1/3rd	2nd Panzer Div	mid-April 1944	22
1/4th	13th Panzer Div	23 Dec. 1943	18
1/6th	3rd Panzer Div	13 Dec. 1943★	19
1/11th	6th Panzer Div	15 Jan. 1944	22
2/23rd	23rd Panzer Div	5 May 1943	ordered
		28 Dec. 1943	17
1/24th	24th Panzer Div	30 May 1944	unknown
1/26th	26th Panzer Div	25 Nov. 1943	19
1/27th	19th Panzer Div	30 Mar. 1944	17
1/25th	7th Panzer Div	30 Jan. 1944	17
1/29th	12th Panzer Div	30 Dec. 1943	22
1/31st	5th Panzer Div	25 Sept. 1943★	17
2/33rd	9th Panzer Div		22
2/35th	4th Panzer Div	15 Nov. 1944	17
		14 Nov. 1943★	14
1/36th	14th Panzer Div	25 June 1944	unknown
		12 Sept. 1943★	17
		8 Dec. 1943★	18

[1] Numbers of tanks per company were determined by dividing total number of tanks shipped by four companies.

13

German Artillery Formations

In World War II German artillery existed in two forms. The first was integral artillery assigned to formations of mixed infantry, artillery, cavalry and/or armor. The other formation where artillery was found was as independent formations that were assigned on the army and corps level. It is the intention of this chapter to address this second type of unit.

Under the Reichswehr, the Weimar Army, all artillery except that organic to the infantry divisions, was assigned to the general headquarters pool. Units were allocated from this pool based on tactical requirements, or on loan to divisions or corps.

Artillery was normally placed under the command of an *Artillerieführer* (Arfü), who was a divisional artillery regiment's commander. When general headquarters pool units were attached, a complete artillery staff came with them. This was under the command of a senior officer, known as the *Artillerie Kommandeur* (Arko). He took command of both the divisional artillery and his specialized artillery units. The Arkos were permanent staffs and were identified as such.

At the general headquarters, the *Artillery Kommandeur* was a general officer. Though he could be referred to as an *Arko*, he was normally called the *General der Artillerie*. He and his staff were part of the general headquarters, which was not normally given an unique number to identify it.

On the level of the army group or army, the artillery commander was the *Höher Artillerie Kommandeur* (HohArko), and was normally a Generalleutnant. These units were numbered 301st and upwards.

The corps and division Arkos were numbered 1st through 44th, and 101st upwards. However, by the end of the war this numbering system was abandoned and the numbers ran from 401st through 500th.

The artillery commanded by these men consisted of several different formations:

Abteilungen[1] *und Batterien* (Detachments and Batteries). These were the smallest artillery formation. They were equipped with a multitude of guns and could be motorized, self-propelled, railroad, horse drawn, or fixed.

Artillerie Regimentsstab (Artillery Regimental Staff). These were staff units organized under the various General Headquarters and allotted to command General Headquarters artillery on loan to an operational formation.

Sturmgeschütz Artillerie (Assault Guns). Though some assault guns were also assigned as integral parts of infantry and armored divisions, a large number served as independent formations. All of them were under the nominal direction of the Army Artillery Staff. These units are covered in Chapter X.

Herresflakabteilungen (Army Flak Detachments). The bulk of the anti-aircraft weapons were under the control of the Luftwaffe, but a large number of army Flak formations existed.

Beobachtungs Abteilungen. (Observation Detachments). These formations were part of the artillery fire control system. The were the flash and sound ranging formations and also performed general artillery intelligence tasks.

Vermessung und Karten Abteilungen (Survey and Mapping Detachments). These units provided materials necessary for artillery support. They were allocated as necessary.

Velocitäts Mess-Zug (Velocity Measuring Platoon). These units were involved in the calibration of weapons. They were numbered 701st and upwards.

Astronomische Mess-Zug (Astronomical Calibration Platoon). These units supported the *Vermessung und Karten Abteilungen* and used stars as infinite fixed points for the calibration of batteries.

Wetter Peilzug (Meteorological Section). These units provided data to support artillery operations. They were numbered 501st to 600th.

Armee Kartenstelle (Army Map Depots). These units provided maps to support the artillery and were numbered 501st through 600th.

Artillerie-Park (Artillery Park). These were formations that controlled artillery equipment not assigned to combat formations.

---

[1] The German word "Abteilung" can be translated either as "detachment" or "battalion". It was normally a battalion-sized formation with two or three batteries.

Artillerie Lehr-Regiment: (Artillery Training Regiment). These were instructional and demonstration units. Their purpose was both to train new artillerists and to evaluate new weapons.

Heeresküsten Artillery: (Army Coast Artillery). This organization commanded coast defense sections under the command of either an Army or Navy headquarters. Most of these units were under the command of Naval Staffs.

HIGHER ARTILLERY FORMATIONS

18th Artillery Division

The 18th Artillery Division was formed in September 1943 from the remains of the disbanded 18th Panzer Division. The 88th Light Artillery Regiment was formed with its 1st Battalion equipped with 105mm leFH-Sfl Wespe self-propelled howitzers; the 2nd, 3rd and 4th Battalions had 105mm leFH (mot). The 288th Heavy Artillery Regiment's 1st and 2nd Battalions were equipped with 150mm sFH (mot) (from the 4/96th and 4/371st), the 3rd Battalion with 210mm mortars (from the 809th Battalion), and the 4th Battalion with 100mm guns (from the old 3/88th AR); the Staff/782nd Artillery Regiment had the 4th Light Observation Battalion, 740th Heavy Artillery Battalion (170mm guns), and 280th Army Flak Battalion. When formed the Division had:

88th Artillery Regiment
1 (mot) Regimental Staff Battery
1st Battalion
  1 (mot) Staff Battery
  2 (mot) Batteries (3 105mm leFH and 2 LMGs ea)
  1 Self-Propelled Battery (2 150mm sFH and 2 LMGs)
2nd Battalion
  1 (mot) Staff Battery
  2 (mot) Batteries (4 105mm leFH and 2 LMGs ea)
  1 Self-Propelled Battery (2 105mm leFH and 2 LMGs)
3rd (RSO) Battalion
  1 (mot) Staff Battery
  3 (mot) Batteries (3 105mm leFH and 2 LMGs ea)
4th (RSO) Battalion
  1 (mot) Staff Battery
  3 (mot) Batteries (4 105mm leFH and 2 LMGs ea)

288th Artillery Regiment
1 (mot) Regimental Staff Battery
1st Battalion (formerly 4/96th Artillery Regiment)
  1 (mot) Staff Battery
  2 (mot) Batteries (4 105mm leFH and 2 LMGs ea)
  1 (mot) Battery (4 100mm K18 and 2 LMGs)
2nd Battalion (formerly 4/371st Artillery Regiment)
  1 (mot) Staff Battery
  2 (mot) Batteries (4 105mm leFH and 2 LMGs ea)
  1 (mot) Battery (4 100mm K18 and 2 LMGs)
3rd Battalion (formerly 3/88th Artillery Regiment)
  1 (mot) Staff Battery

  1 (mot) Battery (3 105mm leFH and 2 LMGs ea)
  1 (mot) Battery (2 105mm leFH and 2 LMGs ea)
  1 (mot) Battery (4 100mm K18 and 2 LMGs)
4th Battalion
  1 (mot) Staff Battery
  3 (mot) Batteries (3 210mm mörsers and 2 LMGs ea)

388th Artillery Regiment
4th Observation Battalion
  1 (mot) Staff (2 LMGs)
  1 (mot) Sound Ranging Battery (2 20mm and 6 LMGs)
  1 (mot) Flash Ranging Battery (9 LMGs)
740th Artillery Battalion
  1 (mot) Staff Battery
  3 (mot) Batteries (3 150mm guns and 2 LMGs ea)
280th Flak Battalion
  1 (mot) Staff Battery
  1 (mot) Battery (9 20mm (mot), 2 20mm quad self-propelled and 2 LMGs)
  2 (mot) Batteries (4 88mm, 3 20mm and 2 LMGs ea)
  1 (mot) Light Flak Column

741st Sturmgeschütz Battery (added later)
(10 sturmgeschützen)

88th Schützen Battalion (added later)

18th Fire Control Battery (added later)

88th Division Signals Battalion (added 7 Sept. 1943)

88th Supply Troop
4 (120 ton) (mot) Transportation Companies (4 LMGs ea)
1 (mot) Supply Company (6 LMGs)
2 (mot) Maintenance Companies

Administrative Troops
1 (mot) Bakery Company
1 (mot) Butcher Company
1 (mot) Divisional Administration Company

Medical
1 (mot) Medical Company (2 LMGs)
1 (mot) Ambulance

Other
1 (mot) Feldgendarme Troop
1 (mot) Field Post Office

The organization of the division was apparently quite variable, as on 16 November 1943 the division was ordered reorganized as follows:

Divisional Staff
88th (mot) Mapping Detachment
88th (mot) Military Police Troop (1 LMG)

88th Artillery Regiment
1 (mot) Regimental Staff Battery

1st Battalion
1 (mot) Staff Battery
2 (motZ) Batteries (6 Wespe SdKfz 124 with 105mm leFH and 2 LMGs ea)
1 Self-Propelled Battery (6 Hummel SdKfz 165 with 150mm sFH and 2 LMGs)

2nd Battalion
1 (mot) Staff Battery
3 (motZ) Batteries (4 105mm leFH and 2 LMGs ea)

3rd (RSO) Battalion
1 (mot) Staff Battery
2 (motZ) Batteries (4 105mm leFH and 2 LMGs ea)
1 (motZ) Battery (4 100mm guns and 2 LMGs)

4th (RSO) Battalion
1 (mot) Staff Battery
3 (motZ) Batteries (4 105mm leFH and 2 LMGs ea)

288th Artillery Regiment
1 (mot) Regimental Staff Battery

1st Battalion
1 (mot) Staff Battery
3 (motZ) Batteries (4 105mm leFH and 2 LMGs ea)

2nd Battalion (formerly 987th Artillery Regiment)
1 (mot) Staff Battery
2 (motZ) Batteries (4 150mm sFH and 2 LMGs ea)
1 (motZ) Battery (4 100mm K18 and 2 LMGs)

3rd Battalion (formerly 1–3rd Btrys, 740th Artillery Battalion)
1 (mot) Staff Battery
3 (motZ) Batteries (3 170mm guns and 2 LMGs ea)

388th Artillery Regiment (formerly 782nd)
1 Regimental Staff and (mot) Staff Battery (2 LMGs)

1/388th Artillery Regiment (formerly 2/262nd Artillery Regiment)
1 Battalion Staff and (mot) Staff Battery
3 (motZ) Batteries (4 105mm leFH and 2 LMGs ea)

2/388th Artillery Regiment (formerly 986th Artillery Battalion)
1 Battalion Staff and (mot) Staff Battery
2 (motZ) Batteries (4 150mm sFH and 2 LMGs ea)
1 (motZ) Battery (4 100mm guns and 2 LMGs)

3/388th Artillery Regiment (formerly 809th Artillery Battalion)
1 Battalion Staff and (mot) Staff Battery
3 (motZ) Batteries (3 210mm mörsers and 2 LMGs ea)

741st Sturmgeschütz Battery
(10 sturmgeschützen)

280th Flak Battalion
2 (motZ) Heavy Flak Batteries (4 88mm, 3 20mm and 2 LMGs ea)

1 (motZ) Light Battery (9 20mm, 2 self-propelled quad 20mm and 2 LMGs)
1 (motZ) Light Battery (12 20mm guns and 2 LMGs)

4th Observation Battalion
1 (mot) Staff Battery (2 LMGs)
1 (mot) Calibration Detachment
1 (mot) Flash Ranging Battery (9 LMGs)
1 (mot) Sound Ranging Battery (6 LMGs)

18th (mot) Fire Control Battery (2 LMGs)

88th Division Signals Battalion (added 7 Sept. 1943)
1 (mot) Telephone Company (5 LMGs)
1 (mot) Telephone Intercept Company (4 LMGs)
1 (mot) Radio Company (7 LMGs)
1 (mot) Light Signals Supply Column

88th Feldersatz Battalion
1 Transportation Company
1 Signals Company
3 Batteries

88th Supply Troop
1/, 2/, 3/, 4/88th (120 ton) (mot) Transportation Companies (4 LMGs ea)
5/88th (60 ton) (horse-drawn) Transportation Company (8 LMGs)
88th (mot) Supply Company (6 LMGs)
1/, 2/, 3/88th (mot) Maintenance Companies
88th (mot) Maintenance Supply Column

Administrative Troops
1 (mot) Bakery Company
1 (mot) Butcher Company
1 (mot) Divisional Administration Company

Medical
1/88th (mot) Medical Company (2 LMGs)
1/88th (mot) Ambulance

Other
88th (mot) Field Post Office

The division's equipment shortages were quickly made up and the division was, to a large degree, re-equipped. The 1/88th was a self-propelled battalion with two light and a heavy battery, each with six guns. The 2/, 3/, 4/88th each had four 105mm leFH and two LMGs. The 1/, 2/288th were equipped with four sFH and two LMGs each. The 3/288th had three 210mm mörsers and the 3/288th three batteries, each with four 100mm K 18 and two LMGs. The 740th Artillery Battalion had three (mot) batteries, each with three 170mm guns and two LMGs. The 280th Artillery Battalion was as shown above, with the addition of a 10th (mot) Battery with 12 20mm and two LMGs. The signals battalion had been armored, but the armored equipment was stripped out and replaced with non-armored equipment. The division was disbanded on 27 August 1944.

309th–312th Artillery Divisions

While serving in Russia, the 310th, 311th, and 312th Höhrer Arkos, part of Army Group South, organized artillery divisions with the same numbers in November 1943. At the same time, the 309th Artillery Division was organized in the west. These divisions had a number of independent artillery battalions assigned to them on a temporary basis. On 20 July 1944 the 310th, 311th, and 312th Artillery Divisions were broken up and their assigned battalions were used to organize the XI, XII, and XIII SS Corps. The staffs of these divisions were organized as follows:

309th Artillery Division Staff
309th (mot) Mapping Detachment
309th Artillery Brigade Staff
  1 (mixed mobility) Telephone Company (6 LMGs)
  1 (mot) Signals Company (4 LMGs)
  1 (mixed mobility) Signals Supply Column (1 LMG)
1/, 2/309th (mot) Maintenance Battalion
1/, 2/309th (mot) Transportation Battalion
310th Artillery Division Staff
310th (mot) Mapping Detachment

310th Artillery Brigade Staff
  1 (mixed mobility) Telephone Company (6 LMGs)
  1 (mot) Signals Company (4 LMGs)
  1 (mixed mobility) Signals Supply Column (1 LMG)
1/, 2/310th (mot) Maintenance Battalion
1/, 2/310th (mot) Transportation Battalion
311th Artillery Division Staff
311th (mot) Mapping Detachment
311th Artillery Brigade Staff
  1 (mixed mobility) Telephone Company (6 LMGs)
  1 (mot) Signals Company (4 LMGs)
  1 (mixed mobility) Signals Supply Column (1 LMG)
1/, 2/311th (mot) Maintenance Battalion
1/, 2/311th (mot) Transportation Battalion
312th Artillery Division Staff
312th (mot) Mapping Detachment
312th Artillery Brigade Staff
  1 (mixed mobility) Telephone Company (6 LMGs)
  1 (mot) Signals Company (4 LMGs)
  1 (mixed mobility) Signals Supply Column (1 LMG)
1/, 2/312th (mot) Maintenance Battalion
1/, 2/312th (mot) Transportation Battalion

Volks Artillery Corps

These formations were organized in September/October 1944 and were given the name Volks-Artillerie-Korps in November. They were numbered 166th, 388th, 401st–410th, 704th, 732nd, 766th, and 959th. In essence, like the 411th and 423th Artillery Corps, they were little more than very powerful artillery regiments. They contained five or six artillery battalions each, about half of them light and the other half heavy artillery. The Volks Artillery Corps were ordered formed on 20 October 1944 as follows:

Volks Artillery Corps	Formed From
388th	388th (mot) Artillery Brigade
401st	401st (mot) Artillery Brigade
402nd	402nd (mot) Artillery Brigade
403rd	403rd (tbew.mot) Artillery Brigade
404th	404th (tbew.mot) Artillery Brigade
405th	405th (tbew.mot) Artillery Brigade
406th	406th (tbew.mot) Artillery Brigade
407th	407th (tbew.mot) Artillery Brigade
408th	408th (tbew.mot) Artillery Brigade
409th	409th (mot) Artillery Brigade
410th	410th (mot) Artillery Brigade
766th	766th (mot) Artillery Brigade

These were not the only artillery corps formed. Others known to have been raised were the 411th, 704th, 732nd, 959th, and 1095th Volks Artillery Corps.

There were two organizations of the motorized Volks Artillery Corps. The first organization contained:

Type I (mot) Volks Artillery Corps
Corps Headquarters
  (mot) Headquarters
  (mot) Observation Battery (12 LMGs)
  (mot) Staff Battery (2 LMGs)
1st Battalion
  1 (mot) Staff Battery (2 LMGs)
  3 (mot) 75mm Batteries (6 75mm FK 40 and 2 LMGs ea)
2nd Battalion
  1 (mot) Staff Battery (2 LMGs)
  3 (mot) 88mm Batteries (6 88mm FK 43 and 2 LMGs ea)
3rd Battalion
  1 (mot) Staff Battery (2 LMGs)
  3 (mot) 105mm Batteries (6 105mm leFH 18 and 2 LMGs ea)
4th Battalion
  1 (mot) Staff Battery (2 LMGs)
  2 (mot) 122mm Batteries (6 122mm sFH and 2 LMGs ea)

5th Battalion
  1 (mot) Staff Battery (2 LMGs)
  2 (mot) 150mm Batteries (6 150mm sFH 18 and 2 LMGs ea)
6th Battalion
  1 (mot) Staff Battery (2 LMGs)
  2 (mot) Batteries (3 210mm mörsers and 2 LMGs ea)
  1 (mot) Battery (3 170mm and 2 LMGs ea)

The Type I Corps had 18 75mm FK 40, 18 88mm FK 43, 18 105mm leFH 18, 12 122mm sFH, 12 150mm sFH, six 210mm mörsers and three 170mm guns.

Type II (mot) Volks Artillery Corps

Corps Headquarters
  (mot) Headquarters
  (mot) Staff Battery (2 LMGs)
1st Battalion (towed by Raupenschlepper Ost)
  1 (mot) Staff Battery (2 LMGs)
  3 (mot) 75mm Batteries (6 75mm FK 40 and 2 LMGs ea)
2nd Battalion
  1 (mot) Staff Battery (2 LMGs)
  2 (mot) 100mm Batteries (6 100mm K 18 and 2 LMGs ea)
3rd Battalion (towed by Raupenschlepper Ost)
  1 (mot) Staff Battery (2 LMGs)
  3 (mot) 105mm Batteries (6 105mm leFH 18 and 2 LMGs ea)
4th Battalion
  1 (mot) Staff Battery (2 LMGs)
  2 (mot) 122mm Batteries (6 122mm (r) sFH and 2 LMGs ea)
5th Battalion
  1 (mot) Staff Battery (2 LMGs)
  2 (mot) 152mm Batteries (6 152mm (r) sFH and 2 LMGs ea)

The Type II Corps had 18 75mm FK 40, 12 100mm K 18, 18 105mm leFH 18, 12 122mm sFH, and 12 150mm sFH. In fact, the Type II Corps had a variation which allocated a 6th Battalion to it. This battalion contained a staff battery with two LMGs, and three batteries each with nine 210mm mörsers and four LMGs.

There were also two formations of the partially motorized (tbew.mot) Volks Artillery Corps. They were organized in the same way s the motorized corps, although the numbers of trucks and prime movers were reduced. The Type I (mot) Volks Artillery Corps had 406 trucks and 111 prime movers, the Type II had 294 and 84, the Type I (tbew.mot) had 157 and 121 and the Type II had 124 and 89 respectively. The (tmot) artillery corps were as follows:

Type I (tmot) Volks Artillery Corps

Corps Headquarters
  (tmot) Headquarters
  (tmot) Staff Battery (2 LMGs)

1st Battalion
  1 (tmot) Staff Battery (2 LMGs)
  3 (tmot) 75mm Batteries (6 75mm FK 40 and 2 LMGs ea)
2nd Battalion
  1 (tmot) Staff Battery (2 LMGs)
  3 (tmot) 88mm Batteries (6 88mm FK 43 and 2 LMGs ea)
3rd Battalion
  1 (tmot) Staff Battery (2 LMGs)
  3 (tmot) 105mm Batteries (6 105mm leFH 18 and 2 LMGs ea)
4th Battalion
  1 (tmot) Staff Battery (2 LMGs)
  2 (tmot) 150mm Batteries (6 150mm sFH 18 and 2 LMGs ea)
5th Battalion
  1 (tmot) Staff Battery (2 LMGs)
  2 (tmot) 122mm Batteries (6 122mm sFH and 2 LMGs ea)
6th Battalion
  1 (tmot) Staff Battery (2 LMGs)
  2 (tmot) Batteries (3 210mm mörsers and 2 LMGs ea)
  1 (tmot) Battery (3 170mm and 2 LMGs ea)

Type II (tmot) Volks Artillery Corps

Corps Headquarters
  (tmot) Headquarters
  (tmot) Staff Battery (2 LMGs)
1st Battalion (towed by Raupenschlepper Ost)
  1 (tmot) Staff Battery (2 LMGs)
  3 (tmot) 75mm Batteries (6 75mm FK 40 and 2 LMGs ea)
2nd Battalion
  1 (tmot) Staff Battery (2 LMGs)
  2 (tmot) 100mm Batteries (6 100mm K 18 and 2 LMGs ea)
3rd Battalion (towed by Raupenschlepper Ost)
  1 (tmot) Staff Battery (2 LMGs)
  3 (tmot) 105mm Batteries (6 105mm leFH 18 and 2 LMGs ea)
4th Battalion
  1 (tmot) Staff Battery (2 LMGs)
  2 (tmot) 122mm Batteries (6 122mm (r) sFH and 2 LMGs ea)
5th Battalion
  1 (tmot) Staff Battery (2 LMGs)
  2 (tmot) 152mm Batteries (6 152mm (r) sFH 18 and 2 LMGs ea)

On 2 November 1944 the 401st Volks Artillery Corps was organized as follows:

Brigade Staff

  1 Brigade Staff
  401st (mot) Staff Battery (2 LMGs)

401st (mot) Observation Battery (6 LMGs)

1st Battalion

1 (mot) Staff and (mot) Staff Battery (2 LMGs)

1st–3rd (motZ) Batteries (6 75mm FK 40 and 4 LMGs ea)

2nd Battalion

1 (mot) Staff and (mot) Staff Battery (2 LMGs)

4th–5th (motZ) Batteries (6 100mm guns and 4 LMGs)

3rd Battalion

1 (mot) Staff and (mot) Staff Battery (2 LMGs)

6th–9th (motZ) Batteries (6 105mm leFH and 4 LMGs ea)

4th Battalion

1 (mot) Staff and (mot) Staff Battery (2 LMGs)

10th–11th (motZ) Batteries (6 152mm 433/I (r) and 4 LMGs ea)

5th Battalion

1 (mot) Staff and (mot) Staff Battery (2 LMGs)

13th–14th (motZ) Batteries (6 122mm Russian howitzers and 4 LMGs ea)

On 2 November 1944 the 388th Volks Artillery Corps was organized as follows:

Brigade Staff

1 Brigade Staff

388th (mot) Staff Battery (2 LMGs)

388th (mot) Observation Battery (6 LMGs)

388th (mot) Control Company (3 LMGs)

1st Battalion

1 (mot) Staff and (mot) Staff Battery (2 LMGs)

1st–3rd (motZ) Batteries (6 75mm FK 40 and 4 LMGs ea)

2nd Battalion

1 (mot) Staff and (mot) Staff Battery (2 LMGs)

4th–5th (motZ) Batteries (6 88mm PAK 43 guns and 4 LMGs)

3rd Battalion

1 (mot) Staff and (mot) Staff Battery (2 LMGs)

6th–9th (motZ) Batteries (6 105mm leFH and 4 LMGs ea)

4th Battalion

1 (mot) Staff and (mot) Staff Battery (2 LMGs)

10th–11th (motZ) Batteries (6 150mm sFH and 4 LMGs ea)

5th Battalion

1 (mot) Staff and (mot) Staff Battery (2 LMGs)

13th–14th (motZ) Batteries (6 122mm Russian howitzers and 4 LMGs ea)

6th Battalion

1 (mot) Staff and (mot) Staff Battery (2 LMGs)

15th–16th (motZ) Batteries (3 210mm mörsers and 4 LMGs)

18th (formerly 2/767th Battalion) (motZ) Battery (3 170mm guns and 4 LMGs)

The identity of the specific units assigned is not known as they lost their original identities and became merely the 1st, 2nd, and 3rd Battalions of a given Corps. The battalions and weapons assigned to some of those corps are shown below, with the effective dates in parantheses after the corps name:

388th (mot) Volks Artillery Corps (on 2 Nov. 1944)

1 Staff and (mot) Staff Battery (2 LMGs)

388th (mot) Observation Battery (12, later 6 LMGs)

18th (later 388th) (mot) Fire Coordination Battery (3 LMGs)

1st (motZ) Battalion (RSO)

1 Staff and Staff Battery (2 LMGs)

3 (motZ) Batteries (6 75mm FK 40 and 4 LMGs ea)

2nd (motZ) Battalion

1 Staff and Staff Battery (2 LMGs)

3 (motZ) Batteries (6 88mm PAK 43 and 4 LMGs ea)

3rd (motZ) Battalion (RSO)

1 Staff and Staff Battery (2 LMGs)

3 (motZ) Batteries (6 105mm leFH 18/40 and 4 LMGs ea)

4th (motZ) Battalion

1 Staff and Staff Battery (2 LMGs)

2 (motZ) Batteries (6 150mm sFH and 4 LMGs ea)

5th (motZ) Battalion

1 Staff and Staff Battery (2 LMGs)

2 (motZ) Batteries (6 122mm sFH 396 (r) and 4 LMGs ea; 122mm guns replaced by 105mm leFH in January 1945)

6th (motZ) Battalion

1 Staff and Staff Battery (2 LMGs)

2 (motZ) Batteries (3 210mm howitzers and 5 LMGs ea)

1 (motZ) Battery (3 170mm guns and 5 LMGs)

401st (mot) Volks Artillery Corps (on 2 Nov. 1944)

1 Staff and (mot) Staff Battery (2 LMGs)

401st (mot) Observation Battery (12, later 6 LMGs)

1st (motZ) Battalion (RSO)

1 Staff and Staff Battery (2 LMGs)

3 (motZ) Batteries (6 75mm FK 40 and 4 LMGs ea)

2nd (motZ) Battalion

1 Staff and Staff Battery (2 LMGs)

2 (motZ) Batteries (6 100mm K18 guns and 4 LMGs ea)

3rd (motZ) Battalion (RSO)

1 Staff and Staff Battery (2 LMGs)

3 (motZ) Batteries (6 105mm leFH 18/40 and 4 LMGs ea)

4th (motZ) Battalion

1 Staff and Staff Battery (2 LMGs)

2 (motZ) Batteries (6 152mm KH 433 (r) and 4 LMGs ea)

5th (motZ) Battalion
  1 Staff and Staff Battery (2 LMGs)
  2 (motZ) Batteries (6 122mm sFH 396 (r) and 4 LMGs ea)
  16th (motZ) Battery (3 128mm guns and 4 LMGs) (added 29 Mar. 1945)

402nd (mot) Volks Artillery Corps (on 2 Nov. 1944)
  402nd Brigade (mot) Staff Battery (2 LMGs)
  402nd (mot) Observation Battery (2 LMGs)
  1st (motZ) Battalion
    1 Staff and Staff Battery (2 LMGs)
    3 (motZ) Batteries (6 75mm FK 40 and 4 LMGs ea)
  2nd (motZ) Battalion
    1 Staff and Staff Battery (2 LMGs)
    2 (motZ) Batteries (6 100mm K18 guns and 4 LMGs ea))
  3rd (motZ) Battalion
    1 Staff and Staff Battery (2 LMGs)
    3 (motZ) Batteries (6 105mm leFH 18/40 and 4 LMGs ea)
  4th (motZ) Battalion
    1 Staff and Staff Battery (2 LMGs)
    2 (motZ) Batteries (6 152mm KH 433 (r) and 4 LMGs ea)
  5th (motZ) Battalion
    1 Staff and Staff Battery (2 LMGs)
    2 (motZ) Batteries (6 122mm sFH 396 (r) and 4 LMGs ea; 122mm guns replaced by 105mm leFH in January 1945)

403rd (tmot) Volks Artillery Corps (on 2 Nov. 1944)
  1 Brigade (tmot) Staff Battery (2 LMGs)
  1st Battalion (RSO)
    1 Staff and Staff Battery (2 LMGs)
    3 (tmot) Batteries (6 105mm leFH and 4 LMGs ea)
  2nd Battalion (RSO)
    1 Staff and Staff Battery (2 LMGs)
    3 (tmot) Batteries (6 88mm PAK 43 and 4 LMGs ea)
  3rd Battalion (RSO)
    1 Staff and Staff Battery (2 LMGs)
    3 (tmot) Batteries (6 105mm leFH and 4 LMGs ea)
  4th Battalion
    1 Staff and Staff Battery (2 LMGs)
    2 (tmot) Batteries (6 150 sFH 18 and 4 LMGs ea)
  5th Battalion (RSO)
    1 Staff and Staff Battery (2 LMGs)
    2 (tmot) Batteries (6 122mm sFH 396 (r) and 4 LMGs ea)
  6th Battalion
    1 Staff and Staff Battery (2 LMGs)
    2 (tmot) Batteries (3 210mm howitzers and 5 LMGs ea)
    1 (tmot) Battery (3 170mm guns and 5 LMGs)

404th (tmot) Volks Artillery Corps (on 29 Sept. 1944)
  1 Staff and (tmot) Staff Battery (2 LMGs)
  404th (tmot) Gunfire Direction Battery (3 LMGs)

1st Battalion (RSO)
  1 Staff and Staff Battery (2 LMGs)
  3 (tmot) Batteries (6 105mm leFH 18/40 and 4 LMGs ea)
2nd Battalion
  1 Staff and Staff Battery (2 LMGs)
  3 (tmot) Batteries (6 88mm PAK 43 and 4 LMGs ea)
3rd Battalion (RSO)
  1 Staff and Staff Battery (2 LMGs)
  3 (tmot) Batteries (6 105mm leFH 18/40 and 4 LMGs ea)
4th Battalion
  1 Staff and Staff Battery (2 LMGs)
  2 (tmot) Batteries (6 150mm sFH and 4 LMGs ea)
5th Battalion
  1 Staff and Staff Battery (2 LMGs)
  2 (tmot) Batteries (6 122mm sFH 396 (r) and 4 LMGs ea; replaced by 6 105mm leFH 18/40 and 4 LMGs ea in Jan. 1945)
6th Battalion
  1 Staff and Staff Battery (2 LMGs)
  2 (tmot) Batteries (3 210mm mörsers and 5 LMGs ea)
  1 (tmot) Battery (3 170mm guns and 5 LMGs)

Note: Field returns from the Battle of the Bulge show that the 150mm sFH were replaced by 12 152mm KH433 (r), that either the 1st or 2nd Battalions had 18 75mm FK40 and that the 6th Battalion was equipped with 12 100mm guns.

405th (tmot) Volks Artillery Corps (on 29 Sept. 1944)
  1 Staff and (tmot) Staff Battery (2 LMGs)
  405th (tmot) Observation Battery (12 LMGs)
  1st Battalion (RSO)
    1 Staff and Staff Battery (2 LMGs)
    3 (motZ) Batteries (6 75mm FK 40 and 4 LMGs ea)
  2nd Battalion
    1 Staff and Staff Battery (2 LMGs)
    2 (motZ) Batteries (6 100mmK 18 and 4 LMGs ea)
  3rd Battalion (RSO)
    1 Staff and Staff Battery (2 LMGs)
    3 (motZ) Batteries (6 105mm leFH 18/40 and 4 LMGs ea)
  4th Battalion
    1 Staff and Staff Battery (2 LMGs)
    2 (motZ) Batteries (6 152mm KH 433 (r) and 4 LMGs ea)
  5th Battalion
    1 Staff and Staff Battery (2 LMGs)
    2 (motZ) Batteries (6 122mm sFH 396 (r) and 4 LMGs ea; on 13 Feb. 1945 the 122mm howitzers were replaced by 10mm leFH 18/40 howitzers)
  Added on13 Apr. 1945
    1 (tmot) Battery (4 100mm K 18 guns and 4 LMGs)
    1 (tmot) Battery (4 128mm guns and 4 LMGs)

406th (mot) Volks Artillery Corps (on 29 Sept. 1944; became tmot on 2 Nov. 1944)

1 Staff and (mot) Staff Battery (2 LMGs)

1st Battalion (RSO)
  1 Staff and Staff Battery (2 LMGs)
  3 (motZ) Batteries (6 75mm FK 40 and 4 LMGs ea)

2nd Battalion
  1 Staff and Staff Battery (2 LMGs)
  2 (motZ) Batteries (6 100mm K 18 and 4 LMGs ea)

3rd Battalion (RSO)
  1 Staff and Staff Battery (2 LMGs)
  3 (motZ) Batteries (6 105mm leFH 18/40 and 4 LMGs ea)

4th Battalion
  1 Staff and Staff Battery (2 LMGs)
  2 (motZ) Batteries (6 152mm KH 433 (r) and 4 LMGs ea)

5th Battalion
  1 Staff and Staff Battery (2 LMGs)
  2 (motZ) Batteries (6 122mm sFH 396 (r) and 4 LMGs ea; on 13 Feb. 1945 the 122mm howitzers were replaced by 105mm leFH 18/40)

6th Battalion (planned to be raised later, but probably not raised)
  1 Staff and Staff Battery (2 LMGs)
  2 (tmot) Batteries (3 210mm mörsers and 5 LMGs ea)
  1 (tmot) Battery (3 170mm guns and 5 LMGs)

407th (mot) Volks Artillery Corps (on 29 Sept. 1944; became tmot on 2 Nov. 1944)

1 Staff and (mot) Staff Battery (2 LMGs)

1st Battalion (RSO)
  1 Staff and Staff Battery (2 LMGs)
  3 (motZ) Batteries (6 75mm FK 40 and 4 LMGs ea)

2nd Battalion
  1 Staff and Staff Battery (2 LMGs)
  2 (motZ) Batteries (6 100mm K 18 and 4 LMGs ea)

3rd Battalion (RSO)
  1 Staff and Staff Battery (2 LMGs)
  3 (motZ) Batteries (6 105mm leFH 18/40 and 4 LMGs ea)

4th Battalion
  1 Staff and Staff Battery (2 LMGs)
  2 (motZ) Batteries (6 152mm KH 433 (r) and 4 LMGs ea)

5th Battalion
  1 Staff and Staff Battery (2 LMGs)
  2 (motZ) Batteries (6 122mm sFH 396 (r) and 4 LMGs ea; on 13 Feb. 1945 the 122mm howitzers were replaced by 105mm leFH 18/40)

6th Battalion (planned to be raised later, but probably not raised)
  1 Staff and Staff Battery (2 LMGs)
  2 (tmot) Batteries (3 210mm mörsers and 5 LMGs ea)

1 (tmot) Battery (3 170mm guns and 5 LMGs)

408th (tmot) Volks Artillery Corps (on 29 Sept. 1944)

1 Staff and (mot) Staff Battery (2 LMGs)

1st Battalion (RSO)
  1 Staff and Staff Battery (2 LMGs)
  3 (tmot) Batteries (6 75mm FK 40 and 4 LMGs ea)

2nd Battalion
  1 Staff and Staff Battery (2 LMGs)
  2 (tmot) Batteries (6 100mm K 18 and 4 LMGs ea)

3rd Battalion (RSO)
  1 Staff and Staff Battery (2 LMGs)
  3 (tmot) Batteries (6 105mm leFH 18/40 and 4 LMGs ea)

4th Battalion
  1 Staff and Staff Battery (2 LMGs)
  2 (tmot) Batteries (6 152mm KH 433 (r) and 4 LMGs ea)

5th Battalion
  1 Staff and Staff Battery (2 LMGs)
  2 (tmot) Batteries (6 122mm sFH 396 (r) and 4 LMGs ea; on 13 Feb. 1945 the 122mm howitzers were replaced by 105mm leFH 18/40)

6th Battalion (raised on 31 Jan. 1945)
  1 Staff and Staff Battery (2 LMGs)
  2 (tmot) Batteries (3 210mm mörsers and 5 LMGs ea)
  1 (tmot) Battery (3 128mm guns and 5 LMGs)

409th (mot) Volks Artillery Corps (on 29 Sept. 1944; downgraded to (tmot) in Jan. 1945)

1 Staff and (mot) Staff Battery (2 LMGs)

1st Battalion (RSO)
  1 Staff and Staff Battery (2 LMGs)
  3 (tmot) Batteries (6 75mm FK 40 and 4 LMGs ea; replaced with 100mm 100mm K 18 guns in early 1945)

2nd Battalion
  1 Staff and Staff Battery (2 LMGs)
  2 (tmot) Batteries (6 100mm K 18 and 4 LMGs ea)

3rd Battalion (RSO)
  1 Staff and Staff Battery (2 LMGs)
  3 (tmot) Batteries (6 105mm leFH 18/40 and 4 LMGs ea)

4th Battalion
  1 Staff and Staff Battery (2 LMGs)
  2 (tmot) Batteries (6 152mm KH 433 (r) and 4 LMGs ea)

5th Battalion
  1 Staff and Staff Battery (2 LMGs)
  2 (tmot) Batteries (6 122mm sFH 396 (r) and 4 LMGs ea; on 13 Feb. 1945 the 122mm howitzers were replaced by 105mm leFH 18/40)

6th Battalion (raised on 9 Jan. 1945)
  1 Staff and Staff Battery (2 LMGs)
  2 (tmot) Batteries (3 210mm mörsers and 5 LMGs ea)

1 (tmot) Battery (3 170mm guns and 5 LMGs; the 170mm were replaced with 128mm guns on 20 Mar. 1945)

410th (mot) Volks Artillery Corps (on 29 Sept. 1944)
1 Staff and (mot) Staff Battery (2 LMGs)
1st Battalion (RSO)
  1 Staff and Staff Battery (2 LMGs)
  3 (motZ) Batteries (6 75mm FK 40 and 4 LMGs ea; re-equipped with 100mm K 18 guns on 20 Jan. 1945)
2nd Battalion
  1 Staff and Staff Battery (2 LMGs)
  2 (motZ) Batteries (6 100mm K 18 and 4 LMGs ea; had 3 100mm K gun batteries on 16 Nov. 1944 and three self-propelled 88mm batteries by 25 Dec. 1944)
3rd Battalion (RSO)
  1 Staff and Staff Battery (2 LMGs)
  3 (motZ) Batteries (6 105mm leFH 18/40 and 4 LMGs ea)
4th Battalion
  1 Staff and Staff Battery (2 LMGs)
  2 (motZ) Batteries (6 152mm KH 433 (r) and 4 LMGs ea)
5th Battalion
  1 Staff and Staff Battery (2 LMGs)
  2 (motZ) Batteries (6 122mm sFH 396 (r) and 4 LMGs ea; on 13 Feb. 1945 the 122mm howitzers were replaced by 105mm leFH 18/40)
6th Battalion (raised on 30 Nov. 1944)
  1 Staff and Staff Battery (2 LMGs)
  3 (motZ) Batteries (3 210mm mörsers and 5 LMGs ea)

411th (tmot) Volks Artillery Corps (on 20 Jan. 1945)
1 Staff and (mot) Staff Battery (2 LMGs)
1st Battalion (RSO)
  1 Staff and Staff Battery (2 LMGs)
  3 (tmot) Batteries (6 75mm FK 40 and 4 LMGs ea)
2nd Battalion (formed on 20 Mar. 1945)
  1 Staff and Staff Battery (2 LMGs)
  2 (tmot) Batteries (6 105mm leFH 18 and 4 LMGs ea)
3rd Battalion (RSO)
  1 Staff and Staff Battery (2 LMGs)
  3 (tmot) Batteries (6 105mm leFH 18/40 and 4 LMGs ea)
4th Battalion
  1 Staff and Staff Battery (2 LMGs)
  2 (tmot) Batteries (6 150mm sFH and 4 LMGs ea)
5th Battalion
  1 Staff and Staff Battery (2 LMGs)
  3 (tmot) Batteries (6 105mm leFH 18/40 and 4 LMGs ea)
6th Battalion
  1 Staff and Staff Battery (2 LMGs)

3 (tmot) Batteries (3 210mm mörsers and 5 LMGs ea)

412th (tmot) Volks Artillery Corps (on 1/20/45)
1 Staff and (mot) Staff Battery (2 LMGs)
1st Battalion (RSO)
  1 Staff and Staff Battery (2 LMGs)
  3 (tmot) Batteries (6 75mm FK 40 and 4 LMGs ea)
2nd Battalion (formed on 20 Mar. 1945)
  1 Staff and Staff Battery (2 LMGs)
  2 (tmot) Batteries (6 105mm leFH 18 and 4 LMGs ea)
3rd Battalion (RSO)
  1 Staff and Staff Battery (2 LMGs)
  3 (tmot) Batteries (6 105mm leFH 18/40 and 4 LMGs ea)
4th Battalion
  1 Staff and Staff Battery (2 LMGs)
  2 (tmot) Batteries (6 150mm sFH and 4 LMGs ea)
5th Battalion
  1 Staff and Staff Battery (2 LMGs)
  3 (tmot) Batteries (6 105mm leFH 18/40 and 4 LMGs ea)
6th Battalion
  1 Staff and Staff Battery (2 LMGs)
  3 (tmot) Batteries (3 210mm mörsers and 5 LMGs ea)

766th (mot) Volks Artillery Corps (on 29 Sept. 1944)
1 Staff and (mot) Staff Battery (2 LMGs)
766th (mot) Observation Battery (12 LMGs)
1st Battalion (RSO)
  1 Staff and Staff Battery (2 LMGs)
  3 (motZ) Batteries (6 75mm FK 40 and 4 LMGs ea)
2nd Battalion
  1 Staff and Staff Battery (2 LMGs)
  2 (motZ) Batteries (6 150mm sFH and 4 LMGs)
3rd Battalion (RSO)
  1 Staff and Staff Battery (2 LMGs)
  3 (motZ) Batteries (6 105mm leFH 18/40 and 4 LMGs ea)
4th Battalion (formerly 2/60th)
  1 Staff and Staff Battery (2 LMGs)
  2 (motZ) Batteries (6 150mm sFH and 4 LMGs ea)
5th Battalion (formerly 3/139th; detached on 25 Sept. 1944)
  1 Staff and Staff Battery (2 LMGs)
  2 (motZ) Batteries (6 122mm sFH 396 (r) and 4 LMGs ea)
5th Battalion (formerly 2/58th; attached on 25 Sept. 1944)
  1 Staff and Staff Battery (2 LMGs)
  2 (motZ) Batteries (6 150mm sFH and 4 LMGs ea)
6th Battalion (raised on 1/9/45)
  1 Staff and Staff Battery (2 LMGs)
  2 (motZ) Batteries (3 210mm mörsers and 5 LMGs ea)
  1 (motZ) Battery (3 170mm guns and 5 LMGs)

88th and 888th (mot) Army Artillery Corps

These two corps were ordered formed on 12 January 1945. Tessin does not mention their existence, but Keilig does, and very precise organizations were found in German records held by the National Archives for 12 January 1945. They were organized from the 88th and 888th (mot) Artillery Brigades. Their organization is typical of the Volks Artillery Corps, which suggests that they existed. If they were formed, they were to be organized as follows:

88th Army Artillery Corps
88th Artillery Staff
88th (mot) Artillery Staff Company (2 LMGs)
1st (mot) Battalion (formerly 12/44th Panzer Artillery Regiment "Brandenburg")
1 Artillery Staff
1 (mot) Artillery Staff Battery (2 LMGs)
3 (mot) 105mm leFH Batteries (6 105mm guns and 2 LMGs ea)
2nd (mot) Battalion (formerly 12/44th Artillery Regiment)
1 Artillery Staff
1 (mot) Artillery Staff Battery (2 LMGs)
3 (mot) 105mm leFH Batteries (6 105mm guns and 2 LMGs ea)
3rd (mot) Battalion
1 Artillery Staff
1 (mot) Artillery Staff Battery (2 LMGs)
2 (mot) 150mm sFH Batteries (6 150mm guns and 2 LMGs ea)
4th (mot) Battalion
1 Artillery Staff
1 (mot) Artillery Staff Battery (2 LMGs)
3 (mot) 210mm Batteries (4 210mm howitzers and 2 LMGs ea)
5th (mot) Battalion (formerly 3/184th Artillery Regiment)
1 Artillery Staff
1 (mot) Artillery Staff Battery (2 LMGs)
2 (mot) 150mm sFH Batteries (6 150mm guns and 2 LMGs ea)

888th Army Artillery Corps
888th Artillery Staff
888th (mot) Artillery Staff Company (2 LMGs)
1st (mot) Battalion
1 Artillery Staff
1 (mot) Artillery Staff Battery (2 LMGs)
2 (mot) 150mm sFH Batteries (6 150mm guns and 2 LMGs ea)
2nd (mot) Battalion
1 Artillery Staff
1 (mot) Artillery Staff Battery (2 LMGs)

2 (mot) 150mm sFH Batteries (6 150mm guns and 2 LMGs ea)
3rd (mot) Battalion
1 Artillery Staff
1 (mot) Artillery Staff Battery (2 LMGs)
3 (mot) 210mm Mrs Batteries (3 210mm howitzers and 2 LMGs ea)
4th (mot) Battalion (formerly 1/344th Artillery Regiment)
1 Artillery Staff
1 (mot) Artillery Staff Battery (2 LMGs)
2 (mot) 105mm leFH Batteries (6 105mm guns and 2 LMGs ea)
5th (mot) Battalion (formerly 4/234th Artillery Regiment)
1 Artillery Staff
1 (mot) Artillery Staff Battery (2 LMGs)
2 (mot) 105mm leFH Batteries (6 105mm guns and 2 LMGs ea)
16th (mot) Artillery Battery
1 170mm (mot) Battery (3 170mm guns and 2 LMGs)

Artillery Brigades

Twelve independent artillery brigades were formed by an order issued on 30 August 1944. They were organized from independent artillery battalions and portions of artillery regiments assigned to the various armies in which they were organized. They were organized on the following schedule and with the indicated organizations:

Date	No of bdes raised	Notes
25 Sept. 1944	1 (mot)	Organization I (2nd Bn, 88mm PAK motZ)
25 Sept. 1944	1 (mot)	Organization I (2nd Bn, 88mm PAK self-propelled)
30 Sept. 1944	2 (mot)	Organization II
25 Oct. 1944	2 (mot)	Organization I (2nd Bn, 88mm PAK self-propelled)
31 Oct. 1944	4 (mot)	Organization II
20 Nov. 1944	2 (mot)	Organization II

Organization I
Staff
  1 (mot) Staff Battery (2 LMGs)
  1 (mot) Observation Battery (12 LMGs)
1st Battalion
  1 (mot) Staff Battery (2 LMGs)
  3 (mot) 75mm Panzerjäger Companies (6 75mm PAK and 2 LMGs ea)
2nd Battalion
  1 Self-Propelled Staff Battery (2 LMGs)
  3 Self-Propelled 88mm Panzerjäger Companies (6 88mm PAK and 2 LMGs ea)
3rd Battalion
  1 (mot) Staff Battery (2 LMGs)
  3 (mot) leFH Batteries (6 105mm leFH and 2 LMGs)
4th Battalion
  1 (mot) Staff Battery (2 LMGs)
  2 (mot) sFH Batteries (6 150mm sFH and 2 LMGs)
5th Battalion
  1 (mot) Staff Battery (2 LMGs)
  2 (mot) sFH Batteries (6 122mm (r) sFH and 2 LMGs)
6th Battalion
  1 (mot) Staff Battery (2 LMGs)
  2 (mot) Batteries (3 210mm mörsers and 3 LMGs)
  1 (mot) Battery (3 170mm K guns and 3 LMGs)

Organization II
1st Battalion
  same as Organization I
2nd Battalion
  1 (mot) Staff Battery (2 LMGs)
  2 (mot) Batteries (6 100mm guns and 2 LMGs)

3rd Battalion
  1 (mot) Staff Battery (2 LMGs)
  3 (mot) leFH Batteries (6 105mm leFH and 2 LMGs)
4th Battalion
  1 (mot) Staff Battery (2 LMGs)
  2 (mot) sFH Batteries (6 152mm (r) sFH and 2 LMGs)
5th Battalion
  1 (mot) Staff Battery (2 LMGs)
  2 (mot) sFH Batteries (6 122mm (r) sFH and 2 LMGs)

The establishing order directed the formation as follows:

766th (mot) Army Artillery Brigade
  766th Army Artillery Brigade Staff
  634th (sFH/mot) Army Artillery Battalion
  2/60th (sFH/mot) Army Artillery Regiment
  3/139th (sFH/mot) Army Artillery Regiment
  2nd Btry/731st (170mm K/mot) Army Artillery Battalion

The 766th Army Artillery Brigade would become the 776th Volks Artillery Corps.

388th (mot) Army Artillery Brigade
  388th Army Artillery Brigade Staff
  2/42nd (sFH/mot) Army Artillery Regiment
  2/43rd (sFH/mot) Army Artillery Regiment
  672nd (210mm mörsers mot) Army Artillery Battalion
  2nd Co/767th (170mm K/mot) Army Artillery Battalion

An order dated 24 October 1944 organized the following army artillery brigades. Each brigade had its elements renumbered as battalions and batteries of an artillery regiment:

959th (mot) Army Artillery Brigade (in Army Group South)
  1/959th Artillery Regiment – formerly 3/140th Regt (sFH/100mm K/mot)
  2/959th Artillery Regiment – formerly 844th Bn (sFH/100mm K/mot)
  3/959th Artillery Regiment – formerly 607th Bn (210mm mörsers)

70th (mot) Army Artillery Brigade (in Army Group A)
  1/777th – formerly 2/67th (sFH/mot) Battalion
  2/777th – formerly 846th (sFH/mot) Battalion
  3/777th – formerly (210mm mörser/mot) Battalion
  10th Btry/777th – formerly 3rd Btry/731th (170mm K/mot) Battalion

288th (mot) Army Artillery Brigade (in Army Group A)
Staff/888th – formerly Staff/288th (mot) Artillery Regiment
1/888th – formerly 737th (sFH/mot) Artillery Battalion
2/888th – formerly 2/388th (sFH/mot) Artillery Regiment
3/888th – formerly 3/109th (210mm/mot) Artillery Regiment

140th (mot) Army Artillery Brigade (in Army Group Center)
Staff/732nd – formerly Staff/140th (mot) Artillery Brigade
1/732nd – formerly 1/108th (sFH/mot) Artillery Regiment
2/732nd – formerly 154th (sFH/mot) Artillery Battalion
3/732nd – formerly 1st Btry/767th (170mm K/mot) Battalion

704th (mot) Army Artillery Brigade (in Army Group Center)
1/704th – 861st (leFH/RSO) Artillery Battalion
2/704th – 934th (leFH/RSO) Artillery Battalion
3/704th –151st (100mm K/mot) Artillery Battalion

Lehr (mot) Artillery Brigade (in Army Group C)
1/Lehr – 3/1st (leFH) Lehr Artillery Regiment
2/Lehr – 4/2nd (sFH/100mm K/mot) Lehr Artillery Regiment
3/Lehr – 1/2nd (210mm Mrs/170mm K/mot) Lehr Artillery Regiment

These brigades had their batteries organized such that the 1st to 3rd were in the 1st Battalion, the 4th to 6th were in the 2nd Battalion, and the 7 to 9th were in the 3rd Battalion. Other brigades known to have been formed were:

77th (mot) Army Artillery Brigade, formed around the 70th Artillery Regiment z.b.V and the Staff/H Artillery Regiment.

412th Army Artillery Brigade. Nothing is known.

703rd Army Artillery Brigade. Organized three battalions, but nothing else is know of its organization or history.

771st Artillery Brigade. Formed from the 77th Army Artillery Brigade. Its 1st Battalion came from the 2/67th Artillery Regiment, its 2nd Battalion was formed from the 846th Army Artillery Battalion and its 3rd Battalion was formed from the 777th Army Artillery Battalion.

845th (mot) Army Artillery Brigade. Nothing is known.

888th (mot) Army Artillery Brigade. Nothing is known, except that it became the 888th Army Artillery Corps on 12 January 1945.

911th Army Artillery Brigade. Nothing is known.

959th Army Artillery Brigade, formed from the 959th Artillery Regimental Staff z.b.V. and three battalions.

OKH records found in T-78, Roll 413, show the existence of the 777th and Lehr Artillery Brigades as well as of the 261st Sturm Artillery Brigade. However, nothing is known about these formations.

On 20 October 1944 the 388th, 401st to 410th, and 766th Army Artillery Brigades were expanded into like-numbered artillery corps. That same order indicates that the 70th, 88th, 140th, 288th, 704th, and 959th (mot) Army Artillery Brigades and the (mot) Army Lehr Brigade were not converted.

A German document dated 23 October 1944 indicates the the army artillery brigades had a standard formation, as follows:

1 (mot) Staff Battery (2 LMGs)
2 Battalions, each with
    1 (mot) Staff Battery (2 LMGs)
    2 (mot) Batteries (6 150mm sFH and 2 LMGs ea)
1 Battalion
    1 (mot) Staff Battery (2 LMGs)
    2 (mot) Batteries (3 210mm mörsars and 2 LMGs ea)
    1 (mot) Battery (3 170mm guns and 2 LMGs)

70th Army Artillery Brigade (on 6 July 1944)
Brigade Staff and (mot) Staff Company (2 LMGs)
1st (motZ) Battalion (formerly 842nd)
    Staff and (mot) Staff Battery (2 LMGs)
    3 (motZ) Batteries (6 150mm sFH and 4 LMGs ea)
2nd (motZ) Battalion (formerly 2/67th)
    Staff and (mot) Staff Battery (2 LMGs)
    3 (motZ) Batteries (6 150mm sFH and 4 LMGs ea)
3rd (motZ) Battalion (formerly 151st)
    Staff and (mot) Staff Battery (2 LMGs)
    3 (motZ) Batteries (3 210mm mörsars and 5 LMGs ea)

70th Army Artillery Brigade (on 10 Aug. 1944; became 777th on 21 Oct. 1944)
Brigade Staff and (mot) Staff Company (2 LMGs)
1st (motZ) Battalion (formerly 1/108th)
    Staff and (mot) Staff Battery (2 LMGs)
    3 (motZ) Batteries (6 150mm sFH and 4 LMGs ea)
2nd (motZ) Battalion (formerly 154th)
    Staff and (mot) Staff Battery (2 LMGs)
    3 (motZ) Batteries (6 150mm sFH and 4 LMGs ea)
3rd (motZ) Battalion (formerly 732nd)

Staff and (mot) Staff Battery (2 LMGs)
3 (motZ) Batteries (3 210mm mörsers and 5 LMGs ea)
1st (motZ) Btry/767th Artillery Batatlion
3 170mm guns and 5 LMGs)

88th (mot) Artillery Brigade (as of 10 Mar. 1945)
1 Staff and (mot) Staff Battery (2 LMGs)
1st Battalion
  1 Battalion Staff and Staff Battery (2 LMGs)
  1 Self-Propelled Battery (6 105mm leFH SdKfz 124 Wespe and 4 LMGs ea)
  2 Self-Propelled Batteries (6 150mm sFH SdKfz 165 Hummel and 4 LMGs)
2nd Battalion
  1 Battalion Staff and Staff Battery (2 LMGs)
  2 (motZ) Batteries (6 105mm leFH and 2 LMGs ea)
3rd Battalion
  1 Battalion Staff and Staff Battery (2 LMGs)
  2 (motZ) Batteries (6 150mm sFH and 2 LMGs ea)
4th Battalion
  1 Battalion Staff and Staff Battery (2 LMGs)
  2 (motZ) Batteries (3 210mm mörsars and 2 LMGs ea)

Note: The 88th (mot) Army Artillery Brigade was organized from the 88th (mot) Artillery Regiment. Its 1st Battalion was self-propelled and became the 1/Brandenburg Panzer Artillery Regiment in early 1945. The remainder of the brigade became the 888th (mot) Army Artillery Corps.

140th (mot) Artillery Brigade (on 14 Aug. 1944; became 732nd on 24 Oct. 1944)
1 Staff and (mot) Staff Battery (2 LMGs)
1st Battalion (formerly 1/108th) (detached on 10/24/44)
  1 Battalion Staff and Staff Battery (2 LMGs)
  3 (motZ) Batteries (6 150mm sFH and 2 LMGs ea)
1st Battalion (formerly 3/36th) (assigned on 10/24/44)
  1 Battalion Staff and Staff Battery (2 LMGs)
  2 (motZ) Batteries (6 150mm sFH and 2 LMGs ea)
2nd Battalion (formerly 154th)
  1 Battalion Staff and Staff Battery (2 LMGs)
  3 (motZ) Batteries (6 150mm sFH and 2 LMGs ea)
    (1 battery detached, date unknown)
3rd Battalion
  1 Battalion Staff and Staff Battery (2 LMGs)
  1 Light (mot) (36 ton) Supply Column
  3 (motZ) Batteries (3 210mm mörsars and 2 LMGs ea)
10th Battery (formerly 1st Btry/767th) (3 170mm guns and 5 LMGs)

288th (mot) Artillery Brigade (on 14 Aug. 1944; became 888th on 2 Feb. 1945)
1 Staff and (mot) Staff Battery (2 LMGs)

1st Battalion (formerly 2/288th) (detached on 7 Feb. 1945)
  1 Battalion Staff and Staff Battery (2 LMGs)
  2 (motZ) Batteries (6 150mm sFH and 2 LMGs ea)
1st Battalion (formerly 737th, formerly 3rd Battalion of Corps; replaced 2/88th on 7 Feb. 1945)
  1 Battalion Staff and Staff Battery (2 LMGs)
  2 (motZ) Batteries (6 150mm sFH and 2 LMGs ea)
2nd Battalion (formerly 3/288th)
  1 Battalion Staff and Staff Battery (2 LMGs)
  3 (motZ) Batteries (3 170mm guns and 5 LMGs ea)
3rd Battalion (formerly 2/288th; became 1st Bn on 7 Feb. 1945)
  1 Battalion Staff and Staff Battery (2 LMGs)
  2 (motZ) Batteries (6 150mm sFH and 2 LMGs ea)
3rd Battalion (formerly 3/109th; assigned 7 Feb. 1945)
  1 Battalion Staff and Staff Battery (2 LMGs)
  3 (motZ) Batteries (3 210mm mörsars and 2 LMGs ea)

388th (mot) Artillery Brigade (14 Aug. 1944)
1 Staff and (mot) Staff Battery (2 LMGs)
2/42nd Artillery Regiment (1st Battalion)
  1 Battalion Staff and Staff Battery (2 LMGs)
  2 (motZ) Batteries (6 150mm sFH and 2 LMGs ea)
2/43rd Artillery Regiment (2nd Battalion)
  1 Battalion Staff and Staff Battery (2 LMGs)
  2 (motZ) Batteries (6 150mm sFH and 2 LMGs ea)
672nd (3rd) Battalion
  1 Battalion Staff and Staff Battery (2 LMGs)
  3 (motZ) Batteries (3 210mm mörsars and 2 LMGs ea)
10th Battery (formerly 2nd Btry/767th; 3 170mm guns and 5 LMGs)

595th Artillery Brigade (on 24 Oct. 1944)
Brigade Staff and (mot) Staff Company (2 LMGs)
1st (motZ) Battalion (formerly 3/140th)
  Staff and (mot) Staff Battery (2 LMGs)
  2 (motZ) Batteries (6 150mm sFH and 4 LMGs ea)
  1 (motZ) Battery (6 105mm leFH and 4 LMGs)
2nd (motZ) Battalion (formerly 844th)
  Staff and (mot) Staff Battery (2 LMGs)
  2 (motZ) Batteries (6 150mm sFH and 4 LMGs ea)
  1 (motZ) Battery (6 105mm leFH and 4 LMGs)
3rd (motZ) Battalion (formerly 607th)
  Staff and (mot) Staff Battery (2 LMGs)
  3 (motZ) Batteries (3 210mm mörsers and 5 LMGs ea)

704th Army Light Artillery Brigade (on 24 Oct. 1944)
Brigade Staff and (mot) Staff Company (2 LMGs)
1st (motZ) Battalion (formerly 861st)
  Staff and (mot) Staff Battery (2 LMGs)
  3 (motZ) Batteries (6 105mm leFH and 4 LMGs)

2nd (motZ) Battalion (formerly 934th)
  Staff and (mot) Staff Battery (2 LMGs)
  3 (motZ) Batteries (6 105mm leFH and 4 LMGs)
3rd (motZ) Battalion (formerly 151st)
  Staff and (mot) Staff Battery (2 LMGs)
  3 (motZ) Batteries (6 100mm K18 guns and 4 LMGs
  ea)

Notes indicate that the third battery of each battalion was deleted, but no date is provided.

732nd Artillery Brigade (on 10 Mar. 1945)
  Brigade Staff and (mot) Staff Company (2 LMGs)
  1st (motZ) Battalion (formerly 3/36th)
    Staff and (mot) Staff Battery (2 LMGs)
    2 (motZ) Batteries (6 150mm sFH and 4 LMCs)
  2nd (motZ) Battalion (formerly 154th)
    Staff and (mot) Staff Battery (2 LMGs)
    2 (motZ) Batteries (6 150mm sFH and 4 LMGs)
  3rd (motZ) Battalion (formerly 151st)
    Staff and (mot) Staff Battery (2 LMGs)
    3 (motZ) Batteries (6 210mm mörsers guns and 5
    LMGs ea)
  10th Battery (3 170mm guns and 5 LMGs)

Note: The 2nd Battalion was replaced by the 3/777th on 1 March 1945. It was equipped with 210mm guns like the existing 3rd Battalion.

766th Artillery Brigade (on 14 Aug. 1944)
  Brigade Staff and (mot) Staff Company (2 LMGs)
  634th (1st) (motZ) Battalion
    Staff and (mot) Staff Battery (2 LMGs)
    2 (motZ) Batteries (6 150mm sFH and 4 LMGs)
  2/60th (2nd) (motZ) Battalion
    Staff and (mot) Staff Battery (2 LMGs)
    2 (motZ) Batteries (6 150mm sFH and 4 LMGs)

3/139th (3rd) (motZ) Battalion
  Staff and (mot) Staff Battery (2 LMGs)
  2 (motZ) Batteries (6 150mm sFH and 4 LMGs)
2nd Btry/767th (later 731st) Battalion (3 170mm guns
  and 5 LMGs)

777th Artillery Brigade
  Brigade Staff and (mot) Staff Company (2 LMGs)
  1st (motZ) Battalion (formerly 2/67th)
    Staff and (mot) Staff Battery (2 LMGs)
    2 (motZ) Batteries (6 150mm sFH and 4 LMGs)
  2nd (motZ) Battalion (formerly 846th)
    Staff and (mot) Staff Battery (2 LMGs)
    2 (motZ) Batteries (6 150mm sFH and 4 LMGs)
  3rd (motZ) Battalion (formerly 777th; detached to
    732nd Artillery Brigade on 1 Mar. 1945)
    Staff and (mot) Staff Battery (2 LMGs)
    3 (motZ) Batteries (6 210mm mörsers and 5 LMGs
    ea)

Artillery Lehr Brigade (on 13 May 1944)
  Brigade Staff and (mot) Staff Company (2 LMGs)
  1st (motZ) Battalion
    Staff and (mot) Staff Battery (2 LMGs)
    3 (motZ) Batteries (6 105mm leFH and 4 LMGs ea)
  2nd (motZ) Battalion
    Staff and (mot) Staff Battery (2 LMGs)
    2 (motZ) Batteries (6 150mm sFH and 4 LMGs ea)
    1 (motZ) Battery (6 100mm K 18 guns and 4 LMGs
    ea)
  3rd (motZ) Battalion
    Staff and (mot) Staff Battery (2 LMGs)
    2 (motZ) Batteries (3 170mm guns and 5 LMGs ea)
    1 (motZ) Battery (3 210mm mörsers and 5 LMGs)

Note: One of the 170mm batteries appears to have been changed to 210mm mörsers on 24 October 1944.

Railroad Guns

Because of its weight, the heavier German artillery had generally abandoned horse- or motor-drawn carriages when it passed beyond the 210mm weapons. The heavier weapons were consigned to the railroad carriage, which was the only method by which they could easily be moved. There were, of course, exceptions.

These massive weapons, ranging up to 800mm (31.5in), were organized into batteries that rarely had more than two guns. The truly large weapons, 240mm (9.5in) and above, were often in batteries of one gun. The crews of these weapons could range up to five officers, 58 NCOs, and 169 men, as served the two guns of a Siegfried (380mm) (E) Railroad Battery. The large weapons batter-

ies, like the Siegfried, contained signals platoons, sound and flash ranging troops, the gun crew, Flak detachments of two single barreled and two quad 20mm guns, maintenance troops and a battery baggage train.

The smaller railroad guns had outriggers and could be fired in any direction from their railroad tracks. However, the larger guns were suspended between two train carriages and had no outriggers. In order to be aimed they required either special turntables, two perpendicular tracks where their carriages ran on different tracks, or a large, sweeping curve of track where the gun could be moved back and forth until it pointed in the desired direction.

The rates of fire for these weapons was generally very slow, but the force with which they hit more than compensated for this slow rate of fire. The longest ranged railroad gun was the 280mm Kanone 5 in Eisenbahnlefette (28cm K5 (E)). This weapon could fire its projectile a maximum of 93.83 miles! In 1941 and 1942 there were nine such batteries. Records indicate, however, that in 1943 only the 686th Railroad Battery continued to be equipped with such weapons.

In 1942 these heavy guns were concentrated before Sebastopol with the 11th Army. After Sebastopol fell they were moved to Leningrad. There are a few instances of them serving elsewhere after that, most notably one serving in Italy against the Anzio beachheads.

Unusual Formations

There were two types of batteries in the German army that require some discussion. The first is typified by the 628th Artillery Battery, which contained two two 600mm self-propelled "Karl" Mortars (Gerät 040) and a reserve gun. This was the largest tracked artillery piece ever built.

An unknown number of these weapons were built in preparation for the French campaign. Their objective was to pulverize the strongpoints of the Maginot Line. After the French campaign, they participated in the Russian campaign, most notably the siege of Brest-Litovsk and Sebastopol. The numbers and organizations of the batteries with these guns is not known, except for the 628th, which appears to have been organized in late 1942.

A second variant of this weapon was built with 540mm guns (Gerät 041). A total of six were manufactured between 1943 and 1944. It is unknown if it was the Gerät 040 or 041 that were used in the Battle of Warsaw, but that was the last major action for these weapons. They were ideally suited for that role and their massive shells pulverized the city with a horrific rapidity.

The second weapon of note was the 800mm "Gustav Gerät". This weapon was designed in 1937 and rolled out of the Krupp factory in early 1942. It was presented to Hitler as a personal present and contribution by Krupp to the German war effort. The gunners assigned to the weapon preferred to call the weapon "Dora", which has often led to the belief that there were two weapons. There was, in fact, only one.

The weapon was so large that it required two parallel railroad tracks to move. It was soon sent to Russia, where it was engaged in the Battle of Sebastopol. It is known to have fired a small number of shells, variously reported to have been 36 or 55. It then went to Leningrad, but had to withdraw before it was overrun by the Russians.

Its fate is not known. It was last seen in 1944 near Warsaw, and after that it disappeared. The Russians make no claim of having captured it and there are some indications that it may have been cut up for scrap: parts were found that appeared to have come from the weapon.

ORGANIZATION OF GENERAL HEADQUARTERS POOL ARTILLERY, 10 FEBRUARY–16 MAY 1941

2/41st, 2/53rd, 2/57th, 2/60th, 2/62nd, 2/64th, 2/68th, 2/69th, 2/72nd, 1/109th and 1/, 2/818th Artillery Regiments
Staff Battery
  (mot) Signals Platoon
  (mot) Calibration Section
3 (mot) Batteries (4 100mm guns ea)
1 Light (mot) Munitions Supply Column (20t)

151st, 153rd, 403rd, 427th, 430th, 445th, 611th, 631st, 633rd, 634th, 709th, 711th, 716th, 842nd, 849th and 852nd Artillery Battalions
Staff Battery
  (mot) Signals Platoon
  (mot) Calibration Section
3 (mot) Batteries (4 100mm guns ea)
1 Light (mot) Munitions Supply Column (20t)

Note: A (10t) supply column was assigned to the 430th, 633rd, 709th, 711th and 716th Battalions.

2/40th, 2/51st, 2/52nd, 2/54th, 2/61st, 2/65th, 2/70th, 2/71st, 1/106th, 1/108th and 4/109th Artillery Regiments; 602nd Artillery Battalion
Staff Battery
  (mot) Signals Platoon
  (mot) Calibration Section
2 (mot) Batteries (4 150mm sFH 18 howitzers ea)
1 (mot) Battery (4 100mm guns)
1 Light (mot) Munitions Supply Column (39t)

Note: The 2/61st, 2/71st, 1/106th, 1/108th and 4/109th had (24t) munition supply columns.

2/37th, 2/38th, 2/39th, 2/42nd, 2/43rd, 2/44th, 2/46th, 2/47th, 2/55th, 2/58th, 2/59th, 2/63rd, 2/66th, 2/67th, 1/77th, 3/818th, 4/207th, 4/213th and 4/221st Artillery Regiments; 101st, 154th, 422nd, 526th, 536th, 646th, 737th, 841st, 843rd, 844th, 845th, 846th, 847th, 848th, 850th and 851st Artillery Battalions

Staff Battery
  (mot) Signals Platoon
  (mot) Calibration Section
3 (mot) Batteries (4 150mm sFH 18 howitzers ea)
1 Light (mot) Munitions Supply Column (48t)

Note: The supply columns were (20t) for 1/77th, (16t) for 737th, and none for 845th or 848th.

3/111th Artillery Regiment

Staff Battery
  (mot) Signals Platoon
  (mot) Calibration Section
2 (mot) Batteries (4 150mm sFH 18 howitzers ea)
1 Light (mot) Munitions Supply Column (48t)

1/, 2/814th Artillery Regiment

Staff Battery
  (mot) Signals Platoon
  (mot) Calibration Section
2 (mot) Batteries (4 240mm Czech howitzers ea)

1/477th Artillery Regiment

4-120mm howitzers and 1 light (mot) munitions supply column

854th, 855th, 856th, 857th, 858th, 859th, 860th, 861st, 862nd and 867th Artillery Battalions

Staff Battery
  (mot) Signals Platoon
  (mot) Calibration Section
3 (mot) Batteries (4 210mm howitzers ea)
2 Light (mot) Munitions Supply Columns

2/, 3/109th and 2/115th Artillery Regiments; 604th, 607th, 615th, 616th, 635th, 636th, 637th, 732nd, 733rd, 735th, 736th, 777th, 808th, 809th, 816th Artillery Battalions

Staff Battery
  (mot) Signals Platoon
  (mot) Calibration Section
3 (mot) Batteries (4 210mm howitzers ea)
1 Light (mot) Munitions Supply Column (48t)

Note: The 635th, 636th, 637th or 777th Battalions had no supply columns.

624th Heavy Mortar Battalion

Staff Battery

(mot) Signals Platoon
(mot) Calibration Section
3 (mot) Batteries (3 305mm Czech howitzers ea)
2 Light (mot) Munitions Supply Columns (34t)
1 Light (mot) Munitions Supply Columns (48t)

641st Heavy Mortar Battalion

Staff Battery
  (mot) Signals Platoon
  (mot) Calibration Section
1 (mot) Battery (1 355mm M1 howitzer)
3 (mot) Batteries (3 305mm Czech howitzers ea)
2 Light (mot) Munitions Supply Columns (34t)
1 Light (mot) Munitions Supply Columns (48t)

815th Heavy Mortar Battalion

Staff Battery
  (mot) Signals Platoon
  (mot) Calibration Section
3 (mot) Batteries (3 305mm Czech howitzers ea)
2 Light (mot) Munitions Supply Columns (34t)
1 Light (mot) Munitions Supply Columns (48t)

511th, 620th, 680th, 731st and 740th Artillery Battalions

Staff Battery
  (mot) Signals Platoon
  (mot) Calibration Section
3 (mot) Batteries (3 150mm guns ea)
1 Light (mot) Munitions Supply Columns (32t)

625th Artillery Battalion

Staff Battery
  (mot) Signals Platoon
  (mot) Calibration Section
3 (mot) Batteries (3 150mm guns on howitzer carriages ea)

821st Battery, 1/822nd Artillery Battalion and 909th Battery

3 150mm guns and (mot) Calibration Section

Note: The 821st Battery had no calibration section.

767th and 768th Artillery Battalions

Staff Battery
  (mot) Signals Platoon
  (mot) Calibration Section
3 (mot) Batteries (3 210mm K38 guns ea)
1 Light (mot) Munitions Supply Columns (48t)

1/84th Artillery Regiment

Staff Battery
  (mot) Signals Platoon
  (mot) Calibration Section

3 (mot) Batteries (3 240mm K3 guns ea)
1 Light (mot) Munitions Supply Columns (48t)

2/84th Artillery Regiment
Staff Battery

(mot) Signals Platoon
(mot) Calibration Section
3 (mot) Batteries (3 240mm Czech guns ea)
1 Light (mot) Munitions Supply Columns (48t)

ORGANIZATION OF GENERAL HEADQUARTERS POOL ARTILLERY, 16 MAY 1941–15 OCTOBER 1942

2/41st, 2/53rd, 2/57th, 2/60th, 2/62nd, 2/64th, 2/68th, 2/69th, 2/72nd, 2/151st, 2/153rd, 1/818th and 2/818th Artillery Regiments; 427th, 430th, 436th, 445th, 611th, 631st, 842nd and 849th Artillery Battalions
1 (mot) Staff Company
3 (mot) Battery (2 LMGs and 4 100mm K18 guns)
1 (mot) Munitions Column (20t trucks)

633rd, 709th, and 711th Artillery Battalions
1 (mot) Staff Company
3 (mot) Battery (2 LMGs and 4 100mm K18 guns)
1 (mot) Munitions Column (10t trucks)

730th Artillery Battalion
1 (mot) Staff Company
3 (mot) Battery (2 LMGs and 4 100mm K18 guns)
1 Towed 105mm Battery (2 LMGs and 4 105mm leFH 18 howitzers)

2/40th, 2/52nd, 2/54th, 2/65th, and 2/70th Artillery Regiments
1 (mot) Staff Company
1 (mot) 100mm K18 Battery
2 (mot) Batteries (4 sFH 18 150mm howitzers ea)
1 (mot) Munitions Column (39t trucks)

2/71st, 1/106th, 1/108th, and 4/109th Artillery Regiments and 602nd Artillery Battalion
1 (mot) Staff Company
1 (mot) 100mm K18 Battery
2 (mot) 150mm (4 sFH 18 150mm howitzers)
1 (mot) Munitions Column (24t trucks)

634th Artillery Battalion
1 (mot) Staff Company
2 (mot) 100mm K18 Battery
1 (mot) 150mm (4 sFH 18 150mm howitzers)
1 (mot) Munitions Column (20t trucks)

1st and 2nd (mot) Artillery Brigades
1 (mot) Staff Company
5 Self-Propelled Companies (6 SP 150mm sFH 13 howitzers and 7 LMGs)

1 Self-Propelled Company (6 105mm leFH howitzers and 7 LMGs)
1 Light (mot) POL Column (15t)
1 Light (mot) Munitions Column (32t)
1 (mot) Maintenance Platoon

Special Service (z.b.V) Self-Propelled Artillery Battalion
2 Companies with
  1 SP Battery (4 SP 105mm leFH 16 guns and 4 LMGs)
  1 SP Battery (4 SP 75mm PAK 40 and 4 LMGs)
  1 SP Battery (4 SP 20mm AA guns)
1 Company with
  1 (mot) Battery (4 88mm guns and 2 LMGs)

Heavy Field Howitzer Battalions

2/37th, 2/39th, 2/42nd, 2/43rd, 2/46th, 2/47th, 2/58th, 2/59th, 2/63rd, 2/66th, 2/67th and 3/818th Artillery Regiments; 101st, 154th, 422nd, 526th, 536th, 841st, 843rd, 844th 846th, 850th and 851st Artillery Battalions
1 (mot) Staff Company
2 (mot) Batteries (4 sFH 13 150mm guns and 2 LMGs ea)
1 Light Munitions Column (48t)

2/61st and 3/111th Artillery Regiments
1 (mot) Staff Company
2 (mot) Batteries (4 sFH 13 150mm guns and 2 LMGs ea)
1 Light Munitions Column (24t)

1/77th Artillery Regiment and 852nd Artillery Battalion
1 (mot) Staff Company
2 (mot) Batteries (4 sFH 13 150mm guns and 2 LMGs ea)
1 Light Munitions Column (20t)

716th Artillery Battalion
1 (mot) Staff Company

2 (mot) Batteries (4 sFH 13 150mm guns and 2 LMGs ea)

1 Light Munitions Column (10t)

506th, 845th and 848th Artillery Battalions

1 (mot) Staff Company

2 (mot) Batteries (4 sFH 13 150mm guns and 2 LMGs ea)

1/814th and 2/814th Howitzer Batteries

1 (mot) Staff Company

2 (mot) Batteries (2 240mm howitzers and 2 LMGs ea)

1 Battery (1 240mm howitzers and 2 LMGs)

458th Howitzer Battalion

1 (mot) Staff Company

1 420mm (mot) Howitzer (and 2 LMGs)

854th, 856th and 859th, Artillery Battalions

1 (mot) Staff Company

3 (mot) Mortar Batteries (3 210mm mortars and 2 LMGs ea)

3 Light (mot) Munitions Columns

2/109th and 3/109th Artillery Regiment, 604th, 607th, 615th, 616th, 808th, 857th, and 858th Artillery Battalions

1 (mot) Staff Company

3 (mot) Mortar Batteries (3 210mm mortars and 2 LMGs ea)

1 Light (mot) Munitions Column (48t)

637th, 777th, and 833rd Artillery Battalions

1 (mot) Staff Company

3 (mot) Mortar Batteries (3 210mm mortars and 2 LMGs ea)

855th Artillery Battalion

1 (mot) Staff Company

3 (mot) Mortar Batteries (3 210mm mortars and 2 LMGs ea)

611th and 612th Light (mot) Munitions Columns

861st Artillery Battalion

1 (mot) Staff Company

3 (mot) Mortar Batteries (3 210mm mortars and 2 LMGs ea)

607th, 608th, 609th and 610th Light (mot) Munitions Columns

624th Heavy Artillery Battalion

1 (mot) Staff Company

624th Light (mot) Munitions Column (48t)

3 (mot) Batteries (2 305mm mortars, 3 210mm mortars and 2 LMGs ea)

3 Light (mot) Munitions Columns (34t)

641st Heavy Artillery Battalion

1 (mot) Staff Company

1 (mot) Battery (2 355mm M1 mortars and 2 LMGs)

2 (mot) Batteries (2 305mm mortars and 2 LMGs ea)

2 Light (mot) Munitions Columns (34t)

1 Light (mot) Munitions Column (20t)

815th Heavy Artillery Battalion

1 (mot) Staff Company

3 (mot) Batteries (2 305mm mortars and 2 LMGs ea)

1 Light (mot) Munitions Column (48t)

511th, 620th, 680th, 740th, and 767th Artillery Battalion

1 (mot) Staff Company, with

1 Calibration Detachment

1 Signals Detachment

3 (mot) Batteries (3 150mm guns and 2 LMGs ea)

1 Light Munitions Column (32t)

625th and 800th Artillery Battalions

1 (mot) Staff Company, with

1 Calibration Detachment

1 Signals Detachment

3 (mot) Batteries (3 150mm guns and 2 LMGs ea)

817th Artillery Battalion

1 (mot) Staff Company

4 (mot) Batteries (2 170mm guns and 2 LMGs ea)

1 Light (mot) Munitions Column (48t)

917th Artillery Battery

1 (mot) Calibration Detachment

1 Self-Propelled Battery (3 194mm guns and 2 LMGs)

768th Artillery Battalion

1 (mot) Staff Company

4 (mot) Batteries (2 210mm guns and 2 LMGs ea)

1 Light (mot) Munitions Column (48t)

1/84th Artillery Regiment

1 (mot) Staff Company

1 Calibration Detachment

1 Signals Detachment

3 (mot) Batteries (2 240mm K3 guns and 2 LMGs ea))

1 Light (mot) Munitions Column (48t)

2/84th Artillery Regiment

1 (mot) Staff Company

1 Calibration Detachment

1 Signals Detachment

1 Self-Propelled Battery (3 240mm Theodor K(E) guns and 2 LMGs)

2 (mot) Batteries (3 170mm guns on mörser carriages
and 2 LMGs ea))
1 Light (mot) Munitions Column (48t)

628th Artillery Battalion
1 Battery (2 Karl guns plus 1 reserve gun)

ORGANIZATION OF GENERAL HEADQUARTERS POOL ARTILLERY, OCTOBER 1942–SUMMER 1943

Motorized Light Artillery

424nd (mot) Artillery Battalion
  (mot) Staff Company
  (mot) Artillery Calibration Section
  3 (motZ) Batteries (4 105mm leFH 18 and 2 LMGs
  ea)
423rd (motZ) Battery (4 105mm leFH 18 and 2 LMGs)
429th (motZ) Battery (4 105mm leFH 18 and 2 LMGs)
433rd (motZ) Battery (4 105mm leFH 18 and 2 LMGs)
443rd (motZ) Battery (4 105mm leFH 18 and 2 LMGs)
1/127th (motZ) Artillery Battalion (4 105mm leFH 18
  and 2 LMGs)
2/140th (motZ) Artillery Battalion (4 105mm leFH 18
  and 2 LMGs)
520th (motZ) Artillery Battalion (4 105mm leFH 18 and
  2 LMGs)
934th (motZ) Artillery Battalion (4 105mm leFH 18 and
  2 LMGs)
935th (motZ) Artillery Battalion (4 105mm leFH 18 and
  2 LMGs)
554th (motZ) Battery (4 105mm leFH 18 and 2 LMGs)
555th (motZ) Battery (4 105mm leFH 18 and 2 LMGs)
556th (motZ) Battery (4 105mm leFH 18 and 2 LMGs)
424th (motZ) Recoilless Artillery Battalion
  (mot) Staff Company
  (mot) Artillery Calibration Section
  3 (motZ) Batteries (4 105mm Recoilless Rifles and 2
  LMGs ea)
423rd (motZ) Battery (4 105mm Recoilless Rifles and 2
  LMGs)
429th (motZ) Battery (4 105mm Recoilless Rifles and 2
  LMGs)
433rd (motZ) Battery (4 105mm Recoilless Rifles and 2
  LMGs)
443rd (motZ) Battery (4 105mm Recoilless Rifles and 2
  LMGs)
1/127th (motZ) Artillery Regiment
  1 (mot) Staff Company
  2 (motZ) Batteries (3 105mm leFH 18 and 2 LMGs
  ea)
2/140th (motZ) Artillery Regiment
  1 (mot) Staff Company

2 (motZ) Batteries (3 105mm leFH 18 and 2 LMGs
  ea)
520th (motZ) Artillery Battalion
  1 (mot) Staff Company
  2 (motZ) Batteries (3 105mm leFH 18 and 2 LMGs
  ea)
934th (motZ) Artillery Battalion
  1 (mot) Staff Company
  3 (motZ) Batteries (3 105mm leFH 18 and 2 LMGs
  ea)
935th (motZ) Artillery Battalion
  1 (mot) Staff Company
  3 (motZ) Batteries (3 105mm leFH 18 and 2 LMGs
  ea)
934th (motZ) Artillery Regiment
  1 (mot) Staff Company
  3 (motZ) Batteries (3 105mm leFH 18 and 2 LMGs
  ea)
2/53rd (motZ) Artillery Regiment (formed 4/15/43)
  1 (mot) Staff Company
  3 (motZ) Batteries (4 105mm leFH 18 and 2 LMGs
  ea)
2/54th (motZ) Artillery Regiment (formed 15 Apr. 1943)
  1 (mot) Staff Company
  3 (motZ) Batteries (4 105mm leFH 18 and 2 LMGs
  ea)
2/59th (motZ) Artillery Regiment (formed 4/15/43)
  1 (mot) Staff Company
  3 (motZ) Batteries (4 105mm leFH 18 and 2 LMGs
  ea)
2/64th (motZ) Artillery Regiment (formed 4/15/43)
  1 (mot) Staff Company
  3 (motZ) Batteries (4 105mm leFH 18 and 2 LMGs
  ea)
1/77th (motZ) Artillery Regiment (formed 4/15/43)
  1 (mot) Staff Company
  3 (motZ) Batteries (4 105mm leFH 18 and 2 LMGs ea)
1/108th (motZ) Artillery Regiment (formed 15 Apr. 1943)
  1 (mot) Staff Company
  3 (motZ) Batteries (4 105mm leFH 18 and 2 LMGs ea)
425th (motZ) Artillery Battalion (formed 15 Apr. 1943)
  1 (mot) Staff Company
  3 (motZ) Batteries (4 105mm leFH 18 and 2 LMGs ea)

425th (motZ) Artillery Battalion (re-formed 15 May 1943)
1 (mot) Staff Company
3 (motZ) Batteries (4 122mm Russian and 2 LMGs ea)

426th (motZ) Artillery Battalion (formed 15 Apr. 1943)
1 (mot) Staff Company
3 (motZ) Batteries (4 105mm leFH 18 and 2 LMGs ea)

426th (motZ) Artillery Battalion (re-formed 15 May 1943)
1 (mot) Staff Company
3 (motZ) Batteries (4 122mm Russian and 2 LMGs ea)

430th (motZ) Artillery Battalion (formed 15 Apr. 1943)
1 (mot) Staff Company
3 (motZ) Batteries (4 105mm leFH 18 and 2 LMGs ea)

616th (motZ) Artillery Battalion (formed 15 Apr. 1943)
1 (mot) Staff Company
3 (motZ) Batteries (4 105mm leFH 18 and 2 LMGs ea)

3/818th (motZ) Artillery Regiment (formed 15 Apr. 1943)
1 (mot) Staff Company
3 (motZ) Batteries (4 105mm leFH 18 and 2 LMGs ea)

851st (motZ) Artillery Battalion (formed 15 Apr. 1943)
1 (mot) Staff Company
3 (motZ) Batteries (4 105mm leFH 18 and 2 LMGs ea)

851st (motZ) Artillery Battalion (re-formed 15 May 1943)
1 (mot) Staff Company
3 (motZ) Batteries (4 122mm Russian and 2 LMGs ea)

855th (motZ) Artillery Battalion (formed 15 Apr. 1943)
1 (mot) Staff Company
3 (motZ) Batteries (4 105mm leFH 18 and 2 LMGs ea)

855th (motZ) Artillery Battalion (re-formed 15 May 1943)
1 (mot) Staff Company
3 (motZ) Batteries (4 122mm Russian and 2 LMGs ea)

860th (motZ) Artillery Battalion (formed 15 Apr. 1943)
1 (mot) Staff Company
3 (motZ) Batteries (4 105mm leFH 18 and 2 LMGs ea)

861st (motZ) Artillery Battalion (formed 15 Apr. 1943)
1 (mot) Staff Company
3 (motZ) Batteries (4 105mm leFH 18 and 2 LMGs ea)

2/46th (motZ) Artillery Regiment (formed 9 May 1943)
1 (mot) Staff Company
3 (motZ) Batteries (4 105mm leFH 18 and 2 LMGs ea)

849th (motZ) Artillery Battalion (formed 9 May 1943)
1 (mot) Staff Company
3 (motZ) Batteries (4 105mm leFH 18 and 2 LMGs ea)

2/72nd (motZ) Artillery Regiment (formed 9 May 1943)
1 (mot) Staff Company
3 (motZ) Batteries (4 105mm leFH 18 and 2 LMGs ea)

2/65th (motZ) Artillery Regiment (formed 9 May 1943)
1 (mot) Staff Company
3 (motZ) Batteries (4 105mm leFH 18 and 2 LMGs ea)

2/818th (motZ) Artillery Regiment (formed 9 May 1943)
1 (mot) Staff Company
3 (motZ) Batteries (4 105mm leFH 18 and 2 LMGs ea)

2/53rd (motZ) Artillery Regiment (15 May 1943)
1 (mot) Staff Company
3 (motZ) Batteries (4 122mm Russian and 2 LMGs ea)

2/64th (motZ) Artillery Regiment (15 May 1943)
1 (mot) Staff Company
3 (motZ) Batteries (4 122mm Russian and 2 LMGs ea)

Heavy Field Howitzer Battalions

2/37th, 2/39th, 2/40th, 2/42nd, 2/58th, 2/61st, 2/63rd, 2/66th and 2/67th Artillery Regiments
1 (mot) Headquarters Company
3 (motZ) Batteries (4 150mm sFH and 2 LMGs ea)
1 Light (mot) Munitions Supply Column (48)

101st, 154th, 450th, 506th, 526th, 536th, 716th, 737th, 841st, 843rd, 844th, 846th, 850th and 852nd Artillery Battalions
1 (mot) Headquarters Company
3 (motZ) Batteries (4 150mm sFH and 2 LMGs ea)
1 Light (mot) Munitions Supply Column (48)

845th and 848th Artillery Battalions
1 (mot) Headquarters Company
3 (motZ) Batteries (4 150mm sFH and 2 LMGs ea)

810th Artillery Battalion
1 Headquarters Company
3 Batteries (4 150mm sFH and 2 LMGs ea)

2/43rd, 2/47th 3/111th, 422nd and 3/818th Artillery
1 (mot) Headquarters Company
3 (motZ) Batteries (4 150mm sFH and 2 LMGs ea)
1 Light (mot) Munitions Supply Column (48)

Note: These units were re-equipped with sFH 18 (mot) howitzers as follows: 2/43rd on 6 May 1943, 2/47th on 13 April 1943, 2/77th on 24 February 1943, 3/111th on 6 April 1943, 422nd on 13 April 1943 and 3/818th on 24 February 1943.

450th Artillery Battalion
1 (mot) Headquarters Company
3 (motZ) Batteries (4 150mm sFH 18 and 2 LMGs ea)
1 Light (mot) Munitions Supply Column (48)

2/37th, 2/39th, 2/42nd, 2/43rd, 2/46th, 2/47th, 2/58th, 2/59th, 2/61st, 2/63rd, 2/66th, 2/67th, 1/77th, 3/818th and 3/111th Artillery Regiments
1 (mot) Headquarters Company

3 (motZ) Batteries (4 150mm sFH 18 and 2 LMGs ea)
1 Light (mot) Munitions Supply Column (48)

101st, 154th, 422nd, 506th, 526th, 536th, 716th, 737th, 841st, 843rd, 844th, 845th, 848th, 850th, 851st and 852nd Artillery Battalions
1 (mot) Headquarters Company
3 (motZ) Batteries (4 150mm sFH 18 and 2 LMGs ea)
1 Light (mot) Munitions Supply Column (48)

1/, 2/814th Artillery Regiment, each with
1 (motZ) Battalion HQ
2 Batteries (2 240mm howitzer and 2 LMGs ea)
1 Battery (1 240mm howitzer and 2 LMGs)

744th Howitzer Battery
3 280mm coastal L12 howitzers and 2 LMGs

458th Artillery Battalion
1 420mm howitzer and 2 LMGs

Armored Artillery Brigade
(appears to have been disbanded on 16 Feb. 1943)
1st Artillery Regiment
1 (mot) Regimental Headquarters
7 Self-Propelled Batteries (6 Sd Kfz 165 Hummel with 150mm gun and 7 LMGs ea)
1 Self-Propelled Battery (6 leFH 18 105mm howitzers and 7 LMGs)
1 Light (mot) Munitions Supply Column (32t)
1 Light (mot) POL Supply Column (15t)
1 (mot) Maintenance Company
2nd Artillery Regiment
1 (mot) Regimental Headquarters
5 Self-Propelled Batteries (6 Sd Kfz 165 Hummel with 150mm gun and 7 LMGs ea)
2 Self-Propelled Batteries (6 leFH 18 105mm howitzers and 7 LMGs ea)
1 Light (mot) Munitions Supply Column (32t)
1 Light (mot) POL Supply Column (15t)
1 (mot) Maintenance Company
Attached Detachment
2 Battalions, each with
1 Self-Propelled Battery (4 leFH 16 and 4 LMGs)
1 Self-Propelled Battery (4 75mm PAK 40 and 4 LMGs)
1 Self-Propelled Battery (6 20mm AA guns)
1 Battery with
4 Self-Propelled 88mm and 2 LMGs
1 Supply Company (mixed mobility)
Heavy (mot) Gun Battalions
2/43rd, 2/47th, 2/52nd, 2/71st, 1/106th, 4/109th and 3/140th Artillery Regiments and 422nd Artillery Battalion
1 (mot) Headquarters Company

2 Batteries (4 150mm sFH 18 howitzers and 2 LMGs ea)
1 Battery (4 100mm K18 guns and 2 LMGs)
1 Light (mot) Munitions Supply Column

Note: The 2/43rd and 2/47th were reduced to three guns per battery on 6 May 1943. The 422nd, 2/43rd and 2/47th had (48t) supply column, 2/52nd and 3/140th (39t); the rest were (24t).

451st Artillery Battalion
1 (mot) Headquarters Company
2 Batteries (4 150mm sFH 18 howitzers and 2 LMGs ea)
1 Battery (4 100mm K18 guns and 2 LMGs)

2/54th, 2/65th, 1/108th, 2/127th and 602nd Artillery
1 (mot) Headquarters Company
2 Batteries (4 150mm sFH 18 howitzers and 2 LMGs ea)
1 Battery (4 100mm K18 guns and 2 LMGs)
1 Light (mot) Munitions Supply Column (39t)

Note: Disbanded or re-gunned during the year.

Heavy (mot) Howitzer Battalions
2/109th, 3/109th, 604th, 607th, 615th, 635th, 636th, 637th, 732nd, 735th, 736th, 809th, 816th, 833rd, 854th, 856th, 857th, 858th, 859th and 867th Artillery Batteries
1 (mot) Headquarters Company
3 Batteries (3 210mm howitzers and 2 LMGs ea)
1 Light (mot) Munitions Supply Column (48t)

Note: The 2/109th appears to have been disbanded on 9 April 1943. The 732nd was converting one battery to 170mm guns. The 833rd had only two batteries. The 667th appears to have been disbanded on 3 February 1943. There were supply columns with the 636th, 637th, 777th, 833rd, 854th, 856th or 859th Artillery Battalions.

951st Coastal Howitzer Battery (3 210mm howitzers and 2 LMGs)

1/814th and 2/814th Heavy Artillery Regiment
1 (mot) Headquarters Company
3 Batteries (3 240mm howitzers and 2 LMGs ea)

774th Heavy Artillery Battalion
1 Battery (3 280mm howitzers and 2 LMGs)

Note: The 774th was reorganized on 1 April 1943 with four 220mm Mrs 531 (f) and two 240mm H39.

458th Heavy Artillery Battalion
1 420mm howitzer and 2 LMGs

624th Heavy Artillery Battalion
  1 (mot) Staff Battery
  1 Light (mot) Munitions Column (48t)
  3 (mot) Battalions, each with
    2 Batteries (2 305mm Czech howitzers and 2 LMGs ea)
    1 Light (mot) Munitions Column (48t)

641st Heavy Artillery Battalion
  1 (mot) Staff Battery
  3 Batteries (2 305mm H M1 and 2 LMGs ea)
  1 Light (mot) Munitions Column (20t)

815th Heavy Artillery Battalion
  1 (mot) Staff Battery
  3 Batteries (2 305mm Czech howitzers and 2 LMGs each)
  1 Light (mot) Munitions Column (48t)

Motorized Heavy Artillery Battalions
2/41st, 2/57th, 2/60th 2/262nd, 2/68th, 2/69th and 2/70th
  Artillery Regiment
  1 (mot) Staff Battery
  3 (motZ) Batteries (4 100mm K18 guns and 2 LMGs ea)
  1 Light (mot) Munitions Column (20t)

Note: The 2/70th had two batteries and no supply column. It was formed on 7 May 1943.

151st, 153rd, 427th, 436th, 445th, 496th, 611th, 633rd, 634th, 709th, 711th, 730th, 1/818th and 842nd
  1 (mot) Staff Battery
  3 (motZ) Batteries (4 100mm K18 guns and 2 LMGs ea)
  1 Light (mot) Munitions Column (20t)

Note: The 496th had no motorized supply column, but did have a motorized calibration platoon. The 730th had no supply column, but had an additional battery with four 105mm leFH and two LMGs. The supply column was a (10t) column for the 633rd, 709th, and 711th Battalions.

2/53rd, 2/64th, 2/72nd, 430th, 631st, 2/818th, 849th Artillery Battalions
  1 (mot) Staff Battery
  3 (motZ) Batteries (4 100mm K18 guns and 2 LMGs ea)
  1 Light (mot) Munitions Column (20t)

Note: These battalions appear to have been destroyed or disbanded in March/April 1943. The supply column was a (10t) column for the 633rd, 709th, and 711th Battalions.

2/127th, 3/140th, 2/40th, 2/52nd, 2/54th, 2/65th, 2/70th, 2/71st, 1/106th, 1/108th, 4/109th, 602nd, 634th, 3/140th and 451st Artillery Battalions
  1 (mot) Staff Battery
  2 (motZ) Batteries (3 210mm howitzers and 2 LMGs ea)
  1 (motZ) Battery (3 150mm K18 and 2 LMGs)
  1 Light (mot) Munitions Column (39t)

Note: The 451st was formed on 20 February 1943. The 634th had one 210mm battery replaced by a second 150mm K18 (mot) battery. The 3/140th was formed on 23 March 1943. The 2/65th had one 210mm battery disbanded or destroyed on 19 March 1943.

934th and 935th Artillery Battalions
  1 (mot) Staff Battery
  3 (motZ) Batteries (4 leFH 18 howitzers and 2 LMGs ea)

Heavy (mot) Gun Batteries with captured Russian equipment
456th, 457th, and 460th Artillery Battalions
  1 (mot) Staff Battery
  3 (motZ) Batteries (4 152mm guns and 2 LMGs ea)

150mm Gun Batteries
767th Artillery Battalion
  1 (mot) Staff Battery, with
    Signals Section
    2 Artillery Calibration Detachments
  2 Batteries (3 150mm guns and 2 LMGs each)
  1 Light (mot) Munitions Column (10t)

1/, 2/, 3/511th, 1/, 2/, 3/620th, 1/, 2/, 3/680th, 1/, 2/, 3/740th, 1/, 2/ and 3/731st Artillery Battalions and 625th Artillery Battery
  3 motorized 150mm guns and 2 LMGs each

Note: Prior to 8 April 1943 the 731st Battalion was organized like the 767th.

170mm Batteries on Mortar Carriages
817th, 763rd and 764th Artillery Battalions
  1 (mot) Staff Battery
  3 (motZ) Batteries (3 170mm howitzers and 2 LMGs ea)

Note: The 817th Battalion was broken up into independent batteries on 27 April 1943.

435th, 1/, 2/, 3/817th, 1/557th and 3/557th Artillery Batteries (3 170mm guns and 2 LMGs ea)

763rd, 764th and 817th Artillery Battalions
  1 (mot) Staff Battery, with

1 Signals Section
1 Calibration Section
3 (motZ) Batteries (3 170mm guns and 2 LMGs ea)
1 Light (mot) Munitions Column (32t)

435th Artillery Battery (3 170mm guns and 2 LMGs)

150mm Gun Battalions

511th Artillery Battalion
  1 (mot) Staff Battery, with
    3 (motZ) Batteries (3 170mm guns and 2 LMGs ea)
  1 Light (mot) Munitions Column (32t)

620th Artillery Battalion
  1 (mot) Staff Battery, with
    1 Signals Section
    2 Calibration Sections
  3 (motZ) Batteries (3 150mm K18 guns and 2 LMGs ea)
  1 Light (mot) Munitions Column (32t)

625th Artillery Battalion
  1 (mot) Staff Battery, with
    1 Signals Section
    1 Calibration Section
  3 (motZ) Batteries (3 150mm K18 guns and 2 LMGs ea)

680th Artillery Battalion
  1 (mot) Staff Battery, with
    1 Signals Section
    1 Calibration Section
  2 (motZ) Batteries (3 150mm K18 guns and 2 LMGs ea)
  1 (motZ) Battery (3 150mm K39 guns and 2 LMGs)
  1 Light (mot) Munitions Column (20t)

731st Artillery Battalion
  1 (mot) Staff Battery, with
    1 Signals Section
    1 Calibration Section
  3 (motZ) Batteries (3 150mm K39 guns and 2 LMGs ea)
  1 Light (mot) Munitions Column (32t)

740th Artillery Battalion
  1 (mot) Staff Battery, with
    1 Signals Section
    1 Calibration Section
  3 (motZ) Batteries (3 150mm K39 guns and 2 LMGs ea)
  1 Light (mot) Munitions Column (32t)

767th Artillery Battalion
  1 (mot) Staff Battery, with
    1 Signals Section
    1 Calibration Section

1 (motZ) Battery (3 150mm K18 guns and 2 LMGs)
1 (motZ) Battery (3 170mm guns on mortar carriages and 2 LMGs)
1 Light (mot) Munitions Column (32t)

800th Artillery Battalion
  1 (mot) Staff Battery, with
    1 Signals Section
    1 Calibration Section
  3 (motZ) Batteries (3 150mm K39 guns and 2 LMGs ea)
  1 Light (mot) Munitions Column (32t)

456th, 457th and 460th Artillery Battalions
  1 (mot) Staff Battery, with
    2 (motZ) Batteries (4 152mm Russian guns and 2 LMGs ea)
  1 (motZ) Battery (4 122mm Russian guns and 2 LMGs)

Note: Formed on 5 December, 25 January and 20 February 1943 respectively.

Other Heavy Artillery Battalions

917th Artillery Battery
  1 (mot) Calibration Section
  1 Self-Propelled Battery (3 French 194mm and 2 LMGs)

768th Artillery Battalion
  1 (mot) Staff Battery
  3 (motZ) Batteries (2 210mm guns and 2 LMGs ea)
  1 (motZ) Battery (3 210mm guns and 2 LMGs)

1/84th Artillery Battalion
  1 (mot) Staff Battery, with
    1 Signals Section
    1 Calibration Section
  3 (motZ) Batteries (2 210mm K3 guns and 2 LMGs ea)
  1 Light (mot) Munitions Supply Column

2/84th Artillery Battalion
  1 (mot) Staff Battery, with
    1 Signals Section
    1 Calibration Section
  2 (motZ) Batteries (3 170mm gun and 2 LMGs ea)
  1 Self-Propelled Battery (3 French 240mm K guns and 2 LMGs)

Note: The self-propelled battery with French guns was replaced by a motorized battery of two 240mm K3 guns and two LMGs, date of change not known.

628th Artillery Battery (2 600mm Self-Propelled "Karl" Mortars and 1 reserve)

ORGANIZATION OF GENERAL HEADQUARTERS POOL ARTILLERY, JANUARY 1944

(tmot) Artillery Regiments

36th (mixed mobility) Artillery Regiment
- 1 Staff Battery
- 2 Battalions
  - 1 Staff Battery
  - 3 Batteries (3 75mm and 2 LMGs ea)
- 1 Battalion
  - 1 Staff Battery
  - 2 Batteries (3 75mmand 2 LMGs ea)
  - 1 (mot) Battery (3 100mm guns and 1 LMG)

1/127th (mot) Artillery Regiment
- 1 (mot) Staff Battery
- 3 (mot) Batteries (4 105mm leFH 18 and 2 LMGs ea)

2/140th (mot) Artillery Regiment
- 1 (mot) Staff Battery
- 3 (mot) Batteries (4 105mm leFH 18 and 2 LMGs ea)

3/999th (mot) Artillery Regiment
- 1 (mot) Staff Battery
- 3 (mot) Batteries (4 105mm leFH 18 and 2 LMGs ea)

520th (mot) Artillery Battalion
- 1 (mot) Staff Battery
- 2 (mot) Batteries (4 105mm leFH 18 and 2 LMGs ea)

555th (mot) Artillery Battalion
- 1 (mot) Staff Battery
- 3 (mot) Batteries (4 122mm howitzers and 2 LMGs ea)

989th (mixed mobility) Artillery Battalion
- 1 (mixed mobility) Staff Battery
- 3 (mixed mobility) Batteries (4 122mm howitzers and 2 LMGs ea)

Light Artillery Battalions (RSO)

2/46th, 2/51st, 2/54th, 2/64th, 2/65th, 2/72nd, 1/77th, 1/108th, 2/109th, 2/818th and 2/818th Artillery Regiments
- 1 (mot) Staff Battery
- 3 (mot) Batteries (4 105mm leFH 18 and 2 LMGs ea)

425th, 426th, 430th, 602nd, 616th, 631st, 733rd, 849th, 851s, 855th, 860th and 861st Artillery Battalions
- 1 (mot) Staff Battery
- 3 (mot) Batteries (4 105mm leFH 18 and 2 LMGs ea)

Garrison Light Howitzer Battalions

1143rd Garrison Artillery Battalion
- 1 Staff Battery
- 4 Batteries (4 105mm French howitzers and 4 LMGs ea)

1146th Garrison Artillery Battalion
- 1 Staff Battery
- 3 Batteries (4 122mm Russian howitzers and 4 LMGs ea)

1148th Garrison Artillery Battalion
- 1 Staff Battery
- 4 Batteries (4 105mm Czech howitzers and 4 LMGs ea)

1162nd Garrison Artillery Battalion
- 1 Staff Battery
- 4 Batteries (4 105mm French howitzers and 4 LMGs ea)

1163rd Garrison Artillery Battalion
- 1 Staff Battery
- 3 Batteries (4 105mm Yugoslavian howitzers and 4 LMGs ea)

1190th Garrison Artillery Battalion
- 1 Staff Battery
- 3 Batteries (100mm Italian howitzers)

Army Heavy Howitzer Battalions (mot u.Sf)

2/37th, 2/39th, 2/61st, 2/66th and 2/67th Artillery Regiments
- 1 Staff Battery
- 3 (mot) Batteries (4 150mm and 2 LMGs ea)

2/40th, 2/63rd and 2/71st Artillery Regiments
- 1 Staff Battery
- 3 Self-Propelled Batteries (4 150mm and 2 LMGs ea)

154th, 450th, 506th, 737th, 841st 526th, 844th, 846th, 848th, 850th, 1151st, 1192nd, 1193rd and 1194th Artillery Battalions
- 1 Staff Battery
- 3 (mot) Batteries (4 150mm and 2 LMGs ea)

101st, 536th, 834th and 845th Artillery Battalions
- 1 Staff Battery
- 3 Self-Propelled Batteries (4 150mm and 2 LMGs ea)

Garrison Heavy Artillery Battalions

929th Garrison Artillery Battalion
- 3 Batteries (4 155mm French and 2 LMGs ea)

1140th Garrison Artillery Battalion
- 1 Staff Battery
- 3 Batteries (4 155mm French howitzers and 4 LMGs ea)

1147th Garrison Artillery Battalion
- 1 Staff Battery

3 Batteries (4 155mm Czech howitzers and 4 LMGs ea)

1149th Garrison Artillery Battalion
1 Staff Battery
3 Batteries (4 155mm French howitzers and 4 LMGs ea)

1150th Garrison Artillery Battalion
1 Staff Battery
3 Batteries (4 155mm French howitzers and 4 LMGs ea)

1180th Garrison Artillery Battalion
1 Staff Battery
4 Batteries (4 105mm Czech howitzers and 4 LMGs ea)

1181st Garrison Artillery Battalion
1 Staff Battery
4 Batteries (4 155mm French howitzers and 4 LMGs ea)

1182nd Garrison Artillery Battalion
1 Staff Battery
4 Batteries (4 155mm French howitzers and 4 LMGs ea)

1195th Garrison Artillery Battalion
1 Staff Battery
3 Batteries (4 155mm French howitzers and 4 LMGs ea)

1196th Garrison Artillery Battalion
1 Staff Battery
3 Batteries (4 150mm Italian howitzers and 4 LMGs ea)

545th Garrison Artillery Battery (4 155mm Polish howitzers and 2 LMGs)

626th Garrison Artillery Battery (4 152mm Russian howitzers and 2 LMGs)

869th Garrison Artillery Battery (4 155mm Polish howitzers and 2 LMGs)

(mot) Heavy Artillery Battalions, Mixed Howitzer and 100mm Gun Units
2/42nd Artillery Regiment
1 (mot) Staff Battery
1 (mot) Battery (4 100mm guns and 2 LMGs)
1 Self-Propelled Battery (4 150mm guns and 2 LMGs)
1 (mot) Battery (4 150mm guns and 2 LMGs)

2/43rd, 2/47th, 2/52nd, 2/58th, 1/106th, 5/109th and 3/140th Artillery Regiments
1 (mot) Staff Battery

1 (mot) Battery (4 100mm guns and 2 LMGs)
2 (mot) Batteries (4 150mm howitzers and 2 LMGs ea)

422nd and 451st Artillery Battalions
1 (mot) Staff Battery
1 (mot) Battery (4 100mm guns and 2 LMGs)
2 (mot) Batteries (4 150mm howitzers and 2 LMGs ea)

(mot) Heavy Howitzer Battalions
1/, 2/814th Artillery Regiment, each with
2 (mot) Btrys (3 240mm Czech howitzers and 2 LMGs ea)
1 (mixed mobility) Btry (3 240mm Czech howitzers and 2 LMGs ea)

744th Heavy Battery
1 Battery (2 240mm Czech howitzers and 2 LMGs ea)
1 Battery (4 220mm French guns)

458th (mot) Howitzer Battery (1 420mm Czech gun and 2 LMGs ea)

(mot) Heavy Artillery Mortar Battalions (210mm and 220mm mortars)
2/2nd ARL, 3/109th,
1 Staff Battery
3 (mot) Batteries (3 210mm mortars and 2 LMGs ea)

604th 607th, 615th, 628th, 628th 635th, 636th, 637th, 672nd, 732nd, 735th, 736th, 777th, 808th, 815th, 857th, 858th, 934th and 935th Artillery Battalions
1 (mot) Staff Battery
3 (mot) Batteries (3 210mm mortars and 2 LMGs ea)

833rd Artillery Battalion
1 (mot) Staff Battery
2 (mot) Batteries (3 210mm mortars and 2 LMGs ea)

854th, 856th and 859th Artillery Battalions
1 (mot) Signals Platoon
1 (mot) Calibration Detachment
3 (mot) Batteries (3 210mm mortars and 2 LMGs ea)

998th (mot) Artillery Battalion
1 Staff Battery
3 (mot) Batteries (3 220mm French mortars and 2 LMGs ea)

951st Heavy (mot) Battery (3 210mm mortars and 2 LMGs ea)

988th Heavy Mortar Battery
1 (mixed mobility) Staff Battery
3 (mixed mobility) Batteries (3 220mm 531(f) French mortars and 2 LMGs ea)

810th Garrison Heavy Artillery Battalion
  1 Staff Battery
  3 Batteries (3 210mm mortars and 2 LMGs ea)

514th Garrison Battery (3 210mm mortars and 2 LMGs)

515th Garrison Battery (3 210mm mortars, 2 20mm Flak and 2 LMGs)

543rd Garrison Battery (3 210mm mortars and 2 LMGs)

546th Garrison Battery (4 210mm mortars and 2 LMGs)

4/255th Garrison Heavy Artillery Regiment
  1 Staff Battery
  2 Batteries (3 280mm French mortars and 2 LMGs ea)

8th Company/355th Artillery Battalion (3 280mm French mortars and 2 LMGs ea)

624th (mot) Heavy Artillery Regiment
  1 (mot) Staff Battery
  3 (mot) Battalions, each with
    1 (mot) Battery (2 305mm Czech howitzers and 2 LMGs ea)
    1 (mot) Battery (3 210mm mortars and 2 LMGs ea)

641st (mot) Artillery Battalion
  1 (mot) Staff Battery
  2 (mot) Batteries (2 305mm Czech howitzers and 2 LMGs ea)
  1 (mot) Battery (2 355mm M1 howitzers and 2 LMGs)

815th (mot) Artillery Battalion
  1 (mot) Staff Battery
  3 (mot) Batteries (2 305mm Czech howitzers and 2 LMGs ea)

(mot) Heavy Artillery Battalions (100mm guns)

2/41st, 2/57th, 2/60th, 2/62nd, 2/68th, 2/69th and 1/818th Artillery Regiments
  1 (mot) Staff Battery
  3 (mot) Batteries (4 100mm guns and 2 LMGs ea)

2/70th A
rtillery Regiment
  1 (mot) Staff Battery
  2 (mot) Batteries (4 100mm guns and 2 LMGs ea)

151st, 153rd, 427th, 436th, 445th, 611th, 633rd, 634th, 709th, 711th, 730th (Czech guns) and 842nd Artillery Battalions
  1 (mot) Staff Battery
  3 (mot) Batteries (4 100mm guns and 2 LMGs ea)

496th Artillery Battalion
  1 (mot) Calibration Detachment
  1 (mot) Staff Battery (2 20mm Flak guns)
  2 (mot) Batteries (4 100mm French guns and 2 LMGs ea)
  1 (mot) Battery (4 170mm guns and 2 LMGs)

Other Heavy Artillery (100mm) Battalions

990th and 991st Artillery Battalions
  1 (mixed mobility) Staff Battery
  3 (mixed mobility) Batteries (4 100mm guns and 2 LMGs ea)

993rd Artillery Battalion
  1 (mixed mobility) Staff Battery
  3 (mixed mobility) Batteries (4 122mm Russian guns and 2 LMGs ea)

708th Garrison Heavy Artillery Battalion
  3 Batteries (4 100mm guns and 2 LMGs ea)

914th Garrison Heavy Artillery Battalion
  3 Batteries (4 105mm Czech guns and 2 LMGs ea)

928th Garrison Heavy Artillery Battalion
  3 Batteries (4 105mm Czech guns and 2 LMGs ea)

1161st Garrison Heavy Artillery Battalion
  1 Staff Battery
  3 Batteries (4 105mm French guns and 4 LMGs ea)
  1 Battery (4 155mm French guns and 4 LMGs)

1191st Garrison Heavy Artillery Battalion
  1 Staff Battery
  3 Batteries (4 105mm Italian guns and 4 LMGs ea)

Other Heavy Artillery (122mm/152mm) Battalions

456th, 457th, 460th Heavy (mot) Battery
  1 (mot) Staff Battery
  2 (mot) Batteries (4 152mm Russian guns and 2 LMGs ea)
  1 (mot) Battery (4 122mm Russian guns and 2 LMGs ea)

985th, 992nd, 997th Heavy (mot) Battery
  1 (mot) Staff Battery
  3 (mot) Batteries (4 152mm Russian 433 (r) guns and 2 LMGs ea)

1/, 2/, 3/511th Heavy (mot) Battalion (3 150mm guns and 2 LMGs ea)

2/260th Heavy (mot) Battalion (3 150mm guns and 2 LMGs ea)

1/, 3/731st Heavy (mot) Battalion (3 150mm guns and 2 LMGs ea)

6/2nd ALR Heavy (mot) Battalion (3 150mm guns and 2 LMGs ea)

143rd Garrison Battalion (4 btrys with 6 155mm French guns and 2 LMGs ea)

289th Garrison Battalion (3 btrys with 6 155mm French guns and 2 LMGs ea)

531st Garrison Battalion (3 btrys with 6 155mm French guns and 2 LMGs ea)

910th Garrison Battalion (3 btrys with 6 155mm French guns and 2 LMGs ea)

Heavy Gun (170mm) Battalions

557th, 763rd and 764th (mot) Artillery Battalions
1 (mot) Staff Battery
3 (mot) Batteries (3 170mm guns and 2 LMGs ea)

435th and 625th Batteries (3 170mm guns and 2 LMGs ea)

1/, 3/620th, 1/, 2/, 3/680th, 2/731st, 1/, 2/767th, 2/800th, and 1/, 2/, 3/817th (mot) Artillery Regiments (3 170mm guns and 2 LMGs ea)

982nd, 984th and 994th (mixed mobility) Artillery Batteries (3 170mm guns and 2 LMGs ea)

503rd and 507th Garrison Batteries (3 170mm guns and 2 LMGs ea)

Other Artillery Formations

917th Self-Propelled Artillery Battalion
1 (mot) Calibration Detachment
1 Battery (3 self-propelled French 194mm guns and 2 LMGs)

9th Btry/355th Artillery Battalion
1 Battery (4 self-propelled French 194mm guns and 2 LMGs)

639th Garrison Artillery Battery
1 Battery (3 French 194mm guns and 2 LMGs)

768th (mot) Artillery Battalion
1 (mot) Staff Battery
2 (mot) Batteries (2 210mm K38 guns and 2 LMGs ea)

659th and 660th (mot) Artillery Battery
1 (mot) Battery (3 210mm Czech guns and 2 LMGs)

508th Garrison Battery
1 Battery (3 210mm guns and 2 LMGs)

1/84th (mot) Artillery Regiment
1 (mot) Company
1 (mot) Signals Detachment
1 (mot) Calibration Detachment
2 Batteries (4 170mm guns and 2 LMGs ea)
1 Battery (2 240mm K3 guns and 2 LMGs)

2/84th (mot) Artillery Regiment
1 (mot) Company
1 (mot) Signals Detachment
1 (mot) Calibration Detachment
2 Batteries (3 170mm guns and 2 LMGs ea)
1 Battery (2 240mm Czech guns and 2 LMGs)

Special Artillery Formations

485th, 836th and 962nd (mot) Artillery Battalions
3 Batteries, each with
1 (mot) Gun Section (number and type of guns not identified)
1 (mot) Security Group
Anti-Tank Battery (3 LMGs and 3 75mm PAK 40)
Anti-Tank Section (6 LMGs and 1 AT rocket launcher)
1 Self-Propelled Flak Battery (2 quad 20mm AA guns)
1 (mot) Light Fuel Column

444th Artillery Battery
1 (mot) Gun Section (number and type of guns not identified)
1 (mot) Security Group
Anti-Tank Battery (3 LMGs and 3 75mm PAK guns)
Anti-Tank Section (6 LMGs and 1 AT rocket launcher)
1 Self-Propelled Flak Battery (2 quad 20mm AA guns)
1 (mot) Light Fuel Column

1/, 2/953rd Artillery Battalion
2 (mixed mobility) Batteries (number and type of guns unknown)

3/963rd Artillery Battalion
1 (mixed mobility) Battery (number and types of guns unknown)

291st, 294th and 311th (mot) Flak Battalions
1 (mot) Staff Battery
3 (mot) Flak Batteries (4 88mm, 3 20mm AA guns and 2 LMGs ea)

Railroad Artillery, 1941–1944

10 FEBRUARY 1941

Railroad Artillery

725th Railroad Battalion
  1 (mot) Signal and Calibration Platoons
  2 Batteries (2 280mm E guns ea)
655th Railroad Battery
  1 (mot) Signals Platoon
  3 150mm E guns
717th and 718th Railroad Batteries
  1 (mot) Signals Platoon
  3 170mm E guns and 2 37mm AA
701st Railroad Battery
  1 (mot) Signals Platoon
  1 210mm K12 gun, 1 210mm K5 gun and 2 37mm AA
644th, 674th and 722nd Railroad Batteries
  1 (mot) Signals Platoon
  2 240mm E guns and 2 37mm AA
688th Railroad Battery
  1 (mot) Signals Platoon
  3 280mm E guns and 2 37mm AA
689th, 695th, 696th, 765th Railroad Batteries
  1 (mot) Signals Platoon
  2 280mm E guns
690th, 694th, 710th, 712th, 713th, 721st Railroad Batteries
  1 (mot) Signals Platoon
  2 280mm E guns and 2 37mm AA

16 MAY 1941–15 OCTOBER 1942

Railroad Artillery Staffs

720th Artillery Regimental Staff
766th Artillery Regimental Staff
781st Artillery Regimental Staff
  1 (mot) Signals Platoon
640th Artillery Battalion Staff
676th Artillery Battalion Staff
  2 20mm guns
679th Artillery Battalion Staff
  1 (mot) Signals Platoon
681st Artillery Battalion Staff
  2 Batteries (4 20mm guns ea)
702nd Artillery Battalion Staff
780th Artillery Battalion Staff
  1 (mot) Signals Platoon

Railroad Batteries

655th Railroad Battery (4 150mm railroad guns)
  1 Calibration Section
717th Railroad Battery (4 170mm railroad guns)
  1 Calibration Section

718th Railroad Battery (4 170mm railroad guns)
  1 Calibration Section
532nd and 687th Railroad Batteries, each with
  4 203mm railroad guns
  1 Calibration Section
  2 quad 20mm guns
685th Railroad Battery (2 203mm railroad guns)
  1 Calibration Section
  2 20mm guns
701st Railroad Battery (2 210mm K 12 railroad guns)
  1 Calibration Section
  2 20mm guns
664th and 674th Railroad Batteries, each with
  2 240mm Theodor Railroad guns
  1 Calibration Section
  2 20mm guns
722nd Railroad Battery (2 240mm Theodor-Bruno railroad guns and 4 20mm guns)
691st Railroad Battery (3 203mm K.(E) railroad guns)
688th Railroad Battery
  1 Calibration Section
  2 K5 280mm railroad guns
  2 20mm AA guns
689th Railroad Battery
  1 Calibration Section
  2 s.Br.K(E) 280mm railroad guns
  2 20mm AA guns
690th Railroad Battery
  2 KB 280mm railroad guns
  2 20mm AA guns
695th Railroad Battery
  1 Calibration Section
  2 KB 280mm railroad guns
  3 370mm railroad guns
  2 20mm AA guns
696th Railroad Battery
  1 Calibration Section
  2 KB 280mm railroad guns
  2 20mm AA guns
710th Railroad Battery
  1 Calibration Section
  2 K5 280mm railroad guns
  2 20mm AA guns
712th Railroad Battery
  1 Calibration Section
  2 K5 280mm railroad guns
  2 20mm AA guns
713th Railroad Battery
  1 Calibration Section
  2 K5 280mm railroad guns
  2 20mm AA guns
721st Railroad Battery
  1 Calibration Section

2 KB 280mm railroad guns
2 20mm AA guns
749th Railroad Battery
1 Calibration Section
2 K5 280mm railroad guns
2 20mm AA guns
765th Railroad Battery
1 Calibration Section
2 K5 280mm railroad guns
2 20mm AA guns
725th Railroad Gun Battalion
1 (mot) Staff Company
1st Battery (2 Bruno "N" 280mm railroad guns)
1st Battery (2 K5 280mm railroad guns)
673rd Railroad Battery (2 340mm railroad guns)
686th Artillery Battery
1 K5 280mm railroad gun
3 400mm railroad guns
1 (mot) "s. Vo." Platoon
693rd Railroad Battery (3 400mm railroad guns)
459th Railroad Battery (420mm Gamma mortar)

OCTOBER 1942–SUMMER 1943

Railroad Artillery
655th Railroad Battery
1 (mot) Calibration Section
4 150mm E guns
717th and 718th Railroad Batteries
1 (mot) Calibration Section
3 170mm E guns and 20mm AA
532nd Railroad Battery
4 (later 3) 203mm guns and 2 quad 20mm AA guns
685th Railroad Battery
3 203mm guns and 2 (later 4) 20mm AA guns
687th Railroad Battery
2 203mm guns and 4 quad 20mm AA guns
701st Railroad Battery
1 (mot) Calibration Section
2 203mm guns and 2 20mm AA guns
664th Railroad Battery
1 (mot) Calibration Section
2 240mm guns and 2 20mm AA guns
674th Railroad Battery
1 (mot) Calibration Section
2 240mm guns and 2 20mm AA guns
664th Railroad Battery
4 240mm guns and 2 20mm AA guns
691st Railroad Battery
3 240mm French guns
692nd Railroad Battery
1 (mot) Calibration Section
3 274mm guns and 2 20mm AA guns

688th Railroad Battery
1 (mot) Calibration Section
2 280mm K5 guns and 2 20mm AA guns
689th Railroad Battery
1 (mot) Calibration Section
2 280mm guns and 2 20mm AA guns
690th Railroad Battery
1 (mot) Calibration Section
4 280mm guns and 2 20mm AA guns
695th Railroad Battery
1 (mot) Calibration Section
3 280mm KB guns, 3 37mm and 2 20mm AA guns (earlier 2 280mm and 1 370mm guns)
696th Railroad Battery
1 (mot) Calibration Section
2 280mm KB guns and 2 20mm AA guns
710th Railroad Battery
1 (mot) Calibration Section
2 280mm K5 guns and 2 20mm AA guns
712th Railroad Battery
1 (mot) Calibration Section
2 280mm K5 guns and 2 20mm AA guns
713th Railroad Battery
1 (mot) Calibration Section
2 280mm K5 guns and 2 20mm AA guns
721st Railroad Battery
1 (mot) Calibration Section
2 280mm K5 guns and 2 20mm AA guns
749th Railroad Battery
1 (mot) Calibration Section
2 280mm K5 guns
765th Railroad Battery
1 (mot) Calibration Section
2 280mm K5 guns
725th Railroad Battery
2 280mm BN guns
2 280mm K5 guns
673rd Railroad Battery
2 340mm French guns
698th Railroad Battery
1 (mot) Calibration Section
2 280mm "Siegfried" K(E) guns
686th Railroad Battery
2 280mm K5 guns
3 400mm French guns
693rd Railroad Battery
3 400mm French guns
459th Railroad Battery
1 420mm Gamma mortar
672nd Railroad Battery
1 (mot) Calibration Section
1 800mm "Gustav Gerät" KE Gun

JANUARY 1944

Railroad Batteries

655th Railroad Battery
  1 (mot) Calibration Detachment
  4 150mm guns and 4 20mm AA guns
717th and 718th Railroad Battery
  1 (mot) Calibration Detachment
  4 170mm guns and 4 20mm AA guns
701st Railroad Battery
  1 (mot) Calibration Detachment
  2 210mm guns, 4 155mm French guns and 4 20mm
    Flak guns
664th and 674th Railroad Battery
  1 (mot) Calibration Detachment
  2 240mm guns and 4 20mm AA guns
722nd Railroad Battery
  4 240mm guns and 4 20mm AA guns
691st Railroad Battery
  1 (mot) Calibration Detachment
  3 240mm French guns and 4 20mm AA guns
692nd Railroad Battery
  1 (mot) Calibration Detachment
  3 274mm French guns, 4 152mm Russian guns and 4
    20mm AA guns
688th and 689th Railroad Battery
  1 (mot) Calibration Detachment
  2 280mm guns and 4 20mm AA guns
690th Railroad Battery
  4 280mm guns and 4 20mm AA guns

695th Railroad Battery
  1 (mot) Calibration Detachment
  1 340mm and 2 320mm guns and 4 20mm AA guns
696th 710th, 712th, 721st, 749th, and 765th Railroad
Batteries, each with
  1 (mot) Calibration Detachment
  2 280mm guns and 4 20mm AA guns
713th Railroad Battery
  1 (mot) Calibration Detachment
  3 280th French guns, 4 155mm French guns and 4
    20mm Flak guns
725th Railroad Artillery Battalion
  1 Battery
    1 (mot) Calibration Detachment
    Gun Section (2 280mm guns, 4 French 155mm guns
      and 4 20mm AA guns)
  1 Battery
    1 (mot) Calibration Detachment
    Gun Section (2 280mm guns and 4 20mm AA guns)
459th Railroad Battery (3 370mm French guns)
698th Railroad Battery (2 380mm Siegfried guns, 4
  152mm Russian guns and 4 20mm AA guns)
686th Railroad Artillery Battery
  1 (mot) Calibration Detachment
  Gun Section (2 280mm guns, 4 40mm French E guns
    and 4 20mm AA guns)
693rd Railroad Battery (4 400mm guns and 2 quad 20mm
  AA guns)

14

German Army Flak Artillery

The Germans first developed their Flak artillery during World War I and it was, at that time, part of the army. On 8 October 1916 a the "Commanding General of Air Combat Forces" (*Kommandierend General der Luftstreigkrafte*) was designated. All Flak artillery was placed under his command. As Germany was prohibited from owning Flak artillery by the Treaty of Versailles, this formation vanished until Hitler tore up the Treaty of Versailles.

Despite this prohibition, in 1928 seven clandestine Flak batteries were formed. In 1932 they were assembled under the name "Transport-Abteilungen". Shortly afterwards Flak machine gun companies were formed under the name "*Deutscher Luftsportsverband*" (German Air Sports Union). In 1934 these units were detached from the army and placed under the *Reichsministerium der Luftfahrt* (Reich Ministry of Air Travel). From here they began to grow.

The Wehrmacht did not, however accept this gracefully and demanded its own Flak artillery units. The Luftwaffe was made public on 1 April 1935 and all responsibility for air defense was formally assigned to them. The growth of Flak units expanded. The 18 present in 1835 became 115 in 1939 and 841 in 1941.

The Wehrmacht remained unsatisfied, and in 1941 they were permitted to organize Flak units for operations with their forces. The *Herresflakbataillonen* were formed and assigned to the infantry, while the *Herresflakabteilungen* were assigned to the artillery. Despite this, all weapons, equipment and ammunition were controlled by the Luftwaffe.

The *Herresflakabteilungen* (Army Flak Detachments) were numbered by the Luftwaffe in the same sequence as their own units. The Wehrmacht's units, however, began numbering at 271st. The army's Flak battalions were originally numbered 22nd through 66th, but this was later changed to 510st and 601st–620th. As the war progressed, however, many unnumbered formations were organized and sent into battle.

On 10 February 1941 the Wehrmacht contained the following independent Flak battalions:

31st, 47th, 55th, 601st, 602nd, 603rd, 604th, 605th, 607th, 610th, 611th and 631st Self-Propelled Flak Battalions
   4 Companies (12 37mm AA guns ea)

612th, 613th and 615th (mot) Flak Battalions
   2 Companies (12 20mm AA guns ea)

46th and 48th Self-Propelled Flak Battalions
   5 Companies (12 37mm AA guns ea)

52nd and 66th Self-Propelled Flak Battalion
   3 Companies (12 37mm AA guns ea)

59th Self-Propelled Flak Battalion
   2 Companies (12 37mm AA guns ea)

1/8th Self-Propelled Flak Battalion
   (88mm guns, number not indicated)

272nd, 273rd, 279th, 280th and 275th Army Flak Battalions
   (mot) HQ Section
   2 Batteries (4 88mm guns and 3 20mm guns ea)
   1 Battery (12 20mm AA guns)
271st, 274th, 276th, 277th and 278th Army Flak Battalions
   1 (mot) HQ Section
   3 Batteries (4 88mm guns and 3 20mm guns ea)

Between 16 May 1941 and 15 October 1942 the army Flak forces expanded and became somewhat inconsistent in their organization. They contained:

601st Flak Battalion
   4 Self-Propelled Flak Companies (12 20mm SP AA guns)
602nd Flak Battalion
   4 Self-Propelled Flak Companies (2 quad 20mm AA guns and 8 20mm AA guns)
604th and 607th Flak Battalions
   3 Self-Propelled Flak Companies (2 quad 20mm AA guns and 8 20mm AA guns)
   1 Self-Propelled Flak Company (8 SP 20mm and 4 towed)
605th Flak Battalion
   3 Self-Propelled Flak Companies (2 quad 20mm AA guns and 8 20mm AA guns)
610th and 616th Flak Battalions
   3 Self-Propelled Flak Companies (12 20mm AA guns)
611th Flak Battalion
   3 Motorized Flak Companies (8 20mm AA guns and 2 quad SP 20mm guns)
614th and 619th Flak Battalions
   3 Self-Propelled Flak Companies (2 quad 20mm AA guns and 8 20mm AA guns)

613th Flak Battalion
  3 Motorized Flak Companies (12 20mm AA guns)
  1 Self-Propelled Flak Company (12 20mm SP AA guns)
615th Flak Battalion
  3 Motorized Flak Companies (12 20mm AA guns)
618th Flak Battalions
  3 Self-Propelled Flak Companies (2 quad 20mm AA guns and 8 20mm AA guns)
  1 Self-Propelled Flak Company (12 20mm AA SP guns)

Independent AA Batteries

503rd, 513th, 523rd, 533rd, 543rd, 553rd, 563rd and 573rd
  20mm Batteries (2 20mm guns each)
436th Motorized Flak Battery (4 20mm guns)

Army Flak Battalions

272nd, 273rd and 280th Army Flak Battalions
  1 Motorized Staff Company
  2 (motZ) Batteries (4 88mm guns and 3 20mm guns each)
  1 (motZ) Battery (12 20mm guns)

275th, 279th, 284th, 286th, 188th and 303rd Army Flak Battalions
  1 Motorized Staff Company
  2 (motZ) Batteries (4 88mm guns and 3 20mm guns each)
  1 (motZ) Battery (12 20mm guns)
  1 Light Motorized Munitions Column (20t)

Between October 1942 and the summer of 1943 the Wehrmacht's Flak forces stood as follows:

601st Flak Battalion
  4 Self-Propelled Companies (12 20mm AA each)
602nd Flak Battalion
  4 Self-Propelled Companies (8 20mm and 2 quad 20mm)
604th Flak Battalion
  3 Self-Propelled Companies (8 20mm AA and 2 quad 20mm ea)
  1 Self-Propelled Company (12 20mm AA each)
605th Flak Battalion
  3 Self-Propelled Companies (8 20mm AA and 2 quad 20mm ea)
607th Flak Battalion[1]
  3 Motorized Companies (12 20mm each)
610th Flak Battalion
  3 Self-Propelled Flak Companies (12 20mm each)
611th Flak Battalion[2]
  3 (motZ) Batteries, each with 8 20mm and 2 SP quad 20mm AA guns)
613th Flak Battalion (disbanded 26 Oct. 1942)
  1 Self-Propelled Company (12 20mm guns)

3 Motorized Companies (12 20mm guns each)
614th Flak Battalion (disbanded 22 Apr. 1943)
  3 Self-Propelled Companies (8 20mm AA and 2 quad 20mm ea)
615th Flak Battalion[3]
  4 Self-Propelled Companies (12 20mm AA each)
616th Flak Battalion[4]
  3 Motorized Companies (12 20mm each)
618th Flak Battalion
  3 Self-Propelled Companies (8 20mm AA and 2 quad 20mm ea)
  1 Self-Propelled Company (12 20mm AA each)
619th Flak Battalion
  3 Self-Propelled Companies (8 20mm AA and 2 quad 20mm ea)
510th Flak Battalion
  1 Company with 8 quad 20mm Flak guns
436th Flak Platoon
  4 20mm AA guns
506th, 516th, and 526th Flak Platoons
  2 quad 20mm Flak guns
503rd, 513th, 523rd, 533rd, 543rd, 553rd, 563rd, 573rd Flak Platoons
  2 20mm Flak guns each

Railroad Flak Artillery

273rd, 275th, 279th, 280th, 284th, 288th, 292nd, 296th, 297th, 291st, 292nd, 294th, 295th, 298th, 299th, 300th, 301st and 303rd Motorized Flak Battalions
  1 Motorized Flak Staff Battery (1 LMG)
  2 Flak Batteries (4 88mm, 3 20mm and 2 LMGs ea)
  1 Flak Battery (12 20mm and 2 LMGs)
  1 Light (mot) Munitions Column (20t)

286th Motorized Flak Battalion
  1 Motorized Flak Staff Battery
  2 Flak Batteries (4 88mm, 3 20mm and 2 LMGs ea)
  1 Flak Battery (12 20mm and 2 LMGs)
  1 Light (mot) Munitions Column

Note: Apparently the 286th was lost or disbanded in May 1943.

304th Self-Propelled Flak Battalion
  2 Self-Propelled Flak Batteries (4 88mm, 3 20mm and 3 LMGs ea)
  1 Self-Propelled Flak Battery (12 20mm and 2 LMGs)

---

[1] It would appear that until November 1942 the 607th Flak Battalion had four self-propelled Flak companies. Each company had 12 SP 20mm guns.
[2] In late 1942 this battalion had three batteries, each with eight motorized 20mm and two quad 20mm Flak guns. It was reorganized in the fall of 1942 and disbanded on 28 November 1942.
[3] Prior to 31 March 1942 the 615th had only three motorized batteries with 12 20mm each.
[4] In 1942 the three companies were self-propelled.

1 Light (mot) Munitions Column (36t)

272nd Motorized Flak Battalion
  2 Flak Batteries (4 88mm, 3 20mm and 2 LMGs ea)
  1 Flak Battery (12 20mm and 2 LMGs)
  1 Flak Battery (2 quad 20mm)
  1 Light (mot) Munitions Column (20t)

By January 1944 the Wehrmacht Flak forces had largely abandoned the use of battalions and had moved towards independent platoons. Those battalions that remained were "garrison" Flak battalions and their role was far more defensive. The deployment of Flak forces on the battlefield had changed, and a considerable number of the larger army formations had Flak platoons integral to their organization. The result was the diminishing of the number of truly independent Flak formations. In January 1944 the independent Flak forces stood as follows:

607th (mot) Flak Battalion
  3 (mot) Btrys (12 20mm AA guns and 4 LMGs)

616th Flak Battalion (forming)
  675th, 676th, 677th, 678th, 679th, and 680th Self-Propelled Flak Platoons (12 Self-Propelled 20mm AA guns ea)

619th Flak Battalion (forming)
  689th, 690th, 691st, 692nd, 693rd, and 694th Self-Propelled Flak Battalions (12 Self-Propelled 20mm AA guns ea)

436th (mot) Flak Platoons (4 light 20mm AA guns and 1 LMG)

506th, 516th, and 526th (mot) Flak Platoons (2 quad 20mm AA guns and 1 LMG ea)

6 Special Self-Propelled Flak Platoons (6 20mm Self-Propelled AA guns and 2 LMGs ea)

3 Special (mot) Flak Platoons (9 20mm (mot) AA guns and 4 LMGs ea)

6 Special Mountain (mot) Flak Platoons (9 20mm (mot) AA guns and 2 LMGs ea)

501st Flak Battalion
  3 Btrys (6 LMGs, 3 37mm AA guns and 8 quad 20mm Flak guns)

958th and 959th Flak Battalion
  3 Btrys (4 LMGs and 12 20mm Flak Guns ea)

519th Garrison Platoon (4 LMGs and 8 quad 20mm AA guns)

1/612nd Flak Battalion (unknown number of 37mm AA guns)

503rd, 513th, 523rd, 533rd, 543rd, 553rd, 563rd, and 573rd Light Flak Platoons (1 LMG and 2 20mm AA guns each)

Army Flak Battalions
275th and 279th Flak Battalions, each with
  1 (mot) Staff Battery (1 LMG)
  3 (mot) Flak Batteries (4 88mm, 3 20mm AA guns and 2 LMGs ea)
307th (mot) Flak Battalion
  1 (mot) Staff Battery
  4 (mot) Flak Batteries (4 88mm, 3 20mm AA guns and 2 LMGs ea)
289th, 292nd, 295th, and 301st Garrison Flak Battalion, each with
  1 Staff Battery (2 LMGs)
  3 Flak Batteries (4 88mm, 3 20mm AA guns and 2 LMGs ea)
300th Garrison Flak Battalion
  1 Staff Battery (2 LMGs ea)
  2 Flak Batteries (4 88mm, 3 20mm AA guns and 2 LMGs ea)
  1 Flak Battery (4 88mm, 2 quad 20mm, 9 20mm AA guns and 2 LMGs)
302nd Garrison Flak Battalion
  1 Staff Battery (2 LMGs)
  3 Flak Batteries (12 88mm and 2 LMGs ea)
306th Garrison Flak Battalion
  1 Signals Detachment
  3 Flak Batteries (4 88mm, 3 37mm AA guns and 2 LMGs ea)
  2 Flak Batteries (12 37mm AA guns and 2 LMGs ea)
308th Garrison Flak Battalion
  1 Staff Battery (2 LMGs)
  2 Flak Batteries (4 88mm, 3 20mm AA guns and 2 LMGs ea)
  1 Flak Battery (6 37mm AA guns and 2 LMGs ea)
  2 Flak Batteries (12 20mm AA guns and 2 LMGs ea)
309th Garrison Flak Battalion
  1 Staff Battery (2 LMGs)
  3 Flak Batteries (4 88mm, 3 20mm AA guns and 2 LMGs ea)
  1 Flak Battery (6 37mm AA guns and 2 LMGs ea)
  2 Flak Batteries (12 20mm AA guns and 2 LMGs ea)
310th Garrison Flak Battalion
  1 Staff Battery (2 LMGs)
  2 Flak Batteries (4 88mm, 3 20mm AA guns and 2 LMGs ea)
  1 Flak Battery (6 37mm AA guns and 2 LMGs ea)
  2 Flak Batteries (12 20mm AA guns and 2 LMGs ea)
316th Garrison Flak Battalion
  1 Staff Battery (2 LMGs)

2 Flak Batteries (4 heavy French AA guns, 3 20mm AA guns and 2 LMGs ea)

1 Flak Battery (2 quad 20mm and 9 20mm AA guns, and 3 LMGs)

On 24 December 1944 Hitler ordered the formation of ten (tmot) light army Flak Artillery Brigades, and directed the formation of the first three on 10 January 1945, three more on 25 January 1945, and four on 15 February 1945. They were to be organized as follows:

Staff

Staff

1 (mot) Staff Battery

1 Munitions Platoon

1 Vehicle Maintenance Platoon

1 Signals Platoon

2 Battalions, each with:

1 (mot) Staff

1 (mot) Staff Company

1 (mot) Supply Platoon

1 (mot) Signals Platoon

4 Batteries (8 20mm triple Flak guns)

1 Battery (6 twin 37mm guns and 12 20mm quad guns)

It is not known how many, if any, of these brigades were organized.

15

German Army Coast and Fortress Artillery

The coastal artillery was generally under the command of the Navy and operated vis-à-vis the Wehrmacht much as the flak artillery operated. In contrast, the fortress artillery was totally under the Wehrmacht. After the signing of the Treaty of Versailles the only fortress artillery was in Königsberg and consisted of about 25 170mm and smaller guns. In 1939 there were a few guns in the Siegfried Line, and as the war progressed large numbers of captured weapons were pressed into service as coastal artillery. The use of captured weapons in coastal fortifications was principally the result of limited supplies of captured ammunition and the ability and willingness of the Germans to invest the industrial capacity in the production of more ammunition.

On 17 March 1941, as the realization dawned that there was a very real threat of an British landing on the Continent, the German high command ordered a strengthening of its coastal artillery. In Norway the number of batteries rose from 13 to 16. On 19 January 1943 Denmark became the recipient of many coastal batteries as the 180th Army Coastal Artillery Regiment was organized. On 10 January 1943 the 971st through 980th Army Coastal Artillery Regiments were organized in Norway. It was in December 1943 that the 1240th, 1245th, 1252nd, 1261st, 1262nd, 1265th, 1287th, 1290th, and 1291st Coastal Artillery Regiments were organized in France.

10 FEBRUARY 1941

Coastal Defense Artillery
523rd, 528th, 529th, 531st and 533rd Coastal Defense Battalions
3 Batteries (6 150mm French guns ea)

3/367th Coastal Defense Artillery Regiment (8 75mm guns)

1/, 2/477th Coastal Defense Artillery Regiment (2 120mm Italian guns and 1 light munitions supply column ea)

1/, 2/510th Coastal Defense Artillery Regiment (4 leFH 16 howitzers ea)

1/, 2/, 3/730th Artillery Regiment (4 105mm Czech guns ea)

907th Coastal Defense Battery (3 170mm guns and 2 LMGs)

903rd, 931st, 932nd and 933rd Coastal Defense Batteries (4 75mm Dutch guns ea)

510th Coastal Defense Battalion
242nd, 252nd, and 262nd Batteries (4 100mm guns ea)

272nd and 282nd Coastal Defense Batteries (4 100mm guns ea)

738th Coastal Defense Battalion
Signals Platoon
3 Batteries (6 150mm French guns ea)

769th Coastal Defense Battalion
Signals Platoon
3 Batteries (4 150mm Czech guns ea)

770th Coastal Defense Battalion
Signals Platoon
3 Batteries (4 150mm Czech guns ea)

778th Coastal Defense Battalion
Signals Platoon
3 Batteries (4 150mm Czech guns ea)

789th Coastal Defense Battalion
Signals Platoon
3 Batteries (4 150mm Czech guns ea)

799th Coastal Defense Battalion
Signals Platoon
212th, 222nd, 232nd Batteries (4 100mm guns ea)

823rd, 826th, 827th, 828th, 829th, 831st, 832nd, 834th and 835th Coastal Defense Battalions
3 Batteries (6 150mm French guns ea)

813th Coastal Defense Battery (6 150mm guns)

928th and 829th Coastal Defense Battalions, each with 3 Batteries (4 150mm Czech guns ea)

541st, 542nd, 543rd and 544th Coastal Defense Batteries (3 210mm Mrs. 18 howitzers ea)

545th, 546th, 547th, 548th, 549th, 550th and 551st Coastal Defense Batteries (4 105mm K13 French guns ea)

552nd, 558th, 559th, 560th, 561st, 562nd, 563rd, 564th, 565th, 567th, 568th, 569th and 570th Coastal Defense Batteries (4 105mm K331 French guns ea)

571st, 572nd, 573rd, 574th, 575th, 576th, 577th, 578th, 579th and 580th Coastal Defense Batteries (4 105mm K331 French guns ea)

581st, 582nd, 583rd and 584th Coastal Defense Batteries (3 210mm Mrs. 18 howitzers ea)

585th, 586th, 587th and 588th Coastal Defense Batteries (3 220mm Mrs. Polish howitzers ea)

589th, 590th, 591st, 592nd and 593rd Coastal Defense Batteries (4 100mm 17/04 guns ea)

594th, 595th, 596th, 597th, 598th, 868th, 869th, 870th, 871st, 872nd, 873rd, 874th, 875th, 876th, 877th and 878th Coastal Defense Batteries (4 155mm sFH 17 Polish howitzers ea)

879th, 880th, 881st, 882nd, 883rd, 884th, 885th and 886th Coastal Defense Batteries (4 155mm K418 Czech guns ea)

887th, 888th and 889th Coastal Defense Batteries (4 120mm K370 guns ea)

890th, 891st, 892nd, 893rd, 894th and 895th Coastal Defense Batteries (4 75mm FK 234 ea)

896th, 897th, 898th, 899th, 927th, 941st, 942nd, 943rd, 944th, 945th, 946th, 947th, 948th, 949th and 950th Coastal Defense Batteries (4 105mm K331 French L13 guns ea)

951st, 952nd, 953rd, 954th Coastal Defense Batteries (3 210mm Mrs. 18 howitzers ea)

955th, 956th, 957th, 958th and 959th Coastal Defense Batteries (3 210mm Czech mortars ea)

960th, 961st, 962nd, 963rd and 964th Coastal Defense Batteries (4 100mm K17/04 guns ea)

965th, 966th, 967th, 968th Coastal Defense Batteries (4 155mm sFH 17 Polish guns ea)

969th, 970th, 971st, 972nd Coastal Defense Batteries (4 105mm K332 French guns ea)

973rd, 974th, 975th, 976th, 977th, , 978th, 979th, 980th, 981st, 982nd, 983rd, 984th, 985th, 986th, 987th, 988th, 989th and 990th Coastal Defense Batteries (4 105mm K332 French L36 guns ea)

991st, 992nd, 993rd, 994th, 995th, 996th, 997th, 998th, and 999th Coastal Defense Batteries (4 155mm K420 French L 16 St Chamant guns ea)

16 MAY 1941–15 OCTOBER 1942

Coast Artillery Staffs
207th, 527th, 643rd, 644th, 645th, 647th, 752nd, 938th, and 940th Coast Artillery Regimental Staffs

404th, 754th, 755th, 756th, 758th, and 759th Coast Artillery Battalion Staffs

Staffs on the English Channel
440th Coast Artillery Battalion Staff
  Signals Section
  Calibration Section
452nd Coast Artillery Battalion Staff
  Signals Section
727th Coast Artillery Battalion Staff (Guernsey)
728th Coast Artillery Battalion Staff (Jersey)

Coast Artillery Batteries
Greece
828th Coast Artillery Battalion
  3 Batteries (6 150mm guns and 2 LMGs ea)
  2 Batteries (4 100mm guns and 2 LMGs ea)
831st Coast Artillery Battalion
  3 Batteries (6 150mm guns and 2 LMGs ea)
835th Coast Artillery Battalion
  3 Batteries (6 150mm guns and 2 LMGs ea)
  1 Battery (4 100mm guns and 2 LMGs)

Other
697th Coast Artillery Regiment
  283rd and 475th Coast Artillery Battalions
    3 Batteries (6 150mm guns and 2 LMGs ea)
    1 Battery (4 100mm K.18 guns and 2 LMGs)
  829th Coast Artillery Battalion
    3 Batteries (6 150mm guns and 2 LMGs ea)
  834th Coast Artillery Battalion
    3 Batteries (6 150mm guns and 2 LMGs ea)
    1 Battery (4 100mm K.18 guns and 2 LMGs)
    1 Battery (4 100mm guns and 2 LMGs)
146th Coast Artillery Battalion
  3 Batteries (4 105mm K33 L113 guns and 2 LMGs ea)
147th, 148th, 149th, 903rd, 914th, 928th and 929th Coast Artillery Battalions
  3 Batteries (4 100 guns and 2 LMGs ea)

338th Coast Artillery Battalion
  4 Batteries (4 107 guns and 2 LMGs ea)
789th Coast Artillery Battalion
  1 Signals Platoon
  3 Batteries (4 100 guns and 2 LMGs ea)
143rd Coast Artillery Battalion
  4 Batteries (6 150mm guns and 2 LMGs ea)

144th, 284th, 287th, 289th, 474th, 531st, 707th, 708th, 772nd, 774th, 901st , 906th and 910th Coast Artillery Battalions, each with
  3 Batteries (6 150mm guns and 2 LMGs ea)

510th, 738th, 769th and 799th Coast Artillery Battalions
  1 Signals Platoon
  1 Battery (4 20mm guns)
  4 Batteries (6 150mm guns and 2 LMGs ea)

823rd, 827th and 832nd Coast Artillery Battalions
  1 Battery (4 20mm guns)
  3 Batteries (6 150mm guns and 2 LMGs ea)

769th and 770th Coast Artillery Battalion
  1 Signals Platoon
  1 Battery (4 20mm guns)
  3 Batteries (6 170mm guns and 2 LMGs ea)

1–9/401st Coast Artillery Battery
  9 Companies (4 75mm guns and 2 LMGs ea)

353rd, 355th, 414th and 415th Coast Artillery Batteries, each with
  1 Battery (4 100mm guns and 2 LMGs)

1–9/745th Coastal Artillery Battalion
  9 Batteries (4 100mm guns and 2 LMGs ea)

3/, 5/, 6/, 8/, 9/, 10/746th Coastal Artillery Battalion
  6 Batteries (4 100mm guns and 2 LMGs ea)

1/, 7/, 747th Coastal Artillery Battalion
  2 Batteries (4 100mm guns and 2 LMGs ea)

2/747th Coastal Artillery Battalion
  1 battery with (6 114mm K365e guns and 2 LMGs)

403rd Coastal Artillery Battery
  1 Battery with 6 122mm K390/2 guns and 2 LMGs

639th Coast Artillery Battery
  1 Battery with 4 107mm K352 guns and 2 LMGs

272nd, 275th, and 282nd Coast Artillery Batteries (6 150mm guns and 2 LMGs ea)

354th, 356th, 461st, 462nd and 463rd Coast Artillery Batteries (4 150mm guns and 2 LMGs ea)

509th and 513th Coast Artillery Batteries (3 150mm guns and 2 LMGs ea)

626th and 629th Coast Artillery Batteries (4 150mm guns and 2 LMGs ea)

3/, 4, 745th and 3/, 4/, 5/, /8/, 9/747th Artillery Battalion (6 150mm guns and 2 LMGs ea)

10/747th Coast Artillery Battalion (4 100mm K35 guns and 2 LMGs)

813th Coast Artillery Battery (6 210mm guns and 2 LMGs)

502nd Coast Artillery Battery (3 170mm guns on mörser carriages, 4 20mm AA guns and 2 LMGs)
503rd Coast Artillery Battery (3 170mm guns on mörser carriages and 2 LMGs)
507th Coast Artillery Battery (2 170mm guns on mörser carriages and 2 LMGs)

464th, 465th, 466th, 467th, 468th, 469th and 514th Coast Artillery Batteries (3 210mm howitzers and 2 LMGs ea)

470th, 471st, 472nd Coast Artillery Batteries (4 210mm 532K guns and 2 LMGs ea)

508th and 515th Coast Artillery Batteries (3 210mm 39 guns and 2 LMGs ea)
2/746th Coast Artillery Battalion (4 220mm K532 guns and 2 LMGs)

Fixed Batteries
141st, 142nd, 159th, 165th, 324th, 343rd, 344th and 345th Coast Artillery Batteries (4 75mm guns and 2 LMGs ea)
347th, 351nd Coast Artillery Batteries (6 75mm guns and 2 LMGs ea)
346th Coast Artillery Battery (3 75mm guns and 2 LMGs)
166th Coast Artillery Battery (2 75mm guns and 2 LMGs)
349th Coast Artillery Battery (4 75mm mountain guns and 2 LMGs)
350th Coast Artillery Battery (2 75mm mountain guns and 2 LMGs)
308th, 309th, 310th, 312th, 313th, 314th, 315th, 316th 317th, 318th and 351st Coast Artillery Batteries (4 100mm guns and 2 LMGs ea)

264th Coast Artillery Battery (4 155mm sFH 414 C17S guns and 2 LMGs)

265th, 266th and 274th Coast Artillery Batteries (4 150mm sFH 25(t) howitzers and 2 LMGs)

1/, 2/, 3/402nd Coast Artillery Battalion (4 150mm sFH howitzers and 2 LMGs)

409th, 410th, 411th, 412th, 413th, 414th, 415th, 416th, 417th, 419th, 420th and 421st Coast Artillery Batteries (4 150mm sFH 155mm 414 howitzers and 2 LMGs)

Denmark

Denmark Coast Artillery Regimental HQ
699th Coast Artillery Battalion HQ
700th Coast Artillery Battalion HQ

521st, 522nd, 524th, 525th, 534th, 535th, 539th and 540th Coast Artillery Batteries (4 100mm 331 guns, 3 20mm AA guns and 3 LMGs ea)

537th and 538th Coast Artillery Batteries (4 100mm 331 guns and 3 LMGs ea)

Norway
Artillery Commands

High Coast Artillery Command Norway (Division)
437th, 438th, 439th, 449th, 824th, 825th, 836th, 839th, 840th and 853rd Regimental HQ

479th, 481st, 482nd, 483rd, 484th, 485th, 487th, 488th, 489th, 490th, 491st, 492nd, 493rd, 494th, 495th, 498th, 499th, 500th, 504th and 505th Coast Artillery Battalion HQ (2 20mm AA guns ea)

486th Coast Artillery Battalion HQ (2 HMGs)

497th Motorized Coast Artillery Battalion HQ (2 20mm AA guns)

7/, 8/, 9/750th Coast Artillery Regiment (4 75mm field guns and 2 LMGs)

890th Coast Artillery Battery
2 Batteries (2 75mm field guns and 2 LMGs ea)

891st, 892nd, 893rd, 895th, and 999th Coast Artillery
Batteries (4 75mm FK 234 (b) field guns and 2 LMGs ea)

930 and 933rd Coast Artillery Batteries (4 75mm field guns and 2 LMGs ea)

444th Coast Artillery Battalion
HQ section
3 Batteries (4 105mm 332 guns and 2 LMGs ea)

1 Battery (4 105mm 331 guns and 2 LMGs)

447th Coast Artillery Battalion
HQ section
4 Batteries (4 105mm 332 guns and 2 LMGs ea)

496th Coast Artillery
Motorized HQ Company (2 20mm AA guns)
985th Coast Artillery Battery (4 105mm guns and 2 LMGs)
986th Coast Artillery Battery (4 105mm guns and 2 LMGs)

3/367th, 1/, 2/.3/, 4/, 5/, 6/750th, 1/, 2/, 3/, 4/, 5/, 6/, 7/ and 8/751st Artillery Regiment; 546th, 549th, 550th, 551st, 552nd, 559th, 560th, 561st, 562nd, 565th, 643rd, 644th, 875th, 878th, 894th, 896th, 897th, 898th, 899th, 927th, 932nd, 941st, 942nd, 943rd, 944th, 945th, 946th, 947th, 948th, 949th, 950th and 950th Coast Artillery Batteries (4 105mm K331/L135 guns and 2 LMGs ea)

960th, 961st, 962nd, 963rd and 964th Coast Artillery Batteries (4 105mm 17/04 n/A guns and 2 LMGs ea)

967th and 968th Coast Artillery Batteries (4 105mm K331/L13S guns and 2 LMGs ea)

969th, 970th, 971st, 972nd, 973rd, 974th, 975th, 976th, 977th, 978th, 979th, 980th, 981st, 982nd, 983rd, 984th, 987th, 988th, 989th and 990th Coast Artillery Batteries (4 105mm 332/L365 guns and 2 LMGs ea)

9/751st Coast Artillery Regiment (4 120mm K370 guns and 2 LMGs)

10/751st Coast Artillery Regiment (4 120mm K390/ 2 guns and 2 LMGs)

887th, 888th and 889th Coast Artillery Batteries (4 120mm K370/31 guns and 2 LMGs ea)

286th Coast Artillery Battalion
2 Batteries (6 155mm K416 guns and 2 LMGs ea)
1 Battery (6 150mm K403 guns and 2 LMGs)

288th Coast Artillery Battalion
3 Batteries (6 150mm guns and 2 LMGs ea)

441st Coast Artillery Battalion
3 Batteries (6 155mm K416 guns and 2 LMGs ea)
1 Battery (6 155mm K425 guns and 2 LMGs)

442nd Coast Artillery Battalion
3 Batteries (6 145mm K405 guns and 2 LMGs ea)

598th, 675th Coast Artillery Batteries (6 145mm K405 guns and 2 LMGs ea)

11/, 12/, 13/751st Coast Artillery Regiment (formed 1 Jan. 1943; 6 145mm K405 guns and 2 LMGs ea)

512th Coast Artillery Battery (6 155mm guns and 2 LMGs)

516th, 519th and 553rd Coast Artillery Batteries (4 155mm K416/L17S guns and 2 LMGs ea)

588th Coast Artillery Battery (3 155mm K425 guns and 2 LMGs)

594th Coast Artillery Battery (4 155mm K425 guns and 2 LMGs)

3/706th Coast Artillery Regiment (6 155mm K425 guns and 2 LMGs)

10/, 11/, 12/750th Coast Artillery Regiment (4 155mm K425 guns and 2 LMGs ea)

14/, 15/751st Coast Artillery Regiment (formed 1 Jan. 1943; 4 155mm K432 guns and 2 LMGs ea)

870th, 872nd, 876th and 877th Coast Artillery Batteries (4 155mm K425 guns and 2 LMGs ea)

879th, 880th, 881st, 882nd, 883rd, 884th and 886th Coast Artillery Batteries (4 155mm K418 guns and 2 LMGs ea)

907th Coast Artillery Battery (3 155mm guns and 2 LMGs)

965th Coast Artillery Battery (4 155mm K425 guns and 2 LMGs)

966th Coast Artillery Battery (4 155mm K403 guns and 2 LMGs)

991st, 992nd, 993rd, 994th, 995th, 996th, 997th and 998th Coast Artillery Batteries (4 155mm K416 guns and 2 LMGs ea)

520th Coast Artillery Battalion
Motorized HQ Company
2 (motZ) Batteries (4 105mm leFH and 2 LMGs ea)
1 (motZ) Battery (3 155mm K416 guns and 2 LMGs)

595th, 596th, 597th and 599th Coast Artillery Batteries (4 155mm sFH 17 and 2 LMGs ea)

13/750th Coast Artillery Regiment (4 155mm sFH 414 and 2 LMGs)

868th, 869th, 871st, 873rd and 874th Coast Artillery Batteries (4 155mm sFH 17 and 2 LMGs ea)

543rd, 544th, 581st, 582nd, 583rd, 584th, 585th, 586th, 587th 951st, 952nd, 953rd and 954th Coast Artillery Batteries; 14/750th Coast Artillery Regiment (3 210mm mörser 18 and 2 LMGs ea)

955th, 956th, 957th, 958th and 959th Coast Artillery Batteries (3 short 210mm mörser and 2 LMGs ea)

OCTOBER 1942–SUMMER 1943

Coastal Artillery
697th Coastal Defense Regiment
283rd and 475th Coastal Defense Battalions
3 Batteries (6 155mm French guns and 2 LMGs ea)

1 Battery (4 105mm Polish guns and 2 LMGs)
829th Coastal Defense Battalion
3 Batteries (6 155mm French guns and 2 LMGs ea)
834th Coastal Defense Battalion
3 Batteries (6 155mm French guns and 2 LMGs ea)
1 Battery (4 105mm Polish guns and 2 LMGs)
1 Battery (4 105mm French guns and 2 LMGs)
1 Battery (4 105mm guns and 2 LMGs)
903rd Coastal Defense Battalion
3 Batteries (6 100mm French guns and 2 LMGs ea)

752nd Coastal Defense Regiment
901st Coastal Defense Battalion
3 Batteries (6 155mm French guns and 2 LMGs ea)

Independent Battalions
101st (Lehr) Coastal Defense Battalion
4 Batteries (4 105mm French guns and 2 LMGs ea)
1 Battery (6 75mm Belgian guns, 4 83.8mm British guns and 2 LMGs)
145th Coastal Defense Battalion
3 Batteries (4 105mm French guns and 2 LMGs ea)
148th and 149th Coastal Defense Battalions
3 Batteries (4 100mm guns and 2 LMGs ea)
338th Coastal Defense Battalion
4 Batteries (4 107mm guns and 2 LMGs ea)
778th Coastal Defense Battalion
1 HQ Battery (20mm guns)
2 Batteries (4 100mm guns and 2 LMGs ea)
1 Battery (4 150mm guns and 2 LMGs)
789th Coastal Defense Battalion
1 HQ Signals Section
3 Batteries (4 100mm guns and 2 LMGs ea)
914th, 928th, and 929th Coastal Defense Battalions
3 Batteries (4 100mm guns and 2 LMGs ea)

Greek Coastal Defense Division
828th Coastal Defense Battalion
3 Batteries (6 155mm French guns and 2 LMGs ea)
2 Batteries (4 105mm French guns and 2 LMGs ea)
831st Coastal Defense Battalion
3 Batteries (6 155mm French guns and 2 LMGs ea)
835th Coastal Defense Battalion
3 Batteries (6 155mm French guns and 2 LMGs ea)
1 Battery (4 105mm French guns and 2 LMGs)

697th Coastal Defense Brigade
Signals Section
283rd Coastal Defense Battalion
3 Batteries (6 155mm French guns and 2 LMGs ea)
1 Battery (4 105mm French guns and 2 LMGs)
829th Coastal Defense Battalion
3 Batteries (6 155mm French guns and 2 LMGs ea)

834th Coastal Defense Battalion
  3 Batteries (6 155mm French guns and 2 LMGs ea; one battery was reduced to 2 155mm guns on 6 Feb. 1943)
  3 Batteries (4 105mm French guns and 2 LMGs ea; one battery was reduced to 3 105mm guns on 6 Feb. 1943)
903rd Coastal Defense Battalion
  3 Batteries (4 105mm French guns and 2 LMGs)

Other Coast Artillery:
145th Coastal Defense Battalion
  3 Batteries (4 105mm K331 (f) L113 guns and 2 LMGs ea)
148th Coastal Defense Battalion
  3 Batteries (4 100mm and 2 LMGs ea)
149th Coastal Defense Battalion
  3 Batteries (4 100mm and 2 LMGs ea; each battery was re-equipped with 3 170mm guns on 14 Apr. 1943)
338th Coastal Defense Battalion
  4 Batteries (4 107mm and 2 LMGs ea)
778th Coastal Defense Battalion
  20mm Flak Battery with HQ
  3 Batteries (4 100mm and 2 LMGs ea)
789th Coastal Defense Battalion
  3 Batteries (4 100mm and 2 LMGs ea)
903rd Coastal Defense Battalion
  3 Batteries (4 100mm and 2 LMGs ea)
914th Coastal Defense Battalion
  3 Batteries (4 100mm and 2 LMGs ea)
928th Coastal Defense Battalion
  3 Batteries (4 100mm and 2 LMGs ea)
939th Coastal Defense Battalion
  3 Batteries (4 100mm and 2 LMGs ea)
101st Coastal Defense Battalion
  4 Batteries (4 105mm and 2 LMGs ea)
  1 Battery (6 75mm and 2 LMGs)
  1 Battery (4 20mm)
143rd Coastal Defense Battalion
  4 Batteries (6 150mm French guns and 2 LMGs ea)
144th Coastal Defense Battalion
  3 Batteries (6 150mm French guns and 2 LMGs ea)
147th Coastal Defense Battalion
  4 Batteries (6 152mm Russian guns and 2 LMGs ea)
284th Coastal Defense Battalion
  3 Batteries (6 150mm French guns and 2 LMGs ea)
287th Coastal Defense Battalion
  3 Batteries (6 150mm French guns and 2 LMGs ea)
289th Coastal Defense Battalion
  3 Batteries (6 150mm French guns and 2 LMGs ea)
474th Coastal Defense Battalion
  3 Batteries (6 150mm French guns and 2 LMGs ea)
510th and 799th Coastal Defense Battalions
  HQ Signals Section
  HQ 20mm Flak Section
  3 Batteries (6 150mm French guns and 2 LMGs ea)
823rd, 826th, 827th and 832nd Coastal Defense Battalions
  HQ 20mm Flak Section
  3 Batteries (6 150mm French guns and 2 LMGs ea)
531st, 707th, 708th 772nd, 774th 906th and 910th Coastal Defense Battalions
  3 Batteries (6 150mm French guns and 2 LMGs ea)
738th Coastal Defense Battalion
  HQ Signals Section
  HQ 20mm Flak Section
  3 Batteries (6 150mm French guns and 2 LMGs ea)
769th and 770th Coastal Defense Battalions
  HQ Signals Section
  HQ 20mm Flak Section
  3 Batteries (3 170mm guns and 2 LMGs ea)
828th Coastal Defense Battalion
  3 Batteries (6 155mm guns and 2 LMGs ea)
  2 Batteries (4 105mm guns and 2 LMGs ea)
831st Coastal Defense Battalion
  3 Batteries (6 155mm guns and 2 LMGs ea)
835th Coastal Defense Battalion
  3 Batteries (6 155mm guns and 2 LMGs ea)
  1 Battery (4 105mm guns and 2 LMGs ea)
2/401st Coastal Defense Field Battery (4 75mm and 2 LMGs)
353rd, 355th, 414th and 415th Coastal Defense Batteries (4 105mm French guns and 2 LMGs)
639th Coastal Defense Battery (4 105mm Russian guns and 2 LMGs)
1/, 2/, 5/, 6/, 7, 8/9/, 10/745th Coastal Defense Battalion (4 105mm French guns and 2 LMGs ea)
1/, 3/, 4/, 5/, 6/, 7/, 8/, 9/, 10/746th Coastal Defense Battalion (4 105mm French guns and 2 LMGs ea)
1/, 6/, 7/747th Coastal Defense Battalion (4 105mm Polish guns and 2 LMGs)
2/747th Coastal Defense Battalion (6 114mm guns and 2 LMGs)
10/747th Coastal Defense Battalion (4 100mm Czech guns and 2 LMGs)
1/748th Coastal Defense Battalion (4 105mm French guns and 2 LMGs ea)
1/, 2/, 18/, 19/920th Coastal Defense Battalion (manned by Italians; 4 105mm French guns and 2 LMGs ea)
3/, 4/, 5/, 6/, 7/920th Coastal Defense Battalion (4 105mm French guns and 2 LMGs ea)
403rd Coastal Defense Battery (4 122mm Russian guns and 2 LMGs ea)
8/, 9/, 10/, 14/, 15/, 16/920th Coastal Defense Battalion (4 122mm Russian guns and 2 LMGs ea; re-equipped from 155mm to 122mm on 28 Feb. 1943)
272nd, 275th and 282nd Coastal Defense Batteries (6 150mm French guns and 2 LMGs ea)
354th, 356th, 461st, 462nd and 463rd Coastal Defense Batteries (4 150mm French guns and 2 LMGs ea)

509th and 513th Coastal Defense Batteries (3 150mm French guns and 2 LMGs ea)

4/706th Coastal Defense Battalion (4 150mm French guns and 2 LMGs)

626th and 629th Coastal Defense Batteries (4 152mm Russian guns and 2 LMGs ea)

4/706th Coastal Defense Battalion (4 150mm French guns and 2 LMGs)

3/, 4/, 745th and 3/, 4/, 5/747th Coastal Defense Battalions (4 152mm Russian guns and 2 LMGs)

502nd Coastal Defense Battery (3 170mm guns, 4 20mm AA and 2 LMGs)

503rd and 10/777th Coastal Defense Batteries (3 170mm guns and 2 LMGs)

507th Coastal Defense Battery (2 170mm guns and 2 LMGs)

470th, 471st, 472nd, 2/746th and 813th Coastal Defense Batteries (4 210mm guns and 2 LMGs ea)

508th Coastal Defense Battery (3 210mm guns and 2 LMGs)

515th Coastal Defense Battery (2 210mm guns and 2 LMGs)

11/, 12/, 13/, 17/920th Coastal Defense Battery (manned by Italians; 2 210mm guns and 2 LMGs ea; upgraded from French 155mm guns to 210mm guns on 5 Feb. 1943)

464th, 465th, 466th, 467th, 468th, 469th and 514th Coastal Defense Batteries (3 210mm howitzers and 2 LMGs ea)

127th, 130th, 135th, 136th, 141st, 142nd, 159th, 163rd, 164th, 165th, 324th, 343rd, 344th and 345th Coastal Defense Batteries (4 75mm guns and 2 LMGs ea)

133rd, 170th, 174th and 347th Coastal Defense Batteries (6 75mm guns and 2 LMGs ea)

346th Coastal Defense Battery (3 75mm guns and 2 LMGs)

166th, 348th and 350th Coastal Defense Batteries (2 75mm guns and 2 LMGs ea)

349th Coastal Defense Battery (4 75mm mountain guns and 2 LMGs)

349th Coastal Defense Battery (2 75mm mountain guns and 2 LMGs)

167th, 308th, 309th, 310th, 312th, 313th, 315th, 316th, 317th, 318th, 351st, 1/401st and 1/402nd Coastal Defense Batteries (4 100mm French guns and 2 LMGs ea)

264th, 265th, 266th, 274th, 314th, 2/402nd, 3/402nd, 405th, 406th, 407th, 409th, 410th, 411th, 412th, 413th, 417th, 418th, 419th, 420th, and 421st Coastal Defense Batteries (4 155mm guns and 2 LMGs ea)

Danish Coast Artillery
180th Coastal Defense Regiment
1/180th Coastal Defense Regiment

4 Batteries (4 100mm guns, 3 20mm AA and 2 LMGs ea)

2/180th Coastal Defense Regiment
4 Batteries (4 100mm guns, 3 20mm AA and 2 LMGs ea)

3/180th Coastal Defense Regiment
2 Batteries (4 100mm guns, 3 20mm AA and 2 LMGs ea)

Norwegian Coast Artillery
971st Coastal Defense Artillery Regiment
1/971st Coastal Defense Artillery Regiment
HQ Company (2 20mm AA)
1st (675)[1] Battery (6 45mm French guns and 2 LMGs)
2nd (897) Battery (4 105mm French guns and 2 LMGs)
3rd (560) Battery (4 105mm Polish guns and 2 LMGs)
4th (868) Battery (4 155mm Polish guns and 2 LMGs)
5th (873) Battery (4 155mm Polish guns and 2 LMGs)
6th (930) Battery (4 75mm Norwegian guns and 2 LMGs)
7th (8/751) Battery (4 105mm French guns and 2 LMGs)
2/971st Coastal Defense Artillery Regiment
16th (933) Battery (4 75mm Norwegian guns and 2 LMGs)
17th (594) Battery (4 105mm French guns and 2 LMGs)
18th (550) Battery (4 155mm Polish guns and 2 LMGs)
19th (549) Battery (4 155mm Polish guns and 2 LMGs)
3/971st Coastal Defense Artillery Regiment
31st (879) Battery (4 155mm French guns and 2 LMGs)
32nd (880) Battery (4 155mm French guns and 2 LMGs)
33rd (2/442) Battery (4 145mm French guns and 2 LMGs)
34th (4/441) Battery (4 155mm French guns and 2 LMGs)
35th (553) Battery (4 155mm French guns and 2 LMGs)
36th (872) Battery (4 155mm French guns and 2 LMGs)
37th (871) Battery (4 155mm Polish guns and 2 LMGs)
38th (870) Battery (4 155mm French guns and 2 LMGs)
972nd Coastal Defense Artillery Regiment
1/972nd Coastal Defense Artillery Regiment
HQ Company (2 20mm AA)
1st (4/442) Battery (6 145mm French guns and 2 LMGs)

[1] The second number is the actual battery, battalion or regiment number of the battery assigned to this unit.

2nd (896) Battery (4 105mm French guns and 2 LMGs)

3rd (886) Battery (4 155mm French guns and 2 LMGs)

4th (874) Battery (4 155mm Polish guns and 2 LMGs)

5th (4/444) Battery (4 105mm French guns and 2 LMGs)

6th (3/442) Battery (6 145mm French guns and 2 LMGs)

7th (559) Battery (4 105mm Polish guns and 2 LMGs)

8th (595) Battery (4 155mm Polish guns and 2 LMGs)

2/972nd Coastal Defense Artillery Regiment

HQ Company (2 20mm AA)

16th (2/444) Battery (4 105mm French guns and 2 LMGs)

17th (582) Battery (3 210mm howitzers and 2 LMGs)

18th (581) Battery (3 210mm howitzers and 2 LMGs)

19th (551) Battery (4 105mm Polish guns and 2 LMGs)

20th (1/444) Battery (4 105mm French guns and 2 LMGs)

21st (552) Battery (4 105mm Polish guns and 2 LMGs)

22nd (3/444)Battery (4 105mm French guns and 2 LMGs)

23rd (876) Battery (4 155mm French guns and 2 LMGs)

973rd Coastal Defense Artillery Regiment

1/973rd Coastal Defense Artillery Regiment

HQ Company (2 20mm AA)

1st (875) Battery (4 105mm French guns and 2 LMGs)

2nd (966) Battery (6 155mm Yugoslavian guns and 2 LMGs)

3rd (965) Battery (4 155mm French guns and 2 LMGs)

4th (544) Battery (3 210mm howitzers and 2 LMGs)

5th (881) Battery (4 155mm French guns and 2 LMGs)

6th (596) Battery (4 155mm Polish guns and 2 LMGs)

7th (599) Battery (4 155mm Polish guns and 2 LMGs)

2/973rd Coastal Defense Artillery Regiment

HQ Company (2 20mm AA)

16th (969)Battery (4 105mm French guns and 2 LMGs)

17th (884) Battery (4 155mm French guns and 2 LMGs)

18th (883) Battery (4 155mm French guns and 2 LMGs)

19th (882) Battery (4 155mm French guns and 2 LMGs)

20th (598) Battery (4 145mm French guns and 2 LMGs)

21st (597) Battery (4 155mm French guns and 2 LMGs)

3/973rd Coastal Defense Artillery Regiment

HQ Company (2 20mm AA)

25th (1/806) Battery (4 155mm French guns and 2 LMGs)

31st (583) Battery (3 210mm howitzers and 2 LMGs)

32nd (584) Battery (3 210mm howitzers and 2 LMGs)

33rd (932) Battery (4 105mm Norwegian guns and 2 LMGs)

34th (870) Battery (4 105mm French guns and 2 LMGs)

35th (561) Battery (4 105mm French guns and 2 LMGs)

4/973rd Coastal Defense Artillery Regiment

HQ Company (2 20mm AA)

46th (3/706) Battery (6 155mm French guns and 2 LMGs)

47th (877) Battery (6 155mm French guns and 2 LMGs)

48th (968) Battery (4 105mm French guns and 2 LMGs)

49th (967) Battery (4 105mm French guns and 2 LMGs)

5/973rd Coastal Defense Artillery Regiment

HQ Company (2 20mm AA)

61st (944) Battery (4 105mm French guns and 2 LMGs)

62nd (898) Battery (4 105mm French guns and 2 LMGs)

63rd (899) Battery (4 105mm French guns and 2 LMGs)

64th (945) Battery (4 105mm French guns and 2 LMGs)

974th Coastal Defense Artillery Regiment

1/974th Coastal Defense Artillery Regiment

HQ Company (2 20mm AA)

1st (3/285) Battery (6 155mm French guns and 2 LMGs)

2nd (566) Battery (4 105mm French guns and 2 LMGs)

3rd (955) Battery (3 210mm howitzers and 2 LMGs)

4th (586) Battery (3 210mm howitzers and 2 LMGs)

5th (1/750) Battery (4 105mm French guns and 2 LMGs)

6th (994) Battery (6 155mm French guns and 2 LMGs)

7th (10/750) Battery (6 155mm French guns and 2 LMGs)

8th (890) Battery (4 guns, type unknown)

9th (2/285) Battery (6 155mm French guns and 2 LMGs)

10th (565) Battery (4 105mm French guns and 2 LMGs)

2/974th Coastal Defense Artillery Regiment

HQ Company (2 20mm AA)

16th (11/570) Battery (4 155mm French guns and 2 LMGs)

17th (891) Battery (4 75mm Belgian guns and 2 LMGs)

18th (927) Battery (4 105mm French guns and 2 LMGs)

19th (943) Battery (4 105mm French guns and 2 LMGs)

20th (1/751) Battery (4 105mm foreign guns and 2 LMGs)

21st (568) Battery (4 105mm French guns and 2 LMGs)

22nd (942) Battery (4 105mm French guns and 2 LMGs)

3/974th Coastal Defense Artillery Regiment

HQ Company (2 20mm AA)

31st (12/750) Battery (4 155mm French guns and 2 LMGs)

32nd (995) Battery (4 155mm French guns and 2 LMGs)

33rd (892) Battery (4 75mm Belgian guns and 2 LMGs)

975th Coastal Defense Artillery Regiment

1/975th Coastal Defense Artillery Regiment

HQ Company (2 20mm AA)

1st (893) Battery (4 75mm Belgian guns and 2 LMGs)

2nd (3/441) Battery (4 155mm French guns and 2 LMGs)

3rd (567) Battery (4 105mm French guns and 2 LMGs)

4th (941) Battery (4 105mm French guns and 2 LMGs)

5th (3/367) Battery (4 100mm Dutch guns and 2 LMGs)

6th (587) Battery (3 210mm howitzers and 2 LMGs)

16th (2/751) Battery (4 105mm Dutch guns and 2 LMGs)

17th (956) Battery (3 210mm howitzers and 2 LMGs)

18th (946) Battery (4 105mm French and 2 LMGs)

19th (1/285) Battery (6 155mm Yugoslavian and 2 LMGs)

20th (997) Battery (6 155mm French and 2 LMGs)

21st (958) Battery (3 210mm howitzers and 2 LMGs)

22nd (588) Battery (3 150mm guns and 2 LMGs)

23rd (998) Battery (4 155mm French and 2 LMGs)

24th (7/750) Battery (4 76.5mm Austrian guns and 2 LMGs)

25th (8/750) Battery (4 76.5mm Austrian guns and 2 LMGs)

26th (9/750) Battery (4 76.5mm Austrian guns and 2 LMGs)

976th Coastal Defense Artillery Regiment

1/976th Coastal Defense Artillery Regiment

HQ Company (2 HMGs)

1st (947) Battery (4 105mm French guns and 2 LMGs)

2nd (571) Battery (4 105mm French guns and 2 LMGs)

3rd (9/751) Battery (4 105mm Belgian guns and 2 LMGs)

4th (572) Battery (4 105mm French guns and 2 LMGs)

5th (573) Battery (4 105mm French guns and 2 LMGs)

6th (574) Battery (4 105mm French guns and 2 LMGs)

7th (13/570) Battery (4 155mm French guns and 2 LMGs)

2/976th Coastal Defense Artillery Regiment

16th (575) Battery (4 105mm French guns and 2 LMGs)

17th (996) Battery (4 155mm French guns and 2 LMGs)

18th (1/288) Battery (4 150mm French guns and 2 LMGs)

19th (948) Battery (4 105mm French guns and 2 LMGs)

20th (959) Battery (3 210mm howitzers and 2 LMGs)

21st (3/228) Battery (4 150mm French guns and 2 LMGs)

22nd (949) Battery (4 105mm French guns and 2 LMGs)

23rd (1/447) Battery (4 105mm French guns and 2 LMGs)

24th (957) Battery (3 210mm howitzers and 2 LMGs)

3/976th Coastal Defense Artillery Regiment

31st (2/750) Battery (4 105mm French guns and 2 LMGs)

32nd (578) Battery (4 105mm French guns and 2 LMGs)

33rd (577) Battery (4 105mm French guns and 2 LMGs)

34th (576) Battery (4 105mm French guns and 2 LMGs)

35th (3/751) Battery (4 105mm Hungarian guns and 2 LMGs)

36th (579) Battery (4 105mm French guns and 2 LMGs)

37th (569) Battery (4 105mm French guns and 2 LMGs)

38th (1/441) Battery (6 155mm French guns and 2 LMGs)

977th Coastal Defense Artillery Regiment

1/977th Coastal Defense Artillery Regiment

HQ Company (2 20mm AA)

1st (14/751) Battery (4 155mm Belgian guns and 2 LMGs)

2nd (950) Battery (4 105mm French guns and 2 LMGs)

3rd (894) Battery (4 105mm French guns and 2 LMGs)

4th (570) Battery (4 105mm French guns and 2 LMGs)

5th (895) Battery (4 75mm Belgian guns and 2 LMGs)

6th (2/228) Battery (6 150mm French guns and 2 LMGs)

7th (644) Battery (4 105mm French guns and 2 LMGs)

2/977th Coastal Defense Artillery Regiment

HQ Company (2 20mm AA)

16th (5/750) Battery (4 105mm French guns and 2 LMGs)

17th (2/447) Battery (4 105mm French guns and 2 LMGs)

18th (645) Battery (4 105mm French guns and 2 LMGs)

19th (590) Battery (4 100mm guns and 2 LMGs)

20th (961) Battery (4 100mm guns and 2 LMGs)

21st (4/750) Battery (4 105mm French guns and 2 LMGs)

3/977th Coastal Defense Artillery Regiment

31st (11/751) Battery (4 145mm French guns and 2 LMGs)

32nd (15/751) Battery (4 155mm French guns and 2 LMGs)

33rd (14/750) Battery (3 210mm howitzers and 2 LMGs)

34th (972) Battery (4 105mm French guns and 2 LMGs)

35th (4/447) Battery (4 105mm French guns and 2 LMGs)

36th (989) Battery (4 105mm French guns and 2 LMGs)

37th (7/751) Battery (4 105mm French guns and 2 LMGs)

4/977th Coastal Defense Artillery Regiment

46th (987) Battery (4 105mm French guns and 2 LMGs)

47th (585) Battery (3 210mm howitzers and 2 LMGs)

48th (960) Battery (4 100mm guns and 2 LMGs)

49th (988) Battery (4 105mm French guns and 2 LMGs)

50th (591) Battery (4 100mm guns and 2 LMGs)

51st (971) Battery (4 105mm French guns and 2 LMGs)

5/977th Coastal Defense Artillery Regiment

61st (6/750) Battery (4 105mm French guns and 2 LMGs)

62nd (970) Battery (4 105mm French guns and 2 LMGs)

63rd (992) Battery (4 155mm French guns and 2 LMGs)

64th (952) Battery (3 210mm howitzers and 2 LMGs)

65th (12/751) Battery (4 145mm French guns and 2 LMGs)

66th (991) Battery (4 155mm French guns and 2 LMGs)

67th (13/751) Battery (4 145mm French guns and 2 LMGs)

978th Coastal Defense Artillery Regiment

1/978th Coastal Defense Artillery Regiment

1st (993) Battery (4 155mm French guns and 2 LMGs)

2nd (990) Battery (4 105mm French guns and 2 LMGs)

3rd (10/751) Battery (4 122mm Russian guns and 2 LMGs)

4th (907) Battery (4 150mm guns and 2 LMGs)

5th (953) Battery (3 210mm howitzers and 2 LMGs)

6th (592) Battery (4 100mm guns and 2 LMGs)

7th (2/441) Battery (4 155mm French guns and 2 LMGs)

8th (962) Battery (4 100mm guns and 2 LMGs)

2/978th Coastal Defense Artillery Regiment

16th (963) Battery (4 100mm guns and 2 LMGs)

17th (974) Battery (4 105mm French guns and 2 LMGs)

18th (3/750) Battery (4 105mm French guns and 2 LMGs)

19th (954) Battery (3 210mm howitzers and 2 LMGs)

20th (964) Battery (4 100mm guns and 2 LMGs)

979th Coastal Defense Artillery Regiment

1/979th Coastal Defense Artillery Regiment

1st (975) Battery (4 105mm French guns and 2 LMGs)

2nd (3/447) Battery (4 105mm French guns and 2 LMGs)

3rd (512) Battery (4 150mm guns and 2 LMGs)

4th (516) Battery (4 155mm French guns and 2 LMGs)

2/979th Coastal Defense Artillery Regiment

16th (4/751) Battery (4 105mm French guns and 2 LMGs)

17th (976) Battery (4 105mm French guns and 2 LMGs)

18th (643) Battery (4 105mm French guns and 2 LMGs)

19th (519) Battery (4 155mm French guns and 2 LMGs)

20th (973) Battery (4 105mm French guns and 2 LMGs)

21st (5/751) Battery (4 105mm French guns and 2 LMGs)

3/979th Coastal Defense Artillery Regiment

31st (997) Battery (4 105mm French guns and 2 LMGs)

32nd (978) Battery (4 105mm French guns and 2 LMGs)

33rd (979) Battery (4 105mm French guns and 2 LMGs)

34th (980) Battery (4 105mm French guns and 2 LMGs)

35th (981) Battery (4 105mm French guns and 2 LMGs)

36th (982) Battery (4 105mm French guns and 2 LMGs)

37th (983) Battery (3 105mm French guns and 2 LMGs)

980th Coastal Defense Artillery Regiment

1/980th Coastal Defense Artillery Regiment

HQ Company (2 20mm AA)

1st Battery (4 105mm French guns and 2 LMGs)

2nd Battery (4 120mm Belgian guns and 2 LMGs)

3rd Battery (4 120mm Belgian guns and 2 LMGs)

4th Battery (4 105mm French guns and 2 LMGs)

5th Battery (4 120mm Belgian guns and 2 LMGs)

6th Battery (4 100mm guns and 2 LMGs)

7th Battery (4 100mm guns and 2 LMGs)

Lapland Coastal Defense Artillery

504th Coastal Defense Battalion

543rd Battery (3 210mm howitzers and 2 LMGs)

546th Battery (4 105mm Polish guns and 2 LMGs)

562nd Battery (4 105mm French guns and 2 LMGs)

580th Battery (4 105mm French guns and 2 LMGs)

869th Battery (4 155mm French guns and 2 LMGs)

999th Battery (4 175mm Belgian guns and 2 LMGs)

951st Battery (3 210mm howitzers and 2 LMGs)

496th Motorized Artillery Battalion

1 Motorized HQ Company (2 20mm AA)

985th Battery (4 100mm French guns and 2 LMGs)

986th Battery (4 100mm French guns and 2 LMGs)

3/520th Battery (4 155mm French guns and 2 LMGs)

520th Motorized Artillery Battalion

1 Motorized HQ Company (2 20mm AA)

2 (motZ) Batteries (4 75mm field guns and 2 LMGs ea)

JANUARY 1944

Coastal Artillery

283rd and 475th Coast Artillery Battalions

3 Batteries (6 155mm French guns and 2 LMGs ea)

1 Battery (4 100mm guns and 2 LMGs)

829th Coastal Artillery Battalion

3 Batteries (6 155mm French guns and 2 LMGs ea)

834th Coastal Artillery Battalion

1st and 2nd Batteries (6 155mm French guns and 2 LMGs ea)

3rd Battery (4 210mm guns and 2 LMGs)

4th Battery (3 105mm Greek guns and 2 LMGs)

5th Battery (4 100mm guns and 2 LMGs)

6th Battery (4 105mm French guns)

7th Battery (6 155mm French guns and 2 LMGs)

903rd Coastal Artillery Battalion

3 Batteries (4 100mm Czech guns and 2 LMGs ea)

752nd Coast Artillery Regiment

801st Coast Artillery Battalion

3 Batteries (6 155mm French guns and 2 LMGs ea)

101st Coast Artillery Training Battalion

1st Battery (4 105mm French guns and 2 LMGs)

2nd Battery (4 100mm Czech guns and 2 LMGs)

3rd Battery (4 105mm French guns and 2 LMGs)

4th Battery (4 170mm German guns and 2 LMGs)

5th Battery (4 83.8mm British guns, 6 75mm Belgian guns and 2 LMGs)

174th Coast Artillery Battalion

2 Batteries (4 105mm Hungarian guns and 2 LMGs ea)

1st Battery (4 122mm Russian guns and 2 LMGs)

338th Coast Artillery Battalion

4 Batteries (4 107mm Russian guns and 2 LMGs ea)

789th Coast Artillery Battalion

1 Signal Detachment

3 Batteries (4 100mm Czech guns and 2 LMGs ea)

144th Coast Artillery Regiment

3 Batteries (4 155mm French guns and 2 LMGs ea)

145th Coast Artillery Battalion

2 Batteries (4 170mm guns and 2 LMGs ea)

1 Battery (4 150mm guns and 2 LMGs)

149th Coast Artillery Battalion

3 Batteries (4 170mm guns and 2 LMGs ea)

284th, 287th, 474th, 707th, 772nd, 774th, 831st, 906th and 906th Coast Artillery Battalions

3 Batteries (6 155mm French guns and 2 LMGs ea)

677th Coast Artillery Battalion

4 Batteries (6 155mm French guns and 2 LMGs ea)

828th Coast Artillery Battalion

3 Batteries (6 155mm French guns and 2 LMGs ea)

2 Batteries (4 105mm guns and 2 LMGs)

835th Coast Artillery Battalion

3 Batteries (6 155mm French guns and 2 LMGs ea)

1 Battery (4 105mm French guns and 2 LMGs)

1st Battery, 804th Coast Artillery Battalion (4 105mm French guns and 2 LMGs)

865th Coast Artillery Battalion (4 100m guns and 2 LMGs)

866th Coast Artillery Battalion (4 100m guns and 2 LMGs)

921st Garrison Coast Artillery Battalion (4 100m Czech guns and 2 LMGs)

509th Coast Artillery Battery (3 150mm guns and 2 LMGs)

2nd and 3rd Batteries, 804th Coast Artillery Battalion (4 155mm French guns and 2 LMGs ea)

1st, 2nd and 3rd Batteries, 805th Coast Artillery Battalion (4 155mm French guns and 2 LMGs ea)

862nd, 863rd, and 864th Coast Artillery Battery (4 152mm Russian guns and 2 LMGs ea)

502nd Coast Artillery Battery (3 170mm guns, 4 20mm AA guns and 2 LMGs)

1011st, 1012nd, 1013th, 1014th, and 1015th Light Tower Howitzer Platoons (unknown number of 75mm howitzers)

1–10th Batteries, 956th Coast Artillery Battalion (4 120mm guns and 2 LMGs ea)

1–37th Batteries, 957th Coast Artillery Battalion (4 120mm guns and 2 LMGs ea)

Danish Coastal Artillery
1/180th Coast Artillery Battalion
  1st–4th Batteries (4 105mm French guns, 3 20mm AA guns and 3 LMGs ea)
2/180th Coast Artillery Battalion
  5th–8th Batteries (4 105mm French guns, 3 20mm AA guns and 3 LMGs ea)
3/180th Coast Artillery Battalion
  9th–12th Batteries (4 105mm French guns, 3 20mm AA guns and 3 LMGs ea)
180th Coast Artillery Battalion
  13th–21st Batteries (4 122mm Russian guns, 2 20mm AA guns and 3 LMGs ea)

Norwegian Coast Artillery
1/971st Coast Artillery Regiment
  Headquarters Flak Battery (2 20mm AA guns)
  1st Battery (6 145mm French guns and 2 LMGs)
  2nd Battery (4 105mm French guns and 2 LMGs)
  3rd Battery (4 105mm French guns and 2 LMGs)
  4th Battery (4 155mm Polish guns and 2 LMGs)
  5th Battery (4 155mm Polish guns and 2 LMGs)
  6th Battery (4 155mm Polish guns and 2 LMGs)
  7th Battery (4 105mm French guns and 2 LMGs)
2/971st Coast Artillery Regiment
  Headquarters Flak Battery (2 20mm AA guns)
  16th Battery (4 155mm French guns and 2 LMGs)
  17th Battery (4 155mm Polish guns and 2 LMGs)
  18th Battery (4 105mm French guns and 2 LMGs)
  195h Battery (4 105mm French guns and 2 LMGs)
3/971st Coast Artillery Regiment
  Headquarters Flak Battery (2 20mm AA guns)
  31st Battery (4 155mm French guns and 2 LMGs)
  32nd Battery (4 155mm French guns and 2 LMGs)
  33rd Battery (6 145mm French guns and 2 LMGs)
  34th Battery (6 155mm French guns and 2 LMGs)
  35th Battery (4 155mm French guns and 2 LMGs)
  36th Battery (4 155mm Polish guns and 2 LMGs)
  37th Battery (6 155mm French guns and 2 LMGs)
  38th Battery (4 105mm French guns and 2 LMGs)
1/972nd Coast Artillery Regiment
  Headquarters Flak Battery (2 20mm AA guns)
  1st Battery (6 145mm French guns and 2 LMGs)
  2nd Battery (4 105mm French guns and 2 LMGs)
  3rd Battery (4 155mm French guns and 2 LMGs)
  4th Battery (4 155mm Polish guns and 2 LMGs)
  5th Battery (4 105mm French guns and 2 LMGs)
  6th Battery (6 145mm French guns and 2 LMGs)
  7th Battery (4 105mm French guns and 2 LMGs)
  8th Battery (4 155mm Polish guns and 2 LMGs)
2/972nd Coast Artillery Regiment
  Headquarters Flak Battery (2 20mm AA guns)
  16th Battery (4 105mm French guns and 2 LMGs)
  17th and 18th Batteries (3 210mm guns and 2 LMGs)
  19th, 20th, 21st and 22nd Batteries (4 105mm French guns and 2 LMGs ea)
  23rd Battery (4 155mm French guns and 2 LMGs)
1/973rd Coast Artillery Regiment
  Headquarters Flak Battery (2 20mm AA guns)
  1st Battery (4 105mm French guns and 2 LMGs)
  2nd Battery (4 155mm French guns and 2 LMGs)
  3rd Battery (6 155mm Yugoslavian guns and 2 LMGs)
  4th Battery (3 210mm guns and 2 LMGs)
  5th Battery (4 155mm French guns and 2 LMGs)
  6th and 7th Batteries (4 155mm Polish guns and 2 LMGs ea)
2/973rd Coast Artillery Regiment
  Headquarters Flak Battery (2 20mm AA guns)
  16th Battery (4 105mm French guns and 2 LMGs)
  17th 18th and 19th Batteries (4 155mm French guns and 2 LMGs ea)
  20th Battery (4 145mm French guns and 2 LMGs)
  21st Battery (6 155mm Polish guns and 2 LMGs)
  25th Battery (4 155mm French guns and 2 LMGs)
3/973rd Coast Artillery Regiment
  Headquarters Flak Battery (2 20mm AA guns)
  31st and 32nd Batteries (3 210mm guns and 2 LMGs ea)
  33rd Battery (4 105mm French guns and 2 LMGs)
  34th Battery (6 155mm Polish guns and 2 LMGs)
  35th Battery (4 105mm French guns and 2 LMGs)
4/973rd Coast Artillery Regiment
  Headquarters Flak Battery (2 20mm AA guns)
  46th Battery (6 155mm French guns and 2 LMGs)
  47th Battery (4 155mm French guns, 2 155mm Polish and 2 LMGs)
  48th Battery (4 105mm French guns and 2 LMGs)
  49th Battery (4 105mm French guns and 2 LMGs)
5/973rd Coast Artillery Regiment
  Headquarters Flak Battery (2 20mm AA guns)
  61st, 62nd, 63rd and 64th Batteries (4 105mm French guns and 2 LMGs ea)
1/974th Coast Artillery Regiment
  Headquarters Flak Battery (2 20mm AA guns)
  1st Battery (6 155mm French guns and 2 LMGs)
  2nd Battery (4 105mm French guns and 2 LMGs)
  3rd Battery (6 210mm Czech guns and 2 LMGs)
  4th Battery (3 210mm guns and 2 LMGs)
  5th Battery (4 105mm French guns and 2 LMGs)
  6th Battery (4 105mm French guns and 2 LMGs)
  7th Battery (4 105mm Hungarian guns and 2 LMGs)

8th Battery (4 75mm Belgian guns and 2 LMGs)
9th Battery (4 155mm French guns and 2 LMGs)
10th Battery (4 105mm French guns and 2 LMGs)

2/974th Coast Artillery Regiment
Headquarters Flak Battery (2 20mm AA guns)
16th Battery (4 155mm French guns and 2 LMGs)
17th Battery (4 75mm Belgian guns and 2 LMGs)
18th Battery (4 105mm French guns and 2 LMGs)
19th Battery (4 105mm French guns and 2 LMGs)
20th Battery (4 155mm French guns and 2 LMGs)
21st Battery (4 105mm French guns and 2 LMGs)
22nd Battery (4 105mm French guns and 2 LMGs)

3/974th Coast Artillery Regiment
31st Battery (4 155mm French guns and 2 LMGs)
32nd Battery (4 155mm French guns and 2 LMGs)
33rd Battery (4 75mm Belgian guns and 2 LMGs)

1/975th Coast Artillery Regiment
Headquarters Flak Battery (2 20mm AA guns)
1st Battery (4 75mm Belgian guns and 2 LMGs)
2nd Battery (6 155mm French guns and 2 LMGs)
3rd Battery (4 105mm French guns and 2 LMGs)
4th Battery (4 105mm Dutch guns and 2 LMGs)
5th Battery (4 105mm French guns and 2 LMGs)
6th Battery (3 210mm guns and 2 LMGs)

2/975th Coast Artillery Regiment
Headquarters Flak Battery (2 20mm AA guns)
16th Battery (4 105mm Hungarian guns and 2 LMGs)
17th Battery (4 88mm Rumanian? guns and 2 LMGs)
18th Battery (4 105mm French guns and 2 LMGs)
19th Battery (6 155mm Yugoslavian guns and 2 LMGs)
20th Battery (4 155mm French guns and 2 LMGs)
21st Battery (6 210mm Czech guns and 2 LMGs)
22nd Battery (3 150mm guns and 2 LMGs)
23rd Battery (4 155mm French guns and 2 LMGs)
24th Battery (4 88mm Rumanian? guns and 2 LMGs)
25th Battery (4 105mm French guns and 2 LMGs)
26th Battery (4 76.5mm Austrian guns and 2 LMGs)

1/976th Coast Artillery Regiment (2 LMGs)
1st Battery (4 105mm French guns and 2 LMGs)
2nd Battery (4 105mm French guns and 2 LMGs)
3rd Battery (4 120mm Belgian guns and 2 LMGs)
4th Battery (4 88mm Rumanian? guns and 2 LMGs)
5th Battery (4 105mm French guns and 2 LMGs)
6th Battery (4 105mm French guns and 2 LMGs)
7th Battery (4 155mm Polish guns and 2 LMGs)

2/976th Coast Artillery Regiment
16th Battery (4 88mm Rumanian? guns and 2 LMGs)
17th Battery (4 155mm French guns and 2 LMGs)
18th Battery (4 155mm French guns and 2 LMGs)
19th Battery (4 105mm French guns and 2 LMGs)
20th Battery (3 210mm Czech guns and 2 LMGs)
21st Battery (4 155mm French guns and 2 LMGs)
22nd Battery (4 105mm French guns and 2 LMGs)
23rd Battery (4 105mm French guns and 2 LMGs)

24th Battery (4 105mm French guns and 2 LMGs)

3/976th Coast Artillery Regiment
31st Battery (4 105mm Hungarian guns and 2 LMGs)
32nd Battery (4 105mm French guns and 2 LMGs)
33rd Battery (4 105mm French guns and 2 LMGs)
34th Battery (4 88mm Rumanian? guns and 2 LMGs)
35th Battery (4 105mm French guns and 2 LMGs)
36th Battery (4 105mm French guns and 2 LMGs)
37th Battery (4 105mm French guns and 2 LMGs)
38th Battery (4 155mm French guns and 2 LMGs)

1/977th Coast Artillery Regiment
Headquarters Battery (2 20mm AA guns)
1st Battery (4 50mm Belgian guns and 2 LMGs)
2nd Battery (4 105mm French guns and 2 LMGs)
3rd Battery (4 105mm French guns and 2 LMGs)
4th Battery (4 105mm French guns and 2 LMGs)
6th Battery (4 155mm French guns and 2 LMGs)
7th Battery (4 105mm French guns and 2 LMGs)

2/977th Coast Artillery Regiment
Headquarters Battery (2 20mm AA guns)
16th Battery (4 105mm French guns, 2 88mm Rumanian guns and 2 LMGs)
17th Battery (4 88mm Rumanian? guns and 2 LMGs)
18th Battery (4 105mm French guns and 2 LMGs)
19th Battery (4 100mm guns and 2 LMGs)
20th Battery (4 100mm guns and 2 LMGs)
21st Battery (4 105mm French guns, 2 88mm Rumanian guns and 2 LMGs)

3/977th Coast Artillery Regiment
Headquarters Battery (2 20mm AA guns)
31st Battery (4 145mm French guns and 2 LMGs)
32nd Battery (4 155mm Belgian guns and 2 LMGs)
33rd Battery (3 210mm guns and 2 LMGs)
34th Battery (4 105mm French guns and 2 LMGs)
35th Battery (4 88mm Rumanian? guns and 2 LMGs)
36th Battery (4 105mm French guns and 2 LMGs)
37th Battery (4 88mm Rumanian? guns and 2 LMGs)

4/977th Coast Artillery Regiment
Headquarters Battery (2 20mm AA guns)
46th Battery (4 88mm Rumanian? guns and 2 LMGs)
47th Battery (3 210mm guns and 2 LMGs)
48th Battery (4 100mm guns and 2 LMGs)
49th Battery (4 105mm French guns, 2 88mm Rumanian guns and 2 LMGs)
50th Battery (4 100mm guns and 2 LMGs)
51st Battery (4 105mm French guns and 2 LMGs)

5/977th Coast Artillery Regiment
Headquarters Battery (2 20mm AA guns)
61st Battery (4 88mm Rumanian? guns and 2 LMGs)
62nd Battery (4 88mm Rumanian? guns and 2 LMGs)
63rd Battery (4 155mm French guns and 2 LMGs)
64th Battery (3 210mm guns and 2 LMGs)
65th Battery (4 145mm French guns and 2 LMGs)
66th Battery (4 155mm French guns and 2 LMGs)
67th Battery (4 145mm French guns and 2 LMGs)

1/978th Coast Artillery Regiment
  1st Battery (4 155mm French guns and 2 LMGs)
  2nd Battery (4 105mm French guns and 2 LMGs)
  3rd Battery (4 122mm Russian guns and 2 LMGs)
  4th Battery (3 150mm guns and 2 LMGs)
  5th Battery (3 210mm guns and 2 LMGs)
  6th Battery (4 100mm guns and 2 LMGs)
  7th Battery (6 155mm French guns and 2 LMGs)
2/978th Coast Artillery Regiment
  Headquarters Battery (2 20mm AA guns)
  8th Battery (4 100mm guns and 2 LMGs)
  16th Battery (4 100mm guns and 2 LMGs)
  17th Battery (4 105mm French guns and 2 LMGs)
  18th Battery (4 88mm Rumanian? guns and 2 LMGs)
  19th Battery (3 210mm guns and 2 LMGs)
  20th Battery (4 100mm guns and 2 LMGs)
1/979th Coast Artillery Regiment
  1st Battery (4 105mm French guns and 2 LMGs)
  2nd Battery (4 105mm French guns and 2 LMGs)
  3rd Battery (6 150mm guns and 2 LMGs)
  4th Battery (4 155mm French guns and 2 LMGs)
  16th Battery (4 105mm and 2 88mm Rumanian guns
    and 2 LMGs)
2/979th Coast Artillery Regiment
  Headquarters Battery (2 20mm AA guns)
  17th Battery (4 105mm French guns and 2 LMGs)
  18th Battery (4 105mm French guns and 2 LMGs)
  29th Battery (4 155mm French guns and 2 LMGs)
  20th Battery (4 105mm French guns and 2 LMGs)
  21st Battery (4 105mm French guns and 2 LMGs)
3/979th Coast Artillery Regiment
  Headquarters Battery (2 20mm AA guns)
  31st Battery (4 105mm French guns and 2 LMGs)
  32nd Battery (4 105mm French guns and 2 LMGs)
  33rd Battery (4 105mm French guns and 2 LMGs)
  34th Battery (4 105mm French guns and 2 LMGs)
  35th Battery (4 105mm French guns and 2 LMGs)
  36th Battery (4 105mm French guns, 2 88mm Ruma-
    nian? guns and 2 LMGs)
  37th Battery (4 105mm French guns and 2 LMGs)

1/980th Coast Artillery Regiment
  Headquarters Battery (2 20mm AA guns)
  Unnumbered Battery (4 83.8mm British guns, 4 155mm
    Polish guns and 2 LMGs)
  1st Battery (4 105mm French guns and 2 LMGs)
  2nd Battery (4 120mm Belgian guns, 2 88mm Ruma-
    nian? guns and 2 LMGs)
  3rd Battery (4 120mm Belgian guns and 2 LMGs)
  4th Battery (4 88mm Rumanian? guns and 2 LMGs)
  5th Battery (4 120mm Belgian guns, 2 88mm Ruma-
    nian? guns and 2 LMGs)
  6th Battery (4 100mm guns and 2 LMGs)
  7th Battery (4 100mm guns, 2 88mm Rumanian? guns
    and 2 LMGs)

Lapland Coast Artillery
999th Coast Artillery Battery (6 75mm Belgian guns
and 5 LMGs)

German Coast Artillery
1230th Coast Artillery Battalion
  1st Battery (4 105mm Polish guns and 5 LMGs)
  2nd Battery (4 105mm French guns and 5 LMGs)
  3rd Battery (4 105mm Czech guns and 5 LMGs)
  4th Battery (4 105mm Polish guns and 5 LMGs)
  5th Battery (3 170mm guns and 5 LMGs)
  6th Battery (6 152mm Russian howitzers and 5 LMGs)
1231st Coast Artillery Battalion
  1st Battery (4 105mm French guns and 5 LMGs)
  2nd Battery (4 105mm French guns and 5 LMGs)
  3rd Battery (6 152mm Russian howitzers and 5 LMGs)
  4th Battery (4 105mm French guns and 5 LMGs)
1/1240th Coast Artillery Regiment
  Headquarters Battery (2 20mm AA guns)
  1st Battery (6 155mm French guns and 5 LMGs)
  2nd Battery (6 155mm French guns and 5 LMGs)
  34d Battery (6 155mm French guns and 5 LMGs)
  4th Battery (2 203mm guns and 2 quad 20mm guns)
2/1240th Coast Artillery Regiment
  5th Battery (6 155mm French guns and 5 LMGs)
  6th Battery (6 155mm French guns and 5 LMGs)
  7th Battery (6 155mm French guns and 5 LMGs)
1244th Coast Artillery Battalion
  1st Battery (6 155mm French guns and 5 LMGs)
  2nd Battery (6 155mm Czech guns and 4 LMGs)
  3rd Battery (6 155mm French guns and 5 LMGs)
  4th Battery (4 76.2mm/88mm guns and 5 LMGs)
  5th Battery (4 76.2mm/88mm guns and 5 LMGs)
  6th Battery (4 76.2mm/88mm guns and 5 LMGs)
1/1245th Coast Artillery Regiment
  Signals Detachment
  Headquarters Battery (4 20mm AA guns)
  1st Battery (4 155mm French guns and 5 LMGs)
  2nd Battery (4 155mm French guns and 5 LMGs)
  3rd Battery (4 155mm French guns and 5 LMGs)
  4th Battery (4 170mm guns and 5 LMGs)
2/1245th Coast Artillery Regiment
  Signals Detachment
  Headquarters Battery (4 20mm AA guns)
  5th Battery (3 170mm guns and 5 LMGs)
  6th Battery (3 170mm guns and 5 LMGs)
  7th Battery (3 170mm guns and 5 LMGs)
  8th Battery (3 170mm guns and 5 LMGs)
3/1245th Coast Artillery Regiment
  9th Battery (4 105mm French guns and 5 LMGs)
  10th Battery (4 105mm Polish guns and 5 LMGs)
  11th Battery (4 105mm French guns and 5 LMGs)
1/1252nd Coast Artillery Regiment
  Signals Detachment
  Headquarters Battery (4 20mm AA guns)

1st Battery (3 170mm guns and 5 LMGs)
2nd Battery (3 170mm guns and 5 LMGs)
3rd Battery (4 150mm Czech guns and 5 LMGs)
4th Battery (4 220mm French guns and 5 LMGs)
5th Battery (4 76.2mm/88mm guns and 5 LMGs)
6th Battery (4 76.2mm/88mm guns and 5 LMGs)
7th Battery (4 76.2mm/88mm guns and 5 LMGs)

2/1252nd Coast Artillery Regiment
Signals Detachment
Headquarters Battery (4 20mm AA guns)
8th Battery (4 155mm French guns and 5 LMGs)
9th Battery (4 155mm French guns and 5 LMGs)
10th Battery (4 155mm French guns and 5 LMGs)

1253rd Coast Artillery Battalion
1st Battery (4 122mm Russian guns and 5 LMGs)
2nd Battery (4 122mm Russian guns and 5 LMGs)
3rd Battery (4 122mm Russian guns and 5 LMGs)

1254th Coast Artillery Regiment
Headquarters Battery (? 20mm AA guns)
1st Battery (4 100mm Czech guns and 5 LMGs)
2nd Battery (4 100mm Czech guns and 5 LMGs)
3rd Battery (3 170mm guns and 5 LMGs)
4th Battery (4 SKC/32 guns and 5 LMGs)

1255th Coast Artillery Battalion
Signals Detachment
Headquarters Battery (? 20mm AA guns)
1st Battery (6 155mm French guns and 5 LMGs)
2nd Battery (6 155mm French guns and 5 LMGs)
3rd Battery (6 155mm French guns and 5 LMGs)
4th Battery (6 155mm French guns and 5 LMGs)

1260th Coast Artillery Battalion
Headquarters Battery (? 20mm AA guns)
1st Battery (6 155mm French guns and 5 LMGs)
2nd Battery (6 155mm French guns and 5 LMGs)
3rd Battery (4 122mm Russian guns and 5 LMGs)

1/1261st Coast Artillery Regiment
1st Battery (4 122mm Russian guns and 5 LMGs)
2nd Battery (4 105mm French guns and 5 LMGs)
3rd Battery (4 105mm French guns and 5 LMGs)

2/1261st Coast Artillery Regiment
4th Battery (4 105mm French guns and 5 LMGs)
5th Battery (4 105mm French guns and 5 LMGs)
6th Battery (6 155mm French guns and 5 LMGs)

3/1261st Coast Artillery Regiment
7th Battery (6 155mm French guns and 5 LMGs)
8th Battery (6 155mm French guns and 5 LMGs)
9th Battery (4 105mm French guns and 5 LMGs)
10th Battery (4 170mm guns and 5 LMGs)

1/1262nd Coast Artillery Regiment
1st Battery (6 155mm French guns and 5 LMGs)
2nd Battery (4 105mm French guns and 5 LMGs)
3rd Battery (2 203mm guns, 4 20mm guns and 5 LMGs)
4th Battery (4 170mm guns and 5 LMGs)

2/1262nd Coast Artillery Regiment
Headquarters Battery (4 20mm AA guns)

Headquarters Battery (4 20mm AA guns)
5th Battery (4 122mm Russian guns and 5 LMGs)
6th Battery (4 76.2mm/88mm guns and 5 LMGs)
7th Battery (4 76.2mm/88mm guns and 5 LMGs)
8th Battery (4 76.2mm/88mm guns and 5 LMGs)

1/1265th Coast Artillery Regiment
Signals Detachment
Calibration Detachment
1st Battery (3 210mm guns and 5 LMGs)
2nd Battery (3 210mm guns and 5 LMGs)
3rd Battery (3 210mm guns and 5 LMGs)

2/1265th Coast Artillery Regiment
4th Battery (4 105mm French guns and 5 LMGs)
5th Battery (4 105mm French guns and 5 LMGs)
6th Battery (4 220mm French guns and 5 LMGs)

3/1265th Coast Artillery Regiment
Signals Detachment
7th Battery (3 210mm guns and 5 LMGs)
8th Battery (3 210mm guns and 5 LMGs)
9th Battery (3 210mm guns and 5 LMGs)

4/1265th Coast Artillery Regiment
10th Battery (4 105mm French guns and 5 LMGs)
11th Battery (4 105mm French guns and 5 LMGs)
12th Battery (4 150mm guns and 5 LMGs)
13th Battery (4 150mm guns and 5 LMGs)
14th Battery (4 150mm guns and 5 LMGs)
15th Battery (4 220mm French guns and 5 LMGs)
16th Battery (4 220mm French guns and 5 LMGs)

1266th Coast Artillery Battalion (St. Malo)
1271st Battery (6 122mm Russian guns and 5 LMGs)
1272nd Battery (4 203mm and 2 20mm quad guns)
1273rd Battery (6 152mm Russian guns and 5 LMGs)
1274th Battery (4 220mm French guns and 5 LMGs)

1280th Artillery Regiment (La Rochelle)
1st Battery (4 105mm French guns and 5 LMGs)
2nd Battery (4 220mm French guns and 5 LMGs)

1282nd Coast Artillery Battalion
1st Battery (4 105mm French guns and 5 LMGs)
2nd Battery (6 114mm British guns and 5 LMGs)
3rd Battery (4 105mm French guns and 5 LMGs)
4th Battery (4 105mm French guns and 5 LMGs)
5th Battery (6 152mm Russian guns and 5 LMGs)

1/287th Coast Artillery Regiment
1st Battery (4 105mm French guns and 5 LMGs)
2nd Battery (6 152mm Russian guns and 5 LMGs)
3rd Battery (4 105mm French guns and 5 LMGs)
4th Battery (6 152mm Russian guns and 5 LMGs)
5th Battery (4 105mm French guns and 5 LMGs)
6th Battery (6 152mm Russian guns and 5 LMGs)

1/1290th Coast Artillery Regiment
1st Battery (4 105mm French guns and 5 LMGs)
2nd Battery (4 105mm French guns and 5 LMGs)
3rd Battery (4 105mm French guns and 5 LMGs)
4th Battery (4 105mm French guns and 5 LMGs)
5th Battery (4 105mm French guns and 5 LMGs)

6th Battery (4 122mm Russian guns and 5 LMGs)

7th Battery (4 122mm Russian guns and 5 LMGs)

2/1290th Coast Artillery Regiment

8th Battery (4 122mm Russian guns and 5 LMGs)

9th Battery (4 105mm French guns and 5 LMGs)

10th Battery (4 105mm French guns and 5 LMGs)

11th Battery (4 105mm French guns and 5 LMGs)

12th Battery (4 122mm Russian guns and 5 LMGs)

13th Battery (4 76.2mm/88mm French guns and 5 LMGs)

1/1291st Coast Artillery Regiment

1st Battery (4 220mm French guns and 5 LMGs)

2nd Battery (4 122mm Russian guns and 5 LMGs)

3rd Battery (4 105mm French guns and 5 LMGs)

4th Battery (4 105mm French guns and 5 LMGs)

5th Battery (4 122mm Russian guns and 5 LMGs)

2/1291st Coast Artillery Regiment

6th Battery (4 122mm Russian guns and 5 LMGs)

7th Battery (4 105mm French guns and 5 LMGs)

8th Battery (4 220mm French guns and 5 LMGs)

9th Battery (3 170mm guns and 5 LMGs)

2/1291st Coast Artillery Regiment

10th Battery (6 155mm French guns and 5 LMGs)

11th Battery (3 75mm French guns and 5 LMGs)

12th Battery (3 75mm French guns and 5 LMGs)

13th Battery (7 75mm guns and 5 LMGs)

16

The Nebelwerfers

When Germany invaded Poland its nebelwerfer force consisted of the 1st, 2nd and 5th Battalions, plus a training and a experimental detachment. Each battalion had three batteries. Initially the nebelwerfer units were equipped with 105mm launchers. However, by 1941 they were upgraded to the 120mm Werfer 41 and in 1942 to the 210mm and 300mm Werfer 42.

At the beginning of the 1940 French campaign the German army had eight battalions of nebelwerfers. Two, the 4th and the 2nd Replacement Battalions, were raised by an order issued on 22 December 1939 and were to be operational by 1 April 1940. The 2nd Replacement Battalion consisted of a staff and three batteries. The 4th (mot) Nebelwerfer Battalion was to consist of a staff, three batteries, and a supply column. They were formed using newly trained troops and drafts from the 5th Battalion. By the invasion of France the nebelwerfer units were assigned to either the Army Group Reserves, or the OKH reserves. Their organization had changed slightly from that ordered for the 4th Battalion:

Battalion Headquarters
  Signals Platoon
    Headquarters Section
    1 Heavy Telephone Section
    1 Light Telephone Section
    6 Pack Radio Sections
    Motorized Weather Detachment
  3 Motorized Rocket Launcher Batteries
    Battery Headquarters
      Headquarters Section
      2 Light Telephone Sections
      3 Pack Radio Sections
    2 Rocket Platoons, each with
      Headquarters Section
      Launcher Section (4 105mm launchers each)

On 10 February 1941 the German army had nine independent Nebelwerfer Battalions, numbered 1st through 9th, and four Nebelwerfer Regiments, numbered 51st, 52nd, 53rd, and 54th. They were organized and equipped as follows:

1st, 2nd, 3rd, 4th, 5th, 6th, 7th and 9th Nebelwerfer Battalions, each with
1 Motorized HQ Signals Platoon

1 Motorized HQ Weather Platoon
3 Motorized Nebelwerfer Batteries (6 launchers each)
1 Light (mot) Munitions Supply Column
8th Nebelwerfer Battalion
1 Motorized HQ Weather Platoon
1 Motorized HQ Signals Platoon
3 Motorized Nebelwerfer Batteries (8 launchers each)
1 Light (mot) Munitions Supply Column

51st, 52nd, and 53rd Nebelwerfer Regiments, each with
1 Motorized Regimental HQ Signals Platoon
3 Nebelwerfer Battalions, each with
  1 Motorized Battalion HQ Signals Platoon
  1 Motorized Battalion HQ Weather Platoon
  3 Motorized Nebelwerfer Batteries (6 launchers each)
  1 Light (mot) Munitions Supply Column
54th Nebelwerfer Regiment
1 Motorized Regimental HQ Signals Platoon
2 Nebelwerfer Battalions, each with
  1 Motorized Battalion HQ Signals Platoon
  1 Motorized Battalion HQ Weather Platoon
  3 Motorized Nebelwerfer Batteries (6 launchers each)
  1 Light (mot) Munitions Supply Column

By 16 May 1941 the 1st (Lehr) Nebelwerfer Regiment had been organized. Earlier there were 1st, 2nd and 3rd Regiments, the 3rd being organized like the 54th (above) and the 1st and 2nd being like the 51st (above). The 3rd was raised at sometime after May. There were also seven other independent battalions, the 101st, 102nd, 103rd, 104th, 105th, 131st, and 133rd. Each had 3 batteries (six launcher and two LMGs each). All of these units vanished before the regiments listed above appear in the document, indicating that they were either renumbered into the above units, disbanded or destroyed. The nebelwerfer force evolved into the following between May 1941 and October 1942:

203rd Nebelwerfer Battery[1]
  6 nebelwerfer launchers, 1 HMG and 2 LMGs

1st, 2nd, 3rd, 4th, 5th, 6th, 7th, 9th and 10th Nebelwerfer Battalions, each with *(see over)*

---

[1] The 203rd Battery was disbanded or absorbed into the other formations prior to the fall of 1941.

1 Motorized HQ Signals Platoon

1 Motorized HQ Weather Platoon

3 Motorized Nebelwerfer Batteries (6 150mm launchers ea)[1]

1 Light (mot) Munitions Supply Column

8th Nebelwerfer Battalion

1 Motorized HQ Weather Platoon

1 Motorized HQ Signals Platoon

3 Motorized Nebelwerfer Batteries (8 150mm launchers each)

1 Light (mot) Munitions Supply Column

51st, 52nd, and 53rd Nebelwerfer Regiments, each with

1 Motorized Regimental HQ Signals Platoon (2 LMGs)

3 Nebelwerfer Battalions, each with

1 Motorized Battalion HQ Platoon[2]

3 Motorized Nebelwerfer Batteries (6 launchers, 1 HMG and 2 LMGs ea)

1 Light (mot) Munitions Supply Column (2 LMGs)

54th Nebelwerfer Regiment

1 Motorized Regimental HQ Signals Platoon

2 Nebelwerfer Battalions, each with

1 Motorized Battalion HQ Platoon

3 Motorized Nebelwerfer Batteries (6 launchers, 1 HMG and 2 LMGs ea)

1 Light (mot) Munitions Supply Column (2 LMGs)

1st Lehr Nebelwerfer Regiment

1 Motorized Regimental HQ Signals Platoon (2 LMGs)

3 Nebelwerfer Battalions, each with

1 Motorized Battalion HQ Platoon

3 Motorized Nebelwerfer Batteries[3] (6 launchers 1 HMG and 2 LMGs ea)

1 Light (mot) Munitions Supply Column (2 LMGs)

70th Nebelwerfer Regiment

1 Motorized Regimental HQ Signals Platoon

1 Nebelwerfer Battalions, with

1 Motorized Battalion HQ Platoon

3 Motorized Nebelwerfer Batteries (6 launchers, 1 HMG and 2 LMGs ea)

1 Light (mot) Munitions Supply Column (2 LMGs)

1 Nebelwerfer Battalion, with

1 Motorized Battalion HQ Platoon

3 Motorized Nebelwerfer Batteries (6 launchers,[4] 1 HMG and 2 LMGs ea)

1 Light (mot) Munitions Supply Column (2 LMGs)

The German army's nebelwerfer forces would consist of the following five nebelwerfer regiments until late 1942:

1st (Lehr), 51st, 52nd, 52nd, 53rd, and 54th Nebelwerfer Regiments, each with:

3 Motorized Battalions, each with

1 Motorized HQ Company with 2 LMGs)

3 Motorized Companies (6 Nebelwerfers, 1 HMG and 2 LMGs)

1 Light Motorized Munitions Column (2 LMGs)

As the utility of the nebelwerfer became more and more apparent, the numbers of their formations expanded. Between October 1942 and 1943 the 1st (Lehr), 51st, 52nd, 52nd, 53rd, and 54th Nebelwerfer Regiments were joined by the 1st, 2nd, and 3rd Heavy Nebelwerfer Regiments, the 70th Nebelwerfer Regiment, the 203rd (Independent) Nebelwerfer Battery, the 224th (Independent) Nebelwerfer Battery, the 10th Mountain Nebelwerfer Battalion, and the 11th and the 56th Nebelwerfer Battalions.

In addition, in 1942 the nebelwerfers were placed under the command of the 1st through 4th Kommandeure der Nebeltruppen . On 1 March 1944 these four units were organized into the 1st–4th Nebelwerfer Brigades, which later rose to the 9th. Finally, in September 1944 the 15th through 20th Volks-Werfer-Brigaden were formed. Each of these brigades contained two regiments.

Between 1943 and 1945 there were eleven heavy nebelwerfer regiments, 20 nebelwerfer regiments, and three position werfer regiments. Each had three battalions with a total of nine batteries. Each battery had six launchers, giving the regiment 324 launch tubes. A few of the regiments were also organized with a 21st and 22nd Battery that was either armored or mounted on the "maultier" half-track truck. These companies had eight 150mm Panzer Werfer 42 launchers.

During 1943 there was an innovation in the equipment assigned to the nebelwerfer units. The standardized organization appears to have been modified on 3 April 1943 and half-tracks equipped with 150mm launchers were standardized in many nebelwerfer batteries.

1st Werfer Lehr Regiment

1st Motorized Battalion

1 (mot) Staff Company (2 LMGs)

2 Nebelwerfer Batteries (6 150mm launchers, 1 37mm PAK 36 and 2 LMGs ea)

1 Nebelwerfer Batteries (6 210mm launchers, 1 37mm PAK 36 and 2 LMGs)

1 Self-Propelled Nebelwerfer Battery (8 150mm launchers and 11 LMGs)

1 Light (mot) Munitions Supply Column (3 LMGs)

---

[1] All these independent battalions were disbanded or absorbed during the summer or fall of 1941.

[2] All the battalion HQs were upgraded from the earlier 1941 structure to this sometime after June. The date is unknown.

[3] The third battery of the 3rd Battalion was added later.

[4] The second battalion was probably equipped with a heavier nebelwerfer launcher than that of the other nebelwerfer battalions.

2nd Motorized Battalion
  1 (mot) Staff Company (2 LMGs)
  3 Nebelwerfer Batteries (6 210mm launchers, 1 37mm
    PAK 36 and 2 LMGs ea)
  1 Light (mot) Munitions Supply Column (3 LMGs)
3rd Motorized Battalion
  1 (mot) Staff Company (2 LMGs)
  3 Nebelwerfer Batteries (6 150mm launchers, 1 37mm
    PAK 36 and 2 LMGs ea)
  1 Self-Propelled Nebelwerfer Battery (8 150mm
    launchers and 11 LMGs)
  1 Light (mot) Munitions Supply Column (3 LMGs)

51st Werfer Regiment
1st Motorized Battalion
  1 (mot) Staff Company (2 LMGs)
  2 Nebelwerfer Batteries (6 150mm launchers, 1 37mm
    PAK 36 and 2 LMGs ea)
  1 Self-Propelled Nebelwerfer Battery (8 150mm
    launchers and 11 LMGs)
  1 Light (mot) Munitions Supply Column (3 LMGs)
2nd Motorized Battalion
  1 (mot) Staff Company (2 LMGs)
  2 Nebelwerfer Batteries (6 150mm launchers, 1 37mm
    PAK 36 and 2 LMGs ea)
  1 Self-Propelled Nebelwerfer Battery (8 150mm
    launchers and 11 LMGs)
  1 Light (mot) Munitions Supply Column (3 LMGs)
3rd Motorized Battalion
  1 (mot) Staff Company (2 LMGs)
  2 Nebelwerfer Batteries (6 210mm launchers, 1 37mm
    PAK 36 and 2 LMGs ea)
  1 Light (mot) Munitions Supply Column (3 LMGs)

52nd Werfer Regiment
1st Motorized Battalion
  1 (mot) Staff Company (2 LMGs)
  3 Nebelwerfer Batteries (6 280/320mm launchers, 1
    37mm PAK 36 and 2 LMGs ea)
  1 Light (mot) Munitions Supply Column (3 LMGs)
2nd Motorized Battalion
  1 (mot) Staff Company (2 LMGs)
  3 Nebelwerfer Batteries (6 150mm launchers, 1 37mm
    PAK 36 and 2 LMGs ea)
  1 Self-Propelled Nebelwerfer Battery (8 150mm
    launchers and 11 LMGs)
  1 Light (mot) Munitions Supply Column (3 LMGs)
3rd Motorized Battalion
  1 (mot) Staff Company (2 LMGs)
  3 Nebelwerfer Batteries (6 150mm launchers, 1 37mm
    PAK 36 and 2 LMGs ea)
  1 Light (mot) Munitions Supply Column (3 LMGs)

53rd Werfer Regiment
1st Motorized Battalion
  1 (mot) Staff Company (2 LMGs)
  3 Nebelwerfer Batteries (6 150mm launchers, 1 37mm
    PAK 36 and 2 LMGs ea)

1 Light (mot) Munitions Supply Column (3 LMGs)
2nd Motorized Battalion
  1 (mot) Staff Company (2 LMGs)
  2 Nebelwerfer Batteries (6 150mm launchers, 1 37mm
    PAK 36 and 2 LMGs ea)
  1 Self-Propelled Nebelwerfer Battery (8 150mm
    launchers and 11 LMGs)
  1 Light (mot) Munitions Supply Column (3 LMGs)
3rd Motorized Battalion
  1 (mot) Staff Company (2 LMGs)
  2 Nebelwerfer Batteries (6 210mm launchers, 1 37mm
    PAK 36 and 2 LMGs ea)
  1 Light (mot) Munitions Supply Column (3 LMGs)

54th Werfer Regiment
1st Motorized Battalion
  1 (mot) Staff Company (2 LMGs)
  3 Nebelwerfer Batteries (6 150mm launchers, 1 37mm
    PAK 36 and 2 LMGs ea)
  1 Self-Propelled Nebelwerfer Battery (8 150mm
    launchers and 11 LMGs)
  1 Light (mot) Munitions Supply Column (3 LMGs)
2nd Motorized Battalion
  1 (mot) Staff Company (2 LMGs)
  3 Nebelwerfer Batteries (6 150mm launchers, 1 37mm
    PAK 36 and 2 LMGs ea)
  1 Self-Propelled Nebelwerfer Battery (8 150mm
    launchers and 11 LMGs)
  1 Light (mot) Munitions Supply Column (3 LMGs)
3rd Motorized Battalion
  1 (mot) Staff Company (2 LMGs)
  3 Nebelwerfer Batteries (6 150mm launchers, 1 37mm
    PAK 36 and 2 LMGs ea)
  1 Light (mot) Munitions Supply Column (3 LMGs)

55th Werfer Regiment
1st Motorized Battalion
  1 (mot) Staff Company (2 LMGs)
  3 Nebelwerfer Batteries (6 150mm launchers, 1 37mm
    PAK 36 and 2 LMGs ea)
  1 Self-Propelled Nebelwerfer Battery (8 150mm
    launchers and 11 LMGs)
  1 Light (mot) Munitions Supply Column (3 LMGs)
2nd Motorized Battalion
  Motorized HQ Company (2 HMGs)
  3 Nebelwerfer Batteries (6 280/320mm launchers, 1
    37mm PAK 36 and 2 LMGs ea)
  1 Light (mot) Munitions Supply Column (3 LMGs)
3rd Motorized Battalion
  Motorized HQ Company (2 HMGs)
  3 Nebelwerfer Batteries (6 150mm launchers, 1 37mm
    PAK 36 and 2 LMGs ea)
  1 Self-Propelled Nebelwerfer Battery (8 150mm
    launchers and 11 LMGs)
  1 Light (mot) Munitions Supply Column (3 LMGs)

70th Werfer Regiment
1st Motorized Battalion

Motorized HQ Company (2 HMGs)

3 Nebelwerfer Batteries (6 150mm launchers, 1 37mm PAK 36 and 2 LMGs ea)

1 Light (mot) Munitions Supply Column (3 LMGs)

2nd Motorized Battalion

Motorized HQ Company (2 HMGs)

3 Nebelwerfer Batteries (6 280/320mm launchers, 1 37mm PAK 36 and 2 LMGs ea)

1 Light (mot) Munitions Supply Column (3 LMGs)

3rd Motorized Battalion

Motorized HQ Company (2 HMGs)

3 Nebelwerfer Batteries (6 150mm launchers, 1 37mm PAK 36 and 2 LMGs ea)

1 Light (mot) Munitions Supply Column (3 LMGs)

Note: The 2nd Battalion seems to have been earlier equipped with 300mm launchers. Date of re-equipping unknown.

1st Heavy Nebelwerfer Regiment

Motorized Regimental HQ Company (2 LMGs)

1st Motorized Battalion

Motorized HQ Company (2 HMGs)

3 Nebelwerfer Batteries (6 150mm launchers, 1 37mm PAK 36 and 2 LMGs ea)

1 Self-Propelled Nebelwerfer Battery (8 150mm launchers and 11 LMGs)

1 Light (mot) Munitions Supply Column (3 LMGs)

2nd and 3rd Motorized Battalions

Motorized HQ Company (2 HMGs)

3 Nebelwerfer Batteries (6 280/320mm launchers, 1 37mm PAK 36 and 2 LMGs ea)

1 Light (mot) Munitions Supply Column (3 LMGs)

Note: The 1st, 2nd and 3rd Battalions appear to have had 300mm launchers prior to 11 April 1943. The self-propelled battery was added to the 1st Battalion around that date.

2nd Heavy Nebelwerfer Regiment (equipped as follows on 22 Feb. 1943)

Motorized Regimental HQ Company (2 LMGs)

1st and 2nd Motorized Battalion

Motorized HQ Company (2 HMGs)

2 Nebelwerfer Batteries (6 300mm launchers, 1 37mm PAK 36 and 2 LMGs ea)

1 Light (mot) Munitions Supply Column (3 LMGs)

3rd Motorized Battalion

Motorized HQ Company (2 HMGs)

2 Nebelwerfer Batteries (6 280/320mm launchers, 1 37mm PAK 36 and 2 LMGs ea)

1 Self-Propelled Nebelwerfer Battery (8 150mm launchers and 11 LMGs)

1 Light (mot) Munitions Supply Column (3 LMGs)

Note: Earlier the third battalion earlier was equipped with 300mm launchers. The date it was re-equipped is unknown. The self-propelled battery was added on 1 April 1943.

3rd Heavy Nebelwerfer Regiment

Motorized Regimental HQ Company (2 LMGs)

1st Motorized Battalion

Motorized HQ Company (2 HMGs)

3 Nebelwerfer Batteries (6 300mm launchers, 1 37mm PAK 36 and 2 LMGs ea)

1 Light (mot) Munitions Supply Column (3 LMGs)

2nd Motorized Battalion

Motorized HQ Company (2 HMGs)

3 Nebelwerfer Batteries (6 280/320mm launchers, 1 37mm PAK 36 and 2 LMGs ea)

1 Light (mot) Munitions Supply Column (3 LMGs)

3rd Motorized Battalion

Motorized HQ Company (2 HMGs)

2 Nebelwerfer Batteries (6 280/320mm launchers, 1 37mm PAK 36 and 2 LMGs ea)

1 Light (mot) Munitions Supply Column (3 LMGs)

Note: The 2nd Battalion was either disbanded or destroyed on 17 March 1943. The 2nd and 3rd Battalions appear to have had 300mm launchers earlier. Date of re-equipping unknown.

203rd (Independent) Nebelwerfer Battery (6 280/320mm launchers and 2 LMGs)

224th (Independent) Nebelwerfer Battery (6 100mm launchers, 1 37mm PAK 36 and 2 LMGs)

10th Mountain Nebelwerfer Battalion

HQ Company (2 LMGs)

3 Mountain Batteries (6 100mm Nebelwerfers, 1 37mm PAK 36 and 2 LMGs ea)

1 Light (mot) Munitions Supply Column (3 LMGs)

11th Nebelwerfer Battalion

1 (mot) Staff Company (2 LMGs)

2 Batteries (6 100mm Nebelwerfers, 1 37mm PAK 36 and 2 LMGs ea)

56th Nebelwerfer Battalion

Motorized HQ Company (2 HMGs)

3 Nebelwerfer Batteries (6 300mm launchers, 1 37mm PAK 36 and 2 LMGs ea)

1 Self-Propelled Nebelwerfer Battery (8 150mm launchers and 11 LMGs)

1 Light (mot) Munitions Supply Column (3 LMGs)

From late 1942 through 1943 a number of new regiments were formed. They were the 56th, 57th, 70th, 71st, 72nd, 81st and 82nd Regiments. Part of the newly formed 71st Nebelwerfer Regiment was sent to Africa. The 2nd and 3rd Companies and the 4th Battalion were lost. The staff, 2nd and 3rd Battalions were still in Sicily when Tunisia fell and were used to reorganize the regiment. Those elements that did arrive in North Africa were lost when Tunisa fell.

The 51st and 53rd Werfer Regiment as well as the 2nd Heavy Werfer Regiment were lost at Stalingrad and rebuilt. On 1 September 1944 the 1/2nd Heavy Nebelwerfer Regiment was rebuilt with 300mm launchers. On 1 October 1944 the 2/51st Heavy Nebelwerfer Regiment was rebuilt with 150mm launchers and on 1 November 1944 the 2/70th Heavy Nebelwerfer Regiment was ordered rebuilt with 300mm launchers. On 28 July 1944 the 2/51st (150mm), 2/70th (300mm) and 1/2nd Heavy (300mm) were refreshed and rebuilt. On the same day the 102nd Position Nebelwerfer Regiment was ordered formed with two 150mm and one 300mm battalion.

By January 1944 the importance of the nebelwerfers and saturation bombardment had grown such that they were organized into brigades. The firepower of these formations was tremendous, yet it was not sufficient to stop the advance of the Allied armies. Though most served on the Russian front, two served in France facing the Anglo-American armies. A total of six brigades were organized that absorbed the existing and some newly formed nebelwerfer regiments. These brigades were organized as follows:

1st Nebelwerfer Brigade
  1st Nebelwerfer Regiment
    1 (mot) Staff Battery (4 LMGs)
    1st Battalion
      1 (mot) Staff Battery (4 LMGs)
      3 (mot) Batteries (6 150mm launchers, 1 50mm PAK 38 and 6 LMGs ea)
      1 (mot) Light Rocket Supply Column
    2nd Battalion
      1 (mot) Staff Battery (4 LMGs)
      3 (mot) Batteries (6 300mm launchers, 1 50mm PAK 38 and 6 LMGs ea)
      1 (mot) Light Rocket Supply Column
    3rd Battalion
      1 (mot) Staff Battery (4 LMGs)
      3 (mot) Batteries (6 300mm launchers, 1 50mm PAK 38 and 6 LMGs ea)
      1 (mot) Light Rocket Supply Column
  57th Nebelwerfer Regiment
    1 (mot) Staff Battery (4 LMGs)
    1st and 2nd Battalion, each with:
      1 (mot) Staff Battery (4 LMGs)
      3 (mot) Batteries (6 150mm launchers, 1 50mm PAK 38 and 6 LMGs ea)
      1 (mot) Light Rocket Supply Column
2nd Nebelwerfer Brigade
  3rd Nebelwerfer Regiment
    1 (mot) Staff Battery (4 LMGs)
    1st Battalion
      1 (mot) Staff Battery (4 LMGs)

3 (mot) Batteries (6 300mm launchers, 1 50mm PAK 38 and 6 LMGs ea)
      1 (mot) Light Rocket Supply Column
    2nd Battalion
      1 (mot) Staff Battery (4 LMGs)
      3 (mot) Batteries (6 300mm launchers, 1 50mm PAK 38 and 6 LMGs ea)
      1 (mot) Light Rocket Supply Column
    3rd Battalion
      1 (mot) Staff Battery (4 LMGs)
      3 (mot) Batteries (6 150mm launchers, 1 50mm PAK 38 and 6 LMGs ea)
      1 Self-Propelled 150mm Launcher Battery (8 half-tracks with launchers, 1 75mm AT gun and 11 LMGs)
      1 (mot) Light Rocket Supply Column
  70th Nebelwerfer Regiment
    1 (mot) Staff Battery (4 LMGs)
    1st Battalion
      1 (mot) Staff Battery (4 LMGs)
      3 (mot) Batteries (6 150mm launchers, 1 50mm PAK 38 and 6 LMGs ea)
      1 Self-Propelled 150mm Launcher Battery (8 half-tracks with launchers, 1 75mm AT gun and 11 LMGs)
      1 (mot) Light Rocket Supply Column
    2nd Battalion
      1 (mot) Staff Battery (4 LMGs)
      3 (mot) Batteries (6 150mm launchers, 1 50mm PAK 38 and 6 LMGs ea)
      1 (mot) Light Rocket Supply Column
    3rd Battalion
      1 (mot) Staff Battery (4 LMGs)
      3 (mot) Batteries (6 300mm launchers, 1 50mm PAK 38 and 6 LMGs ea)
      1 (mot) Light Rocket Supply Column
3rd Nebelwerfer Brigade
  2nd Nebelwerfer Regiment
    1 (mot) Staff Battery (4 LMGs)
    1st Battalion
      1 (mot) Staff Battery (4 LMGs)
      3 (mot) Batteries (6 300mm launchers, 1 50mm PAK 38 and 6 LMGs ea)
      1 (mot) Light Rocket Supply Column
    2nd Battalion
      1 (mot) Staff Battery (4 LMGs)
      3 (mot) Batteries (6 300mm launchers, 1 50mm PAK 38 and 6 LMGs ea)
      1 Self-Propelled 150mm Launcher Battery (8 half-tracks with launchers, 1 75mm AT gun and 11 LMGs)
      1 (mot) Light Rocket Supply Column
    3rd Battalion
      1 (mot) Staff Battery (4 LMGs)
      3 (mot) Batteries (6 150mm launchers, 1 50mm PAK 38 and 6 LMGs ea)

1 (mot) Light Rocket Supply Column

55th Nebelwerfer Regiment

1 (mot) Staff Battery (4 LMGs)

1st Battalion

1 (mot) Staff Battery (4 LMGs)

3 (mot) Batteries (6 150mm launchers, 1 50mm PAK 38 and 6 LMGs ea)

1 Self-Propelled 150mm Launcher Battery (8 half-tracks with launchers, 1 75mm AT gun and 11 LMGs)

1 (mot) Light Rocket Supply Column

2nd Battalion

1 (mot) Staff Battery (4 LMGs)

3 (mot) Batteries (6 300mm launchers, 1 50mm PAK 38 and 6 LMGs ea)

1 (mot) Light Rocket Supply Column

3rd Battalion

1 (mot) Staff Battery (4 LMGs)

3 (mot) Batteries (6 150mm launchers, 1 50mm PAK 38 and 6 LMGs ea)

1 (mot) Light Rocket Supply Column

4th Nebelwerfer Brigade

51st Nebelwerfer Regiment

1 (mot) Staff Battery (4 LMGs)

1st Battalion

1 (mot) Staff Battery (4 LMGs)

3 (mot) Batteries (6 150mm launchers, 1 50mm PAK 38 and 6 LMGs ea)

1 Self-Propelled 150mm Launcher Battery (8 half-tracks with launchers, 1 75mm AT gun and 11 LMGs)

2nd Battalion (seems to have been destroyed)

1 (mot) Staff Battery (4 LMGs)

3 (mot) Batteries (6 150mm launchers, 1 50mm PAK 38 and 6 LMGs ea)

1 Self-Propelled 150mm Launcher Battery (8 half-tracks with launchers, 1 75mm AT gun and 11 LMGs)

1 (mot) Light Rocket Supply Column

3rd Battalion

1 (mot) Staff Battery (4 LMGs)

3 (mot) Batteries (6 210mm launchers, 1 50mm PAK 38 and 6 LMGs ea)

1 (mot) Light Rocket Supply Column

55th Nebelwerfer Regiment

1 (mot) Staff Battery (4 LMGs)

1st Battalion

1 (mot) Staff Battery (4 LMGs)

3 (mot) Batteries (6 150mm launchers, 1 50mm PAK 38 and 6 LMGs ea)

1 (mot) Light Rocket Supply Column

2nd Battalion

1 (mot) Staff Battery (4 LMGs)

3 (mot) Batteries (6 150mm launchers, 1 50mm PAK 38 and 6 LMGs ea)

1 Self-Propelled 150mm Launcher Battery (8 half-tracks with launchers, 1 75mm AT gun and 11 LMGs)

1 (mot) Light Rocket Supply Column

3rd Battalion

1 (mot) Staff Battery (4 LMGs)

3 (mot) Batteries (6 210mm launchers, 1 50mm PAK 38 and 6 LMGs ea)

1 (mot) Light Rocket Supply Column

5th Nebelwerfer Brigade

56th Nebelwerfer Regiment

1 (mot) Staff Battery (4 LMGs)

1st Battalion

1 (mot) Staff Battery (4 LMGs)

3 (mot) Batteries (6 150mm launchers, 1 50mm PAK 38 and 6 LMGs ea)

1 (mot) Light Rocket Supply Column

1 Self-Propelled 150mm Launcher Battery (8 half-tracks with launchers, 1 75mm AT gun and 11 LMGs)

2nd Battalion

1 (mot) Staff Battery (4 LMGs)

3 (mot) Batteries (6 210mm launchers, 1 50mm PAK 38 and 6 LMGs ea)

1 (mot) Light Rocket Supply Column

3rd Battalion

1 (mot) Staff Battery (4 LMGs)

3 (mot) Batteries (6 210mm launchers, 1 50mm PAK 38 and 6 LMGs ea)

1 (mot) Light Rocket Supply Column

71st Nebelwerfer Regiment

1 (mot) Staff Battery (4 LMGs)

1st Battalion

1 (mot) Staff Battery (4 LMGs)

3 (mot) Batteries (6 150mm launchers, 1 50mm PAK 38 and 6 LMGs ea)

1 Self-Propelled 150mm Launcher Battery (8 half-tracks with launchers, 1 75mm AT gun and 11 LMGs)

1 (mot) Light Rocket Supply Column

2nd Battalion

1 (mot) Staff Battery (4 LMGs)

3 (mot) Batteries (6 210mm launchers, 1 50mm PAK 38 and 6 LMGs ea)

1 (mot) Light Rocket Supply Column

6th Nebelwerfer Brigade

81st Nebelwerfer Regiment

1 (mot) Staff Battery (4 LMGs)

1st Battalion

1 (mot) Staff Battery (4 LMGs)

3 (mot) Batteries (6 150mm launchers, 1 50mm PAK 38 and 6 LMGs ea)

1 Self-Propelled 150mm Launcher Battery (8 half-tracks with launchers, 1 75mm AT gun and 11 LMGs)

1 (mot) Light Rocket Supply Column
2nd Battalion
  1 (mot) Staff Battery (4 LMGs)
  3 (mot) Batteries (6 150mm launchers, 1 50mm PAK 38 and 6 LMGs ea)
  1 Self-Propelled 150mm Launcher Battery (8 half-tracks with launchers, 1 75mm AT gun and 11 LMGs)
  1 (mot) Light Rocket Supply Column
3rd Battalion
  1 (mot) Staff Battery (4 LMGs)
  3 (mot) Batteries (6 210mm launchers, 1 50mm PAK 38 and 6 LMGs ea)
  1 (mot) Light Rocket Supply Column

82nd Nebelwerfer Regiment
1 (mot) Staff Battery (4 LMGs)
1st Battalion
  1 (mot) Staff Battery (4 LMGs)
  3 (mot) Batteries (6 150mm launchers, 1 50mm PAK 38 and 6 LMGs ea)
  1 (mot) Light Rocket Supply Column
  1 Self-Propelled 150mm Launcher Battery (8 half-tracks with launchers, 1 75mm AT gun and 11 LMGs)
  1 (mot) Light Rocket Supply Column
2nd Battalion
  1 (mot) Staff Battery (4 LMGs)
  3 (mot) Batteries (6 150mm launchers, 1 50mm 38 and 6 LMGs ea)
  1 (mot) Light Rocket Supply Column
  1 Self-Propelled 150mm Launcher Battery (8 half-tracks with launchers, 1 75mm AT gun and 11 LMGs)
  1 (mot) Light Rocket Supply Column
3rd Battalion
  1 (mot) Staff Battery (4 LMGs)
  3 (mot) Batteries (6 300mm launchers, 1 50mm PAK 38 and 6 LMGs ea)
  1 (mot) Light Rocket Supply Column

The other nebelwerfer units existing at that time consisted of the 1st, 2nd and 55th (Lehr) Nebelwerfer Regiments, the 101st Nebelwerfer Regiment, the 10th Mountain Nebelwerfer Battalion and the 11th Nebelwerfer Regiment. These formations were organized as follows:

1st (Lehr) Nebelwerfer Regiment
1st Battalion
  1 (mot) Staff Battery (4 LMGs)
  3 (mot) Batteries (6 150mm launchers, 1 50mm PAK 38 and 6 LMGs ea)
  1 Self-Propelled 150mm Launcher Battery (8 half-tracks with launchers, 1 75mm AT gun and 11 LMGs)

1 (mot) Light Rocket Supply Column
2nd Battalion
  1 (mot) Staff Battery (4 LMGs)
  3 (mot) Batteries (6 210mm launchers, 1 50mm PAK 38 and 6 LMGs ea)
  1 (mot) Light Rocket Supply Column
3rd Battalion
  1 (mot) Staff Battery (4 LMGs)
  3 (mot) Batteries (6 150mm launchers, 1 50mm PAK 38 and 6 LMGs ea)
  1 (mot) Light Rocket Supply Column

55th (Lehr) Nebelwerfer Regiment
1st Battalion
  1 (mot) Staff Battery (4 LMGs)
  3 (mot) Batteries (6 150mm launchers, 1 50mm PAK 38 and 6 LMGs ea)
  1 Self-Propelled 150mm Launcher Battery (8 half-tracks with launchers, 1 75mm AT gun and 11 LMGs)
  1 (mot) Light Rocket Supply Column
2nd Battalion
  1 (mot) Staff Battery (4 LMGs)
  3 (mot) Batteries (6 150mm launchers, 1 50mm PAK 38 and 6 LMGs ea)
  1 (mot) Light Rocket Supply Column
3rd Battalion
  1 (mot) Staff Battery (4 LMGs)
  3 (mot) Batteries (6 150mm launchers, 1 50mm PAK 38 and 6 LMGs ea)
  1 (mot) Light Rocket Supply Column

2nd (Lehr) Nebelwerfer Regiment
1st Battalion
  1 (mot) Staff Battery (4 LMGs)
  3 (mot) Batteries (6 300mm launchers, 1 50mm PAK 38 and 6 LMGs ea)
  1 Self-Propelled 150mm Launcher Battery (8 half-tracks with launchers, 1 75mm AT gun and 11 LMGs)
  1 (mot) Light Rocket Supply Column
2nd Battalion
  1 (mot) Staff Battery (4 LMGs)
  3 (mot) Batteries (6 300mm launchers, 1 50mm PAK 38 and 6 LMGs ea)
  1 (mot) Light Rocket Supply Column
3rd Battalion
  1 (mot) Staff Battery (4 LMGs)
  3 (mot) Batteries (6 150mm launchers, 1 50mm PAK 38 and 6 LMGs ea)
  1 Self-Propelled 150mm Launcher Battery (8 half-tracks with launchers, 1 75mm AT gun and 11 LMGs)
  1 (mot) Light Rocket Supply Column

101st Nebelwerfer Regiment
1 (mot) Staff Battery (2 LMGs)
1st, 2nd and 3rd Battalions, each with *(see over)*

3 (mot) Batteries (6 280/320mm launchers and 6 LMGs ea)

10th Mountain Nebelwerfer Battalion
Staff Battery (4 LMGs)
3 Batteries (6 100mm launchers and 6 LMGs ea)
1 (mot) Mountain Light Rocket Supply Column

11th Nebelwerfer Battalion
Staff Battery (4 LMGs)
2 (mot) Batteries (6 150mm launchers, 1 50mm PAK 38 and 6 LMGs ea)
1 Self-Propelled 150mm Launcher Battery (8 half-tracks with launchers, 1 75mm AT gun and 11 LMGs)

As 1944 progressed, the numbers of nebelwerfer brigades expanded significantly. An order issued on 30 August 1944 required the formation of 10 nebelwerfer brigades as follows:

No of brigades	Date to be raised
1	15 Sept. 1944
1	30 Sept. 1944
2	15 Oct. 1944
1	31 Oct. 1944
2	15 Nov. 1944
1	30 Nov. 1944
2	15 Dec. 1944

Each brigade was to have two regiments, of three battalions each. Each battalion was to have three batteries of six launchers each. The brigades were to have four battalions of 150mm launchers, one of 210mm launchers, and one with 300mm werfers.

The order of 22 October 1944 directed the formation of the 4th, 7th, 9th, 15th, 18th, 19th, and 20th (mot) Volks Werfer Brigades and the 8th, 16th, and 17th (tmot) Volks Werfer Brigades. An organizational document dated 23 October 1944 indicates that the brigades were organized as follows:

Nebelwerfer Brigade Staff
Staff Company (3 LMGs)
(mot) Weather Company (2 LMGs)
(mot) Signals Platoon

1st Nebelwerfer Regiment
1 (mot) Regimental Staff Battery (2 LMGs)
1st Battalion
1 (mot) Battalion Staff Battery (2 LMGs)
3 (mot) Batteries (6 150mm launchers and 2 LMGS ea)
1 (mot) Supply Company (1 LMG)
2nd Battalion
1 (mot) Battalion Staff Battery (2 LMGs)
3 (mot) Batteries (6 150mm launchers and 2 LMGS ea)
1 (mot) Supply Company (1 LMG)

3rd Battalion
1 (mot) Battalion Staff Battery (2 LMGs)
3 (mot) Batteries (6 210mm launchers and 2 LMGS ea)
1 (mot) Supply Company (1 LMG)

2nd Nebelwerfer Regiment
1 (mot) Regimental Staff Battery (2 LMGs)
1st Battalion
1 (mot) Battalion Staff Battery (2 LMGs)
3 (mot) Batteries (6 150mm launchers and 2 LMGS ea)
1 (mot) Supply Company (1 LMG)
2nd Battalion
1 (mot) Battalion Staff Battery (2 LMGs)
3 (mot) Batteries (6 150mm launchers and 2 LMGS ea)
1 (mot) Supply Company (1 LMG)
3rd Battalion
1 (mot) Battalion Staff Battery (2 LMGs)
3 (mot) Batteries (6 300mm launchers and 2 LMGS ea)
1 (mot) Supply Company (1 LMG)

Each (mot) brigade had 72 150mm, 18 210mm, and 18 300mm launchers, 276 trucks, 109 prime movers, and 2,933 men. The volks werfer brigades were (tmot) and organized identically, except that they had 96 trucks, 54 prime movers, and 2,610 men.

The position nebelwerfer brigade was organized in a relatively similar way: the 210mm battalion was replaced by a second 300mm battalion and the regiment had one supply column instead of two. It contained 72 150mm and 36 300mm launchers, 59 trucks, 18 prime movers, and 1,966 men.

Between late 1944 and early 1945 the Nebelwerfer Brigades were organized and modified as follows:

1st Nebelwerfer Brigade
Brigade Staff
1 Brigade Staff (1 LMG)
1 (mot) "J" Platoon (2 LMGs) (added 5 Oct. 1944)
1st Heavy Nebelwerfer Regiment
1 Regimental Staff and (mot) Regimental Staff Battery (4 LMGs)
1st Battalion
1 Battalion Staff and (mot) Battalion Staff Battery (4 LMGs)
3 (mot) Nebelwerfer Batteries (6 150mm launchers and 6 LMGs ea)
1 (mot) Light Supply Column (3 LMGs)
2nd Battalion
1 Battalion Staff and (mot) Battalion Staff Battery (4 LMGs)
3 (mot) Nebelwerfer Batteries (6 300mm launchers and 6 LMGs ea)
1 (mot) Light Supply Column (3 LMGs)

3rd Battalion

same as 2nd Battalion

57th Nebelwerfer Regiment

1 Regimental Staff and (mot) Regimental Staff Battery (4 LMGs)

1st Battalion

1 Battalion Staff and (mot) Battalion Staff Battery (4 LMGs)

3 (mot) Nebelwerfer Batteries (6 150mm launchers and 6 LMGs ea)

1 (mot) Light Supply Column (3 LMGs)

1 (half-track) Battery (8 210mm launchers and 10 LMGs) (added 28 Sept. 1944)

2nd Battalion

1 Battalion Staff and (mot) Battalion Staff Battery (4 LMGs)

3 (mot) Nebelwerfer Batteries (6 150mm launchers and 6 LMGs ea)

1 (mot) Light Supply Column (3 LMGs)

3rd Battalion

1 Battalion Staff and (mot) Battalion Staff Battery (4 LMGs)

3 (mot) Nebelwerfer Batteries (6 210mm launchers and 6 LMGs ea)

1 (mot) Light Supply Column (3 LMGs)

2nd Nebelwerfer Brigade

Brigade Staff

1 Brigade Staff (1 LMG)

1 (mot) "J" Platoon (2 LMGs) (added 5 Oct. 1944)

3rd Heavy Nebelwerfer Regiment

1 Regimental Staff and (mot) Regimental Staff Battery (4 LMGs)

1st Battalion

1 Battalion Staff and (mot) Battalion Staff Battery (4 LMGs)

3 (mot) Nebelwerfer Batteries (6 300mm launchers and 6 LMGs ea)

1 (mot) Light Supply Column (3 LMGs)

2nd Battalion

same as 1st Battalion

3rd Battalion

1 Battalion Staff and (mot) Battalion Staff Battery (4 LMGs)

3 (mot) Nebelwerfer Batteries (6 150mm launchers and 6 LMGs ea)

1 (half-track) Battery (8 210mm launchers and 10 LMGs)

1 (mot) Light Supply Column (3 LMGs)

70th Nebelwerfer Regiment

1 Regimental Staff and (mot) Regimental Staff Battery (4 LMGs)

1st Battalion

1 Battalion Staff and (mot) Battalion Staff Battery (4 LMGs)

3 (mot) Nebelwerfer Batteries (6 150mm launchers and 6 LMGs ea)

1 (half-track) Battery (8 210mm launchers and 10 LMGs)

1 (mot) Light Supply Column (3 LMGs)

2nd Battalion (lost 11 May 1944, replaced 18 Aug. 1944)

1 Battalion Staff and (mot) Battalion Staff Battery (4 LMGs)

3 (mot) Nebelwerfer Batteries (6 300mm launchers and 6 LMGs ea)

1 (mot) Light Supply Column (3 LMGs)

3rd Battalion

1 Battalion Staff and (mot) Battalion Staff Battery (4 LMGs)

3 (mot) Nebelwerfer Batteries (6 150mm launchers and 6 LMGs ea)

1 (mot) Light Supply Column (3 LMGs)

3rd Nebelwerfer Brigade

Brigade Staff

1 Brigade Staff (1 LMG)

1 (mot) "J" Platoon (2 LMGs) (added 10/5/44)

15th Heavy Nebelwerfer Regiment

1 Regimental Staff and (mot) Regimental Staff Battery (4 LMGs)

1st Battalion

1 Battalion Staff and (mot) Battalion Staff Battery (4 LMGs)

3 (mot) Nebelwerfer Batteries (6 300mm launchers and 6 LMGs ea)

1 (mot) Light Supply Column (3 LMGs) (replaced by mot supply company with 1 LMG)

2nd Battalion

same as 1st Battalion

3rd Battalion

1 Battalion Staff and (mot) Battalion Staff Battery (4 LMGs)

3 (mot) Nebelwerfer Batteries (6 150mm launchers and 6 LMGs ea)

1 (half-track) Battery (8 210mm launchers and 10 LMGs)

1 (mot) Light Supply Column (3 LMGs) (replaced by mot supply company with 1 LMG)

52nd Nebelwerfer Regiment

1 Regimental Staff and (mot) Regimental Staff Battery (4 LMGs)

1st Battalion

1 Battalion Staff and (mot) Battalion Staff Battery (4 LMGs)

3 (mot) Nebelwerfer Batteries (6 300mm launchers and 6 LMGs ea)

1 (mot) Light Supply Column (3 LMGs) (replaced by mot supply company with 1 LMG)

2nd Battalion

1 Battalion Staff and (mot) Battalion Staff Battery (4 LMGs)

3 (mot) Nebelwerfer Batteries (6 150mm launchers and 6 LMGs ea)

1 (half-track) Battery (8 210mm launchers and 10 LMGs; reassigned to 3rd Battalion on 28 Sept. 1944)

1 (mot) Light Supply Column (3 LMGs) (replaced by mot supply company with 1 LMG)

3rd Battalion

1 Battalion Staff and (mot) Battalion Staff Battery (4 LMGs)

3 (mot) Nebelwerfer Batteries (6 150mm launchers and 6 LMGs ea)

1 (mot) Light Supply Column (3 LMGs) (replaced by mot supply company with 1 LMG)

4th Volks-Werfer Brigade (designated "Volks" on 22 Oct. 1944)

Brigade Staff

1 Brigade Staff (1 LMG)

1 (mot) "J" Platoon (2 LMGs) (added 5 Oct. 1944)

51st Nebelwerfer Regiment

1 Regimental Staff and (mot) Regimental Staff Battery (4 LMGs)

1st Battalion

1 Battalion Staff and (mot) Battalion Staff Battery (4 LMGs)

3 (mot) Nebelwerfer Batteries (6 150mm launchers and 6 LMGs ea)

1 (half-track) Battery (8 150mm launchers and 10 LMGs; detached 15 Aug. 1944)

1 (mot) Light Supply Column (3 LMGs) (replaced by mot supply company with 1 LMG)

2nd Battalion

same as 1st Battalion, no half-track battery

3rd Battalion

1 Battalion Staff and (mot) Battalion Staff Battery (4 LMGs)

3 (mot) Nebelwerfer Batteries (6 300mm launchers and 6 LMGs ea)

1 (mot) Light Supply Column (3 LMGs) (replaced by mot supply company with 1 LMG)

53rd Nebelwerfer Regiment

1 Regimental Staff and (mot) Regimental Staff Battery (4 LMGs)

1st Battalion

1 Battalion Staff and (mot) Battalion Staff Battery (4 LMGs)

3 (mot) Nebelwerfer Batteries (6 150mm launchers and 6 LMGs ea)

1 (half-track) Battery (8 150mm launchers and 10 LMGs)

1 (mot) Light Supply Column (3 LMGs) (replaced by mot supply comoany with 1 LMG)

2nd Battalion

1 Battalion Staff and (mot) Battalion Staff Battery (4 LMGs)

3 (mot) Nebelwerfer Batteries (6 150mm launchers and 6 LMGs ea)

1 (mot) Light Supply Column (3 LMGs) (replaced by mot supply company with 1 LMG)

3rd Battalion

1 Battalion Staff and (mot) Battalion Staff Battery (4 LMGs)

3 (mot) Nebelwerfer Batteries (6 210mm launchers and 6 LMGs ea)

1 (mot) Light Supply Column (3 LMGs) (replaced by mot supply company with 1 LMG)

5th Nebelwerfer Brigade
Brigade Staff

1 Brigade Staff (1 LMG)

1 (mot) "J" Platoon (2 LMGs) (added 5 Oct. 1944)

56th Nebelwerfer Regiment

1 Regimental Staff and (mot) Regimental Staff Battery (4 LMGs)

1st Battalion

1 Battalion Staff and (mot) Battalion Staff Battery (4 LMGs)

3 (mot) Nebelwerfer Batteries (6 150mm launchers and 6 LMGs ea)

1 (half-track) Battery (8 150mm launchers and 10 LMGs)

1 (mot) Light Supply Column (3 LMGs) (replaced by mot supply company with 1 LMG)

2nd Battalion

1 Battalion Staff and (mot) Battalion Staff Battery (4 LMGs)

3 (mot) Nebelwerfer Batteries (6 210mm launchers and 6 LMGs ea)

1 (mot) Light Supply Column (3 LMGs) (replaced by mot supply company with 1 LMG)

3rd Battalion

same as 1st Battalion

71st Nebelwerfer Regiment

1 Regimental Staff and (mot) Regimental Staff Battery (4 LMGs)

1st Battalion

1 Battalion Staff and (mot) Battalion Staff Battery (4 LMGs)

3 (mot) Nebelwerfer Batteries (6 150mm launchers and 6 LMGs ea)

1 (mot) Light Supply Column (3 LMGs) (replaced by mot supply company with 1 LMG)

2nd Battalion

1 Battalion Staff and (mot) Battalion Staff Battery (4 LMGs)

3 (mot) Nebelwerfer Batteries (6 150mm launchers and 6 LMGs ea)

1 (half-track) Battery (8 150mm launchers and 10 LMGs)

1 (mot) Light Supply Column (3 LMGs) (replaced by mot supply company with 1 LMG)

3rd Battalion

1 Battalion Staff and (mot) Battalion Staff Battery (4 LMGs)

3 (mot) Nebelwerfer Batteries (6 210mm launchers and 6 LMGs ea)

1 (mot) Light Supply Column (3 LMGs) (replaced by mot supply company with 1 LMG)

Note: Batteries reduced numbers of LMGs from six to two sometime during the year.

6th Nebelwerfer Brigade
Brigade Staff

1 Brigade Staff (1 LMG)

1 (mot) "J" Platoon (2 LMGs) (added 5 Oct. 1944)

81st Nebelwerfer Regiment

1 Regimental Staff and (mot) Regimental Staff Battery (4 LMGs)

1st Battalion

1 Battalion Staff and (mot) Battalion Staff Battery (4 LMGs)

3 (mot) Nebelwerfer Batteries (6 150mm launchers and 6 LMGs ea)

1 (half-track) Battery (8 150mm launchers and 10 LMGs)

1 (mot) Light Supply Column (3 LMGs) (replaced by mot supply company with 1 LMG)

2nd Battalion

same as 1st Battalion, including half-track battery

3rd Battalion

1 Battalion Staff and (mot) Battalion Staff Battery (4 LMGs)

3 (mot) Nebelwerfer Batteries (6 210mm launchers and 6 LMGs ea)

1 (mot) Light Supply Column (3 LMGs) (replaced by mot supply company with 1 LMG)

82nd Nebelwerfer Regiment

1 Regimental Staff and (mot) Regimental Staff Battery (4 LMGs)

1st Battalion

1 Battalion Staff and (mot) Battalion Staff Battery (4 LMGs)

3 (mot) Nebelwerfer Batteries (6 150mm launchers and 6 LMGs ea)

1 (half-track) Battery (8 150mm launchers and 10 LMGs; deleted sometime during the year)

1 (mot) Light Supply Column (3 LMGs) (replaced by mot supply company with 1 LMG)

2nd Battalion

1 Battalion Staff and (mot) Battalion Staff Battery (4 LMGs)

3 (mot) Nebelwerfer Batteries (6 150mm launchers and 6 LMGs ea)

1 (half-track) Battery (8 150mm launchers and 10 LMGs)

1 (mot) Light Supply Column (3 LMGs) (replaced by mot supply company with 1 LMG)

3rd Battalion

1 Battalion Staff and (mot) Battalion Staff Battery (4 LMGs)

3 (mot) Nebelwerfer Batteries (6 300mm launchers and 6 LMGs ea)

1 (mot) Light Supply Column (3 LMGs) (replaced by mot supply company with 1 LMG)

9th Volks-Werfer Brigade (designated "Volks" on 5 Oct. 1944)
Brigade Staff

1 Brigade Staff (1 LMG)

1 (mot) "J" Platoon (2 LMGs) (added 5 Oct. 1944)

14th Heavy Nebelwerfer Regiment

1 Regimental Staff and (mot) Regimental Staff Battery (4 LMGs)

1st Battalion

1 Battalion Staff and (mot) Battalion Staff Battery (4 LMGs)

3 (mot) Nebelwerfer Batteries (6 210mm launchers and 6 LMGs ea)

1 (mot) Light Supply Column (3 LMGs) (replaced by mot supply company with 1 LMG)

2nd Battalion

same as 1st Battalion

3rd Battalion

1 Battalion Staff and (mot) Battalion Staff Battery (4 LMGs)

3 (mot) Nebelwerfer Batteries (6 300mm launchers and 6 LMGs ea)

1 (half-track) Battery (8 150mm launchers and 10 LMGs)

1 (mot) Light Supply Column (3 LMGs) (replaced by mot supply company with 1 LMG)

54th Nebelwerfer Regiment

1 Regimental Staff and (mot) Regimental Staff Battery (4 LMGs)

1st Battalion

1 Battalion Staff and (mot) Battalion Staff Battery (4 LMGs)

3 (mot) Nebelwerfer Batteries (6 150mm launchers and 6 LMGs ea)

1 (half-track) Battery (8 150mm launchers and 10 LMGs)

1 (mot) Light Supply Column (3 LMGs) (replaced by mot supply company with 1 LMG)

2nd Battalion
- 1 Battalion Staff and (mot) Battalion Staff Battery (4 LMGs)
- 3 (mot) Nebelwerfer Batteries (6 150mm launchers and 6 LMGs ea)
- 1 (half-track) Battery (8 150mm launchers and 10 LMGs) (deleted sometime during the year)
- 1 (mot) Light Supply Column (3 LMGs) (replaced by mot supply company with 1 LMG)

3rd Battalion
- 1 Battalion Staff and (mot) Battalion Staff Battery (4 LMGs)
- 3 (mot) Nebelwerfer Batteries (6 210mm launchers and 6 LMGs ea)
- 1 (mot) Light Supply Column (3 LMGs) (replaced by mot supply company with 1 LMG)

Note: Batteries reduced numbers of LMGs from six to two sometime during the year.

15th Volks-Werfer Brigade (established on 5 Oct. 1944)
Brigade Staff
- 1 Brigade Staff (1 LMG)
- 1 (mot) "J" Platoon (1 LMG)

55th Nebelwerfer Regiment
- 1 Regimental Staff and (mot) Regimental Staff Battery (2 LMGs)

1st Battalion
- 1 Battalion Staff and (mot) Battalion Staff Battery (1 LMG)
- 3 (mot) Nebelwerfer Batteries (6 210mm launchers and 2 LMGs ea)
- 1 (mot) Light Supply Column (3 LMGs) (replaced by mot supply company with 1 LMG)

2nd Battalion
- 1 Battalion Staff and (mot) Battalion Staff Battery (1 LMG)
- 3 (mot) Nebelwerfer Batteries (6 210mm launchers and 2 LMGs ea)
- 1 (mot) Supply Company (1 LMG)

3rd Battalion
same as 1st Battalion

85th Nebelwerfer Regiment
- 1 Regimental Staff and (mot) Regimental Staff Battery (1 LMG)

1st Battalion
- 1 Battalion Staff and (mot) Battalion Staff Battery (1 LMG)
- 3 (mot) Nebelwerfer Batteries (6 150mm launchers and 2 LMGs ea)
- 1 (mot) Supply Company (1 LMG)

2nd Battalion
same as 1st Battalion

3rd Battalion
- 1 Battalion Staff and (mot) Battalion Staff Battery (1 LMG)
- 3 (mot) Nebelwerfer Batteries (6 300mm launchers and 2 LMGs ea)
- 1 (mot) Supply Company (1 LMG)

16th Volks-Werfer Brigade (established on 22 Oct. 1944)
Brigade Staff
- 1 Brigade Staff (1 LMG)
- 1 (mot) "J" Platoon (1 LMG)

86th Nebelwerfer Regiment
- 1 Regimental Staff and (mot) Regimental Staff Battery (2 LMGs)

1st Battalion
- 1 Battalion Staff and (mot) Battalion Staff Battery (1 LMG)
- 3 (mot) Nebelwerfer Batteries (6 210mm launchers and 2 LMGs ea)
- 1 (mot) Light Supply Column (3 LMGs) (replaced by mot supply company with 1 LMG)

2nd Battalion
same as 1st Battalion

3rd Battalion
- 1 Battalion Staff and (mot) Battalion Staff Battery (1 LMG)
- 3 (mot) Nebelwerfer Batteries (6 210mm launchers and 2 LMGs ea)
- 1 (mot) Supply Company (1 LMG)

87th Nebelwerfer Regiment
- 1 Regimental Staff and (mot) Regimental Staff Battery (1 LMG)

1st Battalion
- 1 Battalion Staff and (mot) Battalion Staff Battery (1 LMG)
- 3 (mot) Nebelwerfer Batteries (6 150mm launchers and 2 LMGs ea)
- 1 (mot) Supply Company (1 LMG)

2nd Battalion
same as 1st Battalion

3rd Battalion
- 1 Battalion Staff and (mot) Battalion Staff Battery (1 LMG)
- 3 (mot) Nebelwerfer Batteries (6 300mm launchers and 2 LMGs ea)
- 1 (mot) Supply Company (1 LMG)

17th Volks-Werfer Brigade (established on 7 Nov. 1944)
Brigade Staff
- 1 Brigade Staff (1 LMG)
- 1 (mot) "J" Platoon (2 LMGs)

88th Nebelwerfer Regiment
- 1 Regimental Staff and (mot) Regimental Staff Battery (2 LMGs)

1st Battalion

1 Battalion Staff and (mot) Battalion Staff Battery (1 LMG)

3 (mot) Nebelwerfer Batteries (6 210mm launchers and 2 LMGs ea)

1 (mot) Light Supply Column (3 LMGs) (replaced by mot supply company with 1 LMG)

2nd Battalion

same as 1st Battalion

3rd Battalion

1 Battalion Staff and (mot) Battalion Staff Battery (1 LMG)

3 (mot) Nebelwerfer Batteries (6 210mm launchers and 2 LMGs ea)

1 (mot) Supply Company (1 LMG)

89th Nebelwerfer Regiment

1 Regimental Staff and (mot) Regimental Staff Battery (2 LMGs)

1st Battalion

1 Battalion Staff and (mot) Battalion Staff Battery (1 LMG)

3 (mot) Nebelwerfer Batteries (6 150mm launchers and 2 LMGs ea)

1 (mot) Supply Company (1 LMG)

2nd Battalion

same as 1st Battalion

3rd Battalion

1 Battalion Staff and (mot) Battalion Staff Battery (1 LMG)

3 (mot) Nebelwerfer Batteries (6 300mm launchers and 2 LMGs ea)

1 (mot) Supply Company (1 LMG)

18th Volks-Werfer Brigade (established on 4 Nov. 1944)

Brigade Staff

1 Brigade Staff (1 LMG)

1 (mot) "J" Platoon (2 LMGs)

21st Heavy Nebelwerfer Regiment

1 Regimental Staff and (mot) Regimental Staff Battery (3 LMGs)

1st Battalion

1 Battalion Staff and (mot) Battalion Staff Battery (1 LMG)

3 (mot) Nebelwerfer Batteries (6 210mm launchers and 2 LMGs ea)

1 (mot) Light Supply Column (3 LMGs) (replaced by mot supply company with 1 LMG)

2nd and 3rd Battalions, each with

1 Battalion Staff and (mot) Battalion Staff Battery (1 LMG)

3 (mot) Nebelwerfer Batteries (6 210mm launchers and 2 LMGs ea)

1 (mot) Supply Company (1 LMG)

22nd Heavy Nebelwerfer Regiment

1 Regimental Staff and (mot) Regimental Staff Battery (1 LMG)

1st Battalion

1 Battalion Staff and (mot) Battalion Staff Battery (1 LMG)

3 (mot) Nebelwerfer Batteries (6 150mm launchers and 2 LMGs ea)

1 (mot) Supply Company (1 LMG)

2nd Battalion

1 Battalion Staff and (mot) Battalion Staff Battery (1 LMG)

3 (mot) Nebelwerfer Batteries (6 300mm launchers and 2 LMGs ea)

1 (mot) Supply Company (1 LMG)

3rd Battalion

same as 2nd Battalion

19th Volks-Werfer Brigade (established on 10 Dec. 1944)

Brigade Staff

1 Brigade Staff (1 LMG)

1 (mot) "J" Platoon (2 LMGs)

23rd Heavy Nebelwerfer Regiment

1 Regimental Staff and (mot) Regimental Staff Battery (3 LMGs)

1st Battalion

1 Battalion Staff and (mot) Battalion Staff Battery (1 LMG)

3 (mot) Nebelwerfer Batteries (6 210mm launchers and 2 LMGs ea)

1 (mot) Light Supply Column (3 LMGs) (replaced by mot supply company with 1 LMG)

2nd Battalion

1 Battalion Staff and (mot) Battalion Staff Battery (1 LMG)

3 (mot) Nebelwerfer Batteries (6 210mm launchers and 2 LMGs ea)

1 (mot) Supply Company (1 LMG)

3rd Battalion

same as 3rd Battalion

24th Heavy Nebelwerfer Regiment

1 Regimental Staff and (mot) Regimental Staff Battery (1 LMG)

1st Battalion

1 Battalion Staff and (mot) Battalion Staff Battery (1 LMG)

3 (mot) Nebelwerfer Batteries (6 150mm launchers and 2 LMGs ea)

1 (mot) Supply Company (1 LMG)

2nd Battalion

1 Battalion Staff and (mot) Battalion Staff Battery (1 LMG)

3 (mot) Nebelwerfer Batteries (6 300mm launchers and 2 LMGs ea)

1 (mot) Supply Company (1 LMG)

3rd Battalion

same as 2nd Battalion

20th Volks-Werfer Brigade (established on 10 Dec. 1944)

Brigade Staff

1 Brigade Staff (1 LMG)

1 (mot) "J" Platoon (2 LMGs)

25th Heavy Nebelwerfer Regiment

1 Regimental Staff and (mot) Regimental Staff Battery (3 LMGs)

1st Battalion

1 Battalion Staff and (mot) Battalion Staff Battery (1 LMG)

3 (mot) Nebelwerfer Batteries (6 210mm launchers and 2 LMGs ea)

1 (mot) Light Supply Column (3 LMGs) (replaced by mot supply company with 1 LMG)

2nd Battalion

1 Battalion Staff and (mot) Battalion Staff Battery (1 LMG)

3 (mot) Nebelwerfer Batteries (6 210mm launchers and 2 LMGs ea)

1 (mot) Supply Company (1 LMG)

3rd Battalion

same as 3rd Battalion

26th Heavy Nebelwerfer Regiment

1 Regimental Staff and (mot) Regimental Staff Battery (1 LMG)

1st Battalion

1 Battalion Staff and (mot) Battalion Staff Battery (1 LMG)

3 (mot) Nebelwerfer Batteries (6 150mm launchers and 2 LMGs ea)

1 (mot) Supply Company (1 LMG)

2nd Battalion

1 Battalion Staff and (mot) Battalion Staff Battery (1 LMG)

3 (mot) Nebelwerfer Batteries (6 300mm launchers and 2 LMGs ea)

1 (mot) Supply Company (1 LMG)

3rd Battalion

same as 2nd Battalion

In the following list the equipment shown is what was known to be present with the brigades during the Battle of the Bulge in December 1944:

1st Werfer Brigade

1st and 57th Werfer Regiments (equipment unknown)

2nd Werfer Brigade

3rd and 70th Werfer Regiments (equipment unknown)

3rd Werfer Brigade

15th and 52nd Werfer Regiments (equipment unknown)

4th (mot) Volks Werfer Brigade

51st and 53rd Werfer Regiments (72 150mm and 36 210mm werfer launchers)

5th Werfer Brigade

56th and 71st Werfer Regiments (equipment unknown)

6th Werfer Brigade

81st and 82nd Werfer Regiments (equipment unknown)

7th (mot) Volks Werfer Brigade

84th and 85th Werfer Regiments (72 150mm, 18 210mm and 18 300mm launchers)

8th (tmot) Volks Werfer Brigade

2nd and Lehr Werfer Regiment (70 150mm, 18 210mm and 26 300mm launchers)

9th (mot) Volks Werfer Brigade

14th and 54th Werfer Regiments (70 150mm and 54 210mm werfers)

15th (mot) Volks Werfer Brigade

55th and 85th Werfer Regiments (72 150mm, 18 21mm and 18 300mm launchers)

16th (tmot) Volks Werfer Brigade

86th and 87th Werfer Regiment (72 150mm, 18 210mm and 18 300mm launchers)

17th (tmot) Volks Werfer Brigade

88th and 89th Werfer Regiment (72 150mm, 18 210mm and 18 300mm launchers)

18th (tmot) Volks Werfer Brigade

21st and 22nd Werfer Regiment (70 150mm, 36 210mm and 18 300mm launchers)

19th Volks Werfer Brigade

23rd and 24th Werfer Regiments (equipment unknown)

20th Werfer Brigade

25th and 26th Werfer Regiments (equipment unknown)

The designation (tmot) means that the Brigade was partially motorized, which indicates that German industry was having problems providing the vehicles necessary to motorize these formations completely. It is also reasonable to assume that the missing numbers, 1st, 2nd, 3rd, 5th, 6th, and 10th–14th existed and were deployed elsewhere. The order of 9 January 1945 organized the motorized Werfer and Volks Werfer brigade as follows:

(mot) Werfer Brigade

(mot) Headquarters

(mot) Signals Company

(mot) Staff Battery

1st (mot) Regiment

2 (mot) Battalions, each with:

3 (mot) 150mm Nebelwerfer Batteries (6 launchers and 2 LMGs ea)

1 (mot) Light Rocket Supply Column

1 (mot) Battalion

3 (mot) 210mm Nebelwerfer Batteries (6 launchers and 2 LMGs ea)

1 (mot) Light Rocket Supply Column

2nd (mot) Regiment
2 (mot) Battalions, each with:
   3 (mot) 150mm Nebelwerfer Batteries (6 launchers and 2 LMGs ea)
1 (mot) Battalion
   3 (mot) 300mm Nebelwerfer Batteries (6 launchers and 2 LMGs ea)
1 (mot) Light Rocket Supply Column

The order of 9 January 1945 organized the (tmot) Werfer and Volks Werfer brigade as follows:

Werfer Brigade
Headquarters
Signals Platoon

1st Regiment
2 Battalions, each with:
   3 150mm Nebelwerfer Batteries (6 launchers and 2 LMGs ea)
   1 Light Rocket Supply Column
1 Battalion
   3 210mm Nebelwerfer Batteries (6 launchers and 2 LMGs ea)
   1 Light Rocket Supply Column

2nd Regiment
2 Battalions, each with
   3 150mm Nebelwerfer Batteries (6 launchers and 2 LMGs ea)

1 Battalion
   3 300mm Nebelwerfer Batteries (6 launchers and 2 LMGs ea)
   1 Light Rocket Supply Column

In addition, the order of 9 January 1945 established the 300th Position Nebelwerfer Brigade with two regiments. Each regiment had two 150mm battalions and a 300mm battalion, organized as above. Records for 1 January 1945 show the following Werfer Brigades as being operational:

7th, 8th, 9th, 15th, 16th, 17th, 18th, and 19th (tmot) Volks Werfer Brigades
1st, 2nd, 3rd, 4th, 5th, and 6th (mot) Werfer Brigades

As the war began collapsing on Germany the nebelwerfer units began vanishing. On 20 April 1945 the 17th and 19th (tmot) Volks Nebelwerfer Brigades were disbanded. The 19th (tmot) Volks Nebelwerfer Regiment, with two battalions, was formed from the remains of the 17th and 19th Brigades. On 26 April 1945 the 20th Volks Nebelwerfer Brigade was disbanded and its troops absorbed into the 18th Volks Nebelwerfer Brigade. On 24 April 1945 the 4th Volks Nebelwerfer Brigade was re-formed. It contained a brigade staff, two regimental staffs, six battalion staffs, 15 150mm batteries, one 210mm battery, one self-propelled battery, and six supply batteries.

17

Luftwaffe Flak Corps, Divisions and Brigades (Defense of Germany)

I Flak Corps

Established on 28 October 1939 from the Staff/LGKDO III. It was a component of Luftflotte 3 and was assigned to provide anti-aircraft protection for Panzergruppe Kleist during the 1940 campaign. It contained:

I Flak Brigade
  102nd Flak Regiment
    1/18th Flak Regiment
    1/, 2/38th Flak Regiment
    91st Light Flak Battalion
  103rd Flak Regiment
    1/, 4/General Göring Flak Regiment
    1/7th Flak Regiment
    2/43rd Flak Regiment
101st Luftnachrichten (Signals) Battalion
I Corps Supply Commander
Aviation Liaison Squadron

II Flak Brigade
  101st Flak Regiment
    1/12th Flak Regiment
    1/22nd Flak Regiment
    1/51st Flak Regiment
    85th Light Flak Battalion
    3/General Göring Flak Regiment
  104th Flak Regiment
    1/8th Flak Regiment
    2/11th Flak Regiment
    3/9th Flak Regiment
    75th Light Flak Battalion
    3/General Göring Flak Regiment

In addition, under its temporary tactical control were 2 (Light)/L Flak Regiment, 1/36th Flak Regiment, and the 71st, 83rd and 92nd Light Flak Battalions.

II Flak Corps

Established on 1 October 1939 from the Staff/6th Flieger Division. It was a component of Luftflotte 2 and was assigned to provide anti-aircraft protection for the 4th Army (von Kluge) and the 6th Army (von Reichnau) during the 1940 campaign. It contained:

III Flak Brigade
  6th Flak Regiment
    1/, 2/441st Flak Regiment
    741st Light Flak Battalion
    841st Light Flak Battalion
  103rd Flak Regiment
    2 (Light)/General Göring Regiment
  202nd Flak Regiment
    1/23rd Flak Regiment
    1/37th Flak Regiment
    1/61st Flak Regiment
    1/8th Flak Regiment
    74th Light Battalion
102nd (mot) Luftnachrichten (Signals) Battalion

201st Flak Regiment
  1/6th Flak Regiment
  2/26th Flak Regiment
  1/64th Flak Regiment
  73rd Light Flak Battalion
II Corps Supply Command
Aviation Liaison Squadron

III Flak Corps

Formed on 22 February 1944 in France under Luftflotte 3 from the Staff/11th (mot) Flak Division. It was to work with Panzergruppe West against the anticipated Allied invasion. It consisted of:

1st Flak Sturm Regiment (formed from 431st Flak Regiment)
2nd Flak Sturm Regiment (formed from 653rd Flak Regiment)
3rd Flak Sturm Regiment (formed from 37th Flak Regiment)
4th Flak Sturm Regiment (formed from 79th Flak Regiment)
103rd Luftnachrichten (Signals) Battalion

The regiments were trained in mobile warfare and ground combat, then deployed along the English Channel. The 1st Regiment was stationed in Normandy during the invasion and the corps was destroyed in the Falais Pocket. What survived was reorganized and deployed by Cochem in September 1944 as the command staff for the 1st, 18th, 19th and 210th Flak Brigades in the Army Group B Area. In February 1945 the III Flak Corps was stationed by Bonn. At that time it contained:

1st Flak Brigade (by Rheydt; 15th Army)
2nd Flak Division (by Altenahr; 5th Panzer Army)
19th Flak Brigade (by Kyllburg; 7th Army)

The corps was destroyed in the Ruhr pocket. It had served under Luftflotte 3 until September 1944, when it had been transferred to Luftwaffen Kommando West.

IV Flak Corps

Ordered formed in June 1944 in Breslau (Luftflotte 1), but its formation was not executed. It was ordered formed again in September 1944 in the west, deploying in Edenkoben, south of Weiner-Neustadt as part of Army Group G, which was stationed from the Moselle to the Swiss border. It contained:

9th Flak Division (by Landstuhl; 1st Army)
13th Flak Division (by Schlettstadt; 19th Army, later Todtnau/Schwartzwald)

104th (mot) Luftnachrichten Battalion

In January 1945 the 28th Flak Division was added, deploying in the Herrenalb/Schwartzwald (Luftgau V), as were the 21st Flak Division in Darmstädt (Luftgau XIV) and, in March 1945, the the 26th Flak Division in Munich (Luftgau VII).

V Flak Corps

Formed on 15 November 1944 from the staff of the General of Flak Artillery by Luftwaffen Kommando Südost for the southern wing of the Eastern Front (Army Groups E and Süd). It contained:

19th Flak Division (Croatia; Army Group E)
20th Flak Division (by Fünfkirchen; Army Group Fretter-Pico, German 6th Army and 3rd Hungarian Army)
15th Flak Division (by Debreczen; Army Group Wöhler, German 8th Army and 1st Hungarian Army)

Initially the corps was stationed east of Budapest and after December 1944 it was by Pressburg. On 31 March 1945, after being transferred to Wiener Neustadt, the corps was assigned the Flak of Luftgau XVII, which included the 24th Flak Division in Vienna and the 7th Flak Brigade in Linz. It was transferred to St Pölten on 2 April 1945, then to Traun on 13 April. The Corps was taken prisoner on 7 May 1945 near Admont. The VI Flak Corps served under Luftflotte 4, which was redesignated Luftwaffen Kommando IV and assigned to Luftflotte 6 on 21 April 1945.

VI Flak Corps

Formed on 10 February 1945 on the northern flank of the Western Front from the disbanded 16th Flak Division. It contained:

9th Flak Brigade (in Huister Heide; 25th Army)
18th Flak Brigade (in Winkel near Geldern; 1st Fall-schirm Army)
4th Flak Division (by Duisburg)

During the course of the corps' withdrawal from the Rhine to Hamburg, the 8th Flak Division in Bremen and the 3rd Flak Division in Hamburg came under the command of the VI Flak Corps.

Flak Corps z.b.V.

Formed in April 1945 from the staff of the disbanded Luftgau Kommando VI and deployed in northern Germany. It composition is unknown.

1st Flak Division

Formed on 1 September 1941 from the Air Defense Command Berlin. On 1 November 1943 it consisted of:

22nd Flak Regiment
126th Heavy Flak Battalion
211th Heavy Flak Battalion
307th Heavy Flak Battalion
362nd Heavy Flak Battalion
513th Heavy Flak Battalion
979th Light Flak Battalion
53rd Flak Regiment
154th Heavy Flak Battalion
422nd Heavy Flak Battalion
516th Heavy Flak Battalion
855th Light Flak Battalion
126th Flak Regiment
224th Heavy Flak Battalion
437th Heavy Flak Battalion
662nd Heavy Flak Battalion
722nd Light Flak Battalion
104th Barrage Balloon Battalion
172nd Flak Regiment
123rd Heavy Flak Battalion
326th Heavy Flak Battalion
605th Heavy Flak Battalion
733rd Light Flak Battalion
416th Temporary Heavy Railroad Flak Battalion
473rd Temporary Heavy Railroad Flak Battalion
525th Temporary Heavy Railroad Flak Battalion
902nd Temporary Heavy Railroad Flak Battalion
82nd Searchlight Regiment
128th Searchlight Battalion
148th Searchlight Battalion

239th Searchlight Battalion
339th Searchlight Battalion
370th Searchlight Battalion
448th Searchlight Battalion
528th Searchlight Battalion
808th Searchlight Battalion

On 1 March 1944 the division contained:

22nd Flak Regiment
126th Heavy Flak Battalion
211th Heavy Flak Battalion
307th Heavy Flak Battalion
362nd Heavy Flak Battalion
979th Light Flak Battalion
53rd Flak Regiment
154th Heavy Flak Battalion
422nd Heavy Flak Battalion
513th Heavy Flak Battalion
855th Light Flak Battalion
126th Flak Regiment
173rd Heavy Flak Battalion
224th Heavy Flak Battalion
437th Heavy Flak Battalion
662nd Heavy Flak Battalion
722nd Light Flak Battalion
172nd Flak Regiment
123rd (T) Heavy Flak Battalion
326th Heavy Flak Battalion
605th Heavy Flak Battalion
733rd Light Flak Battalion
525th Temporary Heavy Railroad Flak Bn
121st Luftnachrichten Battalion

On 25 August 1944 the staff of the 172st Flak Regiment became the staff of the 6th Flak Brigade in Stettin and was not replaced. During the collapse of the German forces in France a large portion of the staffs and several battalions were "bmot" (*Behelfsmässig motoriziert*, or temporarily motorized) and sent to the Western Front. Most of the batteries remained and some new units were assigned. On 1 December 1944 the 1st Flak Division had:

22nd Flak Regiment
  126th Heavy Flak Battalion
  211th Heavy Flak Battalion
  362nd Heavy Flak Battalion (without staff)
  979th Light Flak Battalion
  1/III Heimat Flak Battalion
126th Flak Regiment
  23rd (T) Heavy Flak Battalion
  224th Heavy Flak Battalion (without staff)
  326th Heavy Flak Battalion
  733rd Light Flak Battalion
53rd Flak Regiment
  154th Heavy Flak Battalion (without staff)
  422nd Heavy Flak Battalion
  605th Light Flak Battalion (without staff)
  4/III Heimat Flak Battalion
82nd Searchlight Regiment
  128th Searchlight Battalion
  148th Searchlight Battalion
  370th Searchlight Battalion
  448th Searchlight Battalion
  528th Searchlight Battalion
  808th Searchlight Battalion
121st Luftnachrichten Battalion

2nd Flak Division

Formed on 1 September 1941 as the command for the Flak defense of central Germany. It was sent into Russia with the invasion of that country and served with Army Group North, Luftflotte 1. Until September 1944 it served near Leningrad. In September 1944 part of the division went to the west and became part of the III Flak Corps. It fought in the defense of Cologne and in the Eifel with the 6th SS Panzer Army. Its known strength was as follows:

Date	Heavy btrys	Medium/light btrys
8 Nov. 1944	20	21
8 Jan. 1945	18	17
8 Feb. 1945	33	38
23 Feb. 1945	19	24

On 1 March 1944 the division contained:

22nd Flak Regiment
  215th Mixed Flak Battalion
  219th Mixed Flak Battalion
  361st Mixed Flak Battalion
  385th Mixed Flak Battalion
  517th Mixed Flak Battalion
  535th Heavy Railroad Flak Battalion
164th Flak Regiment
  341st Mixed Flak Battalion
  214th Mixed Flak Battalion
  431st Mixed Flak Battalion
  834th Mixed Flak Battalion
  2/6th (mixed) Flak Regiment
  1/51st (mixed) Flak Regiment
  1/54th (mixed) Flak Regiment
  92nd Light Flak Battalion
  766th Light Flak Battalion
136th Flak Regiment
  720th Light Flak Battalion
  867th Light Flak Railroad Battalion
  618th Searchlight Battalion
  208th Barrage Balloon Battalion
182nd Flak Regiment
  1/2nd (mixed) Flak Regiment
  2/14th (mixed) Flak Regiment
  2/23rd (mixed) Flak Regiment
  2/32nd (mixed) Flak Regiment
  1/, 3/36th (mixed) Flak Regiment
  1/111th (mixed) Flak Regiment
  617th Mixed Flak Battalion
  75th Light Flak Battalion
  719th Light Flak Battalion
  833rd Light Flak Battalion
122nd Luftnachrichten Battalion

3rd Flak Division

Formed on 1 September 1941 from the 3rd Air Defense Command in Greater Hamburg. On 1 November 1943 it consisted of:

16th Flak Regiment
  601st Heavy Flak Battalion
  602nd Heavy Flak Battalion
  607th Heavy Flak Battalion
  762nd Light Flak Battalion
  205th Barrage Balloon Battalion
51st Flak Regiment
  225th Heavy Flak Battalion
  267th Heavy Flak Battalion
  414th Heavy Flak Battalion
  613th Heavy Flak Battalion
  876th Light Flak Battalion
  201st Barrage Balloon Battalion
60th Flak Regiment
  162nd Heavy Flak Battalion
  674th Heavy Flak Battalion
  208th Barrage Balloon Battalion
161st Searchlight Regiment
  119th Searchlight Battalion
  150th Searchlight Battalion
  368th Searchlight Battalion
  530th Searchlight Battalion
  608th Searchlight Battalion
123rd Luftnachrichten Battalion

On 1 March 1944 the 610st Searchlight Battalion was added to the 161st Searchlight Regiment. Other changes are not known. Later in 1944 the independent Flak Group Mecklenburg was formed in Lübeck (61st Flak Regiment, later 66th) and assigned to the division. During the Allied breakthrough in France the division detached a number of staffs and batteries as "tmot" (*teilweise motorisiert*, or partially motorized) and assigned them to the Luftwaffe Command West (formerly Luftflotte 3). On 1 December 1944 the division had:

16th Flak Regiment
  137th Heavy Flak Battalion (staff only)
  162nd Heavy Flak Battalion
  607th Heavy Flak Battalion
  762nd Light Flak Battalion
51st Flak Regiment
  225th Heavy Flak Battalion
  267th Heavy Flak Battalion
  414th Tower Flak Battalion (1st Company with 16th Regiment and 2nd with 51st Regiment)
60th Flak Regiment
  674th Heavy Flak Battalion
  144th Heavy Railroad Flak Battalion (new)
66th Flak Regiment
  755th Light Flak Battalion
  770th Light Flak Battalion
  916th Light Flak Battalion
  210th Barrage Balloon Battalion
161st Searchlight Regiment
  119th Searchlight Battalion
  150th Searchlight Battalion
  368th Searchlight Battalion
  608th Searchlight Battalion
123rd Luftnachrichten Battalion

4th Flak Division

Formed on 1 September 1941 from the 4th Air Defense Command, Düsseldorf. On 1 November 1943 it contained:

24th Flak Regiment
  151st Heavy Flak Battalion
  177th Heavy Flak Battalion
  244th Heavy Flak Battalion
  383rd Heavy Flak Battalion
  403rd Heavy Flak Battalion
  404th Heavy Flak Battalion
  407th Heavy Flak Battalion
  471st Heavy Flak Battalion
  890th Light Flak Battalion
46th Flak Regiment
  366th Heavy Flak Battalion
  382nd Heavy Flak Battalion
  445th Heavy Flak Battalion
  471st Heavy Flak Battalion
  627th Heavy Flak Battalion
  643rd Heavy Flak Battalion
  881st Light Flak Battalion
  882nd Light Flak Battalion
  248th Searchlight Battalion
  450th Searchlight Battalion
  103rd Barrage Balloon Battalion
74th Searchlight Regiment
  248th Searchlight Battalion
  250th Searchlight Battalion
  409th Searchlight Battalion
  450th Searchlight Battalion
  478th Searchlight Battalion
  518th Searchlight Battalion

581st Searchlight Battalion
648th Searchlight Battalion
650th Searchlight Battalion
124th Luftnachrichten Battalion
44th Flak Regiment
  134th Heavy Flak Battalion
  321st Heavy Flak Battalion
  353rd Heavy Flak Battalion
  462nd Heavy Flak Battalion
  642nd Heavy Flak Battalion
  718th Light Flak Battalion
  748th Light Flak Battalion
  826th Light Flak Battalion
64th Flak Regiment
  305th Heavy Flak Battalion
  394th Heavy Flak Battalion
  401st Heavy Flak Battalion
  447th Heavy Flak Battalion
  472nd Heavy Flak Battalion
  623rd Heavy Flak Battalion
  703rd Heavy Flak Battalion
  838th Light Flak Battalion
  883rd Light Flak Battalion
  884th Light Flak Battalion
  106th Barrage Balloon Battalion

On 1 March 1944 the following changes occurred:

24th Regiment added 474th Heavy Flak Battalion
44th Regiment unchanged
46th Regiment now consisted of:
  366th Heavy Flak Battalion
  382nd Heavy Flak Battalion
  445th Heavy Flak Battalion
  471st Heavy Flak Battalion
  627th Heavy Flak Battalion
  643rd Heavy Flak Battalion
  881st Light Flak Battalion
  882nd Light Flak Battalion
64th Regiment unchanged
74th Searchlight Regiment
  248th Searchlight Battalion
  250th Searchlight Battalion
  478th Searchlight Battalion
  518th Searchlight Battalion
  581st Searchlight Battalion
  648th Searchlight Battalion
  650th Searchlight Battalion

During the summer of 1944 several battalions were detached. On 1 December 1944 the division had:

24th Regiment
  151st Heavy Flak Battalion
  177th Heavy Flak Battalion

  244th Heavy Flak Battalion
  394th Heavy Flak Battalion
  404th Heavy Flak Battalion
  407th Heavy Flak Battalion
  826th Light Flak Battalion
  890th Light Flak Battalion
  941st Light Flak Battalion
  471st Heavy Flak Battalion
64th Regiment
  243rd Heavy Flak Battalion (new)
  305th Heavy Flak Battalion
  366th Heavy Flak Battalion
  401st Heavy Flak Battalion
  447th Heavy Flak Battalion
  472nd Heavy Flak Battalion
  424th Heavy Flak Battalion
  446th Heavy Flak Battalion
  838th Light Flak Battalion (no staff)
  882nd Light Flak Battalion
  883rd Light Flak Battalion
  884th Light Flak Battalion
  106th Barrage Balloon Battalion
44th Regiment
  134th Heavy Flak Battalion (no staff)
  233rd Heavy Flak Battalion
  21st Heavy Flak Battalion
  353rd Heavy Flak Battalion
  462nd Heavy Flak Battalion
  718th Light Flak Battalion
46th Regiment
  382nd Heavy Flak Battalion
  445th Heavy Flak Battalion
  623rd Heavy Flak Battalion (no staff)
  643rd Heavy Flak Battalion
  881st Light Flak Battalion
74th Searchlight Regiment
  248th Searchlight Battalion
  250th Searchlight Battalion
  330th Searchlight Battalion
  478th Searchlight Battalion
  518th Searchlight Battalion
  581st Searchlight Battalion
  648th Searchlight Battalion
  650th Searchlight Battalion

On 1 December 1944 the 103rd Flak Regiment, in Duisberg, consisted of the 146th, 392nd (no staff), 393rd, and 413th (from Lübeck) Heavy Flak Battalions and the 933rd Light Flak Battalion.

5th Flak Division

Formed on 1 September 1941, it was assigned service in the Balkans and northern Italy. At the end of 1942 it was transferred to Rumania and defended Ploesti. In 1943 it was temporarily reassigned to Italy, but in 1944 it returned to Rumania. In June 1944, assisted by Rumanian and Bulgarian Flak, it was under the General Command of Luftwaffe Rumania, defending Bucharest and Ploesti. It was destroyed in August 1944 and the staff was withdrawn to Germany. In March 1944 it contained:

180th Flak Regiment
  183rd Mixed Flak Battalion
  904th Mixed Flak Battalion

166th Heavy Flak Battalion
186th Heavy Flak Battalion
412th Heavy Flak Battalion
622nd Heavy Flak Battalion
230th Searchlight Battalion
509th Searchlight Battalion
202nd Flak Regiment
  156th Mixed Flak Battalion
  118th Mixed Flak Battalion
  187th Mixed Flak Battalion
  913th Mixed Flak Battalion
125th Luftnachrichten Battalion

Date	Heavy btrys	Med/light btrys	Searchlight btrys	Barrage balloon btrys	Smoke companies
8 Jan. 1944	31	16	5	–	4
23 June 1944	34	16	7	–	–
23 July 1944	34	18	11	2	4
23 Aug. 1944	33	23	11	3	6

The division was re-established on 1 November 1944 in Meschede to command the V-1 formations in the West. It served under Luftgau XII, Luftflotte 4, and Korps z.b.V. It contained:

155th (w) Flak Regiment
255th (w) Flak Regiment
155th Luftnachrichten Battalion

6th Flak Division

Formed on 1 September 1941, and assigned to Belgium and northern France with Luftflotte 3. On 1 April 1942 it was sent to Russia. It ended the war in Courland. In March 1944 it contained:

41st Flak Regiment
  645th Mixed Flak Battalion
  843rd Light Flak Battalion
  218th Heavy Railroad Flak Battalion
151st Flak Regiment
  1 (mixed)/13th Flak Regiment

1 (mixed)/50th Flak Regiment
2 (mixed)/11th Flak Regiment
1 (mixed)/411th Flak Regiment
43rd Flak Regiment
  127th Mixed Flak Battalion
  1 (mixed)/291st Flak Regiment
  294th Mixed Flak Battalion
  753rd Light Flak Battalion
  994th Light Flak Battalion
  120th Searchlight Battalion
126th Luftnachrichten Battalion

7th Flak Division

Formed on 1 September 1941 from the 7th Air Defense Command and served in the Cologne area. On 1 November 1943 it contained:

14th Flak Regiment
  146th Heavy Flak Battalion (staff only)

381st Heavy Flak Battalion
666th Heavy Flak Battalion
749th Light Flak Battalion
47th Flak Regiment
  371st Heavy Flak Battalion
  512th Heavy Flak Battalion

101st Barrage Balloon Battalion
203rd Barrage Balloon Battalion (no staff)
84th Searchlight Regiment
    130th Searchlight Battalion
    159th Searchlight Battalion
    270th Searchlight Battalion
    330th Searchlight Battalion
    408th Searchlight Battalion
    438th Searchlight Battalion
    586th Searchlight Battalion
144th Flak Regiment
    135th Heavy Flak Battalion
    245th Heavy Flak Battalion
    331st Heavy Flak Battalion
    666th Heavy Flak Battalion
    784th Light Flak Battalion
    785th Light Flak Battalion
    423rd Temporary Heavy Railroad Flak Battalion
Regiment z.b.V.
    514th Heavy Flak Battalion
    889th Light Flak Battalion
120th Flak Regiment
    137th Heavy Flak Battalion
    389th Heavy Flak Battalion
    886th Light Flak Battalion
127th Luftnachrichten Battalion

On 1 March 1944 the division contained:

14th Flak Regiment
    381st Heavy Flak Battalion
    465th Heavy Flak Battalion
    749th Light Flak Battalion
47th Flak Regiment
    371st Heavy Flak Battalion
    512th Heavy Flak Battalion
    101st Barrage Balloon Battalion
120th Flak Regiment
    389th Heavy Flak Battalion
    886th Light Flak Battalion
    915th Light Flak Battalion (new)
514th Heavy Flak Battalion, with
    889th Light Flak Battalion
144th Flak Regiment
    135th Heavy Flak Battalion
    245th Heavy Flak Battalion
    331st Heavy Flak Battalion
    666th Heavy Flak Battalion
    784th Light Flak Battalion
    785th Light Flak Battalion
    84th Searchlight Regiment
    159th Searchlight Battalion
    270th Searchlight Battalion
    330th Searchlight Battalion
    408th Searchlight Battalion

    438th Searchlight Battalion
127th Luftnachrichten Battalion

During the summer of 1944 the Staff/47th Flak Regiment relieved the Staff/54th Searchlight Reigment (22nd Flak Division) as the Flak Group Münster. The Staff/120th Flak Regiment was reorganized as the staff for the Böhlen-Zeitz Flak Group of the 14th Flak Division. The remaining Flak battalions were concentrated under the staffs of the 14th and 144th Flak Regiments. The staff of the 84th Searchlight Regiment was replaced by that of the 113th Searchlight Regiment (newly formed) on 13 March 1944. On 1 December 1944 the 7th Flak Division contained:

14th Flak Regiment
    331st Heavy Flak Battalion
    371st Heavy Flak Battalion (no staff)
    381st Heavy Flak Battalion
    465th Heavy Flak Battalion
    512th Light Flak Battalion
    666th Heavy Flak Battalion (no staff)
    707th Heavy Flak Battalion (new; no staff)
    749th Light Flak Battalion
    886th Light Flak Battalion
    101st Barrage Balloon Battalion
    415th Temporary Heavy Railroad Flak Battalion
    902nd Temporary Heavy Railroad Flak Battalion
    821st Railroad Light Railroad Flak Battalion
144th Flak Regiment
    135th Heavy Flak Battalion
    222nd Heavy Flak Battalion
    245th Heavy Flak Battalion (no staff)
    784th Light Flak Battalion
    785th Light Flak Battalion (no staff)
    889th Light Flak Battalion
    915th Light Flak Battalion (new)
113th Searchlight Regiment (new)
    159th Searchlight Battalion
    270th Searchlight Battalion
    408th Searchlight Battalion
    438th Searchlight Battalion
127th Luftnachrichten Battalion

8th Flak Division

Formed on 1 September 1941 in the Bremen-Oberneuland region from the 8th Air Defense Command. On 1 November 1943 it contained:

13th Flak Regiment
  117th Heavy Flak Battalion
  262nd Heavy Flak Battalion
  542nd Heavy Flak Battalion
  606th Heavy Flak Battalion
  844th Light Flak Battalion
89th Flak Regiment
  185th Heavy Flak Battalion
  222nd Heavy Flak Battalion
  231st Heavy Flak Battalion
  611th Heavy Flak Battalion
  922nd Light Flak Battalion
  210th Barrage Balloon Battalion
26th Flak Regiment
  390th Heavy Flak Battalion
  531st Heavy Flak Battalion
  879th Light Flak Battalion
160th Searchlight Regiment
  138th Searchlight Battalion
  238th Searchlight Battalion
  268th Searchlight Battalion
  269th Searchlight Battalion
  498th Searchlight Battalion
128th Luftnachrichten Battalion

On 1 March 1944 the division contained:

13th Flak Regiment
  117th Heavy Flak Battalion
  262nd Heavy Flak Battalion
  606th Heavy Flak Battalion
  844th Light Flak Battalion
89th Flak Regiment
  222nd Heavy Flak Battalion
  231st Heavy Flak Battalion
  611th Heavy Flak Battalion
  922nd Light Flak Battalion

  210th Barrage Balloon Battalion
26th Flak Regiment
  390th Heavy Flak Battalion
  531st Heavy Flak Battalion
  542nd Heavy Flak Battalion
  879th Light Flak Battalion
160th Searchlight Regiment
  238th Searchlight Battalion
  268th Searchlight Battalion
  269th Searchlight Battalion
  498th Searchlight Battalion
128th Luftnachrichten Battalion

During the summer of 1944 the Staff/89th Flak Regiment was sent to Narbonne. At that time control of the 9th and 61st Flak Regiments, formerly of the 89th Flak Brigade, was passed to the 8th Flak Division. On 1 December 1944 the division contained:

9th Flak Regiment
  743rd Light Heavy Flak Battalion
  876th Light Flak Battalion
  942nd Light Flak Battalion
26th Flak Regiment
  390th Heavy Flak Battalion
  531st Heavy Flak Battalion
61st Flak Regiment
  879th Light Flak Battalion
  988th Light Flak Battalion
128th Luftnachrichten Battalion
13th Flak Regiment
  117th Heavy Flak Battalion
  262nd Heavy Flak Battalion
  606th Heavy Flak Battalion
  611th Heavy Flak Battalion
  922nd Light Flak Battalion
160th Searchlight Regiment
  238th Searchlight Battalion
  268th Searchlight Battalion
  269th Searchlight Battalion
  498th Searchlight Battalion

9th Flak Division

Formed on 1 September 1941. It served in Western France and later in Russia as part of the I Flak Corps. Most of the division was lost at Stalingrad. It was re-formed on 2 July 1943 and continued to serve in Russia until it withdrew into Germany at the end of the war. In July 1942 this division was motorized and serving in the field. It contained:

9th (mot) Flak Division (Oberst Pickert)
  129th Luftwaffe Signals Battalion
    1 Luftwaffe Telephone Company
    1 Luftwaffe Radio Company
    1 Luftwaffe Signals Supply Column
  1/111th (mot) Luftwaffe Field Hospital

91st Flak Regiment (Oberstleutnant Memmert)
1/9th Flak Regiment
  3 (mot) Batteries (4 88mm guns ea)
  1 (mot) Battery (9 37mm guns)
  1 (mot) Battery (12 20mm guns)
  2 (mot) 600mm Searchlight Batteries
1/12th Flak Regiment
  3 (mot) Batteries (4 88mm guns ea)
  2 (mot) Batteries (12 20mm guns)
77th Light Flak Battalion
  1 (mot) Battery (9 37mm guns)
  2 Self-Propelled Batteries (9 20mm and 3 quad 20mm guns ea)
  2 (mot) 600mm Searchlight Batteries

104th Flak Regiment (Oberstleutnant Schrader)
1/5th Flak Regiment
  3 (mot) Batteries (4 88mm guns ea)
  2 (mixed) (mot) Batteries
  6 (mot) 20mm guns
  6 (self-propelled) 20mm guns
  1 quad (self-propelled) 20mm guns
  2 quad (mot) 20mm guns
  2 (mot) 600mm Searchlight Batteries
1/7th Flak Regiment
  3 (mot) Batteries (4 88mm guns ea)
  1 (mot) Battery (12 20mm guns)
  1 (mot) Battery (9 20mm guns and 3 quad 20mm guns)
  2 (mot) 600mm Searchlight Batteries
3/FAS Flak Regiment
  1 (mot) Battery (9 37mm guns)
  1 (mixed) Battery
  3 (self-propelled) 20mm guns
  3 (mot) 20mm guns
  3 (mot) quad 20mm guns
  3 (mot) 37mm guns
3 (mixed) Batteries
6 (mot) 50mm guns
  3 (self-propelled) 50mm guns

D Supply Regiment (Oberstleutnand Paland)
1/III (mot) Supply Column Staff
  12/VII (mot) Transportation Column
  3/VI Supply Column
  4/VI Supply Column
  2/III (mot)(25t) Transportation Column
  10/IV (mot)(25t) Transportation Column
  10/VI (mot)(25t) Transportation Column
  2/VII (mot) Supply Column Staff
  2/VIII (mot) Transportation Column
  3/VIII (mot) Transportation Column
  5/VIII (mot) Transportation Column
  4/VII (mot)(25t) Transportation Column
  1/VIII (mot)(25t) Transportation Column
  3/VIII (mot)(25t) Transportation Column
  6/VIII (mot)(25t) Transportation Column

Heck (mot) Supply Column Staff
  37/XII Light (mixed mobility) Transport Column
  64/XII Heavy (mixed mobility) Transport Column
  65/XII Heavy (mixed mobility) Transport Column
1/XII (mot) Maintenance Column Staff
  1/III (mot) Maintenance Company
  1/VIII (mot) Maintenance Company
  1/III (mot) Flak Park
  2/XI (mot) Special Maintenance Detachment
  1/XII (mot) Vehicle Park
  1/XII (mot) Vehicle Detachment
  17/III (mot) (?) Detachment

At the end of 1942 it contained:

129th (mot) Luftnachrichten (Signals) Battalion
Staff/91st (mot) Flak Regiment
  1/9th Flak Regiment
  1/241st Flak Regiment
  77th Light Flak Battalion
  774th Light Flak Battalion
  62/VII Flak Transportation Battery
Staff/104th (mot) Flak Regiment
  1/12th Flak Regiment
  1/37th Flak Regiment
  91st Light Flak Battalion
  775th Light Flak Battalion
  38/XI Flak Transportation Battery
Staff/37th (mot) Flak Regiment
  1/8th Flak Regiment
  1/49th Flak Regiment
  3/FAS Flak Regiment
  851st Light Flak Battalion

In early 1943, as part of the 17th Army in the Kuban Bridgehead, it was reorganized and had:

129th (mot) Luftnachrichten (Signals) Battalion
Staff/27th Flak Regiment
  505th Flak Battalion (3 heavy and 2 light batteries)
  297th Flak Battalion (3 heavy and 2 light batteries)
  137th Flak Battalion (3 heavy batteries)
  181st Flak Battalion (4 heavy batteries)
  191st Flak Battalion (4 heavy batteries)
  257th Flak Battalion (4 heavy batteries)
  293rd Flak Battalion (4 heavy batteries)
  734th Light Flak Battalion (4 light batteries)
Staff/42nd Flak Regiment
  164th Flak Battalion (3 heavy and 2 light batteries)
  275th Army Flak Battalion (2 heavy and 1 light batteries)
  279th Army Flak Battalion (2 heavy and 1 light batteries)
  86th Light (sf) Flak Battalion (3 batteries)
  89th Light (sf) Flak Battalion (3 batteries)

1/4th Flak Regiment (4th and 5th Batteries)
3/735th Light Flak Battalion
12. (Fla)/30th Luftwaffe Jäger Battalion
Staff/77th Flak Regiment
  77th Flak Battalion (4 heavy batteries)
  541st Flak Battalion (4 heavy batteries)
  702nd Flak Battalion (4 heavy batteries)
  251st Flak Battalion (4 heavy batteries)
  739th Light Flak Battalion (4 light batteries)
Attached
  3/8th Searchlight Battalion
  3/43rd Searchlight Battalion
  3/321st Flak Battalion (105mm guns)
  1/Lehr Experimental Battalion FAS (128mm gun training battalion)
  4/850th Light Battalion
  2/728th Light Battalion
  Medical Company, 9th Flak Division
  4/II Vehicle Work Shop Platoon
  94/XII Heavy Flak Transportation Battery
  39/XIII Heavy Flak Transportation Battery
  92/VI Heavy Flak Transportation Battery
  125/VI Heavy Flak Transportation Battery

At the beginning of 1943 the Rostov Flak Battalion and 2/43rd Flak Regiment were formed and added to the division.

Date	Heavy btrys	Med/light btrys	Search-light btrys
End 1942	18	21–30	–
Feb. 1943	42	26	8
Army Flak	4	2	–

Oct. 43	28	27	8
9/23/44	28	40	–
10/23/44	33	55	–
11/23/44	36	55	–
12/21/44	28	39	–
1/23/45	32	36	–
2/23/45	30	37	–

In March 1944 the division was organized as follows:

77th Flak Regiment
  254th Mixed Flak Battalion
  373rd Heavy Flak Battalion
  713th Light Flak Battalion
133rd Flak Regiment
  1 (mixed)/33rd Flak Regiment
  96th Light Flak Battalion
  81st Light Flak Battalion
  982nd Light Flak Battalion
  620th Searchlight Battalion
99th Flak Regiment
  1 (mixed)/38th Flak Regiment
  2 (mixed)/38th Flak Regiment
153rd Flak Regiment
  1 (mixed)/7th Flak Regiment
  1 (mixed)/32nd Flak Regiment
  864th Light Railroad Flak Battalion
130th Luftnachrichten Battalion

10th Flak Division

Formed on 1 September 1941 for the defense of the Rumanian oil region and Ploesti. At the beginning of 1942 it was sent to southern Russia and became part of the I Flak Corps, Luftflotte 4. In July 1944 it was in Galicia, and later Silesia, lower Lausitz and Eastern Saxony.

Date	Heavy btrys	Med/light btrys	Search-light btrys
8 June 1944	29	36	4
23 July 1944	40	35	4
23 Aug. 1944	38	32	4
23 Sept. 1944	25	25	4
23 Oct. 1944	25	28	4
8 Feb. 1945	45	29	1 barrage balloon btry

11th Flak Division

Formed on 1 September 1941 from the 11th Air Defense Command II. Initially it was deployed in western France, then from January 1943 it served in southern France. It was fleshed out with Flak battalions from various Luftgau and on 1 December 1944 it had:

106th Flak Regiment
   380th Heavy Flak Battalion
   521st Heavy Flak Battalion
   658th Heavy Flak Battalion
   659th Heavy Flak Battalion
   108th Barrage Balloon Battalion (no staff)
54th Flak Regiment
   374th Heavy Flak Battalion
   383rd Heavy Flak Battalion
   903rd Heavy Flak Battalion

84th Searchlight Regiment
   189th Searchlight Battalion
   379th Searchlight Battalion
   578th Searchlight Battalion
150th Flak Regiment
   109th Heavy Flak Battalion
   570th Heavy Flak Battalion
   653rd Heavy Flak Battalion
   660th Heavy Flak Battalion
   890th Light Flak Battalion
107th Flak Regiment
   702nd Heavy Flak Battalion
   50/VIII Homeland Flak Battalion
   57/VIII Homeland Flak Battalion
   58/VIII Homeland Flak Battalion
131st Luftnachrichten Battalion

12th Flak Division

Formed in early 1942 from the IX Flak Brigade in the center of the Eastern Front, it served under the I and II Flak Corps. It operated solely on the Eastern Front, including the defense of East and West Prussia, under the 2nd Army near Graudenz, Marienburg, Jastrow and Stolp. It contained:

Date	Heavy btrys	Med/light btrys	Search-light btrys
8 June 1944	31	44	8
23 June 1944	33	42	8
23 July 1944	24	30 8	
23 Aug. 1944	6	10	–
23 Sept. 1944	20	22	–
23 Oct. 1944	17	27	–
8 Feb. 1945	50	21	4

In March 1944 the division contained:

10th Flak Brigade
21st Flak Regiment
   1 (mixed)/24th Flak Regiment
   1 (mixed)/26th Flak Regiment
   1 (mixed)/52nd Flak Regiment
   701st Mixed Flak Battalion
   85th Light Flak Battalion
34th Flak Regiment
   2 (light)/411th Flak Regiment
   303rd Mixed Flak Battalion
   853rd Light Flak Battalion
   260th Searchlight Battalion
134th Flak Regiment

1 (mixed)/3rd Flak Regiment
1 (mixed)/11th Flak Regiment
71st Light Flak Battalion
74th Light Flak Battalion
125th Flak Regiment
   783rd Light Flak Battalion
132nd Luftnachrichten Battalion

13th Flak Division

Formed on 1 February 1942 in Western France as part of Luftflotte 3. Part of the division defended Dieppe. At the beginning of December 1944 it was on the Franco-German frontier as part of IV Corps. It contained:

Date	Heavy btrys	Med/light btrys	Searchlight btrys	Barrage balloon btrys	Smoke companies
8 Aug. 1944	60	72	–	0	–
23 Sept. 1944	26	22	–	–	–
23 Oct. 1944	26	25	–	–	–
23 Nov. 1944	15	18	–	–	–
23 Dec. 1944	35	23	–	1	½
22 Jan 1945	37	26	–	1	½
23 Feb. 1945	34	30	–	5	½

In March 1944 the division contained:

15th Flak Regiment
  153rd Mixed Flak Battalion
  441st Mixed Flak Battalion
  596th Mixed Flak Battalion
  98th Light Flak Battalion
  752nd Light Flak Battalion
  852nd Light Flak Battalion
  912th Light Flak Battalion
  991st Light Flak Battalion
30th Flak Regiment
  152nd Mixed Flak Battalion
  24th Heavy Flak Battalion
  835th Light Flak Battalion
  931st Light Flak Battalion
  996th Light Flak Battalion
  298th Searchlight Battalion
133rd Luftnachrichten Battalion

59th Flak Regiment
  344th Light Flak Battalion
  442nd Light Flak Battalion
  683rd Light Flak Battalion
  496th Heavy Flak Battalion
  493rd Heavy Flak Battalion
  859th Light Railroad Flak Battalion
  911th Light Flak Battalion
  997th Light Flak Battalion
  207th Barrage Balloon Battalion
100th Flak Regiment
  193rd Mixed Flak Battalion
  672nd Mixed Flak Battalion
  196th Heavy Flak Battalion
  842nd Light Flak Battalion
  873rd Light Flak Battalion
  984th Light Flak Battalion
  31st Field Flak Artillery School

14th Flak Division

Formed in January 1942 by the relieving of the 2nd Flak Division in Leipzig. On 1 November 1943 it contained:

33rd Flak Regiment
  132nd Heavy Flak Battalion
  406th Heavy Flak Battalion
  433rd Heavy Flak Battalion
  761st Light Flak Battalion
  540th Heavy Flak Battalion
  202nd Barrage Balloon Battalion
140th Flak Regiment
  432nd Heavy Flak Battalion
  736th Light Flak Battalion
300th Flak Regiment
  323rd Heavy Flak Battalion

  568th Heavy Flak Battalion
  430th Temporary Heavy Railroad Flak Battalion
  821st Railroad Light Flak Battalion
73rd Searchlight Regiment
  178th Searchlight Battalion
  199th Searchlight Battalion
  258th Searchlight Battalion
  350th Searchlight Battalion
  500th Searchlight Battalion
  510th Searchlight Battalion

On 1 March 1944 the division contained:

33rd Flak Regiment
  132nd Heavy Flak Battalion

406th Heavy Flak Battalion
433rd Heavy Flak Battalion
540th Heavy Flak Battalion
761st Light Flak Battalion
202nd Barrage Balloon Battalion
300th Flak Regiment
  121st Heavy Flak Battalion
  174th Heavy Flak Battalion
  323rd Heavy Flak Battalion
  568th Heavy Flak Battalion
  729th Light Flak Battalion
  430th Heavy Railroad Flak Battalion
140th Flak Regiment
  432nd Heavy Flak Battalion
  736th Light Flak Battalion
  821st E Light Flak Battalion
73rd Searchlight Regiment
  178th Searchlight Battalion
  199th Searchlight Battalion
  258th Searchlight Battalion
  500th Searchlight Battalion
  510th Searchlight Battalion
134th Luftnachrichten Battalion

During the summer of 1944 the 300th Flak Regiment was redesignated the 90th Flak Regiment, and the 33rd Regiment moved to Central Germany and joined the 21st Flak Brigade. The 120th Flak Regiment was sent to the 14th Flak Division in return. On 1 December 1944 the division contained:

90th Flak Regiment
  121st Heavy Flak Battalion
  568th Heavy Flak Battalion
  729th Light Flak Battalion
  43/IV Homeland Flak Battalion
120th Flak Regiment
  307th Heavy Flak Battalion
  323rd Heavy Flak Battalion
  357th Heavy Flak Battalion
  662nd Heavy Flak Battalion
  525th Heavy Railroad Flak Battalion
  80/XIII Homeland Flak Battalion
140th Flak Regiment
  432nd Heavy Flak Battalion
  722nd Light Flak Battalion
  728th Light Flak Battalion
  664th Barrage Balloon Battalion
  19th Searchlight Replacement and Training Battalion
73rd Searchlight Regiment
  199th Searchlight Battalion
  258th Searchlight Battalion
  328th Searchlight Battalion
  367th Searchlight Battalion
  500th Searchlight Battalion
  510th Searchlight Battalion
134th Luftnachrichten Battalion

15th Flak Division

Formed on 1 March 1942 near Ploesti, Rumania. It operated in southern Russia with Luftflotte 4. The 2nd Flak Division relieved the 15th Flak Division, which was then transferred to Mariupol, in southern Russia, in May 1942, where it supported Army Group A. It then withdrew into Hungary.

Date	Heavy btrys	Med/light btrys	Searchlight btrys	Barrage balloon btrys
23 June 1944	29	27	4	2
23 July 1944	38	32	–	2
23 Aug. 1944	39	34	–	–
23 Oct. 1944	27	28	–	–

In March 1944 the division contained:

7th Flak Regiment
  1 (mixed)/19th Flak Regiment
  1/, 2/I Flak Artillery School
104th Flak Regiment
  181st Heavy Flak Battalion
  91st Light Flak Battalion
  52nd Searchlight Battalion

135th Luftnachrichten Battalion
4th Flak Regiment
  2 (mixed)/24th Flak Regiment
  2 (mixed)/46th Flak Regiment
  147th Mixed Flak Battalion
  236th Mixed Flak Battalion
  77th Light Flak Battalion
  774th Light Flak Battalion

THE GERMAN ORDER OF BATTLE

16th Flak Division

Formed on 1 March 1942, it was assigned to Belgium and northern France as part of Luftflotte 3. In October 1944 it contained the 1st, 18th, and 19th Flak Brigades as well as the 20th Flak Brigade z.b.V. It was engaged at Nijmegen and Arnhem. In February 1945 the division command formed the General Command VI Flak Corps. The Flak Brigade z.b.V. also became the 9th Flak Brigade.

Date	Heavy btrys	Med/light btrys	Notes
9 Sept. 1944	15	7	inc. 5 heavy alarm batteries
23 Sept. 1944	22	49	
23 Nov. 1944	24	38	inc. 1 heavy alarm battery
21 Dec. 1944	26	25	inc. 1 heavy alarm battery
22 Jan. 1945	9	18	inc. 1 heavy alarm battery
6 Feb. 1945	49	66	inc. 7 heavy and 3 light batteries of army Flak

In March 1944 the division contained:

37th Flak Regiment
  2 (mixed)/22nd Flak Regiment
  2 (mixed)/64th Flak Regiment
  141st Mixed Flak Battalion
  242nd Heavy Flak Battalion
  84th Light Flak Battalion
  716th Light Flak Battalion
  978th Light Flak Battalion
  730th Light Railroad Flak Battalion
132nd Flak Regiment
  253rd Mixed Flak Battalion
  266th Mixed Flak Battalion
  501st Mixed Flak Battalion

136th Luftnachrichten Battalion
531st Flak Regiment
  1 (mixed)/20th Flak Regiment
  1 (mixed)/53rd Flak Regiment
  671st Heavy Flak Battalion
  732nd Light Flak Battalion
  773rd Light Flak Battalion
  744th Light Flak Battalion
129th Flak Regiment
  2 (mixed)/52nd Flak Regiment
  252nd Mixed Flak Battalion
  295th Mixed Flak Battalion
  415th Light Flak Battalion
  765th Light Flak Battalion

17th Flak Division

Formed on 1 May 1942 in Russia by the I Flak Corps, Luftflotte 4. In April/May 1942 it was around Stalino. In 1943–44 it covered the withdrawal from the Ukraine as part of I Flak Corps. In March 1944 the division contained:

12th Flak Regiment
  2 (mixed)/251st Flak Regiment
  251st Heavy Flak Battalion
  775th Light Flak Battalion
48th Flak Regiment
  1 (mixed)/25th Flak Regiment

  2 (mixed)/43rd Flak Regiment
  1 (mixed)/61st Flak Regiment
  1 (mixed)/231st Flak Regiment
  375th Mixed Flak Battalion
  541st Heavy Flak Battalion
  724th Light Flak Battalion
137th Luftnachrichten Battalion
17th Flak Regiment
  1 (mixed)/4th Flak Regiment
  1 (mixed)/5th Flak Regiment
  861st Light Flak Battalion

Date	Heavy btrys	Med/light btrys	Notes
8 June 1944	28	31	inc. 4 light alarm batteries
23 July 1944	14	23	inc. 3 searchlight batteries

32 Aug. 1944	27	29	
23 Sept. 1944	37	30	inc. 5 heavy and 1 light alarm/homeland Flak btry
23 Oct. 1944	25	24	inc. 3 heavy and 1 light alarm batteries
8 Feb. 1945	44	22	

18th Flak Division

Formed around 10 April 1942, this was a special force organized in the east. In 1943 it was serving under Luftflotte 6 and operating with Army Group Center. In 1942 it fought in the central sector of the Russian front. In November 1943 it was under the newly formed II Flak Corps. During its campaigning in 1942–43 it contained:

138th Luftnachrichten Battalion
With 2nd and 4th Army
   21st Flak Regiment
   34th Flak Regiment
   101st Flak Regiment
With 3rd Pz Army and 9th Army
   6th Flak Regiment
   10th Flak Regiment
   125th Flak Regiment
   133rd Flak Regiment

In May 1942 the 21st, 34th, and 101st Flak Regiments were detached to the 12th (mot) Flak Division, which operated with the 2nd and 4th Armies. The 18th Flak Division served with the 3rd Panzer Army and the 9th Army. In July/August 1942 the 15th and 125th Flak Regiments fought in the vicinity of Rshev. In August/September 1942, while with the 9th Corps by Rshev, the 10th Flak Regiment destroyed 105 Russian tanks. In March 1943 it fought around Smolensk, Rshev and Wjasma. The 6th, 10th and 125th Flak Regiments were pulled back. The 133rd Flak Regiment was sent to the 12th Flak Division. After Kursk the division was reorganized:

138th Luftnachrichten (Signals) Battalion
6th Flank Regiment – Smolensk Flak Group
10th Flank Regiment – to 3rd Panzer Army

On 12 August 1943 the 35th Flak Regiment was returned from the 12th Flak Division. The 6th and 35th Flak Regiments continued fighting around Smolensk. On 3 November 1943 the division was assigned to the newly organized II Flak Corps. The 6th Flak Regiment was assigned to the 10th Flak Brigade. In February 1944 the Staff/10th Flak Brigade was assigned to the 12th Flak Division. The 6th, 10th, 34th, 35th Flak Regiments remained with the Division during the second winter battle around Vitebsk. On 1 October 1944 the division contained the 6th, 34th and 125th Flak Regiments.

Date	Heavy btrys	Med/light btrys	Search-light btrys
8 June 1944	26	34	4
23 June 1944	36	31	4
23 July 1944	9	10	–
23 Aug. 1944	34	23	–
23 Sept. 1944	37	30	7
23 Oct. 1944	55	39	7
8 Feb. 1945	51	36	7

In March 1944 the division contained:

58th Flak Regiment
   2 (mixed)/12th Flak Regiment
   1 (mixed)/23rd Flak Regiment
   131st Heavy Flak Battalion
   286th Heavy Flak Battalion
   806th Heavy Flak Battalion
   73rd Light Flak Battalion
   777th Light Flak Battalion
91st Flak Regiment
   271st Heavy Flak Battalion
   397th Heavy Flak Battalion
   706th Heavy Flak Battalion
   829th Light Flak Battalion
201st Flak Regiment
   2 (mixed)/25th Flak Regiment
   1 (mixed)/28th Flak Regiment
   143rd Heavy Flak Battalion
   804th Heavy Flak Battalion
   754th Light Flak Battalion
   891st Light Flak Battalion
   449th Searchlight Battalion

19th Flak Division

Formed in June/July 1942 with part of the VII Flak Brigade, which was then serving in Sicily. It served in northern Africa and Tunisia during the end of the African campaign under Rommel in late 1942 and early 1943. It was assigned to Luftflotte 2. It was captured in Tunis in May 1943. Its organization is not known.

The 19th Flak Division was re-formed on 1 November 1943 and was assigned to the defense of Greece. In 1944 it was part of the V Flak Corps in Yugoslavia. It contained:

Date	Heavy btrys	Med/light btrys	Searchlight btrys	Notes
9 Sept. 1943	71	34	3	
23 June 1944	39	23	3	
+ Crete	17	10	–	
23 July 1944	57	36	3	inc. Crete
23 Aug. 1944	57	36	–	inc. Crete
23 Sept. 1944	52	35	–	inc. Crete
23 Oct. 1944	42	34	–	exc. Crete

20th Flak Division

Formed in November 1942. It served at the Straits of Messina and in Sicily during the end of the African campaign in late 1942 and early 1943. It went into Tunisia, where it was captured in May 1943. In January 1943 the following units were assigned:

1/154th Flak Regiment (5 btrys)
2/154th Flak Regiment (5 btrys)
750th Flak Battalion (2 btrys)
243rd Flak Battalion (2 btrys)
277th Flak Battalion (4 btrys)
403rd Flak Battalion (2 btrys)
372nd Flak Battalion (4 btrys)
511th Flak Battalion (3 btrys)
503rd Flak Battalion (4 btrys)
644th Flak Battalion (4 btrys)
5/364th Flak Battalion (1 btry)
15/192nd Flak Battalion (1 btry)
3/452nd Flak Battalion (1 btry)
1/304th Flak Battalion (1 btry)
2/12th Flak Battalion (1 btry)
78th Flak Regiment (7 btrys)
3/932nd Flak Battalion (1 btry)
3/856th Flak Battalion (1 btry)
140th Observation Battalion

While at the Straits of Messina, in January 1943, the 20th Flak Division contained the following units and equipment:

Division Headquarters
Headquarters (mot) Battery (3 20mm guns)

1/154th Flak Regiment
(mot) Signals Platoon (3 LMGs)
1st (mot) Battery (1 88mm and 2 20mm)
2nd (mot) Battery (2 88mm)
3rd (mot) Battery (3 88mm)
4th (mot) Battery (4 88mm, 3 20mm and 5 LMGs)
5th (mot) Battery (4 88mm, 4 20mm and 3 LMGs)
Kol 1/54th (mot) Battery (4 20mm)

2/154th Flak Regiment
(mot) Signals Platoon (3 LMGs)
6th (mot) Battery (4 88mm, 3 20mm and 4 LMGs)
7th (mot) Battery (3 88mm, 1 20mm and 5 LMGs)
8th (mot) Battery (4 88mm, 3 20mm and 4 LMGs)
9th (mot) Battery (3 20mm)
10th (mot) Battery (4 88mm, 3 20mm and 4 LMGs)
Kol 2/52nd (mot) Battery (2 20mm and 4 LMGs)

750th Flak Battalion
3rd Battery (6 20mm)
4th Battery (12 20mm, 6 HMGs and 2 LMGs)

243rd Flak Battalion
3rd Battery (4 88mm and 2 20mm)
4th Battery (4 88mm and 2 20mm)

277th Flak Battalion
1st Battery (4 88mm, 2 20mm and 2 LMGs)
2nd Battery (4 88mm, 2 20mm and 2 LMGs)
4th Battery (12 20mm and 2 LMGs)
6th Battery (15 20mm, 4 HMGs and 2 LMGs)

403rd Flak Battalion
1st Battery (4 88mm, 2 20mm and 2 LMGs)
4th Battery (4 88mm and 3 20mm)

372nd Flak Battalion
1st Battery (2 20mm)

2nd Battery (4 88mm, 2 20mm and 2 LMGs)
3rd Battery (4 88mm, 9 20mm and 2 LMGs)
4th Battery (4 88mm, 3 20mm and 2 LMGs)

511th Flak Battalion
Battery (5 88mm, 2 20mm and 2 LMGs)
Battery (4 88mm, 2 20mm and 4 LMGs)
Battery (4 88mm, 2 20mm and 3 LMGs)

503rd Flak Battalion
Battery (4 88mm)
Battery (4 88mm, 2 20mm and 2 LMGs)
Battery (4 88mm, 2 20mm and 2 LMGs)
Battery (4 88mm and 2 LMGs)

644th Flak Battalion
1st Battery (4 88mm, 2 20mm and 2 LMGs)
2nd Battery (4 88mm, 2 20mm and 2 LMGs)
3rd Battery (4 88mm, 2 20mm and 2 LMGs)
4th Battery (4 88mm and 2 LMGs)

Miscellaneous
5/364th Flak Battalion (12 20mm and 2 LMGs)
15/192nd Flak Battalion (3 20mm)
3/452nd Flak Battalion (4 88mm, 3 20mm and 2 LMGs)
1/304th Flak Battalion (4 88mm, 2 20mm and 2 LMGs)

2/12th Flak Battalion (4 88mm, 2 20mm and 2 LMGs)
78th Flak Regiment
Battery (6 quad 20mm)
Battery (5 quad 20mm)
Battery (5 quad 20mm)
Battery (10 20mm)
Battery (2 20mm)
Eis Afrika Battery (4 20mm)
Mountain Flak Battery (12 20mm and 2 LMGs)
3/932nd Flak Battalion (2 20mm, 3 HMGs and 6 LMGs)
3/856th Flak Battalion (13 20mm, 4 HMGs and 1 LMG)

140th Observation Battalion
1 (mot) Signals Company
1 (airborne) Radio Company (2 LMGs)
1 (airborne) Company (2 LMGs)

The 20th Flak Division was re-formed on 1 October 1943 by Luftflotte 4 and served in the defense of Greece, Albania and Croatia. In the fall 1944 it withdrew into Hungary. It contained:

Date	Heavy btrys	Med/light btrys	Searchlight btrys	Barrage balloon btrys
23 June 1944	51	29	2	1
23 July 1944	51	29	2	1
23 Aug. 1944	45	31	–	1
Bulgarian Flak	17	1	–	– assigned to division
23 Sept. 1944	42	27	–	1
Flak Group Albania	17	2	–	– German units
23 Oct. 1944	34	27	–	1

Between June and the beginning of September one heavy and four to six light/medium Alarm Flak Batteries were added to the division.

21st Flak Division

Formed in June 1943 in Darmstadt from VI Brigade for the defense of the Rhine-Main region. On 1 November 1943 it contained:

29th Flak Regiment
25th Heavy Flak Battalion
291st Heavy Flak Battalion
396th Heavy Flak Battalion
435th Heavy Flak Battalion
715th Light Flak Battalion
49th Flak Regiment
491st Heavy Flak Battalion
492nd Heavy Flak Battalion

636th Heavy Flak Battalion
701st Heavy Flak Battalion
776th Light Flak Battalion
977th Light Flak Battalion
980th Light Flak Battalion
107th Barrage Balloon Battalion
169th Flak Regiment
631st Light Flak Battalion
903rd Heavy Flak Battalion
976th Light Flak Battalion
189th Flak Regiment
322nd Heavy Flak Battalion
637th Heavy Flak Battalion

856th Light Flak Battalion
971st Light Flak Battalion
70th Searchlight Regiment
  8 Searchlight Batteries z.b.V.
109th Searchlight Regiment
  300th Searchlight Battalion
  499th Searchlight Battalion
  908th Searchlight Battalion
119th Searchlight Regiment
  129th Searchlight Battalion
  299th Searchlight Battalion
  399th Searchlight Battalion
  519th Searchlight Battalion
139th Searchlight Regiment
  348th Searchlight Battalion
  349th Searchlight Battalion
141st Luftnachrichten Battalion

On 1 March 1944 the division's organization was relatively unchanged, and consisted of:

29th Flak Regiment
  225th Heavy Flak Battalion
  291st Heavy Flak Battalion
  396th Heavy Flak Battalion
  435th Heavy Flak Battalion
  681st Heavy Flak Battalion
  715th Light Flak Battalion
  987th Light Flak Battalion
49th Flak Regiment
  491st Heavy Flak Battalion
  492nd Heavy Flak Battalion
  636th Heavy Flak Battalion
  701st Heavy Flak Battalion
  776th Light Flak Battalion
  977th Light Flak Battalion
  980th Light Flak Battalion
169th Flak Regiment
  631st Light Flak Battalion
  903rd Heavy Flak Battalion
  976th Light Flak Battalion
Regiment z.b.V. Lothringen
  758th Light Flak Battalion
  857th Light Flak Battalion
  973rd Light Flak Battalion
189th Flak Regiment
  322nd Heavy Flak Battalion
  637th Heavy Flak Battalion
  856th Light Flak Battalion
  971st Light Flak Battalion
70th Searchlight Regiment
  3 Searchlight Batteries z.b.V.
  200th Searchlight Battery
109th Searchlight Regiment
  300th Searchlight Battalion

  499th Searchlight Battalion
  908th Searchlight Battalion
119th Searchlight Regiment
  129th Searchlight Battalion
  299th Searchlight Battalion
  399th Searchlight Battalion
  519th Searchlight Battalion
139th Searchlight Regiment
  348th Searchlight Battalion
  349th Searchlight Battalion
141st Luftnachrichten Battalion

On 1 April 1944 the XII Luftgau in Weisbaden was disbanded. The 21st Flak Division was then transferred to VII Luftgau (München). However, on 6 September 1944 the XIV Luftgau was formed in Weisbaden and the division went back. The 169th Flak Regiment in Saarbrücken and the Regiment z.b.V. Lothringen were transferred to the Western Air Defense Command (9th Division, IV Flak Corps) at about the same time. The 179th Flak Regiment (Würzburg Flak Group) was transferred to the 21st Flak Division from the 21st Flak Brigade. On 1 December 1944 the division had:

29th Flak Regiment
  225th Heavy Flak Battalion
  291st Heavy Flak Battalion
  396th Heavy Flak Battalion
  435th Heavy Flak Battalion (no staff)
  681st Heavy Flak Battalion (no staff)
  715th Light Flak Battalion
  857th Light Flak Battalion (no staff)
  987th Light Flak Battalion
179th Flak Regiment
  451st Light Flak Battalion
  482nd Heavy Flak Battalion
  639th Heavy Flak Battalion
  953rd Light Flak Battalion
  708th Searchlight Battalion
189th Flak Regiment
  322nd Heavy Flak Battalion
  637th Heavy Flak Battalion
  Staff/640th Heavy Flak Battalion
  715th Light Flak Battalion
  856th Light Flak Battalion
  971st Light Flak Battalion (no staff)
  107th Barrage Balloon Battalion
  227th Heavy Railroad Flak Battalion
  430th Heavy Railroad Flak Battalion
  444th Heavy Railroad Flak Battalion
  535th Heavy Railroad Flak Battalion
  536th Heavy Railroad Flak Battalion
49th Flak Regiment
  491st Mixed Flak Battalion
  492nd Heavy Flak Battalion

636th Heavy Flak Battalion
701st Heavy Flak Battalion
776th Light Flak Battalion
418th Temporary Railroad Flak Battalion
423rd Temporary Railroad Flak Battalion
109th Searchlight Regiment
   200th Searchlight Battalion (no staff)
   300th Searchlight Battalion
   499th Searchlight Battalion
   519th Searchlight Battalion (no staff)
119th Searchlight Regiment

129th Searchlight Battalion
299th Searchlight Battalion
348th Searchlight Battalion
399th Searchlight Battalion (no staff)
141st Luftnachrichten Battalion

The numbers of batteries assigned on 25 February 1945 were as follows: heavy—92; medium and light—22; search-light—29; barrage balloon—2½; and smoke companies—2½.

22nd Flak Division

Formed in April 1943 in Dortmund for the eastern part of the VI Luftgau. On 1 November 1943 it contained:

54th Flak Searchlight Regiment
   324th Heavy Flak Battalion
   443rd Heavy Flak Battalion
   625th Heavy Flak Battalion
   737th Light Flak Battalion
   747th Light Flak Battalion
   943rd Light Flak Battalion
   989th Light Flak Battalion
   329th Searchlight Battalion
   358th Searchlight Battalion
67th Flak Regiment
   133rd Heavy Flak Battalion
   301st Heavy Flak Battalion
   463rd Heavy Flak Battalion
   524th Heavy Flak Battalion
   839th Light Flak Battalion
   887th Light Flak Battalion
103rd Flak Regiment
   112th Heavy Flak Battalion
   351st Heavy Flak Battalion
   392nd Heavy Flak Battalion
   393rd Heavy Flak Battalion
   635th Heavy Flak Battalion
   933rd Light Flak Battalion
   941st (?) Light Flak Battalion
   986th Light Flak Battalion
   328th Searchlight Battalion
   367th Searchlight Battalion
   64th Heavy Replacement Battalion
124th Flak Regiment
   146th Heavy Flak Battalion (staff only)
   221st Heavy Flak Battalion
   333rd Heavy Flak Battalion
   446th Heavy Flak Battalion
   477th Heavy Flak Battalion
   745th Light Flak Battalion

   840th Light Flak Battalion
   209th Barrage Balloon Battalion
146th Searchlight Regiment
   158th Searchlight Battalion
   170th Searchlight Battalion
   229th Searchlight Battalion
   230th Searchlight Battalion
   479th Searchlight Battalion
142nd Luftnachrichten Battalion

During the winter of 1943/44 the 54th Flak Searchlight Regiment was redesignated the 54th Flak Regiment. On 1 March 1944 the division contained:

54th Flak Regiment
   324th Heavy Flak Battalion
   443rd Heavy Flak Battalion
   625th Heavy Flak Battalion
   703rd Light Flak Battalion
   737th Heavy Flak Battalion
   747th Light Flak Battalion
   943rd Light Flak Battalion
   989th Light Flak Battalion
103rd Flak Regiment
   112th Heavy Flak Battalion
   146th Heavy Flak Battalion (new)
   351st Heavy Flak Battalion
   392nd Heavy Flak Battalion
   393rd Heavy Flak Battalion
   635th Heavy Flak Battalion
   933rd Light Flak Battalion
   986th Light Flak Battalion
   328th Searchlight Battalion
   367th Searchlight Battalion
142nd Luftnachrichten Battalion
124th Flak Regiment
   221st Heavy Flak Battalion
   333rd Heavy Flak Battalion
   446th Heavy Flak Battalion

477th Heavy Flak Battalion
745th Light Flak Battalion
840th Light Flak Battalion
209th Barrage Balloon Battalion
67th Flak Regiment
133rd Heavy Flak Battalion
301st Heavy Flak Battalion
463rd Heavy Flak Battalion
524th Heavy Flak Battalion
839th Light Flak Battalion
887th Light Flak Battalion
146th Searchlight Regiment
158th Searchlight Battalion
170th Searchlight Battalion
230th Searchlight Battalion
329th Searchlight Battalion (new)
479th Searchlight Battalion

The staff of the 54th Flak Regiment was replaced in July with the staff of the 47th Flak Regiment, 7th Flak Division. The 103rd Regiment was detached from the 22nd Division and on 1 December 1944 it was made part of the 4th Flak Division. On that date the division had:

47th Flak Regiment
323rd Heavy Flak Battalion
324th Heavy Flak Battalion (no staff)
443rd Heavy Flak Battalion
747th Light Flak Battalion
839th (bmot) Light Flak Battalion
943rd Light Flak Battalion
989th Light Flak Battalion
209th Barrage Balloon Battalion
473rd Temporary Railroad Flak Battalion

67th Flak Regiment
273rd Heavy Flak Battalion
301st Heavy Flak Battalion
Staff/402nd Heavy Flak Battalion
463rd Heavy Flak Battalion
524th Heavy Flak Battalion
887th Light Flak Battalion
277th Temporary Light Railroad Flak Battalion
142nd Luftnachrichten Battalion
124th Flak Regiment
221st Heavy Flak Battalion
333rd Heavy Flak Battalion
466th Heavy Flak Battalion (no staff)
477th Heavy Flak Battalion
740th Light Flak Battalion
840th Light Flak Battalion
96th Heavy Replacement Flak Battalion
125th Temporary Railroad Flak Battalion
146th Searchlight Regiment
158th Searchlight Battalion
170th Searchlight Battalion
230th Searchlight Battalion
329th Searchlight Battalion (new)
479th Searchlight Battalion
183rd Flak Regiment
313th Heavy Flak Battalion
737th Light Flak Battalion
892nd Light Flak Battalion
943rd Light Flak Battalion
263rd Heavy Railroad Flak Battalion

The 103rd Flak Regiment no longer was part of the division, but reported directly to the Luftgau.

23rd Flak Division

Formed on 10 October 1943 in the central portion of the Eastern Front from the staff of the 22nd Luftwaffe Field Division and placed under the II Flak Corps. It guarded the rear areas of Army Group Center.

Date	Heavy btrys	Med/light btrys	Searchlight btrys	Barrage balloon btrys
8 June 1944	38	29	4	–
23 June 1944	39	30	4	–
23 July 1944	12	15	5	–
23 Aug. 1944	25	23	–	–
23 Sept. 1944	21	29	–	–
23 Oct. 1944	13	16	–	–
8 Feb. 1945	49	10	–	1

In March 1944 the division contained:

23rd Flak Regiment
  1 (mixed)/8th Flak Regiment
  2nd and 3rd Btrys, 78th Light Flak Battalion
31st Flak Regiment
  235th Mixed Flak Battalion
  494th Mixed Flak Battalion
  802nd Mixed Flak Battalion
  767th Light Flak Battalion

866th Light Railroad Flak Battalion
585th Searchlight Flak Battalion
101st Flak Regiment
  83rd Light 661st Heavy Flak Battalion
  769th Light Flak Battalion
  954th Light Flak Battalion
  995th Light Flak Battalion
  585th Searchlight Battalion
143rd Luftnachrichten Company

24th Flak Division

Formed in December 1943 by redesignating the 16th Flak Brigade. On 1 March 1944 it contained:

28th Flak Regiment
  288th Mixed Flak Battalion
  223rd Heavy Flak Battalion
  532nd Heavy Flak Battalion
  533rd Heavy Flak Battalion
  807th Light Flak Battalion
  145th z. Zt. Railroad Flak Bn
  423rd z. Zt. Railroad Flak Bn
6th Searchlight Regiment
  140th Searchlight Battalion
  338th Searchlight Battalion
  398th Searchlight Battalion
  400th Searchlight Battalion
  529th Searchlight Battalion
  560th Searchlight Battalion
  582nd Searchlight Battalion
76th Flak Regiment
  282nd Heavy Flak Battalion
  336th Heavy Flak Battalion
  516th Heavy Flak Battalion
  615th Heavy Flak Battalion
  644th Heavy Flak Battalion
  803rd Heavy Flak Battalion
  751st Light Flak Battalion
184th Flak Regiment
  285th Heavy Flak Battalion
  289th Heavy Flak Battalion
  189th Searchlight Battalion
  810th Searchlight Battalion
88th Flak Regiment
  284th Heavy Flak Battalion
  290th Heavy Flak Battalion
  543rd Temporary Railroad Flak Battalion
98th Flak Regiment
  288th Heavy Flak Battalion
102nd Flak Regiment
  numbered batteries

536th Temporary Heavy Railroad Flak Battalion
1st Flak Searchlight Regiment
  141st Heavy Flak Battalion
  246th Heavy Flak Battalion
  342nd Heavy Flak Battalion
  372nd Heavy Flak Battalion
  388th Heavy Flak Battalion
  503rd Heavy Flak Battalion
  805th Heavy Flak Battalion
  837th Light Flak Battalion
  188th Searchlight Battalion
  909th Searchlight Battalion
  418th Temporary Flak Battalion
  429th Temporary Flak Battalion
144th Luftnachrichten Detachment

On 1 April 1944 part of the division was detached to form the 7th Flak Brigade in Linz. The 24th Flak Division was then limited to the Vienna Regiments and the Bohemian Flak Group. On 1 December 1944 the division contained:

28th Flak Regiment
  184th Tower Flak Battalion (no staff)
  223rd Heavy Flak Battalion
  532nd Heavy Flak Battalion
  655th Mixed Flak Battalion
  12/XVII Homeland Flak Battalion
  25th Replacement Light Flak Battalion
98th Flak Regiment
  274th Heavy Flak Battalion
  288th Heavy Flak Battalion
  696th Heavy Flak Battalion (new)
  807th Mixed Flak Battalion
  92nd Heavy Replacement Flak Battalion
102nd Flak Regiment
  284th Mixed Flak Battalion
  290th Heavy Flak Battalion
6th Searchlight Regiment
  140th Searchlight Battalion

338th Searchlight Battalion
400th Searchlight Battalion
560th Searchlight Battalion
63rd Flak Regiment
  285th Heavy Flak Battalion
  289th Heavy Flak Battalion
  692nd Heavy Flak Battalion (new)

693rd Heavy Flak Battalion (new)
810th Searchlight Battalion

The 184th Flak Regiment (formerly Bohemian Flak Group) was made the staff of the 4th Dresden Flak Brigade.

25th Flak Division

Formed on 1 April 1944 by reorganizing the General of Flak Artillery South (formerly XVII Flak Brigade). It was deployed in upper Italy.

26th Flak Division

Formed on 1 May 1944 from the 4th Flak Brigade in Munich. After the disbanding of the 21st Flak Brigade in Nürnburg, the division was heavily reinforced. The 130th Flak Regiment, Innsbrück, was transferred to the V Luftgau and replaced by the Staff/148th Flak Regiment. During the summer the 2nd Searchlight Regiment (Augsburg) became the 115th Flak Regiment. On 1 December 1944 the division had:

19th Flak Regiment
  384th Heavy Flak Battalion
  457th Heavy Flak Battalion
  459th Heavy Flak Battalion
55th Flak Regiment
  571st Heavy Flak Battalion
148th Flak Regiment
  577th Heavy Flak Battalion
  768th Light Flak Battalion
  14/XIII Homeland Flak Battalion
93rd Flak Regiment
  484th Heavy Flak Battalion (no staff)
  522nd Heavy Flak Battalion
  634th Heavy Flak Battalion
  682nd Heavy Flak Battalion (new)

951st Light Flak Battalion
198th Searchlight Battalion
439th Searchlight Battalion
72/VII Homeland Flak Battalion
5th Replacement Searchlight Battalion
9th Replacement Flak Battalion
115th Flak Regiment
  453rd Heavy Flak Battalion
  136th Heavy Flak Battalion
  738th Light Flak Battalion
  200th Searchlight Battalion
  228th Searchlight Battalion
  582nd Searchlight Battalion
  15th Heavy Replacement Flak Battalion
8th Searchlight Regiment
  249th Searchlight Battalion
  309th Searchlight Battalion
  370th Searchlight Battalion
  508th Searchlight Battalion
  114th Temporary Railroad Searchlight Battalion
  278th Heavy Railroad Flak Battalion
146th Luftnachrichten Battalion

27th Flak Division

Formed in September 1944 in East Prussia from the Staff/11th Flak Brigade and the units of that brigade, plus some of those from the 15th Flak Brigade. It was assigned to Luftflotte 6. In February 1944 it was in south-east Prussia. The division detached its assigned units to the 18th Flak Division in February 1945 and then moved to assume command of new troops with the 11th Army on the front as part of Luftflotte 6. In September–October 1944 it was assigned the 10th Flak Brigade.

Date	Heavy btrys	Med/light btrys	Searchlight btrys	Smoke companies
23 Sept. 1944	71	19	12	1
8 Oct. 1944	103	28	12	1
23 Oct. 1944	94	25	13	1
8 Feb. 1945	28	2	–	–

These apparently include another 24–29 heavy and 5–8 light and medium Alarm and Homeland Flak Batteries.

28th Flak Division

Formed in October 1944 in Stuttgart from the 9th Flak Brigade. On 1 December 1944 it contained:

68th Flak Regiment
  234th Heavy Flak Battalion
  357th Heavy Flak Battalion (no staff)
  Staff/460th Heavy Flak Battalion
  705th Heavy Flak Battalion
  Staff/691st Light Flak Battalion
  721st Light Flak Battalion
  538th Temporary Heavy Railroad Flak Battalion
  543rd Temporary Heavy Railroad Flak Battalion

130th Flak Regiment
  506th Heavy Flak Battalion
  Staff/681st Heavy Flak Battalion
  71/VII Homeland Flak Battalion
139th Flak Regiment
  241st Heavy Flak Battalion
  436th Heavy Flak Battalion
  460th Heavy Flak Battalion (no staff)
  858th Light Flak Battalion
148th Luftnachrichten Battalion
Staff/69th (mot) Flak Regiment

29th Flak Division

Formed in early 1945 from the staff of the 14th Flak Brigade and the units of the 13th and 14th Flak Brigades then in Norway. It had four Flak regiments.

30th Flak Division

Formed in early 1945 with the staff and units of the 5th Flak Brigade (Railroad Troops), part of the Reich Luftflotte, and assigned to the defense of Berlin. It oversaw all light and medium ETr (railroad troops) Flak Units (50th and 159th Flak Regiments, with about 79 batteries) in the Reich.

I Flak Brigade

Formed on 1 June 19/40 as part of I Flak Corps. It remained in France until October 1940 then returned to Germany. It was disbanded in early 1941 and used to organize a new I Flak Corps.

1st Flak Brigade

Formed in April 1944 in central Germany and then used as the Flak command for Greater Paris and western France as part of Luftflotte 3. In September–October 1944 it was assigned to IV Flak Corps on the Eifel front.

Date	Heavy btrys	Med/light btrys	Searchlight btrys	Barrage balloon btrys
24 Aug. 1944	32	32	–	2
9 Sept. 1944	4	6	–	–
23 Sept. 1944	5	26	–	–
23 Oct. 1944	10	25	–	–
23 Nov. 1944	17	20	–	–
21 Dec. 1944	17	15	12	–
22 Jan. 1945	23	23	12	–
8 Feb. 1945	22	27	–	–
23 Feb. 1945	29	29	–	–

II Flak Brigade

Formed on 1 June 1940 as part of the I Flak Corps. In October 1940 it was around Berlin, and it was disbanded in April 1942.

2nd Flak Brigade

Formed between February and May 1944 in Dessau from part of the Magdeburg Flak Group (52nd Regiment). On 1 December 1944 it contained:

52nd Flak Regiment
  226th Heavy Flak Battalion
  495th Heavy Flak Battalion
  539th Heavy Flak Battalion
  827th Light Flak Battalion
143rd Flak Regiment
  174th Heavy Flak Battalion (staff only)

434th Heavy Flak Battalion
464th Heavy Flak Battalion
727th Light Flak Battalion
108th Searchlight Regiment
  179th Searchlight Battalion
  583rd Searchlight Battalion
  587th Searchlight Battalion
  709th Searchlight Battalion

III Flak Brigade

Formed in June 1940 as part of the II Flak Corps, it served in France and in October 1940 was returned to Germany for the defense of that country. In early 1942 it was used to form the 15th Flak Division.

3rd Flak Brigade

Deployed in January 1944 in upper Italy, near Milan, for air defense under the Commanding General of the German Luftwaffe in Italy, respectively General of Flak Artillery South, Luftflotte 2. From June to October 1944, in the region around Chiusi, near Bambina, Bologna, Prato, Modena and Bologna, it fought with Army Group South.

IV and 4th Flak Brigades

Formed on 1 June 1940 and moved to Munich on 29 September 1942. On 1 November 1943 it contained:

19th Flak Regiment
  457th Heavy Flak Battalion
  459th Heavy Flak Battalion
55th Flak Regiment
  384th Heavy Flak Battalion
  456th Heavy Flak Battalion
  571st Heavy Flak Battalion
  768th Light Flak Battalion
8th Searchlight Regiment
  249th Searchlight Battalion
  309th Searchlight Battalion
  470th Searchlight Battalion
  508th Searchlight Battalion
164th Luftnachrichten Battalion
2nd Searchlight Regiment
  136th Heavy Flak Battalion
  453rd Heavy Flak Battalion
  512th Heavy Flak Battalion
  738th Light Flak Battalion
  876th Light Flak Battalion
  228th Searchlight Battalion
  340th Searchlight Battalion
  825th Light Railroad Flak Battalion
Special Regiment Innsbruck
  577th Heavy Flak Battalion
  730th Temporary Light Railroad Flak Battalion

During the winter of 1943/44 the 130th Flak Regiment was organized out of the Regiment z.b.V. in Innsbrück. On 1 March 1944 the brigade had:

19th Flak Regiment
  405th Heavy Flak Battalion
  457th Heavy Flak Battalion
  459th Heavy Flak Battalion
55th Flak Regiment
  384th Heavy Flak Battalion
  456th Heavy Flak Battalion
  571st Heavy Flak Battalion
  768th Light Flak Battalion
8th Searchlight Regiment
  249th Searchlight Battalion
  309th Searchlight Battalion
  470th Searchlight Battalion
  508th Searchlight Battalion
2nd Searchlight Regiment
  136th Heavy Flak Battalion
  453rd Heavy Flak Battalion
  738th Light Flak Battalion
  228th Searchlight Battalion
  340th Searchlight Battalion
  578th Searchlight Battalion
  825th Temporary Light Railroad Flak Battalion
130th Flak Regiment
  506th Heavy Flak Battalion
  577th Heavy Flak Battalion

On 1 May 1944 the 4th Flak Brigade became the 26th Flak Division.

4th Flak Brigade

Formed in October 1944 in Dresden from the staff of the 184th Flak Regiment. On 12/1/44 it contained:

88th Flak Regiment
  153rd Heavy Flak Battalion
  336th Heavy Flak Battalion
  351st Heavy Flak Battalion
  405th Heavy Flak Battalion

279th Temporary Railroad Flak Battalion
138th Flak Regiment
  403rd Heavy Flak Battalion
  565th Heavy Flak Battalion
  880th Light Flak Battalion
  41/IV Homeland Flak Battalion
  44/IV Homeland Flak Battalion

V and 5th Flak Brigades

Formed in August 1940 in western France out of the Staff/ 209th Flak Regiment (Veith Flak Brigade), covering the Orléans–Nantes–Brest area. In 1943 it became the 5th (mot) Flak Brigade. In May 1944 it was transferred to southern France. It retreated to the Belfort–Strasbourg region and became the 5th Flak Brigade (ETr – Railroad Troops) in October 1944 in Berlin. Luftgau III served as the command staff for all railroad Flak and in March 1945 it was reorganized as the 30th Flak Division (Railroad Troops).

V and 5th Flak Brigades (ETr – Railroad Troops)

Formed in October 1944 from the staff of the 5th Flak Brigade coming from southern France, as the command of railroad Flak throughout the Reich. It was placed under Luftflotte Reich. On 1 December 1944 it contained:

50th Railroad Flak Regiment
  867th Railroad Flak Battalion
  954th Railroad Flak Battalion
  955th FRailroad lak Battalion
  960th Railroad Flak Battalion
  972nd Railroad Flak Battalion
  974th Railroad Flak Battalion

1002nd Railroad Flak Battalion
992nd Light Railroad Flak Battalion
993rd Light Railroad Flak Battalion
159th Railroad Flak Regiment
  952nd Light Railroad Flak Battalion
  956th Light Railroad Flak Battalion
  957th Light Railroad Flak Battalion
  958th Light Railroad Flak Battalion
  959th Light Railroad Flak Battalion
  991st Light Railroad Flak Battalion
255th Flak Regiment
  1003rd Light Flak Battalion

VI Flak Brigade

Formed on 12 January 1939 in Luftgau XI. It was shifted to Munich-Gladbach (Luftgau VI), then Rendsburg (Luftgau XI). It took part in the French campaign with the 40th and 45th Flak Regiments. In December 1940 it was on the Atlantic at Fontenay-le-Comte, under the Flak Commander Paris. It served temporarily in Rumania in 1942. On 28 February 1943 it became the Staff/21st Flak Division.

6th Flak Brigade

Formed on 25 August 1944 in Stettin with the staff of the 172nd Flak Regiment from Berlin, to serve around Stettin and Pölitz. On 1 December 1944 it contained:

3rd Flak Regiment
  154th Heavy Flak Battalion
  325th Heavy Flak Battalion
  337th Heavy Flak Battalion
  437th Heavy Flak Battalion
  Staff/474th Heavy Flak Battalion
  Staff/605th Heavy Flak Battalion
  616th Heavy Flak Battalion
  850th Light Flak Battalion
7th Searchlight Regiment
  180th Searchlight Battalion
  410th Searchlight Battalion
  449th Searchlight Battalion
  3/III Homeland Flak Battalion

Date	Heavy btrys	Med/light btrys	Barrage balloon btrys
24 Aug. 1944	57	48	3
9 Sept. 1944	10	11	–

At the end of March 1945 it was in the II Flak Corps, Luftflotte 6. At the end of the war it was fighting in Stettin and along the Oder.

VII Flak Brigade

Formed on 1 February 1940 from the Flugabwehrkommando (Anti-Aircraft Defense Command) Mosel. In the French campaign it fought in the rear areas, defending them from Allied attacks. In 1941 it served in the defense of the airfields of X Fliegerkorps in Sicily, where, in August 1942, it was organized into the staff of the 19th (mot) Flak Division.

7th Flak Brigade

The 7th Flak Brigade was formed on 1 April 1944 from part of the 24th Flak Division. On 1 December 1944 the brigade contained the following units:

76th Flak Regiment
  358th Mixed Flak Battalion
  516th Heavy Flak Battalion
  803rd Heavy Flak Battalion
  699th Light Flak Battalion
  188th Searchlight Battalion
  10/XVII Homeland Flak Battalion
128th Flak Regiment
  684th Heavy Flak Battalion

695th Heavy Flak Battalion
805th Heavy Flak Battalion
529th Searchlight Battalion
13/XVII Homeland Flak Battalion
118th Flak Regiment
  372nd Heavy Flak Battalion
  388th Heavy Flak Battalion
  503rd Heavy Flak Battalion
  837th Light Flak Battalion
  909th Searchlight Battalion
  16/XVII Homeland Flak Battalion
  429th Temporary Railroad Flak Battalion

VIII and 8th Flak Brigades

Formed on 7 February 1941 from the Staff/26th Flak Regiment to direct the AA defenses along the Weser and Ems, with its headquarters in Bremen. In January 1943 (or earlier) it was shifted to the Rostock–Lübeck area, with its headquarters in Wismar. It served with the VI Flak Corps through the rest of the war. On 1 November 1943 the brigade contained:

50th Flak Regiment
  413th Heavy Flak Battalion
  584th Searchlight Battalion
1st Flak Artillery School
  142nd Heavy Flak Battalion
113th Heavy Flak Battalion
61st Flak Regiment
  232nd Heavy Flak Battalion
  275th Heavy Flak Battalion
  770th Light Flak Battalion
  580th Searchlight Battalion
  105th Barrage Balloon Battalion

In February 1944 the 8th Brigade moved to Oldenburg. On 1 March 1944 it contained:

9th Flak Regiment
  273rd Heavy Flak Battalion
  743rd Light Flak Battalion
  588th Searchlight Battalion
  589th Searchlight Battalion
63rd Flak Regiment
  572nd Heavy Flak Battalion
  942nd Light Flak Battalion
  206th Barrage Balloon Battalion
50th Flak Regiment
  231st Heavy Flak Battalion

61st Flak Regiment
  232nd Heavy Flak Battalion
  413th Heavy Flak Battalion
  770th Light Flak Battalion
  916th Light Flak Battalion
  580th Searchlight Battalion
  584th Searchlight Battalion

On 5 May 1944 the brigade was in Hanover, and on 1 December 1944 it contained:

25th Flak Regiment
  461st Heavy Flak Battalion
  801st Heavy Flak Battalion
  35/XI Homeland Flak Battalion
56th Searchlight Regiment
  139th Searchlight Battalion
  169th Searchlight Battalion
65th Flak Regiment
  165th Heavy Flak Battalion
  216th Heavy Flak Battalion
  218th Heavy Flak Battalion
  772nd Light Flak Battalion
  925th Light Flak Battalion (no staff)

IX Flak Brigade

Formed on 1 April 1941 by Rambouillet from the Staff/129th Flak Regiment for the defense of the rear areas of Army Group Center, in Russia. In March 1942 the staff became the Staff/12th (mot) Flak Division.

9th Flak Brigade

Formed in Stuttgart in July–August 1944 from the Staff/75th Flak Regiment. After some early shuffling of units, the brigade was established with the 68th, 130th, and 139th Flak Regiments.

On 6 September 1944 the Western France Luftgaukommando of Luftgau V was newly organized. The brigade was then moved from Luftgau VII to Luftgau V. In October 1944 it became the Staff/28th Flak Division.

The 9th Flak Brigade was re-formed in January 1945 from the earlier 20th Flak Brigade z.b.V., with the 16th Flak Division, for service on the front. In 1945 it served as a motorized brigade in Holland with the 16th Flak Division.

Date	Heavy btrys	Med/light btrys	Light Alarm btrys
21 Jan. 1945	20	36	1
8 Feb. 1945	22	33	2
23 Feb. 1945	22	34	2

X Flak Brigade

Formed on 1 April 1940 as a Flak Brigade z.b.V. to defend Dortmund. In summer 1941 it became the X Flak Brigade.

10th Flak Brigade

Formed in the summer 1943 in the II Flak Corps, it fought in Russia. It served around Orel, on the Desna and north of Vitebsk, engaging in normal AA activities as well as the anti-partisan war. At the end of July 1944 it was serving with the II Flak Corps, but had no troops assigned to it. On 1 October 1944 it was disbanded and used to build the Staff/116th (mot) Flak Regiment.

Date	Heavy btrys	Med/light btrys	
8 July 1944	10	7	7 heavy and 4 light Alarm Batteries
8 Aug. 1944	24	19	from 2 light and 6 heavy Alarm Flak Batteries
23 Aug. 1944	12	10	

XI Flak Brigade

Formed 19 November 1941 in Luftgau Belgium–northern France. In November 1942 it was deployed in southwest France, between the Gironde and the Spanish border. It served in the Channel Islands (Guernsey) after 1 April 1943. It was redesignated the 11th Flak Brigade in 1942. It became the General of the Luftwaffe, Channel Islands, in November 1943.

Date	Heavy btrys	Med/light btrys	Searchlight btrys	Barrage balloon btrys
15 June 1943	12	7	–	–
26 Nov. 1943	16	12	3	¼
9 Jan. 1944	16	11	–	–

11th Flak Brigade

Organized on 1 June 1944 as the command for Eastern Prussia, Luftflotte Reich, later Luftflotte 6. It was assigned to the II Flak Corps in August 1944. Shortly before becoming the staff of the 327th Flak Division in September, for a short while it may also have been the Staff/15th Flak Brigade.

Date	Heavy btrys	Med/light btrys	Searchlight btrys	Smoke companies
8 June 1944	57	16	–	–
8 July 1944	59	13	–	–
23 July 1944	54	15	–	–
8 Aug. 1944	64	19	–	1
23 Aug. 1944	70	23	17	1
8 Sept. 1944	70	24	12	1

XII and 12th Flak Brigades

Formed in December 1941 in the Channel Islands (Guernsey). It changed places with the XI Flak Brigade in southwest France between the Gironde and the Spanish border on 1 April 1943. In 1943 it was redesignated as the XII Flak Brigade. After the retreat from southern France, it was disbanded and used to form the Staff/145th Flak Regiment. It ended the war in Angermünde.

Date	Heavy btrys	Med/light btrys	Searchlight btrys	Barrage balloon btrys	Smoke companies
15 June 1943	39	27	3	2	3
1 Aug. 1944	36	21	2	1	1
	inc. 1 Alarm Flak Battery				
24 Aug. 1944	26	21	–	2	–
	inc. 2 heavy and 3 light/medium Alarm Flak Batteries				
8 Sept. 1944	2	14	–	–	–

XIII and 13th Flak Brigades

Formed in June 1942 and deployed in northern Finland. It was in northern Norway from July 1944 and was redesignated the 13th Flak Brigade in that period. Most of the troops were returned to Germany and assigned to the 14th Flak Brigade. It was apparently disbanded on 27 January 1945.

Date	Heavy btrys	Med/light btrys	Searchlight btrys	Smoke platoons
9 June 1944	50	32	3	1
23 June 1944	53	32	3	1
23 July 1944	58	32	3	1
23 Aug. 1944	64	34	3	1
23 Sept. 1944	64	32	3	1
23 Oct. 1944	70	36	1	1

In March 1944 the brigade contained:

142nd Flak Regiment
  171st Mixed Flak Battalion
  332nd Mixed Flak Battalion
  426th Mixed Flak Battalion
  527th Mixed Flak Battalion
  359th Searchlight Battalion
181st Flak Regiment
  425th Mixed Flak Battalion

467th Mixed Flak Battalion

72nd Light Flak Battalion

229th Flak Regiment

1 (mixed)/47th Flak Regiment

2 (mixed)/46th Flak Regiment

302nd Mixed Flak Battalion

352nd Mixed Flak Battalion

173rd Luftnachrichten Battalion (not confirmed)

XIV and 14th Flak Brigades

Formed and deployed on 1 June 1942 for the defense of Oslo and assigned to Luftflotte 5. In March 1945 the staff formed the Staff/39th Flak Division. In 1943 it became the 14th Flak Brigade.

Date	Heavy btrys	Med/light btrys	Searchlight btrys	Smoke companies
23 June 1944	70	48	–	1 platoon
23 July 1944	72	49	–	1 platoon
23 Aug. 1944	60	39	–	1 platoon
23 Sept. 1944	60	40	–	1 platoon
23 Oct. 1944	49	34	–	1 platoon

In March 1944 the brigade had:

83rd Flak Regiment

1 (mixed)/15th Flak Regiment

111th Mixed Flak Battalion

421st Mixed Flak Battalion

427th Mixed Flak Battalion

504th Mixed Flak Battalion

725th Light Flak Battalion

152nd Flak Regiment

2 (mixed)/33rd Flak Regiment

265th Mixed Flak Battalion

502nd Heavy Flak Battalion

823rd Light Flak Battalion

174th Luftnachrichten Battalion (not confirmed)

92nd Flak Regiment

515th Mixed Flak Battalion

526th Mixed Flak Battalion

567th Mixed Flak Battalion

641st Mixed Flak Battalion

726th Light Flak Battalion

782nd Light Flak Battalion

162nd Flak Regiment

569th Mixed Flak Battalion

1 (mixed)/611thFlak Regiment

561st Heavy Flak Battalion

562nd Mixed Flak Battalion

740th Light Flak Battalion

781st Light Flak Battalion

XV and 15th Flak Brigades

Formed in Hanover-Burgdorf in June 1942 from part of the 8th Flak Brigade. In 1943 it became the XV Flak Brigade and on 1 November 1943 it contained:

9th Flak Regiment

273rd Heavy Flak Battalion

743rd Light Flak Battalion

25th Flak Regiment

461st Heavy Flak Battalion

521st Heavy Flak Battalion

801st Heavy Flak Battalion

871st Light Flak Battalion

418th Temporary Heavy Railroad Flak Battalion

65th Flak Regiment

216th Heavy Flak Battalion

280th Heavy Flak Battalion

772nd Light Flak Battalion

925th Light Flak Battalion

424th Temporary Railroad Flak Battalion

56th Searchlight Regiment

139th Searchlight Battalion

149th Searchlight Battalion

169th Searchlight Battalion

During the winter of 1943/44 the 9th Regiment was moved to Osnabrück and reassigned to the 8th Brigade. On 1 March 1944 the Brigade had:

65th Flak Regiment
  280th Heavy Flak Battalion
  772nd Light Flak Battalion
  925th Light Flak Battalion
  933rd Light Flak Battalion
  424th Temporary Heavy Railroad Flak Battalion
56th Searchlight Regiment
  139th Searchlight Battalion
  149th Searchlight Battalion
  169th Searchlight Battalion
25th Flak Regiment
  165th Heavy Flak Battalion
  216th Heavy Flak Battalion
  461st Heavy Flak Battalion
  521st Heavy Flak Battalion
  801st Heavy Flak Battalion
  871st Light Flak Battalion

In May 1944 the staff of the 15th Flak Brigade was sent to Upper Silesia to protect the Oder Valley/Heydebreck hydroelectric works and the 8th Flak Brigade took over the defense of Hanover. However, the disbanding was not complete and the brigade, re-established in Luftgau VIII, probably contained:

106th Flak Regiment
  53/VIII Homeland Flak Battalion
  54/VIII Homeland Flak Battalion
  55/VIII Homeland Flak Battalion
107th Regiment
  50/VIII Homeland Flak Battalion
  51/VIII Homeland Flak Battalion
  57/VIII Homeland Flak Battalion
  58/VIII Homeland Flak Battalion

In September 1944 the 15th Flak Brigade was reorganized as the 11th Flak Division. In October 1944 the brigade was re-formed in Danzig from the Staff/62nd Flak Regiment. It served in Pomerania with the 3rd Panzer Division and under the II Flak Corps along the Oder, south of Stettin. At that time it contained the 6th, 138th, and 145th Flak Regiments. On 8 February 1945 it had 12 heavy and nine light or medium Flak batteries.

XVI and 16th Flak Brigades

Formed in September 1942 in Vienna. On 1 November 1943 it contained:

28th Flak Regiment
  223rd Heavy Flak Battalion
  532nd Heavy Flak Battalion
  533rd Heavy Flak Battalion
  263rd Temporary Heavy Railroad Flak Battalion
88th Flak Regiment
  290th Heavy Flak Battalion
  336th Heavy Flak Battalion
  543rd Temporary Heavy Railroad Flak Battalion
98th Flak Regiment
  288th Heavy Flak Battalion
  536th Temporary Heavy Railroad Flak Battalion
6th Searchlight Regiment
  140th Searchlight Battalion
  338th Searchlight Battalion
  398th Searchlight Battalion
  560th Searchlight Battalion
1st Searchlight Regiment
  246th Heavy Flak Battalion
  372nd Heavy Flak Battalion
  388th Heavy Flak Battalion
  503rd Heavy Flak Battalion
  805th Heavy Flak Battalion
  837th Light Flak Battalion
  188th Searchlight Battalion
  909th Searchlight Battalion
  429th Temporary Railroad Flak Battalion
76th Flak Regiment
  282nd Heavy Flak Battalion
  615th Heavy Flak Battalion
  644th Heavy Flak Battalion
  803rd Heavy Flak Battalion
  751st Light Flak Battalion
184th Flak Regiment
  285th Heavy Flak Battalion
  289th Heavy Flak Battalion
  189th Searchlight Battalion
  810th Searchlight Battalion

The Brüz Special Regiment was assigned and reorganized as the 102nd Flak Regiment. On 1 November 1943 the brigde contained:

28th Flak Regiment
  223rd Heavy Flak Battalion
  532nd Heavy Flak Battalion
  263rd Temporary Heavy Railroad Flak Battalion
88th Flak Regiment
  290th Heavy Flak Battalion
  336th Heavy Flak Battalion
  543rd Temporary Heavy Railroad Flak Battalion
98th FlakRegiment
  288th Heavy Flak Battalion

536th Temporary Heavy Railroad Flak Battalion
6th Searchlight Regiment
    140th Searchlight Battalion
    338th Searchlight Battalion
    398th Searchlight Battalion
    560th Searchlight Battalion
76th Flak Regiment
    282nd Heavy Flak Battalion
    615th Heavy Flak Battalion
    644th Heavy Flak Battalion
    803rd Heavy Flak Battalion
    751st Light Flak Battalion
184th Flak Regiment
    285th Heavy Flak Battalion
    289th Heavy Flak Battalion
    189th Searchlight Battalion

810th Searchlight Battalion
Brux Regiment z.b.V. (organization unknown)

In December 1943 the over-strength brigade was re-designated the 24th Flak Division. The 102nd Flak Regiment had:

102nd Flak Regiment
284th Mixed Flak Battalion
290th Heavy Flak Battalion

The brigade was re-formed on 24 October 1944 in East Prussia, from the Staff/110th Flak Regiment, to protect Hitler's main headquarters. It served in Germany in March 1945, deployed along the Elbe by Wittenberge as part of the 14th Flak Division.

XVII Flak Brigade

Formed in the winter of 1943 by the General Command of Flak Artillery South in Italy for the defense of the rear battle area. It then appears to have become the Staff/25th Flak Division. It was re-formed into General of Flak Artillery in 1943 and the 25th Flak Division in 1944.

17th Flak Brigade

Formed in April 1944 in Hungary from the Staff/71st Flak Regiment. It was assigned to the General of the German Luftwaffe in Hungary for the defense of Budapest, under Luftflotte 4 as part of V Flak Corps. It contained a large number of Hungarian Flak units. It was destroyed and disbanded on 1 February 1945. What remained became the 37th Flak Regiment.

Date	Heavy btrys	Med/light btrys	Search-light btrys
24 May 1944	21	6	—
23 June 1944	15	2	—
23 July 1944	15	2	—
23 Aug. 1944	15	2	—
23 Sept. 1944	15	2	3
23 Oct. 1944	15	2	1

XVIII and 18th Flak Brigades

Formed on 27 January 1943 to command the mobile Flak in France. In 1943 it was redesignated the 18th Flak Brigade. It was part of Luftflotte 3. In early 1944 it was in Belgium and northern France and assigned to the defense of the V-1 and V-2 launch sites. In September 1944 it was under III Flak Corps near Culenberg, then in the 16th Flak Division near Sonsbeek, Holland. It fought in Holland as a motorized Flak brigade in the VI Flak Corps. At the war's end it was in Cuxhaven.

Date	Heavy btrys	Med/light btrys	Searchlight btrys	Barrage balloon btrys
9 Sept. 1944	40	27	—	—
23 Sept. 1944	26	14	—	—
8 Nov. 1944	23	12	—	—
8 Dec. 1944	47	34	—	—

| 8 Jan. 1945 | 24 | 13 | – | – |
| 8 Feb. 1945 | 24 | 23 | – | – |

In March 1944 the brigade contained:

694th Flak Searchlight Battalion
656th Flak Regiment

95th Flak Regiment
  402nd Mixed Flak Battalion
  614th Mixed Flak Battalion
  594th Heavy Flak Battalion
  691st Light Flak Battalion
Flak Group Somme
  168th Flak Searchlight Battalion
  369th Flak Searchlight Battalion
  469th Flak Searchlight Battalion

  122nd Mixed Flak Battalion
  417th Mixed Flak Battalion
  694th Heavy Flak Battalion
  880th Heavy Flak Battalion
  345th Heavy Flak Battalion
  157th Light Flak Battalion
  680th Light Flak Battalion
  757th Light Flak Battalion
  993rd Light Flak Battalion

XIX and 19th Flak Brigades

Formed in early 1943 for the defense of Amsterdam. Later in the year it was redesignated the 19th Flak Brigade. On 1 January 1944 it was placed under Luftflotte 3.

Date	Heavy btrys	Med/light btrys	Searchlight btrys	Barrage balloon btrys
9 Sept. 1944	34	32	–	–
23 Sept. 1944	26	38	–	–
23 Oct. 1944	10	28	–	–
23 Nov. 1944	19	52	–	–
21 Dec. 1944	20	27	–	–
8 Jan. 1945	26	47	–	–
21 Jan. 1945	22	44	–	–
8 Feb. 1945	11	48	–	–
21 Feb. 1945	14	46	–	–

In March 1944 the brigade contained:

1/, 2/, 3/, 4/155th Flak Regiment (W)
179th Luftnachrichten Company

8th Flak Regiment
  591st Mixed Flak Battalion
  665th Mixed Flak Battalion
  668th Mixed Flak Battalion
  831st Light Flak Battalion
  847th Light Flak Battalion

111th Flak Regiment
  155th Mixed Flak Battalion
  428th Heavy Flak Battalion
  667th Light Flak Battalion
  764th Light Flak Battalion
  845th Light Flak Battalion

XX and 20th Flak Brigades

Formed in June 1943 in Stuttgart, from the staff of the 75th Flak Regiment. It was quickly redesignated the 20th Flak Brigade. On 1 November 1943 it contained:

75th Flak Regiment
  241st Heavy Flak Battalion
  436th Heavy Flak Battalion

  460th Heavy Flak Battalion
  858th Heavy Flak Battalion
96th Flak Regiment
  455th Heavy Flak Battalion
  705th Heavy Flak Battalion
  932nd Light Flak Battalion
  360th Searchlight Battalion

68th Flak Regiment
  234th Heavy Flak Battalion
  458th Heavy Flak Battalion
  506th Heavy Flak Battalion
  1st z.b.V. Strasburg Heavy Flak Battalion
  444th Temporary Railroad Flak Battalion
  400th Searchlight Battalion
  583rd Searchlight Battalion

The brigade experienced very few changes, and on 1 March 1944 it contained:

68th Flak Regiment
  234th Heavy Flak Battalion

  357th Heavy Flak Battalion
  458th Heavy Flak Battalion
  721st Light Flak Battalion
75th Flak Regiment unchanged
96th Flak Regiment unchanged

At the beginning of 1944, devoid of assigned troops, it was assigned to Luftflotte 3. Tessin says that in July 1944 the brigade staff was sent to Doullens, western France, and the new 9th Brigade took over the defense of Stuttgart. However, it is suggested by Koch that it was then assigned to III Flak Corps in Holland.

Date	Heavy btrys	Med/light btrys	Searchlight btrys	Barrage balloon btrys
23 Sept. 1944	4	24	–	–
8 Oct. 1944	22	32	–	–

XXI and 21st Flak Brigades

Formed on 19 April 1943 in Nürnberg, it was quickly redesignated the 21st Flak Brigade. On 1 November 1943 it contained:

93rd Flak Regiment
  522nd Heavy Flak Battalion
  633rd Heavy Flak Battalion
  634th Heavy Flak Battalion
  951st Light Flak Battalion
179th Flak Regiment
  482nd Heavy Flak Battalion
  639th Heavy Flak Battalion
  906th Heavy Flak Battalion

  953rd Light Flak Battalion
  708th Searchlight Battalion
Regiment z.b.V.
  484th Heavy Flak Battalion
199th Searchlight Regiment
  198th Searchlight Battalion
  439th Searchlight Battalion
  708th Searchlight Battalion
Independent
  342nd Heavy Flak Battalion
  181st Luftnachrichten Battalion

In early 1943 it had:

Regiment	Heavy btrys	Med/light btrys	Searchlight btrys	Smoke companies
93rd	6	2	–	–
93rd in Aug.	3	2	3	–
179th	6	1	–	1
z.b.V.	3	1	–	–

On 22 December 1943 the Regiment z.b.V. Regensburg became the 71st Flak Regiment. On 1 March 1944 the brigade had:

71st Flak Regiment
  484th Heavy Flak Battalion
  906th Heavy Flak Battalion
  822nd Temporary Heavy Railroad Flak Battalion
93rd Flak Regiment

  522nd Heavy Flak Battalion
  633rd Heavy Flak Battalion
  634th Heavy Flak Battalion
  951st Light Flak Battalion
179th Flak Regiment
  482nd Heavy Flak Battalion
  639th Heavy Flak Battalion
  953rd Light Flak Battalion
  263rd Temporary Railroad Flak Battalion

199th Searchlight Regiment
  198th Searchlight Battalion
  708th Searchlight Battalion
  439th Searchlight Battalion

On 1 April 1944 the brigade was transferred to Luftgau VII. During the organization of Luftgau XIV, on 6 September 1944, the 179th Flak Regiment was transferred to the new Luftgau, while the rest of the brigade was transferred to the 26th Flak Division, in Munich. The staff of a re-formed 21st Flak Brigade was organized in October 1944.

On 1 December 1944 the brigade had:

33rd Flak Regiment
  210th Heavy Flak Battalion
  406th Heavy Flak Battalion
  433rd Heavy Flak Battalion
  540th Heavy Flak Battalion
  761st Light Flak Battalion
  46/IV Homeland Flak Battalion
  145th Temporary Railroad Flak Battalion
145th Flak Regiment
  132nd Heavy Flak Battalion
  Staff/185th Heavy Flak Battalion
  Staff/627th Heavy Flak Battalion
  40/IV Homeland Flak Battalion

XXII and 22nd Flak Brigades

Formed in late 1942/early 1943 from the disbanded Staff/VII Flak Brigade. It operated in Sicily until the Allied landings, when it moved to the Straits of Messina. In January 1944 it was in Rome, then in June it moved to Maserata. Despite subsequent moves it remained in Italy until the war's end.

Flak Brigade z.b.V. (Special Assignment)

Formed in October 1944 from the 20th Flak Brigade and other units, it moved to the Rotterdam area. In January 1945 it became the 9th (mot) Flak Brigade.

Date	Heavy btrys	Med/light btrys	Searchlight btrys	Barrage balloon btrys
23 Oct. 1944	25	39	–	–
8 Nov. 1944	24	32	–	–
23 Nov. 1944	19	28	–	–
21 Dec. 1944	16	26	–	–
8 Jan 1945	27	37	–	–

Flak Brigade z.b.V.

In April 1945 it was organized in central Germany as part of Luftflotte Reich.

1st Flak Searchlight Brigade

Formed in July 1940. On 31 July 1941 it operated in north-west Germany in support of night fighter operations. It became the 1st Flak Searchlight Division.

2nd Flak Searchlight Brigade

Formed in July 1940. On 31 July 1941 it operated in Arnhem in support of night fighter operations over Holland. It became the 2nd Flak Searchlight Division.

Bibliography

Bender, D., *Foreign Legions of the Third Reich*. San Jose, CA: R. James Bender Publishing, 1987.

Bender, R. J., *Uniforms, Organization, and History of the Legion Condor*. San Jose, CA: R. James Bender Publishing, 1992.

Deighton, L., *Blitzkrieg: From the Rise of Hitler to the Fall of Dunkirk*. London: Jonathan Cape, 1993.

Guderian, Gen. H., *Panzer Leader*. London: Michael Joseph, 1952.

Haupt, Werner, *A History of the Panzer Troops*. West Chester, PA: Schiffer Publishing Co., 1990.

Hogg, I. V., *German Artillery of World War Two*. London: Arms & Armour Press, 1975. Revised edition, London: Greenhill Books, 1997.

Jentz, T. L., *Panzer Truppen*. Alten, PA: Schiffer Military History, 1996.

Jung, H., *Die Ardennen Offensive 1944–1945*. Frankfurt: Musterschmidt Gottingen, 1971.

Keilig, W., *Das Deutsche Heer 1939–1945*. Bad Neuheim: Verlag Hans-Henning Podzun, 1956.

Koch, H. A., *Flak: Die Geschichte der Deutschen Flakartillerie und der Einsatz der Luftwaffenhelfer*. Podzun, date unknown.

Kurowski, F., *The History of the Fallschirm-Panzerkorps Hermann Göring*. Winnipeg: J. J. Fedorowicz, 1995.

Littlejohn, D., *Foreign Legions of the Third Reich*. San Jose, CA: R. James Bender Publishing, 1987.

MacDonald, C. B., *The Battle of the Bulge*. London: Weidenfeld & Nicholson, 1990.

Macksey, K., *Guderian: Creator of the Blitzkrieg*. London: Macdonald & Jane's, 1975. Reprinted, London: Greenhill Books, 1997.

Niehorster, L. W. G., *German World War II Organizational Series. Vol. 2/II: Mechanized HQ Units and Waffen SS Divisions (10 May 1940)*. Germany: 1990.

Mueller-Hillebrand, B., *Das Heer 1933–1945. Vols I and II: Verband der Truppen der deutschen Wehrmacht und Waffen SS 1939–1945*. Frankfurt am Main: date unknown

Parker, D. S., *Battle of the Bulge: Hitler's Ardennes Offensive, 1944–1945*. Conshohocken, PA: Combined Books Inc., 1991.

Richter, K. C., *Die Geschichte der deutschen Kavallerie, 1919–1945*. Stuttgart: Motorbuch Verlag Stuttgart, 1978. Reprinted, Weltbild Verlag, 1994.

Scheibert, H., *Panzer Grenadier, Motorcycle and Panzer Reconnaissance Units: A History of the German Motorized Units, 1935–1945*, West Chester, PA: Schiffer Publishing, 1991.

von Senger und Etterlin, F. M., *German Tanks of World War II*. London: Arms & Armour Press, 1971.

Spaeter, H., *The History of the Panzerkorps Grossdeutschland*. Winnipeg: J. J. Fedorowicz, 1992.

Tessin, G., *Verbände und Truppen der deutschen Wehrmacht und Waffen-SS im Zweiten Weltkrieg 1939–1945*. Osnabruck: Biblo Verlag, 1977.

Records of Headquarters, German Army High Command, American Historical Association Committee for the Study of War Documents, Washington, DC., 1960

Microcopy No T-78, Rolls 393, 397, 398, 404, 405, 407, 408, 409, 411, 414, 417, 418, 419, 421, 430 and 501.

Microcopy No T-311, Rolls 4, 18, 204

Microcopy No T-312, Rolls 268, 313 and 417

Microcopy No T-312, Roll 123, 427, 516

Microcopy No T-313, Roll 355, 417

Microcopy No T-314, Roll 1194

Microcopy No T-341, Rolls 142, 143, and 146

US War Department Technical Manual TM-E30-451, *Handbook on German Military Forces, 15 March 1945*. Washington, DC: US War Department, 1945.